T5-DHE-142

What's New in Lotus Notes Release 4.0

Tools: User Setup Profiles enable you to predefine the desktop and workstation configuration users will see when they first set up their workstations. **823**

User-Interface: The Ports setup icon is now to be found under File | Tools | Preferences. **815**

Application Development

Action Bars allow a "nonscrollable" region to be added to the top of any Form that contains one or more "buttons" that perform form-level tasks. **485**

Actions: Built-in and custom Actions make forms and views easier to use for end users without having to resort to complicated programming. **290**

Agents with enhanced scheduling, document selection and development options, along with "test" sessions have replaced Release 3 macros. **472**

Environment: Test a form in the foreground without having to leave the edit mode that remains in the background. **273**

Environment: Properties InfoBox, which most objects have, can be displayed by right-clicking the object. **271**

LotusScript, Navigators, Agents, and Simple Actions. **408**

LotusScript: Direct access to ODBC databases from LotusScript classes. **409**

LotusScript: Using LotusScript for programmatic control at the client to implement database integration. **780**

LotusScript: Using LotusScript. **422**

Navigators: Using Navigators, Agents, and Simple Actions. **464**

User-Interface: About document can be made to display every time the database is opened, or every time it is changed. **148**

User-Interface: Layout Regions allow more standard GUI interface entry conventions. **489**

User-Interface: Navigators offer graphical road maps to views in a database. **494**

User-Interface: Twisties to indicate whether a row is expandable or already expanded. **492**

User-Interface: View designers can specify that a column be sorted and/or allow the user to sort the column. **308**

Integration

Internet Web browser permits easy and seamless access to Internet Usenet newsgroups from within Notes. **35**

Internet: Newsletter agent selects news articles per user profiles, then creates a summary as a mail memo with document links to the matching articles. **151**

Internet: The Web browser on the Notes workstation eliminates the need for TCP/IP on the desktop for retrieving HTML pages from the Web. **998**

Internet: WebPub version 4.x supports additional capabilities over WebPub 2.1 intended for Notes Release 3.x. **631**

LotusScript can be used at the client for programmatic control to implement database integration. **780**

Multimedia: Enhancements in the areas of telephony, fax, and image management. **724**

Mail

Adjacent domain documents ensure mail routing does not become global merely because you communicate with a particular domain. **944**

cc:Mail type mail user interface has three adjustable panes showing folders/views, list of mail, and message preview. **21**

Customizable recipient name type-ahead lets you address mail memos, with Notes looking in your address book(s) to find a name and display it. **205**

Mail Create menu, new commands on: Bookmark (for automatic DocLinks), Phone Message, Task (to create a To Do memo), and Serial Routing Form. **157**

Mail Transfer Agents: X.400, SMTP, and cc:Mail, Release 4 is prepared for all three. **1000**

Shared mail can be set up using a single copy object store (SCOS), which holds non-summary data for all messages received by more than one user. **856**

Shared mail database makes it possible to maintain a body of shared e-mail in a single location. **153**

Mobile User

Locations, selectable from a list, allow the mobile user to easily choose from different customized configurations for connection options, and so on. **26, 202**

Mail: customizable recipient name type-ahead lets you address mail memos, with Notes looking in your address book(s) to find a name and display it. **205**

Passthru servers provide a single point of contact for replicating databases across multiple servers. **207**

Remote LAN Service Connection can be used to access network services as if you were connected using a network interface card. **955**

User Interface

What's New in Lotus Notes Release 4.5 and in this Edition

Lotus Notes® and Domino Server 4.5

Second Edition

Randall A. Tamura, et al.

SAMS
PUBLISHING

201 W. 103rd Street
Indianapolis, IN 46290

UNLEASHED

To my wife, Mari, my best friend, and to my son,
Eric, my best pal.

Copyright © 1997 by Sams Publishing

SECOND EDITION

International Standard Book Number: 0-672-31004-X

Library of Congress Catalog Card Number: 96-70718

00 99 98 97   4 3 2

Interpretation of the printing code: the rightmost double-digit number is the year of the book's printing; the rightmost single-digit, the number of the book's printing. For example, a printing code of 97-1 shows that the first printing of the book occurred in 1997.

Composed in AGaramond and MCPdigital by Macmillan Computer Publishing

Printed in the United States of America

Trademarks

Publisher and President	*Richard K. Swadley*
Publishing Manager	*Dean Milller*
Director of Editorial Services	*Cindy Morrow*
Assistant Marketing Managers	*Kristina Perry, Rachel Wolfe*

Acquisitions Editor
Grace M. Buechlein

Development Editor
Sunthar Visuvalingam

Production Editor
Gayle Johnson

Indexers
Erika Millen
Ben Slen

Software Development Specialist
Patty Brooks

Technical Reviewer
Marcia Thomas

Formatter
Katie Wise

Technical Edit Coordinator
Lynette Quinn

Editorial Assistants
Carol Ackerman
Andi Richter
Rhonda Tinch-Mize

Cover Designer
Jason Grisham

Book Designer
Gary Adair

Production Team Supervisor
Brad Chinn

Production
Georgiana Briggs
Cyndi Davis
Ayanna Lacey
Mary Ellen Stephenson

Overview

Contents

Part II Using Lotus Notes

5 The Notes Workspace and Databases 97

Part IV Advanced Development

Foreword

The creation of Lotus Notes more than seven years ago was inspired by the following question: If a personal computer can transform the level of an individual's productivity, what can it do for the productivity of groups of individuals? Why can't the PCs on the desktops of corporate America be used to help teams? The architects of Lotus Notes envisioned employees sharing information, ideas, knowledge, feedback, field data, competitive analyses, and more with their team members via computers rather than exclusively in face-to-face meetings.

It was a groundbreaking idea that led to the sale of millions of copies of Notes and the emergence of a brand-new category of software, dubbed "groupware." However, one of the biggest challenges Lotus faced, as it refined and improved Notes through three releases, was helping organizations find affordable ways to get their employees, suppliers, and customers online so that Notes could fully make its unique impact.

The number one obstacle to the proliferation of Notes disappeared in 1995 as corporations, suppliers, and potential customers the world over became connected via the Internet and the World Wide Web. In July of 1996, Lotus made Web server technology, called "Domino," available for free right on the company's World Wide Web home page. Domino transformed the Notes Release 4 server into an interactive Web application server by combining the open networking environment of Internet standards and protocols with the powerful collaboration and application development facilities already in Notes. And Domino instantly gave organizations the ability to rapidly develop and deploy a broad range of business solutions for the Internet and intranet markets.

The 13,000 Lotus Business Partners who offer products and services based on Notes and other Lotus technologies immediately began to develop Domino-based solutions. The five million users already relying on Notes to help them find and share information wherever it was located—in e-mail, relational databases, desktop applications, or the World Wide Web— immediately became able to leverage the Internet in a truly interactive way.

The story of the Notes 4.5 client and the Domino 4.5 server is the story of a vision fulfilled. Thanks to the Internet, the personal computer is becoming a powerful tool for communication, information sharing, and collaboration. It is as important to teams as it is to individuals, just as the Notes pioneers foresaw. Welcome to Lotus Notes, Domino 4.5, and the fulfillment of your vision.

Steve Sayre
Vice President, Marketing
Lotus Development Corporation

Acknowledgments

When I was just a reader (before I became an author), I knew that there must be a lot of people who contribute to a book. Just look at the page containing the names of editors, managers, and designers. (Notes ACL experts will get the inside joke of the preceding two sentences. Others must buy and read this book first.) But now I realize I didn't know how many people really work on a book.

First, I would like to thank and acknowledge all the coauthors. When you read about their backgrounds, you'll be able to gather what a talented, knowledgeable group of people they are. I suppose this is a good place to have a virtual high-five and breathe a collective sigh of relief. We've done it! Thanks, everyone.

On behalf of all the authors, I'd like to thank our collective staffs, colleagues, and families for their participation. Without their support, we would not have been able to complete this book.

Thanks to Lotus and their Business Partner program. It was through the Lotus Notes Net that I was able to find and initially contact many of the authors.

I'd like to thank all the good people at Sams Publishing, especially Grace Buechlein, our acquisitions editor, who is one of Sams' primary contacts for authors. She always manages to keep in touch and is always friendly and helpful. Thanks also to Sunthar Visuvalingam, the development editor, for his reviews of our drafts and his comments and suggestions. Thanks to our technical reviewers, Marcia Thomas (who reviewed this edition of the book), and Chris Grace and Steven Kern (the technical reviewers for the previous edition). They did a good job of questioning and making us clarify our thoughts so that you would have an easier time understanding. Patty Brooks and Cari Skaggs were responsible for the CD-ROM. Many others at Sams contributed, and the list is much too long to include, but thanks to all of you.

Finally, thanks to you, the reader. We've all collectively worked hard to bring you this book. We all hope you will find it of value. We've created this book for you. Thanks for reading it.

About the Authors

Randall A. Tamura is president of the Graphware Corporation, a consulting company specializing in Lotus Notes and Windows development. He has more than 20 years of experience in the computer field. Before founding Graphware, he was the general manager of Engineering Systems Development in the Application Solutions Division of IBM. He is a Lotus Business Partner and has worked with Notes for several years. Tamura has experience in helping both small and large companies with software development and strategies. Working with Notes as well as other technologies, he has helped his clients plan, implement, and deploy applications. He has helped a variety of companies in the financial, insurance, manufacturing, and high-tech industries. Tamura is a graduate of the University of California at Berkeley and has a master's degree in computer science from Princeton University. He has taught at UCLA and other colleges in the Los Angeles area. He currently is a member of the American Management Association, IEEE, and the Association for Computing Machinery (ACM). You can contact him through CompuServe at 70731,1630, through the Internet at RandyTamura@msn.com, or by phone at (310) 649-0310.

Handly Cameron is a senior consultant with Brainstorm Technology, Inc. He has designed and implemented Lotus Notes databases supporting help desk tracking, customer support, and other workflow activities. He has used LotusScript to automate Notes reporting functions and to integrate Notes with large relational database systems. Prior to working at Brainstorm, Cameron led a software development team for First Data Corporation and NationsBank, implementing Lotus Notes solutions for 401K retirement plans. He holds a B.S. in electrical engineering from the Georgia Institute of Technology. He can be reached at hcameron@braintech.com. To view the latest information on Brainstorm's groupware products and services, see www.braintech.com.

Don Child has worked as a technical writer and trainer in the computer industry since 1982. He currently works as a senior technical writer and Notes trainer for DataHouse, a Premium Lotus Partner and Lotus Authorized Training Center in Honolulu, Hawaii. He is a Lotus Certified Notes Specialist (LCNS) and a Certified Lotus Instructor. He also is a Senior Member of the Society for Technical Communication. Child has a B.A. in humanities from Colorado State University and an M.A. in creative writing from Antioch University. He is a published poet and has edited the *Aspen Anthology,* a literary magazine.

Daniel S. Cooper is president of Beacon Learning, Inc., a Cambridge, Massachusetts multimedia application developer that specializes in interactive multimedia programs for training, marketing, and public information. Prior to founding Beacon Learning in 1990, Cooper spent 12 years at Digital Equipment Corporation, managing educational technology and quality assurance groups. He has worked in multimedia development for more than 25 years. He received a Ph.D. in education and communications from Stanford and an A.B. from Harvard. His publications and trade show presentations have focused on interactive technologies for marketing and training.

Jonathan Czernel is a Certified Lotus Professional (CLP) who has been responsible for the planning, development, and deployment of numerous Lotus Notes applications for several industries. He has also developed Notes database front-ends using a variety of third-party tools, including the Notes API, the VIM API, Lotus HiTest Tools (both Visual Basic and C flavors), and Revelation Software's ViP. In addition to Notes, Czernel has extensive software development expertise using a variety of languages, including C/C++, Visual Basic, QuickBasic, BASIC PDS, LotusScript, and Object Pascal. His significant development experience, especially in the world of BASIC, is especially pertinent to Lotus Notes Release 4.0, which uses LotusScript as its core language technology. Czernel received his B.S. in computer science from the University of Missouri at Rolla. Questions, comments, and criticisms may be sent to jcz@mindspring.com.

Sam Juvonen, currently employed at ENTEX Information Services in Bloomfield Hills, Michigan, holds a B.S. in electrical engineering from the University of Michigan. He is a Certified Lotus Professional and a Certified Lotus Instructor (Level 2) and has worked with Notes since version 2.1. When the LAEC channel opened in the spring of 1993, Juvonen brought ENTEX (then known as The LEAD Group) into the education market as one of the first Lotus Authorized Education Centers. He was among the first 20 people to be certified by Lotus as a Notes instructor. He has assisted numerous companies with administration, migration, and application development projects. Juvonen enjoys using his private pilot license recreationally and, when possible, to visit customers. He can be reached at sjuvonen@entex.com.

Marjorie Kramer's work in encryption as a student at Cornell University attracted the attention of Lotus Development Corp. She was employed by Lotus from 1988 to 1994, where she was a key resource for the Notes product, first in System Engineering and then in the Curriculum Development area. She developed the Instructor Certification Program for Lotus; designed, developed, and delivered Lotus Notes courses; and provided application development, system administration, and technical support for Lotus Notes customers. For the past two years, Kramer has worked as an independent consultant specializing in Notes, providing training, curriculum development, and project management for application development projects to clients such as Lotus, Xerox, IBM, Kellogg's, and various Lotus Authorized Education Centers.

Ralph Perrine is a senior software design engineer and Webmaster for Datahouse Inc. of Honolulu. In this capacity, he serves as Webmaster for several clients and is a Web site development consultant for many of the company's projects. Perrine perfected the two-tier Web architecture method (discussed in Chapter 24) while developing several Web sites for Datahouse, including Datahouse's home page (www.datahouse.com) and CareNet-Hawaii (www.carenet-hawaii.com), which was exhibited at the 1996 Olympics. Prior to working with Datahouse, Perrine was the program manager for Multimedia Research and Development at CAE-LINK Corporation and then at Hughes Training Inc. after its merger. While there, he founded the Multimedia Skunkworks Team, which developed leading-edge Internet applications, interactive multimedia toolsets, and 3D simulation engines for education and entertainment firms. Perrine is also the creator of Cyber Reef (http://www.aloha.net/~perrine), a premier Web resource featured in several Internet books and magazines. Proficient with a wide range of authoring tools and development environments, Perrine is also an accomplished artist. He and his wife, Dina, live in Honolulu.

Wendy Samulski has been in the computer industry since 1988. She graduated from Ryerson Polytechnical University in 1992 with a B.S. in computer science and is a Lotus Notes Certified Consultant. Her experience ranges from C and C++ to PowerBuilder and Notes development. Over the years, she has served as a member of various user groups. Samulski currently is president of the Toronto Notes Users Group (TNUG) and is chair of the Particularly Extraordinary Approach to Notes Utilization of Technical Standards Committee (PEANUTS). In addition, she founded the Gunther Computer Consulting company. She has traveled across North America, South America, Europe, and the Middle East.

Doug Taylor has been working in the field of computer telephone integration for the past four years. He began his computer career at NCR, where he was a technical writer for five years. He then directed the Technical Publications department at Simpact for four years before moving to Big Sky Technologies in San Diego. There he manages technical documentation, develops telephony applications that integrate with Lotus Notes, and assists with product development. He can be reached at dtaylor@bigskytech.com.

Daniel Tyre founded ALI Technologies Incorporated in 1993 with the vision of offering workflow engineering solutions and Lotus Notes products and services to the commercial marketplace. Before that, he was vice president of Sales and Marketing for Copley Systems Corporation, a Massachusetts-based computer reseller and systems integrator. Prior to joining Copley, Tyre was the area director for Businessland, a $1.3 billion dollar microcomputer reseller. He was responsible for sales, marketing, distribution, customer service, advanced systems, training, and operations for a $200,000,000 division. He spent seven years at Businessland in a variety of sales management and executive positions. He holds a B.A. from Colgate University.

Irfan Virk is vice president of development at Brainstorm Technology, Inc. He has designed and implemented several commercial groupware products for Lotus Notes and corporate intranets. His industry experience includes work as both a developer and a manager of client/ server and business process reengineering projects for Fortune 500 companies. He has managed projects for both Andersen Consulting and Brainstorm's Consulting Services division. Virk has extensive project management, technical architecture, and client relationship building experience. He has consulted for firms such as NationsBank, Caterpillar, and Upjohn. He holds a B.S. in industrial and operations engineering from the University of Michigan. He can be reached at ivirk@braintech.com. To view the latest information on Brainstorm's groupware products and services, see www.braintech.com.

Rizwan Virk has been president of Brainstorm Technology, Inc. since founding the company in 1993. Brainstorm is the leading provider of third-party tools to companies developing and deploying groupware solutions utilizing Lotus Notes. His background includes extensive experience consulting with Fortune 500 companies on groupware tools such as Lotus Notes. He has been involved in several high-tech startups, including DiVA Corporation, Sphynx Consulting Group, and Spectra Media, Inc. of Tokyo. He has consulted internationally for firms such as KLM, Reader's Digest, and Fidelity Investments. Virk holds a B.S. in computer science and engineering from the Massachusetts Institute of Technology. While at MIT, he founded SuccessBuilders, a company that marketed leadership and public speaking seminars to youth organizations around the country. He can be reached at `rvirk@braintech.com`. To view the latest information on Brainstorm's groupware products and services, see `www.braintech.com`.

Rob Wunderlich, CLP/CLI, is an instructor and Notes consultant for ENTEX Information Services (formerly The LEAD Group) in Bloomfield Hills, Michigan. He has written numerous articles on groupware in general and Lotus Notes in particular. In addition to doing consulting and development work with Notes, Wunderlich is ENTEX/Michigan's Webmaster and has grown to love the InterNotes products by employing them on ENTEX/Michigan's Web page (`http://web1.leadgroup.com`). He is founder of the Detroit Notes Professionals Association, a user group for Notes developers, administrators, and purveyors in southeastern Michigan. He is also a board member of DANUG, the Detroit Area Network User Group. He can be reached at `rwunder@leadgroup.com`.

Tell Us What You Think

As a reader, you are the most important critic and commentator of our books. We value your opinion and want to know what we're doing right, what we could do better, what areas you'd like to see us publish in, and any other words of wisdom you're willing to pass our way. You can help us make strong books that meet your needs and give you the computer guidance you require.

Do you have access to CompuServe or the World Wide Web? Then check out our CompuServe forum by typing GO SAMS at any prompt. If you prefer the World Wide Web, check out our site at http://www.mcp.com.

NOTE

If you have a technical question about this book, call our technical support line at (800) 571–5840, extension 3668.

As the team leader of the group that created this book, I welcome your comments. You can fax, e-mail, or write me directly to let me know what you did or didn't like about this book—as well as what we can do to make our books stronger. Here's the information:

Fax: (317) 581-4669

E-mail: opsys_mgr@sams.mcp.com

Mail: Dean Miller
            Comments Department
            Sams Publishing
            201 W. 103rd Street
            Indianapolis, IN 46290

Introduction

Lotus Notes has attracted people's attention. Whether you are a current user or a prospective user of Notes, it's clear that something is now happening with Notes. In a sense, it is stealth software. It crept up on us. Although the initial development of Notes started in the mid-1980s, and Notes was first shipped in 1989, it has gradually been developing a following of users. It took approximately six years for this software to develop a user base of approximately 2 million users.

In 1996, Notes really began to skyrocket. In that year, Notes had more than 4 million users, thus doubling its installed base in about a year. Lotus projects that the installed base will double again in the next year, and they want to have 20 million users in the next three years.

What has caused this great interest in Notes? And will this trend continue, or will some other force—such as intranets—kill it off? And what the heck is Notes, anyway? These are some of the questions that this book will answer for you.

A product that has been around since the mid '80s must have an element of value and usefulness. How many products have been around that long? Just as the longevity of Notes implies that it must have value, the recent growth statistics for Notes imply that there are reasons that make it important to look at Notes now.

One of the main reasons for the increasing interest in Notes is the Domino Server. In essence, it lets you set up a World Wide Web server that can be accessed by both Notes clients and regular Internet browsers such as Netscape Navigator and Microsoft Internet Explorer. Although the Domino server was born as the Notes server, it has been transformed into an Internet server. We'll cover Domino as well as the many other aspects of Notes that make it an important tool in today's communication and database environments.

Who Should Read This Book

This book is designed to give you an overview of the broad landscape of Notes. Since Notes has grown, it has developed a rich infrastructure, both within the product and in a thriving third-party add-on environment. This book looks at this environment from four major perspectives: the Notes acquisition manager, the Notes user, the Notes application developer, and the Notes Administrator. For example, you might be one of the following types of readers:

- A manager deciding whether to purchase Notes for your department or company. This book will give you the information you need to make an informed decision. It might come down to this: If you're thinking about putting up an Internet World Wide Web server, you should consider Notes and the Domino server as the core.

- A Notes user. Whether you are a new or experienced user of Notes, you should read this book to find out about the new features of Release 4.x.

- A Notes application developer. As a developer, you should be familiar with the new features of Notes Release 4.x and how to take advantage of them for your users. This book includes not only information on the core aspects of Notes development, but also value-added topics such as improving the look and feel of your forms, using navigators and LotusScript, and advanced API programming.

- A Notes Business Partner. This book was written almost completely by Notes Business Partners. As such, the authors know the kind of information you're interested in, including advice on many third-party integration tools. This book includes advanced topics such as telephony, video, and legacy system integration. The CD-ROM that accompanies this book includes many actual demos of third-party tools.

- A Notes administrator. We have included useful information on configuring your system, upgrading from Release 3 to Release 4.5, and troubleshooting and security concerns when you connect to other companies. This book also tells you how to set up a Web site that is powered by Notes. You might have to implement the Web site that someone else is trying to set up.

Whether you're using Notes now or are trying to decide whether Notes is the right product for your company, this book is for you. It describes why you should consider Notes, how to use Notes, how to develop applications for Notes, and how to administer your Notes network.

How This Book Is Organized

This book is organized into eight parts. Part I, "The Business of Lotus Notes," is a general introduction to Notes. It is designed to help you understand what Notes is and why you should consider it for your company.

Part II, "Using Lotus Notes," describes how to get started with Notes and how to use some of its more important features. Part III, "Developing Applications with Lotus Notes," and Part IV, "Advanced Development," provide you with information about creating Notes Release 4.5 applications. We have tried to highlight the important features of the new release.

Part V, "Domino Server, the Internet, and Intranets," tells you about the new features of Notes R4.5 that let you use Notes as an Internet client and/or server. This part tells you how to set up your own Web site using Domino and how to set up an intranet of your own using Notes.

Part VI, "Integrating and Connecting with Notes," is devoted to connecting your Notes systems with other systems you might have, including the Internet, phones, fax, video, and legacy systems. Part VII, "Setting Up a Simple Notes Network," gives you some core information on setting up and administering a simple Notes network. Part VIII, "Advanced Administration Topics," covers facts you should know when managing a large Notes network.

The following sections discuss each part in more detail.

Part I: The Business of Lotus Notes

Part I covers some basic concepts and information about Notes and the groupware category of software. Chapter 1, "What Is Groupware, and Why Is It Important?," describes why groupware is increasingly important to businesses today. It discusses factors such as global competitiveness, downsizing, virtual corporations, and mobile computing and their effect on our computing infrastructure. It tries to give a business perspective, not just a technical perspective, on why Notes is important.

Chapter 2, "What Is Lotus Notes?," discusses the basic characteristics of Notes. It describes the important features and functions. Chapter 3, "How Does Lotus Notes Work with the Internet?," introduces Notes' new Internet features. It gives you a hypothetical and a real-life example of how Notes is used today on the Internet. Without bogging you down with technical details, this chapter describes not only how Notes might be used tomorrow with the Internet, but how it is actually used today. Chapter 4, "What's New in Releases 4 Through 4.5 of Lotus Notes?," highlights new features of R4 through R4.5. Since the beginning of 1996, Lotus has shipped Release 4, 4.1, 4.11, and 4.5. This chapter describes the new features of all of these recent releases.

Part II: Using Lotus Notes

Part II provides basic information about using Notes R4.5. Whether you are just using Notes, developing applications for Notes, or administering a Notes system, you should read this part.

Chapter 5, "The Notes Workspace and Databases," begins with a discussion of the workspace and covers information you need to know in order to log on to a Notes system and to use databases and SmartIcons. You'll even learn about hieroglyphics and anti-spoofing; even know-it-alls might learn something. Chapter 6, "Views, Documents, and Forms," introduces these fundamental aspects of Notes. You'll learn how to navigate through views, and how to open, print, and save documents. Chapter 7, "Using Applications and Mail on Your Desktop," covers the use of e-mail and general applications. E-mail is now a critical part of business, and with R4.5, Lotus has enhanced the e-mail interface so that it's even more user-friendly than before. The ability to use Notes on a mobile computer or from a remote computer such as one in a home office is a great benefit. Chapter 8, "Using Calendaring and Scheduling," discusses the new R4.5 feature that allows you to keep track of your own calendar as well as that of your workgroup. You can schedule meetings, locate free time, and find an available conference room. Chapter 9, "Using Mobile Notes on the Road," covers the topics you need to know in order to set up replication and usage for your mobile or remote Notes environment.

Part III: Developing Applications with Lotus Notes

Parts III and IV of this book are devoted to application development issues. Part III begins with a description of what type of application is a good candidate for a Notes application. Chapter 10, "What Makes a Good Notes Application?," discusses this topic both from a functional and an industry view. In a nutshell, Notes is a communication database. This means that applications that store information that needs to be communicated to a variety of users are good candidates for Notes. Chapter 11, "Tips on Application Design," gives you an overview of the development process and how to go about designing your Notes application.

Chapter 12, "Developing Forms," Chapter 13, "Developing Views," and Chapter 14, "Making Your Application Look Good and Work Well," use a Sales Automation database example to illustrate many of the concepts of Notes application design. These chapters show you how to develop a Notes application from scratch. Chapter 12 develops three forms for keeping track of companies, contacts, and sales opportunities. Chapter 13 shows you how to build views of your documents. The two views described in Chapter 13 are for your contacts and sales opportunities. Chapter 14 gives you a few tips on form and view design. It shows you some techniques for improving the aesthetic quality of your forms. You'll even learn that reverses and screens are more than football plays.

Chapter 15, "Using Lotus Components," introduces powerful new add-ons for Notes. With them, you can add a spreadsheet to your form, illustrate a project schedule, or use one of several other components to add capabilities that are very useful but would require a lot of effort if you had to build them yourself. Components are lightweight, which makes them ideal alternatives to invoking full-featured applications such as 1-2-3 or Excel. Chapter 16, "Developing a Workflow Application," describes workflow using Notes. In this chapter, you'll use two Lotus-supplied database templates to create two different workflow applications. You'll also learn about the process of creating a workflow application for your own company.

Part IV: Advanced Development

Part IV starts at the surface and dives to the depths of Notes development. Chapter 17, "Introduction to Advanced Development Features," introduces the new, more advanced features of Notes R4.5. It discusses LotusScript, Navigators, Agents, and simple actions. Each of these features is then covered in the next two chapters. Chapter 18, "Using LotusScript," is a tour of LotusScript, the new BASIC scripting language for Notes and many of the other Lotus products. Chapter 18 covers both the fundamental language elements and the classes and objects supplied with R4.5 for accessing Notes data. Chapter 19, "Using Navigators, Agents, and Simple Actions," shows you how to create your own Navigators to make your applications easier to use. It also shows you how to create agents and simple actions, which can automate parts of your application to make it more powerful.

In Chapter 20, "Developing an Advanced Application," you develop a project-tracking application that uses many of the new features of R4.5. You begin with a Notes R3 database and enhance it to use R4.5 capabilities such as actions, layout regions, simple actions, LotusScript, and Agents. Chapter 21, "Advanced Development with the Notes API and HiTest Tools," continues your advanced development theme, but at the next level. It shows you some examples using the Notes API (Application Programming Interface) and the HiTest tools. Chapter 22, "Using Third-Party Development Tools," completes the coverage of advanced development with a discussion of third-party tools. It shows examples using Microsoft's Visual Basic, Borland's Delphi, and Revelation Software's ViP.

Part V: Domino Server, the Internet, and Intranets

Parts V and VI should be of great interest to Lotus Business Partners (and many other readers as well). These parts cover what you need to know about integrating Lotus Notes with other systems. Part V covers Domino, the new name for the Notes server, and shows how Notes and Domino can be used with the Internet and intranets, one of the most important topics for businesses of all sizes.

Part V begins with Chapter 23, "Using the Notes Client on the Internet." With Notes, Lotus has entered the Internet browser war, along with Netscape and Microsoft. You can now use the Notes client for both traditional desktop Notes usage as well as for surfing the Web. Of course, the Notes client has many features that are still lacking in today's traditional Web browsers. For example, Notes now has the ability to cache Web pages, automatically pre-fetch Web pages, categorize and organize the cached pages, and share cached pages among several users. These are just a few of the new Internet client features found in the Notes client.

The rest of Part V concentrates on using the Domino Server as an Internet server. In Chapter 24, "Maximizing Your Domino Web Site and Applications with Advanced HTML," you will learn the fundamentals of building a Web site with Notes. Chapter 25, "Developing Web Applications with Domino.Action," covers the new Lotus technology consisting of frameworks for applications. With these frameworks, it's even easier to create your applications, because much of the more mundane work has already been done for you. Chapter 26, "Connecting Notes to the Internet with InterNotes," covers topics important when you're setting up a Notes server for the Internet. Chapter 27, "Setting Up an Intranet with Domino," tells you the basics of setting up an intranet for your company using Notes.

Part VI: Integrating and Connecting with Notes

Part VI covers the major aspects of integrating Notes with the Internet. This part explores the usage of Notes with other systems. It covers the gamut of topics, including telephony, fax, video, and legacy systems.

Chapter 28, "A Sampling of Third-Party Products for Lotus Notes," provides a taxonomy of third-party applications and gives specific examples of some applications in each of the categories. The categories covered include administration tools, development tools, and data import/export tools, among others. Chapter 29, "Integrating Notes with Phone, Fax, and Image," has information about integrating Notes with telephony applications. You'll see how you can integrate a desktop e-mail system so that a user can have e-mail, phone mail, and faxes delivered to the same inbox. Imagine being able to play your phone messages from your e-mail inbox or being able to view a fax by double-clicking on an e-mail icon. It's all there.

Chapter 30, "VideoNotes and RealTime Notes: Letting Business See What's Going On," discusses VideoNotes and RealTime Notes. These exciting new technologies bring video to the desktop. You can have interactive video conferencing and real-time discussions with colleagues who may be located thousands of miles away. Chapter 31, "Integrating Notes with Legacy Systems," contains important information you should consider when integrating Notes with systems you may currently be using. These considerations are important, because most companies these days have production systems that must be maintained and used in conjunction with Notes. Rarely is Notes used to completely displace a legacy system. Most of the time, Notes is used as a powerful adjunct to existing systems.

Part VII: Setting Up a Simple Notes Network

Part VII discusses the administration of simple Notes networks, which may have up to several hundred users. Chapter 32, "Initial Installation," begins coverage of administration and discusses initial installation. You'll learn about certification, domains, and the initial setup of a server and some workstations. Chapter 33, "Replication and Its Administration," discusses replication, one of the core features of Notes. You'll learn when a database is a replica of another database, how to schedule replication, and some points regarding replication of mail databases and shared mail databases.

Chapter 34, "Security Overview," examines security. You'll learn about cross-certification and the various types of ID files that Notes uses and how to use roles to delegate authority. Chapter 35, "Administering Users, Servers, and Databases," covers the main points you need to know about adding and deleting users, administering and configuring servers, and splitting and merging domains. You'll also get some hints on fixing corrupted databases.

Chapter 36, "Troubleshooting the System," and Chapter 37, "Troubleshooting Networks and Modems," are designed to give you some tools for troubleshooting your Notes system. Chapter 36 discusses system aspects of Notes and tells you how and where to find useful information in the various logs that Notes produces. Chapter 37 considers communication issues in networking and using modems.

Part VIII: Advanced Administration Topics

The last part of this book discusses some advanced administration topics. Chapter 38, "Managing a Large Notes Network," examines many of the issues you need to know and provides hints and tips for managing a large Notes network. Chapter 39, "Migrating from Notes R3 to R4.x," covers migration from Release 3 to Release 4.x of Notes. It gives you the fundamental information you need to begin planning for this major upgrade. Direct communication between companies is becoming more and more common. With this communication comes an increased productivity and better dialog among companies, their suppliers, and their customers. However, with this increasing communication comes the responsibility to ensure that your network security remains intact. Chapter 40, "Using Notes Between Different Companies," discusses this intercompany communication and some of the points you should consider before and while you have these links set up.

How This Book Was Written

This book was the result of a collaborative effort among all the authors. In a sense, we had a "virtual" project team, because the authors are geographically distributed and organizationally separate. As you can tell from the author biographies, all are professionals in the Notes field, and almost all work for Lotus Business Partner companies.

In assembling this team of distinguished authors, Notes was a key tool. I used the Lotus Notes Network and the Business Partner Forum as a means to find interested and qualified authors. Notes, in addition to Internet e-mail, was used to send the chapters to this book's editors.

Here are some interesting facts about this collaboration: The author team never held a single meeting. If you work in a large company, you might consider that amazing. We worked across five time zones in both Canada and the United States—from Toronto, Ontario, to Honolulu, Hawaii, to Clearwater, Florida, and points in between.

Notes, the Internet, and all the new communications technologies are allowing teams like this one to work and produce products such as this book. I hope you will be able to use the information here to decide whether Notes is for you, or to help you maximize and unleash the full potential of Notes in your organization.

Conventions Used in This Book

This book uses the following conventions:

- Menu names are separated from menu options by a vertical bar (|). For example, "File | Open" means "Select the File menu and choose the Open option."
- New terms appear in *italic*.
- All code appears in `monospace`.
- Words that you type appear in regular text in `monospace`.
- Placeholders (words that stand for what you actually type) appear in *`italic monospace`*.
- When a line of code is too long to fit on only one line of this book, it is broken at a convenient place and continued to the next line. The continuation of the line is preceded by a code continuation character (➡). You should type a line of code that has this character as one long line without breaking it.
- An ellipsis (...) in code indicates that the remaining or intervening code required to complete a statement or code structure has been omitted for the sake of brevity.
- The New To 4.0 icon tells you that the feature being discussed is new to Lotus Notes Release 4.x. To simplify matters, the New To 4.0 icon is used for all features in Releases 4.0, 4.1, and 4.11.
- The New To 4.5 icon is used to highlight features new to Release 4.5.

IN THIS PART

I

PART

The Business
of Lotus Notes

What Is Groupware, and Why Is It Important?

by Randall A. Tamura

CHAPTER 1

IN THIS CHAPTER

Groupware is a word that my spelling checker does not recognize. This is an indication, I suppose, that the word hasn't yet officially made it into the English language, but it certainly has made it into the world of business these days. In many ways, the word groupware actually has several different meanings and may mean something different to you depending upon your background and experience.

This chapter explores some of these different meanings, how they came about, how they fit together, and why groupware is important. It covers not only some of the technology questions involved with groupware, but also some of the forces that are becoming important in business and society today.

These topics are discussed before the core topics of Lotus Notes. It is essential to have a solid foundation of the business aspects of Notes to understand not only *what* Notes is, but *why* it's important.

Notes is primarily important because of the expanding, changing business environment. The business environment is becoming more and more competitive, demanding faster response times, higher quality, and increased productivity. The societal environment is also changing, with more people working out of their homes, company outsourcing, and increasing employment of contract labor. Technology is advancing at a dizzying pace. Today's state of the art machine is obsolete in a matter of months.

Changing relationships between companies and their customers and suppliers is becoming more based on technology. The ability to share information between companies is now almost as important as sharing information within your company. Finally, the Internet is rapidly becoming an important aspect of the information infrastructure.

In the short time from the printing of the first edition of this book to the second edition, the Internet has grown tremendously. There have even been Internet "brownouts" due to the enormous demand for communication bandwidth. Support of the Internet has grown from an important component of Notes to a central component. The growth of the Internet makes groupware even more important. Soon, we'll be sending not only e-mail across company boundaries, but our calendars and schedules as well. We're becoming more and more connected within our companies and between companies.

These are just a few of the reasons why groupware, and Notes, are important. With a thorough understanding of groupware, and Notes in particular, you will be well equipped to face today's challenges. You must participate or be left behind.

Groupware and Group Computing

The essence of software for groups is that it makes the group more productive. Management and sharing of information are what makes a group more productive. This idea is at the core of all software within the domain of groupware. Different software products provide features and functions to promote management, sharing, or the dissemination of information. Some packages may handle only one type of task, such as e-mail, and another may be strong in handling discussion databases. The total strength of a software package lies in its ability to handle all the different kinds of information management tasks.

Lotus has developed a model of groupware that defines the broad spectrum of applications of groupware. The Lotus model defines three areas of technology: communication, collaboration, and coordination. *Communication* encompasses electronic mail (or e-mail), *collaboration* involves technology that enables groups to share information in a public forum or workspace, and *coordination* involves the automation of business processes. Coordination is sometimes called workflow automation. (See Figure 1.1.)

FIGURE 1.1.

A groupware model—communication, collaboration, and coordination.

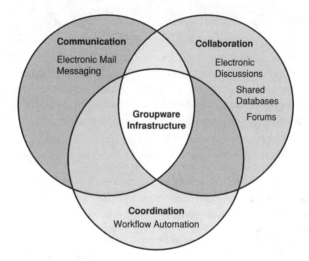

Groupware, by definition, means that the data for an application is used by members of a group. What exactly is the group? Does the group mean a department of 10 people or does it mean a major division of a large corporation? Normally, when you think of group, you tend to think of the departmental size group. This is natural, because while you work, this is the size of the group you most often interact with. Groupware, and Notes in particular, works well in this setting, but is not limited to a small group. Notes works very well in large corporate settings. In fact, a group really can range in size from a small department to an entire major corporation, can cut across departmental boundaries, and can even be used between different companies.

Communication: Electronic Mail and Messaging

One of the earliest forms of group communication was electronic mail. E-mail, as it is sometimes called, enables users to send an electronic version of a message. The system takes care of getting the message to its destination. As a user, you really don't care how it gets to the recipient as long as it gets there in a timely manner.

E-mail is much better than paper mail, mainly because it can reach its destination in seconds rather than days. Also, you can send e-mail to someone down the hall, across the street, or around the world with equal ease.

E-mail has the characteristic of privacy. When you address your message to a particular person, only that recipient receives the message. Of course, you can add a carbon-copy (cc) list to your message to add several other people, but as the sender it's your responsibility to denote exactly who should receive a copy.

NOTE

Carbon paper was used in the days of typewriters, before computers, before copiers, and before carbonless copies. A sheet of carbon paper was inserted between two white sheets of paper, and when the typewriter typed on the top page, the pressure would cause the carbon paper to make a copy on the second page. You needed one sheet of carbon paper and one sheet of white paper for each recipient. For those of you old enough to remember carbon paper, you can marvel at the fact that many young people have never seen or used it.

Using CompuServe, America Online, or another online service, it is easy today for people to have access to e-mail capabilities whether they are at home or at work. In everyday language, the word e-mail has even turned into a verb, as in "I'll e-mail you a document."

Electronic mail is implemented by a network of computers. When the originator of a message sends it, the first computer to receive it stores it, and then checks to see if the recipient is local to that machine. If not, the message is sent on in a chain-like fashion from computer to computer until the message arrives at the recipient's machine. This technology is sometimes called *store and forward* because of the way that the messages are transmitted by intermediate stops from the sender to the receiver.

Another characteristic of e-mail is that it is sometimes called a *push* technology. This means that the sender is "pushing" the message to the receiver. A receiver of e-mail never originates a *pull* of the message. Thus, e-mail is a sort of one-way communication from the sender to the receiver. Of course, once the receiver has received the original message, he or she can send a response, which is essentially another one-way message back to the originator.

When using e-mail it is common to attach separate documents to the mail message. For example, someone may attach a spreadsheet that includes a budget, or may include an image file, or even a document or report. The ability to attach documents to mail is important, and when privacy issues are involved, one can even encrypt the message and document files. On the other hand, when a document should be shared among several people, and when there should be controls on who is able to edit the document, e-mail is the wrong tool.

Collaboration: Shared Information

Collaboration involves shared information. This technology is inherently different from one-way electronic mail. Collaboration relies on a public, shared workspace where information can be created and used by all of the members of a particular group. If you have an account on one of the online services such as CompuServe, America Online, or Prodigy, you may be familiar with their discussion forums. If you use the Internet, you may be familiar with Usenet discussion groups. This section discusses several types of applications for collaborative, shared information.

Electronic Discussions

Electronic discussion databases are sometimes called electronic forums. The forums of ancient Rome (even older than carbon paper) were places where many people could have a spoken dialog on a particular topic. Electronic forums, like their ancient counterparts, provide an opportunity for a group of people to discuss a particular topic or set of topics. An electronic forum is similar to e-mail, but with a public flavor. When you read an e-forum, you can see everyone else's comments, and when you contribute, all other members of the forum can see your words. Also, comments that are contributed are typically kept for longer periods of time as a repository of stored knowledge.

E-forums (discussion databases) have several advantages over their ancient namesakes, and several differences from electronic mail. One difference between an electronic and real forum is that the participants do not all have to be present at the same time. In ancient Rome, to listen, agree, debate, or argue with a person, both people had to be present at the forum at the same time. If your home was located outside of Rome, you had to travel to discuss what was on your mind.

E-forums enable people to participate in an electronic discussion from different locations as well as at different times. The ability to participate in a discussion database with people that you may never meet, see, touch, smell, or hear is actually quite profound, when you think about it. You can still agree, disagree, debate and argue, but need never meet face-to-face.

The public nature of e-forums distinguish them from e-mail. When you post a message to an e-forum, it is available for all the other participants to see. You as the originator do not control who can receive the message. In a way, a message you post to an e-forum is like a radio broadcast and may be heard by many people, or no one. If someone answers your message, it's like a phone caller on a radio talk show, and his or her response is heard by all participants.

In a manufacturing company, a typical discussion database might be for the design of a particular part. In a software company, a discussion database might refer to a software product. In each case, many people can interact together to discuss the topic. Frequently a question is asked by one person and answered by a peer.

More and more companies are collaborating in the design of new products and services. Companies are finding that the old model of complete vertical integration within a single company from design to manufacture no longer makes sense. With all of the partnering, subcontracting, and outsourcing in industry, there is a clear need to communicate between companies.

For example, suppose a major auto manufacturer needs to design windshield wipers for a new car. This task might be subcontracted to a small manufacturing company. The ideal way for these companies to work together would be to have a common electronic discussion database that can include design information. The windshield wipers cannot be designed in isolation from the design of the hood, for example, and the design of the hood must take into account the windshield wipers.

Groupware, and Notes in particular, enable companies both large and small to have electronic discussions that speed the development of products and services.

Management of Quality

The International Standards Organization (ISO) has issued a quality document, usually referred to as "ISO 9000." This document describes a set of criteria for a quality certification. This certification is especially important in countries outside the U.S., but is increasingly becoming important in the U.S. as well.

The essence of the ISO 9000 standard is that it dictates that a company should document the processes that it uses to make its products and/or services, and then the company should follow the documented processes. Although the concept sounds simple, its execution can be surprisingly difficult.

In fact, the documentation of processes, and the implementation of the documented processes, is an ideal application for Lotus Notes and groupware. This is because Notes provides a solid base for creating, maintaining, and managing documents, and its shared information capabilities provide an excellent platform for making the documented processes available to all employees of a company.

There are several third-party applications that help companies implement the ISO 9000 standard with Notes. These products typically provide a framework of Notes databases that a company can use to implement its ISO 9000 program. While Notes provides the platform, the work that a company does to analyze and document its processes is the real benefit to implementing ISO 9000.

Customer Support

One of the ideal applications for groupware is in the area of customer support. The characteristics of this application are that customers (which may be employees within your own company in a PC support application) call in to a call center. The call center retains information about the caller, the transaction, and perhaps a history of previous calls from this person.

For a financial company, a group database may contain customer information about a client's financial account. For example, a mutual fund company, an insurance company, or bank may have records about a customer. These records probably indicate when the customer calls in with questions or requests transactions. The information from previous transactions and calls can be available, no matter which representative answers the call.

Sometimes a representative helps the customer, but may or may not be able to complete the transaction. For example, if the customer is requesting technical help, the technician may ask the customer to try various experiments to see if they fix the problem.

If the caller (customer) hangs up, tries the proposed solutions and they don't work, the customer has to call for additional help. On the second call, a different technician may answer the phone. Here is where a group database can be extremely helpful. If the first technician records the information from the first call, when the customer calls again, the second technician has access to all the information, and the customer does not have to repeat the details of the problem.

To further enhance support, this example can be taken one step further. You could make technical support information available for your customer to access on his or her own. There might be several ways to accomplish this. One way is a fax-on-demand system, which enables a caller to call a computer and request phone documents to be faxed back to his fax machine by touch tone. The customer need only have a phone and fax machine—no special software or equipment.

Another way to make information available to the customer would be to provide the customer with access to a Lotus Notes database or set of databases, such as discussion databases. These discussion databases could contain product support information and could include information from one customer that another customer might find valuable. Support forums are available today on online services such as CompuServe.

Yet another approach would be to make information available with an Internet Web Page. The World Wide Web provides access to information to people who have access to the Internet and a Web browser. It seems as if almost every company these days has a web address: `\\http:www.somecompany.com`.

New with release 4.5 of Notes, the Domino server capability lets you turn your Notes server into an Internet server. The InterNotes Web Publisher provided in release 4.0 (and provided previously as a separate product) is another tool that lets companies leverage their investment in information. By using Notes as your information base, you can selectively publish information you use inside the company to the external world. This saves time and money that would otherwise be spent in rework and administration.

The Mobile Worker

In the 1980s and 1990s a new form of worker began emerging: the mobile worker. The advent of portable personal computers has enabled many professionals to be productive while away from the office. For example, any type of salesperson can use a personal computer to make presentations, perform analyses, and create what-if scenarios while talking directly with customers. The ability to take programs and data to a customer leverages the value of that data. Like a lever, a small amount of valuable information, when available at the right time and place, can provide enormous benefits.

Telecommuting, or working from home by means of telecommunications, is rapidly becoming popular at many companies. In some major metropolitan areas, it is even encouraged by the government as a way to reduce smog. In Los Angeles, for example, major fines have been levied on some companies that did not do enough to reduce smog. Telecommuting is actively encouraged by the Los Angeles government as one means to reduce smog. Telecommuting is also popular with employees because it enables them to spend more time with their families.

While being able to transport information in a mobile computer is valuable, being able to access information while on the road is even more important. For example, a real estate salesman could plug a computer into the phone and download relevant information from a multiple listing service directly from a client's house. An executive could download e-mail from a hotel room and upload answers. With airplane phone service, it's even conceivable that information can be uploaded to a plane flying at 37,000 feet (now that's really uploading!).

What used to be the rare province of astronauts, in terms of computing and communications, is now becoming available to all of us. Although the astronaut is perhaps the ultimate mobile worker, most all professionals take business trips, make sales calls, visit vendors or suppliers, attend conferences, or for some other reason work while away from their desks. With advancing technology, working away from offices will be as normal as working in the office.

Collaboration Review

The main characteristic of all the collaborative applications is that they involve shared information. The information is created by any one of several people that belong to the group and may be used by other members of the group. One reason that groupware has become so popular is that there are many, many applications that can use the information sharing model.

Coordination: Workflow Automation

Workflow automation is a buzzword, but what does it actually mean? In companies these days, a job or task frequently is part of a larger job. In other words, it is part of the bigger picture. For example, take the situation of an employee that would like to be reimbursed for travel expenses. There are likely several people involved, even in small companies.

The travel expense form is filled out by the employee herself. The form is then given to, say, an administrator. The administrator may review the form and, in a small company, create a check and send it to the owner for signature. That's three people and a simple process. In a larger company, the form may travel to the employee's manager, the Human Resources department, the Payroll department, and then be processed by many more people before the final check is received by the employee. (See Figure 1.2.)

FIGURE 1.2.
A workflow process.

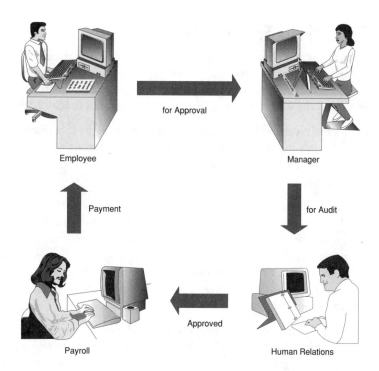

Regardless of the number of people involved in doing the work, there is a process involved, and a flow of the work. For example, in a large corporation the Human Resources department won't process the form unless it is signed by the manager. Payroll won't cut the check unless it's approved by HR. So, the work must flow from the employee to the manager, to HR, and finally to Payroll. It wouldn't make sense to send it to Payroll first.

Workflow automation is the automating of the flow of work from one person or job function to the next. In the preceding example, using software, information is electronically passed from the employee to the manager, to HR, and finally to Payroll. By using groupware, the flow of information can be improved among all the people.

As a very nice by-product of the workflow automation, you can also get improved management reports that can provide information such as: How many items have been processed, how many are left unprocessed, which items are unprocessed, how long does each step in the process take, and so forth.

Why Is Groupware Important?

You've now seen some of the example applications for groupware. But what makes groupware important? The answer lies in several dimensions: the competitive business environment, the societal environment, and technology. First some of the forces at work along these dimensions are covered, followed by discussions about why groupware is important because of these forces.

The Business Environment

The environment for most businesses is very competitive these days. The competition is there trying to make better products more cheaply and quickly, and to provide better service. This intense pressure is in many cases global in nature, so your competitor may be down the street or around the world. You may be unfortunate enough to have both types of competition.

In order to meet and beat the competition, you must be able to cut the time it takes you from the design to the delivery of your product or service. At the same time, you must improve the quality, and in many cases you must provide products that are more flexible and individualized.

One study by an industrial company found that a six-month delay in project completion resulted in a 32 percent loss in after-tax profit. This type of consequence is found in many industries, and arises because the most profitable time of a product's life is the time right after its release. If there is little or no competition at that time, the price and profit can be high. After a very short time, if a product is successful, the competition will arrive on the scene, which will cause prices and profits to lower. It pays to be first, and the longer the lead time, the greater the impact on profitability.

By providing customizable products to market faster, many companies are finding that their customers become more loyal. If you can cement long-term relationships with your customers, it results in longer-term profits. One key to solidifying these relationships, of course, is better communication with your customer.

The Societal Environment

There are several societal forces at work today. Companies are treating the labor pool as much more of a variable cost than a fixed cost. This has resulted in the recent downsizings, rightsizings, or plain layoffs at many companies in the U.S. Following the layoffs, many of these same companies found that they could not do all the work that was required, so they have increasingly turned to contract employees or temporary labor.

This temporary labor may manifest itself in several forms and has many names. Sometimes companies simply hire temporary employees, or "temps." In other cases they subcontract work to an outside company that is responsible for completing a task or project. Other times they "outsource" the work. Sometimes, in the course of outsourcing, employees transfer from the original company to the vendor. This has become quite common in the area of computer information systems support. Large companies such as IBM, EDS, and CSC have major contracts with many companies to provide these services.

Sometimes, in the course of the outsourcing, support transfers to a remote location. While this centralization of support can provide efficiencies of scale, it may introduce an aspect of telecommunications that was not present before the changes.

In an environment where employees are becoming more and more transient, it is important to capture their knowledge of the business in a shared, reusable database. When employees stayed with a company for 25 years, a company could count on the workers' knowledge of the business. With the movement of today's more volatile labor pool, the business knowledge must be captured in a database, and the process knowledge must be captured in a workflow.

In addition to companies changing, individuals are changing their outlook as well. Many of the displaced workers are forming their own companies and/or are working from their homes. This is creating a growing set of small companies, sometimes called the *SOHO* marketplace, for *Small Office/Home Office*. This trend toward SOHO offices is made possible by technology.

Small/home offices can now cheaply buy computers and combination fax/scanner/copier/printer devices. Armed with technology, these smaller companies often can compete well because of their lower overhead and their attention to details that larger companies may sometimes miss. These new small companies are a growing force in America. They are important because either you are one, or you may need to communicate with one.

This movement to smaller, faster-moving businesses means that the number of interconnections a company must deal with is becoming larger. Often these experts are available in small businesses, not necessarily the large ones. To deal with this situation, a company must upgrade its communication infrastructure.

Technology

Technology is improving in almost all dimensions at once. Computing power has been roughly doubling every one and a half years, and has been doing so for the past 25 years. In just the era of the IBM PC, the Intel processors have moved from the original 4.77Mhz 8088 processor to 200MHz Pentium Pro chips. In the time it took to write this book, the upper end of Intel processors moved from 180Mhz to 200Mhz, and by the time you read it, there will probably be an even higher maximum.

Communications at home by modem for PCs used to take place at 300 or 1200 baud and now 28,800 baud is fairly standard. ISDN modems will roughly double this rate again, and for major industrial companies communication rates are measured in the millions of bits per second. The Ethernet standard was 10 Mbits for many years, but recently 100 Mbit Fast Ethernet has become available and is growing in acceptance.

The story is pretty much the same for technology across the board: It will get cheaper, faster, and better. Period.

Speeding Up Processes

These trends are affecting individuals and companies now, and will continue to make changes in the industrial landscape. The companies that survive will recognize the changes and proactively take them into consideration in their strategic planning. Old ways of doing business must make way for new methods.

To improve the time to market, companies can use groupware to change processes that today are serial to processes that are concurrent. Concurrent engineering enables companies to have many people create, review, and update information simultaneously. In a way, this book was created using concurrent techniques. Multiple authors were able to write chapters separately in order to speed the time of development for this book. The authors, in fact, are geographically dispersed across the Western Hemisphere, from Hawaii to the East Coast of the United States, and from Florida to Toronto, Canada. This concurrent development enables the authors to get this information to you faster than if any one of them developed the book individually.

Today, many companies use Electronic Data Interchange (EDI) to exchange business information that was previously exchanged on paper. Transactions such as purchase orders and invoices are today routinely exchanged between large companies. There are great savings to both companies when using electronic exchange because a lot of the manual labor has been eliminated.

In essence, if one company has data in an electronic form, and another company could use this information, exchanging it electronically requires no re-entry of the data. In another example, major manufacturing companies exchange CAD/CAM (Computer Aided Design/Computer Aided Manufacturing) data electronically. This data electronically represents the paper blueprints of previous generations. By exchanging this information electronically, a company can give a supplier the exact specifications of the parts it wishes to buy. This exchange of information not only improves the accuracy, but the timeliness of the data as well.

Changes in the Organizational Structure

Organizations that embrace change empower their employees and move information and decision making lower in the organizations. Layers of management have been removed in the recent downsizings, resulting in flatter, leaner organizations. With this flatter organization come improvements in processes and customer service.

Groupware is a critical technology that enables companies to operate in this flatter organizational structure. In traditional, deeply hierarchical structures, managers play a key communication role, transmitting information laterally between organizational units. When the organization becomes flatter and managers have a much wider span of control, performing this task becomes much, much harder because of the amount of information necessary to communicate.

Groupware enables communication and information to flow directly among the employees without many of the traditional organizational speed bumps. Managers who must be in the communication path just slow the process down. Enabling employees to communicate directly with one another is a key to improving cycle times. Companies that adopt groupware find that it is a key competitive and strategic advantage because of the improved communications paths provided. Those that don't improve their communications will wonder what hit them.

Relationships Between Companies, Customers, and Suppliers

If the people dealing directly with customers can have access to timely and accurate information, they will be able to service the customer better. This is a simple principle, but today, many customer representatives do not have access to the timely information they need to help customers.

Again, a groupware product such as Notes can provide this information to customer support personnel. In addition, Notes can provide management information directly from the support databases, resulting in a better understanding of important issues and problems.

When customers are provided with accurate and timely information, they become more loyal to the company that provides the excellent service. In the long run, this loyalty results in higher revenues and profits for the company.

Suppliers, too, can benefit from improved communications using groupware. Notes databases can be shared with suppliers. The information in the databases could include items such as product specifications, administrative information, and technical support information. The supplier can also add information to the databases so that company employees can benefit from direct input from the supplier.

The benefit of sharing information with suppliers is the shortening of the development cycle and the improvement of quality through improved communication.

The Internet

No discussion of the communication environment could be complete without including the Internet. The Internet is probably one of the most discussed topics in the information processing industry today. In one sense, the Internet is just a bunch of computers (admittedly a very large bunch) that have been linked together with the ability to send information to each other. From a technological point of view, this definition is essentially correct. However, the Internet phenomenon has now reached a different point in its development—it has reached the point where it affects society.

The Internet affects not only the society in the United States, but worldwide. The creation and linking of all these computers is probably one of the most important technological events of this century and will have effects well into the next century. Previous communications vehicles were one-to-one (such as regular mail), or perhaps one-to-many with technology such as radio, television, and the movies. The Internet has now enabled many-to-many discussions, worldwide.

The Internet's World Wide Web capabilities are still in their infancy, but it's already clear, as Bill Gates has said, that the growing Internet phenomenon is the most important event in computing since the introduction of the original IBM PC. The Internet is already affecting every aspect of our lives. Today it is not uncommon for the different forms of communication to interrelate to one another. For example, it is common to see World Wide Web addresses shown on television or printed in newspapers when relevant to a specific topic. In essence, this provides a manual linkage from a newspaper, for example, to a specific page on the Web.

Groupware products must be able to interact with the Internet, be able to use its infrastructure, and finally must be able to leverage the current benefits of the Internet to even higher levels of capability. You'll see in future chapters how Lotus Notes can not only work with the Internet, but can be used as a strategic Internet platform.

With the release of Domino in Notes 4.5, you can create your own World Wide Web site using Notes as the means to create your documents. With the InterNotes Web Navigator, a company can provide Internet access to each employee's desktop while at the same time maintaining central control over content and access. Finally, with the Personal Web Navigator, individuals can now use the Notes client as a browser with capabilities similar to Netscape Navigator or Microsoft Internet Explorer. Now you can use Notes to browse the World Wide Web directly.

Summary

Groupware is a powerful new tool for business. It enables communication, collaboration, and coordination among employees, customers, and suppliers. Applications of groupware include electronic mail, electronic forums or discussions, workflow automation, the management of quality, customer support, support for mobile workers, and many other possibilities.

Communication is the part of the groupware infrastructure that includes e-mail. Electronic mail enables communication from an individual to another individual or group. It's one of the oldest forms of group communication and continues as an important aspect of groupware.

Collaboration involves shared information. This is inherently different from e-mail because of the concept of a shared database. When someone stores information in the shared database, he or she does not necessarily know who will read the document. The document is actually *pulled* by an interested party, rather than being *pushed* from the sender, as in e-mail.

Coordination involves the structuring and automation of work processes. Essentially, the flow of information through a work process is done electronically, rather than by paper, as is frequently done today.

This chapter also discussed some key aspects of the business and societal environment that affect groupware. Business today is moving faster and faster. Competition is rapidly becoming global. The labor pool is becoming more transient. Outsourcing is becoming more and more common. Quality is no longer a buzzword, it's a requirement to be able to compete in the global marketplace. Processes must be improved. Organizations are becoming flatter. Companies must deal with a myriad of customers, suppliers, and sometimes even competitors.

The Internet is changing the communication environment completely, and Notes is an ideal platform to use with the Internet. You can use the Notes server as your Internet server and the Notes client as your Internet client.

Amid all of this change in the environment, a common thread emerges. It is becoming increasingly important for companies to capture and manage the information they control. They must be able to store and retrieve critical business information. They must be able to share their information, in a controlled way, within their company, and among their business partners. Companies that understand these trends will not stand idly by and watch. They will take proactive steps to manage their critical information resources.

The next chapter discusses how Lotus Notes can be used for some of these groupware applications and can help you and your organization improve your productivity, speed your processes, and take proactive control of your company's future.

What Is Lotus Notes?

by Randall A. Tamura

IN THIS CHAPTER

CHAPTER 2

Since the first release of Lotus Notes, any document, magazine article, or book that discusses it must first ask and answer the following question: What is Lotus Notes? I'm sure that in the early 1980s—when electronic spreadsheets were first implemented—people used to ask what Lotus 1-2-3 was. People no longer ask about the nature of spreadsheets, and in the future, a question about the nature of Notes will seem just as superfluous. For now, though, it's an honest question, and one that must still be answered.

People still ask what Lotus Notes is, because the product combines many technologies and does not fit easily into our other categories for software such as databases, word processors, or e-mail. In a sense, Notes is really all of these things, and more. Notes has created a new category called groupware, and Notes is the product that typifies the category. Although there are several other products now implementing some of Notes' capabilities, none of the other products can yet match the broad coverage of Lotus Notes.

Notes itself is also in transition. With Release 4.5, Lotus has split Notes into two pieces: the client, which is still called Notes, and the server, which is now called Domino. For all practical purposes, you can think of Domino as just a new name for the Notes server, but as you'll see in Part V, "Domino Server, the Internet, and Intranets," there is much more to Domino.

Notes as Groupware Infrastructure

As mentioned in Chapter 1, "What Is Groupware, and Why Is It Important?," a groupware infrastructure must be able to support (at least) three types of information management: communication, collaboration, and coordination. You will see throughout this book that Notes provides an excellent platform for these information management models. With these models, it is possible to create a rich set of applications to support business well into the next decade.

This chapter discusses the three types of information management and how they appear to users in Notes. As I take you through a tour of the models, I will point out various items about the Notes user interface and their functions.

Following the description of the user aspects of Notes, some of the features available to developers are described. Developing applications within Notes can be simple and done by experienced users, or can be very complex enterprise-wide development efforts, accomplished by professional programmers.

The last part of this chapter is a brief overview of some of the administrative aspects of Notes, including security and replication. The overview provided here introduces you to some of the important concepts so that you can quickly understand the rich details provided in later chapters.

This chapter, then, is a quick tour of the vast landscape of Notes. It uses the same approach as the entire book, providing you with user information, developer information, and administrative information. Once you have taken this tour, you can explore the depths, the heights, and the nooks and crannies of Notes with the rest of this book.

> **NOTE**
>
> Many of the features available in Notes 4.5 were introduced in Release 4.0, 4.1, or 4.5, so to make things easier, I'll sometimes refer to these releases collectively as R4 or R4.x.

Communication

To support the communication information sharing mode, Notes has electronic mail. In Release 4.5, Notes is building on the highly successful cc:Mail user interface introduced in Release 4.0. Because Notes will now have the cc:Mail interface for mail, it will be easier to train users and to migrate to Notes mail from cc:Mail. Also, with R4, Notes has a new space-saving feature called Single Copy Object Store, or SCOS that allows Notes to store a single copy of the body of a mail document that has been sent to multiple users.

Figure 2.1 shows the new Notes mail user interface. The screen is divided into three panes. The size of the panes is adjustable, and this screen shows the hierarchical folders and views in the left pane, a list of the mail in the right pane, and a preview of the message in the lower pane.

This screen can also be used to illustrate several other aspects of the Notes product. First you'll see that along the top of the screen you find the typical title bar and menu line. In the title line you find the product name, Lotus Notes. In the mail window within Notes, you find another title line, which contains the database name—in this case, the user's name—and finally the current view. In Figure 2.1, the current view's name is Discussion Threads.

With the Discussion Threads view, you can see the thread of conversation on a particular topic, even if the mail for this topic has arrived on interspersed dates. You can see via a note's indentation its reply, the reply to the reply, and so forth. This is a great help in organizing your e-mail.

In Notes, e-mail is handled within a database. This means that most of the features described here are available in other databases as well. For example, Views are a fundamental part of every Notes database. E-mail provides a convenient context to describe views, but they are not unique to e-mail.

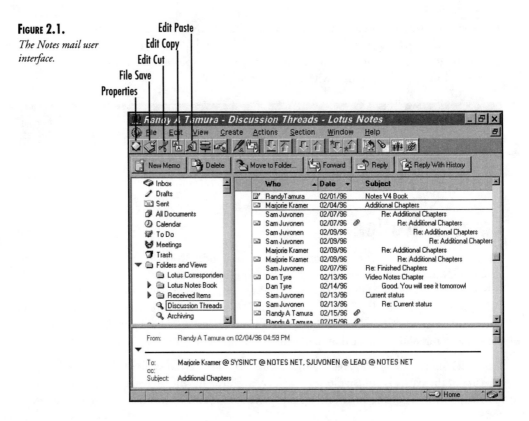

FIGURE 2.1.
The Notes mail user interface.

Edit Paste
Edit Copy
Edit Cut
File Save
Properties

Views and Folders

A view is a way to look at the data in the database. Each database may have several views. For example, Figure 2.1 shows several built-in views (and folders). Each has its own icon, with names such as Inbox, Drafts, Sent, All Documents, Calendar, To Do, Meetings, and Trash. The Calendar and Meetings views are new to Notes 4.5. The others were available in Release 4.

These views represent different ways of looking at different subsets of the same information in the database. The views are set up by the original designer of the database, but you can have your own user-defined views of the database as well. A view is really a predefined query that performs two tasks:

■ Selecting documents that meet specified criteria

■ Sorting documents for presentation to the user

Folders provide similar presentation and sorting options, but do not have selection criteria. As a user, you can put any documents you choose into a folder. The icons to the left of Folders look like a manila folder, and the icons to the left of Views look like a magnifying glass. Folders and Views are discussed in more detail in Chapter 6, "Views, Documents, and Forms", and in Chapter 13, "Developing Views."

The view in Figure 2.1 is Discussion Threads, and you can see in the right pane that the e-mail has been sorted by date. The date used, however, is only for the highest level in the discussion thread hierarchy. This represents the date of the original note. The Discussion Threads view is very useful because it groups e-mail into "threads." That is, if you send an e-mail message to someone, and they reply to you, the reply is stored next to the original message. Keeping all the related messages close to each other enables you to see the history of one topic, or thread, of conversation. Another view such as All Documents does not keep these threads together and instead treats each message as an independent item.

If you think about how a typical e-mail system organizes your messages, you see that having different views of the same information is a powerful organizing tool. In a typical e-mail system today, you must put a piece of mail in a single, specific folder if you want to keep it for future reference. You can organize your folders in any manner that makes sense, but the file itself is treated like a piece of paper you file. It goes into a specific folder. If you filed a document based on the sender but you want to look it up by topic, you're out of luck.

Contrast this with Notes views and folders. With views, you can look at the messages organized by the sender, or you can view by date, or in fact you can make a custom folder that organizes by topics that you select. The data is not duplicated in each of these views; the views only provide different ways of viewing or organizing your data. The ability to view the same data from a variety of perspectives enables you to quickly find the information you're looking for.

Although each database in Notes typically has several views, the views vary from one database to another. For example, the views in the mail database shown in Figure 2.1 are typically not used for a discussion database or a workflow application. Views, then, provide an organizing context for the database to which they apply. They enable you to view your information from different perspectives.

The Preview Pane

In Figure 2.1 you'll see that I sent an e-mail message to coauthors Marjorie Kramer and Sam Juvonen. The bottom pane shows you the first few lines, including the sender and receiver of the message and the subject. If you change the height of the window, it will show the text of the message as well.

In other kinds of databases, the preview pane at the bottom of the screen shows you a Notes document, so this pane is also called the document pane. An e-mail message is just a special kind of document found in e-mail databases. In an expense account database, for example, you might find that an expense account document is shown in the bottom Preview pane.

You can change the size of all of the panes on the screen, and you can even hide one or two of the three panes. The ability to customize the look and feel of each database greatly enhances the ease of use of Notes.

Action Bars

At the top of the mail window in Figure 2.1 is a set of buttons that begins with the button New Memo. This set of buttons is called an Action Bar. The Action Bar is a new feature introduced in R4.0. This button bar appears at the top of the mail view. If you design a Notes application, you can design buttons to go on the Action Bar, but an Action Bar is not required.

In previous releases of Notes, the designer could include buttons that would appear in the document, but if the user scrolled the document, the buttons would move out of sight. With the new Action Bars, the buttons are stationary at the top of the view (or form) and always available.

SmartIcons

Near the top of the screen, just beneath the menu bar, you find a row of Lotus SmartIcons. Lotus uses these icons across its entire line of applications. Notes includes more than 150 icons covering all of the standard operations such as copy, cut, and paste, and most of the Notes menu item commands.

The leftmost SmartIcon that you see is the icon for Properties. Nearly every element in Notes has properties associated with it, and pressing the Properties button displays a tabbed dialog box—called an InfoBox—that enables you to view and change the properties for the object. The next icon is the File Save icon, which is used to save documents. The next three icons are for Edit Cut, Edit Copy, and Edit Paste, which operate on the standard Windows Clipboard.

By now you may have noticed that several of the icons have two-word names, such as File Save or Edit Copy. They have these names so that you can correlate them to their menu counterparts. For example, File Save indicates that this SmartIcon performs the same action as the Save menu option found on the File menu. Edit Copy indicates that the Copy function is located on the Edit menu.

To help you further with the SmartIcons, if you move the mouse pointer to an icon and leave it positioned over the icon for approximately half a second (without pressing any buttons), a balloon help item pops up to tell you what the icon's function is (see Figure 2.2). The icon is a jar of paste, and the function is Edit Paste.

The rest of the SmartIcons are for editing and forwarding mail, navigating through your documents, expanding and collapsing your view, and for searching for documents. You can customize the SmartIcons that appear in your window. In addition, they are context-sensitive, so

Notes displays a set of SmartIcons that is most relevant to the context in which you're working. SmartIcons are discussed in more detail in Chapter 5, "The Notes Workspace and Databases."

FIGURE 2.2.

SmartIcons with balloon help.

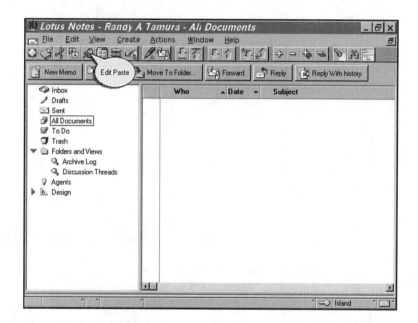

The Bottom Line: The Notes Status Bar

In any business discussion, you should always discuss the bottom line. In Notes, the bottom line is called the Status Bar. In Figure 2.1, you can see that the Status Bar has three sections to the right, containing two icons with the word Home between them. You'll also note that the Status Bar is broken up into several sections, with each section containing a little triangle pointing up. Each of these sections may contain information depending upon your context in Notes. The triangles indicate that by pressing that area, a pop-up list of items appears. The rightmost three sections of the Status Bar are discussed in this section, but all of them are discussed in Chapter 5.

When you click the icon at the far right, which symbolizes an in-box, a selection of mail-related options pops up, as shown in the lower right Figure 2.3. These options include creating, sending, and reading electronic mail. By providing the e-mail options at the bottom right, they become easily accessible from within Notes in virtually any context.

2

WHAT IS LOTUS
NOTES?

FIGURE **2.3.**

Mail options.

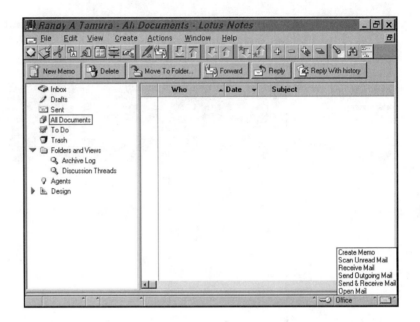

The second section from the right pops up a list of the locations that the user may select, as shown in the lower right of Figure 2.4. The concept of a location is a new, welcome feature to Notes R4. With today's mobile use of Notes on laptops, and when configurations vary depending upon your location, it is desirable for the system to keep track of the differences in the configurations.

FIGURE **2.4.**

Location options.

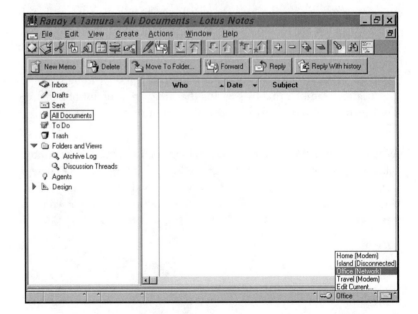

For example, I use a laptop computer in several ways. When I'm in the office, I have it connected with an Ethernet LAN connection to my Notes server. When I take it to a client site, however, I might use the system in a disconnected (Island) mode, or use a Modem to connect to my Notes server. Keep in mind that the Notes server is typically different from your file and print server.

If I'm traveling and using the system from a hotel room, I might need to use special codes in order to use the phone system. By using Notes locations, I can customize each of these situations and have Notes retain all of the configuration information such as port usage, phone numbers, access codes and so forth. In addition, if different people all share the same laptop computer, each person can have a different set of locations that apply to him or her.

The third icon from the right shows a small key. This key represents your access to the database. Notes has seven levels of access for databases. These levels are (from highest to lowest): Manager, Designer, Editor, Author, Reader, Depositor, and No Access. By pressing the small key icon at the bottom of the screen, you can see your access to the database. You should also be aware that your access can vary from one database to another. For example, you could be a manager of one database, but have No Access to another database.

The Personal and InterNotes (Server) Web Navigators

Figure 2.5 shows the three-pane view of R4.5's new Personal Web Navigator. It lets you cruise the Web from your Notes client. It offers the same powerful features as your regular Notes client but adds the capability to view Web sites as well.

FIGURE 2.5.

Personal Web Navigator.

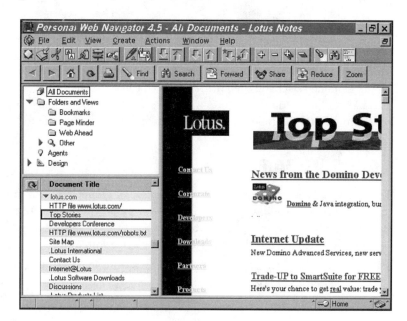

The Personal Web Navigator can also view Web pages in full-screen mode, which is similar to browsers such as Netscape Navigator and Microsoft Internet Explorer. You can connect to the Internet via a phone line, just as you can with other Web browsers. The Personal Web Navigator is covered in more detail in Chapter 23, "Using the Notes Client on the Internet."

Figure 2.6 shows the home page of the InterNotes Web Navigator, also called the server Web Navigator.

FIGURE 2.6.

InterNotes Web Navigator.

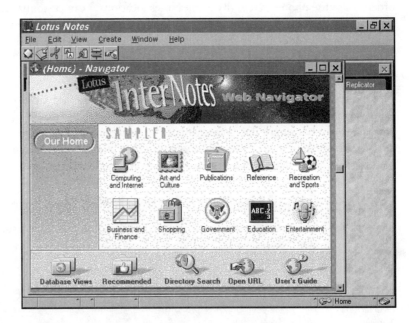

This version of the Navigator allows companies to maintain a single connection to the Internet via the Domino server and then distribute Web pages to Notes users via the Notes network. This allows administrators to maintain Novell's SPX/IPX within their companies without converting to TCP/IP. This powerful feature is described in more detail in Part V.

Collaboration

The idea of collaborative computing is at the core of groupware. It is through collaboration that several people working on an assignment or project can complete the job better, faster, less expensively, and with higher quality than any of them individually. The key concept in collaborative computing is the ability to share information.

To be effective, however, sharing information must be more than placing a file or a set of files on a common disk area of a local area network—we've been able to do that for years. Several key elements are necessary to really take advantage of collaborative computing.

First, users must be able to find the information that they need. These days, companies have gigabytes (billions of bytes) or terabytes (trillions of bytes) of information on their local area networks. An organizing mechanism must be used so that users can quickly access the information that is required for their jobs.

Secondly, users need more than just the data; they need applications that can use the data and turn it into useful information. When a customer or client is on the phone, that person's account number is more than a series of digits, it's the key to unlock the information necessary to provide excellent service for the customer. Applications that are based on the information stored in Notes can provide better service, improve processes and productivity, and can improve the quality of goods you provide to customers.

A third requirement of collaborative computing is security. Information stored in your databases must be protected. Most security needs are much more sophisticated than simple network file sharing enables. For example, users frequently have particular roles within an organization. A role might be a manager, system administrator, or personnel specialist. Although a system administrator typically has access to all files on the network, the company may not want that person to have access to salary information for all of the employees. A personnel specialist, on the other hand, may be authorized for the salary information, but should be limited in his or her ability to grant access to the file to other employees.

To see how Notes organizes data, I will continue this tour with a look at Notes databases. I'll cover the three topics of information organization, applications, and security through the next few sections. These topics are covered in depth in Chapters 5 and 6, but the next few sections give you a brief introduction to some of the important concepts in Notes.

Unstructured Databases Versus Structured Databases

Notes databases are different from typical relational databases with which you may be familiar. The primary difference is that Notes databases are really designed to handle unstructured data, while traditional relational databases are optimized for structured data. This characterization is not absolute because traditional databases can handle unstructured data and Notes can handle structured information. To examine the difference, let's look at some typical structured and unstructured information.

A typical structured, relational database system is good for handling information such as account numbers, account balances, names and addresses, times, dates, and other dollar amounts. The relational database is good for this information because by providing a key, the database system can quickly query the database and retrieve the relevant information for a customer record. These relational systems are in widespread use in financial and accounting applications and any application where discrete, structured information is stored. A primary characteristic of this information is that typically the data fields are fixed-length.

Examples of desktop relational database systems include Microsoft Access, Borland dBASE and Paradox, and Lotus Approach. Client/Server examples include Oracle, Sybase, and similar systems. At the core of these systems is the concept of tables, consisting of rows and columns. Each column typically stores a certain type of information such as Name, Address, or Account Balance. Each row of the database represents one record, grouping the fields from the different columns. As you can tell, the structure of a relational database system is very rigid since the data model is based on rectangular, tabular data.

A typical unstructured database is based more on textual information. This information does not lend itself well to fixed-length data fields. For example, consider a customer support application, where the information stored is a description of the customer's problem or request. This description is narrative in nature and may actually be very long. This description could be stored so that many customer representatives could all access this common knowledge base.

Or consider an application where you want to document procedures for your company. The procedures should all be online, should be searchable, and they should be organized so that an employee could quickly find a required document and read it online. This is a typical document management application and is an important requirement of quality initiatives such as the ISO 9000 quality specification.

Notes databases provide features that are optimized for the handling of textual information. The elements of a Notes database, in fact, are called documents and are the fundamental unit of storage within a Notes database. A Notes document is somewhat akin to a record in a traditional relational database, but because Notes documents can store this unstructured (as well as structured) information, they are very powerful. In addition, you can relate documents from one database to other documents in the same database or other databases.

The Notes Workspace

There are several items to notice about the Lotus Notes 4.5 Workspace, shown in Figure 2.7. First, you'll note that the areas at the top and bottom of the screen contain information similar to the information you have previously seen. The SmartIcons at the top of the screen have changed, however. These icons have changed because our context has changed. Because our focus is now on the Workspace window, the icons have changed to provide features that are useful in manipulating the Workspace, which are different than those provided for e-mail.

The Notes Workspace is actually the starting point for any Notes session. When you initially start Notes, you'll see your Workspace. In the workspace window you can see that there are seven tabs across the top. The currently highlighted tab is labeled Customer Service, and you can see six icons in the workspace area.

Each of the six icons on the page represents one Notes database. You can open the database simply by double-clicking on its database icon. In the example shown in Figure 2.7, the six databases collectively implement a customer service application.

When you initially install Notes, the first six tabs are blank. Each of these six tabs corresponds to a page of icons, or databases. The last tab is reserved for the replicator, which is discussed in Chapter 33, "Replication and its Administration."

FIGURE 2.7.

The Lotus Notes Workspace.

Opening a Database

Figure 2.8 shows the result of double-clicking the Call Tracking Database icon. The first time you open a database, you are usually greeted with a document that is called the About document. This special document, created by the database author, tells you the purpose for the database and who should use it. This About document is usually shown only once, but if you ever wish to see the document again, it is available as an item on the Help menu.

FIGURE 2.8.

The About Document for the Call Tracking Database.

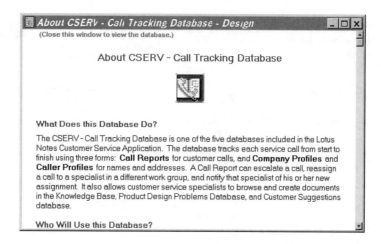

Once you have closed the About document, you see a window similar to the one shown in Figure 2.9, which shows a two-pane view of the Call Tracking Database. In this configuration, the list of Folders and Views is on the left, and the list of documents is on the right.

FIGURE 2.9.

The dual-pane window of the Call Tracking Database.

Notice at the bottom of the database window that there is a double window border. The window actually has three panes in it, but the third pane has been sized so that it is not visible. You can move your mouse to this double border area and resize the third, document preview pane so that a document is visible in it. Figure 2.10 shows the result of resizing the document preview pane so that it is visible. Notice that the bottom of Figure 2.10 has only a single border, not the double border that appears in Figure 2.9. The other border has been moved up so that it separates the two top panes from the bottom pane.

FIGURE 2.10.

The three-pane view of the Call Tracking Database.

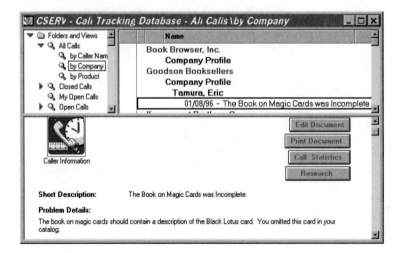

Compare the window format shown in Figure 2.10 with the one you saw in Figure 2.1. Notice how the three panes are available in two quite different contexts in two different databases. The formats shown in both Figures 2.9 and 2.10 are very good for navigating through a database that has many records. Remember that one of the important characteristics of groupware databases is the ability to find what you're looking for. There have been three levels of navigation introduced so far. The first is in the Workspace, where you can navigate between pages, the second level is among databases on the page, and the third level is within a database with the various views.

Once you have found the specific document you were looking for, you probably want to open it up to get as much detail as possible. Figure 2.11 shows the result of double-clicking on the highlighted document in the view shown in Figure 2.10. Double-clicking the document brings up a full page of information.

FIGURE 2.11.

A full window for a particular document in a database.

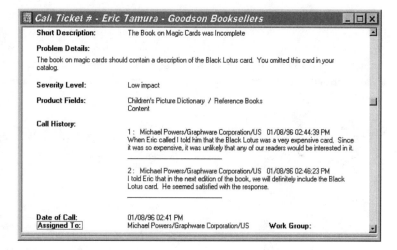

The page shown in Figure 2.11 is the same document shown in the preview pane of Figure 2.10. Notice that when you show the document in a full window much more information is available. You can also scroll the information, so that for this particular document even more information is available above and beneath the window you're viewing.

You can now see the real power of unstructured information in Figure 2.11. The call history has two items in it, but it could have many more. In addition, several people could update this same document, so if different representatives were to work with this customer, all of the call histories would be in one place. Notice that Notes can also store structured information such as the time and dates of the call, the customer name, customer number, and company. The ability to handle both structured and unstructured information at the same time and the ability to present it in a pleasing and easy-to-use format are two of the real strengths of Lotus Notes.

Discussion Databases

Discussion databases provide an opportunity for a group of people to share information with each other and provide support to one another. It is a great way to lower support costs because employees can ask questions and/or provide answers on a completely ad hoc basis. Although discussion databases are not necessarily a replacement for official support channels, they can greatly lower costs because once questions and answers have been logged in to the database, other people who have similar problems can find answers themselves.

This mechanism essentially captures and organizes information that previously may have been lost. It works on the principle that if any one user has a question, it's very likely that another person may have that same question. It's not possible, though, to predict ahead of time what questions people might have. By letting the questions happen spontaneously, the database is filled with relevant questions and answers.

Figure 2.12 shows a typical discussion database. This view shows a section of the database displaying main topics and responses. Main topics are displayed in bold print, and responses are shown indented in normal font without the bold. In this database, each submission shows the author, and for main topics the number of responses is also indicated. In this screen only two levels of indention are shown, but if there were further responses to the first responses, they would be indented at successive levels beneath the topics to which they apply.

FIGURE 2.12.

The main view of a discussion database.

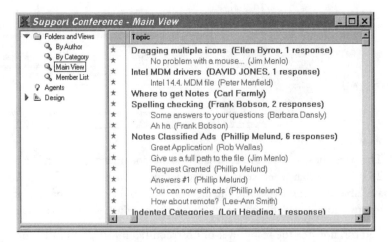

Although this is a typical discussion database, all discussion databases will not necessarily have a structure identical to this one. The structure of the databases can vary depending upon your needs. In your database, for example, you may want to show the date when a particular contribution was made. You may also want to keep track of departments or other organizational information.

In R4.5, the InterNotes Web Navigator (browser) and the Personal Web Navigator browser are included with the client software for Notes. (Refer to Figures 2.5 and 2.6.) By using a Web browser, a user can access Internet Usenet newsgroups from Notes. Notes takes care of the conversion to and from the Internet formats. When they are displayed to the user, they look just like a normal discussion database. This is an important feature because it enables users to access and contribute to electronic discussions using the Internet as the communication vehicle.

Calendar and Schedule Sharing

With Notes 4.5, you can store your calendar online. In addition, you can share your calendar with others so that they can schedule meetings when you're free. With the new free time and meeting room scheduling in Notes, collaboration is even easier.

You can now keep all your correspondence, to-do lists, meeting notices, mail, and calendar all in one place. Notes' calendar feature sports the award-winning Lotus Organizer user interface, so it's easy to use (see Figure 2.13). You can also control who can see your calendar using the built-in security features.

FIGURE 2.13.
The Calendar view of the mail database.

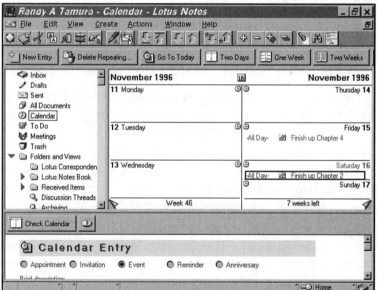
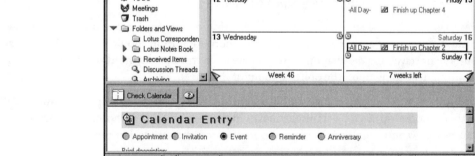

Security

It is important to ensure that information stored in your databases is accessed only by those with the proper authority. Each Notes database has an associated Access Control List (ACL).

The ACL specifies the tasks that are enabled for a particular user with that database. For example:

- A Manager can perform all the tasks for a database, including setting the security (ACL) settings.
- A Designer can modify the database design elements such as Forms, Fields, and Views.
- An Editor cannot modify the design of the database, but can modify all the documents contained in the database.
- Users with Author access may create documents and modify documents that they have created.
- Readers may read documents, but may not create new ones. This access is typically used for reference information databases.
- Depositors can create documents, but cannot see documents in views, even those that they have created. This access could be used to implement a Notes-based survey system, for example.

Coordination

Coordinating the work of a group of people is important in any business. For example, with e-mail, people can attach files to the message, and it is sent to the recipient. Sending attachments is very good for handling ad hoc transmission of information from one person to another. This happens when the type of data to be transmitted is not a recurring transaction.

For recurring transactions, it is better to manage the flow of information from one person to another on the system. This way, each time the process is done, specific, uniform data can be collected and processed by the appropriate people.

For example, take the application of travel authorizations. Suppose a company wishes to automate the process of authorizing travel. The authorization form should include the dates and purpose of travel, the destination, and itinerary. The traveler may need one or more levels of approval depending upon the dollar amount of the travel.

Figure 2.14 shows a sample travel authorization application. In this example you can show the authorizations organized by status (as shown in the figure), or by authorization number. You can also show authorizations by approver or traveler if they are still in process.

In Figure 2.15, the user has changed the window to the three-pane format. Two buttons are shown on the form. These buttons are used by the reviewer after he or she reviews the information farther down in the form. You have control when you design the application about which users you will enable to view which forms. So, for instance, you can prevent nonmanagers from accessing restricted information.

FIGURE 2.14.

A simple travel authorization.

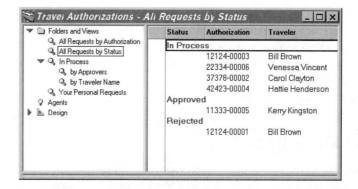

FIGURE 2.15.

The main view of a discussion database.

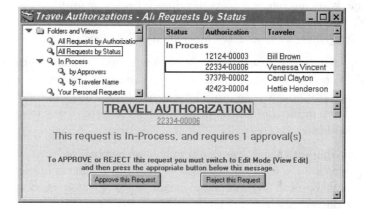

The buttons show how Notes can integrate form filling with process flow. The author of the travel authorization document creates and fills in the form. After the form is filled out, it can be automatically routed to his or her manager. The manager can approve or reject the form. If it is approved, it can go to one of several places, depending upon the logic of the application and company policy. For example, depending upon the dollar amount, another approval may be necessary. If approved, the request could go to the travel department for ticketing, or the request could go back to the traveler so he or she can make the reservations.

All of these scenarios depend upon your company's policies. The policies can be embedded in the Notes application, ensuring by the automatic flow of information that the policies will be followed. If each person sent an ad hoc e-mail message, then some requests might not include all of the information, requiring time-consuming rework. With the Lotus Notes workflow approach, you can arrange the form to ensure that it cannot be sent on to the next stage of the process until all of the required information has been filled out. This infrastructure enables you to have corporate control of the policies, implemented with tools that are very easy for employees to use.

For employees filling out the form, it is as easy as filling out a few blanks on an electronic form. For the manager approving the request, all of the information is guaranteed to be on the form in a uniform format, and approving the request can be as simple as pressing a button on the screen. As each person in the workflow does his or her job, the work gets done in a repeatable, highly efficient manner. It's no wonder many corporations these days are embracing workflow and the structure, control, and efficiency it can bring to work processes.

Designing Forms

I've now covered many of the important concepts involved in using Notes as an end user. How difficult is it to develop applications like I have shown? Actually, developing simple applications is not much harder than using them. There are many tools for developing applications in Notes. Some of these tools can be used without any programming background at all, although others require more advanced programming knowledge.

Before moving on to application development, however, I must first elaborate on the concept of a Notes Form. Forms are similar to their paper counterparts. Forms can contain static information that provides contextual information for the user and is the same on each instance of the form, or they can contain fields, which are allowed to vary from one instance of the form to another.

If you think of a paper form such as an invoice, purchase order, or expense account form, static information is information such as the form name (such as Invoice or Purchase Order), the lines and boxes on the form, and any other preprinted information such as your company name and address.

In Notes, a form is used like its paper counterpart, except that it is on the computer screen. You enter data into the "blanks" of the form. Each of the blanks of the form represents a field.

Fields on the form represent areas that are filled in at the time the form is used. This information might include a customer name and address, a quantity sold, or an item number. In Notes, fields can also include extended textual information. In a discussion database, the text of the message is a field because it varies from one instance of the form to another. The contents of this message field might include several lines, paragraphs, or even pages of text.

In Figure 2.16, the design section of the left pane (of Figure 2.12) has been expanded. After expansion, you can see the items Forms, Views, Folders, and so forth. In Figure 2.12, these terms were collapsed and hidden. The word Forms has been highlighted, and you can see the list of Forms for this database in the right pane.

You can have several forms in a database, each with a separate purpose. For example, in the discussion database, the Main Topic form is for participating in the discussion. A separate form is available, however, to describe information about each member of the discussion database. The member profile could contain information about the person such as name, phone number, e-mail address, and so forth.

FIGURE 2.16.

An example of Forms available for a discussion database.

It is important to stop here and contrast the difference between a Notes database and a traditional relational database table. In a Notes database, each of the forms represents a kind of template. The template is similar in purpose to the definition of the structure of a relational table. That is, to the number and names of the columns found in a relational table. When you have defined all of the columns in a relational table, you have defined the specification for each row of the table. Each row can have different data, but the type of data found in each row is the same.

In Notes, different forms can have completely different formats, fields, and purposes. In other words, you can have different kinds of records in the same Notes database. You can have, for example, a member profile record and a discussion topic record stored together.

In Figure 2.17, you can see that the form includes many fields. Some of the fields, such as the ones that appear above the Subject, are hidden when the user creates a document. Fields on this form are the words that have been enclosed in boxes. Some field names on this form include From, DateComposed, and Body. The last field on this form, Body, is not restricted to the size of the box on the form. The field expands on the form to take as much room as necessary to hold the information typed by the user.

The Form designer is responsible for laying out the form and for defining which areas of the form will be static and which areas will contain fields to be filled in by the user. The form is typically defined when the application is created. Forms for applications aren't usually defined by end-users, although sometimes sophisticated users can create or enhance forms.

FIGURE 2.17.
*The Main Topic form
for a discussion
database.*

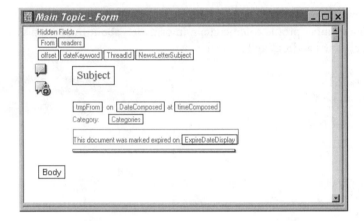

One question that arises, especially with Notes newcomers, is "What is the difference between a Form and a Document?" The simple answer is that the Form is like a template, or as the name implies, a blank paper form. A Document, on the other hand, is like a filled-in Form. Just as you can have many instances of filled-in paper forms, you can have many instances of documents for a single Form.

Compare Figures 2.17 and 2.18. Figure 2.17 is the Form or template to be used, and Figure 2.18 is an example of a document. Note that it is very likely you'll have many, many documents for each unique Form in the database.

FIGURE 2.18.
*A sample document
using the Main
Topic form.*

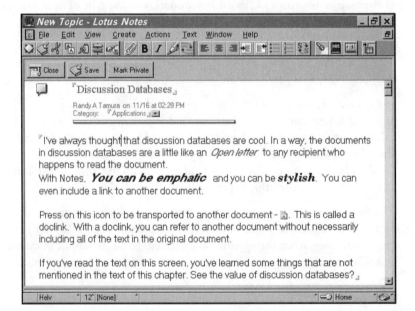

> **NOTE**
>
> Because there will typically be many documents in a Notes database for each form and the information on the form is relatively static, forms and their corresponding documents are typically stored separately from one another. This allows one copy of a form to be used with many separate documents. In special circumstances, though, a Form and Document can be stored together.

Views, Folders, and Navigators

Views provide different points of view on the same data. As we saw in the beginning of this chapter, it is sometimes useful to look at your information from different perspectives, depending upon what you're trying to do. Views are created by the designer of a database. A user with Reader access to the database does not have the ability to change the views in the database, but can create private views that can usually accomplish the same purpose. With Editor, Designer, or Manager access, a user can create shared views for other users of the database.

A folder is similar to a view, but can be created and modified by a user of the database. The ability to create and use folders is new in R4.x of Notes. Because folders and views have a similar purpose and use, they are grouped together in the left pane of the Notes View window. Refer back to Figure 2.16 to see the folders and views pane of a database.

Folders and Views have two major aspects: which documents are included to be shown, and how they are presented. Folders and views have essentially the same presentation characteristics; however, they differ in the selection criteria used to choose which documents are shown. Views use a selection formula that is evaluated for each document to see if it fits the inclusion criteria. If so, it is included in the view.

With folders, the user selects which documents are included, typically by dragging and dropping the documents into the folder. Similar to a view, the folder does not actually store the document; it only provides a reference to it. It is a way of grouping a set of documents together without the need to actually copy the data. This is best explained with an example.

Suppose you have a mortgage on your house, and the lender deducts a portion of your monthly payment and puts it into an escrow account to pay your property taxes. At the end of the year, the lender sends you a statement that indicates the amounts deducted and the amount of taxes paid. Where should you file this statement? It could go in the file with the mortgage information because it is coming from the lender. On the other hand, it could be filed with your property tax information because it deals with your property taxes. To resolve this dilemma with paper, people (including me) usually make copies of the document, filing one with the mortgage information and the other with the property tax information.

With Notes, this is all unnecessary. You can have a single document, but two folders. One folder holds references to mortgage information, and the second holds information about property taxes. There is only a single document, but two different folders reference it. When you open the folder, all the relevant documents are there.

 Navigators are another new feature of R4.x of Notes. They enable designers to add graphically oriented navigation tools to applications. Instead of choosing text-oriented view names, a user can pick from icons or other graphic elements selected by the designer. The view pane on the left is also called the Navigator pane because, in addition to the list of Folders and Views, it can contain these graphical Navigators. Actually, the Folders and Views you see by default are implemented with a built-in Navigator.

 The easiest way to examine Navigators is to look at one. There's actually one close at hand, because the Notes Help file contains a Navigator. If you look at the left pane of Figure 2.19, you'll notice that it looks somewhat different from a normal View pane. First, you can see that the icons in Help are books instead of folders and that the Contents and the How do I? books are open.

FIGURE 2.19.

The Help file navigator.

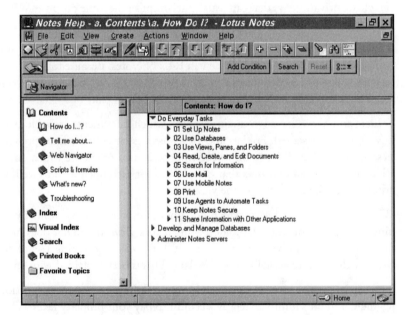

With Navigators, you can use your own icons in the View pane, and you can even use bitmap images and take different actions, depending upon user selections in the navigator area. Some actions are relatively easy to implement (such as opening views or documents), but you can also use the Navigator feature to implement very sophisticated application-dependent functions. Experiment with the Help feature of Notes itself to get an idea about the kinds of things you can do with Navigators. For more information, see Chapter 19, "Using Navigators, Agents, and Simple Actions."

Notes Administration

This book is designed to provide information to users, designers, and administrators of Notes systems. So far, we have covered information about using Notes and some elements of designing applications. We now turn our attention to the administration, or the care and feeding of our Notes network.

The core of administration for Lotus Notes is contained in a Notes database called the Name & Address Book. There are actually two kinds of name and address books. One type is a private address book, called a Personal Address Book, that you can use to store information about your own contacts. This private address book works like the one found in many e-mail systems or, in fact, like your little black book. In addition to the information about your contacts, it also includes information about the locations you've set up and the computers you can contact.

The second type of name and address book is called the Public Address Book. The Public Address Book is very important to Notes, and in addition to keeping information about all of the users, it keeps information about servers, connections, and other important administrative information. You should ensure that this Public Address Book can only be updated by authorized employees for Notes System Administration.

Domino: Notes Server Functions

Notes uses the client/server model of computing and has its own servers. With Release 4.5, Lotus has renamed the Notes server to the Domino server. Don't let this confuse you. The Domino server *is* the Notes server. Lotus renamed it because the Domino server now serves Notes clients and Internet clients as well. Originally, "Domino" referred to just the Internet server part of the Notes server, but because the name is catchy, Lotus broadened the name to include even the non-Internet parts of the Notes server.

Notes (Domino) servers are different from your file servers. Today you may have a network that runs Novell Netware, OS/2, Windows NT, or one of several other networking systems. These systems typically have one or more file and print servers. Client computers, frequently running Windows, OS/2, or DOS, access the file server and access shared data on the file server's disks.

A Notes server normally runs on one of these client machines (not one of your file/print servers), and performs tasks that are specific to Notes. These tasks include the implementation of Notes security and access, mail routing, and replication. Although it might be technically possible to run a Notes server on the same machine as your file and print server, this is not recommended because of performance and other considerations.

Domino: Web Serving

The Domino server can also serve up Web documents to the Internet or to an intranet. The server can convert Notes database documents to HTML, the Esperanto of the Internet. Once the documents have been converted to HTML, they can be viewed by browsers such as Netscape Navigator and Microsoft Internet Explorer. You'll learn much more about Domino and the Internet in Part V.

Replication

One of the most important features of Notes is replication. In its simplest form, replication involves the copying of data from a Notes database on one computer to another. Although this might seem simple, there are many, many complex issues to consider. For example, if you were just to copy a file using a simple DOS command, copying one file from one disk to another, you would get an exact duplicate of the first file.

However, consider the scenario where two files, on two different disks, are updated separately by different people, or perhaps multiple people. Now you have two data files that have both been updated. You cannot really copy either one to overlay the other. If you did, then one set of changes would be lost. Notes Replication is designed to handle exactly this scenario.

 Notes Replication enables multiple users to update information in separate databases, and then update all copies of the database so that the most recent changes to the files are merged. This merging does not happen in "real-time," but during the replication process. For example, if User A and User B, operating on separate computers, have both updated their databases, when replication has completed, User A's database has the latest changes from both A and B, and User B's database has the latest changes from both as well.

You can see that replication involves much more than the simple copying of files. Each document within the database must be separately managed, and with R4 of Notes, even individual fields can be managed and replicated. You can control, for instance, whether individual documents or even fields will be replicated with another computer.

In addition to the implementation details involving the copying and merging of the data, the system must also implement security. Important information must be copied, but only when rigorous security tests have been passed. If the system blindly copied data, unauthorized personnel might be able to access sensitive information just by replicating it. Notes handles the security issues with a very robust implementation.

Security tests included in Notes check both User and Server authentication (you are who you say you are) as well as authorization (you are allowed access). As mentioned, databases also have access control lists (ACLs) that provide an extra layer of security support within databases. Encryption and many other security measures throughout Notes provide mechanisms for developers and administrators to control and enforce security policies.

Replication is used to copy and merge information from server to server, but it is also used for mobile access to Notes. For example, a common usage for replication is to replicate company databases onto a portable PC, which can then be disconnected from the network. You could replicate your e-mail database, work in a disconnected state, and then when you have finished reading and replying to your messages, replicate your database with the master copy on the LAN. This delivers the e-mail messages you have created off-line.

Insurance agents, real estate agents, auditors, adjusters and other types of professionals could use Notes to replicate important business information with the home office while out in the field.

This replication implementation can greatly reduce your phone connect time because you can do a lot of work off-line while disconnected and only pay for phone connect charges to actually send and receive data.

Domains

When I first learned about Notes Domains, it was a very confusing topic, perhaps because I was thinking about physical locations more than logical connections. There is actually a very simple definition of a Domain—it is a group of Notes Servers and their clients that all use a common Public Address Book. If it's the same (replicated) Public Address Book, then it's the same domain. If Servers are using different (for instance, with a different content, not replicated) Public Address Books, they are in different domains. Two servers can be physically in different locations but in the same domain, or they can be in the same location but in different domains.

But why, you ask, should you care? Actually, unless you have a pretty large Notes system, you really don't need to care. The best way for small and medium size Notes networks to be configured is as a single Domain. You can have several servers and can administrate the network from just about anywhere because all the servers use the same Public Address Book. Administration really consists of updating the Public Address Book with the latest information on users, servers, and connections. A single domain can probably work well for up to several hundred users, and the single domain can even handle geographically dispersed servers. Remember that two servers may be in different cities, but if they are using the same Public Address Book, they're in the same domain.

If you have a larger Notes network, then you will care about multiple domains. Because the domain is the context for the Public Address Book, it is essentially the directory for the domain. This means that all of the users within the domain can communicate easily with one another because they're all in the same Public Address Book. This is fine for a small network, but if you have thousands of users, you may wish to partition your network into domains for ease of maintenance. A domain could be organized around geography, or it could be organized around geopolitical boundaries, sometimes called divisions in large companies.

As mentioned, you can start your Notes implementation with a single domain. Within your domain you can add several servers and will be able to handle hundreds of users. As you add more users and servers, you can take comfort in the fact that Notes has all the capabilities to scale up your network into thousands and thousands of users with the use of domains.

Administrative Tasks

Part VII, "Setting Up a Simple Notes Network," and Part VIII, "Advanced Administration Topics," cover administration of a Notes Network in much more detail. Basically, the tasks involved in administering a Notes network are similar to those of administering a file and print sharing (LAN) Network. As an administrator, you must do the following:

- Install and maintain the Notes software.
- Maintain information about physical telecommunication and LANs.
- Add, delete, and update users to the system.
- Certify users to enable them to use the system.
- Schedule replications.
- Perform routine backup and recovery.

The technical aspects of Notes Administration are made pretty simple by the tools provided with the Notes system. In the previously listed tasks, the first three are fairly self explanatory. The certification of users is a concept that may be new to people who are familiar with Network administration, and involves more than just adding a user to a directory.

Certification is required because of the very robust dual-key security system used by Notes. Certification is the process of having an authorized (the certifier) person authenticate the identity of a user (or server). Certification is discussed in detail in Chapter 34, "Security Overview." For now, suffice it to say that the purpose of certification is to provide a robust, high level of security and identity checking within Notes.

Replications, as discussed previously, can take place on either a scheduled or an ad hoc basis. When a remote user dials into the system, replication is considered ad hoc. Servers within a Notes network are typically assigned scheduled replication. With scheduled replication, the server will automatically replicate with other servers, even dialing their phone numbers as required. As the administrator, you can schedule these replications to take place frequently or infrequently, depending upon the needs of your applications, the costs involved, or other factors. The point is that as an administrator, you will be responsible for determining the needs for your organization, and then turning these needs into a replication strategy.

Parts VII and VIII provide you with much more detailed information about how to set up a Notes network, how to schedule and administrate replication, security concerns, and some techniques in troubleshooting the inevitable problems that crop up from time to time. As an administrator, you need to be aware of a lot more of the details on how Notes works in order to properly tune your system for optimum performance. Many people are typically dependent upon your expertise in getting the system running and keeping it running.

Summary

This chapter covered a lot of ground, providing an introduction to some of the more important aspects of Notes. The key concepts of groupware, communication, collaboration, and coordination, are all handled by Notes. You can communicate by means of e-mail and the Internet. You can collaborate with shared databases and implement discussion databases. You can coordinate the flow of work within your company with Notes.

We discussed your workspace, databases, forms, views, and folders. These items are the core of the Notes user interface. Even administration of the Notes system involves the use of these items via the Public Address Book. The Public Address Book is the directory that controls users and servers that are allowed to use the system and is the key database for Notes administration.

Simple administration is really not much more than updating the Public Address Book. You add information about users, servers, and connections. As your network grows, so do the burdens of administration. Of course, administering a large, complex Notes environment is a full-time job. The hardest part is not really the technical work with Notes, but keeping up with the nontechnical demands of your users.

How Does Lotus Notes Work with the Internet?

by Don Child

IN THIS CHAPTER

Not too long ago, pundits were saying that the Internet would kill Lotus Notes. Notes champions responded with what is proving to be an understatement. They said that the idea of the Internet killing Notes was just like saying that the interstate highway system would kill the automobile. The Internet is the "Information Superhighway" and Notes is a vehicle that shares that highway with many others. Notes 4.5 could well turn out to be the pacesetter, staying well ahead of the rest on the quickly expanding Information Superhighway.

Lotus Notes 4.5 has moved beyond that metaphor. With Notes 4.0, Lotus enhanced its recognized workflow strengths and programmability with a Web browser and the InterNotes Web Publisher. This meant that Notes users could develop Web applications in Notes and could use the Web as a team workspace environment. This arsenal has been expanded even further with Notes 4.5.

Added to the Notes Internet family in Notes 4.5 are the following server features:

- Domino: A server task that makes Notes documents into HTML-coded pages on-the-fly.

- Domino.Action: A Notes Internet application that walks the user through the creation of a Notes-based Web site.

- SOCKS version 4 support, HTTP Proxy support, and Notes RPC Proxy support. Native Notes users can access the Internet using HTTP Proxy servers.

On the client side, Notes 4.0 featured the InterNotes Web Publisher and the InterNotes Navigator, which made it possible for any Notes client to access the Internet, regardless of the communication protocol being used. Notes 4.5 puts the Internet right on the desktop by delivering the following additional features:

- The option to retrieve Web pages directly from the Internet instead of retrieving pages that are stored on the InterNotes Web Navigator.

- The Personal Web Navigator, which empowers Notes users by letting them locally manage content retrieved from the Web.

- Web Minder, a Notes agent that automatically updates the contents of locally stored Web pages for fast access to current information.

- Web Ahead, a Notes agent that can download a set number of layers of linked pages before you call them up.

- Advanced features such as Java applet execution, HTML 3.2 support, progressive rendering of text and graphics, SSL, SOCKS, HTTP Proxy and Notes RPC Proxy support, and Netscape Plug-in API support.

- The ability to launch Web pages in a variety of ways—by clicking on URLs within Notes documents, by toggling the Notes search bar so it will accept URLs, from a SmartIcon, or from a menu.

■ Web pages can be launched using the Notes Web Navigator, or you can elect to use another navigator such as Netscape or the Microsoft Internet Explorer.

The application development strengths of Notes as well as its new Web-sensitive features have quickly made Notes into one of the most prolific Web development environments. The installed base of Notes applications has also vastly increased the content available on the Web. Distributed authoring and Web pages on-the-fly minimize the need for people knowledgeable in Web languages such as HTML and Java, and they maximize the widespread Notes development expertise.

In short, both the pundits and the Notes champions were off target. Notes is not just a vehicle for surfing the Internet. With the release of Lotus Notes 4.5, the Lotus Development Corporation must now be considered as one of the leading architects, engineers, and builders of the World Wide Web. It is almost incidental that Notes is also a vehicle for traveling on the Information Superhighway.

Understanding the Internet

Before continuing, let's examine a few Internet terms. These terms are important to an understanding of how Notes uses the Internet:

■ The *Internet* is a worldwide network of computers communicating via TCP/IP protocol. The Internet is frequently depicted as a cloud. Information from the Internet comes out of a cloud. You don't necessarily need to know where the information is stored or how it got to you.

■ The *World Wide Web* (WWW, or simply the Web) is a graphical interface to the Internet. The Web consists of pages coded in HTML (Hypertext Markup Language). HTML provides formatting information and provides links to other Web pages and files.

■ The *Web server* uses HTTP protocol to deliver Web pages over the Internet when someone requests the page via a URL (a Web address) or a hypertext link.

■ A *Web navigator* (or Web browser) is an inexpensive or often free software application that translates HTML coded pages and displays them in graphical format.

■ A *firewall* is a way of making public information accessible over the Internet, while blocking Internet users from gaining access to confidential corporate information that resides on internal networks. An intranet uses Internet technology but uses it behind a firewall so that only corporate users have access to the information. It uses the inexpensive Internet technology to provide a secure private network.

When individual users connect to the Internet, they do so through an Internet Service Provider (ISP). The ISP maintains a full-time TCP/IP connection to the Internet and resells connections to companies and individuals. To connect to the Internet through an ISP, you need one of the following:

- A dial-up telephone connection to the ISP using SLIP or PPP
- Connection to an HTTP Proxy server, which in turn provides connection to the ISP through a firewall
- A dedicated connection through a local area network (LAN)

Figure 3.1 illustrates how this technology is connected.

FIGURE 3.1.

How an individual with a Web browser connects to the Internet.

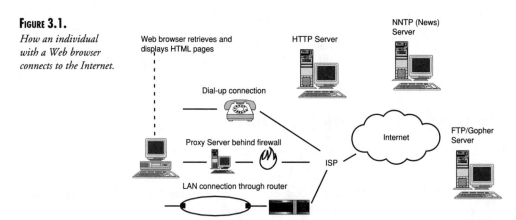

What happens in the real world is that people end up cobbling together a wide area network (WAN) solution that uses several of these elements:

- They use Notes for secure site-to-site replication, but they do it over the Internet using TCP/IP as a communication protocol to cut down on phone costs.
- They either use a commercial firewall, or they use Notes replication strategies to maintain a firewall.
- They use a combination of Notes database design and HTML coding to build Web pages.
- They use Domino to publish Notes databases as HTML pages.
- They use Notes to create Web content in the course of their everyday jobs.
- They use a variety of Web browsers to view data, including the InterNotes Web browser for team or personal Web surfing, Netscape, and the Microsoft Internet Explorer.
- They use Notes to manage data once it comes into the organization over the Internet.

In short, wise businesses use the strengths of both Notes and the Internet. Notes provides an open platform, workflow capabilities, and security. The Internet provides an unstructured surfeit of information and inexpensive technology. Using tools from both camps, businesses build an information-intensive *business solution.* Their aim is to use the Web as an information tool to help achieve their business goals. To go back to the metaphor mentioned at the beginning of this chapter, think in terms of how a long distance truck driver would use the interstate highway system as a tool in his business.

The prevailing paradigm among many organizations, though, is simply to establish a *Web presence.* "If you build a Web site, they will come." It is a seductive proposition because the Web is a hot commodity. But businesses concerned about a Web presence too often do not spend enough effort trying to determine who is the "they" that will come, what will motivate them to come, and what value they will receive from visiting the Web site. Thinking of a Web site as no more than a "presence" on the Information Superhighway results in a marshmallow site—one that looks really sexy and appears to provide something of substance, but in the end leaves you feeling empty. Visitors go away and never come back.

The Notes Internet Paradigm

Lotus started positioning Notes as an Internet player as early as May of 1993. That was when they incorporated native support for TCP/IP in Notes R3. Notes 3.0 had seven months of experience in Internet protocol before the Windows version of Mosaic was launched, marking an early milestone in the development of the World Wide Web.

Lotus is still ahead of the curve. For the cost of a single Notes Server license, you get a bundle that includes a streamlined Web development environment, a Web Server, a choice of methods for publishing information on the Web, and a built-in Web navigator. The Notes installed base of users means that there are already hundreds of thousands of Web-enabled databases, and there are millions of potential Web content creators. But perhaps overlooked in the multitude of Internet options is the workflow function that Notes plays in managing information.

The bottom line is this: There is a lot of information out there on legacy systems and on client/server systems. With all of the Internet functionality that is built into Notes 4.5, users can now tap into all of that information when and where they need it. It doesn't matter what type of network they are using. It doesn't matter what hardware platform they are using. In some configurations, it doesn't even matter which protocol they are using. They can locate and retrieve information, organize it, and then incorporate it into their business processes. That gives them a tremendous advantage over businesses that do not use the Internet, or businesses that have no more than a static Web presence via a canned "home page."

Consider the process of putting together a Web site. For the sake of illustration, we'll follow two fictional companies as they decide to join the Internet revolution. Both organizations have sound business reasons for using the World Wide Web, the graphical interface to the Internet. They need to distribute information widely, and they need to provide a means for interactive communication with their clients.

Abracadaviary Builds a Notes Nest on the Web

The first company is called Abracadaviary, Inc., also known as ABCD. They supply pet stores with exotic birds and bird supplies. They work with breeders, importers, and suppliers from around the world, and they advertise their wares and services to a widely dispersed market. They have two branch offices and one warehouse/aviary. And most important, they have been using Lotus Notes for the past year to track their customers, suppliers, and inventory of birds.

The idea of a Web site at ABCD is first mentioned in an e-mail memo from a field representative in Brazil. He wants to show a potential supplier which birds can be routinely imported, and which ones need special permits. He can have the information e-mailed down to him, but wouldn't it be nice to be able to tap into the Web and access the information online? Probably other people would like the same information, too. He sends the e-mail to the jack-of-all-trades desktop publisher in advertising, because he knows she can quickly find the information he needs. As an afterthought, he also cc's the Notes Administrator in the home office.

Fast-forward a few weeks. All of the employees at ABCD have had a chance to discuss the plans for a Web site. They have inventoried all of the information they store in Notes databases. They have started to categorize the information into what is suitable for public distribution, what can possibly be distributed to a limited audience, and information that is internal and confidential. All of the threaded discussion took place within a Notes database set up explicitly to discuss the issue. There was a company-wide buy in to the idea.

The transition to a Web site is relatively painless. First, ABCD upgrades to Lotus Notes 4.5 so they can take advantage of the POP3 support, the cross-database and cross-server full-text searching, the SOCKS and HTTP Proxy support, and Domino. They put a Web server in front of a firewall and set up replication schedules so that the only information that passes to the outside of the firewall is information that is directed toward the public. Internally, they double-check their standard ACL groups that list clients, distributors, and others who need specific information that is not suitable for full public distribution. They already had a connection to the Internet, because they found it saved money to replicate with the Florida office using TCP/IP rather than calling long distance.

Within 24 hours after they install Domino, they have an intranet site on a Notes server that sits behind the firewall. They spend a week designing and creating graphical navigators for their public databases. Once the graphics are approved, the Notes Administrator activates the link between two computers—one behind the firewall and one outside the firewall. From that moment on, anyone in the world can find out more about exotic birds by tuning in to http://www.abracadaviary.com.

The site gets enhanced with graphics, Java applets, and bird sounds. The Internet connection gets upgraded to a higher speed. But the rest of the work of maintaining the Web site is pure Lotus Notes.

The field rep in Brazil returns from a trip up the Amazon and sends a report about the dwindling habitat for a once-common parrot. Since the e-mail mentions "parrot" and "habitat," it is automatically routed for approval. The approvers include a tropical bird specialist in the Florida office and the Web editor in San Diego. With minimal editing, the story is published to the Web by updating a status field and selecting an appropriate file photo. A link to the new Web page is also forwarded to all clients who have ordered that particular type of parrot.

The parrot story made it from the Amazon to the Web in less than 24 hours, including the routing for approval. And that was just one out of over 75 documents that got added or updated on that particular day, much of it with no intervention by the Webmaster. For example, the accounting office had to change the shipping costs because insurance rates were increased. They made a change in the accounting system. When an order was placed over the Web site by a customer, the system did a lookup in an accounting parameters view and automatically inserted the new shipping costs.

With distributed authoring, built-in workflow capabilities, and the rapid development environment of Notes, the employees of Abracadaviary were able to make feathers fly. It was a no-brainer.

Exploring Familiar Grounds: Lost in Hyperspace

The second company, whose headquarters are located just across town from Abracadaviary, is called Exploring Familiar Grounds, Ltd., commonly referred to as EFG. They organize legal and medical conventions and seminars from three regional offices and publish a quarterly magazine out of their San Diego home office.

The Web is suggested as a way to advertise EFG's seminars, as well as a way to accept online registration and to publish parts of the EFG Journal. The idea is actually just a passing fantasy floated during a phone conversation between the EFG home office and the northwest branch office in Seattle. The VPs on either end of the phone conversation agree that it sounds like a cool idea, but they have no idea where to go from there. The Seattle VP knows someone who has his own Web page, but the Internet is so big and hard to understand. However, by the end of the conversation, he does promise to look into it.

At EFG, the idea of a Web site got dropped after the initial bright idea. It wasn't until a competitor announced their own Web site that the idea was reborn. Then it was a scramble to get the EFG site up as soon as possible. The VP in Seattle called his friend, the one with a home page. This friend became the instant Webmaster, because nobody else had any good ideas about how to do it.

The mechanics of building a web are the same for EFG as they were for ABCD. Well, nearly the same. They need a server, a connection to the Internet, a firewall, and a network of computers running TCP/IP. That last one was not a requirement at ABCD, because Notes users have the option of retrieving Web pages from the Notes server using any of several Notes communication protocols. They need the artwork, and they need to design a site map to identify links between documents.

Also, they need to code all of their documents using HTML. That is something that Domino does on-the-fly, so EFG fell behind ABCD in this phase of the project, just as they did during the planning phase.

The Web Sites Go into Maintenance Mode

To make a long story short, eventually EFG launched their Web site. It was limited in scope, though, because they had to sift through their materials one page at a time and build the links as they went. If a mistake was made, they have to backtrack. If a document was revised, they had to locate the document through a maze of cryptic directories, make revisions, print out the page and forward it to the boss for approval, and then relink the page once it was re-approved. This is an ongoing process, and it takes at least one dedicated full-time person to make sure the links are working, to check for incoming mail, to route the mail to the appropriate person, and so forth.

At ABCD, in the meantime, they were already doing electronic commerce over a secure network. When queries come in from clients, keywords are used to route the queries to the right department without any human intervention. Information gathered in the course of the daily office routine becomes part of the published information on the Web site as soon as it is saved as a Notes document. White papers and topics that may or may not be relevant to the public are routed internally (and automatically) until they have been edited and approved. Work flows through the organization smoothly. The routine means that quality assurance is part of the everyday product, not an afterthought. Also, the Webmaster spends no more than two hours a week reviewing the Web site and adding enhancements. He does not spend any time maintaining links since that is done automatically. ABCD is miles ahead of EFG.

The Cost of Ownership

This scenario I've just described is not just a load of birdseed.

An independent research organization, The Business Research Group (BRG), did a study of the cost of ownership for Notes versus other intranet technologies. They surveyed 100 IT managers, evenly split between Lotus Notes and other intranet technologies, including those from Netscape, Microsoft, Sun, public domain sources, IBM, Oracle, FTP, O'Reilly, and DEC.

The results: Lotus Notes intranet solutions took an average of 53 days to implement, compared to 87 days with other technologies. "Notes demonstrated the lowest cost of ownership among intranet solutions in both the short-term and the long-term," according to Joyce Becknell, Senior Analyst, client/server research.

Lotus Notes proved to be approximately 40 percent more efficient than other solutions on average, in terms of how long it took to deploy. For all types of intranet applications across the board, Notes was clearly the most efficient solution in terms of time invested. That is just one study. If you want to see the entire study, you can contact BRG at `http://www.brgresearch.com`.

If you want to see other reports, check out the Lotus home page at `http://www.lotus.com`. All of the reports say the same thing. Using Notes to build an intranet is economically justifiable for just about any organization. And for someone who is already using Notes, like Abracadaviary in this example, the decision to build an intranet solution using Lotus Notes is a no-brainer.

Putting It All Together with Notes 4.5: A Business Process at Work

Remember those mimeographed bulletins you used to bring home from school when you were a kid? The ones that get crumpled in the bottoms of backpacks and book bags; the ones that are forgotten until the information in them is too old to be of any use? Consider the business process that used to go into creating those bulletins, and then see how Notes 4.5 has been used to transform the process.

If the band teacher wants to announce a special band performance, he writes a note to the school secretary and asks her to put the announcement in the bulletin. If the principal wants to invite the parents to an open house, she asks the secretary to put it in the bulletin. The cafeteria staff creates a menu for the month and has it printed on the second page of the bulletin. If the lunch menu changes, there is no way to tell anyone. Eventually, everything ends up on the secretary's desk. The secretary types everything up, pastes clip art pictures on the bulletin, then runs it through the mimeograph machine or through the photocopier. The teachers distribute the bulletin to the students, who throw it in their backpack. It might get home to the parents, or it might not.

Now look at what the bulletin has become today. As this is being written, there is a beta version of a school bulletin in Notes 4.5 being deployed in Honolulu. The EduSuite Bulletin, as it is called, has turned the old school bulletin into a Web-enabled workflow application that takes advantage of much of the Internet functionality in Lotus Notes 4.5. After reading this, you might want to visit the bulletin's development site to see for yourself at `http://www.edusuite.com`.

Here is how EduSuite uses Notes to create a bulletin—just one of many EduSuite functions.

First, of course, the school must have at least one computer running Notes 4.5, and it must have Internet connectivity available, preferably in the form of a school-wide intranet.

We'll begin in the school cafeteria. The cafeteria manager creates lunch menus in the EduSuite Cafeteria Management database, a Lotus Notes application. If she wants to, she can select from a recipe file that is part of the database to help put together menus. The daily menu is displayed on the computer in a calendar format based on the Notes 4.5 Calendaring and Scheduling interface. In the same database, a daily cafeteria duty roster is maintained.

Thus far, we have a simple, stand-alone application that handles a function that could arguably be done nearly as efficiently without a computer. But the menus and cafeteria duty rosters are destined to become part of the school's bulletin, one that parents can tap into from their home computers. They will be able to see what their child is being served for lunch, and can pack a lunch instead if they know what Johnny won't eat.

The principal (or an assistant) creates the principal's message in another database, the EduSuite Bulletin. This is an article destined for inclusion in the school's published bulletins. In addition to the principal, teachers may also be authorized to contribute articles to the Bulletin database.

Now, this one computer running Notes 4.5 is going to get awfully busy, and it seems that everyone in the school will be using it. That could get tricky. But the Internet connection in Notes 4.5 greatly simplifies the process. If a contributor doesn't have access to the EduSuite Bulletin database, he or she can tap into it using any Web browser and contribute an article over the Internet. When the article is submitted over the Internet, it is routed by the Domino server and ends up as a Notes document in the Bulletin database.

All new articles end up in a Bulletin database view that shows unapproved articles. The articles stay right there until they are approved.

The principal, or whoever is responsible for publishing bulletins, can select articles for specific audiences. For example, suppose a teacher writes an article that he or she wants published in three different bulletins: one for the staff, one for students, and one for parents. However, the bulletin publisher does not think the article is universally applicable and therefore only approves the article for the staff bulletin. The article remains unapproved for the student and parent bulletins.

Using the workflow functionality of Notes, an automatic notification could easily be generated to notify the editor whenever there are new articles that need to be reviewed. Notes security is set up to restrict access to the approval field, so only certain people will be able to approve articles.

The school then defines bulletins for staff, students, and parents. They decide how often the bulletin should be published, and they can customize the layout. Once the bulletin has been defined, a periodic Notes agent checks the Bulletin database for approved articles and creates the bulletin using all of the articles approved for that type of bulletin, as long as the expiration date on the article is not passed. For example, if an article has been approved for students and the date is correct, the article gets published automatically in the student bulletin. The cafeteria menu and cafeteria duty roster are automatically approved and can be included in the bulletin as well.

Within Notes, a Calendar view based on the Notes 4.5 Calendaring and Scheduling interface displays all bulletins that have been published. But not everyone has access to a Notes 4.5 workstation. That is where Domino and the Internet come into play.

Domino is a task on the Notes 4.5 server. Domino makes every Notes server into a Web server, providing on-the-fly conversion of Notes databases into HTML pages. So does the school have to go into the business of publishing its own Web site for this to work? No. What is happening with the EduSuite pilot schools is this: they replicate their Bulletin database to a secure directory on the DataHub, a Domino server run by a subsidiary of DataHouse, which is developing EduSuite. From the DataHub, bulletins are accessible over the Web using any browser.

Most staff members, students, and parents probably do not have full-time access to a Notes 4.5 workstation, but they can still read the bulletins using any Web browser, as shown in Figure 3.2. Over the school intranet, students can view the bulletin online. Depending on how the school is wired, they may see the bulletin in their classrooms, or they might read it at a kiosk in the school library. Staff can read their bulletins by navigating to a private view that requires a user ID and password. Student and parent views are "public"; they are available over the Internet. Of course, the bulletin pages can be set up so that users must register before they use them, to prevent the bulletin from being opened to the entire world.

FIGURE 3.2.

An EduSuite bulletin created in Notes 4.5 and viewed with a Netscape browser.

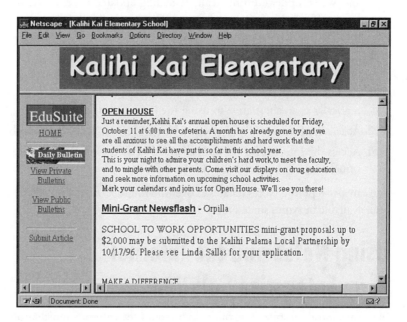

As a backup, schools can always print out copies of the bulletins and send them home in backpacks. Not every household has a computer. Not yet.

The same technology used for the school bulletins can also be used to create other bulletins, such as a French club bulletin, or a student council bulletin. And with the technical infrastructure in place, can distance learning be far behind?

No, as a matter of fact. Some EduSuite pilot schools have already used Notes and Domino for distance learning and collaborative projects. Schools can set up interschool projects, ad hoc discussion databases within the school or district-wide, or they can use other EduSuite modules that build on the strengths of Notes and Domino.

Browsing the Web with Notes 4.5

Within the Notes client, there are several ways you can browse the Web. These are discussed at length in Chapter 23, "Using the Notes Client on the Internet." As a quick preview, you can do the following:

- Launch the Notes Navigator from the search bar, from a pull-down menu, from a SmartIcon, or from a Web Navigator database.
- Manage Web pages, including full-text search, Web Ahead (preloading linked pages), and Web Minder (automatically reloading updated pages in the background), using a Personal Web Navigator or a shared Web Navigator database. Using the Web Navigator database, you can even view Web pages without connecting to the Internet.
- Launch any browser automatically from within Notes documents by double-clicking on URL links.
- Launch third-party browsers such as Netscape or Microsoft Internet Explorer automatically as an alternative to using the Notes Navigator.
- Access the Internet directly from a Notes client or access it through InterNotes.
- Access the Internet from Notes clients that do not use TCP/IP protocol. This functionality was first available in Notes 4.0.

You can also replicate Notes databases over the Internet using TCP/IP, a functionality that has been available in Notes since Notes 3.0.

Using Notes and the Internet in an Enterprise Solution

In today's world, in spite of all of the hype about the Internet, most corporate data still resides on legacy systems. The goal of a good enterprise solution is to be able to integrate all of that data and use it to improve business processes, and ultimately to benefit the business. If you already have the data online and already have audit trails that keep the data sanitized, why mess with it?

Yet, you and your fellow employees need access to that data in order to make decisions. Wouldn't it be nice to have a system that lets you query the data and present it to key executives in summary form? And wouldn't it be nice to be able to do that from a hotel room using your laptop computer, or your Macintosh computer at home, or the PC on your desktop?

With Notes 4.5 and the Internet working together, you can create just such an enterprise information system.

Look at the requirements for an enterprise system. You have both disconnected and proxy users who need to access information stored on legacy systems. The data on the system has to be accessed with real-time client/server SQL queries. The system you are accessing probably has a high volume of complex data, and you do not want to impact performance on that system. In short, you have to be able to access data on the host system, but you must also ensure that the host system continues to perform well.

In a dedicated Notes environment, you can quickly develop applications that have Notes agents to run queries. You can access the data in real-time, but you need a host user ID, a password, a physical connection, and the correct protocol. You can make SQL calls via ODBC/OCI using a LotusScript LSX module, and transactions via MQSeries/CICS using a LotusScript LSX module.

You can also access enterprise data using a Web browser! You still need the host user ID, a password, a physical connection, and the correct protocol, but this is only needed on the Notes Server. And SQL queries and transactions use LSX modules that run on the Notes Server.

Use Domino to publish, as HTML pages, the Notes documents that contain the resultant data. Then all you need to access the enterprise data is a Web browser and an Internet connection.

Use Notes access security and Secure Sockets Layer protocol (SSL) to prevent unauthorized users from accessing the Notes server and keep the legacy data secure. This also opens the doorway to interactive applications requiring secure transactions.

Summary

Notes 4.5 is fully integrated with the Internet. The Notes client can be used to browse the Internet directly or through an InterNotes Web Navigator. The built-in Web Navigator works with many of the latest available features including Java applet execution, ActiveX, Netscape plug-ins, and HTML 3.2. Domino is built into the Notes 4.5 server. Domino translates Notes documents into HTML documents on-the-fly, making the Notes rapid development environment into a Web design tool, and making every Notes server into a Web server. With SSL security and Notes authentication, access to interactive Notes databases can be opened to anyone with an Internet account and a Web browser.

What's New in Releases 4 Through 4.5 of Lotus Notes?

by Randall A. Tamura

CHAPTER 4

IN THIS CHAPTER

One of the biggest and newest changes in Release 4.5 of Notes is that half of it isn't even called Notes anymore! Lotus has split the Notes client and server and has renamed the server. In Notes 4.5, the client is still called Notes, but the server is now called the Domino server. This change is so new that you may still find references to the Notes server in this book. For all practical purposes, though, you can think of the Domino server and the Notes server as being synonymous.

In addition to the server name change, hundreds of new features have been updated or introduced in Release 4.5. As a matter of fact, since the introduction of Release 4, there have been versions 4.0, 4.10, 4.11, and 4.5, each with additional bug fixes and new features. In this chapter, I'll cover the major new features in all of these releases in case you still have not made the jump from Release 3 to Release 4.x of Notes.

Lotus Notes Release 4.x is a major upgrade from Release 3. If you are familiar with R3, you'll be very pleased with the number and scope of the changes that Lotus has made in the product. There are literally hundreds of new features in R4.x (generally referred to as R4 or R4.x). It is easier to use, easier to develop applications, and it is easier to administer in Notes R4.x than R3. In addition to making everything easier, Lotus has added many features that make Notes more powerful as well. Because of the scope and breadth of the changes in R4, in this chapter I'll discuss just the highlights of the new and changed features. This will provide you with a high-level road map for the rest of the book; the in-depth coverage of these features is found in other chapters.

This book uses an icon to highlight new features of Release 4.5. In addition, you'll see an icon for features new to Release 4.0. These icons will help you distinguish features that are new in 4.x, with special emphasis on Release 4.5.

This chapter is organized into six major sections: using Notes, mobile computing, using the Internet, the Domino server, developing applications with Notes, and administration with Notes. The major features of each section are covered through examples.

Using Notes R4.x

I'll begin the discussion of the new features of R4 with user-oriented features. These are the new features that are most visible in the product, and all users will benefit from them whether they are end-users, developers, or administrators. The new user-oriented R4 features are all designed to make Notes easier, more powerful, and more pleasant to use.

The User Interface

One of the themes that you'll find in this chapter about the new features of the Notes user interface is that of simplification. One of the design goals of the new user interface was to make it simpler and easier to use. Because the interface up to Release 3 had been developed over time and several releases, it was soon overtaken by feature after feature of enhancements. This gallery of features eventually lost its coherence, and many times menu options and functions either could not be found or would be found in unexpected places.

The new R4.x interface has not lost any of its power; all the features are still there, along with hundreds of new enhancements. However, many of the menus and operations have been reorganized, prioritized, and configured so that simple things are easy and complex things are still possible.

In addition to the functionality of R4.x, the developers have provided a user interface that is much more pleasing to the eye as well as more powerful and easier to use. Many of the new features, such as Navigators and Action Bars, add beauty as well as elegance to the new Notes interface.

The appearance improvements begin with the desktop, which can now display a marbled look if you have a 256-color display. The icons have a 3-D shadow effect, and when a desktop icon has been pressed, it appears on the screen as without its shadow.

Continuing with desktop niceties, the limit of six pages of icons has been lifted. The new limit of 32 pages, each holding several hundred icons, provides more icons than you could possibly need (or remember). The desktop also contains a new tab, called the Replicator tab, which allows much greater user control over the replication process. I'll cover that feature in more depth under "Mobile Computing" later in this chapter.

Another feature of the desktop is called stacked icons. This feature enables two replica copies of the same database (such as on different servers) to use the same icon. In previous versions of Notes, each replica of a database would be a separate icon; so, if you had a copy of your mail database, say, on your network and a replica on your laptop, two icons would be used.

Stacking icons on the desktop simplifies the user interface and enables you to select the replicas to which you would like the icon to refer. For example, say you have disconnected your laptop from your network and are working remotely. You can click the little triangle in the upper-right corner of the desktop icon and select Local. This tells Notes that you want to work with a local copy of the database. Similarly, when you are connected to the network, you can click on the triangle and select the server copy you wish to access. Stacking icons, although seemingly a small detail, is just one more example of how the user interface for Notes has been improved to make it simpler, less cluttered, and easier to use.

Help Features

One of the handiest new features of R4.x is the new Help facility. Actually, the Help facility has been implemented with a Notes database, so it serves several purposes. Of course, you can use it to look up information, but you can also use the Help facility to see how some of its nifty features have been implemented.

In addition, Lotus has created two versions of Help: one with great taste, and the other less filling. The great-taste version is the full-featured Help facility you will normally use. The less-filling version is called "Help lite" (no kidding). It is a smaller version of the Help facility and is useful for mobile computing on your laptop, where disk space is at a premium. The most important information is in the lite version, but some of the more advanced features have been left out to save space.

In R4.5, the full-flavor version of Help now includes online versions of five manuals: User's Guide, Application Developer's Guide, Database Manager's Guide, Programmer's Guide, and LotusScript Language Reference. It's a great help to have these manuals online and easily accessible, because once they are available in the Help database, they can be searched with the Notes Full Text Search capabilities.

Now, using some screens from the Help facility, we'll walk through some of the new features of Notes R4.x.

Three-Pane Views

Notes R4 has a powerful three-pane view of your data, as shown in Figure 4.1. You can configure these three panes in three different ways. To access this feature, open a database, select View | Arrange Preview, and select the icon that represents the arrangement you prefer.

FIGURE 4.1.

The Preview Pane dialog box.

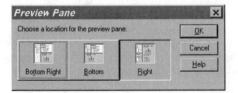

In Figure 4.1, the rightmost icon has been selected. This selects a three-pane configuration with the Navigation pane in the upper left, the View pane in the lower left, and the Preview pane in the right half of the screen. Figure 4.2 shows this arrangement.

Once you have selected the arrangement of the three panes, you can change the relative sizes of the panes, making them larger or smaller by clicking and dragging the borders of the panes.

The three-pane view feature is described in more detail in Chapter 6, "Views, Documents, and Forms," so let's continue with our tour of new features in Notes R4.

Navigators

Navigators are a completely new feature of R4.x of Notes. Navigators are optional, and, if present, they appear in the Navigator pane. The Help database shown in Figure 4.2 has a Navigator. The book icons that appear on the left are actually Navigators. When the mouse is moved over each of the icons, the line will be highlighted. If you select one of the icons, you will be transported to the help information for that topic.

FIGURE 4.2.

The three-pane arrangement with Preview on the right.

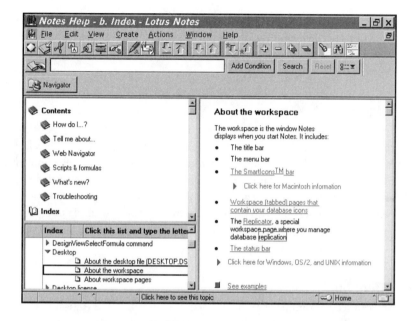

Figure 4.3 shows another Navigator, the Help Visual Index. In this figure you can see that the View Management icon has been highlighted. By moving the mouse, you can select any of the other icons to find help about the specified topic. As you can see, the Navigator feature enables you to create visually appealing applications with Lotus Notes R4.

FIGURE 4.3.

The Help Visual Index Navigator.

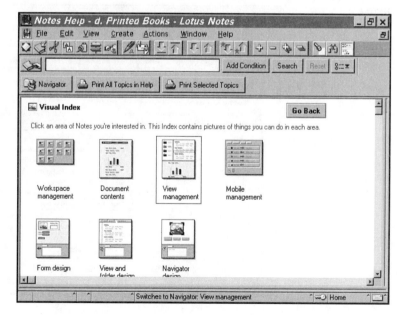

As a database designer, you can supply both the visual images for the Navigators and specify the actions to be taken if the user presses the Navigator hotspot. The hotspot acts like a button. When the user presses it, you can have Notes open other Navigators, open views, or run programs that you supply.

Folders

Folders are another new feature of R4. Folders are similar to views in that they both contain collections of documents, but are different in the method used to select the documents for inclusion. Views have a selection formula. By evaluating the selection formula, Notes determines whether a particular document should be included or excluded from the view. Folders, on the other hand, represent arbitrary collections of documents. As a user, you may place documents in the folder, and you do not have to construct a formula to represent the commonality between the two documents. You can select any documents that are meaningful to you and save them for future reference.

Action Bars

You can see an example of an Action Bar in Figure 4.4. The Action Bar can be in a folder, view, or form. The Action Bar can be used by the Notes database designer to enable commonly used actions to be easily accessible to the user. The actions you see in the Help screen of Figure 4.4 are to ease navigation (Help Topics, Go Back, and LotusScript Tutorial, for example), arrange the screen (Minimize), or to Print the current topic on the printer.

FIGURE 4.4.

A document containing an Action Bar.

Action Bar

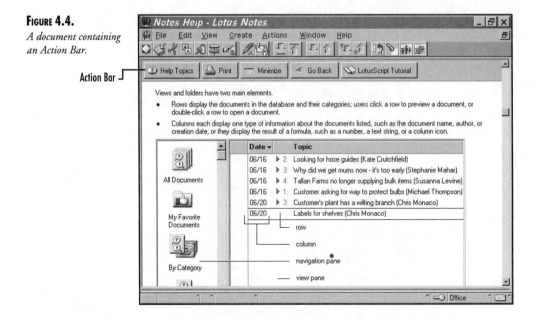

In designing applications, it's usually a good design practice to make all your anticipated actions available on the menus, but to provide Action Bar buttons as a helpful shortcut for users. As a designer, you can design several kinds of actions and show different sets of them to the user depending upon the particular folder, view, or form being viewed by the user. As the user moves through the database, you can provide navigation or application aids. If you experiment with the Notes Help file, you'll get a good idea of how the Action Bar can be used in various contexts.

Calendaring and Scheduling

In Release 4.5, Lotus has added calendaring and scheduling features to the mail database. Lotus has taken the main parts of the award-winning Lotus Organizer and has embedded this user interface into Notes. With these new features, you can schedule your appointments, schedule group meetings, find out about other employees' free time (if they allow it via security), reserve conference rooms, and many other related activities.

In Figure 4.5 you can see the top part of the Calendar profile, which each user will fill out one time. The profile allows you to specify the default length of your appointments, who can view your Freetime schedule, and the range of your Freetime hours. This range is typically your normal workday hours. You'll find out more about Notes' new calendaring and scheduling features in Chapter 8, "Using Calendaring and Scheduling." Figure 4.6 shows a one-week view of the calendar. You use a two-day, two-week, or one-month view.

Column Sorting

Previously in Notes, when a designer wanted to provide different views of a database that differed only in the sorting characteristics, a different view was required for each of the different sorts. No longer. In R4.x, Notes gives the designer the flexibility to allow column sorting. With this feature, Notes attains several desirable traits.

First, because of the column-sorting feature, separate views that differ in sorting characteristics do not need to be created. Only a single view with sorting enabled needs to be created. This greatly simplifies the task of design and development.

FIGURE 4.5.

The Calendar profile.

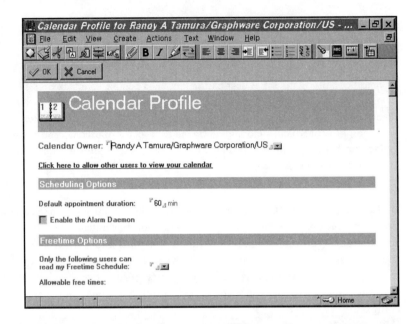

FIGURE 4.6.

The one-week view of a calendar.

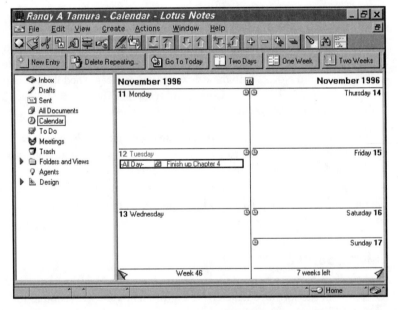

Second, because there are many fewer views, navigation is simplified for the user. Before, the user would have to decide how he or she wanted to see the data and then activate the appropriately sorted view. Now, with the sorting feature, there may be only a single view to work with, so it is much simpler.

Last, because the sorting feature is within one view, the user can dynamically look at the data sorted in different ways without leaving the single view. Again, this simplifies the user interface, making Notes much easier to use and giving the user more flexibility and power over the system.

Sections

Sections in Notes give database designers and users another tool to simplify the interface. Sections are essentially a way to enable users to group information into collapsible sections. Each section has a little triangle, called a "twistie," to its left. If the triangle is pointing to the right, the section is collapsed, and if the triangle is pointed down, the section is expanded.

Sections are very similar to the outline-type features available in many programs such as word processors. One difference is that sections have a bit of programmability to them.

As you can see in Figure 4.7, several options are available for sections. For example, you can specify that you would like sections auto-expanded or auto-collapsed when viewing in preview mode (in the preview pane). Auto-collapsing in this mode may be desirable because the preview pane will typically have less space available on the screen than when the document is opened for reading.

FIGURE 4.7.

Section viewing options.

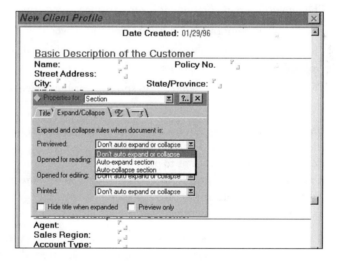

You can also control the expansion status when the document is opened for reading, editing, or is being printed. Separate options for these different cases gives the database designer much more power and flexibility than is typically available in an outliner within an application.

In addition to the standard sections just mentioned, you can also create access-controlled sections. These sections enable the designer to specify a list of authorized users that may edit the section. This feature only works while connected to a server, so carefully analyze your use of this feature.

Access-controlled sections are sometimes used in workflow applications to protect certain areas of a form for authorized signatures. In concept, this is the same idea as a manual signature on a piece of paper. By using access-controlled sections, you can simulate that signature on paper.

Lotus Components

Lotus Components aren't strictly a feature of Release 4.5. They are packaged separately from Notes and Domino, but they work with Notes Release 4.0 and above, so we'll cover them in this book. Components are lightweight versions of application functions that you may want to include in your Notes application. On the one hand, they might be considered a developer's toolbox. On the other hand, regular Notes users can install and use them without doing a lot of application development. So Components can be considered an ease-of-use feature of Notes as well.

The initial release of the Lotus Components contains six components:

- The Chart component is for drawing bar charts, pie charts, and other business graphs.
- The Comment component lets you add comments (with extra security) to rich text fields.
- The Draw/Diagram component is for creating simple artwork.
- The File View component is a generalized file viewer.
- The Project Schedule component is a relatively sophisticated scheduler that can be dropped into other applications.
- The Spreadsheet component can do spreadsheet-type calculations within a Notes document.

The Components are lightweight because they don't contain all the features of a full-function application such as Lotus 1-2-3 or Microsoft Excel. They are typically much faster and smaller, however, which allows applications to perform much better. Components are currently implemented as extensions to Microsoft OCX technology, so they are available only on Windows 95 and Windows NT platforms. Lotus has stated that its strategy is to use Java technology to make components available on other platforms as well.

Lotus has also released a toolkit to help programmers develop custom components. You can develop your own components for use within your company, and you will be able to buy components from Independent Software Vendors as well.

Figure 4.8 shows the spreadsheet component in design mode. You'll notice that the menus at the top of the screen have changed to include the Spreadsheet, and that the Lotus Components button now appears in the title bar of the window. There are many more features that make these components easy to program and use. See Chapter 15, "Using Lotus Components," for more information.

FIGURE 4.8.

A Document with the Spreadsheet component.

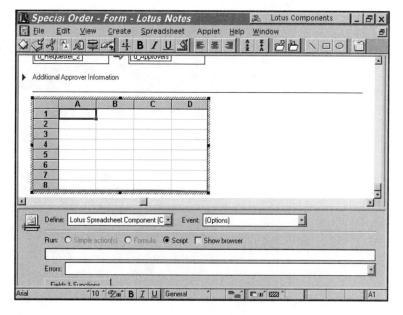

The Right Mouse Button

The features available through the use of the right mouse button have been greatly enhanced. Actually, left and right are relative. With Windows, you can swap the meaning of the left and right buttons so that left-handed people can still use the mouse with their index finger. However, so that you don't get too confused about left and right, I'll use the default, right-handed meanings of the button assignments.

The right mouse button can now be used to bring up a menu of operations that are available in the current context. In Figure 4.9, the right mouse button has been clicked in the workspace context. In this context, several operations are available. The first operation, usually always available, is to find out the properties of the current object. Because in Figure 4.9 the context is the workspace, you see that Workspace Properties is the first selection. In a view or document, for example, Document Properties might be available.

In Figure 4.9, you see some of the other new features of R4. You'll notice that you can create or remove workspace pages, and you are not limited to the six pages of R3. By right-clicking and selecting Open Database, you can conveniently open a database that does not appear on the current page.

As I mentioned previously, you can now stack replica icons. See if you can find the two databases in Figure 4.9 that have stacked replicas. They have little triangles in the upper-right corner of the icon.

FIGURE 4.9.

Right-click in the workspace context.

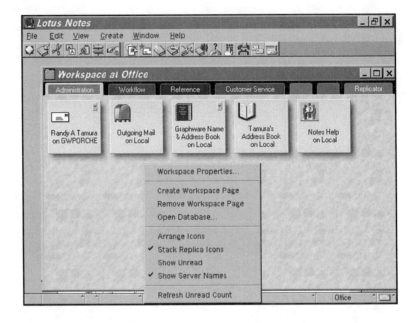

One last feature is the ability to close the current window by double-clicking the right mouse button. This option can be enabled or disabled by selecting File | Tools | User Preferences. Figure 4.10 shows the User Preferences dialog box. You can enable the right mouse button to close windows in the Basics option of User Preferences.

FIGURE 4.10.

The User Preferences dialog box.

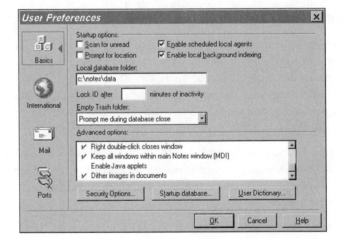

Other User-Interface Features

There are hundreds of other small features that make using Notes R4 much more convenient. You can now resize columns of a view by dragging the column dividers. You can create bulleted and numbered lists, format individual columns or rows of a table, and select from up to 240 colors for text.

You can set the characteristics of a "permanent pen" that you can use for highlighting or annotating a document. By setting the characteristics to Red and Bold, for example, you can go through a document and insert annotations in various spots, but they will all be Red and Bold.

You can add links to views and databases as well as to specific documents, as before. You can search a database without indexing it, and you can save named formulas for later use. If you full-text index a database, you can also have Notes index the contents of attached files. You can use file viewers shipped with Notes to view attached files, even if you don't have the application that created the file.

The list of these features is too numerous to itemize them all, but you get the idea. Notes has made a transformation in its ease of use, and you'll be impressed with its many new features.

Mobile Computing

Lotus has made mobile computing easier by implementing features such as Locations, Passthru servers, and the Replicator tab of the desktop. For mobile computer users there is even a "Help lite," which is the normal Help file that has gone on a diet. It contains the most important and useful information, and omits some of the high-calorie details so that all of those bytes of the file won't weigh you or your computer down. Let's look at some of these features for people on the go.

Locations

Locations are really names for a collection of communication attributes. You can specify a Location such as Office, Home, or Hotel, and have each name represent various communication options. Locations are defined in your Public Address Book. Figure 4.11 shows the Location document in the Public Address Book. In the Location document you can specify whether to use a local area networking port or a modem port. This might be the difference between your Office Location and your Home Location. In addition, you can configure Locations with phone numbers and your server names.

Figure 4.11.

A Location document in the Public Address Book.

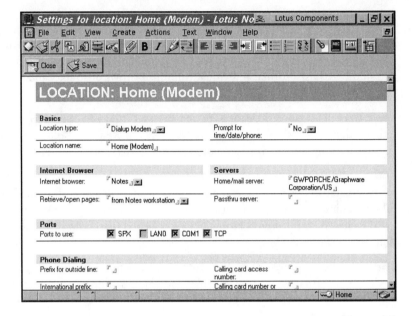

Passthru Servers

R4 has the capability of using Passthru servers to reach your destination server. This capability is especially important when you're on the road. Using a Passthru server enables you to reach several different destination servers, all through a single Passthru server. By using this technique, you can make a single phone call to your Passthru server, and then be connected to several different destinations without making a separate call to each server.

The Replicator

The Replicator tab on the Desktop, shown in Figure 4.12, houses an important new feature for mobile computing.

The Replicator page contains an Action Bar with the most important replication actions. On the Replicator page you can specify which databases you want to replicate by checking the box at the beginning of the row that represents the database. In addition, you can see the direction of replication that will take place. An arrow pointing to the right means sending from your machine to the other server. A left-pointing arrow means pulling data from the other server, and an arrow pointing in both directions signifies a bidirectional transfer.

You can control the order of replication by moving the database lines up or down. You do this by clicking and dragging the line up or down within the list.

With this new replicator capability, you have much more control over which databases will be transferred and the order in which they will be transferred. For example, suppose you're in a hurry or you're on a trip where you must make a long-distance call. You can control the replication so that only your mail database or other critical information will be replicated so that you can save time and money.

FIGURE 4.12.

The Replicator tab.

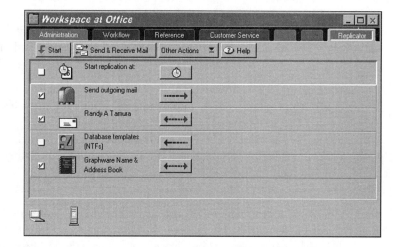

You can easily add databases to be replicated just by dragging a database icon from one of your workspace pages to the Replicator tab. You can remove an item easily just by highlighting the desired line and pressing the Delete key on your keyboard. Replication can't get much easier than this.

Local Security

For mobile users, Notes R4 has added enhanced local security. When connected to a server, Notes provides excellent security. There are logon passwords, database Access Control Lists, and the various access levels such as Author, Editor, and so forth. When you are disconnected from the server, Notes prior to R4 was less secure because a local user was allowed to do almost anything.

In Notes R4, databases can be encrypted with the ID of a particular user. Once this has been done, only a user with the specific ID can access the database. This feature is especially useful for mobile user e-mail databases. Only the authorized user can decrypt the database.

Notes also has a feature to locally enforce ACL settings that have been set on the host. Because local users have complete access to the machine and add-in programs can bypass this access, this feature does not totally secure the database, but it may help provide some additional security.

Using the Internet

The Internet is the hottest thing since a cup of hot, excuse me, Java. Everyone's talking about it; the venture capitalists are falling all over themselves to find the next company that will sizzle. Could Lotus let Notes stand idly by while all this commotion was going on? Of course not. But although many of the other companies are telling us how good it will be, Lotus has delivered the goods. The Internet support in R4 makes Notes the premier authoring and browsing tool.

On December 13, 1995, Lotus unveiled an Internet strategy, coupled with a product-pricing structure that was a preemptive strike in the industry. It took the InterNotes Web Publisher, which previously had an estimated retail price of $2,995 and included it for free with Notes R4. In addition, the InterNotes Web Navigator support is also included in all Notes systems. By dramatically lowering the cost per seat of Notes, by increasing the value of that seat, and by incorporating Internet support as a native feature, Lotus was beginning to make a very compelling case for Notes as an Internet tool.

During 1996, Lotus added many additional capabilities to the Notes server. So many, in fact, that they decided to rename the Notes server the Domino server. At the Lotus Domino Application Developer's conference in November of 1996, Lotus showed how Notes and Domino have become even more Internet-focused.

What exactly is included with Notes now for Internet support? Well, Notes now includes tools for browsing the World Wide Web as well as tools for publishing Notes Documents to the Web. Lotus also has announced products that can be added to other Web browsers, such as Netscape Navigator and Microsoft Internet Explorer. In other words, Notes can now be used as a tool for both viewers and authors of documents, even if you're not using the Notes client. To see why this is important, let's take a look at how you would typically produce documents for the Web today.

Web Clients and the World Wide Web

The World Wide Web is essentially a set of hypertext documents that spans the globe. It can be visualized as a spider web of documents, where each document can link to several other documents. Each document has a home location, or server, and when a user clicks on a hypertext link, he or she is transported to (potentially) another server that houses the destination link. The Web spans the globe because the servers are connected by the Internet and can be located anywhere in the world.

So, you can view a document located on a server in Los Angeles and then click on a link to a document in Paris. From there you can link to a document in Tokyo, and so forth. In addition to the geographical diversity, there is a great topical diversity as well. There are educational institutions, jazz clubs, flower shops, candy stores, manufacturing companies, insurance companies, museums—oh yes, and even a computer company or two. All of these organizations are using the World Wide Web to publish their electronic, interconnected documents. The name "World Wide Web" is an appropriate one, indeed.

In order to view these interconnected documents, you must have some sort of Web browser. Many Web-browsing programs are in use today from companies such as Netscape, Lotus, Microsoft, Quarterdeck, IBM, and many others. With Notes, two different configurations are possible for browsing the Web. The first is by having a server-based program retrieve the pages and then using a Notes client to access them. The second is via a direct connection to the Internet.

To produce pages with the ability to be shown by any browser, standards must be followed. For the World Wide Web, the data standard is called HTML, which stands for HyperText Markup Language. This language includes the text of the document as well as some markup tags. The markup tags of HTML are instructions to the browser that include font and size information, graphics to include, and other information about the presentation of the page.

All of the Web browsers mentioned previously, plus the many others publicly available, can interpret the HTML standard. The data that is sent back and forth over the Internet is sent using this data standard.

One criticism of Notes has been that it is a closed, proprietary system. Pundits have used these adjectives as pejoratives. Although Notes has this reputation, it really is a very open, cross-platform, standards-oriented system. Contrary to other systems, Notes supports not only Windows, but Macintosh, OS/2, UNIX, Novell, Windows NT, TCP/IP, SPX/IPX, and an array of other system and communication standards. Now, with HTML support its standards approach is even more evident. To underscore the openness of Notes, Lotus has recently reached agreements with both Netscape and Microsoft, and will be distributing both Netscape Navigator and Microsoft Internet Explorer with Notes (see Figure 4.13). If distributing your competitor's product isn't the ultimate in openness, I'm not sure what is!

FIGURE 4.13.
News of the Lotus agreements posted on the Web.

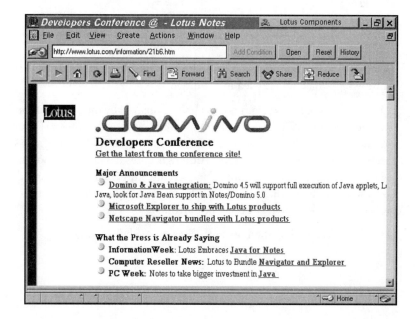

Web Interoperability

One of the main characteristics of the Web is its openness and interoperability. Because of standards in the data format, servers running on one hardware platform can serve information to another platform running one of many Web browsers. As an interesting example of interoperability, look at Figures 4.14 and 4.15. Figure 4.14 shows the Lotus Domino Web site as viewed through Internet Explorer (version 3). The Lotus Domino Web site, as you might expect, is powered by a Domino server.

FIGURE 4.14.

The Lotus Domino Web site as viewed through Microsoft Internet Explorer.

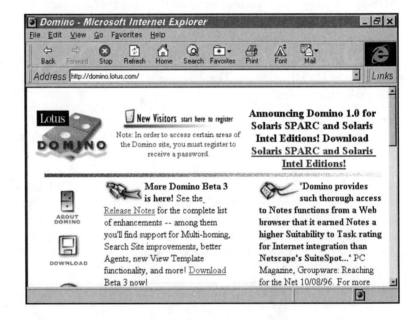

Figure 4.15 shows the Microsoft Web site as viewed through the Lotus Personal Web Navigator browser (which is discussed in a moment).

You have seen the Lotus (Domino) Web site displayed by the Microsoft browser, and you have seen the Microsoft Web site displayed by the Lotus Notes browser. I could have also showed you the Netscape site and browser, but you get the idea. Openness and standards are now a part of the Web development scene. Although Lotus has clearly demonstrated that it is building on a standards-based, nonproprietary architecture, many people still don't understand the Lotus strategy. This situation is probably worsened by Lotus' competitors, who try to paint a proprietary label on Notes at every opportunity.

Let's now take a look at the Lotus offerings for Web browsing.

FIGURE 4.15.

The Microsoft Web site as viewed through the Lotus Personal Web Navigator.

Server Web Navigator

The Server Web Navigator is a program that lets you view the documents that are on the Web, but from within your comfortable, familiar Notes environment. This integration is important because it enables users to access the Internet or the company network with equal ease. Actually, the Server Web Navigator is a client/server application and consists of a server program and the client/user interface. Don't be confused by the name Server Web Navigator. It just means that the Domino server is between you and the Internet.

The program that runs on the Domino server is called the InterNotes Web Retriever. The client program used to be called the InterNotes Web Navigator, but it is now commonly called the Server Web Navigator to distinguish it from the Personal Web Navigator (which I'll cover shortly).

Because the Server Web Navigator is a client/server application, it works differently from most current Web browsers, which are strictly client applications. With the Server Web Navigator, the Domino server is connected to the Internet via TCP/IP; in turn, each client is connected to the Domino server. Notes maintains a cache of recently requested Web pages in the InterNotes database.

When a client requests a Web page, Notes first looks to see if the page is in the InterNotes database. If it is, the request is satisfied immediately, improving performance. Also, it's important to realize that because this cache is shared among all of the Notes users, a Web page requested by any one user becomes cached for all users, again improving performance. If users are grouped by work function, the odds that they will be interested in the same Web pages are increased.

If the requested page is not currently in the InterNotes database, the InterNotes Web Retriever program on the server will go to the Internet and fetch the Web page, optionally convert the HTML codes to Notes document format, and store the page in the InterNotes database. From this point forward, the Web page is treated by Notes as just another document in a database. This architecture is important because now, after the document has been retrieved and stored in the database, the full power of Notes is available to process the Web page. It is not a tool for merely browsing the page, but can be used with all the programmability of LotusScript, Java, and other Notes tools.

In particular, after the Web page has been stored in the InterNotes database, it can also be replicated. Now here is an interesting scenario. You replicate the InterNotes database to your mobile computer. You then disconnect from your LAN, but you can still cruise the Web from your mobile computer because the Web pages are now stored in your replicated InterNotes database. Cruise the Internet without being connected. Now that's flexibility.

Administrators will be happy with this architecture for the Internet because, by going through a central server and repository, they can control access to sites. If administrators would like to deny access to certain sites, they can do so. There may be several reasons for wanting to deny access, including security and productivity reasons. Another major advantage for administrators is that with the client/server architecture, the TCP/IP Internet connection needs to be made only once to the server. TCP/IP does not need to be delivered to each desktop in the company. For example, you can use Novell's SPX/IPX in your internal network and just use TCP/IP to connect to the Internet at one point, not at each desktop.

Notes has had features such as doclinks, the ability to link from one document to another, for a long time. With its new Internet capabilities, Notes now has the ability to link not only to documents contained in the regular Notes database, but to Web pages as well. As a user, you can also forward a reference to a Web page to another user. All hypertext links will be maintained. This seamless integration of Notes databases and e-mail with the Web is unmatched in the industry today.

Personal Web Navigator

Centrally administered Internet access is desirable for companies, but individuals want the same power when they're disconnected from their workplace LANs. The Personal Web Navigator, shown in Figure 4.16, allows you to use the familiar Notes environment as your Web browser. It has much of the same philosophy as the Server Web Navigator.

FIGURE 4.16.

*The Lotus Personal
Web Navigator.*

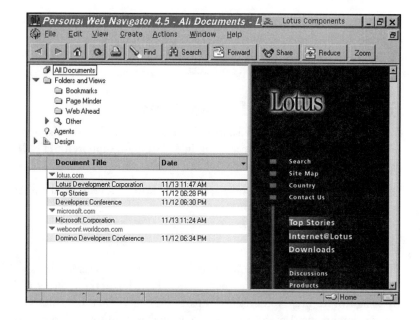

When you use the Personal Web Navigator, you access the Internet directly, but when the pages are retrieved, they are stored in a local Notes database. This lets you later browse offline. With the powerful View capabilities, you can also organize and manage your stored Web pages effectively.

Included with Personal Web Navigator are two useful features: Page Minder and Web Ahead. Page Minder lets you mark certain pages as important. A Page Minder agent checks these pages at certain intervals (which you can specify) and informs you if any of the pages have been updated. You can then choose whether you want to view them or not.

Web Ahead is a useful performance-enhancing feature. It is an agent that checks certain pages that you specify and follows the links located on those pages and fetches them ahead of time so that they will be available quickly when you're browsing.

The Weblicator

At the time of this writing, Lotus had announced but not yet shipped the Weblicator. This exciting new program takes some of the features of Personal Web Navigator and extends them to non-Lotus products. In particular, Netscape Navigator and Microsoft Internet Explorer (IE) are supported.

With the Weblicator, you'll be able to cache Web pages into a Notes database and organize and manage them just as you do with Personal Web Navigator. You can view them later with Netscape Navigator or IE. Lotus has also announced that it will be shipping both of these additional browsers with the Notes product.

Other Internet Client Enhancements

In addition to the features listed above, Lotus has added a laundry list of other features including Java applet execution, Netscape plug-in API support, support for HTML 3.2, and the ability to type URLs in the search bar.

All of these features, and many others, are available in Notes R4.5 and offer users a more friendly and powerful operating environment.

InterNotes News

InterNotes News is an application that runs on a Domino server. It uses the Network News Transfer Protocol (NNTP) to exchange Usenet articles on the Internet with a Notes database. By using this feature, Notes users can participate in Usenet discussions without leaving their Notes environment. Also, because the Notes database is stored on Domino servers, performance for end-users is improved.

This facility will be popular with administrators as well because the InterNotes News program requires only one Internet TCP/IP connection. You do not need to have TCP/IP running at each workstation, which in turn makes cabling and network-server implementations easier. Also, because the service is centrally controlled and administered, you can control the selection of Usenet-newsgroup subscriptions. After the information has been converted to Notes format, you can replicate the databases for use throughout your entire Notes network. You can make Usenet discussions appear just like another Notes database to your users.

Domino: Serving Pages to the Internet

Domino was originally the name for just the Web page-serving program that runs on the Notes server. However, Lotus recognized that the Notes server has become much more than just a Notes server that also serves pages to the Internet. Lotus wants to position its server as the Domino server, which serves pages to Notes and the Internet. Although this might sound like a subtle difference, there can be a great difference in perception, because many people still view Notes as proprietary.

The primary marketing statement that Lotus would like to make is that although people think of Notes as a proprietary system, it isn't. With the name change to Domino, with the ability to serve pages to any Web browser, and with the packaging of Netscape Navigator and Microsoft IE with Notes, Lotus is trying to show that it is completely open to supporting anyone's browser but is more strict about servers.

The two Web server programs for the Internet are the InterNotes Web Publisher and the Domino Web Server. The InterNotes Web Publisher was made available first and has gone through several releases. Domino is the new technology, but both programs remain available. You'll be hearing much more about Domino in the future.

InterNotes Web Publisher

Many companies have decided that the Internet provides an important publishing medium. It enables companies to advertise and market, to provide customer support, and to electronically get closer to their customers and prospects. As Web publishing has started to grow, however, many companies are realizing that the costs of creating and maintaining a Web site are not small. Many times the content for the Web site is created across the company, but must be converted to HTML by a Webmaster. In addition, the power of Web pages is that they contain links to other sites or other documents. Each of the links must be maintained, more or less manually, by the Webmaster.

The InterNotes Web Publisher is a tool designed to make attractive, industrial strength, easy-to-maintain Web sites. It should enable companies with large Web sites to dramatically lower their costs of operation. The principle is simple: Do your Web-page authoring using standard Notes features, and then let Notes automatically convert the documents to Web pages (that is, HTML), including all of the hypertext links.

Notes R4.x has many features for making attractive forms. These same features, as well as all of the user training, are leveraged by allowing them to be used for Web authoring as well. Because of the many features of Notes, you can provide standard templates for your Web site, you can provide common navigational tools, you can provide a common look and feel to your pages, and best of all, you can distribute the authoring of the documents across your company, around the world. Any large company has a lot of information to publish on its Web site. The ability to quickly publish this information should not have to funnel through a guru or department responsible just for creating HTML, because it would quickly become a bottleneck. With the InterNotes Web Publisher, this bottleneck never exists.

The Domino Web Server

With the InterNotes Web Publisher, you can convert your Notes databases to HTML, save them, and then serve them to the Web with any Web server. If you already have a Web server and Notes, this approach lets you flexibly leverage your existing Notes databases and publish them to the Web.

Domino takes this capability and adds to it. For example, wouldn't it be nice to be able to take the contents of a Notes database and make it directly available on the Web without needing another Web server program? Well, now you can. One of Domino's primary functions is to take Notes databases, convert them to HTML on-the-fly, and serve them to a hungry Internet world. So, you could say that Domino delivers (Web pages, not pizza)! This book has an entire mouth-watering part (Part V) devoted to Domino, the Internet, and intranets for your nourishment and enjoyment.

Developing Applications with Notes R4.x

Notes R4.x has many new features for application developers. Most notable, of course, is the addition of LotusScript in Release 4.0, the BASIC language-scripting language now available to handle most programming tasks. In R4.5, Lotus has added more than 100 new classes, methods, and properties to the LotusScript language.

LotusScript

The LotusScript language is the Lotus dialect of BASIC. If you are familiar with Microsoft's Visual Basic, you'll feel right at home with LotusScript. It has many similarities, and if you have existing programs in Visual Basic, a lot of the code can just be cut and pasted into LotusScript. There are a few differences, however, and it is not identical to Visual Basic. One important feature of LotusScript is that it is implemented in a cross-platform manner, meaning you can use it on any of the supported client operating systems such as UNIX, OS/2, Windows 95, Macintosh, Windows 3.11, or Windows NT. This cross-platform capability is not available in Visual Basic.

LotusScript is covered in great detail in Chapter 18, "Using LotusScript"; here I'll just give you an overview of its features and capabilities. Figure 4.17 shows the dialog area where you can input a LotusScript subprogram. The subprogram shown is the Initialize subprogram, which is automatically invoked by LotusScript when a form is initialized. This type of subprogram is handling an event.

FIGURE 4.17.

A LotusScript program entry form.

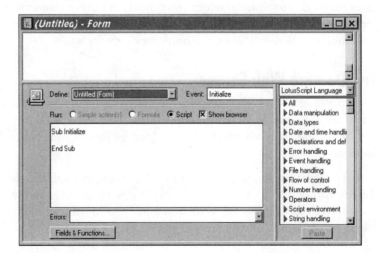

Here are some examples of the types of events that can occur in Notes:

■ A form is initialized or terminated.

■ A button is clicked just before a form is saved.

■ The user enters or exits fields with the cursor in edit mode.

At each of these events (and others), you can attach a LotusScript program to handle the event and perform custom actions. A simple example of a program might be field validation that verifies the appropriateness of values in one or more fields.

At the right side of the screen shown in Figure 4.17, you see a list of some of the features of LotusScript. This list appears if you select the Show browser box. This list is very helpful, especially when you are first learning LotusScript. When you want to add some code to your program but aren't sure of which function you need, you can navigate through the list at the right, and when you find the appropriate function, you double click it. This action will cause the text of the function call to be placed automatically in your code window. You can then use the code as inserted or modify it as necessary.

Notes also defines classes that can be used from LotusScript to manipulate Notes data. The classes are grouped into two categories: database access and user interface. The database classes can be used to manipulate Notes databases, views, documents, fields, and other Notes objects. The user-interface classes enable you to manipulate the workspace and the current document that is open in the user's workspace.

Lotus has also added a debugger to the development environment to make debugging LotusScript programs easier. With the debugger, you can step through your program, examine variables, and perform other tasks that make it much simpler to debug LotusScript programs than the formulas of previous releases.

Now it's also possible to have libraries of LotusScript programs. These libraries are stored in a manner similar to subforms and are accessed from within the Design area of the database. The LotusScript integrated development environment (IDE) now also includes a feature to color-code the LotusScript source. This makes the source program easier to read.

A much-needed feature, find and replace, is now available in R4.5. This feature allows you to look for strings in your LotusScript source code in the current subroutine or other subroutines.

Navigators

Navigators are visual hotspots that users can click. In many ways, they are similar to buttons. You can program the action to take when the user clicks on one of these Navigator hotspots. You can program the Navigator to take one of several possible actions when the user clicks it:

■ Open a different Navigator.

■ Open a view.

■ Act as a folder alias. Clicking the Navigator displays the folder, and documents can be dropped on it to add them to the folder.

■ Open a link to a database, view, or document.

■ Execute a formula.

■ Execute a LotusScript program.

With all of these options, you have a wealth of flexibility in creating an easy-to-use environment for the user.

Subforms, Layout Regions, and Sections

Subforms, Layout Regions, and Sections are all features that can be used to enhance the reuse, aesthetics, and usability of your applications. They are discussed in greater detail in Chapter 14, "Making Your Application Look Good and Work Well." Here are some of the highlights of these features.

Subforms are parts of forms that you can design to be reused. For example, you might have a company logo, Name and Address fields, or other similar information that you would like to have duplicated on several forms. By using subforms and then including them on the various forms, you can reuse your design (thus saving time), and at the same time have more control of common user-interface elements. If you decide to change your design, you'll have to change it only once in the subform and the changes will propagate to the forms that include the subform.

Layout regions can be placed on either forms or subforms. They can contain static text, buttons, graphics, and all field types except for rich-text fields. They can have a 3-D effect associated with them. Layout regions are created with a fixed size, and items that are placed on the layout region remain in a fixed position relative to one another. While you are designing a layout region, you can use drag and drop techniques to place items where you want them.

For example, text on a form or subform that has the Centered attribute will move as the form window is sized. The text will be centered relative to the visible window. Text centered relative to a layout region field, however, will be centered when you create it and will not move as the window is sized. When you understand the differences, layout regions, subforms, and forms give the form designer a lot of flexibility in getting the form to look and behave as desired.

Sections in R4 have been enhanced from R3 and they enable the designer to provide forms that have a great deal of information, but without the necessity of showing it to the user only at once. Sections have a little twistie at the left, which can point either to the right or down. When the twistie points to the right, the section is collapsed. When it points down, the section is expanded. This enables the user to control whether or not the section is displayed.

Sections provide another tool for the designer to simplify the program interface for the user. By displaying the form with sections initially collapsed, the form is greatly simplified. Only when users need to view the information is it necessary to expand the sections, and then it can be done under user control. A great example of this design is in the Server document of the

Public Address Book, as shown in Figure 4.18. Notice how only the main information is shown by default, but each section with a twistie is available for opening under user control.

FIGURE 4.18.

A document with several sections.

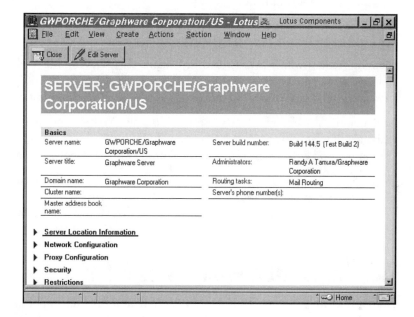

Agents

Agents are another name for the Macros of previous releases of Notes. They are designed to run automatically when a trigger event occurs. Agents can be run automatically based upon a particular time or when an event occurs (for example, when documents are changed in the database). Agents may be private, which means that you create and use them yourself, or they may be shared, which means that they are created by a designer and will be shared by many users.

An agent also has associated with it a selection formula to select the documents that are used by the agent as well as the action to execute. You can associate a formula or a LotusScript program to run on the documents when the event occurs.

Agents are useful tools to do database maintenance, for scanning documents to find important or relevant new information automatically, for responding to your e-mail automatically, or for many other tasks that you would otherwise have to do manually.

As your inventory of databases becomes larger, agents become a more important tool because the information will be too large to effectively monitor manually. When coupled with the InterNotes Navigator support mentioned previously, agents can help you create a system that will go out and automatically search your customer or competitor Web sites for information.

The agent can then download that information into your Notes database automatically, sift through it to look for specific information you identify, and send you an e-mail with just the relevant articles for your review.

Developing Web Applications

Domino.Action, which is described in Chapter 25, "Developing Web Applications with Domino.Action," provides templates for creating Web-based applications. This is an entirely new category of application, but one that is becoming increasingly important.

With traditional Web servers, you must create your own Web site and applications using HTML. Although there are tools for making these applications easier to create, it is still a difficult, time-consuming, and error-prone process. Much of the work still remains manual.

With Domino.Action, a lot of the work of creating a Web site has already been done for you and has been incorporated into the Notes database templates. This approach is much more of a "fill in the blanks" kind of process rather than one that needs a tremendous amount of manual effort.

Administration with Notes R4.x

Administration in Notes R4.x is very similar to that in R3. One important goal of this Notes release was interoperability between the releases, and generally this interoperability is very good. To achieve this goal, Lotus had to keep many of the data formats and structures compatible between the releases. However, they also have improved the interface for the administrative functions.

The Administration Control Panel

Figure 4.19 shows the new Administration control panel. This is the central command center for administrative operations, and it consolidates many of the operations that were scattered across various menus in R3.

The Administration control panel has eight buttons. They are to administer people, groups, servers, certifiers, the address book, mail, and databases. You can also press the console button to issue a console command to a server.

Scalability and Manageability

R4.x of Notes supports symmetrical multiprocessors (SMP). With this new feature, several processors can be managed by the server. By supporting multiprocessors, a single server can now support hundreds of users, a much larger number than with previous releases of Notes. The actual number of processors supported and the maximum number of users supported will depend upon your hardware platform and the operating system you use.

FIGURE 4.19.

The Administration control panel.

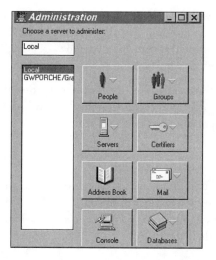

In addition to SMP, Notes 4.5 has added clustering. This is a feature that allows you to group up to six servers. The servers of the group (cluster) all work together to perform load balancing and failover support. In other words, when one of the servers gets too busy, it can hand over work to another server in the cluster. Failover support also means that if one of the servers in the cluster fails for either a software or hardware reason, the other servers in the cluster can pick up the work without affecting the users.

With R4.5, the Domino server can support partitioning. This capability is also sometimes called multihoming or multihosting. This feature allows one physical server to behave as several logical servers. This is particularly useful to the service provider community, which might want to provide partitions for each of its customers. Partitioning is available on the Windows NT/Intel and UNIX platforms.

With R4.5, Notes now has additional capabilities to support billing applications. These features allow customers to measure mail traffic or the way certain applications are used.

Notes R4.5 also supports the searching and browsing of address books of other Notes domains. Of course, these capabilities are subject to the appropriate set of security rules set up by the administrator.

Windows NT Enhancements

There are several new enhancements for clients and/or servers running on the Windows NT platform. The first is called NT single logon. It allows clients running Windows NT to enter only a single password when logging on to Windows NT; they don't have to reenter a password when starting Notes.

4
WHAT'S NEW IN
RELEASES 4
THROUGH 4.5?

Windows NT user management lets administrators automatically create and delete Windows NT user IDs at the time they create them in the Notes Public Address Book. In addition, Notes User IDs can be created at the time a Windows NT user ID is created. This bidirectional capability will greatly ease administration for Windows NT administrators who also support Notes.

R4.5 also includes the capability to save Notes events into the Windows NT event logger. The capability to record Notes events into this log gives administrators a single location to look in for tracking important events on the system.

Security

Event Control Lists (ECLs) are a new feature of Notes 4.5. This feature lets users control what types of programs will be allowed to run in the Notes database. Each user can control various aspects of the ECL by selecting File | Tools | User Preferences | Basics | Security Options. A dialog box will then appear that allows the user to specify execution access.

The Administration Process

The administration process runs on the server and greatly eases the administration of name changes in Notes. Previously, if you wanted to change or delete a user ID from the system, you also had to go through access control lists for all of your databases to change or remove the ID from each one. The administration process of R4.x performs global name changes and deletions for you, as well as several other tasks, automatically.

Document Merging During Replication

When two users modify copies of the same document in different locations and replication occurs, you get a replication conflict on the document. You can specify several options for handling the conflict in Notes. New with R4 is a feature called Merge replication conflicts.

This feature takes advantage of the fact that even though two users are modifying the same document, they may, in fact, be modifying different fields. For example, Sam has modified the Name field, but Sue has modified the Amount field of the same document. In prior releases of Notes, this would cause a replication conflict, even though the data modified was different. Now you can specify Merge replication conflicts (in Form properties, Basics tab at the bottom). Then, if Sam and Sue modify different fields, Notes won't consider this a replication conflict.

This feature will help administrators and users by cutting down the amount of time for replication, since only changes to the fields are updated. It will also cut the number of replication conflicts. Each replication conflict usually must be inspected manually, so this will decrease the amount of time spent investigating the conflicts.

Other Helpful Features for Administrators

There are several other helpful features for administrators in Notes R4.x. The mail-tracing facility enables either a user or administrator to have Notes show the path that mail will take from the sending site to its destination. This will greatly help during troubleshooting sessions.

Passthru servers were mentioned earlier. They enable mobile users to reach a destination server via one or more intermediate servers. With Passthru, replica copies of databases do not have to be on every server. This gives convenience and allows administrators more flexibility in designing their dial-in configuration. Dial-in servers can be like concentrators for other servers, or they may be geographically dispersed to lower telephone costs.

Agents provide a powerful mechanism for administrators to perform routine maintenance and updating of documents and databases. The administration process is similar to an agent, and it is very helpful in handling Public Address Book changes.

The Single Copy Object Store (SCOS) is a very useful e-mail feature. Many times with e-mail, a particular message is copied to several users. This results in the collective mail databases containing many redundant copies of the same message. To cut down on this duplication, Notes now has SCOS. With this feature, only one copy of a document is kept, with separate header information for each recipient.

The users of this feature will not notice a difference, but what is actually happening is that when the user opens a copy of a message that is shared, the user's header information is merged with the text of the message from the SCOS. This merged message is then displayed to the user.

Summary

Notes R4.5 is packed with enhancements and new features. R4.5 adds to this impressive list of enhancements included in R4.0. It's a major upgrade from R3 and R4.x and has something for just about everyone: users, developers, administrators, and Internet cruisers. This chapter was meant to be an overview, and the rest of this book covers many more details about these new features.

The Internet capabilities of the Notes client and the powerful features of the Domino server make R4.5 a compelling upgrade for any company interested in the Internet. There are several options for Internet browsing, including the Notes Personal Web Navigator, the Notes Server Web Navigator, and now, Netscape Navigator and Microsoft Internet Explorer. On the server side, Domino provides a wealth of features unmatched in the industry. With support for replication, workflow, calendars, scheduling, and database management in addition to the traditional serving of HTML pages, Domino is a clear leader.

There are major enhancements in the Notes user interface carried forward from release 4.0. It is more powerful, yet simpler and easier to use. Action Bars and Navigators are used by the built-in components such as Help and NotesMail, but they are also available for use by application developers. Workflow programs are easier to create and use. Mobile users now have location settings as well as Passthru server support. Administration is easier with the Administration control panel and through the use of the administration process and agents.

Notes R4.5 is a major upgrade that brings many new features to existing and new users. The rest of this book will provide you with more information to use this new tool more effectively and enhance your company's productivity.

IN THIS PART

PART

II

Using Lotus Notes

The Notes Workspace and Databases

by Don Child

IN THIS CHAPTER

This chapter describes the desktop environment of Lotus Notes Release 4.5, how to enter a password that identifies you to the system, navigating the workspace—including a quick look at the new replicator tab, how to add a new workspace page (new to Notes R4.x), and how to use SmartIcons. The chapter also briefly describes what a Notes database is, how to add and remove database icons from a workspace page, and how to open a database once it is on the desktop.

For the sake of example, say that you have a private office with a large desk. On top of the desk are most of the tools you need to do your work—for example, sharpened pencils, rulers, white-out, a dictionary.

In addition, there are several neatly stacked folders, each clearly labeled with generalized category names: projects, correspondence, research, and personal. On the desktop there is also an in tray and an out tray, and a ream of paper just waiting for you to start working.

You reach for the projects folder and open it up. Inside are several files, each representing one of the projects you are working on. You thumb through until you locate the project you want to work on right now, and when you open it, there are all of the documents you require—a copy of the contract, a copy of the proposal, spreadsheets, and a diagram illustrating the organization of the project. You sift through all of the papers until you find the one you want, then put aside the remainder of the documents. You push aside the remaining files and folders and set to work without distraction.

Now think about what that desktop would look like if it were a *virtual* desktop.

You have a key to the top center drawer. Inside that drawer, you keep your more important folders, the ones you must keep secure. Because you are sitting at your desk, there is no further need to keep your folders under lock and key. Unlocking that one drawer unlocks all of the drawers, giving you immediate access to all of your private folders. These folders, though, are also ones you share with others. Everyone who needs the folders has their own key.

Your key has also unlocked your electronic communications center. The communications center is a single piece of equipment that provides you with a fax machine, an automatic answer phone, and even a built-in video unit that provides sound and video clips. The communications center can copy single documents or entire files. You can make an exact copy of everything in a file, or even better, just everything that is new and relevant. The copy can be sent off to a co-worker, no matter where their desk is. The co-worker could work in a branch office on the other side of the world, and the task of sending them an exact copy would be fully automated. As long as their name is listed in your address book and they have been authorized to see the file, they can retrieve a copy electronically without even bothering you.

This virtual desk represents some of the more obvious elements of Lotus Notes. For every user, the desktop is stored in a file called *desktop.dsk*. On the Macintosh, the file is simply called *desktop*.

The Notes R4.x Desktop Environment

The Notes R4.x desktop is a graphical workspace that is virtually identical on all Notes client platforms. When Notes is started up, it looks for the desktop file. This file determines how the workspace has been customized by the user. If Notes cannot find a desktop file, it creates a new one.

If a user has his or her own Notes client workstation, the desktop.dsk file can be kept in the default Notes data directory. If, on the other hand, a single workstation is used by multiple Notes users, then multiple desktop files can be kept in different start-up directories, either on the local hard drive or on the network. Then each user can have their own Notes desktop, customized and arranged as they want.

The Notes R4 desktop will look familiar to anyone who has used earlier releases of Notes. In fact, it will probably also look familiar to anyone who has ever used an office desk, whether it be the virtual desk previously described, or a real desk.

Just like the virtual desktop, the Notes R4 desktop has, within easy reach, all of the tools you require to do your job. It has folders, each clearly labeled, with labels that the individual user can define. These folders, referred to as *workspace pages*, have tabs that provide easy access to the databases on that page. To move to a new workspace page, simply click on the tab at the top of the page you want to move to.

Each workspace page can contain one or more database icons, which are synonymous with the files inside a folder on the virtual desktop. And of course, inside each database are the documents that you can work with or refer to in the course of a day.

A Look at the Notes R4 Desktop

When Notes is first set up, the R4 desktop workspace shows one tabbed folder on top, along with five other workspace folders indicated by a tab, plus a tab for the Replicator page. (See Figure 5.1.) Each workspace page (with the exception of the back page, which is the Replicator page) can hold database icons.

The title bar, menu bar, and Status Bar are context-sensitive, displaying information relevant to whatever you are doing in Notes at the moment. For example, the title bar might display the name of a database icon, the name of a document within the database, or it might dynamically display information about the current document by means of a formula.

The SmartIcons change dynamically to reflect your current activity—for example, editing a document, navigating within a database, or dialing up to a remote server each has its own set of SmartIcons. The available SmartIcons depend on what you are doing at the moment. In earlier versions of Notes, you could manually switch between different sets of SmartIcons, but the process was not context-sensitive as it is in Notes R4.

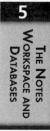

FIGURE 5.1.

*The Notes 4
Workspace.*

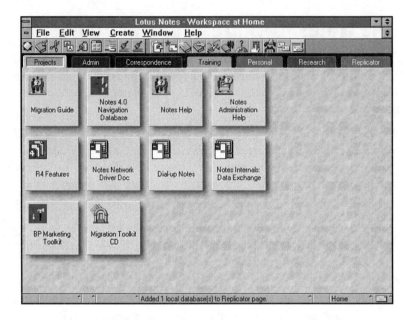

The database icons can be added to or deleted from the workspace, moved between workspace pages, and you can change the amount of information displayed on the icon.

You can add or delete entire workspace pages, and you can change the appearance of the workspace between a three-dimensional marbled appearance, and a more traditional two-dimensional workspace that looks more like the Notes R3 workspace.

> **NOTE**
>
> The desktop shown in Figure 5.1 displays database icons with a three-dimensional texture. This textured desktop can only be displayed if your monitor is configured for 256 colors. If you want to, you can turn off the 3-D display using the Workspace Properties box.

In addition to everything else, the workspace will show vertical and/or horizontal scroll bars if there are too many icons on a workspace page to display on the screen.

Each of these elements is described in detail later in this chapter.

Logging On to Lotus Notes

Logging on means different things to different people. In some environments, you need to log on just to gain access to an application. In others, you never have to log on.

With Notes, you do not technically log on to the Notes network. You identify to Notes which user ID to use when accessing the Notes server, or when accessing certain local databases. You can start up Notes on your local workstation without a user ID. You can move around on certain pages within the workspace, and even within certain databases, without ever having to provide a user ID. But at other times, you will have to provide Notes with a user ID, usually protected with a password, just to work on a local database. It depends on how you have set up individual databases.

Notes sits on top of the local area network, and uses the underlying network infrastructure for communication protocols when a user on a workstation accesses a database or process on the Notes server. The Notes server, however, is distinct from the network file server, and does not usually run on the same hardware as the file server. Therefore, you can work on a Notes network and access the Notes server without being logged onto the local area network, unless you want to use network resources such as shared printers, or you need to access a directory on your file server—for example, you may have Notes user IDs and desktop files stored on the server so users can use Notes from any workstation that has access to the file server. Whether or not you log on to the file server, you do have to provide a valid user ID to use a workstation to access databases and processes on a Notes server, or to access databases on the local workstation that has access control security enforced.

Whether you are logged on to the network or not, you can start up Notes on your workstation by double-clicking on the Notes icon.

Notes opens to the desktop shown in Figure 5.1, assuming initial workstation setup has already been done. You then see the Notes workspace, including any database icons that are on your desktop. You can open and use locally stored databases as long as local security is not being enforced for the database. You can navigate to the various workspace pages, add workspace pages, and create local databases from local templates, all without having to log on.

But Notes has a very secure structure, and requires the use of a password protected ID file when you attempt to access a Notes server or attempt to open a database on which local security is being enforced. The first time any of the following happens, you will be prompted for your password:

- You attempt to open a database on which local security is enforced, a new
  security feature available in Notes R4.

- You attempt to define local security for a database (using the Properties box for
  an existing or new database).

- You attempt to change ID files.

- You attempt to access a Notes server for any purpose, such as opening a database.

- You start up Notes when you have an Island location, new in Notes R4, and
  you have replication scheduled.

- You attempt any other action which requires authentication between a user ID and a
  database or a server.

Each of these activities requires that you have a valid ID file. You are identified to the Notes server or to your workstation as an authorized user by means of an ID file that was created when the system administrator first registered you as a Notes user on the system. The ID file may have a generic name like *user.id.* You also can change the filename to include your name, for example, *djones.id.* The only required part of the ID's filename is the .id suffix, because Notes looks for *.id files when it presents a list of available IDs.

In order to use your ID file, you must first type in one or more case-sensitive passwords to verify that you are the authorized user. The minimum password length is defined by the system administrator. It is advisable to keep a minimum password length of at least eight characters to protect your ID from unauthorized use. The system administrator could set a default password length of zero, which would enable users to clear their passwords; but this circumvents the whole purpose of having IDs, to make access to the server secure.

When Notes requires you to have a user ID, it displays the Enter Password dialog box. (See Figure 5.2.) By entering the password associated with ID, you are demonstrating that you are the legitimate owner of that ID.

FIGURE 5.2.
*The Password
dialog box.*

As you type in your password, Notes displays a random number of Xs to prevent a casual on-looker from guessing the exact length of your password. The Password dialog box also displays "hieroglyphics" as you type in your password. This is called *anti-spoofing* and prevents people from developing programs designed to fool the system by looking like the Password dialog box so they can steal your password.

The password must be entered exactly the same every time, including upper- and lowercase characters. For example the two words "PassWord" and "password" are not interchangeable, because the first word has two characters that are uppercase.

Passwords can be up to 31 characters in length and can consist of letters, spaces, and/or numbers. Examples of valid passwords are:

- lotusnotes
- LotusNotes
- Lotus 123
- 123go notes
- 1#dx85()qwerty
- THEquickBROWNfoxJUMPEDoverTHE

A new feature in Notes R4 is the ability to require more than one password in order to use an ID. This is designed to make the server ID and certifier IDs more secure, but can be used with user IDs as well. To use multiple passwords, you must have a hierarchical name. Multiple passwords are set up using the File | Tools | Server Admin... then by selecting the Certifiers and Edit Multiple passwords. Certifier IDs and hierarchical naming are discussed at length in Chapter 34, "Security Overview."

Once you have correctly entered your password, thereby validating that you are the rightful owner of your Notes ID, you can open databases on which local security is enforced and can access the Notes server at any time during the current session. Your user ID and associated access privileges remains valid until one of the following happens:

- You exit Notes.
- You clear your user ID by pressing F5 or selecting File | Tools | Lock ID.
- You are logged off automatically by Notes (if you or the administrator set your ID to automatically log out after a predefined period of inactivity).
- You change to another user ID file. You will then have the access privileges associated with that new ID, but your previous privileges will no longer be valid.
- The Notes administrator can drop you from the server using a server console command. This is a new administrative capability in Notes R4.

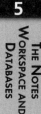

A Closer Look at the Desktop

As already mentioned, the desktop is defined in a file named desktop.dsk (desktop on the Mac). When Notes is started up, it searches the default Notes data directory, then other directories listed in the path until it finds the desktop.dsk file. If the file is not found, Notes creates a new desktop file.

This file contains information such as which database icons display and how they display, which workspace pages are available, and which page is displayed initially (the page that was selected when Notes last shut down).

Each user can customize his or her own desktop. If each user has his or her own Notes workstation, then there is a single desktop file for each registered Notes user. If, however, a Notes client workstation is shared by multiple users, there are a couple of options available.

- Users can share the desktop (with each user having their own workspace pages, for example).
- Users can each have their own unique desktop file.

If users have their own desktop on a shared workstation, they can each have their own startup directory that contains their personal desktop files. Many times, this startup directory will be located on a file server, with each user's desktop and Notes user ID files stored in personal directories protected by network security.

Workspace Pages

By default, Notes displays six tabbed workspace pages, plus the Replicator page, which is always the back page. In addition to the six default pages, you can define up to 26 additional pages, giving you a total of 32 workspace pages. Each workspace page can hold up to 256 database icons. If there are too many icons to see on the desktop, scroll bars will be displayed automatically. In Notes R3, you were limited to six workspace pages, and each page held a maximum of 99 database icons.

The workspace pages are used to organize database icons in any way that makes sense to you. Some people may want to have 26 pages, with one for each letter of the alphabet, just like a filing cabinet might be organized. Notes R3 users may feel more comfortable with six pages, which is the number of pages on a Notes R3 desktop. Other users might want just one or two pages. Whichever configuration is desired, the user can add and delete their own workspace pages. Common ways to organize the desktop are by priority, by type of application (reference, workflow, discussion), by project, or by location—something that is not really necessary with R4 because multiple replicas, residing in different locations, can be stacked. It is really up to the individual user how pages are organized and named, unless corporate policy dictates that databases are organized in a particular fashion.

The Replicator page is an exception. The page cannot be deleted, and database icons can only be placed on the page for the purpose of replication. They cannot be opened or navigated from the Replicator page.

How do you customize your workspace? There are several ways. You can display icons in a three-dimensional motif if you have at least a 256 color display. You can change the color of a workspace tab. You can label tabs. You can add or delete pages. You can compress the desktop to reclaim unused whitespace. Each of these is described in the following sections.

Customizing a Tab

To customize a tab, follow these steps while you are on the desktop:

1. Display the Workspace Properties box. (See Figure 5.3.) This can be done by double-clicking on the tab or by clicking on the tab for the workspace page and selecting Edit Properties from the pull-down menu.

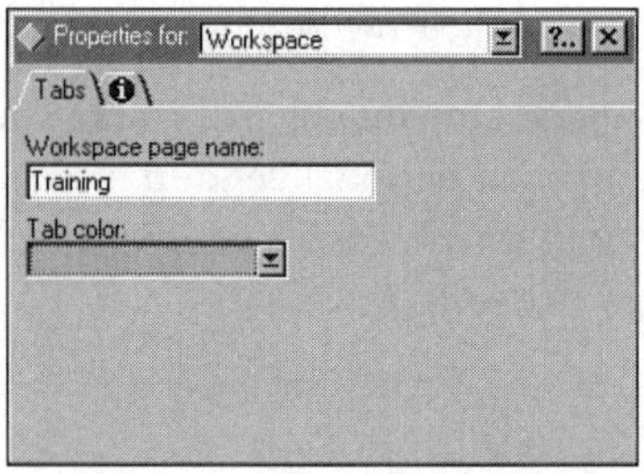

FIGURE 5.3.

The Workspace Properties dialog box.

> **NOTE**
>
> Properties boxes are new to Notes R4, enabling you to change the properties of many elements from a single dialog box. Depending on where you are within Notes, you can at various times display properties for the workspace, for a database, for a document, for selected text, for a view, or for a form or a field. The Properties box consists of multiple tabbed pages where you can set a variety of properties. Once properties have been set, you can close the Properties box by double-clicking in the upper-left corner of the box. Alternately, you can minimize the Properties by double-clicking on the word "Properties" in the box's title bar, then continue editing by clicking anywhere in the workspace outside the Properties box.

2. Add or modify the name for the workspace page. Type in the workspace page name field. The name can be up to 32 characters long. The name you give your workspace page is displayed on the tab for that page.

3. Change the color of the tab at the top of the workspace page by clicking on the small arrow in the tab color field. Notes displays a palette of colors from which to select. Click on the color you want. The tab changes to that color.

   When you use Notes, the tab of the current workspace page is outlined with a gray border. You can move from one page to another by clicking on the tab of the page to which you want to move. The tab for the new page then has a highlighted border. You also can use the keyboard to move to a new page by holding down the Ctrl key (the Command key on the Macintosh) while you press the left or right arrow key.

> **NOTE**
>
> It is possible to add more tabs than will display on the desktop at one time. You cannot use the mouse to scroll to tabs that are off the screen, but you can use the keyboard arrow keys to navigate from tab to tab, including those that are not visible. Therefore, as a general rule it is advisable to keep your tab names as short as possible, well below the maximum length of 32 characters.

Adding a New Workspace Page

To add a new workspace page, highlight the tab to the right of where you want to insert the new page, and select Create | Workspace Page from the pull-down menu or display the Properties box for the workspace page and select Create Workspace Page. In previous versions of Notes, you could not add or delete workspace pages.

Deleting a Workspace Page

To delete a workspace page, something you could not do in earlier versions of Notes, do one of the following:

■ Click with the right mouse button on the tab of the page to be deleted. This displays the workspace page menu. Select Remove Workspace Page to delete the page.

■ Move to the page to be deleted and press the Delete key.

■ Move to the page to be deleted and select Edit Clear from the pull-down menu.

If there are any database icons on the page that is being deleted, the icons are removed from the desktop automatically. This causes private Views and Folders to be lost.

Compacting the Workspace

When database icons are moved around the workspace, or as you add and delete database icons or workspace pages, the workspace eventually accumulates whitespace as the desktop.dsk file gets fragmented. You can regain that whitespace by compacting the workspace periodically, something that could not be done in earlier versions of Notes. A suggested threshold for compacting the workspace is whenever the workspace is more than 15 percent unused. Follow these steps to compact the workspace:

1. Display the Workspace Properties dialog box for any workspace page.

2. Click on the Information tab to move to the second page of the Properties dialog box. (See Figure 5.4.)

FIGURE 5.4.

The Workspace Properties Information page.

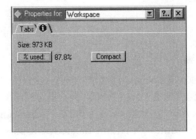

3. Click on the % used button to determine what percentage of the workspace is being used.

4. If the percentage drops below 85 percent, click on Compact.

   Notes compacts the workspace, displaying a Status Bar to indicate how much time remains to complete the process. It may take up several minutes to compact the workspace, depending on the speed of your processor, the number of databases on your desktop, and the amount of whitespace to be freed.

> **NOTE**
>
> You can compact an individual database in essentially the same way. Highlight the database icon, display the Database Properties dialog box, and from the Information page, select Compact. Note that this can take several minutes for a large database. Also, be cautious if you are working in a mixed Notes R3 and Notes R4 environment, because compacting a database using Notes R4 will convert the database to Notes R4 format, which can cause unexpected results for Notes R3 users.

The Replicator Page

The back workspace page in Notes R4 is the Replicator page. This is a new feature that simplifies the management of replication. The Replicator page is described in detail in Chapter 33, "Replication and its Administration." For now, a simple explanation should suffice. The page can hold icons for all databases on your workstation that can be replicated. You can select and change the order in which databases get replicated and initiate replication using the graphical interface on the page. A sample of the page is shown in Figure 5.5.

FIGURE 5.5.

The Replicator page on the Notes R4 desktop.

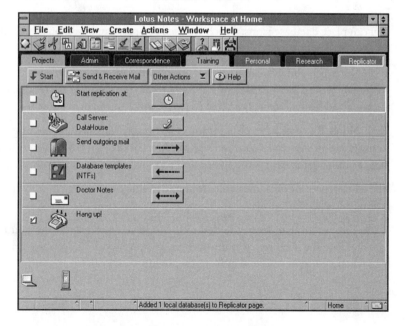

Database Icons

Each database icon on the Notes desktop represents a Notes database, or application. The two words can be used more or less synonymously in Notes, although an application can also consist of multiple related databases. Each database icon is a small square with a graphic image, and certain information about the database is represented by the icon. (See Figure 5.6.)

FIGURE 5.6.

Database icons.

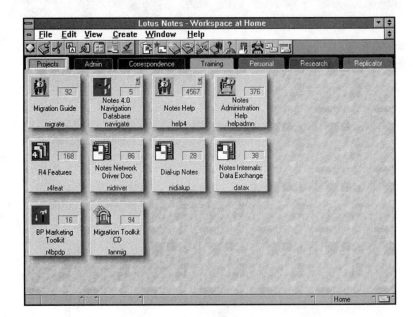

You can place database icons, which are used to open databases, on any workspace page except for the Replicator page.

With Notes R3, you were able to store up to 99 database icons on each of six workspace pages, giving you a maximum capacity of 594 icons on your desktop at any one time. If you wanted to display additional icons, you had to delete some of the existing icons to make room.

With Notes R4, you have 26 additional workspace pages, each holding up to 256 database icons, plus you can stack icons for replica copies of the same database. Therefore, you can display far more database icons on your desktop than you are ever likely to use.

The icons represent databases that are stored as files on the local hard drive, on a Notes server, or even on a network drive.

If you remove an icon from the desktop, you have only deleted the pointer to the database. The database file itself remains untouched. However, you do lose any private views in a database when you remove the icon from the desktop.

The icon can provide several types of information about the associated database:

- The name of the database and the graphic on the icon are always displayed and are part of the database design. The graphic on the icon can suggest the type of application—discussion databases, e-mail, a document library, or a workflow application.

- The location of the database (a server name or *local*) can be toggled on and off by selecting View | Show Server Names.

- The name of the database file can be toggled on and off by holding down the Shift key while selecting View | Show Server Names. By default, Notes databases have a file extension of .nsf (Notes Storage Facility), although the extension is not displayed on the icon. Extensions other than .nsf are displayed on the icon—for example, databases that are used with Notes R3 can be saved with a file extension of .ns3, ensuring that they will not be converted to R4 format.

- The number of unread documents in the database can be toggled on and off by selecting View | Show Unread.

- Icons of replicas of the same database can be stacked on top of each other by selecting View | Stack Replica Icons. To select which replica of the database you want to open, click on the small down arrow in the corner of the icon, and select the replica from a list. Replicas are databases that have the same database ID, meaning that they can be synchronized through the process of replication. This is described in detail in Chapter 33.

Moving Database Icons Around on the Desktop

Icons can be moved around on a workspace page, and they can be moved from one page to another.

- To move an icon to another location on the same page, point to the icon and hold down the left mouse button while you drag the icon around the desktop. Release the left mouse button to drop the icon. The icon is automatically aligned with other icons above or below it and to the left or right.

  If the icon does not fit into the display area on your screen, a scroll bar is displayed so you can move to the parts of the page that are off the screen.

- To move more than one icon at a time, hold down the Shift key and click on the icons you want to move. Continue to hold down the left mouse button on the last selected icon, and drag the icons to their new location. Release the left mouse button to drop the icons.

- To move one or more icons to another workspace page, drop the icon(s) on the tab of the page to which (they) are being moved. You must place the pointer directly on the tab until you see a white box outlining the title of the destination tab before you drop the icon.

You cannot copy an icon the way you do in regular Windows. The nearest equivalent is to copy an entire database, including its icon.

> **NOTE**
>
> You cannot store icons on the Replicator page. See Chapter 33 for information about using the Replicator page.

Adding Database Icons to and Removing Database Icons from the Workspace

Before you can use a Notes database, you must first add it to your workspace. You can add to your desktop the icon of any database to which you have authorized access.

Adding a Database Icon to the Workspace

To add a Database icon to the workspace, follow these steps:

1. Select File | Database | Open (Ctrl+O). Notes displays the dialog box shown in Figure 5.7.

FIGURE 5.7.

The Open Database dialog box.

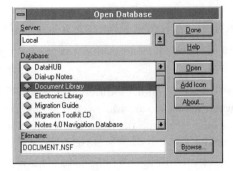

2. Select the Server (or Local) where the database is located. Notes displays a list of available databases. Local refers to a local drive (including network drives), as contrasted to a directory on the Notes server.

3. Locate the database you want by navigating through the Notes directory structure, or select Browse to look through non-Notes directories on your local drive. If you know the correct path- and filename, you can type in the path- and filename in the Filename: field at the bottom of the dialog box. Notes lists databases in the default data directory in alphabetical order by database title, followed by an alphabetical list of all directories beneath the default data directory. If you are not in the default data

directory, the last item in the list of databases and directories will be an arrow pointing upward. Double-click on the arrow to move to next higher directory level.

4. When you locate the file you want, press About to view the About Database page to verify that you have selected the correct database.

5. Click on Add Icon to put the icon on the desktop. If you want, you can add several icons by selecting a database and clicking on Add Icon, then selecting another database and adding that icon.

6. Click Done when you are through adding icons.

   Alternatively, instead of steps 5 and 6, you can open a database directly by clicking on Open to open the database, or double-clicking on the database title. When you exit the database, the icon remains on your desktop.

Removing a Database from the Workspace

To remove a database (or databases) from the workspace, follow these steps:

1. Click on the database icon to select it. (Hold down the Shift key while selecting databases if you want to select multiple database icons.)

2. Press the Delete key or select Edit | Clear.

The database icon is removed from the desktop. Removing the icon does not delete the database itself, but results in the loss of any personal database settings and private views or Folders—information that is stored in your desktop.dsk file for the database icon.

Opening a Database When the Icon is Already on the Desktop

To open a database when the icon is already on the desktop, follow these steps:

1. Locate the database icon on your desktop.

2. Double-click on the icon, or highlight the icon by clicking on it once, and select File | Open, or press the Enter key. You can also select Open Database from the database Properties box, displayed by clicking with the right mouse button on the database icon.

   The database opens. Depending on how the database has been designed, the database may display an About Database document or may go directly to the default View. If the About Database document is displayed, you can close the document by pressing the Esc key.

Using SmartIcons

SmartIcons are buttons that perform simple actions when you click on them, providing a shortcut for navigating through the pull-down menus or using keystrokes. You can also create custom SmartIcons that run macros.

To determine what a particular SmartIcon does, point to the icon, and Notes displays what the SmartIcon does in a small bubble. (See Figure 5.8.)

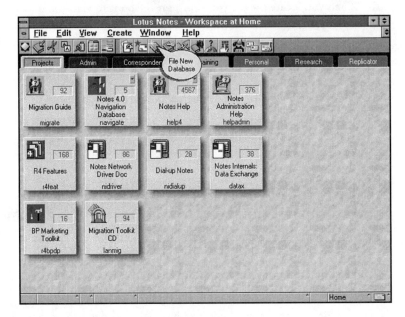

Notes R4 provides more than 150 predefined SmartIcons, as well as over a dozen custom SmartIcons that you can use to define your own macros.

Many of the SmartIcons are context-sensitive, and you can elect to have the SmartIcons display only when they are relevant to what you are doing. For example, you cannot format a paragraph of text when there is no document open for editing. You cannot modify the design of a database if you do not have designer access. Notes recognizes the current context and does not display those icons except at the appropriate time.

Notes provides two sets of SmartIcons, and you can create additional sets that can be used for specific tasks, such as editing a document or designing a database. You can switch between sets by selecting File | Tools | SmartIcons and selecting a new set, or you can choose to have Notes display *context icons*, SmartIcons that change depending on what you are doing within Notes.

To modify the way SmartIcons are displayed or to customize individual icons or sets of SmartIcons, select File | Tools | SmartIcons... to display the SmartIcons dialog box, shown in Figure 5.9.

In the SmartIcons dialog box, you have the following options:

■ Switch to another SmartIcon set in the drop-down list above the second column.

■ Change the position of the SmartIcon bar. Options are floating, left, top, right, and bottom.

■ Show the SmartIcon bar or hide it. The icon bar is not displayed if you are not using a mouse. If you have checked the icon bar box and still cannot see your icons, you may have them stored in the wrong location.

■ Display context-sensitive SmartIcons by selecting context icons. If you select this, you do not need to change between sets of SmartIcons—Notes does this for you automatically.

■ Select Descriptions to turn on the automatic bubble help for SmartIcons. If you have not selected this option, you can still view bubble help by clicking on a SmartIcon with the right mouse button.

■ Select Icon Size to switch between small and large icons. The small icons display nicely on VGA screens, but the large icons may be needed on a super VGA screen.

The other options are used to customize SmartIcons and SmartIcon sets.

FIGURE 5.9.

The SmartIcons dialog box.

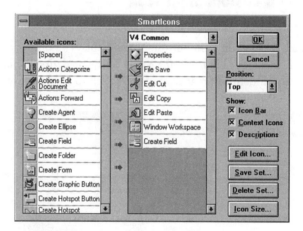

Customizing a Set of SmartIcons

To customize a set of SmartIcons, follow these steps:

1. Select a set that is similar to the custom set you want to create.

2. Name the new set by clicking on Save Set. Give the new set a name of up to 15 characters.

3. Give the new set a filename with an .SMI file extension. On the Macintosh, the set name is the filename.

4. Click on OK to accept the information and close the dialog box.

5. Remove icons from the set by clicking on the icon to be removed and dragging it to the left (Available Icons) column.

6. Add icons to the set by locating the icon you want in the Available Icons column and dragging it to the right column. You can drop icons wherever you want on the bar, or you can drag them to a new location within the set. You can also add spacers to group similar functions together.

7. Click on OK to accept the changes to the set, or click on Cancel to return to the workspace without saving your changes.

Deleting a Set of SmartIcons

To delete a set of SmartIcons, follow these steps:

1. Switch to another set of SmartIcons. You cannot delete the currently selected set.

2. Click on the Delete Set button. Notes displays a list of sets that can potentially be deleted.

3. Click on the set you want to delete, and click on OK. The set is deleted.

Creating a Custom SmartIcon

To create a custom SmartIcon, follow these steps:

1. Click on the Edit Icon button. Notes displays a number of SmartIcons that are undefined. (See Figure 5.10.) Many of the predefined SmartIcons cannot be edited, but the undefined SmartIcons can be used to create customized SmartIcons.

FIGURE 5.10.

The Edit SmartIcons dialog box.

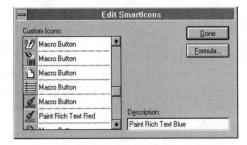

2. Click on the SmartIcon graphic that you want to use, and enter an Icon description. This description is what will be displayed as bubble help later on.

3. Click on Formula to display a SmartIcons Formula dialog box. Create a formula by adding @Commands and @Functions. (See Figure 5.11.)

FIGURE 5.11.

The SmartIcons Formula dialog box.

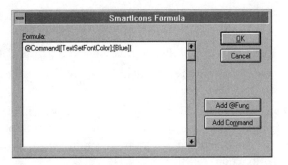

> **NOTE**
>
> For information on how to create valid Notes formulas, refer to Chapter 12, "Developing Forms."

4. Click on OK and Done to save the formula and save the SmartIcon.

5. Add the SmartIcon to a SmartIcon set by selecting the new SmartIcon from the Available Icons column and dragging it to the set.

Using the Notes Status Bar

The Status Bar at the bottom of the Notes R4 workspace provides status information regarding the current document and the current Notes environment. The Status Bar, with most elements showing, is shown in Figure 5.12.

FIGURE 5.12.

The Status Bar.

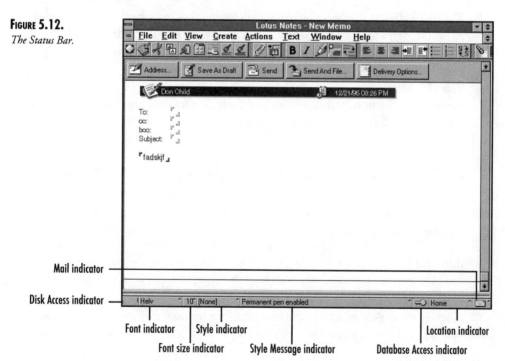

Elements on the Status Bar include:

- Disk access indicator (indicates when Notes is busy accessing a disk or server by network or modem)

- Font indicator (visible when editing in a Rich Text field. Rich Text fields are defined in Chapter 6, "Views, Documents, and Forms."

- Font size indicator (visible when editing a Rich Text field)

- Style indicator (visible when editing a Rich Text field)

- System message indicator

- Database access indicator

- Location indicator

- Mail indicator

The Status Bar provides you with another alternative to using SmartIcons and pull-down menus for certain functions.

- The disk indicator displays a lightning bolt when accessing a local drive or a Notes server through a local area network. When you have a remote connection, the Status Bar displays a small modem with blinking lights to indicate that your workstation is busy accessing the Notes server via a modem connection.

- You can change the current font, font size, and style by clicking on the appropriate boxes on the Status Bar while editing in a Rich Text field within a document. Notes displays a list of available alternatives, and you can pick from the list.

- Notes displays system status messages on the Status Bar. You can view up to the last nine messages by clicking on the System Message portion of the Status Bar. Examples of common system messages include "Checking for new mail…" or "Connected to Server Excalibur."

- You can determine your database access privileges for a particular database by highlighting the database icon and clicking on the key icon (in the example shown in Figure 5.12), which indicates database access privileges. Your access privileges are displayed in the message portion of the Status Bar. If the database is already open, the indicator on the Status Bar shows an icon that represents the level of access you have been granted.

- Clicking on the key or access icon also displays a window that shows your current level of access and lists any other groups or roles you belong to.

- You can change your location setting by clicking on the location portion of the Status Bar. Notes displays a list of all the location setup documents you have defined. To change to a new location, click on the name of the location and Notes will use your location setup document for that new location. See Chapter 9, "Using Mobile Notes on the Road," for more information.

■ You can manage your mail from the Status Bar without having to go to your mail database or to the drop-down Mail Menu, as in Notes R3. When you click in the right hand corner of the Status Bar, a list of mail options is displayed. These options include the following:

  ■ Create Memo

  ■ Scan Unread Mail

  ■ Receive Mail

  ■ Send Outgoing Mail

  ■ Send and Receive Mail

  ■ Open Mail

These options are described in Chapter 7, "Using Applications and Mail on Your Desktop."

Customizing Display Characteristics of the Workspace

Notes R4 provides several options that enable you to change the way Notes is displayed and operates in your environment. You can do the following:

■ Use only typewriter fonts. Typewriter fonts are monospaced so that all characters line up when you select this option.

■ Use large type. This can be used to assist those who have difficulty seeing smaller type or those who are using a monitor (such as an SVGA monitor) that displays everything smaller than they may be used to.

■ Display a marbleized workspace with 3-D database icons. This option is not available if you use large type.

■ Display the workspace in monochrome.

■ Double-click the right mouse button to close the current window. This was the default in Notes R3, but in R4 the right mouse button displays a context-sensitive floating menu from which you can make selections such as displaying the Properties box.

You can select these options in the Advanced Options window on the Basics page of the User Preferences dialog box. This is displayed by selecting File | Tools | User Preferences.... This dialog box is shown in Figure 5.13.

FIGURE 5.13.

The User Preferences dialog box.

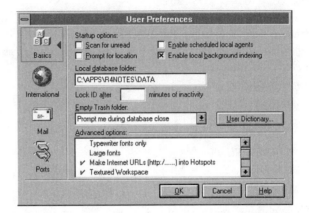

Summary

The Notes workspace described on the preceding pages is what you see when you use Notes as an end user. The same Notes workspace environment is used by application developers and system administrators, who can also benefit from the shortcuts that come from being familiar with the workspace. The Notes interface uses a desktop metaphor, with one or more folders that hold database icons. You can customize many of the features on the desktop. The desktop also provides easy access to common functions through SmartIcons and the Status Bar, as well as through the Properties dialog box. The Properties dialog box lets you define properties for a variety of elements, from the Notes workspace to databases to elements within the database. The Notes workspace can be customized so it is organized in a way that makes sense to the individual user.

Views, Documents, and Forms

by Don Child

IN THIS CHAPTER

CHAPTER

6

This chapter describes Views, documents, and forms from an end-user perspective. It shows you the integrated view of R4, and how R4 is different from R3. The chapter also will demonstrate how to show a Form and View at the same time and how to scroll and pull up a document so it fills the screen. In addition, this chapter shows you how to fill in various kinds of fields and how to import graphics data and OLE data.

If you are a Notes R3 user, the first time you open a Notes R4 database you might feel like you opened the wrong application. It's as if you had been reading a magazine and suddenly found yourself sitting at your computer, staring at an electronic version of the same publication on the World Wide Web. Some of the labels are the same, and the principles are pretty much the same, but it's an entirely different medium, one that literally opens new windows, new opportunities, and new ways to use Notes.

The news magazine is a good metaphor for the earlier versions of Notes. You could look at the front cover (a *view* of the magazine) to tell where to find the major articles, the ones the publisher thinks you will be interested in. Look at the inside table of contents (another *view*) to see a complete listing of all articles and columns in the magazine. It's still the same magazine, but the table of contents provides completely different information. Now turn to the back and look at the index of advertisers. This is yet another view of the magazine, one that guides you to an entirely different type of information.

This same metaphor can still work for Notes R4.x, but the metaphor needs to be expanded.

If you are used to a text-based environment, you can look at a *View* (a list of *documents*, or *notes* that you can open and read or edit) that is primarily text-based. If you are used to a graphical interface with hyperlinks, like you might find on the Internet's World Wide Web, Notes developers can create a View that uses graphical navigators. If you are accustomed to using applications like cc:Mail or msMail that have multiple panes, then you will feel right at home with the new interface of Notes R4.

Figure 6.1 shows what the default view of a Notes R4 database looks like.

The standard Notes R4 database View is a three-pane window with considerable flexibility. You can choose to view all three panes, or you can expand one pane until it fills the entire screen. You can rearrange the panes on the desktop. Sometimes you can even sort a View by clicking on a column head.

The Navigation menu, shown in the left pane, contains elements that used to be part of the View menu, as well as elements that used to be in the Design menu. The Navigation pane is used to navigate between Views and folders in the database, to run agents (macros), or to access *design elements* used to create or modify the design of the Notes database if you have sufficient database access privileges.

FIGURE 6.1.

View panel of a Notes R4 database.

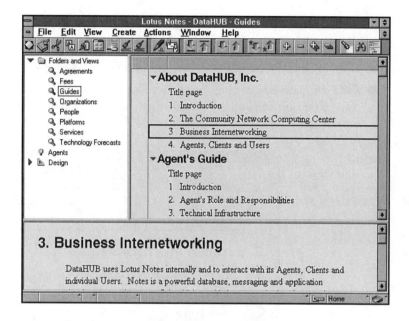

The View pane, the top right of the three panes shown in Figure 6.1, is closer to what a view was in Notes R3—a list of documents available for reading or editing.

But the Notes 4.x View pane is simpler to use. A single click of the mouse expands and collapses categories, and you can view documents in the Preview pane at the bottom of the screen as you scroll through the list of available documents. And depending on how a View is designed, you sometimes can select a different sorting order for the View by clicking on a column title.

The Preview panel, shown as the bottom of the three panels in Figure 6.1, has no counterpart in earlier versions of Notes, but will look familiar to those who have used other software packages, such as cc:Mail.

In this chapter, all of the permutations of the View screen are explained, but only as a prelude to the true purpose of the View screen, which is to provide a means of easily viewing documents (also referred to as *notes,* hence the name of the product) and creating or editing documents.

The main point about the Notes R4 View window is that it provides a variety of ways to navigate within the database.

The three-paned View window is new to Notes R4.x. The standard window has a Navigation pane at the top left of the screen. At the top right is a View pane that is used to display selected information about the documents in the database and to provide a way to open the documents for reading or editing. At the bottom of the screen, a Preview pane lets you read a document as you are navigating through the list of documents in the View pane.

You can modify the layout of the three panes in the following ways:

■ Change the arrangement of the three panes by selecting View | Arrange Preview.

■ Open or close the Preview pane by selecting View | Hide Preview Pane SmartIcon.

■ Resize the pane by grabbing one of the adjoining edges of the pane and sliding it. If you grab the intersection between all three panes, you can resize all three at the same time, as shown in Figure 6.2.

FIGURE 6.2.

A resized Preview pane makes it easier to read documents.

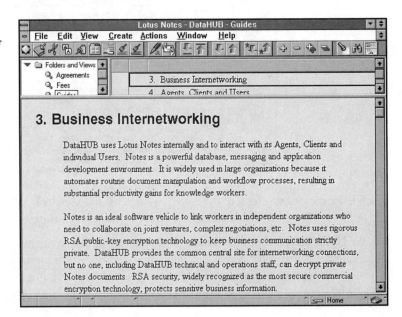

The Navigation Pane

The Navigation pane is more flexible than it might first appear.

There are four standard icons that represent common navigation features:

■ A folder icon will navigate to a *folder*. A folder is similar to a View, but can contain views or documents that you have moved into the folder. Folders can be public (displayed in yellow and shared by different people) or private (displayed in gray, available only on your desktop). You can create private folders by selecting Create Folder, clicking on Private Folders, and then entering the name of the new private folder.

■ A magnifying glass navigates to a View.

■ A light bulb navigates to an agent (the Notes R4 term for macros).

■ A triangle navigates to a *design element*, if you have at least designer access to the database.

6

VIEWS,
DOCUMENTS,
AND FORMS

Another marker, new to Notes R4, is the small triangular arrowhead that is called a *twistie*. A twistie indicates that the current entry is categorized and can therefore be expanded or collapsed. If the twistie points to the right, you can expand the category by clicking once on the twistie. If the twistie points downward, you can collapse the category by clicking once on the twistie.

There are other possibilities with the Navigation pane, depending on the design of the database. The designer may have created what are called *Navigators*—graphical elements that make navigation more intuitive. These new graphical Navigators can be simple, as seen in the Notes R4 Help database shown in Figure 6.3, or they can be as complex as a map that lets you click on a location to display information relating to that location.

FIGURE 6.3.

The Notes Help Index View showing simple graphical Navigators.

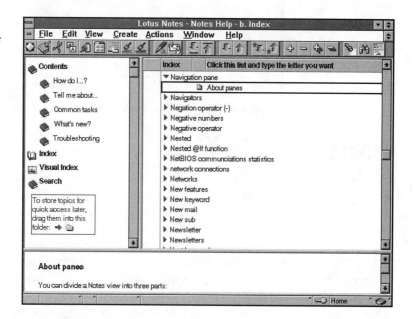

Although the Navigation pane has simple graphical devices to assist with navigation, if you click on the Visual Index icon, shown in Figure 6.3, you will see an interface that is entirely graphical and guides the user to help on several common types of screens, including Views, documents, and the workspace. For example, Figure 6.4 shows the graphical Navigator that provides help on editing a document.

In sum, you can move around in the Notes database from the Navigation pane, whether it is graphical or text-based, by clicking on the element you want to display.

FIGURE 6.4.
*Graphical Edit
Document Navigator
shows a full-screen
graphical Navigator
using hotspots.*

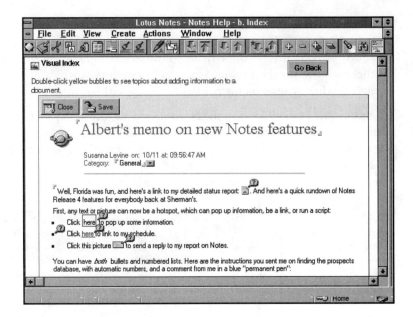

Navigating in the View Pane

The View pane is more analogous to the Database view seen in Notes R3. You see a list of available documents, and you can move work from those documents from the View or you can open the documents from the View. There are normally multiple views of the database. The Views may be categorized, or they may simply be a listing of selected documents within the database. Views will normally have columns, rows, and a marker column. There are differences, however, between the View pane in Notes R4 and Views in Notes R3 that vastly simplify navigation within the database. Most of these differences are optional, but commonly used. Their use depends on how the database developer designed a particular View. Refer to Chapter 13, "Developing Views," if you are interested in changing the design of a View.

 Alternating lines can be displayed in different colors. This new feature makes it easier to read through a list of documents.

 A View can now be designed so that an individual document can be displayed on multiple lines, making it possible to display more information about a document in a View than was possible in earlier versions of Notes.

 A column can be resized by pointing to the edge of a column heading and dragging it to make the column wider or narrower.

 Columns can be dynamically sorted within the View. By clicking on a column header for a column marked by a small arrowhead, the column is instantly sorted by different criteria.

In Figure 6.5, you can see all of the documents listed in alphabetical order. Figure 6.6 shows the same View in the same database, only now it displays collapsed categories, which were obtained by clicking on the column header. The small arrowheads in the column header indicate that the column can be re-sorted by clicking on it. Another click, and the same documents would be displayed in reverse alphabetical order.

FIGURE 6.5.

R4 Features by Focus Area View sorted alphabetically.

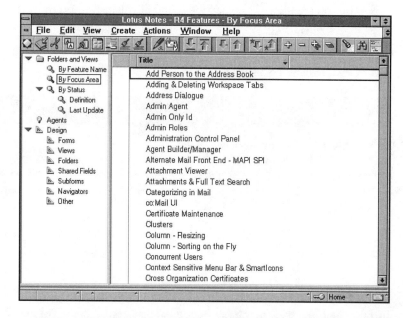

FIGURE 6.6.

R4 Features by Focus Area View categorized.

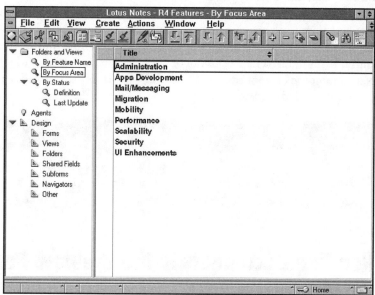

Within earlier versions of Notes, it would have taken three separate Views to display the information in the same three ways.

Categories in a View may or may not have twisties beside them. If they do not have twisties, you can still expand or collapse categories by double-clicking on them, or you can select one of the following:

■ + or - on the numeric keypad to expand or collapse, respectively

■ View | Expand All

■ View | Collapse All

■ View | Expand | Collapse

> **NOTE**
>
> Documents can also be expandable or collapsible, appearing as if they were categories. If you attempt to expand them by double-clicking on them, the document will open rather than expanding to show other documents beneath it. You therefore have to expand collapsed documents using the + key or using one of the options from the View menu.

To switch to another View, click on the View title in the Navigator pane or select the new View from the View menu.

Actions and the Action Bar

In some databases, there may be an Action Bar displayed at the top of the View screen or within documents. The Action Bar contains buttons that perform View- or document-specific common functions, such as adding a new document to the database, toggling between a standard View window and a graphical View window, or forwarding documents to another user via e-mail. Many of the same actions can be performed using menus or by selecting Actions in the Navigation pane or from the Actions menu. The Action Bar provides a place where buttons can be permanently displayed as long as you are in the View window or in a document.

> **NOTE**
>
> Buttons on the Action Bar also give Internet users access to document editing features when the documents are published by the Domino 4.5 server. They can interact with the Notes documents using any common Web browser.

Reading Documents in the Preview Pane

You can view documents in the Preview pane as you scroll through the View to find a document that you want to see. If you know the first few characters of the document's title

6
VIEWS,
DOCUMENTS,
AND FORMS

(actually, whatever is displayed in the first column of a particular View for a document), you can find the document by typing in the first few characters. Notes displays a search box, shown in Figure 6.7, when you type the first character. When you are done typing in characters, click OK to move to the first document that begins with whatever characters you typed.

FIGURE 6.7.

The Quick Search dialog box for finding documents in a View using Type Ahead.

Once you find the document you want, you can preview it before opening it. Point the mouse to the bottom of the View pane and pull up the Preview pane, or click on the View Show | Hide Preview Pane SmartIcon. The document you have highlighted in the View is then displayed for viewing. Scroll up or down to view one document at a time, and the document in the Preview pane changes, always showing what you have highlighted.

When you view a document in the Preview pane, some of the header information may be summarized or may remain undisplayed so you can see the body of the document.

You also have the option of fully opening the document by double-clicking on the document title in the View, highlighting the document, and selecting File | Open, or highlighting the document and pressing the Enter key.

You can view documents from within the Preview pane, as long as the pane is open. By default, this leaves the documents unread. (Within Notes, many databases are designed to display a star next to documents that have not yet been read by you.) However, you have the option of marking documents as having been read after previewing them in the Preview pane.

Use the following steps to mark documents as read after previewing:

1. Select Mark Documents Read When Opened in Preview Pane from the Advanced Options box on the first page of the User Preference dialog box (File | Tools | User Preferences…).

2. Open the View screen and make sure the Preview pane is displayed.

3. As you move down through the list of documents in the View pane, the documents are marked as having been read.

In Notes R3, you had to actually open a document before it was marked as having been read.

You also can manage unread marks using Edit | Unread Marks to mark all documents or selected documents as being read or unread, as you could in Notes R3.

Using the View to Open, Copy, Delete, or Print Documents

You use the View pane to access documents, but you can also copy and paste documents or print them from the View pane. To perform an action on a single document, highlight the document and select the action from the menu, or click on the appropriate SmartIcon. The options include:

■ Edit Copy to copy a document, and Edit Paste to paste the document that is currently in the Clipboard.

■ Edit Cut to delete a document. A garbage can icon will be displayed beside the document, but the document will not actually be deleted until you exit the database or until you refresh the View by selecting View Refresh (F9).

■ Print a document by selecting File | Print. In the dialog box that will be displayed, you have the option of printing the document or printing the entire View.

■ Open a document for viewing by selecting File | Open, by double-clicking on the document, or by pressing the Enter key. Once the document is open, you can edit it (assuming you have editor privileges) by double-clicking anywhere in the workspace, or by using Ctrl+E on the keyboard.

> **NOTE**
>
> You also can edit a document in the Preview pane by double-clicking on the document to place it into the Edit mode. Some features may not be available if you edit in the Preview pane; for example, parts of the document can be selectively hidden during preview reading and editing that may be visible if you edit the document while it is open.

You can perform functions such as printing, copying, and deleting documents on more than one document at a time from a View. To select multiple documents, click within the View pane to the left of the desired document. A check mark indicates that a document has been selected. You can select several documents in a row by holding down the left mouse button and dragging the cursor up or down the screen. To unselect a document, click on it again.

Viewing Attachments

Files of various types can be attached to a Notes document within a Rich Text field—a field within a Notes document that can hold various attachments and text that has attributes such as bold and italics. Notes R4 provides viewers so that you can see attached files in over 100 native formats, even if you do not have the original application on your computer. If you do have the original application, you can launch the file in that application and work with the file

within the application, or you can detach the attached file from a local drive, then open it in its original format. This makes a convenient way for Notes users to share non-Notes files with other Notes users.

Viewing, launching, and detaching are available by double-clicking on the attachment. When you elect to view or launch an attachment, you can return to Notes by closing the attachment's application.

Besides the extended ability to view file attachments, Notes R4 also provides the option of searching for specific text within attached files using full-text searches, described later in this chapter.

Putting Documents into Folders

You can group documents into folders—if you find documents that you want to refer to fre- 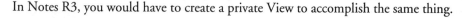 quently, for example. To place a document in a folder, highlight the document in the View pane. While keeping the left mouse button depressed, drag the document to the desired folder in the Navigation pane. You can also place documents into folders from the Action menu or from a button on the Action Bar, depending on the design of the application. Once a document is in the folder, the folder is essentially a private View that contains the documents you want to read. The documents put into the folder are still available in Views. If you delete a document from within a folder or from within a View, it is deleted from the entire database. If you move a document out of a folder, however, it is still available in other folders or Views, as long as it has not been deleted from the database. To remove a document from a folder, click on the document and drag it to another folder or View.

In Notes R3, you would have to create a private View to accomplish the same thing.

Navigating in Documents

The Preview pane lets you browse through documents, but many times you will want to actually open the document to work on it. You can open a document in any of the following ways:

- Double-click on the document in the View pane.
- Select File | Open when the document is highlighted.
- Press the Enter key when the document is highlighted.
- Select one of the following SmartIcons: Navigate Next Main, Navigate Previous Main, Navigate Next, Navigate Previous, Navigate Next Unread, or Navigate Previous Unread, when you already have a document open for reading. From the View pane when the Preview pane is not open, selecting these SmartIcons moves you to the next document, but does not open the document for reading.
- Select Edit | Unread Marks | Scan Unread to view the first unread document in the database.

- Select Edit | Unread Marks | Scan Preferred to view the first unread document in a list of preferred databases.
- Press the Enter key to open the next document when you already have a document open for reading.
- Press the Backspace key to open the previous document when you already have a document open for reading.

Once you are in the document, you can move up or down the page using arrow keys, PgUp or PgDn keys, or using the scroll bar. If you encounter a collapsed section (indicated by an arrow icon), you can open the section by clicking on the section marker.

Scanning Preferred Databases

If your job means that you have to keep track of new documents in several databases, you can set up Notes to automatically scan those databases. You mark the databases you want to read as *preferred* databases. This saves you the trouble of having to open each database separately to look for unread documents.

To set up scanning for preferred databases:

1. In the Notes workspace, be sure that no database is selected.
2. Choose Edit | Unread Marks | Scan Unread. Notes displays the Scan Unread dialog box.
3. Select Choose Preferred.
4. Select the names of the databases you want to scan regularly.
5. Click OK.
6. Click Done.

The next time you scan for unread documents, Notes scans your preferred databases, unless you select other databases to scan. Notes also scans the preferred databases if you select Scan Unread as a startup option on the User Preferences screen.

Searching for Specific Text in Documents

You can search for text within a document using Edit | Find | Replace. The same function can be used to locate a specific word within a View. However, Notes provides a much more powerful tool for locating documents—the Full-Text Search.

Any Notes database can be full-text indexed. Notes creates an index of the database that, depending on the options selected, can index every word by case, and in Notes R4, can even index text contained in attachments and encrypted fields. Notes can exclude from the index any words contained in a predefined stop file, and can index by word break or can identify a word's location within a sentence and paragraph, thus enabling proximity searches.

Imagine having to sift through 100,000 articles from five different publications, looking for articles about client/server systems and electronic mail, with an emphasis on the Internet and Lotus Notes. Using Notes full-text search engine, you can search five databases simultaneously, looking for multiple phrases or words, giving more weight to some terms, and less to others. In a matter of seconds, you will have a list of all the articles that match your search criteria, with the most likely matches located at the top of the screen.

You can create an index using the Database Properties dialog box. Select the last page in the Properties box (the Full-Text page), and select the options you want for your index.

You can also create an index by selecting View | Search Bar. If the database has not yet been indexed for full-text searching, a button will be displayed from which you can create an index. To index a database on a Notes server, you must have Designer or Manager access to the database. On a local database, you can create an index if access control is not enforced or if you have Designer or Manager access.

The index creation may take several minutes, depending on the size of the database and where the database is located. It makes a difference, for instance, if the database is on a busy server, rather than on a local workstation.

You can also control the size of the index. The index can be as much as half the size of the entire database, depending on the options you select. To create the smallest possible index, select the following options at the time you create the full-text index:

- Do not create a case-sensitive index.
- Do not index attachments.
- Do not index encrypted fields.
- Exclude words in a stop file, an ASCII text file that contains a list of words that should not be indexed—for example, "the," "an," and numbers.
- Index on word breaks only.

By creating a smaller index, you lose some precision in your search abilities. Users will have to weigh whether this loss of precision is offset by the decreased size of the index and the increased speed and ease of searching.

Once the index is created, it is stored in a subdirectory beneath the directory where the database file is located. The index subdirectory is given the name of the database with an .FT file extension, such as /TRACKING.FT.

If you move the database to another location, the index can no longer be used. This is true whether you move the database by copying it or through replication. The index will have to be re-created at the new location before you can search for documents using a full-text search. However, if you delete a database icon, the index is not affected. To delete an index, you must click on the Delete button on the Full-Text page of the Database Properties box, or delete the index subdirectory at the operating system level.

Once the database has been indexed, you can perform boolean searches from a search bar or build a query in the Search Builder dialog box displayed by pressing the Add Condition button. A boolean search enables you to search for combinations such as documents that must contain both word A and word B, documents that contain either word A or word B, or you can search for documents that contain word A but not word B. The Search Builder that guides you through building a boolean search is displayed at the top of the screen in Figure 6.8.

FIGURE 6.8.

Entering a boolean search string in the Search Builder dialog box.

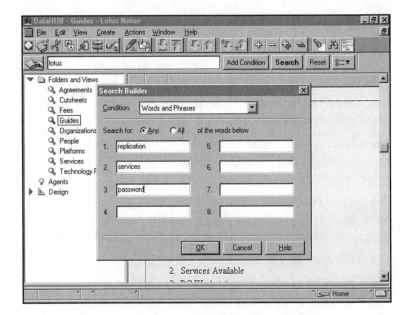

Enter the words that you want to search for. Click OK to return to the Search Bar, and then click on Search to conduct the search. Documents selected by the full-text search are displayed ranked by relevance (by default), or by date, or selected in a View (marked by check marks). When you open a document that was selected in the full-text search, the words that match the search criteria are highlighted. You can navigate to the matches using Ctrl+ to move down through the document, or Ctrl- to navigate up through the document.

Explore the Search Bar. The icon at the far right of the Search Bar displays a drop-down menu that lets you select different display and search options. Using the Search Builder, you can search for any of the following:

- Documents created by a specific author.
- Documents created or modified in relation to a specific date. For example, you can search for a document modified on or after the 15th of November, 1995.
- Text in a specific field on any form in the database. If you select this option, Notes displays the selected form in the Search Builder, and you can type the search text into the field you want to search on.

- Text in a specific field on a specific form.
- Text anywhere in a specific form.
- Text anywhere within the database.

When you use the Search Builder, Notes will create a query using the proper boolean search context. Once you have learned the correct format for a boolean search, you can build searches without the help of the Search Builder by typing a boolean search directly in the Search Bar.

You can save a search with the Options button on the right side of the Search Bar. Perform a search, then click on the Options button and select Save Search As.... Enter a name for the search; and if you want others to be able to use this search, click on Shared Search, and then click on OK to save the search. The search will be listed as a menu option on the Options menu. To run the saved search, click on the Options button and select the saved search.

Using a Notes Crawler to Search a Notes Database, Directory, Server, or Domain

In Notes 4.5, you can search all databases on an entire site using a Notes crawler multidatabase search, which is similar to a Web crawler but is designed to work on Notes databases instead. The databases may or may not be full-text indexed. You search a Notes site using a special search database (with the new database type Multi DB Search) created from a Search Site template.

> **NOTE**
>
> In Web terms, a *crawler* is a process that automatically explores the Web in the background and gathers data based on a complicated set of rules. The Notes crawler explores a collection of Notes documents and returns them based on the same boolean search rules that apply to full-text indexes. Notes databases do not have to be full-text indexed to be included in the collection, but the search is faster if the databases are indexed. The Notes crawler process runs in a Multi DB Search database on a Domino server, retrieving Notes documents that may reside on any server in the Notes Domain. Notes users can perform searches as long as they have at least editor access to the database that performs the search.

To use the Search Site database, you must have at least editor access. You can then set up search parameters by creating a Search Scope Configuration document from the Create menu. On this document, you will have the option of specifying a database, a directory, a server, or an entire Notes domain on which to conduct a search.

You can also define the level of search. Options include searching with no index, with a summary index (in other words, the search does not include the content of rich text fields), a full document index, or a full document index including file attachments. The search returns links to any documents you would normally have access to, as long as the documents match the search criteria. The Search Site database can be used for simple searches (for example, all documents that contain the word "Search") or advanced searches. The Advanced Search screen is shown in Figure 6.9.

FIGURE 6.9.

The Advanced Search screen in the Search Site database.

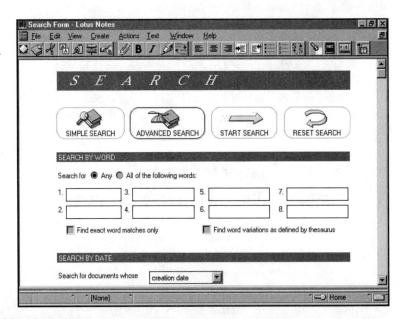

With an advanced search, you can search for documents containing any or all occurrences of up to eight words, their variants, or their equivalents from a thesaurus. You can also narrow the search by creation or modification date or by specifying which categories to search. You can also define how the search results are sorted.

Creating a New Document

New documents can be created in a database in three primary ways: They can be added to the database from an external source (for example, mailed into the database automatically from a workflow application or imported into the application from a non-Notes source), they can be pasted into the database from another Notes database, or they can be created within the database using a Notes form designed to accept data input from users.

The primary focus for many Notes users is reading documents or creating new Notes document within the database. In Notes R4, you create a document by selecting one of the forms available on the Create menu. In Notes R3, you *compose* a document. The process is the same, but the menu option has changed.

Depending on how a database is designed, you may also be able to create a new document by clicking on a button, either from within a document or by using the Action Bar from a View.

Entering Data into Notes Documents

Data is entered into predefined fields on a form. And a form is just what it sounds like—a form. Think about the various forms you use in daily life. You use forms while filling out a credit application, applying for jobs, ordering items from catalogs, addressing envelopes, and, every April, filing income taxes. Everywhere you turn, there are forms for you to fill out, and all of them have one thing in common. They provide enough information to help you fill in the information that is required.

A form is blank. When you have entered information into the fields, it becomes a document.

Notes pretty much follows the same logic. The database has one or more forms that can be filled out, thereby creating documents (the "notes" that give Lotus Notes its name). The forms consist of static text and fields into which data is entered.

The documents can originate in a number of ways. For example, they can be created by automated agents that scan other databases and gather information. They can be created manually by typing data into blank fields—and in some cases, certain fields can inherit data from another document or from an environment variable.

The Notes form in many database designs has a field that can be used as a document title in Views to indicate what the document contains. But the design of the form is really up to the database designer, who determines which fields accept data input from the user and which fields are filled in by the system.

Fields aside from user input fields may have data entered automatically from any of the following places:

- Inherited from another document in the database (the document that was selected at the time you created this new document)
- Computed by the system (such as the current date and time)
- From environmental variables, which can be stored in the NOTES.INI file and shared between Notes databases
- Calculated using information entered in other fields

You can enter data into several types of fields, including fields you type in, fields where you can select from a list of keywords (either predefined or retrieved by a lookup), by clicking on a radio button or checkbox, or by typing data into a window that pops open on the screen.

There are eight different data types in Notes R4. The database designer determines what type of data can be entered into a field. Data types include the following:

- **Text**: Text fields contain letters, punctuation, space, and numbers that are not used mathematically. Examples are names and addresses, telephone numbers, or short descriptive fields. You cannot format the text in a text field, and you cannot include file attachments or hotspots such as DocLinks or buttons.

- **Rich Text**: Rich Text fields enable you to insert pictures or graphs, hotspots, attachments, or embedded objects. Text can be manipulated and displayed in different styles, such as bold, italicized, or underlined, with different fonts and sizes, or even in a different text color. One caveat about Rich Text fields, though—they cannot be displayed in a View, and the contents of the field cannot be used in most formulas.

- **Keywords**: Keyword fields provide predefined text choices that make it easier to enter consistent data to documents. Lists of keywords can be generated in several different ways and can be displayed in a variety of styles. For example, keywords can be selected from a drop-down list, they can be displayed using a type-ahead lookup, they can be displayed as mutually exclusive radio buttons, or they can be displayed as a number of checkboxes.

- **Number**: Number fields are used for information that can be used mathematically. Number fields can include the characters 0, 1, 2, 3, 4, 5, 6, 7, 8, 9, -, +, ., E, and e and can be formatted as decimals, currency, or in scientific notation.

- **Time**: Time fields are used to define time and date information and are comprised of letters and numbers separated by punctuation. The format of time fields depends on the level of detail that needs to be displayed and the type of operating system on the workstation. For example, on a Windows 3.1 or Windows 95 workstation, a date might be displayed 03/26/96, while on an OS/2 workstation, it would be displayed as 03-26-96. Valid time entries include hours, minutes, and seconds, and keywords such as "today."

- **Authors**: Authors fields are used for text lists of names (user names, group names, and access roles) used for giving people Author access to documents, whether they actually created the document or not. A user must have at least Author access to a database before he or she can be given the right to edit a document, but the Authors data type lets multiple users with Author access edit the same document.

- **Readers**: Readers fields enable you to restrict who can read documents created with a particular form. If there is a Readers field on a document, then only users who are listed in the field (or in an Authors field) can read the document, even if other users have Reader or higher access in the access control list. If there is a Readers field and it is blank, then anyone with Reader access or higher can read the document.

- **Names**: Names fields display user or server names as they appear on Notes IDs. Names fields are useful for displaying names in fields that do not affect document access rights, such as the To: field on a mail memo.

NOTE

R4 enables Sections within a document, but Sections is no longer a data type, as it was with Notes R3.

Importing Rich Text Data from Other Sources

Rich Text fields enable you to create, embed, or import a variety of information, including formatted text, graphics, attachments, tables, and hotspots. You can also link or embed text, graphics, and spreadsheets as objects in Rich Text fields.

Information from many external applications can be imported directly into a Rich Text field. Applications include popular word processors and spreadsheet programs and graphics applications that create formats such as TIFF, PCX, BMP, and JPEG.

If a document was created in a word processor supported by Notes, you can import the document directly into a Rich Text field and retain most of the formatting attributes, or you can import ASCII text or a binary file with text. The text can then be formatted in Notes.

Supported graphics formats can be imported directly into a Rich Text field, and then they can be resized by dragging the lower-right corner.

Spreadsheets can be imported into the Rich Text field and then modified within the Notes document. Columns in the spreadsheet are delimited by tabs once the spreadsheet has been imported into Notes.

Pasting Objects into a Rich Text Field

Text, graphics, and spreadsheets can also be pasted into a Rich Text field using a regular clipboard cut and paste, or they can be pasted as a linked or an embedded object. Linked objects in Notes documents can optionally be updated whenever the original file, created and maintained in another application, gets updated. Embedded objects, on the other hand, are stored within the Notes document and have no link to the original object, but you can edit the objects using the applications with which they were created, if you have those applications available from your workstation.

Use linking if all users have access to the original file on a network, and the file will be updated on the network. This enables all users to see the latest data in the file. Use embedding if some users do not have access to the original file on the network. Embedding has no connection to the original document, so it can be mailed to users in other locations, for example.

There are two ways to create linked or embedded objects within a Notes document:

■ Select Create | Object and select the type of object you want to create.

■ Copy the object to the Clipboard from an open application and select Edit | Paste Special, and then indicate the type of object you want to paste. The Paste Special dialog box is shown in Figure 6.10.

FIGURE 6.10.

The Paste Special dialog box.

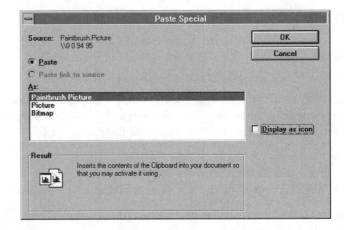

■ Select Paste to embed the object. Select Link to link the object.

TIP

If you click on Display As Icon in the Paste Special dialog box, the object displays the icon you select, rather than displaying the full object. This can make the document considerably smaller and makes opening the document quicker.

Attaching Files to a Document

You can attach virtually any type of file to a Notes document. Anyone reading the document will be able to view an attachment using one of Notes 100+ viewers if the application used to create the file is not available, launch the application to work with the attachment if the original application is available, or detach the file to a local drive and use locally available applications to edit the detached file. Attached files can include data files, Notes ID files, executable files, and even Notes database files.

> **TIP**
>
> You can view a Notes database file that is attached to a document using the attachment viewer. You can also detach it from a local drive. This makes attaching Notes databases to a document a convenient way to share a database with users in another location.

To attach a file, select File | Attach. A standard windows Navigator will be displayed so you can select the file to be attached. You can also attach a file by dragging it from File Manager and dropping it into the Rich Text field in a Notes document, if you have both applications open at the same time.

Note that attaching a file to a Notes document does not affect the original file. The Notes attachment is a copy of the original file and remains a part of the Notes document. Likewise, when a Notes user detaches a file from within a Notes document, the attachment is not affected, but a new copy of the file is created on the user's destination drive.

Attachments can also be sent to users of many non-Notes mail systems. The attachments do not have to be formatted specially when being sent to non-Notes users; for example, you do not have to *uuencode* a file before sending it.

> **NOTE**
>
> You cannot attach one Notes document to another because the document is just one part of a Notes database file. To refer to another Notes document, you must use a Document Link, described later.

Linking to Other Notes Documents, Views, and Databases

Although you cannot include one Notes document as an attachment in another Notes document, you can create a pointer to another Notes document. The pointer is called a Document Link (also referred to as a *DocLink*).

You also can create links to other Notes databases or Views. You cannot link to non-Notes applications. Within Notes R3, users had to be knowledgeable enough to create buttons if they wanted to link to a View or open another database.

Use the following steps to create a link:

1. Do one of the following:

   To create a Document Link, open the document to which you want to link or highlight the document in a View.

   To create a View Link, select the View to which you want to link in the Navigation window.

   To create a Database Link, highlight the database icon or open the database to which you want to link.

2. Select Edit | Copy as Link, and then select Document Link, View Link, or Database Link, depending on the type of link you want to create.

3. Open the document where you want to place the link. Make sure you are in the Edit mode and that you are in a Rich Text field.

4. Select Edit | Paste or press Ctrl+V to paste the link.

The link is displayed as a small icon in the document where it is created. The icon looks like a small document if it is a Document Link. It looks like a row and a column on a View if it is View Link, and looks like a small container if it is a Database Link.

Point to the link and hold down the left mouse button to see where the link leads you. To activate the link, double-click on the icon. The linked document, View, or database opens. When you close the document, View, or database, you are returned to the document you were in when you activated the link.

The Notes Text Editor

The Notes text editor is very similar to most graphical word processors, so most functions can be skipped over quickly. For example, in Notes R4, you can do the following word processing functions within a Rich Text field:

- Change the typeface
- Change the font size
- Change the font characteristics (bold, underline, italicize, and so forth)
- Change the line spacing
- Change the tabs and margins using a ruler displayed across the top of the screen
- Change the alignment
- Enlarge or reduce text

- Create bulleted or numbered text
- Select from a list of Named Styles

- Change the color of text

These functions can be accessed from the Text menu, from SmartIcons, from the Text Properties box, or on the Status Bar at the bottom of the screen.

Named styles are defined in the Text Properties box.

Another editing feature that is new to Notes R4 is the Permanent Pen, which can be used for marking up or commenting on text. When you select the Permanent Pen, everything you type is in the font and color defined for the pen, no matter where you are in the text. So you can move from paragraph to paragraph in a document, adding your comments with a unique font or a unique color.

To define the Permanent Pen font characteristics, display the Text Properties box, select a font, type size, font characteristics and font color, and then click on Set Permanent Pen font. After that, you can toggle the Permanent Pen feature on and off using the Permanent Pen SmartIcon or by selecting Permanent Pen from the Text menu.

Using Tables in Notes R4

You can create tables in Notes Rich Text fields, as with most graphical text editors.

Tables are created by selecting Create | Table. A dialog box is displayed so you can enter the number of rows and columns in the table; then the table is displayed.

You can enter text and format text in the table, attach files, or even paste graphics into a cell. You can format the text in individual cells, you can highlight a range of cells, or you can format the entire table.

To change the size and format of the table, display the Table Properties box, shown in Figure 6.11.

FIGURE 6.11.

The Table Properties dialog box.

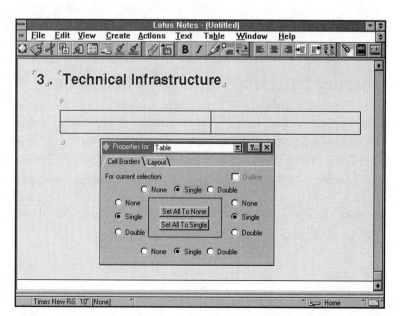

To change the border around one or more cells, highlight the cells and select None, Single, or Double for each edge of the cell, or click on the button in the middle of the Table Properties box to set all edges of the highlighted cells to single or none.

The second page of the Table Properties box is used to determine whether the table will be resized to fit the current window, or remain a constant size. If you check the box indicating that you want the table to be resized, the width of the table is always resized to fit the current window, no matter what type of display is being used. If you do not check the box to resize the table, you can define the left margin of the table, the width of each column, and the amount of gutter between rows and columns.

You can add or delete rows and columns from the Table menu, or you can add a row or column from the Table Properties box. When you insert a column, it is placed to the left of your current position in the table. When you insert a row, it is placed above your current position in the table. To add a column to the right side of the table or a row to the bottom of the table, select Append. If you select Insert Special, you can insert more than one row or column at a time.

You can also cut a table from another application and paste it into Notes, and then modify the table properties within Notes. Another alternative to creating a table is to copy a range of cells from a spreadsheet application such as Lotus 1-2-3, and then paste it into Notes. The cells will be formatted as a table in Notes if the spreadsheet application is left open while you are pasting the cells.

> **TIP**
>
> You can achieve the effect of columnar text in Notes by creating a table and setting all lines to none. A two-column table with one row gives you a page with two columns.

Enhancing Document Readability with Sections

Notes documents can contain Sections, which can be collapsed or expanded and can be selectively hidden, for example, while the document is being edited. In Notes R3, Section was a data type, which meant that a section could only be defined by an application developer. In R4, any user with editing rights to a document can define a section.

Sections enable you to hide part of the text (including graphics, because Sections can only exist in a Rich Text field) until a reader decides to open it or until the right conditions exist for the section to be displayed. For example, the section could be displayed only when the document is opened for editing.

6

To create a section while editing a document:

■ Highlight the portion of the document to be included in the Section.

■ Select Create | Section.

The section is created and displayed as a twistie with the first line of text in the section as the section title.

To change the section attributes, point to the section and display the Section Properties box. Enter a new section title and section color on the first page, and then move to the second page of the Section Properties box, as shown in Figure 6.12.

FIGURE 6.12.

The second page of the Section Properties box.

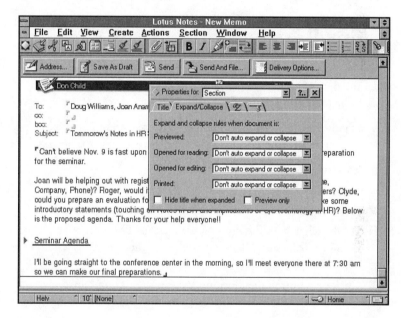

On the second page of the Section Properties box, you can set the display characteristics for the section. You can leave it so readers have to expand/collapse the section by clicking on the twistie, or you can have the section automatically expand or collapse on previewing, opening the document for reading, opening the document for editing, or printing the document.

The third page of the Section Properties box enables you to change the font for the section header.

The fourth page of the Section Properties box enables you to determine when the section is visible. You can hide the section at any of the following times:

■ When the document is displayed in the Preview pane

■ When the document is edited in the Preview pane

■ When the document is opened for reading

■ When the document is opened for editing

■ When the document is printed

■ When the document is copied to the Clipboard

■ When the conditions of a formula evaluate to true

The last option can be used to hide the section unless certain conditions exist. For example, you could create a section that is confidential and is only to be seen by particular individuals, and then create a formula to compare the user's name on his or her Notes ID to a name entered in the formula. The Formula Window button at the bottom of the formula box expands the Formula window so that you can work more easily on longer formulas.

Saving Documents

When you create or edit documents, Notes automatically prompts you to save the document when the document is closed. You also can save a document while editing, by selecting File | Save, or by pressing Ctrl+S.

You can close the document in a number of ways, depending on how you are used to working, how your Notes desktop is set up, and how the document is designed. You can:

■ Press the Esc key.

■ Select File | Close.

■ Press Ctrl+W.

■ Double-click with the right mouse button. This only works if you have selected Right Double-Click Closes Window in the advanced options window on the User Preferences dialog box.

■ Click on a button in a document or on the Action Bar to save and close the document, if such a button was created by the application designer for your use.

Editing an Existing Document

You can only edit documents within Notes if you are an authorized editor for that particular document. Authorized editors include the following:

■ Any user with at least Author access to the database, if he or she created the document or is listed as an author in an Authors field on the document

■ Any user with Manager, Designer, or Editor access to the database, as long as he or she has not been excluded from editing the document unless he is excluded from editing the document in a Readers field on the document

> **NOTE**
>
> Authors and Readers fields are optional and can be defined by the database designer for some documents.

In addition, some portions of the document may be hidden when editing attributes are set, so you can only edit the parts of the document you can see; and Sections within the document can have their own security that prevents reading or editing for some users.

Any fields that can be edited, aside from checkboxes and radio buttons, are displayed inside small corner brackets when the document is opened for editing.

There are several ways to open an existing document for editing:

- From View, highlight the document and press Ctrl+E.
- From a document that is open in the Read mode, press Ctrl+E.
- From View, highlight the document and select Actions | Edit Document.
- From a document that is open in the Read mode, select Actions | Edit Document.
- From a document that is open in the Read mode, double-click anywhere in the document.

Summary

In this chapter, we have looked at how a person actually uses Notes, including how to navigate within the Notes database, how to work with Notes documents in a View, how to read documents, and how to create and edit documents. You can copy, print, delete, and preview documents all from the View screen within a Notes database. When creating a Notes document, you have at your disposal a variety of tools, including a text editor with much of the functionality of many graphical word processors. Think of the Notes documents that you create as ways of sharing information with other Notes users, whether that information originates within Notes or comes from another application and is shared as imported text or graphics, as a linked or embedded object, or an attachment. The document is a fundamental element within Notes, and the View window is how you access Notes documents.

Using Applications and Mail on Your Desktop

by Don Child

IN THIS CHAPTER

This chapter describes how to use Notes applications on the desktop. The About Database document is described, and several Notes applications are used as examples, demonstrating how Notes can be used in different contexts. This chapter also describes in detail how to use Notes Mail in Notes R4.5, including sending and receiving mail, and using the public and personal address books.

Lotus Development Corporation describes the types of Notes applications as components of the three C's—communication, collaboration, and coordination. The three C's represent increasingly complex interactions between Notes users, from a simple communication tool to a fully automated workflow application.

Think of Notes applications as a scatter graph. The vertical axis on the graph represents increasingly complex applications. The horizontal axis represents increasingly complex interaction between Notes users. Therefore, the simplest application would be one with simple, unchanging documents, and a user community that does nothing but read the database. The most complex applications would be highly automated workflow applications involving multiple databases with multiple data sources (for example, information captured from legacy systems or the Internet, as well as from other Notes applications), and a variety of Notes users in multiple locations. To understand Notes, this chapter looks at examples of each type of application.

The final section of this chapter focuses on Notes Mail from the perspective of the end user. By the end of this chapter, you should realize that Notes Mail is just one tool in a much more comprehensive workgroup paradigm.

Communication

Communication applications are those applications that have the simple function of communicating information to Notes users. Collaboration applications are those that promote workgroup computing, helping people share their knowledge and expertise with other members of their work team. And coordination applications automate workflow within the workgroup by mailing information to other databases, including to users' personal mailboxes.

In reality, though, no application fits neatly into just a single category. There are elements of coordination involved in even a simple document-library application, as you shall soon see.

The document library is probably one of the simplest types of Notes application, used to store documents that may need to be referred to occasionally, such as an online employee handbook.

 Open the application, and you will see the About database document for the database. In Notes R4.5, the database designer can cause the About database document to be displayed every time the database is opened, or every time the document is changed, whereas in earlier versions of Notes, the document was only displayed the first time the database was opened. The About database information is stored as a special document in the database, and can be used as sort of a splash screen (the first screen a user sees when they open an application) for the database. The About database document for the *Acme Employee Handbook* is shown in Figure 7.1.

FIGURE 7.1.

The About database document, displayed (optionally) when the database is first opened.

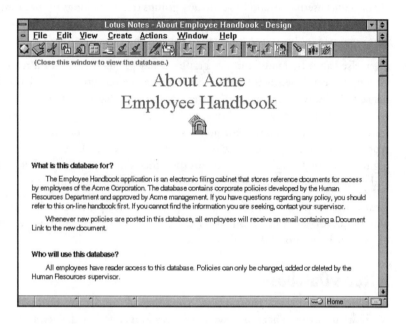

After the About database document is closed, the View window is displayed.

In a simple library application, the only interaction takes place between the individual user and the Notes database. The user navigates the database, locates a specific document, and opens it to read it. The user needs to make a copy of a document, or print a document, but beyond that, there is virtually no activity in the database. The documents cannot be edited by most users, and new documents are seldom added. The purpose of the database is to communicate a particular type of information.

Even with that simple database—a virtual book that can be taken off the shelf, glanced at, and returned to the shelf—there is a lot that can be done in Notes R4. For example, consider how sections are used in R4.

A section can be hidden when a document is being previewed, edited, and read, but in Notes R4.5, it can also be hidden by formula. Suppose your company offers a menu of benefits that the employee can choose from. An employee, Alvis James, has been promoted to Junior Partner and gets additional benefits that are not available to other employees: Life insurance. An option to use a company car. When Alvis looks at the Employee Benefits document for the first time, there is a Junior Partners section that was not previously visible. When the section is expanded, he can see his new benefits listed.

This can easily be done in Notes R4, because sections can be hidden using a formula. The Notes application developer can create a formula that makes the section readable only by those who are either in the Human Resources department management group (so the document can be read and changed, if necessary) or in the Junior Partners group. Notes looks at Alvis's Notes ID to get his username, and looks up any groups that he belongs to. Because he has been added to the Junior Partners group, he can now see the Junior Partners section in the Employee Benefits document. This is just one way to expand the functionality of a Notes document in R4.

How else can it be modified? Try graphical navigators. Instead of a text-based menu for reviewing the employee menu, imagine a graphical menu. A time-clock icon can represent attendance policies. A beach and a palm tree can represent vacation policies, whereas a doctor with a stethoscope can represent sick-leave policies. Or your company may require a different approach. One icon can represent policies for employees in your home office, and other icons represent the Tokyo office, the Paris office, and the Rio de Janeiro office, with each icon leading to a localized employee manual in the office's native language. Let your imagination go, and even this simple application can come alive with excitement.

That is the simplest form of document library. Notes provides a document library template with Notes R4.5, but that template is described in the section entitled "Coordination" because of its built-in, approval-cycle functions.

A News Database

Another common application within Notes that falls under the heading of "Communication" is a news database. There are several services available that deliver a variety of news to your desktop, including Lotus's own NewsStand, as well as DowVision and NewsEdge. These services deliver newspapers such as the *Wall Street Journal* and *USA Today*, as well as a number of monthly publications, to your desktop in the form of Notes documents. Services also provide news based on a user profile. For example, the DowVision's HiTech News provides news related to the computer industry, culled from something in the neighborhood of 10,000 articles that are published electronically every day. If your company subscribes to any of these electronic publications, then the database is probably replicated overnight so that when you sit down at your computer, the news is available.

So how do you read the newspaper when it's on your computer? You can't fold it in thirds and read it while holding onto a strap on the subway or on the bus, that's for sure. You could read it by opening to the first article, reading it, then pressing the Enter key to move on to the second article, until you were to the back page, but…Notes sorts articles by various criteria, such as alphabetically, or creation or modification date, but it doesn't organize by any sort of editorial priority the way the newspaper does. So you might get a stock quote, then an article about Aardvark technologies, and another 75 assorted articles before you get to the one you really wanted to read, the one where IBM and Lotus announce that Notes is becoming the preferred front end for legacy systems. You need a way to drill down and get the news you want.

You can do this in one of the following ways:

- Index the database for full-text searching, then search for keywords when you need the information. You can save your full-text queries and reuse them, or you can use your saved queries as part of an agent that searches your database.

- Browse through a view, reading the titles of the articles and previewing or opening the articles that look interesting. You can also put them into a folder for later reading.

- Run a Newsletter agent, new to Notes R4. This agent will read through news databases and select articles on the basis of user profiles. The agent then creates a news summary in the form of a mail memo with document links to the articles that match the user's profile. It is like having a clipping service that finds the articles you want, cuts them out, and mails them to you.

TIP

You can also obtain news and other information from the Internet. A simple but inelegant example of obtaining Internet news is the Listserv. You can subscribe to lists that interest you, and have them mailed directly to your mail database.

The Employee Handbook and the News database are databases whose primary purpose is to communicate information. With these databases, the primary differences from earlier versions of Notes are cosmetic to the end user. Beneath the surface, however, they are likely to be more sophisticated, for example, by using LotusScript to define some of the more complex functions.

Note that the databases previously described, as well as those that follow, depend on Notes database security for their operation. Most users will have reader access to databases where they look up information, or author access to databases where they have the ability to create response documents. However, they will not be able to edit other people's documents, and will probably be restricted in the types of documents they can create. In the *Employee Handbook*, for example, only individuals working in the Human Resources department are likely to be able to create documents. Others will be able only to read the documents, or maybe post questions to the HR department. Notes database security, which determines what a user can do within the database, is described in Chapter 34, "Security Overview."

There is, of course, another side to the communications paradigm. Users can actively communicate using e-mail. In the preceding examples, the communication is essentially passive. The corporation puts information into a Notes database that is accessible to all users, and the users are expected to know that the information is available. Also, they are expected to know when they need to go out and search for the information, unless the information is being posted in their mailbox via a Newsletter agent. But to communicate directly, e-mail is used.

New To **4.0**

7

USING
APPLICATIONS
AND MAIL

Consider the differences between *pushing* and *pulling* information. The topic will come up again when discussing database replication, so it may help to think in those terms as an end user. You can pull information out of a database if you know that it is there. But if you want to make sure that information reaches another user, you can push the information through the network to the user by addressing an e-mail memo to them.

If your Notes network has an Internet connection, then you could even develop a push-pull combination that produces customized newsletters. You send out queries to the Internet (push) until your query agent finds the information you want. That information would then be pulled into Notes, and mailed to your mailbox. Or you could publish a home page on the World Wide Web using Notes R4's built-in Internet Web Publisher, gather the information you want via a form, then display the information as a Notes document that is mailed to your database. If you have sufficient analytical and programming ability, the complexity of communication applications within Notes R4 is limited only by your imagination.

The Notes mailer is not used just in e-mail. It is an essential component of workflow applications, bringing information to the electronic mailbox of users through automated, just-in-time delivery. Because e-mail is such an important component of Notes, and one of the components that most users will become familiar with quickly, it is covered in detail later in this chapter.

Collaboration

It is in the areas of collaboration and coordination that Notes really begins to earn its position as the premier workgroup-computing platform. Five years ago, the prevailing workgroup paradigm was the project team, the conference room, the one-on-one meeting, the phone call, and mail. Everything had to be scheduled by location, by who was available. Meetings had to be scheduled, travel plans made. If you were not available to meet with others, you were at best a peripheral part of the team.

Today, the word "team" has been transformed to "workgroup," and location has become comparatively irrelevant. A workgroup can be scattered across the globe, and they can still collaborate using Notes.

Take the example of a simple discussion database. An ad hoc discussion database can be created for a specific project, and access to the database can be granted for all members of the workgroup. Any one person can create a topic for discussion. Other members of the workgroup in the same location can respond immediately with their comments. And as soon as the discussion database has been replicated to other locations, members of the workgroup in those locations can comment on the topic. Another replication, and their responses become available to all others in the workgroup. It doesn't matter whether the workgroup members are in the same office, in a nearby branch office, or in an office on the other side of the globe. After the discussion has evolved, the various discussion points can be consolidated into a white paper or a proposal, members of the workgroup can contribute their comments and edits to the document, and a final version can be created. After the discussion is completed and the desired product has been created, the database can be archived or deleted.

The standard discussion-database template in both Notes R3 and Notes R4 provides three forms—one for main topics, one for responding to a main topic, and one for responding to either a response or to a main topic. There are standard folders to place documents into, and within R4 there are buttons on the Action Bar for composing documents.

But there are additional features that are new to R4. For example:

- You can create anonymous responses by selecting Create | Other and selecting either Anonymous Response or Anonymous Response to Response.

- You can set up a Newsletter function by creating an Interest Profile from the pull-down Action menu. Then, once a day, a Newsletter will be mailed to you with links to any documents or conversations (documents and responses) that were added or updated that match your profile (for example, the author, category, or a phrase within the document matches your profile).

- You can establish criteria for archiving obsolete documents, copying them to an archive database, and deleting them from the original discussion database.

Also note that when a document is created, it can be marked as private by clicking on an action button. Marking the document as private inserts a Reader Name field, with the author's name as the only authorized reader. In that way, you can create a draft of a document in the database, and not publish it until you are ready.

Let's look at a real-world example of how a discussion database is being used.

In Hawaii, the state Department of Education is using Notes to discuss curriculum issues. The discussion database used for this forum on curriculum issues is replicated from the central DOE office in Honolulu to District offices on Oahu, Maui, Hawaii, and Kauai, and from the District offices to those schools who have implemented Notes. The workgroup, in this instance, can range from Superintendent of Schools Herman Aizawa to a resource teacher in Kau, a remote town near the southern tip of the island of Hawaii. That resource teacher may never have a chance to meet the Superintendent face to face, but she can participate in the curriculum discussion workgroup without having to make the long and expensive commute to Oahu.

Perhaps, as an example, there is a discussion track in that database concerning the curriculum for the Hawaiian Language Immersion Program. When a particular discussion point is concluded and a policy decision is made, then that discussion thread is no longer needed. It can be archived, and the new policy can be published in the online *Policies Handbook*. The curriculum discussion database continues on other topics, because it is an active database with a widespread workgroup.

Collaborating with other users on the same local area network presents another interesting opportunity in Notes R4. With Notes R3, you could define a single database as a repository of large documents and create document links to that database. This enabled you to keep the size of the main database to a minimum, making it easier to replicate, if need be, and quicker to open. But the e-mail application in R4 has a facility that makes it much easier to maintain a body of shared e-mail in a single location. The shared mail database, new to Notes R4, gives you the option of collaborating more efficiently through e-mail on certain types of projects where it is not important to maintain a single source of information for tracking a project.

For example, imagine a project where there is a single point of contact for a project, although the project may involve numerous team members. Say the public relations department has developed a new corporate logo, and they want everyone in the organization to have a chance to comment on it anonymously, without others seeing their comments. Jane, the point of contact in public relations, sends a copy of the new logo along with a short survey to everyone in the organization. The memo has a response button that the reader clicks on after filling out the survey, ensuring that only the substance of the response—not a copy of the original document—gets returned to Jane in the mail. Jane can place all of the surveys in a unique folder in her mail database, then consider all of the comments at one time.

With most e-mail packages, this would be an inefficient approach, because there would be an identical memo, including the memory-hungry graphic, going to everyone's mailbox. With Notes R4, however, a single copy of the body of the message is stored on the server (in a database called a Single Copy Object Store, or SCOS). Each user gets his or her own e-mail message, which looks like the full message, but in reality he or she is looking at that single shared object stored on the server. The only information that is unique is the header information. This facility is described in greater detail later in this chapter, where Notes mail is discussed as a separate application.

Coordination

Coordination uses elements of Notes' document-management capabilities, elements of its collaborative environment, elements of its e-mail-communication capabilities, and elements of the Notes application-development environment.

We will begin looking at coordination with a simple application, the Notes R4 Document Library template, which provides a good model for a simple workflow operation—an application where coordination between members of the workgroup is paramount. Using the template as it comes straight out of the box, we will look at how the Acme Corporation creates a catalog of its products and services.

The Acme Corporation specializes in computer graphics and printing. It sells hardware and software for use in the graphic-arts industry, as well as providing graphical-arts consulting and education, with branch offices in several cities. It has a project to develop and publish a full description of each of its products and services on one-page cutsheets, and the same information will be published on its home page on the Internet's World Wide Web. It is developing the information using Notes R4.

A draft document is created by Steve, the individual on the project team who is responsible for all of the information that goes into the "Services" part of the catalog. Steve creates a document, marking it as Private until his draft is complete, so that others cannot edit the document until he gives them permission. The others on the team can enter responses to the document, if they want.

After Steve is done with his work on a document—for example, the one on Desktop Publishing Design—he wants the document to be reviewed by others on the workgroup team. He uses the Action button to toggle the document so that it is no longer private, then sets up a review cycle (because he knows they are busy and won't get the review done unless they are reminded). The document-review cycle is a Notes R4 feature that automatically routes the document to members of the workgroup for review.

The document Review Cycle dialog box is shown in Figure 7.2.

FIGURE 7.2.

Setting up an automatic document-review cycle in a document-library application.

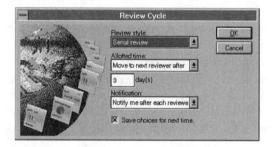

When you want a document reviewed, you set up a review cycle by selecting the Setup Review Cycle action. A Review Cycle dialog box will be displayed. In this dialog box, you can define the type of review (one of the options listed later), the time allotted for review, and how the person defining the review cycle should be notified. Review options include the following:

- Serial Review sends a single copy of the original document to a series of reviewers, forwarding the same copy to the next reviewer as soon as the first reviewer is done, until all reviewers have seen the document and had a chance to make their edits or comments within the document. There is a time limit for each person to review the document, ensuring that it doesn't get stuck in limbo.

- Serial Review (keep all revisions) is similar in that a copy of the document is routed to selected reviewers in sequence, but a copy with each subsequent reviewer's edits is saved as a response to the original document.

- Document Reservations sends out the document for review in parallel to selected reviewers. When a reviewer has the document open for editing, it is locked so the other reviewers have to wait until it is available. All edits are made within the same document, and a clean copy of the original is kept.

- Response Review sends the document out to selected reviewers in parallel, but there is no document locking. Each reviewer's edits and comments are saved as a response to the original document.

After the review cycle is completed, the document can be finalized and marked as Private so it can no longer be edited by others, and all responses and earlier versions can be archived if necessary.

The review cycle process described here is part of the Document Library template. It is not necessarily a part of all Notes databases.

This is a workflow application at its simplest. The possibilities for more complex applications are boundless. Imagine what you could do with various data sources that are available to Notes.

For example, here's a system that may not yet exist but could easily be imagined. The weather watchers track temperature and snowfall in various mountain passes. That information is fed into a computer system, either automatically or manually. A spreadsheet is created and updated once an hour, then gets imported into a specially designed Notes database. Another Notes database, a road-condition monitoring database, uses the first Notes database as a source of information for doing lookups. Periodically, road-condition reports are created automatically by the system based on those lookups. If certain thresholds are exceeded, then an e-mail message is sent through a pager gateway, and the snowplow driver gets word that it is time to warm up the snowplows and sanding trucks. The entire process is automated, with Notes used as the communication agent to coordinate everything.

Another application ideal for a Notes deployment is a sales-force automation application. You keep track of customer information, sales-team members in diverse locations, plus product information and inventory.

A member of the sales team visits a customer, carrying along a laptop computer. When the customer wants information on a product, the information is available right there in the Notes database. When the customer wants to place an order, the salesperson creates an order. The order form uses lookups to get the price and product description from the product view, and gets customer information from the customer view. Calculations are performed right within the order form.

Later, back at the branch office, the sales person's orders are replicated to the main office for billing, and the order also gets mail to the warehouse, where an automatic pick ticket is created. The customer's order gets filled, with the entire process coordinated through Notes. When the accounting office receives payment, a notification is automatically created and mailed to the sales person's Notes mailbox indicating how much commission they can expect from the sale during the next pay period.

At the same time, new leads are received by the main office, and when members of the sales team replicate, they receive all of the new sales leads for their region. The replication is selective, so each member of the team ends up only with the information pertinent to his or her own clients.

The story can be further rolled out to include discussions among the sales force of potential new products. Incentive programs and personnel action forms can be added to the formula, and so forth. What was a single Notes database can eventually span several different databases and numerous replicas, becoming much more than just a desktop document-storage application, much more than an e-mail application. It becomes a client/server system that extends to the entire enterprise.

Notes Mail as an Application

Notes is considerably more than just another e-mail application, but the e-mail component is sufficiently important to warrant close examination. When you understand how Notes Mail works in R4.5, you will understand how to use most Notes applications.

First, let's look at the options for creating new documents. The pull-down Create menu shows the following forms:

- Memo, used to create standard mail messages
- Reply, used to create a reply to a memo
- Reply with History, used to create a reply to a memo with the text of the memo included as part of the message
- Workflow documents, new in Notes R4, include the following:

  - Bookmark, which creates an automatic Document Link in a memo
  - Phone Message, used for taking phone messages
  - Task, used to create a To Do memo, which can be saved as a reminder to yourself or sent to other members of your workgroup by clicking on an Assign to Others action button. When you are done with the task, click on Completed and the task will be moved to the "completed" category.
  - Memo to Database Manager, used to send a memo to the person listed as the manager of the current database. This is useful when creating a mail memo regarding a database—for example, to request a higher level of access in the database, without having to look at the Access Control List to see who the database manager is.
  - Serial Routing Form, used to route a memo to a series of individuals one a time, as shown with routing applications earlier in this chapter.
- Appointment documents, new to Notes 4.5. These documents are used to create appointments, events, and anniversaries using the new Calendaring and Scheduling functions. These functions are described in detail in Chapter 8, "Using Calendaring and Scheduling."
- Temporary Export Certificate document, which allows Notes users to carry a computer with the North American Notes license while traveling in most countries outside

of North America on a temporary basis. The certificate is necessary because Notes encryption algorithms are powerful enough to be restricted from export by the government.

As with any Notes database, forms have two uses: to display documents and to create them. Mail forms are available for creating new memos from within the Mail database, but they are also available as an option on the Create menu from anywhere within Notes. This makes forms like the Bookmark form very useful for referencing information and mailing to another user who has access to the referenced database.

CAUTION

The availability of mail forms assumes that you have your mail set up correctly for your current location. If mail is set up incorrectly, Notes may not be able to locate mail forms from the pull-down Create menu except while you are in the mail database.

Information is entered into fields on the various forms in essentially the same manner as with earlier versions of Notes. See Chapter 6, "Views, Documents, and Forms," for information on creating documents within Notes.

The Views and folders available in Notes Mail suggest the type of workflow that one would normally follow when reading e-mail. These views and folders are seen in the navigation window shown in Figure 7.3. The navigation window closely resembles the cc:Mail interface, with three panes: the Navigation pane, the View pane, and the Preview pane.

FIGURE 7.3.

The Notes R4.5 Mail navigation window.

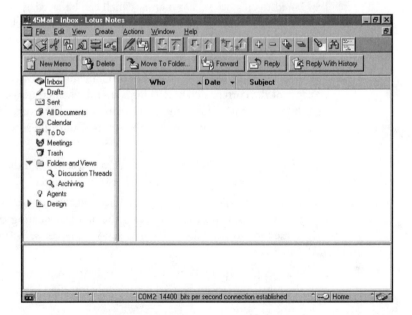

The navigation options include the following:

- Inbox, a folder that holds new messages. The messages are stored in the Inbox until you delete them or move them to another folder. You can move them to another folder by dragging them to another folder and dropping them, or you can highlight the documents, then select the Move to Folder button on the Action Bar or from the pull-down Action menu.

- Drafts, a view that holds messages you have created and saved without sending. The messages can later be edited and sent, moved to another folder, or deleted. When a message is sent to an addressee, it is automatically moved from the Draft folder to the Sent folder.

- Sent, a view that stores all messages you send, as long as you select "save" when you send them. You can move the messages to another folder if you want to.

- All Documents, a view that displays all documents in the database, regardless of which other folders they may be stored in. Using on-the-fly sorting (by clicking on the column heads), you can view the documents alphabetized, listed by ascending or descending date, or alphabetized ascending or descending by author.

- Calendar, which displays appointments in calendar format, as described in Chapter 8.

- To Do, a view that holds tasks. Tasks are workflow documents that you created yourself, or that were mailed to you by other users in a workgroup. They can be used to keep track of a specific task until it has been completed. When the task is completed, you can check it as completed and its status will change in the view.

- Meetings, which shows all appointments scheduled through the new Calendaring and Scheduling feature.

- Trash, a folder that holds messages you want to delete. The messages are not marked for deletion, but when you close or refresh the mail database, you will be asked if you want to delete any documents that are in the folder. If you select Yes, then the documents will be deleted from the database. The folder is handy for placing any documents that you might possibly want to delete, even if you are not sure. Then when you are ready to close the database, you can reconsider whether you want to delete the documents.

In addition to these Notes-defined folders and views, Notes contains the following standard Views, which can be displayed by clicking on the view name in the Navigator panel or by selecting the view from the pull-down View menu:

- Discussion Thread, which shows messages grouped by discussion. A discussion is a memo along with any replies exchanged in relation to that original memo. They are displayed with replies indented beneath the original document, the same way responses are displayed in a discussion database.

- Archive Log, which displays a list of documents that have been transferred to an archive database. An archiving profile is set up by selecting Actions | Mail Tools | Archive Profile. A window will be displayed on which you can define an archive database, and define parameters for archiving documents in the database. Archiving removes the document from the mail database, places it into the archive database, and creates an entry in the Archive Log.

In addition to these standard folders and views, you can create your own folders, or you can have the system administrator run the mail conversion utility to have Notes create folders based on categories assigned in earlier versions of Notes when your mail is upgraded to Notes R4 mail. The categories are stored in a hidden field in each Notes document.

You can also create your own private views.

Creating a Mail Memo

Creating a memo (an e-mail message) addressed to another user is probably the number-one activity for most people using e-mail, aside from reading messages that get sent to you. Here are a few fundamentals about how to create a memo.

First, from within your mail database, select Create | Memo. From any other application select Create | Mail | Memo or click on the mail icon in the lower-right corner of the screen, and then select Create Memo. Notes displays a memo screen. The appearance of the memo form depends on which letterhead you have selected (under Actions | Mail Tools | Select Letterhead in the Mail database), but the basic layout will be similar to that shown in Figure 7.4.

Figure 7.4.

Creating a new mail memo.

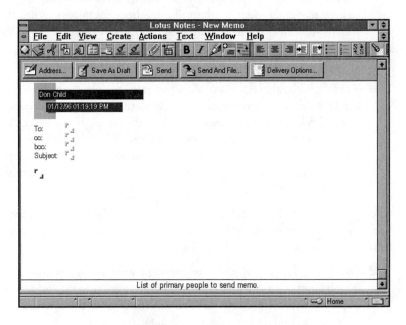

Creating the basic memo is fairly simple, after you master how to address other users. You enter the following information in the memo:

- ■ *To:* The e-mail address of the primary person(s) and/or groups to whom the memo is being sent. If there are multiple addressees, they should be separated by commas.

- ■ *cc:* The e-mail address of the primary person(s) and/or groups to whom the memo is being sent as a courtesy copy.

- ■ *bcc:* The e-mail address of people to whom a blind courtesy copy is being sent. The other addressees will not see any names listed in the BCC: field, but the BCC recipient will be able to see who was addressed in the To: and CC: fields.

- ■ Subject: The subject of the e-mail. The subject will be displayed in the View, so this should give the addressee some idea of the subject of the message.

The field beneath the Subject field is a Rich Text field that contains the body of the memo. In this field, you can do all sorts of things—create or import documents, change the formatting of the documents, insert graphics, attach files or create links, and create buttons.

After you complete the memo, you are presented with a variety of options that can be accessed from the Action Bar at the top of the memo form. These are described in detail here.

To Address the memo:

1. Select the Address button to look up the correct mail address of the individuals or groups to whom the memo is being sent. Notes will display the Mail Address dialog box.

2. Select the address book you want, then select individuals or groups to whom you want to address the memo. Drag and drop the names or groups on the appropriate field in the Addresses window, or highlight names or groups and click on the button for the field you want. (See Figure 7.5.) The names will be transferred to that field. When you are done, click on OK to close the dialog box; Notes places those names in the appropriate field on the memo.

FIGURE 7.5.

Dragging and dropping a name onto the To: field on a mail memo.

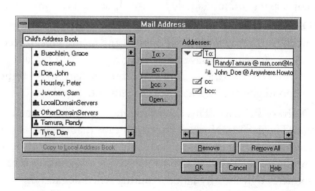

Alternatively, you can type in the name of the person to whom you want to send the memo, and Notes will look for that name in the Public Address Book, then in your Personal Address Book. If Notes cannot find the name, one of two things will happen. An error message will be displayed informing you that the name does not exist, or an ambiguous Names dialog box will be displayed with two or more names that match the information you have entered. You can then select the person you intended.

Depending on how much detail you have entered in the Public Address Book and Personal Address Book, you may be able to type just a nickname, a first name, a complete first and last name, or an explicit mail address to a user in another mail domain, indicated by an @ symbol in the address.

Selecting Delivery Options

Select Delivery Options from the Action Bar to display the Delivery Options dialog box, shown in Figure 7.6.

FIGURE 7.6.

The Delivery Options dialog box.

The Delivery Options dialog box presents the following options:

- **Importance**: If you select High, Notes will display a red envelope icon next to the memo when in the recipient's Notes mailbox to indicate that the memo is important.

- **Mood Stamp**: This will personalize the memo with a graphic to indicate the mood of the memo. For example, you can stamp a memo as confidential (a "Confidential" icon), as a good job (a gold star icon), or even as a joke (Groucho glasses).

- **Delivery Report**: You can have Notes confirm that the memo reached the recipient's mailbox or provide a message only if the memo fails to reach the recipient's mailbox, or you can select to have no delivery reports. You can also ask for a trace report, which provides confirmations from every intermediate server to help you determine why a memo might not be reaching the recipient.

- **Delivery Priority**: This determines how quickly the memo gets routed to the recipient. The default, Normal Priority, means that the message will be routed to the recipient during the next scheduled mail routing or as soon as a minimum threshold for the number of messages to the recipient's location is reached, whichever comes sooner. High Priority ignores routing schedules and thresholds, sending the memo immediately. Low Priority memos get sent only if there is a scheduled mail-routing connection to the recipient's location between the hours of midnight and 6 a.m.

You also have the following delivery options, available by clicking on a checkbox:

- ■ **Sign** attaches a digital signature to the memo, verifying that it was indeed created with your Notes User ID.

- ■ **Encrypt** causes the memo to be encrypted. If you send encrypted mail to another user who shares the same Public Address Book, he or she can read the encrypted memo automatically, since he or she can get your public encryption key from the Public Address Book. If you send an encrypted memo to a user in another mail domain, you must also provide him or her with your public encryption key so he or she can decrypt the memo.

- ■ **Return Receipt** generates an e-mail memo back to you as soon as the recipient opens the memo for reading.

- ■ **Prevent Copying** makes the memo more confidential by ensuring that it cannot be copied to the Clipboard, forwarded, included in a Reply with History, or printed.

Mail Send and Save Options

When you are through creating your memo, you have three options for sending and/or saving it—four options if you count discarding the memo without sending or saving it. You can do any of the following:

- ■ Save the memo as a draft. It is not sent at this time, but is saved so you can continue to work on it later. It will be saved in the Drafts View. If you decide later that you want to mail the memo, open it up and select the Send action button.

- ■ Send the mail. If you select this option, the memo will be sent immediately. You will be asked if you want to save it.

- ■ Send and File. If you select this option, the memo will be sent, and Notes will present a choice of folders in which the memo can be saved.

- ■ To discard the memo, close the new document by pressing Esc or selecting File | Close, and click on the Discard radio button.

Keeping in mind the types of documents that you can create, and the available Views and folders, consider a scenario for using Notes Mail. Keep in mind that, as with most things in Notes, there is no one correct way to do things.

You are reading the *Wall Street Journal* online when you learn that you have incoming mail. You know, because the computer makes a chiming noise. You could click on the mail icon in the lower-right corner of your screen, and select Scan Unread Mail. Notes would display the first unread document, and when you close that, open the next unread document. But you don't want to read the daily announcement of a lunchtime expedition by members of the walking club.

Instead, you select Open Mail to open the mail database on your desktop. You look in your inbox, move the message from the walking club to the trash folder, then look at the next message. It is from your co-worker who works in the consulting office. You double-click on the message title, and the entire message fills the screen so you can read it. She has written an executive summary for a proposal, and wants your comments before she finalizes it. The proposal is for the Western Commerce Bank, who may want you to develop a loan-tracking application.

As you read your co-worker's summary, you realize that you will have to look at the proposal more closely before you can make any comments. You click on the Reply button on the Action Bar. A response-document form is displayed, already addressed to your co-worker who sent the memo. You write a response to tell her that you'll comment on the executive summary as soon as you read the rest of the proposal in greater detail, and you ask her for a deadline.

Before you send the memo, you click on the Delivery Options button on the Action Bar and select a new mood stamp—for example, "good job" or "question."

You then send your reply by clicking on the Send and File action button, and put the document into your personal edit/reread folder when prompted by Notes. It will also be in the Discussion Threads view, along with the original memo. With the reply saved and filed, you can keep track of all activity relating to the proposal.

After you reply, you decide to look for any earlier documents from the same person to see if any of them are relevant to this proposal. You look in the All Documents view and click on the column header to re-sort the view by author. You find a document from six months earlier by the same author, saying that she had met someone in the MIS department at the bank, and thought he or she might be a good candidate for Notes. She said she would try to nurture her contact at the bank to see if anything comes of it. Good job!

You can perform a lot of mail functions from the Navigation window of the Mail database, or from within documents, using the buttons on the Action Bar at the top of the screen. And you can manage your mail without ever having to directly open your mail database from the desktop by accessing your mail using the mail icon on the status bar at the bottom of the screen.

Click on the right-hand corner of the status bar to display a list of mail options, including:

- ■ **Create Memo**: Displays a blank memo form so you can create a memo and send it.
- ■ **Scan Unread Mail**: Opens up the first unread mail in your mailbox. Navigate to the next unread document when you are done by clicking on the Scan Next Unread SmartIcon, or by closing the open document. If there are no more unread documents, you are returned to where you were within Notes.
- ■ **Receive Mail**: Used when you have a local replica copy of your mail database. For example, you can use this when you are a mobile user and have a copy of your mail database on your laptop computer. Selecting Receive Mail establishes communication with the replica of your mail database on your Home server (the one that holds your mail database, according to the Public Address Book) and retrieves any messages that have been sent to you.

- **Send Outgoing Mail**: Used when you are working on a local copy of your mail database, and have mail in your outgoing (store-forward) mailbox. Selecting this option establishes communication with the server so mail can be sent out. Think of it as putting up the flag on the mailbox out by the curb to tell the mail carrier to pick up the mail you want to send.

- **Send and Receive Mail**: Combines the two previous options.

- **Open Mail**: Opens the mail database on your desktop, no matter where you are in Notes. When you close the mail database, you will be returned to wherever you were when you opened your mail database.

> **NOTE**
>
> You can have up to nine Notes documents (including Views) open at one time. If you try to open more than nine, you will receive an error message and will have to close a window before you can open another.

Other Mail Options

There are a few other Notes Mail options that are worth noting.

You can forward any Notes document to another user by selecting Actions | Forward from the pull-down menu. Notes will place the document into the body field of a mail memo. You can then address the memo and mail it with any of the normal mail options previously described.

You can have Notes automatically mail a response to people when you are out of the office. Select Action | Mail Tools | Out of Office to create a message that will be forwarded to anyone who sends you mail, using their return address to determine where to send the memo. You can specify a special message for specific individuals, and you can specify individuals to whom an out-of-office memo should not be sent.

You can automatically add a sender's name to your Personal Address Book by selecting Actions | Mail Tools | Add Sender to Address Book.

You can archive selected messages by selecting the documents you want to archive and selecting Actions | Mail Tools | Archive Selected Documents, or you can have them archived automatically by setting up an Archive Profile under the Mail Tools menu.

And finally, if you find yourself repeatedly having to create the same memo, you can save it as stationery by highlighting the document and selecting Actions | Save as Stationery. This option is like saving a document template. Every pay period, for example, payroll may send out a memo saying "Don't forget, timesheets are due tomorrow. All projects must have a valid project code, and all hours during the pay period must be accounted for."

Collaborating with External Applications

Notes by itself can be used for powerful workflow applications. Much more powerful applications can be built by reaching outside of Notes using functions such as importing and exporting, object linking and embedding (OLE), and Notes/FX.

Sharing Information with Import and Export

There is a lot of information that resides on external systems. Some of it can be shared through Notes by attaching a file and mailing it to another user, or by using linking or embedding, but there are times when neither of these alternatives are viable. For example, a user may have access to Notes, but not have access to the application used to create a file. If the application does not have a cut-and-paste option—with a DOS-based program, for example—the only alternative aside from attaching the file is to import it into Notes, or into another application that does have more connectivity with Notes. Even if the file could be attached and viewed using Notes' built-in attachment viewer, the user would be unable to edit the data if he did not have access to the original application.

Importing the file into Notes provides an alternate way of making it available to another user, either through e-mail or via a mutually accessible Notes database. The other user could edit the information in Notes, and it could then be stored in Notes or exported to another application after it had been edited. In a heterogeneous environment, this may be a good way to share information.

A more robust scenario would have data being imported into a Notes view, making information available within Notes, then using the Notes replicator and e-mail to distribute the information. In this way, you can access large volumes of information, and maintain formatting by selecting the correct import filter. Conversely, information within Notes can be formatted in a specially designed View, then exported to another application—such as a spreadsheet—as a way of consolidating and reporting on the information.

To import files into a View, you have to prepare your Notes database by designing a View that will accommodate the data and a form that contains fields to hold the data. If necessary, you then will have to define what is called a .COL file (column descriptor file), which defines which columns will be imported or modifies data as it is imported from worksheets and tabular text. Then you can import the file. If you attempt to import data to a View without planning the import, you will get unpredictable results.

There are four types of file that can be imported into a View:

- Worksheets (defined by the View, by the .WKS file, or by a .COL file)
- Tabular Text (defined by the View or by a .COL file)
- Agenda (.STF files, defined by COL-type file with a .AFF extension)
- Structured Text (you can define your own inter-document delimiter)

The .COL file is an ASCII text file with a .COL file extension. The file specifies the data type of the field into which you are importing data, and has the basic format of "FIELD NAME: DataType Keyword Data." If you do not specify which type of data to use, Notes will determine the data type based on the contents of the field. For example, you might define a line as "Amount: type number WKSCOL E" where the Amount field will will be populated as a number field using data from column E in a worksheet file. Refer to Lotus Notes documentation for details on how to create .COL files.

To import the data, display the View and select File | Import. Select the type of file you are importing, along with other options that identify how to import data. If appropriate, enter the name of the .COL file to use. When you select OK, the data will imported.

When you import files into a View, the data in each row becomes a separate document in the Notes database, and each column in the View defines a field that contains the contents of the original cell being imported.

Sharing Information with Object Linking and Embedding

Notes R4 supports OLE and OLE/2. This means that you can link or embed a variety of objects in Notes documents, including word processing documents, spreadsheets, graphics, sound objects, and a variety of multimedia objects. An object, as used here, can be an entire file, or a part of a file that has been linked or embedded in a Notes document. Those using Notes will be able to see on their desktop a rendition of the object, or an icon representing the object. The object can be opened for editing or viewing in its original application by double-clicking on it.

The following are key Notes R4 features for handling OLE/2 objects:

- You have the option to include OLE objects in full-text indexes so you can extend text searching beyond Notes.

- You can edit OLE objects from within Notes or by launching the application with which the object was created. To edit an object in-place, click the object, select the object type, and select Edit In-Place.

- You can have an object that launches automatically when a document is first opened by defining a launch parameter in the Form Properties dialog box. In this way, you could conceivably use Notes security features to contain documents and use the Notes interface to navigate, but use other editors (such as AmiPro, Lotus 1-2-3, and so on) to work with the documents.

- You can work with objects in various ways (for example, creating or activating objects) using LotusScript.

There is a distinction between linking and embedding that must be understood if you are to use OLE successfully in a Notes application. Linking maintains a link between the object within a Notes document and the original file that was used to create the object. Therefore, when you double-click on a linked object, you start up the application used to create the object and open the original file used to create that object. If that original file has been changed since you last looked at the linked object, those changes will be reflected when a user opens the object. The person who created the link may have elected to have the link refresh automatically, in which case changes to the original will be seen in the rendering of the linked object every time the Notes document containing the link is opened. Otherwise, the user will have the option to refresh a link when they open the Notes document.

An embedded object, on the other hand, has no link to the original file used to create the object. When a user double-clicks on an embedded object, the application used to create the object is opened locally, and the embedded object is displayed and can be modified. However, when the user saves changes to the object, those changes are saved only to the object embedded in the Notes document.

If all users of a Notes application have access to the original linked file, then a linked object can be used to great advantage. For example, imagine an organization with a large Human Resources Department, one that must handle numerous forms. The HR department will have authorizations, benefit elections, even Fax cover pages that in the past have been printed and stored until they were needed. Some of the forms change frequently, while others seldom change.

Notes has been successfully used as a repository for such forms using object linking. All of the forms are maintained by a forms specialist in the Human Resources Department, and they are stored in word processing documents, or in the format of some sort of form layout. When a user needs a form, they can do a full-text search within Notes to locate the appropriate form, double-click on the linked object, then print it out on their local printer. In this way, the users are assured of having the latest revisions, and the organization saves a mint on printing and storage costs for forms that absolutely have to be created on paper. Notes is used as a container for data that is created and maintained in another application.

There are a couple of ways to create a linked object in Notes.

- Copy a saved file from any OLE server application; for example, Lotus 1-2-3 Release 5, Approach, and Freelance Presentation are all OLE applications. The data must come from a saved file so that Notes knows what to link to. You can do the same from a DDE application, but you must keep the DDE application open while creating the linked object in Notes. Switch to Notes. Make sure the cursor is in a Rich Text field, and select Edit | Paste Special. Notes will give you a choice. You can link the file or simply paste it. And you can display the information in a variety of formats, depending on the type of application. For example, you can display in native format, as Rich Text, as plain text, as a picture, or as a bitmap image. If you elect to display the object as a bitmap, or elect to display it as an icon, then only an icon will be displayed in the Notes document. The object can still be launched by double-clicking on it.

- Place the cursor in a Rich Text field, and select Create | Object, and select Create an object from a file. Locate the file you want to link, and click on OK. Depending on the type of file, and whether you elect to, the object may be displayed as an icon.

Embedded objects have a slightly different focus. You would embed an object if the data is going to be used by someone who does not have access to the file in which the original data is stored. Imagine, for example, that you are on the West Coast, and you are collaborating with a Notes user in another organization on the East Coast to create a new logo. You can create the original version of the logo and store it on your local file server, but the other user does not have access to it. You could attach a file and e-mail it back and forth. But an easier alternative is to embed the logo as an object. The user on the other end can double-click on the embedded object, thus opening the object's native application (an *OLE server*) and editing the embedded object, which is a copy of the original logo. There is no need to leave Notes and hunt for the OLE server on the other end. Notes does it automatically.

To embed an object, you can copy all or part of the data from an open file and paste it into Notes in the same way a linked object is pasted in. You can also embed a blank object, then create data in the object. To create the object, you select Create | Object, then select the type of object from a list of available applications. Notes creates an embedded object and opens the selected application so you can create or edit the object.

Sharing Information with Notes/FX

Notes/FX (Field Exchange) is closely related to OLE, with a taste of importing and exporting thrown in. Notes/FX-enabled applications can exchange information with Notes at a field level. This enables Notes users to see information from other desktop applications in a Notes View and in fields in Notes documents.

Notes/FX is enabled on a form-by-form basis. If a form is to be used for field exchange, verify that Disable Field Exchange is not selected on the Defaults page of the Form Properties dialog box. The form must contain fields with the same name as the field in the Notes/FX-enabled application with which data is to be exchanged. For example, if you have a field called Summary on your Notes form and you want to exchange data with a Lotus 1-2-3 spreadsheet, you must define a range called Summary on the spreadsheet, which can then be correlated to the field with the same name on the Notes form.

In Notes/FX, Notes displays certain information about objects that are embedded in documents, such as the author, date, file size, and number of pages. Other fields can also be displayed, such as named ranges in spreadsheets, slide titles, and paragraph headings. With this type of information available in Notes, it is easy to see how an application could be built to store information as an index to worksheets, slide presentations, and a variety of word processing documents. Information can be exchanged through one-way fields that send information, two-way fields that send and receive information, and user-defined fields that send and receive information.

The field exchange takes place in two directions. For example, you can trigger a Notes macro based on changes to information in certain fields in Notes documents. Therefore, when a field in a worksheet or a word processing document changes and is exchanged with Notes, it can trigger a workflow process.

Notes/FX is an excellent tool for integrating a variety of desktop applications. Notes becomes a shared container for information, and distributes the information through replication and mail routing. But the information comes from common desktop applications, is moved into the Notes database seamlessly, and can again be moved out of Notes into a different word processing or spreadsheet application. The secret to successfully setting up a Notes/FX application is creating common definitions of fields in the Notes/FX applications and in Notes.

An example borrowed from Lotus is a travel authorization, reporting, and reimbursement application. You have to submit a travel authorization request in order to receive a cash advance and budget approval when you are going on a business trip. You begin the process by filling out a Travel Authorization Request in Notes. Notes/FX automatically launches Ami Pro, letting you fill out the form in the word processing environment you are accustomed to. Notes then forwards the document for approval, sends a confirmation back to you, and sends a cash advance request to the finance department.

You do the same thing when you return to the office after your trip. You fill out a reimbursement form starting in Notes, which opens a Lotus 1-2-3 document that contains specific trip information passed through Notes/FX from the Ami Pro document. Notes acts as the container for the shared information, and contributes its workflow capabilities to create an integrated process. The end result is a robust application that lets everyone use the desktop applications with which they are familiar, and provides a centralized reporting application (Lotus Notes) that also provides built-in security for the consolidated information.

How you create Notes/FX applications is dependent on the application you are integrating with Notes. Applications with the Lotus SmartSuite are Notes/FX enabled, as is Microsoft Word for Windows and Windows 95. Microsoft applications for the Macintosh are not Notes/FX enabled. Refer to the documentation that comes with your applications to determine if and how to Notes/FX enable them and start to share data between applications.

Summary

In this chapter, we have looked at a variety of applications in Notes R4, including applications that help users communicate information, coordinate activities, and collaborate with each other. Finally, we took an in-depth look at Notes Mail in R4, including how to create an e-mail message using one of several different mail forms, how to address a memo, and how to send it using a variety of options.

Notes Mail is just one type of application possible within Notes. It is, however, probably one of the most commonly used applications because it brings information directly to the attention of the person who needs to know that information. Therefore, it is well worth examining in detail from an end user's perspective.

In addition to applications that run entirely within Notes, you can also build applications that share data with other applications using importing and exporting, object linking and embedding, and Notes field exchange. These applications let you maintain data in its native application but make the information available to Notes users. This method of making information available to users in your organization has the added advantage of using Notes security features, such as access control, authentication, and data encryption to protect the data.

Using Calendaring and Scheduling

by Handly Cameron

IN THIS CHAPTER

This chapter describes the new calendaring and scheduling features in Lotus Notes release 4.5. It details how to set up and use the calendar integrated with your mail database and how to use group scheduling to view other people's free time and invite them to meetings.

In today's hectic business environment, time management is an important part of your daily work. You have to keep track of appointments, events, and anniversaries, and you have to schedule meetings with other people. Many times, your schedule changes, and you can't contact everyone attending to determine a new time to meet.

In the past, several applications, including Lotus Organizer, have had strong group scheduling features. Now, with the release of Lotus Notes R4.5, group scheduling can be integrated with workflow and information databases.

The group scheduling features in Notes are based very closely on the same group and resource features in Organizer. This means that you can easily schedule a meeting by checking other people's schedules for free times and find a room that is available when you want to meet. Notes will send out invitations to the attendees and automatically reserve the room for you.

Lotus Development Corporation is developing a plug-in API that can be used to create links to allow Notes users to share free time information and group scheduling with users of other time management systems. Currently, Lotus is working on calendar connection software for Lotus Organizer and IBM OfficeVision. This chapter describes how to link Notes with another calendar system.

The calendaring and scheduling features in Notes R4.5 allow the mobile user to create appointments and meetings while disconnected from the network. The Free Time database can be replicated to your local machine to allow you to easily schedule meetings while you are traveling.

An Overview of Scheduling in Notes

 The calendaring and scheduling features of Notes are integrated into your personal mail database. You use the new features by creating appointment documents in your mail databases and viewing your schedule using the new calendar view, shown in Figure 8.1.

The new features in your mail database include the following:

- Calendar view lets you view appointments and events using Two Days, One Week, Two Weeks, and One Month formats.
- Calendar Profile form lets you set scheduling options, such as default length of appointments and access for other people to view your free time.
- Calendar Entry form is used to create personal appointments, meeting invitations, events, reminders, and anniversaries.
- Invitation form is used to accept or decline meeting invitations and to request to reschedule a meeting.

FIGURE 8.1.

You can view your appointments using the new calendar view.

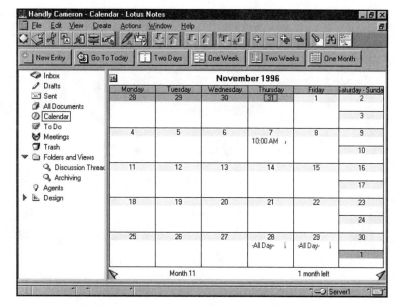

You manage your schedule by creating appointments, inviting others to meetings, and responding to invitations to meetings. If you invite other people to a meeting, Notes will mail the invitation to the attendees who, in turn, can choose to accept or decline the meeting. Notes can also automatically reserve a room and resources, such as an overhead projector.

Setting Up a Calendar Profile

Before you start using the new calendaring features, you must fill out a calendar profile document in your personal mail database to set your user preferences. The calendar profile allows you to set default information that is used when you schedule meetings and events. Examples of settings in the calendar profile include the following:

- Default appointment duration
- Enable alarms for appointments, events, and anniversaries
- Restrict access for other users to see your free time
- Set when your valid free time occurs

Notes will automatically ask you to fill out a calendar profile the first time you use the calendar features in your personal mail database. Alternatively, you can choose Actions | Calendar Tools | Calendar Profile to complete your profile before you start scheduling. Figure 8.2 shows what the calendar profile looks like.

FIGURE 8.2.

You must complete a Calendar Profile before using the new scheduling features.

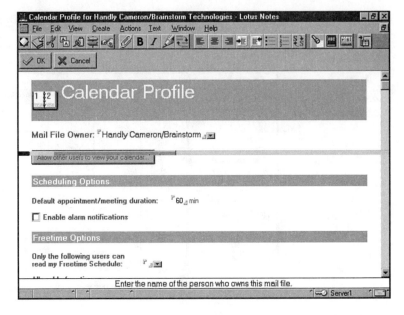

In the first section of the calendar profile, you should set the Calendar Owner field to your Notes user name, which will be the default value. Next, you can choose to allow others to view your calendar by clicking on the button below the Calendar Owner field. This will open a Delegation Profile document.

Delegation Profile

You can use the delegation profile document to allow other users to read and edit your calendar and e-mail. This access is in addition to the ability to view your free time, which is configured in the calendar profile. Figure 8.3 shows the Calendar Access section of the delegation profile.

You can choose to allow everyone to read or manage your calendar, or you can specify individual people or groups who should have that access. If someone is granted read access to your calendar, he or she will be able to open your mail database and read your appointments and meetings. This feature is useful if someone needs to find you, but does not know where you are at a given time. A person with manager access to your calendar can create, modify, and delete entries from your calendar. For example, this access would be used by an administrative assistant who needed to maintain a manager's schedule.

NOTE

Users with reader or manager access to your calendar will not be able to read or edit your personal mail, or any calendar entries which are marked "Not for public viewing."

FIGURE 8.3.

The Delegation Profile allows other users to read your calendar.

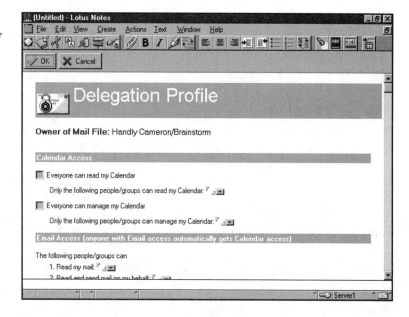

Scheduling Options

The Scheduling Options section of your calendar profile allows you to set a default duration for your appointments and meetings, to turn on alarms, and to automatically set alarms for certain types of calendar entries. Figure 8.4 shows the Scheduling Options section of the calendar profile.

FIGURE 8.4.

Use the Scheduling Options to set a default duration and to turn on alarms.

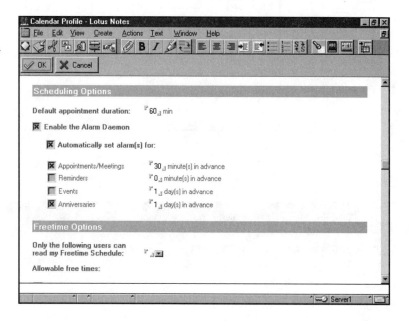

You can enable alarms by checking the Enable the Alarm Daemon box. This will enable the alarms and make the checkbox to automate alarms appear. Checking the automatic alarms box will cause a configuration section to appear. This section lets you enable automatic alarms for each calendar entry type and set a default time for the alarm.

Free Time Options

The free time options allow you to restrict access to other people who want to view your free time and to set which times are considered valid free time. If you do not want everyone to be able to check your free time, you can enter a list of individuals or groups who should be allowed to see when your schedule is free. If you do not enter any names, Notes will allow access to everyone. A person with access to see your free time cannot read your calendar directly; they will only see the times you are available while using the Free Time dialog box, which is described later. Figure 8.5 shows the Free Time Options section of the calendar profile.

FIGURE 8.5.

Use the free time options to set up your allowable free time.

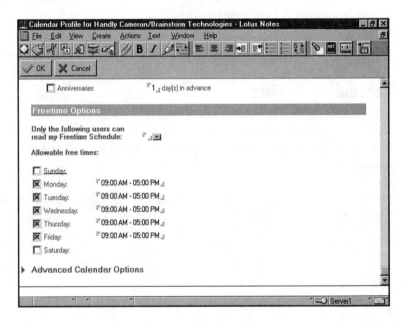

To set up allowable free time, you can check on any of the days of the week and enter a time range in the field that appears.

> **TIP**
>
> Multiple times within a given day can be set by separating the time ranges with a comma.

Advanced Calendar Options

The advanced calendar options allow you to configure automatic calendaring features, to set default calendar types, and to enable conflict checking. Figure 8.6 shows the Automated Calendar Options section of the calendar profile.

FIGURE 8.6.

Automated calendar options help you easily manage your schedule.

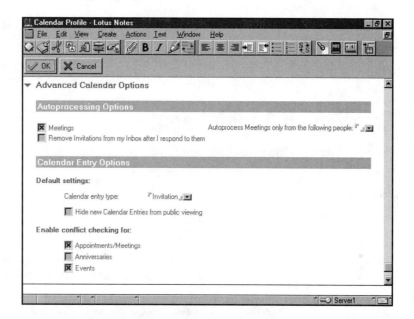

Using the autoprocessing options, you can tell Notes to automatically accept meeting invitations. You can choose to accept all invitations, or only those from certain people or groups. For instance, you might want to accept all invitations from your manager, but manually accept meetings from other people. You also have the option to automatically remove invitation messages from other people after you have accepted or declined their meeting. If you do not use this option, Notes will leave the invitation in your mail file so you can decide whether to keep the invitation or delete it yourself.

The calendar entry options allow you to configure defaults for new calendar entries. Choose from the Appointment, Invitation, Reminder, Event, or Anniversary types to set the default calendar entry type to the type you will use most often. You can also choose to make all new calendar entries hidden from public viewing. This selection has the effect of checking the "Not for public viewing" option on all new entries.

Finally, you can choose to enable time conflict checking for each of the calendar entry types. Reminders are not included on this list, as they occur at a single time and do not have a duration. If you choose to use conflict checking, Notes will check your free time whenever you create a new calendar entry or accept a meeting invitation. If there is a conflict, Notes will warn you and ask if you want to reschedule the new entry.

Saving the Calendar Profile

Click OK to save and close your calendar profile. Notes will present a dialog box, shown in Figure 8.7, in which you choose which server should run the autoprocessing agent. You should enter the name of your home mail server and click OK.

FIGURE 8.7.

Choose your home mail server to run the auto-processing agent.

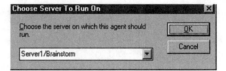

Creating an Appointment

Once you have completed a calendar profile, you are ready to start creating your schedule. You create a new calendar entry using any of the following methods:

■ Open your mail database and choose Create | Calendar Entry.

■ Click on the New Entry button on the calendar view of your mail database.

■ Choose Create | Mail | Calendar Entry from within any other Notes application.

Notes will display a new calendar entry form, using the default configuration you set up in your calendar profile. Figure 8.8 shows the Calendar Entry form when it first appears.

FIGURE 8.8.

Creating a new calendar entry.

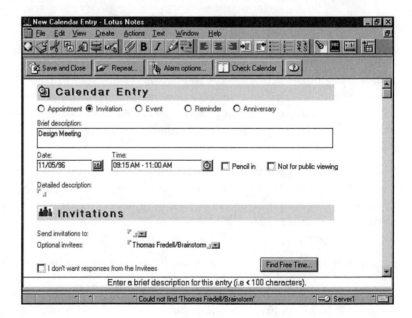

Next, you must decide what type of entry you want to create. You can choose from the following types:

- Appointment is used to create an appointment with yourself.
- Invitation is used to create a meeting appointment, invite others, or reserve a meeting room.
- Event is used to record single-day or multiday events.
- Reminder is used to remind yourself of a task or appointment without reserving any time.
- Anniversary is used to create yearly events, such as holidays and birthdays.

After entering a brief description, which will be used to display the appointment in a view, you can choose the date and time the appointment occurs.

To enter the date, you can type the date manually or you can click on the button next to the date field to use the new calendar control, shown in Figure 8.9. This control displays a small monthly calendar that let's you quickly and easily choose a date for your appointment.

FIGURE 8.9.

Use the new calendar control to easily select dates.

You choose the time for your event by entering a time range manually, or using the new time duration control by clicking on the small clock icon next to the Time field. This control, shown in Figure 8.10, allows you to easily set the time for an appointment with the mouse by sliding the control up or down as needed.

FIGURE 8.10.

Use the time duration control to easily select a time for your appointment.

8

USING
CALENDARING
AND SCHEDULING

After choosing a date and time for your appointment, you can select from the following options:

- Pencil in is used to create a calendar entry without reserving free time. This is useful if you have an unconfirmed appointment; using Pencil in will allow other users to see that you are free during the appointment time. When you confirm your appointment, simply deselect the Pencil in box to reserve the time.

- Not for public viewing is used to mark this appointment as private, and keep others from seeing it when they view your calendar.

If you do not want to invite other people to a meeting, set an alarm, or make the appointment a repeating appointment, you can click on the Save and Close action button to finish editing the document and save the entry in your calendar.

Inviting Other People to a Meeting

Use the Invitation Calendar Entry type to create a meeting and invite people to it. Selecting Invitation will cause two new fields to be displayed on the form, Required Attendees and Optional Attendees. You can enter names in these fields or click on the small button next to the field to bring up the Address Book dialog box to easily select people or groups to invite to your meeting.

If you want to find a time when all attendees can meet, you can click on the Find Free Time button below the Optional Invitees field. This will bring up the new Free Time dialog box. Figure 8.11 illustrates the use of this dialog box to view free time and adjust your meeting time. The dialog box shows a chart of free time either by day or by person. Busy times are indicated by a light blue color, while free time is indicated with white. A bar shows when your meeting is scheduled and will be colored green if the meeting time is available for all attendees or red if someone is busy. On the left side of the dialog box are recommended meeting times based on the attendees' free time.

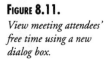

FIGURE 8.11.

View meeting attendees' free time using a new dialog box.

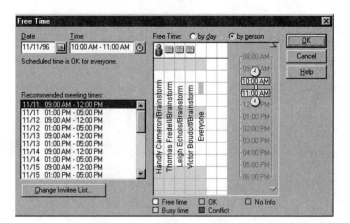

If you need to change the time of your meeting, you can use the date and time controls in the Free Time dialog box to update your meeting and see if the new time has any further conflicts. You can click on the Change Invitee List button if you want to adjust the attendee list, for instance if you need to have the meeting at a certain time, but one person is busy and does not need to receive an invitation.

TIP

You can schedule a meeting any time, even if one of the attendees is busy during the meeting. The busy attendee will still receive an invitation and can decide to modify his or her schedule to accommodate your meeting, decline your meeting, or accept the meeting as a time conflict. Notes can display time conflicts in the new calendar view so the attendee will know when he or she is scheduled for concurrent appointments.

Setting a Reminder Alarm

You can set an alarm to remind you before (or after) your appointment by clicking on the Set Alarm button on the action bar. A dialog box will appear, and you can enable the alarm and set the number of minutes before or after the appointment for the alarm to trigger. You can also enter a message that will appear when the alarm triggers. Figure 8.12 shows how you set the alarm.

FIGURE 8.12.

The SetAlarm dialog box.

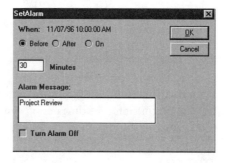

When the time comes for the alarm, a dialog box will pop up to remind you about your meeting, as shown in Figure 8.13. The alarm has a snooze button so you can delay the alarm for 10 minutes or for a period you define.

FIGURE 8.13.

A reminder alarm.

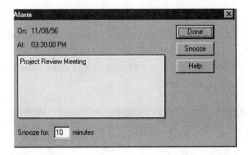

Creating Repeating Appointments

You can create a repeating appointment by choosing the Repeat button on the action bar. This will display the Repeat Rules dialog box, shown in Figure 8.14. Next, you should choose a repeat frequency. You can choose between daily, weekly, monthly, and yearly settings. For instance, you can set an appointment to occur weekly, on every Tuesday and Thursday. You should set a starting date and an ending date or duration for the appointment. Click OK to return to editing your calendar entry.

FIGURE 8.14.

Create repeating appointments with the Repeat Rules dialog box.

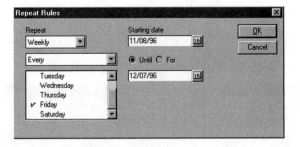

When you save a repeating appointment, Notes will automatically create calendar entries for all occurrences of the appointment for the time period you specified. Later, if you need to move or delete a single occurrence of the appointment, Notes will ask you if you want to apply the change to all of the repeating appointments, update all future or all past occurrences, or only change a single occurrence.

Checking for Time Conflicts

If you have set your calendar profile to enable time conflict checking, Notes will automatically check your schedule when you save a new appointment or accept a new meeting invitation. If a time conflict is found, Notes will inform you that there is a conflict and ask you if you want to schedule the new appointment anyway.

If you do schedule a time conflict, the calendar view will indicate the conflict by placing a red line next to the conflicting entries to remind you that the appointments overlap.

What to Do When You Receive an Invitation

When another person invites you to a meeting, you will receive an invitation in your mail like the one shown in Figure 8.15. If you need to check your calendar before accepting or declining the invitation, the Check Calendar action button will display the calendar view of your mail database.

FIGURE 8.15.

Meeting invitations are sent through Notes mail.

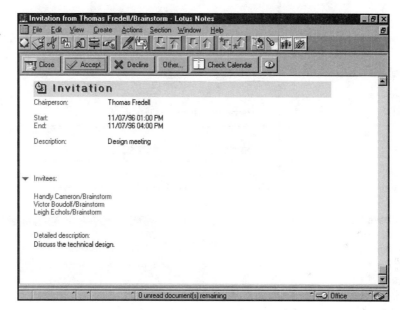

Rescheduling Meetings

You can send a request to reschedule the meeting back to the chairperson by clicking on the Other action button and choosing Propose Alternative Time/Location. Notes will convert the invitation into a reschedule request form, shown in Figure 8.16. Using this form, you can choose a new date and time, enter a reason for the reschedule request, and propose a change of location. Click on the Send Counter Proposal button to return the request to the chairperson.

Delegating Meetings

Sometimes important meetings cannot be moved to fit your schedule. In this case, you can delegate the meeting invitation to another person. To delegate a meeting, click on the Other action button and choose Delegate. Notes will ask you who to delegate the meeting to using the dialog box shown in Figure 8.17. Choose a person to go to the meeting in your place and click OK to send the invitation to the new person and to inform the chairperson that someone will be attending in your place.

FIGURE 8.16.

You can request to reschedule meetings.

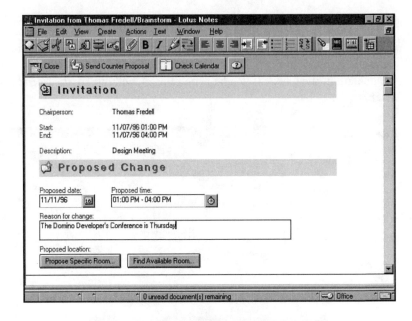

FIGURE 8.17.

You can delegate meetings to other people.

Calendar Views

Notes 4.5 introduces a new view type. You can use this view to see your schedule using four calendar types: Two Days, One Week, Two Weeks, and One Month. The view is similar to the interface of Lotus Organizer or your notebook planner. Figure 8.18 shows the new calendar view using the One Week display.

You can choose which view type you want to see by selecting it from the buttons on the view action bar or choosing View | Calendar and selecting a type.

The calendar view allows you to easily change your schedule using drag-and-drop. If you want to move an appointment, simply click on the entry in the calendar view and drag it to the new day. Notes will automatically move the entry, check for time conflicts, and send reschedule notices to meeting attendees if necessary.

You can also create new appointments in your calendar by double-clicking on the day in which the new entry will be scheduled. Notes will display a new Calendar Entry form on which you can type the details of your new entry.

FIGURE 8.18.

The new calendar view lets you see appointments using a standard calendar format.

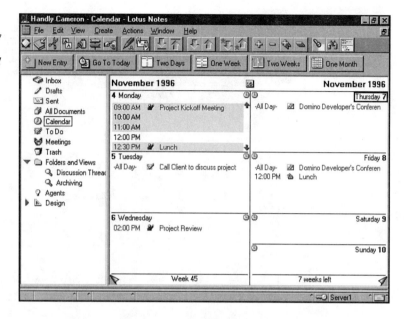

Calendaring and Scheduling While Traveling

The calendaring and scheduling features can be used by the mobile user while disconnected from the network. You can create new calendar entries, including invitations while traveling. The invitations will be stored in the outgoing mail database and be routed to the attendees when you perform your normal mail replication. Your schedule will also be updated in the Notes server Free Time database during replication.

One unique feature of Notes calendaring and scheduling is the ability to check other people's free time while disconnected. You can create a replica of the Free Time database on your local computer that will be used when displaying the Free Time dialog box. The information reflects the other user's free time at the time you last replicated with the server. Figure 8.19 shows how you can easily replicate the Free Time database using the Replicator workpage.

You can edit the free time replication options to set which user's free time is reflected in your local Free Time database, the amount of free time information that is stored, and how often the local free time is updated. Figure 8.20 shows the free time replication options dialog box.

8

USING
CALENDARING
AND SCHEDULING

FIGURE 8.19.

The Replicator work page allows you to use free time information while traveling.

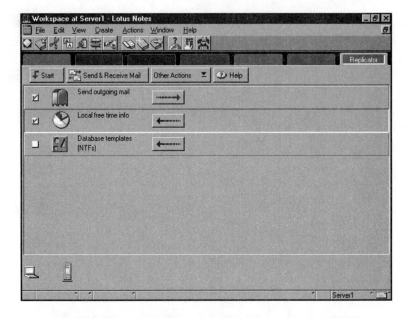

FIGURE 8.20.

You can configure how free time information is stored locally.

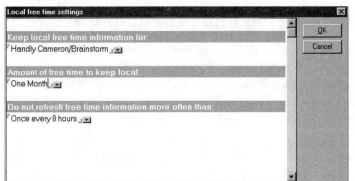

Using the Resource Reservations Database

Lotus Notes automatically tracks room and resources using the Resource Reservations database. The Notes administrator creates this database on the server using the RESRC45.NTF database template. This database is used to create site, room, and resource documents, and can be used to directly enter a reservation without using the standard invitation process.

Before using the Resource Reservations database, you should choose Create | Site Profile to compose a site profile document. This document contains information about your office and domain, as shown in Figure 8.21. Enter a site name and the Notes domain name on the document and click Save Profile to save and close the site profile.

FIGURE 8.21.
*The site profile
document.*

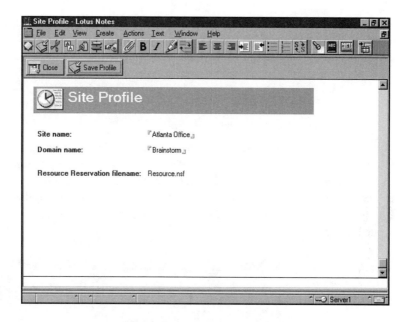

Choose Create | Resource to enter a new room or resource into the database. Figure 8.22 shows the resource document being used to create a new room. To create a room, enter the room name and capacity. Click the Site button to indicate which site contains this room. You can then enter time ranges when the room is available for reservations. Click on the Done action button to save the resource document. Notes will automatically create a request for the administration process (adminp) to enter a resource document into the Name and Address Book.

FIGURE 8.22.
*Use the Resource form
to create new rooms
and resources.*

8
USING
CALENDARING
AND SCHEDULING

To enter a resource, choose Other for the resource type. An example of a resource might be an overhead projector or a VCR. After entering a name for the resource, click on the Categories key to group the new resource with existing resources. Notes uses resource categories when multiple resources are available. For instance, you might have three overhead projectors available. The person reserving a projector does not care which projector they use; he only cares that one is available. Notes will randomly reserve a projector out of all of the projectors available to balance the resource usage.

Rooms and resources are normally reserved as part of creating a meeting invitation in your mail database. If you need to reserve a room or resource without creating a meeting, you can use the Resource Reservations database directly. Choose Create | Reservation to compose a new reservation form, as shown in Figure 8.23. Notes will guide you through the reservation process, asking you to choose a resource type and then requesting more details after you click the Continue button.

FIGURE 8.23.

The reservation form.

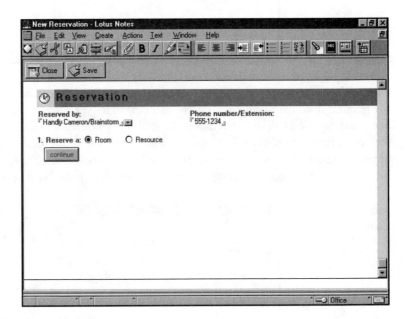

Using Calendaring and Scheduling with Other Software

Notes can communicate with other calendaring and scheduling applications such as Lotus Organizer and IBM OfficeVision using special Calendar Connectors developed with the plug-in API. You set this up by creating a Foreign Domain document in your Public Name and Address Book. Choose Create | Server | Domain to compose a new domain document.

Figure 8.24 shows the domain form. Select Foreign Domain for the domain type and enter a domain name and description. Enter the name for the server and the calendar system that will process the scheduling requests for the other scheduling application. If a Notes mail user is using a different scheduling application, enter the name of the foreign domain in the Calendar Domain field of the user's person document in the Name and Address Book. Notes will automatically route invitations and free time requests to the server defined in the foreign domain document.

FIGURE 8.24.

A foreign domain is used to link Notes and other scheduling software.

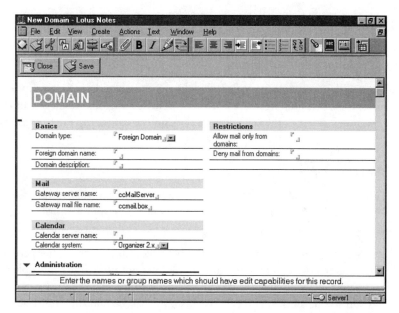

New Server Tasks

Two new server tasks have been added in Notes 4.5 to support the calendaring and scheduling process. The first of these, the Schedule Manager, automatically creates the Free Time database (BUSYTIME.NSF) and updates the database as users create new calendar entries. When a user requests to view free time, the Schedule Manager references the Free Time database to populate the Free Time dialog box. The Free Time database is a special database that can only be accessed by the Schedule Manager task.

The second task, the Calendar Connector, is used when a server receives a free time request for a person whose mail is located on another server. The Calendar Connector will automatically communicate with the other server in real time to retrieve the free time information and display it to the current user.

Using Calendaring and Scheduling in Other Notes Databases

All the new calendaring features in your mail file are available to you while you're designing new Notes databases. You can create special calendar entry forms, check free time, and display your Notes documents using the new calendar views.

There are many potential uses of these features in Notes design. For example, a customer service application could display customer orders by order date or ship date using the new calendar view. Managers and production staff would be able to easily see which orders needed to be shipped in the next day or week.

The new date and time controls will make any time-based application more user-friendly. Your Notes users will no longer need to waste time figuring out which day of the week the 15th of next month falls on; they can simply click on the date using the new calendar control.

Summary

This chapter introduced you to the new calendaring and scheduling features of Lotus Notes 4.5. We reviewed the new calendar documents, date/time controls, and calendar views. We also looked at how they can be used to create calendar entries and manage your schedule.

Using these features, you will easily be able to coordinate with other people. You can schedule a meeting, reserve a room, and send invitations without making multiple phone calls trying to track down every attendee and find an empty conference room. By creating repeating meetings and setting alarms, you can keep a complex schedule and continue to be organized.

Using Mobile Notes on the Road

by Don Child

CHAPTER 9

This chapter discusses the use of Lotus Notes R4 for mobile users. You can use multiple locations in Notes, setting up a laptop computer to work from a variety of locations such as airports or hotel rooms, in addition to the work Notes can already do in the office or at home. Included in the setup is the use of modems and communications ports, the setup of Location documents, and planning for replication when you are on the road.

Working as a Mobile User

When you think about it, the Notes workgroup exists in virtual space. The members of workgroup team might all work in the same office and might be constantly connected to the same local area network, at least from 8 a.m. until 5 p.m. But then again, they might be scattered around the globe, and connections between team members might take place once a day or once a week, and users might be replicating at noon in Bangalore, India, at midnight in Paris, or at 8 a.m. in Boston.

Notes users might well say that they carry their office desk with them on their laptop computer. For example, imagine a busy sales representative, Janet Aubrey, who travels to visit several sales areas, and occasionally visits a regional office. At the company headquarters in San Diego, she is connected to the local area network. She reads her Notes mail, which is stored on the Notes server, and works with several of the corporate databases on a daily basis.

We will follow her on one of her sales trips. On the morning before she is scheduled to leave, she updates a local replica copy of her mail database and a few other vital databases, such as her company's customer-tracking database, an online sales brochure, and a travel planner that lists good places to visit in the cities she will be visiting. If she made full replicas of all the databases she used in the office, her laptop computer would quickly run out of storage space, so she creates a replication formula that collects only those documents that might be relevant to her during her travels. Then she leaves with her entire desktop stored on her laptop computer.

The first hop of her journey is a short one to Los Angeles, where she has a connecting flight to Honolulu. She visits the Los Angeles office for a meeting before her continuing flight, and connects to the office LAN and selects LA OFFICE as a location. Notes has already been predefined, so she doesn't have to define the protocol she is using, doesn't have to tell the computer that her home/mail Notes server is in San Diego.

After her meeting, she heads to the airport. Just as she is going toward her departure gate, her beeper goes off. She has urgent Notes mail waiting for her. She finds a pay phone, connects a phone line to the laptop, and plugs the other end into a jack on the bottom of a pay phone at the airport. She changes the Location setting to LA MOBILE. Then she goes to the replicator page and selects Send and Receive Mail. As soon as Notes is finished, the phone connection is ended. Janet puts her laptop back in her briefcase and heads for the plane.

The call from the airport didn't dial directly to her home/mail server. Instead, the LA MOBILE location record in her Personal Address Book calls the LA branch office, which has a passthru server that puts her through to San Diego. Because her company takes advantage of the passthru-server feature, she was able to connect to her personal-mail file directly, using a local call even though the mail file was on a Notes server in San Diego.

After replicating her mail database, she boards a flight for Honolulu. As soon as the plane is airborne, somewhere high above the Pacific Ocean, she has an opportunity to open the laptop replica of her mail database. She reads through her correspondence and creates responses to some of the mail when necessary. She selects Send and File as soon as she is done with creating a memo. The outgoing mail is held in a store/forward mailbox right on her laptop computer. She sends another memo to coworker Wally Takayama, who had asked her where on the network she had placed a word-processing file. She addresses the memo simply to "Wally," knowing that Notes will look up the correct address in her Personal Address Book.

One of the memos she received, the urgent one that had activated her beeper, mentioned an additional client for her to visit in Honolulu, with a meeting set up for half an hour after she arrived. No problem. The client is in the Client Tracking database, which she now has on her laptop. She opens the client's profile to brush up on their background, then examines past orders and develops a brief proposal for them, including a Freelance presentation. When she gets to the client's office, she will be able to launch the application from within the proposal in Notes.

She continues to read and respond to her e-mail, takes time out for lunch, then has a nap. After all, this will be a 27-hour day when the time zones are factored in.

When she lands in Honolulu, she goes directly to the client's office, the one for whom she has just prepared a proposal. She shows them her proposal online, then hooks up her laptop to a phone line in the client's office and changes the location to Honolulu Fax, one of the locations she has predefined on her laptop. From the replicator page, she selects Send Outgoing Mail from the Other Actions button. Notes calls a local business associate who has a Fax gateway. The result is that the mail in her store/forward mailbox is sent, including the proposal, which she has addressed to the client's Fax number. The proposal is printed on the client's Fax machine while she is showing the clients her Freelance presentation. The result is another sale.

When she finally reaches her hotel, she hooks up her modem line to the hotel telephone, starts up Notes, switches her location to Hotel, and clicks on Start from replicator page. Notes prompts her for the telephone number to call. She selects the home office, since there are no passthru servers any closer than San Diego. By the time she sits down to dinner, she has current data on her laptop computer, her order has already been sent to the fulfillment clerk, and she is ready to enjoy a stroll down Waikiki beach.

Notes Release 4 deserves a lot of the credit. It was virtually effortless to work as a mobile user.

Setting Up the Workstation for Mobile Computing

There are several necessary steps to set up for all of the events in the scenario described here. You need Notes 4.0 and a valid Notes User ID. You need a Notes compatible modem set up to use with your workstation. You need to know the phone numbers of the Notes servers you want to contact, or alternately, the phone number for an Internet provider and the IP address of the Notes server. You need an analog phone line to connect to, plus a phone cord, extra batteries, a power adapter, and so on. And you will probably want to include a copy of Notes Help Lite on your mobile computer, rather than carrying the full help database.

Within Notes itself, there are four items that need to be set up properly before you can take full advantage of Lotus Notes on the road (at least as described in the preceding scenario). You need to set up and define ports. You need to set up and define locations. You need to set up and define replication schedules. The Notes Administrator needs to set up passthru servers if necessary, and you need to identify the passthru server you will be using if appropriate. Defining passthru servers and replication schedules are both done on the Location document.

Many of the mobile options can be initiated from File | Mobile. The options on this menu include the following:

- **Choose Current Location** displays a list of available locations from which you can select. The same list is available from the Locations section of the status bar, found near the bottom-right corner of the Notes workspace.

- **Edit Current Location** displays the Location record for the currently selected location. You can also edit the location record from the Locations section of the status bar.

- **Edit Current Time/Phone** displays a dialog box so you can enter specific dialing information for the current location, including the current time, the number to dial to get an outside line, and the country and area codes.

- **Locations** displays the Locations view in the Personal Address Book; from here you can select location records for editing or create new locations.

- **Server Phone Numbers** displays the Server view in the Personal Address Book so you can edit existing server connection records or create new records. The server connection records hold the phone number to call for a specific server.

- **Call Server** lets you select a server from a list of those servers for which a connection record exists, and initiate the call so you can directly access databases on the server (assuming you are authorized to do so).

- **Hang Up** disconnects your modem from the server.

Setting Up Ports

All of the discussion about how to use Notes R4 as a mobile computing platform depends on your ability to establish communications between your workstation and the Notes server with which you are replicating. That means either configuring a network connection or a connection through a modem via a modem.

You can set up multiple ports and then enable specific ports for use at different locations, depending on the type of physical connection you have. Each port uses a specific communications protocol, which must match one of the protocols being used by the server that you are communicating with.

Communication Protocols

All connections between a Notes client and a Notes server are classified as either a network connection or a dial-in connection, regardless of whether the connection is made locally or from a mobile computer. Although one usually thinks of network connections as being local, physical connections to a network, the link could also be via a wide area network with a link to the server through a bridge or router, or the connection could be over the Internet via TCP/IP.

Notes provides several communications drivers (in other words, protocols), including the following:

- AppleTalk is used to communicate with Macintosh clients or with other Notes servers using AppleTalk.
- Banyan VINES is used for communication over a Banyan VINES network.
- DECnet Pathworks uses a NetBIOS driver to communicate.
- Lotus Notes Connect for SNA is used to communicate across IBM SNA networks using either the OS/2 Communications Manager or DCA Communications software for the server or workstation, and the associated hardware. Both the server and workstation must use Lotus Notes Connect for SNA, which is available as an add-on product.
- NetBIOS is used to communicate over any network that uses NetBIOS. There is a separate NetBIOS driver for IBM Extended Edition LAN Requestor.
- NetWare SPX is used to communicate over a Novell network using native SPX protocol rather than NetBIOS.
- TCP/IP is used to communicate between client and server and between Notes servers across all supported Notes hardware platforms. Because of its cross-platform capabilities, TCP/IP is widely used. TCP/IP is, of course, also the protocol used on the Internet. This means that you can connect to a Notes server via the Internet as if you were making a local Internet connection, no matter what your location.

9

USING MOBILE NOTES ON THE ROAD

> **TIP**
>
> Although one of the banner applications in Notes R4.5 is the InterNotes Browser and the InterNotes Server, which combine to make it easy to publish and view information on the Internet's World Wide Web, you do not need to use TCP/IP on your workstation to navigate on the Web. The InterNotes server handles all of the communication with the Web, but you can communicate with the InterNotes server using any of the Notes-supported protocols, and read Web pages as Notes documents. Browsing the Web while on the road is discussed in greater detail near the end of this chapter.

- XPC is built into every Notes client and server, and is used to communicate over dial-up or null-modem connections when no other communication drivers are available. You can also use the XPC driver's asynchronous communication scripts to dial into an X.25 Packet Assembler Disassembler (PAD). This gives you the ability to issue commands to communicate with any X.25 address.

- Lotus Notes Connect for X.25 is an add-on product so that Notes can communicate directly with X.25 private or public networks. The Lotus Notes Connect for X.25 driver can be used to communicate over X.25 leased lines using Eicon hardware and software, although the Eicon Technology components are not included with Notes. They must be obtained from Eicon. If a server supports X.25, PAD-connected users do not need Lotus Notes Connect for X.25 to communicate.

Defining a New Port

You can define multiple ports. Each one is associated with a particular communications protocol.

Communication protocols are set on the User Preferences screen, displayed by selecting File | Tools | User Preferences, and clicking on the Ports icon on the left of the dialog box. (See Figure 9.1.)

FIGURE 9.1.

Setting up Ports in the User Preferences dialog box.

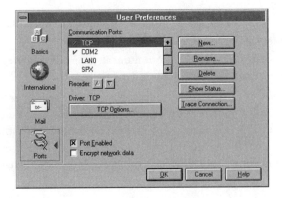

Click on the New button to display a dialog box where you type in the name of the new port (for instance, COM2), select the protocol, and specify at which locations you will use this protocol.

Each port name is associated with a single communication protocol. You can rename or delete a port, but you cannot change the protocol assigned to that port. If you want the port to have a different protocol, you must delete the port, then create a new port by the same name using the new protocol.

After you name the port, select a protocol and identify locations where the port will be used, you can define additional optional information by clicking on the Options button beneath the protocol name, as listed:

- **TCP/IP:** You can define the duration of a connection-attempt time out.
- **NetBIOS:** You can choose between automatic or manual setup. If you choose manual setup, you can specify the NetBIOS unit/Lana number.
- **IPX/SPX:** You can choose between automatic or advanced configuration for NetWare Services. The advanced configuration lets you choose between NetWare Directory and Bindery Services, NetWare Directory Services (NDS), or Bindery Services. You can also define a Fallback Name Server for the workstation.
- **VINES:** There are no additional options when you set up the VINES protocol.
- **XPC:** For all COM ports, the default protocol is XPC, which depends on having a modem connected to the COM port (either internally or externally), or a null modem that connects one computer to another directly via a null modem cable.

Setting Up a Modem

Since we are talking about the mobile use of Notes, you will need a modem and a phone connection in order to communicate with the Notes server. Setting up a modem is done when you select the XPC protocol. In fact, if you select XPC, you have to define the type of modem you are using before you can use the port.

Since we created a new port named COM2, the User Preferences dialog box will display a button labeled COM2 Option. Click on this button to display the Additional Setup dialog box, shown in Figure 9.2.

9

USING MOBILE NOTES ON THE ROAD

FIGURE 9.2.

The Additional Setup dialog box, used to define modem communications for a COM port.

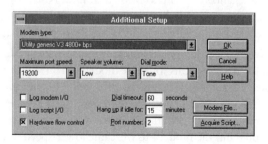

In this dialog box, you select a modem type from among the nearly 150 modem files that ship with Notes. If you cannot find a file that matches your modem, there are some utility generic modem files available. If your modem is a 100 percent Hayes-compatible modem, you can select Auto Configure near the bottom of the list of modems, and Notes will select the file that most closely matches your particular modem. The modem files are placed in a Modem directory in Notes' default data directory on installation, so if you have moved the modem files to another location, Notes may have a hard time locating the files.

Once you select a modem type, you can select the following options for the modem:

- **Maximum Port Speed:** Select the first speed above the highest rated speed for your modem, since Notes will use the lesser of the Maximum Port Speed and your modem's maximum speed. For example, if your modem is rated at a port speed of 14400, select 19200 as your maximum port speed, and your modem can then operate at its highest rated speed. If you are having problems with a noisy phone line, try dropping back to a lower speed.

CAUTION

Some modems may not connect if the Notes speed is set too high. You may have to experiment if you are having trouble connecting with your modem.

- **Speaker Volume:** Set the speaker volume on your modem to off, low, medium, or high.
- **Dial Mode:** The dial mode can be Tone or Pulse, depending on the type of phone system you have. Normally, this should be left on Tone.
- **Log Modem I/O:** If you select this option, then modem-control strings and responses will be recorded in the Miscellaneous Events view of your local Notes log database. Keep this selected only if you are troubleshooting suspected modem problems. Otherwise, leave it deselected; the logging adds a lot of extra information to the log files.
- **Log Script I/O:** If you select this, asynchronous script-file responses get recorded in the Miscellaneous Events view of your local Notes log database. Keep this selected only if you are troubleshooting suspected problems with a script file. Otherwise, keep it deselected, since this also adds a lot of extra information to your Notes log.
- **Hardware Flow Control:** This controls the flow of data between your computer and the modem. Select this for most modems. You want to deselect this only if your modem doesn't support flow control, or if you are using certain null-modem connections or some types of add-in equipment, such as older versions of DigiBoard. If a modem doesn't support flow control, you will want to set the maximum speed for the computer and the modem to the same lower-speed settings to reduce CRC errors.

- **Dial Time-Out:** This is used to tell the modem to pause for a set length of time before trying again, if a connection cannot be made with the server. It keeps the modem from dialing constantly, and it gives the server a better chance of being available on the next try. You may want to increase the time-out to 120 or 180 seconds to minimize the number of retries.

- **Hang Up If Idle:** This setting tells the modem to hang up if there is no activity on the phone line for a set length of time. If the phone line is idle for too long, the connection is broken and the modem hangs up the phone. This will greatly reduce the cost of long distance calls if you are away from the computer when your call is finished.

- **Port Number:** This is the COM port that is being used by the modem.

- **Modem File:** This button displays the modem text file for the selected modem. If you are familiar with modem drivers, you can edit and customize the modem file.

The Acquire Script button opens up a box that lists available acquire scripts. An acquire script is a text file used to acquire a communication device such as an ISDN modem before the modem script is run. For example, you may need an acquire script to connect to one of the modems, or connect to a PAD device. The acquire script is stored in the modem directory and has a filename extension of .SCR. When you select an acquire script, it is permanently associated with that COM port. To disconnect from the script, edit the port, select the Acquire Script button again, and select NONE as the script that you want to associate with the port. If you need to create or edit a script file, you should refer to the Administrator's Guide that comes with Notes. The guide provides sample files and definitions of script file keywords and script command lines.

> **NOTE**
>
> The Lotus Notes Technical Support knowledge base, which can be accessed on the World Wide Web via the InterNotes Browser or other Internet browsers, has this to say about using Notes over an ISDN phone line:
>
> "A number of customers have reported successful use of Notes over an ISDN phone line. However, Notes currently does not have a native ISDN driver, like X.25 or X.PC.
>
> "Currently, you can use Notes to communicate over an ISDN phone line provided the ISDN device you use, like a digital modem, supports the standard AT command set. Since Notes does not have a native ISDN driver, you must communicate to the ISDN device via the X.PC driver, thus the need for support of the AT command set. It is also recommended that the ISDN device on each end of the connection be identical. This is due in part to interoperability issues that exist with the use of various ISDN devices. Generally speaking, if the ISDN devices on both ends of the connection can communicate successfully, Notes
>
> *continues*

continued

can leverage that capability with a little effort on the part of the Notes user. That is to say, you may need to create an acquire script to setup the ISDN device, or, in some cases, incorporate the ISDN device setup in the Notes MDM file."

The Lotus Home Page address is URL `http://www.lotus.com`, then follow links to Customer Service.

There is one other selection near the bottom of the port selection dialog box you should be aware of—the Encrypt Network Data checkbox. If you select this option, then all communication through the port will be encrypted, no matter whether it is implemented on the workstation end or on the Notes server end. If you elect to encrypt data through the port, then the other end will also be forced to encrypt the data. This will slow down the transmission of data slightly.

Setting Up Location Documents

Workstation setup automatically creates a Personal Address Book with four default locations already defined:

- **Office** (network connection), which you would use when you are directly connected to the Notes network in your office
- **Home** (remote connection), which would use a modem to dial into a Notes server
- **Island** (no connection), which lets you work as an isolated workstation with no connection to a Notes network
- **Travel** (remote connection), which lets you define how to connect to the Notes server when you are on the road

You can edit the definitions for these locations, and you can create additional location documents. For example, you might want to define a Hotel location document that automatically enters your phone card number when you dial.

A location document defines where to find your mail file, how to make a connection to your home server (the one that holds your mailbox), and other specifications for the location.

The Location Document

Each location has its own Location document, as shown in Figures 9.3 and 9.4. The document is divided into five information areas—plus, there are two collapsible sections. The information areas include basic information, server information, phone-dialing information, mail information, and replication information. The two collapsible sections are Advanced and Administration.

FIGURE 9.3.

The Location document (top half).

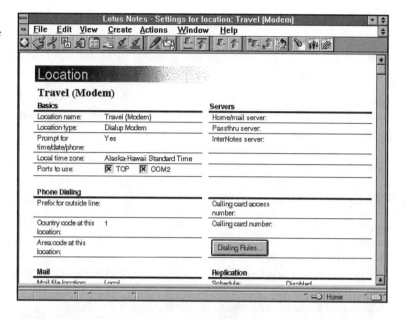

FIGURE 9.4.

The Location document (bottom half).

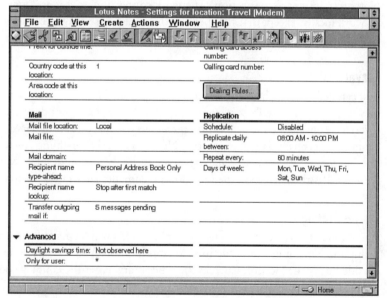

To create a Location document, select File | Mobile | Locations and select the Add Location action button. To edit a location, highlight the location on the File | Mobile | Locations screen and select the Edit Location action button. The Location document will be displayed. You can also add a new Location document from the Create menu in the Personal Address Book.

Basics

The information that goes into the Basics part of the document includes the name of the location document, the type of connection (Local Area Network, Dialup Modem, both, or no connection), and, depending on the type of connection, which ports to use.

Select for use at this location one or more ports from all ports you have set up and enabled. If a connection cannot be made from the first enabled port, Notes will try the next one until a successful connection is made. In addition, you can specify whether or not Notes should prompt for the time, date, and phone number each time when you use this location. This might be necessary for a location document if you travel between time zones and don't want to create a separate location document for each place that you travel to. The default time zone is Eastern Standard Time, but you can define the time zone for anywhere in the world.

Depending on the type of connection specified in the Basics portion of the document, there may be small differences in the remainder of the document. One notable difference is in the Advanced section of the document. There are two additional fields that can be defined if you specify a network connection. The two additional fields let you enter a secondary Domain Name Server if you use TCP/IP as a communication protocol. TCP/IP is the protocol used when you connect to the Notes network via the Internet. Even though you are connecting remotely, Notes recognizes the connection as network connection, so it is as if you were using the Notes network locally, except that the speed of the network is likely to be slower than if your workstation were a node on the local area network.

Servers

You can define three different servers for a location. The home/mail server is the Notes server on which your mail database is stored. The passthru server is your default Notes passthru server, if you have one defined. The passthru server lets you dial one Notes server, and from that single connection, get passed through to other Notes servers, thus enabling you to make a single phone call and replicate all of your databases, even if they reside on different servers. Refer to "Verifying the Passthru Server in the Location Document" later in this chapter for details.

Phone Dialing

The Phone Dialing section defines how phone calls will be made from a location, assuming a dialup modem connection is defined for this location. You can enter the prefix for getting an outside line at the location (such as 9). If necessary, enter the country code for the location as well as the area code.

If you want to use a calling card to charge all of your dialup modem calls from a particular location, enter the calling card access number (the number you dial before a phone number to indicate that you want to use a calling card). Then, in the calling card number field, enter the calling card number to use. You can use an alternate phone number for a server by clicking on the Dialing Rules button and selecting the server, then entering a different prefix, phone number, and/or suffix for the server.

> **TIP**
>
> Commas can be entered into a phone number or dialing prefix to force a delay, if necessary. Each comma forces a two-second delay.

Enter commas to force the modem to pause while dialing. For example, consider the following number: 9,0,8082345678,,,,,480834565678789. This will dial 9 to get an outside line, pause, dial 0 to get the long distance carrier, pause, dial the phone number, pause long enough for the number to dial and for the carrier to request your telephone credit card number, then dial your credit card number.

Mail Options

For each location, you can specify the type of mail you are going to use—server-based or workstation-based. If you have server-based mail selected, you will have to connect to the server either remotely or via a Local Area Network in order to access your mail. If you have workstation-based mail selected, then you can perform functions such as composing mail or forwarding documents without having to connect to the server. The difference between the two types of mail is that, with server-based mail, documents are immediately routed to the user's mailbox on the Notes server. With workstation-based mail, documents are held locally in an outgoing mailbox and are transferred later, when a connection is made to the home-server.

Recipient name type-ahead lets you address mail memos using a type-ahead, with Notes looking in either your Personal Address Book or the Public Address Book on your mail server to find a name and display it as soon as you type enough letters to uniquely identify the addressee. You can limit the type-ahead feature so that it looks only in your Personal Address Book if you want, or you can turn the feature off completely from the Location document. And you can determine whether Notes will look in all address books for name matches, or stop after a single match is made. Notes will not let you send a mail message unless there is a valid mail address—that is, unless a matching name is found in a personal or public address book. If the address has an @ symbol in it, indicating that the message is being sent to another domain, then the address book is not available to the sender and Notes will allow the message to be sent without first validating the address.

The final field in the Mail section of the Location document has to do with mail routing. If you have set up a location with the mail file defined as local, then you can have your workstation dial the server automatically when a certain number of outgoing messages are waiting. As soon as the minimum threshold is reached, your workstation automatically calls the home server and transfers outgoing mail.

Replication

The process of replication is described in detail in Chapter 33, "Replication and its Administration," but basically, it is the process of synchronizing databases that have a single, identical ID, but that reside on different systems. Replication takes place between two servers, or between a workstation and a server. There is, however, no peer-to-peer replication between workstations.

The replication that is initiated from the Location document is workstation-to-server replication. You can enable a schedule, and when the scheduled replication time arrives, the workstation will automatically call the server and replicate. The process takes place in the background so you can continue working without interruption.

Replication will take place in the background. On Windows workstations, you have to run the program SHARE.EXE before Windows is started. Otherwise, the background program cannot run. Running in the background means that you can continue doing other work while replication is taking place.

The Replication section on the Location document gives you the option of enabling or disabling replication by toggling with the spacebar or pressing the Enter key to display a list of options. In this instance, however, the only options are enabled or disabled.

You can set up a schedule that includes a range of times during which scheduled replication will take place, or you can set specific times for replication, with times separated by commas. If you define a range of times, then you can also enter a repeat interval. A repeat interval of 360 minutes, for example, means that the workstation will dial the server 6 hours after the last successful replication completed.

Normally, you will want to set up scheduled replication only for time-sensitive databases. You can then select a repeat interval that is appropriate for your situation. Note that you can also set the schedule up so it works only on specified days of the week.

Advanced Options

The Advanced Options section has two fields for dial-in and unconnected locations, and four fields for network locations. All location records let you specify whether or not daylight savings time is observed at the location, so Notes can coordinate differences in time between the server and the mobile workstation. If a workstation is being used by more than one user, you can specify which user or users are authorized to use a particular location record in the Only for user field.

If the location record is for a network location, you can enter the name of a secondary Notes name server. The Notes name server provides a list of server names that are available to the user, such as computers to which you can potentially connect based on available communications protocols. When the primary Notes name server is not available, Notes searches for the secondary name server to provide this list of names.

Depending on the type of network connection you have, Notes finds the secondary name server in different ways. Over AppleTalk, Notes searches the AppleTalk zone in which the workstation resides, looking for servers defined through the Macintosh Chooser or in the Additional Setup dialog box. Over Banyan VINES, a datagram is broadcast over a well-known port, and other Notes servers send a datagram back to the client. Over NetBIOS, each Notes server has a thread that listens for the NetBIOS groupname IRISNAMESERVER. Any server can respond with a list of servers. In NetWare SPX, the client sends a SAP broadcast. Local servers respond, and NetWare routers send requests to other LANs. In TCP/IP, you have to configure a specific secondary server with a valid address. You can enter the server address in IP address format (such as 193.94.222.65), in fully qualified DNS format (such as ServerName.companyname.com), or in host-name format (ServerName). The third format is not recommended because the TCP/IP stack cannot query multiple servers in a network.

Administration Options

There are a couple of administrative fields on the Location document. The Owner field lets you enter the name of the person who owns the Location document. If access control is being enforced, then the owner is the person or persons who have the right to edit the document.

If you have delegated local administration of the location, enter the name of the document administrator in the Administrator field.

Setting Up Passthru Servers

Passthru servers provide a single point of contact for users who want to replicate databases and therefore may need to contact multiple servers. Instead of calling each server separately to replicate one or two databases, you can call a single passthru server, and it will forward-link you through itself and possibly through other intermediate passthru servers until you are in contact with the destination server.

Passthru provides a couple of advantages. First, the passthru server can act as a conduit for all requests to a number of servers in an organization. All of the external communication comes through a communications hub server, which passes users through to the server they want to contact. The passthru server does not need to hold replica copies of the databases users want to access. Instead, it has to provide only the connection to the destination server. Second, the passthru server can handle multiple protocols, thus enabling connection from a variety of users. The destination servers need only a single protocol, one that can communicate with the passthru server, and the users need only a single protocol that can communicate with the passthru server. The server provides the connection between the different protocols.

The mobile Notes R4 user in the example at the beginning of this chapter was able to call a local passthru server in Los Angeles. The server passed her through to her home server in San Diego. In this way, all of the communication costs were incurred through the corporate WAN, which is a fixed cost to the corporation, rather than through a long-distance telephone call at much higher rates.

9

USING MOBILE NOTES ON THE ROAD

Setting up the passthru server is an administrative function, and requires the correct documents in four locations:

- A passthru Connection record has to be created for each server in the Public Address Book.
- The passthru Restrictions for each server record must be properly filled in.
- Users must verify that they have the correct information in a passthru Server Connection document in their Personal Address Book.
- The Default passthru Server field in the location document must correctly identify the passthru server that will be used from that location.

Each of these steps is described here.

Passthru Connection Record

In the Public Address Book, the system administrator should create a Connection document, and in the Connection Type field, select Passthru Server. An example of the Passthru Server Connection document is shown in Figure 9.5.

FIGURE 9.5.

A Passthru Server Connection document.

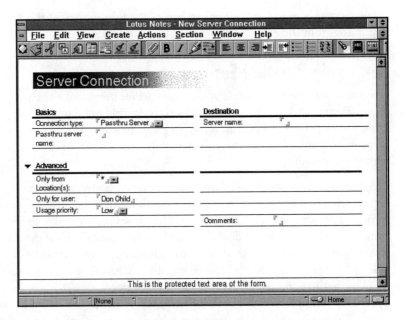

Enter the following information for the connection document:

- The name and domain of the Passthru Server (the Source server).
- The name of the intermediate passthru server to use to get to the destination server.

- The Usage Priority of the passthru server. Notes uses the most direct route to reach a server, so if you want Notes to give priority to the passthru for connections (even though a dialup connection directly to the server might be more direct, for example), this should be set to Normal.

- The name and domain of the destination server. If the passthru server does not have a normal connection to the destination server, and you are not passing through an intermediate server, you may also need to create another connection document to that server—for example, a dialup Connection document.

The remaining fields on the form can be used to set up scheduled replication and mail routing with the destination server, but they are not required for passthru.

Passthru Server Restrictions

In the Public Address Book, there are four new fields that define access security for passthru servers. These four fields—Access this server, Route through, Cause calling, and Destinations allowed—define which people, servers, and groups can use the server for passthru connectivity. The four fields are found in the Restriction section on the Server form. You may have to switch from the Location form to the Server form to see these fields.

The effect of these four fields is as follows:

- **Access this server:** Determines who may access this server via a passthru server. Only those servers, persons, or groups listed in this field can access the server via passthru. You can press Enter or click on the keyword indicator to display the Public Address Book to assist in selecting names to include in this field.

- **Route through:** Determines who may use this server to route through to another server. Only those servers, persons, or groups listed in this field can pass through this server on their way to another server. In other words, these are the people, servers, or groups who can use this server as a passthru server.

- **Cause calling:** Determines who (usually another server) may tell this server to call another server. The server has to be able to call other servers so it can build a passthru route to the destination server. This is usually a server routing through the passthru server, seeking to replicate with the destination server. Only servers, persons, or groups listed in this field can cause calling.

- **Destinations allowed:** Determines which destinations a server can route to. If the field is blank, there are no restrictions, and the server can route to any server to which it has access. If there are any servers listed in the field, then only those servers can be routed to.

If you switched to the Server form to view these fields, be sure to switch back to the Location form before saving the record.

Mobile-User Passthru Connection Documents

Mobile users have to set up a Connection document for the Passthru server in their Personal Address Book. To do this, open up the Personal Address Book and compose a Server Connection document.

Select Passthru Server as the connection type. Enter the name of the destination server, and the name of the passthru server that will be used to connect to the destination server.

In the Advanced section of the Connection document, you can specify which locations can use this passthru-server connection. For example, suppose the mobile user has a laptop that they take to client sites, and a docking station with a modem at home. They can define two Location records (such as Home and ClientSite) to use the same passthru server. But if they are staying in a hotel in another city, it may be more economical to dial the destination server directly. You can restrict the use of this Connection document so that it is valid only for certain locations.

Verifying the Passthru Server in the Location Document

On each Location document in the user's Personal Address Book, there are three server fields: the Home/Mail Server, the Passthru Server, and the InterNotes Server. The mobile user should verify that the correct server is named in the Passthru Server field, and that the server name is spelled correctly. Use the fully distinguished name of the passthru server—for example, Server1/Sales/Acme.

The end result of setting up a passthru server is that the entire process is automated. The mobile user selects a replica of a database that is on the destination server, then selects replicate. Assuming that they are hooked up to a telephone at some mobile site, Notes asks if they want to call the passthru server. After they say yes, Notes automatically calls the server. The passthru server will authenticate with the user, then call the destination server, authenticate with the server, then pass the user through to their destination. It is all more or less automatic. Note that authentication takes place at every step of the way, so users cannot use passthru to gain unauthorized access to another Notes server.

Selecting Databases for Replication

The primary tool that gives the mobile user access to data is Notes database replication. As a mobile user, there are a couple of things you should consider: which databases you will need to have available locally, and which documents within those databases you will need.

A corollary to those two considerations is to determine when you should replicate. As a rule, you will want to make an initial replication before you leave; the initial replication is much quicker over the local area network, and you don't have to tie up the telephone lines as you would if you decided later to replicate from somewhere on the road.

For a database to replicate, there have to be at least two replica copies of the database—one on the workstation, and one on the Notes server. You create the replica on your workstation by adding the icon for the server-based database to your desktop, highlighting the icon, and selecting File | Replication | New Replica. Make selections in the dialog box that is displayed to create the new replica on your local workstation. Replication is discussed in detail in Chapter 33.

If you have icons for the original database and its replica on your desktop, you can stack the icons by selecting View | Stack Replica Icons. You will then have only one icon showing on the desktop at a time. You can switch from one replica to another by clicking on the small arrowhead in the corner of a stacked icon, and selecting the replica you want. Whichever icon is on top is the currently selected version of the database. So, if the top icon is the server-based replica of the database, when you select it, Notes will attempt to contact the server. If it is a local replica, Notes will open the replica that is on your workstation. The stacked icons are location-sensitive, so if you have a mobile location selected, local replicas of databases should be on the top of the stack.

Notes determines which databases are replicas of each other by comparing each database's replication ID to see if they are the same. The replica ID can be seen on the information page of the database Properties box. If the replica IDs are the same on two databases, then they are replicas of each other, even though you might have renamed one of the databases. The databases may even contain a different subset of documents as the result of selective replication. And of course, you can always tell if they are replicas by stacking replica database icons on your desktop. If they are stacked on top of each other, they are replicas. If they are not stacked, they are not replicas.

Initiating Replication

To replicate a local database from a mobile location, the database with an icon on your desktop must have a replica copy of the database on the server you call, or on another server that can be reached using a passthru server.

There are several ways to initiate a replication from a mobile workstation:

- Highlight the workstation-based icon and select File | Replication | Replicate.
- Click on the small arrow on a stacked icon, ensure that you have the local replica selected, and click on "Replicate."
- Set up scheduled replication on the Location record.
- Use the Replicator page to manually initiate replication.

The Replicator page consolidates all of the replication options in a single location. (See Figure 9.6.) This page holds icons for all of the databases that can be replicated. You can select specific databases for replication by clicking in the checkbox to indicate that those databases should be replicated during the next replication with the server. Note that you can select replicas that are on different servers if you are using a passthru server for replication.

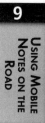

FIGURE 9.6.

The Replicator page.

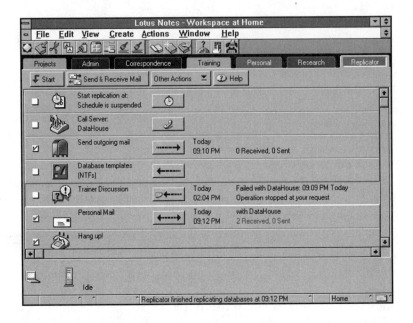

If you check the first item, Start Replication At:, any replication schedules you have enabled will cause replication to occur in the background.

If you check the second item, Call Server:, Notes will call the selected server even if the replica is not on that server. For example, you could specify a passthru server to call.

If you check Send Outgoing Mail, Notes will check your store/forward mailbox and send any outgoing mail messages at the same time it replicates.

If you check Database Templates, template files will be replicated.

If you check any databases, those databases will be replicated. Notes automatically puts databases on the replicator page the first time the database is replicated. If you want to remove an icon from the replicator page, you can select the icon and press the Delete key. If you want to put the icon back onto the replicator page, you can locate the icon on the workspace, then drag and drop it onto the replicator tab. Note that you can set replication settings for an individual database by selecting File | Replication | Settings. This lets you specify which documents will get replicated before replication actually takes place.

CAUTION

If you use the Single Copy Object Store feature of Notes mail on your home server, you must be sure to create a *replica* copy of your mail database on your workstation. Creating a replica means that the full document will be copied to your workstation. If you accidentally select copy instead of *replica copy*, you will end up with nothing but summary data in your

> mailbox. Pointers to non-summary data can be resolved only if your mailbox is on the same server as the Single Copy Object Store.

If you check Hang Up, Notes will hang up as soon as the replication is completed. If the Hang Up icon is not checked, Notes will remain in communication with the server after the replication is completed.

You can manually initiate replication from the replicator page by selecting the Start action button. You can manually initiate sending and receiving mail without replication by selecting the Send and Receive Mail action button. You can specify which databases you want to replicate, or just send mail, from the Other Actions action button.

Finally, for each row on the replicator page except for the Hang Up row, you can click on the button to the right of the descriptive text to change settings for the action or database. For example, you could change a database's replication settings to send documents but not receive any new documents.

NOTE

Replication is discussed here in the context of the mobile user. However, there are instances where a user might use replication over a local area network. For example, a designer may want to make design changes on a replica of a database, rather than making modifications directly on a production database. When the design changes are completed, they can be replicated back to the production database.

Using Mobile Notes After It Is Set Up

So far, the focus of this chapter has been how to get set up as a mobile user. Now let's assume that everything is set up correctly, and you are ready to work as a mobile user. There is no single correct way to work with Notes. How you manage your databases and your connections to the Notes server depends on the type of data you are using, and the type of organization you are working with. The options described in the following sections are, therefore, just some of the ways you can work with Mobile Notes.

Establish a Telephone or Direct Connection

Depending on the type of communications you have set up, you need to connect to a telephone outlet, or to some sort of device that provides a connection to the server via a wide-area network. If you are on the road, take along a phone cord that you can use to connect your computer's modem to a phone jack, either on the bottom or back of a telephone, or a wall jack. You can then communicate with your server via the telephone line.

Select a Location

As a mobile user, you select a location to work from by selecting the appropriate Location document. This can be done in either of two different places:

- Select File | Mobile | Choose Current Location then select the location you want from a list.

- Click on the location button (located near the right hand side of the Status Bar at the bottom of the Notes workspace) and select the current location from a list.

The Location document contains relevant information for each location, such as what type of connection you have to the server (if any), whether your outgoing mailbox is local or on your home server, and which databases should be replicated on what sort of schedule. You can edit the current location document so replication and mail parameters suit your particular needs. Once it is set up the way you want it, all you have to do is select the location, and Notes takes care of everything else. Notes knows whether to dial the server directly or use a passthru server, which databases should be replicated, which phone numbers to dial, and so on, all based on the Location document for that location.

Connecting Over the Internet

To connect to Notes over the Internet, you have to have your server set up with a direct connection to the Internet, the server has to be running TCP/IP, and must have its own IP address. Once everything is set up, you have to do the following:

Establish either a direct or dial-up Internet connection using either a Serial Line Internet Protocol (SLIP) or a Point-to-Point (PPP) protocol. This gives your workstation the equivalent of TCP/IP functionality.

Once you have a SLIP or PPP connection, start Notes and switch to a Location document that uses a TCP/IP port. You are then seen by the server as a node on the local Notes network, and can open databases or replicate databases from the server, just as you would if you were in the office working over the local area network.

According to Lotus Notes Internet Cookbook (available from Lotus at http://www.lotus.com), these are the acceptable SLIP/PPP protocol stacks you can use with Notes:

- IBM TCP provides SLIP (for OS/2)
- LAN Workplace for Windows 4.2 (for Windows 16)
- FTP Software (for DOS, Windows 16, and OS/2)
- NetManage Chameleon (Windows 16 and Windows 32)
- Trumpet WinSock shareware (for Windows 16)

To set up SLIP/PPP on your Notes server, follow the instructions provided with the SLIP/PPP protocol stack that you choose.

The Internet Cookbook should answer most of your questions regarding how to connect to a Notes server via the Internet.

Connecting Over a Modem

There are a couple of ways you can connect over a modem, depending on the type of work you are going to be doing. If you are always working with a particular subset of documents that you carry around with you on your laptop, then you will want to connect to the server to replicate those databases, either on a regularly scheduled basis, or on an as-needed basis. On the other hand, if you are looking something up in a large database that you do not need to access routinely, you can stay connected to the Notes server for a few minutes, open the database to find the information you want, then disconnect from the server.

To replicate a single database, you can do the following:

1. Highlight the local replica of the database you want to replicate.
2. Click on the arrowhead on the icon to display stacked icons list, and select Replicate...; or

   Highlight the icon and select File | Replication | Replicate...; or

   Locate the database icon on the replicator page, and make sure it is the only database with a checkmark beside it. Then click on the Start button.
3. Notes will display a dialog box that lets you decide between background replication or replication with options for this one-time replication. Options include which server to replicate with, whether to send documents, whether to receive documents, and whether to receive whole documents, summary information plus 40KB of rich text, or summary information only.
4. Click on OK to begin replication. When replication is done, Notes will disconnect from the server connection automatically.

To replicate multiple databases, display the Replicator page, make sure the databases you want to replicate are checked, and click on the Start button. Databases will replicate one at a time, with a pointing hand indicating which database is currently being replicated. You can also edit the Location document to enable automatic replication, as described earlier in this chapter.

You also have a couple of options if you want to connect to the server so you can work with databases online, or so you can add new databases to your desktop.

■ Double-click on the icon for a database that is on the Notes server. A list of phone numbers that can be called to connect to the server will be displayed. Select or type in the number you want to call and click Auto-Dial. Notes will call the server and open the database on your desktop. You will remain connected to the server when you are done working with the database, so remember to hang up (described later) when finished.

- Select File | Mobile | Call Server.... A list of phone numbers that can be called to connect to the server will be displayed. Select or type in the number you want to call and click Auto-Dial. Notes will call the server. You can then work with any databases to which you have access on the server. When you are done, remember to hang up.

- Click on the File Mobile Call Server SmartIcon (the finger pressing a button on a phone dialer). Everything else is the same as calling the server from the drop-down menu.

To hang up when done connecting to a server, select File | Mobile | Hang Up... or click on the File Mobile Hang Up SmartIcon (a hand placing a handset back onto a phone). Notes will display a list of COM ports. Select the port that is currently connected and click on Hang Up.

Sending Mail as a Mobile User

To send mail, create a memo just as you would if you were directly connected to the office LAN. Notes can look up names for addressing in any address books you have defined under File | Tools | User Preferences | Mail. Outgoing mail is placed into your outgoing mailbox, and is sent to the Router on the server when you replicate with the server from the Replicator page if you have Send Outgoing Mail checked, or you can select Send Outgoing Mail from the Action menu, or click on the Send and Receive Mail button on the Replicator page. You can also open the outgoing mail database and click on the Send Mail button.

You can replicate your mail database with your mail database on your home server, just like with any other database.

Database Security for Mobile Notes

The one problem with using Notes on the road has always been the fact that a laptop computer can be lost or stolen. That means that databases on the laptop can also be stolen, and those databases may contain valuable information that you don't want to fall into the wrong hands. Notes R4 provides two security features for databases that the mobile user should be aware of.

- Local enforcement of the Access Control List. The Database Manager can elect to enforce a consistent Access Control List across all replicas of a database. With this feature turned on, replica databases on your laptop cannot be accessed unless the user has a valid ID (and a password that lets them use that ID).

- Encryption of local databases. You can elect to encrypt local databases, thereby making the database unusable to anyone unless they have the proper user ID and its associated password(s). This is set up by clicking on the Encryption button on the first page of the Database Properties box, and selecting the options you want.

Browsing the Web While on the Road

With Notes 4.5, you have several options if you want to browse the Web while on the road.

You can replicate a copy of the Web Navigator database from the Notes Server in your office before you go on the road. Then, you can browse the downloaded Web pages at your leisure when you are disconnected from the network. This option has been available since the release of the InterNotes Web Browser, and many Notes users have happily browsed the Web on their laptop computers while 30,000 feet in the air.

With Notes 4.5, this option is actually considerably more appealing because of the Personal Web Navigator and an option called Web Ahead. You can define the number of layers of links you want Notes to download to your computer. Theoretically, you could download an entire site such as the Lotus site (`http://www.lotus.com`) just by typing the home page's URL and defining a large number of Web Ahead links. This isn't very practical, but the point is, instead of downloading the corporate pages from your Server Web Navigator, you could instead connect directly to the Internet using your Personal Web Browser and save the pages you want for later perusal.

Other options are just as interesting but require a telephone connection and a modem. If the long distance charges aren't too steep, you can dial into your home Notes Server and retrieve Web pages directly from the Server Web Navigator. You can do this with any communications protocol as long as you can access the Notes Web Navigator. The Server Web Navigator is the only machine that must have TCP/IP protocol running. It will download the pages you request and pass them to you as Notes documents.

If you have TCP/IP running on your laptop, you can connect to any Web server using a SLIP, PPP, or remote LAN service connection. Since you can launch the Personal Web Navigator or another Web Navigator from within Notes, all you need is a way to connect to the Internet. If you have a mobile account, this can mean loading Trumpet Winsock or a Windows 95 connection and dialing an ISP near wherever you are. Or, you could dial your regular Internet connection, make a TCP/IP connection, and then browse as usual—maybe a bit more slowly, though. However, you're still connected directly to the Internet and can download Web pages directly from within Notes.

When you get set up with a remote LAN service such as Microsoft RAS, you can work as if you were in your office. When you type a URL in the Search Bar, your computer will dial up the Web server using the RAS connection, and you will find yourself in cyberspace.

All of this assumes a couple of things. First, you must have your Personal Address Book connections set up correctly. And you must have some sort of connection to the Internet, either directly through an ISP or via an HTTP Proxy Server. Notes 4.5 offers numerous alternatives (as described earlier). For a more detailed description, refer to Chapter 23, "Using the Notes Client on the Internet."

Summary

Once properly set up, Mobile Notes automates many of the variables that are specific to different locations where you work with Notes, such as the office, at home, or on the road. Notes R4 has been optimized for the mobile user through Location records in the Personal Address Book, which make it possible to switch from one location to another with a single click of the mouse. Notes for the mobile user can be further automated by setting up replication schedules and taking advantage of passthru servers, whereby the user can communicate with multiple servers using a single connection.

Setting up Notes for the mobile user involves setting up communication ports, defining location records, setting up replication of databases on your desktop, and taking advantage of the option of using passthru servers.

Once Mobile Notes is set up properly, there are a variety of ways you can work, depending on the type of information you are working with. You can determine how often Notes calls a server to replicate databases, which documents to replicate to a particular location, and how your mobile workstation should communicate with Notes servers.

In addition, with Notes 4.5, you now have several options for browsing the Web, even while on the road. You can browse the Web while disconnected, you can browse through an HTTP Proxy server, or you can browse directly on the Internet—all from within Notes.

IN THIS PART

Developing Applications with Lotus Notes

CHAPTER 10

What Makes a Good Notes Application?

by Sam Juvonen

IN THIS CHAPTER

Okay, so Notes looks easy enough to use. But what is behind these applications? How hard are they to build, really? And most importantly, when should Notes be considered the ideal platform to build a new application, as opposed to one of the more traditional database-development tools on the market?

This chapter kicks off the development section of this book. You will gain an understanding of Notes' position in the application-development arena. There are essentially two types of database applications: data-centric, where the focus is on small, often numeric, information that is voluminous, often segmented into multiple related tables and that is used to generate large, complicated reports; and communication-centric, where the focus is on information that is organized around forms and documents, often using unstructured formats such as paragraphs and rich text objects. Lotus Notes is, first and foremost, a communications tool; it is also a database. Think of it as a "communications database," because the types of information you store in Notes are typically used to help people communicate more effectively, as opposed to merely logging data.

For instance, a hotel or an airline reservation system stores complex relationships between resources and reservations. The information must be current at all times. While Notes wouldn't be used to develop a system of this type, it can be used effectively to communicate a periodic summary report such as the average bookings per day for the last month to management (as opposed to the typical paper report). These reports can be accumulated over time and staff members can generate comments and brainstorm new ideas alongside these documents in the same database.

You'll find in this chapter that as you ponder (or receive requests for) new ideas for applications, you should focus on the communication-centric aspects, for this is the area where you will achieve the greatest success with Notes.

Notes is also an excellent prototyping tool. By offering a design platform that is easy to learn and use, it is possible to cost-effectively prove new ideas. For example, you may have a process in place to handle expense reports. Individuals fill out by hand a multipart form and submit it to accounting. The form is separated into several forms and routed to different individuals for approval. By using Notes, you can quickly develop a system that uses spreadsheets and routes them for approval.

Notes R4 offers complete programmability through its inclusion of the LotusScript language. Yet it also offers simple actions that can perform sophisticated tasks without programming, such as routing documents. The formula language that makes use of the famous Lotus @functions still remains and has been enhanced with more functions. This all means that Notes now scales easily for the new developer and the seasoned programmer. Even without knowledge of LotusScript it is easy to develop prototypes that include much of the logic you'd like or need in the final version.

The Notes Paradigm

A few years ago, Lotus introduced Notes as a new application-development platform that promised rapid development and answers to problems that had been difficult to solve with the tools of the day. Notes has proven itself to be a leading-edge product, so this claim remains true. The term *groupware* has been bandied about and perhaps diluted by a variety of vendors, but it has had the positive effect of differentiating Lotus Notes from relational tools.

Although some applications can be developed with Notes as well as tools such as Approach, Access, or Paradox, most Notes applications would simply cost too much if developed with the relational tools. Why? Their highly structured environments require more effort and custom programming to achieve the same effects as Notes, especially when geographical dispersion and security concerns are important.

Ask one simple question: at first blush, is the information you wish to capture better aligned into documents, or into tabular records? Answer this question from a distant perspective, looking at the whole picture, not at one portion.

Realize that documents are used for communication (think memo), whereas records are used for logging and storage (think ledger). Lotus Notes is a document-centric application environment. Documents can be *compound*—that is, they can contain very rich types of data such as formatted text, images, bitmaps, even sound objects. Records tend to be homogeneous, containing simple information.

Lotus Notes solves a different array of problems. Though most systems tend to bring to mind tabular structures of information, a "softer" class of information goes uncollected, missing the opportunity for true collaboration.

The quickest and biggest buy-in from the user community comes about through a groupware application when users can see that vital information and knowledge is being shared, processes that used to be agonizingly slow and painful can be improved in such a way that their daily work lives are better. Customers experiencing such benefits often voice testimonials such as "We can't imagine working without Notes." They once did, of course, but the introduction of groupware significantly improved their processes.

Communications-Centric Opportunities

Notes excels in solving communications problems, where information isn't reaching the necessary individuals appropriately. A customer-tracking system that enables and communicates activities taken with clients (such as phone calls, written correspondence, and meetings) is a wonderful use of Notes. The information varies in length, often consisting of paragraph-oriented documents.

Figure 10.1 shows a sample communications-centric environment. Another metaphor for this model is "sometimes connected." The network users in the two offices work with their local copies of the Customer Tracking application. The Notes servers replicate to keep the documents synchronized. At the top of the diagram is the remote user, who dials into a Notes server to synchronize the laptop copy of the database. This enables the user to work offline—adding, modifying, and perhaps deleting documents, then replicating (this is the "sometimes connection") to become up-to-date with the server's copy.

FIGURE 10.1.

The Notes environment uses a sometimes-connected model.

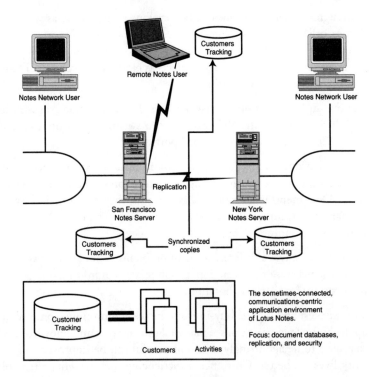

With the additional capabilities of Release 4.5 and Internet integration, communications applications can become even more powerful. For example, in prior releases of Notes, the user had to dial in directly to a Notes server. With the new Internet capabilities, a user can connect via an Internet Service Provider (ISP) and a local phone number and route communications through the Internet rather than calling the server directly. This lets companies save money on phone bills and eases connection configurations for IS departments.

One of the templates that ships with Notes is the Customer Tracking database. It contains many forms such as Customer and Contact Profiles along with Activity records (meeting reports, action items, and phone calls). For a consultant, even documents that need simple numeric data, such as time-billing sheets, may be recorded in this database. Users in your department, your regions, or from around the world can contribute to the same customer information, often helping each other with information that otherwise wouldn't have been communicated. A representative in San Francisco can see the letters and phone calls that have taken place with an account's Washington, D.C. office; when that rep visits the San Francisco site, they can speak knowledgeably about current events.

Data-Centric Opportunities

Standard database tools excel at storing data, usually in tabular form, and modeling relationships between portions of that data. A sales-tracking system models customers, products, and sales of products to customers. To do this requires tight relationships that preserve the information's integrity. For instance, a customer with outstanding invoices should not be deleted. Relational integrity ensures that such an event cannot happen.

Such systems often involve large numbers of users entering new records and modifying existing records on the same network. Sophisticated locking, logging, and transaction-based devices have been implemented to ensure the integrity of the information, even in cases of power loss during updates.

A common element that is evident from these important systems is that they usually contain numeric or short alphanumeric fields of data. Although it can be said that the information is being communicated because it can be retrieved by another individual, such communication is often ineffectual. It has been said that there is too much information in relational systems that cannot be easily consolidated and disseminated.

Figure 10.2 depicts a data-centric application environment: a relational database system. This environment relies on constant connections; if the network goes down, the expectation is that it will be brought back to life quickly. A central database server maintains the integrity of the line-of-business tabular data (for instance, a customer, orders, and inventory-control system).

The remote user shown in Figure 10.2 uses a remote access server to become a network user to interact with the database. The user works with the data online, then hangs up when finished. No local copy of the data exists. A typical call might be made to enter new orders or check an order's status.

The data in the database is highly structured; it is tabular in format, so a change to a table affects all of the records. Design changes cannot be made easily. This structure provides excellent integrity and allows for useful roll-up reports. Current inventory levels can be obtained at any time, for instance.

FIGURE 10.2.

A traditional relational database is constantly connected and centralized.

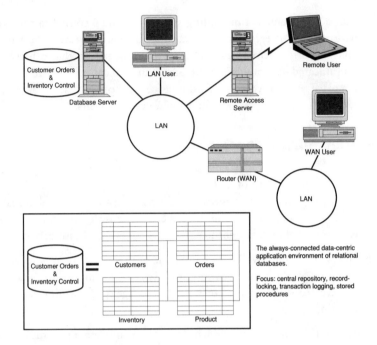

Can Notes "Act" Relational?

Lotus Notes, with Releases 3 and 4, has brought about the ability to develop somewhat relational databases. Although the heavy-duty relational engine was never intended to exist in Notes, simple lookups can be performed that can "relate" or use information in one document from that of another. Release 4, with LotusScript and the LotusScript:Data Object (LS:DO), moves this further along and offers more control over relational data from within Notes.

It is possible to write a pseudo-relational database with Notes, but because that isn't its strong suit, the results will probably be disappointing when compared to a relational system. If the volume of data is low, then the performance will be acceptable; however, if the volume is expected to be large, then it is best to turn to a relation tool to build that system.

Notes has a part in a mixed-data environment, where some data belongs in a relational system, but some of the "softer" information would be better suited for Notes. Using the LS:DO scripting power, it is relatively easy through ODBC to make the two coexist. Use the relational system for the relationships, record locking, and storage of bulk data, but use Notes for the summarization and dissemination of extracts of that data to field personnel or regional offices.

If you aren't familiar with ODBC, let's quickly look at what it means. The acronym stands for Open Database Connectivity, and it is a standard developed by Microsoft for establishing communications between a wide variety of data sources, such as dBASE, SQL Server, and Paradox. You use ODBC by configuring a specific connection to a data source, giving this connection a name and also specifying the particulars to connect to the data source.

LS:DO gives you the ability to communicate ODBC data sources from within LotusScript. You can fully control this data source, and you can perform SQL (Structured Query Language) queries, getting the results back in memory where you can browse them and base decisions on these results. Use LS:DO to integrate with another data source on an as-needed basis, for instance, making changes in a Paradox database upon a status change in Notes.

Remote Users

It seems that Lotus likes laptops. As the proverbial salesman travels the globe, the laptop is used to dial in from a wide variety of locations. Much of Notes' design stems from the remote users' perspective. For instance, it doesn't use record locking, but seen from the travelers' perspective this makes sense; with a plethora of roving users, each of whom is working standalone, locking these documents is impossible. Instead, resolution of document conflicts occurs during replication.

Two factors that weigh heavily in favor of Notes when choosing a development platform are: Notes provides an extremely sophisticated replication engine, and it offers excellent security. These two feature sets must be developed independently under another development environment, such as Microsoft Access or Borland's Paradox. This isn't to say that Notes is only useful if you have remote users, but if you do, then these benefits will save you much time, effort, and money.

Notes applications can be used to bring remote users into "local" workgroups, disseminate timely information to field, collect field information, and also reduce or ease field-reporting requirements.

What Is Notes Good For?

Let's summarize: Lotus Notes is an excellent platform for developing multiplatform, communications-related applications that:

- Utilize rich objects
- Require easy routing via e-mail
- Require tight, granular security
- Require easy searching through stored information
- Need to offer easy remote access, replication, and security to remote users

Putting all of these factors together into one package is what gives Notes its punch. Even combining other off-the-shelf products, it is nearly impossible to reach the sophistication of the replication and security engines that you can take for granted with Notes.

Multiplatform compilers exist for C++ and other languages. But those languages have a high entry cost, especially in terms of their learning curves. Notes offers immediate cross-platform solutions regardless of the platform used to develop the application. In fact, one of its drawing features is the common interface across platforms and across multiple applications. Learn Notes on a Windows machine and you will feel right at home using the Solaris version (while in Notes, at least).

In addition, bear in mind that today's business world is a rapidly changing environment. Business-process reengineering is the hottest topic in large companies as they move toward greater profitability. Software applications can no longer be put in place with the expectation of longevity; they need to be able to change as the processes evolve.

Relational platforms, using more rigid table structures, resist large or frequent design changes. Notes, which does not force a rigid form-to-document relationship, can change quickly as the need arises. Agents that rework the existing documents into the new design (if necessary) are easy to write.

If you are wondering about the power available to you to program the Notes environment, consider that with the advent of LotusScript, you will now have full control over the environment, both at the user interface level as well as the back-end level. LotusScript is built into Notes and available in many of the places where you can write formulas, such as behind fields and buttons.

How Can Notes Help You?

The easiest way to illustrate this is to ask a question: With whom does your job require you to communicate?

You might have regular communication channels and protocols established with suppliers, contractors, government agencies, law firms, or partners. How do you formulate and track these communications? It is usually important, and often required, to record and file business communications. In many instances, specialized forms have been developed that give structure and method to these communications. Certain protocols must be followed. For example, you originate a document that is passed to your contractor, who in turn uses that document to receive approval from another agency for work to be performed.

Where do you file them? As forms are filled and routed, they must be filed. File cabinets and folders with various labeling mechanisms have been developed to accurately store documents. For example, a work order is filed under the customer's name or number.

Yet, how do you cross-reference them for retrieval at a later date? Someone asks you to find a work order, and they know who created it, but not the customer number. Because it was not filed under the author's name, you have some work to do. If you decide to copy and file documents in multiple files, or create a cross-reference log, you realize that much effort is extended just to retrieve these documents later. You hope that no one asks for one of them by another entry, such as the date. Using Notes, however, a document can be retrieved by any of the fields that were entered, essentially cross-referencing it for you automatically.

How efficient are these communications? For your processes, define the reasons for the inefficiencies. Where could they be improved? Where are the biggest breakdowns? Often the answers to these questions indicate that documents in process are hard to find because they are in one individual's file, or in a file that passes along a line of communication (and no one ever knows just where that folder is at the moment).

A paper process usually hinders productivity; no one but the person holding the folder can contribute to its contents. Notes alleviates this bottlenecking because all of the related documents can be entered into a database at any time (depending on the nature of the work) and each participant can see and interact with them. Documents are no longer lost in one agent's customer file, for instance.

In business, you wish to avoid miscommunication and misplaced documents, and you would like to shorten cycle times on your current paper-based or even e-mail-based processes. One of the best tools to enable these benefits is Lotus Notes.

Features of a Good Application

A good Notes application succeeds for a variety of reasons. Which features ensure such a win?

In R4, with many new features as tools, there is more potential to create a shiny application. But aside from appearance, you can succeed with a Notes project by keeping things simple, employing measures such as context-sensitive action buttons to ensure proper use of the application, making it easy to create and find documents, and creating useful summary views.

Keeping Things Simple

Extend effort on your code on the back end to simplify steps for the users. Make use of "hide when" features and sections to streamline the appearance of the documents, showing only pertinent information.

The "hide-when" feature is an attribute connected to paragraphs and objects that enables you to selectively hide (or display) certain portions of a form. Six options (in the form of checkboxes) control the appearance at times such as when a document is opened for editing, opened for reading, or printed. A seventh option lets you write a formula (as opposed to LotusScript) to control the display. Using hide-when, you can create one form that drastically changes appearance based on the value in one field. To see an example, take a look at the Connection form in the R4 Public Address Book.

Ensuring Proper Use

Use action buttons and navigators to provide access to features when they are appropriate. Instead of instructing users to first highlight the appropriate document, then create a response, allow the creation of the response to occur only through a button that appears when the main document is open.

Perform extensive validations to ensure that what is entered will not be inappropriate at a later time.

Easy Creation

Provide action buttons and navigators that make document creation easy. For instance, in a Customer Tracking application, let users create Activities for a particular contact without making them find the contact first. Present dialog boxes for making the choices that will place the document correctly in the database when they save it.

Easy Retrieval

Use Notes' full-text search capabilities so that documents can be quickly retrieved. Use the new view-sorting capabilities so that users can accomplish more while using one view by resorting those documents, as opposed to using multiple views.

Balance

Provide a balance between ease of use and quick access to information. It is easy to overemphasize one side or the other. Lean applications require more knowledge to use them, but they often provide quick and easy access through standard features to their documents. On the other hand, making an application too user friendly will please newcomers but distract and frustrate experienced users. The visual aids may actually slow down an advanced user by requiring too many "easy" steps to actually reach a desired document.

Provide easy access to quicker methods so new users can use graphical methods initially, but as they become accustomed to the database they might choose to use a quicker, less graphical, method.

For instance, let's say you decide to use a series of maps to navigate a user into a piece of "local" information. You start with a map of the United States, then navigate to a regional map, then to a state map, then a county map, and then a city map. After the second or third time through these navigators, the average user might wish for a simple list of cities to choose from in a dialog box. A good database will provide both methods.

Make Use of Add-On Products

Wait! Before you skip this paragraph as a sales pitch for more products you must purchase, consider this—Lotus Notes is a rich multimedia object container, but it does not actually create these rich objects. Other products, when appropriately applied, can yield an entirely new and productive application.

For instance, consider the telephone. You may have used a pay phone between flights on a business trip. How would you like to use that phone as a Notes client? By using the PhoneNotes product, you can do just that. PhoneNotes lets users interact with your Notes databases through any touch-tone phone. You might provide users the ability to look up (or, hear it, in this case) the status of an order or register for a training class, or listen to their mail messages.

Lotus Notes is a great tool. But don't miss exciting new opportunities that are appearing rapidly on the horizon. These technologies can help you to be even more productive with Notes than you will be with Notes-only solutions.

Types of Applications

As already mentioned, most Notes databases have something to do with communication. The following sections will look at the various ways Notes databases interact with communication, such as discussions, libraries, and workflow applications.

Tracking

A tracking application is identifiable by its usage. Typically a large number of users create the documents, and they are used to track conditions or trends over time. A customer-tracking application is useful to trace back through the relationships that have developed, looking at the meeting records, action items, and correspondence items that have been recorded.

Broadcast

A broadcast application is one in which there are only a few creators of the documents in a database. Most users read documents on either a regular or *ad hoc* basis to read the latest news or find new updates in the Policy Manual.

Discussion

E-mail provides you the ability to send messages, potentially multiple times on the same topic to and from multiple people. These extended conversations tend to break down quickly, however, as individuals manage their own mail files. Also, for e-mail conversations that take place over an extended period of time, it becomes more difficult to piece together the past memos that form the conversation.

A discussion database in Notes solves this problem and enables multiple extended conversations in tidy threads that are easy for everyone to participate in and to follow. Response documents that are always bound to their "parent" topic remain together, forming a thread over time. Participants have one place to attend to hold a conversation; the problem of mail-file management is gone, because one database (not mail) contains the thread.

The components of a discussion, the Topic and the Response, can often be included in other types of applications to further enable their potential as communication tools. Pertinent discussions about a client, for example, might take place in the Client Tracking application so that anyone new to that account can read this history and quickly become aware of important issues.

Approval

Approval applications often include mail-routing logic to move documents through an approval process, collecting changes from a series of approvers.

Examples of approval applications include loan approvals and travel-expense approvals. ISO 9000 is a process which relies primarily on documentation and approvals. Notes is an excellent platform for creating and/or deploying an application which can help you reach or maintain certification.

Workflow

Workflow applications closely map a business process, usually with a final sign-off or closure point to the process. A help-desk escalation procedure might specify that a problem be moved up a hierarchy of support specialists, with each specialist adding more information along the way.

Workflow applications that actually move documents tend to rely either on e-mail or replication. Mail-based designs route documents along an approval chain, for instance, then mail the final document back to the originating database. A replication-based design lets users modify documents in-place in a database, often using views that segment documents based on their status to move documents through various stages.

Prototypes/Proof-of-Concept

The application-development environment offered by Notes lets you quickly build applications, some even considered throw-away, to test the viability of new business processes. These applications may not have the polish of a production application, but that can be added later if the application proves worthy.

Some legal firms have found it prudent to develop applications this way for individual cases. Once a case is over, the application can be archived. Once the process has been proven, then a finely tuned template may be created from the application and used repeatedly for a series of cases, perhaps being modified somewhat for each case as needed.

World Wide Web–Related

With the advent of Lotus InterNotes Publisher, creating World Wide Web pages is a snap. This type of database could be a special type of broadcast application that advertises your marketing literature. Typically, the design will have two forms: one for Notes usage, and one with extra HTML codes for optimal appearance on the Web.

Applications using InterNotes can also accept feedback in documents that are filled out using Web browsers live on the Internet. Use these to capture surveys or even orders!

With Domino and Release 4.5, Notes has become the premier application platform for both serving documents and viewing documents. These topics will be discussed in greater detail in Part V, "Domino Server, the Internet, and Intranets."

Object Libraries

Notes' rich-text-object storing capability makes it a great place to store all types of objects: file attachments, OLE objects, and even images (using Lotus Notes:Document Imaging, or LN:DI, for instance).

Embed OLE objects that originated with another Windows application, such as a Visio file or an Excel spreadsheet. Using Notes Field Exchange (FX), you could even embed Expense Reports and use fields like the daily, weekly, and grand totals for use in summary views in Notes.

Notes R4 ships with three different object library templates. Two of them are specific: one is for Microsoft Office objects, and the other for SmartSuite objects.

You can also use Notes to store file attachments; you will get the benefits of extra fields such as the author and the subject of the file. Categorize them or store them in folders for easy retrieval. The files can be stored in compressed format, so you save disk space.

Notes is an excellent container for all types of multimedia objects and files, from graphics to sound and even to movies.

Imaging: Small Scale

Using Lotus Notes:Document Imaging, an add-on product, you can use Notes for low- to medium-volume imaging projects. LN:DI uses a separate Mass Storage server to house the images, and it interfaces with various scanners for capturing them.

You can store the images in a rich text field in any type of Notes database, using them for workflow and approval or tracking applications.

Information Warehouses

Often useful in help-desk scenarios is the capture of valuable knowledge gained from troubleshooting or consultative engagements into a KnowledgeBase application for use by your whole team or organization. Lotus distributes the Lotus Notes KnowledgeBase that helps consultants with Notes technical support issues, store answers and even various files for retrieval later.

Executive Summaries

You could make use of the LS:DO scripting tools to build summary reports from your legacy systems, accruing the reports over time in Notes for quick and easy distribution (actually, the users will come to the reports as opposed to sending them out, but it has the same effect) to networked or traveling users.

Things to Avoid

Lotus Notes is an extremely useful tool. Relational databases are also extremely useful tools. Some things are best left to the relational systems, whereas others are best accomplished with Notes. Let's look at some of the things *not* to do with Notes.

Real-Time Needs

Lotus Notes is not appropriate for designing systems that accept real-time feeds (such as a stock-market analyzer) or are expected to be constantly accurate (such as an airline-reservation system). These are quintessential transaction-processing systems.

Does this mean, then, that Notes is useless for a stock broker? Not at all. A broker doesn't use the last 15 seconds of trading activity for making decisions. Rather, trend analysis is key; this requires historical information, often in document form. Although Notes would not suffice for the stock-market analyzer, it would excel in collecting company-behavior information from a wide array of analysts for use in future analyses.

Heavy Reporting Needs

Notes uses views to collect documents for easy retrieval and limited summaries. Because they can be printed, they can be looked at as reports, but that is the extent of the power in Notes itself. Other tools offer better report-design mechanisms so that real reports can indeed be generated from Notes databases.

When data needs to be heavily cross-tabulated, joined, and summarized on a regular basis, especially if these activities take place on large quantities of numeric data, a relational database is called for.

Relational Data

The general rule is: the more relational the data, the less appropriate Notes becomes. This is not to say that relational-like databases cannot be accomplished with Notes, but that if they are, they are likely to be underused due to poor performance.

Large Numbers of Users Accessing the Same Documents

This is an area where record locking is a vital component. Because Notes does not have it, another tool would be better. However, databases that merely have large numbers of users adding information work as expected, with the exception that as complex views grow in size, they slow down. This caveat can easily be circumvented by employing simpler data-entry views.

Human Resources Solutions

Let's look at how Notes benefits a company's Human Resources department. Perhaps through these examples, new ideas will form in your own mind. We'll look at the areas of resume tracking, performance reviews, benefits, policies, job postings, and training.

Human Resources

A Human Resources department tracks many things for and about employees. Some of this information is more relational in nature, but a majority of it is document-oriented and could really use a convenient mechanism for storage, cross-reference, retrieval for the HR personnel, and broadcast to employees.

Companies such as PeopleSoft and Skillset offer Notes-based solutions that cover many important areas of an HR department.

Resume Tracking

Seeking and hiring new employees can be a monumental job. At large firms, where there may be many advertisements on the market, resumes enter the HR department in great volume. Each resume must be visually scanned for applicability for the position sought, and frequently it is stored in a file. When a department wishes to fill an opening, it contacts HR and someone must rifle through the resumes to find matches for the current position. Any extra submissions, such as writing samples, must be filed with the resume so as to be available to the hiring party for review.

A Notes-based, resume-tracking application will be able to store the resume and any additional documents from an applicant. The resumes can be scanned, run through an Optical Character Recognition program, and stored in both formats. Particular fields can specify skill levels and applicability for various areas. When a position becomes available, a quick search can be performed based on categories or keywords, revealing all applicants who meet these basic requirements. This query can be performed from the requesting manager's desk, where they will also have the ability to review the supplemental materials (such as writing samples).

Performance Reviews

Notes fits well in keeping track of performance reviews, which may contain lengthy descriptions, as well as fielded information such as salary, ranking information, skill sets, and goals.

Standard appraisal forms can be used to collect this information, and managers can complete and then route them electronically through their approval sequence.

Management-level views can summarize particular information, such as salaries, offering quick review and comparison of salaries versus budgets allocated. Anomalies such as low performance with high merit raises can be detected and handled as appropriate.

Benefits and Compensation

With standard company policies documented online, employees can easily find answers to their questions. The documents can show the date they were last updated to give credence to their contents.

Employed change forms can be filled out by employees regardless of their location, and the requests can be routed for approval or handling. If certain forms require actual signatures, then the forms can be made available for printing; the employee can print, sign, and mail the information on the most up-to-date form.

Job Postings

New job openings can be posted for internal review by employees; if a requisition-review process is needed before a posting is official, workflow features can be used to route for approval, then change the posting's security status so that it is readable by all users.

Employees interested in positions can respond to postings through a button which routes the inquiry back to the appropriate department(s).

Training Administration

Courses available for internal consumption can be broadcast and updated as needed. Employees can review prerequisites and available dates.

Workflow features can route a request to attend a class through the approval chain.

Confirmation in a particular class can be generated from this database and mailed to the attendee. Managers can be notified automatically of their employees' upcoming training.

Policies and Procedures

Large corporations normally provide large binders with company policies and procedures, then follow up with periodic updates to the contents. This paper-intensive, costly process can be streamlined by putting the documents into Notes.

Users can review up-to-date policies at any time. Discussion features enable employees to pose questions that can be answered by HR just once in this database. The answers then benefit everyone, because another user browsing that section will see not only the policy, but any discussion on that topic.

Industry-Specific Solutions

Let's look at how Notes benefits particular industries. We'll look at some topics in the pharmaceutical, healthcare, legal, banking, and telecommunications industries.

Pharmaceuticals and Healthcare Providers

With the protocol and government regulations that encumber this industry, Notes can provide information management through a variety of applications to streamline and perhaps reduce duplication of efforts spent in research, product development, regulatory approvals, and education.

As pressures occur from managed-care organizations, pharmaceutical companies can use Notes to track current challenges, enabling quick response to changing market influences.

Lab Notebooks

Product development often occurs in multiple countries, even within the confines of one company. Coordinating research and testing efforts globally is a challenge, and often work is duplicated unnecessarily. Shared laboratory notebooks can help scientists leverage the work of their colleagues. They can communicate effectively over any distance or time zone without traveling to do so.

Standardized result-collection forms can be offered so that understanding of theories and results can best be leveraged.

The security built into Notes can be used to assure privacy of the documents, and field encryption can be used when particular information is deemed extremely proprietary. Electronic signatures can be used to authenticate documents along with the associated time and date.

Authorized users can pose questions about current studies and offer suggestions from field-level contacts.

Protocol Analysis and Management

Processes that require input from large numbers of people can take inordinate amounts of time. Pharmaceutical companies develop standard operating procedures using word-processor technology, then send these documents through interoffice mail for approvals and revisions.

Notes can speed this process and reduce the time required to develop new protocols by offering documents for review at any time by involved participants. Documents can be secured appropriately for visibility and editing. Responses can be offered in one place, under consideration of peer comments, as opposed to being created alone and routed slowly around the company.

Protocols can be categorized efficiently under many appropriate categories so that related protocols can be found and reviewed quickly and easily.

FDA Correspondence

Another communications-intensive process is acquiring regulatory approval for new products. The communications with the FDA and other regulatory agencies is voluminous and difficult to manage in a way that keeps many people aware of the current status.

Tracking these communications in a Notes database can achieve this, plus it will enable feedback to be gathered in one place where it might be beneficial as the approval moves ahead.

News of pending or actual approval can be posted on the Internet or intranets using the InterNotes publisher so that a wider audience learns the details of the developments.

Pharmaceutical Industry News

News feeds from provider companies such as Sandpoint (with its Hoover product) or Desktop Data (with NewsEDGE) can be captured and disseminated in Notes on a daily basis, providing researchers and marketing personnel with timely information of industry events.

Total Quality Management

Companies focused on quality can use Notes to collect information from quality audits. Laptops can be used by traveling auditors, and they can feed results back into server-based databases for use by other QA staff.

Legal Contracts and Case Management

Contracts can be stored and retrieved easily in document libraries after going through review processes in Notes to arrive at final wording.

As legal situations arise through litigation involving pharmaceutical products, the cases can be managed through Notes. Preparation and research for courtroom appearances can be conducted, allowing for feedback from experts inside the company that can help the case.

Product Launch, Development, and Changes

As new products arrive on the market, InterNotes can be used to disseminate the information over the Internet. Notes users in the company can receive information about the new products as they reach the market. Corporate policies regarding the handling of new products, including any caveats, can be discussed and disseminated prior to launch to streamline the introduction process.

Field-level requests for new products or variations on packaging can be recorded and used by marketing and development staff to quickly react to market conditions, increasing profitability.

Product-change requests can be discussed, and standardized forms can be used to get approval for them. Field representatives can receive early notice of the coming changes.

Legal Industry

Products from business partners such as ELF Technologies can be used to track and coordinate efforts on matters. Instead of using piecemeal word-processor technology, Notes can be used to collect and categorize legal documents for any phase of litigation or research.

Typically, a pre-Notes system will have consisted of documents created in word processors and stored on file-based servers, or information entered into larger mainframe applications. The ELF system consists of "elves," or electronic processes that retrieve this information and centralize it in Notes databases, bringing to the system the automation and ties between the legacy systems and Notes. The original systems are not replaced, but the "elves" repeatedly find and migrate new information into Notes. In some cases, the "elves" modify data and change status of legal documents. The effects of their work can be seen in Notes.

Document Libraries

Discussion features included in a Notes document library can enable legal professionals to research and develop briefs. Large legal firms can benefit greatly from the ability of distanced individuals to contribute to this development.

Time Management and Tracking

Legal professionals bill handsomely for their time, so tracking time spent on various activities is a crucial aspect of this business. Notes can enable collection of time spent on documents either through dedicated time-tracking applications or through stop-watch features which can easily be put into form design to track editing time.

Banking

Much of the information tracked in the banking industry is back-room transactional data. Yet many aspects of this industry are communications-intensive, and Notes can enable collection and approvals of many document-oriented transactions such as loans.

For example, Nationsbank sells a Notes application for field auditors and the Arkansas State Bank uses Notes to perform field audits.

The use of PhoneNotes can greatly enhance customer service by offering touch-tone feedback on loan status or account information.

Mergers and acquisitions generate mountains of paperwork as the two institutions figure how to merge information systems and products, many of which might overlap. Notes can help the merger teams determine the methods for reconciling these differences into a cohesive set of offerings for their new combined customer base.

Industry Analysis

As the financial wizards of the world move with the market, Notes can enable the tracking of industry-specific information to better understand those clients and ultimately offer solutions that will win their current and future business.

News-wire feeds and industry reports can be collected, and online discussions can lead to new ideas and products before the competition develops the same.

Loan Requests and Approvals

As loan requests are received, demographic information entered on standardized forms can be used to watch trends and use demographic information to develop strategies.

Notes can route loans for approval, collecting digital signatures from the various authorities, notifying the loan officer of the status along the way.

Account Tracking

A customer represents more than an account balance. To win repeat business, recording information about a customer's interests and business methods can help account managers anticipate their needs and keep managers aware of the activities taking place with these customers.

Specialized forms can track specific information about phone calls, meetings, and action items. Unresolved action items can be sorted in their own view to prevent embarrassing mishaps in delivering services.

Specialists in other departments can team up online using Notes to cross-sell other products and services to a common customer base.

Regulations

Notes can help departments and employees in financial institutions keep abreast of new and changing regulations which could affect their customers or procedures.

Telecommunications and Utilities

These industries have several things in common: they own assets that are used to provide services to the public, they must track and resolve conflicts and problems with their customers, and they must respond to emergency situations.

Notes helps to manage the documents related to these activities. Again, geography plays a significant role, because these companies have multiple offices and common functions are often split across them. These disparate team members would do well to collaborate on common problems for the betterment of customer service company-wide.

Asset Tracking

Tracking the assets of a utility or telecommunications company is a multifaceted task. Not only are the numeric data required, but other "soft" information is invaluable as well, such as maps and historical information regarding particular assets. A line that has a history of documented problems can help an engineer better determine the cause, especially with surrounding documentation about this and other related assets.

Maintenance schedules and history for various assets can be tracked, letting management view the assets by any number of criteria for planning purposes and trend analysis.

Engineering Service Work Orders

As new services are planned and existing assets are maintained, engineering work orders can be scheduled and completed using a Notes database. Commentary regarding changes or problems can be recorded for the current issue; these documents can be used to prevent the recurrence of the same types of problems in the future.

PhoneNotes can enable field personnel to give feedback, with their voice annotations being stored in related documents, or laptop-enabled field users can enter complete documents including any applicable diagrams or voice annotations. Portable digital cameras can be used to record images of a site, and they can be stored with the related work order.

Technical Standards

Like policies and procedures, changing standards can be referenced in a common, up-to-date repository of documents as needed.

Notes' rich object store is a great way to store related diagrams and photographs.

Product and Troubleshooting Manuals

Having these manuals online and available, especially for those who travel, can be an invaluable time-saver, because the most up-to-date information can be found there. As the information changes, updates are made to these databases and they are replicated to other offices and to the field.

Notes' rich text capabilities are invaluable here, enabling the storage of high-quality photographs, schematics, and diagrams. Even movie files and voice annotations could be included to help those who are troubleshooting.

Service Change Requests

As customers request new services or changes to existing services, keeping track of the requests and the expectations can enable excellent customer satisfaction. This is especially true when a large number of people interact with a request. Having the same information presented to each of them will give the customer the impression that there is a high amount of teamwork involved to satisfy their request.

Views of requests by customer or demographic information can be used to monitor response in various sectors, enabling decisions to be made to bolster any lagging areas. By logging request fulfillments, satisfaction surveys can be scheduled (and also logged) to ensure high customer satisfaction.

Proposal Generation

As new services are marketed, especially to large corporate customers, using Notes to collaborate on the generation of proposals from team members within different departments can lead to high-quality documents that directly target the customers' needs.

Managers can review the progress of the proposal-generation process, offering feedback and assistance, and also gaining timely knowledge that can be used to correctly set expectations for the customer.

The proposal library can be used to build new documents by leveraging pertinent sections from past proposals. Hindsight and experience from past proposals can also be used to improve on the methods for new proposals. Discussion documents surrounding these historical proposals can also lead to more targeted results.

Large Account Management

Tracking documents and discussions relating to the largest customers, who may account for a large percentage of profitability, will enable proactive management of these accounts.

Some of the documents that may be used are status reports, meeting reports, phone calls, and even specific information about the customers' organizational charts.

New employees assigned to a large customer can benefit from the past experiences that can be read in the database, thereby enabling them to more quickly provide good customer service.

Travel Requests

When employees need to make travel arrangements and get approval, they can fill out their request online and route it for approval. Standard request forms can be used to ensure that specific information required by your company gets entered.

Views can be used to review travel itineraries and expenses over time, revealing trends in travel that can be used to plan future negotiations with travel providers.

Summary

It is evident from the successful Notes applications developed under the R2 and R3 platforms, as you've seen from these and perhaps other industry examples, that the issues most directly improved through Notes are those that are communications-centric. Although many applications lean on data-centric systems or require the adaptation of Notes into this area, sharing information with team members worldwide provides the biggest return.

Notes R4 builds on this foundation, offering more intuitive methods and tools for building efficient groupware applications. Many industries have already seen wonderful benefits from using Notes, and many more will do so in the future as the awareness in this market grows and more applications are developed.

Tips on Application Design

by Sam Juvonen

IN THIS CHAPTER

CHAPTER 11

In this chapter, you will learn how to write a good Notes application from a project perspective. More than slick design techniques are required for success; planning the team, taking the right approach toward data gathering, choosing the right tools in addition to Notes, and following a methodology of design and delivery help ensure that the application meets the needs of the end users and ultimately improves the communication process.

Determine the Applicability of Notes

Before jumping into the design of a new database, first find out whether Notes is really the correct platform on which to develop the application. If you read Chapter 10, "What Makes a Good Notes Application?," you will have a good idea of what makes a good Notes application.

Notes solves communication-related problems. Qualitative information that is difficult to track with other systems often finds a home in a Notes database. For example, keeping track of activities with your clients involves such information as call reports, letters, and future actions; this information doesn't fit well in a highly structured relational database, but Notes handles this nicely. Add to this some requirements for traveling sales representatives, and another database platform can't easily handle the replication requirements; Notes can.

By proceeding to this chapter, you have determined that your application is a fit for Notes. Given that, let's have a look at how you might actually go about the design.

Plan for the Application

After you learn your way around the Notes interface and poke at the design features a bit, you might be tempted to jump right in and solve all those data and communication problems that have been stacking up in your mind waiting for an answer. Go ahead. Jump in. If the application is for you alone, you really can't get into too much trouble.

If the application is for your team, department, or company (or your customer's, if you are of the consultant persuasion), however, think a bit before proceeding. The more widespread the application and the more complex the problem being solved, the more you need to plan ahead.

For this discussion, and if you are a corporate developer who will write applications for your company, let's consider how to tackle your first application. If your intent is to be a consultant who will develop applications for other customers, you can also consider how to approach a project from that perspective. Because the process is similar, and because even as an internal developer you will be in the role of a consultant, let's use that point of view.

Build Your Design Team

As with launching a spacecraft, a significant application development project isn't accomplished by one person, or even two. Instead, a well-balanced team representing the many aspects of a

Tips on Application Design

CHAPTER 11

247

11

TIPS ON
APPLICATION
DESIGN

communications opportunity (we've all heard the motivators: problems are bad, opportunities are good) should be active in developing a solution.

You should make every effort to include individuals from the various aspects of the business process. In addition to management, pull in end users, who are using the process daily and can provide invaluable insight into the changes that are needed to streamline the operation. Because they will be using the application, their cooperation will determine its ultimate success. Getting their buy-in early in the process, and giving them the opportunity to help during the design process, increases the chances for success, because they will have invested much energy in the process themselves.

Determine the Scope of the Application

For a team-developed application, the resources at hand must be considered to determine whether they are sufficient to accomplish the desired result. The most important resources to consider are people, their available time and the skills they bring, and their associated costs.

Your first job is to align the resources with the desired scope for the project, which is often the most flexible aspect to schedule. Low available time or budget constraints may limit the application.

Consider phases: write a pilot application first, test it against a small group (as compared to the full deployment population), then build the full-scale application using what you've learned from the pilot. Perhaps some portions of the application are cumbersome or develop bottlenecks; these can be redesigned while the application still has low visibility.

Scope of Notes Design

Your team needs to evaluate the features that should be considered for the project, given the constraints you face. The Notes interface in R4 can be used in many different ways. Applying highly graphical elements such as Navigators and layout regions often requires graphical arts skills; this increases the scope, requires more time, and brings a higher cost. Using a simpler interface saves time and money at the expense of appearance.

Scope of External Data

Consider the information requirements for the application. Do you need access to data from a mainframe or relational database? If so, in which directions? Consider the tools you have available and the associated cost of purchasing or using these tools.

Notes R4 can access any ODBC data source from LotusScript, so you may not need to use some of the tools that you have used in R3 applications. Weigh the costs of writing your own scripts versus using a high-level tool.

Consider the effort required to access this external data along with the benefits to the application. If the information is not critical, perhaps mocking up the data or delaying this access until a later time will reduce the scope, saving time and money.

Scope of Connectivity

How many departments, sites, and users will use the application? The costs associated with large numbers of sites include the costs of including them in the design, deploying the application, and supporting the users with the production application. If any of these costs are too much to bear, reducing the numbers for a pilot phase can still prove your concept, but at or under budget.

Will this application involve other companies?

Rollout and Support Requirements

Once you develop the application, you need a plan for deploying it to user desktops and supporting the users as they learn it. Training, although often deemed unnecessary, is extremely important; in fact, although the cost of training is very visible and occurs early, it may save you plenty in support costs later, especially if travel is required to solve the problem. Often, field users have to wait months for another face-to-face meeting where they can get their problem fixed or their questions answered; this bears a hidden productivity cost.

Model the Current Processes

After determining the scope for the project, the first item on your agenda is to understand the current process or problem in detail. Only through a thorough understanding can you hope to improve it sufficiently to have an impact on productivity or even save money.

There are many methods and tools available for mapping processes. Each has its merits, and you should weigh your own experience and methods against these when deciding how to tackle this. For instance, Action Technologies has a Windows process-mapping tool called Action Workflow that enables you to create detailed, meaningful flow diagrams. You might consider a product like Inspiration for Windows, which enables you to capture ideas by creating independent "sticky notes" on the screen and then linking them together in a meaningful sequence; it generates an outline from the linked boxes. There are also many flow-charting tools available that can help you create traditional flow diagrams.

Let those individuals engrossed in the current business practice explain in their own terms their observations and their ideas for improving the process. As they explain, develop a process map that matches their experience.

Tips on Application Design
CHAPTER 11

249

11
TIPS ON
APPLICATION
DESIGN

In the process map, include any practices that are not part of the "authorized" methods—that is, any of the additional work that is done as needed. Determine and indicate as you draw the map whether these additional steps occur frequently, along with their relative importance.

Most processes involve people and their agreements with one another. These agreements may be dictated by the business practice, or they may be developed between the individuals as necessary. Each agreement is reached through a process of negotiation. The agreement normally includes work to be accomplished. The performer of the work, after agreeing to perform the work, completes it, and a review process takes place. Either the work as performed is satisfactory and the process ends, or it is deemed unsatisfactory and a renegotiation takes place for the resolution of the problem (usually requiring rework on the part of the performer).

Determining whether to include the minutia of such processes depends on the significance to the business practice. Your map may show only the steps and the desired handoffs, with the negotiation and agreements being assumed. Usually, a standard flow diagram with annotations works well to represent the current practice.

Your map should at least show every step where data is created or modified. Indicate clearly where external data enters or exits the process. Show points where reports are generated, who receives them, how often, and why they receive them.

A map gives everyone the same perspective on the process, and enables communication among your team members. Once you reach agreement on the current process, you're prepared to improve on it.

Make Improvements to the Current Process

Once you draw a comprehensive process map, you can use this to make improvements. Usually the people involved in the current process will have plenty of feedback.

Work through the process map again, offering all parties the opportunity to give their suggestions. During this brainstorm session, let every idea be recorded in plain sight. Consider using Post-it notes and a thick marker. Each note can contain one idea, and it can be easily moved to the appropriate point on the map. Use a different color marker to indicate any steps in the process map that are duplicated or in some way deemed unnecessary.

After everyone has contributed, use the suggestions and work through the map again. This time, focus on streamlining the suggestions and arranging them in the optimal order.

Pay special attention to the reports you indicated during the development of the map. For each of these, in light of the entire process, determine the applicability of these reports. At this point, don't eliminate every report, but do scale down to just those that are truly beneficial.

Now redraw the map again, including the suggestions that have been agreed upon.

Analyze the completed map and look at the data requirements. Some areas may exist entirely in other systems. Determine those areas that need to be modeled using Notes. Processes that involve remote users are the most likely candidates for a Notes implementation. Show the places where data will need to be brought into or extracted from Notes.

The Design Process

Consider using an iterative process as you plan for and design the application. Notes is an excellent platform for using this type of process, because it has a lower learning curve and is thus accessible to a broader range of designers. Applications can quickly move from prototype to pilot to production. Consider using three design iterations:

- Data collection, look and feel, simulated flow
- Refining appearance, implementing logic details
- The final version for this scope

The Basic Tasks

The following are the jobs that you'll accomplish as you complete the application:

- Designing forms
- Designing views
- Designing folders
- Implementing actions, buttons, and workflow
- Designing simple Navigators
- Applying LotusScript
- Adding final logic and refining design
- Designing final artwork for Navigators and layout regions

Collect Design Specifications from the Customers or Users

Once you work through the process map, you are ready to focus on the actual fragments that make up the application. Typically, the current process is being handled on forms or in another database. There is some dissatisfaction with the current process, but there is also something from which to build.

Collect all the forms being used, regardless of their importance. Collect any reports that are being generated. Once you have them, you need to look them over for issues that either require extra work or are difficult to accomplish with Notes. These issues may force you to approach the design in a different manner or even scale back the application.

What to Look for on Forms

Most forms are easily designed in Notes. Under R4, in fact, using layout regions, you can even scan a form and use it in Notes. By placing this scanned image into a Layout Region, you can then create actual fields in the proper positions on the form, essentially creating an online form that can take advantage of the power of Notes—by using the Notes mail engine for workflow routing, for instance.

However, let's talk about some things that might cause your application to be less than stellar because they are best handled with a relational database.

Dynamic Tables

Dynamic tables are an advanced concept, but they're mentioned here as a tip. You need to know about this now—not how to create them, but to notice the need for such a design so that you can plan around it.

A form such as a purchase order might contain a table with a varying number of rows. Per document, the table might be very small or very large. It is possible to create such a table in Notes by controlling input and editing in a series of fields so that you always work with an entire row of data.

For example, let's say that the table contains three columns: quantity, part number, and price. To create a "table" in Notes that accepts varying numbers of rows, you might create three fields side by side. The fields would be defined so that they each accept multiple values (defined in the field properties box).

To ensure the integrity of the table, however, you need to ensure that something is written to each of the three fields for every modification; otherwise, the rows would become skewed and they would form a false representation of the information.

Tables of this sort are manageable, and you will see them in various applications. With LotusScript, even more can be done with them than before.

In addition to this concern, however, comes another issue. Because a filled-out table exists entirely within one document (because it is designed into a form), its rows cannot be used to summarize their contents across many documents. They are not true records as documents are; a view can show one document per line.

In other words, you cannot create a view that sorts and categorizes by part number and displays the corresponding quantity sold for each part number. Why? Because there is no way for you to programmatically know which of the multivalue entries the view has just categorized so that you can associate that to another corresponding element.

One workaround to this lack of reporting capability is to use response document hierarchy where you create a response document for each row of the table instead of designing it into a form. These documents can then be used in views to summarize their contents.

Another workaround is to use the Notes Reporter tool, which has a feature specifically for dealing with related multivalue fields as mentioned here.

What is the bottom line? Use dynamic tables if you will not need to build views from them. Knowing this now can save you much trouble later, because you can present this during your planning meetings. If this behavior is of utmost importance to the application, either plan to use Notes Reporter or export this information to an ODBC data source and create reports from there. If this is still not acceptable, this functionality should be written in a relational database.

Complex Relationships

Notes is not a relational database, yet it can be made to act like one. The normal way to reuse information is to use *inheritance,* where the entry of a field (Customer, for example) is used to populate a similar field on a new document at the time the second document is created, but no linkage is established between them.

In R4, two new @functions, @SetDocField and @GetDocField, enable you relatively easy access to fields on other documents. With this functionality, given the unique identifier to a document, you can relate values between those on that document and those on the current document. This unique identifier (called the UNID) is not readily available; you must create a mechanism for inheriting and keeping track of it.

Realize, however, that this solution does not address the concern of speed. An application that relies heavily on this type of behavior is likely to be a disappointment due to slow performance. LotusScript can help this situation somewhat if you script access to this information through the Notes ODBC driver and work with relational result sets in your scripts.

If your application needs to keep all entries synchronized when one entry changes, performance will suffer. For instance, you have a field called CustomerAddress on a Customer Profile form, and you also use this field on a Contact Profile form. When a user changes the address on the Customer Profile, you would like all the Contact Profiles to reflect that change. This does not happen automatically. It is possible to write formulas or scripts that ensure this behavior, but the application will probably be a bit slower.

Identify during the planning process whether this behavior is a requirement in the application. Knowing this right away will help you as you plan the design.

What to Look for on Reports

As you work through the reports that are needed, you are thinking about using views to provide them. More formal reports can be generated using add-on products from Lotus or other

Tips on Application Design

CHAPTER 11

253

11

TIPS ON
APPLICATION
DESIGN

third parties. The Notes Reporter, for instance, lets you create nicely formatted reports, whereas views are rather limiting in the sense of traditional reports.

Relationships and Cross-Tabulation

Reports that rely on table joins that create specific result sets for those reports cannot be done with views. Likewise, cross-tabulation is a feature that requires a report-writing tool.

If your application requires these features, plan on using such a tool. The benefits will be nice-looking reports, but they are not as quickly generated as a view. Many users appreciate being able to work with a report in the form of a view; it doesn't have to be printed and it can be called up on demand.

Try to use views to eliminate existing reports where you can. This alone can help streamline the business process. Often, in other applications, work stops until a report is generated and reviewed by management. Perhaps the report is generated every Friday; with Notes, the current information can be found any day right on the manager's desk.

Specifications

Decide on and document the specifications for your application. Use the iterative design approach to make changes to the specifications at design reviews, but expend sufficient energy initally to define the application fully so that changes will be minor. If you rush into the design, you may find yourself rewriting the application—the changes people want are major because they weren't considered early.

Decide on the Scope for Each Form

For your application, you will want to determine the scope for each form in the database. Using the tips listed previously, determine just how complex you need to get for the pilot application versus the final, production application. It might be prudent for the proof-of-concept or pilot version to create mockups of the eventual features to get feedback before you spend a lot of time writing them and then rewriting them after the pilot phase.

Determine Input Needed (Forms) and Output Desired (Views)

Now that you have mapped the process and analyzed the current documentation, use this information to formulate the Notes design. Because the basic building blocks are forms and views, focus on these two items first. An application is "complete" with a form and a view; enter data through the form and see the results tabulated in the view. Most applications, however, require many forms and views. It is when multiple items must be designed that you need to spend time considering how to structure them.

Determine the Hierarchy and Appearance of Forms

Using the current paper-based forms, first design any hierarchies, then focus on appearance. Forms (eventually documents when data is entered) can be designed using a main-document-to-response-document hierarchy. A response document is one that contains a reference pointer to its parent, which is the main document that was highlighted or open when the response is created. In a view, response documents are usually shown in a hierarchical fashion, and they are indented in outline fashion under their parent document. Each response's pointer references the same main document; it never references another response document. In an outline, where the first level is represented by Roman numerals (I, II, III) and the second level by capital letters (A, B, C), response documents all exist at this second level:

I. Main document 1 (MD1)

    A. Response document 1 (points to MD1)

    B. Response document 2 (points to MD1)

    C. Response document 3 (points to MD1)

II. Main document 2 (MD2)

    A. Response document 1 (points to MD2)

On the other hand, a response-to-response document contains a reference pointer either to a main document or to another response. It may live at the second, third, or lower level, using the outline analogy:

I. Main document 1 (MD1)

    A. Response document 1 (MD1-RD1, points to MD1)

        a. Response to response 1 (RD1-RR1, points to MD1-RD1)

        b. Response to response 2 (RD1-RR2, points to MD1-RD1)

            i. Response to response 3 (RR2-RR3, points to RR2)

    B. Response document 2 (points to MD1)

    C. Response document 3 (points to MD1)

II. Main document 2 (MD2)

    A. Response document 1 (MD2-RD1, points to MD2)

        a. Response to response 1 (RD1-RR1, points to MD2-RD1)

Why might you use a response-to-response hierarchy? Consider the Customer Tracking template that ships with Notes. It contains the following hierarchy:

    Customer Profile

        Contact Profile

            Activity: Phone call

            Activity: Meeting

Tips on Application Design
Chapter 11

255

11

**Tips on
Application
Design**

The Activity forms create response-to-response documents. This hierarchy allows them to "belong to" the Contact Profile documents, not the Customer Profiles. If the Contact Profile is modified so that the contact changes companies, all the Activities stay with that document when it appears in the view under the new company name.

Examine your set of forms to determine whether you need your documents to fit into such a hierarchy. Consider the relationships between the forms; you may find that where you can make a statement such as "each contact can have multiple phone calls," you have just established the possibility for a response hierarchy.

Once you have determined the hierarchical structure, you have determined the *inheritance path,* the path where information can be copied from an existing document into a new one, because the subordinate document (for example, Phone Call) is always generated from the form just above it in the hierarchy (for example, Contact Profile). The Phone Call can inherit the name of the contact, for instance.

Appearance

Now you can spend some time deciding how you want the forms to look. You might consider developing the ultimate appearance but targeting a simpler interface for the pilot application and saving the harder work for the production version, or the appearance might make or break the application and you'll need to extend energy right away to ensure success.

Browse the templates that are shipped with Notes. Compare those to the layout of the forms in the Address Books. You'll notice various techniques for creating nice-looking forms; you can borrow these features and modify them to fit your needs. Study these ahead of your planning meetings so that you'll have suggestions ready for others to consider.

Determine the Views You Need

Using the reports that will be needed, specify the various views that will be needed. Define the columns for each view. If you need to have a particular view sorted different ways, look into the sort-on-the-fly feature, whereby you can enable sorting on multiple columns. Users can click on a column title to see the documents sorted by that column, in effect decreasing the number of views you need to create.

Views have the capability of performing simple math on numeric columns. You can total, average, or compute percentages. If you have anything more complex, you should head for a report-writing tool such as Notes Reporter. Because these features also compute at the category and subcategory levels, though, you'll likely find what you need.

Determine Ease-of-Use Features

Notes R4 provides some very graphical tools for creating truly beautiful applications (such as a kiosk) that can help users find their way around the application and fill out information easily.

Navigators

R3 designers attempted various methods to provide button-driven menus from forms, but they were always a touch kludgy. R4 gives you Navigators, which are screens where you can put buttons, hotspots, and graphics (that is, maps) that can lead users around the application.

A marvelous example of the use of Navigators can be found in the Web Navigator database that ships with R4. As you open the database, you are not presented with a view, but instead see a beautiful gradient-background pallet of choices for browsing the World Wide Web.

As you build your application, however, it's a good idea to implement any Navigators with buttons only, to prove the concept. Then return later and have a person specializing in graphic arts design create useful artwork for them.

Navigators can occupy the entire screen, or they can appear in the pane normally occupied by the views and folders outline. Experiment with both of these and realize that, in cases where you want users to drag documents into a folder on the Navigator, you want to use the latter.

Dialog Boxes from Layout Regions

A new @function, @DialogBox, enables you to capture a layout region designed into a form and present it in a dialog box. This can be seen in the Delivery Options action in NotesMail in R4. Use this feature to lead users through data entry of an application, splitting larger forms into several dialog boxes. Use it also, as in NotesMail, for fields that have sufficient default values and are not that important to the document in general.

This feature, not being part of standard form design, can initially be thought of where you are considering a standard prompt dialog box (@Prompt). It gives you much more flexibility and can have a much nicer appearance (depending on your graphic artist).

Determine Security Features Desired

If your application contains sensitive information, or if you want to segregate documents based on visibility by regions or groups, consider using some of the finer points of security.

Should You Plan It All at the Start?

Security features, although possible to define loosely at the beginning of the project, should be defined throughout the iterative development cycle. These features could easily be the last to be implemented before delivery.

How Low Do You Go?

Notes provides security at many different levels. You do need to set security rights to the database through its Access Control List (ACL), but other measures are optional. You may want to see Chapter 34, "Security Overview," which covers security in more detail.

Database

Every database has an Access Control List, or ACL. This defines what the listed members (users, servers, or groups) can do in the database. Seven levels of access are available, but the most common levels assigned to users are Author and Reader. Reader access is granted in databases where users need only to read documents, such as a technical knowledge base or an on-line policies and procedures manual. Author access is the most common level granted for applications where there is much interaction. This enables users to create documents and modify them, without being able to edit other users' documents.

Three levels of access exist above Author: Editor, Designer, and Manager. These are all granted sparingly. Editor access enables a user to edit any document in a database. Designer additionally grants the capability of modifying the design of a database. Manager access additionally grants the capability of modifying the security settings (ACL) of a database.

In addition, R4 enables you to enforce local security of a database even if it resides on a remote workstation (such as a laptop). This feature is designed not as true security, but as a measure that helps this type of user by indicating to them what they can do to the server's replica of the database.

While an educated or determined user can find ways around local security, it is intended to avoid the problems found in R3 where users made changes to their local copy fully expecting these same changes to affect the server's replica. Since the ACL on the server's copy didn't allow them to make such changes, however, there was a disjoint between the user's expectations and reality.

This R4 feature helps that user understand what they can expect the server to accept since the local copy behaves in accordance with the settings on the server's replica. Through education it should be explained to these users how this helps them avoid confusion and frustration. Even if they do "break" the local security, they still cannot harm the server's replica.

Form

You can also set two ACLs for a form: the Read Access List and the Create Access List. These lists are initially empty, allowing everyone access. Read access allows the listed users, servers, and groups to read documents that were created with or that use that form. If a list is present and you are not in it, any document that uses that form to display its contents is not visible in any view of the database. Create access enables the listed users, servers, or groups to create documents using the form. You can selectively choose who can see this form on his or her create menus; it also affects any commands that create a new document with this form.

View

Like a form, views have a Read Access List. This limits who sees the view on his or her view menu. It also controls any formulas that attempt to use that view. If you are not listed, you cannot use the view. If there is no list, everyone can use it.

This is not secure, however, as users can still create private views or folders that show the same documents. It is intended as a means to streamline the views that users see in their list, tailoring the choices available to the appropriate people.

Document Author

By using a field with the special type Authors, you can define which users with the Author ACL access are allowed to edit the document. This does not block the document from viewing or printing. To enable these authors to modify their documents, Notes has to know who the authors are, so you must use a field of this type. Typically, this is taken care of by creating a field to capture the author's name using @Username. This feature refines the ACL, and it applies only to those users who have been granted Author access. It cannot promote a user who has been given Reader access such that they can edit the document.

You might even create a subform that captures the author's name and displays the creation date, then use that subform on each form.

Document Reader

By using a Readers field, you can control the list of users, servers, or groups that can see this document in the database. This is like a form's Read Access List, but it is more selective: you can specify per document (as opposed to a whole class of documents, by form) who is allowed to see it.

If a Readers field is present on a document, but is left blank, then it behaves as though it were not there, enabling anyone with Reader access or higher to read the document. If one or more entries reside in the list, however, the document is limited to the individuals who meet the criteria (either by name or by group).

Encryption

By creating and applying encryption keys, you can prevent certain fields from appearing on a document. Only those users with the encryption key see the data. All other users see an empty field; any attempt to pry into the data using the properties box reveals an encrypted mass of data that is unreadable. This might be used to protect information such as employee review comments, salary data, or minutes from a closed meeting.

What Should You Do About All This?

To take advantage of these security features, you should plan to create one or more test databases to prove to yourself exactly how they work. Don't worry about planning these right away for your application, but keep the possibilities in mind as you work through your planning stages. As the application design reaches maturity, discuss and plan where to use the applicable features. Don't think that they are necessary. With the exception of the Authors field type, all other settings are optional.

Develop Design Standards

As you know or will soon discover, you have a great deal of flexibility when writing Notes applications. Within your company, you may have now or in the future many application developers. Users of your applications benefit greatly, especially in terms of training, if the applications you write contain familiar elements. Standards make the business of writing and using Notes applications easier.

Why Standards?

Standards are often thought to be a hindrance to creativity. If misapplied, they can be. However, certain decisions are arbitrary, yet important. For instance, imagine reading this book if the heading styles were different for each chapter. You would quickly tire of figuring out the new style as you moved through the book. You wouldn't be able to open to Chapter 37, "Troubleshooting Networks and Modems," and browse it quickly.

Likewise, users benefit when they know for certain that, on a form, text with certain attributes (maybe green, underlined as in Windows help files) represents a piece of help when clicked. They benefit when they know that text of a certain color or marked with a certain icon represents a field that requires an entry.

Developers also benefit from standards, because they will be able to move from application to application with ease, making maintenance much easier; they will understand why things have been arranged as they are, and changes they make will make sense to others. For new applications, decisions that are made ahead speed up the process.

What Should You Standardize?

You shouldn't create standards for every possible choice in the Notes interface; this would stifle creativity. Besides, you can't presume the entire spectrum of usage. Certain elements, however, should be standardized; the precise elements that fit in this category may differ between companies, depending on their styles of development.

Stay Flexible

Just because you decide on a certain standard today doesn't mean that you shouldn't change it if a better idea comes along. It does mean that you shouldn't change it willy-nilly, however. You should also take it seriously, and treat changes to larger features with care. Remember, it is ultimately your users who will be frustrated by misapplied or nonexistent standards; as they visit your library of applications, they will be unnerved to know that they have to remember a different set of codes for each database.

Naming Conventions

Using standard names for items in Notes makes design and maintenance much easier for you and your fellow developers. It often means that you don't have to open another window to hunt down the meaning of a certain reference.

Forms and Views

Alphabetical sorting often doesn't match the hierarchy of forms and views. Consider making it a standard to number each of them. This will also make it easier for users who like the keyboard. They will be able to reference them by number.

Standardize the use of synonyms so that a reference is instantly recognizable from your formulas. Rather than using random abbreviations, for instance, you might include an F or V in the synonym name (such as NameLookup_V or Cust_F).

Though case doesn't matter except for readability, it is a good idea to standardize on a convention, nevertheless.

Fields

You might consider setting aside certain field names that will be used consistently throughout your applications. For example, using "Subject" consistently enables you to create folders and views that show the title of a document.

For other fields, you might adopt a standard naming convention that defines the type of data in the field in addition to its name (txtCustomer or Customer_txt).

Tips on Application Design

Chapter 11

261

11

TIPS ON
APPLICATION
DESIGN

Form Layout

There are two very common areas on the forms of most Notes applications: the header computational fields and the footer computational fields. These fields are hidden from view at all times but perform critical calculations that are used by visible fields.

Between these two regions, you might standardize other header areas, body regions, and tracking regions. Notes R4 makes this process much easier, because you can create a standard set of subforms for use on your forms. To enable mail routing on a form, for instance, you might use a standard routing subform among all your applications.

Some of your fields will be designed to require input. It's a good idea to standardize on a color or some other attribute (perhaps an icon) that indicates that a value is required.

By using a design template with design elements that have been agreed upon as a basis for new databases, your designers can leverage these agreements with ease, making it more likely that they will conform to the standards.

View Layout

R4 has added new standard methods that are easy to turn on, making your views easy to standardize. One such setting is called the *twistie,* and you can enable this for any column you design. If that row in the view becomes expandable because it is a category or a response document, the twistie shows up automatically. Users can click on this arrow to expand or collapse that entry. This is standard behavior in any application.

You should consider standardizing the various colors you use, such as for the background of the view, the first categorized column, or alternate row colors.

Folders Layout

Folders should be designed with a flat hierarchy—that is, without using categorization. Because folders accept any kind of document that is dragged into them, you won't know how to categorize them. Design the columns so that only generic information is shown—perhaps the date, the author, and the subject.

Navigators

Because Navigators are limited only by your imagination, any standards you apply should be broad-based. For instance, you might require your company logo to always be placed in the lower-right corner.

Script Variable and Object Names

As your various developers write LotusScript, you may want to standardize the names of general variables that are dimensioned repeatedly, such as "doc" for a reference to a single NotesDocument or "collection" for a reference to a NotesDocumentCollection in Agents.

Documentation and Help

Your methods of providing help should be standardized. Written documentation can be standardized easily by using a word processing template. For on-line help, develop a common method of providing help documents. You might use DocLinks liberally on your forms and have them all lead to a central help database, or you might create a standard set of help forms that you include in each database so that the help documents reside in the relevant application. You might also consider using DocLinks to documents that can easily be printed out, such as a manual.

Notes R4 enables you to cause the About document to reappear to users each time a modification to that document is made. This is a good place for your developers to document their conventions; as they make changes, the users will be made aware of them, lowering frustration levels proactively.

Plan Training and Rollout

Training philosophies differ widely between organizations. Some feel strongly that training should be provided to ensure the success of deployment, and others feel that Notes is easy enough to use that a few printed pages will suffice.

Whatever your philosophy, plan to provide something that explains in detail how to use the application. Often, a short session of an hour or so is enough to train users sufficiently to use it.

The more complex the application, especially if it involves special customization by the users, the more likely it is that you should actually deliver a training session.

Plan Future Enhancements and a Development Schedule

Notes is a flexible tool. You can use this to your advantage; don't try to tackle a huge application in one pass. The longer it takes to deliver, the more anxious users will be. If you can deliver useful functionality and build on a strong foundation, the application can start strong and get better with time. Consider also that a small but extremely useful application will often have high participation, and this will enable you to leverage the opportunity to provide even more features.

Put enhancement requests into a queue and schedule further development cycles. Consider publishing the current status to the user population to give a sense of forward movement. Provide an easy method for users to provide feedback as they use the tool.

Summary

Lotus Notes continues to grow into a corporate-strength application development platform. With the exception of small applications, you should plan to attack development efforts rigorously, using a solid methodology to define and develop the application iteratively.

By choosing the right team, you increase the chances for success, because end users will have much invested with you in making it right.

By proving your concept with simple functionality, then building extra features and graphical capabilities, you avoid rework and arrive at a deliverable sooner.

Above all, enjoy the Notes development platform and its plethora of opportunities!

Developing Forms

by Randall A. Tamura

IN THIS CHAPTER

CHAPTER 12

This chapter explores Notes forms and how to create them. If you have a Notes system, you can follow along and create the forms as we progress through this chapter. Although you can read about forms here, the best teacher by far is experience. Just creating a few forms, exploring the menu options, and trying various experiments will be both fun and educational. So I encourage you to follow along and also to diverge a little and add your own flair to the forms presented here.

In this chapter, you'll design some new forms for a Sales Automation application. Because you'll be creating this application from scratch, it won't be a complete, full-featured application, of course, but by employing a real-world example, I hope to illustrate several of the Notes features and provide you with some ways to use them.

This application will consist of three forms, which you'll create in this chapter, and two views, which you'll create in the next chapter. In Chapter 14, "Making Your Application Look Good and Work Well," you will enhance the forms and views with aesthetic appeal. The purpose here is to track sales opportunities and contacts with this application. The forms that you'll create in this chapter will be the Company form, the Contact form, and the Opportunity form. For each company there may be several contacts. An opportunity will be linked with a particular contact and company, and there may be several opportunities for each company and contact. See Figures 12.1, 12.2, and 12.3 for examples of each of the forms as they will appear when we have finished with Chapter 14.

FIGURE 12.1.

The Company form.

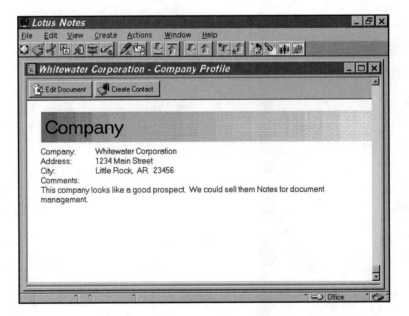

FIGURE 12.2.
The Contact form.

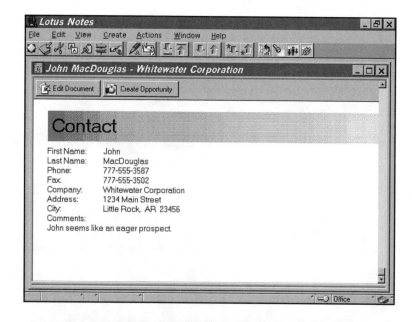

FIGURE 12.3.
The Opportunity form.

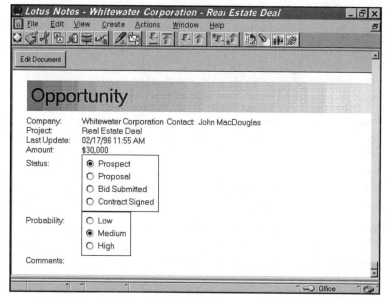

Creating the Database

If you have not yet logged on to Notes, do so now. Enter your password into the password dialog box. You will see your Notes workspace.

As you know, forms are always created in the context of a Notes database. This application will be built with a single database. Your first task will be to create a new, empty database to house the forms, views, and your application. You do this by first starting from a workspace page and then using the File menu option: File | Database | New. (See Figure 12.4.) In the dialog box, enter Sales Force Automation for the database title, and use Salesfor.nsf for the filename. Use the -Blank- template.

FIGURE 12.4.

The New Database dialog box.

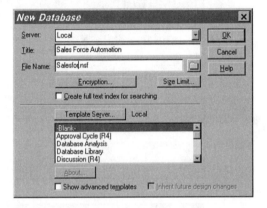

You'll notice in Figure 12.4 that there are several other templates you can use besides the -Blank- template. The -Blank- template is like a clean sheet of paper; you must supply all the information. The other templates provide a framework for an application. A template is not necessarily an application by itself, but it is the starting point and has many or most of the features common to a particular type of application.

Many times the templates supplied by Lotus will be useful for your own purposes. For example, you may want to create a discussion database that contains discussion about new product or service ideas. You may want to create a Database Library of all your Human Resource documents describing benefits and policies, or you may want to create a database that has an expense reimbursement-approval cycle. Chapter 16, "Developing a Workflow Application," will show you how to use two of the templates supplied by Lotus to develop workflow applications.

You can create your own templates if you will be creating databases that fit a generic mold. You can turn any database into a template. Also, if you are creating a new database you can copy the design of a previous database as a starting point. These various options enable you to reuse the design work you have done before.

In the New Database dialog box, shown in Figure 12.4, there are several other options. Encryption enables you to locally encrypt this new database. You may wish to consider this option if you will be replicating the database to a local or mobile computer. If you do not encrypt the database, anyone can access your data without being required to type in a valid password for your user ID. If you lose your laptop computer, for example, anyone that finds it will be able to access your data.

In R3 of Notes, databases were limited to 1GB. In R4, you can specify via the Size Limit button size limits of up to 4GBs in 1GB increments.

By checking the full text index box you can request that Notes create a full text index for this database. Although it is not required for searching the database, a full text index will greatly speed searches and is very useful if you will be searching the database frequently. You can also do more advanced searches if the database has a full text index. If you do not specify the option now you can index the database later via the Database properties InfoBox.

Now, back to the Sales Force Automation example. After you enter the information in the New Database dialog box and press OK, a new icon is placed on your workspace page. Click the "twistie" triangle (not the drafting triangle icon) to the left of the word Design in the Navigator pane; you will see a screen like that shown in Figure 12.5.

FIGURE 12.5.

*Sales Force Automation
initial view.*

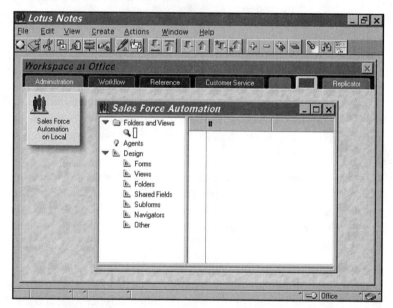

All Notes databases must have at least one view, so one is automatically created for you. Because Notes doesn't know what to call your view, the view has no name. Let's give the view a name while we're here. Right click on the black rectangle just below the words Folders and Views. When the menu comes up, pick Rename. Now type the word `Contacts`.

Creating the Company Form

You're now ready to create our first form, the Company form. From the menu, select Create | Design | Form. You should see a screen similar to that shown in Figure 12.6.

This new form will be a company record for your Sales Force Automation application. This application will help you keep track of the companies you're working with, your contacts (maybe several) within each company, and your opportunities at each company. This is obviously a very simplified application, but it will illustrate several of the capabilities of Notes.

FIGURE 12.6.

The initial screen in creating a new form.

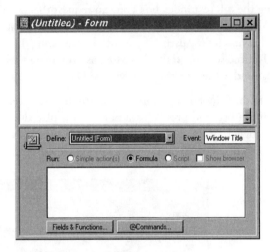

Move your cursor to the top input area of the form and enter the word **Company** on the form. See if you can figure out how to select a font you like (I used Helv), pick a size (preferably about 24 points or so), and then see if you can left justify the word within the form. I'll wait here while you do that.

Dum, ta-dum, dum. Oh? You're finished? Good. I must say, your form looks pretty good so far. Not. If you're like most people, you probably just read straight through and didn't create the form as I suggested. That's OK, you don't have to feel too guilty. I'd like to reemphasize, though, that practice in creating the forms is both fun and calorie-free. Next time you reread this chapter, try creating the form, OK?

If you actually have been following along and did create the form, good for you! In Figure 12.6 you'll notice that there are two input areas in the dialog box. The top one, as we've seen, is for the main form definition. In that area, you essentially get what you see. You can add text and change fonts, sizes, and colors. You can add background colors and fields for information. As a matter of fact, we'll be doing some of these things later in this chapter.

The bottom text-entry field is for defining actions that should take place when certain events occur on this form. The Window Title event that you see in Figure 12.6 is to define the text string that should appear in the window title area for this form. It's not really an event, but this is a convenient place to define the title. Other kinds of events that can occur on the form are, for example, when the form initializes or terminates.

Creating a Field

Let's add some more information to the form. Switch to a 10-point font by pressing the font size button on the status bar at the bottom of your screen. In Figure 12.7, it is the button between the Helv button and the button that says (None). Select 10. By the way, if you were having trouble creating the 24-point size font large word Company, you can use this same technique to change the point size to 24.

Now, move your cursor a couple of lines below the large word Company and type the word `Company:`. Tab once. Then from the menu select: Create | Field. Your screen should now look like Figure 12.7.

FIGURE 12.7.

Creating a Field dialog box.

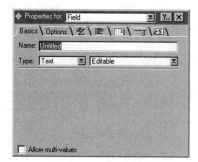

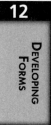

You should replace the name Untitled with the name CompanyName in the Name field of the Properties dialog box for the field. Leave the type Text and Editable. In Windows 95, you can close the Properties InfoBox by pressing on the X in the upper right corner. In Windows 3.1 (and Windows 95), you can close the window by pressing on the diamond in the upper left corner and selecting Close, or by double-clicking on the diamond in the upper left corner. Close the Properties box now.

Property InfoBoxes

One point to notice here is how, by right-clicking, you can bring up the Properties InfoBox for an object. In Notes R4, most of the objects you encounter have a Properties box. For example, forms, views, fields, databases, the workspace, and many other objects have properties in Notes. Properties include the visible characteristics of an item, such as its font, color, or size. Other properties include items such as the object's name, security attributes, or initialization values. Right-clicking on an object is a good way to find out about the object. You can find out what its current attributes are, and you can find out about some of the other properties that you can modify for the object.

Right click on the field CompanyName now. When the menu comes up, select Field Properties. You should see the same Properties InfoBox that you see in Figure 12.7 (but with the field now named CompanyName).

Within the InfoBox you'll notice that in the window title line there is a pull down box following the text Properties for:. This shows you the element type you are examining. Frequently there will be more than one object that is available for query. For example, while you can query the Field properties, you can also query Form or Database properties.

Each object will typically have several tabs in the Properties box. Each of the tabs is used to separate the various object properties. The specific tabs and properties available will vary from one object to another. For example, the properties available for Fields differ from the properties available for Forms.

To illustrate this point, move the Properties box to the right and move the form to the left to a location where you can see all of the information on your form and the Properties box at the same time. Now, using your mouse, select various areas of your form. First, click in the large word Company and see what the Properties box contains. (See Figure 12.8.) Notice that properties such as font and size information are available. Next, click in the formula window at the bottom of the form. (See Figure 12.9.) Look at just a few of the properties available for forms. Next, click in the CompanyName field. Click on the Basics tab to see the field type.

FIGURE 12.8.

Properties for the static text Company.

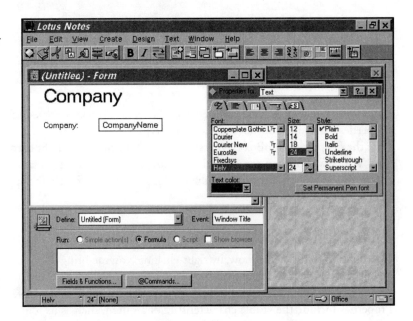

You'll see that as you click on each one of these areas in turn, the Properties InfoBox changes to show you the properties of the object you have selected. Notice how the tabs and fields of the dialog box change for the different types of objects. As mentioned previously, Figures 12.8 and 12.9 show examples of the Properties InfoBox for the large word Company and the properties for the form itself.

This is a good point to stop and describe what we have done so far on this form. We have entered the word Company twice on the form. We have specified the font size and placement of the text on the form. This type of information is called *static text*. Static text is typically used to provide information to the user about the form being used or the information to be filled in within the fields on the form.

FIGURE 12.9.

Properties for the form.

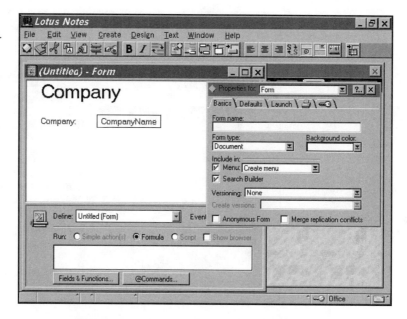

We have also created one field. The field we have created is called CompanyName. As you can see in the Properties box on your screen, the field has a name and a type. In this case the type is Text. You can press on the drop-down button next to Text to see the other types of fields that are available. I will describe these shortly.

Testing Your Form

Now let's test our form. Before we can test it, however, we need to give the form a name. Click on the drop down box in the Properties InfoBox title. Select Form Properties. Your Properties InfoBox should switch to Form Properties. Click on the Basics tab. Under Form name, enter the name **Company**. Note that form names may contain spaces and are case-sensitive, so company and Company are two different forms. As a good programming practice, you should avoid using only capitalization to distinguish two forms with the same name.

Now from the menu, select Design | Test Form. You will be asked whether you want to save the form. Select Yes. After you do this, you will see your form displayed. (See Figure 12.10.)

Notice in Figure 12.10 that the form is still available in Edit mode in the background and in the foreground we see our actual form available for use. This testing without leaving edit mode is a new feature of R4 of Notes. Close the test form now without entering any data. You can do this by double clicking on the upper-left corner of the window, or on Windows 95 by pressing the X in the upper-right corner.

FIGURE 12.10.

Testing the Company form.

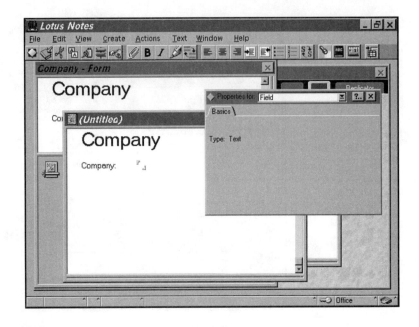

Adding More Fields

Now, let's continue with our form definition. On the next two lines, enter the static text Address: followed by a tab and then a Create | Field with the name CompanyAddr. Following this, enter the word City:, followed by a tab (or two) and a field named "CompanyCity", then a comma (,), then the field CompanyState, then a space, then finally the field CompanyZip. Your screen should now resemble Figure 12.11.

FIGURE 12.11.

A Company form with fields.

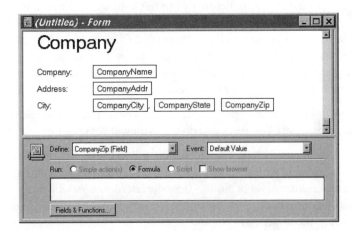

Figure 12.11 displays five fields and several static text constants. These fields are where variable data will be stored in the Notes database. You can think of the form like a paper form such

as your expense-account form, an invoice, or a similar form. The fields that you have just put on the form represent the "blanks" of the form. When a user fills in the form, they will be filling in these blanks. Each of these field blanks is given a different name so that you can refer to them in formulas and scripts.

When a user wants to add information to a Notes database, Notes displays an empty form for the user to fill out. After a form has been completed, the data is stored in the Notes database. Since you will typically have many sets of data for each form, the data is usually stored separately from the form itself and each set of data is known as a *document*. When you open the document, the data is retrieved from the database and displayed in the fields of the form.

There are several kinds of fields that can be placed on the form. Probably the most common is the type we have used, which is called the Text type field. If you look back to Figure 12.7, shown previously, you can see that the type of the CompanyName field is Text. You'll also notice that the field has the property of being Editable. This just means that a user can edit this field in this document. Although many fields will be editable by the user, you may want to create some fields that are based on other, known information in the database, making it easier for the user to use the system. These fields are called *computed* fields in Notes, because they are computed by the system based on other known data.

Field names must begin with a letter and can be up to 32 bytes long. After the initial letter, you may use any letters, numbers, or characters. Field names may not contain spaces. Field names must be unique within a form (and any subforms), and are not case-sensitive. That means that "FiElD1" and "field1" are the same field name. Please contrast this with form names, which *may* contain spaces and *are* case-sensitive.

Before finishing, let's add one last field of a different type. Just below the City line on the form, add the label Comments: on a line by itself. Just below that, add a new field with Create | Field. This time, name the field Body and make the type Rich Text. Rich text fields enable users to enter any type of information, including text, graphics, OLE objects, and so forth. A convention sometimes used is to name the field Body if it is the main rich text field of the form.

This rich text field has been added at the bottom of the form to handle any type of input that the user may want to include in the document. Because this field is a powerful rich text field, the user can enter a spreadsheet, a map on how to get to the company, facts about the company's history, or any other important information. This is a way to add flexibility for the user without knowing exactly what type of data the user may want to save.

Rich text fields are very useful on forms for handling extended text, descriptive information, and long narrative type information. They are good for storing, for example, customer descriptions or for discussion database fields. Rich text fields are not ideal for all situations, however, because they cannot be used in views. Only regular text fields, such as our CompanyName field, number fields, and some others that we will be discussing shortly may be used in views.

Formulas

Formulas are a powerful programming tool in Notes. Prior to R4, they were the main way to program Notes. In R4, LotusScript may begin to overtake formulas as the most effective way to program Notes, but formulas are still with us and retain a lot of their power in R4. You can attach either formulas or LotusScript scripts to many objects. Some objects can attach both, some only formulas, and others only scripts. You can usually tell which applies by seeing what is available in the formula window at the bottom of the design window.

If you look back at Figure 12.11 you'll see that you can use a formula as a default value for a field. In Figure 12.6, shown previously, you saw that a formula could also be used as a Window Title. Formulas can be used in these contexts and many others.

Formulas are sometimes used for computing a result. Formulas also can contain limited logic and conditional execution. You can access features of the Notes system itself from formulas by using `@functions`. These functions can retrieve information from Notes and send information back to Notes for either control or data storage purposes. I'll show you two of these `@functions` in the next section.

As other examples, formulas with Boolean (such as true/false) results may be used to determine security access, whether to show or hide information, and whether documents should be shown in views or not. Other types of formulas return text strings for display. So, you can see that formulas are very versatile and essential tools in Notes programming.

Setting the Window Title Formula

The formula area that you have seen at the bottom of the form design window is used to set the window title when the form is being used. A formula that returns a text string is used for the window title. You can simply specify a constant string such as Company, or you can supply a more complex formula based on some of the fields in the form. Let's use the window title as a simple example of our first formula.

Make sure that the design window is open and the Define field specifies Company (Form). The event should be Window Title. Move your cursor down to the bottom part of the screen and enter the following for the Window Title event:

```
@If(@IsNewDoc;"New Company Profile"; CompanyName + " - Company Profile")
```

If the entire line does not fit within one line, just press Enter at a convenient spot and continue typing the line on the next line of the screen. In Figure 12.12, the line has been continued after the semicolon.

The formula that you see in the formula box looks rather bizarre, but it's actually quite simple. Because this is the Window Title event, you are specifying what should appear in the window title line when a document using this form is shown on the screen. The formula is evaluated and the result is used as a text string for the window title.

FIGURE 12.12.

The Company form with Window Title formula.

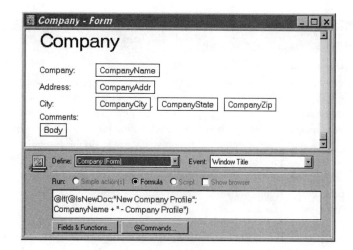

The formula in English means: If the document is a new document, the window title should be the constant New Company Profile. Otherwise (if it's an existing document), use the field named CompanyName, followed by a constant text string of - Company Profile. For example, suppose the CompanyName field was Ajax Corporation. Then the title would be Ajax Corporation - Company Profile.

The function @IsNewDoc is very useful in Notes and can be used in many places to choose whether to have the title be a constant (for a new document) or somehow be related to the existing document. Likewise, the @if function is also very useful; the first parameter to the function is a Boolean true/false expression, and the second is the value to return if true. The third parameter is the value to use if false.

Making an Alias for a Form

Okay, you have completed your first form. You have one last task to do before we move on. Please select from the menu: File | Document Properties. You can also press the Properties SmartIcon. In Figure 12.12 it is the leftmost icon, but your setup may be different. You can find it by placing your cursor over the icons and waiting for the balloon help to tell you which icon it is.

You should now see the Form Properties dialog box. For an example, you can refer back to Figure 12.9, shown previously. Enter the value Company ¦ CPY in the Form name field. The field should already contain the word Company, so you will be adding the vertical bar and the CPY. This rather unusual name is actually two names in one. The first is the common name that will appear on menus and so forth, and is the word "Company." The second name, "CPY," is called an *alias*. We will use the alias in our internal formulas.

> **TIP**
>
> Using an alias enables you to write programs and formulas that do not need to change if you modify the user interface. Using an alias is not required, but is generally considered good programming practice. If you use the alias "CPY" in all of your formulas, then if the user interface changes, you do not need to change your formulas. For example, suppose you decided to change the menu item and the form so that the word "Company" was changed to "Organization." Maybe you want to do this because sometimes you work with nonprofit organizations that are not really companies. Using an alias enables you to continue to use the word "CPY" in your formulas, but in menu items that are shown to the user and on forms, the word "Organization" is displayed.

If you haven't closed the Form properties box, do so now. Save your form by issuing the menu commands File | Save. Congratulations. You have just created and saved your first form. If you close the form, then click on Forms under Design in the Navigator pane, you will see that your form Company is now available.

Testing the Company Form

You're now ready to test your first form. Select the Create menu item. Notice that directly under the Mail option a new option, called Company, is now available. This menu option really means Create a new document using the Company form. Select the Company option.

You will see a blank version of your form. Notice first that the title line says New Company Profile. This is because of the window title formula we entered previously. Your static text labels appear on the left and surrounding each of the text fields are L-shaped field markers at the upper left and lower right of each field.

Enter sample data now in each of the fields on your form. Note that you must use the tab key to move from one field to the next. If you press the Enter key, it will create a new line within the same field. See Figure 12.13 for an example.

FIGURE 12.13.

*The Company form
with sample data.*

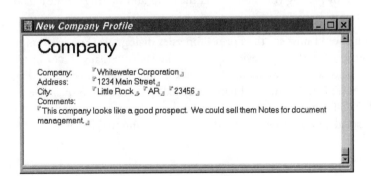

After you have filled in your data, close the form by selecting File | Close from the menu. Press Yes when Notes asks you if you want to save the new document. Once you have closed the document, you will see your default view. Since Notes does not know what information to provide in the view, it just shows you the document number. Chapter 13, "Developing Views," will show you how to make more useful views, but for now you can refer to Figure 12.14 to see what your view should look like.

FIGURE 12.14.

The default view with one document.

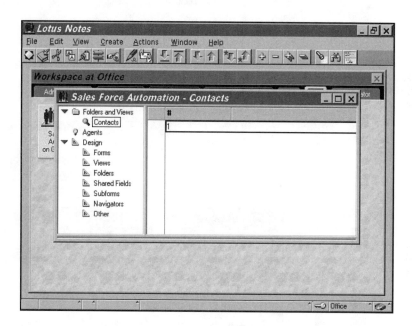

You see in your view that there is only one document, and that its document number is 1. Double click on the view line that contains this document number. Your document should appear again, this time in read mode instead of edit mode. After you have perused your handiwork, you can close the document and we'll go on to creating our second form.

Creating the Contact Form

Now that you have the idea, we'll create a second form—this time moving a little quicker. From the menu, select Create | Design | Form. Again, in the upper-left corner of the form enter the name in 24 point font, which in this case will be Contact. Enter the constants and fields as shown in Figure 12.15. All of the fields should be normal text fields except the last one, called Body, which is a rich-text field.

Now, before we save the form, we must change some of the form and field properties. Make sure that you're showing the bottom part of the form design pane, the area where you can enter a formula. If the area is not visible (as in Figure 12.15), you can press the View Show/Hide

Design Pane SmartIcon button as seen in Figure 12.16, you can select this command from the menu with View | Design Pane, or you can drag the border of the design pane upwards to expose its contents.

FIGURE 12.15.

The Contact form.

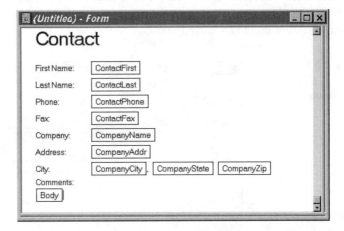

FIGURE 12.16.

The View Show/Hide Design Pane SmartIcon.

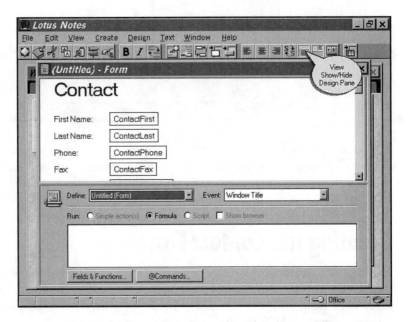

Open the Field Properties box. To do this, right-click on the CompanyName field and select Field Properties. Alternatively, you could just double click on the CompanyName field, press the Properties SmartIcon, or use the menus. With the mouse, move the Properties box to the right so you can access all of the fields and see the Properties box at the same time.

For each of the five Company fields—CompanyName, CompanyAddr, CompanyCity, CompanyState, and CompanyZip—perform the following steps:

1. When the dialog box comes up, change the type from Editable to Computed.

2. In the bottom part of the Form definition dialog box, press the Fields and Functions button. Select the Fields radio button. (See Figure 12.17.)

FIGURE 12.17.

The Fields and Functions dialog box.

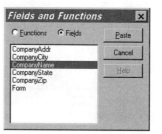

3. Find the field name that you are defining, and press Paste. This defines the Value event as the same name as the field name. The name will appear in the bottom formula area and the Fields and Functions dialog box should close.

4. Click on the next Company field in the form window (such as CompanyAddr, CompanyCity, CompanyState, or CompanyZip), leaving the Properties dialog box open. Go back to Step 1.

Once you have followed steps 1–4 for CompanyName, CompanyAddr, CompanyCity, CompanyState, and CompanyZip, then the field name will appear in the formula area at the bottom. See Figure 12.18 for an example of the CompanyName field. The other fields will have their respective names in the formula area.

Computed Fields

When you changed the field property from Editable to Computed, the pull-down list had four choices: Editable, Computed, Computed when Composed, and Computed for Display. Editable is obvious; with this setting, the field is editable by the end user. None of the computed types are editable by the user. Each computed field has an associated formula, which is evaluated to compute the value of the field. The types differ only in the timing and frequency of the recalculation of the formula.

For *Computed when Composed* fields, the formula is computed only once, at the time the document is composed (created). This type of field is good for information that you want to capture once and will not change during the life of the document. For example, you could use this type of field for an invoice or document number, to save the original document author, or location of creation. Use this field type carefully because once the value has been determined, it will never be recalculated. The value for this type of field is stored with the document.

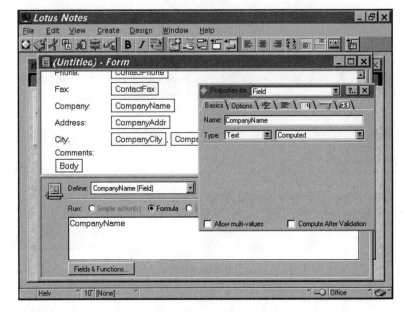

The *Computed* type is used for formulas that must be recalculated when the form is created and each time the form is saved or refreshed on the screen. You can use F9 or View | Refresh to update fields on the current form or view. This is the most frequently used computed type because it is the most flexible. The value for this type of field is stored with the document.

A *Computed for Display* field is recalculated each time the document is opened. This type of field has the most overhead, and it should be used for fields where values frequently change and you must display the most recently calculated result. Values for this type of field are not actually stored with the document, so there is a slight savings of storage space for this field type.

The Compute after validation checkbox in the Properties dialog box enables you to specify that the field should be computed after all of the fields have been validated. This is useful in cases where some fields are dependent upon the values of other fields, and enables you to defer the computation until the fields have been validated.

Now you can also see what we were doing with the company Value formulas. Remember that we used the type Computed. Computed field formulas are reevaluated whenever the form is created, saved, or refreshed.

Setting Form Properties

If you have been following along, you may be wondering why you made the Value formula for CompanyName as CompanyName. It may seem funny that the value of the formula is the field name itself. This seems like a circular definition, but in fact is not. Now we'll see why.

First show the form properties by selecting Form from the properties InfoBox drop down list. Click the Defaults tab and select Formulas inherit values from selected document. (See Figure 12.19.)

FIGURE 12.19.

The Form Properties InfoBox showing the Defaults tab.

Selecting the Inherit values from selected document checkbox activates the copying of the Company values from the Company form to the Contact form. So, you see that when we entered the formula for the field, we are actually specifying that we want to take the CompanyName field from the Company form and use this value as the computed value for the CompanyName field on the Contact form. This enables you to alleviate typing for the end user.

The definition seems circular, but it only looks this way because we are using the same field names on both the Company and Contact forms. We use field name CompanyName on both forms to show their relationship to one another. We could, in fact, use different names on the different forms, but this could be very confusing later on when someone is doing maintenance on the application.

Now select the Basics tab on the Form Properties box. In the Basics tab, enter the form name `Contact ¦ CON`. As before, Contact will be the name the user sees and CON will be our alias name.

Set the Form type to Response. A response document is associated with a main document. In this case our main form will be the company form and documents created with the contact form will be associated with a particular company. Another document type called the response-to-response is useful in discussion databases. It enables a document to be associated with either a main document or another response document. We do not use this type of document in this example.

Now click on a white-space (empty) part of the form. In the bottom pane you should see the form name and the event Window Title. In the formula area type this formula:

```
@If(@IsNewDoc;"New Contact Profile";ContactFirst + " " + ContactLast + " - " +
➥CompanyName)
```

This window title formula serves the same purpose as the formula for the Company form. In this case, if you are creating a new document, the title will be New Contact Profile, but for an existing profile it will include the contact's first name, last name, and company name.

You can close the Properties dialog box and issue the menu command File | Save. Close the Contact form, and press Yes when asked whether you want to save the form.

Testing the Contact Form

We're now ready to test the Contact form that you have just created. In the Contacts view, make sure record 1 (the only record) is highlighted with the black rectangle and then from the Create menu select Create | Contact. A new Contact document will appear. (See Figure 12.20.) Notice that the company fields have been filled in because of our Computed fields. Also notice that the window title shows the text New Contact Profile which is what we said should be displayed for a new document.

FIGURE 12.20.

Testing the Contact form.

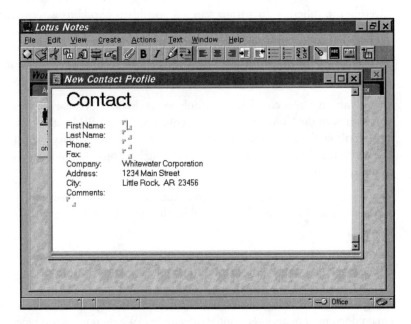

Fill in the rest of the fields with sample data. Remember that you must use tab to move from one field to another. See Figure 12.21 for an example.

After you have entered your sample data, close the Contact form and say Yes when prompted to save the document. Notice in your view you now have two documents, one called 1 and the other called 2. Since Notes does not know what information to display in the view, it is just showing you the document number. The 1 document was your Company document, and the 2 document is our Contact document.

FIGURE 12.21.

The Contact form with sample data.

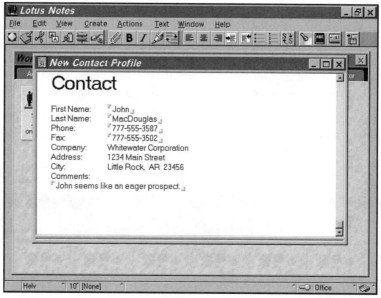

Before moving on to the Opportunity form, you should understand by now how to create fields and forms. If you want to customize the two forms we have created, you can do that now. For example, suppose that you have customer numbers associated with each company. You may want to add the customer number field on the Company form. You may have other information that you want to include for each contact. For example, you may want to record the contact's home address and/or telephone number.

Creating an Opportunity Form

The Opportunity form will be used to store information about each opportunity. For the purposes of this simplified application, an opportunity will consist of the Company involved, the Contact, a project title, and then information about the project such as the amount of the opportunity, the phase of the selling cycle, and the probability of success.

To create the form, you start out the same as with your other two forms: Create | Design | Form. You can fill in your Window Title event formula in a manner similar to the other forms:

```
@If(@IsNewDoc;"New Opportunity"; CompanyName + " - " + OppName)
```

This title will include the company and project name. If you wanted to be more creative and/or include more information on the title, you could add the contact name as well.

Now, in the Form area, create a 24-point title called Opportunity. By now you have noticed that we include the form name in large letters at the top of the form. This is not required, of course, but is a good programming practice. It enables the user to quickly see which form is being displayed. Also, you'll notice that I've used the Helv font, left justified. This is a matter of taste, but it is done so that the form looks "modern"; the left justification is currently used in the more modern operating-system windows such as Windows 95 and OS/2. Left justification, as opposed to centering, allows the title to remain stationary, even if the window is resized. This is just a small, human-factor consideration, but these small items can make it easier for your users. These considerations are described in more detail in Chapter 14.

Refer to Figure 12.22 as you go through the fields to create the Opportunity form. For the CompanyName, ContactFirst, and ContactLast fields, the type should be Text and they should all be Computed fields. Remember to type the field's name into the Value Event formula box in the lower pane. These fields are similar to the ones in the Contact Form.

FIGURE 12.22.

The Opportunity form.

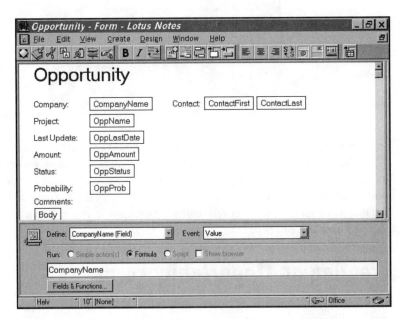

Time and Number Fields

The OppName field is the project name and should be a text field that is Editable.

The OppLastDate is a new type of field that has not yet been discussed. It is a Time field. Although it is called Time, these types of fields can hold dates and/or times. In this case, it will display the date and time the document was last modified. This is done so that if multiple people are modifying this opportunity information, they can see when the last modification occurred. (See Figure 12.23.)

FIGURE 12.23.

The field definition for a Time field.

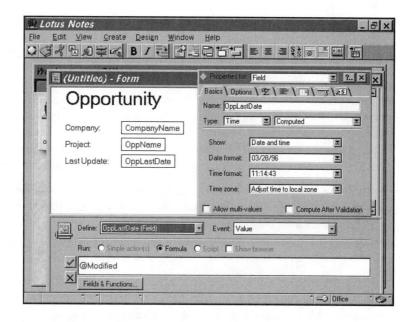

After you have created the field from the menu with Create | Field, fill in the name as OppLastDate, use the type Time with the Computed attribute. You will see additional options at the bottom of the dialog box. You can choose to show both the date and time as in this case, or just the date or just the time. You can choose formats for the date and time and also specify whether you want adjustments for time zones.

The Allow multi-values checkbox option enables the user to enter several data items into one field. Allow Multi-values does not apply to this field, but may apply, for example, to a text field such as a cc: list for e-mail. Compute After validation enables you to have fields validated before an attempt is made to compute this field's value. This is important if a field is dependent on other fields which may or may not contain valid data.

Choose the options as shown in Figure 12.23, or choose other display options if you like.

At the bottom of Figure 12.23, you'll note that we have our friend the formula window. In this case, we're specifying a Value event and the formula is @Modified. This function is a built-in function of Notes that will return the time/date of the last time this document was modified (and saved). This is just what you want to display in the form. There are other related functions available for other uses: the @Accessed function, which will return the last time the document was accessed either for reading or writing; and the @Created function, which returns when the document was created.

Moving on, you should create the OppAmount field as type Number with the Editable attribute and specify that it will hold Currency values with zero (0) decimal places. You can also specify punctuation at thousands if you like.

Keyword Fields

The next two checkbox fields, OppStatus and OppProb, are both specified as Keyword fields. Keyword fields are somewhat like text fields, but are designed for use where you want to constrain the options for the end user. For example, if you use a text field, such as CompanyName, the user can enter any name and it will be valid. However, for the status field you want to restrict the choices to Prospect, Proposal, Bid Submitted, and Contract Signed. These four represent the business process of your company. Of course, your real sales process may have more or less phases, but the point is that you really don't want to enable the user to enter any sort of word here because you want to enforce a consistency among all of your users.

Keywords can be used to enforce consistency with a (relatively) small number of choices. You don't have to make keywords mutually exclusive as we did with these fields. You can use keyword fields where multiple choices are allowed. This is more like the supermarket approach—you provide all of the various options and the user can select among them, essentially filling his or her shopping cart with several items from those offered.

In addition to whether one or multiple choices are allowed, you have several options on how the choices are generated. The most straightforward method is where each option is just typed into the list. Other options include using a formula to generate the list or, for example, using the access-control list to generate the option list. There are several other choices, including obtaining data from a database as well.

The user interface for keyword fields is also flexible. You have three choices: dialog list, checkboxes, or radio buttons. The dialog list is just a list of text strings that a user can select. The checkboxes allow multiple choices, and the radio buttons force a mutually exclusive selection of a single item from the list.

The OppStatus field will be your first Keywords type field. Make it Editable. In the scrollable field of the Dialog box enter the following words, each on a separate line: **Prospect**, **Proposal**, **Bid Submitted**, and **Contract Signed**. These will be the sale phases that you will define for this application. (See Figure 12.24.)

Keyword fields enable users to select from a list of items. Normally the list is predefined, but you can also enable a user to enter additional keywords at the time the form is filled out. If you display the list of keywords to the user as a dialog list (such as a list of text items) you may additionally specify whether or not you want to enable the user to add items. You may also specify whether the user may select more than one item from the list. We will not allow this option.

Now, choose the second tab of the Field Properties dialog box. It is between Basics and Options and has an icon on it. The icon looks like a small rectangle being chased by little line.

In the Interface field, specify Radio Button and in the Frame field specify Standard. There should be one column. (See Figure 12.25.) At a later time you can try the various user interface options to see if you like the look of different styles.

FIGURE 12.24.

OppStatus keyword field definition.

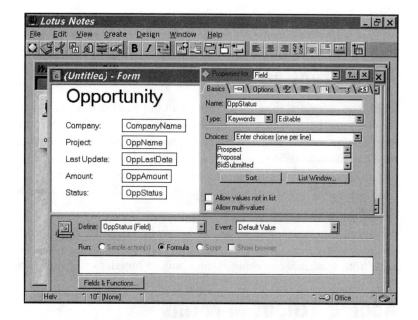

FIGURE 12.25.

OppStatus keyword interface definition.

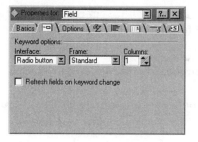

Click on the Basics tab again. Notice that because you have selected the radio button user interface choice, you may no longer have multiple values. Compare your screen now with Figure 12.24. In Figure 12.24, the default user interface of a dialog list was in effect, so you could have multiple values. When you picked the radio button user interface style, multi-values is no longer an option.

The OppProb (Probability) field will also be specified as a Keywords type, Editable field. Make the choices Low, Medium, and High. Choose the second tab and specify Radio Button, Standard, and one column. Moving on to the last field of the form, we find our old friend, the Rich Text Body field. Create a label called Comments: and then create the field named Body and give it the Rich Text type and make it Editable.

Before you save this form, you must change a few of the Form properties. From the menu choose: File | Document Properties. In the dialog box, give the form the name Opportunity ¦ OPY, and make the type of the document a Response. On the Defaults tab, turn ON the On Create Formulas inherit values from selected document. These are the same type of options used for the Contact Form. Finally, select File | Save from the pull-down menu. Close the Properties InfoBox. Close and save the Opportunity Form.

Form Creation Summary

Great, you've created three forms. You're an old hand at this now. Let's review a few of the major points about what you've done before we move on. First, forms are like empty paper forms, or documents with "blanks" on them. Fields on the forms represent the "blanks" or areas that users can fill in. You give each of these fields a different name so that you can refer to them in your formulas. There are several types of fields: Text fields, Rich Text fields, Keyword fields, Time fields, and Number fields. You can specify the type of the field in its Properties InfoBox.

Forms can have a title, which you can specify by a formula. Also, fields can be computed as well as edited. A computed field must have a formula, which can be as simple as inheriting a value from another form or may involve built-in functions such as the @Modified function.

Adding Actions to Forms

 Actions are a new feature of R4. They enable you, the application designer, to make your forms and views easier to use for end users without resorting to a lot of complicated programming. There are several built-in actions, and you can also create your own custom actions as well.

Actions can be invoked from the Action Bar, which is the bar located just below the SmartIcons, or they can be invoked from the Action menu item. Let's see how to customize our forms with actions. Don't confuse actions with Agents, which are the new name for Notes macros. Agents are form or view specific, while macros are not.

From the main view of your database, show the Forms view under Design. You should see the names of your three forms in the right pane under the word Title: Company, Contact, and Opportunity. Double-click on the Company form. Your Company form should now be activated in design mode.

Adding a Built-In Action

You may not have noticed this before, but the right border of your design window actually has a double border. Right now it is all the way to the right and is hiding the Action pane. You can open the pane in one of several ways: Click the View Show/Hide Action Pane SmartIcon. It should be the third icon from the right. (See Figure 12.26.) Another way to open the pane is to check the menu option View | Action Pane. A third way is to drag the border of the window to the left to expose the action pane.

Several actions are built into Notes. These include Categorize, Edit Document, Send Document, Forward, Move To Folder, and Remove from Folder. Categorize is used with a built-in feature of Notes that enables documents to be grouped into categories. To use this feature, you must have a field in your document called Categories. In it you can fill text or keywords that will group the documents. We will not be categorizing our documents in this example.

FIGURE 12.26.

The Company form with the Action pane visible.

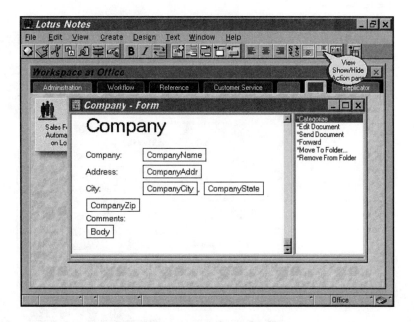

Edit Document makes the current document editable if the proper security authorizations are met. Send Document and Forward are mail options so that you can send documents to others. Send Document looks in the current document for a field called SendTo, extracts the name found there, and sends the document to the recipient. The Forward action enables you to forward a document from a folder or view. You type in the name of the recipient.

The Move To Folder and Remove from Folder actions enable you to manipulate documents by adding or removing documents from folders.

All the built-in actions described here, as well as custom actions that you create, can appear on the Notes Actions menu and/or the new Action Bar that appears above Forms and Views. By default, the built-in actions appear on the menus but do not appear on an Action Bar. When you create your own custom action, you can enable either or both options for your custom action. You're now going to enable one built-in action on the Action Bar and create a custom action as well.

After the action pane is visible, double click on the *Edit Document line. This brings up a dialog box of properties for the action. Turn on the checkbox entitled Include action in button bar. For the Button icon, press the drop-down button and select an icon that you feel represents the editing of a document. The third icon in the second row is one pretty good choice. Remember which icon you choose, though, because you will need it again later. (See Figure 12.27.)

Now, select the Hide tab and turn on the checkboxes for Previewed for editing and Opened for editing. This will disable the edit button if the document is already being edited. (See Figure 12.28.)

FIGURE 12.27.

Action Properties and icons available.

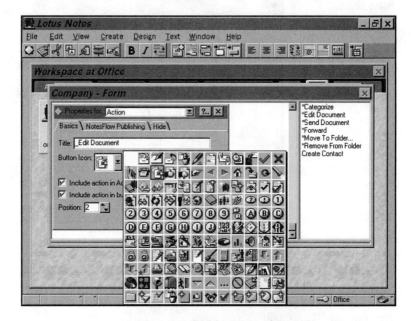

FIGURE 12.28.

Action Hide properties.

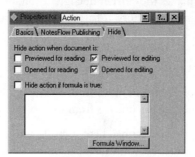

In the Hide tab, you can specify when the action should be hidden (in other words, not made available to the user). In this case, we are hiding the action if the document is either being previewed for editing (it is in edit mode in the preview pane), or if it's opened for editing in its own window. We disable the edit action because if it is already previewed or opened for editing, it doesn't make much sense to have the edit button available.

You can now close the dialog box.

Adding a Custom Action

We're now going to add one of our own actions. From the menu, select Create | Action. In the Title field enter Create Contact. Both of the checkboxes should be on. For the Button icon, select an icon that suggests to you creating a contact record. I chose the first icon in the third row; you can choose another one if you like. (See Figure 12.29.)

FIGURE 12.29.

Custom Action Properties and icons available.

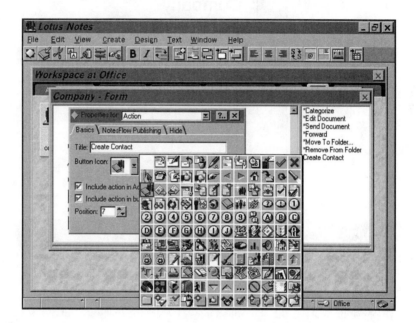

On the Hide tab, turn on the checkboxes for Previewed for editing, Opened for Editing. You can close the dialog box. Notice that your new action appears in the Action pane.

You will now specify what should happen when the custom action button is pressed. You do this in the formula pane at the bottom. (See Figure 12.30.)

Now, in the bottom pane specify the formula to execute when the action button is pressed. In the formula window, enter:

```
@Command([Compose];"";"Contact")
```

This is called an @Command function. It is similar to the other built-in functions, but @Command enables you to programmatically simulate menu sequences. In this particular case, you're simulating the user composing a new Contact document. This is how to let users create the Contact document. The second parameter in the @Command is specified as " " and represents the database in which to compose the document. The empty string means that the current database will be used. You may now close the dialog box and the form. Be sure to say Yes when asked whether to save the form.

FIGURE 12.30.

Custom Action formula.

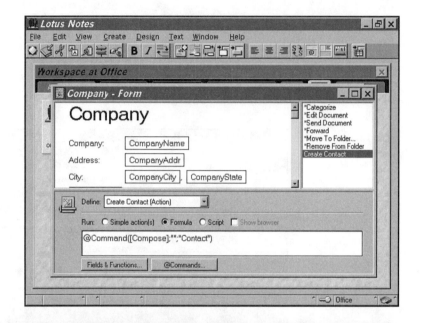

The terminology changed slightly from R3 to R4 of Notes. In R3, when you created a document, Notes used the terminology "composing" the document. The @Command function that appeared previously, called [Compose], was actually a menu option of R3, but it no longer appears as a menu option in R4. For compatibility so that old programs would continue to run, they kept the word "compose." You'll also recall that one type of computed field was called Computed when composed. This type of field is computed only when the document is created. In R4, the more common word "create" is used in the menus and mostly throughout the rest of the user interface. The word "create" is more generic and is now used for all objects, whereas the term "compose" previously was used mainly in the context of documents.

Adding Actions to the Contact Form

You're now going to add actions to the contact form. Go to the design view and double click on the Contact form. When it comes up, show the Action pane as before. Double-click on the Edit Document action and enable the Include action in button bar option. On the Hide tab, enable the Previewed for editing and Opened for editing options. For the Button Icon, use the same icon that you used before for the edit document of the Company form. I used the third icon in the second row. Close the dialog box.

To create your custom action from the menu, select Create | Action. The title of the action should be Create Opportunity. Make sure that both options are enabled. For the icon, I chose the "thumbs up" icon for the opportunity, which is the fourth icon in the second row. On the Hide tab, enable Previewed for editing and Opened for editing. You can now close the dialog box.

For the Create Opportunity formula, you should enter:

```
@Command([Compose];"";"Opportunity")
```

This formula is similar to the one previously added to the Company form.

Bring up the properties box for the Contact Form. In the Basics tab, turn off the Include in Menu option. We turn this option off because now that we have actions enabled, we want to force the end user to create contacts via our actions, not from the menu.

Finishing Up Actions

We now need to update the Opportunity form with a single action. This action will be the Edit Document action. See if you can do this by yourself. Remember to enable the button in the Action Bar and hide it when the document is already being edited. Be sure to save the form after you have made the changes. If you're having some problems doing this, go back in the chapter and review how it was done on the other two forms. You do not need to do another Create button for the opportunity form.

Bring up the properties box for the Opportunity form. In the Basics tab, turn off the Include in Menu option. You turn this option off because now that you have actions enabled, you want to force the end user to create opportunities via your actions, not from the menu.

Close the Properties InfoBox and close and save the Opportunity Form.

Testing Your Forms

Well, we've come to a good point to do some more testing of forms. Go back to the main view of your database. Double-click on the line that just contains a 1 in the first column. This represents the document that you previously saved in the database. It should bring up the Company form you entered. (See Figure 12.31.)

See if you can notice a subtle change in the form. There should now be an Action Bar above the form, and it should have two buttons in it. The first is called Edit Document and the second is Create Contact. These are the two action buttons we created.

Try pressing the Edit document button. The document should enter into edit mode, and you should be able to edit the fields. Do you notice that the Action Bar disappears after it goes into edit mode? Why does that occur?

Close the document for editing.

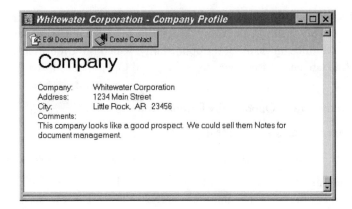

At this point you can test your Contact document. Double-click on the 2 document. You should get the contact with the information that you previously typed. Notice that the Action Bar appears in your form because it is in view mode, not edit mode. From the Action Bar, press Create Opportunity. You can now see your Opportunity form. The appropriate fields have been already prefilled in. You can fill in the other fields. (See Figure 12.32.)

FIGURE 12.32.

The Contact and Opportunity forms.

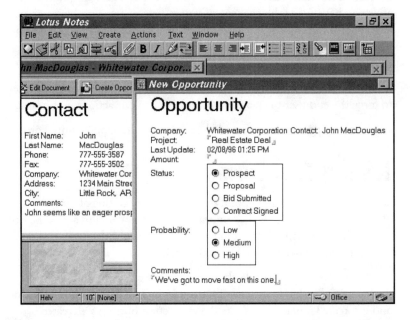

In Figure 12.32 you'll notice that the Keyword fields are shown as radio-button boxes. Try picking various selections in the radio-button boxes. Notice that as you pick one choice, your previous choice is deselected. Radio buttons operate like the radio buttons of your car radio; when one is selected, the previous one is deselected.

Close and save your opportunity document. When you do this, you will be returned to your contact document. Close your contact document. When you close this document, you will see your main view again. Notice that there are now three documents in your database. The last document is your opportunity document. You can verify this by double-clicking on the document labeled 3. Close the document when you have finished.

Summary

We've reached the end of our tour of Notes forms. I've tried to give you an introduction to some of the most important features of Notes R4. You now know how to create a new form, and how to fill in static text labels and fields. You know how to give each field the proper type and, for computed fields, how to enter the formula to be evaluated.

We've covered Property InfoBoxes and have shown how you can use them to change the properties of your fields, forms, databases, and actions.

This chapter covered actions, including the built-in actions and how to create your own action. You put one of each kind on an Action Bar and used them to essentially link the forms to one another.

As I mentioned at the outset, one of the best ways to learn about Notes is to explore. Take the database that you have created and experiment. Create additional forms and add additional fields. Who knows? Maybe you can even take this sample application and turn it into a useful tool for you and your business.

In the next chapter, we'll cover views. I'll show you how to create views and how to use them to summarize your data. You'll find out about columns, selection formulas, and even how to put icons in your views.

CHAPTER 13

Developing Views

by Randall A. Tamura

IN THIS CHAPTER

This chapter continues the Sales Automation example from the previous chapter. If you followed along and created the database from Chapter 12, "Developing Forms," you can continue using the same database. If you're jumping in fresh and you haven't done the previous chapter, you can copy the database SALESF12.NSF from the CD-ROM which accompanies this book. This file can be found in the subdirectory called \SOURCE\CHAP12. This database is a sample from the end of Chapter 12.

Every Notes database has at least one view. In fact, if you'll recall from Chapter 12, when the initial, empty database is created by Notes, it also creates a default view. We used that default view several times in that chapter.

The purpose of a view is to give the user an easy way to see a related subset of the documents in a Notes database. It is displayed in a tabular fashion with both rows and columns. The rows usually represent one document from the database. The information displayed in each column for that row is typically extracted from fields in the document. For example, if the documents contained a field called Name, then the Name field from each document would be retrieved and displayed on the corresponding row of the view.

In addition to showing information from fields within the form, Notes enables you to display a simple function such as the document's number within the view, the document creation date, last modified date, size, or one of several other document attributes. You can also specify more complex information using Notes formulas and/or simple functions.

As the designer of the database, you have the flexibility and the responsibility to choose which fields to extract from the database for display within the view. In our simplified example we will be creating two views for use with our Sales Automation example.

Setting Up the Sales Force Automation Database

Open the Sales Force Automation database that you created in the last chapter, or open the database SALESF12.NSF that is supplied on the CD-ROM. In order to use the SALESF12.NSF database, you must first:

- Copy the database to your Notes data directory.
- With the Windows file manager or other utility make sure that the Read-only attribute has been turned off. In Windows 95 you can use the Explorer, right-click on the file, and then select Properties. Deselect the Read-only checkbox.

After you have copied the database to your Notes data directory, you should add the icon for the database to your desktop. You can do this as follows:

- First select the workspace page on which you want the icon to appear.

- Right-click on an empty area of the page.
- Select Open Database.
- Make sure you have selected the "local" server.
- Scroll through the list of databases until you find the Sales Force Automation database.
- Click Add Icon.

Finished Views: Our Target

By the end of this chapter, you will have created two views of the forms you made in Chapter 12. The two views will be called Contacts and Opportunities. The Contacts view will contain information about both companies and people. Opportunities will contain information about the specific business opportunities you're working on.

In Chapter 14, "Making Your Application Look Good and Work Well," you will enhance your views with additional color and actions. In Figure 13.1 you see the Contacts view showing company information as it will appear after you have completed Chapter 14.

FIGURE 13.1.

Finished Contacts view showing company information.

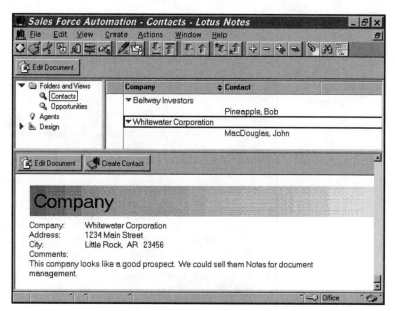

In Figure 13.2 you see the same view as it appears when showing contact information. Notice that the same view can be used to consolidate both company and contact information.

FIGURE 13.2.

*Finished Contacts view
showing contact
information.*

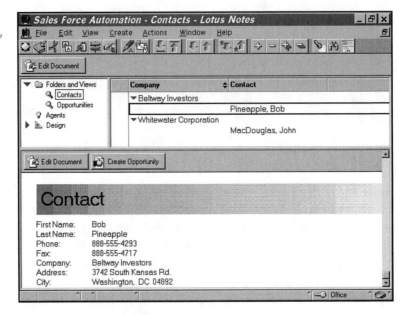

In Figure 13.3 you see the Opportunities view with the list opportunities sorted by the status phase. Notice that this view contains alternating background colors and icons. You'll be adding the icons in this chapter and the alternating background colors in the next chapter.

FIGURE 13.3.

*Finished Opportun-
ities view.*

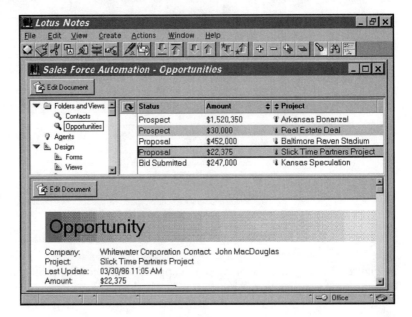

Working with the Contacts View

Let's get started. After the database has been added to your desktop, double-click the database icon to open it. After you have opened the database, click on the twistie next to the Design line to expose the design elements. Click on Views. You should have one view called Contacts. Double-click on this view. Your screen should now resemble Figure 13.4.

FIGURE 13.4.

The View dialog box.

Notice that in the upper-left corner of the dialog box there is a curled arrow next to the number sign (#). This curled arrow signifies that this view contains information that has not yet been refreshed. Depending on the status of your database, your view may or may not display this arrow. If it does, press it and watch what happens. Your view should be updated with the documents that were present in the database but not displayed. If you're using the database created from Chapter 12, you'll see that the view now contains three lines with the numbers 1, 2, and 3. These represent the document number within the view.

Refreshing Views

As you look out at a panoramic ocean view, with the waves rolling and the sun rising, you may find your view very refreshing. However, in Notes, refreshing views has quite a different meaning. You must occasionally refresh views because sometimes the information in a view may be out of date.

How, you may ask, can the information get out of date? Doesn't Notes always keep fresh data? Can I really trust the information in my view? Well, you can relax. There are options to have the information always up to date in your view, but you may not necessarily always want to use them.

The reason is performance. Notes keeps an index, called the view index, of the information in a view. Any time documents change, the view index must be updated to correctly show all the information in the view. Now, if you have a database of say 30,000 records, and someone else has changed a document that you don't really care about, do you want to wait for Notes to update the view index? Well, maybe and maybe not. This is the reason why Notes enables you to determine for each view whether or not the views will be refreshed automatically or will wait for users to refresh them when they want to. You can set these options in the View Properties InfoBox in the Options tab.

As a user, you can refresh a view by pressing F9 or by using the View | Refresh option from the menu. I've mentioned refreshing views early in this chapter because it is important to realize that changes you make to documents may not be immediately reflected in your view. If you were not aware of this feature of Notes, it may be very mystifying to see that your updated information is not reflected in your views.

View Selection Formulas

In the View selection box in the lower part of the dialog box shown in Figure 13.4, notice that there is no formula shown. This means that the view will display information for all documents in the database. If you want to selectively show only some of the documents in the database, you can do this by making a selection formula. Notes will test the formula using data for each document. If the selection formula evaluates to true for a particular document, then the document is selected and will be shown in the view. If it is false, the document will not be shown within the view.

In this case, you are going to be defining the Contacts view, so you should display information only from the Company and Contact forms. You can restrict which documents will be displayed based on the form that was used to create the document. Select the Formula radio button and then enter the following line in the formula box:

```
SELECT (Form="CPY" ¦ Form="CON")
```

This formula will now be used for view selection. In English, this formula means, select documents for this view if the form associated with them is either "CPY" or "CON". The vertical bar means OR. As mentioned, Notes will evaluate this formula for each document, and if the formula evaluates to true, the document will be selected for display and otherwise not.

Do you remember the symbols CPY and CON? They were used as aliases for the Company and the Contact forms back in Chapter 12. We used form alias names so that the view formula can refer to them.

We could also refer to the forms by their main names of Company and Contact, but as I mentioned previously, if you want to change the user interface, then you would need to go through the database and change all references in all formulas. That could be a time-consuming, nonproductive task. By using aliases, you can change the user interface without changing your formulas. Remember also that form names and alias names are case-sensitive, so be careful how you use capitalization, and use it consistently.

By changing the selection criteria, only Company and Contact documents will be included in this view. Opportunity documents will not be included.

In addition to using the form type to select the documents, you can use other criteria such as the document date, the author, a status field (for example, all "Open" problem reports), or by checking any of the fields of the document for conditions that you specify. This selection mechanism using formulas is the heart of the view mechanism. You can create several views of the database, each with a different purpose, and each showing a different subset of the database sorted in a different order.

Here are a few sample formulas:

```
SELECT Sales>=10000

SELECT ProbStatus="OPEN"

SELECT Priority="HIGH"
```

These are just a few examples of the kinds of formulas you can create. You can also create much more complex selections involving two or more field values, such as (`InvoiceAmount>=1000 & Status="NOTPAID"`).

Defining a Column in a View

Okay, now we're ready to change the view to contain more useful information. Let's change the definition of the first column. You can do this by selecting the Define drop-down listbox at the top of the formula pane and selecting the item that says `# (Column)`. After you have done this, your screen should look something like Figure 13.5.

FIGURE 13.5.

Modifying the first column definition.

Notice in Figure 13.5 that the scroll box has been scrolled down within the Simple Functions. The highlighted line # in View (eg 2.1.2) represents the Notes default for the first column. You can define columns by Simple Function, Field, or Formula. As you can see from Figure 13.5, there are many simple functions that you can use. For example, you can make the column contain the last date modified, the creation date, the document size, the document author, or one of several other functions. You can use these definitions without writing any formulas or LotusScript scripts.

If you choose a Field type, then the column will contain the contents of the field you specify for each record. In this example, since all of the documents contain a CompanyName field, you could use a field definition. In this case, for example, if there were three documents—one each of a Company, a Contact, and an Opportunity document—then each of the three consecutive rows would contain the same CompanyName information. To make this view a little easier to read, you're going to use a formula instead of a field.

Selectively Displaying Information in a Row

Our purpose with the formula will be to selectively display information in some rows, but not others. Because you're going to change the first column to a Formula, select the Formula radio button.

You will see that the default value is the built-in function @Docnumber. Please change this formula to the following:

```
@If(Form="CPY";CompanyName;" ")
```

This formula says (in English): If the form used to create the document was the "Company" form (via the alias CPY), then display the CompanyName field from the form. Otherwise, display a blank for this column. Now, why the heck are you doing this? Well, remember that you first modified the selection formula, so that for this view only Company and Contact documents will be selected. This @If statement really means: If it's a Company form, display CompanyName; otherwise, it's a Contact form, so don't display anything. Ah ha! You'll selectively display information depending upon the type of document that is being displayed in the row. So, the first column will either contain the Company name (for company documents) or it will be blank (for contact documents). Okay, that's pretty easy.

Look back at Figure 13.1 and notice that for Company records, the first column contains the company name. You can also see that although Contact records are shown in the view, the first column contains a blank for them. The @if statement is a powerful tool that enables you to have different information displayed for different document types within the same view.

Column Properties

For the last piece of definition for this column, you need to change some properties of the column. First is the column title because the # really doesn't apply any more. To change the title, you must open the Column properties InfoBox. There are several ways to do this. You can do any one of the following:

- Double-click on the column header now displaying #.
- For the next three methods, first select a column by single clicking on the header, and then:
    - Click on the Properties SmartIcon.
    - Select Edit | Properties from the menu.
    - Press the Alt+Enter keyboard combination.

Choose a method (or try them all out) and bring up the Column Properties InfoBox. In the Title field, change the # to Company. (See Figure 13.6.) Also enable Show twistie when row is expandable.

FIGURE 13.6.

Column properties for the first column of Contacts view.

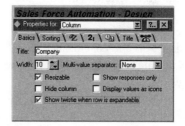

Using twisties on expandable rows is a new feature of Notes R4. In previous versions of Notes, the programmer had to add additional logic to the Notes program in order to implement a similar feature. Now, twisties can be used in a manner similar to twisties next to sections. In Figure 13.1, shown previously, you'll notice that the twisties have been expanded so that the contents of the indented lines are visible. If the twistie were pointing to the right, then the indented lines would be collapsed and would be hidden. This feature enables a user to expand or collapse information in the view making it easier to navigate through the view.

Main and Response Documents

In order to discuss the Show responses only checkbox of Figure 13.6, you must first understand the relationship of main and response documents. If you recall from Chapter 12, we specified that the Company documents would be main documents and that the Contact documents would be response documents.

Notes differentiates between main and response documents. A response document is always associated with a main document. One convention in views is that response documents are shown indented underneath their main document. In our example, this means that the contacts will be shown indented underneath the appropriate company.

13

DEVELOPING
VIEWS

In the example we are building, we will be using formulas to implement this indention so I can show you how formulas work. However, there is actually a built-in feature that almost makes this indention automatic. You may have guessed by now, it is the Show responses only checkbox shown in Figure 13.6.

Although we won't be using it for this example, here's how you can use this feature: By adding a column of width 1, and checking this checkbox for the column, you can have responses displayed under their respective main documents. You must still specify the information you want to extract and show from the response document via the display simple function, field, or formula.

Sorting Information in a Column

We will be discussing all of the other options in the Basics property tab later on in this chapter as we progress through our views. For now, after you have completed the changes for the Basics tab, click on the Sorting tab. With R4 of Notes, you can now specify that you would like the column to be sorted and/or you can enable the user to sort the columns. For this column, select the Ascending Sort and enable Click on column header to sort Both. This will bring up the column in ascending order, but enable the user to sort the column in descending order if so desired. (See Figure 13.7.)

FIGURE 13.7.

Sorting tab in Company Column Properties InfoBox.

The options you have just picked will cause the initial sorting of the Company name column to be sorted in ascending order. After the view is displayed, though, the user can manually sort the column either in ascending or descending order. With only one Company document, this is not necessarily important, but if you had hundreds or thousands of documents, this feature could be a handy time saver for the user.

In the Sorting dialog box you'll notice that there are several other options besides the ascending or descending nature of the sort. Standard is a normal alphanumeric sort, as you have used here. Categorized is a special kind of sort for the Categorizing feature of Notes. By placing a special field on documents called Categories and by enabling a category sort, the documents will be sorted into categories. Note that a single document can belong to more than one category, which is not possible with a standard sort.

Case-sensitive sorting will differentiate between upper- and lowercase words that are otherwise the same. Normally you'll want this option turned off, but there may be some cases where you would like to distinguish between two identical words with different capitalization. Accent-sensitive sorting is mainly for non-English language sorting. Languages other than English may sometimes have accents over or under letters; checking this box will distinguish these letters.

You may now close the Properties dialog box.

At this point you may notice the curled arrow in the upper-left corner of the view. Press it and see what happens. You should see the name of the sample company you entered. You'll also notice that the first column title has changed to Company and that there are up and down arrows to the right of the word Company. These arrows are for sorting the column in ascending or descending order.

Defining the Contact Column

You're ready to proceed by defining the second column in your Contacts view. To do this, double-click on the column to the right of the first column. By double-clicking on the area to the right of the first column you are essentially performing an Append of a new column. This double-clicking technique is a shortcut. You could perform the same operation from the menus with Create | Append New Column, which will add a column to the far right. Create | Insert New Column will insert a new column to the left of the selected column.

When the Properties box is displayed, enter Contact for the title of the column on the Basics tab. On the Sorting tab, enable Sort Ascending. You don't have to enable column header sort because you don't anticipate that many contacts within each company. There will be a few, but an ascending sort is probably sufficient. You can now close the Properties dialog box.

In the bottom part of the Contacts - View dialog box, you should see Define Contact (Column). Enable the Display Formula radio button. In the Formula area, enter the following:

```
@If(Form="CON"; ContactLast + ", " + ContactFirst; " ")
```

See Figure 13.8 for an example of how your screen should look.

This formula means, in English: If the form associated with the document is the Contacts form, then the view should display the Contact's last name, followed by a comma, followed by the Contact's first name. If it is any other form, display a blank for this column.

Notice that in the formula, you are using the last name for the contact, followed by a comma, followed by the first name. The contents of this column of the view, then, will be a computed formula rather than a single field. Also notice that by using the last name to begin the string, you can sort the column in ascending order and they will be alphabetized by last name. If you had started the strings with the first name, then all of the contacts would be sorted by first name. Although possible, this is not normally how to view lists of names, so use the last-name-first approach to obtain a last-name-sorted list.

FIGURE 13.8.

*The Contacts View
Contact Column
formula.*

This is a good point to clarify how response documents are sorted. When the main documents are sorted, the response documents that are associated with the main document move along with the main document. Thus, even though the contact documents all have blanks in the company column, they will not all sort together at the top of the list. Each contact will be listed under its associated main company document.

Press the green check mark to the left of the formula to enter the formula to Notes. Now press the Refresh button (the curled arrow in the upper-left corner of the view) to see the results of your formula.

You should now see the name of your contact displayed in the line below the company name. You may also notice that the columns are a little bit too small to contain all of the information you would like to display. There are a couple of ways to make the columns wider. First, you can move your mouse cursor to the dividing lines between the column headers and simply click and drag them to the size you would like. This is probably the easiest way.

The second way, if you're more precise about things, is to double-click on the header to bring up the Column properties InfoBox and change the column width numerically in the InfoBox. You can, for example, make both columns exactly 15 instead of 10. Use this third method to make both columns have a width of 15.

Once you have set the width, you can allow the column to be resizable by the user, or you can fix the width of the column so the user cannot change it. You do this with the resizable checkbox in the Basics tab.

Moving, Copying, and Deleting Columns

Before I finish with this first view, let me describe some of the other editing features for columns. Editing columns is actually rather simple. You can treat columns as you treat many other objects in Notes.

To move, copy, and delete columns you can just use the normal edit cut and paste operations. For example, to move a column, first click on the header of the column while in edit mode. After the column has been selected, from the menu select Edit | Cut. You will be prompted that you are permanently deleting the column. Press Yes. Click on the header of the column where you would like to move the old column and from the menu select Edit | Paste. Your old column will be pasted in front of the column you had selected.

To copy a column, first click on the header and from the menu select Edit | Copy. After this, click on the header where you would like your new copy to appear and from the menu select Edit | Paste. A copy of your column will appear in front of the selected column.

You can delete a column with Edit | Cut from the menus. So, moving, copying, and deleting columns is as easy as cutting and pasting. Of course, you could also use the equivalent SmartIcons for each of the cut, copy, and paste operations.

Finishing Up the Contacts View

Okay, you're done with your first view. Close the View editing dialog box and save your changes.

Take a moment to admire your handiwork. In the main view, select (under Folders and Views) the Contacts view. Notice that a twistie is available to the left of the company you entered. Try pressing the twistie a couple of times and watch the contact below disappear and reappear. Enlarge the preview pane in your view. You should now have three panes visible: the Navigator pane in the upper left, the view pane in the upper right, and the preview pane on the bottom. Click on the company name and watch the preview pane. Click on the contact name and watch the preview pane. See Figure 13.9 for a view of our contact.

FIGURE 13.9.

*Contact information
displayed in the preview
window.*

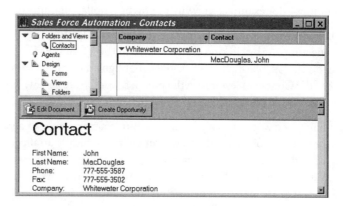

Notice that the Opportunity document created previously is now not shown. Compare this view with the view of Figure 13.5, shown previously. In that view, all three documents in the database were shown (although they were only represented by their document numbers). In this view, only the first and second documents are shown.

The Opportunity document is not shown because our view selection formula now selects only documents that are associated with the Company form or the Contacts form. Since the Opportunity document was created with the Opportunity form, it is not now shown in the view. We'll remedy this by showing the opportunities in their own view.

Adding the Opportunities View

You're now ready to add the Opportunities view. In the Opportunities view, you'll be able to see all the current (and/or past) opportunities. If you'll recall from Chapter 12, you created the Opportunity form with several fields that might be of interest to sales people. For example, if you were a salesperson, you might be interested in the sales amount, especially if you are paid on commission.

Another field that might be of importance is the current status of the opportunity. Our model had a phased sales cycle that went through the phases: Prospect, Proposal, Bid Submitted, and Contract Signed. Your sales process may be different, and you can use different words, but you get the idea.

As a salesperson, you might also be interested in the probability of winning the order, expressed as low, medium, or high. Those high-amount, high-probability orders are the best, but what about a high amount, low probability? By using these different fields, you can sort the data in a variety of ways and see where you can best spend your time.

For the second view, use four fields from the Opportunity form: Status, Amount, Probability, and Project name. These should give an overview in the view of the opportunity. You'll also enable sorting so that the user can re-sort the view on different fields to highlight different priorities—for example, showing the highest dollar amounts or the highest probabilities.

Okay, let's begin. From the main view of your database, open up the design section in the Navigator pane by clicking on the twistie to the left of the word Design. Select Views by clicking on it. The black rectangle should highlight the word Views. You should see one existing view, the Contacts view. From the menu, select Create | View. When the dialog box comes up, change the view name from Untitled to Opportunities and click the Options... button.

Although we won't use this feature for our example, you can also create views that are within other views. In other words, views can be hierarchically arranged. To do this, instead of highlighting the word Views, you would highlight a particular view, and the new view will be created under the selected view. When the user sees the views in the Navigator pane, they will be displayed in the typical, indented hierarchical fashion.

In the Options dialog box, select the -Blank- view under Inherit design from: and press OK. This will cause Notes to inherit the view from a blank view rather than the Contacts view. The Contacts and Opportunities views do not have much in common, so it is easier to start this view from a blank one. Sometimes in Notes you will have views that are very similar to one another. If so, it is more convenient to inherit view attributes from an existing view than to start from a blank one. You can now close the dialog box.

Back in the Create View dialog box, select the Shared box near the middle of the dialog box. (See Figure 13.10.) The Shared box is used to differentiate between private and shared views. If you leave the box unchecked, then you will create a private view. As you might expect, private views are not available to all users, just the user who creates the view. Shared views, on the other hand, are shared among all users of the database.

FIGURE 13.10.

*The Create View
dialog box.*

The Personal on first use checkbox enables you to create a view that will initially be shared, but will become private for each user as he or she uses the view. Suppose you wanted to create a central database of to-do items. You would like each user to have a view with only to-do items relevant for him or her. Rather than create 100 different views, one for each person, you could create a single view, based on @UserName that turns private as each user uses the database. We will not be using this feature in our example.

You may now click OK. You have now created the Opportunities view.

Adding Status to a View

You must now customize the Opportunities view to add the view columns and selection formula. Double-click on the Opportunities view in the view pane on the right. You will get the Opportunities - View editing dialog box. As a new view, your screen should now look as it did in Figure 13.4, shown previously.

In the View Editing dialog box, you'll notice that there are two radio buttons just above the formula area. You can select either Easy or Formula. The Easy option enables you to add conditions by example. You could press the Add Condition button at the bottom and add selection conditions by field or form. Since the formula is so easy, however, it's just as convenient to type it directly into the box. Select the Formula button so you can enter the formula. In the formula area near the bottom of the box, replace the existing formula `Select @All` with the formula:

```
Select Form="OPY"
```

This formula will select only Opportunity documents. Company and Contact documents will be ignored and not displayed in this view.

Now, double-click on the first column header (the one with "#"). This brings up the same box seen earlier in this chapter. Change the title from # to Status. Close the Properties dialog box.

You now see the column definition area. You have three choices: Simple Function, Field, or Formula. These are three mutually exclusive choices. If you choose one, it will disable the others. The choices are related, however. For example, when the dialog box first appears, you see that Simple Function is selected. Select Formula. You now see the formula equivalent for the Simple Function that was selected.

Each of the radio buttons will actually generate a formula, so the formula option is actually the most general choice of the three. If you select Simple Function, Notes just substitutes the corresponding `@function` name for you in the formula, as you have seen. If you choose field, then the field name is used as the formula.

You should note, however, when you change your choice from one radio button to another, you will be deleting the old definition and replacing it with a new one. For example, the default formula is `@DocNumber`. If you choose the field button, you will be deleting this definition and replacing it with a field name. Because Notes does not want you to lose data inadvertently, it will show you a dialog box warning you that you will lose your current definition.

To see this in operation, select the Field radio button. A dialog box appears, warning you that you will lose your current action data (for instance, your current formula). Press Yes when asked to confirm losing action data. Select the field name OppStatus. (See Figure 13.11.)

FIGURE 13.11.

Defining the Status column of the Opportunities - View.

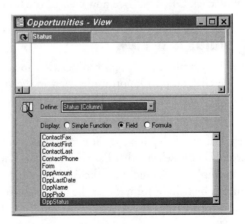

Enhancing Our Status

Your status column will display one of our predefined status values: Prospect, Proposal, Bid Submitted, or Contract Signed. It might be nice to sort the rows so that all the opportunities with the same status will sort together. This is fairly easy, as seen with your Company view, you can just enable sorting by the contents of the column and all of the groups will sort together.

Wait a minute, though. If you think about it, when you sort the records in alphabetical order (either ascending or descending), they are not in the normal order in which we think of the sales process. What we would really like is to be able to sort the columns in order, either ascending or descending in terms of the sales process, not the particular words that are used. When sorted in ascending sequence, Bid Submitted should not come before Prospect even though this is the alphabetical order. The preferred sequence is the one that appears on the form, namely: Prospect, Proposal, Bid Submitted, and Contract Signed. A descending sort could be in the reverse order. How do you do this?

The essential trick to sorting in this manner is to add an additional, hidden column that will be used for sorting. The visible column just defined will not actually be used for the sorting. Let's see how this is done.

In order to accomplish the special sorting, we must insert a new column. So, while the Status column is highlighted, select Create | Insert New Column. You could also use the equivalent SmartIcon.

> **NOTE**
>
> If the Insert New Column option is not enabled in your menu, the changes in your Status column definition have not been saved. Click on the header line, to the right of the word Status, then click on the Status column again to highlight it. Now go back up to the menu and try Create | Insert New Column again.

The new column should be inserted to the left of the Status column. In the View editing dialog box, select the Formula radio button. Replace the @DocNumber formula with this formula:

```
@if(OppStatus="Prospect";"1";OppStatus="Proposal";"2";OppStatus="Bid
➥Submitted";"3";"4")
```

This rather daunting formula is actually quite simple. Remember, our goal is to get the rows to sort in the order: Prospect, Proposal, Bid Submitted, Contract Signed. Because this order is not in alphabetical order, we associate a number with each of these types of status. By associating a number with each one, we can then sort on the number as a proxy for the text string.

So, if you look back at the formula, it simply says, if the status is Prospect, assign the proxy number 1. If it is Proposal, then assign 2; Bid Submitted is assigned a 3; and since Contract Signed is the only remaining option, it is assigned a 4. Now, each text string is associated with a number, and the column can be sorted based on this number. You can use this trick to assign a sorting sequence to any arbitrary set of strings if you want them to sort in an order other than ascending or descending alphabetical order.

Now, open the Column Properties box by pressing the Properties SmartIcon or selecting Edit | Properties from the pull-down menu. Do not enter a title for this column. Make the column width 1 character. Enable the Hide column option. (See Figure 13.12.)

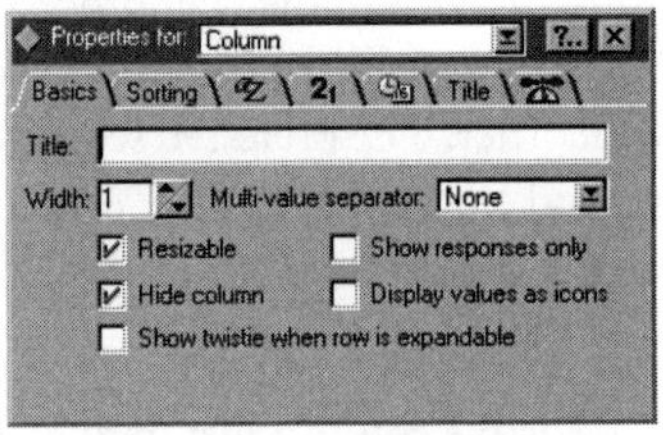

FIGURE 13.12.

Column properties for the hidden Status column.

In the sorting tab, select the Ascending radio button for the Sort: option. This completes your definition of the hidden column.

Adding Money to Our View

Of course, one of your main interests as a salesperson is the amount of money this project might be worth. Let's add the amount field.

To add a new column, from the menu select Create | Append New Column. As you saw in the first view, an alternative to the menu method is to double-click on the header area to the right of the last column. This performs the same operation as appending a new column.

Now, select the Field radio button. A dialog box appears, warning you that you will lose your current action data (your current formula). You'll remember from the previous column that this is just a warning that we are about to change the definition of the column. Press Yes when asked to confirm losing action data. Select the field name OppAmount.

Bring up the Properties InfoBox by pressing Alt+Enter. This is another alternative method to show the Properties InfoBox. In the Title area, enter the word `Amount`.

In the Sorting tab, select Descending. You want to have all of your opportunities sorted from the largest opportunity to the smallest. Also, enable Click on column header to sort both.

In the 21 tab, enable currency formatting. Enable Punctuated at thousands. This property tab can be used to format numbers. It is the same property box used to format the amount field within the form. (See Figure 13.13.)

FIGURE 13.13.

The Amount column properties in the Opportunities view.

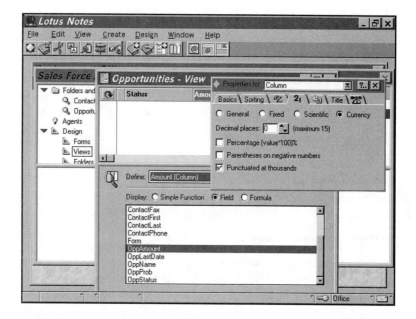

In addition to the currency formatting option, there are several formatting checkboxes. You can show the value as a percentage, which just multiplies the value by 100. You can show parentheses around negative numbers, which is an accounting convention, and you can add punctuation at thousands. In the U.S., this just adds commas at every three places, so 1 million is 1,000,000. The reason for this odd phraseology (punctuated at thousands) is that in countries outside the U.S. sometimes a period is used as the thousands separator and a comma is used as the decimal point.

Now close the Properties dialog box.

Showing the Project Name

Adding a column to show the project name is a simple task. Double-click to the right of the amount field in the View title bar to bring up the Column Properties box. This is a shortcut that appends the column and brings up the Properties box at the same time. In the Title field, enter the word Project, make the width 15, and close the Properties box.

Back in the Opportunities - View dialog box, select the Field radio button. Confirm the loss of action data. Then select the field called OppName. You won't sort on this field because you will be typically looking at your Opportunities based on their potential, not based on the project name. If this is something important to you, see if you can figure out how to do it.

Showing the Probability as an Icon

There are several characteristics of the probability field. First, it is similar to the status field because it is stored as a set of keywords. If you were just to sort on the words High, Medium,

13

DEVELOPING VIEWS

and Low, you would not get the list sorted in the proper order. In fact, you'd either get High, Low, Medium for ascending, or Medium, Low, High for descending. Neither of these sorts is appealing.

You could use the hidden column trick that we used for the status field. If so, you'd insert a new column, add a formula, and hide the column. In this case, though, to add variety, let's use a different technique. You're going to display this column with icons.

Three different icons will be used, one each for Low, Medium, and High. Let's see how we can do this.

With the Project column highlighted, from the menu select Create | Insert New Column. The inserted column should appear to the left of the Project column. In the column definition at the bottom of the screen, select Formula. Replace the @DocNumber formula with:

```
@If(OppProb="Low";88;OppProb="Medium";89;90)
```

Don't worry right now if you don't understand this formula. It will be explained shortly. For right now, just notice that we are creating a correspondence between the words Low, Medium, (and High) with the numbers 88, 89, and 90. The number 88 will substitute for Low, 89 for Medium, and 90 for High. This correspondence will be explained later.

Press Alt+Enter to bring up the Column Properties box. Leave the Title field blank. Change the width to 1. Turn off the Resizable attribute. Enable Display values as icons. (See Figure 13.14.)

FIGURE 13.14.

The Probability column properties.

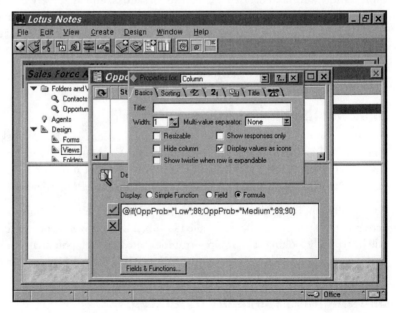

In the Sorting tab, select Descending and enable Click on column header to sort both. Enable a secondary sort column and select the Amount column with a descending sort. (See Figure 13.15.)

FIGURE 13.15.

Sorting properties for the Probability column.

Close the Properties box.

Okay, now that you've entered all the information into the property boxes, go back to the column formula. What on earth can it mean? Why are these arbitrary numbers like 88, 89, and 90 used? Well, I'm glad you asked. Built into Notes is a set of 170 icons that can be used instead of column values. Notes converts an integer number in the range of 1–170 to one of these icons. See Figure 13.16 for a display of these icons.

FIGURE 13.16.

Table of column icons.

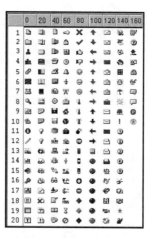

Figure 13.16 shows the values for the various icons. The way to read the table is to first find the icon you're interested in. Then add the column header and the row value to the left. For example, the very first icon in the upper-left corner of the table has a value of 0+1=1. The icon to its immediate right has a value of 21. Find the icons for values 88, 89, and 90. These are the three thermometers in the middle of the table. Now you can see what we were doing with the values. When a value of Low is in the probability, it is translated to an 88, which in turn

translates to the first thermometer with a low value. The values 89 and 90 represent the Medium and High values.

If you want to specify a blank for the column, you should use the value zero (0).

If you take a close look at the icons in Figure 13.16, you'll notice that icon number 5 is a paper clip. This is useful for denoting attachments to documents. The first 10 or 20 icons, in fact, are useful for denoting ideas such as folders, people, groups, reports, graphs, and so forth. Many of these icons can be used as flags to show in the view that a particular document has some attribute—for example, an attachment. In developing your view, you may want to show the user some other attribute of the document.

Now, because of a quirk in some early releases of Notes, we need to verify our columns before we finish up our view. You should now be viewing the Opportunities - View dialog box. Click on the header of each of the following columns in turn. Start with the Status column. Verify that the display type has Field selected and that the field name is OppStatus. Next, click on the Amount header. Verify that it is also a field and the field name is OppAmount. Lastly, click on the Project header and verify that the field name is OppName.

If any of the fields were incorrect, fix them and then close the Opportunities - View dialog box. You're now ready to test your view. Click on the Opportunities view in the Navigator pane; your screen should look similar to Figure 13.17.

Figure 13.17.

The Opportunities view.

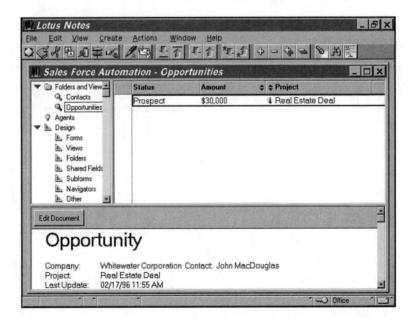

Notice in Figure 13.17 that there are three visible columns, but actually there are five columns. The first column is the hidden column that sorts the status column in Status order instead of alphabetical order. Then the Status and Amount columns follow. The amount column can be sorted by the user by pressing on the arrows. The next column holds your probability. This can be either Low, Medium, or High, and is signified by three different types of thermometers. This column can also be sorted. The last column is the Project name column. It appears as though the Probability column with its icons is part of the Project name column, but it actually isn't.

A copy of the database for this chapter as it appears following all of the editing done in this chapter can be found on the CD-ROM in the directory CHAPTER13. The file in this directory is SALESF11.NSF. You can open this file if you don't want to go through all of the editing done in this chapter.

Summary

This concludes your tour of Lotus Notes views. You have created two views, but have explored a variety of the features that are available to you as a view designer. In the Contacts view, I showed how to create a view with main and response documents. I also showed you how to conditionally include information for a row of the view. In the Contacts view, you can sort the companies in either ascending or descending order just by clicking on the header. You can also expand or contract all the contact records so that only company names appear.

In the Opportunities view, I showed you how to sort columns by an invisible, associated column. This is useful when the field is a keyword field because usually the priority order for the keywords is not the alphabetical order. I also showed you how to include numerical fields, format, and sort them. Finally, I showed you how to make the values of a column appear as icons. Again, this is useful for keyword-type fields because you will usually have a small number of choices.

The next chapter will show you pointers on making your forms and views look good and work better, too. The aesthetics of your forms and views is becoming more and more important these days. Users want and expect professional-looking forms and views. Chapter 14 will give you some tips on how to create more compelling forms and views.

Making Your Application Look Good and Work Well

by Randall A. Tamura

IN THIS CHAPTER

Designing Forms and Views in Notes entails more than just defining the static text and fields to be used. There is an aesthetic component to designing a compelling user application as well as the functional component. Sometimes this aesthetic aspect is called the "fit and finish" of a product; sometimes it is called the "form" of a product as opposed to the product's "function." Think about any product you use: a coffee maker, a stereo receiver, your automobile. If you think about these products, you buy them not only for their functional characteristics, but also for their aesthetic appeal.

A product, whether it is an automobile or a computer application, must function correctly and perform well, but its look and feel is important, too. The way your application looks makes a difference in how it is perceived by users as well as affecting its usability. It may even affect how well your users accept and like using your application.

Lotus has recognized the increasing importance of these perceptions. Take a few moments to flip through this chapter and other chapters in this book and review some of the new forms Lotus has provided with this release. They clearly have spent a great deal of time updating their forms to make them more visually appealing. The new forms in the Public Address Book are much nicer and easier to use than before. In the mail functions, clip art and even mood stamps add visual zest to Notes. The great news is that Lotus has also provided tools for you to do the same.

This chapter covers some aspects of form and view design that are really borrowed from desktop publishing. If you have a book on desktop publishing or graphic design, it will be an excellent additional source of suggestions for your Notes forms.

Usability in many ways is related to the aesthetic design. Think back about your car and about using its controls. In your car, there are lots of things to control: your head lights, inside lights, radio, windshield wipers, turn signals, air conditioning, defrosters, fog lamps…and the list goes on and on. A challenge to the designer is to make all of these controls easy to use; actually, they should be so easy to use that their use is transparent. In other words, you shouldn't even have to think about how to do something; it should be automatic. Your challenge as an application designer is really the same.

In designing an application, it should be almost automatic for the user. The user should be able to concentrate on the "driving"—in other words, the business task at hand. The interface should look good and work well. The user should be able to perform the business task without even thinking about the user interface. Many of the usability enhancements available in R4 of Notes can improve the visual appeal of the application as well.

This chapter will cover some usability improvements in your application as well as the aesthetics of your application. The purpose of this chapter is not to turn you into a graphic artist or a usability expert, but to give you some introductory ideas and concepts that you can easily use to improve the overall effectiveness of your designs.

General Aesthetic Observations

The visual appeal of your forms and views is affected by several components: the fonts you use, the layout of the form, and additional features such as white space, rules (lines), reverses, drop shadows, and boxes.

To illustrate some of these concepts, I'll be showing you some of the detail that has gone into Notes R4.

Fonts

One of the most obvious and important characteristics affecting the look of your form is the selection of fonts you use. This decision is affected by technical as well as aesthetic considerations. For example, do you expect your documents to be used across different platforms? If so, carefully select your fonts; the latest, fanciest true-type font for Windows may not be available for use on UNIX or the Macintosh.

If you're familiar with the editing capabilities of Notes or a word processor, you know that you can select a font by its name. In most text-editing programs, you can usually also select the type size and attributes such as bold, italic, and/or underlining.

What exactly is a font? Actually, in publishing, the name of the font is actually called the *typeface name*. A couple of common typeface names are Times Roman and Helvetica. In Notes, these are abbreviated to Tms Rmn and Helv.

The weight is the letter width and stroke thickness. For example, the Helvetica typeface family comes in several weights such as Helvetica Light, Helvetica Condensed, Helvetica Black, and Helvetica Black Condensed. The full Helvetica family includes 20 or 30 variations, mostly in the weight of the font. The font weight should not be confused with the type style.

The type style is used to add emphasis to the typeface. Typically the styles include the four styles: Normal, Bold, Italic, Bold Italic. Helvetica Bold, for example is the Helvetica type face with a bold style. Any particular typeface family may have various combinations of weight and style.

A Serif typeface is commonly used for text. This sentence, for example, is set in a Serif typeface. Serif typefaces have small lines at the tops and bottoms of the letters. For example, look carefully at the letter "i", "d", "b", or "l" in this sentence. You'll see that there are small lines, called serifs, at the top and bottom of the letters. Serif typefaces work very well for longer passages of text. They are easy to read in long blocks.

A Sans-Serif typeface has no serifs. Look carefully at the section headings within this chapter. They are set in Sans-Serif type. Look for the same letters "i", "d", "b", and "l" in various headers. You'll notice that a lowercase "l" in Sans-Serif type looks a lot like a capital "I." Sans-Serif fonts are very good for headers and short sequences of text.

The Workspace Drop Shadow

To see a simple example of visual effects in Notes R4, open Notes to your workspace. Figure 14.1 is an example of your workspace with the Textured Workspace option turned on.

FIGURE 14.1.

A workspace with the Textured Workspace option on.

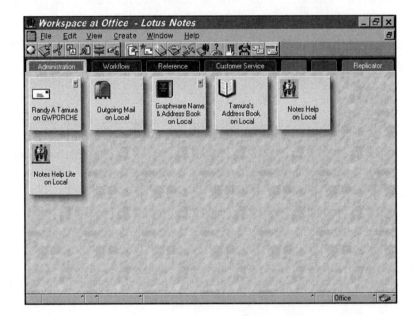

Now select File | Tools | User Preferences. In the basics icon, select the Textured Workspace option under Advanced Options. If it was previously off, you can turn it on. If it was on, turn it off. (See Figure 14.2.)

FIGURE 14.2.

User Preferences options.

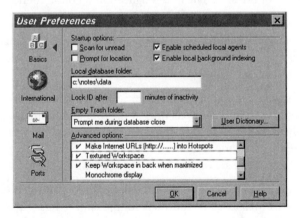

Several of the Advanced options in the User Preferences dialog box are related to the visual characteristics and usability of Notes. If you have turned off the textured workspace option, your screen should look like Figure 14.3.

FIGURE 14.3.

A workspace without the Textured Workspace option.

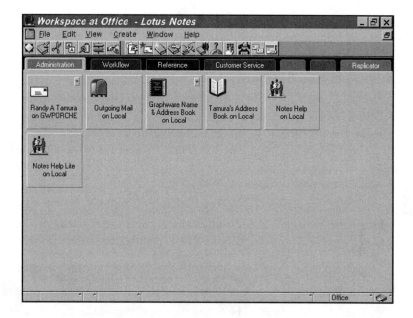

Now, compare the screen shots of Figures 14.1 and 14.3. You'll notice at once that Figure 14.1 is much more appealing. In Figure 14.1, the icons seem to have a 3-D look about them. This effect is created by the drop shadows of the icons. In this case, the shadows are actually very complex shades of gray. The slight irregularity of the drop shadows gives it a more realistic look than a typical drop shadow in a publication.

Look at Figure 14.4 to see an 8× magnification of the shadow itself. You can see from Figure 14.4 that individual picture elements (pixels) have been modified in a sort of random manner to achieve this look on the desktop. It's clear that someone spent a significant amount of time adjusting individual pixels for this look. You can also now see why this feature is only available if you have a 256 color monitor and adapter card.

FIGURE 14.4

Zoomed-in view of the shadow effects of the Workspace.

14

MAKING YOUR APPLICATION WORK WELL

Your efforts don't have to be this intense, but you can see the importance that Lotus has placed on the look and feel of the product.

Reverses and Screens

If you're a football fan, you know that reverses and screens are two types of plays on the football field. Both of these types of plays involve trying to trick the opponent with the unexpected. They involve a contrast to the normal. In publishing, they also involve a contrast to the normal by highlighting words or phrases. A *reverse* highlights the word or phrase by using white type against a black background. In a world of color, this definition can probably be extended to be a light color against a dark, solid color.

A *screen* is a variation of a reverse. The major difference between a screen and reverse in publishing is that the screen is used with shades of gray instead of a solid, black color. Also, with a screen, the text color may be light or dark depending upon the shade of the background.

> **NOTE**
>
> This note is a self-referential Note. The top line of this note contains a reverse of the word "NOTE". The rest of this note is in a screen. Notice that in the reverse, the text is white; the background is very dark gray, but it is not completely black. In this screen, the text is black. If the background of the screen were a darker color of gray—say, like the top line—then the actual text of the note could be in white. In general, however, you should avoid long sequences of text such as this in a reverse. Reverses should be reserved for single words or very short phrases.

In Figure 14.5, the highlighting on the word "Person" would generally be considered a screen. Also, the background for the word "Person" is called a *gradient*. A gradient is the gradual changing of shade from one color to another. If you view the document on a color screen, the background changes from a dark blue-black to a dark blue, to a purple, to a pink, and finally to a white.

FIGURE 14.5.

The Person document in the Public Address Book.

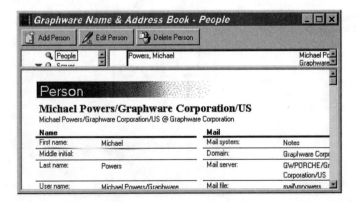

When using screens and reverses, you should typically use a Sans-Serif font (such as Helv), as Lotus has done for the Public Address Book. The reason is that any fonts with thin lines do not work well with reverses. You should also avoid reversing a large amount of text. Headlines, form names, section titles, and so forth are ideal for reversing.

Looking at Letterheads

This is a good time to take a look at the letterheads that are supplied with R4. From the workspace, select your mail database icon. It is typically the icon with your name on it and a picture of an envelope. You do not need to open the database—just select it. Select Actions | Mail Tools | Choose Letterhead. Your screen should resemble Figure 14.6.

FIGURE 14.6.

The Choose Letterhead dialog box.

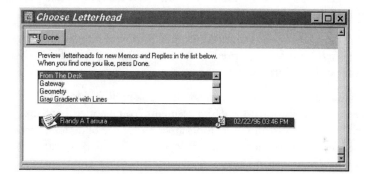

Choosing a letterhead enables you to customize the look of your correspondence. On your system now, choose various options for the letterheads. You'll see that several of the options include gradients, and one is entitled Reversed Teal. This, as we now know, is a letterhead with a solid teal bar with white letters displaying the username.

After you have gone through the list of letterheads, pick one that you like, and set it to be your default letterhead.

Rules

Rules in publishing don't represent the regulations you must abide by. In publishing, rules are just lines. They can be thick or thin, horizontal or vertical. In fact, rules in forms are all around us. If you look back at Figure 14.5, you'll notice that the Person document is full of rules.

You'll also notice that Lotus has divided the form into various areas by using a table. This is a good human-factors technique as well. In general, people can work well with about seven items (plus or minus two). If you open up the Person document in the Public Address Book, you'll find that most of the areas contain five to nine fields. Each area is headed by a keyword with a heavy rule. Each field within the area is separated from others with a thin rule. This makes

14

MAKING YOUR
APPLICATION
WORK WELL

each area easy to differentiate from the others and makes each field separate from the other fields. You can find out more about this form by editing the Person form and seeing how Lotus has defined the various fields. Lotus has used a table for defining many of the fields. This is convenient because the table can automatically generate lines (rules) between rows and columns.

Contrast

A general recommendation for your forms is to use contrast. The reason for this is that items that contrast stand out. You want the titles of your forms to stand out from the rest of the form so that the purpose of the form is clear. Think back to the Person document that Lotus created in Figure 14.5, shown previously. Notice how it uses a reverse with a screen to make the form title really stand out.

You can also introduce contrast through the use of different fonts. For example, you can use a Sans-Serif font for your titles to contrast with Serif fonts for body text. You can use a larger point size to create a size contrast.

Take a moment to browse through this book itself, just looking at the formatting, the headers, reverses, screens, and other design elements. You'll notice that Sans-Serif fonts are used in titles, while normal Roman (Serif) fonts are used for the body text. Notice how different fonts are used for examples such as code listings and how the contrasting fonts make them stand out. You may be able to observe some characteristics that you'd like to use in your own Notes forms and views.

Simplicity and Consistency

In addition to contrast, you should keep your forms and views simple. In general, simple forms are easier to use. When you have a lot of information to display, you can use sections, described later in this chapter, to simplify your form.

Consistency might seem to be in conflict with my recommendation for contrast. However, you should use consistency across forms. For example, pick a format for your form titles. After you have picked the format, use it for all your forms. Look again at the Lotus Public Address Book. You'll find that the titles for each of the different types of documents—Person, Server, Location, and so on—has a consistent look to it. You know, after looking at a few forms, what the title format looks like and can spot the title in the various forms. Each title, however, contrasts with the other items within the form so that the title stands out. So, you should use contrast to differentiate the elements from one another, but you should use consistency for the same type of element across forms.

Enhancing Your Forms

For some practice, you'll now use some of the techniques you learned in this chapter along with the example from Chapter 12, "Developing Forms," and Chapter 13, "Developing Views." If you'll recall from Chapters 12 and 13, we built a small sales-force automation example from scratch. If you built that example, you can use the database that you constructed. If you didn't follow along in Chapters 12 and 13, don't worry—you can pick up where we left off.

In order to complete the examples in this chapter, there are some files on the CD-ROM. They are a set of gradients that have been created for your use. You can also create your own gradients using a desktop graphics program such as CorelDraw!. You will also need a copy of the Microsoft Paintbrush or Microsoft Paint program. MS Paintbrush is normally distributed with every copy of Windows and MS Paint with Windows 95, so you should have a copy either on your hard disk or on your computer network.

You can either use the files directly from the CD-ROM that accompanies this book, or you can copy the files to a working directory on your hard disk. The files are stored on the CD-ROM in a subdirectory called CHAP14. If you want to work from your hard disk, copy all of the files that have names GR*xxxxxx*.PCX to your working subdirectory.

Open the Sales Force Automation database that you created in the last chapter, or open the database SALESF13.NSF that is supplied on CD-ROM. This file is in the \SOURCE\CHAP13 subdirectory. In order to use the SALESF13.NSF database, you must first:

- Copy the database to your Notes data directory.
- With the Windows File Manager or other utility, make sure that the Read-only attribute has been turned off. In Windows 95 you can use the Explorer, right-click on the file, and then select Properties. Deselect the Read-only checkbox.

After you have copied the database to your Notes data directory, you should add the icon for the database to your desktop:

1. Select the workspace page on which you want the icon to appear.
2. Right-click on an empty area of the page.
3. Select Open Database.
4. Scroll through the list of databases until you find the Sales Force Automation database.
5. Click Add Icon.

After the database has been added to your desktop, double-click the database icon to open it. After you have opened the database, click on the twistie next to the Design line to expose the design elements. Click on Forms. One of the forms should be called Company. Double-click on this form. Your screen should now resemble Figure 14.7.

FIGURE 14.7.

Editing the Company form.

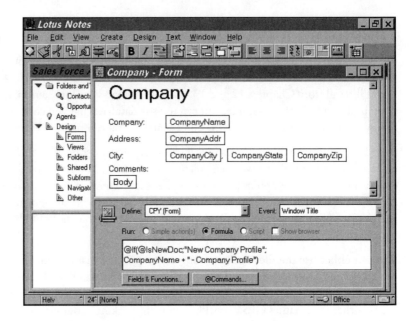

Layout Regions

Layout regions are a type of element new to R4 of Notes, designed to help you lay out your forms. Layout regions are fixed in size and position on your form. Other than rich text, a layout region can contain graphics, buttons, static text, and any other type of field. Also, within a layout region you can easily drag and drop your fields and text to get just the look you want.

You cannot add the following types of fields to a layout region:

■ Attachments

■ Hotspots

■ Links

■ Objects

■ Pop-ups

■ Rich-text fields

■ Sections

■ Tables

You can add fields to the form within or outside a layout region. One major difference between these situations is what happens when the document window is resized. Take, for example, an input field that is placed normally on a form. If you resize the right side of the window to the left so that it comes in contact with the field, Notes will automatically wrap the field to the next line in the window. This way, the field is still visible. The fields are very dynamic. Another example is if a text field is centered. The text within the field is centered relative to the window, so when the window is resized the text moves back and forth to remain centered within the new window size.

Contrast this with the operation of fields within a layout region. In this case, text fields are centered relative to the text box. Resizing the window does not move centered text, and it does not move fields on the form. This is one reason why these regions are called layout regions, because they enable you, the form author, to lay out the form so that it will not change dynamically depending upon user action.

With R4, you now have the best of both worlds. You can make text that moves dynamically depending on user action by putting fields directly in the form. You can also have fields remain static so that you can create a nice-looking form that does not change when resized.

Adding a Layout Region to the Sales Automation Example

Now that you know some basic facts about layout regions, let's create one. You should now be editing the Company form, shown in Figure 14.7. If it is not open, from the Navigator pane click on Design-Forms then double-click on the Company form.

In this section, we'll be adding a gradient screen background to the word Company. If you'd like to see where we're headed, look ahead to Figure 14.12 for an example.

Delete the large word Company from the first line of the form. Delete all extra spaces so that the small word Company: is at the very top of the form. You can ensure this by just deleting characters until you have deleted the C of the small Company:, then reinsert it.

Move the cursor so that it is before the initial C of Company:. Now select Create | Layout Region | New Layout Region. You should see a large, white rectangle with several small black sizing boxes at the sides and bottom of the layout region.

Now we're going to add a graphic to the layout region. Unfortunately, Notes does not provide a direct import option. The only way to import a graphic is to go to another application, copy the graphic to the clipboard, then go back to Notes and paste it into the layout. Although it's a little cumbersome, it works.

If you want, you can now minimize the whole Notes window, but don't close it completely. Start the Microsoft Paint application—or, if you have another graphics application, you could use that instead. In Windows 95, the application is called Microsoft Paint; in Windows 3.1, it is called Paintbrush. Either one should work, but I'll be describing the MS Paint of Windows 95.

Start MS Paint. The icon for the application is generally in the Accessories group. After the application has started, open one of the gradients that was supplied on the CD-ROM that accompanies this book. They are found in the CHAP14 directory. The file type is .PCX, and all of the filenames begin with GR, for gradient. The next six letters are a code to tell you the colors involved. The abbreviations are:

BLU: Blue

CYA: Cyan

PUR: Purple

RED: Red

GRE: Green

YEL: Yellow

ORN: Orange

Load some of them (or look at all of them) into the Paint program and select one that you like. For this example, I have used the Cyan-Yellow gradient. This file is named GRCYAYEL.PCX. (See Figure 14.8.)

FIGURE 14.8.

The Cyan-Yellow gradient loaded into MS Paint.

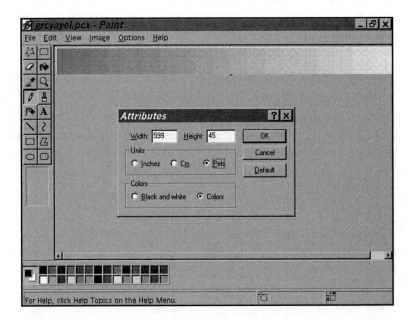

After you have opened the file into Paint, select Edit | Select All. A dotted line should surround the gradient. Select Edit | Copy. The image has now been copied to the clipboard.

Now go back to the Notes workspace. You can do this by pressing Alt+Tab until the Notes workspace appears. Click on the title bar of the Company-Form window to select it. Make sure your layout region is still highlighted within the window. Now select Edit | Paste. You will get a dialog box asking you to paste as either a Graphic or a Graphic Button. Select Graphic and press OK. (See Figure 14.9.)

FIGURE 14.9.

The layout region with the graphic pasted in.

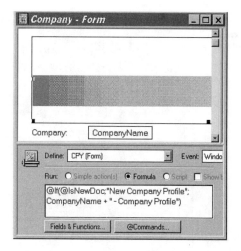

As you can see from Figure 14.9, the gradient and the layout region take up a lot of space. Let's edit this layout a little bit. Click on the gradient. You should see the little highlight black boxes jump and now surround the gradient rather than the layout. Now take your mouse and click on the gradient and drag it up so that it is at the top of the layout region. Make sure it is flush with the top and left boundaries. Now click outside the gradient, but inside the layout region. The layout region should now be highlighted. Click on one of the sizing boxes of the layout region and drag it up so that it is almost flush with the gradient. It doesn't have to be absolutely flush.

Click on the gradient item again to select it, and then press the Design Send to Back SmartIcon. (See Figure 14.10.)

In Figure 14.10, to the left of the Design Send to Back SmartIcon, there are four other icons that become available while you are in the layout editing context. These SmartIcons enable you to bring a design to the front, create a graphic button, create a textbox, and create a hotspot button. These SmartIcons appear in addition to the buttons that create fields and set other properties.

In this case, we're using the SmartIcon to send the design element to the back, but we could also use the menu options to accomplish the same task.

You send the gradient design to the back because you're about to add some text to the layout area, and you want the text to be on top of the gradient. Select Create | Layout Region | Text. A small field called Untitled will appear in the middle of the region.

Drag the field to the left and double-click it. In the Control properties box, change the text to Company. Click on the AZ tab. Change the font size to 24.

Notice that some of the word Company has been clipped so that all of the characters are not visible. This is because the text box was originally sized for much smaller characters. (See Figure 14.11.)

FIGURE 14.10.
The gradient selected and Design Send to Back pressed.

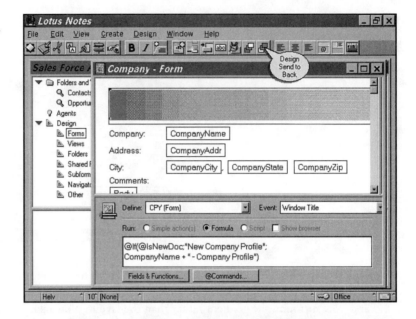

FIGURE 14.11.
The Company text field before resizing.

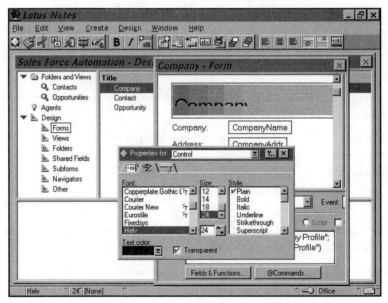

Close the Properties box now.

You can enlarge the text box now by clicking on one of its corners and dragging it to enlarge it. When you have done that, move the word Company so that it is positioned near the left edge of the gradient and vertically centered.

See Figure 14.12 for the final company form title.

FIGURE 14.12.

The Company text field after resizing.

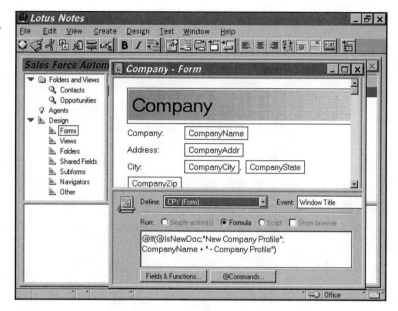

To make your work consistent across the various forms, it is easiest if you copy and paste the work already done. Select the layout region by clicking on one of the borders. You can ensure that it is selected by looking for the dark sizing boxes around the layout outline. Make sure you select the layout region and not just the gradient. If you click on the inside of the layout region you're likely to select either the text Company or the gradient. Try clicking in a few different spots and then make sure that you have selected the full layout region.

Before saving, you must modify one last property of the layout region. Press Alt+Enter or press the Properties SmartIcon button. In the layout properties, make sure Show border is *not* selected. Close the Properties box.

With the layout region selected, choose Edit | Copy. Close the Company form and save it.

Now, double click on the Contact Form to edit it. Delete the large word Contact at the top of the form. Delete everything up to and including the F of First Name. Then replace the F. This ensures there is nothing at the top of the form. Now move your cursor before the F of First and select Edit | Paste. This should paste in the Company header.

Click on the word Company in the layout region to select it. Press Alt+Enter to bring up the Properties box for the text. Replace the text with the word Contact. Press the check mark to the left of the text after you have entered it. After you press the checkmark, it will disappear to indicate Notes has accepted your entry. Figure 14.13 shows the properties box after Notes has accepted your entry.

Close the Properties box, close the form, and save it.

FIGURE 14.13.

The Contact Form with header.

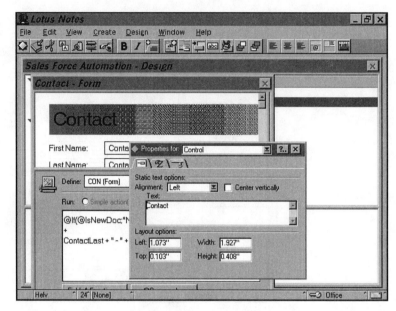

We're on a roll now. Double-click on the Opportunity form. Delete the large word Opportunity at the top of the form. Delete everything up to and including the C of Company. Then replace the C. This ensures there is nothing at the top of the form. Now move your cursor before the C of Company: and select Edit | Paste. This should paste in the Company header.

Click on the word Company in the layout region to select it. Press Alt+Enter to bring up the properties box for the text. Replace the text with the word Opportunity. Press the check mark to the left of the text after you have entered it. (See Figure 14.14.)

You can now close all the dialog boxes and look at the documents you have previously created. They should be using the reversed titles you created.

Subforms

Subforms are another new feature of R4 of Notes that can be used to improve the look of your forms and to promote consistency. Subforms can contain all the same elements as forms, such as fields, rich-text fields, layout regions, and so forth. With subforms, you have a lot of new flexibility in designing your forms. Subforms can be directly included to promote consistency, and you can also use a feature called *computed subforms* to dynamically pick the subform to show to the user.

You can use computed subforms, for example, to pick between a detailed loan application for high-credit risks, or an abbreviated loan application for low-risk applicants. The basic data on the form can remain the same, but you can switch to a more-or-less detailed subform. You could use computed subforms in many applications where you have some data that is the same on several forms, but detailed information varies by process, applicant, user, or some other characteristic.

To examine a real application of computed subforms, take another look at the e-mail application that Lotus distributes with Notes. Open up your mail database, click on the design twistie in the navigation pane, then double-click on the Memo form. You will get a warning message about editing the form. Click Yes to close the warning dialog box. You won't be editing this form; we just want to take a look at it.

FIGURE 14.14.

The Opportunity Form with header.

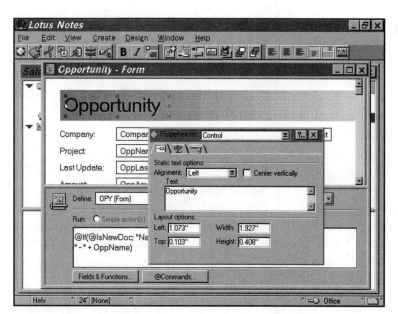

In Figure 14.15 you can see the highlighted line Computed Subform. This is an indication that this area of the form is to contain a computed subform, so it cannot be shown because the text editor does not know which form to show. If you look at the formula area you can see the formula used to select which subform will be displayed. The result of the formula is the name of the subform to display. You can see from the formula that the default subform is StdNotesLtr16.

Actually, this computed subform is used by Notes to select the letterhead used for your memos. A similar technique is used to implement the mood-stamp feature of Notes. Scroll down in the memo-form definition to see if you can find the mood-stamp implementation. You can now close the memo form.

In Figure 14.16, you can see the subform list shown with the Choose Letterhead dialog box. It's fairly clear where the letterhead choices are coming from: subforms. You can easily implement a similar feature for your applications with computed subforms.

FIGURE 14.15.
Inside the Memo form.

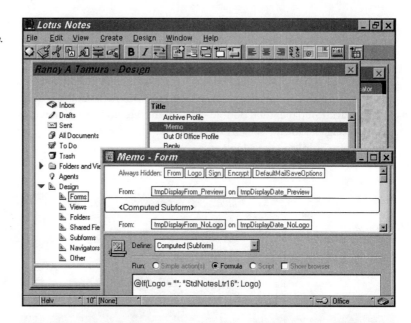

FIGURE 14.16.
Subform list with Choose Letterhead dialog box.

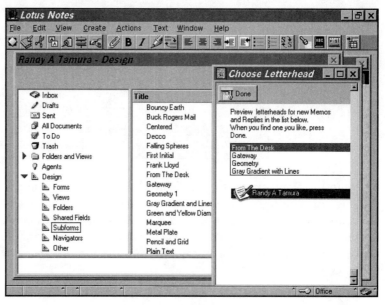

You create a subform in a manner very similar to creating a regular form. You can create it from the design menu with Create | Design | Subform. After the Design dialog box opens, you add fields the same way as you do for forms. One point to remember, though, is that when a subform is inserted into a form, the field names must be unique. Be careful when naming your fields, so that you don't get a conflict between fields on your subform and fields on the main form or other subforms.

For a similar reason, you cannot insert the same subform into a form more than once. One reason for this is that the names of the subform are sure to conflict with the previous instance of the same subform. You probably wouldn't do this directly, but you must be careful about this happening with computed subforms where the user may have some part in selecting the subform to be shown.

To summarize, subforms are useful tools that you can use to get a consistent look to your forms. You can create subforms, and spend a significant amount of time to get just the right aesthetic look to them. Once you have invested this time, you may use them over and over throughout the forms for your applications. You must, however, make sure that you carefully watch your naming conventions so that you will not get conflicts when you start to use the subforms from many different forms.

Sections

Sections are a feature of Notes that can be used to improve both the usability and aesthetic quality of your forms. As a general rule, users will have difficulty when forms display too much information. This information overload means that it takes users much longer to fill out forms when creating them, and it takes them longer to find important information when viewing them.

Sections are a way to simplify the user interface. Remember that one of the most important design rules to follow is to simplify the interface. After you have done that, simplify it again. To paraphrase an old saying, simplify the interface so that it is as simple as possible to get the job done, but no simpler. Easier said than done. (See Figure 14.17.)

FIGURE 14.17.

A Server document in the Public Address Book.

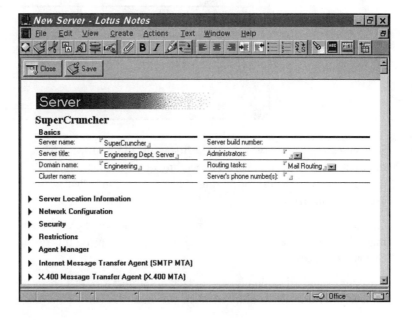

If you look at Figure 14.17, you notice that Lotus has used sections very effectively in the Server document of the Public Address Book. Notice that there is just basic information at the top of the form. This basic information is the main information for the server and so should be available all the time.

The rest of the information in the document is fairly specialized and unless you happen to be interested in it would just clutter up the document with a lot of extraneous information. Within each of the sections, there can be a lot of extra information.

In Figure 14.18 you see the first section of the server document expanded. Notice that this one section fills the entire screen. This information is probably the second most important information (after the basic information) and so it is found in the first section. Notice that although this is important information, it does not necessarily change frequently. For example, a server is unlikely to frequently change its local time zone.

FIGURE 14.18.
Server Location Information.

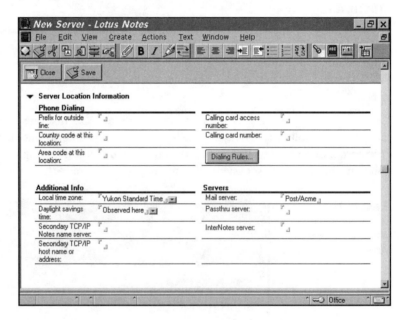

Sections can be used in two ways. The first is just to simplify the form. With a twistie at its left, the section can be open or closed depending upon various conditions. The second use for sections is to control access for editing. These access-controlled sections can be edited only by users that you enable.

Controlled-access sections are not a true security measure because the fields within the section might be modifiable via some other form, but you can use this feature to make inadvertent changes less likely.

Creating a standard section is easy. In fact, it's almost fun. Just create the lines and areas of the form as you normally would. Highlight the lines that you would like to make into a section;

then select Create | Section | Standard. Your lines will be collapsed into a section.

As a Notes user, you can use the same technique within a rich text field while you are editing a document to create a section. In fact, you can even create sections that contain other sections.

After you have created the section, right-click on its header line. Select Section Properties. This will bring up the Properties box. You can then change the title of the section and the Expand | Collapse properties. For the Expand | Collapse properties you can control whether the section is automatically (in other words, initially) expanded or collapsed in the following situations:

- When the document is in the preview window
- When the document is opened for reading
- When the document is opened for editing
- When the document is printed

In addition, you can control whether the title line is visible when the section is expanded, and you can specify that the section is expandable only in preview mode. If you choose this last option, when the document is in read or edit mode the section twistie is not shown and all of the fields look as if they are just normal parts of the form.

Shared Fields

The name "shared fields" in Notes is almost a misnomer. From the name you might expect that shared fields are used for sharing data, but they're not. Shared fields are actually used for sharing the properties of a field. For example, suppose you have a field called CompanyName that you have defined as a text field. If you define this field as a shared field, you can share the field properties such as the data type, the font, size, help description, and so forth among several forms.

If you define the field CompanyName as a shared field, and then use it on several forms, the data contents of the CompanyName field are *not* shared from one form to another. Again, a shared field means that the definition of the field properties is shared, not the data itself.

In order to share data between forms, you must program the forms or fields to transfer the data. In the example from Chapters 12 and 13, this was done by defining formulas that would transfer the information from one form to another. You can review those chapters to see how that was done.

For an example of shared field properties, look at Figure 14.19. You'll notice that for the CompanyName shared field, it is type Text and is Editable. There are a variety of other properties, such as fonts, alignments, and so forth within the Shared Field property InfoBox.

Also notice that shared fields can have events, such as the Entering Event and the Exiting Event. These events occur when the user's cursor enters or exits the field. If you program some

FIGURE 14.19.

Shared Field Properties and Events.

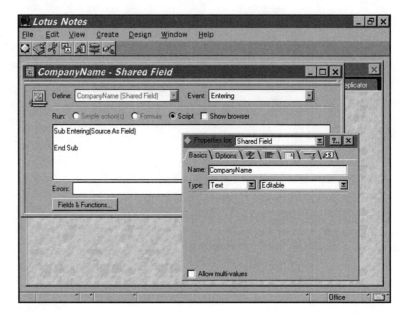

LotusScript code for these events, by using shared fields you can have a consistent set of actions for your fields across all of your forms. For example, on the CompanyName field you may want to do validity checking when the user exits the field. By coding this checking once and making the field a shared field, all forms that include the field gain the advantage of the validity checking.

The main reasons for using shared fields are:

- To promote consistency in both visual appearance and user interaction when the same field is used on multiple forms
- To save some space in the database because the field definition needs to be stored only once for all forms
- To make maintenance easier because only one definition will need to be changed for all forms if the field definition changes

NOTE

If you are just beginning to design your database, you can make all your fields single-use fields. After you have laid out all of your forms and fields and have gone through some of the inevitable iterations, it will be easier to decide which fields to make shared fields. You can convert a single-use field into a shared field as your design matures.

The reason why shared fields are important when considering the aesthetic appeal and usability of your forms is that they are a tool to promote consistency. When the same field is used on several forms, it should look the same each time. It should use the same font and size and if there are usability characteristics (such as entering or exiting events), these should also be shared so the user has a consistent experience with the field on all forms where it is used.

Enhancing Your Views

You can improve the usability of your views in several ways. This section covers some of these features. I'll show you how to add color and actions to your views. Actions, as you saw in Chapter 12, enable you to make your forms easier to use. Actions can also be used with views to make common user activities more accessible from the menu and from action buttons.

Colorful Views

New with R4 of Notes is the ability to have alternating colors on every other line of your view. In addition, you have control over a variety of other features as well. To see how this works, open the Sales Force Automation database you have created and used before. See Figure 14.20 for an example of how our view will appear after we have made some changes.

FIGURE 14.20.

Alternating colors in lines of a view.

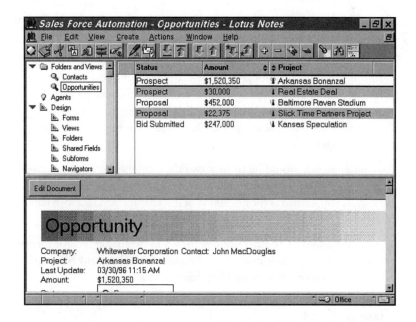

Open the Opportunities view by doing the following. Select View | Design. Click on Views in the Navigator pane, then double-click on Opportunities. When the

Opportunities view appears, select Edit | Properties. When the Properties box appears, click on the S tab. (See Figure 14.21.)

FIGURE 14.21.

The View Properties dialog box.

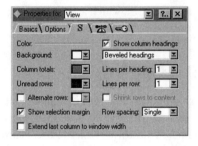

As you can see, there are several options for adjusting the way your view appears to the user. Under the Color section, you can select the background color. If you would like a solid light-yellow background, you can press the pulldown button next to the background color and then select it.

The Column Totals color is used for the text color of fields that are totaled. Note that it is the color of the detailed rows, not the total row that is affected by this setting. The Unread Rows color, as you might imagine, is the color of text for rows that have not yet been read.

To enable alternate row coloring, you must first select the checkbox that appears just before Alternate Rows. After you select the checkbox, the color pulldown will be enabled. Click on the pulldown and select a color.

When picking color combinations for your views, it's best to avoid dark color backgrounds. White and Cyan are a pleasing pair, as are white and pale yellow. If you think about it for a moment, the colored rows behave like the screens mentioned at the beginning of this chapter. Because you will likely be using black text, you want to pick two background colors that contrast well with black.

Another approach would be to pick two dark colors and have a light color as the text color. This method is not recommended, however, because typically the fonts used for text will be narrow. As you learned at the beginning of this chapter, reverses with narrow, stroked text should be avoided.

You can try some of the other options shown in the dialog box for formatting the View. They each operate pretty much as you would expect. If you have any other questions about the properties, you can access the Notes Help feature.

View Actions

In Chapter 12, you added action buttons to the forms created for the Sales Automation application. You can also add action buttons to Views. Actions that you add to views will typically be of a different type than form actions. This is because form actions are always acting in the context of a specific document. View actions do not necessarily (although they might) have a specific document context.

Let's create a View action now. We'll create an action using one of the built-in actions of Notes. To create the view action, from the Navigator pane select Design | Views. Then in the right-hand view pane, double-click on the Contacts View. After the View has been opened, open the action pane by using the SmartIcon, by using the mouse to adjust the pane, or from the View menu. (See Figure 14.22.)

FIGURE 14.22.

Contacts view with the action pane open.

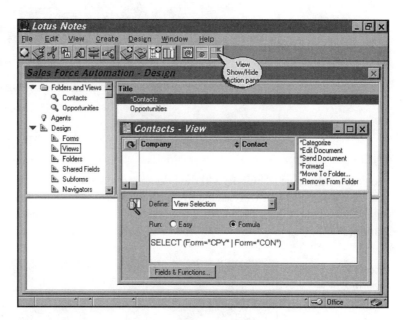

Notice that there are several built-in actions that you can use with your views. As with forms, you can also specify your own custom actions as well.

Double click on the *Edit Document action. When the dialog box appears, enable the Include action in button bar option. Select an icon to represent editing the document. You can use the same one you did for Chapter 12, which was the second row, third icon. (See Figure 14.23.)

NOTE

You should note that although I've been using the second row, third icon to represent the "Edit" action, Notes uses the icon at the first row, sixth position. It is a red pencil with a curl next to it. You can use the Notes default if you would prefer to be consistent with Notes. I've only used a different icon for illustrative purposes.

14

MAKING YOUR
APPLICATION
WORK WELL

FIGURE 14.23.

Action View icons.

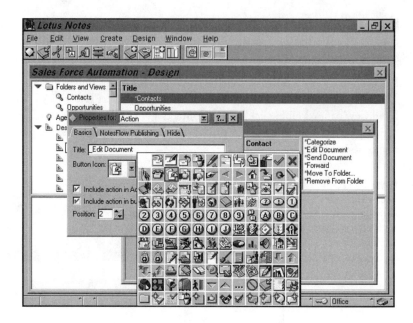

Now, using the same technique, add the Edit action to your Opportunities view as well. Once you have done this, you will be able to go directly into edit mode on any of the documents in either of your Views. Figure 14.24 shows the Contacts View with the new edit action button.

FIGURE 14.24.

Contacts View with edit action.

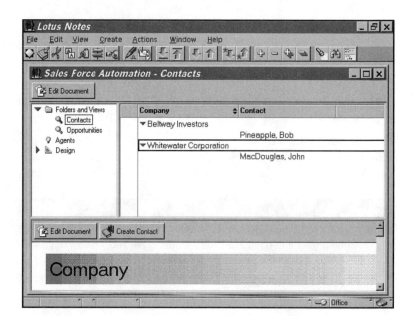

You can also create custom actions for Views. We will not be doing this for our example, but if you want to do this you can select Create | Action (you must already be editing the view). You will be shown the Properties box for the action. You should add a name for the action, an icon, and you can decide whether the action should be included in the action menu and/or the action button bar. Once you have done this, you can specify a simple action, formula or LotusScript program to be executed when the action is invoked.

Summary

In this chapter, I've covered some fundamentals of desktop publishing as they apply to designing your Notes Forms. Many of the concepts that I've described are exemplified in the new Notes databases and templates. Take some time to review the databases supplied with Notes. They provide a wealth of information and are generally very good examples of application design.

Some of the fundamentals I've covered include fonts, reverses, screens, and rules. I've also covered contrast, which should be used on your forms to highlight and create interest. Contrast can occur between large and small, between light and dark, and between various colors. After using contrast to highlight elements, use consistency when formatting similar objects. However you decide to format your titles, use the same formatting for all of your titles.

Keep it simple.

I've covered many of the tools you can use on your Forms and Views: subforms, layout regions, sections, and shared fields. You can also use color now on your views on alternating rows. This produces a very pleasing effect and makes it easier to read Views, especially if there is a lot of white space on some of your lines.

I've also covered view actions. They are very similar to form actions. Several of the most common and useful actions built into Notes. You can also create your own custom actions and associate a simple action, formula or LotusScript program to be run when the user activates the action. Actions are important to aid in the usability of your Forms and Views.

Spend some time on the aesthetics and usability of your Forms and Views. Although it may mean a few extra minutes or hours for you as a designer, your users will be using these applications for days, months, or years. Make your applications compelling, vibrant, and beautiful as well as functional.

14

MAKING YOUR
APPLICATION
WORK WELL

Using Lotus Components

by Thomas L. Fredell

IN THIS CHAPTER

Years ago, Apple released the AppleWorks software package for the Apple II series of computers. AppleWorks was unique because it provided all of the essential "office productivity" tools within a single, easy-to-use interface. It contained a simple spreadsheet tool, database, and word processor; other software vendors such as Microsn8d and Borland followed the lead with similar integrated application packages. With the addition of the Lotus Components, Lotus Notes can serve as a modern, turbo-charged version of the integrated software package concept.

Lotus Components allow Lotus Notes to perform the task of all of the typical office productivity applications. The components are OLE servers that also function as ActiveX controls. This means that you can embed the components as objects within Notes, WordPro, Microsoft Word, or any OLE object container. But it also means that you can plug the components into a Visual Basic program, or into an ActiveX template for use with Web browsers.

This chapter covers how to install these components, how to include them within your applications, and how to customize them. Examples are given for each of the components available in the current release.

The Components

The current Lotus Components release includes the following components:

- Chart allows you to create charts and graphs in numerous formats.
- Comment allows you to create formatted comments with access control.
- Draw/Diagram can be used to generate drawings or diagrams.
- File Viewer provides the capability to include a file within a viewer window inside a Notes document.
- Project Scheduler allows you to generate a project with tasks and display them using a GANTT chart.
- Spreadsheet allows you to enter numbers and perform calculations.

This chapter describes the process involved in installing the components, inserting the components into a document, and performing tasks using the components.

The components are conveniently available from a small toolbar that floats in the Lotus Notes workspace menu bar.

Lotus Components can be used to significantly enhance your Notes applications by adding functionality that was only available in other applications. For example, a budgeting application built in Notes can now have built-in spreadsheets and pie charts. An expense report database can have a custom component that guides a user through filling out expense reports, including such things as automatic totaling. Previously, the user had to attach spreadsheet files or use the clumsy Notes F/X interface.

Getting Started with Lotus Components

You can acquire the Lotus Components distribution from the Lotus Web site at `http://www.lotus.com`. Information about the components and licensing options is also available online at this site.

Lotus Components are very easy to use. Installing the components is simple, and adding them into a Notes document is also very easy. The following sections give brief instructions about installing and inserting Lotus Components.

Installing Lotus Components

Installing the components is very easy; Lotus provides an excellent setup program that does almost all of the work for you. When running the setup program, you only need to specify the path to your `notes.ini` file. The components add a `AddInMenus=` line to your `notes.ini` file. The change to the `.ini` file provides the hook used by the Lotus Components toolbar to display itself when Notes is launched.

The `AddInMenus=` line contains a pointer to the Lotus components DLL. The default points to the components directory, c:\lotusc~1\runtime\lcpln10.dll.

Inserting a Component in a Document

To insert a component in a Notes document, put your cursor in a rich-text field and then click on the Lotus Components toolbar. When you click on the toolbar, a list of available components will appear. Figure 15.1 shows the Lotus Components toolbar with the expanded component list.

FIGURE 15.1.

The Lotus Components toolbar.

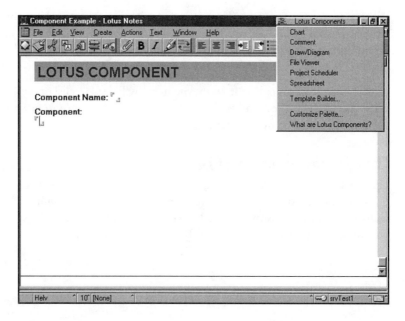

15

USING LOTUS
COMPONENTS

The Lotus Components toolbar is sensitive to the current context. The two Notes containers that can handle OLE objects are rich-text fields and form designs. If you click on the toolbar when you aren't in a rich-text field or form design, the toolbar will display the component names in grayed text.

Component Behavior

Lotus Components use all of the useful features of OLE in-place editing to integrate seamlessly into the Notes environment. When a component is selected, the SmartIcons will change to reflect component actions. The menu bar will also change. When you insert a chart, for example, the menu bar changes from File, Edit, View, Create, Actions, Text, Window, and Help to File, Edit, Chart, Applet, Help, and Window. The contents of the Help menu also change. For the chart, the Help menu options are Using the Chart Component, Programming with the Chart Component, and About the Chart Component.

Online Component Help

All of the components provide excellent online help with Windows 95 standard table of contents and keyword search functionality. Each component has two help files: one contains detailed usage information and the other contains programming information.

The Chart Component

The Chart component allows you to create charts using a variety of formatting styles. You can insert a chart in a document by clicking on the Lotus Components toolbar and selecting Chart. Figure 15.2 shows a Chart component that has been inserted in the body of a Notes mail message.

When you create a chart in a Notes document, it will be displayed in a three-dimensional bar chart format with some default data. You'll notice that the SmartIcons change to reflect the various options available for the chart object. The menu bar also changes to exclude irrelevant options, as well as to include the new Chart option.

Clicking on the Chart option from the menu bar will display a list of the various characteristics of the chart that may be modified. It also provides the Edit Data option, which is used to change the data series plotted by the chart.

Changing the Format of a Chart

Literally every visual detail for a chart can be controlled and modified. To change chart options, you can use the aforementioned Chart menu, or you can right-click on the chart object to display a context-sensitive menu. The context-sensitive menu will display the Chart Properties option. Figure 15.3 shows the InfoBox that is displayed when this menu option is selected.

FIGURE 15.2.
The Chart component.

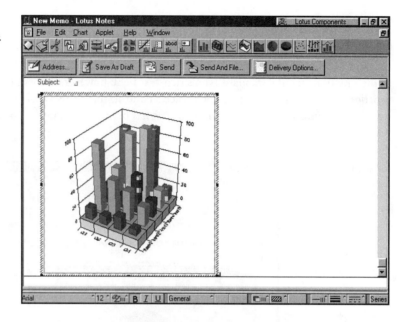

FIGURE 15.3.
The Chart Properties option's InfoBox.

There are many different chart types: bar charts, line charts, area charts, pie charts, hi/low/close charts, scatter charts, and mixed charts.

After you select a chart type, the InfoBox will display several small squares containing icons that represent different charting options. For example, if the bar chart type is selected, the icons will change to represent various bar chart formats, including two-dimensional and three-dimensional bar charts.

NOTE

One of the best chart formats is the pie chart. If you are charting multiple data series, you can select the multiple pie chart option. Each pie chart will represent one data series. You do this by selecting pie as the chart type and selecting the picture of multiple charts on the left. It's particularly neat because the overall size of each pie chart is determined relative to the other pie charts.

15

USING LOTUS COMPONENTS

The Comment Component

The Comment component allows you to create a rich-text comment within the body of a Notes rich-text field. In many respects, it's like a document within a document. It doesn't provide all of the functionality of a standard Notes rich-text field; however, it does provide some unique functionality, such as an icon view and access control, that is unavailable with standard rich-text fields. Figure 15.4 shows a comment that has been inserted in the body of a Notes rich-text field.

FIGURE 15.4.

A Comment component within a rich-text field.

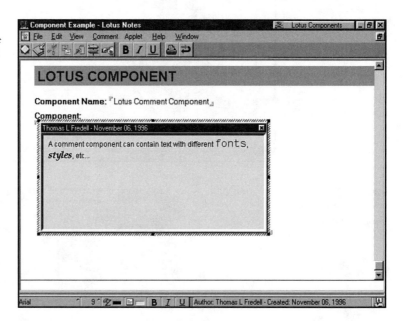

The contents of a comment can use different fonts, character styles, and character sizes. The fill color for the entire text body can be set from the properties box. The properties box also provides the capability to set access levels for the comment. Access levels may be set to No Protection, Private (so that the comment can only be read or edited by the original author), Protected (so that the author can read and edit and all others can read), or Custom (which allows the comment creator to specify access on a user-by-user basis).

When comments are minimized, they are displayed as small icons that look very similar to Notes document links. Figure 15.5 shows a minimized comment and a Notes document link.

Comments can also be printed as individual documents. To do so, select Comment | Print Comment.

FIGURE 15.5.

A minimized Comment component.

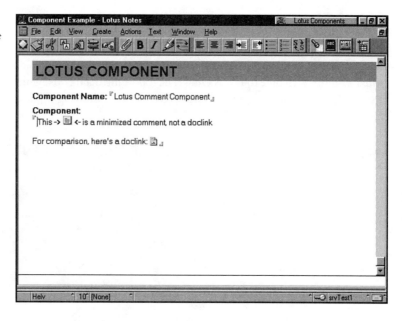

Specifying Custom Comment Access Control

The levels of access control available for comments are very similar to the standard Notes access control levels. The types of access are

No Access

Depositor

Reader

Editor

Manager

Pvt Manager (Private Manager)

Default access can be specified using the [All Others] setting.

The access control features of the comment object make it very useful for adding annotations to sensitive documents, such as documents in Human Resources' databases. In a Human Resources database, comments about salary, bonuses, and vacation time could be incorporated into a comment object that is only available to authorized personnel.

The Draw/Diagram Component

The Draw/Diagram component allows you to create a drawing or diagram within a Notes rich-text field. When you insert a Draw/Diagram component into a Notes document, you are presented with the Welcome to Lotus Draw/Diagramming dialog box, which asks you if you want to start with a template diagram or begin from a blank drawing. Figure 15.6 shows the Welcome dialog box.

FIGURE 15.6.

The Draw/Diagram component Welcome dialog box.

Using a Draw/Diagram Template

If you select the option labeled Use a ready-made diagram, you will be presented with a dialog box that prompts you to select a diagram or clip art, as shown in Figure 15.7.

FIGURE 15.7.

The ready-made diagram-selection dialog box.

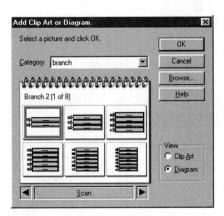

The Draw/Diagram component comes with an extensive variety of standard diagram templates. The templates are listed in the following categories:

- Branch diagrams can be used to illustrate processes that have multiple outputs or parallel paths.

- Flow diagrams illustrate various types of process flows, ranging from standard sequential processes to feedback loops.

■ Standard graph layouts include bubble graphs, which can be used to illustrate relationships between items based on attributes, bell-curve charts, and so on.

■ Hub diagrams provide layouts that correspond to various types of hub-oriented topologies. Most of the hub charts include a central shape that has connecting lines to surrounding shapes.

■ Pyramid diagrams provide the capability to illustrate hierarchical data relationships.

■ Section diagrams can be used to illustrate various types of relationships between objects in a system. Some section diagram types include donuts and three-dimensional cubes.

■ Timeline diagrams show the sequence of events that occur over a time range.

■ Venn diagrams can be used to illustrate the relationships between sets of items.

Each template category provides a number of different diagram styles. There are a total of 99 standard styles available from the Draw/Diagram component.

Figure 15.8 shows a diagram that was created using one of the standard branch diagram templates.

FIGURE 15.8.

A standard branch diagram.

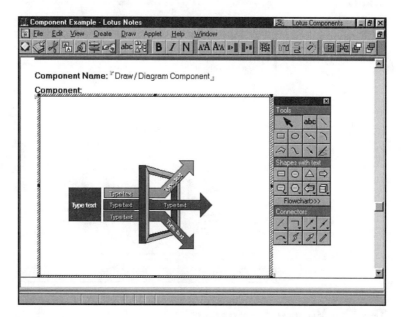

Using a Blank Drawing

If the standard Draw/Diagram templates don't fit your needs, you can begin with a blank drawing pad. All of the shapes used in the standard templates are available from a floating tool palette that appears to the right of the drawing pad.

The drawing component provides clip art that can be used in your drawing or diagram. The two clip art categories that are standard in the Draw/Diagram component are Network, which provides pictures of computers and other hardware, and People, which includes pictures of people in various poses.

> **NOTE**
>
> If you decide to use a standard template, you aren't forced by the Draw/Diagram component to utilize the specific look provided by the standard template. You can modify the generated diagram in whatever manner is necessary, including deleting drawing elements. It is frequently useful to start with a template that approximates your needs and then modify the auto-generated result.

Figure 15.9 shows a diagram that was created without using a diagram template. Some standard diagram clip art has been added to illustrate what's available using the component.

FIGURE 15.9.

A diagram with clip art.

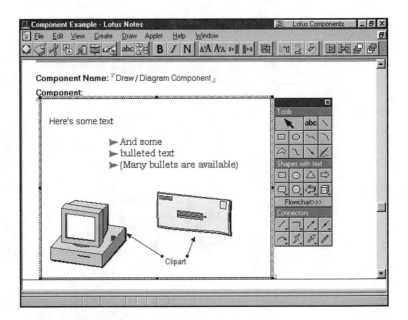

The File Viewer Component

The File Viewer component can be used to include a file within the body of a Notes rich-text field. The File Viewer can handle a variety of file formats, including standard graphic and document formats. It provides zooming capabilities and integrated printing capabilities that preserve the original look of the associated file. Figure 15.10 shows a File Viewer component that displays a Microsoft PowerPoint file within a rich-text field.

FIGURE 15.10.

A File Viewer component in a Notes document.

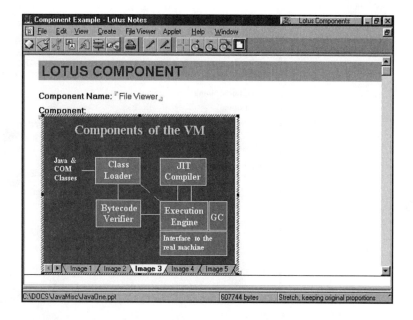

Using the File Viewer component provides somewhat more functionality than the standard viewer that is integrated with Notes version 4. Within Notes, you can select an attachment and use the View command to display it using the Notes viewer. Within the document containing the attachment, the only visible indicator is an attachment icon. However, if you use the File Viewer component, the body of the file is displayed within the Notes rich-text field. It's also better than using an embedded OLE object because other users only require the File Viewer component—not a number of different applications—to interact with the file.

The Project Scheduler Component

The Project Scheduler component provides a fully functional project scheduling management tool within a small, lightweight OLE object. The project scheduler breaks down projects into tasks with designated durations. The tasks are displayed in a table format with a dynamically updated GANTT chart displayed to the right of the tasks. Figure 15.11 shows a project that has been created in a Notes document.

Adding Tasks to a Project

To add a task to a project, enter the task name in the Tasks column. Press Tab to move to the Start Date column. When you press Tab, the date will default to the current date. The Duration column will also default to one day.

FIGURE 15.11.
A Project Scheduler component in a Notes document.

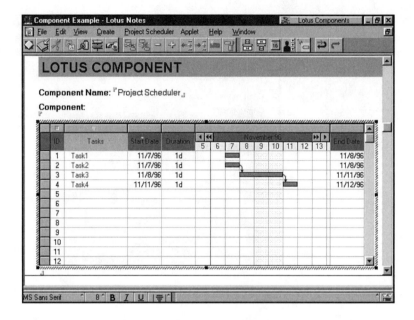

To add another task, go to the next row in the Tasks list and perform the aforementioned steps. When you enter the second task, you will notice that it is automatically linked in sequence to the first task. To insert a task between existing tasks, right-click on the task that you wish to follow the new task. A context-sensitive pop-up menu will appear. Select Insert New Row from the menu. When you've defined the task name and duration, you'll notice that the new task will automatically be linked to the tasks between which it was inserted.

> **NOTE**
>
> Most of the functions that are listed in the menu bar are also available from the context menu, depending on the target of your right-click. Using the context menu can save time because it presents less choices and the menu appears where you click. However, if you prefer, you can use the menu option on the menu bar to perform the same functions.

Working with Subtasks

To create subtasks, define the supertask the same way that you would define a standard task. Next, create a task that you want to be a subtask. As previously described, the second task will automatically be linked to the supertask. To indicate that the second task should be a subtask of the supertask, right-click on the second task and select Demote Task from the context menu.

After you select Demote Task, the second task will become indented, and the supertask will now have down-arrow indicators that enable you to collapse and expand its subtasks. The shape of the supertask's bar in the GANTT chart will also change to reflect its status as a supertask. Figure 15.12 shows a project after a task has been demoted to a subtask.

FIGURE 15.12.

A task that has been demoted to a subtask.

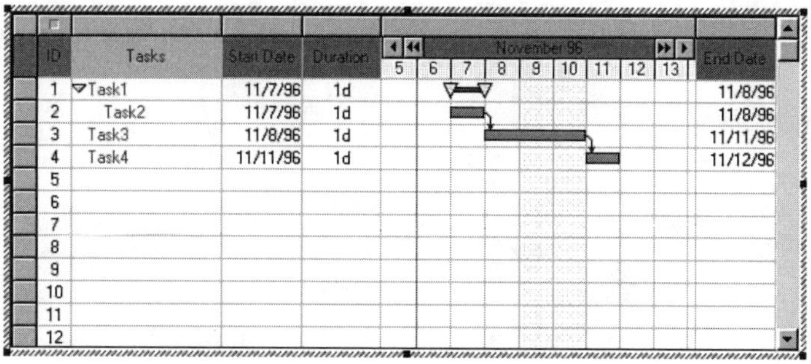

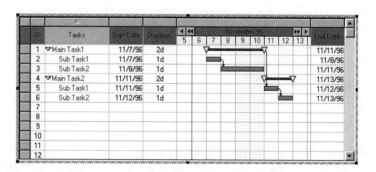

You'll notice that the supertask's duration is dependent on the subtask. As you add more subtasks, the length of the supertask will increase, and visa-versa if you delete subtasks. To add additional subtasks, you can go to the row underneath the first subtask and enter the new task. It will automatically be indented and listed as a subtask of the supertask. If you don't want it to be a subtask, you can promote it by using Promote Task from the context menu or menu bar (under the Project Scheduler menu option).

To link two supertasks together, you can link a subtask of the second supertask to the first supertask. Figure 15.13 shows a link between the first subtask in a supertask and a preceding supertask.

FIGURE 15.13.

A link from a supertask to a subtask.

Creating Milestones and Milestone Lines

To create a milestone, enter a task with the name of the milestone. The task will appear as a standard task. Change the duration of the task to zero days. When you change the duration, the task will be displayed using a diamond shape. You can link milestones to following tasks; this allows you to define the structure of your schedule without being dependent on links between individual subtasks.

You can also create *milestone lines*. Milestone lines appear as colored, vertical lines in your schedule. Unlike milestones, you can't create links between milestone lines and project tasks. However, they can be very useful to reflect strict calendar deadlines that are independent of project tasks. Figure 15.14 shows a project that uses milestones and milestone lines.

FIGURE 15.14.

A project with milestones and milestone lines.

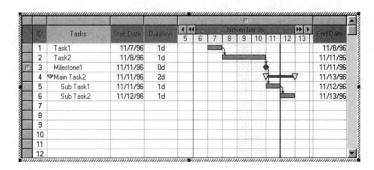

Limitations of the Project Scheduler Component

Unfortunately, the current release of the project scheduler does not provide the capability to add resources to a project and assign resources to project tasks. As the Project Scheduler component is updated, it will no doubt become more useful and fully functional. Already it represents a lightweight solution that easily allows you to share a schedule among people who use Lotus Notes.

The Spreadsheet Component

The Spreadsheet component provides a very functional spreadsheet within the body of a Notes rich-text field. When you create a spreadsheet, you'll be presented with a numeric row, alphabetic column layout that will be immediately familiar to you if you have previously used a spreadsheet program. Figure 15.15 shows a Spreadsheet component that has been inserted in the body of a Notes document.

As you can tell from the picture, the Spreadsheet component provides most standard spreadsheet functionality including multiple worksheets, cell formulas, and various cell formatting options.

CAUTION

As bizarre as it may seem, the Lotus Spreadsheet component provides no undo capability. Be very careful when you make changes that affect a large number of cells! You will have to manually undo any of your changes.

FIGURE 15.15.

A Spreadsheet component in a Notes document.

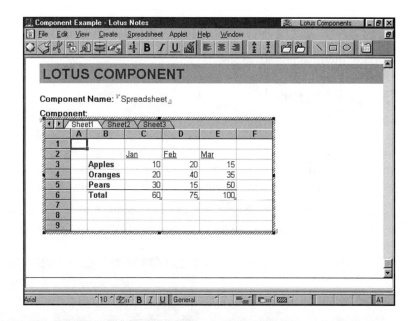

> **NOTE**
>
> In order to view a cell formula, you must press the F2 key while the cursor is in the cell you want to view. The cell will display a small gray square as an indication that it contains a formula.

Cell Validation

It's possible to specify validation formulas within cells in a Spreadsheet component. To enter a validation formula, highlight a cell and select Spreadsheet | Range Properties. An InfoBox containing cell information will appear. Click on the key icon to display the page containing the validation formula. Figure 15.16 shows a cell's property page with a validation formula that ensures that only numbers are entered.

FIGURE 15.16.

A cell validation formula.

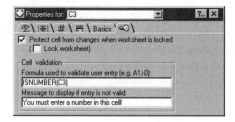

The validation formula is not as sophisticated as Notes, but it does provide support for basic data validation. You can use any standard worksheet function, including functions that use ranges of information such as SUM.

Using Fill-by-Example

One of the useful timesavers built in to the spreadsheet component is the fill-by-example capability, which allows you to fill a range of cells based on a short sample. It's very useful for month names; for example, in one cell enter the month January. Select the cell containing January and the adjacent cells that you would like to autofill. Next, select Spreadsheet | Fill By Example. The adjacent cells will automatically be filled with month names.

You can add additional fill-by-example lists by selecting Create | SmartFill Lists. You will be prompted with a dialog box that displays the currently available lists, as shown in Figure 15.17.

FIGURE 15.17.

Default SmartFill lists.

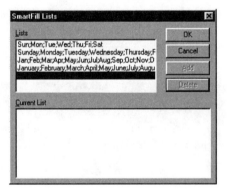

To add a new list, enter the list elements in the text box titled Current List. Use a semicolon to separate list elements. When you've finished, click the Add button to save the new SmartFill list. When you return to the spreadsheet, you will be able to use the same automatic fill capability that you use with month names, and so on.

Changing Spreadsheet Scrollbars and Other View Parameters

The spreadsheet component allows fine-tuned control over the display of the worksheet. You can determine whether or not scrollbars are allowable, which enables you to create a spreadsheet that can only be used to display a certain number of rows and columns. You can also hide column and row headings, and combined with the ability to lock cells, this allows you to create spreadsheet-based data entry forms.

Creating Charts Using Spreadsheet Data

To create a chart using data from a Spreadsheet component, insert a Chart component into a rich-text field. Next, select the information you want to plot from the Spreadsheet component. Choose Edit | Copy or select Copy from the context menu. Next, select the chart and choose Edit | Paste. Figure 15.18 shows a chart that has been filled using data from a Spreadsheet component.

FIGURE 15.18.

Charted data from a Spreadsheet component.

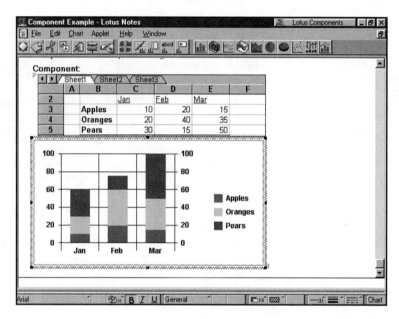

You'll notice that the chart has changed to reflect the pasted information. The data in the spreadsheet doesn't maintain any connection to the data plotted in the chart; to create a dynamically updated chart, you must use a link to the spreadsheet data.

Before you can create a link to a spreadsheet, you must name the spreadsheet object. You can do so by selecting Spreadsheet | Spreadsheet Properties. The Spreadsheet InfoBox will appear. Enter a name for the spreadsheet in the text box next to the Object name: label. Figure 15.19 shows a spreadsheet object that has been named using the InfoBox.

Next, select the data that you want to plot. Copy the data using the menu bar, context menu, or keyboard. Next, select the chart and then select Edit | Paste Link. Test the connection from the spreadsheet to the chart by changing information that's used for the plot.

FIGURE 15.19.

A named spreadsheet object.

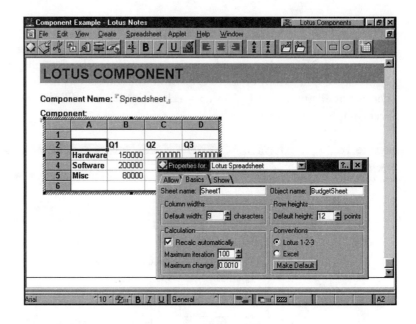

A somewhat faster alternative is to drag and drop a link from the spreadsheet into the chart. To do so, select the desired data in the spreadsheet. Next, move the pointer to the edge of the data selection until the pointer changes into a small hand. Hold down the Ctrl and Shift keys, press and hold the left mouse button, and then drag the mouse pointer to the chart. When the mouse is over the chart, it will change to an arrow with a square drag indicator to let you know that the chart is a valid drop target. Release the mouse button when the mouse pointer is over the chart, and the chart will change to reflect the newly linked information.

Exporting and Importing Spreadsheet Component Data

The Spreadsheet component supports exporting and importing in a variety of data formats. Available export formats include standard spreadsheet types such as Lotus 1-2-3, Microsoft Excel, and Formula One, various text formats, and a special Lotus Spreadsheet component format. The Spreadsheet component also provides the capability to import using any of these formats.

NOTE

When you import into a Spreadsheet component, the entire contents of the component spreadsheet will be replaced with the imported data.

Using Component Templates

Lotus Components also comes with a tool called the Template Builder, shown in Figure 15.20. The Template Builder allows you to create a standard layout using any of the Lotus Components. You can launch the template builder from the Lotus Components toolbar using the Template Builder option.

Figure 15.20.

The Lotus Components Template Builder.

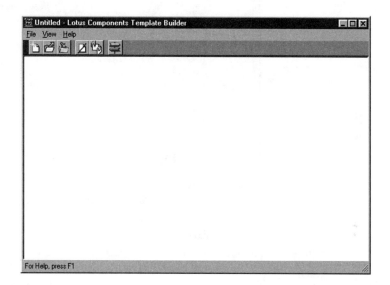

The Template Builder is extremely useful for customizing a component. For example, you could take the Lotus Spreadhseet Component and create a custom Expense Form Component or a Sales Commission Calculator component. Developers could then insert the custom component into their applications. This makes the components object-oriented to some degree, because you can define your own custom "classes" from existing "classes."

Saving a Template

When you save a template, you are prompted for the following items:

- The descriptive name is the name of the template as it shows up in the Create Objects dialog box.

- The LotusScript name is the internal name of the object that is created using the template; you use this in LotusScript to get the object and manipulate it programmatically.

- The text specified in the Quick Steps dialog box is displayed when a user creates an object using the template. It should specify simple instructions for using the object.

Figure 15.21 shows the dialog box that appears when you save a template. The template is a sample expense report generated using the Spreadsheet component.

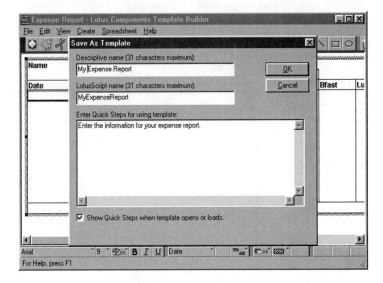

After you save a component template, you have the option to add it to the list in the Lotus Components toolbar. To do so, select the Customize Palette option from the components toolbar. The Customize Component Palette dialog box, shown in Figure 15.22, will appear. Under the list of available components, you'll notice your template object. You can add it to the toolbar list by dragging it from the available components list to the list underneath. Figure 15.22 shows the Customize Component Palette dialog box with the My Expense Report template object.

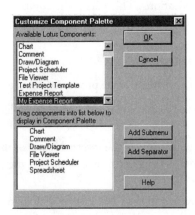

Distributing Component Templates

The Lotus Template builder has the capability to create a "distribution pack" that contains one or more component templates within an executable file. To give someone else a template, you need only create a distribution pack using the template builder.

The distribution pack is an executable file, much like an install program, that can be run by an end user to install your component templates. The executable file takes care of putting the components in the right place and performing all the steps necessary to register your component template and make it available on the Lotus Components menu.

Creating a Distribution Pack

To create a distribution pack, launch the Template Builder. From the Template Builder menu bar, select File | Create Distribution Pack. You see the Create Distribution Pack dialog box, shown in Figure 15.23.

FIGURE 15.23.

The Create Distribution Pack dialog box.

Select the templates that you want to include in the distribution pack by highlighting them in the Select Templates list. Next, select the pack path and filename. When you have selected the templates and pack file, click the OK button to generate the distribution pack.

The distribution pack is created as an executable file. You can send it to other people as an attachment using e-mail, or you can distribute it via a shared network directory, and so on. The user who receives the file only needs to run it to install the component templates.

Summary

The Lotus Components provide excellent, lightweight applications that satisfy a number of standard office application needs. Installing the components is simple and the disk space requirements are minimal; they can be an excellent solution in an environment where more fully functional office applications are overkill.

15

USING LOTUS
COMPONENTS

You can generate templates using the components, and you could use this capability to create standard expense reports, secured comments, project plans, and so on. Distributing customized templates is easy using the distribution pack capability from the Template Builder; once you create the distribution pack, you can send it to others using standard Notes file attachment capabilities.

Developing a Workflow Application

*by Randall A. Tamura
and Wendy Samulski*

IN THIS CHAPTER

In this chapter, you'll learn how to design and implement a workflow application within the Notes R4 environment. It covers a basic description of workflow and gives you some real-world examples, and then you'll construct two workflow applications using database templates supplied with Notes R4. The end of the chapter presents an outline of how you should go about planning and implementing your own workflow application using Notes.

It's usually easier to understand a new concept by working from examples. As a first example of workflow, consider the process of an employee travel expense-account reimbursement application. If you are an employee, and if you occasionally get reimbursed for travel expenses, I'm sure you're interested in getting timely, accurate reimbursement without a lot of hassle.

On the other hand, if you are a manager, in addition to ensuring prompt payment for your employees, you have the obligation to ensure that the expense-account mechanism is being used correctly and is not being abused. You have a financial responsibility to the company and are responsible for approving the payments to employees.

This is a good example of an application that can use Notes to expedite the process, ensure auditability, and make the whole process easier for employees, managers, and others involved in this process.

If you think about how this process is typically handled in many companies, as an employee you must fill out an expense-reimbursement paper form. This form is typically routed to your manager (and perhaps to a finance department) for approvals, and then on to payroll to produce a check for your reimbursement. With a paper form, and the shuffling from department to department, this process can take several days or even weeks in large companies.

Notes automates the flow of this work (hence the name *workflow*) by substituting an electronic form for the paper equivalent. By using Notes forms and documents, an electronic version of the form can be routed from person to person as fast as e-mail. This results in a faster, more reliable process flow.

Workflow Applications

Of course, expense-account reimbursement is not the only workflow in your company. There are typically many, and, depending upon the nature of your business, they can be simple or very complex. Another example of a workflow application is equipment-purchase requisitions. These requests would flow from the person needing the equipment, to a manager or finance department, to a person in the actual purchasing department.

A workflow in the software-development area might be for the process of fixing bugs in software. One possible scenario is from the person discovering the bug, to the customer service agent, to a quality-assurance tester to validate the bug. From there a developer fixes the bug and integrates the fix. Finally, a tester assures that the bug was fixed. A sample of this workflow can be found later in this chapter.

A company might have a process for marketing a product. The product manager sends a request for a campaign to the marketing department, which might send it to management for funding, and then send it outside the company to an advertising agency. The flow then continues with management approval of the ads, and finally to outside mass communication companies such as magazines, radio, or television.

Even mundane correspondence can have a workflow. In an organization that receives thousands of pieces of mail a day, such as an insurance company, a bank, or a credit card company, mail processing can be a workflow. Upon receipt, the mail might be logged and sorted. From there, the sorted mail might fan out to several departments, such as quotes, general inquiries, payments, or other departments. Each department might handle the relevant requests and/or pass the requests on to other departments within the company. The customer correspondence at the beginning triggered a flow of work throughout the company.

The list of these examples can go on, of course. Other examples include a product-design workflow, a loan-approval process, documentation development, ISO9000 processes, and even a process for approving new World Wide Web pages to be published on your InterNotes Web Publisher Site.

So, workflow is included in all of these examples. What qualifies these as examples of workflow, and what is common among all of these diverse applications? In a word, *process*. Workflow is process, and process is workflow. Within a company, a process or workflow is the handling of a job or task by a group of people. Typically, a process is sequential. In other words, it has a start, a middle, and an end.

In the preceding examples, the processes are started by employees that have a job to do. For example, the employee receives a letter that starts the process. Or, the employee has just received a loan application to process, a software-bug report, or expense account to process. After an employee has the information to start the process, there is typically a form that must be filled out. This form then flows through the corporation. The activity of starting a process is sometimes called *opening* it. For example, you might speak about "opening a bug report."

The start of a workflow is called opening it because, although the process may be a continuous workflow, there are discrete items of work flowing through the system. Each item has a unique character and must be tracked individually. It must be tracked while it is in the open state. This item might be called a job, a task, a loan application, or be given a company-specific acronym. What you are doing at the start of the process is actually opening the specific item or job itself.

The middle of a process is where the main activity takes place. It is the authorization of your expense account, or the fixing of the bug, or the approval or denial of the loan. The people performing these tasks must have certain information and typically are making decisions while they perform their tasks. When the system is automated, it is important that these people have the information they need, and that they can handle the decision-making process easily.

Just as each workflow or process has a beginning, it also has an end. In the jargon, the activity of finishing up the process is sometimes called *closing* it. After an item is closed, it can be considered historical information, but it does not need to be tracked.

Although a single person might handle the start, middle, and end of a task or job, this kind of job usually isn't considered workflow. Another aspect of the essence of workflow is that the job is too big for one person to handle, so the job flows through the company, from person to person or from department to department, each person adding value to the job until it is complete. This group processing of the task is what makes Notes an ideal platform to handle the job.

A Sample Workflow

To see how one workflow might be diagrammed on paper, look at Figure 16.1. This example shows a very abbreviated version of a software bug-fixing process.

FIGURE 16.1.

A sample workflow of the software bug fix process.

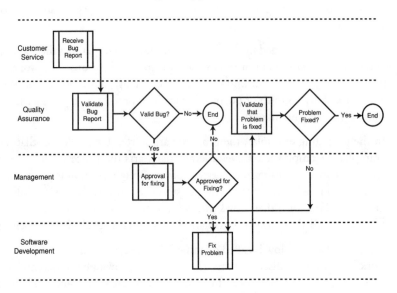

Figure 16.1 is a typical workflow diagram. Although it can be viewed as a standard flow chart, there are some important differences. The first point to notice is that there are four roles portrayed in this diagram: Customer Service, Quality Assurance, Management, and Software Development. The activities of each role are illustrated on one horizontal line.

I use the word *role* because, for example, one person may actually be performing more than one role within the workflow. A role does not necessarily represent a single person or a department—it could actually represent either. In this example, Customer Service, Quality Assurance, and Software Development might be departments, but the Management role is typically played by an individual.

Developing a Workflow Application

CHAPTER 16

377

16

DEVELOPING A
WORKFLOW
APPLICATION

The workflow starts when Customer Service receives a phone call, e-mail, or other notification of a problem or bug. Customer Service enters the problem into a database and notifies Quality Assurance that there is a problem report to process.

The Quality Assurance department receives the bug report and tests the scenario provided by the customer. This test is performed to ensure that the bug is indeed a valid bug. If the bug is determined to be a user error or is not reproducible, then the process is finished. By having a separate group validate the bug, valuable software-development time is saved; the developers know that all bugs they receive have been previously tested and can be reproduced in-house.

If the bug has been reproduced, it goes to management for work scheduling. The current development team may be in the middle of an important development cycle. Resources to fix the bug may or may not be available immediately. If resources are not available or the problem is not too severe, the bug report may be filed for fixing in the next release rather than providing an immediate fix for the problem now. If it is not approved for fixing right now, it will be filed away and the current bug report closed.

If the bug has been approved for fixing immediately, it will be passed on to the software-development group. This group uses the information provided by the customer and also the information found by Quality Assurance during their testing. Software Development will then try to find the cause of the problem and provide a fix. After the fix has been developed, the fixed code is sent back to Quality Assurance for validation.

Notice that the Quality Assurance group has two tasks to perform in this workflow. They validate that the bug is indeed valid on the incoming side, and they validate that the bug has been fixed before the problem is closed. They are first testing for the presence of the bug, and then they are testing for the absence of the bug. If the bug has been fixed by development, the bug report is closed and the process is complete.

If the testing for the bug determines that the bug still exists, then the Quality Assurance group will send it back to the Software Development group for more development. Ideally, the bug will be fixed the first time, but this process ensures that an independent group is testing the code and validating the quality of the resulting programs. After the code has been approved by the Quality Assurance group, the problem is closed.

What have you learned in this example? Well, you learned that each bug report that flows through this company goes through a repeatable, documented process. This is an important aspect of most quality programs in companies today. Each bug report in the system may be at a different stage in its workflow life cycle. There may be several bugs in this process at different stages.

We also learned that some departments (Quality Assurance in this example) can participate more than one time on the same project or workflow. By showing the workflow in a diagram where each role is on a separate line, it becomes clearer where information flows within a role and also between roles. When you begin to outline your workflow projects, use a diagram similar to Figure 16.1 to illustrate not only what is being done, but which roles are performing the tasks.

Workflow Models

Lotus defines three important abstract information models. They call these models Communication, Collaboration, and Coordination. In workflow, all of these concepts come together. The word *coordination* is actually representative of workflow. It means coordinating the work of a group of people electronically. You start, perform, and end a process within the Notes environment; not only can you perform your processes, but you can now have management information about the work you are performing. Information is available to answer questions: How many work items have we delivered? How long does it take to perform each step? Where are the bottlenecks? In essence, when you begin to manage processes electronically, you begin to have the information necessary to improve them. Management from this information is usually much more effective than management by instinct.

To implement workflow, you can use one of the other two models: Communication or Collaboration. Communication is related to e-mail and can be considered an information model that *pushes* information from one step to the next. Communication is always triggered from the sender, never the receiver. This is why this model is also sometimes called the *send* model.

Alternately, you can implement workflow using the collaboration model. This model is sometimes called the *share* model because it involves putting information about the process in a common database and then sharing the information among all the parties. Each participant in this type of model must *pull* the information from the common database.

The models are not necessarily pure or mutually exclusive. For example, the software bug-fixing example shown previously may actually be implemented as a *hybrid* model; notifications are sent from one person to the next via e-mail, but the actual bug reports are stored in a central repository. Using the Notes doclink capability, you can provide a linkage from the e-mail note to the data about the bug report that is stored in the repository.

Using the Approval Cycle Template

Let's use some of the concepts that you've learned and actually create a workflow application. For this application, you'll use one of the built-in templates provided with Notes R4. This template is called the Approval Cycle (R4) template. The filename for this template is APPROVE4.NSF and should be available in your Notes directory.

> **NOTE**
>
> Notes has several levels of user licenses. The most restricted type of license is a Notes Mail license. The next level up is called the Desktop license, and the type with no restrictions is called a Notes license, a full license, or a full client license. In order to design a new database or modify the design of an existing database, you must have a full license. The

Developing a Workflow Application

CHAPTER 16

379

16

DEVELOPING A
WORKFLOW
APPLICATION

Desktop license enables you to use applications derived from any template (including the Approval Cycle template), but you cannot perform design or administrative tasks. The Notes Mail license allows use of the e-mail features of Notes and a few selected templates. It is not sufficient to be able to use the Approval Cycle template; you must have at least the Desktop license.

Using Workflow Database Templates

Templates in Notes are like skeleton databases. They contain the structure of the database, but they don't contain any "meat." Although they can have some content, usually they don't; most of the time they are used as a starter database, so that you don't have to build each application from scratch.

Several templates are shipped with Lotus Notes, each for a different generic application type. For example, in addition to the approval template (seen shortly), there is a discussion database template, a document library template, and several others. You can also make your own templates if you anticipate creating several databases of a similar type.

Templates can contain views, forms, and the other design elements covered in previous chapters. To distinguish templates from normal databases, templates use the file suffix NTF, whereas regular databases use the file suffix NSF.

Templates promote reuse because the databases you create from them can also inherit future design changes. This means that after you have created a template and a set of databases from the template, you can update the template once and then propagate the changes to all the databases very easily.

Creating an Approval Workflow Database

The approval database template is very general; you should be able to use it for a variety of applications in your company. In fact, you can use it to implement several applications in the same database, or use different databases for different applications.

NOTE

In order to really test this application, you will need access to several Notes User IDs. When you simulate the flow of work among several people, each is represented by a different User ID. If you have access to an administrator ID for Notes, you can create some extra IDs to complete the exercises here. If not, you can either have your coworkers join you or ask your Notes administrator to create the IDs for you.

This example continues with a Sales Force Automation example: the approval of a special bid for a customer. To begin, select a workspace page on which you'd like to create your new workflow database. Then, select File | Database | New. In the title field of the New Database dialog, enter **Special Bid Approval**. In the File Name field, enter **SPECBID.NSF**. In the list box at the bottom, select Approval Cycle (R4). At the bottom, select Inherit future design changes and leave Show advanced templates deselected. Figure 16.2 shows an example of your screen, just before you press OK.

NOTE

If you are using Windows 95, the default filename for your file will be the same as the database title. Windows 95 can use this name on disks that have been enabled for long filename support. Not all network disks can support long filenames and Windows 3.1 users cannot use long filenames, so I have used a filename for this example that conforms to the old 8.3 naming convention. If you'd like to use a long filename instead of the name I've shown you, and your operating system supports it, feel free to do so. It will not affect the operation of your database.

FIGURE 16.2.

The New Database dialog box for Approval cycle workflow.

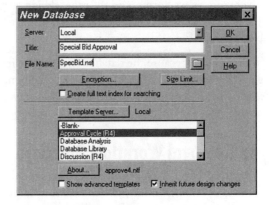

Inheriting future design changes enables you to create a set of databases from a single template, and then in the future make changes to them all by changing the master template. This example doesn't use that feature, but in general you should probably enable it to obtain the maximum reuse from your templates.

Several of the templates supplied with Notes are categorized as Advanced templates. They are templates that are system-oriented or use advanced features that many users may not need. When you open a new database, you can check Show advanced templates to indicate that you want to view the advanced templates. We do not need to use this option for our example.

After you press OK, information about using this template should be displayed by Notes. Read through this online document to find out more about the Approval process template.

Developing a Workflow Application

CHAPTER 16

381

16

DEVELOPING A
WORKFLOW
APPLICATION

The Special Bid Approval Process

This example looks at the approval process for a special bid in a manufacturing company. The Friendly Widget company produces Fwidgets. These are new and improved versions of those widgets commonly available everywhere. Fwidgets can accommodate much more capacity than regular widgets, they have improved safety features, new ergonomic design, and come in a variety of colors.

Even with all of the improvements provided by Friendly Widgets, though, some customers would like special features installed on their Fwidgets. For example, some customers want more gizmos, others would like special sockets, and still others want a special order color such as fuchsia.

To accommodate these customers, Friendly Widgets has a special bid process. This process is designed to provide its customers with the best products and services at the lowest prices while still maintaining profitability for the company. If customers would like to order a Fwidget with special features, they contact their sales representative and initiate a special bid. See Figure 16.3 for the workflow of the special bid process at Fwidgets, Inc.

FIGURE 16.3.

The special bid process at Fwidgets, Inc.

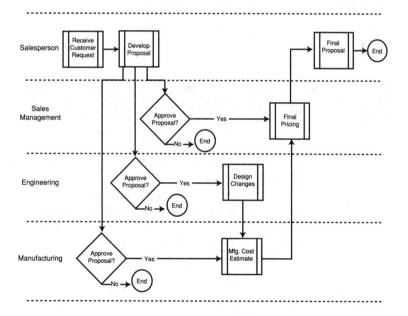

As you can see from the process flow, after the customer submits the request for additional gizmos on their Fwidget, the salesperson develops a proposal that includes the requested product enhancements. This proposal is sent to the various organizations in the company for approval and as the basis for the actual engineering and design work to be performed.

In this flow, the proposal is actually simultaneously sent to sales management, engineering, and manufacturing. This is a form of concurrent engineering and allows a faster response time to the customer. Because all of the departments can access the information more quickly and simultaneously, the overall time is reduced.

If all of the departments approve of the special bid, they perform additional work to actually create the final proposal. For example, the engineering department may need to make design changes in the Fwidgets to accommodate more gizmos. They may need to readjust the timing of other internal operations.

Manufacturing will take the proposal input and also the proposed design changes from engineering and will estimate the additional cost to manufacture the Fwidget. For simple changes such as a fuchsia Fwidget, there may be very little additional cost. Adding two wingdings and a fruzenblat may double or triple the cost.

After the additional costs have been estimated, the final pricing to the customer can be determined. Sales management takes all of the information and works up this price. The sales person then updates the proposal and delivers it back to the customer. If all goes well, this process can proceed very quickly because it all has been automated with Notes.

Using the APPROVE4.NTF Template

Now that you have created your approval-process database and you understand the process at Fwidgets, Inc., let's see how to automate this process using the APPROVE4.NTF template provided with Notes.

> **NOTE**
>
> When you are using databases created from this template, it is important that all users be limited to Author access, as opposed to Editor access or higher. This is also specified in the information provided with the template. The reason for this restriction is that, because the application is fundamentally for approval, it is important that unauthorized users cannot edit documents without the controls provided by the application. If an unauthorized user is granted access at a high level, then approvals may be granted improperly and without an audit trail. If you will be using this application in any type of financial situation, please take great care to map out the appropriate security classifications for users of the database.

The approval database template enables you to create many approval processes and place them all in the same database. All of the approval logic for this database is handled by a subform called ApprovalLogic and by LotusScript programs. Using one set of logic for all of your approval processes enables employees to become familiar with the database and user interface. Approval processes are handled in a uniform manner resulting in easier training and maintenance. If you decide to change the approval logic or corporate approval policies, you will have a single, central place to change rather than have to update many different systems.

In order to accommodate the handling of many diverse processes, each different approval application is given an application profile. You could have, for example, a profile for this special bid process, a different one for employee travel expenses, another for purchase requisitions, and so forth. All of these approval processes can reside in the same database with different sets of approvers and users.

An application profile is stored in the database as a Notes document. The document contains, for example, the approval form name, how the approval document is routed, the names of the approvers, and so forth. Each different approval process will have a different application profile document. To change the approver for a particular process, all you have to do is change the application profile for that process.

> **NOTE**
>
> This database has been named Special Bid Approval and SPECBID.NSF because it will include only one workflow. If you decide you would like to have more than one workflow in your database, you may want to consider naming your database with a more generic name (for example, Approval Processes). Alternatively, you could create a separate database for each workflow, using the APPROVE4.NTF template to create each one. You will still be able to change the design for each database in the future by changing the template and propagating the changes to the individual databases.

Highlight the Application Profile view in the navigation pane of the Special Bid Approval database. In the view on the right side of your screen, you should see a column called Workflow Object, which is discussed shortly. (See Figure 16.4.)

FIGURE 16.4.

The Application Profile view before adding a profile.

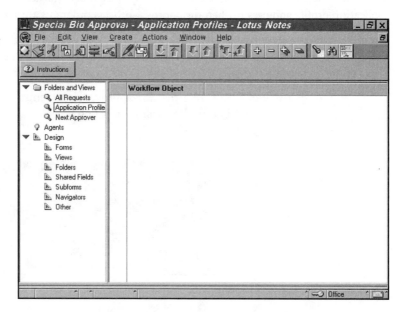

Select Create | Application Profile. On the resulting form, enter **Special Bid** in the Approval form name. Click the down-arrow next to routing type and select All at Once. Leave the routing delivery Doclink and change the number of approvers to 3. (See Figure 16.5.)

FIGURE 16.5.

The Application Profile form for the Special Bid Process database.

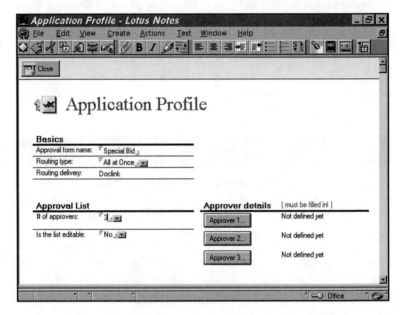

In just a few moments, you will be creating the actual form used for the approval process: Special Bid. It is important that the name you fill in on the application profile form matches the actual form name you use. This is because the LotusScript program extracts the form name from the application profile and uses it when the approval-process programs are actually running.

The All at Once type routing has been selected. Look back at Figure 16.3. You'll notice that after the proposal has been developed, it is routed to the three other organizations all at once. If any of the organizations denies the proposal, it will be considered disapproved.

Notice on the right side of Figure 16.5 that the approver details must be filled in. Do that now. Press on the Approver 1 button. You will see a dialog box similar to the one shown in Figure 16.6.

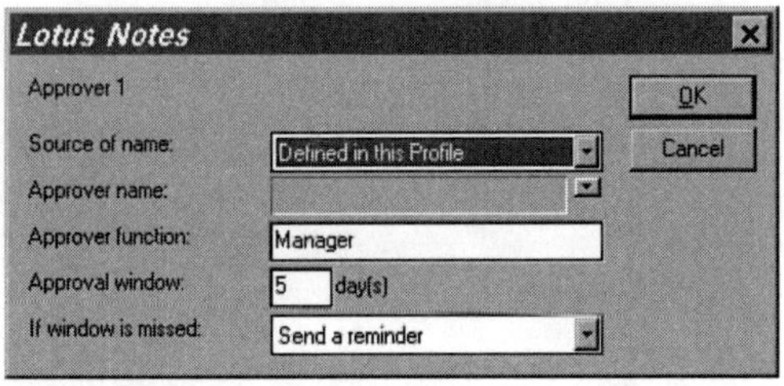

FIGURE 16.6.

The Approver details dialog box.

16

DEVELOPING A
WORKFLOW
APPLICATION

Click on the down-arrow for Source of name. You'll see that you have three options: Defined in this Profile, Entered on the form by the submitter, and Retrieved from a database. These options give you a lot of flexibility in determining how to specify your set of approvers. For example, you may already have a database that lists your managers or approvers for your process. The third option enables you to take advantage of your existing data. The second option enables the creator of the form to specify the approver. Normally you would not use this option for financial types of approvals, but if the approval process were a technical review, you might want to allow the submitter to specify a colleague as the technical approver.

This example uses the Defined in this Profile choice. Now, press the down-arrow on the Approver name. When you do this, names from your Public Address Book should appear in a dialog box. Select the name of one of the users you have set up for this exercise or else pick the name of one of your colleagues. In the Approver function, change the word `Manager` to `Sales Management`. Leave the Approval window at 5 days and the action If the window missed to Send a reminder. When you have finished, press OK.

Press the Approver 2 button. Fill in the approver name from your Public Address Book, but this time make the approver function Engineering and press OK.

Press the Approver 3 button. Fill in the approver name from your Public Address Book, but this time make the approver function Manufacturing and press OK. When you have finished, your screen should look like Figure 16.7 (of course, the names in your organization will be different).

FIGURE 16.7.

The Application Profile with Approver details filled in.

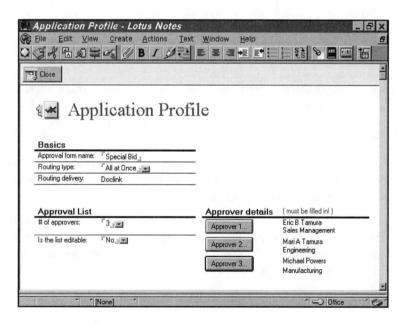

You're now ready to create the actual Special Bid form, so close the application profile by pressing the Close action bar button and, when prompted, say yes to save the new document. After your form has been saved, the application profile should show one workflow object called Special Bid.

Now open the Design twistie and select Forms in the Navigator pane. Your screen should look like Figure 16.8.

FIGURE 16.8.

The Forms view before creating the special bid form.

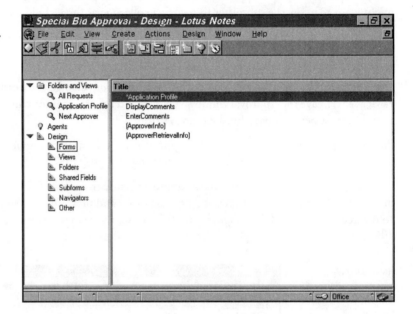

Select Create | Design | Form. You will see a dialog box entitled Insert Subform. Press OK to insert the ApprovalLogic subform. This is the subform that contains the main approval logic for the workflow. Your screen should now contain the subform within the new, untitled form. (See Figure 16.9.)

Scroll down to the bottom of the form; you will notice a rule (a line) that extends across the form. This line is at the bottom of the subform; below it, you can insert several fields that will be used during your workflow process.

Just below the line, enter the static text description `Customer Name:`. Following this text, select Create | Field. At the dialog box, give the field the name txtCustomer; leave its type text and editable. Choose the Options tab, enter `Sales: Enter customer name.` in the Help description field, and close the dialog box.

FIGURE **16.9.**

*The new form with the
ApprovalLogic subform
inserted.*

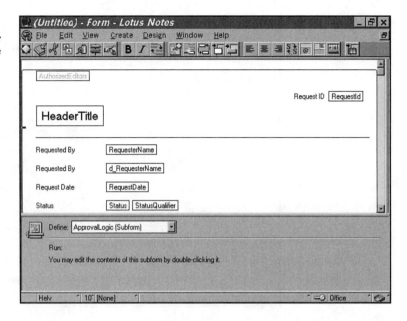

On the next line, enter the text description **Special Order Description:**. Following this text, select Create | Field. At the dialog box, give the field the name rtSpecOrd. Change the type to Rich Text and leave it editable. Choose the Options tab, enter **Sales: Enter description of special order.** in the Help description field, and close the dialog box.

On the next line, enter the text description **Engineering Notes:**. Following this text, select Create | Field. At the dialog box, give the field the name rtEngNotes. Change the type to Rich Text and leave it editable. Choose the Options tab; in the Help description field enter **Engineering: Enter design change engineering notes.**, and close the dialog box.

On the next line, enter the text description **Mfg. Cost Estimate:**. Following this text, select Create | Field. At the dialog box, give the field the name nCostEst. Change the type to Number and leave it editable. Choose the Currency type, zero decimal places, and select Punctuated at thousands. Choose the Options tab, and in the Help description field enter **Manufacturing: Enter cost estimate.**. Close the dialog box.

On the next line, enter the text description **Final Price to Customer:**. Following this text, select Create | Field. At the dialog box, give the field the name nFinalPrice. Change the type to Number and leave it editable. Choose the Currency type, zero decimal places, and select Punctuated at thousands. Choose the Options tab and in the Help description field enter **Sales Management: Enter final price to customer.**. Close the dialog box.

See Figure 16.10 for a view of the field properties of the nFinalPrice field.

FIGURE 16.10.

Fields on the Special Bid form.

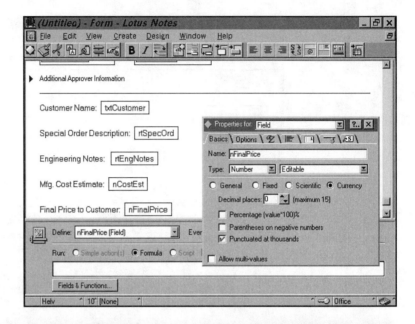

TIP

Note that I have used a field-naming convention in which I prefix each field with an abbreviation for its field type. For example, text fields are prefixed by txt, Rich text fields are prefixed by rt, and number fields are prefixed by n. This type of convention makes it easy to see at a glance the types of fields you are working with. When dealing with these fields in LotusScript, it also makes it easier to ensure that you are working with fields of the appropriate type and to know when you will need to make conversions from one type to another.

Now look in the definition area in the bottom of the screen. In the first drop-down box (following Define:), select Untitled (Form) and for the event Window Title. In the formula area just below, enter **"Special Bid Form"** (including the double quotes). From the menu, select File | Document Properties or press the properties button in the SmartIcon bar. You should get the Form properties InfoBox. Under Form name, enter **Special Bid**. Remember that this name must be the same name specified for Approval form name on the application profile form, as shown previously in Figure 16.5.

Deselect the Include in menu option. (See Figure 16.11.)

Close the Form properties InfoBox. Close the form by selecting File | Close. Save the new form.

Congratulations: you have created your first workflow application.

FIGURE 16.11.

*The Special Bid Form
properties and Win-
dow Title.*

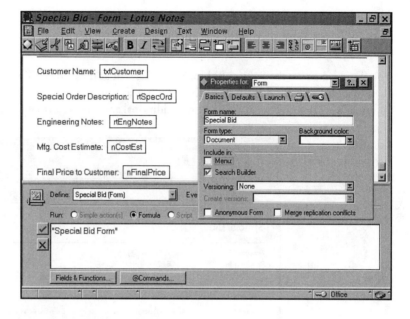

Using the Special Bid Application

Now that you have created the Special Bid workflow application, let's try it out to see how it actually works. From the main Navigator pane, select the All Requests view. You should have no requests initially. Now, press the Create New Request button in the action bar. (See Figure 16.12.)

FIGURE 16.12.

*The All Requests view
after the Create New
Request button is
pressed.*

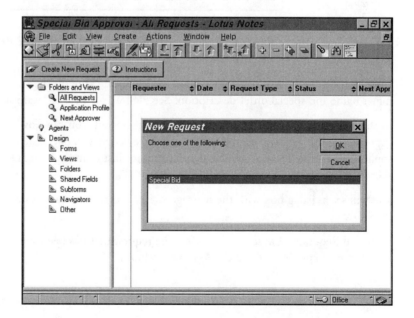

After you have pressed the Create New Request button, you will get a dialog box with a list of all the different Approval workflows contained in the database. For now, you just have the one called Special Bid. Press OK to select it.

You should then see the Special Bid form. Notice that at the bottom of the form are the fields that we added, and in the middle of the form is a section that is entitled Additional Approver Information. Press on the twistie to see the additional approver information. (See Figure 16.13.)

FIGURE 16.13.

The Special Bid form with additional approver information.

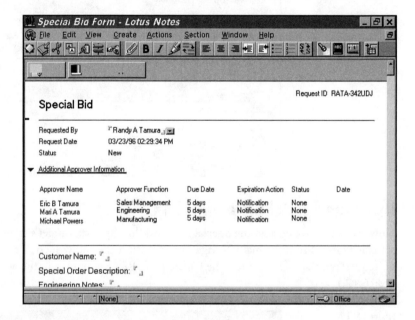

On the left side of the form you'll see the names of the people you specified to be approvers and the three approver departments that were created.

Close the additional approver information section by clicking on the twistie. Fill in the Customer name and special order description. See Figure 16.14 for an example.

At this point, because you are simulating the sales person, you can now press the Submit for approval button. This will send e-mail to the three people you have listed as approvers in your application profile. If these are actual users and not just dummy User IDs, you should probably tell them to expect some e-mail from you.

You will see a dialog box with the message `Notification has been sent to all Approvers`. Press OK.

In the All Requests view you will now see the request that has been submitted. The name of each approver appears in the Next Approver column.

FIGURE 16.14.

The Special Bid form with customer and special order description.

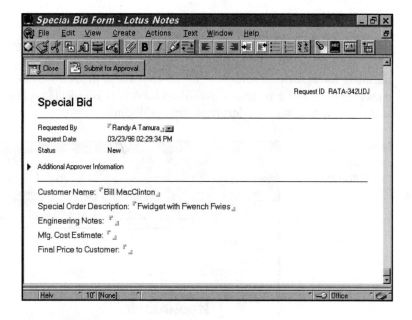

Performing an Approval

Let's see what this application would look like to an approver. In the Next Approver view, you see an entry for each approver. See Figure 16.15 for the Next Approver view.

FIGURE 16.15.

The Next Approver view.

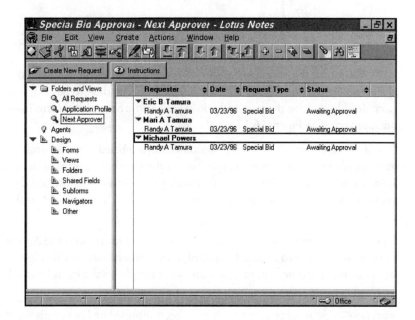

If there were more than one action for a particular approver, the list of documents for the approver would be longer.

Take a look at the e-mail inbox for one of the approvers. If you look at Figure 16.16, you'll see the inbox for the first approver. The document pane at the bottom shows the content of the e-mail message, which is just a bookmark. A bookmark is really like a place holder and serves as the launching point for a document link, or doclink.

FIGURE 16.16.

The e-mail message received by one of the approvers.

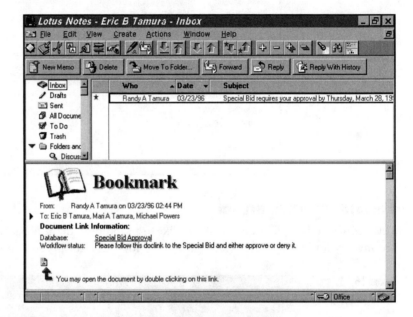

At the bottom of the message is an icon; by double-clicking on that icon, the user will be shown the actual Special Bid form. Because you're now pretending to be an approver of this application, double-click on the icon and take a look at the Special Bid form from the perspective of an approver. (See Figure 16.17.)

In Figure 16.17, you'll notice two action buttons labeled Approve and Deny. These buttons appear only to the users who are specified in the Current Approver box. If you have been following along, you'll notice that your window probably does not contain the Approve and Deny buttons, unless you switched IDs to one of the User IDs specified in the Current Approver box.

As you might imagine, the approver in this case simply can press the Approve or Deny button to perform the desired action. If enabled, e-mail will be sent to the originator, informing him or her of the outcome. Approval for the other people on the list is handled similarly.

This wraps up the discussion of the Special Bid example. Let's move on to another example of workflow using another template that has been supplied by Lotus with R4 of Notes: the Document Library template.

FIGURE 16.17.
*The Special Bid form
from an approver
perspective.*

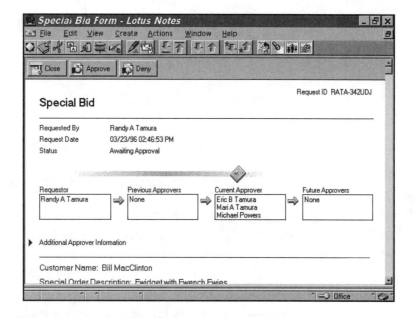

Using the Document Library Template

The document library template is used to create databases that can store documents that must be tracked and managed. This template has some basic workflow functions built in. When you create a document, you can specify the reviewers that you would like to have review the document. Thus, each document can have a separate set of reviewers. This is in contrast to the Approval cycle template, where you define a fairly static process and handle many documents using the same process.

> **NOTE**
>
> As with the Approval cycle database, users of databases created from the document library template should have Author access. Editor access or higher may compromise the security of the application and/or cause errors.

To create a document library database, first select an appropriate workspace page, and then select File | Database | New. In the title field, enter **Document Library**. In the File Name field, enter **DOCLIB.NSF**, and in the template area at the bottom choose the template Document Library (R4). Press OK when done.

From the All Documents view, press the New Document button in the Action Bar. A new document will be created. (See Figure 16.18.)

FIGURE 16.18.
*A New document
created in a document
library database.*

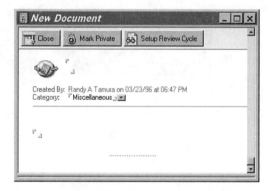

For this example, let's simulate an employee who would like to have a proposal reviewed. The documents that are routed in the document library database can be typed in directly, or they can be attached files. This example shows an attached Microsoft Word document.

Setting Up a Document-Review Cycle

After the document has been entered, attached, or otherwise imported, it can be routed and reviewed. Press the Setup Review Cycle button. Notes will show you a dialog box similar to that shown in Figure 16.19. Notice the Microsoft Word document icon at the bottom of Figure 16.19. This icon shows that a Word document has been attached to this Notes document. You can attach any kind of file to your Notes document by using the menu option File | Attach while the document is being edited. Notes prompts you for the name of the file to be attached.

FIGURE 16.19.
*The Review Cycle setup
in the Document
Library database.*

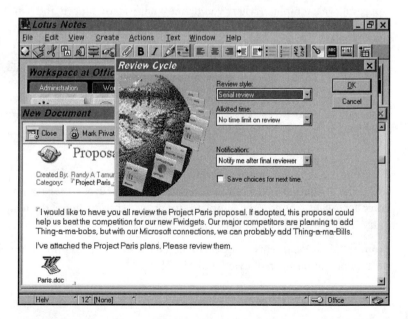

Review Style

For review-cycle style, you can choose the following:

■ *Serial Review.* The document is routed sequentially to each reviewer. As the author, you can choose to whom to route the document. As each reviewer looks at the document, he or she may make changes; the changes are incorporated into the document. A copy of the original document is saved, but separate copies for each reviewer are not saved.

■ *Serial Review* (keep all revisions). This case is similar to the regular serial review, but as the document is routed, all versions of the changes are kept as response documents. Each reviewer can see the comments of previous reviewers. A copy of the original document is kept.

■ *Document Reservations.* Requests for review are sent out to all reviewers in parallel. Each reviewer may make comments in a copy of the original document. A copy of the original document is kept. For document reservations, a type of file lock will be placed on the document on the server. This will not prevent another user from editing the document, but it will issue a warning message telling a second user that a previous user is currently reviewing the document.

■ *Response Review.* Requests for review are sent out in parallel, as in document reservations. There is no file lock, and each response will be saved as a separate response document. Because each response is saved separately, there is no need for the lock. A copy of the original document is also kept.

Allotted Time

As with any workflow, you must have a policy to deal with cases where a document has been routed to someone, but no action has been taken. To handle this situation, you normally set a time limit for some action to be taken. After the time limit expires, you can trigger an event to occur. For example, you can automatically approve, automatically disapprove, or you can send reminders or take some other action.

For the document library, you have three choices in dealing with nonaction. You can ignore it, which means that there will be no time limit. You can do this, for example, if you want to send out a document for review to a lot of reviewers, but do not require that every one of the reviewers responds.

You can also set a time limit for review, expressed in days. At the end of the time limit, you can have the document automatically move on to the next reviewer, or you can have the system send a reminder to the reviewer to take action. Your choice will depend upon the type of document that you are reviewing.

Notification

As the author of the original document, you naturally will be interested in the progress of the review. You can choose to be notified once only at the end of the review cycle, or you can choose to be notified after each reviewer. You will be notified by an e-mail from the system.

When you have made your choices, you can also check the box to save your choices for the next time you set up a review cycle.

Reviewers

After you have set up the initial parameters for your review cycle, an area will be added to your document that specifies the selections you have chosen and enables you to add the names of the reviewers. (See Figure 16.20.)

FIGURE 16.20.

Specifying reviewers in the Document Library.

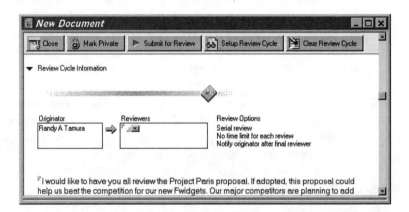

In Figure 16.20, notice the small down-arrow within the Reviewers box. If you click on this down-arrow, you will be presented with names from your Public Address Book. Choose the names of the reviewers you would like to have review this document. In the case of a serial review, the order in which you select the names will be the order in which the documents are routed.

Notice also the appearance of a Clear Review Cycle button in the action bar. If you have made a mistake and would like to reset the review cycle, you can press this button; the review cycle will be canceled. You can then go back and specify different routing options and/or reviewers.

You can use the document library template to route documents to groups of people sequentially or in parallel. It can be a useful tool in managing documents in many different scenarios. A publisher, for example, might use this mechanism for routing chapters from authors to reviewers and then back to the author for update after the reviewers have made comments.

A legal firm may use this template to route draft documents among several lawyers working on a single case. An insurance company might use this mechanism to route the text of an insurance policy among legal, actuarial, operations, and management employees before they send the document to the government for approval. If your company routes documents among several people for review, comment, or approval, you should consider using this template before embarking on your own development efforts.

This completes the discussion of the document library template. There are a couple of other useful features of this template, including the ability to mark documents private and to automatically handle the archiving of documents. If you are interested in using these features, consult the About document and the Using document of this database.

Mail-In Databases

Mail-in databases are not strictly a workflow tool, but they can be valuable in the workflow context, so they are explained here. The concept of a mail-in database is very simple, and it uses Notes' e-mail features.

If you recall, your e-mail is contained in a mail database. Notes takes care of delivering documents from remote sources and placing them in this database. Notes looks in the Public Address Book to find your mail database location and then deposits the document in that database.

Mail-in databases operate very similarly, except that rather than storing documents into e-mail databases, Notes can store documents in arbitrary databases. You can give any database a name, enable it to receive documents, and then local or remote users can send documents to the database.

For example, you might design a Sales database and then have remote salespeople mail in their sales orders into the database. You might have an inquiry database that you'd like to have receive documents from your World Wide Web page. In an insurance company, a Mail-in database might serve as the recipient of insurance quote requests. There are a variety of reasons to have a mail-in database.

After you have created a mail-in database, you can create agents to process incoming mail. These agents can then initiate workflow processes. For example, suppose you created a Mail-In database for your sales orders. When the sales order comes into the Mail-In database, you might have an agent start a sales-processing program to process the sales order. It could perform some tasks and route documents to various people in your organization as required.

The main step necessary to enable Mail-In databases is to add an entry into the Public Address Book. See Figure 16.21 for an example of a Mail-In Database entry in the Public Address Book.

FIGURE 16.21.

The Mail-In Database entry for sales orders.

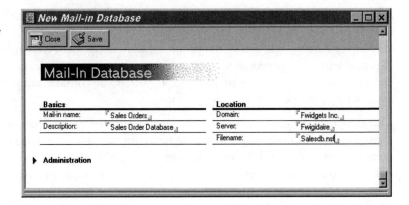

The Mail-In name you see in this example, Sales Orders, is used as the e-mail address when sending mail. For example, to send a document to this database, you would address it to `Sales Orders @ Fwidgets Inc.`

Steps in Workflow Development

Now that you understand the thought process behind developing a workflow process, I'll cover specific steps that you can follow to successfully develop and deploy your own workflow application. The following section provides a framework for application development. There are four phases in developing a workflow application:

- Determining the business process
- Developing the prototype application
- Deploying the prototype and refining the application
- Managing and rolling out the real application

You can equate developing a workflow application to building a house. The foundation for the house is "the business process" (phase I); building the house is equivalent to "developing the prototype application" (phase II); the little extras and fix-ups required just before moving into the house are equivalent to "deploying the prototype and refining the application" (phase III); and, finally, moving into your house is equivalent to "managing and rolling out the application" (phase IV). If you don't have a strong, well-structured foundation for your house, it will fall apart; this applies to your application also.

If the business-process definition is not solid for your application, it may exhibit plumbing problems in communication, which in turn can cause stoppages and workflow backups. You may see workflow blackouts or brownouts in your workflow electrical current. Structural problems may cause your house to eventually become uninhabitable. It is therefore essential to take the time necessary to clearly define your goals and your business processes. We'll cover this most important aspect first.

Phase I: Determining the Business Process

It is important to take your time when defining the business process, because this is the basis from which you will develop the rest of your application. This section will describe the critical elements of this phase. You should: Decide on the roles, define the tasks and flows, decide on the forms and reports to automate, and review the workflow and specifications.

Decide on the Roles

Before you can automate the process, it is important to understand who will participate in it. You don't necessarily need names, you need roles. In other words, which job are the various people doing? Which role are they playing in the workflow process? In some of the previous examples, you have seen roles such as Customer Service, Engineering, Management, Sales, and so forth. These are typically the roles you find in companies today.

Get the necessary details from the manager of the process and the users of the system. During this information-gathering phase, you should try to narrow down the number of roles to as few as possible, while still making the flow work. If you have started with a very large workflow task, try to break the task up into possibly smaller, more self-contained workflows.

For example, a major workflow may involve five different departments, but there may also be several workflows within each of the five departments. Try to analyze these workflows separately so that you don't end up with a workflow diagram that is too large.

After you have decided on the roles, you can start the creation of your workflow diagram. Look back at Figures 16.1 and 16.3. You'll notice that each role is represented by a horizontal line of tasks. The flow of information between roles takes place as information passes from one horizontal line to another.

Define the Tasks and Flows

After you have defined the roles and begun the workflow diagram, draw the boxes and arrows. The boxes in your workflow diagram represent the job or tasks to be done in the workflow, and the arrows represent the flow of information.

Information flows from one task to another. The tasks may be performed by the same role, in which case they'll be on the same horizontal line. They may be performed by different roles, in which case a task on one line will flow to a task on another line.

Decide on the Forms and Reports to Automate

You should obtain a copy of all the hard-copy forms that are currently used. You should obtain both the blank and filled-in copies of the forms. You can use these forms for guidance as you are preparing the online versions of these forms.

The forms will contain the information that must flow from task to task in your workflow. All of the information required for a task must have been gathered in some previous step, or must be gathered in the current step.

Look at all of the reports that are currently generated by the system. Do you really need all of this information, or can you now use the online system for query purposes so that users can dynamically determine information that previously was in a report? Can you think of additional or different information that might be useful to users of the system that can now be generated because the system is online?

You should also carefully review your security requirements and the access levels that will be required for each of the databases in your application.

Review the Workflow and Specifications

After you have completed your analysis, your workflow diagram, and your specifications, schedule a meeting with the manager and users of the prospective system. Show them the diagram you have created and verify that the flows are accurate. After everything has been written down (perhaps for the first time), you may be surprised to discover quicker or easier ways of accomplishing your goals.

Make sure that your users agree with your workflow! This cannot be emphasized too much. They will be the ultimate users of the system. Frequently, automating the existing process will not be the best automated process. This is because sometimes extraneous steps are taken, improper procedures followed—or worse, done in manual systems because it may be the only way for the users to accomplish their tasks.

Finally, when the users are involved in the design of the process, they have much more of a feeling of ownership of the system. It's not just a system that someone has dropped in from the sky and told them to use. It becomes a system to enhance their jobs and make it easier for them to get their work done.

Phase II: Developing the Prototype Application

Design the forms that will be used in your application. Review Form components (like buttons, reserved fields, Author, Reader Names, and sections) to confirm you have covered all the details necessary in creating a well-designed form layout. Good form design promotes ease of use and readability for users.

Next, design the views that will be used in your application. Some tips in view layout include the following:

- Try to include document status in one or more of your views (useful for the reviewers of documents).

■ Include age of document as one of the columns (useful for editing purposes).

■ If applicable, include views by next reviewer (this is especially useful for managers who want to glance at what stage of review a process is in).

Finalize the design of your agents. A good rule of thumb is: the less experienced the user base, the more your users will need help to guide them through the process. Background agents are especially useful for the following:

■ Processing documents in batch mode (saves time for database managers)

■ Sending notifications for delays in the workflow process (helping to keep the flow of information moving along)

■ Using agents to extract information from other applications (to accomplish this you may need to use Notes/FX, DDE or OLE)

Finally, you may consider using agents for the processing of multiple documents.

Phase III: Deploying the Prototype and Refining the Application

Before rolling out an application, it is important to test its functionality on a smaller user group rather than large-scale deployment all at once. This is a good time to refine button formulas and LotusScript programs, and to fix any other major bugs. During this phase, you will be testing your prototype and refining it into the final application.

It is important to provide as much help as possible. Help comes in many shapes and sizes:

■ Policy documents (About and Using documents)
■ Help buttons on forms
■ Field level help
■ Pop-up help

Policy documents are created in the design view of the database in the Other section. You can enter text graphics or other information in the policy documents. The About document is typically displayed when a new user first opens the database. This document should tell the purpose of the database, who should use the database, and describe the major functions. The Using database should describe "how-to" information. It should tell the user how to perform the major tasks in the database. You can think of this document as a very abbreviated help file or user manual.

Help buttons are just buttons that can be activated by the user and that you associate with a dialog box or other help message.

Field-level help can be created for editable fields in the field properties InfoBox. Select the Options tab and enter text into the Help description field.

Pop-up help can be created while designing your forms by first highlighting some text on your form and then selecting Create | Hotspot | Text Pop-up. You can then enter a long help message, which will be displayed if the user clicks on that area of the form.

While pilot testing your application it is important to get feedback from your testers. This can be accomplished with a "Comments" form and view. You can make the Comments form specifically for development feedback. You can enable a button on the application form to activate the Comments form. The Comments form can be kept in the database (so all users can read it and comment), or it can be sent to a Mail-In database (which you can check for your user feedback).

Request feedback on the usability of the application. Find out which features are used and which are not. You should also see if there are any missing features that should be added before the final application is rolled out.

Fix any problems that have been discovered on your forms and views. Make sure that all the management information is available in views or reports generated by the system.

Phase IV: Managing and Rolling out the Real Application

Before deploying your application, it is important to do a spot check on your security. Check that your ACL is correct, and that Author and Reader access lists are accurate. Assign manager access to the person responsible for maintaining the replication schedule and the Access Control List.

If your application will be utilized on multiple servers, it is important to check your ACLs to confirm the correct setup for the servers you will be replicating with.

Be sure to have some level of training available for your users. Documentation is always a good solution, but additional user aides are helpful. Using ScreenCam (for Windows only) may be another form of help that you can provide along with classroom seminars.

Summary

This chapter has covered the basics of workflow. You have learned about workflow diagrams and how they can help you illustrate a workflow process. You can illustrate various roles on horizontal lines, the tasks to be performed in boxes, and flows of information with arrows.

You created a sample workflow application using the APPROVE4.NTF template supplied with Notes R4. This template is useful for approval types of applications, such as travel expense accounts and other simple financial or management approvals. You can have up to five approvers, and they can approve sequentially or in parallel. You can also control what happens if an approver does not take action within a specified amount of time.

The Document Library template supplied with Notes allows another kind of workflow application. This template can be used for reviewing documents. The documents may be legal drafts, insurance policy drafts, project proposals, company plans, or any type of document where you might want to have peer or management review and approval. Reviews using this template can also occur serially or in parallel.

Mail-In databases can be useful as trigger mechanisms for some types of workflows. For example, you can create a Mail-In database that triggers a Sales Order process.

Finally, I covered the generic process you should take when designing a workflow program. You don't have to use the built-in templates supplied with Notes; you can design a much more complex workflow if your needs dictate. When designing your own workflow, you should follow the normal design guidelines as you would with any type of Notes application. In workflow, though, you may be working with several departments within your company, so design reviews with all of the applicable people become even more important than with simple applications used only within your own department.

Workflow can be a powerful tool to simplify processes within your company. It can make the work in your company flow faster, with fewer errors, less paper, and make the job simpler for employees. You should investigate within your company whether you can use Notes technology to give your company a new competitive advantage.

IN THIS PART

IV

PART

Advanced Development

Introduction to Advanced Development Features

by Jonathan Czernel

IN THIS CHAPTER

Lotus Notes R4 introduces several new advanced development features that bring a great deal of flexibility and scaleability to the experienced Notes applications designer, eliminating many of the development barriers that existed in Release 3.x.

In this chapter we will introduce some of the most significant new development features found in R4. Later chapters address all of these enhancements in a much more hands-on fashion.

This chapter is aimed at experienced Release 3.x developers that wish to gain a fundamental understanding of what each of these new features bring to the development table. New Notes developers already armed with basic design skills will find this chapter a refreshing precursor to the rigorous, in-depth discussion of design issues that are found in subsequent chapters.

The development enhancements discussed in this chapter include:

- **LotusScript**. This powerful object-oriented BASIC-compatible scripting language enables direct access to virtually any Notes object.
- **Navigators**. These are graphical "road maps" that may be used to step a user through database forms and views.
- **Agents**. Formerly referred to as Macros, these have been significantly enhanced to enable more versatility.
- **Simple Actions**. An alternative to both Formulas and Script, a Simple Action is perhaps the easiest way to write code in R4.

Lotus has taken great strides to make Notes a more powerful development environment. With these additions, compounded with the additional design features described in earlier chapters, Lotus has indeed succeeded.

Because the Notes development environment has matured, the developer must also learn to use these tools in a reasonable and effective fashion. For this reason a brief section on general development tips has also been included. This section should be mandatory for developers that do not have experience taking on large development projects.

Without further ado, let's dive headlong into this vast ocean of advanced Notes development tools!

LotusScript: the Lotus Scripting Language

LotusScript Version 3.0, the most anticipated new addition to the Notes development toolbox, is a feature-rich BASIC-compatible object-oriented language. First introduced in Lotus Visual Programmer, or ViP (now owned by Revelation Software), LotusScript provides the developer with benefits that far outweigh the minor growing pains associated with learning this new, powerful scripting language.

NOTE

From this point forward, the terms LotusScript and Script are used interchangeably. I will also use the term Formula to refer to the Lotus Notes Formula macro-language. Formulas encompass @Functions and @Commands, when applicable.

First, let's discuss some of the benefits and shortcomings of LotusScript.

LotusScript is all of the following:

- An ideal scripting tool used to significantly enhance the programmability and functionality of Lotus Notes databases by providing a modern, structured programming language. The language may actually be readable, unlike most complex Formulas.

- A language that contains built-in classes that enable direct access to servers, databases (including the Access Control List, views and collections) and documents. The extensive built-in class list includes the ability to directly access ODBC-compatible databases, a long awaited feature.

- A (99 percent) platform-independent language that enables a database with included LotusScript code to be executed on any platform that is supported by Lotus Notes, including Windows 95, Windows NT, OS/2, Macintosh, and AIX.

- The common scripting language that Lotus uses in its entire SmartSuite line of desktop products, including WordPro, 1-2-3, Approach, and Freelance.

LotusScript, however, is not any of the following things:

- A language that enables developers to write complete, stand-alone applications.

- A replacement for Notes formulas. Rather, it complements the use of Formulas and Simple Actions.

- A replacement for other more advanced front-ending utilities, such as Microsoft Visual Basic, Borland Delphi, or C/C++ with appropriate VBXs, OCXs, and/or DLLs necessary to tap into the Notes API.

Where Are Scripts Used?

In Release 3.x, inserting Formulas to handle various events was a straightforward matter—simply double-click on a field, then click on the Formula button to add one or more formulas to handle various tasks, such as input validation and input translation. In the latest Notes release, the development environment has a vastly different look and feel.

You can see the Print Database Information Form in the Design Mode in Figure 17.1. Note the following features in this figure:

- **Programmer's Pane**. The lower portion of this screen replaces the pop-up dialog box that enables formula-based code to be inserted in Release 3.x.

- **Define**. The Define pull-down list box enables the developer to select the object for which code must be inserted. An *object* is a screen element, such as a field or a button on a Notes form.

- **The Run Section**. Right above the code window, the developer may select one, and only one, development option for the particular object and event selected: Simple Action(s), Formula, or Script. Depending on the event and object selected, one or more Run choices may be unavailable.

- **Event**. This pull-down list box, only present when Script is chosen in the Run Section, presents a series of events and/or procedures that are associated with the object selected in the Define field. Each event in this box may have script associated with it.

- **The Code Section**. The largest multiline text box contains the Simple Action(s), Formula(s) or Script code that will be executed if the selected Event is trigged for the selected Object.

FIGURE 17.1.

Designing a Form in Release 4.x.

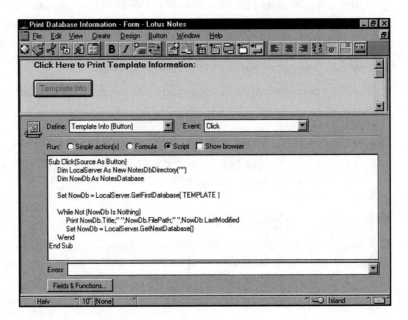

To insert Script, simply select the Script button in the Run area of the Programmer's Pane when an object that enables Script coding (and an event, in some cases) is selected.

Scripts may not be used in place of Formulas in all areas, however. Lotus has put up a fence over which Scripts may not hurdle. The following list indicates, for various selected Notes objects, where Scripts may be used:

- Agents
- View actions
- Form actions, events, buttons, and hotspots
- Navigator hotspots
- Field events
- Rich text field buttons and hotspots

Formulas Versus Scripts

Formulas, used along with @Commands in Release 3.x, are now complemented and enhanced through the use of Scripts. In some cases, a one-line Formula may exist to perform a particular function that would require several lines of Script. In other cases, Scripts might perform tasks that are impossible to perform using Formula(s) alone.

For any given task, the developer must select the option that best suits the needs of the task at hand. In some cases, Lotus Notes disallows the use of Scripts with certain object/event combinations. For example, a Script cannot be used when defining Input Validation or Input Transformation formulas for a field—this particular event must use a Formula.

Generally speaking, use Formulas when they make sense. Yes, "making sense" is a subjective and extremely vague expression. However, guidelines for when and when not to use Formulas cannot be cast in stone; a set of rules cannot be defined for all instances. After developing a few R4 applications you will strike a natural balance between Simple Actions (discussed later), Formulas, and Scripts.

At the risk of contradicting my earlier statement, I recommend the following very general guidelines. Use Formulas when a few @Functions or @Commands can be strung together to accomplish a given task, or when complex logic is not required. Use LotusScript in almost any other situation.

Added Functionality of Scripting Over Functions

The LotusScript language enables several features that are not available through the use of Formulas alone. It is for this reason that it will become mandatory for developers to jump onto the Script bandwagon.

These features include the following:

- **Exploring Database Internals.** Script enables several internal database structures to be read, and in some cases set. These structures include the Access Control List (ACL), the date the database was created, the filename of the database, whether or not the database is a Public Address Book, and a list of groups or individuals that have Manager access to the database.

  Access to databases, fields and other Notes specific structures are performed through the use of classes and associated properties and methods.

- **Access to external Dynamic Link Libraries (DLLs).** Through the use of function declarations, calls to external DLLs, such as the Windows or Notes API, may be performed.

- **Document Collections.** All documents or a subset of documents in an entire database may be scanned and modified through an iterative looping mechanism.

- **ODBC Links**. Through the ODBC-related Classes, ODBC connections, queries, and look-ups may be performed directly from Notes Scripts.

Other Products that Use LotusScript

Lotus Notes R4 is not the only product that includes LotusScript. LotusScript is a significant desktop integration strategy implemented by Lotus to compete head to head with Microsoft's Visual Basic for Applications, or VBA.

Besides Notes R4, LotusScript is found today in Lotus WordPro, the revolutionary collaborative word processing system, and Lotus Approach 96, a desktop database package that competes with Microsoft Access. Lotus Freelance 96 also includes LotusScript. Lotus 1-2-3 will be retooled in 32-bit form along with LotusScript functionality in 1996. It is obvious that LotusScript will play a significant role as the glue that binds the Lotus product suite (as well as other OLE 2.0 Windows server and client applications) together.

Each implementation of LotusScript may be tailored somewhat by Lotus to better suit the needs of the application in which it is included. For example, various classes are built into LotusScript in Lotus Notes R4 to enable Notes data access. These classes are not likely to be very useful in Lotus WordPro. However, rest assured that the core syntax and functionality of the LotusScript language will remain the same from one product to the next.

In addition to Lotus products, through a technology sharing agreement, Revelation Software's Visual Programmer, or VIP, will also include complete compatibility with LotusScript 3.0 in an upcoming release. This compatibility is discussed further in Chapter 22, "Using Third-Party Development Tools."

LotusScript Compared to Visual Basic

Developers with experience using Microsoft Visual Basic (VB) 3.0 or 4.0 will feel right at home when they use LotusScript. With the notable exception of complete object orientation that is built into LotusScript (in the form of several predefined Notes and ODBC-related classes), a majority of the data types and keywords found in VB are identical to those found in LotusScript.

LotusScript is derived from a BASIC standard aggressively developed by Microsoft over the past several years. The most recent Microsoft incarnation of their BASIC language is Visual Basic 4.0. Visual Basic for Applications (VBA) is more akin to LotusScript than the stand-alone Visual Basic product because it is used as an internal scripting tool within a significant desktop application, such as Microsoft Word or Microsoft Access.

One of the most significant advantages of LotusScript is platform independence, a feature that enables developers to forget about the unique characteristics of different target environments. A sophisticated Notes database may be designed and used on all platforms supported without change, including Windows 95, OS/2, Macintosh, Sun Solaris, and AIX. While some may argue that platforms besides Windows are irrelevant (in particular, Bill Gates and party), other platforms, in particular Apple Macintosh and IBM OS/2, host a significant number of Notes clients.

For those experienced with VB/VBA development, some of the most notable differences between the languages follow:

■ **Directives**. Compiler directives, such as the INCLUDE directive, are preceded by a % instead of a $. For example, to include a LotusScript file (that incidentally uses the LSS extension), LotusScript uses the statement %INCLUDE "Test.Lss". Additional directives are added, such as %REM…%END REM.

■ **Typical Constant Declarations**. As a standard, you should include the file LSCONST.LSS in the global declarations section of any Notes database that you create. This file is similar to the Visual Basic 3.0 CONSTANT.TXT file. Peruse the LSCONST.LSS file to acquaint yourself with the constants that are defined within.

■ **I/O Functions**. In LotusScript, the MessageBox() function is used instead of the MsgBox() function in VBA. Most of the command line parameters for these functions are identical.

■ **Printing at Runtime**. In LotusScript, a printer object is not defined—direct printing to a Windows default printer is not possible. The Print statement in LotusScript prints output to the standard Lotus Notes status bar at run-time (when not in Debug mode and when running on a standard client system).

- **Matrix-Like Operations**. The `ForAll` statement enables one or more statements to be executed for each element of a given array, collection or list. A collection may be a set of documents in a database, or a set of databases on a server. The Visual Basic equivalent of this command is the `For Each` statement.

- **Notes Formula Evaluation**. The `Evaluate()` function enables a Notes Formula to be executed from within a Script.

As a VBA developer, you will undoubtedly discover other differences between the two development systems. However, in most cases your experience with VBA or VB will only help to better your understanding of LotusScript.

Navigators

Navigators are another significant front-end tool added to the Lotus Notes R4 development tool chest. Navigators are graphical road maps that enable the developer to create an application that is extremely easy to use. If designed properly, a Navigator, or group of Navigators, may be used to step the user through an entire Lotus Notes workflow application—without requiring the use of any pull-down menus.

Navigators are displayed in the left-side pane in an open database. A Navigator may consist of one or more *hotspots*, or predefined graphical regions, that trigger an action. Unique actions may be defined for each hotspot. Actions that correspond to hotspots may, for example, present a new Navigator or open a new database View.

Perhaps one of the most significant aspects of Navigators is that, in many cases, they require little programming effort. Simple Actions may be used to define what happens when a user clicks on a hotspot. For more complex requirements, Formulas or Scripts may be activated when the user triggers a hotspot.

Figure 17.2 shows a Navigator being used in the standard Room Reservations template that is shipped with Lotus Notes R4. The graphical Navigators appear to the left of the screen. Note that a box appears around the user's current selection, based on a predefined hotspot drawn on the screen during Navigator development.

> **TIP**
>
> Need to impress someone? One of the most dramatic front-end development offerings in R4, Navigators enables you to perform a "face-lift" on any Release 3.x database. Navigators are easy to develop, and enable you to visibly illustrate one of the many aesthetic advantages of R4 for your users.

FIGURE 17.2.

A room reservations Navigator example.

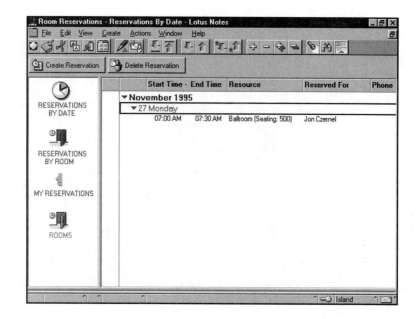

Agents

Replacing Lotus Notes Release 3.x Macros, Agents have been expanded dramatically in R4. When combined with the powerful scripting and database access capabilities of LotusScript, agents may be used to perform tasks that previously may have required the intervention of alternative development packages, such as C or Visual Basic. It is now possible, for example, to write import agents that run on a nightly basis that will update data residing in a Notes database based on information from either ODBC-compatible data sources or simple ASCII files. Try to do that using a macro in a Notes Release 3.x database!

Both Public and Private Agents may be created for a database, enabling the end-user to create their own personal agents to perform tasks such as automatic mail routing. Additionally, new searching criteria has been added that enables agents to run on documents that adhere to a variety of date, author names, or field specifications within a form.

Figure 17.3 shows the design screen that is used to define agents tasks in R4. Note that either Simple Actions, Formulas, or Scripts may be executed when an Agent is triggered.

With agents, combined with the advanced capabilities of LotusScript, developers are able to write complex maintenance agents that perform various database actions, such as automatic document archival.

In many ways, the advanced characteristics of agents may prove to be the most important new tool provided to Notes R4 developers, second only to LotusScript.

FIGURE 17.3.

The Agent design screen.

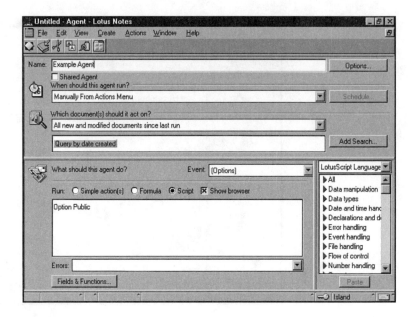

Simple Actions

While this chapter has devoted a significant amount of time to LotusScript and, to a lesser extent, Formulas, there is yet another simple method provided in Lotus Notes R4 to respond to triggers and events: Simple Actions. With virtually no coding effort, Simple Actions enable a variety of tasks to be easily performed.

Simple Actions are a set of predefined routines (15, to be exact) that execute specific tasks. When using a Simple Action, context sensitive entry screens in the Simple Action dialog box appear that guide you through the process of completely defining the necessary attributes of a selected action, eliminating the need to write Script or Formula code in most cases.

> **TIP**
>
> Due to the simplicity of Simple Actions, as well as the need to produce Notes applications as quickly as possible, Simple Actions should be the first line of attack selected to handle any coding task. If a Simple Action cannot be found to perform a particular task, move to more advanced Formulas or Script.

Figure 17.4 depicts the selection of a Simple Action to define an action associated with a button. In this example, the Simple Action has been defined to modify the value of a field when a button is pressed.

FIGURE 17.4.

Simple Actions in action.

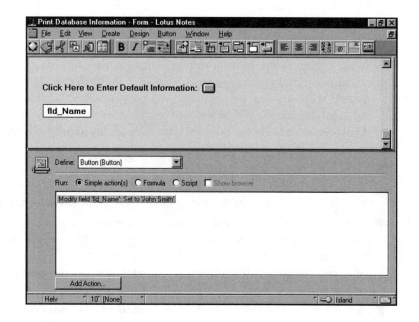

Multiple Simple Actions may be defined for one event. The order of multiple Simple Actions may be altered easily by cutting a Simple Action from one location and pasting it to its new location.

Simple Actions provide a convenient way for designers to develop seemingly advanced databases with minimal effort and time.

Designing an Application with Lotus Notes R4

With new development capabilities, the software life cycle under Lotus Notes R4 has been altered significantly.

While it is true that one of the strengths of Lotus Notes has been its RAD (Rapid Application Development) cycle, not all applications can still be developed with a cavalier attitude.

With the additional capabilities of LotusScript, in particular the definition of classes, subroutines and functions, it is important for the developer to break down a complex project into bite-size, easily maintainable pieces.

Here are some general development guidelines that should be followed when designing any application for R4:

- Write a project scope prior to writing a single line of code. Make sure that your scope document includes, at a functional level, all of the goals that your new system must meet. Verify your final project scope with your customer. With LotusScript, Navigators, and Agents, you will be tempted to add "cool" features on-the-fly that might not have been included in the initial project design. This strategy will undoubtedly lead to an application that never sees the light of day.

- Create functional prototypes for entry screens, and (most importantly) demonstrate these prototypes to the customer. Oftentimes a customer may reject your system if it doesn't look the way they think it should—right down to the font size and color.

- Throughout the development process, especially when using LotusScript, break down complicated tasks into short, concise subprograms or functions. Use subprograms or functions to define script logic that is repeated more than once anywhere in your program. You may wish to place common procedures and/or class definitions used for several projects into a LotusScript Include file, for simple inclusion in new projects.

- When using variable names, make them meaningful, but not ridiculously long. This applies to field names on forms as well. For field names, consider using a prefix, such as "fld." Additionally, always assign synonyms to form and view names.

- Use comments to ensure that your script is readable, but don't go haywire. If your application uses a fair amount of subprograms or functions, insert a common comment block after the procedure definition describing, in plain English, the exact role of the procedure, return values (if any) and passed values (if any).

- When estimating project times, take into account Murphy's Law. Estimating the length of a development project is perhaps one of the most difficult tasks that developers face. It requires years of real-world experience and expertise in several areas.

These rules are not all encompassing, and do not cover all of the issues associated with large-scale advanced development. Simply remember that the advanced development features that Lotus Notes R4 enables may mean that more planning and effort is needed to ensure that applications developed today are delivered on schedule and are easily maintained in the years ahead.

Summary

Lotus has made some great strides in the Notes development arena with R4. For the developer that has grown accustomed to Release 3.x limitations, these additions will undoubtedly induce a sigh of relief.

In this chapter we have discussed, in broad terms, a majority of the new development Lotus Notes R4 tools. It is important for a developer with Release 3.x experience to be aware of these substantial offerings before becoming bogged down by details.

Here is a summary of the most significant topics covered in this chapter:

- LotusScript, or Script, is a BASIC-compatible, object-oriented scripting language that enables direct access to Notes database, and user interface elements. Additional capabilities, such as external ODBC connectivity, provide necessary links to other RDBS.

- The learning curve for LotusScript is quite reasonable, especially for developers with Microsoft VisualBasic experience.

- Navigators enable the design of an easy-to-use front-end for any existing or new database. The developer may either use built-in drawing tools or import bitmap images to create appealing Navigator panes. Simple Actions, Formulas or LotusScript may be triggered when a hotspot on a Navigator is selected.

- Agents, formerly referred to as Macros, have been significantly enhanced to enable a great variety of scheduling and document selection choices. Simple Actions, Formulas or LotusScript may be triggered when an agent is executed.

- Simple Actions, used as an alternative to Formulas and Scripts, enable a variety of basic Notes tasks to be initiated with virtually no coding effort. If you want to create Notes applications quickly, Simple Actions is your answer.

- The new development capabilities introduced in this chapter, particularly LotusScript, force database designers to adhere to more principled, rigid development guidelines. The promise of Rapid Application Development (RAD) and maintainable code under Notes is lost if new high-level development skills are not acquired.

17

INTRODUCTION TO
ADVANCED
DEVELOPMENT

Using LotusScript

by Jonathan Czernel

IN THIS CHAPTER

CHAPTER 18

Our in-depth discussion of LotusScript Version 3.0, the scripting language built into Lotus Notes R4, begins in this chapter. LotusScript, or "Script" in Lotusese, enables Notes databases to contain underlying logic and data-access capabilities that bring a tremendous amount of power to Notes applications development.

The first portion of this chapter is written for the experienced Lotus Notes Release 3.x developer who has not had a great deal of exposure to "modern" programming languages, such as C, Pascal, Visual Basic, or FORTRAN. I *do*, however, assume that the reader is familiar with general terminology that would be expected of any Release 3.x developer. We will begin with the very high-level concepts that are essential in providing a basic foundation, then work our way down to the more detailed subtleties of the LotusScript language. Real-life examples will be provided as often as possible to demonstrate the principles being discussed.

The center cut of this chapter, "Common Tasks," describes how to perform activities that are commonplace in the world of LotusScript, including basic user input and output. This section is intended for all developers new to LotusScript or BASIC.

The final portion of this chapter, "Advanced LotusScript," is intended for those already familiar with languages such as Visual Basic, C, or Pascal, as well as experienced Release 3.x developers who have reviewed the basic features of LotusScript. This section discusses the object-oriented extensions and built-in classes that are used to extract information from, and add information to, Notes databases (as well as other external objects, such as ODBC databases).

NOTE

This chapter should not be considered a replacement for documentation included with Lotus Notes R4. If you need further information on a particular subject discussed, use the Lotus Notes R4 online help or hard-copy documentation provided with Notes.

LotusScript is a powerful language, providing an incredible amount of flexibility to the Lotus Notes applications developer. After reading this chapter, I hope you will continue to use it to supplement your Lotus Notes R4 documentation.

NOTE

From this point forward, the terms *LotusScript* and *Script* will be used interchangeably. The term *Formula* is used to refer to both @Functions and @Commands, the macro language available in both Lotus Notes Release 3.x and Release 4.x.

LotusScript Essentials

This section discusses some of the basic tools that will be necessary to efficiently write LotusScript code in a Notes database.

Here is a brief description of the topics that follow:

- *Handling events.* Events trigger Script; a discussion of events, therefore, is mandatory.
- *Procedures.* Both functions (not to be confused with @Functions) and subprograms may be added and called from event handlers.
- *Conditionals.* Use the If...Then...Else statement to perform one or more tasks based on the value of an expression.
- *Program flow.* Several methods are now available to assist the developer in iterating through a series of Script statements two or more times.
- *Variables and constants.* This section discusses the different variable types and pre-defined constants that are available in LotusScript.
- *Operators.* Several numeric operators are available in LotusScript. This section introduces these operators.
- *String operations.* How do you parse a string using LotusScript? Answers to this and other common string-related questions are presented in this section.
- *Other features.* This section presents other commonly used features of the LotusScript language.

Handling Events

Script is written to act as a response to *events* that are initiated by the user or by the Lotus Notes system itself. As it is through events that all Scripts are executed, it is important to understand the various events that exist in Notes, and how these events may be used in a typical Notes database.

Events are actually Notes system "triggers" that initiate a specific subprogram (or *sub*) that contains Script.

Examples of events include:

- *Clicking on a button:* When a user clicks on a Form button, you might want to fill in one or more fields on the form with default values.
- *Entering a field:* When the user moves focus to a new field on a form, the Entering event is triggered.

Figure 18.1 illustrates the use of the Entering event in a database. In this example, a user is asked to enter the value for the Name field when input focus is received. The LotusScript InputBox() function is used to present the pop-up dialog box that will accept user input.

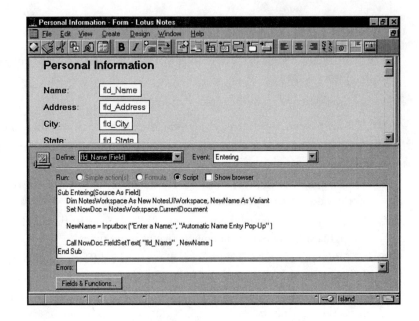

FIGURE 18.1.
Using the Entering
event.

Table 18.1 enumerates the events that are built-in for various objects utilized in Notes. For some events, an example of a "real world" use is provided.

Table 18.1. Notes events.

Event Name	Object(s)	When It's Triggered
Initialize	Form, Agent	When form or an agent is created.
QueryOpen	Form	Before a form is loaded. The Continue parameter may be used to halt the form from loading by setting its value to False.
Initialize	Field, Action, Button, Hotspot	When an object is loaded from the database.
PostOpen	Form	After a Form is opened. This event may be used to set default field values on a form.
PostRecalc	Form	After a Form is refreshed. A refresh is triggered when the user selects View | Refresh (F9) or a Refresh agent is executed on the document. When filling out a Form, the user may be asked to press F9 to optionally fill out default information on a Form.

Event Name	Object(s)	When It's Triggered
QuerySave	Form	Immediately before a document is saved. If desired, Script in this event may be used to perform complex input validation. To halt the save operation, set the Continue parameter to False.
Click	Button, Hotspot, Action	When one of the objects listed is selected with a mouse click.
QueryModeChange	Form	The mode is toggled between Edit mode and Read mode (Ctrl+E). To disallow the mode change, set the Continue parameter to False.
Entering	Editable Fields	When a field on a Form receives focus. (See Figure 18.1.)
PostModeChange	Form	After the mode is changed from Edit mode to Read mode, or vice versa.
Exiting	Editable Fields	When a field on a Form loses focus.
QueryClose	Form, Agent	Immediately prior to a form or agent being closed. Set the Continue parameter to False to disallow the close action.
Terminate	Form	When a Form is being closed.
Terminate	Field, Button, Hotspot, Action	When one of the objects listed is closed. Note that the Terminate event for a Form is triggered prior to the Terminate event for one of these objects.

> **NOTE**
>
> For all events listed in Table 18.1, with the exception of Initialize and Terminate, you may use formulas instead of Script. In most cases, however, Script will provide a tremendous amount of flexibility, and should be used to handle all event logic.

If you have been briefly exposed to Notes R4, you've probably noticed that we have omitted several "events" that appear in the Event pull-down list box at design time, such as Default Value, Input Validation, and Input Translation. It is true that, in the traditional sense, these events are triggered by the Notes system, and therefore may be considered legitimate events. However, unlike the events listed in Table 18.1, these events do not enable LotusScript to be executed—only Formulas. The inclusion of these "events," therefore, enables Release 3.x databases to be easily migrated to R4.

18

Additionally, a (Declarations) or (Options) selection may appear in the Event list box, depending on the current context. These are not really events; their inclusion in the Event list box is somewhat misleading. Here is a brief description of what these choices represent:

- The Declarations section is used for *nonexecutable* script, such as variable- and user-defined, data-type declarations.
- The Options section is used to define constants, external LotusScript eXtensions (LSX), and compiler options.

For either one of these events, when used with the (Globals) object, the Declarations and Options sections pertain to all of the event scripts contained within the database. Otherwise, they pertain only to the object that is selected.

> **NOTE**
>
> The Event list box contains not only events, but also Formula-only Release 3.x-compatible events (such as Default Value), a Declarations section, and an Options section, as well as user-defined procedures.

> **TIP**
>
> It is possible to use Script-based events, such as QueryClose(), to replace the functionality of Release 3.x-based events such as Input Validation, Input Translation, and Default. Use Script when more complex logic is required to properly validate or translate the value of a field.

Procedures: An Introduction to Subprograms and Functions

One of the advantages of LotusScript over the formula system of Release 3.x is that more complicated routines can be broken down into simple, reusable pieces. This slice-and-dice process is facilitated through the use of *procedures*.

One type of a procedure is a *subprogram*. An example of a subprogram follows:

```
Sub SayThis( SayString$ )
    'Presents a dialog box to the user
    MessageBox ( SayString$ )
End Sub
```

To execute Script in a subprogram, the Call statement is used. For example, to begin execution of the preceding subprogram, use the statement Call SayThis("Hello").

When a subprogram is called, control is returned to the caller when an End Sub or an Exit Sub is encountered. Optionally, the Call statement may be omitted when a subprogram is called.

> **NOTE**
>
> The events discussed in the previous section, are, in essence, predefined subprograms. (Refer back to Table 18.1.)

> **NOTE**
>
> This chapter uses the term *subprogram* to define a block of Script sandwiched between the Sub and End Sub keywords. However, Lotus documentation uses the terms *subprogram* and *subroutine* interchangeably. We'll define a subroutine as a block of code that is called with the Gosub keyword, described later in this chapter.

The second type of procedure is a function. The only difference between a function and a subprogram is that a function returns a value to the caller. In the following sample function, note that the return data type is specified (in this case a Variant).

```
Function GetResponse ( AskString$ ) As Variant
     'Presents an input box, and returns the user entry
     GetResponse = InputBox( AskString$ )
End Function
```

To call the preceding function, use the statement Response = GetResponse("Enter a String, Fred!"). *To properly return a value, the function must contain an expression that sets the function name to a return value.*

Procedures may contain zero or more *parameters*. A parameter is a value that is passed to a procedure, such as the AskString$ string variable in the preceding example. The variable *type* for each parameter must be specified.

Creating New Procedures

To create a new procedure (either a subprogram or a function), you must first determine what other sections of Script need access to the procedure.

To enable a new procedure to be "seen" by *any* other procedure in the database, including all of the predefined event procedures (such as the Entering() subprogram), make sure that the object (Define) is set to the (Globals) choice prior to creating the new procedure. If the (Globals) object is *not* selected when a procedure is created, only other procedures defined within the context of the object selected will be able to reference the new procedure. This process of defining where an object is visible is known as defining a procedure *scope*.

After selecting an appropriate object that will provide the procedure visibility, or scope, that you require, you must select an event that allows Script, such as (Declarations).

Finally, after an appropriate object and event have been selected, simply move the cursor to any blank line in the script text editor and type in the first line of the procedure. Figure 18.2 illustrates a new function being defined that will be visible to every other procedure in the database. Note that the object selected is (Globals), enabling this new procedure to be called anywhere in the database.

FIGURE 18.2.

Creating a new global procedure.

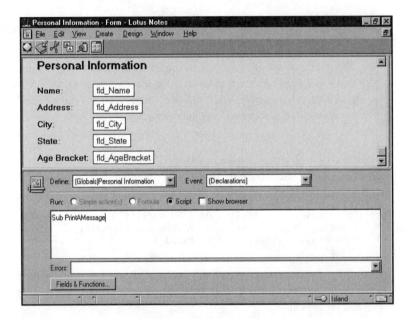

After typing in the procedure name, pressing Enter automatically adds an End Sub statement. From this point forward, the procedure will appear in the Event list for the object selected.

TIP

To exit a subprogram before the End Sub statement, use the Exit Sub statement; to exit a function prematurely, use the Exit Function statement.

This feature may be useful, for example, to terminate the execution of the current procedure while deeply nested in several levels of If...End If statements. Without the Exit statement, one would either need to rework the logic of a procedure to "gracefully" fall to End Sub as needed, or use Goto to branch to a label just before the natural End Sub. This is considered terrible programming practice for reasons described later in this chapter.

Here are some guidelines to follow when creating a new procedure:

- ■ Be sure the name makes sense, like PrintMessage() or AskForName().
- ■ When called, procedure names are not case-sensitive.

- The first character must be a letter; the remaining characters may be any letter or number, including the underscore (_) character.

- If the parameter list for a procedure is empty, the parentheses ( ) after the procedure name may be omitted—they are optional. Parentheses around the parameter list are mandatory only when one or more parameters are specified.

- A procedure name cannot exceed 40 characters in length.

TIP

After developing several Lotus Notes R4 applications, you may have a library of procedures that you use in each one of your databases. Instead of cutting and pasting procedures from existing databases to new ones, insert all of your common procedures into one or more text (ASCII) files, one after the other, using your favorite text editor. While not mandatory, for the sake of consistency it is best to use the extension LSS (LotuSScript) for the text file that you create. Save this text file in the directory that contains Lotus Notes R4 executable files, not your database files (Data directory).

To use the procedures in this file in any database, insert the line `%INCLUDE "filename.LSS"` into the `(Globals)` object in the `(Declarations)` section, where `"filename.LSS"` is the name of the file that contains your procedure(s). At compile time, LotusScript loads and compiles the contents of the file specified. After successful compilation, procedures contained in this file will be visible to any other procedure in the database.

Note, however, that distribution of databases that uses the `%INCLUDE` directive also requires the distribution of all text (*.LSS) files used in the database.

Conditionals

Much to the joy of Release 3.x developers who have lived through the agony of debugging nested `@If()` functions, Script allows fully formatted, easily understood nested conditionals through the `If` statement.

The following example illustrates a nested `If...Else...EndIf` block structure in R4:

```
If NewName = "Fred" Then
  MessageBox("His Name is Fred.")
Else
  If (City = "Clearwater") And (Age >= 50 ) Then
    MessageBox("He is in Clearwater, FL")
  End If
End If
```

In this example, if the variable `NewName` is equal to `"Fred"`, a message is printed to the user indicating that, indeed, `"His Name is Fred."` Otherwise, script execution proceeds to the line after the `Else` statement. If the individual lives in the city Clearwater and his or her age is greater than or = to 50, a dialog box is presented that indicates this match to the user.

After typing an `If` statement in LotusScript, followed by Enter, the text editor automatically adds a terminating `End If` statement. This is the case for virtually all block-oriented LotusScript statements, including `Do...Loop`, `While...Wend`, and `ForAll...End ForAll`.

> **TIP**
>
> Indent script statements within an `If...Then...Else` block in a consistent fashion. Proper and consistent indentation allows the logic of the script to be easily understood by any developer.
>
> Due to the automatic block termination performed in the text editor, the default indentation level should be used.

The `If...Else...Endif` statement is able to perform one or more condition evaluations. In the preceding example, `NewName = "Fred"` is the first condition evaluated. In this case, the equal sign is the *comparison operator*.

A list of the most common comparison operators in LotusScript in shown in Table 18.2. Note the inclusion of the `Like` operator, a unique member of the operator family that is sure to be used in a number of situations.

Table 18.2. LotusScript comparison operators.

Comparison Operator	*Description*	*Example*
=	Equal to	`NewName = "Fred"`
<>	Not equal to	`NewName <> "Fred"`
>=	Greater than or equal to	`Age >= 50`
<=	Less than or equal to	`Age <= 50`
Like	Used to compare one string with a provided string pattern	`NewName Like "Jo*"`

You may string together several comparisons, as in the second `If...Then...Else` block in the preceding example. The Boolean operators `AND` and `OR` are most commonly used in multiple comparisons.

The following `If` statement provides an example of a more complex comparison operation:

```
If (NewName Like "Jo*" OR State = "FL") AND (Age > 50 OR State <> "MI") Then
```

> **TIP**
>
> For more complex `If...Then...Else` blocks (in particular, those involving a long conditional expression), after several indentations you may run out of room on the screen to contain one full statement.
>
> To continue evaluation of a script statement on the following line, append a space or tab, followed by an underscore (_), to the end of the current line. You may then continue the statement on the following line.

Program Flow Control: Repetition Statements

There are several mechanisms in LotusScript that allow *blocks* of script to be repeated several times. A block of script is defined as one or more LotusScript statements.

Fixed Repetition

To repeat a block of Script a *fixed* number of times, use the `For...Next` statement, as in the following example, which pops up a dialog box five times in a row:

```
For Count% = 1 to 5
    MessageBox ("We are in the loop, Count: " + Str$( Count%) )
Next Count%
```

Note the following points about our example:

1. We started at one and "counted" to five. The 1 and 5 may be replaced by variables, constants, or other expressions.

2. The variable used in the `For` statement—`Count%` in this example—may be referenced within the `For...Next` loop. However, do not modify this value manually!

3. To exit a `For...Next` loop prematurely, use the `Exit For` statement. Never use the `Goto` statement to break out of a loop—it's bad programming practice.

4. To count backwards, add the `Step -1` option to the end of the For statement. In this example, you would use the statement `For Count% = 5 to 1 Step -1` to count from five to one.

5. In this example, the `Count%` variable in the `Next` statement is optional. For readability purposes, however, the variable name should be included, especially in nested `For...Next` loops or loops that embody several lines of script.

After you type in the `For` statement and required arguments, pressing Enter automatically adds the `Next` statement to your procedure, and properly indents the first line between the `For` and `Next` statements.

Variable Repetition with Conditional Looping

Other methods of looping allow a group of Script statements to be repeated while a particular condition evaluates to `True`. Evaluations used in these loops are identical to those used in an `If...Then...Else` statement.

The two statement blocks that allow logical iterations are `Do...Loop` and `While...Wend`. The `Do...Loop` statement is the most versatile of the two. In fact, one form of the `Do...Loop` statement allows it to clone the operation of the `While...Wend` statement.

The `Do...Loop` statement is discussed first. Examine the following code fragment:

```
...
ContinueProcess% = True
...
Do While ContinueProcess% = True
    ...
    If NewName = "End" Then ContinueProcess% = False
    ...
Loop
...
```

Note that the condition (`ContinueProcess% = True`) is checked *before* executing any script contained in the loop. If `ContinueProcess%` is set to `False`, program execution will continue after the `Loop` statement, skipping all script within the `Do...Loop` block. This type of looping construct is referred to as a *pretest* loop.

Here is another form of the `Do...Loop` statement, with a minor alteration:

```
...
ContinueProcess% = True
...
Do
    ...
    If NewName = "End" Then ContinueProcess% = False
    ...
Loop While ContinueProcess% = True
...
```

Notice the difference? In the second example, the script contained within the loop is *always* executed *at least* once, because the `While` evaluation occurs in the `Loop` statement instead of the `Do` statement. This type of loop is referred to as a *posttest* loop.

The alternate form of the `Do...Loop` statement replaces the `While` keyword with an `Until`. Here is another example of a posttest loop that uses the `Until` keyword.

```
...
Do
    ...
    If NewName = "End" Then ContinueProcess% = False Else ContinueProcess% =True
    ...
Loop Until ContinueProcess% = False
...
```

Note the following about the preceding example:

1. Instead of using `While`, we have used the `Until` keyword. The statement block within the loop is repeated *until* the evaluation is `True`. To achieve the same functionality as the other examples, the logic in the "posttest" changed.

2. In the other examples, we set the value of `ContinueProcess%` to `True` before the `Do...Loop` block. This is referred to as a loop *primer*, and may be required to allow the `Do...Loop` block to execute at least once in the case of a pretest loop. This example sets the value to either `True` or `False` *within* the `Do...Loop` block. In most cases I recommend the use of a primer, enabling you to simply change the state of a variable once to terminate a loop, avoiding unnecessary CPU cycles within the loop (resulting in slower execution).

The second repetitive looping construct, `While...Wend`, is identical in nature to the `Do...Loop` statement when used as a pretest with the `While` keyword.

An example of a typical `While...Wend` loop is found here:

```
...
ContinueProcess% = True
...
While ContinueProcess% = True
    ...
    If NewName = "End" Then ContinueProcess% = False
    ...
Wend
...
```

To wrap up this section on repetitive structures in LotusScript, here are some final notes:

■ To prematurely break out of a `Do...Loop`, use the `Exit Do` keyword within the body of the loop. The `While...Wend` construct does not have an equivalent mechanism.

■ Just as with the `If...Then...Else` statement, you may build more complex comparison operations.

■ Loops may be nested within each other.

Program Flow Control: Jumping To and Fro

To detour script execution within a procedure from one location to another, two statements are provided: `Goto` and `Gosub`. To use either of these statements, a *label* somewhere in the *current* procedure must be defined. Remember that a `Call` statement, unlike `Gosub`, is used to branch to a completely *different* procedure defined elsewhere in an application, using a `Sub` instead of a label.

A label is like a bookmark in the procedure. Examples of labels include `PrintAMessage:`, `PhaseI:`, `PhaseII:`, and `ErrorTrap:`. A label must be by itself on a line of Script, and should be meaningful to the reader. Labels are always followed by a colon.

NOTE

It is very, very important to remember that a label is only "visible" in the procedure in which it is defined. That is, it has only procedure scope.

The Curse of BASIC: Goto

The Goto statement is used to *unconditionally* branch from one location to another. In older BASIC dialects, such as those distributed in the early 1980s, the Goto statement was a necessary evil, required to compensate for the lack of sufficient block structures and procedure declarations. However, its use over the years has dwindled. Some computer scientists argue that it should be excluded from any modern programming language.

The most significant problem with the Goto statement is that it creates code that is very difficult to read, and therefore difficult to maintain. Under normal circumstances, when reading a procedure, a developer begins on the first line and proceeds line by line, following program logic until the last statement is reached. Because Goto statements can jump to labels *anywhere* in the current procedure, either below *or above* the current statement, the ideal of top-to-bottom program readability is thrown by the wayside when a few unwisely placed labels and Goto statements are used. The term *spaghetti code* was originally coined to define a program that contained numerous intertwined labels and Goto statements.

One of the more common uses of the Goto statement has been to branch out of a looping structure, such as a Do...Loop or For...Next, prematurely. This is no longer required, due to the addition of the Exit statement with the Do and For keywords, respectively.

TIP

The Goto statement should be avoided like the plague, unless you enjoy being ridiculed by experienced software developers worldwide.

"Come Back Real Soon, Y'all!": Gosubs

The Gosub statement, like Goto, is used to branch program execution to a label. Unlike Goto, however, a Return statement may be executed to resume operation at the line immediately following the last Gosub. In this respect, a Gosub is similar to a procedure (a subprogram or function), in that control is *temporarily* passed to another block of script.

The following LotusScript code fragment demonstrates the use of the Goto and Gosub statements.

```
...
MessageBox ("We begin our travels here.")
Goto GotoLabel
ProceedAfterGoto:
MessageBox ("We are home, but what a nightmare!")

MessageBox ("Now let's try a Gosub...")
Gosub GosubLabel
MessageBox ("We have been safely returned home!")

Exit Sub   'Get out of this subprogram

GotoLabel:
    MessageBox ("How do we return?  Only through another Goto!")
    Goto ProceedAfterGoto

GosubLabel:
    'This is a Subroutine...
    MessageBox ("How do we return?  Like this...")
Return

...
```

NOTE

From this point forward, we will call any block of code that begins with a valid label and ends with a Return statement a *subroutine*. A subroutine is *not* the same as a subprogram, which is a procedure that begins with a Sub statement and ends with an End Sub statement. This may not be consistent with all Lotus documentation, but it is consistent in the more universal world of modern BASIC.

In some cases, it is more desirable to create a new procedure (subprogram or function) instead of a subroutine that is called with the Gosub statement. Here are some guidelines to follow when deciding whether to create a new subroutine or a new procedure (subprogram or function).

Create a new subroutine (that may be Gosubed) if:

- The new routine will be used only by the current procedure. Because subroutines are visible only within the procedure in which they are defined, they may not be called from any other procedures in the database.

- Several (for example, more than five) parameters would need to be passed to any procedure that is created. Because a procedure falls outside of the variable scope of the current procedure, all variables that are required in the new routine would need to be included as procedure parameters.

> **NOTE**
>
> Although the use of the Gosub statement is not nearly as controversial as the use of the Goto statement, it should be noted that more advanced developers always lean toward the creation of procedures (subprograms and functions) over subroutines.

Holding Data with Variables

Just as in a Release 3.x formula, *variables* are used to hold data. However, variables in LotusScript are much more versatile and powerful. This discussion of variables begins by describing how variables are declared, as well as the different types of data that variables may contain.

Variable Declarations: Implicit and Explicit

Under normal (read: default) circumstances, as LotusScript interprets a procedure it automatically allocates memory to accommodate the storage requirements of variables *as they are encountered.* Thus, variables may be used "on-the-fly" in any procedure, without any prior declaration. This is known as *implicit declaration* of a variable. For Release 3.x developers, *temporary variables*, to a certain extent, are examples of implicitly declared variables—they do not require a formal "declaration" prior to use.

In some cases, however, it is desirable to declare a variable *before* it is used. A variable declared in this fashion is said to be *explicitly declared.* The Dim statement is used to explicitly declare a variable.

The following procedure fragment illustrates explicit and implicit declaration of variables:

```
Sub IllustrateVariables()
    'Here are explicitly declared variables
    Dim I%, NewPrice@
    ...
    ...
    'This is an implicitly declared variable -
    'A DIM statement is not used to declare the variable
    TempHolder% = 4
    ...
    ...
End Sub
```

To an inexperienced developer, the difference between implicit and explicit declaration might seem trivial. Because more effort is involved in declaring variables explicitly, why not just use implicit declaration? The answer, like so many other situations discussed in this chapter, involves the long-term maintenance of your database.

In the previous example, is TempHolder% used elsewhere in the database? If you allow implicit declaration, there is no way of telling the difference between a variable used for the first time in a procedure or a variable that is specified as being globally accessible to all procedures in your database. For a developer reading this script for the first time, it is much more straightforward to see a list of all variables and their associated types defined near the beginning of each procedure.

> **TIP**
>
> Although implicit declaration is easy in the short haul, it may manifest itself into a dangerous maintenance issue in the long haul. For databases that survive the times, use explicit variable declaration.

> **TIP**
>
> To force all variables to be explicitly declared with the `Dim` statement, include the compiler directive `Option Declare` in the `(Globals)` object and `(Objects)` event in your database. Any reference to a variable that has not been properly declared will produce an error at compile time.

Now that you know the difference between explicit and implicit variable declarations, we will now focus our attention on the different variable types that are at your disposal in LotusScript.

LotusScript Data Types

Throughout several examples provided thus far, you've probably noticed characters, such as % and @, attached to variable names. These characters are referred to as *variable suffixes*. Because LotusScript allows for a variety of *data types*, these characters are used to define the type of data that a specific variable is equipped to store.

Table 18.3 enumerates all of the data types available in LotusScript, along with appropriate variable suffix characters.

Table 18.3. LotusScript data types.

Type Name	Variable	Value Limits	Common Usage Suffix
Integer	%	−32,768 to +32,767	Counters in For...Next loops, array indexes, various flags (True/False).
Long	&	−2,147,483,648 to +2,147,483,647	When the capacity of a standard integer is insufficient.

continues

Table 18.3. continued

Type Name	Variable	Value Limits	Common Usage Suffix
Single	!	–3.402823E+38 to +3.402823E+38	To hold values stored in various computations.
Double	#	1.7976931348623158E+308 to +1.7976931348623158E+308	When the capacity of single precision is insufficient.
Currency	@	922,337,203,685,477.5807 to 922,337,203,685,477.5807	To hold monetary values, especially in monetary calculations when proper rounding is required.
String	$	From 0 characters to 32KB characters.	To hold various non-numeric data, such as names and addresses.
Variant	None	Any of the preceding data types, plus object references and LotusScript date/time values.	To hold data whose type is unknown at design time.

When a variable is implicitly declared, the variable suffix determines the type of data that the variable can hold.

NOTE

If a variable type is not defined either explicitly or implicitly, a *variant* data type is assumed.

When a variable is explicitly declared, either the variable suffix or the variable type in conjunction with the Dim statement and As keyword may be used. Here is a code fragment that explicitly declares variables using the Dim statement:

```
...
Dim Astring as String
...
'More than one variable may be declared with one Dim statement.
Dim NumberOne as Long, NumberTwo!
...
'The variable here will be declared a Variant, since no suffix or As is specified...
Dim SomeValue
...
```

After a variable is declared, a Type Mismatch error will occur at runtime if an illegal assignment, such as an attempt to store a string value into an integer variable, occurs. For example, the following code block generates a Type Mismatch error.

```
Dim HeavyOne%, AnyValue as Variant
AnyValue = "This is a string!"
'This statement attempts to store a variant containing a string
'expression into a variable designated as an integer! Type Mismatch all the way!
HeavyOne% = AnyValue
```

Variable Scopes

As a final note, remember that variables declared in one procedure may not be referenced by any other procedure. Just like procedures, variables have a *scope* to their existence.

To declare a variable that is visible to all procedures, referred to as a *global* variable, explicitly declare variables using the Dim statement in the (Declarations) event in the (Globals) object.

Using Arrays

We will now focus our attention on *arrays*. An array is a *collection* of zero or more values that are all referenced through a single variable name, along with one or more *dimensions*. A data type is assigned to an array, just like regular variables.

An array and its corresponding size may be declared either with a Dim statement or a ReDim statement. After an array is declared with the Dim statement, its size cannot be adjusted at runtime—it is referred to as a *static*, or *fixed*, array. *Dynamic arrays*—specified with the ReDim statement—may be resized with subsequent ReDim statements.

The following script block illustrates the declaration and use of a static and a dynamic array:

```
...
'Declare a static integer array
Dim A%(10), Count%
Redim B%(0)
...
A%(1) = 1
A%(2) = 2
For Count% = 3 to 10
    A%(Count%) = Count%
Next Count%
...
'This is a dynamic array; we can resize it any time!
Redim B%(20)
B%(20) = 20
...
```

In this example, both arrays contain one *dimension*. That is, the collection of integers contained within the array are referenced by one index value. In LotusScript, up to eight dimensions may be specified. Therefore, the following statements are completely acceptable:

```
Dim PriceMatrix@( 5, 4 )
ReDim SeatInformation%( 10, 10, 5, 2 )
```

At runtime, two functions are available that allow the determination of the upper and lower bounds of a particular dimension of an array: Ubound() and Lbound().

TIP

It is sometimes necessary to dynamically change the size of an array at runtime while retaining the values already stored in an array. To perform this operation, use the `Preserve` keyword with the `ReDim` statement. Without the `Preserve` keyword, the `ReDim` statement causes all values in the array collection to be reset.

Constants

Like variables, *constants* contain values that may be used in any LotusScript expression. Unlike variables, however, the value of a constant cannot be changed.

Constants are typically used to define either values passed as parameters to procedures, or to define return values from procedures, replacing cryptic numerical values with more user-friendly, English-like variables. They may be defined within a procedure or as global constants in the `(Globals)` object using the `Const` statement.

One example of how constants are used involves the `MessageBox` function, a built-in procedure that presents a simple dialog box to the user. This function requires various parameters that indicate what the message box will look like at runtime. The following example illustrates how constants are used to make LotusScript, in this case the `MessageBox` function, more readable. Note the difference between the first and second `MessageBox` parameter list.

```
...
'Here is a call to MessageBox without using constants
'What does the 32 mean???
MessageBox( "Hello, World!", 32, "Hello Title Bar")
...
'Here is a call to MessageBox with constants.  Everything is clear!
MessageBox( "Hello, World!", MB_OK + MB_ICONQUESTION, "Hello Title Bar")
...
```

Lotus Notes R4 contains the predefined constants listed in Table 18.4.

Table 18.4. LotusScript constants.

Constant	Usage
NULL	Used when data is either unknown or missing. Only variant values can hold a NULL value. The IsNull operator may be used to test for a NULL value.
NOTHING	The value initially assigned to a variable used as an object reference.
TRUE	Equal to −1.
FALSE	Equal to 0.
PI	3.141592654 (a)

NOTE

Other predefined constants also exist for Notes classes described later in this chapter. Because they are not a part of the LotusScript Version 3.0 product, and are considered language "extensions," Notes class-specific constants have not been included in this discussion.

In addition, the file LSCONST.LSS, shipped with every copy of R4, contains a number of additional constants that may be used in conjunction with any one of the following LotusScript functions. Either values returned from or values passed to the functions shown may use constants defined in this file, making your code significantly more readable.

- `DataType`: Used to determine the data type of a given expression.
- `MesssageBox`: Used to present a simple dialog box to the user.
- `SetFileAttr`, `GetFileAttr`: Used to set and get attributes for a given file.
- `Dir`: Used to get a directory listing.
- `FileAttr`: Used to obtain the access type for the file number specified.
- `Shell`: Used to launch another application.

TIP

For most databases, it is always good practice to include the file LSCONST.LSS using the `%Include` directive.

Other included .LSS files that contain several useful constants include:

- LSXBEERR and LSXUIERR: Define constants returned by various errors triggered by Notes-related methods.
- LSCERR and LSSTR: Define error constants returned at compile time.

Constants, like variables, have data types associated with them. The variable suffixes defined in Table 18.3 all apply to constants, with the exception of the Variant type. However, unlike variable declarations, if a type is not explicitly specified in a Const statement using a constant suffix (such as % or @), LotusScript automatically determines an appropriate type, based on the value specified. The following rules apply when a constant suffix is not defined:

- For all floating-point values, such as 3.2234 or 4329685.09432, the double type is used.
- For integer values, such as 324 or 3, the Integer type is used. If the value is larger than 32768 or less than −32767 (the limits on a standard integer data type), a long integer is used.

Numerical Operators and Functions

What can be done with numerical variables after they are defined? Anything, of course! Table 18.5 contains common *numerical operators*, operators that act upon numerical values.

Table 18.5. Common numerical operators.

Operator	Example	Description
+	A% = B% + C%	Simple addition
–	A! = 20 – C!	Simple subtraction
/	A# = B# / 405.4	Division
\	A% = B% \ C%	Integer division
^	A# = 2 ^ C%	Exponentiation

In addition to operators, other mathematical functions are built into LotusScript, such as `Sin()`, `Cos()`, `Tan()`, `Acos()`, `Asin()`, and `Atn()`.

> **NOTE**
>
> All of the angles passed to trigonometric functions should be expressed in radians, not degrees.

With respect to numerical calculations, make sure that the destination variable type is large enough to contain the result of the calculation being performed. For example, the following code fragment will return an `Overflow` error at runtime:

```
...
'These are both valid integer values...
A% = 32000
B% = 10000
...
'This operation results in an Overflow error!
'42000 is too large for an Integer data type!
C% = A% + B%
'However, this statement would work fine,
'storing the result in a Long Integer...
C& = A% + B%
...
```

It is the responsibility of the developer to ensure that runtime errors due to numerical calculations do not occur.

String-Related Functions

Through illustrating the outcome of most of the common string-related functions in LotusScript, Table 18.6 demonstrates how functions may be used to modify and extract information from string variables. Remember that each of these functions will also work with variables of the variant data type that contain a string.

Table 18.6. Common string functions.

Example	Returns	Explanation
Ucase$("Fred A")	"FRED A"	Capitalizes all letters.
Trim$(" Alpha Beta ")	"Alpha Beta"	Removes leading and trailing spaces from a given string, but *not* embedded spaces.
Ltrim$(" Alpha Beta ")	"Alpha Beta "	Removes only leading spaces.
Rtrim$(" Alpha Beta ")	" Alpha Beta"	Removes only trailing spaces.
Left$("Jonathan",3)	"Jon"	Returns the specified number of characters, starting with the left-most position.
Right$("Wilson",2)	"on"	Returns the specified number of characters, starting with the right-most position.
Mid$("Apple",2,3)	"ppl"	In this example, returns three characters, starting with the second character.
Mid$("Apple",2)	"pple"	In this example (without the third parameter specified), returns the string starting with the second character.

To determine the length of a string, use the Len() function.

Common Tasks

This section demonstrates, using examples of LotusScript, two commonly required tasks undertaken in LotusScript:

- Screen input and output
- File input and output

As these capabilities existed only in primitive form in Release 3.x formulas, we will discuss some of the LotusScript statements and built-in functions that enable these capabilities to take place.

18

USING
LOTUSSCRIPT

Screen Input and Output

LotusScript provides two functions that enable a standard Windows dialog box to be presented to the user at runtime. These dialogs may be used to warn the user of an event, such as the activation of an agent running on their desktop, or to request the entry of a value (perhaps for a field in a database).

> **TIP**
>
> Always use the constants declared in the file LSCONST.LSS to specify command-line options for the procedures described in this section, instead of hard-coding cryptic numbers into your procedure calls. Remember to use the %Include "LSCONST.LSS" directive in your database to include these constant definitions.

> **NOTE**
>
> In all code examples in this section, it is assumed that the constants defined in LSCONST.LSS are available.

Simple Dialogs Through MessageBox

The MessageBox procedure can be referenced like a subprogram or a function. Both forms of the MessageBox procedure enable three parameters to be specified; the first parameter is required, whereas the second and third parameters are optional.

We'll begin our discussion with the MessageBox subprogram.

The first parameter is the message that will be printed in the dialog box itself, such as "Hello, World!" For multiline messages, embed the line-feed (LF) character using the function CHR$(10). Optionally, LotusScript enables vertical bars (¦) to be used instead of quotes in a string assignment, allowing strings to contain embedded line-feed characters directly in Script itself. For example, the following string assignments are equivalent:

```
...
NewString$ = "This is the first line." & CHR$(10) & "This is the second line."
...
NewString$ = ¦This is the first line
This is the second line¦
```

The third and last parameter of the MessageBox function is the title of the dialog box. This parameter should indicate to the user, at a quick glance, what type of information is provided in the dialog box.

The second parameter, a numeric value, enables one or more properties for the dialog box to be specified. This parameter is simply the numerical addition of one or more constants that may be classified in the following categories:

- *Buttons*, enabling the buttons appearing at the bottom of the dialog box to be specified. Options available are MB_OK, MB_OKCANCEL, MB_ABORTRETRYIGNORE, MB_YESNOCANCEL, MB_YESNO, and MB_RETRYCANCEL. If a button type is not specified, MB_OK is assumed.

- *Icons*, enabling a system standard icon to appear in the dialog box. Available options are MB_ICONSTOP, MB_ICONQUESTION, MB_ICONEXCLAMATION, and MB_ICONINFORMATION. If an icon is not specified, no icon will appear.

- *Default buttons*, enabling the default button position (one, two, or three from the left) to be specified. Options include: MB_DEFBUTTON1, MB_DEFBUTTON2, and MB_DEFBUTTON3. The first button is always the default, if not overridden by a value in this category.

- *Mode*. Application Modal (MB_APPLMODAL) indicates that the current application (Notes database) will not continue until the dialog box has completed processing. System Modal (MB_SYSTEMMODAL) forces all applications to halt until the dialog box has been terminated. Application Modal is the default value; modeless dialogs are not allowed.

Note that only one value in each category may be specified.

The following statement produces a dialog box that displays multiline text and an exclamation-mark icon. You can see the dialog box in Figure 18.3.

```
MessageBox "About to process" & Chr$(10) & "all new entries...",
MB_ICONEXCLAMATION, "Process Status"
```

FIGURE 18.3.
A multiline dialog box with an exclamation icon.

The function form of the procedure, like any user-defined function, enables a value to be returned. Return values from the MessageBox function are fairly self-explanatory, enabling you to determine the button selected by the user. A return value will be one of the following: IDOK, IDCANCEL, IDABORT, IDRETRY, IDIGNORE, IDYES, or IDNO.

The following function produces a dialog box in which the user is asked whether or not a process should continue:

```
ret% = MessageBox( "Continue processing?", MB_YESNO + MB_ICONQUESTION, "Process
↪Status" )
If ret% = IDYES Then
    ... Perform processing here...
End If
```

TIP

MessageBox is sometimes useful during script debugging. It may be used to trace the execution of code, or to display the value of one or more variables at a specific location.

Text Input Through `InputBox`

To present a dialog box in which text may be entered, use the `InputBox` function.

NOTE

There are actually two forms of the `InputBox` function: one that returns a variant data type, and one that returns a string data type. We will discuss only the variant form of the function in this text, although the difference between the two is minimal.

The `InputBox` function has five parameters. Only the first parameter is required; the other four are optional. This discussion will omit an explanation of the last two parameters, used to specify an X and Y screen position for the input dialog box; in most cases the default position is adequate.

Here is a description of the first three parameters specified on the `InputBox` command line:

- `Prompt`: A string that specifies the message to be displayed in the dialog box, such as `"Enter a new value:"`.
- `Title`: The caption for the dialog box, such as Field Entry.
- `Default`: The default value for the input field on the dialog box.

The following example illustrates a typical use of the `InputBox` function:

```
ret = InputBox( "Enter a new value:", "Field Entry", "100")
```

Figure 18.4 shows the dialog box that results from running this statement.

FIGURE 18.4.

A typical InputBox *at runtime.*

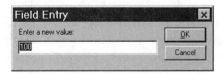

The return value from this function is either the value of the text in the entry box or an empty string (`""`) if the Cancel button was selected.

File Input and Output

In some cases, you may be required to save information to or retrieve information from a text (standard ASCII) file. This need may arise if:

- Another application that is not capable of reading Lotus Notes databases directly needs access to documents stored in your database. However, this application *is* capable of importing data contained in text files. Therefore, using LotusScript, you may create a text file that contains essential elements of your Notes database for use by this application.

- You have been tasked to read data from a text file that is generated by a mainframe application on a nightly basis, using a Lotus Notes Agent. The Agent will contain LotusScript code that reads the contents of this text file, converting it to Lotus Notes documents.

- Your Lotus Notes database needs to store the values of several variables for use by a second Lotus Notes application. Instead of storing all of these values as "environment variables" in the NOTES.INI file, the typical solution in Lotus Notes, you may create your own text file and access it to store and retrieve values between applications as necessary.

This section demonstrates, through two code examples, how to take on the task of reading from and writing to text files using LotusScript.

> **NOTE**
>
> It is beyond the scope of this section to provide an in-depth discussion of all of the Lotus-Script statements that are used to perform file input and output. These examples are pro-vided only as a very basic starting point.

Reading from Files

We will now step through the statements required to open up and read all of the lines in a text file, TEXT.TXT, that consists of several lines of values that must be read and manipulated.

1. A file *handle* must be defined. This file handle, which is actually just a numeric value, will be used to reference the file after it is opened. Always use the `FreeFile()` function to determine a file handle; never hard-code a file-handle number.

   ```
   f% = Freefile()
   ```

2. Next, open the file in input (read) mode. Various command-line options on the `Open` statement enable other types of files, including binary, to be accessed.

   ```
   Open "Text.Txt" For Input As #f%
   ```

3. We will now step through all of the lines in the file using the `Do...Loop` statement, with a check for an End Of File (`EOF`) before each new line read.

```
Do While Not EOF(f%)
    Line Input #f%, NewLine$
    ...
    'Process the line as required here...
    ...
Loop
```

4. After reading and processing the contents of the file, we need to close the file-handle reference.

```
Close #f%
```

Writing to Files

Now that you've read information from a file, you will step through the creation of a simple LotusScript block that saves several lines of text to a file. We'll throw in a few twists here and there, utilizing the `InputBox` function to enable the user to enter text that will be saved to our new file.

1. Just as in the previous reading example, you must first define a file handle.

```
f% = Freefile()
```

2. Open a file, selected by the user with the `InputBox` function, for output (writing). The `Output` option on the `Open` statement will create the file specified. If the file already exists, current contents will be destroyed and overwritten. An `Append` option also exists, enabling the contents of the file to remain intact.

```
UserFile$ = InputBox ("Enter a filename, please: ", "Filename Entry")
Open UserFile$ For Output As %f
```

3. Now step through a loop that enables the user to enter names of individuals to be stored in the output file. The loop will terminate when the Cancel button is selected. Note that the `Print` statement used in the following code snippet automatically adds both the carriage-return (CR) and line-feed (LF) characters to the end of each line in the output file; adding a semicolon (;) to the end of the `Print` statement suppresses this action.

```
Do
    NewName$ = InputBox("Enter a new name:", "New Names")
    If NewName$ <> "" Then
        Print #f%, NewName$
    End If
Loop Until NewName$ = ""
```

4. Now that you've stopped writing to the file, you need to close the file-handle reference.

```
Close #f%
```

Advanced LotusScript

As foreshadowed by the title, this section discusses some of the more advanced features found in LotusScript. The topics discussed herein include:

- "Object Orientation: The Basics." One of the defining characteristics of LotusScript is the ability to develop an application using the principles of object orientation. This section discusses object-oriented basics.

- "Predefined Notes Classes." This section discusses several of the classes that are built into LotusScript.

- "LSX and ODBC." One of the characteristics of LotusScript is the ability to add classes to the base LotusScript language. This section discusses LotusScript eXtensions (LSX) and the LSX for ODBC access that ships with Notes R4.

Object Orientation: The Basics

So far we've talked a lot about LotusScript, but haven't mentioned anything about Notes-specific capabilities. This section will open several new doors to uncharted worlds, including the world of the Notes Application Programming Interface (API), through LotusScript.

A Simple Introduction to the Notes API

The Notes API is a set of system-level functions that are called from various programming languages to access Notes databases and Notes system functions.

Figure 18.5 illustrates how the Notes API acts as a middleman between various high-level languages and Notes databases and system functions.

FIGURE 18.5.
The Notes "middle-man" is the Notes API.

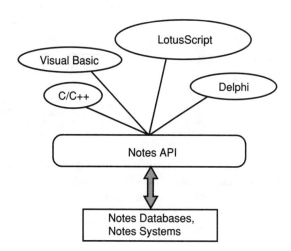

At this point, don't get bogged down with questions about *how* the Notes API works. Chapter 21, "Advanced Development with the Notes API and HiTest Tools," gets down and dirty with this technology. The details aren't important here. Simply keep in mind that all Notes database and system access is performed through a set of Notes functions collectively referred to as the Notes API.

API Access Through LotusScript

Lotus has embraced the most important principles of *object-oriented programming* (OOP) in LotusScript, allowing all Notes-specific data access to occur through the use of *classes, events,* and *methods.* All of the Notes-specific classes that are included in R4 *encapsulate,* or allow access to, one or more Notes API functions.

It is through the use of classes in LotusScript that functions in the Notes API are accessed.

Figure 18.6 illustrates the preceding sentence.

FIGURE 18.6.

LotusScript Notes Classes allow Notes API Access.

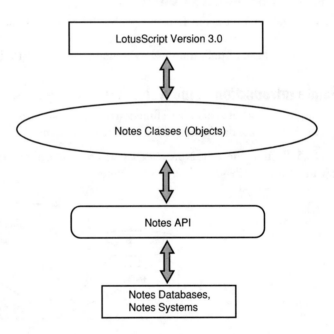

For many Release 3.x developers, the introduction of LotusScript, let alone the OOP capabilities of LotusScript, may be intimidating. Take a deep breath, relax, and proceed one step at a time—things are not as difficult as they seem.

Developers already wise in the ways of OOP, especially languages such as C++ or Object Pascal, will find the object-oriented facilities in LotusScript easy to pick up. However, some object-oriented principles that some might consider essential to any object-oriented language have been stripped from LotusScript, including function overloading, multiple inheritance, and polymorphism.

> **NOTE**
>
> If you don't have OOP experience, patiently read through this material until you have a firm understanding of classes, objects, and, more importantly, how they are used in LotusScript. Because all Notes data access is performed through objects, this material is quite important.

Classes, Objects, Properties, Methods, and Events

The world of OOP revolves around classes and objects. A class is a definition, and an object is a physical entity that may be manipulated, such as a Notes database or a specific field within a database. To further illustrate classes and objects, I will refer to an object that most people use every day: a car.

The definition of a car would be its class definition. For example, you could define a car as having doors, tires, and a steering wheel. This definition is separate from any particular car, such as your friend's white Ford Bronco.

A particular car is an object. You can have several objects of the same class. For example, you can have many Ford Broncos. Each may be in a different state (dual meaning intended), but all the Broncos will behave similarly, because they come from the same class—the car class.

Each class has properties, methods, and events associated with it. It is these characteristics that define the properties of the object, what it can do, and how it will react to different situations. It is up to the developer of a particular class to create properties that may be set and methods that may be initiated.

Properties are used to set various attributes of an object. In a car, you might want to define the number of doors on a car, the license number, or the color of the seats.

Methods are similar to subprograms. However, methods deal specifically with objects and are used to initiate a task that an object of a particular class can perform. For example, a `Car` class might include methods such as `StartTheCar`, `ApplyEmergencyBrakes`, or `TurnOnLights`. A user of a car object would be able to invoke one of these methods.

18

USING
LOTUSSCRIPT

An *event* is a "trigger" that is set off by an object under specific circumstances, often requiring some type of reaction on behalf of the developer. For the Car object, for example, events may be defined for the opening or closing of a door. However, the developer cannot create "trigger" events in LotusScript. The sole provider of events in LotusScript is the Notes system itself.

Creating and Using Objects

Let's move one step further, and begin to describe how classes are actually defined in LotusScript and how they can be used to create objects.

In LotusScript, you use the reserved word Class to define a new class. Classes must always be defined at the module level, in the (Declarations) section. They cannot be defined within a procedure.

Listing 18.1 is a class definition for the Car class.

Listing 18.1. Car class definition.

```
Class Car
    'Member variables for the class (properties)
    Public NumberOfDoors As Integer
    Public SeatColor As Integer
    Public LicenseNumber as String

    Sub New
        'The class constructor
        'Set some default values:
        NumberOfDoors = 4
        LicenseNumber = "ABC123"
        SeatColor = 16
    End Sub

    Sub Delete
        'The class destructor
        ...
    End Sub

    'Here are the Methods for this class:

    Sub StartTheCar
        'Insert code required to start the car here
    End Sub

    Sub ApplyEmergencyBrakes
        'Insert code required to apply emergency brakes here
    End Sub

    Sub TurnOnLights
        'Insert code required to turn on lights here
    End Sub
End Class
```

This class definition contains all of the properties and methods for the `Car` class discussed earlier, in addition to two new methods—`New` and `Delete`. These methods will be explained later.

With respect to properties, or *member variables*, note the following:

- Member variables are not declared using the `Dim` statement.

- Variable suffixes designating the scalar data type, such as `%` for integer or `$` for string, cannot be used. The full type must be spelled out (such as `Integer` for all integer variables). See Table 18.3 for names of data types.

- Member variables are visible to all member procedures (subprograms) within the same class. In this example, the `New` procedure can access the variable `NumberOfDoors` directly.

- To enable a member variable to be read and set directly from outside of a class, use the keyword `Public` before each member variable declaration. If `Public` is not specified, `Private` is assumed, allowing only member procedures within the class to get or modify the value of a member variable.

After a class has been defined, there is a two-step process required to use a class in a procedure:

1. First, create a variable that will be used to refer to the class. This variable will represent a particular instance of the class, and thus is an object. Instead of declaring a data type for a variable (such as `Dim A as Integer`), simply use the class name as the data type:

    ```
    Dim Car_A as Car
    ```

2. Next, use the `Set` statement to *create* and *bind* an object to the variable declared previously. The `Set` statement is analogous to the `Let` statement, the only difference being that `Set` deals with objects, whereas `Let` deals with standard scalar variables (integers, strings, and so on):

    ```
    Set Car_A = New Car
    ```

From this point forward, the `Car_A` is referred to as an *instance* (that is, an object) of the `Car` class. Because we can include any number of `Dim` statements that bind variables to the `Car` class, multiple instances (objects) of the `Car` class may exist, independently of each other, in memory at the same time.

18

USING
LOTUSSCRIPT

> **TIP**
>
> It is also possible to condense the two statements shown previously into one line: `Dim Car_A as New Car`. The `New` keyword, followed by the class name, automatically binds the variable to a new instance of the specified class.

After a variable has been bound to an object using the Set statement, the properties and methods for the class are referenced through the newly bound variable. The following code fragment demonstrates how properties and methods for an object are accessed:

```
...
'First, create a variable for the Car object:
Dim A_Car as Car
...
'Now, create a new instance of Car and bind it to the variable A_Car:
Set A_Car = New Car
...
'Here we access two of the member variables for the A_Car object:
'Note that this would not be possible if the Public keyword was not used in our
'class definition!
A_Car.SeatColor = 10
A_Car.NumberOfDoors = 4
...
'Here we initiate a method from the Car object:
A_Car.ApplyEmergencyBrakes
...
'Note that the a Call may be used as well, but is seldom used to differentiate
'standard subprograms from methods:
Call A_Car.TurnOnLights
...
```

Constructors and Destructors

It's now time to explain the meaning of the Sub New method in the Car class. When a new instance of a class is created, the New method is automatically executed. This method, known as the class *constructor*, may be used to assign default values to properties or to initiate other methods defined within the class.

Similarly, the Sub Delete method, referred to as the class *destructor*, is automatically executed when an instance of a class is removed from memory. An instance of a class may be deleted using the Delete statement anywhere within a procedure. However, an instance of any class is automatically removed from memory when it falls out of the scope of a given procedure—that is, when it is no longer visible to the procedure that initially bound it to a variable.

NOTE

The inclusion of New and Delete member procedures is optional.

"He Has His Father's Smile": Inheritance

In the example object, you created a class from scratch—that is, you defined all of its characteristics within the Class...End Class structure. However, one of the advantages of OOP is that a new class definition may inherit the attributes of an existing class. This practice is known as *inheritance*. The class from which properties are inherited is referred to as a *base class*.

To inherit the properties of an existing class, use the As keyword when defining a class (for example, Class MiniVan As Car). The following example declares a new class, referred to as MiniVan, that inherits all of the member variables and procedures of the Car class.

```
Class MiniVan As Car
    Public HasRoofRack as Integer
    ...
    Sub New
        'Insert initialization code here
    End Sub

    Sub SlideOpenDoor
        'Insert code required to slide a door open here...
        ...
    End Sub
End Class
```

When a new instance of MiniVan is created, you will have access to all of the member variables defined in the Car class, such as NumberOfDoors, in addition to the HasRoofRack variable. Similarly, the member procedures, such as TurnOnLights, are accessible.

To make matters a bit more complex, the chain of inheritance can continue through several iterations. For example, in this chain of car-related classes, let's say you want to create a new class that represents custom vans. This class will inherit all of the characteristics of a MiniVan class, which in turn inherits all of the characteristics of the Car class. The new class definition for a custom van would begin with the line Class CustomVan As MiniVan.

What about class constructors and destructors? You may have noticed that a New subprogram was defined in the MiniVan class definition. When a new instance is created, the New member procedure in the base class (Car) is executed first, followed by the New procedure in the immediate class (MiniVan). When an instance of a class is destroyed, the order is opposite—delete is executed first in the MiniVan class, followed by the Car class.

You may also create a new class that is inherited from another class that in turn has inherited the properties of a base class, allowing for multiple "levels" of class inheritance. In your chain of classes, let's say you want to create a new class to represent custom vans. This class will inherit all of the characteristics of a MiniVan class, which in turn inherits all of the characteristics of the Car class. Your new class definition for a custom van would begin with the line Class CustomVan As MiniVan.

Classes: A Quick RunDown

This concludes the discussion of classes in LotusScript. You may find it surprising to learn that many Lotus Notes R4 developers may *never* find the need to create new classes. Instead of creating classes, most developers will take advantage of predefined classes that are included in R4, discussed in the next section.

Here are some points to remember:

- A class is a definition. It describes properties, methods, and events. It describes the characteristics of objects that will be created from that class. You create a class using the keyword `Class`.

- An object represents an entity that may be manipulated through LotusScript. An object is an instance of a particular class. You create an object by using the keyword `New`.

- A class may be defined from scratch or, through *inheritance*, inherit all of the attributes of another class (for example, `Class MiniVan As Car`).

- A *method* is a subprogram that may be referenced through any variable that has been bound to a class. Parameters may be used with any method, including `New` and `Delete`. Methods are referred to as *member procedures*.

- *Properties* of a class, referred to as *member variables*, are variables that are declared and used within a class.

- User-defined classes cannot initiate or control system *events*. Events are associated only with predefined classes, such as Notes-specific classes.

- The `Dim` statement is omitted when declaring member variables within a class. Always use the full data type name in a declaration; the use of variable suffixes is not allowed. Use the `Public` keyword when variables require direct access from outside of the class (for example, `A_Car.NumberOfDoors = 5`). If the `Public` keyword is not used, `Private` is assumed, allowing only member procedures within the class to access the value of a member variable.

Predefined Notes Classes

Lotus has provided a variety of predefined classes. These classes present a multitude of features, including:

- Modification of the Access Control List (ACL)
- Viewing the properties of agents
- Modifying the value of fields in a document
- Initiating a full text search

To use classes in LotusScript, two things are required:

- Knowledge of object orientation in LotusScript, including the definition of an instance of a class, properties, and methods
- Some basic understanding of the Notes-specific class structure provided in R4

This section will address the latter of the two. First, a road map to all Notes-specific classes will be introduced. You will then delve into some of the most common tasks that need to be initiated through Notes classes, studying code examples when appropriate.

Unfortunately, it is impossible to include a discussion of each and every Notes class, property, and method in this text. However, after understanding the basic concepts discussed here, you will be equipped to handle most class-related, application-development tasks.

The Notes Class Road Map

Figure 18.7 represents some of the Notes-specific classes available in R4.5.

FIGURE 18.7.
Meet the Notes class family.

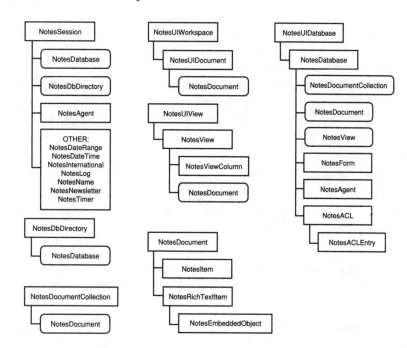

NOTE

Seven new classes and more than 100 methods have been added to Notes in R4.5. The new classes are NotesUIDatabase, NotesUIView, NotesDateRange, NotesForm, NotesInternational, NotesName, and NotesTimer. I don't have room to discuss all the new methods and properties, but suffice it to say that all the new classes, methods, and properties make it easier than ever to program the Notes environment.

Not included in this diagram are standalone classes that assist in performing "utility" functions: NotesDateTime, NotesNewsletter, and NotesLog.

Here are a few notes regarding Notes classes:

- Some Notes classes are said to be *contained* within other classes. This means that some classes require at least one instance of another class to exist prior to being used. For example, a NotesDocument must be contained by a class that contains Notes documents, such as a NotesDatabase or a NotesView. Classes that act as "containers" for other classes are also indicated in Figure 18.7 through indentation in the tree-like structure.

- The NotesRichTextItem is the only Notes class that is actually derived from a base class—in this case, NotesItem. Therefore, all of the properties and methods associated with the NotesItem class also apply to the NotesRichTextItem class.

- The NotesUIWorkspace, NotesUIDatabase, NotesUIView, and NotesUIDocument classes may be used only on a client, where a user interface (UI) exists. Because the Notes Server task does not have a graphical interface, these classes cannot be used in agents that utilize LotusScript on a server.

Basic Database Control

Before accessing anything within a database, including agents, Access Control Lists, and documents, it is first necessary to create an instance of a Notes class (that is, an object) that references a Notes database.

The NotesDatabase class allows more properties and methods than virtually any other Notes class, including the ability to create a new database. To create an instance of a Notes database class that refers to the database NEWNAMES.NSF on server Notes1, use the following statement:

```
Dim NewNamesDb as New NotesDatabase("Notes1", "NEWNAMES.NSF")
```

After a database object is created, various properties of a database—the size of the database, the title of the database, or a list of views in the database, for example—may be accessed. Methods enable the database to be searched using the full-text engine and are used to initiate replication with a specified server.

The following block of script demonstrates some NotesDatabase properties and methods in use:

```
...
'First, collect and print some information about this database
FilePath = NewNamesDb.FilePath
ReplicaID = NewNamesDb.ReplicaID
DbSize = NewNamesDb.Size
...
MessageBox "FilePath: " & FilePath & ", Replica ID: " & ReplicaID & ", Size: " &
➥DbSize
...
```

```
'Now replicate this database with a replica (that already exists) on server Notes2
ret% = NewNamesDb.Replicate("Notes2")
if ret% = False Then MessageBox ("Replication failed!", MB_OK+MB_ICONSTOP,"Oh oh!")
...
'Create a new replica on server Notes3
Dim DbReplica as NotesDatabase     'Need a reference to a new database object for the
                                   'replica
Set DbReplica = newNamesDb.CreateReplica("Notes3", "NEWNAMES.NSF")
...
```

The `NotesDatabase` class may also be used to physically create a new database. There are two steps involved. First, create a new instance of a `NotesDatabase` object, passing empty strings for both the server and the filename:

```
Dim NewDb as New NotesDatabase("", "")
```

Next, use the `Create` method to physically create a database. In this example, you will create the database file NEWDB.NSF residing on server Notes3.

```
Call NewDb.Create ("Notes3", "NEWDB.NSF", True)
```

How to Modify the Current Document

It is fairly simple to modify fields within the current document using Notes classes. The two classes required to read or modify the value of fields in a document are `NotesUIWorkspace` and `NotesUIDocument`.

First, the `NotesUIWorkspace` class is used to reference the current Notes workspace window (User Interface - UI), in which the current document resides.

```
Dim NotesWorkspace As New NotesUIWorkspace
```

Next, a variable that will be used to reference the Notes document is created.

```
Dim NowDoc as NotesUIDocument
```

At this point, all that remains is a binding of the current document in the workspace to the Notes document variable (`NowDoc`):

```
Set NowDoc = NotesWorkspace.CurrentDocument
```

`NowDoc` may now be used to refer to the current document. All properties and methods of the `NotesUIDocument` class may be used. Properties include the ability to determine if the document is new, or to access the current Window Title. Methods enable field values on the document to be read and set, in addition to hard-copy generation of the document.

To change the value of the field `fld_Name` in the document to the value contained in the variable `NewName`, the following method call is used:

```
Call NowDoc.FieldSetText( "fld_Name" , NewName )
```

18

Iterating Through Documents in a View

Through the use of the NotesView class, all of the documents that exist in a particular view may be retrieved and manipulated through LotusScript.

Alternatively, the Search method of a NotesDatabase class may be used to create a collection of documents that are accessed through the NotesDocumentCollection class.

If at all possible, always use the NotesView class to iterate through documents. NotesViews are more efficient (indexes are created and maintained automatically), and they enable response hierarchies to be easily identified through the child and sibling related Get methods of the NotesView class.

The following subprogram example iterates through all of the documents in the Personal Info view that exists in the current Notes session. For each document in the view, the value contained in the field fld_Name is displayed using a call to MessageBox.

```
Sub Click(Source As Button)
    Dim NowSession As New NotesSession
    Dim NowDb As NotesDatabase
    Dim NowDoc As NotesDocument
    Dim NowItem As NotesItem
    Dim View As NotesView, Temp As Variant

    Set NowDb = NowSession.CurrentDatabase
    Set View = NowDb.GetView("Personal Info")

    Set NowDoc = View.GetFirstDocument
    While Not (NowDoc Is Nothing)
        Temp = NowDoc.GetItemValue("fld_Name")
        Messagebox ("Name is: " & Temp(0) )
        Set NowDoc = View.GetNextDocument( NowDoc )
    Wend
End Sub
```

Obtaining Current Session Settings

A *session* in Notes R4 is defined as the current Notes environment, with respect to the current script. The NotesSession class allows access to the attributes of the current session, such as:

- The database currently being used
- User information
- Environment variable access
- The current operating platform and Notes version number
- The names of the Public Address Books and Personal Address Books available

To access the current session, use the following statement:

```
Dim NowSession as New NotesSession
```

After a session instance is created, several properties and methods may be used that define the characteristics of the current session. The following block of script demonstrates how some of these attributes may be accessed:

```
...
UserName$ = NowSession.UserName
MessageBox ( "The current user is: " & UserName$ )

UserName$ = NowSession.EffectiveUserName
MessageBox ( UserName$ & " created this database!" )

NowPlatform$ = NowSession.Platform
MessageBox ( "The current Notes platform is: " & NowPlatform$ )

'Now get an environment variable:
EnvVal = NowSession.GetEnvironmentValue( "Counter" )
...
```

> **TIP**
>
> The NotesSession class enables the functions of the @SetEnvironment and @Environment formulas to be duplicated in LotusScript using the GetEnvironmentValue, SetEnvironmentVar, and GetEnvironmentString methods. In all three methods, the $ character, used before an environment variable in Release 3.x, is automatically appended to the name of the variable specified. However, the concatenation of this character may be eliminated by setting the second parameter in each method to True.

LotusScript Extensions (LSX) and ODBC

The Notes-specific class extensions that are built into Notes are actually examples of Lotus-Script eXtensions, or LSX. Lotus has provided a method of enabling LotusScript to be extended through the use of these extensions, allowing access to objects originally not included in LotusScript to be easily added by either Lotus or third-party tool providers.

This feature enables the core LotusScript product to be bundled with a variety of products, allowing access to application-specific data to be performed through classes defined within an LSX module.

It is clear that the ability to extend the power of LotusScript through LSXs will become a significant factor in the Notes development universe.

ODBC Classes

Besides the Notes classes that are automatically made available to a Notes R4 developer, Lotus has provided a set of three classes that allows access to standard ODBC databases.

Before using one of these classes, however, the following statement must be inserted into the (Global) object in the (Options) event:

`UseLSX "*LSXODBC"`

This statement makes the classes in the LSXODBC extension immediately available to LotusScript. A path name should never be included; doing so might make your database workstation-specific. The UseLSX statement will automatically search through the system registry to determine the location of the DLL that has been specified.

After this statement is inserted, the following new classes become available:

- ODBCConnection, used to establish a connection to an ODBC data source.
- ODBCQuery, used to define and execute a query for an established connection.
- QDBCResultSet, used to access the results of a query, as well as to add or modify entries in the data source.

TIP

The file LSXODBC.LSS contains constants that may be used to handle ODBC classes. It is recommended that you use the %Include "LSXODBC.LSS" statement to enable these constants to be utilized in your LotusScript code.

Summary

Despite the volume of information unearthed, you've only just begun to discover the vast and powerful features of LotusScript. Clearly, it will take a significant amount of effort for a Release 3.x developer to come to grips with the new influx of technology that Lotus has provided in Notes R4.

It is impossible for printed material to replace hands-on, down-and-dirty experience. However, printed material, including the book you are holding, does provide some necessary pieces to the vast development puzzle.

For many Release 3.x developers, LotusScript may seem quite overwhelming. Indeed, there is an ocean of new information to absorb. However, by including support of formulas in R4, Lotus has provided a stepping stone that will enable you, the developer, to learn LotusScript as specific needs arise.

Using Navigators, Agents, and Simple Actions

by Jonathan Czernel

IN THIS CHAPTER

The new development capabilities in R4 don't stop with LotusScript. Although the experience of using Lotus Notes has been improved dramatically for the end user through a retooled user interface, developers have at their disposal new instruments that bring much-needed excitement and life to any bland, but entirely functional, Release 3.x database. These new capabilities can bring any Notes database to the graphical and functional level that today's users expect.

This chapter discusses three new concepts introduced in Lotus Notes R4:

- *Navigators*, or graphical "road maps" that enable views and folders to be accessed through simple point-and-click bitmaps. Navigator objects also enable other features, including the initiation of an Action.

- *Agents*, enabling formulas or LotusScript code to be executed at predefined intervals on selected documents. (Yes, Release 3.x developers, these are really macros—with extra *zip!*)

- *Simple Actions*, a programming alternative to LotusScript and formulas that may be used to react to system actions in some cases.

You may be wondering why we've included these items in the Advanced Development section. What, exactly, is so "advanced" about Navigators, Agents, and Simple Actions? For all practical purposes, an entry-level developer (or even an experienced Notes Release 3.x developer) may choose not to use Navigators, Agents, or Simple Actions. These are all add-ons introduced in Lotus Notes R4 that are not mandatory in a database. Unlike forms and views, the two most essential elements of a database, these features may be considered "icing on the cake" (albeit *necessary* icing, in many cases).

> **NOTE**
>
> A discussion of two important design elements, *action bars* and *form layout regions*, is excluded from this chapter. It is not because these elements are unimportant—on the contrary, they both dramatically improve the usability of a database. They are, however, fairly simple to use. For this reason, they are not discussed in this chapter. They will be used in Chapter 17, "Developing an Advanced Application," as you design a database application.

I know you're excited to get down to business, so let's start dancing with Notes!

Navigators: Road Maps for Notes

Humankind has always had the desire to make the world in which we live a beautiful place. Works of art, including sculptures, paintings, poetry, and music, tap the hidden worlds within our souls, enlightening us with a sense of tranquillity and deeper understanding.

This love of beauty extends to the realm of the computer. Much of the success of the most widely accepted software, from operating systems to applications, can be attributed to the aesthetic nature of the user interface. Is the interface *appealing*? Is it *intuitive*? Is it *color coordinated*? In some cases, the determination of market winners in the software arena is partially decided by the aesthetic, as opposed to the technical attributes of a product.

Using (arguably) one of the crudest interfaces in town, Release 3.x databases have relied on two menus—View and Compose—to view documents and to create new documents. Although the underlying technical attributes of Lotus Notes are awesome, it has been lacking in the areas of elegance and charm.

With Lotus Notes R4, however, databases can take on new shapes and forms that make it an altogether different product. Of course, the developer must be aware of and utilize the new "Wow" design capabilities of the product.

Just like Forms, Views, and Folders, *Navigators* are new database elements that, in many cases, enable the mostly unappealing View menu to be completely replaced by a graphical interface. A Navigator is a free-form area upon which various objects may be drawn.

Figure 19.1 illustrates a Navigator that contains all of the objects available:

FIGURE 19.1.

The objects of a Navigator.

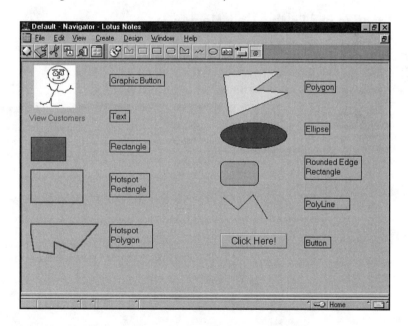

When the user clicks on an object in a Navigator, various actions may be defined, such as opening a new database view.

> **CAUTION**
>
> Notice the lack of artistic talent demonstrated in Figure 19.1, most notably in the Graphic Button object. Although Navigators offer a significant design advantage, the use of either Graphic Buttons or Graphic Backgrounds should be undertaken when presentable bitmaps are available or a graphic artist is on your design staff.

Designing a Navigator

Navigators are designed in four easy steps:

1. First, create a new Navigator in your database.
2. Next, decide whether or not you would like to use a Graphic Background.
3. Next, create one or more Navigator objects. Objects include lines, ellipses, and hotspots.
4. Last, actions must be defined for one or more objects that have been created.

Creating and Setting Up a Navigator

To create a new Navigator in your database, choose Create | Design | Navigator. The *Navigator designer* appears, presenting you with a blank slate from which to work. (See Figure 19.2.)

FIGURE 19.2.

A blank Navigator.

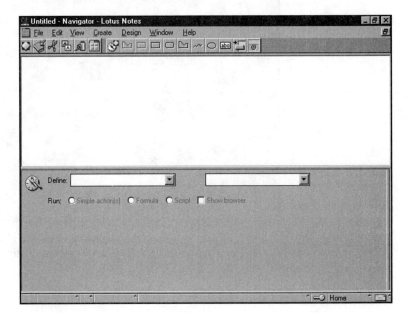

After a Navigator is created, options may be configured by bringing up the InfoBox. Click on the right mouse button anywhere in the new Navigator pane, and select Navigator Properties.

The Basics tab in the InfoBox (properties box) contains four settings:

- The *Name* of the Navigator should be entered. Give the Navigator a name that will immediately identify the contents of the Navigator, such as "DefaultNavigator." This is especially important when multiple Navigators will be created in a single application.

- *Initial view or folder* enables you to select the first view or folder that will appear in the View pane to the right of the Navigator pane.

- If *Auto adjust panes at runtime* is selected, the right and bottom Navigator pane boundaries will be determined based on the rightmost object and the bottommost object in the Navigator. This is a good option to enable in most cases.

- A *Background color* can be chosen to match conventions used elsewhere in your database.

The Grid tab in the InfoBox enables objects to be "snapped into place." This enables multiple objects to be visually aligned at design time without requiring the steady hand of a brain surgeon. In most cases, the grid should be enabled and set to a granularity of at least five pixels.

Graphic Backgrounds: Are They for You?

Before drawing any objects onto your new Navigator, decide whether or not you wish to use a *Graphic Background*. Use a Graphic Background if you have at your disposal an image that contains areas that the user would immediately identify as discrete objects that may be selected to initiate an action.

For example, the image of a bookcase may be used as a Graphic Background. Each shelf, or book, on the Graphic Background may be used as a launching pad for a particular view in the database. Another obvious example of a Graphic Background is a map, where particular regions may be used to initiate actions.

If you intend to use a Graphic Background, first paste a bitmap to the clipboard from another application. Unfortunately, Notes does not enable bitmapped files to be loaded directly from disk. Next, select Create | Graphic Background. Graphic Backgrounds are always "anchored" in the upper-left corner of the Navigator screen. If the size of your Graphic Background is larger than the viewable area of the Navigator, scroll bars will automatically appear and your image will *not* be cropped.

TIP

To remove a Graphic Background, select Design | Remove Graphic Background.

Drawing Navigator Objects

After you have chosen to insert a Graphic Background (or have decided to skip this step), Navigator objects may now be inserted.

Navigator objects include the following:

- Standard shapes, including rectangles, ellipses, lines (referred to as polylines) and polygons. All of these shapes, with the exception of lines, are automatically filled with a user-defined color.

- Hotspots, either in the form of a rectangle or a polygon. A hotspot is simply an outline that may be used to identify a particular region of a graphic background. Because hotspots are only outlines, they are never filled with a color. Hotspots may be used, for example, to outline geographical regions, such as cities, on a state map.

- Text boxes, enabling text to be displayed anywhere on a Navigator. Font, size, and color area all configurable.

- Two varieties of buttons: graphic buttons, which are essentially rectangular clipboard objects (such as a bitmap pasted to the clipboard); and hotspot buttons, which are standard buttons that contain a single line of text.

Objects may be created using either the Create menu or the second set of SmartIcons that represent various objects that may be created. The easiest way to create an object is through the use of these SmartIcons.

The first click of a particular object on the SmartIcon bar enables object-creation mode, represented by a crosshair cursor when the mouse pointer is over the Navigator design pane. The second click of the same SmartIcon object turns off creation mode and enables object-manipulation mode. In this mode, you may manipulate objects that have been drawn; they may be moved, resized, or deleted.

After an object has been selected, drawing it is fairly straightforward—especially to those already familiar with other drawing programs. Here are some quick drawing tips:

- To draw an ellipse, rectangle, rounded rectangle or a hotspot rectangle, move the cursor to the anchor point in the Navigator, then click and hold down the mouse button. With the mouse button depressed, move the mouse pointer to size the object. Let go of the mouse button to complete your drawing.

- To draw a polygon, hotspot polygon or a polyline, move the cursor to the first point, then click once on the mouse button to begin your drawing. Each subsequent, single, mouse-button click adds a new point to your polygon. To complete drawing a polygon-type object, double-click the mouse button. For polygons, a double-click automatically draws a line from the last point to the first point, closing the bounds of the object.

- To move several objects simultaneously, hold down the Shift key and click once on each object that must be moved. When the last object is selected, continue holding the Shift key, press the left mouse button and move the mouse to relocate all selected objects. Let go of the mouse button when the new positions are satisfactory. Moving groups of objects in a Navigator is similar to moving desktop icons in the Notes workspace.

- To draw a circle or a square, hold down the Shift key, then begin drawing an ellipse or rectangle. This trick also works after an object is drawn, when one of these objects is resized.

After an object has been drawn, properties for each object may be modified. The *InfoBox* is used to manipulate properties. To make the InfoBox visible, click on the right mouse button over any object, then select Object Properties.

Each object will have different properties that pertain to it. For example, a text object will allow for the selection of a font and point size. However, the HiLite tab applies to all Navigator objects. (See Figure 19.3.)

FIGURE 19.3.

The HiLite tab exists for every Navigator object.

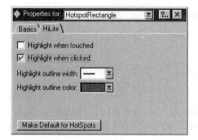

For objects that will trigger events, one or both of the options presented in this screen should be selected:

- *Highlight when touched.* Enabling this option will draw the border for the object, as specified by the Highlight Outline Width and Highlight Outline Color settings, whenever the user moves the mouse over the Navigator object. This option should typically be selected for hotspot polygons or hotspot rectangles.

- *Highlight when clicked.* Enabling this option will flash the border for the object, as specified by the Highlight Outline Width and Highlight Outline Color settings, when the user clicks on the Navigator object.

TIP

See a Navigator in another database that you would like to use in your database? No problem! Navigators may be "cut" and "pasted" to and from databases just like forms and views. Simply highlight the source Navigator in Design Mode and select Edit | Copy (Ctrl+C). Next, open the destination database, select Navigator from the Design folder (from Design Mode), then select Edit | Paste (Ctrl+V).

Acting on Clicks

Now that objects have been drawn, you must determine how an object will react to a `Click`, the one and only event that Navigator objects can "react to" at runtime.

When the user clicks on a Navigator object, one of the following may occur:

- A Simple Action may be initiated, enabling common Navigator functions, such as opening a new view, to be developed with no programming effort.

- A formula may execute, for those that are comfortable with Notes Formulas.

- Script may execute, enabling simple or complex LotusScript statements to be executed.

- Nothing, nada, zip. Objects do not necessarily have to initiate one of the previous actions. They can be included in the Navigator for artistic reasons alone.

To designate an appropriate action for Navigator objects, first select the object whose action(s) need to be defined. Next, in the lower design pane, select the programming method that you wish to use for this object (Simple Action, Formula, or Script).

In many cases, Simple Actions are the most appropriate way to deal with Navigator events. The four Simple Actions available for each object include the following:

- *Open another Navigator.* Use this choice to link one Navigator to another. When selected, a combo box will appear containing a list of available Navigators.

- *Open a view.* This option is used to display a new view in the view pane. When selected, a combo box will appear containing a list of available views.

- *Alias a folder.* This particularly useful option does two things. First, it switches the view pane to the folder specified. Second, it enables objects from other views and folders to be dragged and dropped into the Navigator object itself. When selected, a combo box will appear containing a list of available folders.

- *Open a link.* This choice enables a document, view, or database link to be opened. When selected, a button will appear that will enable a link to be pasted. First, however, you must switch to a database, document, or view, then choose Edit | Copy as Link for the appropriate object. After a link is copied to the clipboard, switch back to the Navigator designer and click on the Paste Link button.

> **NOTE**
>
> In the context of Navigator design, only a few very straightforward Simple Actions are available. The discussion of Simple Actions later in this chapter focuses on the use of this new programmability feature in forms and agents, where a multitude of Simple Actions are available.

How to Use Navigators in a Database

When a Navigator has been created, the Database must be told how it should be used. To configure the use of a Navigator in a database, select File | Database | Database Properties to present the InfoBox. The Launch tab contains settings that need to be modified for Navigators.

In the On Database Open list box, there are two choices that may be used to present a Navigator when a database is opened:

- *Open designated Navigator.* This choice opens the default three-pane (Navigator, View/Folder and Document) screen when a database is opened, with the Navigator chosen appearing in the Navigator pane.

- *Open designated Navigator in its own window.* This choice opens the chosen Navigator in full-screen mode, without the View/Folder or Document panes.

When the On Database Open selection has been made, the Navigator itself must be chosen from the Navigator list box that appears in the InfoBox.

Agents: Your Personal Assistants

They never get tired, are always available, and never complain. Agents are your personal database assistants, ready and willing to perform complex tasks at your command.

Agents may be used to

- Automatically copy old documents to archive databases on a nightly basis.
- Send all mail posted to a specific mailbox to a forwarding address.
- Change the value of a field in selected documents.

> **NOTE**
>
> The word *macro*, used in Release 3.x, has been struck from the vernacular of the Notes world, replaced by *agents*. Agents provide all of the features of macros, and more. Release 3.x developers will find that many of the limitations of macros have been stripped. The process of creating agents has changed dramatically in R4, enabling significantly more scheduling, document selection and development options. Agent "test" sessions are also now available, enabling the developer to determine what an agent will do when it is executed before valuable data is accidentally destroyed.

This section steps through the process of creating a new agent, defining the options that are available to the developer (or the end user, in the case of private agents) every step of the way.

Creating an Agent

> **NOTE**
>
> This discussion assumes that you have Designer access rights to a database, enabling both shared and personal agents to be created. To create a personal agent, either Editor, Author or Reader (or above) database access is required.

To create a new agent, select Create | Agent from the Design screen in your database. A blank agent template will appear, as displayed in the Figure 19.4.

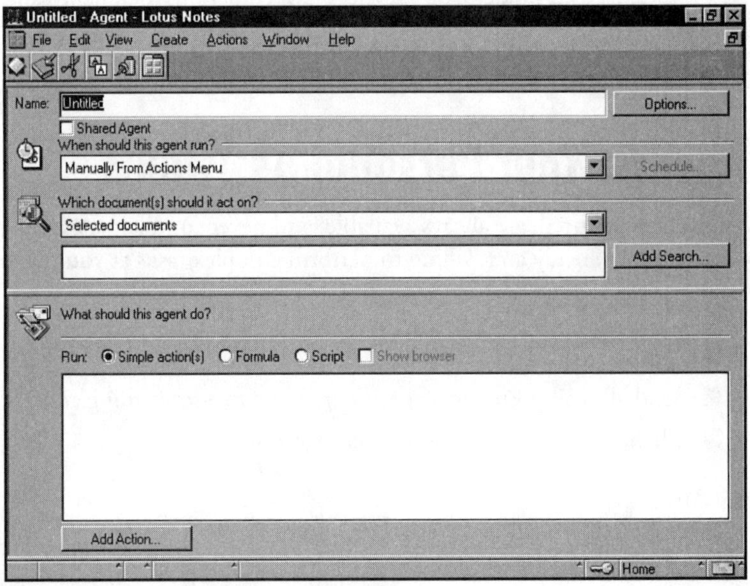

FIGURE 19.4.

The birth of an agent.

> **TIP**
>
> Agents may also be "cut" from other databases and "pasted" to your new database using Edit | Cut or Edit | Paste.

The first entry in this agent-design screen enables a name to be given to an agent. An agent name should be meaningful to the end user, especially if the agent is to appear in the Actions menu. Agent names can be cascaded to one level, just like form names, using the backslash character (\). This enables agents with similar functions to be grouped together in the Actions menu. An agent name cannot contain more than 64 characters, or 127 characters when the name includes a cascaded menu item. As a final note, agent names may contain spaces.

Right below the agent name field, check the Shared Agent checkbox if the agent you are creating may be used by every user of the database with appropriate access. To create a *public agent*, synonymous with the term *shared agent*, check this box. To create a *personal agent*, an agent that will only be accessible on your personal workstation, do not check this box.

With respect to access rights, remember that only a database designer may create shared agents. Database editors, authors, and readers (or higher) may create personal agents.

The Options button, the next choice on the new Agent screen, presents a dialog box in which two new choices appear:

- *Show search in search bar menu.* Select this option to enable a user to view the search criteria used by an agent after it has been executed.
- *Store highlights in document.* Select this option to retain keyword highlights for all matches in a document after an agent has been executed.

In addition, a Comments field in this dialog box enables a full description of the agent to be documented for future reference. This is a tremendous feature that should be utilized to enable others to easily determine the purpose of an agent when it is not readily apparent with the agent name alone. The value placed in the Comments field is also displayed when the *agent list* for the database is displayed, immediately under the agent name.

The entry of these fields completes the first phase in the creation of an agent.

Scheduling Agents

After a name has been chosen for an agent, and you have chosen whether the agent should be made public or is to remain in your personal domain, the agent must be told when it needs to execute; the agent must be scheduled.

The choices available for scheduling appear in Table 19.1.

Table 19.1. Agent-scheduling options.

Scheduling Option	Description
Manually From	Adds the agent name to the Actions menu, enabling a Actions Menu user to run it at any time.
Manually From Agent List	Creates a "hidden" agent, often used to create an agent that is initiated by another agent.
If New Mail Has Arrived	This type of agent acts upon documents that are mailed to the user's mail database.
If Documents Have Been Created or Modified	Initiates the agent on all documents that are either new or have been modified since the last agent execution. The Schedule button allows more options when this agent type is used. Search criteria may also be specified.
If Documents Have Been Pasted	Initiates the agent action on all documents that have been pasted to a database that match the desired search criteria.
On Schedule…Hourly, Daily, Weekly, Monthly, Never	Runs an agent on a scheduled basis. The Schedule button enables the precise time of agent execution to be set, including the possible exclusion of weekends.

The dialog box that is presented when the Schedule button is clicked is fairly straightforward, enabling a scheduled agent's execution time to be refined. However, two choices in this dialog box deserve further clarification:

■ The *Run only on* selection enables you to choose the server that will execute the agent. Any server that replicates this database is a viable candidate; the default choice is the system that houses the database.

■ If the *Choose when agent is enabled* checkbox is selected, a prompt is presented to the user when the agent is initiated that enables the server to be selected.

Defining Your Agent's Playground

The next phase in the development of an agent is to define which documents your agent will act upon, and which search criteria, if any, should be used.

First, select an option from the *Which document(s) should it act on?* list box. The choices in this list box will vary depending on what was selected in the *When should this Agent run?* list box.

If either Manually From Actions Menu or Manually From Agent List is selected, the following choices will appear:

- All documents in database
- All new and modified documents since last run
- All unread documents in view
- All documents in view
- Selected documents
- Run once (@Commands may be used)

The last choice, Run once, executes the agent only once on the current document, whether it is being edited, read, or highlighted in the current view.

If an agent that has been defined as an On Schedule (Hourly, Daily, Weekly, Monthly, or Never) agent, the following choices will appear:

- All documents in database
- All new and modified documents since last run

If the scheduling choice is either If New Mail Has Arrived, If Documents Have Been Created or Modified, or If Documents Have Been Pasted, the scheduling definition itself defines which documents the agent will act upon; no definition for this entry is required.

> **CAUTION**
>
> If either All Documents in Database or All Documents in View is selected, a Full Text Index must exist for the database in order for the agent to execute.

Refining the Playground with the Search Builder

After selecting the general type of documents that an agent should act on in the last step, the Add Search button may be used to further narrow down the list of documents that will be affected by a rampant agent.

When the Add Search button is pressed, the Search Builder window will appear. The Search Builder may be initiated several times for a single agent, enabling a search criteria with numerous rules to be constructed. Figure 19.5 shows a typical Search Builder screen, in which a date-based search is being defined.

Each time the Search Builder is used to add a new search criteria, a summary of the criteria is added to the text box to the left of the Add Search button. To remove a criteria that has been selected, highlight the criteria summary in this text box and press the Delete key. In some cases, conjunctions, such as the AND operator, may also need to be removed when a summarized search criteria is eliminated.

The Search Builder is capable of defining a wide variety of search rules in an extremely easy to use fashion. After a general search type is selected, the user is literally walked through the remaining portion of the search setup.

FIGURE 19.5.

The Search Builder being used to define a search based on the date a document was created.

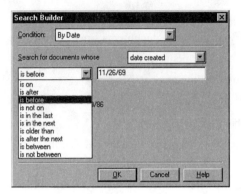

Table 19.2 lists the conditions for which the Search Builder is capable of generating Notes search queries.

Table 19.2. Search Builder conditions.

Condition Name	Description
By Author	To select documents in which the Author field either contains or does not contain a specific person.
By Date	To select documents in which the creation or modification date adheres to specified settings, such as "Created On 11/26/96" or "Modified Between 1/1/95 and 6/1/96."
By Field	To select documents that contain or do not contain a value in a particular field.
By Form	This choice enables values to be typed into one or more fields on the form used to create a document. If the values match in a document, it is selected.
By Form Used	To select documents that use one or more forms.
In Folder	To select documents that belong to a particular folder or view.
Words and Phrases	To select documents that contain up to eight words or phrases.

Instructing Agents

Now that your agent knows *when* and *with whom* to play, it must be told *how* to play. The lower pane in the agent Design screen, appropriately titled *What should this agent do?*, enables either Simple Actions, formula, or LotusScript (Script) to be used to program the action(s) that an agent will take on each document that matches the search criteria that has been established.

If at all possible, first attempt to use one or more Simple Action(s), since no programming is involved. Simple Actions are described in detail in the next section.

If a Simple Action is not available to perform the necessary agent instructions, try to use Notes formulas. For example, the following Notes formula is used to change the value of a field to 1 in all selected forms:

```
FIELD fld_Counter := 1;
```

If the logic required to complete a formula is difficult to follow, or if a formula does not have a feature that is required, use LotusScript. LotusScript provides more features than the other programming options, allowing an abundance of flexibility. If LotusScript is to be used, select Script, then the Initialize event. When an agent executes on each document, the code in the Initialize subprogram executes first, followed by script in the Terminate subprogram.

Testing an Agent

After an agent is created, it may be tested using a new agent-simulation tool built into R4. Testing agents using this method does not alter the contents of the database; it simply reports the following statistics at the end of a test run:

- The number of documents that were included in the agent session.
- The number of documents that matched the search criteria.
- The number of documents modified by the agent.

To begin an agent test, first select the agent that you wish to test from the agent list. Next, choose the Test option from the Actions menu. The results from a typical agent test can be seen in Figure 19.6.

FIGURE 19.6.

Results of an agent test run.

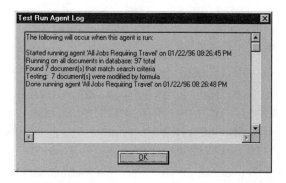

> **Test Run Agent Log**
>
> The following will occur when this agent is run:
>
> Started running agent 'All Jobs Requiring Travel' on 01/22/96 08:26:45 PM
> Running on all documents in database: 97 total
> Found 7 document(s) that match search criteria
> Testing: 7 document(s) were modified by formula
> Done running agent 'All Jobs Requiring Travel' on 01/22/96 08:26:48 PM
>
> OK

If the agent appears to function appropriately, you should consider running the agent using a copy of the database, enabling the agent to run in a "real" environment.

Simple Actions: Programming Made Easy

Lotus Notes R4 includes LotusScript Version 3.0, a powerful BASIC-compatible, object-oriented programming language. This language enables virtually any task to be accomplished through Script statements, combined with several Notes classes that enable nearly full database and environment access.

At the other end of the development spectrum, R4 introduces *Simple Actions*, a set of common routines including many commonly performed tasks that act upon documents. The use of Simple Actions is ridiculously easy—choose a desired action, and Lotus Notes automatically requests information required to perform the action in an easy-to-understand dialog box, as shown in Figure 19.7.

FIGURE 19.7.

A typical Add Action dialog box, used in Simple Actions.

Where and How to Use a Simple Action

Although Simple Actions are extremely easy to use, offering a bountiful number of features, they may only be used where they make sense—when an action occurs, as the name "Simple Action" implies.

Simple Actions may be used instead of formula or LotusScript (Script) in the following areas:

- During form design, Simple Actions may be used to designate action(s) that occur when the user clicks on a form button.
- Simple Actions may be used to define how an agent acts upon each document that meets specified search criteria.

When using Simple Actions, remember that multiple actions may be defined, one after the other. Simply use the Add Action button to add one Simple Action after another.

As Simple Actions are added, they will appear in the code window of the design pane, one after the other, in blocked text with a gray background. To remove a Simple Action, click on the action to be removed so that it is highlighted, then select Edit | Cut.

Simple Actions Unleashed

Table 19.3 contains all of the Simple Actions that may be used to define an action in Lotus Notes R4.

Table 19.3. Simple Actions.

Simple Action	Description
Copy to Database	Copies the current document to the selected database on the selected server.
Copy to Folder	Copies the current document to the selected folder.
Delete from Database	Deletes the current document from the database.
Mark as Read	Marks the current document as "Read."
Mark as Unread	Marks the current document as "Unread."
Modify Field	Enables the value of a selected field to be replaced or concatenated with a new value.
Modify Fields by Form	Enables more than one field to be replaced by a new value.
Move to Folder	Moves the current document to the selected folder.
Remove from Folder	Removes the current document from the selected folder.
Reply to Sender	Creates and mails a Reply document to the name listed in the Sender field. A copy of the document may also be included.
Run Agent	Runs the selected agent.
Send Document	Mails the document to the appropriate individual(s) as defined by mail-specific fields in the document, including SendTo, CopyTo, and BlindCopyTo.
Send Mail Message	Creates and mails a new message to the individual(s) or group(s) specified. This choice also enables a full mail body to be created at design time, and enables either the document to be sent along with the mail message or a doclink to be sent.
Send Newsletter Summary	Sends a newsletter summary to the individual(s) or group(s) specified.
@Function Formula	Enables formula statements to be embedded within a set of Simple Actions, allowing the flexibility of both programming features to be fully exploited.

19

NAVIGATORS, AGENTS, AND SIMPLE ACTIONS

Summary

This chapter discussed two new features (Navigators and Simple Actions) and one fundamentally new feature (agents) introduced in Lotus Notes R4. These items address many of the shortcomings of Lotus Notes Release 3.x.

Here is a brief overview of the topics discussed in this chapter:

- Navigators, new design elements in a Lotus Notes R4 database, enable road maps to views to be created.

- A Navigator may include a graphic background, enabling an existing image that represents a real-world object to be used as the background for a Navigator, upon which hotspots may be created.

- In most cases, a Simple Action is used to define an appropriate response to a user event in a Navigator.

- Agents are your personal assistants. They may be used to perform various functions on one or more documents that match your search criteria.

- The scheduling, search, and programming options (either Simple Actions, formula, or LotusScript) available in agents eliminate many, if not all, of the limitations of the Release 3.x era.

- Simple Actions, while extremely limited in design scope, enable commonly used procedures to be easily used by the most inexperienced developer.

Developing an Advanced Application

by Jonathan Czernel

IN THIS CHAPTER

This chapter puts to test many of the principles discussed in the last several chapters by converting a fairly simple Release 3.x database into an application that utilizes several of the more important R4 features, such as:

■ New Form and View design tools—including Navigators, form layout regions, and Action Bars—that allow a pleasant sense of aesthetic responsibility to be brought to your Notes database.

■ LotusScript, including automatic field entries and input validation, to replace typical formula-based functions.

■ Notes-specific classes, enabling you to manipulate data stored in a Notes database.

■ A nightly agent that uses LotusScript and Notes Classes to create an ASCII export file.

As you can see, your database will include most of the advanced development features that are found in R4 of Lotus Notes. We will proceed through the development process in a real-world fashion.

Included in the development of any application is the process of *debugging*. In most cases, it is best to test "chunks" of code as they are written, in piecemeal fashion. While writing the application included in this chapter, I've already gone through the painstaking code-test cycle, enabling us to concentrate on the task at hand without jumping off on tangent discussions. However, the end of this chapter includes a discussion of the exceptional debugging tools introduced in R4. This discussion of the new debugging facility will be extremely important to any high-end developer.

This chapter assumes that you are familiar with most basic design techniques in Lotus Notes R4; that is, you should already know how to design basic forms and views. You should also feel comfortable with using the InfoBox to set properties for various objects.

> **NOTE**
>
> The CD-ROM included with this book contains both the original database and the final database that we'll create in this chapter (PROJ1.NSF and PROJ_FIN.NSF, respectively). Like the infamous "Before" and "After" images of those who have successfully (and miraculously) completed weight loss programs, the difference between these two applications is absolutely incredible.

If you prefer to learn by example, this chapter is for you!

About Your Application

Because this chapter homes in on the advanced development features of Lotus Notes R4, we'll begin with a rough template developed with Lotus Notes Release 3.x capabilities.

This chapter assumes that you have been tasked to expand an existing application to take advantage of a variety of Lotus Notes Release 4 features. The application that you'll be expanding is the Simple Project Tracking database.

The Release 3.x database has the following capabilities:

■ New projects may be composed, consisting of: project name, inception date, estimated completion date, project manager, brief description, full description (a rich text field), current status ("In Progress" or "Completed"), and an actual completion date.

■ For each project, one or more activities may be composed, consisting of: activity name, start date, estimated time (in days), assigned to, activity description (a rich text field), status ("Not Started," "Started," and "Completed"), actual time, and closing comments. These documents are responses to each project document.

■ For each project or activity, other users of the Notes database may compose their own comments to interject their own experiences. In this sense, the database is a discussion-like application surrounded by a shell of projects and activities. These documents are classified as "response to response" documents.

■ When a new activity is created, a mail notification with a doclink to the activity is sent to the individual that has been assigned to perform the activity.

■ Each form has some standard buttons, such as an Edit button (to enable edit mode) and a Save & Exit button.

■ A variety of useful views are built in, including "All Projects," "Projects In Progress," "Projects Completed," and "Projects by Individual." A private view is also available, which lists all projects and activities for the current user.

Figure 20.1 depicts the Projects\All View in the R3 database with four projects shown, as well as corresponding activities and associated comments.

You will be modifying virtually every aspect of this database, starting with forms in the next section.

FIGURE 20.1.

*The Projects\All view
in the R3 database
with four projects.*

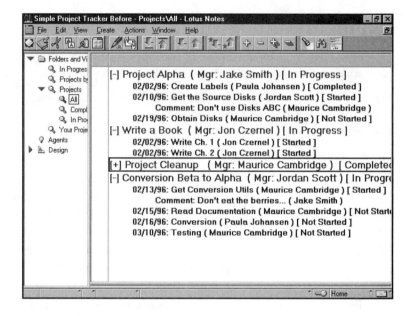

Actions in Forms and Views

The forms that your Simple Project Tracker database uses are completely respectable for a Lotus Notes Release 3.x database. However, there are some "annoyances" with our current form design that we can easily remedy using new R4 features.

Figure 20.2 represents the default New Project form.

FIGURE 20.2.

*The default New
Project form.*

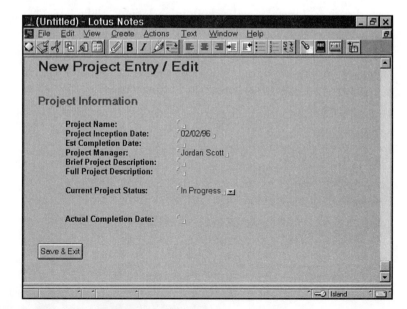

The bottom of the screen contains a Save & Exit button, to be used after the fields on the form have been successfully completed. When a form is being read, an Edit button appears towards the top of the form, used to switch to Edit Mode.

One problem with design is that buttons are anchored to a particular location on a form. If a form is more than one page long, the user may have to scroll up or down on the page to find a particular button, making data entry a cumbersome process.

Action Bars enable a nonscrollable region to be added to the top of any form or view, containing buttons that perform document-level tasks, such as saving the current form or switching the current form to and from Edit mode. You'll add Action Bars to all three forms that your database uses.

First, to add an Action Bar to your New Project form, switch to Design Mode for this form, then select Create | Action. Figure 20.3 depicts the design screen when a new action is being defined.

FIGURE 20.3.

Adding a new action.

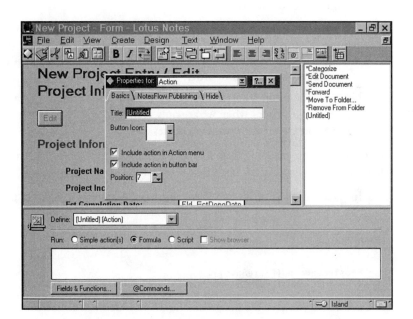

Note that a new window pane has appeared containing several system-defined Actions, noted by an asterisk (*) next to the action title. These actions automatically appear in the Action menu, depending on the state of the current form. The title for these actions may be modified, but they may not be deleted from the Actions list, nor may their particular operations be modified.

To define a new action, use the InfoBox to define the following:

1. For the Title, use Save and Exit. This action will replace your Save and Exit form button. Note the intentional inclusion of an underscore character. The purpose of this is simple: The character immediately following this character will be underlined in the Action menu at runtime, enabling a hotkey for the menu item to be defined. By default, the first character of the title is underlined—you are simply forcing this assignment.

2. A *button icon* is a small icon that will appear next to the title of any action that is included in the Action Bar. Several icons are available to represent a variety of actions. Select an icon that implies acceptance of the current form, such as a "thumbs up."

3. Make sure Include action in Action menu is checked, enabling those without a mouse to easily use your form actions.

4. Ensure that Include action in button bar is checked. This selection adds the current Action to the Action Bar.

5. The *Position* choice indicates the absolute position of this action with respect to other actions. Actions that appear in the Action menu and in an Action Bar will appear in this order. In this case, move the Save and Exit action to Position #1. Note that the Actions Pane lists actions in order.

6. Next, switch to the *Hide* tab in the InfoBox. Because you don't want the Save and Exit Action to appear when we are only reading a document, select the Previewed for reading and Opened for reading choices.

The final step required is to create a simple action, script, or formula that should be executed when this Action is initiated. In this case, you will use two formulas.

1. In the lower pane, make sure Save and Exit (Action) is selected in the Define pull-down list box.

2. Select Formula for the Run type.

3. Type in:

```
@PostedCommand([FileSave]);
@PostedCommand([FileCloseWindow]);
```

You have now completed the design of a new action that will appear both in the Action Menu and the Action Bar.

To make your form easier to use, disable any system-defined actions that are not appropriate for it. Using the InfoBox, disable Include action in Action menu for each system-defined action listed *with the exception of* Edit Document.

Next, modify the Edit Document action as follows:

1. Select an appropriate button icon, such as a pencil.

2. Ensure that the choices Include action in action menu and Include action in Action Bar are selected.

3. Move the *Position* to #2, right below Save and Exit.

4. Switch to the Hide tab, and check Previewed for editing and Opened for editing. Make sure the other choices are not checked.

You now have finalized your Actions for this form. To complete the design process, delete the Edit and Save and Exit buttons that were previously used from the New Project form. Your Actions have replaced these buttons.

Figure 20.4 depicts a New Project form with your new Action Bar. Note also the contents of the Action menu.

FIGURE 20.4.

New Project Entry with appropriate actions.

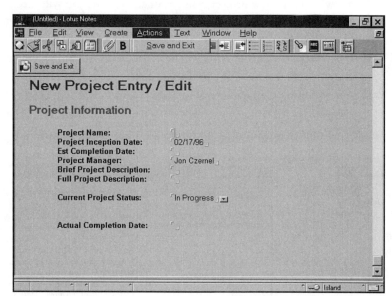

The other forms in the database should be modified in a similar fashion.

TIP

It was previously mentioned that a new window pane with actions appeared when Create | Action was selected. Actually, this pane is always present in Form Design Mode, the left border is simply pushed to the rightmost border of the screen, shrinking this pane to minimal width. To view actions at any time, move the cursor just to the right of the Form scroll bars. When the pointer switches to a "left-right resize" pointer, press the left mouse button and drag the pane to a reasonable size. You may also double-click on any action listed in this pane to present the properties of an action in the InfoBox.

By including Action Bars and limiting the choices on the Action menu from your forms, you have made your database slightly more useable. However, Actions may also be altered at the

20

DEVELOPING AN
ADVANCED
APPLICATION

View level. This process is very similar to altering actions in forms. The most apparent difference is that the *Hide* tab in the InfoBox for a view action contains only a formula-based choice. The reason for this limitation is obvious; from a view, you can never be in edit or read mode for a document.

For your database, you will use the following actions on all of the views in the database. We'll begin with a modification of the Projects\All View:

■ You will retain the system-defined Edit Document Action, adding it to the Action Bar.

■ A new Action, New Project, will be added. This Action will execute the formula `@Command([Compose]; ""; "NewProj")`. Note that `NewProj` is the synonym for the New Project form.

■ A new Action, New Activity, will be added. This Action will execute the formula `@Command([Compose]; ""; "NewAct")`.

■ A new Action, Comment, will be added. This Action will execute the formula `@Command([Compose]; ""; "AComm")`.

With these additions, your Projects\All View looks like that shown in Figure 20.5.

FIGURE 20.5.

Your new view with Action Bars.

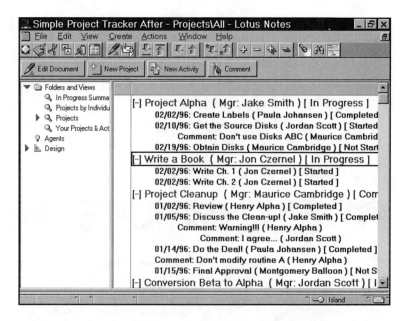

All views in the database have been altered to use these new actions (both bars and menu items).

Layout Regions: Making Forms Shine

On many occasions I've heard Lotus Notes customers comment that Lotus Notes Release 3.x databases look "DOS-like" or "mainframe-ish." Although this comment may be seriously argued, their primary concern is that entry forms do not adhere to standard Graphical User Interface conventions (Windows, OS/2 PM, and so on). Instead of appearing within a dialog box, fields in forms are surrounded by tiny brackets. This is a unique convention that is unfamiliar to a majority of non-Notes users. Similarly, keywords fields are not presented as standard checkboxes or radio buttons.

In addition, due to the fluid nature of data entry in Notes and the manner in which forms are designed, it is difficult to control the screen layout of a form. One problem is the fact that text fields cannot be limited to a specific number of characters, which may result in static text and fields being shifted to the right or down on the screen one or more lines during data entry, resulting in screens that have seemingly lost all sense of order. This typically results in user confusion.

To remedy this problem, Lotus Notes Release 4.x introduces layout regions, allowing more standard GUI-interface entry conventions. A *layout region* is a "free-flow" portion of a form that may contain any of the following items:

- Any type of field (with the notable exception of rich text fields). Fields may be simply "drawn" on a layout region. For keywords fields, the designer may choose to display keyword choices as checkboxes, radio buttons, a standard list box or a combo list box.
- Static text, typically used as layout region titles or titles for fields.
- Standard buttons.
- Buttons that contain a graphical image in the background, or *Graphic Buttons*.

Keep in mind that a layout region is just one rectangular area on a form. Forms may contain all of their typical objects surrounding the layout region. Also remember that several layout regions may be created on one form, spread out wherever you choose to place them.

In your Project Tracking database, your users have complained numerous times about the user interface, resulting in a high turnover rate among your developers. To pacify users, you will create a layout region in each of your forms, transferring as many controls as possible from standard form objects into layout region objects.

First, load the New Project form in Design Mode. Position the cursor on the line immediately following the Project Information blue title. To create a layout region, select Create | New Layout Region. A rectangle will appear on your form at the current cursor position. This rectangle is your layout region. You may resize the layout region using the mouse, or move it up and down on your form by adding or deleting blank lines above the region.

NEW TO 4.0

Unlike standard Notes forms, objects in a layout region may appear anywhere by dragging them around with the mouse. To make alignment easier, a snap to grid is available. To activate a grid in a layout region, open up the InfoBox and display Layout properties. Select the Show grid and Snap to grid options. I recommend altering the grid size to 0.100".

Adding objects to a layout region is similar to adding objects to a standard form. When the layout region is selected, the SmartIcon set will switch to a series of objects available in a layout region. You may select a SmartIcon that represents a new object to be drawn, or select any one of the available object choices from the Create menu. When a new object is created, it is automatically inserted at the center of the layout region.

In this database, you need to shift as many fields as possible from the standard Notes form area into the layout region. The easiest way to do this is to simply highlight all of the fields, Edit | Cut them into the clipboard, select the layout region with the click of a mouse button in the rectangle, then select Edit | Paste. When this is done, all of the pasted fields will appear, one on top of the other, in the center of the layout region. Simply use the mouse to grab and drag each field to a new location in the layout region.

Note that standard form text cannot be pasted to a layout region. Instead, a *Text Box* object must be created to label various layout region fields. Text boxes are used only to place static text on a layout region. For each field in your layout region, create a new text box that appropriately identifies the field.

The only keywords field on the form, `Fld_BigProjStatus`, was changed to two radio buttons using the InfoBox for this object.

Since rich text fields are not allowed in a layout region, the full-description RTF will remain just below the layout region. As fields on layout regions look substantially different than those in a standard Notes form, you want to make the RTF that lies just below the layout region *look* like a field in a layout region by enclosing it in a 1×1 table with single borders. Additionally, since it helps to eliminate the separation between the layout region and the rest of the form, layout region borders were disabled from the Layout properties InfoBox (Show border was deselected).

The result of your conversion from a standard form to a layout region is shown in Figure 20.6.

At runtime, your New Project form looks much more like a typical, GUI entry form. (See Figure 20.7.)

The other forms in the database have also been converted from standard Notes forms to forms that use layout regions in the After database.

FIGURE 20.6.

The New Project form with a layout region in design mode.

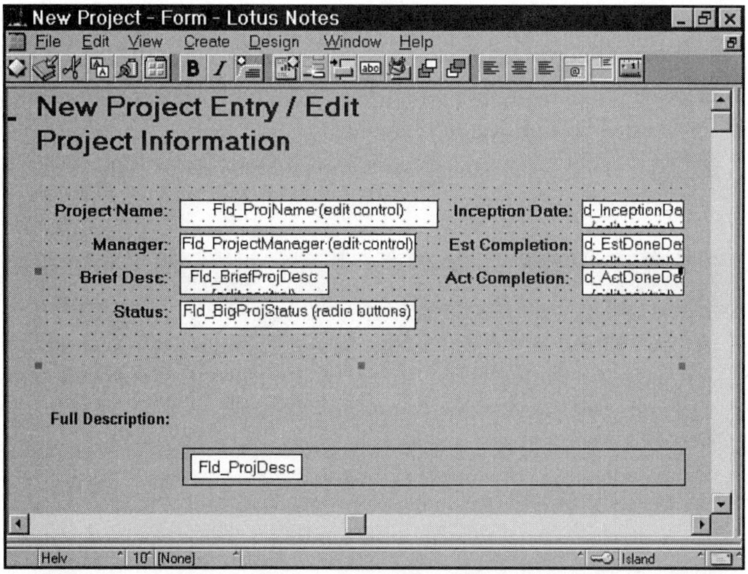

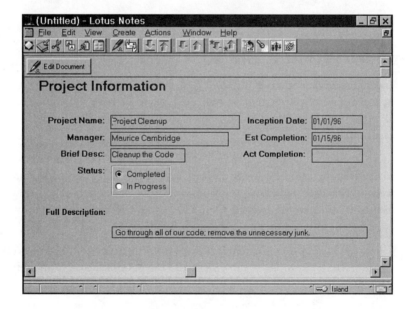

FIGURE 20.7.

The New Project form at runtime with a layout region.

Here are some tips that apply to layout-region design:

- Enable the grid and Snap to choices when you are adding objects to a layout region.
- Because the number of items in a keyword list varies, allow for ample room below a keyword field for expansion at runtime. For keyword lists with several entries, increase the number of columns for the keyword list (when using checkboxes or radio buttons) to spread the choices out from left to right.

- The background color of a layout region inherits the background color for the form that it is drawn upon.

- A graphical background may be pasted to the background of a layout region, using Create | Layout Region | Graphic.

- After any design change, test your layout region to make sure it looks correct at runtime.

TIP

A form that contains a layout region may also be used in conjunction with the @DialogBox formula or the DialogBox method of the NotesUIWorkspace class to present a "standard" dialog box that contains the contents of a layout region on a form, as well as OK and Cancel buttons that are automatically added. To use these new DialogBox routines with a layout region, you must pass as a parameter the name of the form that contains the desired layout region for inclusion in the dialog box. It is best to use the AutoHorzFit and AutoVert-Fit options to automatically fit the dialog box to the size of the first layout region on the form.

A Different Point of View

Your current database uses [+] and [–] in each view to indicate when a row is expandable and when it may be collapsed. This requires logic to be built into your view columns using the @IsExpandable formula. This section shows how to replace your view-column logic by activating simple *twisties*.

If a particular view row is expandable, a *twistie* will appear to the left of the first character in the row. If the row may be expanded, the twistie will look like a triangle pointing to the right; if a row is expanded (and may be collapsed), the twistie will look like a triangle pointing downwards. In other words, twisties are used to indicate whether or not Response or Response to Response documents are linked to a particular row.

First, let's examine your primary views: Projects\All, Projects\In Progress, and Projects\Completed. All of these views use the @IsExpandable formula in the first column as follows:

```
NewLine := @If(Form = "AComm"; "Comment: " + Fld_Subject + " ( " +
➥Fld_CommentAuthor + " )"; Form = "NewAct";  @Text(Fld_ActivityDate) +": " +
➥Fld_Activity + " ( " + Fld_PerformedBy + " ) [ " + Fld_ProjStatus + " ] "; "");
@IsExpandable( "[ + ] "+NewLine; NewLine)
```

This formula simply adds a [+] to the beginning of a row in a view if there are response documents.

The second column of these views contains a similar formula:

```
@If(@IsResponseDoc; ""; @IsExpandable("[+] " + Fld_ProjName + "    ( Mgr: " +
➡Fld_ProjectManager + " )  [ " + Fld_BigProjStatus +" ]"; "[-] " + Fld_ProjName + "
➡( Mgr: " + Fld_ProjectManager + " ) [ " + Fld_BigProjStatus +" ]"))
```

The ultimate beauty of twisties is that most of the @IsExpandable logic, which is often confusing when embedded in a formula, may be completely removed; the expandability and collapsibility of a particular row are *automatically* indicated.

To enable twisties, use the Column Properties InfoBox and select the choice Show twistie when row is expandable for each column that may contain documents that have links to response documents. Figure 20.8 depicts an InfoBox with this choice selected.

FIGURE 20.8.

A View Column InfoBox with twisties activated.

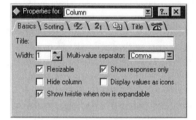

Of course, with twisties activated, the @IsExpandable logic can be removed from the column formulas. With these changes, Figure 20.9 shows an image of a typical view that uses twisties.

FIGURE 20.9.

The new Projects All View using twisties.

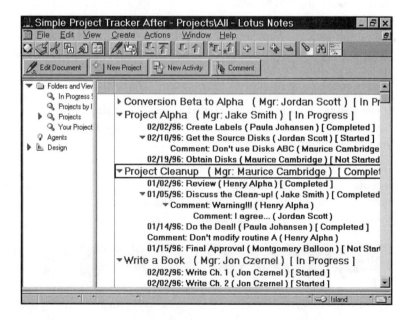

All of the other views in the Project Tracking database have been modified to use twisties.

In addition to the use of twisties, the column headings for the views `Projects\All`, `Projects\In Progress`, and `Projects\Completed` were disabled using the Style (S) tab in View Properties (deselect Show column headings).

Navigating Through Views

The final visual change that will be made to the Project Tracking database will be the inclusion of a Navigator.

Navigators are like graphical road maps to views in a database. For a detailed description of Navigators, see Chapter 19, "Using Navigators, Agents, and Simple Actions."

You will add a Navigator to replace the default set of views and folders that appear in the Navigator pane. This Navigator will enable all built-in database views to be accessed, in addition to a hotspot that enables the database window to be closed.

There are generally two approaches to designing a Navigator. If you have a bitmapped image that may be used as a background, or a series of bitmaps that may be used as graphic buttons, by all means use them. If bitmaps are not readily available, however, and you are artistically challenged (we do want to be politically correct), you may utilize the easy-to-use, built-in design tools in Notes to obtain extremely acceptable results.

Nobody is forcing you to create beautiful Navigator bitmaps that rival those found in professional software packages (or even the Release 4.x templates that ship with Lotus Notes, like `Room Reservations`). Remember that the idea of creating a Navigator is to make the selection of views or the initiation of actions (formula or script) simple and straightforward, perhaps replacing the need for menu items. This can be accomplished very easily using standard, simple objects, such as rectangles.

If you will be using prepackaged bitmaps, remember that Lotus Notes Release 4.0 does not have a facility to load bitmaps; the desired bitmap must first be placed in the clipboard *before* you create a graphical object.

If you would like to try creating bitmaps for your application, you may use Microsoft Paint included in Microsoft Windows 95 or a variety of Windows, OS/2, or UNIX-based drawing utilities. If you plan on using Microsoft Paint, change the drawing area to roughly 32×32 (Pels) using Image | Attributes, then Zoom in and enable Gridlines.

> **TIP**
>
> If you'd like to use bitmaps in your Navigators (or forms, for that matter) and have access to the Internet and the WWW (World Wide Web, for those who have been living in a barrel for the last year or so), search for the words "Icon" or "Bitmap" using one of the

Internet search sites, such as Yahoo! (www.yahoo.com), Excite (www.excite.com), WebCrawler (www.webcrawler.com), or Magellan (magellan.mckinley.com). You may also purchase a CD-ROM that contains a slew of bitmaps that may apply to your application.

Because I do not have bitmaps that would be particularly useful in your database, we will use built-in Navigator objects to create a Navigator for the Project Tracking database.

To create a Navigator for your database, follow these steps:

1. First, select Create | Design | Navigator. A blank Navigator window will appear, and the SmartIcon set will change to a set of objects that may be added to a Navigator.

2. Now, define some basic Navigator properties by bringing up the Navigator InfoBox. Click on the right mouse button anywhere in the blank Navigator, and select Navigator Properties.

3. In the Basics tab, give the Navigator a name, such as Default. For the Initial view or folder, always choose the most common view or folder. In this case, Projects | In Progress will be selected. Next, select Auto adjust panes at runtime. This property automatically adjusts your Navigator view pane to fit all of the objects that you draw in the Navigator. Choose a background color that suits your taste.

4. In the Grids tab, select Snap to grid, and bump up the grid size to about five pixels.

5. Next, create one Rectangle object (*not* Hotspot Rectangles) for each View in your database (there are six views). For now, don't worry about exact placement of these objects or the definition of their actions—this will be handled later.

   For each Rectangle, change the Caption (found in the Basics InfoBox tab for Rectangle Properties) to the name of the view that the object will present. You will also change the Fill Color to a different color for each rectangle, and increase the Outline Width slightly (the default is a very thin line). Using the HiLite tab, we'll enable the Highlight when touched option, which will present a red (by default) outline around an object when the mouse pointer moves over it.

6. To add some usability to the database, also create a final Rectangle with the Caption set to Exit. Use a formula to terminate the database when the user clicks on this object.

7. Now that all objects have been created, you can deal with object placement. In this particular database, it would be good to enable the use of the Document Preview pane, enabling individual documents to be viewed while navigating through a view. Your Navigator must be designed in such a way as to allow a reasonably sized Document Preview pane to exist in the lower portion of the screen. If this pane is too small, it will be essentially useless. There are several approaches to this problem. With your database, I've chosen to create two columns of rectangular objects, resulting in a table-like Navigator. This is shown in Figure 20.10.

FIGURE 20.10.

The Navigator in Design Mode.

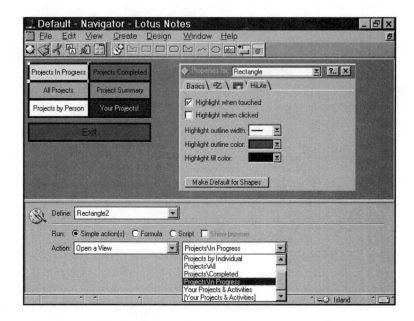

FIGURE 20.10.

The Navigator in Design Mode.

Note the placement of the objects in Figure 20.10, all shifted to the upper-left portion of the Navigator to allow room for the Document Preview pane.

TIP

When you are satisfied with the placement of an object, I suggest enabling the Lock size and position option in the Basics tab for each object. Without this option enabled, simply selecting an object with the mouse click may move the object ever so slightly, resulting in a great deal of frustration.

---

8. The final step in creating a Navigator is to assign an action to each applicable object. In most cases, a Simple Action will suffice, enabling you to easily open a view, folder, link, or another Navigator. In this database, you'll use Simple Actions for each object, with the exception of the Exit object (to be defined in the next step).

   For each object, select Simple Action, then Open a View for the Action selection. From the second list box, select the view that should be opened for the object. Note that in the case of Private on First Use views (Your Projects & Activities in the Project Tracking database), always select the original view name—*not* the view name enclosed in parentheses, which represents the actual Private View.

9. For the Exit object, select Formula, then type in the command `@Command([FileCloseWindow])`. This formula closes the current window, which will result in closing the current database.

10. Now that your objects have been created and defined, the last step is to tell our database to open this Navigator when the database is opened instead of the default Folder Navigator. Use the Launch tab in the Database Properties InfoBox to specify "Open designated Navigator" for the On Database Open setting, then select the Navigator created previously. Do not select "Open designated Navigator in its own window." This choice will open the Navigator as a full-screen image, without the View and Document Preview panes. This might be useful in some applications but definitely does not apply to our Project Tracking database.

Now that your Navigator has been created, let's look at your database (the Document Preview pane is activated here). (See Figure 20.11.)

FIGURE 20.11.
The After database, with new views, a Navigator, Action Bars, and a Document Preview pane.

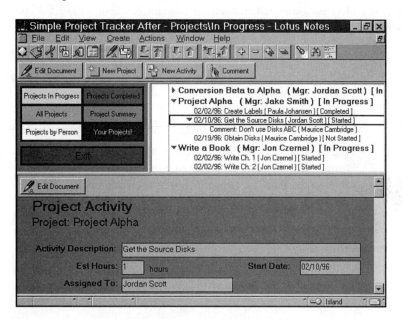

Using LotusScript and Simple Actions

Now that you have a good-looking database, we'll focus our efforts on the following programmatic changes to the Project Tracking database:

■ You will add some buttons that use Simple Actions and LotusScript that were left out during the conversion from standard forms to layout regions.

■ Using LotusScript, you will add several input validations and translations to various fields.

Buttons and Actions that Use Simple Actions and LotusScript

Since our database was originally written using Release 3.x of Lotus Notes, all of our event handling routines utilize Formulas. While this is completely acceptable, Simple Actions enable common programming tasks to be completed with minimal programming effort.

When Layout Regions were added to our forms, the buttons used to "automatically" set various fields were not converted. We will now add these buttons, using Simple Actions instead of Formulas.

The first change will be made to the New Project form, where you will add a hotspot button to the layout region (*not* to the nonlayout region portion of the Form!) that automatically marks the project as Completed and sets the Actual Completion Date field to the current date.

1. First, enter Design Mode for the New Project form.

2. Click once anywhere on the Layout Region to select it.

3. Select Create | Hotspot | Button. The new button will appear in the center of the Layout Region. Move it underneath, or somewhere near, the Status field (use your best judgment).

4. For the Button Label property of the button, type in Mark as Completed.

5. Finally, assign a set of Simple Actions to this button. First, change the Run type from Formula (the default) to Simple Action. Next, select Add Action, and change the values in the Edit Action dialog box as shown in Figure 20.12.

FIGURE 20.12.

Defining a Simple Action to change the value of a field.

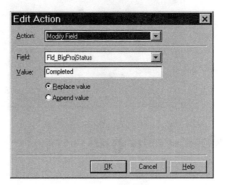

6. The final Simple Action that you need to add changes the value of the field Fld_ActDoneDate to the current date. However, there is no Simple Action that sets a field to the current date. Do not fear! One of the Simple Actions that is available is the execution of a formula. This enables predefined Simple Actions to be easily mixed with @Functions. To complete the second Simple Action for your button, change the fields in the Edit Action dialog box as shown in Figure 20.13.

FIGURE 20.13.

Defining a Simple Action that uses a formula to set a field to the current date.

Save the new form and test the new button. Make sure the fields in the Layout Region are properly placed, and that the button functions properly. Remember that the button can be executed only when a document is being edited.

Next, modify your Save & Exit Action in the New Activity form to use LotusScript to mail the New Activity form to the individual to whom the activity is assigned, in addition to saving the form and closing the window:

> **NOTE**
>
> Due to the way the `NotesUIDocument` and `NotesDocument` classes work in LotusScript, this is not as trivial as it sounds. I would have liked to simply send a doclink in the mail message; alas, doclinks are not supported with the `Send` method.

1. First, open the New Activity form in Design Mode.

2. Next, select the View | Action pane to view all Actions defined for this form. Select the Save and Exit Action.

3. The current Save and Exit Action contains the formula:

```
@PostedCommand([FileSave]);
@PostedCommand([FileCloseWindow])
```

4. Change the Run selection to Script.

5. Before typing any script, you will need to add a few hidden fields to our New Activity form. Towards the bottom of the form (*not* in the Layout Region), add the text fields SendTo, Body, and Subject. Do the names of these fields ring a bell? They are fields that allow this form to be mail enabled. *Make sure these fields are hidden.*

6. Now you can begin typing in some script. The first thing that is necessary is to declare variables that will be used to reference the current document, and to bind the variable NowDoc to the current document. Note that the classes NotesUIWorkspace and NotesUIDocument refer to the current user-interface workspace and the document that the user is currently viewing in the interface. The NotesDocument class is used to reference a document that has already been saved to the database; it will be used later.

```
Dim NowWorkspace As New NotesUIWorkspace
Dim NowDoc As NotesUIDocument
Dim NowDocStd As NotesDocument
Set NowDoc = NowWorkspace.CurrentDocument
```

7. Now, place values into the hidden mail-related fields that were added previously. But first, use the `FieldGetText` method to save the value in the field `Fld_PerformedBy` into the string variable `ToName$`.

```
ToName$ = NowDoc.FieldGetText( "Fld_PerformedBy" )
Call NowDoc.FieldSetText( "Subject", "A new assignment...")
Call NowDoc.FieldSetText( "Body", "Here is a new assignment for you!")
Call NowDoc.FieldSetText( "SendTo", ToName$)
```

8. Now the *real* fun begins. The `Send` method for the `NotesUIDocument` class allows only a simple message to be mailed, consisting of "standard" fields, such as a subject and body. The `Send` method for the `NotesDocument` class, however, allows a complete form to be mailed. Therefore, you need to reference the current document using the `NotesDocument` class, so that you can initiate a `Send` method that mails the final form.

    The `NotesDocument` class can be used only on documents that are in a database. At this point, your document has not been *saved*; it is only on the screen (it is, after all, a `NotesUIDocument`). Therefore, you will first save the current document, then bind a new `NotesDocument` variable, `NowDocStd`, to a reference to the saved back-end document. This reference to the back-end document is accessed through the `Document` property of the `NowDoc` variable (a `NotesUIDocument` class).

```
Call NowDoc.Save
Set NowDocStd = NowDoc.Document
```

9. Now that you have a reference to a saved document with a variable bound to a `NotesDocument`, you can initiate a `Send` method that sends the whole form to the individual listed in the `SendTo` field.

```
Call NowDocStd.Send(True)
```

10. The final step required is to close the current window. However, due to the operations that were performed previously, LotusScript feels that you have changed your document since the last save. If you issue a `Close` method alone, you'll be prompted if you want to save the current document. Because you want this entire process to be completed "behind the scenes," simply save the document again before closing it.

```
Call NowDoc.Save
Call NowDoc.Close
```

Now you may save the new form and test it. Try to create a New Activity and assign it to you. When the Save and Exit Action is selected, you should receive a mail message that includes the New Activity form.

The previous example illustrates both the power and complexity of LotusScript. It also provides at least one valuable lesson. Before undertaking any task using LotusScript, first see if the same function may be performed using Simple Actions or formulas. In this case, due to a bug in Lotus Notes Release 4.0, I was unfortunately unable to use Simple Actions. The `Send Mail`

`Message` Action works marvelously, but the `@Command([FileCloseWindow])` crashes Notes with an infamous "red box" error, requiring system shutdown.

However, a simple set of formulas would be able to accomplish virtually the same tasks as shown previously, with one exception: Instead of sending the whole form, a DocLink will be sent. This formula may be used instead of the script shown previously:

```
@MailSend( Fld_PerformedBy; ; ;A new assignment; ; Click here -> ;
➥[IncludeDocLink] );
@Command( [FileSave] );
@Command( [FileCloseWindow] );
```

As you can see, three statements replace all of the script used in the example database.

However, remember that Script does have significant advantages over formulas. For example, the built-in debugger, a new feature in R4, can only be used with Script, not formulas. Additionally, the preceding Script may be modified to perform virtually any task, so expansion to include new features that are supported through LotusScript (Script) is possible.

Input Validation Using LotusScript

The current database does not contain any input validation or translation mechanisms. We will focus our attention here on the New Project form, adding input validation for four fields.

Before allowing a New Project form to be saved, you will first ensure that appropriate values have been entered for various fields. The `QuerySave` event for the NewProj (the synonym for the New Project form) object is triggered before the form is saved. If the Script in this subprogram sets the `Continue` variable to `False`, the Save operation is canceled.

1. Open the New Project form in Design Mode.
2. Use the `%Include` directive to load various constants that will be used in your validation routines for the `MessageBox` statement. In the Programming pane, select the `(Globals)` NewProj object and the `(Declarations)` event. Type in the statement

   `%Include "LSCONST.LSS"`

   Remember that any variables declared in the `(Globals)` object in the `(Declarations)` event are visible to any procedure (subprogram or function) in the current database. Therefore, all of the constants defined in the file LSCONST.LSS may be accessed from any procedure.
3. Before proceeding, you must correct a slight problem in the form. Using the current Save and Exit Action, the `QuerySave` event is initiated when `@Command([FileSave])` is executed. However, because this command is immediately preceded by `@Command([FileCloseWindow])`, it is possible for the user to be confused by a dialog box asking whether or not the document should be saved, even after the script in the `QuerySave` event has set `Continue` to `False`.

To eliminate this confusion, rename the Save and Exit Action to Done, and change the formula to:

```
@PostedCommand([FileCloseWindow]);
```

This change will force the database to always prompt the user whether or not to save the document before closing the document window. If the user chooses Yes, the QuerySave event will be initiated, enabling us to properly terminate a save action.

4. Now select the NewProj(Form) object, followed by the QuerySave event.

   You will use the variable Source, an instance of the current NotesUIWorkspace class, to reference the fields on the current form. This variable is passed as a parameter to the QuerySave subprogram.

5. The first validation performed will be to make sure text entries have been entered for text-only fields. The following code fragment first copies the value from the field Fld_ProjName into the variable TempVal$. The Trim$ function is then used to eliminate all leading and trailing spaces from the string. If this trimmed string is equal to an empty string (""), the field is empty—the Continue variable is set to False, forcing the save operation to terminate. The MessageBox statement is then used to warn the user of the invalid entry, and focus is set to the offending field with the GotoField method. Since an invalid entry has been found, the Exit Sub is executed to leave the QuerySave subprogram so that no further processing is initiated.

```
TempVal$ = Source.FieldGetText( "Fld_ProjName" )
If Trim$(TempVal$) = "" Then
     Continue = False
     Messagebox "A Project Name must be entered before proceeding!", _
          MB_OK+MB_ICONEXCLAMATION, "Missing Value"
     Call Source.GotoField("Fld_ProjName")
     Exit Sub
End If
```

6. The same general block of statements are repeated for Fld_ProjectManager.

```
TempVal$ = Source.FieldGetText( "Fld_ProjectManager" )
If Trim$(TempVal$) = "" Then
     Continue = False
     Messagebox "A Project Manager must be entered before proceeding!", _
          MB_OK+MB_ICONEXCLAMATION, "Missing Value"
     Call Source.GotoField("Fld_ProjectManager")
     Exit Sub
End If
```

7. Next, verify that correct dates were entered in the fields Fld_InceptionDate and Fld_EstDoneDate. The LotusScript function IsDate will be used to determine if the dates entered are valid. The remaining portion of the logic is similar to the script from Step 5.

```
TempVal$ = Source.FieldGetText( "Fld_InceptionDate" )
If Not Isdate(TempVal$) Then
     Continue = False
     Messagebox "The Inception Date is invalid!", MB_OK+MB_ICONEXCLAMATION,
```

```
    "Invalid Date"
        Call Source.GotoField("Fld_InceptionDate")
        Exit Sub
    End If
```

8. A check for the field `Fld_EstDoneDate` is similarly performed:

```
TempVal$ = Source.FieldGetText( "Fld_EstDoneDate" )
If Not Isdate(TempVal$) Then
    Continue = False
    Messagebox "The Estimated Completion Date is invalid!",
_MB_OK+MB_ICONEXCLAMATION, "Invalid Date"
    Call Source.GotoField("Fld_EstDoneDate")
    Exit Sub
End If
```

Once again, this simple exercise proves to be more complicated than the use of standard Input Translation and Input Validation formulas. However, due to the flexibility of Script, it is possible to apply significantly more complicated translation and validation routines that are not possible, or extremely cumbersome, using formulas alone. For example, using the ODBC classes, you may use Script to perform a database lookup and translation based on an external data source. Remember also that Script, unlike formulas, may be debugged with the built-in R4 debugger, an option not available to formulas.

Adding an Agent that Uses LotusScript

For the most part, your database is complete. However, it has come to your attention that you need to save, in a comma-delimited ASCII file, all In Progress projects on a nightly basis. This file will be read by another project-tracking application, which will eventually feed this data to a mainframe somewhere in Michigan.

A typical agent that uses formulas is fairly simple to create, especially using the advanced Agent Builder of Lotus Notes R4. When Script is used, however, the only filtering assistance available is through the `UnprocessedDocuments` *collection*, a subset of documents in a database.

In an agent, the contents of this collection varies depending on the selection Which documents should it act on? in the Agent Builder. For a complete table of collection contents based on different settings, look up "Collecting all documents and unprocessed documents" from `Help Topics` in Lotus Notes Release 4.0.

For your agent, choose All documents in database, which enables you to specify search criteria. Using these settings, the `UnprocessedDocuments` collection will contain all documents in the database that match the search criteria specified.

To create an agent that performs the Text Dump task, you need to first create an agent by selecting `Create...Agent`. In the Agent Builder, define an agent as shown in Figure 20.14.

20

DEVELOPING AN
ADVANCED
APPLICATION

FIGURE 20.14.

The Text Dump Agent.

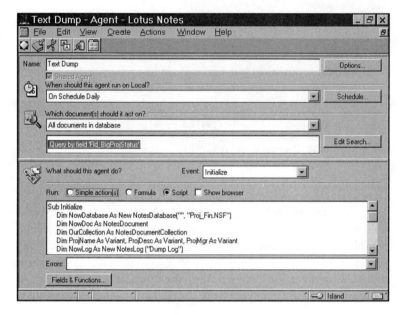

The settings for the Schedule should be set as shown in Figure 20.15.

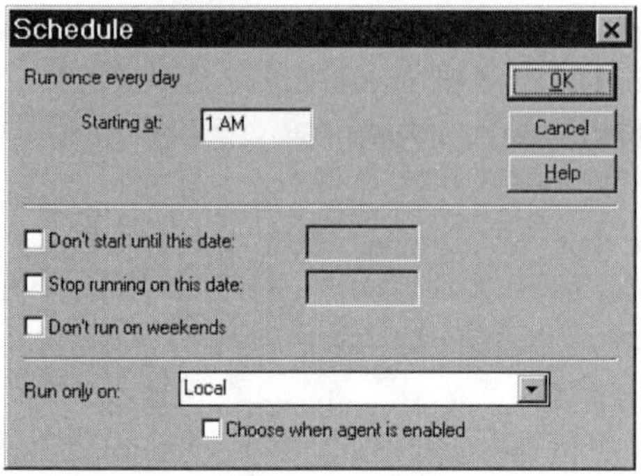

FIGURE 20.15.

The Schedule for the agent.

The settings for the Search Builder should be defined as shown in Figure 20.16. Note that the Agent requires a Full Text Index for this Search to be properly executed. Because a Full Text Search is utilized when the Agent is executed, you will search for the word "Progress" in the field `Fld_BigProjStatus`, which will find all documents that contain "In Progress."

Now that the basics for this Agent are defined, you will now write Script to take care of the following tasks:

- Obtain a collection of documents from the database that comply with your search criteria.

- Create a text log file using the `NotesLog` class that will allow for progress tracking if this Agent is run later on a server. The log filename will be called DUMPLOG.TXT.

■ For each project that is "In Progress," as defined by our Search Builder, write one line to the file PROJECTS.TXT that lists the Project Name (Fld_ProjName), the Project Manager (Fld_ProjectManager), and a brief description of the project (Fld_BriefProjDesc).

FIGURE 20.16.

The Search Builder for the agent.

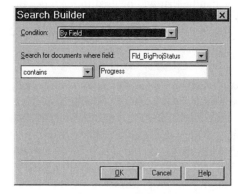

You will now begin to write LotusScript statements that accomplish these tasks:

1. Switch to the Initialize event in the Programming pane. This script in this subprogram is executed when the Agent is triggered.

2. Begin by declaring variables that will be used in your endeavor. This includes the declaration of a variable that will be used to access the database itself (NowDatabase), a document collection (OurCollection), and a Notes log file (NowLog).

```
Dim NowDatabase As New NotesDatabase("", "Proj_Fin.NSF")
Dim NowDoc As NotesDocument
Dim OurCollection As NotesDocumentCollection
Dim ProjName As Variant, ProjDesc As Variant, ProjMgr As Variant
Dim NowLog As New NotesLog ("Dump Log")
```

3. Bind the collection of unprocessed documents to your collection variable, OurCollection. Remember that, based on your agent definition, the "Unprocessed Documents" collection refers to a subset of database documents that adhere to the search criteria specified—in this case, documents that contain the word "Progress" in the field Fld_BigProjStatus.

```
Set OurCollection = NowDatabase.UnprocessedDocuments
```

4. Create a new log file DUMPLOG.TXT using the OpenFileLog method of the NotesLog class, then add a log entry using the LogAction method indicating that the dumping agent has been initiated.

```
Call  NowLog.OpenFileLog("DumpLog.txt")
NowLog.LogAction("Text Dump started")
```

5. To trap any unforeseen errors in your script, such as a problem during the creating of the text file, add a general error-trapping mechanism. When this statement is executed, any LotusScript error will cause program execution to branch to the

AgentError label, defined later in your script. The script starting at this label will be responsible for handling all errors.

```
On Error Goto AgentError
```

6. Open the text output file PROJECTS.TXT. The FreeFile function is used to obtain a valid file handle that will be used to reference the output file. The Open statement actually opens the file using the file reference. The Output keyword forces the creating of a new file. That is, if the file exists, it is overwritten.

```
f% = Freefile
Open "Projects.txt" For Output As #f%
```

7. Your main loop through all documents in the collection now begins. The Count property indicates the number of documents in OurCollection. Bind the variable NowDoc to each document in the collection, using the GetNthDocument to indicate a document position in the collection.

```
For i=1 To OurCollection.Count
    Set NowDoc = OurCollection.GetNthDocument( i )
```

8. Continuing in your loop, extract necessary values from each document using the GetItemValue method. Note that in the case of text fields, the GetItemValue method returns an array of strings, allowing for multiple values stored in fields to be returned. In this case, however, you can assume that your fields contain only one value.

```
ProjName = NowDoc.GetItemValue("Fld_ProjName")
ProjDesc = NowDoc.GetItemValue("Fld_BriefProjDesc")
ProjMgr = NowDoc.GetItemValue("Fld_ProjectManager")
```

9. Finally, write the field values to the file referenced by the variable f%. Because the field values returned are all single values, you use the array index 0 for each variable. The Write statement adds commas between each field and encloses each value in quotes in the output file. With the Next statement, you continue to the next document in the collection.

```
    Write #f%, ProjName(0),ProjDesc(0),ProjMgr(0)
Next i
```

10. With the successful completion of your loop, you can close the handle to the file f% and add a positive entry to your log file. The Exit Sub statement is then used to terminate execution of the Initialize subprogram.

```
Close #f%
NowLog.LogAction("Dump completed successfully")
Exit Sub
```

11. What about the error handler described in Step 5? It is found in the following code snippet. The handler first closes all files with the Close statement, then logs the LotusScript error number (Err) to the log file. It then terminates the execution of the subprogram with Exit Sub.

```
AgentError:
    Close
    NowLog.LogAction("An error occured in Text Dump, #" + Str$(Err))
    Exit Sub
```

Listing 20.1 includes the final listing of your Terminate subprogram for this agent, in complete form for ease of reading.

Listing 20.1. Terminate subprogram for the Text Dump agent.

```
Sub Initialize
    Dim NowDatabase As New NotesDatabase("", "Proj_Fin.NSF")
    Dim NowDoc As NotesDocument
    Dim OurCollection As NotesDocumentCollection
    Dim ProjName As Variant, ProjDesc As Variant, ProjMgr As Variant
    Dim NowLog As New NotesLog ("Dump Log")

    Set OurCollection = NowDatabase.UnprocessedDocuments
    Call  NowLog.OpenFileLog("DumpLog.txt")
    NowLog.LogAction("Text Dump started")

    On Error Goto AgentError

    f% = Freefile
    Open "Projects.txt" For Output As #f%

    For i=1 To OurCollection.Count
        Set NowDoc = OurCollection.GetNthDocument( i )
        ProjName = NowDoc.GetItemValue("Fld_ProjName")
        ProjDesc = NowDoc.GetItemValue("Fld_BriefProjDesc")
        ProjMgr = NowDoc.GetItemValue("Fld_ProjectManager")

        Write #f%, ProjName(0),ProjDesc(0),ProjMgr(0)
    Next i

    Close #f%
    NowLog.LogAction("Dump completed successfully")
    Exit Sub

AgentError:
    Close
    NowLog.LogAction("An error occured in Text Dump, #" + Str$(Err))
    Exit Sub
End Sub
```

In this example, standard Notes formulas could not have accomplished the tasks required. This example clearly illustrates some of the advanced capabilities that LotusScript brings to the development table.

The Debugging Cycle

Besides the striking development capabilities found in Lotus Notes R4, Lotus has provided developers with a significantly advanced script-debugging aid that will assist any application designer having difficulties getting his Script events to execute properly.

As debugging options are not available using formulas, this feature alone provides a significant argument in favor of switching any complex formulas to LotusScript.

To enable the LotusScript Debugger, select File | Tools | Debug LotusScript. When Debug LotusScript is enabled, the *Script Debugger* will appear any time event handlers that utilize LotusScript are executed. Figure 20.17 represents a typical Debugger screen.

FIGURE 20.17.

A typical Script Debugger.

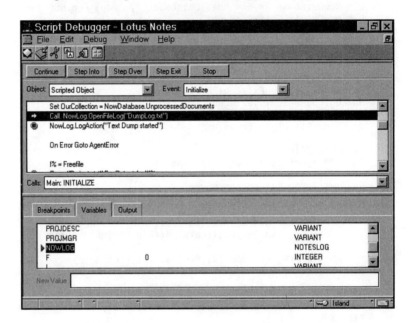

When the Script Debugger is activated, you will notice the following three distinct screen areas:

- *A Stepping Buttons Bar.* This area contains five buttons: Continue, Step Into, Step Over, Step Exit, and Stop. These buttons are used to control Script execution during the debugging phase.
- *Script Pane.* This area contains script for the current object and event, as indicated in the Object and Event list boxes.
- *Debugging Tools Pane.* This area contains breakpoints, variables, and output that will assist tremendously in the debugging process.

The Stepping Buttons Bar

The buttons on this bar enable Script execution to continue in slightly different ways.

Use the Continue button to resume Script execution as normal until the next breakpoint is encountered. The F5 key duplicates this function.

The Step Into button is used to execute the current statement. If the current statement is a call to a subprogram, the debugger will jump "into" the statements listed in the called procedure, enabling it to be traced as well. The F8 key duplicates this function.

The Step Over button is used to execute the current statement. If the current statement is a call to a subprogram, the statements in the procedure will be executed *without* being traced (the debugger will step "over" the procedure), and debugging will resume with the line immediately following the current statement. Shift+F8 may also be used to initiate this function.

Use the Step Exit button to enable execution of the current subprogram to resume until the next Exit Sub or End Sub is encountered. Ctrl+F8 may be used to initiate this function.

For those without the benefit of a mouse, or for those who feel that the mouse is the physical incarnation of Satan himself (*you* know who you are), the Debug Menu lists all of the preceding options.

The Script Pane

This pane contains Script. By default, the current Object and Event Script will be displayed, with a yellow arrow to the immediate left of the current statement. This yellow arrow indicates the *next* line that will execute, should execution continue.

In addition, any *breakpoints* that have been set will be indicated by a small red stop sign to the left of the breakpoint line.

To a set a new breakpoint in the Script, either double-click on the Script line, or highlight the desired line and press F9.

The Tools Pane

This pane contains three tabs. The first tab, Breakpoints, lists all stop points that are currently enabled. When a breakpoint is defined, Script execution will automatically terminate up to the specified breakpoint statement. Breakpoints enable the developer to focus debugging attention on a particular portion of Script, instead of stepping through Script that has already been tried and proven. Breakpoints are listed with the format *Object:Event:Line Number*.

The second tab, Variables, lists all variables that are visible to the current subprogram. In other words, all variables that exist within the scope of the current subprogram are shown. The variable type and value are listed. For variables that are types or arrays, an expansion arrow is shown next to the variable name; clicking on this arrow presents more detailed variable information.

When a variable is selected, it may be possible to change its value using the New Value entry box that appears underneath the variable list.

The last tab, Output, enables the developer to easily trace program execution. All output from the `Print` statement is sent to this window during execution. Note that `Print` statement output is normally sent to the Notes Message Bar when the Debugger is *not* active.

A Typical Debugging Procedure

When problems are experienced in Script, the first step is to enable the debugger by selecting File | Tools | Debug LotusScript. With this option enabled, the next time any Script statements are encountered the Debugger will appear. Because all Script in Notes is executed based on the trigger of an event, after the LotusScript Debugger is enabled you may select the event that needs to be examined.

After the Debugger appears, Script for the current event will appear. Additionally, any variables that exist within the scope of the current subprogram will be displayed in the Variables tab. At this point you have three options:

1. To debug the current Script, you may execute line-by-line with the Step Over or Step Into buttons, watching the value of variables and/or output from `Print` statements in the Output tab.

2. If the section of buggy Script appears several lines (or pages, perhaps) down into the current subprogram, it may be cumbersome to repeatedly hit one of the Step buttons. In this case, you may move down in the current Script and set a breakpoint by double-clicking on a statement just before the known "infested" (with bugs) area. When a logical breakpoint is set, click on the Continue button. When the Script requiring debugging is finally displayed, use the procedures described in Step 1.

3. If the current subprogram is not problematic, but a problem area exists in a subprogram that the current subprogram (or any other subprogram, for that matter) *calls*, you may switch to the called subprogram using the Event and Object list boxes, then set logical breakpoint(s) just before the section of problem Script. To resume execution to the next breakpoint, click on the Continue button. When the Script requiring debugging is finally displayed, use the procedures described in Step 1.

Note that Script itself may not be altered while in debug mode. To modify Script that contains errors, you'll need to return to database design mode.

Using the debugger will require some practice for those that have never used a true debugging system. However, with some practice you will find the debugging tools an irreplaceable instrument in your development arsenal.

Safe Deployment of Notes Applications

As a final subject in this chapter, I'd like to briefly touch on a new capability introduced in R4: The ability to completely hide the design of a database. This feature enables Notes developers to deliver "shrink-wrapped," protected applications to their clients while protecting all of their design secrets. With the addition of LotusScript, a truly wonderful and full-featured programming language, the ability to hide design attributes is a welcome addition.

The steps involved in hiding all of the design elements of a database are as follows:

1. First, thoroughly test your database. Remember that after the database design elements are hidden, you will no longer be able to make design changes "on the fly" once your application is rolled out.

2. Create a new copy of your database using File | Database | New Copy. For the database title, insert the word "Template" somewhere for easy identification. Also, use the file extension .NTF instead of .NSF (NTF is a Notes Template File).

3. Using the new copy created, switch this database to a template by using the Design tab in the Database Properties from the InfoBox, as found in Figure 20.18.

FIGURE 20.18.

Converting your database to a template.

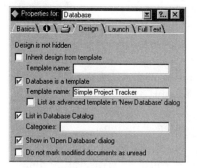

4. Next, create a new database using File | Database | New. As the template, choose the template file created in Step 2. You may select the box Inherit future design changes if this feature is required.

5. When this database is created, close it, then make sure it is selected. Use File | Database | Replace Design to (finally) hide your database design. In the Replace Database Design dialog box, make sure the template was created in Step 2, and select the option Hide formulas and LotusScript. (See Figure 20.19.)

FIGURE 20.19.

The choices that need to be selected in the Replace Database Design dialog box.

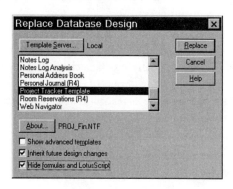

6. Finally, click on the Replace button, then click on Yes to enable the replace process to continue.

Go ahead, try to change the design attributes of this new database. They are completely hidden, and may not be viewed, protecting your design secrets indefinitely!

Summary

This chapter discussed several of the new development capabilities introduced in Lotus Notes R4. The following is a summary of the most important points mentioned:

■ Actions, in the form of both Action Bars and Action menu items, enable form-level formulas, Simple Actions, or script to be executed without the need to add hotspot buttons to a typical form. The advantage of Action Bars is that they appear in a nonscrollable region near the top of any form. In addition to programmed actions, several predefined actions may also be used.

■ Layout regions, free-form design areas created in a standard form, enable more traditional GUI-interface features to be utilized. All standard fields may be used in a layout region with the exception of rich text fields (RTF). Note also that the @DialogBox formula or the DialogBox method in the NotesUIWorkspace class may be used to display a form that contains a single layout region as a standard dialog box with OK and Cancel buttons.

■ Views may now use twisties to indicate if a particular document listed in a view may be expanded or collapsed. This feature simplifies the user interface significantly, and simplifies View Column programming.

■ To assist the user in moving from one view or folder to another, Navigators have been introduced. Navigators are used to open views, folders, or other Navigators in the database. In creating a Navigator, remember that even the built-in design tools will enable you to create an acceptable Navigator screen.

■ When programming any event, attempt to use Simple Actions before formulas or script. They are especially useful in Actions, where most of the functions that might be required at the form level are included, such as mailing the current document and forwarding a document.

■ Several Notes classes have been provided in R4, allowing a variety (correction: a *huge* variety) of database-related tasks to be performed through LotusScript. The most important are the NotesUIWorkspace class, allowing access to the current Notes workspace (user interface); the NotesUIDocument class, enabling access to the document currently displayed; and the NotesDocument class, which is used to represent a document saved in the database.

■ To perform input translation or validation using LotusScript instead of Formula, use the QuerySave event. If the value of various fields does not meet required criteria, simply set the Continue variable to False to terminate the save operation.

■ The Agent Builder in R4 has been significantly enhanced, enabling either Simple Actions, Formula, or LotusScript to be used during execution of the agent. If LotusScript is used, the UnprocessedDocuments collection may provide a great deal of assistance.

■ The all-new debugging capabilities in R4 are a welcome addition to the Notes product. The Script Debugger is a full-featured, LotusScript-debugging utility that will assist any developer writing complex Script routines. Unfortunately, there is still no tool provided to debug Formula.

■ R4 brings developers one step closer to developing native "shrink-wrapped" Notes applications, enabling design elements to be completely hidden. Use File | Database | Replace Design to facilitate this process.

Advanced Development with the Notes API and HiTest Tools

by Irfan Virk

IN THIS CHAPTER

Lotus provides two alternatives for API (Application Programming Interface) development: a low-level C Notes API and a higher level C API, called HiTest. Although both APIs are C level interfaces, the low-level C Notes API will be referred to as the Notes C API and the HiTest C API will be referred to as the HiTest API.

Both APIs are a set of function calls and data structures that enable programmatic access to Notes functionality. These functions are written in C and are usually called from C programs. This gives API programs the capability of accessing and modifying a wide range of information about Notes databases. This includes details about Notes documents, design information (views, forms, macro/agents, and so forth), security (field level, document level, database level, and so on), and replication (such as selective replication formula).

One of the most popular uses of the APIs is to create custom data transfer programs. For example, a company enters new sales leads into an existing mainframe system. These leads need to be distributed to the sales force, which uses Lotus Notes. The company might write a custom API program to retrieve all new sales leads from the mainframe system and import those leads into a Notes database. All salespeople will receive new leads when they replicate the Notes database.

Another example is a company that requires specialized reports about help desk calls. It uses Lotus Notes to manage all incoming calls to its help desk. It could write an API program (using either API) to query the Notes database, compute the needed information, and then output specialized reports. It could even use Lotus Notes to distribute those reports to all managers.

This chapter discusses the C Notes API first, walks you through a simple C Notes API program, then redevelops the same program using the HiTest API.

The fundamental difference between the two APIs is that HiTest currently provides access to less Notes functionality, but is far easier to use. As you will see from the examples developed in this chapter, HiTest API programs require significantly less code and are easier to develop. Consequently, API programmers should always try to use HiTest first. If HiTest does not have the required functionality, only then should the programmer resort to using the C API.

Types of Notes C API Programs

The Lotus Notes C API can be used to manipulate databases (such as consolidating two departmental databases into one database), perform system administration (monitor server statistics, create new user IDs), and even to extend the Notes software (add menu options on the client using Add-Ins). Generally, Notes C API programs can be grouped into the following categories:

■ *Stand-alone applications.* These are stand-alone applications that make calls to the API for Notes-specific tasks. Although Notes does not need to be running, the Notes client libraries must be installed and on the path.

■ *Notes server add-in tasks.* These are API programs that are automatically launched from the Notes server. The Notes server consists of a number of server tasks (such as the replicator, the mail router, and so forth). The Notes API gives the capability of creating additional custom server tasks (named Server Add-In Tasks) that will be executed alongside the existing server tasks. These custom server add-ins can be scheduled to run every night at 1:00 am, for example, or every time the server is started.

■ *Notes workstation menu add-ins.* API programs that can be launched from the Notes client menu. They appear in the Tools menu in Notes R3 and in the Actions menu in Notes R4.

■ *Notes workstation import and export libraries.* Notes provides a set of libraries to import data into a Notes field. Using the File-Import menu option, users can import a variety of data (for example, Microsoft Rich Text, ASCII Text, BMP Image). This menu option uses import libraries provided by Lotus. API programs can serve as custom import/export libraries that also can be called from File | Import or File | Export.

■ *Database hook drivers.* Database hook drivers are API programs that are called each time a document is opened, updated, or categorized.

■ *Drivers for external (non-Notes) databases.* External Drivers enable access to data in non-Notes databases from a Notes by using @DBLookup and @DBColumn. In addition, this type of API program can be used to define custom @Functions. Notes applications can call these custom @Functions via parameters of the @DBCommnad function.

The set of available API functions is essentially the same for all types of API programs. The differences between each type of program are the entry points, exit points, and startup methods. In all the types of programs except stand-alone programs, the custom API code is executed as a result of something happening in Lotus Notes. Notes calls the entry points, often waits for the custom API code to execute, then resumes its normal functioning.

Getting Started with the C API: Notes Concepts

Logically speaking, a Notes database contains several types of information: header, design, document, and collection. (See Table 21.1.)

Table 21.1. Types of information in a Notes database.

Type of Information	Examples
Header	Database Title, Replication Settings, Access Control List, Replication History, User Activity Log, and some other header data
Design	Icon note, Policy note, Help note, View note, Form note, Filter note, and Macro/Agent notes
Document	Data notes
View Collections	Indexes of data note IDs

The *header information* contains the Database Title, Replication Settings, Access Control List, and other database details. The API does enable selective access to header information, but it does not enable programs to modify the replication history, user activity log, or database icons directly.

The *design information* includes details about views, forms, icons, and so forth. Most information in a Notes database is stored in a generic data structure referred to as a *note*. There are two types of notes: *design notes* and *data notes*. All design information is stored in design notes. For example, the Policy note contains the Help | About information for a Notes database. Each document in a Notes database is stored in a data note (that is, document). Within a data note, each field is stored as an *item*. The API provides a very large number of functions to read, modify, and write notes (both design and data) and items.

To avoid confusion, all references to the generic data structure will be lowercase (note), and all references to the software will be capitalized (Notes). Document and data note are the same and will be used interchangeably in this chapter.

A Notes database has the extension NSF, which stands for Notes Storage Facility. The Notes API has a set of functions for accessing data notes and design notes. These functions are prefixed with NSF—NSFSearch, for example.

From the Notes user interface, every view has a view definition (design information) and a set of documents. Because the same document is usually in multiple views, Notes does not maintain multiple copies of the document. Instead, Notes maintains an index to all the documents that are part of each view, called a *collection*. Although the design of a view may remain constant, the collection changes as documents are added or removed from the view.

From the API, every view has a view note and a collection. The view note describes the design of the view. For example, the selection formula used to filter documents is part of the design. The view collection describes the set of documents that currently qualify for a view. Because documents are stored as data notes, a collection is a list of note identifiers or *note IDs*. The note IDs in a collection appear in the exact same order as the documents in the view. API functions relating to views have the prefix NIF, which stands for Notes Index Facility.

API programs often use collections when the following are true:

- Parent/child relationships need to be maintained.
- Documents need to be sorted. The sorting order can be designed into the view.
- Performance is a key issue. Using a view collection to locate a particular document is usually much faster than searching the entire Notes database.

Sample Application Using the C API

This section walks you through the creation of a C API sample application. Assume that a company creates new orders in Notes. Each new order document contains an Order Status field whose value is defaulted to New. However, the actual orders are processed in some other non-Notes mainframe system. Once the order has been submitted to the mainframe system, the Order Status must be changed to Processed.

An API program to accomplish this task has three steps:

1. Get a list of all new orders.
2. Submit each new order to the mainframe system.
3. If successfully submitted, change the Order Status to processed.

There are a number of different ways to get a list of all new orders. In order to demonstrate the processing of views, assume that a New Orders View exists in the Notes database. Depending on the situation, using a view to process all new orders may not be the best solution. A discussion of why it may not be the best solution is beyond the scope of this chapter. An alternate way to find new orders is to search the entire database for data notes that have the Order Status field equal to New. This would be done using the NSFSearch() function, but is not demonstrated here.

This chapter's sample program, ViewTest, completes only the first step mentioned previously. ViewTest is not a functionally complete application, but it is intended to give the reader a flavor of Notes API programming. ViewTest prints all note IDs in a specified view. Once the note IDs have been retrieved, it is very easy to add functions to process and update each document. In this section, ViewTest is created using the Notes C API. In a later section, the HiTest version of ViewTest is developed.

Opening the Database

Notes API programs can have several entry points: NotesMain(), Main(), or WinMain(). ViewTest uses the traditional entry point for C programs, Main(). (See Listing 21.1.) Programs using either Main() or WinMain() must call a function to initialize the Notes runtime system. Programs that use NotesMain() are called by the Lotus Notes runtime system, so they do not need to initialize that system explicitly.

Listing 21.1. Opening the Notes database.

```c
#define NOTES_SERVER            "LOCAL"
#define NOTES_DATABASE              "test\\viewtest.nsf"
#define NOTES_VIEW          "Main View"

main()
{
        STATUS    error = NOERROR;      /* Return status from API calls     */
        FILE          *OutputFile;          /* Ouput filename          */
        DBHANDLE dbHandle;              /* Database identifier        */
        char     FullDBPath[256];        /* Pathname of the database */


dbHandle = NULLHANDLE

    /* Open the output file */
    OutputFile = fopen (FILENAME, "w");

    if (!OutputFile)
        {
        return (-1);
        }

    if (error= NotesInit())
          {
          ProcessNotesError( error );
          return(error);
        }


    if (NOTES_SERVER == "Local" || NOTES_SERVER==NULL)
        {
        strcpy( FullDBPath, NOTES_DATABASE );
        }
    else
        {
        /*    This is a Server Database, therefore we need to call
            OSPathNetConstruct(). */
        if (error = OSPathNetConstruct(
            NULL,
            NOTES_SERVER,
            NOTES_DATABASE,
            FullDBPath ) )
            {
            ProcessNotesError( error );
            return(error);
            }
    }


/* Open the database. */

    if (error = NSFDbOpen (FullDBPath, &dbHandle))
        API_RETURN (ERR(error));
```

```
/*        . . .    Additional Notes API code will be here    . . .    */

if (error = NSFDbClose (dbHandle))
        {
        ProcessNotesError( error );
        return(error);
            }

    error = NotesTerm();
    fclose (OutputFile);



    return(0);
}
```

For release 3.x of the C API, `NotesInit()` should be used on Windows and OS/2 and `NotesInitExtended()` for UNIX and Netware. Starting with release 4.x of the C API, `NotesInitExtended()` is used for all platforms.

`NotesInit()` (or `NotesInitExtended()`) work correctly only if the Notes runtime libraries and/ or DLLs are on the system search path. This function establishes a session by locating the Notes data directory, reading the notes.ini (or the Notes Preferences on Macintosh), and finding the user's ID file.

After establishing a session, the sample application must construct a path to the Notes database. If the database is LOCAL, the path is the same as the local path and filename. However, if it is a database on a Notes server, the program must call `OSPathNetConstruct()` to construct a server path to the database. This path is used by `NSFDbOpen()` to return a handle to the opened database. This database handle and other Notes-specific data structures are defined in the include files that come with the Notes API.

After completing all API calls, the application must call `NSFDbClose()` and `NotesTerm()` to close the Notes database and session.

Finding and Opening the View

Now that the database is open, the next step is to find and open the view. (See Listing 21.2.) `NIFFindView()` takes a handle of a database and the name of a view in the database and returns the note ID of the view design note. Remember that each view is stored as a design note and every view has an associated collection. A collection is an index to the document and category notes that currently qualify as part of the view.

Listing 21.2. Finding and opening the view.

```
    NOTEID ViewNoteId;                  /* Note id of the view      */
    HCOLLECTION hCollection;            /* Handle to the collection  */

/* Find the view by retrieving the view note id.      */
   if (error = NIFFindView (dbHandle, NOTES_VIEW, &ViewNoteId))
        {
        NSFDbClose (dbHandle);
        ProcessNotesError( error );
      return(error);
        }

/* Open the collection associated with this view */
 if (error = NIFOpenCollection(
        dbHandle,
        dbHandle,
        ViewNoteId,
        0,
        NULLHANDLE,
        &hCollection,
        NULLHANDLE,
        NULL,
        NULLHANDLE,
        NULLHANDLE))
   {
        NSFDbClose (dbHandle);
        ProcessNotesError( error );
      return(error);
      }



/*            . . .    Remaining Notes API code will be here   . . .    */


   /* Close the collection. */
   if (error = NIFCloseCollection(hCollection))
   {
        NSFDbClose (dbHandle);
          ProcessNotesError( error );
      return(error);
        }
```

Once the view note ID has been identified, the collection is opened using `NIFOpenCollection()`. This function returns the memory address of the handle to an open collection of notes (`hCollection`). If this function is unable to open the collection, `hCollection` is set to `NULL`.

Notes creates the collection the first time a view is opened and stores it to disk so that future retrieval will be very fast. If the on-disk collection is out-of-date with the documents in the database, `NIFOpenCollection()` updates the collection before returning.

Reading the Entries in a Collection

Once the collection has been opened, every note in this collection can be identified by using
NIFReadEntries(). The code in Listing 21.3 reads the note IDs from the collection and copies
them into a memory buffer with the handle hBuffer. The read flag is set to READ_MASK_NOTEID
to retrieve only the note ID in Listing 21.3. It could have been set to request the field values
displayed in the view. Entries displayed in a view can be read, but not modified. To modify a
document, the program has to open the data note using the note ID. ViewTest does not do
this.

Listing 21.3. Reading the entries of a collection.

```
COLLECTIONPOSITION CollIndexPosition; /* Position within the collection */
DWORD EntriesReturned=0;          /* Number of entries returned     */
HANDLE hBuffer=NULLHANDLE;        /* Handle to buffer of note ids */
WORD   ViewSignalFlag;            /* Flag for View navigation     */
WORD   BufferLength=0;            /* Length of the buffer         */



    CollIndexPosition.Level = 0;
    CollIndexPosition.Tumbler[0] = 0;

/* Get a buffer with information about each entry in the collection.
   Perform this routine in a loop.  Terminate loop when SignalFlag
   indicates that there is no more information to get.    */

    do
    {
       error = NIFReadEntries(
               hCollection,        /* Handle to this collection    */
               &CollIndexPosition,/* Where to start in collection */
               NAVIGATE_NEXT,      /* Order to use when skipping    */
               1L,                 /* Number to skip                */
               NAVIGATE_NEXT,      /* Order to use when reading     */
               MAXDWORD,            /* Maximum Entries              */
               READ_MASK_NOTEID,   /* Return only NoteId            */
               &hBuffer,           /* Handle to return buffer       */
               &BufferLength,       /* Length of returned buffer    */
               NULL,               /* Skipped Entries               */
               &EntriesReturned,   /* Number of entries read        */
               &ViewSignalFlag);    /* Flags for looping            */

       if (error)
          {
               NIFCloseCollection (hCollection);
               NSFDbClose (dbHandle);
               ProcessNotesError( error );
          return(error);
          }

/* Verify that a buffer was returned                        */
       if (hBuffer == NULLHANDLE)
```

continues

Listing 21.3. continued

```
           {
             NIFCloseCollection (hCollection);
             NSFDbClose (dbHandle);
             ProcessNotesError( error );
         return(error);
           }


if (EntriesReturned==0 || BufferLength== 0 )
    /* No entries returned ...          */
      {
      OSMemFree(hBuffer);
      NIFCloseCollection (hCollection);
       NSFDbClose (dbHandle);
         ProcessNotesError( error );
      return(error);
      }


/*     . . .          . . .        . . .              */
/*     . . .          . . .        . . .              */
/*     . . . The buffer can be processed   . . .    */
/*     . . .          . . .        . . .              */
/*     . . .          . . .        . . .              */


      } while (ViewSignalFlag & SIGNAL_MORE_TO_DO);
/*  If the end of the collection has not been reached, then call NIFReadEntries
again */
```

COLLECTIONPOSITION is a data structure used to specify the position of a note in a view. The settings of IndexPosition.Level and IndexPosition.Tumbler[0] instruct NIFReadEntries() to start at the beginning of the collection.

If the collection contains more information than this function can return, the SIGNAL_MORE_TO_DO bit of the SignalFlag will be set to true and the function will not return an error. Because there is no way to predict how large the collection will be, NIFReadEntries() should always be called in a loop.

NIFReadEntries() never returns a truncated entry at the end of the buffer; it always returns up to the last complete entry. If NIFReadEntries() is called multiple times, the last complete entry from the previous call should be skipped on the next call to NIFReadEntries(). The fifth parameter is set to NAVIGATE_NEXT to ensure that the same entry is not reread.

Printing the Note IDs

The code in Listing 21.4 prints all the note IDs. The code first locks the memory allocated by NIFReadEntries(). Then it iterates through all the notes in the collection. The collection contains both category and data notes. This application skips the category notes and prints the note ID of the data note.

Listing 21.4. Printing the Note IDs.

```
        NOTEID      *NoteIdList;        /* Pointer to a note id */
        DWORD       i;                  /* Counter for looping  */
        DWORD       NoteIdsFound;       /* Another counter */



        NoteIdList = (NOTEID far *)OSLockObject(hBuffer);
/* Loop through all the note ids and print all only document  */
        NoteIdsFound=0;
      fprintf (OutputFile,"\n");
      for (i=0; i<EntriesReturned; i++)
      {
         if (NOTEID_CATEGORY & NoteIdList[i]) continue;
         fprintf (OutputFile,"Note count is %lu. \t Note ID is: %lX\n",
              ++NoteIdsFound, NoteIdList[i]);
      }

      /* Unlock and free the memory allocated by NIFReadEntries */
   OSUnlockObject (hBuffer);
   OSMemFree (hBuffer);
```

ViewTest shows how to retrieve all the note IDs in a view using the C API. With the note ID, the program can process every document as desired (read, modify, or delete).

As this example shows, even the relatively simple task of printing all the note IDs requires significant knowledge of Notes data structures. The Notes C API is very powerful because it gives low-level access to a wide variety of Notes information. However, the vast majority of API programs do not need this level of granularity. For this reason, Lotus has provided a simpler alternative, the HiTest API.

HiTest API

The HiTest API was developed by Edge Research (a wholly owned subsidiary of Lotus/IBM). It is a higher-level API that is built on top of the low-level C API. Rather than directly calling the C API, applications can call HiTest functions, which in turn call C API functions. One HiTest API function often replaces multiple calls to the C API. HiTest makes all the C API function calls needed to manage the opening and closing of low-level Notes structures (for example, view collections in the previous example).

Both HiTest and the C API consist of a set of functions that are usually called from C programs. Instead of exposing low-level Notes data structures, however, HiTest abstracts Notes information into functional classes. These are not actual C++ classes (because it has a C interface), but are functional groupings. This provides many benefits to the API developer, resulting in shorter development cycles.

The HiTest API is easier to learn and easier to use than the Notes C API. It shields the programmer from the low-level understanding of Notes that is required for the C API. For example, the HiTest API programmer does not need to know about callback functions, ID tables, and collections. Instead, the HiTest programmer works primarily with objects that are exposed in the Notes user interface, such as views, columns, documents, agents, servers, databases, and so forth. The same object model is also used by LotusScript in Lotus Notes Release 4.x. Please see Figure 21.1 for the object model used by HiTest.

FIGURE 21.1.

The HiTest object model.

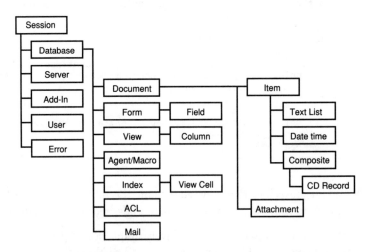

HiTest API programs usually require significantly less code than their C API equivalents, because HiTest encapsulates Notes functionality so well. Consequently, HiTest programs are easier to maintain and debug, and they take less time to develop.

HiTest API programs can call C API functions when needed. Starting with Release 2.2 of HiTest, Lotus added interoperability between HiTest and the C API. This is accomplished through two bridge functions that convert HiTest identifiers to C API identifiers and vice versa.

Although the HiTest API programs are usually written in C, the HiTest API can also be called from Visual Basic and LotusScript.

HiTest Classes and Functions

Because the function calls in HiTest have been matched so well with Notes functionality, simply reviewing the function names gives an excellent overview of the breadth of functionality exposed by HiTest. To see a complete list of HiTest functions, please refer to the HiTest API *User's Guide.*

The functional classes available in HiTest have consistent actions across classes. For example, there is a `HTDocumentGetProperty()` and a `HTServerGetProperty()`. Although the first requires

Advanced Development with the Notes API and HiTest Tools

CHAPTER 21

527

21

THE NOTES API
AND HITEST
TOOLS

a document handle and the second requires a server name, both function prototypes look very similar.

All HiTest functions also maintain the same general structure. The prefix is always HT, followed by the class name (for example, View), a verb (for example, Locate), and an option modifier (for example, ByName). This enables the developer to understand a new function quickly.

Now, let's rewrite ViewTest using HiTest. Instead of printing out the note IDs, this version of ViewTest prints out the HiTest document IDs.

Opening the Database

All HiTest API programs must initialize and terminate the HiTest API. This is accomplished by calling HTInit() to establish a HiTest session. (See Listing 21.5.) After establishing the session, the database is opened using HTDatabaseOpen(). This is simpler in HiTest than the C API, because there is no need to call OSPathNetConstruct() for server databases. HiTest calls this OSPathNetConstruct() function if it is needed. After completing all HiTest API function calls, the session must be terminated using HTTerm().

Listing 21.5. ViewTest implemented using the HiTest API.

```
#include "htnotes.h"

#define NOTES_SERVER          NULL
#define NOTES_DATABASE        "test\\viewtest.nsf"
#define NOTES_VIEW            "Main View"
#define FILENAME              "htview.txt"


main ()
{
  FILE          *OutputFile;
  HTSTATUS      ErrStatus;
  HTDATABASE    DatabaseId;

      /* Open the output file */
      OutputFile = fopen (FILENAME, "w");
      if (!OutputFile)
          return (-1);

      /* Initialize HiTest API */
      if(ErrStatus=HTInit (0))
          return ( ErrStatus);

      /* Initialize HiTest API */
      ErrStatus = HTDatabaseOpen (NOTES_SERVER, NOTES_DATABASE, 0, &DatabaseId);
      if (ErrStatus)
          return (ErrStatus);
```

continues

Listing 21.5. continued

```
/*      . . .               . . .         . . .    */
/*      . . .               . . .         . . .    */
/*      . . .  Additional HiTest Code     . . .    */
/*      . . .               . . .         . . .    */
/*      . . .               . . .         . . .    */


     /* Close the database    */
     HTDatabaseClose (DatabaseId, 0);

     /* Terminate HiTest and close the output file */
     HTTerm (0);
     fclose (OutputFile);

}
```

Opening the View and Printing the Entries

The next step is to locate the view using HTViewLocateByName(). As is obvious from Listing 21.6, retrieving the entries in a view is as easy as opening a view-based index and then navigating to a particular document in the index.

Listing 21.6. Opening the View and printing entries.

```
HTVIEWID      ViewId;
HTINDEX       ViewIndex;
HTDOCID           HTDocumentId;
HTINT         Indent;

    /* Obtain the view id by locating with the View Name */
    ViewId = HTViewLocateByName (DatabaseId, NOTES_VIEW);

    /* Create the view-based index */
    if (ErrStatus= HTIndexOpen (DatabaseId, &ViewIndex))
        return (ErrStatus);

    /* Open the view-based index */
    if (ErrStatus= HTIndexOpenView (ViewIndex, HTNULLHANDLE, ViewId, 0))
        return (ErrStatus);

    while (!HTIndexNavigate (ViewIndex, HTNAV_NEXT, HTNAVF_NO_CATEGORY,
    ➥&HTDocumentId, &Indent))
        {
        /*   Now that the application has the HiTest document id, it can
             perform any operation on that document.  In this example
             the program will simply output the id to a file.           */
        fprintf (OutputFile,"High Test DocId is %lu  \n " ,HTDocumentId) ;
        }

    /* Close the index and database.  This will automatically free memory */
    HTIndexClose (ViewIndex);
```

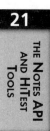

Within HiTest, an index means more than it does in the Notes C API. A HiTest Index is a generic class used to manage temporary result sets. Although the example uses a view-based index, index result sets can be created by executing macros/agents, performing full text searches, or performing database searches. In all cases, HiTest provides a consistent and easy way of navigating and manipulating the result set. For example, one part of an API program needs a list of agents, and another part needs a result set of all the documents in a view. Both result sets are created and managed using index functions.

Summary

This chapter introduced the Notes API. Both the Notes C API and the HiTest API were examined. A simple program to print the ID of every entry in a specified view was developed using both APIs.

The strength of the C API is that it provides the most comprehensive and detailed access to Notes information. Because it is so powerful, programmers who use this API are required to learn Notes concepts, such as ID tables, collections, and callback functions.

The alternative is to use the HiTest API. This is a higher-level API that makes function calls to the C API. It is very easy to learn, because it uses objects that are exposed in the Notes user interface. Unfortunately, some API programs may require Notes functionality that is not yet available in HiTest. However, for most API programmers, HiTest has enough benefits to outweigh its limitations.

Using Third-Party Development Tools

by Jonathan Czernel

IN THIS CHAPTER

The tools provided in Lotus Notes R4 allow the development of fairly advanced and fully functional Notes-native applications. Certainly, the advanced programmability provided through LotusScript Version 3.0 and corresponding Notes database classes allow Actions, Agents, and other Notes-triggered events to initiate virtually any required function that interfaces with Notes databases.

Even with these advanced development capabilities, however, there may be situations that arise requiring an application to be created outside of the Notes environment, while retaining the ability to access data stored in a Notes database.

This chapter includes a discussion of the following:

- The advantages and disadvantages of non-Notes native development solutions
- Using three popular third-party development platforms, we'll step through the creation of the same Notes front-end application in each environment
- Lotus NotesSQL, an ODBC driver available for both Windows and OS/2 platforms, is discussed briefly. This driver allows Notes data to be accessed from any standard ODBC-compliant design environment.

This chapter is not intended to provide complete and detailed explanations of third-party development tools or Notes-related add-ons. It is provided merely to introduce the capabilities of some of the alternative development platforms and drivers that are available. It is ideally suited to those that are contemplating the use of a third-party, front-end tool for either user interface design or reporting purposes.

> **NOTE**
>
> If you plan on using the sample source files included on the CD-ROM, first copy the files SDATAR3.NSF and SDATAR4.NSF to your Notes program directory so that you can access them as local databases. These files are in the Source\Chap22 directory.

Why Use Third-Party Development Tools?

Lotus Notes R4 provides a plethora of design features that are surely superior to those found in its previous incarnation. Unfortunately, user-interface options in this new and powerful release still do not approach those that are found in more universal development platforms such as Visual Basic and Delphi—that is, development systems that are not necessarily catered to the development of Notes applications, but instead are used to create full-blown Windows applications that may suit a wide array of tasks.

Although the interface capabilities of Lotus Notes R4 are sufficient in a majority of cases, you may consider an alternative development environment if

■ You require a low-profile, stand-alone application that is extremely easy to use, severely limiting choices available to the user.

■ You have been asked to create an extremely robust and flexible user interface that front ends an existing Notes database, taking advantage of features such as spinners, scroll bars, and view lists that are unavailable even in R4.

■ You'll be adding Notes data-access support to an existing product written using a development tool such as Microsoft Visual Basic, which currently acts as a front end to other data sources such as Informix, Oracle, or InterBase.

■ You need to create a data-migration utility that "manually" replicates or synchronizes information between an existing data source, such as SQL Server, and a Notes database. A Notes agent might not provide all of the capabilities or the speed that you require.

■ You require an extremely quick database front end, and find that the interpreted nature of LotusScript is not adequate.

Unfortunately, all of the development environments discussed in this chapter exist only as native Microsoft Windows applications. Third-party development options for the other platforms supported by Lotus Notes R4—such as OS/2, UNIX (the many varieties) and Macintosh—are virtually nonexistent. In these cases, the best alternative development approach is through the use of the Notes C HiTest Tools or the Notes C API directly, in conjunction with a popular C/C++-based development environment used on the target platform. Unlike the development options discussed in this chapter, these tools enable Notes server add-in tasks to be developed. In addition, development using the Notes C API may be rendered in a fairly cross-platform fashion, allowing one common code base to be used on a variety of operating systems. Development using the Notes C API and Notes HiTest tools is discussed in Chapter 21, "Advanced Development with the Notes API and HiTest Tools."

Optionally, the Lotus NotesSQL ODBC drivers, discussed in the last section of this chapter, are available in both Windows and OS/2 flavors. This driver presents a higher-level interface to Notes database information for those who are familiar with SQL using a standard ODBC interface.

A Comparison of Three Development Platforms

We'll now step through the development of a fairly straightforward Notes front-end application, using three of the more popular development tools around: Microsoft Visual Basic, Borland Delphi, and Revelation Software Visual Programmer (ViP).

> **NOTE**
>
> In the development sections of this chapter, I'll assume that you are somewhat familiar with each environment discussed. Even for those that are unfamiliar with these systems, however, you will get a general feel for the Notes-related capabilities of each package by reviewing the front-end development steps that are outlined herein. Additionally, the most significant highlights of each system are described for each environment, enabling you to get a brief summary of the features of the included packages.

As Revelation's ViP is geared towards Notes development, it contains built-in support for Notes database access in addition to generic ODBC support. Visual Basic and Delphi, on the other hand, require add-ons to strike data oil while drilling into a Notes database. We will use the Lotus HiTest Tools for Visual Basic in conjunction with Microsoft Visual Basic, and Brainstorm Technologies' VB/Link with Delphi. Due to the importance of these add-ons, without which there would be no method by which to access Notes databases, they will be discussed in a fair amount of detail.

The application that will be developed in each of these environments is used to front end a simple Notes database that acts as a miniature address book. The database has the following design properties:

- One form, Names Entry, allows the entry of the following text fields: Fld_Name, Fld_Addr, Fld_City, Fld_State, Fld_Zip, and Fld_Description.
- One view, Names, contains two columns: Name (Fld_Name) and Description (Fld_Description).

This database may be found on the CD-ROM in two flavors: SDATAR3.NSF, a Release 3.x database, and SDATAR4.NSF, an R4 database that takes advantage of action bars and the @DialogBox function. The source code and final executables for all three of the examples is also included. Due to limits imposed by HiTest Tools for Visual Basic, the Visual Basic example uses SDATAR3.NSF, an R3 database, and the other two examples use SDATAR4.NSF, a full-fledged R4 database.

The goal of this application is simple: to display documents in the database one at a time, and to enable text in any field to be easily modified and saved back to the source Notes database. The user will not be able to add documents to the database using our front-end. I'll leave this functionality up to you as an entertaining development exercise.

In addition to the development of a database front end, this section discusses scalability and distribution requirements for each environment.

> **CAUTION**
>
> Regardless of the third-party development tool selected, a client copy of the Notes system is required on any workstation that will be running a Notes front-end utility, allowing the true utilization of the Lotus Notes client/server mechanism. The DLLs found in the Notes program directory are used by the third-party development tool or add-on to attach to the Notes server and to perform all database-access actions. Because all access to databases is performed through Notes DLLs, a user ID file that has proper server and database authorization is required when accessing a database stored on a server; the user ID file used with the workstation's copy of Lotus Notes is automatically used. This, in turn, implies that a password for server access is also required when server access is initiated; this is handled automatically by the Notes DLL itself, in the form of a password-entry dialog box, when server access is requested.

Microsoft Visual Basic with the Lotus HiTest Tools

Visual Basic is considered to be the "king of the hill" by many in the development community. Although many professional developers and "hard core" computer scientists thought of BASIC as a "brainless" language, Microsoft continued to defy common logic by enhancing its BASIC products through the years, introducing structured language enhancements, optimizing compilers and debugging tools that rivaled those found in more accepted development environments such as C/C++.

The latest incarnation of Microsoft Visual Basic is found in Microsoft Visual Basic 4.0, which supports either 16-bit or 32-bit development. For reasons described later in this chapter, this project uses the 16-bit version. Some highlights of the Visual Basic family include

- OLE 2 Automation support.
- An extensive library of third-party add-ons. Support for VBXs in the 16-bit version and OCXs in the 32-bit version is included.
- A highly structured programming language that includes limited support for classes. VB is more of an "object-based" language than a true object-oriented language. For example, two fairly standard OOP mechanisms, inheritance and function overloading, are not allowed in VB.
- Visual Basic is an interpreted language, like LotusScript. The result is an inherently slower executable that cannot match the speed of executables created with true compiled languages, such as C/C++ or Delphi.
- Executables created with VB require the VB runtime DLL, which consumes about 720KB for 32-bit VB executables, and 935KB for 16-bit VB executables. In addition, any other VBXs, OCXs, or DLLs used by the application must be distributed with the executable for proper execution.

About HiTest Tools for Visual Basic

To access any data source from the VB environment, an add-on component is required. This example uses the Lotus HiTest for Visual Basic product. For any developer familiar with the Notes HiTest for C tool, this add-on will be very easy to pick up—it is, in fact, a subset of the most important API calls found in the HiTest for C product.

Using the HiTest tools, there are fundamentally two ways to tap into a Notes database:

- Using Notes-specific controls, referred to as htVisual Controls, that are added to the VB toolbox. Twelve controls are included, such as Server Selector, Database Selector, and Omni Selector (used to view and select a variety of items, including views, forms, agents and document items).

- Programmatically, through calls to the HiTest API (Applications Programming Interface). The HiTest tools include most, but not all, of the functionality of the HiTest for C product.

Of course, a combination of the preceding two methods may also be used.

Interestingly, when htVisual Controls are used, one object may be "piped" to another object at design time; that is, the output of one object may be routed to the input of another object while controls are drawn on forms used in the VB application. For example, the server chosen using the Server Selector may be automatically sent to the Database Selector if the two controls are piped. This unique design-time feature, referred to as Piped Properties, allows for a variety of tasks to be accomplished with little programming effort. While Piped Properties may take some getting used to (there are several nuances, and they act unlike most other VB add-ons), they are a unique and welcome addition to any VB toolbox.

Alternatively, calls through the HiTest Basic API may be used. Due to the breadth of this API, developers not familiar with Lotus Notes nuts-and-bolts internals may find that tapping directly into Notes is a slightly daunting task. To create an application that uses the HiTest Basic API, the files HTNOTES.BAS and HTFUNC.BAS should be included in your project. These files contain structures, constants, and function declarations that are used in HiTest API function calls.

To distribute an application that uses the HiTest Basic API, you will need the following:

- An executable copy of your application.
- The appropriate Visual Basic runtime library and any VBXs that your application uses, including the HiTest VBXs. These files should be copied to the WINDOWS\SYSTEM directory.
- The HiTest API DLLs, W3HTAPI.DLL and W3HTGLVB.DLL. These files should be copied to the WINDOWS\SYSTEM directory.

As of this writing, plans for an OCX or ActiveX version of the Lotus HiTest Tools for Visual Basic are unclear. The current version, which utilizes VBXs, will only work with 16-bit Visual Basic 4.0. Due to this limitation, you will use 16-bit Visual Basic 4.0 to develop your front end. These 16-bit controls will work with any R3.x or 16-bit R4 client.

> **TIP**
>
> Edge Research, the Lotus subsidiary that develops the HiTest line of products, might release a 32-bit control in the near future, sometime after the release of Notes 4.5. For the latest information on HiTest tools, see the Edge Research Web site at `http://www.edge.lotus.com`.

> **NOTE**
>
> If you are interested in moving up to the 32-bit version of Visual Basic 4.0, or you need to access Notes data on a system that is running the 32-bit version of Notes, take a look at VB/Link from Brainstorm Technologies. VB/Link is discussed in the next section, where it is used in conjunction with Borland Delphi 2.0. It offers a set of ActiveX controls that may be used with either VB 4.0 16-bit or 32-bit.
>
> Alternatively, if you are comfortable with interfacing Visual Basic applications with lower-level APIs, you may use the latest Lotus HiTest Tools for C, calling the HiTest API functions directly from Visual Basic. For information on the latest Lotus development tools, see `http://www.lotus.com/devtools`.

Your Front End in Visual Basic and HiTest for VB

For your database front end, skip all of the htVisual Controls and instead access your database using the HiTest Basic API. This is done for two reasons. First, user interaction will be minimal; the server is fixed (local), as is the database. Second, using the HiTest API illustrates, to a certain extent, how the Notes API itself works. Using the HiTest API to develop your "applet" might give you some insight as to the inner workings of Notes that would not be possible using just the htVisual Controls.

The first step in creating a VB application is to design the user interface. Figure 22.1 shows the preliminary interface in VB Design Mode. Note the 12 HiTest controls loaded in the Toolbox.

FIGURE 22.1.
Our Microsoft Visual Basic database front end in Design Mode.

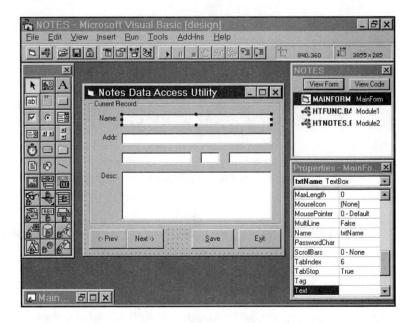

Your front end will consist entirely of one form, MainForm, and the two HiTest modules HTFUNC.BAS and HTNOTES.BAS. The form is fairly simple. The edit fields are named txtName, txtAddr, txtCity, txtState, txtZip, and txtDesc. The buttons are named btnPrev (Previous Document), btnNext (Next Document), btnSave (Save Current Document) and btnExit (Exit).

Because you are using calls to the HiTest Basic API, the inclusion of htVisual Controls in your VB Control Toolbox is unnecessary for this application. However, they have been included for instructional purposes.

Before doing any API-related coding, you will first define four global variables that will be used to reference various elements of your Notes database throughout your application:

```
Dim HTDbHandle&  'Used as a handle to our opened database, SDATAR3.NSF
Dim FormId&  'Used to identify a Form in our database
Dim DocId&  'Used to identify a specific document in our database
Dim HgIndex&  'Used to point to an index that will be used to navigate
              'through our database
```

When your application opens, you'll first need to take care of some API "housework":

1. The Notes API must be initialized using the HTInit() function.

2. The database that you'll be accessing must be opened with the HTDatabaseOpen() function. This function returns a handle to the open database; this handle will be stored in the global variable HTDbHandle&.

3. The Notes Form that is used as a filter between the database and our application must be located; the `HTFormLocateByName()` function is used. This function returns a Form identification; this value will be stored in the global variable `FormID&`.

4. Next, create an index that you can later (in Step 5) use to navigate through documents in the database. The `HTIndexOpen()` function will be used; the return value, `HgIndex&`, refers to this new index.

5. Using `HTIndexSearch()`, populate the index created previously with all documents in the database. The `""` in the call is equivalent to the Notes formula `SELECT @All`. Using this index, you may "navigate" from one document to the next using `HTIndexNavigate()`.

6. Move your index "pointer" to the first document available using `HTIndexNavigate()` with the `HTNAV_NEXT` flag. Note that each time this function is called, `DocId&` is set to reference the current document.

7. Populate the text fields in your main dialog box with values at the current document by calling a subprogram, `FillInValues()`, that will be created later.

The following block of code will be added to the `Form_Load()` event of your Start-Up Form to facilitate the preceding steps:

```
Sub Form_Load()
    Dim ret%, Status&, hgbegin_datetime As HTDATETIME
    ret% = HTInit(0)      'Initialize the HiTest API
    Status = HTDatabaseOpen("", "SDATAR3", 0&, HTDbHandle&) 'Open the database
                                                            'and set HTDbHandle&
    FormId& = HTFormLocateByName(HTDbHandle&, "Name Entry") 'Find the form
                                                            'we'll use
    Status = HTIndexOpen(HTDbHandle&, HgIndex&) 'Create a new index
                                                'in the database
    Status = HTIndexSearch(HgIndex&, "", ByVal FormId&, hgbegin_datetime)
                                                'Populate the index
    Status& = HTIndexNavigate(HgIndex&, HTNAV_NEXT, 0&, DocId&, hgindent&)
                                                'Go to the entry #1
    FillInValues      'Fill in current values from DocId&
                      'This is a routine we've added
End Sub
```

Next, add the routine `FillInValues` to your form. This routine performs the following tasks:

■ The current document in our database is "opened" using `HTDocumentOpen()`. This function sets a handle to an opened document, `DocHandle&`.

■ For each text field in your dialog box, you will call a routine that will be added later to your program called `TextItemFetch`, passing the document handle (`DocHandle&`) and the corresponding Notes field name.

■ As a final step, close the opened document with a call to `HTDocumentClose()`.

The subprogram described previously is found here:

```
Sub FillInValues()
    'Fill in all values from the current record into screen
    'text fields...

    Dim Status&, FldLen%, DocHandle&, hglength&, ItemName$, InBuffer$

    Status& = HTDocumentOpen(HTDbHandle&, DocId&, 0&, DocHandle&)

    txtName.Text = TextItemFetch(DocHandle&, "Fld_Name")
    txtAddr.Text = TextItemFetch(DocHandle&, "Fld_Addr")
    txtCity.Text = TextItemFetch(DocHandle&, "Fld_City")
    txtState.Text = TextItemFetch(DocHandle&, "Fld_State")
    txtZip.Text = TextItemFetch(DocHandle&, "Fld_Zip")
    txtDesc.Text = TextItemFetch(DocHandle&, "Fld_Description")

    Status& = HTDocumentClose(DocHandle&, 0&)

End Sub
```

You'll now add the `TextItemFetch()` function that extracts the value of a field from a Notes database. This function is fairly straightforward. The `HTItemGetLength()` API function is first called, returning the length of the required text buffer to hold the contents of the specified field (`ItemName$`). You then ensure that your string buffer, `InBuffer$`, is large enough to hold the return value using the VB `String` function. If the buffer is not large enough, it is likely that the application will crash with a general protection fault.

The last step is to call the `HTItemFetch()` API function, which returns the value of the designated field in the format specified—in this case, `HTTYPE_TEXT` for a text value. Note that the buffer, `InBuffer$`, is passed with the `ByVal` keyword.

```
Function TextItemFetch(DocHandle&, ItemName$)
    'Use two HiTest API calls to get ItemName$ from
    'the document referenced by DocHandle&.  Return
    'the text value as a string.

    Dim Status&, hglength&, InBuffer$

    Status& = HTItemGetLength(DocHandle&, ItemName$, 0&, 0&, hglength&)
    InBuffer$ = String(hglength& + 1, 0)
    Status& = HTItemFetch(DocHandle&, ItemName, HTTYPE_TEXT, 0&, HTTYPE_TEXT,
    ➥ByVal InBuffer$)

    TextItemFetch = InBuffer$

End Function
```

Now you will add a subprogram that stores values into a Notes database. This subprogram, TextItemPut, simply calls HTItemPut(). Here is the definition for TextItemPut:

```
Sub TextItemPut(DocHandle&, FieldName$, FieldVal$)
    'Use HTItemPut API call to place FieldVal$ text into
    'the Notes field FieldName$ in DocHandle&.

    Dim Status&

    Status& = HTItemPut(DocHandle&, FieldName$, HTTYPE_TEXT, 0&, HTTYPE_TEXT,
    ➥ByVal Trim$(FieldVal$), 0&)

End Sub
```

Now, add Click event-handler code for the Save button. This code performs the following tasks:

- Verifies that the user wants to overwrite data stored in the Notes database.

- In order to act upon a document in a database, you must first open it using the HTDocumentOpen() API function. This function sets a document handle that refers to the current Notes document, DocHandle&.

- For each field requiring an update, calls the TextItemPut routine (described previously). This routine requires the current document handle (DocHandle&), the Notes field name, and the text value to save in the field.

- When values have been copied to the document, you need to commit changes using HTDocumentSave().

- Closes the document using HTDocumentClose().

Here is the subprogram that handles the preceding described tasks:

```
Private Sub btnSave_Click()
    Dim ret%, Status&, DocHandle&, FieldName$, FieldVal$

    ret% = MsgBox("Continue to save information to Notes database?",
    ➥vbYesNo + vbQuestion, "Are you sure?")
    If ret% = vbYes Then
        Status& = HTDocumentOpen(HTDbHandle&, DocId&, 0&, DocHandle&)

        TextItemPut DocHandle&, "Fld_Name", txtName.Text
        TextItemPut DocHandle&, "Fld_Addr", txtAddr.Text
        TextItemPut DocHandle&, "Fld_City", txtCity.Text
        TextItemPut DocHandle&, "Fld_State", txtState.Text
        TextItemPut DocHandle&, "Fld_Zip", txtZip.Text
        TextItemPut DocHandle&, "Fld_Description", txtDesc.Text

        Status& = HTDocumentSave(DocHandle&, HTDOCWRITEF_FORCE_OVERWRITE)
        Status& = HTDocumentClose(DocHandle&, HTDOCWRITEF_FORCE_OVERWRITE)
    End If

End Sub
```

22

THIRD-PARTY DEVELOPMENT TOOLS

You'll now add code to the Click events for the Previous and Next document-navigation buttons. These routines are fairly straightforward, using the HTIndexNavigate() API call. The only difference between the two routines is the use of the HTNAVF_BACKWARD flag, when you need to traverse backwards through the index. Both routines are finalized with a call to FillInValues, taking values from the current document (DocId&) and placing them into text fields on your form.

Here are the two routines that handle navigation:

```
Private Sub btnNext_Click()
    Dim Status&

    Status& = HTIndexNavigate(HgIndex&, HTNAV_NEXT, 0&, DocId&, hgindent&)
                                            'Navigate to first entry
    If Status& = HTFAIL_END_OF_DATA Then
        'We're at the end of the line... pop to the last item
        Status& = HTIndexNavigate(HgIndex&, HTNAV_END, 0&, DocId&, hgindent&)
                                            'Navigate back to #1
        Beep
    End If

    FillInValues    'Fill in current values from DocId&

End Sub

Private Sub btnPrev_Click()
    Dim Status&

    Status& = HTIndexNavigate(HgIndex&, HTNAV_NEXT, HTNAVF_BACKWARD, DocId&,
    ➥hgindent&)
    If Status& = HTFAIL_END_OF_DATA Then
        'We're at the beginning of the line... pop to the first item
        'Note the use of HTNAVF_BACKWARD to actually move us to the 1st
        'entry with HTNAV_END
        Status& = HTIndexNavigate(HgIndex&, HTNAV_END, HTNAVF_BACKWARD, DocId&,
        ➥hgindent&)
        Beep
    End If

    FillInValues    'Fill in current values from DocId&

End Sub
```

The final step in the development process for your database front end will be to properly close all Notes-related references before terminating your application. The most important of these calls is HTTerm(), which terminates the HiTest Basic API. These closing statements will be handled by the Unload event for your form:

```
Private Sub Form_Unload(Cancel As Integer)
    'Terminate the HiTest API
    Dim Status&

    Status& = HTIndexClose(HgIndex&)
    Status& = HTDatabaseClose(HTDbHandle&, 0&)
    ret% = HTTerm(0)
End Sub
```

This simple example merely scrapes the surface of the HiTest Basic API. Perhaps more than any other add-on, the Lotus HiTest Tools for Visual Basic provide a microscope into the inner workings of Notes itself.

Borland Delphi with Brainstorm Technologies' VB/Link

Borland Delphi has taken the development world by storm, offering the combined benefits of front-end prototyping and code simplicity of products such as Microsoft Visual Basic, combined with a true 32-bit compiler that produces executables approaching the speed of other compiled languages, such as C/C++.

The underlying language used by Delphi, Object Pascal, is based on tried and proven Borland Pascal technologies, with fairly complete object-oriented programming (OOP) extensions. Object Pascal provides developers with features such as dynamic memory allocation, pointers and exception handling—features not found in the other products discussed in this chapter.

For your database front end, you will use Borland Delphi 2.0 along with VB/Link 4.2.

The feature set of Borland Delphi 2.0 includes the following:

- A native, optimizing 32-bit compiler, producing tight and fast executables that do not require a corresponding runtime library.
- Full support for Windows 95/NT controls and features such as tree views, status bars, multiple threads, and long filenames. Complete access to the Windows API is also supported.
- OLE Automation, including support for OCX controls.
- The Object Pascal programming language, featuring support for the most important characteristics of object oriented programming, including inheritance.
- A set of professional tools that assist in code reusability, software distribution, and team development (including source code versioning).
- Easy executable distribution. After an application is compiled into an executable (.EXE), it may be shipped without any additional runtime files. Any OCXs or DLLs referenced, however, must be distributed with the executable.

About VB/Link

VB/Link, produced by Brainstorm Technologies, is an add-on in the form of three ActiveX controls:

- NotesData, which provides full access to Notes servers and database elements, including the creation of result sets based on forms, views, or selection formulas.

22

THIRD-PARTY
DEVELOPMENT
TOOLS

■ NotesView, which provides an easy way to display Notes views in a Delphi application, including view features found in Notes itself, such as collapsing/expanding categories and parent/child document relationships. This control nearly replicates the look and feel of a native R4 view.

■ NotesRichText, which enables any Notes rich text field to be displayed in its intended form. This control includes support for OLE, file attachments and other Notes-specific rich text field items. Rich text fields may be viewed and easily edited using this control.

These controls are remarkably easy to use, requiring very little experimentation to master. The NotesData control enables a Notes database to be referenced like a typical database result set. Documents are represented in result set rows, and fields within a document are represented in columns. The combination of these controls provides access to virtually every element in a Notes database.

However, the "pseudo" result sets referenced through these controls are not the same as real database result sets in Delphi, so the data-aware components of Delphi can't be used in conjunction with VB/Link components. In other words, you can't link a VB/Link `NotesData` object to Delphi data-aware controls such as `TDBEdit` and `TDBGrid` through a data source.

> **NOTE**
>
> The name VB/Link is a misnomer. VB/Link consists of three ActiveX controls that may be used in a variety of development environments, including Microsoft Visual Basic or Visual C++, Borland Delphi or C/C++, and Powersoft Optima++.

The Front End in Delphi and VB/Link

The development of a front end using the VB/Link product proved to be remarkably simple. First, define the user interface. Figure 22.2 shows your application in design mode. Note the inclusion of a NotesData control that will be invisible at runtime.

FIGURE 22.2.

*The Borland Delphi
database front end in
Design Mode.*

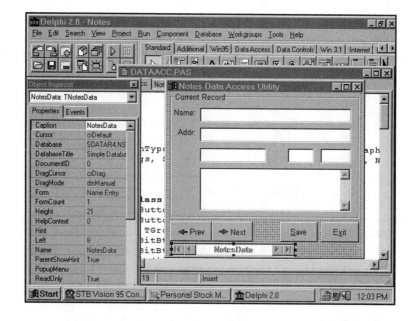

The one and only form (frmMain) used in this application contains the following objects:

- Four TEdit objects: editName, editAddr, editCity, and editState. These text edit fields correspond to the Fld_Name, Fld_Addr, Fld_City, and Fld_State Notes database fields, respectively.

- One TMemo object: memoDesc. A memo edit is like a multiple-line-aware version of the TEdit object. This object will contain the Fld_Description Notes database field.

- Two TBitBtn objects: btnPrev and btnNext. These buttons will enable your database to be navigated. Glyphs representing a forward and backward arrow have been specified.

- Two TButton objects: btnSave and btnExit. These buttons are clicked to save the current form contents to the Notes database and to exit the application, respectively.

- One TNotesData object: NotesData. This VB/Link object is used to accomplish all Notes access required in your application.

Due to the simplicity of your front-end application, it is possible to set up the NotesData control completely at design time, specifying the server (LOCAL) and the database (SDATAR4.NSF). Instead of using the Delphi Object Inspector to fill in these values, you may double-click on the NotesData control to present a configuration dialog box that lets you select the server, the database, and the default form and view.

In your application, however, these properties will be set using Object Pascal, to illustrate what information VB/Link requires to perform the various tasks at hand. You will see that Notes database access through VB/Link is equally simple to understand at this level.

The following preliminary steps are required to initialize the NotesData object in the FormShow procedure:

1. First, NotesData needs to know the name of the server that you'll be accessing, as well as the name of the database. In this case, you're using your local system (Local); the database should be set to SDATAR4.NSF.

2. Next, we must define the Notes form that we would like to use as a "window" to our Notes data. In our example, the form name is Name Entry.

3. We can now log into the Notes database using the Logon method.

4. Next we may execute a query to obtain a result set using the RunQuery method. The only parameter required will indicate the type of data "window" that should be used to represent each Notes document in the result set. In our case, we will use a form, Name Entry, as our data "window." Therefore, the query method type will be set to QueryTypeForm.

5. When RunQuery has completed its task, a result set will be available. We will call the procedure PopulateFields (it's shown next). This procedure displays information from the result set at the current record position on our form.

Here is a listing of the TfrmMain.FormShow procedure that performs the aforementioned tasks:

```
procedure TfrmMain.FormShow(Sender: TObject);
begin
    NotesData.Server := 'LOCAL';
    NotesData.Database := 'SDATAR4.NSF';
    NotesData.Form := 'Name Entry';
    NotesData.Logon;
    NotesData.RunQuery(QueryTypeForm);
    PopulateFields;
end;
```

The procedure PopulateFields, which, as just described, places values from the current position onto the form, is shown next. The FieldValue method allows access to a string value for a named Notes field.

```
procedure TfrmMain.PopulateFields;
begin
    editName.Text := NotesData.FieldValue['Fld_name'];
    editAddr.Text := NotesData.FieldValue['Fld_Addr'];
    editCity.Text := NotesData.FieldValue['Fld_City'];
    editState.Text := NotesData.FieldValue['Fld_State'];
    editZip.Text := NotesData.FieldValue['Fld_Zip'];
    memoDesc.Text := NotesData.FieldValue['Fld_Description'];
end;
```

Now you'll insert code that reacts to the Previous and Next buttons, updating the screen with values from the new current document. The code required in these events is fairly straightforward. The `MoveNext` and `MovePrevious` methods are used to traverse the result set. The `PopulateFields` routine, just shown, is then called to update the user interface. Here are the procedures required in the Previous and Next button click event handlers:

```
procedure TfrmMain.btnPrevClick(Sender: TObject);
begin
     NotesData.MovePrevious;
     PopulateFields;
end;

procedure TfrmMain.btnNextClick(Sender: TObject);
begin
     NotesData.MoveNext;
     PopulateFields;
end;
```

Now you'll take care of cleaning up your `NotesData` object when your application is closed. Simply log off from the database when the `FormDestroy` event is triggered:

```
procedure TfrmMain.FormDestroy(Sender: TObject);
begin
     {Log off!}
     NotesData.Logoff;
end;
```

The final action that needs to be dealt with is the Save button. To perform this task, simply copy the contents of the various Delphi Form objects into their corresponding `FieldValue`, and then trigger the NotesData `Commit` method to save changes to the current document. The following procedure handles this task:

```
procedure TfrmMain.btnSaveClick(Sender: TObject);
var
   ret: Integer;
begin
    {Save the contents of the current text fields}
    {We now have data available, so let's update the screen}
    ret := Application.MessageBox('Continue to save information to the Notes
    ➥database?', 'Are you sure?',
        mb_YesNo + mb_IconQuestion);
    if ret = IDYES then begin
        NotesData.FieldValue['Fld_name'] := editName.Text;
        NotesData.FieldValue['Fld_Addr'] := editAddr.Text;
        NotesData.FieldValue['Fld_City'] := editCity.Text;
        NotesData.FieldValue['Fld_State'] := editState.Text;
        NotesData.FieldValue['Fld_Zip'] := editZip.Text;
        NotesData.FieldValue['Fld_Description'] := memoDesc.Text;
        NotesData.Commit;
    end;
end;
```

This brings to a conclusion the development of your Notes front end using Borland Delphi and VB/Link.

Revelation Software ViP

The third product included in our discussion of third party development tools is Revelation's ViP 2.0. The development environment found in ViP is remarkably easy to use, offering visual, point-and-click "programming" that requires minimal coding effort in many cases, as well as a full set of both standard Windows and Windows 95 dialog controls.

Unlike Microsoft Visual Basic and Borland Delphi, ViP caters exclusively to the Lotus Notes developer. The core programming language used in ViP is LotusScript Version 3.0, the same language used in Lotus Notes R4. Additionally, third-party "add-ons" are not required to access Notes databases—extensive support for both Notes databases and ODBC data sources is seamlessly built into the product through the use of a dialog control called a data object.

The most important features of ViP are:

- A full set of Windows and Windows 95 controls, including support for Lotus Components and ActiveX Controls.
- Built-in support for Lotus Notes R4 databases. Although the ViP Designer, the tool used to create applications, can only access Notes databases through 32-bit R4, both 16-bit R4 and Release 3.x access is available through a 16-bit runtime option.
- LotusScript is used as the ViP programming language, giving experienced Lotus Notes R4 developers a familiar working environment. Like R4, LotusScript in ViP is an interpreted language, not compiled.
- The same Notes classes available in Lotus Notes R4 are included in ViP, allowing for Notes programmability through LotusScript exclusively, bypassing the use of the ViP data object.
- Full support for OLE 2 Automation.
- Visual Linking from data objects to other objects, enabling the flow of data from a database to other objects to be "drawn" instead of programmed at design time.
- Built-in, comprehensive and easy to use charting and report generation capabilities based on the query results of ViP data objects. Like other objects, Visual Linking may be used to easily define source data for charts.
- The distribution requirements for ViP applications are fairly hefty. The 16-bit runtime files consume approximately 10MB of disk space, while the 32-bit runtime files consume approximately 13MB. These runtime files may be distributed free of charge. They're available from the Revelation Software Web site at `http://revelation.com`.

Your Front End in ViP

ViP is dramatically different than most other development packages. As you will see, your database front end requires only a fraction of the coding required using traditional environments. The principal interface design is straightforward, not unlike either Microsoft Visual Basic or Borland Delphi. Objects such as text fields and buttons are simply drawn onto a blank form.

After the main interface components are drawn and properly configured, a data object is added to the Form. This data object appears as a spreadsheet-like control at design time that contains a collection of documents, one per row, as well as the fields from each document that you specify. The importance of a data object in ViP cannot be underestimated; it is the cornerstone for all visual database access.

Each data object may have a "connection" to a database associated with it. A single ViP application may have one or more connections associated with it; each connection points to a specific data source, which may be an ODBC data source or a Notes database.

In this case, you'll create one connection that points to the R4 version of your database: SDATAR4.NSF. In ViP this connection is done from a page in the Connection Manager dialog box, as shown in Figure 22.3.

FIGURE 22.3.

Configuring a connection.

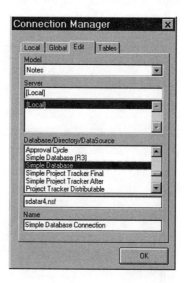

You may now configure the data object to use the defined connection. In this step, you'll also select the Notes document fields that will appear as column headers in the data object. The page used to perform these tasks is shown in Figure 22.4.

FIGURE 22.4.

Specifying Connection and Notes document fields to be included in the data object.

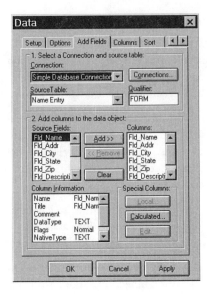

At this point, the main form used in your application contains the basic end-user interface, as well as your defined data object. The contents of the form are shown in Figure 22.5.

FIGURE 22.5.

Your nearly complete user interface in ViP.

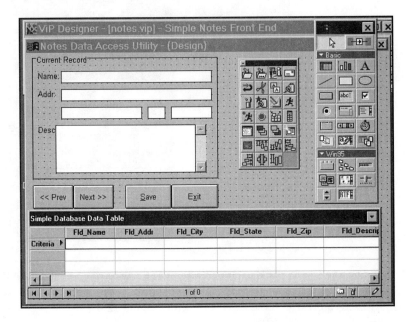

Now you'll use the Linking Tools in ViP that make this programming environment so unique. Using most development tools, at this point you would begin to write code that extracts data from your "data object" and inserts it into appropriate text-edit fields. In ViP the strategy is remarkably different. You simply "draw" links from various columns in the data object that contains field values to their corresponding text edit fields on your main user interface. Each link is indicated at design time by a red line connecting the source and destination object; an arrow in the center of the line indicates the direction of data flow.

Links may be assigned a "behavior" that varies depending on the source and destination objects. Behaviors tell ViP which task the link should perform. A link between a data object column and a text-edit box uses the default behavior `TextCopyFromCell`, for example.

In your front end you'll create links that connect each column in the data object to corresponding text-entry fields in the user interface. For example, the Fld_Name column will be linked to the `txtName` edit field. For each of these links, the `TextCopyFromCell` behavior will be retained, copying text in the data object automatically to appropriate fields at the user-interface level.

You'll also create links from the Next and Prev buttons to the data object itself. These links will be used to initiate specific actions through changing the behavior property to Next Row and Previous Row, respectively.

Figure 22.6 shows your application in design mode with all appropriate links drawn. Note that as of this point, the application can be used to effectively navigate through your entire database, even though you have not written a single line of code.

FIGURE 22.6.

Our final interface, with all necessary links.

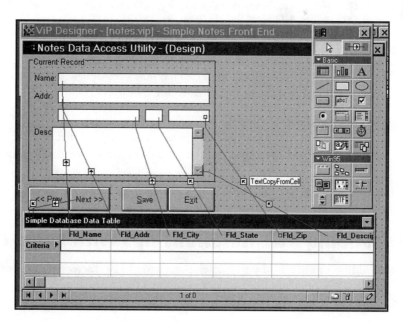

One of the final tasks required to complete your application is the development of code used with the Save button. Of course, links may be created from your interface text-edit boxes to appropriate columns in our data object. However, to include logic that prompts the operator to verify an update, as well as to illustrate at least some of the capabilities of the ViP programming language, LotusScript Version 3.0, you'll simply write the 12 lines of code that are required to complete the application.

This block of code must first place the current data object row in an "open" state, enabling edits to be performed. The RowOpen method of the data object (named SData) is used to perform this task. Next, simply copy values from user-interface edit fields into corresponding columns in the data object. Remember that each column represents a field in the current Notes document. The CellSetData method is used to perform this task. The final step is to update the data source using the ExecuteUpdate method.

The following code block is inserted in the Save button's Click event to accomplish the functions described previously:

```
dim ret%, row&
ret% = MsgBox( "Continue to save information to Notes database?",
➥MB_YESNO+MB_ICONQUESTION, _
      "Are you sure?")
if ret% = IDYES then
     row& = SData.RowOpen (SData.CurrentRow)
     ret% = SData.CellSetData( row&, 1, txtName.Text )
     ret% = SData.CellSetData( row&, 2, txtAddr.Text )
     ret% = SData.CellSetData( row&, 3, txtCity.Text )
     ret% = SData.CellSetData( row&, 4, txtState.Text )
     ret% = SData.CellSetData( row&, 5, txtZip.Text )
     ret% = SData.CellSetData( row&, 6, txtDesc.Text )
     ret% = SData.ExecuteUpdate( )
end if
```

For the most part, your Notes front end has now been designed and is completely functional. Some brushing up of the front end is required, however:

- The data object must be made invisible at runtime using data object settings.
- The size of your form must be altered as necessary so that only required user-interface elements are shown, hiding even the data object during design time.

When these changes are made, your ViP application will perform all of the tasks required of your database front end, with minimal coding effort.

Building SQL Relationships with Lotus NotesSQL

In addition to the third-party development tools just discussed, Lotus offers NotesSQL, an ODBC 2.0-compliant driver that allows Notes databases to be accessed in a more traditional relational database format. This driver allows any third-party development environment that has ODBC "hooks" to read data from and write data to a Notes database.

This section takes a very brief, introductory look at NotesSQL. The following topics will be addressed:

- The pros and cons of using NotesSQL as a Notes database access option
- How Notes database elements translate into SQL
- How to make a Notes database "ODBC-ready"

You should supplement the information covered in this section by reviewing the Lotus NotesSQL Driver Documentation, a Notes database included with each copy of NotesSQL. It discusses the installation and configuration of the NotesSQL driver, as well as SQL statements that are supported in a given release of the driver.

> **NOTE**
>
> NotesSQL is available for download from the Lotus Corporation Web site at `http://www.lotus.com` in the downloads section. It is available in 16-bit Windows, 32-bit Windows (Windows NT and Windows 95), and OS/2 Warp flavors.

> **TIP**
>
> To demonstrate the use of NotesSQL in a standard development environment, the simple front-end developed in the first part of this chapter in Visual Basic, Delphi, and ViP has been rewritten in Borland Delphi 2.0 using native data-aware controls. Because the development of this front-end using these controls is quite easy to do, I won't explain here so that we can concentrate our efforts on the high-level aspects of NotesSQL. However, the source code for this example is included on the CD-ROM for your viewing pleasure. To use the source code, make sure an ODBC data source using the NotesSQL driver is defined that points to the SDATAR4.NSF database, using the name SDATAR4.

The Pros and Cons of NotesSQL

Remembering that Notes is *not* a relational database, NotesSQL does a fairly decent job of hiding this fact from developers who prefer to work with a relational model. When you view a Notes database through this ODBC 2.0-compliant driver, a Notes database really does look like a standard relational database. Forms in Notes are translated into tables in SQL, documents are translated into rows, and fields are translated into columns. More details surrounding the translation of Notes to SQL elements are given later, in the section "NotesSQL to SQL: Element Mapping."

The principal advantage of using NotesSQL in conjunction with a development environment such as Visual Basic or Delphi is that the *data-aware* controls that are built into these environments may be fully utilized. These data-aware controls allow an ODBC *data source* to be tied directly to user interface controls, such as edit boxes, list boxes, and check boxes. Once a control is bound to a data source, changes to the database, such as moving from one record to the next, are automatically reflected in the user interface. Minimal coding is required to populate fields on the user interface and to save changes to new or edited records.

Another significant advantage of using NotesSQL lies in the area of generating reports based on data residing in a Notes database. By using NotesSQL, you may format reports and generate graphs using third-party applications that are not available in Notes itself, such as Access and FoxPro.

Before you throw away your copy of VB/Link or HiTest, however, you should be aware of the following significant disadvantages of using NotesSQL:

- Only the text portion of rich text fields may be accessed. Any attachments (such as OLE objects) or text formatting is lost in the ODBC translation.

- Since Notes is not natively a relational system, there may be serious performance penalties if you do not set up your database properly.

- Unlike the HiTest and VB/Link tools, you cannot retrieve other Notes-related information that may be necessary in your application, such as a list of available servers, databases, or agents in a database. NotesSQL deals exclusively with elements of a specific database that can be mapped directly to standard SQL.

> **TIP**
>
> NotesSQL, like any other tool that hits a Notes database, uses the Notes client software to access a Notes database. Therefore, Notes will still exercise user privileges as defined in the database ACL, and the user will still be required to log into the Notes server by entering his or her password. A password entry prompt will appear automatically when a new session through the NotesSQL driver is opened.

NotesSQL to SQL: Element Mapping

The NotesSQL driver has specific rules that define how Notes data elements map to and from SQL data elements. Table 22.1 defines Notes-to-SQL element mapping. Table 22.2 defines field-specific mappings.

Table 22.1. Mapping Notes Forms and Views to SQL.

Notes	*SQL*	*Description*
Form, View	Table	All forms and views are mapped to tables.
View	Index	A view is mapped as an index if a single form is utilized for all documents in the view, and at least one column in the view is sorted.
Form Fields and View Columns	Column	
View	View	All Notes views are treated as SQL views, with the exception of private views. When a view is created using SQL, a view based on one form is created in Notes.

Table 22.2. Mapping Notes data types to SQL data types.

Notes Data Type	*SQL Data Type*
Text	SQL_VARCHAR
Keyword	SQL_VARCHAR
Multivalue list	SQL_VARCHAR
Rich text field (text portion only)	SQL_LONGVARCHAR
Number, fixed or percent	SQL_DECIMAL
Number, general or scientific	SQL_FLOAT
Time	Depends on format. May be SQL_TIME, SQL_DATE, or SQL_TIMESTAMP.

Making an ODBC-Ready Notes Database

Although a Notes database looks like a relational database through NotesSQL, it is important to remember that the *perception* of a relational system does not jibe with reality: *Notes is not a relational database.* It's still Notes underneath the veil of the relational model. This simply means that there are limitations to using NotesSQL that are directly inherited from the nonrelational nature of Notes, as well as from the nature of SQL itself.

Due to this "Notes to SQL" translation, several nuances are involved with the development of a Notes database and SQL statements that hit a database through the driver. Some of these subtle issues are covered in the following list. Refer to the NotesSQL documentation for full details.

- Since views are grouped separately from forms in a Notes database, there may be a view that has the same name as a form. NotesSQL doesn't allow access to forms that have identically named views, and vice versa.

- If any of the following characters appear in a view or form name, they are translated into an underscore character (_) automatically: space . \ [ ] - ! ' ". For example, a view named 1. Solutions\All would be translated into 1__Solutions_All.

- Always use views instead of forms in your queries. In Notes, view indices are prebuilt. Queries based on Forms will result in significant performance penalties.

- A Notes view may be treated as an SQL index if the selection formula for the view includes all documents (SELECT @All) or all documents based on a specific form, if view columns are not mapped to formulas, and if at least one column in the view is sorted.

- View columns that contain @functions such as @All, @DocLevel, @DocNumber, and @IsExpandable are ignored by the driver. Refer to the NotesSQL documentation for other @functions affected by this rule.

- Do not use column names in views that are equivalent to ODBC or SQL reserved words. Also, avoid characters that are not alphanumeric.

TIP

If you're running into problems with NotesSQL, performance or otherwise, refer not only to the Lotus Web site but also to the newsgroups that are dedicated to Lotus Notes: comp.groupware.lotus-notes.* (apps, misc, admin, and programmer). It is likely that others have run into the same problem that you are experiencing.

Summary

This chapter introduced you to three Notes data-access development options outside of the Notes environment. In addition, a brief introduction to Lotus NotesSQL was provided. There are definite, unique advantages to each of the third-party development tools presented in this chapter. In some cases, it may be appropriate to utilize the NotesSQL driver. An analysis of your specific needs, as well as the features of each of these tools, will enable you to choose a development platform that is right for you. When you're choosing a third-party platform or add-on that allows access to Notes data, here are some questions to ask:

- What are the distribution requirements for the final deliverable application?
- How extensible is the environment itself? Can I add additional controls as necessary?
- How quickly are Notes queries performed? Are full-text searches and other Notes-specific options available?
- How fast does the final executable need to be? Is the language interpreted or compiled into a true executable?

Remember that each Notes access tool has its own trade-offs—you must choose the right tool for the task at hand.

A variety of additional third-party development tools are available—far too many to include in this chapter. One source for alternative or add-on development tools is The Lotus Notes & cc:Mail Guide, published by Lotus. Other sources include the Lotus Web site (`http://www.lotus.com`) and Lotus Notes periodicals, such as the Notes Advisor.

Here is a summary of the main points presented in this chapter:

- The use of a third-party development tool may arise depending on a variety of circumstances, including the need for a quick, easily distributed front end for a Notes database.
- Always remember that a copy of Notes client software must be installed on any computer that uses a third-party tool to access a Notes database.
- Microsoft Visual Basic is one of the more popular development environments at this time. VB 4.0 offers support for all Windows 95 controls and full OLE 2 Automation. Visual Basic is the name of both the design environment and the programming language used in this package.
- The Lotus HiTest Tools for Visual Basic offer both a set of 12 extensive custom controls and a rich API that is nearly as powerful as the HiTest Tools for C. The htVisual custom controls offer a feature known as piping, which enables the output of select objects to be connected to object inputs at design time.
- Borland Delphi, a rising star in the development community, offers a true compiled executable along with the simplicity of interface prototyping found in packages such as Visual Basic. Borland Delphi 2.0 supports 32-bit development, support for OCXs, and full OLE 2 Automation. The underlying language used by Delphi is Object Pascal.
- Brainstorm Technologies offers VB/Link, a Notes add-on for the Borland Delphi environment. VB/Link is an easy-to-use, yet powerful, set of ActiveX controls.

- Revelation ViP is an outstanding product that allows for virtually "codeless" programming through the use of graphical object linking. Full runtime support for both Lotus Notes R4 and R3 databases is "in the box." LotusScript Version 3.0 is the programming language used in ViP, the same language used in Lotus Notes R4.

- If you're comfortable with Structured Query Language (SQL), you should review the Lotus NotesSQL ODBC driver. It allows Notes databases to be accessed using any development environment that allows hooks into ODBC data sources, with some Notes and SQL limitations. Performance penalties may apply if you're not careful. NotesSQL is available for Windows (3.1, 95, and NT) and OS/2 platforms.

V

PART

Domino Server, the Internet, and Intranets

Using the Notes Client on the Internet

by Don Child

IN THIS CHAPTER

In this chapter we'll explore the use of the Notes client on the Internet. First you'll be introduced to the Personal Web Browser in an overview; then you'll learn how to set up and customize the navigator so it does what you want it to. Finally, once you get the navigator set up, you'll be able to take a small tour of the World Wide Web.

An Overview of the Personal Notes Navigator

Consider how you have used the Internet in the past. Within Notes 4.0, you had two choices. You could open the InterNotes Web Browser, which resided on the Notes Server, and request Web pages from the server. The server would go out and retrieve pages that you could then view as Notes documents in the InterNotes Web Browser database. The other alternative was to toggle over to a dedicated Web browser, such as Netscape, and access the Internet directly.

Both alternatives had their strengths. Many people prefer the freedom of a direct connection to the Internet, as afforded by a stand-alone product. However, with the InterNotes browser you could handle the data in Web pages using the strengths of Notes (for example, the built-in full-text searching and workflow processing) and you could share your favorite Web pages with members of your workgroup.

 Lotus Notes 4.5 has now combined the best of both worlds. With the Personal Notes Navigator, you have direct browser access to the Internet from within Notes. When this is combined with the already strong document and workflow capabilities of Notes, you have a tool that introduces you to the future of the Internet as a business solution.

The Personal Web Navigator demonstrates how businesses will be using the Internet in the future. The Web will cease to be an exciting toy full of promise and will become a strategic information tool used to deliver potent business solutions.

For example, with the Web Navigator on your desktop you can transform a URL or a Web link into a Notes document in a number of ways. You can click on a link within a Notes document. You can click on a SmartIcon or select a URL dialog box from a menu and then type in a URL. You can transform the search bar (used for full-text searching) into a URL launching pad. Or you can browse through a list of Web pages that are stored as Web pages in the Personal Web Navigator database and open them as Notes documents.

You can have Notes automatically refresh selected Web pages that are stored as Notes documents. An agent handles this task, scanning the Web for changes to the databases that you want to keep refreshed. The agent will even notify you when a page has been changed. Another agent will automatically load all links on a Web page for you. For example, if you had enough disk space available, you could point to `http://www.cnn.com` and tell the computer to load links three pages deep. You now have your own electronic newspaper fully loaded, and all you had to do was point to a single page on the Web to do it. This can be particularly handy if you are getting ready to unplug your computer to take on the road with you, and you want to browse a favorite Web site while on the airplane. This is described in Chapter 9, "Using Mobile Notes on the Road."

Consider how you can use the Web as a workgroup! When you locate a new document you want to share, you can use NotesMail to forward the entire document (or you can forward a URL link) to others on your work team. You can have Notes automatically forward documents to a shared Web database such as the InterNotes Web Browser (which is now called the Server Web Browser to distinguish it from the Personal Web Browser). Also, you can create Web Tours, which are links that record an entire navigation session on the Web so it can be replayed at a later time. You can edit the session and move links around to create the Web Tour you want to recall.

If you think that a tool with this much versatility must have a lot of options, you're right. Follow along and learn how to customize the Personal Notes Navigator for your work environment as well as for your needs.

Setting up the Personal Web Navigator

As you set up the Personal Notes Navigator, you'll have occasion to touch the following screens:

- ■ The Location document in your Personal Address Book
- ■ The Internet Options document in your Personal Web Navigator database
- ■ The Properties box for your Personal Web Navigator database
- ■ The User Preferences screen under File | Tools

Set up Your Location Document

There are fields on the Location document specifically to define your Internet setup. To ensure that you set up Personal Web Navigator correctly, we'll begin there. Later, you'll return to look at advanced setup features on the Location document (you need to get your connection set up correctly).

The Notes 4.5 Location document is shown in Figure 23.1. Note that the location is set up using a TCP/IP connection, which is necessary if you want to connect directly to the Internet.

You have to pay attention to two parts of the Location document:

- ■ In the Internet Browser fields, specify "Notes" as the Internet browser that you want to use and that you want to retrieve Web pages from the Notes workstation.

> **TIP**
>
> You can select Netscape or the Microsoft Internet Explorer as a browser if you want to use these browsers when you retrieve URLs from within Notes. However, only the Notes navigator saves documents in the Personal Web Navigator database, which gives you the ability to work with the content of Web pages using the Notes client.

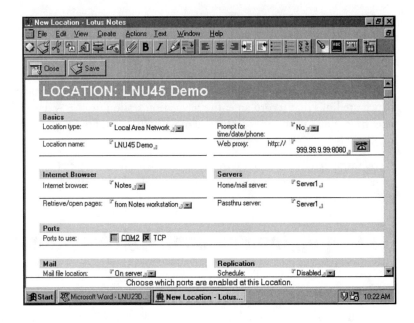

■ If you are using a proxy Web server rather than connecting directly through an ISP or over a corporate LAN, enter the proxy setup information in the Web Proxy field. A proxy server provides an extra layer between the Internet and the user, thus offering additional firewall security. When the user requests a Web page, that request is intercepted and reissued by the proxy server. Since there is no direct connection between the user and the Web, external users can't use a Web connection to steal data from corporate networks.

To set up a Web proxy, click on the button in the Web Proxy field (the button that looks like a propeller hat). The Proxy Server Configuration dialog box, similar to those found in other Web navigators, appears, as shown in Figure 23.2.

You can enter separate proxies for different application services, including FTP, Gopher, and SSL security, or you can use the same proxy for all Internet protocols. Separate proxies provide additional security by limiting what can be done through any one proxy. You can also set up a Notes RPC proxy, which is used for all Notes-to-Notes communications, such as replication over the Internet.

You can enter a SOCKS proxy as well. This is a proxy server for IP hosts behind firewalls. In other words, it intercepts and reissues requests to an Internet provider when you use a dial-up connection from your server. If you use a SOCKS proxy, it will override an HTTP proxy, but it does not override a Notes RPC or SSL Security proxy.

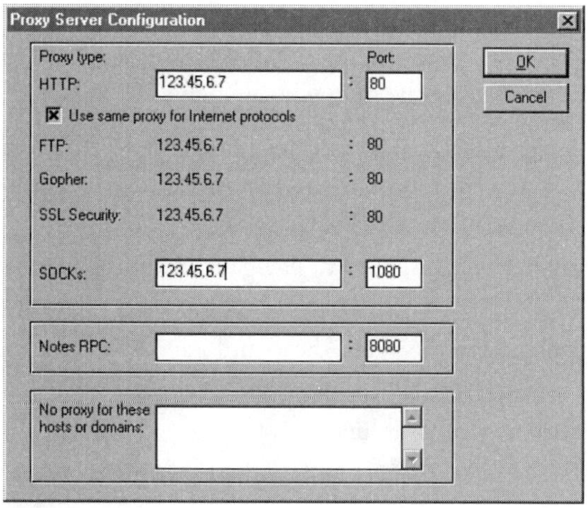

FIGURE 23.2.

The Proxy Server Configuration dialog box, used to set up a proxy server for use with the Personal Web Navigator.

The Personal Web Navigator

To put the Personal Web Navigator database on your desktop, select Open URL from the File menu on your Notes desktop. In the Open URL dialog box, type the URL of one of your favorite Web sites. For example, type the following:

```
http://www.lotus.com
```

Notes will create and open a Personal Web Navigator database using PERWEB45.NTF and will display the Web page. The Personal Web Navigator database is shown in Figure 23.3.

FIGURE 23.3.

The Personal Web Navigator has a view pane, a navigation pane, and a document preview screen like any other Notes database.

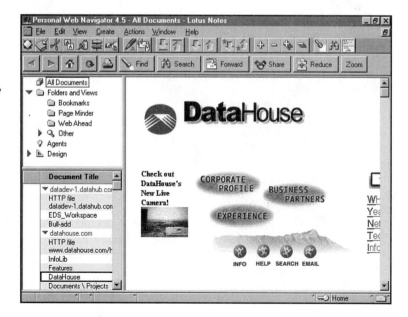

When you open a URL, the Web page will fill the entire screen. You can resize the screen by dragging the left edge to display the navigation pane and the view pane, as shown in Figure 23.3. What you see are the following elements:

- An Internet search bar, used to type in a URL that you want to retrieve. This is the same search bar (at the top of the screen) used for full-text searching, only now it has been enabled to accept URLs.

- Action bar buttons, used to navigate on the Internet

- A navigation pane, which lists available views and folders, including special folders associated with the Web Ahead and Page Minder agents

- A view pane, which lists all of the Web pages available as Notes documents or links in the current view or folder

- A preview pane, which displays the currently selected Web page

The Internet Search Bar

 In previous versions of Notes, the search bar was used only for full-text searching. Within Notes 4.5, the search bar has the additional function of letting you type URLs that are then retrieved by the Personal Notes Navigator.

The search bar now has a button on the left side that, when the search bar is enabled for the Web, displays a hand pointing to a globe. When the search bar is enabled for full-text searching, this button displays a hand pointing to a book. From anywhere within Notes 4.5, you can click on the button to toggle so the search bar is Web-enabled and then type in a URL to open a Web page.

Action Bar Buttons in the Personal Web Navigator

The buttons on the action bar are the same buttons that are available on the Server Web Navigator. Here they are (from left to right):

- Go to the previous page in the history list.

- Go to the next page in the history list.

- Go to the Home page (defined on the Internet Options screen, described in a moment).

- Reload the current page from the Internet.

- Print the current page.

- Find. The Find button is dependent on the context. If you have a document open, you can search for text in the document. If you are in a view, you can search for occurrences of a word in the view.

- Use the Internet search engine defined on the Internet Options screen.

- Forward the Web page to others in a workgroup via e-mail.

- Share the Web page by forwarding it to another database, such as the Server Web Navigator database, as defined on the Internet Options screen.

- Reduce the Web page to a URL link rather than storing the entire Web page in the Personal Web Navigator database.

- Zoom the current Web page so it fills the entire Notes workspace.

Views and Folders in the Personal Web Navigator Database

You can navigate through the Personal Web Navigator database just as you would with any other Notes database. Click on a view or folder in the navigation pane to display a list of documents (that is, Web pages) in that view or folder.

The views and folders available in the database include the following:

- All Documents view. This view contains all of the Web pages you have retrieved in the database.

- Bookmarks folder. You can drag your favorite Web pages into this folder for quick retrieval at a later time.

- Page Minder folder. You can drag Web pages into this folder to be notified when they are updated. This is set up on the Internet Options page.

- Web Ahead folder. You can drag Web pages into this folder to start an agent that will retrieve all linked pages, as defined on the Internet Options page.

- File Archive view. This view displays all Web pages that contain attachments.

- House Cleaning view. This view displays Web pages sorted by size. You can choose which ones you want to delete or reduce to URLs.

- Web Tours view. Web tours enable you to replay a Web navigation session. Later in this chapter, you'll get to take a Web tour.

The Internet Options Screen: Customizing Your Setup

Now that you know your way around the Personal Notes Navigator screen, it is time to customize the screen with your personal preferences. Your navigator is customized using the Internet Options document. You can display this document, shown in Figure 23.4, by selecting Actions | Internet Options in the Personal Web Navigator database.

On this document, you can specify the following options:

- Startup options. The name of your home page, and whether you want it to be displayed automatically when you open the Personal Web Navigator database.

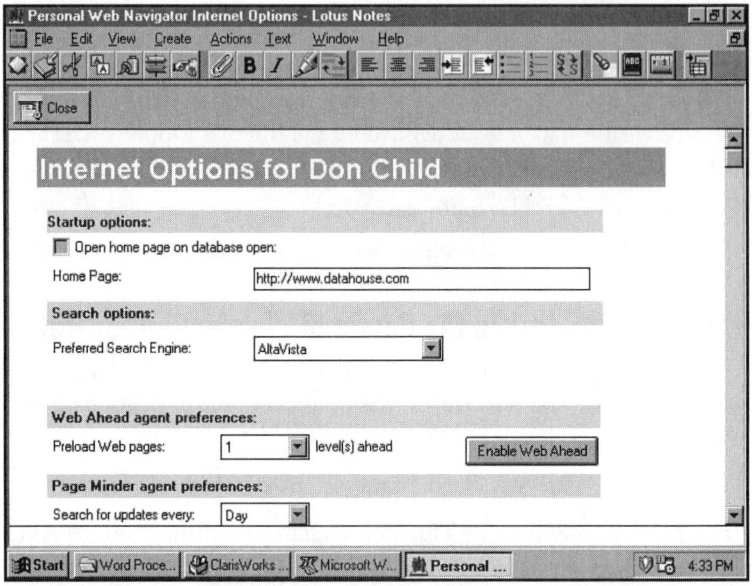

FIGURE 23.4.

The Internet Options screen, used to customize options in your Personal Web Navigator database.

[Screenshot: Personal Web Navigator Internet Options - Lotus Notes]

Internet Options for Don Child

Startup options:

☐ Open home page on database open:

Home Page: http://www.datahouse.com

Search options:

Preferred Search Engine: AltaVista

Web Ahead agent preferences:

Preload Web pages: 1 level(s) ahead   [Enable Web Ahead]

Page Minder agent preferences:

Search for updates every: Day

TIP

On the Basics page of the User Preferences dialog box, under File | Tools there is the Startup Database button, which lets you specify a database that is opened automatically when you start up Notes. If you specify the Personal Web Navigator database and indicate on the Internet Options document that you want your home page opened when you first open the database, then you'll see the home page every time you start up Notes.

TIP

Do not enable a home page on startup if you'll be using the Web Navigator when disconnected. The Web Retriever will try to locate the home page and will eventually return an error message since the home page cannot be located.

■ Search options: Select the Internet search engine you want Notes to use by default.

■ Web Ahead agent preferences: Notes will preload Web page links up to four layers deep if you activate this option. Enter the number of pages you want to preload and then click on the Enable Web Ahead button. To preload pages, drag and drop a Web page into the Web Ahead folder.

■ Page Minder agent preferences: If you enable Page Minder, Notes will, at the interval you select, browse (from the Internet) Web pages that have been dragged and dropped into the Page Minder folder. If a page has changed, you or whomever you designate will be mailed a summary of the page or a copy of the full page, depending on the options you select.

■ Database purge options: You can specify that documents are automatically deleted or reduced to links if they have not been read in 30, 60, or 90 days. You can also have Notes warn you when the Personal Web Navigator reaches 5, 10, 25, or 50 megabytes in size. To reduce the size of the database, you might want to go to the Housecleaning view and delete pages that you no longer want to save.

■ Collaboration options: You can specify a server and a shared Web Navigator database where Web pages and your personal ratings are sent when you click on the Share button on the action bar.

■ Presentation preferences: You can specify how the Personal Web Navigator displays text that is defined using different HTML tags, such as body text, address text, and anchor text (that is, links). You can also specify that you want to save the raw HTML text in Web pages, if you need the code for programmatic purposes.

Advanced Setup Options

The Advanced section of the Location document provides further control over the Personal Web Navigator. There are three types of parameters that can be set up in the Advanced options.

Images

You can define how images are loaded. First, you must select "Store images so that they are loaded asynchronously" on the Basics page of Database Properties for the Personal Web Navigator. This stores each image as a separate document in the database. Then, in the Advanced section of the Location document, select Always as an option to load images—the images will be loaded automatically after a page is loaded. If you select On Request, you can open images one by one as you click on them.

Web Retriever Configuration

The Web Retriever Configuration section of the Advanced options in the Location document lets you work with how the Personal Web Navigator is configured on your system. The "Web Retriever" is the process that retrieves Web pages so that you can view them with the Notes Web browser. The fields that you can set include the following:

■ Web Navigator database: This field holds the name of the Web Navigator database. You have the option of quitting Notes and using DOS to change the name of your

Web Navigator database, but then you must enter the new name of the database in the Web Navigator database field so that Notes can find the database to use for retrieving Web pages.

■ Concurrent retrievers: You can set up to six concurrent retrievers and then open multiple documents and cascade them in your Navigator. In other words, you can have up to six Web pages visible at one time.

■ Retriever log level: You can determine how Web Retriever events are recorded in your LOG.NSF file. Options include None, Terse, and Verbose.

■ Update cache: When you open a Web page that is already stored in your Personal Web Navigator database, you can determine how often Notes refreshes the stored document from the Internet. Options include the following:

Never: Notes opens the locally stored version.

Once per session: Notes reloads pages only once during a session.

Every time: Notes always downloads pages from the Web, even if they are already stored in the Personal Web Navigator database.

■ Accept SSL site certificates: SSL is a Secure Socket Layer, a type of secure data transfer that is used on the Internet. Notes has RSA security built in. RSA security uses a public key in the Public Address Book and a private key (part of the Notes User or Server ID) to solve mathematical algorithms to ensure that communications are authentic. However, when navigating the Web, you'll encounter secure Web sites that require a certificate (such as a public key) from a Certificate Authority (CA) other than RSA in order to authenticate communications. These sites can be handled in one of two ways.

The first method of handling certificates from SSL sites, which negates the security afforded by certificates, is to say Yes in the "Accept SSL site certificates" field in the Location document. This basically tells Notes that you don't want to take advantage of certificates, so just go ahead and accept all certificates without authenticating.

The second, more secure method entails adding a new certificate from a CA before accessing a secure Web site using that CA's certificates. To get a certificate, open the SSL Certificate database (SSLCERT.NSF) from the Home/Notes/Net server. From the Certificates | Internet Certifiers view, select the certificate you want and then paste it into the Server | Certificates view in your Personal Address Book. Once you have the certificate in your Personal Address Book, you can access any secure Web site as long as you share a certificate. When you select this option, you do not have to open your workstation to all certificates as you do with the first option.

Java Applet Security

With Notes 4.5, you can run Java applets on your system if you are running Notes under any of the following platforms: Windows 95, Windows NT/Intel, Sun Solaris (SPARC and *x*86), HP-UX, and AIX. Other Notes platforms will support Java applet execution in the future.

When a Java applet runs on your workstation, you run the risk that someone may have hidden destructive code in the Java applet. In other words, you are opening up your system to computer viruses. Although Notes 4.5 does not let Java applets access your operating system, by including files, environment variables, password files, and so on, you can still decide exactly how much risk you are willing to take with outside Java hosts.

In order for Java applets to run on your system, you must enable Java. To do this, open the User Preferences dialog box (under File | Tools). In the Advanced Options box, select Enable Java applets. You also must specify a proxy server, if you are using proxies.

Once Java applets have been enabled, you can determine the level of access of any host that runs Java applets. For example, you can allow a corporate server from behind your firewall to run Java applets, while denying Java access from hosts outside of the firewall.

By default, any host system can run Java applets on your workstation. But you can limit which hosts have access using the following Advanced fields on Location documents in your Personal Address Book:

- Trusted hosts. In this field, you can enter the IP address or domain name of all hosts that you trust to load Java applets onto your workstation. You can enter any HTTP address (for example, `www.lotus.com`, and you can use wildcards such as `999.888.77.*` or `*.lotus.com`. If this field is blank, then all hosts are considered "untrusted" hosts and will be subject to whatever security level you select for untrusted hosts.

- Network access for trusted hosts. Use this field to define the level of network access you want to give to trusted hosts, defined in the previous field. Network access options include the following:

  Disable Java: Trusted hosts cannot run applets on your system.

  No access allowed: Trusted hosts can run applets on your workstation but cannot make network HTTP connections.

  Allow access to any originating host: Applets can make network HTTP connections only on the host from which the applet was retrieved.

  Allow access to any trusted host: Applets can make network HTTP connections on trusted hosts.

  Allow access to any host: Applets can make network HTTP connections on any host.

- Network access for untrusted hosts: Use this field to define the level of network access you want to give to untrusted hosts. Untrusted hosts include any host not specified as a trusted host. Network access options include the following:

  Disable Java: Untrusted hosts cannot run applets on your system.

  No access allowed: Untrusted hosts can run applets on your workstation but cannot make network HTTP connections.

  Allow access to any originating host: Applets can make network HTTP connections only on the host from which the applet was retrieved.

  Allow access to any trusted host: Applets can make network HTTP connections on trusted hosts.

- Trust HTTP proxy: Use this field only if you defined an HTTP proxy, through which Java applets are run. "Yes" in this field means that you want your HTTP proxy to resolve the host name for you because you do not have a direct connection to the Internet.

TIP

You can troubleshoot Java applet execution by displaying a Java console. The option to display the Java console can be found under File | Tools.

A Summary of the Personal Web Navigator Setup

To use the Personal Web Navigator you need to be connected to the Internet. This connection can be over a network or via a dial-up connection. Also, the connection can be direct to the Internet, or it can be through an HTTP proxy server.

You need to set up your location to recognize the HTTP proxy server if that is how you are connecting, and you have to define Notes as the Internet Browser. You also have to define Web retrieval as being from the Notes workstation as opposed to retrieving Web pages from the server. In effect, this says that you want to connect directly to the Internet instead of sharing a Web Navigator database with others in your organization.

In the Location document you can also configure advanced options, such as logging and how to handle SSL certificates, and Java options if you are running Notes under Windows 95, Windows NT/Intel, Sun Solaris (SPARC and *x*86), HP-UX and AIX platforms. Java applets must also be enabled in the advanced options on the User Preferences page.

Finally, you can determine how the Personal Notes Navigator displays and handles documents using the Internet Options page, opened from the Actions menu when you are in the Personal Notes Navigator database.

A Web Tour Using the Personal Notes Navigator

Now that the Personal Web Navigator is configured to run under Notes 4.5, let's look at how it might be used in the real world.

Opening a Web Page from the Notes Desktop

Begin by calling up the Lotus home page. You can do this by toggling the search bar so that it shows a Web icon and then typing in a URL, or you can select File | Open URL or click on a URL in a Notes document (but in this case, you are on the Notes desktop, so you click on the Open URL SmartIcon). In the dialog box, type the URL. You'll notice in Figure 23.5 that all you need is www.lotus.com because the default protocol is HTTP. You can, if you want, type the entire address (for example, http://www.lotus.com).

FIGURE 23.5.

Entering a URL to retrieve a Web page within Lotus Notes 4.5.

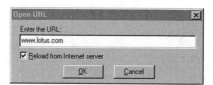

If you specified in your Location document that Web pages should be retrieved from the Notes workstation, then the Web Retriever process on the workstation will retrieve the designated page from the Internet. If you had specified that you wanted to retrieve Web pages from the InterNotes server, then you have the option of retrieving a version of the page that is saved on the InterNotes server or retrieving the document directly from the Internet.

When the page is retrieved, it is displayed on a full screen, as shown in Figure 23.6. You have just retrieved a Web page directly from the Internet. The page will also be saved in your Personal Web Navigator database.

Opening a Web Page from the Personal Web Navigator

Now that you have seen how to open a Web page from anywhere in the Notes 4.5 workspace, it is time to explore the Web from within the Personal Web Navigator database. Double-click on the Personal Web Navigator icon to open the database. The system will display in the Preview pane whichever page was last selected in the Navigator pane, as shown in Figure 23.7.

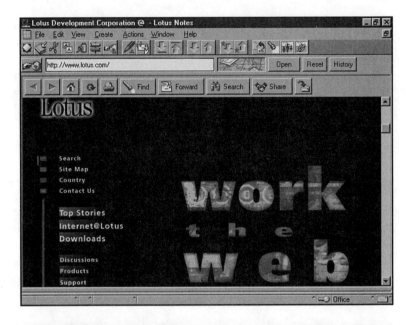

FIGURE 23.7.
Opening the Personal Web Navigator database.

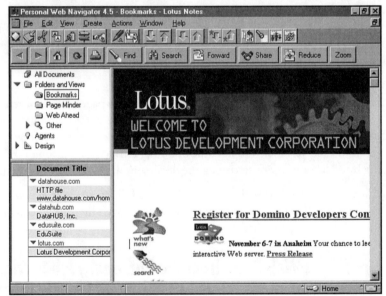

You can retrieve a page directly from the Web by entering a URL, or you can retrieve a Web page that is stored as a document in the database. Select a view or folder that contains the document you want and click on the document to load it into the Preview pane. For example, in Figure 23.8 the EduSuite home page was opened from within the Personal Web Navigator as a Notes document.

FIGURE 23.8.

The EduSuite home page, retrieved as a Notes document from the Navigation pane.

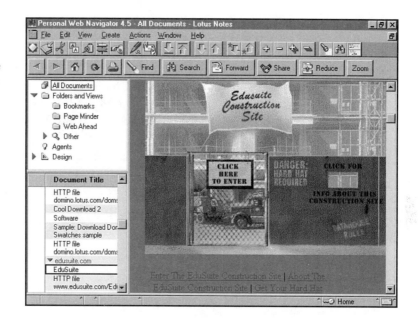

Note that the EduSuite home page has three links to other pages. If you want to retrieve all of these linked pages and you have Web Ahead enabled to retrieve one level of links, retrieving is a snap! Click on the document title in the Navigation pane and then drag and drop it onto the Web Ahead folder. That's all. The pages will be loaded in the background while you are working.

If not, you'll have to do it the old-fashioned way—by clicking on a link. Now, let's enter the "construction site" and see what's going on.

Exploring a Web Site Published by Domino

Inside we see two menus: one for educators and one for developers (see Figure 23.9). These menus are graphical navigators in a Notes database. If you were using a frames-capable browser such as Netscape, these two menus would be displayed in frames on the left of the screen. Since the Notes browser does not display frames, the navigators become image maps inside the Web page.

Parts of the EduSuite database are open to any casual user. However, parts of the database utilize Notes security to limit access. For example, when you click on one of the Discussion options, the Web Retriever displays a security dialog box asking for your user name and password. Once you gain access to the Discussion database, you can navigate through documents as you would with any Web browser looking at a Domino database. You can add new documents to the discussion, and you can expand and collapse categories.

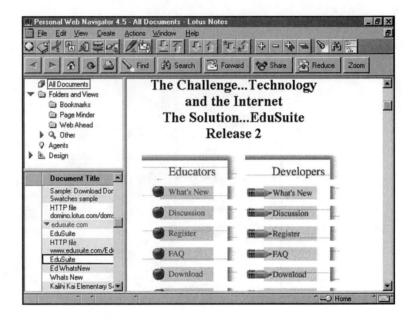

Sharing Web Pages with Others

When you are done browsing through the database, you have all of the Web pages saved as Notes documents. If you elected (in your Internet Options document) to save HTML code with the documents, you can view the HTML using the Document Properties info box and looking for the HTML field. But regardless, you have all of the Web pages you visited saved as documents. Now the power of Notes comes into play.

As an ordinary Web browser, the Notes browser does not necessarily outshine dedicated browsers such as Netscape. But with Notes, you can copy the database to a laptop computer, generate a full-text index, and then perform powerful Boolean searches on the Web pages, even when you are disconnected from the network.

You can open a Web page from the Personal Web Navigator, then forward it to a work colleague by clicking on the Forward button, which includes the Web page in a Notes e-mail memo. A better solution, however, might be to click on the Share button to share a copy of the Web page with others via the Server Web Navigator. While you are at it, you can rate the screen and enter your comments so that anyone accessing the Server Web Navigator can decide for themselves if the page is valuable. The process of sharing a Web page is illustrated in Figure 23.10. Note that you have the option of sharing the Web page as a link or as a full page. Remember, you also have the option of saving space by reducing pages in your Personal Web Navigator to links using the Reduce button.

FIGURE 23.10.

Rating a Web page before sharing it with others in the Server Web Navigator database.

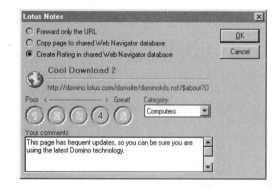

If you are familiar with Notes workflow applications, you'll recognize how easily Notes could be set up using features such as Page Minder and full-text searching agents to automate the process of distributing new information from the Web. You are not restricted to the Forward and Share buttons when it comes to sharing information with others. The workflow capabilities of Notes demonstrate a new paradigm for using the Internet as a business tool.

Saving a Tour of the Web

Sometimes you may have an especially fruitful tour of the Web, and you want to return at a later time to many of the same documents. You can save a session, or part of a session, as a "Web tour." Select Action | History and then click on the Save button. You can then edit the list of URLs that will be saved in the Web tour and save the URLs from your present history file on the screen (see Figure 23.11).

FIGURE 23.11.

Saving a Web Tour so you can return at a later date.

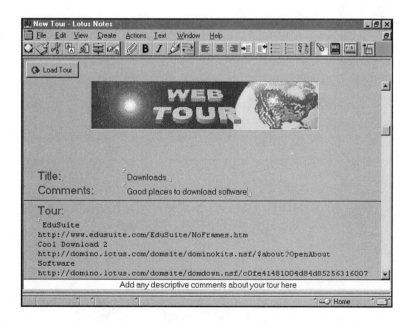

Summary

The Personal Web Navigator lets you connect directly to the Internet from within Lotus Notes. The Notes browser has many configuration options that let you adapt it to any Notes 4.5 environment. Depending on the platform you are using, you can even allow Java applets to execute within the Notes browser. You can take advantage of the strengths of the Notes environment, such as workflow processing and security, to enhance the way you do business on the Internet. The Personal Web Browser saves Web pages as Notes documents and then lets you work with the pages as you would work with any Notes document. This introduces a new paradigm for Internet computing—combining the power of groupware and document sharing with the rich content of the World Wide Web.

CHAPTER 24

Maximizing Your Domino Web Site and Applications with Advanced HTML

by Ralph Perrine

IN THIS CHAPTER

Today's global corporations face the challenge of managing and distributing timely information across a confusing landscape of incompatible platforms, varying network protocols and different clients. Notes and the Domino server work together to help users meet this challenge, allowing them to distribute information not only to Notes clients and browsers but also to non-Notes browsers such as Netscape Navigator and Microsoft's Internet Explorer.

Lotus Notes and the Domino server have a number of powerful capabilities that can drastically streamline the development and maintenance of a Web site. They greatly simplify networking and support issues for small companies seeking to collaborate with outside partners, customers, and suppliers, and for larger corporations seeking to open up communication across disparate environments within their enterprise.

However, it should be pointed out that, despite the unquestionable advantages, developing a Notes/Domino Web site requires a carefully planned approach. Not all HTML functions are supported in the Notes environment. This has been a source of frustration for some HTML composers and Web page designers. You can avoid this problem by following the two-tiered site architecture described in this chapter (see the section "Advanced HTML Functions"). This architecture was perfected in the development of several corporate Web sites I worked on. These sites are published by Domino and rely heavily on Notes databases but implement a good deal of advanced HTML functionality. Two of these sites are good examples: the DataHouse home page at `http://www.datahouse.com` and the CareNet-Hawaii home page at `http://www.carenet-hawaii.com`.

This chapter focuses on designing your Web site to take maximum advantage of Notes functionality. This chapter is not intended to serve as a detailed guide for Domino and Notes functions. Instead, you'll see how to extend the power of Notes by incorporating advanced HTML functionality into the design of your Web site. This chapter takes you through the design and planning stages, discusses important organizational considerations, and describes the two-tiered site architecture just mentioned. In addition, several paragraphs are devoted to the subject of incorporating graphics into your site.

The Internet and Notes/Domino

Since the World Wide Web burst onto the mainstream scene in 1994, industry pundits and corporate prophets have spun dozens of different visions of how the Web will emerge and whisk us all into the twenty-first century ahead of schedule. As we all know, most of these visions are quickly discarded as the true nature of the Web becomes more and more apparent. Companies tailor their strategies and offerings to meet the new demands driven by the Internet's popularization. This chaotic process often produces widespread notions that seem obvious, but soon turn out to be misconceptions.

One misconception prompted many to think of Notes as somehow a competitor with the Internet. On the one hand, you had a free browser (Mosaic or Netscape) along with a host of free Web development tools that could be quickly downloaded from many FTP sites. These tools arose out of an online community that provided generous documentation and resources for fledgling developers all pretty much for free. Supposedly pitted against all these was Notes, which was pretty expensive and which required you to learn a proprietary development environment. In these terms, there seemed to be no comparison.

But as the true nature of the Internet became clearer, and as Lotus retooled its approach, Notes and Domino began to make a lot of sense. Today's Web sites have a relentless need for interactivity, fresh content, and the latest information. The "traditional" Web development tools are becoming increasingly inadequate to meet the demands of maintaining a continually updated Web site. Manual HTML coding is too time-consuming and labor-intensive to be practical. Developers are now looking for ways to automate the development and maintenance of interactive Web pages.

Enter Domino, which goes much further than simply automating the process of updating a Web page. Domino makes updating virtually invisible to the Webmaster (the person managing the content and structure of the Web site) while adding a number of great functions that are not even possible with other solutions.

How Domino Works

Domino is an integrated HTTP/Notes server developed by Lotus that allows any Web browser (client) to request and receive information from Notes databases. You can download the latest version of Domino and find a wealth of Domino documentation at the Lotus Domino home page (http://domino.lotus.com/). You should also refer to Chapter 27, "Setting Up an Intranet with Domino," for more information about setting up a Domino server.

Domino can interface with HTTP, parse URLs, and perform a number of other Internet-related functions. Here's a real-world scenario: you're surfing the Web and click a hyperlink to a home page served by Domino. Your Web browser sends a request for that home page to the Domino server. When it receives your request, Domino first determines if the requested information (the home page, in this case) resides in a Notes database or in the server's file system.

It's possible that the home page you've requested doesn't reside in a Notes database but rather sits on the server as an existing HTML file. If this were true, Domino would, in typical Web server fashion, simply send this HTML file to your Web browser.

However, if the requested information resides in a Notes database, it gets a little more interesting. Depending on the URL you clicked, Domino could do one or more of the following: dynamically construct an HTML file from components (known as Notes constructs) in a Notes database, open a database for you, or even take information from a form you filled out and save it in a Notes database.

Notes constructs such as documents, links, views, navigators, and formulas are used by Domino to dynamically generate HTML files and provide advanced Web functionality to users. All this occurs in split-second timing at the moment a request is made. Domino takes the right combination of constructs, generates the HTML file, and sends it out to the requesting Web browser.

Getting Started

This chapter assumes that you have Lotus Notes 4.5 and the Domino server installed. If you're familiar with Lotus Notes 4.x, you should be ready to understand the items discussed in this chapter. It is also assumed that you have a working knowledge of HTML and are familiar with Web and Internet terminology.

Designing Your Web Site

As a first step, Web developers must sit down and determine the purpose of the site. What is this site supposed to do? Who will it serve? What are the objectives of this Web site? How will you know if the site is meeting its objectives? These are some of the hard questions that need to be answered before the work begins.

The next step is to think about how best to implement Notes and the Domino server to meet the site's objectives. Certain Web site designs are better suited to leveraging the power of Notes and Domino than others. A Web site that is either very small or contains rarely updated information is not going to leverage the power of either Notes or Domino. Also, if for some reason you are required to use a Mac Web server (such as Webstar), Notes and Domino will not be of much use to you. Other poorly suited designs would include sites with a lot of components that are incompatible with Notes or Domino. An example would be sites that are primarily graphical in nature (online art museums) or sites that contain extensive Virtual Reality Modeling Language (VRML) environments. This brings up an important principle that will be elaborated on later: concentrate non–Notes-compatible items in the top layers of the site and use Domino to publish information-intensive material in the lower layers of the site.

If your site is large, contains text-intensive content, requires constant updating, and needs to facilitate collaboration, then Notes and Domino will be of great value to your development and maintenance efforts.

A good way to find the best design is to think through the different pieces and components of your Web site. Take into consideration who will manage the site, who will maintain the site's content, and how often things will need to be updated. Chart out the various user groups who will be visiting the site and decide what they will or will not have access to.

Think about how information is generated in your organization. Plan to use Notes to shorten the lines of communication between information generators and information processors. You may want to organize your content into various categories such as graphical, internal, data-intensive, for customers only, and so on. Having a plan for all these issues will help you determine the best use of Notes and Domino in your Web development efforts.

Web Site Architecture

Your site needs an organized architecture to make development, maintenance, and user navigation easier. It's always a good idea to develop a site map showing each of the levels in your site as well as the Web pages that will appear in each level. From this, plan out the paths that users will take as they navigate through your site. This will help you determine how to make the best use of navigation buttons.

At a minimum, it is a good idea to provide a home, or back button, along with some basic choices on every page. Think about what your user will expect to see and how they will try to move through the site. In some sites, users may tend to move laterally through material, clicking along through similar documents on the same hierarchical level. In this case, a lateral-navigation scheme would be very helpful. This would require a navigator to appear on every page and provide links to all the other pages on the same level.

In other sites lateral-navigation would be irrelevant. If, for example, your site primarily provides data that users pinpoint through either a search or by quickly drilling down through the levels on your site, then lateral navigation buttons might simply add more clutter to the page and more unnecessary work for the developer. Figure 24.1 shows a simple site map with lateral and vertical navigation.

FIGURE 24.1.

Lateral and vertical navigation through a series of Web documents.

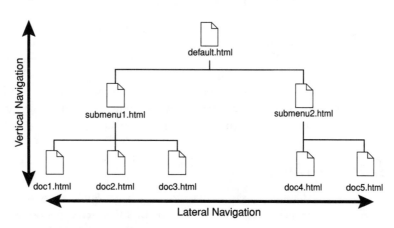

Planning Organizing Notes Databases

Because the Notes database(s) will be the primary source of your Web site's content, it is important to consider beforehand which Notes databases you will publish from and how you will manage their content for Web publication.

You can create a new database that will contain all the Web site content. But you'll probably want to be able to publish content from an existing database onto the Web. It is extremely important to carefully plan out what content will and will not be published, who will manage it, and how it will be approved for publication. Carelessness in this area can result in sensitive data being published inadvertently on the Web.

In some cases, you may want to have your Web site draw from more than one Notes database. One reason for doing this might be to allow different groups within your organization to take responsibility for different sections of your Web site. For example, a Human Resources department could publish job openings from its database in your corporate Web site, while the Public Relations department publishes press releases from its database to the same Web site. The two departments could each easily manage their respective portions of the Web site from within Notes. No HTML, no uploading, no mess, no fuss.

Planning for Maintenance

Maintenance is also something you should give a good deal of attention to in the planning stages. Too often, Web development teams underestimate either the importance of planning for maintenance, or the amount of effort involved in maintaining a Web site. In fact, many companies with Web sites have discovered only too late that the ongoing process of maintaining the Web site is a far greater task than the initial challenge of developing and launching the site. Typically, these companies then face the dilemma of either allowing their Web site to become more and more outdated, or watching the Web site budget balloon out of proportion as maintenance requirements absorb increasing amounts of time and energy.

With proper planning and foresight, Notes can help prevent this dilemma by facilitating a "distributed Webmaster" model. Your Web site maintenance can be shouldered by a group rather than a single Webmaster. Instead of the company's information being bottlenecked by a single Webmaster, the Domino server allows those who generate the information to automatically publish the information on the Web. As soon as new information or data is generated by the various parts of your company, it is quickly and automatically made available to the users, no matter what client or browser they are using.

Development

For most, the development stage of a Web site never quite comes to an end. In addition to routine maintenance of the site, Webmasters find themselves periodically needing to redecorate or overhaul their site to meet new requirements or provide a fresh updated image. Developing your site in Notes can save you from having to manually move files around in your site whenever you reorganize. This section goes through the basic (and some not-so-basic) aspects of developing your Web site. Toward the end of this chapter, the section "Advanced HTML Functions" deals with how to implement some HTML functions that are difficult or currently unsupported in Notes and Domino.

Creating Your Home Page

Every Web site needs a home page to serve as its "front door" for visitors to acquaint themselves with the site and decide what parts of it they will want to explore. Your home page should probably include some sort of table of contents or menu element, as well as some identity items that let the user know what kind of organization this is, and what resources are available in this Web site.

When your home page is requested, your home database opens automatically and launches the items you've designated to serve as the home page. Your home page can be the About page of your home database, or a navigator you've created.

The first step in creating a home page is establishing your *home database.* If you have more than one database to be published on the Web, the home database will be the database that contains your home page. Remember, this will be the first thing seen by visitors to your Web site. If your Web site will only use a single Notes database, then of course it will be your home database.

Next, you need to create either an About page or a navigator to serve as a home page for your Web site. About pages and navigators can both contain links and hotspots, but navigators have an advantage: they allow you to use image maps that graphically depict the content in your Web site and let users click on the areas they wish to explore further. For detailed instructions on creating navigators, see Chapter 19, "Using Navigators, Agents, and Simple Actions."

In the following step-by-step instructions, we'll assume that you've created a home database named home.nsf and that you've created a navigator that will serve as your Web site's home page.

1. After creating a database named home.nsf, open its properties and click on the Launch tab, shown in Figure 24.2. Set the On Database Open option to Open Designated Navigator. Then, in the Navigator option, specify the Navigator you've created. By doing this, you are specifying which item Notes will launch as your home page. You could set the About Page instead, but let's assume you chose to specify the Navigator.

FIGURE 24.2.

Configuring the database properties.

> **NOTE**
>
> One quick note: In the Launch options list, you'll probably notice these two options: Launch 1st attachment in About database and Launch 1st doclink in About database. Ignore them—they are not supported by Domino.

2. In your Public Address Book's Home URL setting, specify home.nsf as the database to be automatically launched when your Web site is visited. To do this, you must have Domino already installed on your Notes server. Open your Public Address Book's server record. Find the section titled "HTTP Server." In this section you'll see the Home URL setting, as shown in Figure 24.3. This setting basically tells Domino, "When you see this URL, it means go and open this particular database." In this case, you want home.nsf to be opened, so in the Home URL field, type `/home.nsf?OpenDatabase`. What you're saying is, "When Domino receives a request for the URL www.yourhomepage.com, it will open the home.nsf database."

FIGURE 24.3.

Configuring the Public Address Book's Home URL setting.

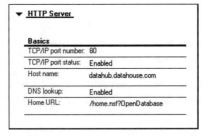

Let's look at what we've done so far: You've created a home database named home.nsf and a navigator that will serve as your home page. You've told Notes to respond to a browser request by automatically opening your home database (step 2) and automatically opening the navigator you specified as your home page (step 1).

Therefore, when a user clicks on the URL of your Web site, Domino takes the URL and appends the command to open the home.nsf database. Notes opens the home.nsf database, which in turn automatically launches your navigator. Domino sends the result to the user, who is delighted (hopefully) to see your home page!

Creating Links

Most Webmasters will agree that one of their biggest headaches is managing the many links scattered throughout their Web site. Anytime a file or folder is updated, renamed, removed, or relocated, dozens of links in the Web site may be left pointing to items that are no longer there.

Someone then has the unpleasant task of finding and repairing all these invalid or "broken" links in the Web pages. This is one area where the power of Notes and Domino really becomes apparent.

Domino recognizes the same link hotspots used by Notes. This means that you can use all of the Notes link types (Document, View, and Database links) to connect the documents in your `home.nsf` database and any others you decide to use in your Web site. When Notes creates a link to a document, it gives that document a unique identifier. Because of this Domino will always recognize all your links, even if you move things around in the database. This means Webmasters can say good-bye to hours and hours of mending broken links.

Making links between documents, views, or databases within Notes is very simple. Here's a quick example.

1. Let's say you wanted to link from your home.nsf database to another database named other.nsf. In your Workspace, select the database you want to link to. Select Edit | Copy As Link. A submenu will appear with three choices; choose the Database Link option. If you wanted to link to a document, you would follow the same steps, but open or select a document and choose the Document Link option instead.

2. Now let's create a hotspot for the link. This could be a graphic or a portion of text. Open a document and make sure that it is in edit mode. Now highlight a line of text. Then select Create | Hotspot | Link Hotspot.

But what if you need to link to something outside your Notes database, such as another Web site? Let's say you want to link to an associate's Web site on your home page. Here are the steps to follow:

1. Open the navigator (the one you created to be your home page) in the design view. Decide what the user will click on to activate the link. This could be a graphic or a portion of text. Select this item, and then select Create | Hotspot | Action Hotspot.

2. Go to the formula editing panel and add the @URLOpen function, as shown in Figure 24.4. Type in the URL of the Web site you wish to link to. Now you have a hotspot on your home page that, when clicked, will take the user to the Web site you specified.

FIGURE 24.4.

Creating links to other Web sites.

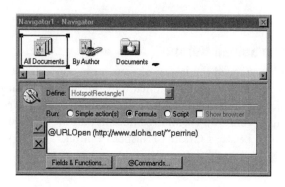

24

MAXIMIZING
YOUR DOMINO
WEB SITE

Forms

As with most Web sites, you'll probably need to incorporate a form to gather feedback from users who visit your Web site. Domino supports input forms that allow users to enter information via their Web browser and then save this information to a Notes database. This means your input forms can take advantage of Notes application development resources such as input validation formulas and computed fields. Your form can also run CGI scripts to provide customized responses to users who submit information.

For additional information on forms, see Chapters 12, "Developing Forms," and Chapter 14, "Making Your Application Look Good and Work Well."

Adding HTML to Your Forms

You can also add HTML functionality to these forms. If you chose to add HTML to your forms, keep in mind some of the differences in formatting capabilities between Notes and HTML. HTML doesn't support tabs, indents, spaces, justification, or "no wrap" alignments. HTML supports a limited number of font sizes, and until recently did not allow you to specify a type font.

So if you have a document that relies on tabs, justification, and so on, it's best to let Notes handle it. This includes any tables, columns, or indented outlines you want to add. The most common reason for adding HTML to a form is to add a hyperlink to a non-Notes URL. Try to avoid integrating large portions of HTML text that require precise spacing and formatting. If you're in the unenviable position of having to transpose a group of existing HTML files to Notes, see the section "Porting an Existing Web Site to Notes." The main point here is to be aware of the limitations of both Notes and HTML, and to use the best tool in each situation.

> **TIP**
>
> Netscape 3.0 and Microsoft Internet Explorer 3.0 both support the `<font face="">` tag, which allows you to specify one or more fonts for the browser to choose from. The browser will use the first font it finds on its local system.

Creating a Submit Button

Once you've designed the layout of your form, you may want to add a customized Submit button to the form. Domino automatically puts a Submit button at the bottom of each form as it is converted to HTML. In many cases this button is adequate, but sometimes you may want to create your own customized Submit button. To do this, place your cursor where the button should be select Create | Hotspot | Button. Then type in the name or label for your button.

> **NOTE**
>
> Don't try to create multiple Submit buttons; Domino will only recognize the first button. Also, adding button formulas won't work either because Domino thinks every button is a Submit button.

Creating a Customized Response

Whenever a user clicks the Submit Button on an input form, Domino lets the user know their input has been received by sending a default response of "Form processed." This is fairly bland compared to what could be done, so here's how to create your own customized response. The Notes Documentation database recommends adding a computed $$Return field to your form and including HTML code as part of the formula for the field. You could also use a $$Return field to run a custom CGI (Common Gateway Interface) program immediately after the user submits the form and Notes creates the document. For instance, a CGI program could use the Notes API to further process the input data. The user would see a display of the CGI script's output on his or her browser screen.

Here's a simple example of what the CGI-related code would look like:

```
[http://your.URL.here/cgi-bin/CGIprogram.exe?" +
FieldValue1 + "&&&" + FieldValue2 + "&&&]
```

Notes enables you to run CGI scripts by simply including the URL of the CGI executable along with its necessary arguments inside brackets. Arguments can come from different sources, including your form's field values. Sometimes you can simplify things by using a LotusScript agent rather than a $$Return field to process the user's input. This would particularly apply in cases where the forms could be batch processed without the requirement for extensive return messages.

The Notes Documentation database has a couple of excellent examples, which are included here in a somewhat condensed form:

> Here's how to create a personalized thank-you message for users who submit forms. The following $$Return formula returns a thank-you message and appends the user's name:
>
> ```
> who:= @If(@Left(From; " ") = ""; From; @Left(From; "
> "));
> @Return("<h2>Thank you, " + UsersName + "</h2><br><h4>
> <a href=/register.nsf/Main+View?OpenView>Main
> View</a>");
> ```
>
> You can also suggest a URL for the user to visit, based on field values in the submitted form. The following $$Return formula returns a response based on the region the user

selects. For example, if the user selects Europe, a message saying "Visit our site in Italy" is sent with a link to the Web site in Italy.

```
@If(Region="Asia"; stdAnswer + "<h2>Visit our site in
<a href=\"http://www.japan.lotus.com\">Japan</a></h2>"
+ stdFooter;
Region="Europe"; stdAnswer + "<h2>Visit our site in
<a href=\"http://www.lotus.com\it_ciao/it_ciao.htm\">
Italy</a></h2>"+ stdFooter; stdAnswer + stdFooter);
```

For more information on CGI, see NCSA's CGI documentation Web site at `http://hoohoo.ncsa.uiuc.edu/cgi/`.

Fields

Because fields play an important role in gathering and maintaining data in your Web site, it is important to be familiar with the types of fields you can use on the Web. Table 24.1, which comes from the Lotus Notes Documentation database, shows which field types and properties do not apply to the Web or are not supported.

Table 24.1. Understanding fields on Web forms.

Notes Design Feature	*Supported for the Web?*
Field Types	
Keyword fields	Supported, except for the keyword entry helper option. You can control the number of visible rows by adding HTML code to the Help field in the Field Properties dialog box.
Name fields	Supported, except for the following options: Use Address dialog for choices, Use View dialog for choices, Use Access Control List for choices, User access to databases is based on the authenticated name.
Computed-when-	Supported. Avoid values based on time computations, such composed fieldsas @Now and @UniqueID, that may be updated a second time during a Web transaction. To simulate an @UniqueID formula, use @DocUniqueID and compute an extra value, such as an incremental integer.
Notes/FX fields	Not applicable.
Field Formulas	
Default value formulas	Supported. Because document selection isn't applicable to the Web, default value formulas cannot reference a selected document in the view.

Notes Design Feature	Supported for the Web?
	Field Properties
Compute after validation	Not supported.
Field help	Not supported. Use the Help field input box to add HTML code to fields.
Field-level encryption	Not applicable.
Give this field default focus	Not supported.
Signed fields	Not applicable.

Creating a Navigator

Chapter 19 does a great job of describing the ins and outs of navigators. It might be a good idea to familiarize yourself with that chapter before proceeding. In this chapter we'll cover the Web-specific issues surrounding the use of navigators.

Creating a navigator is fairly simple: Create a bitmap image that will serve as your background image map. This image map should include all of the visual elements in a single image. In other words, all buttons and menu items should be contained within this single graphic. In the Create menu choose Graphic Background. This creates your image map. Now you can specify hotspots on this image as well as where the hotspots will take you when they are clicked.

Here are some guidelines for creating a navigator for your Web site. Try to make your image map as compact as possible while retaining legibility and clarity. Often an image map on a Web site will include the company logo surrounded by icons that represent the various parts of the site. For more information on designing graphics for your Web site, see the section titled "Including Graphics." From a user interface standpoint, the clearest method of representing a menu choice is embodied in these three basic principles:

■ If you want users to click on it, make it look like something that should be clicked. One common fault of image maps is that, while they look great, they don't give the user any clues about where to click. Experience with computers and home electronics has taught most users to look for raised buttons or items surrounded by boxes. On the Web, a good combination is to provide an icon with descriptive text placed immediately below or beside it, or sometimes around it.

■ Provide a graphical icon that represents each section of the Web site choice. Giving the icon some kind of 3D "pressable" look is always a good idea, but not absolutely necessary. Once the section is entered, it's a good idea to have that icon persist throughout that section as part of each Web page's header. This goes a long way toward helping your users stay oriented as to their location in the site.

■ In addition to the icon, have a bold title and a short plain text description of what the user will get if he or she clicks this icon. Web users prefer to get information about the choices before they make the choice. Descriptions can be witty and should be written to pique the reader's interest. You should make sure your description provides an accurate view of the section or item it represents. Remember, many Internet users are paying for dial-up Internet access time; help them navigate quickly to the desired items. Don't make them waste time going down through unnecessary layers in order to figure out what things are.

Incidentally, there is a fourth principle: feedback. Currently it does not apply to image maps in Notes navigators. Most buttons in computer programs immediately give the user some kind of feedback when pressed. The button may visibly depress, make a noise, or display a message. This lets the user know that the computer has acknowledged the request and will begin processing it. Most Web sites, because of limitations in HTML, have had to violate this because there was no way to make a button respond to user input. But now it's possible to implement feedback in your Web site using Java applets. In order to implement a Java applet, you'll have to place it in an HTML page. This would more or less preclude the use of a navigator. For a more detailed discussion, see the section titled "Advanced HTML Functions."

Including Graphics

There are two graphical file formats used on the Web: GIF and JPEG. Fortunately there is no shortage of very good graphic design software available that can help you develop very impressive graphics for your Web page. Some of these tools include Adobe Photoshop, CorelDRAW, GifConstruction, and many more.

The challenge of developing graphics for your Web page is how to have the coolest, sharpest, most interesting graphics with the fastest download time. It is quite a difficult balancing act. In traditional graphic design or painter software it is common for decent-looking images to be several megabytes in size. On the Web, these graphics would take hours to download to most of the typical connections.

However, a new art form has developed within the realm of computer graphics—the art of creating better and better Web graphics with increasingly smaller file sizes. It is definitely an art and somewhat of a science.

When developing from a Notes environment, remember that publishing on the Web means your audience will probably not have the same kind of connection speed that you may enjoy inside your organization. Graphics that load quickly in Notes at your office might be frustratingly slow to someone with a modem connection elsewhere. Do *not* assume that users will just wait for your graphics to download. No matter how cool or hip or hot your graphics are, if they take too long, most of your intended audience will be clicking their way through someone else's site long before your page can even get to their screens.

The principle to follow is this: try to get something visible and significant downloaded as quickly as possible to the user. Then give them choices about downloading larger files, advising them about the size of the file they are about to download. If a 140KB file comes down the pike, it should be because the user knowingly chose to request that file.

File Sizes

What is the optimal file size for Web graphics? The smaller the better, but a general rule is to keep most graphics under 20 KB. For a large masthead or similar graphic, you should shoot for something between 40 and 60KB. Try to keep the total combined graphic file sizes on any given Web page under 100 KB. A page with 100 KB worth of graphics will load in a few seconds over a 28.8Kbps modem connection, but will be exponentially slower if your users are running slower connections. This could conceivably mean one 80KB graphic and two 10KB graphics, but you'd better have a really good reason for the 80KB graphic! Sometimes, due to the content on the page, its impossible to stick with these guidelines. However, it's good to impose some discipline on the size and quality of your Web graphics.

Here are some tips on reducing the sizes of your graphics files while maintaining good image quality:

- Always resize the image to as small as possible, making critical judgments about how big a graphic really needs to be. It is surprising how many sites have huge (and quite meaningless) header graphics loading on their home page.

- Make sure all graphics are cropped as closely as possible. Again, this is a simple principle: shave as many kilobytes off the file size as you possibly can. Every unneeded byte just takes more download time.

- Reduce the colors as much as possible. Try to do this while the graphic is in the design stages, not after you've finished. Often an artist creates a beautiful graphic, but when it's reduced to 256 colors it looks horrible. There's just too much color in it, so reducing the colors ruins it. Many image manipulation software packages (such as Photoshop) have a "layers" feature that can help with this. Let's say you have a background layer and foreground layer. Because things appear to fade as they get farther and farther away, you can eliminate as much color as possible from the background. Your background could be reduced from several thousand colors, down to four to six shades of light blue, and still look good. It will make a difference when you go to reduce the colors for GIF conversion, or if you decide to use JPEG.

  Here's another related idea: When you're choosing icons or objects for a Web page, look for objects that have as few radically different colors as possible. A graphic of a bronze sculpture is excellent, because all the shades are variations of a few colors. A picture of a jungle dominated by greens would be excellent, too. But a green jungle on the edge of a white beach with blue waves and hula dancers wearing red, pink, purple, and yellow leis—well, that would be a challenge.

- Reduce the bit depth. A 4-bit graphic can be a lot smaller than an 8-bit (256-color) graphic. This can work if you've been careful to minimize your colors in the creation of the graphic. Usually graphic software packages will allow you to reduce the bit depth in conjunction with either saving the file or converting it from an RGB file to an indexed color file.

- Try turning your image into a grayscale image and then using a "colorizing" tool (found in most image-editing software). This essentially puts your graphic on a grayscale setting but allows you to give the grayscale image color, brightness, and saturation settings. This makes for realistic, sharp icons that have only a few colors (because they're all different shades of the same color). The fewer the colors, the smaller your file size.

- Test to see whether a JPEG or a GIF version of the graphic will be smaller.

- Experiment with the four JPEG quality settings to see which one best serves the graphic you're making. When you save a JPEG file, the program will ask you which quality level you want to use to save the file. There are four options from Lowest to Highest. The Highest option will retain amazing image quality, but with very little reduction in file size. The Lowest option reduces files to a fraction of their original size, but often the result is too blurry or mangled to be of much use.

- Try saving an image as a GIF and then reopen it and save it as a JPEG. You may get better results than if you had simply saved it as a single file type.

NOTE

On the Web you have a choice between using either the JPEG or the GIF file formats for graphics. There are some differences between the two, and understanding these differences can pay off in terms of better quality images with smaller file sizes.

There are a number of white papers and documentation on the Internet describing these file formats in detail. But for the Webmaster or Web artist, here are the basic need-to-know facts:

JPEGs compress files using an "averaging" technique. The color values of four pixels may be averaged to create a single pixel whose color value represents the original four pixels. As you can imagine this could work very well in many instances, but very poorly in others. JPEG can often compress images to lower file sizes than GIFs can, while retaining good quality. JPEG does best with photographs or complex patterns. Graphics containing text or high contrasts between solid panels of color will usually be unsatisfactory. Small text will often appear mangled, and straight lines will sometimes appear wobbly. If you have a brightly colored icon that sits against a black background, you'll see little squiggly blobs of color in the black area around the icon. These blobs, referred to as *cosine artifacts*, mark the areas where the JPEG compression technique didn't do the pixels justice.

The GIF file, on the other hand, uses a "lossless" compression technique. Because GIF files do not "average" pixels the same way JPEGs do, GIF files can often do a better job of handling graphics containing text, straight lines, or high-contrast areas. With complex patterns or photographs, GIFs do fine, but they probably won't be able to get the file size down as low as a JPEG file would.

Handling Different Users and Clients

Domino's security features combined with its unique capability to dynamically transform Notes constructs (documents, links, views, navigators, and even formulas) into HTML files means that you can dynamically customize your Web pages to individual users and clients. You can also exercise complete control over who gets to see what in your Web site. Notes provides a number of formulas you can use to customize the contents of your Web pages. You can tailor your Web site's content to different users based on the user's identity, the time a document was created, or the type of client being used to view the content. There are a number of helpful resources on this topic at the Domino home page at `http://domino.lotus.com`.

Different Clients

There are several scenarios where you might want to customize your content for different users or clients. One scenario might be where you want Notes users to see one thing while Web users see something different. Adding HTML code to Notes documents or forms can greatly enhance their appearance and usefulness to Web users, but can clutter up the page for Notes users. One solution is to have two separate databases. Another is to have Notes provide a different subform depending on the user's client type.

Here is a simple example using the `@UserRoles` function. Basically, you insert a computed subform that looks at the client type and decides which subform to use. If the user's client is a Web client, then the appropriate subform is used. If it is a Notes client, the other subform will be used. Follow these steps:

1. Open a form in edit mode.
2. Select Create | Insert Subform. The Insert Subform dialog will appear.
3. Be sure to check the checkbox labeled Insert subform based on formula. This tells Notes to look at your formula in order to determine which subform to use.
4. Decide on the names for your subforms. Name them so that one is obviously the Web subform and the other the Notes subform.
5. Add your subform formula. Basically it looks to see if `$$WebClient` is a member of `@UserRoles`. It should look something like this:

```
IsWebClient:=@IsMember("$$WebClient";@UserRoles);
@If(IsWebClient;"Name of your Web subform";"Name of your Notes subform")
```

6. Now you can create your two subforms to be used.

24

MAXIMIZING
YOUR DOMINO
WEB SITE

Controlling Access

In another scenario, you could use Notes' dynamic tailoring capabilities to control access to different pages or sections of your site. Domino makes this simple for you. Perhaps you want anonymous visitors to be able to access a general interest section of the Web site, while giving employees access to confidential information.

Controlling access to various levels or sections of your Web site involves the following three procedures:

1. You need to decide who should have access to what. You should define all the potential users for your Web site, including anonymous users, and determine what kind of access you will allow each of them to have.

2. Once these decisions have been made, you can then set up each user's record in the Public Address Book. You also decide if you will allow users who have no record in the Public Address Book (in other words, anonymous users) to see documents in your Notes databases. If you decide to prohibit anonymous users, Notes will always ask for a login and password before allowing access.

3. Set up access control lists in all of the Notes databases associated with your Web site. *Access control lists* allow you to assign a level of access to each user (including anonymous) or "Default" users.

Domino's flexible security measures let you control your documents based on a variety of factors. Typically, you'll want to follow a principle of granting "author" or "creator" rights to the creator of a document, and lesser rights to readers or users of documents. Therefore, if you create a document in a Notes database, you have the right to edit or delete it. If you are not the document's creator, you shouldn't have these rights. This would also apply if you had a discussion database incorporated into your Web site. This topic is discussed further in the next few paragraphs.

Colors, Text, and Fonts

This section, which deals with different users and clients, is probably as good a place as any to mention the importance of planning your colors, text, and fonts for use on a vast array of client operating systems and display hardware. In the development stages, you should try to look at your pages on as many different types of computers and clients as possible. What looks good on your computer might look terrible on someone else's. There are some items you should consider especially when preparing Notes documents for publication on the Web.

For most intranet and Web publication scenarios, it would be wise to stick with the standard VGA 640×480 resolution and no more than 256 colors for your initial development. If people with laptop or portable computers will be using your pages, you should test them using a laptop to make sure text is legible and colors aren't clashing. Make sure your color combinations have the right amount of contrast so people will not have difficulty seeing the various elements and text of your pages.

Fonts should be easy to read. It has become fashionable to use tiny fonts in a number of Web sites. Tiny fonts are fine for unimportant items or for disclaimers, and so on, but if you want people to read through a segment of text, it needs to be legible to people with all types of vision. Also, beware of italic fonts: In many Web browsers, they are very difficult to read.

> **TIP**
>
> Netscape and Microsoft Internet Explorer now allow you to specify different fonts in your HTML code, using the `<font face="fontname1, fontname2,">` tag. The browser checks the user's system to see which font is available and uses it to set the text on the browser screen. This can give you a measure of control over the appearance of the text in your pages, but remember, some users might have their preferences set to override a page's fonts with their own fonts.

Discussion Databases

The Domino discussion database is an interactive Web application with extremely powerful potential for collaboration over the Internet. Both Web and Notes users can participate in threaded discussions, add items to a database, search each other's comments, and view database contents in the way that is most intuitive for themselves.

A couple of recommendations are in order for discussion databases. First, your discussion database should be a separate database. Also, it should require all users to be registered in the Public Address Book. By default, Domino prohibits all access to the discussion databases without a name and password.

Using the customization features discussed in previous sections, you can give the creator of a document the right to edit or delete that document, while prohibiting non-creators from doing the same. This can be accomplished through the `@UserRoles` function described previously in the section titled "Different Clients." As Figure 24.5 illustrates, authors will see one subform that contains an Edit or Delete button, while non-authors would see a different subform without these two buttons, as shown in Figure 24.6. Users cannot delete or modify documents they did not author.

24

MAXIMIZING
YOUR DOMINO
WEB SITE

FIGURE 24.5.

The Domino discussion database as it would be seen by a person who has author's rights.

FIGURE 24.6.

What a non-author sees in a Domino discussion database. (Notice the absence of the Edit and Delete buttons.)

On the Domino home page (`http://domino.lotus.com`), you can find a paper titled "Getting Started Creating Web Applications with Domino!", which has a number of helpful explanations about the various features of the Domino discussion databases.

Advanced HTML Functions

Earlier in this chapter I mentioned an important design principle: concentrate non-Notes compatible items in the top layers of the site and use Domino to publish information-intensive material in the lower layers of the site. In this section, I discuss exactly what that means and how to do it.

Figure 24.7 shows a suggested directory structure that places HTML files in the top level and has Domino publishing in the lower levels. What this boils down to is placing an HTML "front end" onto your Web pages published from Notes databases.

FIGURE 24.7.

A suggested directory structure for implementing HTML functionality that is either unsupported or unfeasible with Domino/Notes. (Note the contents of the HTML directory to the right.)

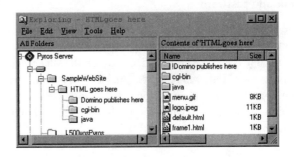

In case you're wondering why the HTML should go on the top level and the Domino documents on the lower levels, there are several good reasons.

First of all, most of the jazzy HTML special effects and functionality you would probably want to utilize are designed for the front page of a site. Many Web sites start off with glamorous front pages featuring frames, scrolling signs, animations, and interactive rollover menus. These items are intended to arouse curiosity and prompt the visitor to explore the site further. People also seem to have a tendency to show off a little, using the latest HTML tricks to prove that theirs is a leading-edge Web site from a leading-edge company. The front page items don't contain deep content; they simply point to it and promise that it will be empowering, helpful, and exciting. The information-intensive documents that Domino manages so well typically aren't found on this top level. The user locates the desired documents by drilling down a level or two in the Web site or by performing a search that does essentially the same thing.

Second, if you decide to use frames in your site, you can establish your frame design in the top level of your site, and it will persist throughout the entire site structure.

Last, and perhaps most important, this two-tiered hierarchy greatly simplifies the site's management and maintenance, because all the HTML functions are kept to a minimum, concentrated in one place, and managed by one HTML composer. On the other hand, the Domino documents can be managed by secretaries, managers, and salespersons in different departments, companies, and continents. Imagine the Webmaster's nightmare of having to keep track of advanced HTML functions scattered throughout dozens of documents being continuously updated by many different users!

Currently there are a number of HTML functions that Domino and Notes do not recognize or handle. However, these unsupported functions can still be implemented in your Web site by using this split-level design. Place all your non-Domino pages in the top level and then let their menus point down to the lower levels where the more information-intensive material (published by Domino) resides.

On the CD-ROM included with this book are several sample HTML files that incorporate frames and are designed for use with the split-level folder structure described here. I'll discuss frames in further detail in the next few paragraphs. The top-level folders (where these HTML files would reside) contain your fancy HTML, frames, Java, and so on. The sublevel folders contain the files published by Domino. This design is consistent and compatible with most Web sites; typically, the higher level pages in a Web site are mostly menus and glitz anyway, with the lower levels providing more detailed information.

Doing the Split-Level Design

Here are some instructions on setting up a split-level folder structure in your Web site:

■ Develop a top-level folder and decide what content should reside in it. The top-level pages of a Web site are typically menus and "identity" material that make a first impression on visitors and orient them with the site's contents. These are great places to use fancy animations, JavaScript, Java applets, server push tricks, and other whizbang effects. You should plan to put your raw HTML, JavaScript, and frames files here.

■ Decide the names of the HTML files in this page. Remember, when the user jumps back to the top-level page from somewhere down in the site, Domino will have to have that filename handy in order to provide the page for the user. You'll have to give these files "static" filenames.

Static Filenames

Why static filenames? The Domino server by default does not use or need preexisting HTML files in the same sense that other Web servers do. Instead, Domino waits for a request and then in response to a request for a specific file, dynamically generates that file from its database and sends it to the requesting client. The dynamically generated Web page that arrives on the user's computer will have a name that might look something like 100234mh24311.htm. If you access that same Web page five minutes later it will have a totally different name.

Now, let's suppose you wanted three files that were filled with custom HTML, JavaScript, or other advanced Web functions. Let's assume that they are named default.htm, contents.htm, and Webcam.htm. If you want these filenames to stay the same, you'll need to assign them as static filenames in Domino. This lets the Domino server know that it does not need to generate a Web page when these files are requested; instead, Domino will simply point to the preexisting HTML page that was requested. Use the `@URLOpen` formula to specify the name of a nondynamic HTML page. For example, if you want to return to your home page you could use `@URLOpen("http://www.yourWebsite.com")`.

Using Frames

For detailed instructions on using the frames feature as implemented by Netscape and Microsoft's Internet Explorer, take a look at "An Introduction to Frames" on Netscape's site (`http://home.netscape.com/assist/net_sites/frames.html`). This section has some tips for getting frames to work with your Domino-served Web pages.

The frames feature allows the window of your Web browser to be divided into several subsections instead of being viewed as a single framed area. Figure 24.8 shows a typical view of frames as they would appear in a Web browser. Here's how it works: The default.html file (the first file accessed in a Web site) sets the boundaries of the framed areas and also says which files will appear inside each of the framed areas. The frame file doesn't contain any graphical or textual content (well, it actually can, but don't worry about that now). Instead it simply describes the boundaries for two or more separate HTML files to be displayed on the browser screen at once.

For example, let's suppose your home page, named default.html, is a frame file. The inside of the file looks like this:

```
<HTML>
<HEAD>
<TITLE>Welcome to Frames</TITLE>
</HEAD>
<FRAMESET ROWS=70,*>
<NOFRAMES>
Items placed between these tags will be displayed to
users whose browsers do not support frames.
</NOFRAMES>
<FRAME SRC="banner.htm" NAME="Banner">
<FRAME SRC="home.htm" NAME="Area">
</FRAMESET>
</HTML>
```

FIGURE 24.8.

An example of frames in a browser, with recommendations of documents and elements best suited for each frame.

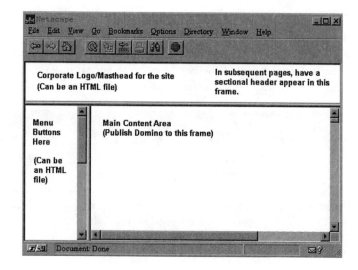

In the <FRAMESET ROWS> tag, the number 70 indicates that 70 pixels of this browser screen will belong to the first frame and the rest (the * next to the 70) will belong to the second frame.

Notice the <NOFRAMES> tag and its corresponding </NOFRAMES> tag below it. If your browser did not support frames, then it would simply display whatever was placed between these two tags. This is an important provision for those users who have older versions of Netscape or other nonframes-capable browsers. However, tags like this get really tricky when you're working with Domino. That's why I'm describing a safe way to proceed.

Targets

At the time I wrote this chapter, Domino still couldn't dynamically generate a frame file. However, you can still use frames quite handily with Domino by "targeting" Domino to appear in the desired frame. Let's suppose you have one small frame named "smallframe" that contains your menu buttons, and one larger frame named "largeframe" that displays the documents in your Web site. Place your frames file (usually the default.html file) in the top-level folder of your folder hierarchy. Include in the same folder the two or more subframe files to which it refers.

So far, so good. Now, here's where Domino comes in. It's all in the hyperlinks: when you're using frames, your hyperlinks must specify which Web page to display as well as which frame to display it in. This is done using the "target" tag.

Since you want the Domino documents to appear in the large frame, you add HTML code that specifies that when the Domino database is requested, it should appear in the frame titled "largeframe." Here's an example:

```
<A HREF="Domino Database URL" TARGET="largeframe">
Hyperlink to the Domino Database</A>
```

24

MAXIMIZING
YOUR DOMINO
WEB SITE

Reference your Domino documents or databases from your menu hyperlinks. These documents will in turn reference their subordinate documents not with HTML links, but with Notes links. By setting the target for the top-level documents, you are setting a precedent that will cause the lower-level documents published by Domino to appear in your frames. In this example, the Domino database appears in the frame called "largeframe."

CAUTION

Not everyone is enthusiastic about the use of frames. Many Web browsers, including older versions of Netscape, do not support frames. In Netscape versions prior to 3.0, frames appear on the screen but can be extremely difficult to navigate in. Users who attempt to navigate back to a previously viewed frame by pressing the Back button will find themselves tossed out of the entire site to the previous URL they visited! These bugs have been fixed in both Netscape 3.0 and Internet Explorer 3.0.

There are obvious advantages to using frames. If implemented correctly and viewed by 3.0 version browsers, frames can streamline and simplify navigation through a Web site.

For example, every Web page within a well-designed site will have a number of common elements that remain the same from page to page. Perhaps the company logo appears on every page, or maybe a set of menu buttons. Placing these items in a frame allows them to be downloaded only once, thus reducing download time.

Frames also give users immediate and convenient access to the menu buttons no matter where they go in the site. And they won't have to scroll up or down the page to reach the menu buttons.

If you are thinking about using frames, consider your target audience and what version of browser they are likely to be using. If you are fairly sure that your audience will be using the latest browsers, frames may be a good idea. But be sure to make provisions for browsers that do not support frames.

Java and CGI

Some developers have found it to be less complicated just to relegate all Java applets to a top-tier folder in the Web site, while publishing Domino pages at the lower levels in the site. This method was described previously in relation to using frames, but it applies here as well. The sample HTML files on the CD-ROM that comes with this book feature a frames-based layout that can be used to display a Java applet in one frame while simultaneously displaying a Domino database in another frame. A frame that contained a Java applet would be a simple HTML file that is not published by Domino. It has a static filename and resides in the server file system, as opposed to residing in a Notes database. You would simply include the applet code in the body of the HTML file.

Your Notes users should be able to view your Java applets using the Web Navigator. Notes has its own Java interpreter that copies applet code into memory and executes the applet.

A number of companies have developed "applet generators," which ask you how you want your applet to work and then generate the needed applet code for you. You can then copy and paste this code into your HTML file. Macromedia makes a very handy one called Applet Ace. It can be downloaded from their Web site at `http://www.macromedia.com`.

While there are many simple Java applets floating around on the Web, making sense of them and being able to use Java for your own Web site requires some study. The quintessential `comp.lang.java` FAQ is available from a number of Web sites. Here are a couple to try:

```
http://funrsc.fairfield.edu/program/java/javafaq.html
http://cuiwww.unige.ch/db-research/java/doc/javafaq/javafaq.html
```

You may also want to consult Sun's JavaSoft home page (`http://java.sun.com`) and the Gamelan site (`www.gamelan.com`), which contains a myriad of samples and explanations. JavaSoft recently designated Gamelan as the official directory for Java.

CGI can be implemented using the two-tiered approach described here; it can be implemented in Notes databases as well. To use CGI in an input form, you include a computed `$$Return` field with the appropriate HTML code to provide a return message to the user. See the section titled "Creating a Customized Response."

Porting an Existing Web Site to Notes

While entirely possible, this scenario is possibly one of the most difficult, especially if it requires converting hundreds of HTML files into Notes documents. One recommendation is to simply start managing all new information in Notes while retaining a hard-coded link to the old HTML files. Either the new pages published from Notes will make the old HTML files unnecessary, or the old HTML files will gradually become so outdated that no one will miss them anymore.

In the unfortunate cases where this live-and-let-live approach won't work, here are some ideas for facilitating the process of porting an existing site to Notes:

■ Cut and paste the text from all HTML files directly from Netscape (or your preferred browser) into the appropriate Notes forms. This saves you from going through every file and stripping out all the unusable HTML tags.

■ Use common forms for as many of the different Web pages as possible. In a single form you can set a navigator and whatever additional elements (for example, formulas and HTML tags) for all the Web pages (or as many as you want). Notes will follow this template for any pages it sends out on the Web.

■ If feasible, try to implement the two-tier folder structure described earlier. This will allow you to retain the top-level features of your existing Web site while leveraging the power of Notes in managing your Web site's content.

Summary

This chapter introduced the power and flexibility of Notes and Domino to help you meet the challenges of managing and distributing timely information across different platforms, protocols, and Web clients.

The power of Notes and Domino lies in their collective capabilities to streamline the Web site development and maintenance process, deploy interactive Web pages, and facilitate collaboration among user groups and developers alike.

Notes and Domino also have the flexibility to allow you to leverage their capabilities while taking advantage of non-Notes features such as frames, advanced HTML functions, and more.

This chapter also provided a number of recommended approaches for getting the maximum use out of Notes and Domino in your Web site. Properly integrating Notes and Domino into your Web development efforts will transform your Web site from a marginally useful "billboard in cyberspace" to an indispensable resource of timely information and collaboration.

Here are some Web sites that have been developed using Notes and Domino:

- Lotus Notes site: `http://www.lotus.com`
- Lotus Domino site: `http://domino.lotus.com`
- CareNet-Hawaii: `http://www.carenet-hawaii.com`
- Datahouse Inc.: http://www.datahouse.com

Developing Web Applications with Domino.Action

by Thomas L. Fredell

IN THIS CHAPTER

Lotus took the world by storm when they introduced the Domino software for use with Lotus Notes servers. Domino combines the ability to dynamically render Notes documents and forms as HTML with a robust HTTP server. With Domino, a Notes server immediately becomes a functional Web server.

Domino provides a powerful tool for the development of a corporate Web site. However, it doesn't provide a Notes application framework as a foundation for Web site development. Lotus has supplemented Domino with a Notes application called Domino.Action that provides a robust, comprehensive framework for Web site development.

Domino.Action is a comprehensive corporate Web site development framework for use with Lotus Notes and the Domino server version 1.5. You can download Domino.Action from Lotus at `http://www.lotus.com`.

> **NOTE**
>
> Domino.Action was previously referred to as Net.Action. The figures of the Action applications in this chapter show the application as Net.Action. Lotus will update the name soon.

> **NOTE**
>
> At the time this book was written, Domino.Action was still in beta. This means that many of the screens represented in the figures might look slightly different in the final release.

Installing Domino.Action

The Domino.Action distribution is currently a single executable file slightly less than 2 MB in size. The file is a compressed executable that contains the following three files:

- LibAct.NTF, a Notes template containing design elements for a Web site generated using Domino.Action
- Readme.TXT, a file that contains information about Domino.Action and installation instructions
- SiteAct.NTF, a Notes template that will guide you through the creation of a Web site using Domino.Action

To install the Domino.Action framework, place the executable in your Notes data directory. Run the executable to expand its compressed contents. After doing so, you will have two new templates in your Data directory. Go to the Notes workspace and select File | Database | New. You'll notice two new database templates; Figure 25.1 shows the New Database dialog.

FIGURE 25.1.

Domino.Action templates.

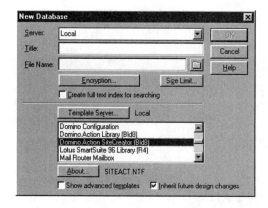

Create a database using the Domino.Action SiteCreator template and a database using the Domino.Action Library template. You can use any database name you wish; you'll need to enter the names when you configure Domino.Action. The SiteCreator database contains the interactive Notes application that's used to setup your Domino.Action Web site. It also contains an additional tool, the AppAssembler, that generates the Notes databases for your Web site. The Library database contains the design elements that will be used to create your Web site.

When you create a Web site using the Domino.Action tools, your Web site will be divided into *site areas*. Each site area provides a specific type of site information and is contained within a single Notes database.

Domino.Action Site Areas

The Domino.Action Web site framework contains the major areas that you would expect in a comprehensive corporate Web site. It provides all of the following site areas:

- Home Page
- About the Company
- Corporate Policies and Procedures
- Discussion
- Document Library
- Feedback
- Frequently Asked Questions
- Job Postings
- Products
- Registration
- Search
- White Paper

The following sections describe the various site areas and provide some examples of the look and feel of site pages as seen through a Web browser.

> **NOTE**
>
> Only some of the possible formatting combinations are listed. Various options are available for page layout, and the contents of each page may be specified using Notes rich-text formatting and embedded HTML codes.

Home Page Area

The Home Page area is the root of your Web site. It contains a list of the information available at a site and provides links to navigate to other site areas.

Figure 25.2 shows a simple home page for the fictitious ACME corporation, maker of fine widgets, as seen through the Microsoft Internet Explorer.

FIGURE 25.2.

ACME Corporation's Domino.Action home page.

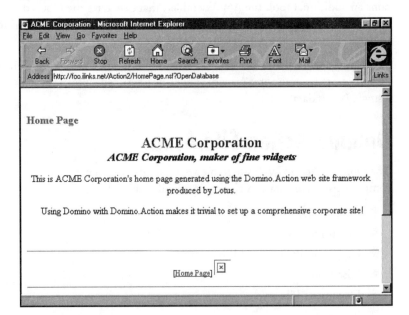

About the Company Area

The About the Company area contains general information about your company, employees, products, and services. Its purpose overlaps to some degree with the Home Page area.

Figure 25.3 shows the ACME Corporation's About the Company area as viewed through the Internet Explorer.

FIGURE 25.3.
ACME Corporation's About the Company home page.

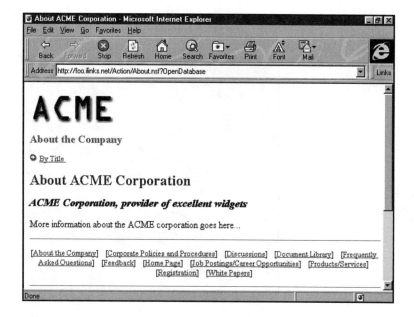

Corporate Policies and Procedures Area

You can use the Corporate Policies and Procedures area to disseminate information that is relevant to all company employees such as employee manuals. It's probably more useful for an intranet rather than a public Web site due to the sensitive nature of the information.

Figure 25.4 shows the ACME Corporation's Corporate Policies and Procedures area as viewed through the Internet Explorer.

Discussion Area

You can use the Discussion area to host discussion threads. Use of the Discussion area is very similar to the use of a standard Notes discussion database. You create a main discussion topic and people can respond to your topic or to subsequent responses.

Figure 25.5 shows the By Title view of the ACME Corporation's Discussion database.

Document Library Area

The Document Library area can be used to store any type of document. It performs a similar function to the White Paper area; you can determine your own rules for the distribution of documents between this area and the White Paper area.

Figure 25.6 shows the Document Library page as viewed by someone with access to modify the page. The top of the page has graphic buttons that can be used to change the contents of the page.

FIGURE 25.4.
*ACME's Policies and
Procedures area.*

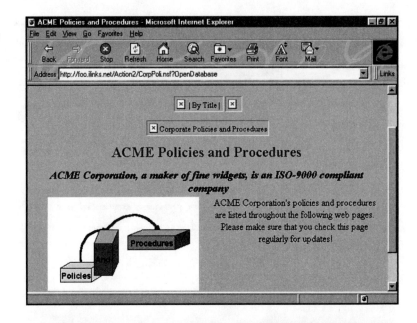

FIGURE 25.5.
*The ACME Discussion
topic's By Title view.*

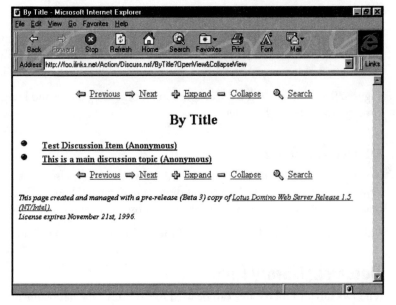

FIGURE 25.6.
*ACME's Document
Library page.*

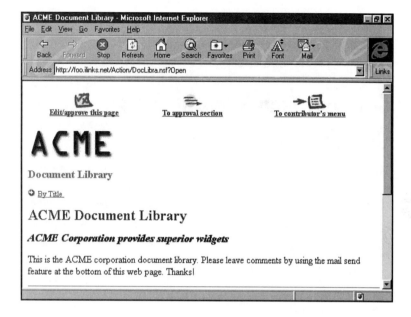

Feedback Area

You can use the Feedback area to provide a means by which site visitors can submit comments about your Web site.

Frequently Asked Questions Area

The Frequently Asked Questions area can be used to provide answers to the questions that are most commonly asked of customer service, marketing, technical support, or other relevant corporate departments.

Job Postings/Career Opportunities Area

The Job Postings/Career Opportunities area provides a forum for you to publish information about current employment opportunities within your corporation.

Products/Services Area

The Products/Services Area can be used to provide product descriptions, pricing information, and other associated product materials such as demos or product updates.

Registration Area

The Registration Area provides the ability to allow visitors to register with your site. Information captured during registration can be used to control access to the areas within your site.

White Paper Area

The White Paper area can be used to store "white papers" that describe the details of your companies' products, business approach, and so on.

Creating Web Site Databases Using Domino.Action

To create a Web site using Domino.Action, you must first create the SiteCreator and Library databases in accordance with the aforementioned installation instructions. Once you have created the databases, you'll use the SiteCreator database to follow these steps:

1. Configure your site.

2. Design your site.

3. Install AppAssembler.

4. Generate your site.

5. Finish your site.

To begin, open the SiteCreator database from the Notes workspace. When you open it, you'll see the dialog shown in Figure 25.7.

FIGURE 25.7.

The SiteCreator database opening dialog.

After you dismiss the dialog, you'll see the three-pane SiteCreator interface. Figure 25.8 shows the SiteCreator interface and SiteCreator overview document. The bottom-left section of the screen contains the steps that you will follow to define and create your Web site.

To begin creating your Domino.Action Web site, select Step 1: Configure Your Site from the Quick Start: SiteCreator list.

FIGURE 25.8.

The SiteCreator three-pane interface.

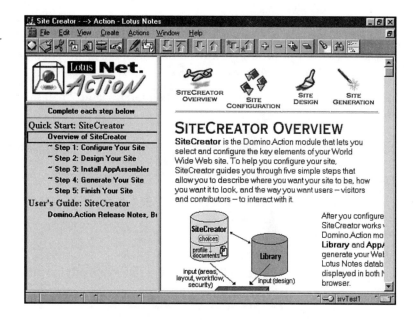

Step 1: Configure Your Site

After you select Step 1, the right half of the screen will change to a description of the configuration process and an associated Configure Your Site button, as shown in Figure 25.9.

FIGURE 25.9.

Step 1: Configure Your Site.

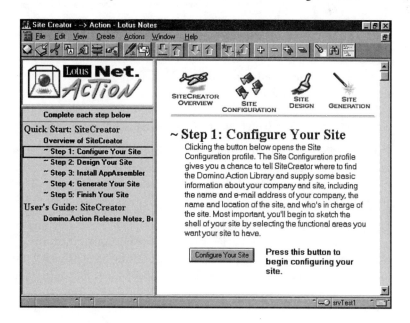

25

DOMINO.ACTION

To start the configuration process, click the Configure Your Site button. You'll notice that one or more Notes agents will run; this is very typical for interaction with the SiteCreator database. Literally all actions are performed with button clicks, and many actions involve agents that the SiteCreator uses to cause the regeneration of databases and so on.

The screen will change to a Site Configuration form. Figure 25.10 shows the top portion of the form.

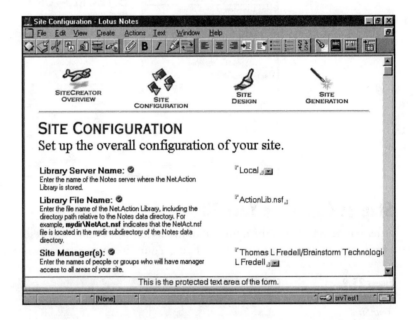

You will use the Site Configuration form to set various parameters for your Web site. Each of the editable fields in the form has a description underneath the label next to the field. Most of the fields are straightforward; however, it is important to make sure that the library filename corresponds to the database filename that you created during the installation process.

Various actions are available from the Site Configuration form. At the top of the form, you'll notice a row of graphics with captions (such as SiteCreator Overview). Each graphic above the captions is a hotspot; if you click on one, various actions will occur. The same row of graphic action buttons will appear within each configuration document in the Site Creator database.

Further down in the Site Configuration form, you'll notice several buttons. (If you're in Notes, you can use the scroll bar to navigate to the lower portion of the form.) The first button from the top, labeled Attach Image, is next to the Company Image(s): label. If you click on the button, you'll be brought to a New Site Image document, as shown in Figure 25.11.

FIGURE 25.11.

Site Design: New Site Image document.

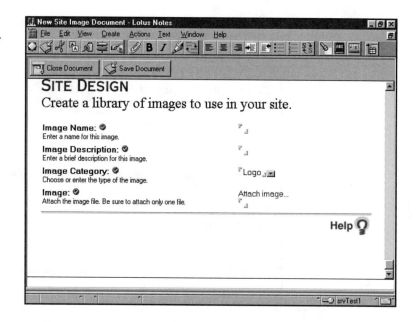

You can add as many graphics as you require. After you finish the configuration process and generate your Web site using the AppAssembler, you'll be able to use the graphics to customize the generic templates that it creates.

Toward the bottom of the Site Configuration form, there's a small button underneath the Site Areas label. The button and text immediately precede a set of check boxes that you'll use to specify the site areas that you want to create. By default, the only selected area is the Home Page. You can use the small button to see a description of each site area. If you click it, the display will change as shown in Figure 25.12.

The last section of the form contains custom setup settings. The custom setup settings can be used to specify the Site Directory and Image Directory for the Notes databases generated using Domino.Action. You can maintain multiple Domino.Action Web sites by specifying different site directories.

When you've finished filling the requisite configuration fields, you can click the Continue> graphic button at the bottom of the Site Configuration form. The configuration document will be saved and you will be returned to the SiteCreator menu. You'll notice that the menu has changed; a small thumbs-up icon should appear next to the Step 1 menu item. The selected menu option will also change automatically to Step 2.

25

DOMINO.ACTION

FIGURE 25.12.
Site descriptions.

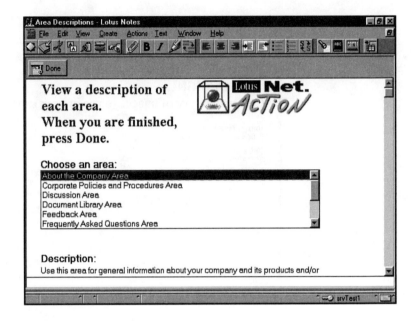

Step 2: Design Your Site

When you've finished Step 1, you'll be returned to the SiteCreator action menu. Step 2 will be highlighted, as shown in Figure 25.13.

FIGURE 25.13.
Step 2: Design Your Site.

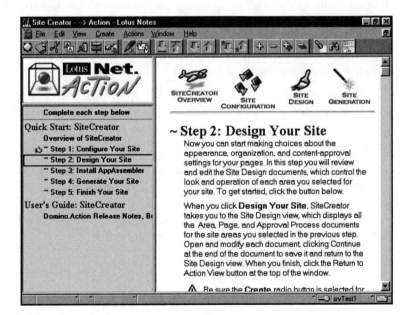

To begin the design process, click the Design Your Site button, which is located near the bottom of the Step 2 form. The screen will change briefly to a list of document titles, and you'll notice that a Notes agent will run. After a few moments, the screen will change to the Site Configuration menu, as shown in Figure 25.14.

FIGURE 25.14.

The Site Configuration menu.

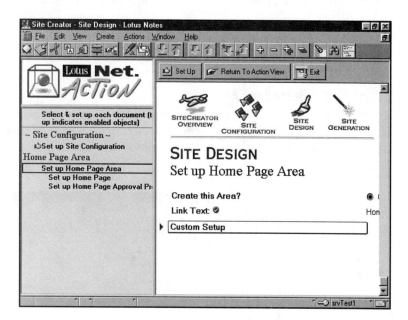

The Site Configuration menu has a three-pane style that is similar to the Site Action interface. The first document in the Site Configuration menu, titled Set Up Site Configuration, should be adjacent to a thumbs-up icon. The Site Configuration document contains the information that you specified in Step 1.

When you enter the Site Configuration menu, the selected menu entry is positioned to the first unapproved document. Approved documents are distinguished from unapproved documents by a thumbs-up icon that appears to the left of the document description. During Step 1, I specified that I wanted to generate only the Home Page area. Consequently, the only area that is visible in the Configuration menu is Home Page. If I had selected additional site areas, they too would appear in the Configuration menu.

Setting Up Site Areas

Each Site Area has at least the following setup documents:

Set up Area

Set up Page

Set up Approval Process

For example, the Home Page Area might have the documents Set up Home Page Area, Set up Home Page, and Set up Home Page Approval Process.

Some site areas have additional setup documents. For example, the About the Company area has an additional Set Up About the Company Main Page document.

When you set up an area, you will configure settings in each document sequentially. To begin the setup process, click the Set Up button in the action bar above the document displayed on the right side of the screen. The Set Up button places the document in edit mode.

Setting Up the Home Page Area

The first step in the Home Page area setup process is to refine the settings in the Set up Home Page Area document. To do so, select the document in the menu and click the Set Up button in the document action bar. Figure 25.15 shows the document after the Set Up button has been clicked.

FIGURE 25.15.

The Set up Home Page Area document.

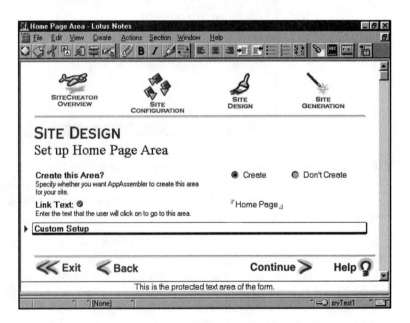

You need to specify the following three options in the Home Page Area setup document:

- Create this Area?: Indicates whether or not the Home Page area should be created when the AppAssembler tool is executed.

- Link Text: A list of links to other site areas appears near the bottom of each site area page created using Domino.Action. The Link Text setting allows you to specify the descriptive text for links to the Home Page area.

■ Custom Setup: There's only one setting in Custom Setup—the Area Database File Name. Change this setting if you need to use a different database for the Home Page area.

After you've modified the options as necessary, you can proceed to the next step in the setup process by clicking the Continue> graphic button at the bottom of the setup form. You will return to the Site Configuration menu, and the next item in the menu, Set Up Home Page, will be highlighted.

Setting Up the Home Page Document

Click the Set Up action button to edit the home page. Figure 25.16 shows the Home Page Set Up form in edit mode.

FIGURE 25.16.

The Home Page Set Up form.

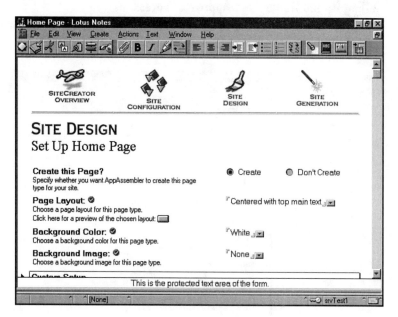

The options within the Home Page Set Up form are basically used to control the visual layout of the page. The following Home Page options may be set:

■ Create this Page? indicates whether or not the Home Page document should be created when the AppAssembler tool is executed.

■ The page layout field controls the visual layout of the Home Page. Several page layout options are available; you can preview a page layout by clicking the preview button underneath the Page Layout label.

■ The background color controls the background color of the Web page rendered by Domino.

- The background image will appear tiled across the back of the home page when it is viewed as through a Web browser.

- The Custom Setup section contains custom options for the home page; for the Home Page document, there's only one option, Display Copyright, which determines the copyright message that is displayed.

When you've finished changing the options for the Home Page document, click on the Continue> button at the bottom of the form to proceed to the next step in the setup process. You will return to the Site Configuration menu, and the next item in the menu, Set Up Home Page Approval Process, will be highlighted. Click the Set Up action button to edit the Home Page Approval Process document.

Setting Up the Home Page Approval Process

After you click the Set Up action button on the Home Page Approval Process document, you'll see the document shown in Figure 25.17.

FIGURE 25.17.

The Set Up Home Page Approval Process document.

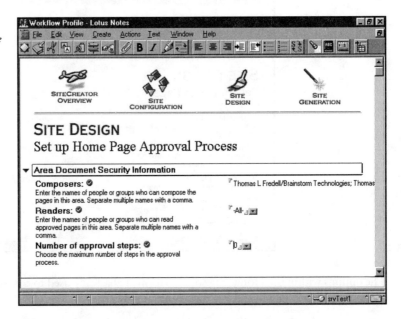

The options within the Home Page Approval Process Set Up form are used to control the access for people to create and read pages within the area, and to determine the number of approval steps and required approvals. The following approval process options may be set:

- The Composers field is used to specify the people and/or groups that are allowed to compose pages in the Home Page area.

- The Readers field specifies the people and/or groups that should be allowed to read approved pages in the Home Page area.

■ The Number of approval steps is used to determine the number of people that need to review and approve documents in the Home Page area before they are published to the Web site. By default, the number of approval steps is zero. If you increase the number of approval steps, the form will change to reveal additional setup fields.

Figure 25.18 shows the Home Page Approval Process Set Up form after the number of approval steps has been changed from zero to two.

FIGURE 25.18.

Approval setup form with two approval steps.

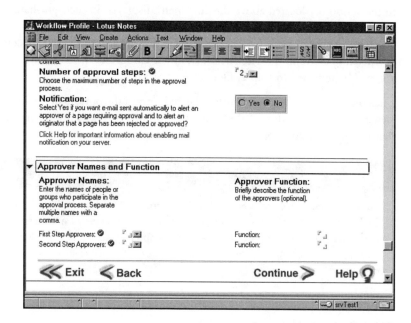

When the number of approval steps field is greater than zero, the following fields are displayed for modification:

■ The First Step Approvers field allows you to specify users or groups that should be first in the approval process. Multiple Approvers fields will appear depending on the number of approval steps you specify.

■ Each approvers field has an associated function field. The function field can be used to briefly describe the role of the approvers.

To finish the setup process for the Home Page area, click the Continue> button at the bottom of the form. You will return to the Site Configuration menu.

Site Area Setup Summary

The example used to illustrate Site Area setup was the Home Page area. It's representative of the amount of effort necessary to set up any of the site areas, but it should be noted that each of the site areas may have additional documents, and each document may have additional custom setup fields. Lotus provides documentation within the form that explains the purpose of additional setup fields.

Adding an Area to Your Site

If you would like to add an area to your site, you can click the Return to Action View button in the action bar located above the document displayed in the right-hand side of the screen. When you return to the Site Action view, select Step 1: Configure Your Site. Click on the Configure Your Site button on the right-hand side of the screen; then select the additional areas by checking boxes in the Site Areas list. Click Continue> when you're finished, after which you will be returned to Step 2: Design Your Site.

Click on the Design Your Site button located toward the bottom of the Design Your Site overview text. You will return to the Configuration menu. You'll notice that the additional areas that you selected now appear in the Configuration menu.

> **NOTE**
>
> Sometimes the list of site areas in the Configuration Menu won't be properly refreshed. Selecting View | Refresh won't help. I've found that you may be able to force it to refresh if you leave the Site Creator database, then re-open it and click the Design Your Site button in Step 2. Lotus probably will have this fixed either in the first release or a point release thereafter.

Step 3: Install AppAssembler

The AppAssembler is a program that uses the Notes HiTest API to read the configuration settings from the SiteCreator database and create the Notes databases for your site using components contained within the Domino.Action Library database.

Step 3 of the SiteCreator process involves the installation of the AppAssembler; Figure 25.19 shows the Step 3 instructions.

To install the AppAssembler, click the Install AppAssembler button. After doing so, you'll see the AppAssembler menu, shown in Figure 25.20.

Click the Install button in the right-hand side of the screen. You'll be prompted for the destination directory for the AppAssembler program. I suggest that you specify the directory containing the notes.exe file; if you do so, you don't need to worry about having the Notes executable directory specified in your system PATH variable.

After installing the AppAssembler, click the Return to Action View button. You will return to the SiteCreator menu.

FIGURE 25.19.

Step 3: Install AppAssembler.

FIGURE 25.20.

AppAssembler 32-bit.

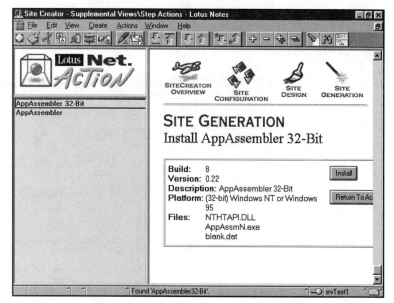

25

DOMINO.ACTION

Step 4: Generate Your Site

When you've finished Step 3, you'll be returned to the SiteCreator action menu. Step 4 will be highlighted, as shown in Figure 25.21.

FIGURE 25.21.

*Step 4: Generate
Your Site.*

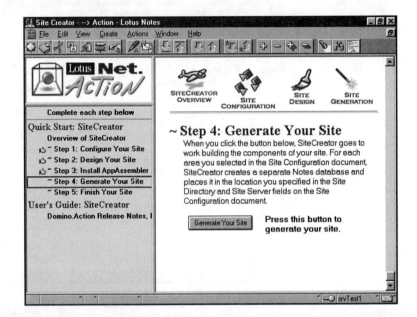

To begin the site generation process, click the Generate Your Site button located in the right-hand portion of the screen.

FIGURE 25.22.

*The Run AppAssembler
document.*

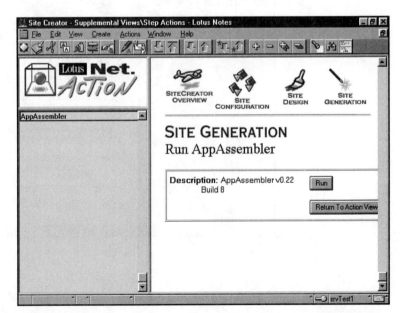

A Notes agent will run to refresh your site configuration documents. When the agent is finished, the Run AppAssembler document, shown in Figure 25.22, will appear.

Click the Run button to execute the AppAssembler program. The AppAssembler will display a progress dialog box indicating the percent of the site that has been generated, as shown in Figure 25.23.

FIGURE 25.23.

The AppAssembler Progress bar.

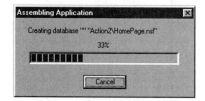

When the AppAssembler has finished running, you'll notice that a new subdirectory has been created in your Notes data directory; the default name of the subdirectory is Action, but it will be different for you if you changed that option during Step 1 of the setup process.

The new subdirectory will contain several new databases. Each database contains a different site area. The name of the database, as presented in the Notes Open Database dialog box, describes the site area.

After the AppAssembler has finished, click the Return to Action View button to return to the SiteCreator menu.

Step 5: Finish Your Site

Step 5 is the final step involved in generating the basic Site Area application databases. For each site area, you will still need to customize the contents of the database to include your company's information. Instructions on customizing the auto-generated site databases is provided later in this chapter.

Click the Finish Your Site button in the Step 5 overview document, shown in Figure 25.24.

A Notes agent will run to refresh various documents and modify certain database Access Control Lists (ACLs) to set the appropriate security levels. When the agent is complete, a dialog box will be displayed indicating that your Web site has been successfully generated.

FIGURE 25.24.

Step 5: Finish Your Site.

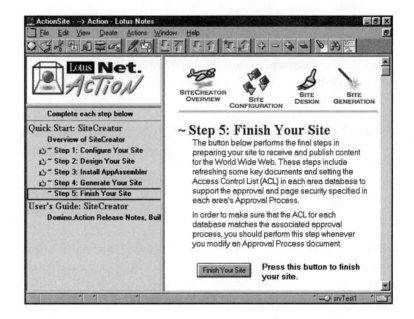

Customizing Domino.Action Site Databases

After you complete the steps listed in the section "Creating Web Site Databases Using Domino.Action," you should have a subdirectory containing a number of auto-generated site area databases. Each of the databases has the layout, color, and approval process attributes that you specified during setup. However, none of the databases contain your corporate information; you need to modify them to add the necessary information.

Add the databases to your Notes workspace by selecting File | Database | Open. You will need to open each database, one after another, and modify the contents.

For example, if you open a freshly generated Feedback Area database, you'll see a document that looks like the one shown in Figure 25.25.

You'll notice that the document contains default headings such as "Enter the Area Main Page title here." To modify the headings, place the document in edit mode by clicking the graphic button labeled Edit/approve this page. Figure 25.26 shows the document in edit mode.

FIGURE 25.25.

The default Feedback Area document.

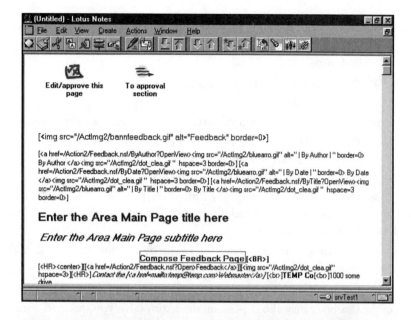

FIGURE 25.26.

The Feedback Area document in edit mode.

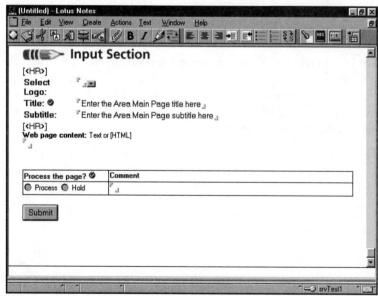

You can modify the following fields in the Feedback Area document:

- The Logo field specifies the name of the graphic image that appears at the top of the Web page.
- The Title field specifies the text title that appears near the top of the Web page underneath the logo.
- The Subtitle field specifies the text that appears in a smaller font underneath the title.
- The Web Page Content field is a rich-text field that can contains graphics and other Notes formatting information such as fonts and tables. It can also contain embedded HTML codes enclosed in square brackets.
- There are two choices for the Process the page? field: Select Process if you want Domino to go ahead and display your changes on the Web, or Hold if you want to delay the update.
- You can use the Comment field to specify a comment that will not appear on the Web page. It may be used to provide information about the current status of the page.

The editable fields may vary, depending on the document that you're editing. The formatting of the text body may also depend on the settings that you specified during configuration.

Summary

The Domino.Action Web site framework provides an excellent, comprehensive framework that you can use to easily create a corporate Web site. It has support for key business functions including recording of user registration information and dissemination of essential information such as policies and procedures, and it provides an interactive framework that you can use to support discussions and feedback.

The development of the Domino.Action framework is currently in progress; when it is released, it will no doubt include even more functionality and ease-of-use improvements.

Connecting Notes to the Internet with InterNotes

by Rob Wunderlich

IN THIS CHAPTER

Two years ago, a book like this wouldn't have mentioned the Internet—and Lotus wouldn't have had a product like Domino, either.

It seems as though the Internet has become an overnight sensation and that the rush of software companies to embrace the Web has become a literal stampede. At trade shows such as COMDEX, new features have taken a backseat to "Internet awareness." Word processors are expected to support output to HTML formats, graphics packages are expected to support Web standards, everything is supposed to be able to open files from Internet sites, and so on.

One of the basic truths about "Internet-ready" software is that whatever that means today, that phrase will mean something different tomorrow. Even browsers, for example, have been a moving target. In a scant six months, browsers that supported Java went from unheard-of to commonplace.

As discussed in Chapter 3, "How Does Lotus Notes Work with the Internet?," the Internet revolution at first seemed to challenge Notes. Lotus moved quickly to integrate Notes and the Internet—to have them work together rather than competing with each other. That was when the InterNotes Family of products came into being.

With the release of Notes 4.5 and Domino, the challenge has not only been met, but Notes itself has raised the bar. The Notes 4.5 client has capabilities that other browsers don't have, and Domino server has capabilities that other HTTP servers don't have.

What This Chapter Doesn't Cover

A quick comment here about Internet connectivity issues. For the purpose of this chapter, the assumption is that your organization is already talking to the Internet in some way, shape, or fashion.

We'll spend a little time at the end of this chapter on general connectivity, but, although these may be fascinating topics, it is beyond the scope of this chapter to cover the pros and cons of SLIP versus PPP, T1 versus ISDN hookups, and so on.

The following topics are not covered in this chapter:

- In order for any of the Notes Internet products to operate, you need to have a live Internet connection. I'll make the assumption that your organization is hooked up and you've managed to deliver the Internet to the Domino server. If you haven't done this already, this chapter will be interesting theory, but little else. Domino and InterNotes features will not work on a dial-up connection.

- Also, even though the InterNotes Web Publisher product needs a Web HTTP server to be in place, this chapter will not discuss setting up the HTTP server itself. I'll assume that if you need one, you've got one. Web Publisher will work happily with a Domino server, so use it!

Connecting Notes to the Internet with InterNotes

CHAPTER 26

631

26

CONNECTING
NOTES TO THE
INTERNET

■ Additionally, there are serious considerations regarding security whenever a computer in your organization connects to the outside world. While we'll take a quick look at the Notes security aspects (in the discussion about skeleton servers), the greater security issues, such as firewalls, are also beyond the scope of this chapter. That's not to say they should be ignored. You might want to refer to a book such as *The Internet Unleashed 1996* (Sams Publishing, 1996).

A Word About Lotus's Position

The Internet aspect of Notes is probably the area most likely to undergo changes over the life of Notes 4 and, as such, some of the details you're about to explore are subject to change. There were some major changes between Notes 4.0, 4.1, and 4.5, and no doubt, such changes will continue. Lotus is continually refining its Internet strategy; as more features are developed, they will be rolled into interim versions of Notes 4.

A perfect example of this changing scene is the InterNotes Web Publisher. Originally a $7,500 separate product, it became a $3,500 separate product, then a "free" separate product (assuming the correct combination of support contract and/or product version), and then a free, included-in-the-package product. Now, with the release of Notes R4.5 with the Domino HTTP server capabilities, Web Publisher is all but obsolete. All this in the span of less than a year!

TIP

One of the best ways to keep abreast of Lotus's evolving Internet strategy and product line is to check in frequently with the Lotus Web site (http://www.lotus.com/). This site is a great source of information about Lotus's Internet product line. It features downloadable beta versions of products as well as numerous links to Lotus Business Partners and others who've employed the InterNotes products and can offer assistance.

Additionally, many of the individual product lines have either their own site or area of the main site. Domino information, for example, can be found at http://domino.lotus.com and Web Publisher information can be found at http://www.lotus.com/inotes/.

From an outsider's perspective, Lotus appears to be succeeding in the attempt to integrate Notes with the Internet. Its position is going to continue to grow and change (much like the products themselves), and as the Internet itself evolves, Lotus Notes will evolve right along with it.

The InterNotes Family

As discussed in Chapter 3, Notes databases can now be tightly integrated with the Internet, and there are several Lotus products that can assist.

The various Internet products surrounding Lotus Notes (originally called the InterNotes products, although that moniker seems to be going away) can be split into two general categories: Publishing (providing information to the Web) and Retrieving (getting information that's on the Web).

There are four individual members in the InterNotes family. The first two involve publishing:

- Domino Server is the new name for the Notes 4.5 server with built-in HTTP services.
- InterNotes Web Publisher is a Notes server application that provides Web site content from Notes databases and also captures information from Web visitors into Notes databases.

The next two involve retrieving:

- Web Navigator is a Notes client feature that enables direct Internet access from within Notes itself. InterNotes Web (or Web Retriever) is the server task that facilitates the Navigator.
- InterNotes News is another Notes server application that captures Usenet news articles and enables Notes users to participate in newsgroups from Notes databases.

Although each of these products has merit in its own right, the product garnering the most critical acclaim is the Domino server. We'll look at each of the individual products, but Domino comes first and will get most of our attention.

The two products that "publish" are Domino and Web Publisher.

Both WebPub and Domino take Notes databases and make them available to Web users, although they accomplish this in totally different ways.

Let's take a look at each individually; then we'll take a closer look at some of the similar things they can do to make Notes databases available to the Web.

Domino Close Up

Of all the Notes-related products that interact with the Internet, none has generated the amount of interest that Domino has. Countless articles have appeared in the press recently; a veritable furor has risen in the Business Partner community. And for good reason: Domino has totally redefined what a Notes server is capable of doing and, therefore, what a Notes database can do.

In this chapter, when I use the term "Domino," I'm referring to HTTP services, not to the Domino server itself. My use of the term "Domino" should be taken to mean the Web-enabling capability that Notes servers didn't previously have.

Connecting Notes to the Internet with InterNotes

CHAPTER 26

633

26

CONNECTING
NOTES TO THE
INTERNET

What Domino Does

Domino was the code name for the beta versions of a Notes server add-in task called HTTP Services. The Domino name seems to have stuck, and the Notes 4.5 server is officially known as "Domino."

Domino brings HTTP services to Notes. That is, it allows a Notes server to function as a Web server, offering Notes databases and/or HTML documents to users hitting the Notes server via a Web browser, not just via a Notes client. Put more simply, it allows users to access your Notes server with a Web browser such as Netscape Navigator, Mosaic, or Microsoft's Internet Explorer.

The ramifications of this capability are astronomical. Suddenly, the Notes databases in your company can form the basis for an Internet or intranet Web site without any HTML coding at all. Just let Domino do it.

Domino takes a Notes database and translates it—on-the-fly—to HTML for a browser. Unlike Web Publisher, discussed later in this chapter, there is no HTML file created—there's no database "cloning." Therefore, the interaction is instantaneous—the moment a document has been saved (whether in Notes or from the Web), Domino makes it available to the next visitor.

Domino handles all the linking chores. Anything you throw into a Notes database is instantaneously made available to a Web visitor. Add a new document—it's in the view and Domino makes it available to a browser. Domino also translates DocLinks, ViewLinks, and so on, with ease.

Domino also takes graphics that have been pasted into Notes forms and documents and seamlessly translates them into GIF or JPEG formats and serves them as well.

In addition, Domino can serve HTML documents, so a Web site with hard-coded HTML documents can coexist with a Notes-driven database via Domino.

Features and Functions

Although the Domino HTTP function works strictly as a server task, it's a tremendously powerful one. Domino can do the following:

- Translate Notes databases into HTML on-the-fly for Web browsers
- Translate images to GIF or JPEG formats
- Serve HTML documents to Web browsers
- Extend Notes access control to Web visitors, allowing an author to edit a document from a Web browser, for example
- Support file attachments, Notes tables, Hide When attributes, and other typical Notes application design elements

- Offer SSL (Secure Sockets Layer) transactions for high-security Web commerce
- Offer Notes application development capabilities to Web applications, allowing functions not available in any other fashion (such as collapsible views)
- Leverage Notes' graphical capabilities, such as navigators and backgrounds, and extend them with view layouts
- Allow Web clients to search Notes databases

Domino does all this automatically; there's no need for any special talents to make it work. (In other words, you don't need anything more than Notes application development experience to build a Domino application—you don't need to be an HTML expert.)

Benefits of Domino

I've been working with Domino since its inception and have come to appreciate Domino's special characteristics. It falls halfway between a "regular" Notes setup and a hard-coded HTML Web site.

It brings all Notes capabilities (security, replication, navigation, and so on) to the Web world, yet it offers the simplicity of access from a Web browser. It obviates the need for learning HTML or, for that matter, Java or CGI or Perl scripting, yet it supports all of them. It offers Webmasters the ability to manage a dynamic site with ease; Domino takes care of maintaining all the links and references. It also supports file attachments, Notes tables, and even full-text indexes (enabling Web visitors to search a database). The combination of all these makes Domino a potent Web development tool that surpasses the capabilities offered by many other products.

Here's a case in point. The Southeast Michigan Computer Organization (SEMCO), a computer user group, asked me for assistance in setting up their Web site. They were being hosted by a local university and wanted some sort of online discussion. The university Webmaster hemmed and hawed, and, to his delight, I offered to host it on my firm's Domino site. I set up the discussion in (quite literally) 10 minutes, and it's happily chugging away today (check it out at `http://web1.leadgroup.com:8080/semco.nsf/`). A simple Notes discussion database, "published" to the Web by Domino, did something the university's Web site was unable to do—provide true interactivity.

Requirements

The requirements for a Domino server are much the same as for other Notes servers, only slightly more robust. Lotus recommends 64 MB of memory and a 1 GB hard drive—however, the more the merrier.

Platform is a consideration. Currently, Domino is available only for Windows NT, a couple of the UNIX flavors, and OS/2. At the time I wrote this chapter, the OS/2 version was one revision behind (in other words, the OS/2 version was Domino 1.0, while the other platforms were at 1.5).

Connecting Notes to the Internet with InterNotes

CHAPTER 26

635

26

CONNECTING
NOTES TO THE
INTERNET

In particular, note that NetWare is *not* a potential platform for Domino.

Check the Domino Web site for the latest platform information and availability.

As hinted at earlier, connectivity is a big issue. The only protocol that browsers speak is TCP/IP, so your machine must support TCP/IP. If it's going to be used as an Internet server, it needs Internet connectivity as well.

Some sections later in this chapter discuss hardware requirements and connectivity issues.

Getting Domino Working

Although the Domino HTTP service is merely an additional Notes server task, there are several important steps to consider in getting it to work. You've got the ingredients; all you need is the recipe.

The Recipe for Domino

There are a series of steps that you'll need to perform to get Domino installed, configured, and running properly. Here's the quick outline (detailed explanations follow):

1. If necessary, procure and install Domino (if you're using Notes 4.5, Domino is already installed).
2. Configure the Public Address Book (again, if you're using Notes 4.5, this has already been done).
3. Update the Server document and person documents as appropriate.
4. Start the HTTP server task.
5. Test connectivity.
6. Modify database ACLs if appropriate (see "Domino and the Database ACL" for a discussion of Domino security).
7. Check to make sure that the paths are correct for your icons.

These steps will ensure that Domino gets installed and configured properly and that your Web visitors will be able to use the databases with ease. Details for each of the recipe items are discussed in the following sections.

TIP

If you have problems with any of these steps, check out the Domino Discussion database on the Domino Web site at `http://domino.lotus.com/`.

Most likely you'll find that whatever the problem you're experiencing, someone has already asked a question about it. Although it's not an official "support site," the discussion is monitored by the Domino team at Lotus.

Installing Domino

If you're already working with the Notes Domino 4.5 server, the Domino HTTP service is already installed. Skip the next few paragraphs and go directly to the section titled "Configuring Domino."

> **TIP**
>
> Even if you are using Notes 4.5, you should check the Domino Web site anyway.
>
> The Lotus Domino Team is committed to providing fresh versions of Domino frequently; you may find an incremental build or a beta of a newer version.

If you're using Notes 3.x or a 4.x version below 4.5, you need to actually install the product. It's a three step process: you need to download the product, install it, and then modify your PAB (Public Address Book).

If you don't already have Domino, it can be downloaded for free from the Domino Web site at `http://domino.lotus.com/`.

The download file is DOMINO.EXE, a single, executable zip file that needs to be expanded in an installation directory. Typing `DOMINO` extracts the files and automatically runs Setup.

As shown in Figure 26.1, you simply need to follow the prompts. You'll be asked to confirm where your Notes program directory and data directory are. Setup will create the additional directories and copy the appropriate files.

FIGURE 26.1.

The installation screen.

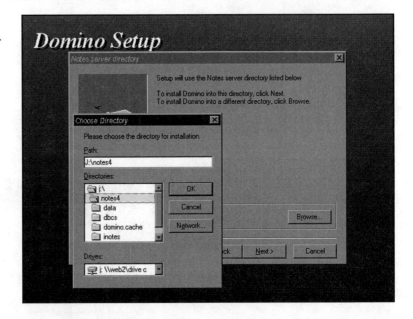

26

CONNECTING
NOTES TO THE
INTERNET

> **TIP**
>
> Because running DOMINO.EXE results in the actual "install kit" for Domino, you should copy the file to an appropriate temporary directory rather than running it from something like your Notes program directory. Create a directory called DomKit (or something similar) and run it there; this then becomes your Domino install directory, and subsequent versions can be run in a similar fashion.

The Setup program copies the appropriate files and creates a series of subdirectories off your Notes Data directory, as shown in Figure 26.2.

FIGURE 26.2.

Subdirectories created by the Domino Install program.

The Domino subdirectory serves as Domino's *home base*. CGI-Bin is used for any CGI programs that you may want Domino to run, HTML becomes the root directory for any HTTP services, and Icons is where Domino stores (and looks for) standard GIF files.

The Setup program automatically installs NHTTP.EXE (the actual Domino "executable") into the Notes program directory, along with a couple DLL files, the DOMGUIDE.NSF and SSLADMIN.NSF files (Domino documentation and SSL security documentation, respectively) into your data directory, and a bunch of GIF files into the Icons directory.

> **TIP**
>
> In addition to the other valuable information available, the Domino Web site also has "server tuning" information in the form of a database with performance tuning tips.
>
> This information will help you optimize the server you're using for Domino. Check it out at `http://domino.lotus.com/domsite/dominotuning.nsf/`.

Configuring Domino

If you're using Notes 4.5, or if you've just performed the installation outlined in the preceding section, you need to configure Domino to run properly.

There are two forms in your PAB that need modification. If you're running Notes 4.5 (and have refreshed the design of your 4.1x PAB), these two modifications have already been made. If you're not, you need to open the PAB template in design mode and add the `HTTPServerFormSubForm` to your server form. You also need to add the `HTTPPassword` field to the person form; you can find that field on a form in the HTTPCFG.NTF template that is installed with Domino.

Either way, once the forms have been modified and the design of your PAB refreshed, you need to edit the Domino server's Server document (as shown in Figure 26.3) and edit any person documents for people who you want to allow Web access to.

FIGURE 26.3.

The HTTP section of the Server document.

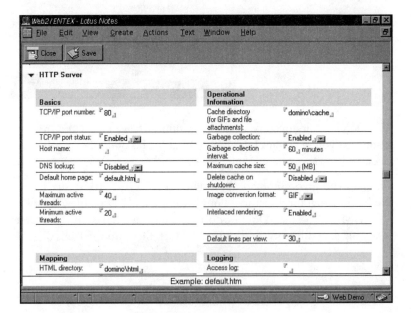

Opening Your Server's Server Document in Edit Mode

Even if you're willing to accept all the default settings, you need to edit the document in order for the settings to take effect.

> **TIP**
>
> There are certain settings that you'll probably want to change, such as the Home URL field. This field controls what Domino will offer when a Web client hits your site. It defaults to /?Open, which is the equivalent of File | Database | Open. You might want to point this at a particular database or HTML document that will serve as your site's home page.
>
> The Domino Documentation explains the various fields at great length; be sure to consult it.

In addition to the Server document, you'll also need to modify one or more person documents. As noted previously, the person document now has a new field called HTTPPassword. This field is necessary if you want to extend Notes access control to Web visitors (see the section "Domino Security"). When the administrator or a user types a password into the field, as soon as the document is saved the field automatically encrypts the password, rendering it illegible to casual viewers.

> **CAUTION**
>
> The HTTPPassword field is tremendously important if you want to authenticate Web visitors. If the field is empty, a Web visitor will not be able to access a restricted database, even if he or she is listed as manager on the database's ACL.
>
> See the section "Domino Security" for more information.

Start the HTTP Server Task

You can start the Domino HTTP services by simply typing Load HTTP at the server console. As shown in Figure 26.4, a message will appear on the server console stating that Domino has been successfully loaded (if you get an error message, double-check the error against the trouble-shooting section in the documentation).

As with most Notes server tasks, you can add HTTP to the Server Tasks= line in the server's NOTES.INI file. This will automatically load Domino each time the server starts.

Figure 26.4.

The Notes server screen showing the Domino message.

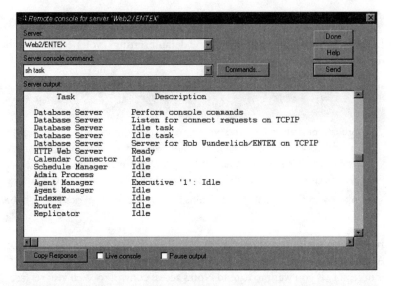

CAUTION

Notes administrators instinctively reboot the Notes server (often referred to as "bouncing the server") whenever changes are made to the Server document. Note that anytime you make changes to the HTTP section of the Server document, you only need to bounce Domino, not the entire server. Simply type Tell HTTP Quit at the console prompt to unload Domino, and once it has successfully been unloaded, type Load HTTP and Domino will restart with the new settings.

Testing Connectivity

Using your Web browser, access your Notes server from your workstation. The syntax should be something similar to this:

http://servername/?open

Depending on your TCP/IP setup, you might need to access the server using the IP address, rather than the server name.

By default, Domino will open with the equivalent of File | Database | Open a listing of the databases available. You can configure what Domino opens first by editing the Home URL field in the HTTP section of the Server document. For example, you could create a Home Page database and have Domino open its About document by entering Homepage.nsf/$About. This prevents people from snooping through the files on your server.

Connecting Notes to the Internet with InterNotes

CHAPTER 26

641

26

CONNECTING
NOTES TO THE
INTERNET

TIP

In the 4.5 PAB server document, there's now a new field that disables "browsing." But you can do it for Domino on a Notes 4.0 or 4.1 installation, too.

There's an undocumented way to prevent people from "browsing" through the databases on your 4.0 or 4.1 server. This is from the Domino Web discussion database:

"Add a keyword field in the Server document (or in the HTTPSettings subform) with the following characteristics:

```
Name: http_databaseBrowsing
Type: Keyword
Keywords:
Enabled ¦ 1
Disabled ¦ 0
```

"`Enabled` works as it does today. `Disabled` will not allow the `/?Open` command."

Be aware that this is an undocumented, unsupported function—but it works!

Again, with the Domino 4.5 server, this is built into the server document.

Modifying Database ACLs

Keep in mind that Domino, by definition, allows Web access to your Notes databases. Web users, until authenticated, fall into the default access of a database. That is, Web visitors will be able to access your databases at whatever access you've assigned to default.

You should go through all your databases and make sure that you don't have the default set too high (Editor, for example, on certain databases). Refer to the section "Domino Security."

Double-Check Paths, WebPub, Incompatibilities, and More

One of the potential problems you may have out of the box is incorrect pathing. Often Domino either can't find the database or graphic file that you've designated, or it's missing altogether.

Double-check that a typical database opens correctly and that you have no "broken icon" symbols (for such things as twisties in a view, for example). Domino automatically drops the necessary icons in the DOMINO/ICONS directory off the DATA directory, but your Server document may need to be changed to reflect this.

Also, if you've used Web Publisher, be careful—some of the views you modified for WebPub might not display correctly under Domino. (The WebPub discussion template, for example, hard codes some HTML in the views that Domino cannot interpret correctly.)

If you find that some of your paths need to be modified, simply change the HTTP section of the Server document and bounce Domino.

> **TIP**
>
> Use Domino's ICONS subdirectory for corporate logos and other similar graphics.
>
> You can add HTML image references to such icons and have much more responsive Web applications, and you've got a central place to put all of them!
>
> A company logo can be added to a Notes form, for example, by adding an HTML image reference like this to the top of the form:
>
> `[<img src = /icons/complogo.gif>]`
>
> If you reuse a graphic with such a reference in multiple databases, the Web browser would cache that image, making the response time for your user dramatically quicker.

What Domino Doesn't Do

As noted at the beginning of this chapter, the Internet capabilities of Notes are undergoing huge changes as this book goes to print.

As such, this list might quickly be obsolete as the Lotus folks make Domino more functional. Lotus has publicly repeated that WebPub will eventually be made obsolete by Domino, so any interim build of Domino may add one of these "missing" features.

With that caveat, here are some of the things that Domino doesn't do right now:

■ Support layout regions. They are literally ignored.

■ Support LotusScript behind buttons, fields, and so on.

■ Support anything on a navigator other than what was initially added as the navigator background graphic (that is, text boxes, buttons, and so on). The multitude of navigators in Notes help, for example, are rendered useless.

■ Allow only certain views to be made available (as WebPub does).

■ Support HTML heading tags (H1, H2, and so on), although it does support font size.

■ "Publish" a Notes database as HTML files (that is, you can't use Domino to publish a Notes database into a series of HTML files that you can FTP to another Web site).

Domino Security

One of the biggest benefits of Domino is its capability to extend Notes' much-heralded security to a Web browser. This is no idle comment—a typical Web server can only restrict users based on a directory on the server. Domino extends database ACLs, author access, user roles, and a multitude of other things that typical Web servers can't offer.

Connecting Notes to the Internet with InterNotes

CHAPTER 26

643

26
CONNECTING
NOTES TO THE
INTERNET

There are two pieces to Domino security. The first is what you need to do to a database ACL to enable Web security, and the second is what you need to do to the Public Address Book to facilitate this.

An Overview of Domino Security

Domino is able to handle database ACL security from a Web user just as it does from a Notes client.

The difference, of course, is that a Notes client needs to have already authenticated with a Notes server just to be working with the server. Web clients are anonymous until they're challenged by Domino.

When a Web user attempts to access the database, he or she will be challenged by Domino to provide a name and password. If the name and password matches someone who's in the appropriate group, then the user is allowed in with author access to the database. The user can edit his or her own documents and so on, just as though they were coming in from a Notes client.

Domino and the Database ACL

Working with the database itself is easy. The manager of the database merely needs to work with the database's ACL in order to facilitate security from the Web. What you want to do is challenge the browser user to find out who they are, as shown in Figure 26.5.

FIGURE 26.5.
Domino challenging a previously anonymous Web user.

To accomplish this, you set the database ACL such that the default level is relatively low (that is, No Access or Reader). Then add whatever groups you want to in your database's ACL.

For example, let's say you have a group called Domino Users, and you've set their access to Author. Default access is set to Reader.

A Web user will be allowed to read all the documents in the database without a problem. However, if you have an Edit action or a "Respond to this topic" action on your action bar and the user clicks on the action, he or she will be challenged by Domino to enter a name and password. If valid entries are submitted in those fields, the user will be allowed to continue. If not, he or she will get an error message.

Be aware that Domino will typically only challenge a user once during a session. The combination of the browser information and Domino security will keep track of who the user is and whether he or she has been authenticated during this session.

Once someone has been allowed into a database, the normal Notes ACL security takes over. If a user is an author in the ACL, he or she can create new documents, edit his or her own, and so on. If a user is an editor, he or she can edit other people's documents and so on, all from a Web browser.

The catch to all this is that the person or group in the ACL needs to exist in the PAB, and the individual needs to have a Web password.

Domino and the PAB

Earlier in this chapter, I discussed the changes to the Server document in the PAB.

In order to enable the database's ACL-level security, two specific things must be done in the PAB. First, there must be a person document for anyone who wishes to be authenticated from a Web browser (in the previous example, a person document isn't needed to merely read a document but is needed to compose a new one). Second, that person document needs to have a value in the HTTPPassword field.

The HTTPPassword field must be filled in to authenticate a Web visitor. If this field is blank, a user will not be able to authenticate from a browser. If this field is missing (if you didn't modify the PAB as discussed earlier in this chapter), a user will not be able to authenticate from a browser.

HTTPPassword is not the same thing as your Notes password (although you could certainly use the same word for both). The only place it exists is in your person document, so even bona fide Notes users will not be able to authenticate from a browser until they fill in this field.

This means you need a person document for everyone you want to authenticate from the Web, and even your existing Notes users need to update their person documents! Luckily, you can employ the Sample Registration database to automate this process. The Sample Registration database can be downloaded from the Domino Web site.

The combination of database ACLs and person documents makes Domino security more robust than anything else in the market. See the "Skeleton Server" section later in this chapter for additional thoughts about Domino security.

A Word About SSL

Within the Web world, security is a tremendous concern on another level. If you were to purchase a product, you would have a legitimate concern about entering your credit card number on an order form on the Web. Where's that number going to go? Who's going to see it? How many computers will it travel through? Can someone along the line "grab it" with a sniffer? These are all valid concerns.

SSL (Secure Sockets Layer) was developed specifically to answer such concerns. Essentially, when you're ready to enter that credit card number, your browser drops into a different mode and submits the data in an encrypted manner.

SSL is a tremendously complex topic and far beyond the scope of what this book intends to cover. However, suffice it to say that Domino, like most good Web servers, supports SSL. An entire, separate SSL documentation database ships with Domino that explains SSL as well as offers installation and implementation instructions and troubleshooting information.

> **TIP**
>
> Like many other topics, SSL has been discussed at length in the Domino Discussion database on the Domino Web site at `http://domino.lotus.com/`. Check it out!

WebPub Close Up

You've met Domino. Before Domino was released, InterNotes Web Publisher (WebPub) was the only way to "publish" Notes databases to the Web. Although it has most certainly been eclipsed by Domino, WebPub will likely stay around for some time. There are still features in WebPub that Domino doesn't have. Let's spend some time with this other "publishing" product.

What WebPub Does

WebPub takes Notes databases, publishes them as HTML-coded documents, and makes them available to specialized servers on the World Wide Web. Unlike Domino, WebPub needs to work in conjunction with an HTTP Web server; it cannot serve the HTML document itself. WebPub, quite literally, takes a Notes database and "clones" it in a series of HTML files that are used by a Web server.

WebPub, by default, takes the database's About document and turns it into the home page, and the database's views become the way to navigate through the documents.

On a scheduled basis, WebPub will publish new documents and modifications to existing ones, as well as remove individual documents or even entire databases from a Web site. Like Domino, it supports Notes DocLinks, so just as a Notes user can easily reference another Notes document with a simple DocLink, WebPub publishes those databases so that a visitor to a Web site can click on the same DocLink and jump to another document.

WebPub also supports file attachments, Notes tables, and even full text indexes (enabling Web visitors to search a database). Like Domino, WebPub enables users to paste a bitmap on a Notes document, and it automatically converts it, regardless of original format, into GIF format for publication on the Web.

The transformation of a document in Notes to a Web-published document is seamless, automatic, and painless. The document on the Web appears virtually identical to the original document in Notes, as shown in Figures 26.6, 26.7 (the WebPub version), and 26.8 (the Domino version). Note that there's some HTML code written on the Notes document in an effort to facilitate faster graphic loading.

FIGURE 26.6.

A document in the Notes database.

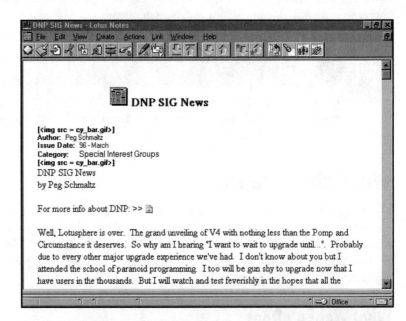

FIGURE 26.7.

The same document published via InterNotes (shown through Netscape Navigator).

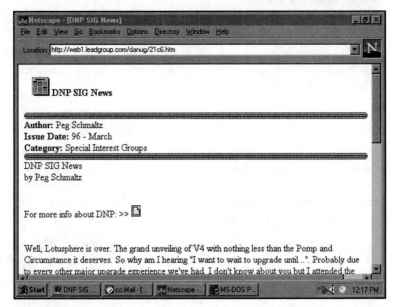

Connecting Notes to the Internet with InterNotes

CHAPTER 26

647

26
CONNECTING
NOTES TO THE
INTERNET

FIGURE 26.8.

The same document published via Domino.

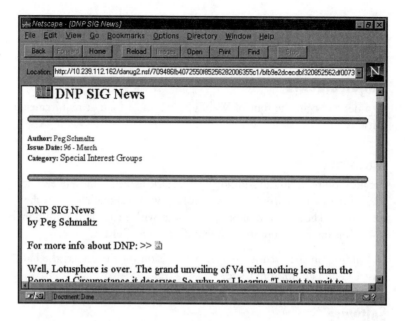

The three versions of the document are startlingly similar; all contain headings, graphics, and text, and even the DocLink at the bottom is supported on the Web.

The document shown in Figures 26.6 and 26.7 was published to the Web via InterNotes, yet other methods could have been employed. The biggest difference is that the person who composed the document was able to compose it in Notes. It also can be edited and even deleted in Notes. In essence, the content side of the database is easy—if you're familiar with Notes, you're a potential content provider. The changes are done automatically in Notes.

If you've ever tried keeping a Web site current, you can appreciate the automatic feature. Even the slightest change requires major work. Fire up the HTML editor, load the document, make the change, save the document, transfer it to your Web site, and so forth.

InterNotes Web Publisher handles all this automatically.

There are two versions of InterNotes WebPub: WebPub 2.1, a Notes 3.x version, and WebPub 4.0, a Notes 4.x version. Each runs as a server add-in task and obviously requires the appropriate version of Notes server to be running.

Although the actual functionality between the two is similar, there are some notable additional capabilities of WebPub 4:

- WebPub 4 supports publishing navigators as image maps.
- Link hotspots can be used for URLs and other links.
- Subforms, both computed and named, can be used and published.
- Bullets and numbered lists can be used.

- Formulas can detect whether the document is being viewed in Notes or on the Web.
- Folders as well as views can be published.

Requirements

In order to begin the tour of WebPub, you must look at requirements, both hardware and software.

Hardware

Because you're adding an additional server task, as well as most likely adding the Web site server itself, this is a true case of "you can't have a powerful enough box." At the very least, the WebPub server should be a 486DX or better machine, with an absolute minimum of 32 MB of memory (64 MB is better, and more than that if you can afford it.

Depending on the eventual usage you envision for the server, the hard drive should start at least 1 G and go up from there.

Software

Whatever the operating system, the necessary network and/or Internet connections need to be in place, along with whatever gateways and so forth that may be needed. Even though this is about WebPub, just like a typical Notes server, the box itself needs to be configured for whatever protocol and network are in place. The assumption is that the box itself is up and running, happily communicating with the network and the Internet. See "The Connectivity Issue" for a discussion of connectivity.

In addition, the Notes 4 server needs to be installed and running. Typically, this Notes server is similar in setup to other Notes servers in your organization. See the section "Skeleton Server."

CAUTION

Keep in mind that if you're placing this server on the Internet, it's in a position to be accessed by the outside world. Couple that with the fact that Notes 4 enables "anonymous access" and there's a huge potential security problem.

If you haven't thought through the security aspects, don't set up the server.

Typically, an organization that connects to the Internet will implement a firewall—a computer that allows people on the inside to get out, but people on the outside can't get in. Setting up a Notes server outside your firewall (that is, directly connected to the Internet and not "protected" by the firewall computer) is not to be taken lightly; there are serious security considerations. In addition, keep in mind that there are unsavory types in the world who would like nothing better than to use a Notes/Web server to shoehorn their way into your network.

See the section "Skeleton Server" for thoughts about security.

Connecting Notes to the Internet with InterNotes

CHAPTER 26

649

26
CONNECTING
NOTES TO THE
INTERNET

Typically, the WebPub server is also the Web site server (that is, the box that is actually serving the HTML documents to the Internet). In addition to the operating system and the Notes server, a Web HTTP server needs to be in place. The HTTP server is what actually "serves" your HTML documents to the Internet; for the purposes of this chapter it's assumed you've got one up and running.

Keep in mind that Domino can function as a Web site server for HTML documents as well as handle Notes databases. However, if Domino isn't appropriate for your site, there are other options.

There are several well-known and easily configured Web servers. Netscape (http://www.netscape.com) offers a robust Web server for Windows NT and UNIX; O'Reilly and Associates (http://www.ora.com) offers a product (called Web Site, of all things!) for NT and Windows 95. Microsoft's Internet Information Server (http://www.microsoft.com/) has been making major inroads recently. The major PC magazines frequently run comparison articles; check your recent past issues.

> **TIP**
>
> A quick search at Yahoo (http://www.yahoo.com), AltaVista (http://altavista.digital.com), or WebCrawler (http://www.webcrawler.com) for "Internet" and "servers" will yield a lengthy list of products you can check out. There are sites for the major commercial publishers, as well as numerous shareware products. In most cases, you can download a demo version to try out for 30 or 60 days.

To review, here are the requirements that must be met:

- The hardware component is purchased and of sufficient horsepower.
- The operating system of the box is in place and operating smoothly.
- Connectivity with the local network and/or Internet is working.
- The Notes server is installed and running.
- The Web site server is installed and running.

It's now time to install WebPub.

Installing WebPub

There are two separate server components to WebPub, as well as several client pieces. First, the server side: If you have Notes 4.1 or later, WebPub is already installed, and you can skip to the "Configuring WebPub" section.

If not, WebPub needs to be installed. You may have downloaded it or gotten a diskette. (The downloadable version needs to be unpacked before it can be installed, so copy the downloaded executable into a temporary directory and unpack it there—usually by clicking on the file itself.)

Either way, you type INSTALL or click on the INSTALL.EXE executable, and the Install program takes over. It asks only a few questions: where's your Notes program directory, where's your Notes data directory, and where's your Web server's CGI directory? CGI (Common Gateway Interface) is a protocol used between the HTTP server and external programs. There's a special directory on your HTTP server where these CGI files are stored.

When you install Web Publisher, it copies several files into the server's executable directory—notably, the WebPub and INOTES server tasks—and a couple of files into the server's data directory (the Web Config database, a Web guide online documentation, and Web Toolkit, a series of how-to documents about HTML and the Web, not specifically about WebPub). In addition, there are a couple of sample databases, including the full-blown Mercury Sports Web demo (which is worth its weight in gold to see what Lotus people who really know what they're doing have put together). There are a couple of templates specific to InterNotes as well.

Double-check that the INOTES.EXE executable file has been correctly copied into your server's CGI directory. During the Install routine, you are asked in what directory to put CGI. The default is to put it in the CGI-BIN directory, but your server might not have such a directory (Web Site, for example, has CGI-DOS, CGI-WIN, and CGI-SHL directories, but no CGI-BIN). Consult the online documentation for a chart that shows the correct directory, depending on what Web server you're using.

It's important to note that the INOTES program is a DOS-based executable; therefore, it needs to be dropped into the CGI directory on your machine that handles DOS programs (for example, not CGI-WIN). If you're not sure, copy it into a couple of directories and experiment (you won't cause any harm by having it where it isn't needed).

> **NOTE**
>
> INOTES, incidentally, is the server task that gives InterNotes its interactivity. That is, INOTES lets visitors to your Web site fill out forms and so forth, which are deposited back in your Notes database. Without INOTES, WebPub would be strictly a one-way street, publishing Notes databases to the Web. With INOTES, it's a two-way street, publishing to the Web but also capturing information from the Web. A Web discussion database isn't possible without INOTES—nor is searching a database.

> **TIP**
>
> Check in frequently with Lotus's InterNotes Web site (http://www.lotus.com/inotes/) for the latest information about things such as CGI mappings. There's a lively discussion database, and any problems you're having with such subjects have probably already been addressed at length.
>
> In addition, Lotus's InterNotes Web site has a series of Tech Notes that give tips and tricks as well as answers to common questions.
>
> This Web site, not surprisingly, is totally run by InterNotes, so you also have a chance to take a close look at a full-blown InterNotes site.

Configuring WebPub

Once WebPub is installed, edit the Web Publisher Configuration database. There are two types of documents to be concerned with here: the Webmaster Options form and the database publishing records.

The Webmaster Options form, shown in Figure 26.9, is where the overall InterNotes configuration is set; the database publishing records, shown in Figure 26.10, tell InterNotes what to publish. Note that the record in this figure lists how often to publish, which specific views to publish, heading font mappings, and so on.

FIGURE 26.9.

A Webmaster document in a configuration database.

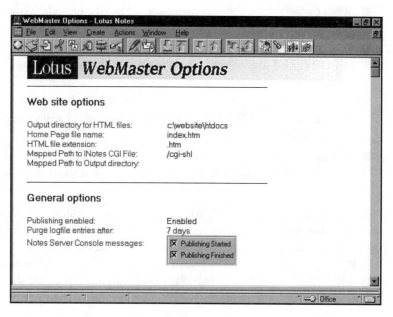

FIGURE 26.10.

A database publishing record for DANUG database.

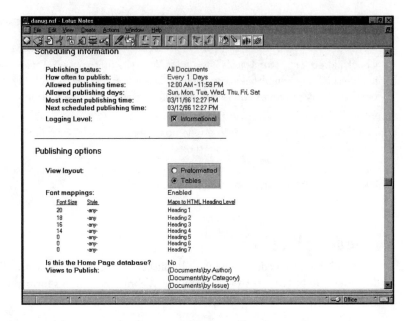

The Webmaster Options form is relatively straightforward, although the fields for mappings can be a bit confusing. Simply tell InterNotes via the Webmaster form what to do:

- Which directory to publish in.

- What the default for the home page should be (the filename WebPub will give the home page in each database it publishes).

- What HTML extension you're using (typically .HTM or .HTML—it's often easiest to use .HTM if you work with a "normal" Windows client, because it won't support the extended extension).

- Where your CGI directory is (that is, where the Install program placed INOTES or the manually-placed INOTES executable is located) as well as where the mapped output to the HTML directory is.

- Whether or not publishing is enabled. You may opt to turn off publishing during heavy server load times, when to purge log files, and whether or not to have server console messages.

Note that both the CGI and HTML listings require mappings relative to the Web server's document directory, rather than a system mapping. That is, if your directory structure had the Web server's executables in the directory C:\WEB and the CGI files in C:\WEB\CGI-BIN, your CGI entry is simply /CGI-BIN. In the preceding example, the actual CGI directory is C:\WEB\WEBSITE\CGI-SHL, but relative to the server's home directory, the path is .../CGI-SHL.

The other documents that need to be created are database publishing records, which tell InterNotes what to publish. You need at least one for every database you intend to publish.

The database publishing records give InterNotes information about the database(s) you want to publish. Specifically, you tell InterNotes information that includes the database to publish (the filename with complete with path, if necessary), how often to publish it, which views to publish, and so forth.

Note that you could conceivably publish once every second, although that hardly makes sense. A lively Web discussion database might be appropriate to publish once every minute or two, but it might make sense to publish a product information database once a day.

TIP

You can have multiple database publishing records for a particular database. As such, it might make sense to have one record for updates only that publishes every five minutes, and another that publishes all documents once a day. In this manner, new or modified documents would find their way to the Web quickly, but all documents would be refreshed on a daily basis (in case forms or formulas are time-sensitive—for example, a document that says the time created was "10:05 a.m. Today").

This is also where you can specify to WebPub how to handle HTML headings. In the HTML world, font sizes aren't specified—information is sent that merely says "this is a Heading #1." The font mappings section of the publishing record enables the Webmaster to specify which font sizes in Notes equate to which heading marks in the HTML document. The default is that anything with a 20-point font or better is mapped as an H1 heading (the largest), 18-point font for H2, 16-point for H3, and so on. If you've created styles in your Notes database, they can be used in this dialog as well.

Additionally, you can specify which views you want to publish. A developer can create two similar views in a database—one for use in Notes itself, another for publishing to the Web. The second view can be hidden in Notes itself yet specified on the Views To Publish field so that WebPub publishes the second view. This is a great way to include formulas that might contain icons (a formula that displays a "new" bitmap next to documents that are less than a week old, for example) or put other bits of HTML code into a view that would make little sense if seen from Notes itself.

CAUTION

Be careful about answering Yes to the "Is this the Home Page database?" question. If you answer Yes, InterNotes may wipe out your main home page. A good rule of thumb is to set up the Webmaster Options form with DEFAULT.HTM as your home page filename and leave INDEX.HTML as the name of your actual main home page. This way, even if you answer this question incorrectly, you won't blow up your entire site.

The third manual task is to modify the server's NOTES.INI file to include WebPub and INOTES on the `ServerTasks =` line, as shown in Figure 26.11. The server either needs to be "bounced" at this point or WebPub and INOTES need to be loaded at the console (type LOAD WEBPUB and LOAD INOTES at the console).

FIGURE 26.11.

A portion of the server's NOTES.INI file showing server tasks entries.

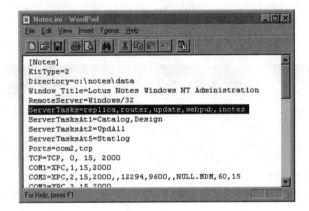

After you modify the NOTES.INI file, each time you restart your server, both WebPub and INOTES will automatically load as a server task. Note that if you change the information on the Webmaster Options form, you need to shut down WebPub and INOTES (type TELL WEBPUB QUIT and TELL INOTES QUIT) and then restart those two processes.

At this point, everything should be up and running. Typically, there will be some troubleshooting necessary the first time you attempt to publish something. For example, your pathing might be wrong, INOTES might be in the wrong directory, incorrect databases or views might be specified, and so on. A lengthy amount of troubleshooting may be necessary to get WebPub working correctly initially, but once your configuration is in place, everything should publish just fine.

TIP

If you have checked all there is to check and everything seems perfect, yet WebPub and InterNotes aren't doing what you think they're supposed to be doing, shut down the entire box (not just the Notes server, but the entire machine).

Both NT and OS/2 are notorious for hanging onto things in a memory cache long after they should have let them go.

There have been numerous times when, during a troubleshooting session, a problem has mysteriously disappeared after I rebooted the machine (not just bouncing the server).

In other cases, you may find that deleting the published database and republishing it solves a problem.

Connecting Notes to the Internet with InterNotes

CHAPTER 26

655

26

CONNECTING
NOTES TO THE
INTERNET

If things are seriously wrong, try retracing your steps, paying close attention to any error messages you might be getting. Also, check the Lotus InterNotes discussion.

One additional consideration is that what looks great in Notes may not work on the Web. Typically, Notes databases have views laden with column headings and so forth. On a Web site, those headings end up making things look cluttered. Therefore, you may find that everything works perfectly, but you're not happy with the result for aesthetic reasons.

WebPub and Domino: Working Together

Although Domino and WebPub are different, they are certainly complementary. Many Web sites may want to employ both.

Domino, for example, can be the Web server that WebPub uses. You can use a mixture of WebPub-published databases and Domino-published databases and simply use links to hand off users seamlessly between the two.

Publishing Notes Databases with Either WebPub or Domino

Regardless of which you use, there are a number of factors regarding application development that you need to take consideration.

Considerations About What to Publish

There are numerous ways to control what gets published by Domino or WebPub, assuming you don't want every view and every document in your database to be exposed to the public.

For the purpose of this discussion, let's assume that you're working in a product information database. Not all the product information you're currently storing in this database is for public viewing; some information is strictly for your salespeople, whereas some strictly for the production department.

There are several things you can do to restrict what gets published to the product information that is for the public. One potential way is to build a form with a field called Approved, and then build a view with a selection formula that allows only those documents marked "approved." With WebPub, you could publish only that view. You would have all the documents in a central database, but only documents that show up in certain views would be made public. With Domino, it's slightly more complicated, but a combination of navigators leading only to the "approved" view and a view access on the "unapproved" views will have the same effect.

One of the benefits of handling the publication control this way is that the documents become available quite quickly once they're marked approved (no need to wait for a replication to take place in the middle of the night, for example).

In addition, the particular view you've chosen to publish might be formatted specifically for Web publishing, and you might have gone so far as to hide it from view of normal Notes users. As stated earlier, a column in a view might contain some code to display an icon if the document is newer than 10 days old:

```
REM "setting temporary variables to work with";
NewDate := @Adjust(@Today; 0; 0; -10; 0; 0; 0);
UpdatedDate := @Adjust(@Modified; 0; 0; -10; 0; 0; 0);
REM;
REM "Here's the statement that does the work";
REM "It'll display a NEW bitmap if the document is newer than ten days old";
REM "or a UPDATED bitmap if modified in the past ten days";
REM;
@If(@Created >= NewDate; "[<img src=../graphics/new.gif>]";
➥@If((@Modified >= NewDate) & (UpdatedDate > @Created);
➥"[<img src=../graphics/updated.gif>]"; ""))
REM;
```

By publishing the database with such a formula in a hidden view, the Web version of the database correctly identifies which documents are new. If you had left this formula in the column in a view visible to a Notes user, they would see the formula (although the Notes version could substitute the word NEW for the IMG code). The Web view is shown in Figure 26.12. Note that in order for a formula like this to work effectively, you need a database-publishing document that is set to publish all documents at least once a day.

FIGURE 26.12.

The resulting view from the formula.

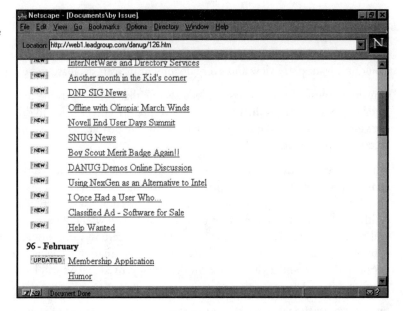

Another way to achieve control is to have two copies of the database: one on an internal production Notes server and the other on your Domino or WebPub server. Using a method similar to the preceding one, you can create a selective replication formula that restricts any document not marked "approved" from even making it into the InterNotes database.

The benefit of doing it this way is the increased security of knowing that only the public documents are available to be published.

Yet another way is to eliminate the selective replication and to substitute a Mail macro that, for example, runs once a day and sends all approved documents to the second database. Again, this is more complicated, but virtually ensures that only the appropriate documents are transmitted and published.

> **CAUTION**
>
> Before attempting any of the preceding methods in a database that contains sensitive information, do a dry run with a couple of innocuous documents. Just as you would test agents (or macros), make sure your formulas select the correct documents and replicate them (or display them) properly. Nothing is worse than seeing the wrong set of documents on a Web site!

Both Domino and WebPub 4.x enable you to write formulas that can detect whether or not they are running in Notes using a new, Notes 4-specific @function: @UserRoles, which returns a list of all roles that the current user has in a database. If WebPub is evaluating this function, one of the values that will be returned is $$Web. (The current version of the product returns $$WebPublisher, but Lotus suggests testing for a string of $$Web because future versions may change that.) If Domino is evaluating the formula, it returns $$WebClient.

Using @UserRoles, a formula can be built that brings up a computed subform or various Hide When options based solely on whether this document is in Notes or is on the Web.

Here's a sample chunk of code that conditionally inserts one of two subforms based on whether or not the client was visiting via a Web browser or a Notes client:

```
@If(@Contains(@UserRoles; "$$Web"); "SubFormWeb"; "SubFormNotes")
```

This formula inserts the Web subform if Domino or WebPub are evaluating the formula; if not, it inserts the Notes subform.

Such a formula could control the display of computed subforms, HTML code, Hide When formulas, input translation and validation, default values (if you're in Notes, default to your UserName or else default to Please Type Your Name Here), and even keyword formulas.

Using Objects, Attachments, DocLinks, and Popups

Both Domino and WebPub cater to the use of attachments, objects, document links, and other Notes features. The most obvious of these is the capability to convert graphics (see the discussion later in this section about graphics), but there are numerous other examples as well.

Notes has often been called the database into which you put stuff for which you don't have databases. As such, Notes often becomes the depository for files, forms, and so forth. With an InterNotes database, those items can be put into normal, everyday Notes documents, and Domino or WebPub will take care of the dirty work.

For example, if you had a WAV file, you could embed this object in a Notes document, and Notes would interpret it correctly, leaving a file in the HTML output directory and a hotlink on the document itself.

Likewise, both Domino and WebPub will automatically take care of file attachments, creating a link at the bottom of a Web document that can be clicked on to download a file. Once again, from a user perspective, this is considerably easier than hard-coding an HTML document and then transferring the file to whatever directory the Web visitors can access.

Linking to Other Documents

Recall that servers on the World Wide Web are called HTTP servers. One of their main features is the capability of offering links between documents. These links, called *hypertext links*, enable a user to click on a highlighted word and have the server send the new document, graphic, or whatever to the user's browser.

Typically, to facilitate this within normal HTML coding, you have to put in a Uniform Resource Locator (URL), a direct reference to the other document (for example, `http://web1.leadgroup.com/lnu/index.htm`). With an InterNotes database, you merely need to create a DocLink within Notes from the document to which you want to link. Figures 26.6 and 26.7, shown earlier, feature DocLinks in action.

One of the key benefits of using DocLinks is that users don't need to know anything about the directory structure and so forth of the HTTP server. They simply need to be able to create DocLinks within Notes itself.

Popups are another way to create links. If you want to create a link to another Notes document, you can highlight some text and create a text popup (select Create | Hotspot | Text Popup). The text of the popup is the URL of whatever you want to link to, surrounded by brackets (that is, you could enter the preceding reference as the text of a popup: `[http://web1.leadgroup.com/lnu/index.htm]`). Note the brackets surrounding the URL of the document. This is particularly useful if you want to do something other than a strict document reference (for example, `[mailto:webmaster@leadgroup.com]` inserted as a popup to create an automatic `mailto` reference).

Yet another way to create links is to put the URL in brackets immediately next to whatever you want to have create the highlighted link. For example, you can insert a graphic and, immediately next to the graphic, put a URL in brackets. Notes will display the graphic with a blue box around it; clicking on the graphic will trigger the link to the new document.

Navigators

With Domino and WebPub 4, you can use navigators as image maps. A navigator in Notes is the same thing as an image map on the Web—they're both graphic images with embedded hotspots that trigger links when certain regions are clicked.

There are multiple ways to use navigators. In WebPub, the easiest is to create a field on your Notes form called $$ImageMapBody, where the help description is the name of the navigator. If your hotspot link in Notes is an Open A Link action, the image map will point to the document, view, or database.

In Domino, you simply "open" the navigator, either by setting the database launch properties or by opening it via a command such as

```
@URLOpen(http://server/database/main+navigator?OpenNavigator)
```

Graphics

One of the truly frustrating things about working on the Web is the limitations placed on graphics. They have to be in one of two formats in order for Web browsers to access them—GIF or JPG. Neither of those formats is supported by typical user graphics tools (Windows Paintbrush, for example), so rendering graphics on Web documents could be a chore.

Domino and WebPub make life much simpler by enabling users to paste a graphic—a Windows BMP or PCX file, a scanned image, or whatever—on a Notes document. Domino and WebPub take care of the rest.

As WebPub publishes the Notes document, it automatically "tears off" the graphic, converts it to a GIF format, places a copy of the .GIF file in the appropriate directory on the Web server, and creates a link on the document to display the graphic in the right spot. If you can import or paste it onto a Notes document, you can now publish it to the Web. Domino does the conversion on-the-fly, but essentially does the same thing.

This is a tremendous benefit, because users have no need to have any graphics packages available to them other than Paintbrush. Forms can be created with company logos, bars, and other graphic elements, and Domino and WebPub will translate all of these into nice-looking Web documents. Figures 26.6 and 26.7 show some of the graphic elements transferring nicely between Notes and the Web.

> **TIP**
>
> If you have a graphic element that you'll be using over and over within a database (such as a corporate logo), use an HTML code on your Notes form rather than pasting the graphic directly onto your Notes document.
>
> The rationale behind doing it this way is that both Domino and WebPub will see the graphic on each document in your database as a different graphic, and will republish it for each document. If you had a 50-document database, you'd have 50 identical GIF files. As users move between your documents, their browsers would need to reload that graphic each time, slowing down access time. If you merely reference the graphic, their browsers will have cached the graphic image, and the document will come up much more quickly.
>
> Note that the two bars (above and below the Author, Issue Date and Category headings) in Figure 26.7 don't exist in the Notes version in Figure 26.6, but an HTML code points to the graphic for the bars. The use of the HTML code facilitates reuse of graphics loaded into memory, thus increasing the loading speed of the Web page.
>
> The downside to doing this is that some HTML coding will be necessary on your Notes form, although minimal. On the Notes side it will look clumsy unless you are extremely good with formulas and extremely careful with Hide When statements.

HTML Coding on Forms

Even though one of the key benefits of employing Domino or WebPub is the capability of avoiding HTML coding, there are numerous places where a little HTML code might be worth it.

In the graphics arena, it makes a tremendous amount of sense to reference a graphic with an HTML tag rather than force a user to reload the same image over and over. Figures 26.6 and 26.7, for example, show the graphic bars being put on via an HTML code (`<img src = cy_bar.gif>`) that loads a GIF file of the cyan bar. Once the bar has been loaded into memory the first time, the browser loads it quickly the next time, rather than needing to "fetch" it from the Web site again.

Likewise, there are subtle things you can do with HTML code placed on a Notes form that make the form far nicer visually once published to the Web.

A perfect example is document backgrounds. Although this seems to have shifted dramatically over the past year or two, many Web sites have adopted a style of "embossed" logos for backgrounds on their documents, or of various graphic textures or plain colors.

WebPub doesn't support backgrounds directly (Domino does), but there's no reason not to put the appropriate HTML codes on your Notes form to facilitate a background when viewed on the Web.

With Domino 4.5, background graphics are supported within Notes itself, and the Domino server supports them too. Simply add a background for a form in Notes, and Domino will serve it as a Body Background Image to a Web browser.

Any HTML code you want to put in a Notes form or document needs to be surrounded by brackets, so the HTML code for centered text, <CENTER>, appears on a Notes form as [<CENTER>]. Both Domino and WebPub understand that anything within brackets is HTML code and translates it appropriately, making it invisible when published.

To drop in a logo for a background, you use a line such as the following:

```
[<BODY BACKGROUND= "graphics/logo.gif">]
```

To use a color for a background, you use a line such as the following:

```
[<BODY BGCOLOR="#ffffff">]
```

One of the HTML codes you may want to use that WebPub doesn't currently support by itself is centered text, so you can add the [<CENTER>] tag before a heading to turn on centering and the [</CENTER>] tag after it to turn it off again. Domino does support centered text.

> **TIP**
>
> There are numerous books on HTML coding, but there are also numerous online references available. Quite a few seasoned HTML coders have put together how-to sites on the Web. Try a Yahoo or WebCrawler search on HTML and see what you come up with.

One Form for Notes, Another for the Web

As has become apparent, you've suddenly gone from simply publishing a Notes database as-is to making major alterations for the Web.

There are several things you can do to simplify the situation. First, if you're working strictly with one database and merely choosing which view to publish, a form formula could be written in both MainView (the Web version, with no space between the words) and Main View (the Notes version, with the space), which will bring up different forms for the same documents. You can then have a Web version of your main topic form with HTML code all over it, but the form formula in the other view will bring up a clean version for the Notes users' consumption.

Another option is to have different forms altogether in two different databases. One database is used strictly for publishing purposes, and it has the HTML-coded forms. The other database has the clean version of the form. The Notes users use the second database, and you set up the access control between the two so that they readily transfer new and modified documents, but design changes don't replicate.

The advent of the new @UserRoles function mentioned earlier in this chapter also offers the developer the capability of controlling the display of subforms and so forth. By creatively using this capability, you can bring up certain subforms only on the published documents, not on their Notes-side counterparts.

Yet another consideration is then creative use of Hide When attributes. You can use Hide When attributes to create a different look for forms being filled out and documents being read, although they're the same form.

Interactive Forms in Web Publisher

Since Domino works directly with a Notes database, using interactive forms is a snap. But it's not all that tough with Web Publisher, either.

Many sites on the Internet are interactive in one form or another. You can order products, you can ask questions, you can request more information, and so forth. The trouble in many of the existing systems is that the information gathered is dropped into a big DAT file on a UNIX server, and you practically need a Master's in computer science to decipher and use the information. Wouldn't it be nice to be able to capture information from a Web site and drop it directly into your prospects database in Notes? You bet!

With the advent of version 2, Web Publisher became interactive. That is, not only can InterNotes publish to the Web, but it also can capture information from the Web. Better yet, the data it captures is dropped directly back into a Notes database.

The simplest example of this is an information request, such as the Mercury Sports sample database with which InterNotes ships. In the Mercury Sports example, an interactive form is published to the Web, enabling visitors to the Web site to request information, order products, ask for a salesperson to call, and so forth. If taken to the next level, a workflow application can be built into Notes, automatically routing that new document to the appropriate person. If the Web visitor checks "request information," the document gets routed to the mail room for fulfillment. If "have salesperson call" is checked, it goes directly to the sales coordinator. The Mercury Sports sample database is a combination lead generation, product information, and product-ordering database.

In addition to that type of database, there are numerous other uses for the interactive aspects of InterNotes.

You can set up a discussion database, enabling Web visitors to participate in a discussion. You can have a class registration database or an automatic fax-back system. You can create an online help system with knowledge base documents already in place, and yet enable users to ask questions or request further information.

Full text searching falls under the heading of interactivity, too. You can index your Notes database and enable Web visitors to type in a search criteria, just as users do within Notes itself, and they'll receive a list of documents in the database that meet their criteria.

> **CAUTION**
>
> Searches work only if all the various components are on the same machine—that is, the Notes server, InterNotes Web Publisher, Web server, and database must all reside on the same physical computer.
>
> Users have the same search options during Web searches that they would have during a normal Web search (complex query statements, limiting the number of responses, and so forth).

Creating the Interactive Form

Unfortunately, although you can publish to the Web by simply filling out a database publishing record and telling Notes to do it, making things interactive takes a bit more intervention on the part of the developer.

Suppose you're putting together the simple product information request form from the Mercury Sports sample database. There are several steps involved in making this form interactive. First, build the form itself in Notes. The form can be a normal Notes form, and all the normal things you might do with a form in Notes can be done with a form that will be put out on the Web, such as input validations (@If(Name - "", "Please Enter a Name", @Success)), input translations (@ProperCase(Name)), and default values. There are a number of subtle extra things you can do to the Notes form that will customize its appearance on the Web. You can, for example, control the size of text fields by specifying a row and column length in the Help Description. Figure 26.13 shows a field description that results in a field that will be 20 rows deep by 80 characters wide.

Second, give the form the synonym $$WEB. Once the form has been created, the $$WEB synonym tells Notes that this is a form that's to be made available to the Web. You may have multiple forms in a database with the $$WEB synonym. Typically, because this form will be heavily formatted for Web use, you would deselect the Include in compose menu option so that the form is available only on the Web.

Notes creates an HTML form with the real name of the form. So, if your form is called Product ¦ $$WEB, Notes will create an HTML document called PRODUCT.HTM that you can reference.

Third, you need to create the HTML links to this form. That is, you need to access this form from the Web site. The easiest way to do this is to create a text popup hotspot on the home page that references the HTML name for the document. You could have a sentence such as "Click here for more INFORMATION," with the word *information* highlighted as a popup. The text for the popup would be [PRODUCT.HTM]. Notes knows that when this is clicked, the Product Info form is to be brought up. (See Figures 26.14 and 26.15.)

FIGURE 26.13.

Field description with Help Description set to control the size of the field in the published Notes document.

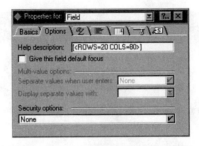

FIGURE 26.14.

The interactive form in Notes.

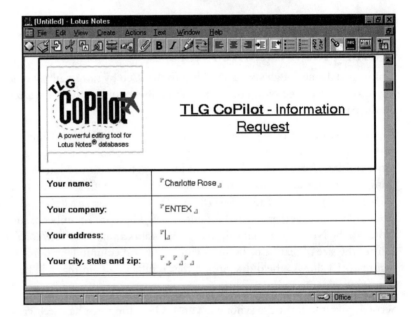

There are numerous subtleties involved in making a Notes database truly interactive.

- You can create a response formula that displays a "Thanks for your request" message after someone saves a request.

- You can include a search bar in a home page document, enabling people to search for documents in your database.

- You can create a discussion-type database, with true parent-child relationships between documents.

- Most importantly, you can create a complete workflow application in Notes. Then, when someone enters information on your Web site, Notes will handle routing and so forth so that the information gets to where it needs to go.

Lotus has done an admirable job of documenting the nuances of creating a truly interactive Web site in both the documentation and the information available at their Web site. Read the documentation and give it a try; check the Web site for troubleshooting information.

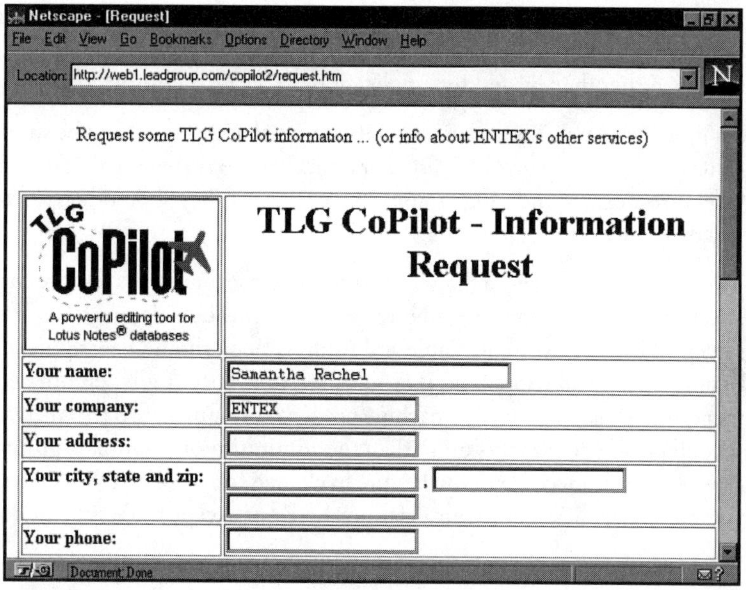

FIGURE 26.15.

The interactive form shown on the Web.

Skeleton Server

This book does not delve deeply into Web security, but it would be a serious oversight to ignore this subject altogether.

There are several things to be aware of when you place any machine outside your organization's firewall. First, any actual connection between that machine on the outside and your network on the inside needs to be secured. Second, the machine itself needs to be secured. Third, the software, databases, and so forth on that machine need their own security.

The first issue becomes a matter for the firewall experts. One of the easiest ways to guarantee a secure connection from your outside server is to set up a "poor man's firewall"—a modem setup. Hook up your outside machine to the Internet via a network card, but hook it up to another internal Notes server via a modem. Notes can communicate via LAN ports or COM ports; users reaching your InterNotes server are coming in over the Internet on the LAN port. They may conceivably be able to do some damage on that machine, but there's no way they can configure the box to do damage to your network over a modem that's attached only to the COM port of an internal Notes server. There's no shared protocol, no common port. It's about as safe as you can get.

At my office, we took this method a step further. We literally hooked up the outside machine to an inside machine via a LapLink cable. There wasn't even a real modem; the LapLink cable serves as a null modem (the transmit and receive pairs are reversed). The phone number you put in the connection document: Ring.

The second issue is equally complicated. How do you secure the box itself? There are a couple of obvious things to do. Run Notes, the Web server software, and any other applications as services rather than as desktop applications. This further protects them.

Set up an extremely limited user population on that machine, and be sure the password is something other than "password." Use user limitations to make sure that unauthorized people won't be electronically wandering around the machine if they should happen to stumble in over the Internet.

The third issue is largely a matter of common sense, but needs to be mentioned in this context. Because there is going to be a Notes server on this outside machine, it should be a "skeleton server." That is, the public Name and Address Book should be stripped of all documents other than those critical to making that machine run. Specifically, eliminate all connection documents other than the one the machine needs to communicate back with the inside world. Eliminate all person documents other than the administrator. Eliminate groups, servers, and certificates that are unnecessary (and be sure to change your replication settings appropriately so that you neither replicate out your deletions here nor accept those type of documents back).

Keep the mission-critical, company-secret databases off this server. Use selective replication formulas to replicate only subsets of databases; keep the internal stuff off this machine.

Check your ACLs carefully. Eliminate individual names and triple-check the default access on every database and database template. Be sure to break the replica IDs of anything that's out there, even if it's Help itself. To "break" the IDs, simply make copies of the databases from within Notes (File | Database | Copy) and delete the originals. The new copies will have different replica IDs than the originals.

By doing this, if someone should figure out a way to break into Notes, there's nothing much they could find. Keep in mind that Notes 4 supports anonymous users, so, conceivably, people could be lurking about, exploring, trying to see what they can uncover.

Using a Home Page Database

Sam Juvonen, one of my clever compatriots and a fellow author of this book, hit upon the idea of creating a home page database. The idea, in its fullest implementation, is twofold.

First, you create a database that will be your site's main home page. Use this database strictly as a jumping-off point for the other databases you want to publish.

This part is relatively easily done. An About document can be created with a two-column table. A skinny left column holds a series of icons, and the right column holds a series of database names. Both the icons and the database names are highlighted with text popups that contain the URLs of the individual databases.

This is insanely easy to create, maintain, and update. Our home page database is still in place today; when you hit our Web site, a Notes About document answers, as shown in Figure 26.16.

It's a spiffy document, complete with backgrounds and other graphics, but it was created completely within Notes itself.

Figure 26.16.
A home page document created from a Notes About document.

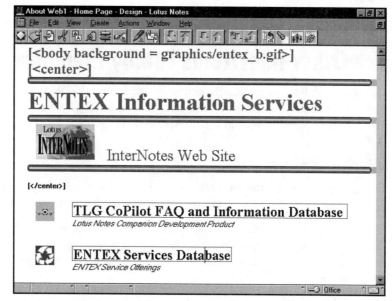

The second part of the home page database idea has yet to materialize fully on our site, but it's a perfect opportunity for enabling users to create personal home pages in this database.

The database, obviously, won't be used for anything other than InterNotes publishing. Why not enable users to create personal home pages there using a tool they're already familiar with: Notes?

We offer them a Create menu with a single option: Home Page. The Home Page form consists of three fields: an author name field, a date field, and a rich text field into which they can put anything they want. Users can insert pictures, stories, files, jump links—anything they want.

Web Publisher Limitations

There's a risk when writing about a product like WebPub that does so much—you might begin to think it does everything. It doesn't; there are some limitations as to what it can and cannot do. Here's a quick sampling of things that you can't do with WebPub:

- Certain HTML codes are not supported (WebPub won't center text, for example, and Domino doesn't support heading tags).

- Many HTML extensions are not supported (Netscape, Microsoft, and others have proprietary extensions, such as frames and backgrounds, that their browsers recognize but WebPub doesn't).

- Certain Notes functions and formulas are rendered ineffective (@DbLookup and @DbColumn, for example). This restricts some of Notes' lookup capabilities from being used on the Web.

As the entire InterNotes family matures, some of these restrictions may go away.

The Other InterNotes Family Members

Despite the amount of excitement generated by the InterNotes Web Publisher product, it's only one member of the family. There are two other client-oriented products that deserve mention: InterNotes News and InterNotes Web Navigator.

InterNotes News

Newsgroups are one of the most talked-about aspects of the Internet. You can subscribe to a newsgroup on literally every imaginable subject (and many unimaginable, I suspect).

One of the problems with the newsgroups—or Usenets, as they're called—is managing the flood of material that comes through. Users typically lose the "threads" because things don't arrive sequentially, and often it's tough to separate the worthwhile information from the worthless.

Lotus took aim at the newsgroup problems with InterNotes News, a product that grabs the newsgroups and dumps the content into the Notes database. Users can then read and respond to articles from within the familiar confines of Notes itself.

One of the main selling points of both InterNotes News and the Web Navigator is that they enable Internet connectivity through the Notes server. Individual users no longer have to be connected to the Internet directly to access the services; the server has the TCP/IP connection, not the user.

Another key benefit is that administrators can control what newsgroups people have access to by filling out a configuration database similar to that of WebPub. It enables administrators to subscribe to individual newsgroups, create custom Notes databases, and control their replication. ACL settings further the administrative options by restricting which users have access to the newsgroup database.

Additionally, full text indexes can be created for the InterNotes News databases, meaning that users can search for material of interest, rather than having to dig through themselves. They can create macros and mail-forward scenarios to assist in disseminating news through their organization.

InterNotes News is a server process combined with a couple of new database templates. If your server has Internet access, you can set up InterNotes news in half an hour.

Configuring InterNotes News

Just as with WebPub, there is a server add-in task for InterNotes News. You can either load it manually at the server console (by typing LOAD INNEWS) or you can add INNEWS to the ServerTasks line in your server's NOTES.INI.

After you install the software and get INNEWS running, you need to set up a few configuration documents:

- News Gateway form
- News Server form
- News Connection form
- News Database form

Each of these forms, in succession, creates a step of the setup needed to get Usenet news to your Notes server.

The Gateway form determines which Notes server will function as the news gateway. The News Server form tells the gateway machine what new server to connect to, either within your own organization or at your Internet provider.

The News Connection form tells Notes how often to make a connection with the news server, and the News Database form tells Notes in which database to store retrieved articles.

Once INNEWS is running, new Usenet articles will automatically be added to the various Notes databases you've specified. At this point, you can create a full-text index to facilitate searching the database, create signature files to facilitate posting on the news groups, create macros to filter and/or block entirely certain subjects, and even send mail back to the author of an article.

INNEWS is merely an easy way to get Internet news into Notes, but, like the other InterNotes products, it takes much of the confusion of the Internet and eliminates it, substituting the familiar ground of Notes.

InterNotes Web Navigator

The final member of the InterNotes family has two parts: the Web Navigator itself (the client portion of the program), and Web or Web Retriever (the server add-in task). The Web Navigator, shown in Figure 26.17, lets users visit Web sites with ease. (You access the Open URL dialog box shown via a SmartIcon.)

Just as InterNotes News brings Internet newsgroup content and dumps it into Notes databases, the Web Navigator (WebNav) brings Web site content into Notes databases. When a user accesses an Internet site via Navigator, Notes retrieves and converts the content into Notes documents in the Navigator database. Subsequent users can access the content from the Notes database, and users can create DocLinks to Web pages and so forth. Users can even create Web tours, where they can keep track of a certain series of Web pages as they're visited and replay the series.

FIGURE 26.17.

The Web Navigator's main screen.

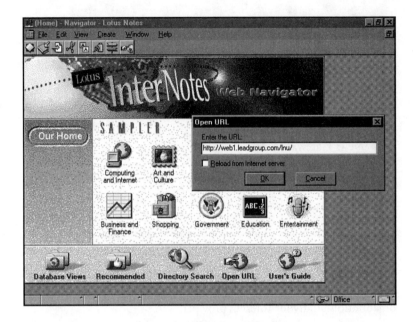

In action, Web Navigator is similar to any other browser, enabling users to open URLs, back up through previously visited Web pages, and so on. As you can see in Figure 26.18, the Web page looks virtually identical viewed through Navigator as through other browsers.

FIGURE 26.18.

Viewing a Web page through Web Navigator.

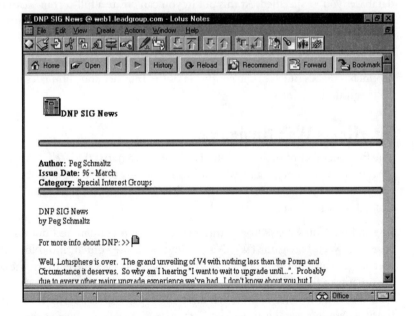

Connecting Notes to the Internet with InterNotes

CHAPTER 26

671

26

CONNECTING
NOTES TO THE
INTERNET

A key Navigator selling point is the capability of accessing Internet Web sites without needing to bring TCP/IP to each client workstation. Administrators can also deny access to certain Web sites, thus limiting users access to "questionable" spots on the Web.

In addition, agents or macros can be created to visit competitors' or suppliers' sites regularly, sending colleagues a DocLinked summary on a regular basis showing changes.

Full-text search of the Navigator database enables searching of the Web sites for content.

A side benefit of having Web Navigator running is that URLs included in any Notes document (mail, discussions, or news articles) are highlighted and can be accessed with a click of the mouse.

Installing Web Navigator is a simple task. Web Retriever needs to be installed on the Notes server as a server add-in task (modify NOTES.INI to add `WEB` to the server's `ServerTasks =` line). Retriever automatically ships with Notes 4, as does the Web Navigator database template. They're there, but they need to be added manually.

TIP

Lotus maintains a special section of its Web site strictly for information about the InterNotes Web Navigator. You can either open the URL of this site directly (`http://www.lotus.com/webnav.htm`) or click on the Go to template resource site reference on the Administration document.

This site offers new Navigator templates, tech tips, and other information that you'll find useful—this is recommended reading!

The WebNav Client

This topic is covered extensively in other parts of this book, but here's a quick overview to round out our discussion.

The InterNotes Web Navigator client is actually a central, shared database. This database resides on a Notes server that is connected to the Internet and running the WEB server task. The client does not need TCP/IP; it can connect to its InterNotes server via whatever network protocol it normally uses. (Users can access the Internet via modem if they're dialing in to an InterNotes server.)

Each time a user accesses a Web page, WebNav actually translates it into a Notes document and dumps it into a Notes database. If several users are accessing the same site, their access to the page is increased because they're accessing a local Notes database instead of transferring all the data over the Internet.

There are a couple of simple steps to configure WebNav on a client. First, in your personal Name and Address Book, edit the current location document to include the name of the InterNotes server (use the hierarchical name!).

Next, select File | Tools | User Preferences and check the Basic options enabling Make Internet URLs into Hotspots. This enables you to click and open a Web page if someone sends you a URL reference in a document or e-mail.

When you first open WebNav, you see a Notes navigator that will assist you in your travels on the Internet. Administrators can easily modify this document to give one-click access to the organization's home page, certain vendor or customer sites, and so on.

In addition, by clicking on the Database Views on the Home Navigator, Notes opens up another navigator that enables users to create their own bookmarks and so forth.

Users can also mark a site as "recommended" by simply clicking on a button of the action bar as they browse Web sites. In addition to recommending the page, users can give it a rating! The page they're recommending could be "live" (in other words, they accessed it for the first time just then), or it could be that they were simply looking through the database to see what other people had visited. To see the pages others have marked as recommended, click the Recommended Views icon from the Home Navigator.

Users can also create a Web tour—a collection of Web pages. Essentially, it's nothing more than a history of Web pages you've visited that you can share with others. You save the history of the sites you've been visiting and then enter the title of your tour. You can modify your tour by changing the order of the URLs, adding or deleting additional ones, and so forth.

Currently, the feature set of the actual Web Navigator browser is similar to other browsers, but it adheres fairly closely to the vanilla HTML coding standards. It does not support some of the new extensions, but it does a passable job. By default, WebNav looks in its own database before actually accessing the Web, but administrators can set the configuration automatically to refresh pages stored in the database.

With the Notes 4.5 client, the actual Notes client handles more of the chores itself.

WebNav Administration

There are several important requirements for the WebNav server:

- Hardware: The typical "robust" Notes server specs (as noted earlier in this chapter) are 486DX or better, 32 MB of memory, and at least a 1G hard disk.
- Notes 4 server (WebNav is strictly an R4 process), though not limited to NT and OS/2.
- TCP/IP connection to the Internet (either leased line or via a proxy Web server that is connected via an Internet provider—dial-up won't work).

Connecting Notes to the Internet with InterNotes

CHAPTER 26

673

26

CONNECTING
NOTES TO THE
INTERNET

WebNav ships with Notes 4, so it's available for your use out of the box. Type LOAD WEB at the server console to get it started. (Once again, in order to automate this process each time the server restarts, enter WEB on the ServerTasks line in the NOTES.INI. Once WEB is running, a SHOW TASKS command at the console will report that Web Retriever is loaded.)

There are a couple of configuration issues to take care of:

■ You need to specify the location of the Web Navigator database by specifying an InterNotes server. Typically, this is done on the client workstation in the location documents, but if those fields are blank, Notes checks the Server document in the Public Address Book.

■ Because WebNav is really a Notes database, you need to specify the ACL for WebNav itself. Both the local InterNotes server and other Local Domain Servers are recommended to have manager access to the database.

When WebNav is installed, a configuration document is created in the WebNav database. It's created with a number of defaults for items such as the maximum size of the database and so forth.

Controlling Access to Certain Sites

Administrators can grant or limit access to certain Web sites easily using the WebNav administration document.

There are two fields on the admin document, Allow Access and Deny Access, which enable the administrator to control the user's capability of navigating in WebNav. There's an implied "all" in the blank Allow Access field that enables users to access all sites unless restricted by entries in the Deny Access field.

These access fields can contain wildcards, specific IP addresses, or site names. Wildcards, for example, can be used to allow access to FTP or WWW servers at a site by listing *.site.com. Organizations can screen out specific Web sites by a listing such as www.playboy.com in the Deny Access field.

The combined client and server portions of Web Navigator bring various Web services to the Notes client. It brings FTP, Gopher, and HTML access to Internet sites directly into Notes databases.

The combination of InterNotes News with Web Navigator round out the InterNotes family, allowing access to both Web sites and newsgroups from within the normal Notes 4 client. Users can have full Internet functionality without the additional protocol being needed on each desktop, and they can access Internet resources from the familiar confines of Notes.

The Connectivity Issue

All of the various InterNotes products discussed in this chapter—Domino, WebPub, InterNotes News, WebNav—require live, full-time Internet connections at the server, if not elsewhere. If your organization is not already attached to the Internet, you should be!

The first step is to find an Internet Service Provider (ISP). In one form or another, an ISP will bring the Internet to your firm, typically in the form of a 56KB or better line that attaches to a router somewhere on your network. This Internet line allows you TCP/IP access to Web servers, FTP sites, and so on, on the Internet.

Finding the right ISP is a process similar to finding a spouse; you may not be able to tell whether you made the right decision for some time. There are a few obvious questions to ask before signing up:

- What speeds can we connect at? (The faster the better, naturally.)
- Do we get our own domain? Also, who "owns" the domain registration?
- Can we get mail services, as well as other options?

You might also check a couple sites that the ISP is already responsible for. Check response times, and so on, to see whether the provider has the bandwidth to add your organization to its list.

Once the ISP has been chosen, you need to take additional items into account, such as IP addressing internally, firewall considerations, TCP/IP protocol on client desktops, and more.

If you're new to this topic, your best bet is to find a consultant or business partner who can help you sort through all the issues and challenges.

Summary

We've taken an in-depth look at Domino from system administration, application development, and security points of view. Domino is still incredibly new, and it continues to grow and evolve daily. Its powerful features will continue to be augmented, and those of us in the trenches will continue to exploit them. In a very real sense, Domino is the beginning of an entirely new era for Notes.

The InterNotes family of products—Domino, Web Publisher, InterNotes News, and Web Navigator—offers Notes users, developers, and administrators an impressive arsenal of tools to work with the Internet.

Domino opens up your Notes server directly to the Web. Web Publisher enables Notes databases to be published to the Web, as well as capturing information from visitors to your Web site. Web Navigator gives Notes users a built-in browser, and InterNotes News brings newsgroup articles into the Notes database.

The InterNotes family brings full Internet integration to Notes 4. The products will continue to mature and change, and as the market continues to evolve, additional capabilities will be added.

Keep checking with Lotus's own Web site; it's your best source for up-to-date information.

As I stated at the outset of this chapter, the entire area of the Internet and Notes is changing rapidly. Domino, barely in the design stage at the beginning of 1996, was a dominant Web server force by the end of the year.

Lotus has publicly stated that Domino will make InterNotes Web Publisher obsolete, and development has been halted on that product, even though there are still some things that you can do with WebPub that you can't do with Domino.

My prediction is that Domino will not only become the prevalent Notes server platform, but that it will quickly become a Web server standout. The HTTP services rolled into the Domino server make it a potent force. I'd bet the farm on it.

Setting Up an Intranet with Domino

by Rob Wunderlich

IN THIS CHAPTER

CHAPTER 27

Here's an oft-told story (the authenticity of which I have no reason to doubt), recently repeated by Mike Zisman, Lotus Vice President:

> The chairman of Stanley Tools was set to address the yearly sales meeting. The various sales staff members had been assembled, and there was an air of jubilation. This had been a banner year—tool sales had set records—and everyone was in a great mood.
>
> The chairman entered the room with a doleful expression. He was obviously glum. He was slated to present a "fire-them-up" sales motivation speech—yet something was obviously amiss.
>
> He approached the podium. "Ladies and gentlemen," he solemnly began, "we have a problem. People don't want our drills."
>
> The sales folks were taken aback. How could this be? Murmurs were heard throughout the assemblage: "People don't want our drills? This was our best sales year—what's he talking about?"
>
> The chairman went on: "People don't want our drills. What they want are *holes.*"

Just as Stanley's chairman discovered that people want holes, not his company's product, the truth is that today people really don't want Lotus Notes, Netscape, Microsoft Access, or any other *product*—what they want is information.

Within the corporate environment, there is a lot of information. There's product information, sales information, Human Resources information, supplier information, customer information, and so on.

Some of the information is appropriate for dissemination via the Internet—corporate information that has a marketing orientation (I recently heard a speaker refer to most Web sites as "brochure-ware" since so much of what's on an Internet site tends to be static marketing information). Many sites have some interactivity involved—you can order a product or you can ask the tech staff a question, but it's still "public" information. This isn't really internal corporate information.

That's where intranets come in. Intranet sites are—at the same time—both the same as and totally different from Internet sites.

In one sense, there's no difference between the Internet and an intranet site. They both use the same hardware and software setups, they use the same protocols, and you use the same tools to access them. But often, that's where the similarities end.

Intranet sites tend to offer a totally different type of information than Internet sites. Where the Internet is aiming at information that is to be shared with the public, the intranet site often has information that is of interest only to people within a corporation. Instead of the glossy "brochure-ware" of the Internet site, the intranet site tends toward Human Resources information, internal project tracking, employee expenses, and insurance forms.

Just like Internet sites, intranet sites require a lot of consideration, from the physical setup point of view and the content side as well.

This chapter covers both aspects of intranets. First I'll cover what's involved in setting things up to begin with (and the challenges of an intranet site versus an Internet site), and then I'll spend some time on the content side of the equation as well.

I'll provide a lot of examples of intranet-type applications and how to facilitate them. I'll also focus on a couple of in-depth examples that leverage Notes databases for use on an intranet site.

Chapter 26, "Connecting Notes to the Internet with InterNotes," looks in depth at Internet sites utilizing Domino. This chapter, on the other hand, brings the discussion back inside the firewall.

Domino is the perfect tool for a corporate intranet site. Many corporations already host intranet-specific information in Notes databases. Opening the Notes server to Web browsers makes corporate information easily available to more employees than deploying Notes clients.

Within many corporations, Netscape and Internet Explorer are becoming ubiquitous. As such, deploying Domino applications that the browsers can access, rather than setting up Notes users and creating and disseminating Notes IDs, is an attractive proposition.

Domino is a far better tool than the current crop of "normal" HTTP servers. Using the Notes databases' ACL, with Domino an organization can create secure Web applications, right down to letting individual users access individual documents—a feat no "normal" Web server can accomplish.

An Intranet Primer

As I mentioned, an intranet site is largely identical to an Internet site. Both utilize HTTP servers, users access both with Web browsers, and both serve HTML pages.

But, as stated previously, there are differentiations. Let's look at the physical differences and then compare and contrast against Notes itself.

The physical setup is much the same whether you're talking Internet or intranet. You need an HTTP server (a Domino server, naturally) and TCP/IP connectivity. Although there are some "protocol tunneling" products available, the bottom line is that you need TCP/IP.

The biggest difference is that an intranet site is *inside* the firewall, whereas the typical Internet site is outside. Simply stated, the intranet site is accessible only to people on your network; people from the outside can't access the server.

NOTE

Although an in-depth discussion of firewalls is beyond the scope of this chapter, a quick explanation is appropriate.

If a corporation is attached to the Internet, typically a firewall is installed. This firewall, generally nothing more than a computer somewhere in the organization's network, is the entry point for the Internet. There are usually two network cards in this machine—one attached to the outside world, and one attached to the internal network.

This machine is responsible for keeping the corporate network secure. It protects the network from being accessed by people on the outside.

In most cases, a firewall is set up to give people on the inside access to the outside world, but block requests from the outside do get inside. This allows corporate users to browse the Web while protecting corporate assets from outside eyes.

When I said that an intranet is set up with the HTTP server inside the firewall, I meant just that—the server is accessible only to people within the company.

Unfortunately, in real life the inside/outside firewall discussion isn't quite this simple. There are many firewall products that, if properly configured, could let certain outsiders through your firewall, and thus give access to specific servers inside. At my company, for example, our firewall allows my department to access our internal Notes servers over the Internet from our homes, despite being inside our firewall. As discussed in Chapter 26, the security issue is incredibly important if you're implementing either an Internet or intranet site. Be sure to work with someone who understands firewall and security issues.

For the purposes of this discussion, the intranet server sits inside the firewall, and the Internet server sits outside, as shown in Figure 27.1.

FIGURE 27.1.
A typical firewall setup.

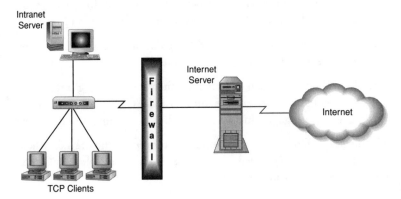

The firewall in this example prevents the outside world from getting to the intranet server, thus allowing the company to put information on it that is for internal consumption (in other words, material that is relevant to the organization's employees rather than the outside world).

But, why would a company use a Domino-powered intranet site when, obviously, they're already running Notes? A quick look at the pros and cons follows.

Intranet Pros and Cons

If you're already running a Notes server, why would you turn it into an intranet server?

Certainly, Notes has more robust security. Certainly, the Notes client has more capability (such as entering rich text, attaching files, embedding objects, and so on). But for some users that may not be enough. There are some challenges to implementing Notes. For starters, many companies are loath to go through a Notes rollout, replete with creating IDs, installing software, and so on. They figure that deploying browsers to employees is an easier means to the same end.

Some organizations, even if they use Notes throughout the organization, will still find that Domino offers some benefits. They might find that a Domino application accessed by Web browsers augments the Notes infrastructure nicely.

Additionally, since this intranet site is internal, security itself might not be a compelling reason. Table 27.1 shows how a Domino-based intranet site falls roughly halfway between a traditional Notes installation and a traditional Web site.

Table 27.1. Security comparison table.

	Web/HTTP	*Domino*	*Notes*
Access Control	Via operating system or Web server index	ACL, groups, roles. Control access from the server down to the field.	ACL, groups, roles. Control access from the server down to the field.
Authentication	Name and password only	Client: Name and password only	Notes ID, secure authentication, digital signatures
Encryption	SSL via SSL browser and server	SSL via SSL browser and server	SSL, encrypted fields, encryption keys

As Table 27.1 shows, Domino security strikes a balance between the relatively insecure HTTP server and the ultra-secure Notes server. For example, as the first row indicates, the only way to control user access in a standard HTTP server is either via the OS itself or the server index, a complicated method of giving access to individual subdirectories only to certain users.

If a database were in a restricted directory, you'd need a password to get in. But once you were in, you were in. Notes allows access to go far beyond the simplistic approach of a typical HTTP server, with access restrictions all the way from the server (that is, who can access the server itself) through database access, through view and form access, through reader and author access.

In a very real sense, Domino offers the best of both worlds. A Domino-powered intranet site offers the robust development capabilities of Notes, along with extending the Notes ACL security model to the Web. At the same time, it offers the simplicity of a browser client. If corporations feel that Notes is too cost-prohibitive (although Lotus has come a long way in removing that roadblock) or labor-intensive to roll out company-wide, they can roll out browsers for clients and still get the best of Notes.

NOTE

Although it's highly unlikely, you could actually run Domino without deploying Notes clients.

Lotus is shaping the pricing for Domino in such a way that, after the server itself and whatever clients you might need for application development and/or system administration purposes, the user community could use only Web browsers. There's a mail access license that would allow users to access mailboxes on a Domino server without having a Notes client.

However, corporations probably will still find the Notes client compelling for users who will be actively involved with a Notes application. They'll need a Notes client if they're going to be involved in developing the application or if they're going to be a major content contributor (remember that browsers don't understand text formatting, OLE, or embedding objects).

Setting Up an Intranet

Just as with an Internet site, there are numerous requirements for setting up a Domino intranet site.

Physical Setup

The hardware requirements are the same for an Internet or intranet site. You need a robust Domino server. The official Lotus recommendation is for a Pentium machine, 64 MB of memory, and a 1GB hard drive. Quite bluntly, this would be a good starting point, but the hard drive will probably become woefully inadequate very quickly. In particular, if this machine is serving as a "normal" Notes server as well as an intranet server, you may need to up the ante.

Depending on the activity you anticipate, this machine could easily evolve into a multiprocessor box with a ton of memory and a huge hard drive. You'll be able to tell quickly if your box is underpowered.

As this book goes to print, Domino is available for NT, OS/2, and a couple flavors of UNIX. As such, the server machine needs the appropriate OS on it, with the appropriate connectivity.

> **TIP**
>
> The list of available platforms is constantly changing, as are the supported versions of each OS.
>
> Keep checking with the Domino Web site at `http://domino.lotus.com` for the latest information on platforms, availability, and so on. Generally, beta versions of future platforms are available for download from there.

Network Considerations

Regardless of platform, there are several network considerations concerning an intranet server. Virtually all of these mirror the considerations concerning an Internet server; therefore, much of what was discussed in Chapter 26 is applicable here, and much of what's discussed here is applicable in Chapter 26.

The browser world works on the TCP/IP protocol. Therefore, your Domino server needs to have both TCP/IP connectivity and some sort of usable IP address. That is, your users need a way to find this machine in your network environment, via TCP/IP.

The protocol issue is important, but so is the naming issue. A perfect case in point is the server in one of the classrooms at my office. A browser cannot access the machine, known by its network name of Leader, if you use that name. If a user in the classroom attempts to type `http://leader` in the location bar in the browser, he or she will get back a message that says "Bad IP address Leader." Or, if the user attempts to access that machine via a Notes client, he or she will receive a message that says either "Server not responding" (a rather cryptic Notes message that really means "I can't find a server by that name") or "Host Unknown."

Either way, what the user is being told is that the internal network doesn't know that Leader is a valid network name for this machine. A DNS (Domain Name Server) machine or a DHCP machine is needed somewhere in the network to provide the directory services required to access the machine by name.

Otherwise, the user could access the machine, as is done in my classroom, via its IP address: 10.245.1.240. This works fine. The user simply types http://10.245.2.140 in the browser, and the server opens. Or, the user tells Notes that the server is at that address, and Notes is happy. However, the IP address is the key—the "name" of the machine or the Notes server is insufficient. (Before any network geeks jump in my face, this particular machine is on an isolated segment of our network, hence the "prime" IP address. It only has that IP address within that room.)

> **NOTE**
>
> Even in an intranet, naming conventions are critical.
>
> In the example just mentioned, I discussed the methods for distributing network names in an organization. Most TCP/IP networks have a DNS (Domain Name System) server and/or a DHCP (Dynamic Host Configuration Protocol) server somewhere.
>
> The DNS server is responsible for assigning network names within an organization. The DHCP server is responsible for assigning IP addresses if they aren't specified in the individual machine's network properties.
>
> In the classroom example, we have a DHCP server but not a DNS server. This means that the individual workstations on the classroom network receive their IP address automatically, but the users can't use a common name to access the HTTP or Notes server machines.
>
> As I mentioned, assigning and maintaining IP addressing schemes within a network is a task not to be taken lightly. If you or your organization aren't comfortable with the ins and outs of IP deployment, get some assistance.

Even in an intranet situation, you need to make sure that your users have a way to access the machine by address. If you aren't set up to do network-wide DNS or DHCP services, you'll need to resort to the clunky IP address scheme.

Also, the protocol issue remains. Most corporate networks today are running on NetWare, and therefore most are running SPX as the network protocol. SPX will not work in a browser/HTTP server scenario. The browser needs TCP/IP, and that means adding an additional protocol in order for people to access the intranet machine via their browsers. Once again, this is a serious challenge to many corporations. Many machines suffer from RAM-cram already, and many IS departments are overloaded—they don't need an additional protocol to manage.

One of the reasons the server-based Notes Web Navigator has been successful is because it allows corporations to offer Internet access without IP. Here we go again.

CHAPTER 27

NOTE

Several products available today (Microsoft's Catapult, for example) "tunnel" IP. That is, they allow an SPX protocol client to access a Web site by "tunneling" the IP packets inside SPX.

While this sounds great at first, it still requires an agent running on the client PC, so the potential RAM savings of not running the additional TCP/IP protocol is somewhat blunted. Also, you still need to visit every PC in the corporation to make this work. In the long term, you're probably better off going ahead with IP deployment.

Regardless of whether your company is interested in Internet or intranet sites, TCP/IP is important. As discussed previously, there are numerous challenges to deploying the protocol. This is certainly an area in which you should hook up with a knowledgeable consultant who can lead you through the morass.

Accessing the Site Physically

Once you've tackled the protocol issues and have gotten the naming conventions correct so that those users can see the intranet server machine, there are still some challenges.

One has to do with your company's wide area network (WAN). If your company has multiple sites and you're connected over bridges, routers, or dial-up or leased lines, all of the communication devices also need to know about the TCP/IP protocol and need to be able to route your client's PCs to your intranet site. This is not as simple as it may seem at first glance.

If you're running an SPX WAN, your routing configuration might be totally inappropriate for TCP or your routers may need to be updated or reconfigured to accept the protocol. Routing tables may need to be built. And then there's the firewall...

If that weren't enough, your WAN may be powered by an Internet Service Provider (ISP) who sells you T1 or T3 leased line service between branches. The ISP may also have some concerns about the additional protocol you want to carry.

Additionally, the ISP may have differing dial-up options. My firm has about 60 branches throughout the United States. Yet, *our* branch uses a WAN configuration to connect the corporate WAN with our four satellite offices in our area. Technically, they aren't part of the corporate WAN—they're serviced by our local LAN via an ISP provider who allows our field staffers to call a local number and connect via IP to our local RAS server. It gets complicated, but it works.

TIP

One of the questions you should ask your ISP when you begin to discuss Internet connectivity is whether he can set you up so that not only does your network have access to the outside Internet world, but that far-flung users on your network have access to your intranet site.

That is, can your ISP allow users in other cities to have dial-in access, but in effect be inside your firewall?

This gets tricky, but it can be done!

The physical problems involved with setting up a workable TCP/IP network within an already functioning corporate network are numerous, but the benefits are there as well.

None of this is intended to talk you out of the idea—just be aware that there are a lot of "challenges" to be overcome before this will be successful.

The Content Side of an Intranet

Once the physical side is handled, it's time to tackle the content. In this section, we'll take a look at the differences between Internet content and intranet content, and we'll take a look at some case studies.

What Are Companies Using Intranets For?

While the physical considerations are largely the same between Internet and intranet sites, the content side is likely quite different.

Internet sites are public sites, and their content is appropriately public. You'll find product specifications, press releases, samples, order forms, and other types of public information.

Many Web sites are referred to as "brochure-ware." They have static, marketing-oriented pages for public consumption.

Intranet sites, by contrast, are typically populated with information that's designed for in-house consumption. Instead of glossy product information, the intranet site is likely to have sales figures or part number listings. Instead of press releases, the intranet site is likely to have Human Resources information such as insurance plans, forms, and the like.

If Internet sites are often brochure-ware, intranet sites are often company handbooks online.

The intranet site might have databases containing corporate policies or proposals. It might have customer tracking or lead tracking. Instead of "services offered" as might be found on the Internet, it might have a corporate resources guide.

Where Was This Information Before the Intranet?

This type of in-house, employee-oriented information isn't a new data type that was dreamed up in the past 18 months.

Prior to utilizing some form of electronic dissemination, most companies provided this type of information in their employee handbook. Often, during new employee orientation, people were handed a three-ring binder that had everything from insurance forms to a list of paydays to vacation schedules.

In some companies, this type of information might have been stored electronically on public bulletin boards. This might have been within an e-mail package such as Beyond Mail or cc:Mail. (One of cc:Mail's biggest claims to fame was the invention of the bulletin board, where many companies put information.) Or the information might have simply been put on the network in a series of files in a common directory.

A few firms I've worked with put this type of information out in file in a common directory on the network. While workable, this method was always clumsy. Finding the latest template for expense tracking ended up in a conversation like this: "Okay, go to drive M on server CorpApps2. There's a subdirectory called EMP. In the EMP subdirectory there's another subdirectory called FORMS and a subdirectory there called EXP96. Look for a file called EEXPTMP6.WK5." This worked, but it was clumsy at best and unmanageable at worst.

As corporations began to employ Lotus Notes, many of these bulletin boards and files began migrating themselves to Notes. Many firms realized it was much simpler to have an Expense Tracking database in Notes and do all the work there (including the workflow behind expense approvals) than to expect employees to keep going out to some unknown destination on the network to continually grab an updated template for the expense worksheet.

Corporations began migrating Human Resources information to Notes, as a way to centralize storage of insurance information and forms, benefit information, 401K offerings, and the like.

Notes had already begun to be the perfect repository for this type of information; an intranet Web site is the perfect dissemination tool. Domino is the logical extension of the combination of the two. An added benefit is that even if the information *was* stored in files on the network, either Notes could become the repository for those files (as file attachments to documents in Notes databases), or the information could be imported into individual documents.

Are There Administration Concerns?

One of the benefits of employing Domino is that Notes ACL security can be extended to these databases. If I had a 401K database, for example, I could do the following:

- Look up 401K account balances.
- Look up my contribution percentages.
- Change contributions.

■ Change my investment strategies.

■ Change allocations.

Obviously, I would want this information to be secure. I wouldn't want other people to be able to access my information.

With a "normal" intranet site, this would be impossible. But with Domino, you can take the database and employ both Notes ACL and Reader Name access within the database so that the information is secure.

Security is critical for some of these databases within a firm, and Domino brings Notes security to the browser world.

Are These Databases Different from "Normal" Notes Databases?

We've been talking about a lot of different ideas for intranet databases, and it brings up the question of whether these databases are any different than "typical" Notes databases.

In a sense, they aren't, because as stated previously, many companies are already using Notes databases for this type of information. But, because these databases are going to be accessed by a browser, they do have to be different from a UI (User Interface) standpoint. You have to configure the user interface in such a way that things can be easily done from a browser client, which has far fewer resources than a normal Notes client.

> **TIP**
>
> Many Lotus Authorized Education Centers are now offering a one-day class focusing on Application Development for Domino databases. This class discusses issues such as presenting a different UI to the Web user than a Notes client and using HTML codes on forms. Check the schedule of your local LAEC and see whether it offers the class.

In other chapters in this book (notably Chapter 26), much has been said about customizing Notes databases for Domino use. As shown in Figure 27.2, you need to give the Web client options the browser doesn't have. For example, creating actions for navigation, since they don't have the Esc key to use to back out of a document in a browser, and a CREATE action to replace the missing Create menu option. All of these tips and tricks need to be employed in an intranet situation, just as in an Internet site. The content is different, but the context is the same.

Setting Up an Intranet with Domino

CHAPTER 27

689

27

SETTING UP AN
INTRANET WITH
DOMINO

FIGURE 27.2.

A Domino database showing "navigational actions" at the top of the form.

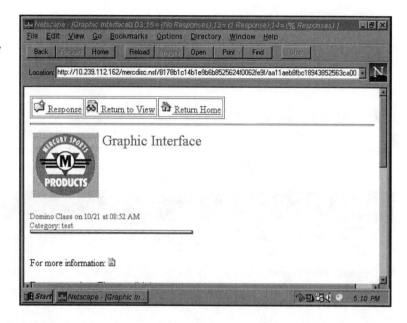

As with any other discussion of Notes databases being used on the Web, you can do a lot with special @Functions (such as @UserRoles and @URLOpen), which lend themselves to intranet usage. In Chapter 26, I discuss using @UserRoles to conditionally call subforms for a database destined for Web usage; just because an intranet site is inside the firewall doesn't mean similar subform manipulation wouldn't be just as useful.

Graphics are another concern—databases that will be served to browser clients need to handle them differently for performance optimization.

All in all, the intranet databases are "typical" Notes databases, optimized for Domino usage, just as they would be for Internet usage. The only real difference is who they're aimed at. The only real difference is the content.

Case Studies

I've been talking around the subject of content for the better part of this chapter, and the truth is that this is the area that truly delineates the Internet site from the intranet site.

Let's take a look at a fictitious company, Ridge Communications. Ridge Communications is a media/advertising/marketing conglomerate, with twelve branches throughout the United States. It has just under 1,000 employees.

Ridge Communications has set up an intranet site to complement their Internet site. Their Internet site is a showcase of their work—an electronic portfolio that people can access to see samples of Ridge's work. They can visit the Internet site and find links to their customers, product offerings from the company, press releases, and the like. All the "public" stuff is on the Internet site.

Their intranet site, by contrast, has been neglected. Ridge has fallen into "shoemaker's kids" syndrome—they've expended themselves on their paying customers and left nothing for in-house. Therefore, Ridge sets up a Domino intranet site and attempts to employ some of the excellent Domino.Action applications and/or some of the Instant Inet stuff.

> **NOTE**
>
> Domino.Action and Instant Inet are both prefab sets of applications that can be implemented to jump-start a Web site.
>
> Domino.Action is offered by Lotus. At the time this chapter was written, a sample was available for downloading from Lotus' Domino Web site. Lotus is planning not only Domino.Action but also a series of more content-specific applications.
>
> A similar offering is Instant Inet from InfoImage. This series of databases has consistent graphics and user interfaces and is linked with an attractive home page database. You can download a sample of Instant Inet from `http://download.infoimage.com`.

Now let's take a look at Ridge Communications' Domino intranet site, shown in Figure 27.3.

FIGURE 27.3.

Ridge Communications'
intranet home page.

The Home Page

Although the sample mockup here probably won't win any design competitions, it gives you a sense of the organization of the site. (Keep in mind, their *real* design efforts are lavished on the paying customers.)

There are some obvious divisions within the types of information on the site, and the home page attempts to point that out with simple graphics. They've subdivided the site into four major categories: Corporate Communications, Human Resources/Benefits, The Company's Business, and Miscellany (which becomes the catch-all for stuff that doesn't fit within the other three categories).

By a simple mouse click, employees can get information on benefits, find the expense worksheets, or check out information on the company picnic. Let's take a closer look.

Corporate Communications

Within the corporate communications section of their intranet site, Ridge has placed a number of useful databases, including (but not limited to) press releases and company backgrounds that might be useful to employees.

They've also created databases for things such as employee phone listings, branch phone numbers and addresses, the corporate organizational chart, and supplier and customer contact numbers.

HRB: Human Resources and Benefits

The HRB section of Ridge's intranet site is where employees can go to find all sorts of employment-related information.

This is where Ridge keeps a lot of their benefit stuff: information regarding the medical plan, 401K and profit sharing plans, benefit listings, vacation policies, employee referral programs, loans, employee purchase plans, employee stock options, and insurance claims.

This is also where Ridge keeps all its forms, so the employees know where to go for everything from expense forms to medical claim forms as well as leave-of-absence forms to payroll deduction forms. The forms database has become one of the most popular databases over the course of time, because it consolidates the many disparate forms that abound throughout the firm.

There were several benefits. A form had to be changed in only one place (and therefore paper waste was cut dramatically). And since employees were accustomed to looking in the form database for whatever it was they were searching for, it quickly became the automatic repository for all the new forms, even incidental ones ("The picnic potluck sign-up sheet can be found..."). One place to look, and only one place to administer.

This is also where Ridge maintains an active job posting database, where regional, branch, or departmental managers can post job offerings. A simple click of a mouse is all it takes for employees to indicate their interest in a posted position.

The Job Posting sample shown in Figure 27.4 was loosely taken from the Domino.Action samples. The Job Posting database is probably one of the most interesting databases within the Human Resources area of Ridge's intranet site. Within the Job Posting database, regional and departmental managers can post job openings. As shown in Figure 27.4, the main view of the database is a simple listing of open positions, categorized by location.

FIGURE 27.4.

The main view of the Job Posting database as viewed in Netscape.

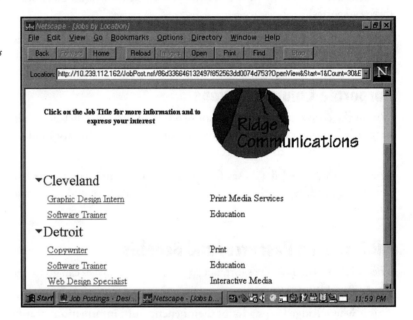

Although Ridge hasn't done so, it wouldn't be too hard to build in some additional approval workflow behind this application to make it both the place where managers go to request additional positions and where they post them once they're approved.

What Ridge *did* do, however, was equally interesting. They built a different type of workflow behind this application so that any employee accessing the job posting list could indicate his or her interest in the position by simply clicking on the Apply button, as shown in Figure 27.5. The Apply button triggers the composition of an "interest" form, which is automatically sent to the appropriate manager once the candidate has submitted it from his or her browser.

FIGURE 27.5.

A typical document in the Job Posting database as shown from a browser.

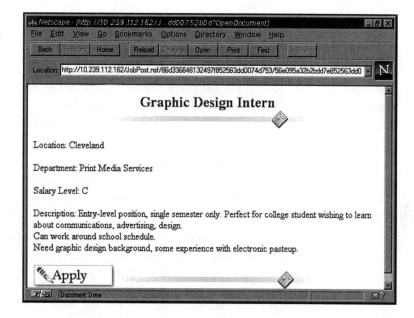

As with all databases, these job posting documents could be made to disappear automatically after a certain number of days (some companies require that job postings be available for a given time period—this could be easily made part of the application).

This database is the perfect combination of Lotus Notes and the Web. Notes builds the workflow into the database, yet the capability to access the database and be active in it from a browser extends the potential reach of the application tremendously.

Other databases within the Human Resources/Benefits area include the following:

- Insurance Info: This lets employees easily see all the insurance options available, see rules and additional information, find updated and approved doctor listings, and so on.

- 401K: Here the employee can see his or her deduction percentages, change investment options, see individual plan backgrounds, and so on.

- Payroll Deduction Tracking: The employee can find out what all his or her deductions are, what the maximums are, and so on.

- Benefits: Here the employee can keep track of all of the numerous benefits Ridge offers.

- New Employee Information: The entire "What we're all about" kit is kept online so that employees—both old and new—have one place to turn for everything from holiday schedules to vacation days to employee parking regulations.

The Company's Business

One of the things that Ridge realized they needed to disseminate to employees was some of the critical but hard-to-capture information about customers and suppliers.

Therefore, under the general heading of TCB (The Company's Business), fall a number of databases that address corporate information. This is where Ridge employees go to check corporate policies, corporate asset management, vendor tracking, customer tracking, sales forecasts and actuals, legal policies and agreements, product management, and training.

Ridge keeps its proposal database here, too, so that if you're about to pitch a big account, you can see the pitch that some other branch may have made in a similar situation. They also keep a "brag book" online, so you can quickly find out what similar customers they're working with. This information can be sorted by industry, by state, or by whatever you want.

The most active database within this area is the expense tracking database, and Ridge managers have been delighted with doing their expenses electronically. Although receipts are still needed, the company has already instituted an "only over $20" rule, which means that for all smaller expenses, simply marking it on the expense spreadsheet is sufficient. On large expenses, the receipts are still to be sent to the accounting department. Also, by using controlled access sections, employees' expense reports can be approved by their managers and automatically sent through the system.

Here are the other databases in this area of the intranet site:

- Product Management: Ridge keeps track of the various product management assignments in this database; employees can check in to see how a project is progressing.

- Corporate Assets: Ridge keeps an online "asset management" database, tracking everything from office equipment to computers.

- Project Tracking: As the various media projects work their way through the stages of proposal to work order to completion, the Project Tracking database logs their progress. Most of the people who are actually inputting this information use Notes clients, but anyone involved with a project can view its progress with a browser.

Miscellany

This division of the intranet site was originally intended to stay private, but a couple parts of the site were quickly replicated to the public Domino site as well. For example, Ridge decided to offer the employees the ability to have their own home pages. It proved so popular that they replicated the People Pages database to the Internet server so that the world could see what their employees were up to.

This is also the area in which Ridge placed the "Soapbox" and "Suggestion Box" databases, which allow employees to chat about things and to offer anonymous suggestions to management.

Although not necessarily applicable to all of Ridge's branches, this is also where a "What's on this week" database resides for employees at the home office, covering everything from special presentations and programs to the weekly menu at the corporate canteen. The company offers special after-hours exercise programs as well as employee activities (such as the upcoming skating party). This section is where all this type of information goes.

> **TIP**
>
> What draws people to sites (regardless of whether they're intranet or Internet) are things that are fun.
>
> Perhaps a weekly contest is appropriate, or some sort of company trivia database. Maybe a "bad joke of the day" database. Perhaps scanning in the weekly Dilbert cartoon from the Sunday newspaper.
>
> This is a great draw for this site, particularly if it can be done in a way that is visually appealing and mentally entertaining.

In the view of Ridge's management, it is infinitely simpler to have a database that people can refer to rather than having bulletin boards or paper memos that have to be created, printed, distributed, and ultimately discarded.

Some Final Considerations

As this case study points out, an intranet site is truly just like an Internet site, except with different content.

One of the concerns of many corporations, however, is that with the proliferation of browsers and Web sites, the actual business of the company is suffering. Too many people, they feel, are doing too much surfing.

Personally, I'm not sure that's the case. My company allows unlimited Internet access through our network. However, I understand the concern. In a well-documented case in 1996, a certain firm found that over 40 percent of the IP requests went to a *Sports Illustrated* Web site that offered sports scores. This company cut off access to the site. I'm not sure this proved that 40 percent of an employee's time is spent doing something extraneous, and it might not have even meant that the SI site was being accessed during business hours. It might have been during lunch hours. Who knows? Let's be honest: We've all kicked back and played Solitaire at one time or another. Regardless, we should not let some of those concerns thwart the construction of an intranet site.

The next sections cover a couple of final considerations.

Security

Just because this intranet site is inside the firewall doesn't mean you should be lax about security. You should employ all the normal Notes ACL and other security measures to make sure that unwanted people aren't getting into your site. Just because it's a Web site doesn't make it less important.

> **NOTE**
>
> This is a reminder that the ?Open command given to a Domino Web site will have the same effect as File | Database | Open—meaning that all the databases on your site are exposed.
>
> As discussed in Chapter 26, you should either disable the ?Open command or prevent it from returning a list of databases (by setting fields in the server document to open a given database).
>
> In Domino 4.5, you can easily disable browsing with simply setting a server document field.

Quite honestly, the types of information outlined in this chapter are actually of greater importance to a corporation than the stuff they put out for public consumption. It's important to keep it under a tight rein.

Mind your ACLs and the maintenance of your groups. Be sure to check that you haven't inadvertently left open a back door somewhere so that the wrong employee can access the wrong information.

Administration and Upkeep

Another concern is ongoing administration and upkeep. Just as with a normal Notes setup, you need to make sure that the proper system administration functions are being handled on a Domino intranet site. You need someone to manage the PAB, and you need someone to manage the ACLs on the databases.

Additionally, there's nothing worse than a stale Web site—you need someone assigned to periodic updates and cleanup.

Summary

In this chapter, we looked at the intranet site—the "internal Web site."

The setup considerations are essentially identical to the ones for an Internet site, as discussed in Chapter 26, but the content is of a different sort.

We looked at the physical side of the intranet site in this chapter, and we ended with a hard look at the content, including a case study of a firm employing Domino to power a substantial intranet site.

As you've seen, Domino provides the perfect engine for an intranet site.

27

SETTING UP AN
INTRANET WITH
DOMINO

VI
PART

Integrating and Connecting with Notes

CHAPTER 28

A Sampling of Third-Party Products for Lotus Notes

by Rizwan Virk

IN THIS CHAPTER

The rise in the number of seats of Lotus Notes over the past several years has led to a proliferation of third-party companies that provide services and shrink-wrapped, add-on products for Notes. In order to "build an industry around Notes," Lotus has made a concerted effort to recruit and train business partners who can provide value to the companies that use Notes. The Lotus Business Partner program had grown from a few hundred to over 12,000 companies by the end of 1995. It's continuing to grow by 2,000 to 3,000 business partners per year.

Although most of the companies in the Business Partner program provide services (installation, application development, and so on) around Notes, a growing number have encountered the same problem often enough to realize that a generic tool or application would solve the problem once and for all for all of their customers. The result is a vibrant third-party industry around Lotus Notes.

With each release of Notes, including R4, new companies have entered this marketplace. At Lotusphere in January 1996, several hundred press announcements were made for new products or new releases of existing products. At Lotusphere in January of 1997, with the advent of Domino, there will be even more products—many of them Internet-related. These products range from administrative utilities to full-blown, sales-force automation packages that are used to help sell Notes to a customer.

Many of the companies that make third-party products for Notes are quite young and entrepreneurial. Each has its own mix of product-versus-services revenues, and each can provide a different level of support for its products. This chapter provides a sampling of the third-party products available for Lotus Notes.

Types of Third-Party Products

I like to divide the third-party industry for Notes-related products into three general categories. Although there are numerous subcategories within these major groupings, each one represents a group of solutions focused at a different segment of the Notes industry:

- Shrink-wrapped tools
- Links to Notes
- Near shrink-wrapped applications

Shrink-wrapped tools are products directed primarily toward Notes administrators and developers, although a few are also targeted toward end users. These tools help to build Notes applications, help administer Notes servers, or otherwise arm a company to fully deploy and utilize Lotus Notes as a strategic information platform. They are typically developed using the Notes API, and are rarely customized. In the future, a growing number of these tools may be developed entirely in LotusScript.

Links to Notes are products that help an organization leverage its existing information technology investments by linking them to Notes. These products help use the strengths of Notes while interacting with other desktop and/or client server environments (for example, Microsoft Visual Basic). In some cases, these products may link Notes to mainframe systems.

Near shrink-wrapped applications are usually marketed by companies that provide Notes-related, application-development services. These fully functional Notes applications can save an organization thousands of dollars in development costs. Notes-based applications are developed using the Notes scripting languages (Notes macro and LotusScript) and can help jump-start a Notes deployment. The companies that sell these applications usually also provide customization services to tailor the application to the specific need of the customer or, in some cases, enable the customer to perform the customization themselves.

Types of Third-Party Companies

Today, the companies that provide Lotus Notes-related products have one of the following business models. The initial surge of Lotus Business Partners consisted of companies providing Notes installation and application development companies. Many of these companies branched out and created Notes-related products as a complement to their services. More recently, many small companies have appeared that only provide Notes-related products. Today, the number of product and service companies is growing at an alarming rate. Over the next few years, I expect companies to specialize in either services or products, along with a general consolidation of the number of independent players in the Notes third-party industry.

- Software vendors providing links to Notes
- Product-based companies dedicated to Notes
- Service-based companies dedicated to Notes

Software vendors providing links to Notes are usually big software companies who believe that support for Notes enhances their existing product line. These companies may have found that a large portion of their existing customer base also happens to be using Lotus Notes. Sometimes, these software vendors believe that they can open up entirely new markets for their products by linking them to Notes. Examples include Gupta (now Centura Software), Powersoft (now Sybase), Borland, and yes, even Microsoft.

Product-based companies dedicated to Notes have grown up in the Notes space by developing and marketing Notes-related tools and applications. Although many of these companies started by providing Notes consulting services and may continue to do so, their primary business is the development, marketing, and support of their Notes products. Examples include Brainstorm Technologies, Casahl, Quality Decision Management, Application Partners, Inc. (API).

Service companies dedicated to Notes provide consulting services around Notes as their main line of business. They have developed a product, usually a near shrink-wrapped application, that provides a generic solution for a problem or need that they have seen again and again. Examples include ALI Technologies, The Lead Group (acquired by Entex), MFJ International, and InfoImage.

28

THIRD-PARTY
PRODUCTS FOR
LOTUS NOTES

Shrink-Wrapped Tools

The number of shrink-wrapped tools for Notes has grown considerably over the last 12 months. These tools and utilities help a user, developer, or administrator of Notes save time and money by simplifying critical tasks. The resultant savings usually more than justifies the cost of the product. The tools mentioned here are horizontal—they apply equally to companies in all industries using Notes. I have divided shrink-wrapped tools into three groups:

- Administrative tools
- Development tools
- Miscellaneous tools

Choosing the Right Tool

Because Notes is a client/server system that runs on many platforms, it is important to check the compatibility of each tool with the operating systems that you are using. As of this writing, most Notes servers run on OS/2 (although Windows NT servers are catching up fast) and most Notes clients run on Microsoft Windows (3.11 or Windows 95). As might be expected, server-based tools most often support OS/2 as their main platform. However, more and more companies are adopting a client-based approach to their tools. By running a utility on a client machine, the problem of buying multiple versions of software for the different operating systems is solved. I know of many companies that use both OS/2 and Windows NT for their Notes server. A client-based tool, which usually supports Windows, will run against any Notes server, whether it is running on OS/2, Windows NT, HP-UX, NLM, or Solaris.

Lotus Notes shrink-wrapped tools have three types of user interfaces. One type of tool is just an Agent that monitors a Notes database. This type of tool uses Notes as its interface, and generally runs on a server machine. Another type of tool is the workstation menu add-in product. This type of product adds a menu item into the Tools menu of Notes. When the user clicks on this new menu option, the application pops up. The third type of tool is a standalone application that has its own custom user interface.

A tool that uses a Notes database as its user interface might seem cross-platform, but usually the Agent has been written with the Notes API—so different versions are necessary for different operating systems. Client-based tools are also platform-specific—except they run against any Notes server.

Administration Tools

The first set of tools that we'll look at are administrator productivity tools. Because of its distributed nature, Lotus Notes can be a difficult platform to monitor and maintain. On any given day, Notes administrators find themselves performing a multitude of tasks, including moving and compacting Notes databases, changing access control lists (ACLs), troubleshooting replication schedules, generating user IDs, maintaining the Public Address Book, and so on. The Lotus Notes Administrator's Guide has a nice, exhaustive list of tasks that a good administrator must be prepared to do.

On top of all that, when Notes is first deployed in many companies, one person is often responsible not only for administration of Notes servers but also for development and deployment of Notes applications. This tends to work effectively for organizations that have 10 or fewer users of Notes. After the numbers move beyond 10, this task can be monumental for a single person. Luckily, many of the tools mentioned here make it possible for a single administrator to perform tasks more quickly and efficiently. I divide these administrative tools into two subcategories:

- Server and replication monitoring and management
- ACL and security management

Server and Replication Monitoring and Management

Perhaps the most critical situation that can occur for a Notes administrator is for a server to go down. Equally important are problems with replication, mail routing, and monitoring disk space on the server. Knowing about and troubleshooting any of these tasks can bring even an experienced administrator to his knees. Yet another constant task that an administrator needs to do is to monitor the disk space on the server and manage it appropriately. The following tools help an administrator deal with all of these problems and more:

- *CleverWatch*, from CleverSoft in Portland, Maine. This neat product advertises "lights-out system management." It has the ability to not only detect if a server is down, but also bring the server back up. Unlike many other utilities, which are written exclusively using the Notes API, CleverWatch operates at the network level. This means that CleverWatch Agents can keep going even if Notes is not up.

  CleverWatch has Agents that must be installed on each server that is to be "watched." These Agents are quite powerful and perform a variety of tasks in addition to bringing the server back up. Through a Lotus Notes database, an administrator can specify a set of rules and steps to follow if disaster occurs—for example, if a server goes down, bring it back up and call the administrator's beeper. These triggers follow a similar style to alarms that can be defined in Notes R4. The Notes R4 version of Cleversoft is currently available.

- *Server Admin Plus* from Brainstorm Technologies, in Cambridge, Massachusetts. Server Admin Plus is a point-and-click tool that can cut administration time in half. The product contains a collection of utilities (all run from a single GUI console) that can save an administrator many hours of tedious tasks. Server Admin Plus works with Notes R3 and Notes R4 servers all from a single console.

  One of the components of Server Admin Plus is the Database Workbench, an easy-to-use, point-and-click way to manage databases and disk space on your server. The

Database Workbench lets administrators find databases that are taking up too much space or are replicating inappropriately and, with the click of a button, correct the situation. Databases can very easily be made to begin replicating with one another, or one master database can be used to copy ACLs to other databases. Figure 28.1 shows the Database Workbench screen for Server Admin Plus.

FIGURE 28.1.

The Database Workbench of Server Admin Plus.

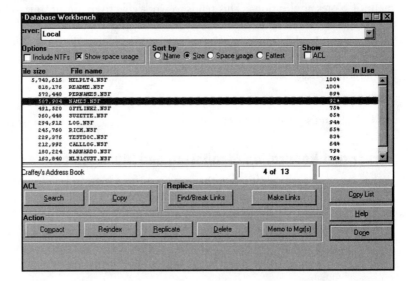

Another of the components of Server Admin Plus is a statistics-graphing module. Although many organizations have statistics reporting turned on with their Notes databases, very few administrators find useful information in them because there is no visual representation. By looking at the graphs provided with Server Admin Plus, you can get a bird's eye-view of the problems that may be occurring on your server over a chosen period of time.

Server Admin Plus runs on a Windows client machine and can be pointed at any and/ or all servers on all platforms.

■ *DYS Analyzer* from DYS Consulting in Brookline, Massachusetts. DYS Analyzer is a highly focused tool that deals with one of the most powerful and complicated issues in Notes: replication. When Notes servers replicate, the status information about that replication can be buried deep in the Notes log or in other locations. DYS Analyzer provides a client-based, easy-to-use interface that shows graphs and summary data about replication events. Administrators can, upon coming to work in the morning, see a quick summary of all of the replication events that occurred the previous night, including the number of successful and unsuccessful replications, the number of retries, the connect time for each server, and so on. This summary report is the beginning of a set of informational utilities for making sure replication is working correctly, and for troubleshooting when it isn't.

ACL and Security Management

Nothing can be more time-consuming for an administrator than managing server- and database-security access. The proper way in Notes to simplify this task is to put individual users into groups only within the company's Public Address Book. Then, only groups should be given an access level in database Access Control Lists (ACLs). However, many organizations find names creeping into the ACL for a variety of reasons. After a while, it becomes very difficult for an administrator to know which databases contain individual groups and which also contain names.

After some time, as the number of databases on each server grows and users move between departments and companies, an administrator can be hard pressed to keep up with all of the security implications. ACL cleanup and enforcement is a major issue, and the companies listed here all have elegant solutions to help the administrator:

■ *Server Admin Plus* (SAPlus) from Brainstorm Technologies in Cambridge, Massachusetts. A Notes administrator's desk usually has a large number of little yellow stickies posted on it and on the computer monitor. Each of these is a task that someone in the organization wants done. Oftentimes, these notes contain items such as, "Please give Fred access to this database," or "Fred has access to these three databases but shouldn't," or "Remove Sharon from this group, she's moving to another department," and so on. SAPlus is a point-and-click tool that can be an administrator's salvation. Each of these tasks can be done with a couple of button clicks from the SAPlus user interface.

For managing ACLs, SAPlus has three features: Purge User, ACL Search, ACL Replace, and the Database Workbench. When a user leaves a company, there are six steps that an administrator should perform for that user. Notes R3 left it to the administrator to do all of these manually, and so many of them never got done. Even Notes R4 automatically does only three of the six steps that should be performed, and these steps are performed only on databases that have the AdminServer property set appropriately. An organization migrating to Notes R4 is in for a surprise if they expect to count on Notes for removing users across databases—setting the AdminServer property for each database is just as tedious as manually going through each database to remove the user. SAPlus's Purge User function takes care of all of these steps, across all databases, on all servers. The ACL Search feature can be used to find out places where synonyms or aliases of a user reside and remove them. The six steps are:

1. Remove Person from ACLs.
2. Remove Person from Groups.
3. Remove Person Record from the Public Address Book.
4. Delete Person's Mail File.
5. Add Person to DenyAccess Group.
6. Remove Synonyms from ACLs.

28

THIRD-PARTY PRODUCTS FOR LOTUS NOTES

The ACL Search is an interactive way for an administrator to query which databases a user has access to. When a search is complete, an administrator can change the ACLs with a simple button click. For example, a search on the word "default" would reveal what the default access level is in each database ACL. The Database Workbench provides a quick way to navigate around all of the databases so that their ACLs can be changed quickly. The Database Workbench also lets an administrator create one master ACL and then copy that ACL to a number of other databases. This greatly reduces the burden of maintaining a separate ACL for every database.

■ *J&T Shell* from J&T Associates, Inc., in Saline, Michigan. The J&T shell takes a different approach to system administration from all of the other tools mentioned. This product does provide its own user interface, but the user interface consists of a set of command-line utilities for taking care of a variety of tasks, including Address Book management, access control list maintenance, replication monitoring, and more. Based upon the UNIX shell in some ways, this product is for power administrators who prefer command-line utilities to point-and-click solutions. Administrative tasks are accomplished by typing (or selecting) a command and waiting for a response.

■ *ACL/Reporter* from DSSI/QXComm in Los Angeles, California. ACL/Reporter was actually one of the first third-party tools available on the market. ACL/Reporter is an Agent that runs on a Notes server, and is available for OS/2 and Windows NT. ACL/Reporter is an elegant way to capture and store information about which users have access to which databases. ACL/Reporter runs every so often on the Notes server and produces a Notes database as its output. This database can then be reviewed from time to time to see who has access to what. One of the more exciting features is the ability to specify exception rules. ACL/Reporter will find those databases having ACLs that don't match the rules, and then write the output to a Notes database. DSSI QXComm also has ACL/Updater, a batch utility for making changes to ACLs.

■ *Essential Tools* from InfoImage in Phoenix, Arizona. Essential Tools (ET), most recently marketed by GroupQuest, is now back in the hands of its original developer, InfoImage. ET is a product that uses Lotus Notes forms as a way to manage users, access control lists, and groups. ET consists of a set of server-based Agents that monitor a control database. An administrator fills out forms in the control Notes database for each action that needs to be performed, such as, "Remove this user from all groups." The server-based Agents monitor the database at predefined intervals and fulfill the requests.

Development Tools

Lotus Notes is a rapid application-development environment that is well suited for prototyping. Unlike other prototyping tools, however, the robust infrastructure of Notes makes it easy to turn prototypes into production applications. The savvy Notes developer must be part database designer and part application developer, managing a collage of design elements in each database. Each Notes database contains multiple forms, views, Agents, and Navigators. Each of these design elements and their sub-elements have multiple patches of code associated with them. The development tools sampled in the following list simplify the process of maintaining, developing and deploying Lotus Notes applications.

■ *TLG CoPilot* from Entex Information Services of Michigan in Bloomfield Hills, Michigan. TLG CoPilot is one of my favorite development tools for Notes. (See Figure 28.2.) CoPilot is an easy-to-use tool for maintaining Notes databases that have a large number of design elements and code snippets. CoPilot arranges all of the design elements of a database in an outline format so that any design element is only a simple click away. The outline goes all the way down to the field level. Even Notes 4 design outline doesn't come close to CoPilot's complete design element outline. On the right-hand side, whenever a design element is selected, a property box displays all of the relevant properties for that item. Following an approach that is used by development tools like Microsoft Visual Basic, CoPilot lets the developer quickly change a number of properties, including code, data type, etc. of Notes fields. This type of property box is one that is sorely needed for Notes objects.

FIGURE 28.2.

The outline structure of CoPilot.

Perhaps one of its most useful features is the ability to search and replace across multiple formulas and code snippets at once. As in any software project, changing the name of a field or variable can have repercussions elsewhere in the code. CoPilot lets developers quickly find all of the places in a database that are affected by a design change. Another major area of usage for CoPilot is when a new developer comes aboard on a project. It can take hours of navigating around the Notes 4 interface for a developer to understand how a database works, and how the design elements interact with one another. Using the CoPilot interface, it takes only minutes; each snippet of code is available with the click of a button. Yet another feature is the ability to open multiple databases at once. A developer can look at two databases to find similarities, fix inconsistencies, copy and paste code, and so on. CoPilot is a client-based tool that runs on Windows platforms but can access databases on any server platform. The Notes R4 version of CoPilot will be released in mid-1996.

■ *RADD Toolkit* from Workgroup Productivity Corporation in OakBrook, Illinois. The RADD Toolkit is a set of Notes databases that provides the necessary tools for planning, installing, developing and deploying Lotus Notes enterprise-wide. Unlike the other tools in this category, RADD does not actually assist in developing applications or writing code—it helps you in *planning* the development, deployment, and maintenance of Notes applications. The Toolkit includes a Systems Standards and a Development Standards database, to help members of a Notes development team or roll-out team stay on the same page and add consistency to their applications. The RADD Toolkit was put together by Workgroup Productivity Corporation after years of compiling their "best practices" during consulting engagements. Design standards, development methodology, quality assurance, change control, and data libraries and dictionaries are all included. These databases can be populated with data from your company. The RADD Toolkit is a set of Notes databases that can reside on any Notes server.

■ *ALI Design Analyzer* from ALI Technologies Incorporated in Needham, Massachusetts. The ALI Design Analyzer (DA) is a useful utility for Notes developers that is kicked off from the Tools menu on the Notes client. As its name suggests, this product analyzes the design elements of the current Notes database. It might be viewed as an enhanced design synopsis. The DA compiles all of the relevant attributes of the design elements of a Notes database and outputs them to another Notes database. This second Notes database then can be used to quickly peruse design elements and their attributes in predefined Notes views. The database contains a separate Notes document for each design element in the source database. Design Analyzer works on a Windows client against any Notes database, and produces a Notes database as its output. The R4 version of Design Analyzer should be released by publication date.

■ *TILE* from the Shelby Group in Bethesda, Maryland, is similar in some ways to the Lotus InterNotes publisher. It is an extremely powerful tool for publishing documents on the World Wide Web. TILE converts any Notes database into HTML, the language of the World Wide Web, keeping all of the elements and doclinks of the Notes database intact. TILE turns Notes into a development environment for the Web. Because a Notes database is a self-contained unit, you can use it to organize the different elements of your Web pages, including doclinks and hypertext. And because Notes databases can be replicated, Web pages can be designed collaboratively by people in different locations. TILE doesn't just export to HTML, it incorporates many unique features of Notes, including collapsible Notes views. TILE reproduces them in the Web environment.

■ *WIT: The Notes Author* from Application Partners, Inc. in Iselin, New Jersey, is a unique tool for developing Notes applications without actually writing any code. The WIT control database contains WIT "programs," which are executed by the WIT engine, an Agent developed using the Notes API that resides on the server. Rather than programming using the Notes macro language or LotusScript, a user (the programmer) of WIT fills out forms. Each form can have a certain number of pre-defined actions, which represent the programming language of WIT. By filling out the form and putting these actions into a logical order, powerful applications can be built, including workflow applications, archiving applications, and more.

■ *Formula One Toolkit* from Groupware Concepts, Inc. in Irving, Texas. This product, more relevant to Notes R3 developers than Notes R4, is a set of add-on functions for Notes developers. The folks at Groupware Concepts used a "back-door" way to extend the Notes macro language. The Notes macro language, you'll recall, is a set of `@func-tions` that can be used to perform operations within Notes. Many developers, when they become proficient with the given set of `@functions`, find themselves wanting more `@functions`, but without the ability to extend the language. The Formula One Toolkit uses the `@DbCommand` function as a door to a whole new set of functions. The `@DbCommand` function was originally meant to send database commands to external databases such as Sybase's Oracle. In order to do this, the command calls a DLL in the Notes directory. The Formula One Toolkit uses its own DLL to execute the additional functions. These functions can be put into your code anywhere that `@functions` can be. Sample functions include the ability to modify ACLs, mathematical functions such as sine, cosine-sine, database actions such as compact, copy, pop-up windows, list functions, and more. `@functions` continue to be supported in many places in Notes R4. However, the introduction of LotusScript in Notes R4, a more powerful and extensible programming language allays some of the shortcomings of the R3 macro language, making the additional `@functions` provided by this product less relevant.

Miscellaneous Tools

In addition to developer and administrator tools, there are quite a few widgets and end-user tools that do not fit nicely into any category. I will give one example:

■ *Network Based Training for Lotus Notes* from ReCOR in Evanston, Illinois. One of the best ways to train end users on Notes is to use an online, on-demand training tool. Network Based Training (NBT) for Lotus Notes is one of the best available tools for this. By making the training program available across the network, individual users can progress at their own pace. NBT for Lotus Notes contains 29 different lessons, covering the fundamentals of using Notes, including Notes Mail, Notes Databases, and Remote Notes operation. Throughout the course, users are asked to perform tasks

28

THIRD-PARTY PRODUCTS FOR LOTUS NOTES

using a simulated version of Lotus Notes. Many Notes administrators have found NBT to be a cost-effective way to deliver Notes training to their end users.

Links to Notes

This general category of products includes a collection of tools that were designed to link Lotus Notes with existing information systems. For Lotus Notes to be truly successful, it cannot be an island—it will need to leverage and integrate with all of the other products that a company uses to store, share, and organize information. I divide these software systems into three groups, and then sample tools for linking them to Notes:

- Client/server development tools
- Legacy databases
- Desktop applications

Links to Client/Server Development Tools

The client/server revolution has produced a host of rapid application-development environments to enable an MIS organization to quickly create front-end, data-entry and business-process applications connected to relational-database servers. These application-development environments are a mixture of a 4GL language and a visual GUI builder. The most popular of these tools is Microsoft Visual Basic, with more than 2 million users. Visual Basic has become the *de facto* standard for rapidly building client/server applications and GUI front ends for databases. On the higher end, tools such as PowerBuilder from Sybase and SQLWindows from Gupta (now Centura Software) provide more sophisticated database-linking and display capabilities.

Many of these environments now have some way of linking with Lotus Notes databases. Sometimes these links, which can take the form of a set of objects, function calls, or drivers, are included in the box. Using these linking tools, an organization can create a front-end application that brings data from Notes and other databases together on the same screen. Alternately, an organization can implement a complicated workflow process that needs to update information in multiple databases using these tools.

Third-party products for linking to client/server development tools include:

- *VB/Link for Lotus Notes* (for Visual Basic) from Brainstorm Technologies in Cambridge, Massachusetts. One of the first third-party development tools available for Lotus Notes, VB/Link was a pioneer in creating front ends for Notes databases. Introduced in 1993, VB/Link consists of a set of objects that can be used to connect to Notes databases, read and write data, and display Notes-specific features. Originally, VB/Link was implemented as a Visual Basic custom control (VBX), but it is now also available as a set of OCX controls (both 16-bit and 32-bit). Because it is available in OCX form, VB/Link can now be used in other environments that support

OCX controls. The current or next release of most major application-development environments will support OCX controls.

VB/Link consists of three main objects: a Notes data control, a Notes view control, and a Notes rich text control. By using the Notes data control, an application can connect to a Notes database, read a result set, pipe the results to other visual controls, create new Notes documents, or edit existing Notes documents. By using the other two controls, an application can display a Notes view with its hierarchical outline structure intact, including categories and response documents, or can display a Notes rich text field as it would appear in Notes, with all fonts, colors, file attachments, doclinks, and so on showing properly. Figure 28.3 shows an example application built using VB/Link for Lotus Notes.

FIGURE 28.3.

A front end to Notes developed using Visual Basic and VB/Link for Lotus Notes.

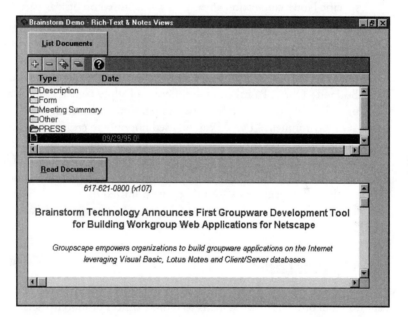

■ *QuickObjects for Lotus Notes* (for SQLWindows) from Gupta in Menlo Park, California. The QuickObjects for Lotus Notes, which ship with the enterprise version of SQLWindows, provide one of the quickest methods for building a front end to Notes, and one of the most powerful methods of integrating Notes data with data from relational sources.

The QuickObject architecture (Gupta has QuickObjects for SQL database access, for Graphing, for e-mail, and for various other functions) consists of three parts: data sources, visualizers, and commanders. The QuickObjects for Lotus Notes have a data-source object for connecting to a Notes database and displaying the result set in a grid. The commanders are command buttons that have specific functions, such as Navigate Next, Add Record, Navigate Previous, Delete, and so on, for the currently selected record. Visualizers are ways to display and edit the data in the fields of the current record. In SQLWindows, the Data Source can be configured using wizards, and visualizers and commanders can be hooked to data sources in minutes. A complete data-entry application can be created without writing a single line of code!

■ *PowerBuilder Library for Lotus Notes (PLAN)* for PowerBuilder from Powersoft (recently acquired by Sybase) in Concord, Massachusetts. Powersoft sells this class library as one of the ways to get at Notes databases from PowerBuilder applications. Other ways include OCX controls (such as VB/Link for Lotus Notes) and custom DLLs (written using the Notes API) that can be called from PowerBuilder applications. The class library is actually an external program that is used to connect to Notes databases and configure a DataWindow object. The DataWindow object (which has a specific Notes connection already wired) is stored on disk as part of a PowerBuilder library. This DataWindow object can then be included in a PowerBuilder application.

■ *Delphi/Link for Lotus Notes* (for Delphi) from Borland in Scotts Valley, California. Released from Borland in 1995, Delphi is one of the most powerful development tools available for Windows. Delphi is a visual-development environment based upon Borland's Object Pascal compiler. Because Delphi code is compiled and not interpreted, it can usually run from two to ten times faster than code developed in other 4GL environments. Delphi can be used not only to create applications, it can also create DLLs, VBX, OCX and OLE servers. Delphi/Link for Lotus Notes is a product distributed by Borland that provides a set of objects for accessing Lotus Notes databases. Delphi/Link was originally developed by Brainstorm Technologies and provides similar functionality to VB/Link, only optimized for the Delphi environment. Delphi and Delphi/Link are discussed in Chapter 22, "Using Third-Party Development Tools."

Links to Databases

Notes databases often need to be linked to other database systems. This can be to distribute data stored in other database systems to remote offices or mobile users, or it can be to collect information in Notes and move it into other database systems. For example, a purchase-order approval system built on Notes may need to transfer the PO information into the accounting system after a PO has been approved. For a more thorough discussion of the reasons and methods for integrating Notes with other database systems, please see Chapter 31, "Integrating Notes with Legacy Systems." This section gives a quick overview of database-integration products for Lotus Notes.

■ *DataLink for Lotus Notes* from Brainstorm Technologies in Cambridge, Massachusetts. DataLink is a point-and-click tool for migrating and synchronizing data between existing database systems and Lotus Notes. DataLink is a client-based solution, so it can work with Notes servers on any platform, including OS/2, Windows NT, Solaris, NLM, and HP-UX. DataLink's user interface qualifies as one of the gems of the

Notes third-party industry—using three panels, DataLink lets a user choose from a set of source and destination fields, and maps the two via a panel in the middle. (See Figure 28.4.) DataLink can export data from or import data into Notes. On an ongoing basis, DataLink can be scheduled to update or synchronize records from one data source to another. DataLink's field mappings between a source and destination database can be stored as a .TPL (transfer template) file and scheduled to run later, or can be used as the starting point for another template. Brainstorm received the 1995 Lotus Business Partner Beacon award for Best Application Development Tool for DataLink and VB/Link.

FIGURE 28.4.

Mapping relational fields to Notes fields in DataLink.

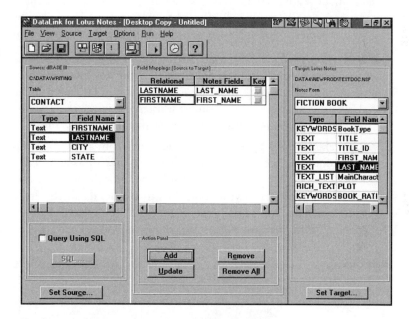

Of the solutions presented here for database linking, DataLink is the most cost effective because of its client-based approach. DataLink provides native drivers for desktop databases, including Microsoft Access, Borland Paradox, and others, and will work with any ODBC-compatible data source, including Sybase's Oracle, and so forth.

- *Replic-Action* from Casahl in Danville, California, is a high-end database integration product that is used to replicate data between relational databases and Lotus Notes databases. The user interface is a set of Lotus Notes forms in a Notes database that are used to specify which are the source and destination databases. Replic-Action engines then are launched to perform the data transfers. Replic-Action is licensed on a per-server basis, and it uses ODBC for its database access.

- *Notrix Composer* from Percussion Software in Stoneham, Massachusetts. Notrix Composer is a server-based Agent for OS/2 servers that uses a Notes database to define

28

THIRD-PARTY
PRODUCTS FOR
LOTUS NOTES

its data-migration events. An organization can extend the Composer by purchasing Notrix, a language based on REXX. Notrix Composer is sold on a per-server basis, and will work with ODBC sources. Percussion, however, recommends that companies purchase its dedicated drivers to get better performance than ODBC drivers alone can give.

Links to Desktop Products

Users of desktop-productivity applications, such as spreadsheets and word processors, often need to link their applications to Notes. This might be to store data in Notes, so that it can be shared across a workgroup or distributed to remote sites. The following tools provide user-friendly and sophisticated approaches to integrating desktop applications with Lotus Notes.

■ *OfficeLink for Lotus Notes* from Brainstorm Technologies. OfficeLink for Lotus Notes provides a method for users of Microsoft Word and Excel to stay within their favorite desktop applications. OfficeLink turns Notes into an extended network file server. Using this file-server model, different users within the same workgroup can share files, offer suggestions, or collaborate to make modifications to files.

OfficeLink adds a Notes menu to Microsoft Word and Excel. This menu contains three options: Open From Notes, Save To Notes, or Save As To Notes. Below these three are the most recently used files. Using OfficeLink, a user can create a memo in Microsoft Word and save that memo into a Notes database. Other users of OfficeLink can then open that memo. Version 2.0 of OfficeLink lets the user save the memo as a rich text field in Notes. Figure 28.5 shows the OfficeLink menu placement.

FIGURE 28.5.

The Notes menu provided by OfficeLink in Microsoft Word.

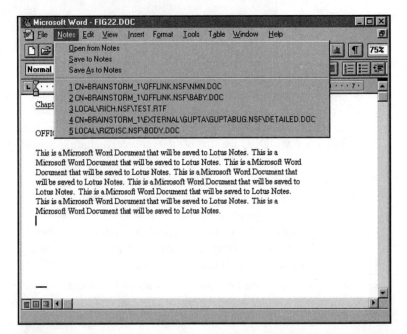

- *ProjectLink* from CamBridge Publishing Group, Inc. in Columbus, Ohio. This product is a combination of a Notes application and a utility for data migration. Although OfficeLink could be used to store Office files into any Notes database, this product contains one specific Notes database that can be used for project management. This database can be used for data input and review functions that are now done in the Microsoft Project environment.

- *Intell*Agents from Intell*Agent,* Inc. in Dallas, Texas. This product is an Agent to move data between ACT, the popular contact-management product for sales people, and a specific Notes database. The Notes database is part of the Intell*Agent* sales-force automation package described later in this chapter, under "Sales-Force Automation Applcations."

Near Shrink-Wrapped Applications

Lotus Notes ships with a set of sample applications. These application templates serve as good examples of how to build Notes applications, but they are not typically used in production. Many companies hire consultants to build applications to their specification from scratch. However, it may be much more cost effective for a company to buy a near shrink-wrapped application and add a few company-specific customizations.

The following categories represent only a fraction of the types of Notes applications that are available today on the market. I will list a few applications in each of these categories:

- Sales-force automation
- Help desk
- Human-resource applications
- Project management and scheduling

Factors to Consider Before Purchasing Applications

The main issues you need to be aware of while evaluating and/or purchasing Notes-based applications are platform support, pricing model, customizability, licensing and maintenance.

- **Platform support.** Many of these applications are implemented as Lotus Notes databases. That means that each one will work on any Notes server or local Notes client. However, some applications also include Agents or add-in DLLs, which are usually written using the Notes API, making them platform-dependent. If the application has Agents included in it, you must be sure that it works on your server platforms.

- **Pricing model.** There are two basic pricing models for Notes-based applications: per end user and per server. The server model is usually easier to implement, and may be more cost effective. The per client must be clarified, because a mobile user might need two copies—one on his/her desktop machine and one on a laptop.

■ **Customizability and licensing.** An important factor to ask about before purchasing any application is the level of customizability. Some application vendors hide the design of the Notes database, so you will not be able to modify it in any way. Many times, these same vendors will sell you a design version of the application at a higher price. Some applications are licensed so that you can freely make modifications. Others, however, are licensed so that *only* the application vendor can make modifications.

■ **Maintenance.** Another factor to consider is maintenance—please be sure of the maintenance terms and conditions before customizing an application. Some companies will no longer provide support for an application if it is modified. Also be sure to ask about the pricing of upgrades to Notes R4, as well as point releases if the applications were first developed for Notes R3.

Sales-Force Automation Applications

Perhaps one of the most compelling applications for Lotus Notes is contact management. Particularly for a mobile sales force with regional and district offices, Notes is the perfect way to share and consolidate lead and status information. Many companies buy Notes in order to provide a way for their salespeople to share information while traveling. Here are a few packages:

■ *Intell*Agent *Control* from Intell*Agent,* Inc. in Dallas, Texas. The Intell*Agent* Control system is a Notes database that can be used to track leads, organize sales information, and provide summary reports. The system is divided into four databases that form the hub of this sales management system:

   ■ Intell*Agent* Control: Master database for viewing customer, prospect, and project information.

   ■ Sales Intell*Agents*: A database that keeps track of all of your pricing, discount, and specification information.

   ■ Intell*Agent* Document Control: A database that keeps track of various documents needed in the sales cycle, including marketing materials, slide shows, contracts, proposals, and more.

   ■ Competitive Intell*Agents*: A database used to store information about competitors and the industry.

These databases work together to form the basis for a very powerful sales-force automation system.

■ *OverQuota* from MFJ International in New York, New York. OverQuota is a popular sales-force automation package that can be used by different parts of an organization to work collaboratively on sales opportunities. OverQuota consists of a set of databases that are not just used by sales people for contact management—they are used by marketing, administration, management, and product development. Over-Quota is also designed to work with your sales channels and partners by utilizing Notes replication. It can act as an effective focal point for your company's sales process.

Help Desk Applications

Most Notes consulting firms have some template that they use to quickly build customer-service applications. Lotus Notes is an excellent tool for tracking customer issues and, in the process, creating an effective knowledge base. This class of applications, which I will call Help Desk, can be used to service customers or internal end users. Here are two shrink-wrapped applications that can be used out of the box for this purpose:

- *Visual Help Desk* from Brainstorm Technologies in Cambridge, Massachusetts. The Visual Help Desk is the first help-desk application built entirely for Notes R4. Visual Help Desk streamlines the process of entering, tracking, and closing support issues. For example, when a call comes in from a new customer, the Visual Help Desk can automatically populate the request and the employee database in one step. The Visual Help Desk consists of an issue-tracking module, a customer/employee tracking module, a knowledge base, and an inventory-tracking module. Used together, these components can be used to track an issue from the initial call through resolution, and into the Knowledge Base if the user desires. Using Brainstorm's VB/Link technology, the product ships with "visual" components as well. The statistical views are represented dynamically with charts and graphs. Through the Notes R4 Navigators, the Visual Help Desk lets support personnel navigate seamlessly with an intuitive user interface.

- *Corporate HelpDesk* from Trellis Network Services in Bellevue, Washington. The Corporate HelpDesk from Trellis was originally released for Notes R3, but it still serves as a powerful customer service-tracking application. The Corporate HelpDesk provides similar features to the Visual Help Desk, including an issue-tracking module and an employee module. One of its features is the ability to track the number of hours spent by multiple technicians on a single call request. It is like many other Notes applications in that it is completely configurable by the end user. This is important for users who have Notes-development capabilities, yet lack the time to develop a solution like this from scratch.

Human-Resource Applications

Lotus Notes databases, unlike other databases, are well suited for storing textual information stored in documents. This makes Notes an ideal platform for storing and organizing human-resource-related information. Here are some of the better-known HR packages for Notes:

28

THIRD-PARTY PRODUCTS FOR LOTUS NOTES

- *Desktop Recruiter* from SkillSet Software in Menlo Park, California. SkillSet software is a company dedicated to human resource services and applications built on Lotus Notes. Their set of human resource applications cover the entire spectrum, from recruitment, training, and development to succession planning. Usually, they will analyze your HR workflows and customize their applications to make your human resource processes more efficient. Examples of HR databases include corporate policies, HR benefits matrix, job descriptions, job posting, resume books, recruiting, company phone book, and many more.

- *HRQuest Professional* from InfoImage in Phoenix, Arizona. HRQuest is a series of menu-driven applications that encompass all the functions of an HR department. These functions include recruitment, job postings, skills, employee profiles, course descriptions, policies, and call tracking. HRQuest was previously marketed by GroupQuest software, which is now a part of InfoImage.

Project Management and Scheduling Applications

Lotus Notes is best known for its ability to help groups of people share information and work together more effectively. The following products are Notes applications that enhance interaction and coordination between coworkers. This category of applications includes project management, scheduling, and workflow databases.

- *Quality at Work* from Quality Decision Management (QDM) in North Andover, Massachusetts. Quality at Work (QAW) is a set of Notes applications and Agents that help manage work and workflow. Currently, QAW consists of two parts: QAW Business Utilities and QAW Business Builder. QAW Business Utilities are ad hoc workflow forms that enhance your Notes databases and mail messages. The package contains forms for assigning action items, for brainstorming with colleagues, initiating a dialog, conducting an opinion poll, and request approval. The Agents automatically update the original document as it progresses through the workflow. QAW Business Builder is a set of development tools for a Notes developer or administrator. These tools help you synchronize nonreplica Notes databases, automate recurring macros, archive documents, and assign sequential numbers. These tools also tie to QAW Business Utilities by capturing and graphing statistics information for workflow applications.

- *Project Gateway for Lotus Notes* from Marin Research in Mill Valley, California. Project Gateway imports, exports, and synchronizes changes between Notes and leading project-management applications, such as Microsoft Project. Project Gateway contains a Notes template that can be used to create project-management databases. When users make changes to the project database, the changes can be automatically synchronized with the Microsoft Project file. The Notes database contains forms and views for project and action-item tracking, including periodic tracking of actual versus budgeted time, and so on. The database can also be used on a standalone basis.

■ *@ScheduleBase* and *@PlanMan*, from Workflow Designs in Dallas, Texas. These two products provide a solution for individual and group scheduling, and individual- and group-activity management. @ScheduleBase specifically lets a group of people coordinate their schedules by finding shared free time. The application, built in Lotus Notes, contains sophisticated Notes forms that display calendars and scheduled events. Users can quickly scan shared databases to check for conflicts before setting the time and place of meeting. @PlanMan is an action-item–tracking application that enables organizations to define workflow roles and actions, in order to request, assign, manage, track, and record action items. The database contains views that can be quickly scanned to find the status of individual- or group-action items. The result is better coordination among the members of a workgroup.

How to Contact These Companies

The Lotus Notes Guide, published quarterly by Lotus, contains a list of companies that make add-on products for Notes, and a complete list of companies that provide services for Lotus Notes. An online version of the Business Partner Catalog, which always contains the latest contact information on these companies, is available over Notes Net, or directly from Lotus.

Most of the third-party products mentioned in this chapter are sold only by the software manufacturer. However, some of them are available through resellers like Egghead. To make it easier to order Notes-related products, several organizations have developed catalogs that you can order from. *Just Notes* is a catalog created in Europe by the UK Notes User Forum that contains tools and applications for Lotus Notes. The *Brainstorm Buyers Guide* from Brainstorm Technologies is one such catalog in the U.S. Stream International (formerly Corporate Software) will soon be creating a project called NotesStore to resell the most popular Notes third-party products. Many of these third-party companies also have home pages on the World Wide Web.

Summary

The third-party industry around Notes has grown considerably to include a rich set of tools and applications. These products can help to jump start a deployment of Notes, or can save your Notes administrator or developers many hours in performing their daily tasks. Because the list of products is growing monthly, it is impossible to know everything that is available. However, if you want your Notes deployment to be successful, you should investigate the third-party tools and application markets very seriously.

Integrating Notes with Phone, Fax, and Image

by Doug Taylor

IN THIS CHAPTER

CHAPTER 29

Having established itself as an essential workgroup tool in major corporations and small businesses, Lotus Notes is now reaching beyond its traditional roles of handling shared databases and providing workflow management. Third-party vendors, along with Lotus and IBM, have been steadily opening up Notes databases to offer new ways of accessing and distributing information. In the most revolutionary development, Notes is now being used as a simple, yet powerful telephony platform, a role traditionally reserved for expensive, proprietary systems. New telephony tools have empowered the average Notes programmer with the means to rapidly roll out low-cost Interactive Voice Response (IVR) applications. These applications can enable any touch-tone telephone to access any Notes database; suddenly Notes has been extended to millions of new users who may not even be aware that they are tapping into Notes.

Corporate fax management has also come to Notes. The departmental fax machine, which has come to rival the water cooler as a social gathering place, may rapidly be eclipsed by the Lotus Fax Server. Both incoming and outgoing faxes can now be handled directly from any Notes desktop.

These telephony and fax enhancements have been combined to usher in a much anticipated communications tool: unified messaging for Notes mailboxes. Now, in addition to e-mail, a standard Notes mailbox can contain voice messages and faxes. The e-mail can be reviewed in the traditional way from the desktop, and it can now also be accessed by telephone; the message text is "read" to the caller using text-to-speech technology. Likewise, voice mail that has been accessible only by phone can now be accessed from the desktop as well. Simply clicking on a message icon will play back the recorded voice.

In another development, Lotus has added image handling to the list of Notes capabilities. A single scanner can be shared by many Notes users. The scanned images can be attached to any Notes document and can then be viewed or printed with versatile imaging software that includes optical character recognition.

This chapter takes a closer look at these enhancements, along with other tools that extend the power of Notes in the areas of telephony, fax, paging, and image management.

Telephony Access Comes to Notes

Have you ever been on the road and needed up-to-the-minute information from one of your company's Notes databases? Notes provides excellent support for remote access through database replication, but perhaps you don't have your laptop with you. Even if you do, you may find yourself in a hotel room without a phone jack, or it may be that you simply don't have the time to make a connection and perform the replication procedures. It's situations like these when a Notes telephony application can be invaluable. By dialing in and responding to simple voice prompts, you can get the database information you need, and you can even update the database with new information. There's no need to use a computer; you can call from a pay phone, a car phone, or an air phone, from a client's office or your living room. Phone Notes, a telephony-development language from Lotus, makes this type of database access possible.

Phone Notes can "phone enable" any Notes database. Prime candidates include databases frequently accessed by mobile users. Phone Notes is also a good method for enabling customers to obtain product information; customers appreciate the convenience of telephony access and do not need to be Notes users. Here are some real-world examples of Phone Notes applications:

- A marketing hotline that enables callers to receive product information through faxback or listen to demonstrations.

- A course registration line that lets students check course schedules and sign up for classes.

- A help desk application that employees can use for reporting problems and listening to troubleshooting tips.

- A human resources support line that supplies answers to commonly asked questions about company benefits.

- An inventory and pricing application that is used by sales associates in the field. Valued clients also have access to the application so they can check the inventory themselves.

Phone Notes ships with the following sample applications that you can use as a starting point for developing your own programs: a customer support help desk, a faxback hotline, a human resources benefits help line, and a demonstration of how to validate a user ID. Also included is a sample auto-attendant application that answers the phone, transfers calls, records messages, and plays back company information.

Two Ways of Accessing Notes Data

The real power of Phone Notes is that it provides a completely new way of interfacing with Notes databases. They can still be accessed from the desktop in the traditional way, but they can now be accessed from a telephone as well. This dual view of a database opens up many possibilities. Take, for example, a Help Desk application. Customers who call into the application can record help requests and check on the status of existing requests. These callers are probably completely unaware that they are accessing a Notes database; they are simply responding to voice prompts. The system administrator, on the other hand, checks on the help requests directly from the Notes desktop. This visual perspective on the requests enables the administrator to prioritize items, add written comments, and so on. The administrator can also take advantage of the telephony access to the database. When out of the office, the administrator can phone in, listen to the pending requests, and respond as needed, all without the use of a PC.

Phone Notes Telephony Architecture

Phone Notes programs are controlled by Remark! PhoneClient, a telephony application engine from Big Sky Technologies. PhoneClient accesses Notes databases on behalf of the application, reading and writing information as required. The databases do not need to be local; they can reside on any Notes server on the network. PhoneClient also communicates with the Remark! Voice Server, which is responsible for managing the call session and caching voice objects. Both PhoneClient and the Voice Server are software products that run in an OS/2 environment; they usually run on the same machine but can run on separate machines with a LAN connection. Supported transport types include NetBIOS, TCP/IP, SPX/IPX, Banyan VINES, and local. Figure 29.1 shows a typical Phone Notes system architecture using a Remark! Server. Table 29.1 summarizes the basic components needed for running Phone Notes applications.

Lotus has indicated that it will allow other vendors to develop software for running Phone Notes applications, but currently Big Sky's Remark! products are the only Phone Notes engines.

FIGURE 29.1.

Phone Notes system architecture using a Remark! Voice Server.

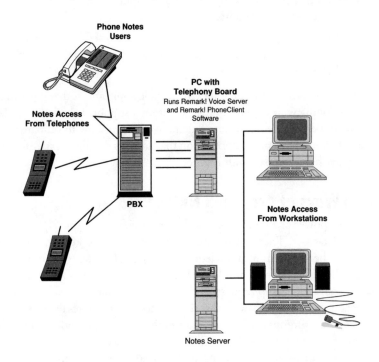

Table 29.1. Summary of Phone Notes telephony components.

Hardware	*Description*
Telephony Boards	Connected via analog phone lines to the PBX. Boards from Dialogic and Natural MicroSystems are supported.
Voice Server PC	Standard IBM compatible PC that contains telephony boards and runs Remark! Voice Server and Remark! PhoneClient software. This PC acts as a bridge between the PBX and LAN. It is connected to the PBX via telephony boards and is connected to the Notes server and Notes clients on the LAN.

Software	*Description*
Phone Notes	Forms-based language used to write telephony applications that access Notes databases.
Remark! PhoneClient	Engine that runs Phone Notes applications and accesses Notes databases on behalf of the applications.
Remark! Voice Server	Controls the telephony boards and communicates with Remark! PhoneClient.
Remark! LanClient	Workstation software that allows playback and recording of voice objects embedded in Notes databases.

To manage call sessions, the Remark! Voice Server uses telephony boards from Dialogic or Natural MicroSystems. Phone lines connect the telephony boards with a PBX or Centrex. The boards answer incoming calls, transfer calls, play and record voice objects, and perform other telephony functions. The boards are available in two-line versions for development. For production installations, boards come in four-line, eight-line, and 24-line configurations. A single Voice Server can handle multiple boards and a total of 24 lines. Large installations can use multiple Voice Servers to accommodate an unlimited number of lines.

Analog Lines

The phone lines used by the Voice Server must be analog. That is, they must use Dual Tone Multi Frequency (DTMF) signals for dialing and controlling call sessions. DTMF signals are more commonly known as touch-tones; they are the tones you hear when dialing on an ordinary touch-tone telephone. Many PBXs now use digital lines that are more sophisticated than the older analog lines. Unfortunately, these digital interfaces are highly proprietary and vary significantly from one manufacturer to the next. Despite the talk of industry standards, there are hundreds of different digital interfaces for PBXs, and they are rarely documented to the point where third parties can create add-on products that speak the same digital language. In the world of PBXs, analog touch-tones remain the only truly universal language. To accommodate third-party products, almost every PBX maker allows analog lines to be added alongside their digital lines. By taking advantage of these analog lines, the Remark! Voice Server can be installed with virtually any PBX.

Typical Call Flow

Consider a typical call session for a Phone Notes application. An incoming call arrives at the PBX and rings the extension of one of the lines connected to the Voice Server. The Voice Server answers the phone and notifies PhoneClient of the incoming call. The Phone Notes application that is running on that line under PhoneClient then takes control. Normally, the application starts by playing a greeting to the caller, and then enables the caller to make a selection from a menu. If the caller requests information from a Notes database, PhoneClient accesses the database and retrieves the information. The Voice Server "reads" text information to the caller using text-to-speech software. If the information is in the form of a voice object, the Voice Server plays the recorded voice to the caller. When the caller inputs information in the form of touch-tone strings, PhoneClient stores the strings in the appropriate Notes document. The Voice Server can also record a message from the caller; PhoneClient stores the voice object in a Notes document. When the call session is complete, the Voice Server hangs up and the Phone Notes application resets so that it is ready to accept the next call.

Client Software

One advantage of phone-enabling a Notes database is that callers can easily leave voice messages, which are embedded in a Notes document. Notes users within the company can then access the document from their Notes desktop and play back the recorded voice. Likewise, a Notes user can record a message at the desktop and embed it in a Notes document; a caller can then listen to the voice message over the phone.

Recording and playback at the desktop is performed with Remark! LanClient. Instead of using a sound board for this function, LanClient uses the telephone next to the workstation. For example, suppose a Notes user double-clicks on an icon representing a voice message. The workstation connects with the Remark! Voice Server across the LAN and instructs the Voice Server to play back the voice object. The Voice Server is connected to the PBX so it can dial the telephone next to the user's workstation. When the phone rings, the user picks up the phone and hears the voice message being played back by the Voice Server. LanClient can also be used in a similar way to record voice messages. In other words, by acting as a bridge between the

PBX and LAN, the Voice Server enables a workstation and nearby telephone to work together for the purpose of recording and playing back voice objects. This arrangement avoids the need to install sound boards in every workstation at a site—a significant savings.

For workstations that already contain sound boards, LanClient includes a configuration option that allows it to use the sound board's microphone and speakers for recording and playing back messages rather than using the telephone. This multimedia option supports mobile users who want to record and play back messages from a laptop when they are out of the office.

Voice Object Compression

Voice objects recorded by the Voice Server are either embedded in Notes documents or stored as files with a .RMK extension. The objects are stored in a proprietary format determined by the make of the voice board that performed the recording (Dialogic or Natural MicroSystems). That is, a standard .WAV player cannot be used to play back the objects. Instead, LanClient is used as described previously. To save disk space, the recorded speech is highly compressed using the Adaptive Differential Pulse Code Modulation (ADPCM) standard. Each minute of recorded voice occupies only about 180K of disk space (11 Megabytes per hour). This level of compression provides very good sound quality. The system can be configured for lower compression rates with even higher sound quality, but the tradeoff will be larger voice files. The compression and decompression process is completely transparent to the user.

Writing a Phone Notes Application

Anyone who has developed a Lotus Notes database will have little difficulty learning how to write Phone Notes applications. The Phone Notes language consists of 25 commands that perform various database and telephony functions. (See Table 29.2.) Each command is stored as a document in a Notes database. A view of the database shows the flow of the application. Figure 29.2 is a partial view of a sample Help Desk application that is included with Phone Notes. The program answers the phone and enables the caller to enter a new request for help, or check on the status of an existing request. The Help Desk administrator can also call into the program to check the queue of requests and archive requests that have been taken care of. The complete application contains about 50 commands.

Table 29.2. Summary of Phone Notes commands.

Command	Description
Assign	Assigns variables.
Call Subroutine	Branches to a subroutine within the application.
Case	Compares a variable with up to five different conditions and branches accordingly.

continues

Table 29.2. continued

Command	Description
Convert DTMF to String	Converts touch-tones entered by the caller to a string.
Copy Document	Copies a Notes document.
Create Document	Creates a Notes document.
Decision	Evaluates an expression and branches accordingly.
Delete Document	Deletes a Notes document.
Dial	Dials a phone number.
Execute Notes Macro	Executes a predefined Notes macro in the specified Notes database.
Execute OS Task	Executes a task with the operating system.
Forward Document	Mails a specified document to a Notes user.
Get Next Document	Retrieves the next document ID in the list of document IDs created by a Select command.
Hang Up	Hangs up the phone.
Play	Plays a voice object or uses text-to-speech to "read" text in a synthesized voice.
Record Voice	Records the caller's voice and stores it as a voice object.
Restart Application	Terminates the application. Then restarts it or starts another application.
Select Documents	Uses a Notes formula to select a list of document IDs within a specified view. Usually followed by a Get Next Document command.
Touch-Tone Menu	Plays a menu to the caller and then branches according to the caller's touch-tone input.
Touch-Tone String Input	Plays a prompt to the caller requesting touch-tone input and then stores the input in a variable.
Trigger Event	Causes the application to branch when certain events occur, such as the caller hanging up.
User Info	Accesses Phone Person documents that are used to authorize callers.
User Lookup	Retrieves an ID from a Phone Person document.
Wait for Call	Causes the application to wait in an idle state until a phone call is received.
Wait Time	Causes the application to wait in an idle state for a specified time.

FIGURE 29.2.

A sample Help Desk application written in Phone Notes.

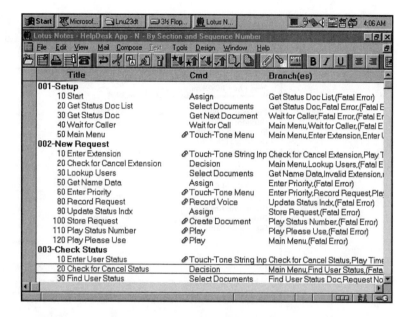

The first step in writing a Phone Notes program is to create a new source application database using the supplied template. The Compose menu in the source database lists the available forms; each form corresponds to a Phone Notes command. To start writing an application, select a form in the Compose menu and fill out the required fields.

Most Phone Notes applications begin with an Assign command that establishes local variables. This is usually followed by commands that read in configuration information from a Notes database. When this setup is complete, the Wait for Call command is executed; it causes the application to wait on the line until a call is detected. The Wait for Call command from the Help Desk application is shown in Figure 29.3. As with all Phone Notes commands, the bottom of the form contains branching fields that control the flow of the application. These fields specify which command to execute next, depending on various conditions. In this case, after the application answers the phone, it branches to the command titled Main Menu, which is shown in Figure 29.4.

In the Help Desk application, Main Menu is a Touch-Tone Menu command that plays a prompt to the caller ("Welcome! Press 1 to enter a new request..."). The command then branches based on which key the caller presses. Note that Main Menu is a command title that was assigned by the programmer who created the Help Desk application. It uniquely identifies this occurrence of a Touch-Tone Menu command within the program. The Help Desk application contains several Touch-Tone Menu commands; each one is uniquely identified by its command title ("Main Menu," "Enter Priority" and so on.)

FIGURE 29.3.

The Wait for Call command.

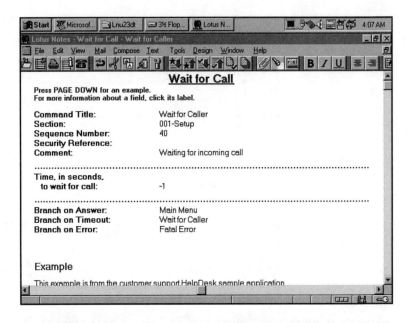

FIGURE 29.3.

The Wait for Call command.

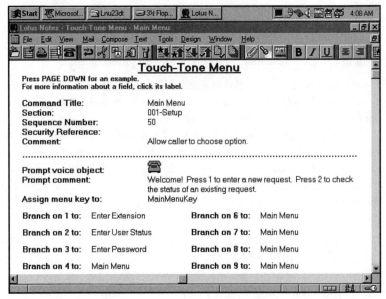

FIGURE 29.4.

The Touch-Tone Menu command.

The small telephone icon in Figure 29.4 is a voice prompt recorded by the programmer using Remark! LanClient. Most Phone Notes commands can include a voice prompt, which the voice server plays to the caller before the command is executed. When the prompt has been recorded, it can be copied into other forms if a similar prompt is needed elsewhere in the application.

The programmer can also check the prompt by double-clicking on it to play it back at the desktop. The comment under the voice prompt usually contains the text of the prompt; this text is for ready-reference only and is not used by the application.

Phone Notes Command Set

Phone Notes commands enable your applications to manipulate Notes forms in most of the same ways that a Notes user can while sitting at the Notes desktop. A program can select documents, extract information, assign variables, and so on. Phone Notes commands also include telephony functions that answer the phone, transfer calls, and record and play back voice. Following is a summary of the most frequently used commands:

- *Wait for Call.* Causes the application to wait on the line and then answer the phone when an incoming call is detected.

- *Dial.* Dials out or transfers a call. For example, an automated receptionist application can answer the phone, ask the caller to enter the desired extension, and then use the Dial command to transfer the caller to that extension.

- *Touch-Tone Menu.* Branches to the next command depending on the key pressed by the caller.

- *Touch-Tone String Input.* Accepts a string of touch tones entered by the caller and assigns the string to a variable. For example, the command may be used to accept a user ID number from a caller.

- *Play.* In the case of a voice object, this command plays back the recorded voice to the caller. In the case of text, this command uses text-to-speech technology to "read" the text to the caller.

- *Record Voice.* Sounds a beep and then records the caller's voice. The recording ends after a period of silence or when the caller presses a defined key.

- *Select Documents* and *Get Next Document.* These commands are used together to pass information to and from Notes databases. The Select Documents command first selects a list of documents based on a selection formula specified in the command. Notes programmers will be familiar with this type of formula, which is used throughout Notes databases. The Get Next Document command then gets the first document in the list. Subsequent commands can then assign variables in the document (for example, touch-tone input from the caller) or extract information from the document (for example, text or recorded voice.)

- *Create Document.* Creates a new document in a Notes database.

- *Forward Document.* Forwards a document using Notes mail in the same way that a document is forwarded from the Notes desktop. The command specifies the Notes mail address of the recipient.

Compiling and Running a Phone Notes Application

A completed Phone Notes source application must be compiled before it can be run. Compiling the application improves performance and, more importantly, protects the programmer's intellectual property; the compiled application can be shipped without giving up the source code. Like the source application, the compiled application resides in a Notes database that can easily be installed in any Notes environment.

In most installations, the compiled Phone Notes database is accompanied by one or more "target" databases. These contain configuration information and the working data accessed by the application. For example, the Help Desk application has a target database called "Help Desk Data." It is used to store the help requests submitted by callers and information about the Help Desk administrator.

The PhoneClient application engine is used both for compiling and running the application. A special Notes database is supplied for storing your compiled Phone Notes applications. You can store multiple applications in a single compiled applications database. To compile an application, you simply start PhoneClient and open the Compiler Window. You specify both the source application and the destination compiled applications database. PhoneClient then compiles the source application and places the resulting compiled code in the compiled applications database. The compile process produces messages and a log that can be used for troubleshooting.

After the application is compiled, it can be configured within PhoneClient. The Voice Server must be identified, as well as the phone lines on which the application will run. There is also a provision for assigning initial variables to be used by the application (for example, the location of the target databases). You could set initial variables within the application, but it is often more convenient to set them in PhoneClient; there is no need to recompile if you want to change the variables. This feature is especially useful for application developers who want to ship only the compiled version of an application; their customers can set site-specific variables without the need to have the source code.

When bringing up a Phone Notes application, the Voice Server should be started first so that it can make the necessary phone lines available. Next, PhoneClient is started and is then used to launch the Phone Notes application. (The entire process can be configured to auto-start from a cold boot.) When the Phone Notes application starts, it connects with the Voice Server and reserves the phone lines it needs. The system is designed to run unattended. The Voice Server and Phone Client screens show the status of each application and the phone lines they are using. Logging facilities provide historical and debugging information. A statistics tool gathers call data that can be used for billing purposes.

Setting Up Hunt Groups

A single session of the Voice Server and PhoneClient can run multiple Phone Notes applications that are assigned to different phone lines. For example, with an eight-line system, a Help

Desk application could run on three lines and a Human Resources application could run on the remaining five lines. For this configuration to work, the person in charge of the PBX would need to set up two different hunt groups to support the two different applications. A *hunt group* is a logical group of lines that is configured on a PBX. If the first line in a hunt group is busy, a new incoming call rolls over and is answered on the next line in the hunt group. If that line is busy as well, the call rolls over to the next line, and so on. In this example, users of the Help Desk application would be given one number to call into—for example, 555-1000. This number would ring on extension 1000, which would be answered by the Voice Server. If another caller dialed in to 555-1000 while extension 1000 was busy, the call would roll over to 1001, and an additional call would roll over to 1002. The Human Resources application would be set up in a similar way, but in this case the number to call would be 555-2000, which would ring extension 2000 and roll over to extensions 2001, 2002, 2003, and 2004. By using a hunt group, a Phone Notes application can be accessed through a single telephone number but can be running on as many lines as needed to handle the expected call volumes.

Although Phone Notes applications make use of hunt groups, they are strictly a function of the PBX. That is, you configure hunt groups on your PBX, not within Phone Notes. Check your PBX documentation for instructions on how to set up hunt groups.

Unified Messaging for Notes Mailboxes

Until recently, voice mail and Notes e-mail have been worlds apart. For Notes users to keep pace with their messages, it was necessary to check their Notes mailbox for e-mail and then dial in to their company's voice-mail system to check voice mail. However, the traditional boundary between voice mail and Notes e-mail has been removed by Remark! MessageCenter, a new, unified messaging product from Big Sky Technologies.

MessageCenter was written using the Lotus Phone Notes telephony language described previously. The application comes precompiled and can be run "off-the-shelf" following a routine software installation and some simple configuration procedures. MessageCenter comes bundled with the Remark! Voice Server and Remark! PhoneClient. As described in the previous sections, the Voice Server manages the phone lines, and PhoneClient runs the MessageCenter application.

A User's View of MessageCenter

After MessageCenter is installed at a site, Notes users have two new perspectives on their messages:

- All voice messages and e-mail are in one place: the user's standard Notes mailbox.
- All voice messages and e-mail can be reviewed in two ways: from the Notes desktop or by telephone.

For example, consider a Notes user who has opened his Notes mailbox after MessageCenter is installed. The mailbox will contain the usual e-mail, but it will also contain voice messages. To play back a voice message, the user double-clicks on the small telephone icon. This launches a player that lets the user listen to the message. Buttons for rewind, fast forward, and pause provide control during playback. The player, called Remark! LanClient, is described earlier in this chapter. The user can send e-mail in the usual way or can use LanClient to record and send a voice message. Figure 29.5 shows a typical Notes mailbox after MessageCenter has been installed. Note that one of the voice messages in the mailbox is being played back.

FIGURE 29.5.

Notes mailbox containing voice messages.

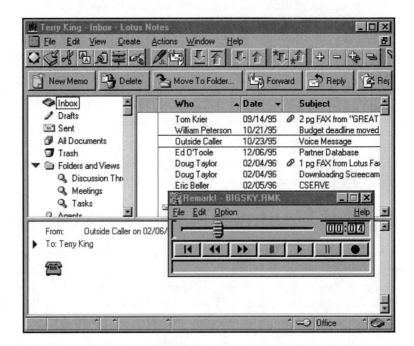

Also consider a Notes user who is out of the office on a business trip. She could check her messages by replicating her Notes mailbox, but an easier way is to call into MessageCenter. After she enters her password, MessageCenter accesses her Notes mailbox and plays back her messages. Her voice messages are played back just as they would be on a familiar voice-mail system. However, she can now also "listen" to her e-mail messages. They are read to her by MessageCenter using text-to-speech technology. She can respond to both e-mail and voice messages with her own voice messages.

MessageCenter Features

In addition to unified messaging, MessageCenter has the following features:

- *Auto-attendant.* MessageCenter includes a full-featured auto-attendant that can answer the phone in place of a live operator. The auto-attendant transfers calls, takes messages, and sends pages if the optional pager gateway is installed. When the auto-attendant records a voice message from an outside caller, it places the message in a memo and sends it to the Notes mailbox of the appropriate person.

■ *Fax support.* MessageCenter supports the Lotus Fax Server, which is described later in this chapter. When the server is installed, fax messages will be included in a Notes user's mailbox along with e-mail and voice messages. When a user is reviewing messages over the phone and encounters a fax message, it can be forwarded to any fax machine. E-mail messages can also be forwarded to a fax machine. This is useful for e-mail messages that cannot be easily read to the caller with text-to-speech—for example, messages containing tables or graphics.

■ *Workgroup support.* In keeping with the Notes workgroup philosophy, MessageCenter extends workgroups from the desktop to the telephone. For example, a technical-support workgroup could be defined to handle support calls. A logical telephone extension is defined for the workgroup. When a customer calls the workgroup, MessageCenter transfers the call to the first person in the workgroup. If that person is unavailable, MessageCenter transfers the call to the next person, and so on. If no one in the workgroup is available, MessageCenter will record a voice message from the caller and mail it to designated members of the workgroup.

■ *Easy Configuration.* All MessageCenter configuration is performed in a Notes database. Each MessageCenter user has a Subscriber profile that defines his or her Notes username, telephone extension, mail address, and so on. Figure 29.6 shows part of a typical subscriber profile. Other forms in the configuration database are used for defining workgroups and for specifying information needed for MessageCenter to interface with the PBX.

FIGURE 29.6.
Typical MessageCenter subscriber profile.

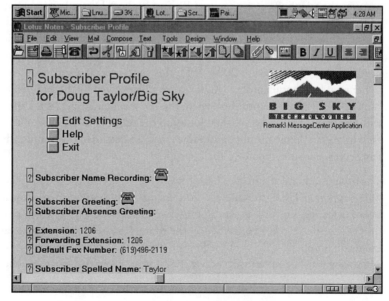

Faxing with Notes

The Lotus Fax Server enables Notes users to send and receive faxes from within Notes. Sending an outgoing fax is a simple matter. The user composes a Notes memo containing the information to be faxed and then addresses the memo with the recipient's name, fax number, and the domain name of the Fax Server—for example, Tom Jones @ 1-619-555-1212 @ LFS. Receiving faxes is also easy. If the proper fax hardware and PBX support are present, each fax can be automatically routed directly to the recipient's Notes mailbox. Alternatively, all faxes are routed to a central, inbound fax mailbox; the Fax Server administrator then manually forwards each fax to the appropriate recipient's Notes mailbox.

One or more fax boards or modems must be installed in the Fax Server machine. When an incoming fax is received, the Fax Server converts it to an image file and attaches it to a Notes memo. The image file can be in TIFF, PCX, or DCX format. When a Notes user receives a memo with an attached fax, he or she can use the Lotus Image Viewer to display or print the fax. This viewer, which runs under Windows 3.1 or higher, is bundled with the Fax Server. Because it has an unrestricted license, the viewer can be freely installed at each workstation where faxes will be received. When the viewer is properly configured in the registry, it will launch automatically when a Notes user clicks on the icon representing an attached fax. Alternatively, a Notes user can view faxes with the more sophisticated Professional Edition viewer, which is described later in this chapter.

Automatic Routing for Inbound Faxes

The Fax Server supports two methods for automatically routing inbound faxes. The first method requires the telephone company and PBX to support Direct Inward Dialing (DID). This is a method by which outside calls can be routed directly to an extension without the need for the call to be handled by an operator or auto-attendant. For example, an outside caller dialing 555-1000 is connected directly to extension 1000. Another outside caller dialing 555-2000 is connected directly to extension 2000. If DID is supported at a site, each Notes user can have his or her own fax phone number. All faxes are still received by the Fax Server, but the Fax Server "knows" the fax phone number where the fax was being sent (this number is received along with the fax). The Fax Server then looks up the number in a configuration table that contains each user's fax phone number and Notes mail address. After attaching the fax to a memo, the Fax Server sends the memo to the appropriate recipient.

The other method for automatic fax routing requires that the sending and receiving fax hardware support DTMF (touch-tone) addressing. This method of addressing a fax is supported by some fax machines. The sender must use touch-tone keys to enter a routing address while the fax is being sent (for convenience, the routing address is usually the same as the recipient's extension number). If the fax board or modem in the Fax Server machine also supports DTMF addressing, the Fax Server will receive the address. From this point on, the routing is similar to the DID routing described previously; the Fax Server uses a configuration table to determine the fax recipient.

If automatic routing is not available at your site, all faxes will be sent to a single infax Notes mailbox. They can then be manually distributed to the recipients. This is analogous to the situation that exists with most paper fax machines. Faxes are stacked next to the machine, and recipients must go to the machine and look through the stack or wait for the mailroom to deliver the faxes. The situation is actually somewhat improved with the Fax Server. Because the infax mailbox is a standard Notes database, Notes users can put it on their desktop. Users who are expecting faxes can generally check the infax mailbox more easily than they can walk to a departmental fax machine. In addition, the Fax Server administrator can periodically cull through the infax mailbox and forward faxes, usually with greater frequency and efficiency than the mailroom.

Attachment Support for Outbound Faxes

The Fax Server has been designed with excellent support for attached files. When composing a memo to be faxed, the user can attach a file. If the Fax Server supports the file format, the file will be "rendered" and sent at the end of the fax memo; the recipient receives a printed copy of the file. For example, you can attach a Microsoft Word 6.0 document to a memo that you want to fax. The attached document appears only as an icon in the memo when you send it, but the person who receives the fax will also receive a complete printout of the Word document. The Fax Server supports attachments of image files in PCX, BMP, DCX, and TIFF formats. It supports attachments of files in the following formats: ASCII, Microsoft Word for Windows 2.0, Microsoft Word 6.0, Microsoft Word RTF, WordPerfect 5.1, and Lotus AmiPro.

Print-to-Fax Driver

The Lotus Print-to-Fax driver comes bundled with the Fax Server. This handy application enables you to send faxes via the Fax Server from within any Windows program (as long as your machine can also send Lotus mail). The driver works in a way that is similar to most PC fax software. After you install the driver, the Fax Server will be displayed in the Print Setup dialog boxes of your Windows applications. If you specify the Fax Server as your "printer" and then request that a document be "printed," it will actually be mailed to the Fax Server. The Fax Server, in turn, will fax the document to the fax phone number you specified in the Print Setup dialog box.

Fax Server Databases

The Fax Server includes a number of databases that are installed onto a Notes client desktop. The databases enable the Fax Server administrator to configure and monitor the server. One database contains information about the current queue of outbound faxes, another database displays an historical log of all inbound and outbound faxes, and so on.

Phone Notes Faxback Applications

By using the Fax Server together with Phone Notes, you can create faxback applications that will fax documents out of any Notes database. (Phone Notes is a telephony-application development language that is discussed at the beginning of this chapter.)

For example, you may have a Notes database containing documents that describe your product line. Your customers who use Lotus Notes can replicate the database and view the documents, but you would like to make this information available to a much wider audience. Without making any changes to the database, you can "telephone enable" it by writing a simple Phone Notes application. Anyone can dial in to the application. The caller hears a greeting and is then asked to enter a document number and a fax phone number. The specified document is immediately faxed to the caller. Callers who are not familiar with the document numbers can request that a list of available documents be faxed to them. A faxback application of this type usually contains no more that twenty or thirty Phone Notes commands.

The key to a faxback application is the Phone Notes Forward Document command. Again consider our example. After a caller enters the number of a document, the application retrieves the document from the product information database. The application then executes the Forward Document command, which mails the document to the Fax Server along with the fax phone number of the caller. The Fax Server then sends the fax.

If you plan to develop a faxback program, you may find it useful to look at the sample faxback application that is shipped with Phone Notes.

Paging with Notes

The Lotus Pager Gateway is a simple application that enables Notes users to send pages to numeric or alphanumeric pagers. To initiate a page, a Notes user sends a memo to the Pager Gateway. The To field in the memo contains the PIN number of the person to be paged, along with a domain name that has been configured for the paging service, for example, `123456 @ SKYTEL`. In the case of an alphanumeric page, a short message can be included in the subject or body field (depending on how the gateway has been configured). To simplify addressing pages, aliases can be added to the Notes Public Address Book. For convenience, the alias is usually the person's name followed by the word `Pager`. For example, `Linda Smith Pager` could be created as an alias for `123456 @ SKYTEL`.

In addition to sending pages manually from the desktop, it is also possible to write background macros that will send pages. This can be useful for databases in which urgent requests are logged. For example, a paging macro could run every fifteen minutes against a customer-support database. The macro could detect when a new problem is logged and send a page to a support technician. If the pager is alphanumeric, it could display information about the nature of the problem as supplied by the macro.

The Pager Gateway runs in an OS/2 environment. When installed, it adds forms to the Notes Public Address Book that are used for configuration. Pager information messages and summary statistics are logged in the Pager Gateway Log database.

Phone Notes Paging Applications

You can use the Pager Gateway along with Phone Notes to create telephony applications that send pages. The approach is similar to that used for faxback applications as described earlier. A Phone Notes application initiates a page by using a Forward Document command, which mails a memo to the Fax Gateway. This simulates the way in which a Notes user sends a page from the desktop.

Note that a Phone Notes application can also perform numeric paging on its own without the Pager Gateway. The application simply uses the Dial command to call the pager service and enter touch-tones, just as a person would.

Managing Images in Notes

Lotus offers a group of sophisticated image-management tools known as the Lotus Notes: Document Imaging product suite. This name is usually shortened to LN:DI which is pronounced "Lindy." The LN:DI tools currently consist of four separate products:

- *LN:DI Professional Edition.* This is an enhanced version of the Lotus Image Viewer described earlier. In addition to the basic display and print features provided by the Image Viewer, the Professional Edition enables users to annotate images electronically, take advantage of "smart" storage options, and scan in documents from a wide selection of popular scanners. The Professional Edition also includes a shared scanner utility that makes it easy for any Notes user to capture images. The user goes to the machine that is running the shared scanner utility and enters her Notes mail address. When scanning is complete, the image is automatically mailed to the user.

- *LN:DI Image Processing Server.* This server queues up image-processing requests from the Lotus Image Viewer and Professional Edition clients. When the server receives a request, it determines the appropriate software to handle it and places the request in a queue. When the processing software is available, the request is sent. The results are returned to the Image Processing Server. The server is required to support image-processing products like the LN:DI Workgoup OCR.

- *LN:DI Workgroup OCR.* This product adds the capability for optical-character recognition to the LN:DI Professional Edition and the Lotus Image Viewer. The Workgroup OCR resides on the network and is shared by the client viewers. To perform OCR processing on an image, the user opens the image using one of the client viewers. The user then sends the image to the OCR software, which returns the processed text via Notes mail.

■ *LN:DI Mass Storage System.* Designed to improve the performance of Notes databases by managing the storage of large images, this software can operate with most popular "optical jukeboxes." It automatically stores frequently accessed objects on the server's hard drive where they can be quickly retrieved, and it moves less frequently accessed objects to slower optical storage devices.

Notes "Call Centers" on the Horizon

The release of Notes 4 was accompanied by many powerful enhancements in the areas of telephony, fax, and image management, but there is still much room for growth. One of the most anxiously anticipated developments was software and hardware that would more closely integrate Notes with PBXs and Caller ID. This integration should enable Notes databases to act as "call centers." Phone-number fields in Notes databases will be universally enabled for autodialing so that outbound calls can be placed more efficiently. Inbound calls will trigger screen pop-ups containing important information about the caller that has been automatically extracted from a Notes database. This information can be used to intelligently route the call to the person who can best respond to the caller's needs, and all this occurs in an instant—before the phone has even been answered!

Summary

Telephony access to Lotus Notes is here now and waiting to be exploited. By setting up a voice server and writing some simple Phone Notes applications, you can "telephone enable" your Notes databases. Callers can access the databases from any touch-tone phone without the need to use a workstation or laptop. This makes it much easier for your mobile Notes users to retrieve and enter information. It also enables you to open up your Notes databases to non-Notes users, such as your customers and suppliers.

Other companion products such as the Fax Server, Pager Gateway, and Document Imaging suite further extend the reach of Notes databases. Each of these tools adds a significant dimension to the core Notes product, and as they are combined in innovative ways, their effect will tend to be synergistic, providing a new generation of information services that have only just begun to reshape the workplace.

VideoNotes and RealTime Notes: Letting Business See What's Going On

by Daniel Tyre and Daniel S. Cooper

IN THIS CHAPTER

Lotus Notes is all about using valuable information in new and meaningful ways. The beauty of Lotus Notes is the capability of dealing with information on an individual user's terms—when, where, and how the user perceives it to be most useful. The use of Lotus Notes has expanded exponentially over the last few years because it enables organizations to organize, distribute, analyze, and share information in ways that are meaningful beyond traditional electronic communications. Lotus Notes Business Multimedia products, specifically Lotus VideoNotes and Lotus RealTime Notes, extend communication capabilities one step further by providing a powerful development environment that enables video to be included as a cost-effective alternative for everyday business communications and information transference.

Lotus Notes has become the preferred means of sharing and storing information within workgroups or throughout the enterprise for employees of many companies. Numerous studies have shown an extraordinary return on investment for large-scale Lotus Notes users. Many Notes users have become used to working efficiently with different data types, such as text, hypertext, graphics, and compound documents. Therefore, Notes has become a natural extension for these users to demand the full spectrum of available data types to better express information in its most powerful form. Stored digital video (VideoNotes) and real-time conferencing (RealTime Notes) Business Multimedia products are great improvements and essential steps to realizing this vision. These products enable business users to utilize advanced multimedia technology and to make knowledge available to workers enterprise-wide. These new products provide significant value by providing visually oriented information in a way that is immediately recognizable. Effectively deployed, real-time and stored digital video can provide an easy way to develop and exploit a competitive advantage.

Video technology is beneficial to business today because it is immediately useful, easy to use, and fun. Typically, most information is displayed as boring old text and graphics. Captured video and real-time video data is futuristic information that can turn traditional information sources into powerful, easy-to-use presentations. The full impact of video is immediately apparent—very few people complain about receiving information when it is presented to them like their favorite television show. The critical issues with video usage have traditionally been cost, ease of use (for the video producer and user), and a reasonable return on investment. However, the introduction of Lotus VideoNotes and Lotus RealTime Notes removes the obstacles for Lotus Notes environments.

There is nothing that will ever replace the power of face-to-face communication. Looking directly at the individual and seeing, smelling, feeling, touching, and sensing what is going on is the most efficient way of communicating. Video (as a stored digital image or in real time) is not as good as shaking someone's hand, but it has more advantages than traditional communications methods for many types of information.

No one can dispute the power of multimedia technology or its ability to facilitate better business communications. In an electronic and phone mail age, the value of "looking someone in the eye," hearing it "from the horse's mouth," or observing the messenger as well as the message carries the tremendous benefits of portraying increased customer satisfaction and a sense of commitment directly to your employee, customer, or prospect. In today's wired world, it can actually become a crucial competitive advantage. Ancient history (five years ago) taught us that if a business was connected to a client with electronic mail, it would be in a position to conduct business with the client forever. This connection ensures that you can exchange information back and forth, ask questions, provide answers, and establish or enhance a long-term relationship based on more frequent communications.

In summary, Lotus VideoNotes and Lotus RealTime Notes provide several significant benefits:

- The high impact of visual presentations for explaining and persuading.
- The widespread preference for viewing many kinds of information as video or graphical images.
- The capability to establish trust and rapport in business relationships rapidly through face-to-face contact without being present in person.
- Exceptional ease of use for video applications such as video mail, within the popular Notes user interface.
- Integration with other familiar Notes functions, such as document creation, mail, and information retrieval.
- Reduced cost for applications like videoconferencing, video mail, and live screen sharing, through integration of the Intel ProShare technology with the existing Notes architecture.

This chapter reviews the trends in the video marketplace that make stored video and real-time video technology affordable and cost-effective within the Lotus Notes framework. It looks at the architecture of Lotus VideoNotes, its features and benefits, some of the challenges with implementing the technology, and some basic applications and systems requirements. It also discusses Lotus RealTime Notes, including the Intel ProShare upgrade for live two-way video, reviews its features and benefits, and describes some of the most beneficial uses. Finally, this chapter deals with the effect of these technologies on business applications.

The Business Case for Digital Video

With the advent of Lotus Notes solutions, communications standards are being taken an additional step forward. Now groups of people share information and check it when they need to on their own personal terms. Lotus Notes allows for the documentation of problems and solutions, and archives how the relationship evolved. Many businesses have established internal and external Lotus Notes databases to facilitate this type of communication.

Now with cost-effective video solutions, the bar has been raised on valuable communication standards. An Internet or electronic-mail connection does not provide the same value proposition, especially if your competitor is able to establish a video connection with your customer that provides more accurate or timely information. While you are sending static text information, your competition may be communicating with a personalized video. While you are sending "Dear Client" messages, your competition can be updating the client in real time. Since you are limited to traditional data types, your competition has an advantage by providing a face-to-face interaction in addition to the standard text.

With the increased use of the Internet for business use, the personal computer has become more of a communication device than a personal productivity tool. The introduction of these two Lotus Notes business multimedia products, Lotus VideoNotes and Lotus RealTime Notes, can assist in moving Lotus Notes users to this new mode of communication, which makes client contact even more personal.

Business applications of these new products will undoubtedly evolve over time, but many are obvious from the beginning, including:

- Conducting "virtual focus group" research with key customers.
- Training customers, employees, and resellers. Training materials can be accessed through Notes (including video materials on CD-ROMs, for isolated users), and live training can be provided through RealTime Notes.
- Customer Service calls can be initiated (and possibly completed) through RealTime Notes, giving customers a sense of exceptionally high support, while using Notes databases to optimize service operations.
- Customer retention can be maximized without exorbitant cost or time demands by having senior executives at your company deliver regular briefings to key customers over VideoNotes (for recorded general messages) and RealTime Notes (for live, customer-specific information).

VideoNotes: Notes Enters the Video Age

In the late 1990s and beyond, words are not enough. Today, information is passed from person to person—or from person to persons—in multiple data types. Information loses some of its inherent value if it is not presented in its native form. Information delivered with its original essence, feeling, and meaning (untouched by outside influence), retains a powerful energy. There is no parallel to providing information directly from the original source, especially if that information remains true to form. Video clips can often meet this need, and VideoNotes brings video clips into Notes.

Background and Industry Trends

Most industry visionaries would agree that the golden age of multimedia, forecasted throughout the late 1980s, never materialized. There were several reasons for this, but an overriding factor may have been the cost and difficulty of supporting hardware and software designed to provide multimedia solutions. Certainly there were always many business uses for multimedia—

presenting educational content for training purposes, personalizing information, and recording video for archiving purposes are a few that provide business productivity improvements. Perhaps the most important business use of multimedia applications has always been to increase effective communications—the essence of business. The effective use of audio and video was never "plug and play." Most multimedia projects required extensive resources to produce and deliver. Traditionally, multimedia applications required expensive, complex business equipment to produce content, trained professionals to produce applications, and extra hardware and software to deploy them. Video was impossible to implement into older legacy systems because of the data structure, and it was difficult to run at the desktop level because of system requirements. Even the most successful multimedia applications were pilot applications with specialized uses—not widely deployed business applications.

What Is Lotus VideoNotes?

Lotus VideoNotes is a Lotus Notes Business Multimedia product that enables Notes users to build compound documents, including digital video. Lotus VideoNotes also provides services for managing video distribution across local area networks (LANs) and wide area networks (WANs), using Lotus Notes as a vehicle for transporting the video files.

Lotus VideoNotes provides an efficient way to capture, store, transport, use, update, and manage digital video data while eliminating many of the traditional bottlenecks, including large amounts of data storage required to store video on workstation hard drives. It divides the storage, playback, editing, management, and coordination functions necessary for stored digital video usage among clients and servers.

To handle the storage and transfer of large video objects efficiently, the VideoNotes architecture uses the concept of a site. A Lotus VideoNotes site consists of a collection of Notes client workstations with the Video Client software, one or more video servers, a VideoNotes Site Manager Server, and conventional Notes database servers. (See Figure 30.1.) A site boundary is independent of a Notes-named network; servers from multiple Notes-named networks may be members of the same VideoNotes site. Each VideoNotes site requires only one Site Manager server (which can be the same computer as a video server, in small sites).

FIGURE 30.1.

Possible Lotus VideoNotes site configuration.

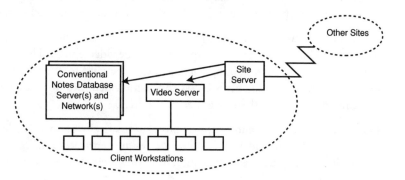

30

VIDEONOTES AND REALTIME NOTES

Lotus uses the concept of sites to minimize the impact of video on the personal computer workstation, LAN, and WAN. This is an important consideration when you are dealing with large files and especially when you want to provide users with easy and efficient access to video, stored throughout the enterprise in a common, easy-to-use fashion. The idea is to minimize the storage of large video objects on networked servers and to manage the network bandwidth to allocate resources to both constant bit-rate video streams and data traffic that occurs in bursts, which is the most frequent problem in deploying video.

The Lotus Notes Site Manager is an OS/2 or Windows NT-based Notes server that coordinates the delivery of video to client workstations. A video server can be either specialized hardware, or standard server-running system management software that prioritizes disk I/O and manages network bandwidth to guarantee multiple, uninterrupted video streams on the LAN or WAN. With VideoNotes Release 1.1, the video server and the Site Manager Notes Server functions can be shared. A site can have multiple video servers to permit growth and flexibility in distributing and partitioning content within the workgroup. Although Lotus indicates that each video server can support 20 to 40 users who are simultaneously accessing video clips, the actual number is highly dependent on the type of operating system and type of video clips, as well as the available capacity of the LAN or WAN (bandwidth).

A Lotus VideoNotes workstation is a Windows-based Notes workstation running VideoNotes client software. This software provides utilities to monitor, capture, and digitize full-motion video in real time from any video source, including VCRs and video cameras. VideoNotes provides basic editing utilities to mark sections and cut and paste. Using object linking and embedding (OLE) technology, which is already available in Lotus Notes, VideoNotes users can embed video references within Notes documents while the video itself is stored separately on video servers. This saves drive space and provides more efficient throughput on the LAN. When users view the Notes document, they see a still video "poster" (bitmap picture) in the document. When you double-click on this icon, it launches the VideoNotes client application, which starts the playback on the video server and delivers it to the desktop.

The video server, Site Manager, and VideoNotes clients communicate through NT file services or through the Novell NetWare network operating system. Client workstations can communicate with the Site Manager server or other Notes servers via any Notes-supported protocol. The Site Manager needs TCP/IP to connect to other sites exchanging video data types.

The greatest advantage of Lotus VideoNotes is that it uses the full range of powerful Notes services, including replication and e-mail, to manage video objects. Users or administrators can mail Notes documents containing references to video clips to other sites. However, when the Notes documents are sent, VideoNotes copies the video files to a video server at the remote site, rather than sending them to a user's hard drive.

Notes administrators can allow clips to move automatically or on a scheduled set to maximize LAN and WAN bandwidth. Of course, Notes authenticates replication of databases that contain video by requiring authentication from sites requesting video. Notes then forwards the video clips only if the site has the required key.

Features and Benefits of VideoNotes

The most outstanding feature of VideoNotes is that a Lotus Notes user does not have to learn complex multimedia software to become proficient in the technology. One of the obvious benefits of Lotus VideoNotes is the capability of giving every Lotus Notes user on a network access to video, without requiring additional storage space on the user's hard drive. Using Notes to distribute the video ensures that it is easily managed and controlled by the systems administrator.

Another key benefit to Lotus VideoNotes is that the application can be accessed, distributed, and managed just like any other Lotus Notes application. Everyone with access to a Lotus Notes license can potentially use video applications. Users can distribute documents containing video references through normal Notes mail routing and replication, over both LANs and WANs.

VideoNotes provides full-function video. Through a single convenient application, users can capture and play video, make any video, frame the poster that represents the video in the Notes document, and edit videos. VideoNotes provides full editing functionality, including cutting and pasting and trimming. (See Figure 30.2.) By making video easy to create, capture, and play back, VideoNotes increases the accessibility and usability of video.

FIGURE 30.2.

VideoNotes showing the standard menus, toolbar, and so forth.

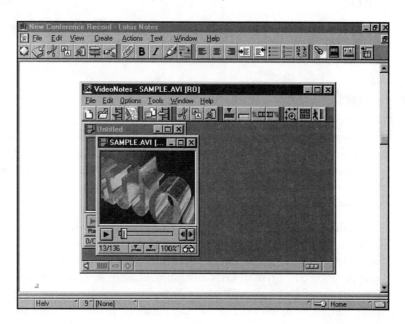

VideoNotes supports playback of all industry-standard video and audio file types. Users can embed or play back any clip compatible with Windows MCI device drivers, including Video for Windows, MPEG, and QuickTime video files, as well as MIDI and .WAV sound files.

Users can transfer selected video clips to their local workstations or laptops for use when disconnected from the network, increasing their productivity while reducing network access charges. Users can also customize interfaces by using SmartIcons. For example, users can create one toolbar for editing, another for recording, and another for playing video.

VideoNotes can be administered by the Lotus Notes administrator with very little incremental education. In addition, because VideoNotes provides an intuitive interface, most users find that embedding video in Lotus Notes documents is an easy extension of traditional Lotus Notes concepts. A special feature of Lotus Notes (Lotus Notes Field Exchange, also referred to as Lotus Notes/FX) enables users to update video clip statistics easily in fields contained in Lotus Notes documents, such as an on-line catalog of available video clips with information about each clip's topic, creator, and format.

A flexible replication model enables administrators to balance user demand for immediate access to video with the need to minimize the impact of large video transfers on the network. Bandwidth management schemes enable administrators to manage the transmission of both real time video and traditional data simultaneously on the network. Lotus VideoNotes uses industry-standard network management protocols supported today by network router and hub vendors.

VideoNotes conserves system resources. Multiple documents can reference the same video, but only one copy of the video clip is stored at each site. This enables organizations to leverage system resources efficiently.

Barriers to Digital Video

The decision to implement video on a LAN or WAN is not simple because of the characteristics of video technology. Although video technology may be more complex than other data types, it does not involve mystical properties found only through years of diligent study. Digital video is simply another data type. Like most data types, video can be entered, stored, edited, processed, and distributed through Notes. Because of its characteristics, however, video is more complex for users, administrators, and developers.

For one thing, video data files are typically very large compared to standard text files. This requires additional planning for storage space on individual workstations and servers. In certain cases, video files may require special video-ready disk drives that meet the demands of interactive applications. In a typical LAN environment, a single minute of compressed digital video results in a file of 8MB to 12MB in size. Fortunately, smaller-format, higher-density drives are rapidly coming to market at dramatically declining prices. The advent of LAN-based video servers has decreased the cost of storing digital media assets by amortizing the cost of high-capacity disk storage forms over a community of users. Even more importantly, video servers enable multiple users to access a single copy of the video object, thus minimizing overall storage requirements.

When digital video is used over a network, it requires network bandwidth management control to ensure that LAN resources are allocated and shared with other applications. Obviously, this affects network performance. Although dedicated networked digital video servers can minimize storage demands by enabling users to share video content, this strategy creates its own set of challenges for the corporate computing environment. Even with the most sophisticated compression encoding, a single video stream can average 1 to 1.5MB/s (megabits/second), sustained for the duration of the video clip or segment. Fortunately, video server and network infrastructure providers are developing standards for network bandwidth management and control to ensure that LAN resource distribution reflects the requirements and priorities of different applications and users.

Most LANs can accommodate video streams. The aggregate number of streams that a segment can support increases dramatically with proper planning and utilization of switching technology. Switching technology on 10MB/s LAN media can guarantee that users streaming real-time video from a shared video server do not compete with each other for network resources. A single user on a switched Ethernet segment can simultaneously subscribe to multiple video streams. Advancing technology will make it easier. Solutions such as 100 Megabit Ethernet increase overall capacity. Emerging protocols and new communications media will dramatically increase the options for managing networked digital video in the very near future.

Digital video requires specialized tools for capture, editing, and playback. The need to synchronize sound and images for playback also presents a few minimal additional requirements at the workstation level. For a Microsoft Windows 3.1 environment, these requirements include Video for Windows and QuickTime for Windows support, available through Lotus VideoNotes and a sound card.

Software-based decompression on a typical desktop personal computer is available immediately in the most popular video-encoding formats. Dataquest, in a recent survey, indicated that more than 10 million units shipped in 1994 met this criteria. The most popular software compression/decompression units (codecs) are included with new Windows systems. The Indeo (Intel-developed video-encoding scheme for real-time software playback on a wide range of desktop clients) decompressor is bundled with Video for Windows, which comes standard with Windows 95. MPEG software is available for Video for Windows under Windows 95, and MPEG hardware support is available for an increasing number of machines.

The sharp drop in the cost of networked "video-capable" storage, the increasing availability of network infrastructure to support the management of networked digital video, and the powerful components at the desktop level are rapidly eliminating the obstacles to video-ready applications in an enterprise network.

The Business Advantage of Lotus VideoNotes

Costs and complexity have restrained the business use of video in the past. However, the cost of creating digital video is dropping rapidly, approximately tenfold in the last two years alone.

30

VIDEONOTES AND REALTIME NOTES

The costs of video playback and storage for video (including CD-ROM drives) have also dropped considerably. At the workstation level, more and more workstations are shipped video-ready with on-board sound, 256-color display, and graphics acceleration. In 1996, the infrastructure for desktop video is becoming the de facto configuration for business computers. As these component prices decline, digital video becomes a more attractive alternative for business. Lotus VideoNotes enables businesses to take advantage of these trends rapidly and easily.

Lotus VideoNotes offers effective and robust digital video communication, distribution, and management services within the familiar and productive environment of Lotus Notes. By building on the Notes interface and management architecture, on industry standards for network protocols, and on video/audio file management features within commercially available video servers, VideoNotes overcomes the most frequently encountered obstacles to adopting digital video in the workplace. VideoNotes efficiently leverages existing networks and systems while providing a flexible means of managing video at a level that businesses can support and quickly enhancing productivity in an increasingly complex business environment.

VideoNotes commands a unique position in the business information systems market. It makes applications such as video databases (with RealTime Notes) and video mail available with only a few clicks inside an interface that is already familiar to millions of users. Many businesses are discovering compelling reasons to incorporate these capabilities into existing commercial applications. The following are among the most obvious examples:

- *Video E-Mail.* Sending video messages to clients that personalizes interactions and builds relationships by visual aids. When VideoNotes is combined with RealTime Notes, video mail becomes as easy to use as text mail.

- *Insurance.* Insurance claims adjusters and claims analysts can review embedded video in Notes documents, along with standard text files about properties, vehicles, or events for which claims have been filed. Video clips can clarify claims evidence significantly, compared with typical text descriptions.

- *Advertising.* Media and advertising agencies can use Lotus VideoNotes documents during the approval and review process, ensuring that the visuals in a campaign are effective. An advertising agency can distribute updates to employees directly. Sharing video clips can also improve collaboration within the creative team.

- *Public Relations.* Public relations managers who store video with printed media can organize, analyze, distribute, and control their media exposure. Lotus VideoNotes enables the convenient categorization of documents by topic rather than data type.

- *Real Estate.* Brokers and agents can provide a better description of properties by combining video clips with data, still pictures, and floor plans. The video clips can be seamlessly integrated with other types of data in a Notes database.

- *Education.* Business education can be made much more cost-effective by providing video on demand combined with a full range of classroom support materials. Notes can be used to handle communications and collaboration among students and instructors who are at different sites.

■ *Retail.* Corporate headquarters can provide video clips of new ad campaigns, featured products, promotional displays, and sales strategies so that sales personnel, customer service reps, and store managers anticipate customer demand and make appropriate preparations. Again, integration with other types of data in Notes databases (such as current availabilities, rollout schedules, marketing messages, and pricing) makes VideoNotes clips much more valuable than traditional video tapes.

■ *Sales and Customer Service.* Companies can provide video clips of products and services, along with detailed, written product descriptions, so that sales and customer service representatives can respond to customer inquiries and leverage interests. Distributing video to customers through VideoNotes can increase product awareness and understanding dramatically, with little investment of labor.

Lotus VideoNotes Application Development

VideoNotes comes with all the utilities necessary to capture, record, edit, and play video within the Lotus Notes development environment. (See Figure 30.3.) Users who can create a Notes document can potentially create video-enabled Notes applications, as long as they have the authority from the systems administrator. Any field that can contain rich text can contain embedded video.

FIGURE 30.3.

A typical VideoNotes editing session.

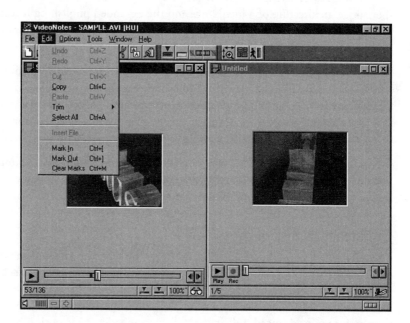

In addition, the current release of VideoNotes supports Notes/FX (Notes Field Exchange), which enables the exchange of data between fields in Notes documents and other Notes/FX-enabled OLE server applications. An external player or recorder can receive messages about VideoNotes objects through the Notes/FX interface. Examples of useful information about video objects include encoding scheme, codec version, frame rate, bandwidth, and resolution. These parameters are user-definable and extensible. For example, authoring applications can make use of the Notes/FX interface to communicate revision control and author attribution for royalty payments, as well as to insure that any required special video playback software or hardware is available.

The VideoNotes API is available to third parties upon request. This API consists of a library of C-callable functions that gives developers of video applications access to the video/data management services of VideoNotes. Developers can use this API to build multimedia applications that take advantage of, but are not limited to, Notes user interface conventions. In addition, this API makes the fundamental VideoNotes storage, distribution, and management capabilities available to any video player.

Publishing with VideoNotes

For a Lotus Notes user looking to incorporate video, Lotus VideoNotes is a clear choice, but the unique architecture of VideoNotes and the expanded publishing features of VideoNotes Release 1.1 enable content developers to distribute their digital video assets to VideoNotes users at reduced cost, with greater flexibility and impact.

Any authorized user can publish a CD-ROM designed for use with VideoNotes by using standard OLE commands to embed video in Notes documents, also stored on the CD. Once the CD is delivered to a site and Notes documents containing video are copied to a Notes server at that site, the VideoNotes Site Manager automatically transfers video from the CD to a video server and makes the new content available to any VideoNotes client.

This publishing feature also has many noncommercial applications. For example, users can easily update, create, and maintain training materials, reference guides, and new on-line digital marketing collateral when new source video is all managed within Lotus Notes.

Implementing VideoNotes

Organizations that have advanced Lotus Notes installations will find the implementation of Lotus VideoNotes uneventful. Many organizations have experienced excellent success by introducing Lotus VideoNotes in stages so that users can begin to experience the benefits of video in small increments. This enables the network administrator to learn the technology and paves the way for more advanced, full-frame, full-motion video. One option is to enable individual VideoNotes users to make local copies of small video objects for direct playback from their workstations, although that can potentially tie up excessive hard drive storage. The users can access video even when the network doesn't support video streaming.

Another option is to use a single system for both the Site Manager and video server. This enables an organization to test video with a less expensive targeted number of users. Although this is not a suitable long-term solution, it works for a pilot project. Companies that want to provide access to a larger number of users want to install a separate video server to guarantee optimal allocation of network resources and robust performance (including glitch-free, full-motion video).

Lotus currently supports video-server systems, such as the IBM Ultimedia, Starlight Network's StarWare and First Virtual Corporation Media Server, and NetWare Video Services. It is reasonable to expect that the list of supported video servers will expand with the industry.

System Requirements for Lotus VideoNotes

Lotus VideoNotes is currently available for Windows client workstations using either an OS/2 or Windows NT Notes server for the Site Manager. The following are the systems requirements according to Lotus Development Corporation:

VideoNotes client workstation

- 486 or Pentium processor
- 8MB memory (12MB recommended)
- 6MB hard disk space free for installation
- 256-color graphics adapter
- Windows-compatible sound board
- Windows 3.1 or later
- Lotus Notes 3.2 or later client software
- (Optional) Intel Smart Video Recorder board or ATI Video-It!
- Allow 10MB (we recommend 20MB) free disk space for each minute of video captured

VideoNotes Site Manager Server

- 486 or Pentium processor
- 4MB minimum memory (32MB or more recommended)
- OS/2, version 2.1 or later (we recommend Warp or later) or Windows NT 3.5 or later
- Notes 3.2 or later server software

VideoNotes Site Manager Server Options

- IBM OS/2 LAN Server Ultimedia
- Windows NT 3.5
- Novell NetWare with Novell Multimedia Server NLM

30

**VIDEONOTES AND
REALTIME NOTES**

■ Novell NetWare with Starlight StarWare NLM

■ First Virtual Corporation's Media Storage Server and Media Switch

Lotus RealTime Notes: Going Live with Video Technology

The key to the information age is the availability of information and how quickly it can be accessed. Without information, business professionals are at a competitive disadvantage. When it comes to information transfer, however, there is nothing like being present at an event for effectiveness. Everyone has experienced being part of an important business event or transaction, where participating in or observing what was going on defined the event and made a lasting impression. There is nothing like being where the action is, watching an event as it unfolds, to understand its impact. The benefits of immediate information can be greatly enhanced by video. By definition, watching a live event provides the most accurate portrayal of what happens in an event or through a series of events. Observing in real time creates a level of excitement that is impossible to reproduce.

For instance, if a Lotus Notes user needs to understand the concept behind a major company strategy speech, there are several ways in which the user can learn that information. At the very least, a Lotus Notes user can read the text of the speech, and if it is well written, understand the information as it was presented in print. To gain a greater understanding of the information, perhaps the Lotus Notes user can launch an attachment to see the graphics that went along with the presentation. The benefit of graphics is that the text is supplemented with important information that may not be emphasized in the text. A further enhancement of the information is a replay of a digitally stored video of the speech. This provides additional information above the text and graphics. The reader is able to see the speaker's specific emphasis and can get a sense of the overall mood and atmosphere via intonation and pacing. The viewer can also see the body language and other subliminal aspects that add substance to the message.

The ultimate expression of this information is real-time video. Real-time video creates an immediacy and sense of urgency that cannot be duplicated in any other data form. It creates a personalized atmosphere that enhances the message. Real-time video can emphasize important points and reduce confusion. It commands attention and therefore provides a distinct advantage over all other types of communications for important events.

With the advent of RealTime Notes, a Lotus Notes Business Multimedia product, Lotus Notes users can take advantage of easy-to-use, easy-to-learn applications that incorporate real-time multimedia into mainstream business communications.

RealTime Notes incorporates Intel's ProShare technology seamlessly into the Notes framework. It is a separate product from VideoNotes, and each may be used alone or in combination with the other. The most powerful uses come from the combination. For example, video mail is available at a click of a SmartIcon to users who have VideoNotes, RealTime Notes, and the Intel ProShare Video upgrade to RealTime Notes.

Background and Industry Trends

There are common communication characteristics that span every industry and company. Communications occur as either real-time communications or stored-data communications. Real-time communications consist of face-to-face meetings, phone conversations, shared computer conversations (on-line communications), and any other event that involves two or more human beings communicating with each other at the same time. Stored-data communications are characterized by information that is read, reviewed, or processed at different times or different locations—text, graphics, audio cassettes, video cassettes, and much more. Most business people rely on stored-data communications today, not because it is necessarily more efficient as a data source but because it is often easier to use, manage, and share on desktop computers.

Productivity is lost in the move from using one type of communications to the other. Unless real-time and stored-data communications are available in the same physical location, with standard telecommunications and computer equipment, the physical location and daily processes are disrupted. In these cases, even if the method of communications can be shown to have a clear benefit, it simply becomes too difficult. The telephone is a great example of technology that seamlessly supports both levels of communication. A telephone supports a real-time conversation or a recorded phone-mail message. The explosive growth of phone mail is a direct result of the unobtrusive process of using the technology for productivity improvements.

The requirement to stay connected has driven a variety of communication technologies, ranging from phone mail to electronic mail. The resulting cost savings and productivity improvements have built a multibillion-dollar communication infrastructure that makes a variety of data types accessible to expedite the decision-making process. The standard lifecycle will evolve to a point where this communication infrastructure will get more powerful and less expensive. The infrastructure will carry more information for less cost and it will pave the way for "advanced communications" such as real-time video.

The basic infrastructure is the first step. Business people will continue to participate in real-time exchanges only when they can be completed in a low-cost, convenient fashion. Lotus RealTime Notes offers a whole new class of desktop conferencing tools based on existing networks and desktop personal computers. For significant productivity increases to occur, a large-scale adoption must take place. This universal adoption will take place only when all the technology is in place and users feel comfortable using the technology as a natural extension of their current arsenal of personal productivity tools.

Most business communications are a combination of real-time and stored-data. With the advent of advanced telephone communications, contact can be easily made to all parts of the world. Modern travel has reduced distance considerations to doing business, but the method of conduct

30
VIDEONOTES AND
REALTIME NOTES

is still the same. A business person can fly anywhere in the world, but he must still shake hands with the client when he gets to the destination. With the advent of RealTime Notes, these communications can be further enhanced by providing more frequent, inexpensive, face-to-face communications. The results provide better productivity and higher-quality decision-making because better informed people make better decisions.

Productivity improvements come from ease of information access, reduced travel, higher frequency of client interactions, and even having fun. There are also many competitive advantages. For instance, in many industries, such as financial service, brokerage, and media, viewing information as it happens is a critical competitive advantage that has a direct correlation to the organization's bottom line.

What Is Lotus RealTime Notes?

Lotus RealTime Notes is a Lotus Notes Business Multimedia product that provides real-time desktop conferencing. Real-time conferencing enables users to connect live to other users' desktops—sharing data and applications with (optional) real-time video.

Lotus Notes users can communicate with others, sharing their information, perspective, and expertise, regardless of location. The real-time desktop conferencing functionality is based on Intel Corporation's ProShare desktop conferencing product line. RealTime Notes also provides Notes-based applications and tools to integrate the powerful groupware and messaging functionality of Lotus Notes with the innovative real-time data sharing and desktop videoconferencing of Intel ProShare.

RealTime Notes is included at no charge with all Notes R4 Desktop and Full Client licenses and quarterly maintenance updates. Standard RealTime Notes delivers full data and application sharing to the Notes desktop and requires no additional hardware beyond that which is required for local area network or modem connectivity.

RealTime Notes also supports optional Intel ProShare desktop videoconferencing in addition to data and application sharing. Notes users can incorporate live desktop videoconferencing through the purchase of additional hardware from Intel.

The three fundamental levels of real-time desktop conferencing in RealTime Notes are:

- *Data Sharing* is shared use of the RealTime whiteboard, which provides a common notebook-like interface for displaying text, drawings, or material copied from other desktop sources. Data sharing provides the ideal environment for ad hoc brainstorming, review, or process synchronization.

- *Application Sharing* enables users to share desktop applications live, in real time. Both users work on one version of the data, utilizing the full power of the application and eliminating multiple copies of the information. For example, both users can see and edit one of the two users' Notes documents, as if they were both working at the same computer. Any other Windows application can also be shared.

■ *Videoconferencing* involves using Lotus RealTime Notes and the optional Intel Pro-Share desktop videoconferencing to provide live two-way video and audio between two (or more) personal computers. Each system has a small camera and speaker, as well as add-in hardware boards. Users see each other in on-screen windows that can be set from icon size to full-screen size (with appropriate graphics cards).

Lotus RealTime Notes enables business people to document meetings automatically and quickly distribute meeting notes, action items, participant lists, and essential information throughout the network. The technology works directly from the desktop, taking advantage of personal computer networks and phone lines. RealTime Notes provides robust data synchronization and includes the replication features of Notes, which ensures enterprise-wide information access.

RealTime Notes Architecture

The RealTime Notes architecture (see Figure 30.4) provides the most common conferencing functions directly from the Notes desktop, with very little user setup activity, including:

■ Shared whiteboard with live markup and editing

■ Shared Notes desktop (and other Windows applications)

■ Live two-way videoconferencing (with ProShare Video upgrade)

■ Video mail (with VideoNotes and ProShare Video upgrade)

FIGURE 30.4.

RealTime Notes architecture.

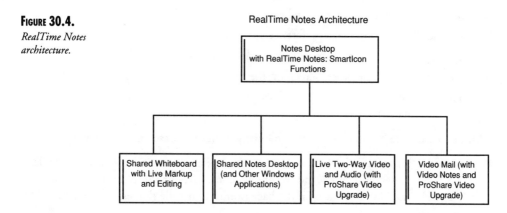

The architecture also encompasses all other conferencing functions, from call initiation to transparent access control over applications, as well as address books and logging facilities.

Establishing a call with another ProShare-enabled system is quite simple, because RealTime Notes helps coordinate the management of connections, initiate session-level conversations, and launch applications to support the conversation. RealTime Notes performs essential auditing functions for these connections.

RealTime Notes provides access to conferencing applications through new macro facilities and Notes API calls. The core architecture is the Dynamic Data Exchange support provided in both Lotus Notes and Intel ProShare products. Developers may also use these calls to access the set of directory services and real-time events.

Features of RealTime Notes

One of the main features of RealTime Notes is that the software is free, easy to use, and integrated into the Lotus Notes Desktop. The features discussed in this section are standard.

RealTime Notes includes a customized conference-enabled *SmartIcon Palette*, providing integrated access to ProShare's desktop conferencing facilities directly from within the Notes environment. This direct integration simplifies access and use of the new real-time conferencing facilities, lowering the learning curve and accelerating adoption by end users. The following SmartIcons are available in support of real-time activities:

- Initiate a ProShare data conferencing session
- Initiate a ProShare video session (requires optional Intel ProShare Video System)
- Share the Notes desktop
- Hang up the current conferencing session
- Open the active RealTime Notes conference address book
- Open the conference journal database
- Open the conference audit log database
- View and modify conference preference settings
- Share the ProShare whiteboard during a video conference session
- Place a snapshot of the Notes screen on the ProShare whiteboard
- Compose a conference-enabled mail message (support for optional VideoNotes messages included)

In addition, RealTime Notes includes the following Notes databases for conferencing:

- *Conference Preferences* help the user manage the available connectivity options (modem or LAN for whiteboard and Windows applications, LAN or ISDN for live video) while RealTime Notes operates in the background to handle the rest of the data connection.
- *RealTime Notes Conference Address Book* fills an important role in the Notes integration of real-time conferencing by organizing conference connection information and providing automated call initiation directly from Notes. RealTime Notes address books are the primary source of real-time connection information, accommodating the variety of conference connection methods available, including standard modems, LANs, and integrated services digital network (ISDN). RealTime Notes address books

follow the familiar Public Address Book format and are easily populated from existing corporate or private Notes name and address databases. Users can have multiple conference address books, both server-based and local, to reflect different sources of information.

■ *Conference Journal Databases* are designed to facilitate the tracking and summarization of real-time conference sessions. Conference Journal documents represent personal records or accounts of individual conference sessions. A Journal document is created automatically when a user initiates a conference connection from RealTime Notes, or it can be composed manually when receiving a conference call from another party. For users who do not wish to summarize conferences, automatic creation can be disabled. Journal information can be stored in a server database or locally, in a more private setting.

■ *Notes Conference Audit Log Database* provides system administrators and management with an audit trail of conference activity by the account code, person, date, and connection method. The audit log database is a valuable tool for tracking the effectiveness and utilization of supporting resources. In an account billing environment, the audit log summarization can be of assistance in generating periodic statements to clients or internal charge-back allocations.

An important additional feature of RealTime Notes is the capability to create conference-enabled mail messages. Conference-enabled Notes mail contains a "Return Conference Call" button to establish a return real-time conference with the composer of the message automatically. The conference-enabled mail form automatically stores the composer's available connection address information inside the form, presenting the reader with the appropriate options for a successful conference connection. If the Lotus VideoNotes application is available, the conference-enabled Notes mail form can automatically embed a recorded video message to be mailed along with any additional text, images, or file attachments.

The combination of these features enables the user to respond to business opportunities faster and better than ever before. For example, suppose you are suddenly asked to prepare a proposal, and you need help from an expert in a distant city. If you and the expert have RealTime Notes, you both can view what is written while it is being worked on, simply by sharing the desktop. The expert can actually take the keyboard and mouse and make changes to your document, as if you both are working on the same computer. The expert can also show anything that can be placed in front of a camera (or played from a VCR), as well as transfer any relevant files at high speed.

The same features enable you to give an on-screen presentation, complete with sophisticated graphics, audio, and video, to several people at once. All of this can be done simply by using RealTime Notes, ProShare Video, and a multi-point video bridge service (available from AT&T and other companies).

RealTime Notes Benefits

RealTime Notes' most important benefit is its incorporation into Lotus Notes, the industry standard groupware product. RealTime Notes' feature set is specifically designed to address ease of use and simplified access to new technology using existing tools, and to provide a seamless transition to minimize the transition to new technology.

The ease of use begins with convenient call initiation. RealTime Notes leverages the familiar Lotus Notes desktop and information in the Public Address Book to enable conference initiation direct from within Notes. A Lotus Notes user, system administrator, or developer will find familiar surroundings consistent with the main Lotus Notes product.

Simplified access of the technology makes collaboration with another person who has ProShare installed as simple as pressing a SmartIcon from a menu. If the user is not in a conference-enabled file or database at the time, RealTime Notes displays a dialog box populated from the conferencing address book. This easy extension to standard Lotus Notes system administration databases saves hours of time and makes the transition easy.

RealTime Notes enables users to enhance their existing collaborative applications' environments to include real-time desktop data or video interaction with minimal disruption. Further integration of real-time desktop conferencing with customized groupware and messaging is possible through the conference API provided with RealTime Notes.

The Business Case for Lotus RealTime Notes

The business advantage of Lotus RealTime Notes is growing as fast as the need for real-time information. Lotus RealTime Notes increases workgroup spontaneity, facilitates more frequent meetings or periodic visits, and makes face-to-face communication as easy as electronic mail. There is a tremendous productivity advantage resulting from an electronic conference with two associates working on the same information or document, especially when it takes place without the people leaving their desks. A Lotus RealTime Notes user can increase productivity by reducing or eliminating the time-consuming disruption of travel. Complex information can be explained directly by the experts and questions can be asked directly by interested parties, rather than archived and relayed back, and follow-up questions can be answered on-line.

Because Lotus RealTime Notes is built into the Lotus Notes format, business users can share all data and information and perform all functions from within the Notes desktop. Lotus RealTime Notes enables greater productivity because it is a natural extension of a user's desktop.

There are a variety of uses for Lotus RealTime Notes that enhance information sharing within a workgroup, throughout an enterprise, or between strategic partners, clients, or vendors.

Real-time video can assist in adding urgency and importance to important events or presentations. Meetings can be facilitated more easily between team members who are geographically dispersed and then documented through the built-in conference journal feature, which makes it easy to distribute meeting notes and action items and to create an audit trail.

Marketing teams can share product and customer information, review ad campaigns and promotions, and analyze research directly with the clients or with creative associates throughout the world. Software engineers or CAD designers can share designs, drawings, and specifications in real-time conferences through brainstorming about design changes, working together to solve complex issues, and proposing alternative solutions.

Sales managers can review proposals and contracts, plan sales strategies, and update or review sales tools and materials with sales people in the field, or use Lotus RealTime Notes to talk directly to top clients. By extending RealTime Notes to suppliers, partners, associates, and clients, managers can cultivate and enhance relationships and resolve problems quickly and easily.

Product development organizations can utilize the power of Lotus RealTime Notes to hold conferences with experts from all over the world so that teams can share ideas on whiteboards, brainstorm new ideas, coordinate diverse activities, and even review stored digital video application files on-line. Customer service managers can resolve customer service and quality problems directly with the customer, quickly and efficiently without costly, time-consuming travel and in-person meetings. Workgroups of all types can improve their effectiveness and increase productivity by enabling close collaboration without the time, expense, and delay of travel meetings.

RealTime Notes Application Development Resources

RealTime Notes supports the sharing of all data types, including video through VideoNotes. In addition, application developers can incorporate desktop conferencing into their custom Notes applications.

RealTime Notes includes a Conference API that is provided via a dynamic link library (DLL) and a Notes database driver. The API is a custom Notes `@DBCommand()` function designed to facilitate management of RealTime Notes video functions. Software engineers can use the Conference DLL to add ProShare desktop conferencing to their new or existing custom Notes applications. The functions that can be added are very similar to those available through SmartIcons, and they allow custom Notes applications to incorporate these functions into their own interfaces. In addition, the ProShare Development Kit, available separately from Intel, enables developers to tailor the look and feel of the live video windows to suit their own applications. The kit includes extensive sample applications in Visual Basic and C, as well as thorough documentation.

Implementing Lotus RealTime Notes

The basic functionality of RealTime Notes (shared whiteboard and shared Windows applications) is a free upgrade to Notes Desktop or Full Client licenses. It installs automatically in a few minutes. It uses the existing Notes LAN and/or modem connections for communications. In other words, there is no reason why most Notes users should delay installing it!

The video upgrade requires additional hardware (camera, headphone/microphone, and one or two ISA [Industry Standard Architecture] add-in circuit boards—one for LAN-only configurations, two for ISDN) at extra cost. The costs are likely to drop considerably over time. All the hardware and associated software come in a kit box from Intel with excellent documentation. Ordinary users with no experience at hardware installation report easy installation in less than one hour. Intel provides first-class technical support, and ProShare Video vendors can help arrange for the installation of ISDN phone lines.

System Requirements for Lotus RealTime Notes

RealTime Notes' hardware and software requirements are divided into three groups: software requirements for workstations *without* the video upgrade; hardware requirements *without* the video upgrade; and additional hardware and software requirements to add the video upgrade. The primary software requirements for RealTime Notes workstations without the video upgrade are:

- Microsoft Windows 3.1
- Lotus Notes desktop or full client, version 3.15 or higher

The required hardware for workstations without the video upgrade is:

- CPU: 486/33 or faster
- Memory: 8MB
- Storage: 14MB
- Display: VGA

Additional requirements for workstations with the video upgrade include:

- Intel ProShare Personal Video Conferencing System 150 (LAN) or 200 (LAN and ISDN) version 1.9 or higher, which includes hardware and software (available from Intel resellers)
- CPU: 486/66 or faster (Pentium recommended)
- Memory: 16MB
- Display: Minimum 256 colors, local bus graphics
- Storage: 17MB
- Slot(s) for ISA circuit board(s): Two for ProShare 200, one for ProShare 150
- ISDN and/or LAN connections (ProShare 150 assumes separate LAN card)
- Lotus VideoNotes version 1.1 (optional—only required for video e-mail)

Summary

VideoNotes and RealTime Notes extend the power of Lotus Notes in two of the most important directions for business communications in the future: video and live electronic interaction. VideoNotes brings stored video into the standard Notes architecture, whether the video is distributed over servers or from local CD-ROMs. RealTime Notes incorporates live interaction in any of three forms: live review of a shared whiteboard, live interaction with a shared Windows application (including the Notes desktop), and live two-way video and audio. When the two Business Multimedia products are combined, additional applications like video mail are automatically enabled. Together, they truly bring Notes into the Video Age.

Integrating Notes with Legacy Systems

by Rizwan Virk

CHAPTER

31

Lotus Notes is an information platform that is fast becoming the primary means of information distribution in many organizations around the world. This new type of database system does more than just store data. Notes organizes the data in meaningful ways to provide information to end users, making it one of the first information platforms for corporate use.

Although Notes is a database itself, it is quite different from the other databases. In particular, the type of data that is best suited for Notes is more textual and free-form than the type of data that is suited for traditional database systems. Lotus Notes complements these solutions, and is most powerful when it is used in combination with these systems, which I will refer to as "legacy systems."

One of the key measures of the success of Notes at major organizations around the world has been its Return on Investment (ROI). However, most MIS managers are not as concerned with the ROI of a particular database or technology as they are with the overall ROI of information technology spending for the company, a large part of which is taken up by the legacy database system. By integrating Notes with existing MIS database systems, organizations realize a higher ROI from their MIS investments, and can begin to use their information systems to gain a competitive advantage.

This chapter explores the integration of Notes with other database systems, and it is broken into several parts. The first part gives an overview of reasons and methods for integration of Notes and legacy systems, the second part gives the details of different implementation methods, and the third part runs through a detailed example that uses Notes as a front end to a relational database.

An Overview of Notes-Legacy Integration

This section explores the background of Notes and legacy systems, details the reasons for integration, and summarizes the questions you need to ask in preparing to implement an integration solution.

Legacy Systems

A typical organization that implements Lotus Notes will have information and data stored in many formats in many different places. The storage mechanism is usually determined by the type of data that needs to be stored and how often it needs to be accessed. Table 31.1 shows how different types of information are typically stored in corporations.

Table 31.1. Storage mechanisms for corporate data.

Type of Information	Storage Mechanism
Unstructured files, memos	Local hard disks, file servers
Small number of structured records	Flat file, desktop databases
Large number of structured records	Client/server relational databases mainframe systems

This chapter does not deal with memos, reports, and spreadsheets that are stored on individual workstations or on file servers. Migrating those bits of information into a corporate knowledge base such as Notes is a topic unto itself. *Legacy systems* are existing database systems that a company has been using for storing and organizing its data.

These systems typically have a number of highly structured records of data and enable users to perform transactions against this data via applications. Often, these databases are at the heart of a company's mission-critical processes and need to be kept running at all costs. As Lotus Notes becomes the preferred method for distribution and collection of information among employees, links between these database systems and Lotus Notes will also become mission-critical.

This definition of legacy systems can be divided into three categories:

- **Desktop Databases.** These databases, primarily relational, reside on end-user desktops and usually include a front-end development environment. Examples include Microsoft Access, Borland Paradox, Microsoft FoxPro, and Gupta SQLBase. These databases can also reside on a LAN file server, where they are accessed by multiple users. End users access the database on the file server by using a network drive mapping. Because this is analogous to local file access, it does not scale when there are a large number of users. Some of these databases also have client/server versions for use by a workgroup. They typically run on a PC running Microsoft Windows or Macintosh.

- **Client/Server Databases.** These are the industrial strength, relational database servers being used in production environments at major companies. Examples include Oracle, Sybase, Ingres, and Informix. These servers are at the heart of the client/server revolution, and migration of mainframe applications to run against these servers has followed the growth in scalability and reliability of these database servers and their front-end application development tools.

■ **Mainframe Databases.** These are the heavy transaction-oriented systems that still contain most of the world's data. In the traditional data processing model, only certain clerks were given access to the database on the mainframe, and everyone else had to get and give information via these clerks. The clerks were responsible for all data entry and reporting on a regular basis. Mainframe systems are extremely reliable and might host millions of records of data in one central database.

Most MIS departments in large corporations have systems in all three categories. Small to mid-size companies might have a combination of the first two types. When deploying Notes across an enterprise and planning a Lotus Notes database integration strategy, it is important to consider all three types of databases.

Structured Versus Unstructured Data

Traditional databases are best at storing what might be termed structured data—records of information with fixed-length columns—such as name, address, phone number, and so on, of customers, prospects, vendors, and so forth. Desktop applications (including word processors, presentation software, and spreadsheets), on the other hand, are best at creating and managing documents that would be considered unstructured data—memos, reports, budgets, forecasts, and so forth.

Unstructured data is usually stored in documents or files, and structured data is usually stored as records in tables in a database. Lotus Notes combines the benefits of these two types of data into a semi-structured format. Lotus Notes documents are semi-structured records.

Each Notes record contains a collection of fields. Each field has a data type, such as date-time, text, or rich text. Unstructured data (such as the body of a memo) is stored in rich text fields within a Notes record. The fields that are contained in one Notes document depend on the form that was used to create the document. Using this approach, documents can be organized based upon the value of their non-rich text fields.

For example, although a memo might be considered unstructured, most memos do have a definite structure. They have a place for the recipient's name, the sender's name, the subject, the date, and the body of the memo. In Notes, a database to store memos has a memo form. The memo form has fields for the author's name, the recipient's name, the subject, the date, and the body of the memo. Notes documents are unstructured because the body field is of data type rich text, which enables a user to type using different fonts and bitmaps, and embed objects within it.

A Complementary Fit: Different Types of Applications

Lotus Notes and traditional database systems are complementary. Because of its specific semi-structured database architecture, the types of applications that are best suited for Notes are quite different from the types of applications that run against most existing database systems.

The types of applications that work best against a structured database are those in which the following are true:

- A large number of records are constantly changing.
- All end users need up-to-the-minute information.
- Multistep transactions need to occur, with locking, commit, and rollback capabilities.
- Data consists of a large number of records, each with a fixed structure.
- Queries need to be performed on an ad hoc basis.
- Financial data needs to be stored, manipulated, or processed.

In contrast, the types of applications that are more suited for Lotus Notes include those in which the following are true:

- Groups of people in different locations (including mobile users) need to share information.
- The data is highly textual or consists of rich text elements.
- Documents need to be reviewed, shared, and organized in workgroups.
- Documents need to be routed to different individuals for approval.
- The number of records is not unusually large (25,000 records or less works best in Notes database).
- Reporting format is standardized and doesn't change often.
- Data needs to be published, and changes are made daily.

Here are some examples of how customers are using Notes today:

- Lead-tracking databases for mobile sales force
- Project- and status-tracking databases
- Travel authorization databases
- Expense report submission and approval databases
- Discussion databases
- Knowledge capture and knowledge base
- Customer support and help desk applications
- Document storage and distribution
- Corporate policies and other reference information

Although many of these example applications might also be built using client/server databases, they would be difficult to implement and maintain. The unstructured nature of data being captured and routed through an organization makes Notes a better choice for these and many other types of applications.

However, when they first deploy Notes, many companies attempt to use it for applications that require near real-time data access, or highly normalized data. These attempts tend to push Notes to its limits and often end in failure. For these types of applications, a much better solution is to separate the structured data and the unstructured parts of the application and link them via the methods described in this chapter.

Reasons for Integration of Notes and Legacy Systems

As you've seen, Notes excels at a class of applications that are slightly different from the ones being built by using traditional client/server tools. However, the users of Notes applications are typically the same people who need access to the data stored in client/server databases, and many companies moving to Notes have existing applications that need to be maintained and improved.

Rather than trying to force Notes to look like a relational database, the two can and should be used together. A very practical method to achieve MIS goals is to divide a business process into its respective pieces, implementing some of the process in Notes and leaving the rest in the existing system.

For example, accounting and/or financial applications are not well suited for Notes. However, a credit and collections application that tracks the status of each collection case over a period of time is well suited for Notes. For this collection case-tracking application to be truly useful to an organization, however, the data must somehow find its way back into the accounting system. This can be done by integrating Notes closely with legacy systems.

Here are some additional examples of why Notes and legacy systems might need to be linked:

■ *Migrating Data from Existing Systems.* Often, as a new application is deployed in Notes, the developers come close to the deployment deadline and realize that, before they can roll out the application, they need to get historical data into the new Notes database. This type of one-time transfer is very typical in Notes organizations.

■ *Business Process and Workflow Integration.* In the example of collections being tracked in Notes, a business process was defined that went beyond the boundaries of the systems used to implement specific pieces of functionality. Often, a company analyzes its critical business processes and, upon reengineering them, discovers that implementation of the new process is not very easy. The main reason is usually incompatibility between disparate data sources. By writing part of the application in Notes and the rest against the existing accounting databases, the problem is solved and everyone is happier.

Another example is a company that wants its expense reports to be tracked and authorized in Notes, but as they are approved, needs them to be deposited into the company's financial systems, which are implemented on a relational database. An expense report authorization implemented in Notes alone will stop with the final

Integrating Notes with Legacy Systems

CHAPTER **31**

773

31

INTEGRATING
NOTES WITH
LEGACY SYSTEMS

approval or disapproval. However, with Notes-legacy integration, the application can follow the logic of the process all the way into the accounting system so that a reimbursement check is issued. Then it can come back to mark the status not only as approved but reimbursed, if appropriate.

- *Distribution of data to remote locations.* Because of its capability of maintaining and synchronizing multiple copies of data via replication, Notes is an excellent tool for distributing information to users in remote offices or locations. For example, one accounting firm uses Notes to replicate changes made to the federal tax laws from Washington D.C. to each of its offices around the country. Previously, this was done via a tedious and labor-intensive process of sending large binders with appendixes to the tax laws to all of its offices. Another company publishes its company-wide employee phone directory in a Notes database that is replicated to all of its offices.

  Similarly, if information stored in a company's legacy systems needs to be distributed to employees in other offices or to employees that are mobile, Notes can do the job effectively. However, strong links between the legacy system and Notes need to be up and running for the data to get from one system to another. For example, one high-technology company uses its Oracle system to track prospects who call in to ask about its products. In order to get these leads to a mobile sales force, a Notes-Oracle link was used to migrate the data from Oracle into Notes, which then replicated the data to its traveling sales force.

- *Data Collection.* Another company uses a Notes application on laptops to enable its salespeople to enter product orders and lead-tracking information while on the road. This information is then replicated to the Notes server in the home office and, using a Notes-legacy link, is brought into the company's order processing system.

- *Ad Hoc Reporting.* Yet another reason to integrate Notes with legacy systems is to do ad hoc reporting on the data in Notes databases. Many companies regularly dump a snapshot of their Notes databases into relational tables so that reports can quickly run against the data. As a simple example, a software company uses Notes to track all its leads. It uses a Notes-Microsoft Access link to migrate information from Notes into Access, and then prints out mailing labels and performs ad hoc reports on the data.

- *Archiving.* Because of their indexing capabilities, relational databases are better at storing and sorting large numbers of records. Many companies prefer to migrate Notes documents that are no longer being used into relational databases for archiving purposes.

How to Build an Integration Solution

In order for you to design, implement, test, and deploy an integration strategy, it is helpful to answer some basic questions about your application. The answer to each question will suggest a slightly different approach to the implementation of the Notes-legacy integration and will require a different set of tools:

- What will be the user interface?
- Where is the data stored today?
- Where will the data be stored in the future?
- Which direction does the data need to move (one-way, or two-way)?
- How often does the data need to be synchronized (one time, scheduled, or real-time)?
- Where will the data be updated?
- How often will the data be updated?
- If necessary, how will conflicts be resolved?
- How complicated is the logic of integration?

What Will Be the User Interface?

Perhaps the most important question to ask when implementing a Notes-legacy integration is about the presentation of the data to the end user. If Notes is the primary environment that the end user will live in to read, create, and update information, the details of the integration plan will be quite different than if the user wants to see a custom Windows front end.

Sometimes, it makes more sense to use Notes databases as a repository for the data, leveraging Notes security and replication features while presenting the data as part of a custom client/ server user interface built in a 4GL development environment, such as Visual Basic or PowerBuilder, rather than using the Notes user interface. At other times, the Lotus Notes user interface is the ideal solution for presentation of data to the end user. The operating systems that are being used by the members of the workgroup affect this decision. If your users are running many different operating systems, Notes may be the ideal cross-platform application development environment for the presentation.

Where Is the Data Stored Today?

Before starting to build a workgroup application with Notes that will tie into legacy systems, you should do a thorough analysis of all the places where the data is stored today. Are expense reports currently kept in the accounting system? Are they submitted manually today? Which databases are they stored in? Perhaps they are not even in a database.

By analyzing the structure and location of the data before you build your application, a coherent data migration strategy can be planned. Far too often, an organization will deploy Notes and build an application, but put little thought into how the historical data will get into the Notes database. For example, one consulting firm wanted to put its historical project information into a new Notes database to make it available to its consultants worldwide. Four days before going live it realized that it had no reliable way to migrate the data from its existing location, a Filemaker Pro database on a Macintosh, to a Lotus Notes database running on an OS/2 server. A third-party tool for data migration did the job.

Where Will the Data Be Stored in the Future?

After understanding the location and disposition of the data before the Notes application is rolled out, it's important to map out a detailed data architecture for the final application. This data architecture consists of the following pieces:

- Which subset of the data will reside in Notes database(s)?
- Which subset will reside in a relational database?
- Where will the master Notes database reside?
- Where will the Notes database(s) be replicated to (servers, desktops, and so on)?
- Will there be more than one Notes database? What data elements will tie them together?
- How will data integrity problems in the distributed database architecture be resolved?

For example, one company currently had all its information in an Oracle database, mapped out in a relational schema of many tables. A sales application had already been developed (in PowerBuilder) that relied on these relational tables in a WATCOM database.

Because Notes was the corporate standard for data distribution, the company decided to use Lotus Notes as a way to distribute data to its mobile sales force utilizing Notes replication. Once the data moved to a remote laptop via Notes, an Agent on the remote client migrated the data out of the Notes database and back into a WATCOM database. The salesperson then was able to use the sales application already developed against the WATCOM database. In this example, Notes was used only for distribution of the data, since there was no way for the WATCOM database to mirror the Oracle database while the salesperson traveled.

The final database architecture consisted of several different databases in different locations. It also consisted of a field-by-field mapping. Table 31.2 provides a quick overview of the database architecture used by this company.

Table 31.2. Sample database architecture.

Location	Format
An Oracle server in corporate headquarters	Relational tables
A Notes server in corporate headquarters	Notes database (db)
Notes servers in regional offices	Notes db replica (subset)
Laptop computer	Notes db replica (smaller subset)
Small-footprint relational database	

This particular company also had a detailed mapping of the fields, and in this case, there was only one Notes database. Some applications require multiple Notes databases, each linked to a legacy database.

One-Way or Two-Way?

In the preceding example, the information was centrally maintained in an Oracle database. The members of the sales force used this application to receive product and pricing information while on the road. The salespeople never modified the pricing information in Notes. A one-way transfer on an ongoing basis like this usually represents either a distribution or collection application.

Another company wanted its salespeople to take orders while at customer sites (using Notes), then replicate them back to the home office, where they were migrated into the company's order entry system. The copies in Notes were promptly deleted. In this case, the application could be considered an information collection application. One-way movement of data is much easier to implement than a bidirectional model, because you don't run into data integrity problems and conflicts to resolve.

One Time or Scheduled?

When an organization is abandoning its current system in favor of a Notes application to do the same thing, not only will the data only go one way, it will do so only once. In such a model, after the initial migration, the data is modified only once and maintained in Notes. Tools that are most useful in accomplishing a one-time, one-way movement of data are referred to as *ad hoc data migration tools*.

If, however, the migration will happen on an ongoing basis, it is important that the solution provides data propagation capabilities. Data propagation takes the changes in the source (master) database and propagates them to databases on the other system(s). If a record does not exist in the destination system, a new record is created. If it does exist, the old record is updated. Propagation of deletes are also important for some applications.

Where Will the Data Be Updated, and How Will Conflicts Be Resolved?

If the data needs to move both ways on an ongoing basis, and it is to be modified in both places, synchronization needs to occur. If the data is only modified in one place, then only one-way updates need to occur to keep the data in sync.

This is analogous to how Notes uses replication to maintain different copies of the same database. Under such a system, however, the integrity of the data across systems may be compromised. One employee may modify the data in Notes, and another employee may change it on the legacy system, causing a *conflict* to occur. In this model, data not only needs to be propagated; it also needs to be synchronized. A conflict-resolution strategy should be thought out before proceeding on this dangerous path.

There are three basic ways to accomplish data propagation and/or synchronization on an on-going basis:

- Scheduled (this is how Notes does it)
- Ad hoc (Notes does this for remote users)
- Real time (this is close to how a transaction-based system might work)

Applications where integrity and up-to-the minute information are critical are better suited for a host or relational system. If the databases must always be connected, Notes cannot be used for one of its biggest strengths: sharing between occasionally connected users. In a real-time implementation, the link between Notes and the other database system can lock the record in the legacy system, update it there, and then enable the update to proceed in Notes. Even this can lead to deadlock in complicated situations.

How Complicated Is the Logic of the Integration?

In the simplest one-time, one-way migration case, a Notes form has the same fields as a relational database table. All the records in the source database are moved to the destination database system. However, as the application and data transfers become more complex, more effort is required to get the system to do the right thing. In particular, the number of conditions on processing records are the biggest factor in how much a data integration solution costs.

In a simple case, some subset of the records in one database are moved to another. However, in the relational database world, data is stored in multiple tables, which are joined in order to get meaningful reports. If you need to migrate records from multiple relational tables to an equal number of Notes forms, this works smoothly. However, if, for example, you need to make response documents based upon certain criteria, or migrate multiple joined records into multivalue fields in one Notes document, the logic becomes more complicated, and you may have to do some scripting or programming.

Furthermore, if you actually have multiple legacy systems that need to be integrated with one Notes application, the system not only becomes more complicated, but also more expensive in terms of development time. For example, a request that is in different states of completion may need to be linked into different corporate systems.

Mapping Structured Data to Semi-Structured

As a final note in this overview, before a relational database can be integrated with a Notes database, the intricacies of the data model need to be fleshed out and translated into each system. Without an understanding of the differences in data types, a data integration project between Notes and legacy systems will not go smoothly.

Relational data does not always map one-to-one with Lotus Notes data. For example, Lotus Notes has the following data types:

- Text
- Number
- ...Time-Date
- Rich Text
- Keywords
- Author Names
- Reader Names
- Section

Relational databases have their own basic data types, such as char, varchar(x), and so forth. Each database server also has its own special data types, but rarely will you find a rich text or keywords data type in a database other than Notes (or Reader Names or Section, for example).

A feature of Notes that has no counterpart in the RDBMS world is multi-value fields. Each value of the multi-value field in Notes may need to map to a separate relational record. It is up to the designer of the integration strategy to map fields from one place to another. A graphical tool can help in this mapping. Figure 31.1 shows the main screen of DataLink, a third-party tool for migrating data between Notes and relational databases. The screen is divided into three parts, with relational fields listed on one side, Notes fields listed on the other side, and mappings in the middle. Such an interface makes it easier for an administrator or designer to set up a data mapping.

Furthermore, character fields in traditional databases (particularly in host-based systems) are typically limited in size to a certain number of characters. This makes finding data in the database more efficient. However, in Notes, a standard text field can have a variable number of characters. Migrating data from the other system to a Notes text field usually works fine, but going from Notes to these other areas is not as easy. The data gets truncated. Certain relational databases have memo fields that can have up to 64KB of data. Memo fields are also the logical place for Notes rich text fields to go—although you lose all your formatting and embedded objects.

Mainframe files do not always have nicely structured records. In some cases, a special character at position *n* in a record designates the format for the rest of the characters in the record. For example, if the 30th character is a Y, characters 31 through 50 might be the person's phone number to which this record belongs. However, if that 30th character is an N, characters 31-50 might be the person's address.

FIGURE 31.1.

The main screen of DataLink, a third-party tool for migrating data between Notes and relational databases.

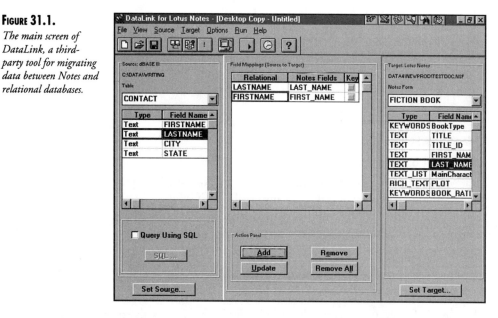

Lastly, the data format may cause problems. For example, you may have dates stored in a database that stores them as 3-5-96, and the destination system may require the inputs to have slashes instead of dashes (3/5/96). Given the content of your application, you may want to combine several fields or otherwise massage the data along the way. These parameters are referred to as data translation or cleansing, and they should be part of your requirements analysis for Notes-legacy integration.

The Details: Implementation Tools and Methods

Once you answer the questions about the type of application, the type of database integration, the database architecture, and the specifics of mapping the database fields, you are ready to explore implementation options. This section describes the ways of implementing a Notes-to-external-database solution.

Build Versus Buy Versus Both

Once the parameters of a Notes-legacy system integration have been identified, the next step is to take stock of the tools available to implement a solution and to select the best method to proceed. Today there are many choices on how to integrate Notes with legacy systems. You can buy an off-the-shelf tool, build your own integration, or do some combination of the two.

Building it yourself means designing, implementing, testing, and deploying software modules that are written in one of the following programming languages. Each offers a different level of complexity and flexibility:

■ Lotus Notes database design and macro language

■ LotusScript

■ Notes C low-level API

■ Notes HiTest API

■ Visual Basic or other 4GL environment

However, even if you purchase a generic solution for Notes-DB integration, you may still find yourself doing a good deal of coding. Many off-the-shelf solutions are not point-and-click and require you to write script. A third-party tool from Trinzic (now a part of PLATINUM technology) called InfoPump is a high-end server-based tool that requires a good deal of coding.

Most likely, you need to customize your Notes application and the fields that exist in your forms and views to make the integration proceed efficiently, combined with an Agent or a third-party tool to execute the transfer.

The arsenal of tools that you can select from to integrate Notes with existing databases is quite large. Lotus and numerous third parties offer products and services to help in the database integration arena. Lotus Notes R4 also has some new features that ease the data migration process. This section lists the different ways of implementing a solution, based upon the method of data access and given the tools available. A later section in this chapter, "A Detailed Example of Bringing Relational Data into Notes," shows some of these methods at work.

The examples of how and why Notes should be integrated with legacy systems are wide and varied. However, for the developer, all these examples can be divided into three different methods of data access, each with its own implementation styles. The questions that were listed earlier in this chapter should suggest which of the three methods your application needs:

■ Using the Notes client for integration

■ Background Agent integration (real-time and batch)

■ Bringing Notes data into client/server tools

Using the Notes Client for Integration

In this method of data access, the Notes client "looks up" data that is stored in legacy systems, presents it to the user for selection or manipulation, and may initiate update commands in that system.

For example, the user might press a button on a Notes form that brings up a list of part numbers (which are read from a relational database). When the user chooses a part, more

Integrating Notes with Legacy Systems

CHAPTER **31**

781

31

INTEGRATING
NOTES WITH
LEGACY SYSTEMS

descriptive information from that part can be read from the relational database and filled into fields of the Notes form. The following tools can help you implement this type of integration:

- Notes Lookups (@Db functions)
- LotusScript
- OLE/Notes Field Exchange (Notes F/X)
- Dialog boxes to launch from Notes
- Importing to a Notes View

Notes Client Tool #1: @Db Functions for Lookup

The most common way to implement this type of data access is to use the @Db functions that are provided in the Lotus Notes macro language. Although these functions have been available since Notes R3, most Notes developers have used the @Db functions only for looking up data from other Notes databases. Because of the special way Lotus has implemented these functions, they've been designed to work across different database systems. The @Db functions can read data from (and sometimes write data to) other databases.

These functions can be embedded in almost any place where you can use the Notes macro language. The most frequent use of these is to populate the possible values of the keyword field by reading them from another database. This other database might be a Notes database or, using the cross database functionality, a relational table. Another example is to look up information once a value is chosen.

@Db Functions for Database Access

There are three @Db Functions that can be used to access ODBC databases:

- @DbColumn() is used to read one column of a table.
- @DbLookup() is used to locate rows matching a key value and return more information about that row.
- @DbCommand() is used to execute a command, such as a SELECT command (for retrieving a set of records), or a stored procedure on a database system.

The @DbColumn() function is most useful when you want the user of a Notes application to pick from a list of choices that are stored in a relational database. Here is the syntax of the @DbColumn() function:

```
@DbColumn( "ODBC": "NoCache"; data_source; user_ID; password; table;
➥column:null_handling; "Distinct": sort)
```

This syntax is used when looking up data from a non-Notes data source. The @DbColumn has a slightly different syntax when looking up from another Notes database. For an example of how to use this function, please see the example section. Parameters are the following:

The ODBC parameter is a required keyword that indicates that this is an ODBC data source, and not a lookup to another Notes database.

The NoCache keyword, which is optional, tells whether Notes should cache the information the first time it is fetched. If the data is being updated constantly, you should not cache the information, but you should always read it from the external database.

The *data_source* parameter is the name of the ODBC data source, as defined in the ODBC.INI file. This is a required parameter and is only used for non-Notes lookups.

Both the *user_ID* and *password* parameters can be blank if security is not required. If these two parameters are blank and a logon is required, ODBC prompts the user. This parameter is also only used for non-Notes lookups.

The *table* parameter is the name of the table in the database from which data will be read. Again, this parameter is used only for non-Notes lookups.

The *column* parameter is the name of the column from which data will be retrieved. Again, this parameter is used only for non-Notes lookups.

The *null_handling* parameter is optional and tells Notes how to handle null values in this column. This parameter can be one of the following three values: Fail, Discard, or a replacement value. If it is Fail, then Notes will display a failure message if any null values are found. If it is Discard, then null values are ignored and not presented in the result set. If a replacement value is indicated, then the null value will be replaced by the replacement value. The Distinct keyword, which is optional, removes duplicate values from the list being retrieved. If the Distinct keyword is being used, the *sort* type parameter can be Ascending or Descending.

The @DbLookup() function is useful when the user has chosen a value, such as a part number or a customer name, and you want to retrieve more information about that choice. It can be quite powerful, as when used in conjunction with the @DbColumn() function (see the CONTACT example at the end of this chapter). A user might choose from a list provided by @DbColumn(), then the @DbLookup() can find more information on the choice.

For example, a lead-tracking system in Notes might be combined with an order processing system in a relational database. If the salesperson is working on a lead in Notes and wants to know what orders the current customer has made in the past, a simple click of a button might execute an @DbLookup() to find those orders. If the logic is more complicated than looking up the value from a single relational table, you can run a select statement using @DbCommand() or use LotusScript for full programmatic control.

The syntax of the @DbLookup() function for looking up data from external (non-Notes) databases is the following:

```
@DbLookup("ODBC": "NoCache"; data_source; user_ID; password; table;
↪column:null_handling; key_column; key; "Distinct": sort)
```

Integrating Notes with Legacy Systems

CHAPTER 31

783

31

INTEGRATING
NOTES WITH
LEGACY SYSTEMS

For an example of how to use this function, please see the example section at the end of this chapter. The first six parameters work in almost the same way as in @DbColumn(). As in @DbColumn(), the sixth parameter, *column*, is the name of the column that should be retrieved. The only difference is the column values are retrieved only for records that match the key value.

The *key_column* parameter is the name of the column that is being used to locate records in the data source.

The *key* parameter is the value that should be matched. Only those records whose *key_column* matches the key will be retrieved.

The Distinct and *sort* parameters are used in the same way as in @DbColumn().

The @DbCommand() is useful when you want to run a select statement from within the Notes macro language or want to invoke some other database command, such as a stored procedure. A stored procedure is a routine that runs on a database server. Most client/server database servers, such as Oracle and Sybase, have stored procedures. This is a useful way to invoke processing on the database server without tying up the workstation from which the user is running Notes.

Unlike the other two @Db functions, which work with Notes and ODBC databases, the @DbCommand() function can be used only with non-Notes databases. The syntax of the @DbCommand() function is the following:

```
@DbCommand("ODBC": "NoCache"; data_source; user_ID ; password;
➥command_string:null_handling)
```

The first four parameters of @DbCommand() work the same as in the other two functions. The *command_string* parameter is passed to the data source to execute. This *command_string* can be a SQL statement, command statement, or the name of a stored procedure to be executed.

Notes Client Tool #2: LotusScript for Programmatic Control

LotusScript is a full, object-oriented programming language, first introduced to Notes in R4, that provides more control and flexibility than the Notes macro language. Because it supports all standard programming constructs, including loops, exception handling, and so on, it can be used to embed complex logic easily into your Notes applications. LotusScript is cross-platform and can run on both a Notes client and a Notes server. There are three ways to implement database integration using LotusScript at the client.

The first method, which is also the most difficult, is to use LotusScript to call an external program. LotusScript, like Visual Basic and other fourth-generation programming languages, can call functions exposed in dynamic link libraries (in Windows, or their equivalent in other platforms). If your company already has routines (usually written in C or C++) that perform functions such as logging onto the accounting system and extracting reports, those functions can be called from a LotusScript program. This gives you the flexibility to implement a standard data access method for all your client/server applications. The standard methods can return result values to LotusScript.

The second method is to use OLE Automation. LotusScript, like Visual Basic, can call any application that is an OLE2 server and supports OLE Automation. Many database vendors (such as Oracle) have released OLE Automation APIs for accessing database functions.

Making OLE Automation calls for databases is not unlike making calls to an OLE server application such as Microsoft Excel, for example. Utilizing this technique (again, for only those platforms where OLE is enabled), your Notes application can use OLE2 servers to read from and write to external databases. Because these OLE Automation API's are usually provided by the database vendors themselves, they usually offer better performance than ODBC-based data access.

The third method is to use the LotusScript data object, a new set of LotusScript classes that can be used to access databases. This is probably the easiest method because it doesn't rely on external programs or DLLs, except the ODBC driver for your database and the ODBC driver manager that comes with Windows.

The LotusScript data object is a set of classes that serves as a logical interface to other database systems. These classes use the ODBC standard for database access. Using standard SQL, these classes can be used to read and write to any database that has an ODBC driver. It works on all platforms where ODBC is supported.

Using LotusScript for Database Access

LotusScript is a fully object-oriented language where new classes can be defined and treated as part of the language. Lotus has defined the LSX standard (LotusScript eXtension) so that standard components can be imported into other LotusScript applications. This is not unlike the VBX standard that Microsoft used to help spread the popularity of Visual Basic. One of the LSX modules that Lotus provides with Notes is the ODBC LSX, which gives developers the capability of incorporating data from external databases into their Notes application.

To use the ODBC LSX in your application, you must put the following statement into the (Options) event of the (Global) object:

```
UseLSX "*LSXODBC"
```

The UseLSX statement is the standard way of including LSXs within your LotusScript code. The "*LSXODBC" tells Notes which LSX to load.

The ODBC LSX has three public classes that can be used to build database-aware applications from within Notes: ODBCConnection, ODBCQuery, and ODBCResultSet. You need to declare variables of all three classes in order to use the LotusScript data object. New instances are declared by using a Dim statement in the following format:

```
Dim <varname> as New ODBCConnection
Dim <varname> as New ODBCQuery
Dim  <varname> as New ODBCResultSet
```

The `ODBCConnection` class is used to establish and maintain a connection with an external database. To use the `ODBCConnection` class, you should first have an ODBC data source defined. It is possible to define an ODBC data source on the fly if you have an ODBC driver installed for that type of database; however, the procedure is not well documented and not recommended. It is best to have the ODBC data source defined for use by your application. For more information on defining an ODBC data source, please see the detailed example at the end of this chapter.

The methods that are most important for the `ODBCConnection` class are the `ConnectTo` and `Disconnect` methods, which connect to an ODBC data source and disconnect from the data source. The `ExecProcedure` method also can be used to execute a stored command or procedure in the external database system, much like the `@DbCommand()` function. If you want the user to choose the data source, the `ListDataSources` method gives a list of available data sources.

The `ODBCQuery` class is used to create a query against an ODBC data source. The format for the query is always SQL. The `SQL` property is used to store the text of the query, and the `Connection` property stores a reference to the `Connection` that it is with; one `ODBCConnection` object can have multiple `ODBCQuery` objects referencing it.

Once you have created a query, you run it against a database to get a result set of records that match the query. This is done via the `ODBCResultSet` class. Of the three ODBC classes, the `ODBCResultSet` class is the one with the most properties and methods.

The Query property of the `ODBCResultSet` object should be set to an `ODBCQuery` object, and then the `Execute` method should be called to run the query. If the query is successful, the `ODBCResultSet` object has a valid result set of records from the external database. The result set is like a grid—it contains records that match your query. The columns of the grid are the fields of each record. Once you have a result set, you can navigate through it, get values from it, update records, add new records, and so forth.

For a list of all the properties and methods of the ODBC classes, please refer to Table 31.3. For more information on each of these properties and methods, please refer to the Lotus Notes on-line help.

Table 31.3. Properties and methods of ODBC classes.

Class	Properties	Methods
ODBCConnection	DataSourceNameString	ConnectTo
	DisconnectTimeOut	Disconnect
	Exclusive	ExecProcedure
	IsConnected	GetError

continues

Table 31.3. continued

Class	Properties	Methods
	IsSupported(option)	GetErrorMessage
	IsTimedOut	GetExtendedErrorMessage
	SilentMode	GetRegistrationInfo
		ListDataSources
		ListFields
		ListProcedures
		ListTables
ODBCQuery	Connection	GetError
	QueryExecuteTimeOut	GetErrorMessage
	SQL	GetExtendedErrorMessage
ODBCResultSet	Asynchronous	AddRow
	AutoCommit	Close
	CacheLimit	DeleteRow
	CommitOnDisconnect	Execute
	CurrentRow	FieldExpectedDataType
	FetchBatchSize	FieldID
	HasRowChanged	FieldInfo
	IsBeginOfData	FieldName
	IsEndOfData	FieldNativeDataType
	IsResultSetAvailable	FieldSize
	MaxRows	FirstRow
	NumColumns	GetError
	NumRows	GetErrorMessage
	Override	GetExtendedErrorMessage
	Query	GetParameter
	ReadOnly	GetParameterName
		GetRowStatus
		GetValue
		IsValueAltered
		IsValueNul
		lLastRow
		LocateRow

Integrating Notes with Legacy Systems

CHAPTER 31

787

31

INTEGRATING
NOTES WITH
LEGACY SYSTEMS

Class	*Properties*	*Methods*
		NextRow
		NumParameters
		PrevRow
		RefreshRow
		SetParameter
		SetValue
		Transactions
		UpdateRow

Notes Client Tool #3: OLE and Notes/FX

Perhaps the simplest way conceptually to access external data from the Notes client is to have some other application do all the work. Lotus touts Notes as the ultimate "container," which means that OLE objects (documents created in another application) can reside within Notes documents. More specifically, a Notes user can embed an OLE Object (for example, a 1-2-3 spreadsheet or a Microsoft Word document) directly into a rich text field in a Notes document. The designer of a Notes form can also put an OLE object inside a form so that it activates automatically. Because Notes supports OLE2, this can include in-place editing so that the embedded document really looks like it's part of the Notes document.

Using this approach, an application such as 1-2-3 or Microsoft Excel, which has the capability of reading data from existing data sources, is embedded in a document. The spreadsheet reads data from a legacy system.

Taking this approach even further, a client/server reporting product that is also an OLE server (such as Quest from Gupta or Business Objects), can be embedded into a Notes document to provide a real-time report. When users double-click on the report, they can modify the parameters or do other such end-user things to the report.

Using Notes Field Exchange (Notes F/X), information from the embedded object can be linked to other Notes fields in the same form. For example, a Notes form called Expense Report might have three standard fields (Name, Date, and Total Amount) and one rich text field to contain the embedded Excel Spreadsheet. Using Notes F/X, the TotalAmount field can be linked to a particular cell in the embedded spreadsheet, so that whenever it changes, the Notes field changes. This makes the value visible in a Notes view, so that it can be used as a sort criteria or simply provide summary information. Notes F/X is used when every document created with a given Notes form needs to launch an external application, such as 1-2-3.

Notes Client Tool #4: Launching Dialog Boxes

The last way to implement bringing legacy data into Notes in a real-time interactive way is more of a trick. The idea is to have the user click on a button and have a complex dialog box pop up. That dialog box can read and write data to and from external database sources. It might enable users to browse a list of customers, for example, then select the right one and modify the record. When the users are finished, they click on OK and end up back in the Notes space.

The most effective way to do this from the Notes client is to extend the Notes client by bringing up another application and trick users into thinking they are still in Notes. Perhaps the best example of this is a Visual Basic application that looks like dialog box popping up from a Notes database.

The dialog box, which can be built using a variety of tools, is highly customizable. It can process as well as display data from legacy systems and other Notes databases at the same time. Depending on the users' choices, the dialog box can pass information back to the Notes form, which can then fill in fields of the form.

Notes Client Tool #5: File Import to a Notes View

Notes has the ability to import files which can be a basic method for importing records into a Notes database. The Notes import function (located in the File menu) has two modes:

■ Import to a document. This option is activated when the user is editing a document and wants to import a file into a rich text field. This option can import files in formats such as Microsoft RTF, Lotus AmiPro, etc.

■ Import to a view. This option is activated when the user is looking at a Notes view and wants to import records from a file and compose multiple Notes documents.

For our purposes, the second option (import to a view) is relevant. Notes can import records from one of three file formats:

■ Lotus 1-2-3 worksheet
■ Tabular text
■ Structured text

In order to bring database records into Notes, you can export from the database (usually this only works with desktop databases) into a 1-2-3 worksheet. Or, you could export it to a tabular text or a structured text file, and import it into Notes.

For more complete import functionality you can use an ad hoc data migration tool (such as DataLink for Lotus Notes).

Integrating Notes with Legacy Systems

CHAPTER 31

789

31

INTEGRATING
NOTES WITH
LEGACY SYSTEMS

Background Integration (Batch or Near Real-Time)

The second way to implement Notes-legacy integration is to have the data integration and/or synchronization done in the background. The user continues to work in Notes without any knowledge of how the data is moving back and forth between the Notes database and the external database system. This is the best solution for applications where data needs to be kept synchronized across database systems, or when requests are being made in Notes to fetch data from other systems and the requests do not need to be filled in real time.

A data-propagation or request-processing Agent can be implemented using a combination of third-party products and LotusScript Agents. A special type of Agent, available from IBM, can be used for integration of Notes with mainframe-based database systems. There are two basic options for background Agents:

- Notes data migration products
- Building your own Agents using LotusScript

Background Tool #1: Notes Data Migration Products

Since the introduction of Notes, a plethora of third-party products have cropped up to help the adventurous Notes developer build an application that works seamlessly across database systems. In 1995, Lotus released its own high-end product to help with this task, Lotus NotesPump. In selecting a product or Agent to help you with your database integration strategy, you should keep two decisions in mind.

Batch Versus Real Time

The first is to decide what type of database integration you will need on a regular basis. Most of these products are geared toward batch processing of records. For example, each night an Agent in the background finds all the changes made in a Notes database and propagates them back to a legacy system. Changes may also be propagated in the reverse direction, from the legacy system to the Notes database.

If, however, you want the changes to propagate to the other system at the time they are made, you face several constraints. Although some of these products can do real-time updates (including NotesPump), enforcing a real-time paradigm limits your Notes application to one server. By the definition of replication, Notes does not synchronize different copies of the same databases on a real-time basis. Having a criterion that the changes must be made in real time forces all the users to work off one server—unless you want each server always to be connected to the legacy system. The "occasionally-connected" model of Notes is compromised under these circumstances.

However, almost all the products on the marketplace can be invoked from some event, such as the user pressing a button or saving a change; so it is possible to catch a transaction at the source and automatically update the other system. Another possibility is to have an Agent always running at the server that is looking for changes in a particular database.

Client-Based Versus Server-Based Tools

The second decision about the tools to use is whether to use a server-based tool or a client-based tool. There are pros and cons to each. A server-based tool tends to offer better performance, because it is running locally against a Notes database rather than going across the network. However, server-based tools are not always as scalable as you might want to believe—server performance can suffer if the server task is taking up too many cycles, causing user complaints.

Unless they can be absolutely certain no bugs are in the software (which they can't be), many Notes administrators are hesitant to put a third-party tool on their servers.

Client-based tools are generally easier to use and are usually implemented on a Microsoft operating platform, where multiple ODBC driver managers and ODBC drivers are more mature. However, they may not always be as fast as some of the server-based tools. Of course, the resource and cost tradeoffs are important, too. Client tools tend to cost less and also work with 16-bit drivers and desktop databases.

Server-Based Tools

Lotus NotesPump 1.0 was introduced in late 1995. Lotus is promising version 2 in the summer of 1996. NotesPump was designed and built by the folks at Edge Research, which Lotus acquired in 1994. NotesPump is Lotus' solution for enterprise-wide, ongoing data synchronization between relational database servers and Notes. NotesPump works by having the administrator fill out forms in a Notes database. The NotesPump Agent, which can run on one server or many servers, reads this database and executes a data transfer activity at the appropriate time on the appropriate records.

Other server-based tools, which follow an approach similar to NotesPump's, include Replic-Action from Casahl, Notrix Composer from Percussion Software, and InfoPump from Trinzic. Future versions of NotesPump will provide an API so that third-party companies can build their own custom activities to run on the NotesPump architecture. Future versions of NotesPump also will use LotusScript as a scripting language to implement complex logic during data transfer activity.

For integration with mainframe systems, IBM provides products called MQ Series and CICS Link that can be used to build applications with host systems. These Middleware products provide a reliable way to queue transaction requests to a mainframe host system. These transactions then become part of the normal transaction queue that the host system will process. Using these products, an OS/2 Notes Server can be used to take requests of mobile and geographically separated users and integrate them into an enterprise-wide workflow.

Integrating Notes with Legacy Systems
CHAPTER **31**

791

31

INTEGRATING
NOTES WITH
LEGACY SYSTEMS

Client-Based Tools

The most widely known and used client software for database integration with Notes is DataLink, from Brainstorm Technologies, Inc. DataLink is a point-and-click solution for ad hoc and scheduled data migration that requires no scripting or programming. Because it is client-based, DataLink can be used against a Notes server on any platform, including OS/2, Windows NT, and the various flavors of UNIX. As client-based programs mature, their performance will match those of server-based tools. Figure 31.1 shows the data mapping screen in DataLink.

Other client-based solutions include Zmerge from Granite Software. Client-based solutions are best suited for ad hoc and scheduled batch updates, and they are the only solution for many desktop databases such as Microsoft Access.

Background Tools #2: Build Your Own LotusScript Agents

If the off-the-shelf solutions won't work for your particular application, you may need to implement your own custom Agents to bridge the gap between Notes databases and other database systems.

The Agents that you build may mimic the functionality of the off-the-shelf products, but with a heavy amount of custom business logic added into the solution. The way to build server-based Agents is either to use LotusScript or the Notes API and build an Agent in C or C++. LotusScript has the following advantages:

- Gives your Agent the capability of running on multiple platforms
- Takes less time to develop

An Agent written with the Notes API has the following advantages:

- Gives you more flexibility
- As a general rule, runs faster than the LotusScript Agent

For most custom Agents in Notes R4, LotusScript is powerful enough to do the transfer, so it is the preferred method. Avoid going to the API unless it's absolutely necessary.

Once you are implementing your own Agent, you have embarked on a custom software development module. A typical data propagation Agent might have the following structure:

- A control Notes database or .INI file to keep track of the integration parameters.
- Startup Module: This module calls the Transfer Authorization Module to see whether anything needs to be done, then calls the process module to run the transfer and the status module to report on the results.
- Transfer Authorization Module: This module usually answers the question, "Is there anything that needs to be done?" This is done by monitoring the control information, which might be stored in a custom file or in a Notes database.

■ Process Module: This module runs the transfer, getting the changes that need to be propagated by calling both the Notes Module and the DBMS module. On a record-by-record basis, this module performs the processing by writing each field to the destination.

■ Status Reporting Module: This module simply reports success or failure information, typically by adding control information to a Notes database, by sending mail, or by displaying it on the screen.

■ DBMS Module: This lower-level module is used to read and write records to the legacy system and is called by the other modules.

■ Notes Module: This lower-level module is used to read result sets from Notes and is called by the other modules.

LotusScript Agents can have access to all the documents in a database and should use the ODBC LSX as the preferred method for ODBC database access. If ODBC access is not available on the platform you wish to run your Agent on, you may need to implement custom routines calling the Database API and call these custom routines from LotusScript.

Although simple Agents are relatively straightforward to implement, they can grow in complexity very fast, and you may soon find yourself on a project that is overdue and over budget. Use an off-the-shelf solution first, then add any customization you need via LotusScript.

Notes Data in Client/Server Tools

The final method of implementation of Notes-legacy integration is to utilize Notes as a database and not as the user interface. This is usually appropriate when the main reason for using Notes is for distribution (via replication), organization, and storage—not presentation. The main benefit of this approach is that it provides a way to leverage the client/server applications that many companies are already building, and it gives the developer a way to present both Notes and relational data on the same screen in a highly interactive way. Although Notes R4 does provide the capability of doing some of this within Notes, the high level of interactivity that users may need for the presentation of data from multiple sources may dictate that a client/server tool be used. If reporting needs to be done against a Notes database and another database at the same time, a client/server tool is the best choice.

For example, one company had a master customer database on a relational database system, and Notes was used for lead-tracking and contact management. A custom application by this company could provide the user with a list of customers (from SQL database) and with the click of a button could show, on the same screen, a list of the orders (from SQL database) and the call reports for further sales activity with this customer (perhaps from the same or another Notes database). This type of select-and-fetch information is extremely useful in real-time call scenarios or in Executive Information Systems, where ad hoc reporting may be critical.

Integrating Notes with Legacy Systems

CHAPTER 31

793

31

INTEGRATING
NOTES WITH
LEGACY SYSTEMS

There are two basic toolsets for bringing Notes data into client/server tools:

- Ad hoc reporting tools
- 4GL Link tools

Client/Server Option #1: Ad Hoc Reporting Tools

Lotus provides NotesSQL, an ODBC driver for Notes that can be used to give Notes data a "relational" feel so that it can be reported on by client/server reporting tools. These tools include Microsoft Access, Lotus Approach, Forest & Trees, Crystal Reports, and many others.

Although massaging Notes data to look like a relational database may not be appropriate for building most Notes applications, it may be a good move to provide a bird's eye view of data stored in the Notes database. Large Notes databases in particular can benefit from this approach, because the fewer views a Notes database has, the smaller it is on disk.

Some of these tools, such as Lotus Approach, actually let you join Notes data with relational data so that you can do a customer analysis to find out what issues and records might exist for that customer across all your systems. To use Notes with these tools, you must get the NotesSQL ODBC driver from Lotus (available from CompuServe and other on-line Lotus locations). Follow the procedure for creating an ODBC data source, then use Notes like any other source database.

Lotus has also released Notes Reporter, which provides a subset of the reporting capabilities available in Approach. Lotus Notes ViP, which Lotus sold to Revelation Technologies, also has a reporting module that can be used to generate reports against Notes.

Client/Server Option #2: 4GL Link Tools

Since 1993, when Brainstorm introduced VB/Link for Lotus Notes, corporations around the world have been incorporating data stored in Notes databases into their custom Visual Basic applications. The rapid development capabilities of a fourth-generation language such as Visual Basic, combined with its capability of accessing corporate databases and rich user interface design elements, provide an excellent cross-database front-end environment.

Tools, such as Visual Basic—including SQLWindows from Gupta, PowerBuilder from PowerSoft (since acquired by Sybase), and Delphi from Borland—have added development modules to access Lotus Notes databases. Most of these development environments have both ODBC and dedicated links to a variety of data sources, ranging from desktop databases to host systems. The importance of the front-end application development environment for databases was underscored when Sybase acquired Powersoft.

Many of these modules not only give access to textual data stored in Notes, but they also bring in some native Notes data types into the client/server environment. For example, an application developed in Visual Basic with VB/Link can incorporate a Lotus Notes View directly into the window, Notes Rich Text fields (including objects such as file attachments), and so on.

The products for accomplishing this type of integration include VB/Link for Lotus Notes from Brainstorm, Powersoft Class Library for Lotus Notes, Gupta QuickObjects for Lotus Notes, Delphi/Link for Lotus Notes from Borland, Notes ViP from Revelation Technologies, and, of course, the HiTest Tools for Visual Basic from Lotus. (See Chapter 21, "Advanced Development with the Notes API and HiTest Tools," for more information.) You can also use the NotesSQL ODBC driver from Visual Basic and other 4GL tools, but they limit the amount of interactivity available with the Notes database.

A Detailed Example of Bringing Relational Data into Notes

This section contains an example Notes database that you can use as a starting point for your Notes-legacy systems integration. This section walks you through creating the Notes database that reads information from this database and brings it into the Notes environment. For the sake of simplicity, this example works against a dBASE III database, which you can easily create using a spreadsheet such as Microsoft Excel.

> **NOTE**
>
> Both the dBASE file and the Notes database you will build in this example are included on the CD-ROM.

Alhough the code shows the basic method for accessing this data from Notes, you can add functionality to the code provided here to achieve any level of complexity you like. Any database that is ODBC-compliant, including Oracle, Sybase, FoxPro, and so forth, can be accessed in the same way from Lotus Notes. Simply set up an alternate ODBC data source and change the data_source parameters in the code.

This example is implemented in two ways: using @Db functions to look up data and bring it into a Notes form, and using LotusScript to read all of the records via ODBC. A description of how the code could be modified to work as a background Agent follows.

Working with This Example

This example runs on Windows 3.1, Windows for Workgroups 3.11, Windows 95, or Windows NT using Notes R4. While the Notes code will work in OS/2 Notes R4, the ODBC administration must be done differently. It contains one external database, a dBASE file that

Integrating Notes with Legacy Systems

CHAPTER 31

795

31

INTEGRATING
NOTES WITH
LEGACY SYSTEMS

contains a list of contacts. It also contains one Notes database with a single form. All the code is contained within that form.

In any case, you have to follow the steps to set up an ODBC data source on your machine if you do not have any ODBC sources to work against already.

Setting Up the Relational Database

The database contains one table, which is a list of contacts. For each contact, the following information is stored in the columns of the table:

- Last name
- First name
- City
- State

Creating the dBASE III File

This table can be created using Microsoft Excel. Create a new spreadsheet and type the sample information as shown in Table 31.4. The first row should have the column names. Beginning with the second row, type the sample rows. Do not leave any blank rows between the column titles and the data.

Table 31.4. The data for the CONTACT table.

FIRSTNAME	LASTNAME	CITY	STATE
Fred	Flintstone	Bedrock	MA
Barney	Rubble	Bedrock	MA
Bill	Clinton	Washington	DC
Ray	Ozzie	Cambridge	MA

Then, save the file. In the Save File dialog box, choose dBASE III as the file type and save the file as CONTACT.DBF in a directory of your choosing. Figure 31.2 shows the spreadsheet in Excel.

FIGURE **31.2.**

*The CONTACT table
in Microsoft Excel.*

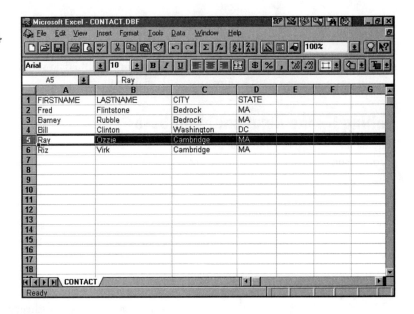

A Word About ODBC

The Open Database Connectivity standard, defined by Microsoft in the early 1980s, has become the de facto standard for building database-independent applications. To use the ODBC standard, your program needs to have an ODBC driver for the database you are using (dBASE III driver comes with Windows) and a data source defined for the specific database and/or tables you are accessing. This can be done by running the ODBC administrator program available in the control panel for Windows (you can also run it by double-clicking on ODBCADM.EXE in the WINDOWS\SYSTEM directory).

ODBC drivers are available from the database manufacturer and from third parties such as InterSolv, and some ship with Microsoft Windows. A list of the database drivers installed on your system is available in the ODBCINST.INI file in your Windows directory or can be viewed by running the ODBC administrator. For example, Oracle provides ODBC drivers for Oracle databases.

A driver still relies on having the right network connections to be able to talk to a database server. Sometimes, ODBC drivers take databases that are not relational and make them look like relational databases so that you can issue SQL statements against them. For example, there are ODBC drivers for Text Files and for spreadsheet files.

An ODBC data source is a logical name for a particular database or table to which you want to have access. For example, your customer database might be implemented by using Microsoft SQLServer—you need a SQLServer driver, and you need to define a data source for your customer database. When an application wants to reach that particular database, it specifies the name of the data source you have defined. The list of available data sources is stored in the ODBC.INI file in the Windows directory.

Integrating Notes with Legacy Systems

CHAPTER 31

797

31

INTEGRATING
NOTES WITH
LEGACY SYSTEMS

ODBC support is available on Windows 3.1, Windows 95, Windows NT, and most drivers now available for OS/2, and support may soon be available on other platforms. The drivers are needed only on the client. For example, a Windows client can use the Oracle ODBC driver to read and write to an Oracle server running on UNIX.

Creating the ODBC Data Source

In order to access the dBASE file from Notes, you need to define an ODBC data source on your machine. This is a relatively easy process. Run the ODBC Administrator program (either from the control panel in Windows or, from the File Manager, find ODBCADM.EXE, which is usually located in the WINDOWS\SYSTEM directory).

When you run the program, you see a list of ODBC data sources that are available from your machine. Choose the New button to create a new ODBC data source. You are prompted with a list of drivers that are installed in your machine. Choose dBASE III as the driver choice, and you will go to the dBASE data source setup screen. (See Figure 31.3.) Fill in the name of the data source as CONTACTS. Click on the select directory button and choose the dBASE file that you saved earlier (CONTACT.DBF). Select dBASE III as the type and then click on OK.

FIGURE 31.3.

Creating a data source for the dBASE file.

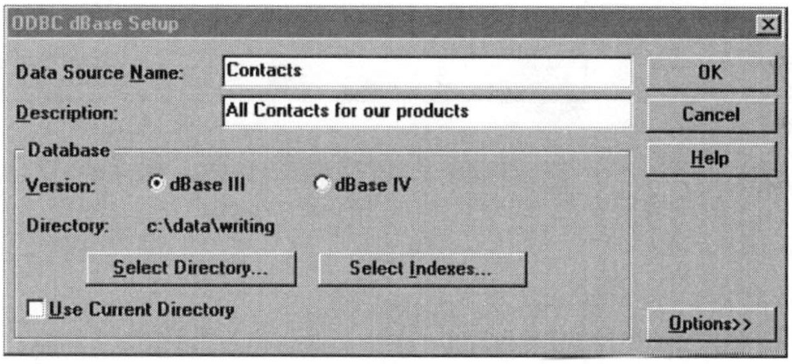

You should now see CONTACTS as one of the ODBC data sources on your workstation in the main ODBC administrator screen.

Setting Up the Notes Database

The example database is called DATABASE TESTING, the filename is DBTEST.NSF, and the single form it contains is called DATABASE TEST FORM. If you are creating this from scratch, create the database without using a Notes template and add a blank form called DATABASE TEST FORM:

1. Create a New Notes database, called Database Testing.
2. Create a New Form, called DATABASE TEST FORM.

Figure 31.4 shows this form in Design Mode. Figure 31.5 shows this form being used.

This form demonstrates using both @Db lookup Functions and LotusScript to read data from the CONTACT table.

FIGURE 31.4.

The DATABASE TEST FORM in Design Mode.

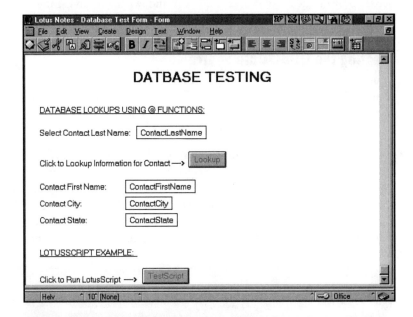

FIGURE 31.5.

The DATABASE TEST FORM in action.

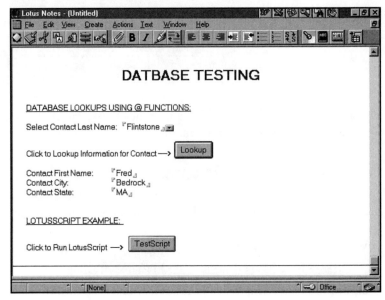

The DATABASE TEST FORM has four fields and two buttons. Table 31.5 has a description of each field, and Table 31.6 has a description of the two buttons. The ContactLastName field is a field of data type keywords. When the user puts the cursor in this field and presses Enter, the field reads a list of the last names of the contacts from the external database and puts them in a pick list for the user. This is a simple example of an @DbColumn().

Table 31.5. Fields in the sample Notes form.

Field Name	Field Datatype	Field Description
ContactLastName	Keywords	Enables the user to choose one of the contacts from a list read from the CONTACTS data source
ContactFirstName	Text	Field to receive the first name from the external database
ContactCity	Text	Field to receive the city of the contact from the external database
ContactState	Text	Field to receive the state of the contact from the external database

The form contains two buttons. The first button demonstrates how to use @DbLookup() to find out the first name, city, and state of the contact that was chosen. The second button demonstrates using LotusScript to read all the records from the CONTACT database and present them to the user field-by-field. (See Table 31.6.)

Table 31.6. Buttons used in the sample form.

Button Name	Button Purpose
LookupButton	For the chosen contact, retrieves the values of the first name, city, and state, and fills in the appropriate fields here.
TestScriptButton	This button demonstrates using LotusScript to read all of the records from the CONTACT table and displaying the fields of each one.

Writing the Code for the Example

The code for this example, which is available on the CD-ROM, can also be typed into each field and button on the DATABASE TEST FORM.

Writing the @Db Functions

The Database Test Form in our example uses two of the @Db functions to bring data into Notes from the CONTACTS dBASE III table: @DbColumn() and @DbLookup(). They are used in conjunction with each other.

The first field, ContactLastName, is a field of type Keywords, so it can present the user with a list of choices from which to select. In this example, it gives a list of the last names of the contacts.

If you are creating this field from scratch, create a new field called ContactLastName and make it editable, choosing the data type Keywords in the properties box. In the properties box, choose Use Formula for choices, and type the following formula:

```
@DbColumn("ODBC";"Contacts";"";"";"CONTACT";"LASTNAME";"":"Ascending")
```

This code uses the @DbColumn() function to read a column from the CONTACTS dBASE table. It says to make a connection to the ODBC data source called CONTACTS, open the table called CONTACT (which is in the dBASE file CONTACT.DBF), and retrieve all values in the column labeled LASTNAME. All the values in that column (Flintstone, Rubble, Clinton, Ozzie) are retrieved and presented to the user in a pick list.

The second snippet of @Db function code is behind the button called ButtonLookup. Based upon the choice made by the user for the ContactLastName, this button goes back to the CONTACT table, finds the chosen record, retrieves the other values in that record, and then fills in the remaining fields on this form with those values. If you are creating this from scratch, Create a New button, select it, choose formula as the type of code, and enter this code into the Click event:

```
FIELD ContactFirstName := @DbLookup( "ODBC" ;   "CONTACTS" ;
➡"";"";"CONTACT";"FIRSTNAME";"LASTNAME"; ContactLastName);
FIELD ContactCity := @DbLookup( "ODBC" ;   "CONTACTS" ;
➡"";"";"CONTACT";"CITY";"LASTNAME"; ContactLastName);
FIELD ContactState := @DbLookup( "ODBC" ;   "CONTACTS" ;
➡"";"";"CONTACT";"STATE";"LASTNAME"; ContactLastName);
1;
```

Each of the first three lines connects to the ODBC data source called CONTACTS, opens the table called CONTACT, matches the LASTNAME column with the value in the ContactLastName field in this form, and retrieves the appropriate value. The first line of code retrieves the FIRSTNAME column from the external table and puts it into the ContactFirstName field of Notes. The second line of code retrieves the CITY column of the external table and puts the value into the ContactCity field in Notes. Similarly, the third line gets the STATE column and puts it into the ContactState field in Notes. The last line is simply to give the formula a return value—it is arbitrarily set to 1.

Writing the LotusScript Example

The TestScript button on the form demonstrates using the three LotusScript ODBC classes to set up, execute, and then process the result set of a query to the CONTACTS data source. The button cycles through all the records in the CONTACT table and shows the user the value of each field via message boxes. Although putting up message boxes is not a typical application of retrieving a result set, the structure of code to get to external databases from LotusScript is always similar:

1. Connect to external database.
2. Construct query.
3. Run query to get result set.
4. Cycle through result set, processing each record.

For navigation, this example uses the FirstRow and NextRow methods of the ODBCResultSet class. The GetValue method of the ODBCResultSet class can be used to retrieve the value of a particular column of the current record. The GetValue method can specify the column name or the ordinal number of the column in order to get values. Both are demonstrated in the example.

Although it is not shown in this example, the SetValue method could be used to update the values in the result set, and the Transactions method could be used to commit or discard the changes.

Initially, in the options event of the globals object, you need a Uselsx statement for the ODBC LSX. Select (Globals) from the Define dropdown list and Options from the Event dropdown. You should type the following line of code into the script editor:

```
Uselsx "*LSXODBC"
```

Although this LotusScript code is behind a command button on a form, the same code could be put into a LotusScript Agent. Listing 31.1 is the code behind the button.

Listing 31.1. The code behind the TestScript button.

```
Sub Click(Source As Button)
    'Sample Code for Reading Data
    'From a dBASE table via ODBC

    Dim Conn As New ODBCConnection
    Dim Qry  As New ODBCQuery
    Dim CResult As New ODBCResultSet

    'Note: You must know the name of the ODBC data source
    'Connnect to ODBC data source
    result = Conn.ConnectTo("Contacts")

    'Check for Errors
    If Not result Then
```

continues

Listing 31.1. continued

```
            Msgbox "Failure connecting to ODBC data source: Contact "
            Goto endit
      End If

      Msgbox "Connected successfully!"

      'Use connection for query
      Set  Qry.connection  = Conn

      'Create SQL statement for query
      Dim qSQL As String

      qSQL = "Select * from Contact"
      Qry.SQL = qSQL

      Msgbox "Query is: " + Qry.SQL

      'Attach query to Result set
      Set  CResult.query = Qry

      'run query
      result = CResult.Execute

      If Not result Then
            Msgbox "Failure executing query"
            Goto EndConnection

      End If

      CResult.FirstRow

      'cycle through rows in the result set
      While Not CResult.isendofdata

            'Get Last Name
            Msgbox CResult.GetValue("LASTNAME")

            'Get FirstName
            Msgbox CResult.GetValue(1)

            'Get City
            Msgbox CResult.GetValue("CITY")

            'Get State
            Msgbox CResult.GetValue(4)

            CResult.Nextrow

      Wend

endConnection:

      result  = Conn.Disconnect

      'Check for Errors
      If Not result Then
```

Integrating Notes with Legacy Systems

CHAPTER 31

803

31

INTEGRATING
NOTES WITH
LEGACY SYSTEMS

```
        Msgbox "Failure disconnecting from ODBC data source "
        Goto endit
    End If

endit:

End Sub
```

Using the Example

To use this example, go into the Database Testing Notes database and Create a New DATA-BASE TEST FORM. Put the cursor into the Contact Last Name field and press Enter. The disk will whirr for a second, and a pop-up list box will show—if everything has been set up correctly—the last names of all the records in the CONTACT table.

After choosing a last name, click on the button marked Lookup, and the formula code behind the button will go to the CONTACT table. Find the contact that was chosen, and fill in the First Name, City, and State fields.

Finally, click on the button marked Test Script, and the LotusScript behind the button will cycle through all the fields of all the records of the CONTACT table.

This example is a simple one, but the techniques are powerful, and the code here shows all the building blocks needed to build applications integrating Notes with relational database systems. Of course, if you want to avoid programming, you can always choose one of the third-party tools for database Integration.

Building a LotusScript Agent

An Agent built using LotusScript can run on either the client or the server. There are some restrictions to an Agent that runs on the server. For example, when an Agent is created, the Agent knows who its author is and runs with the security privileges of that ID. The default database is also set to the server on which it was first created.

A LotusScript Agent running on a server gets access to relational databases in the same way as the script we used in our button in the example. The Agent uses the ODBC LSX. The same three classes, ODBCConnection, ODBCQuery, and ODBCResultSet can be used on the server. The ODBC data sources, of course, need to be defined on that server.

Summary

Lotus Notes is a powerful platform for storing, organizing, collecting, and most importantly, distributing information. If it is to fit smoothly into the landscape of your current information infrastructure, it must be integrated with existing database systems.

A distribution mechanism is no good if it is an island. For Notes to be successful in its role of the primary information dissemination vehicle, Notes applications must integrate with your other database system. As you have seen, there are a multitude of approaches you can take to do your database integration with Notes, from buying third-party tools to creating your own.

Notes 4 offers some enhancements in the way you can use Notes as a front end for relational systems and as a back end for client/server applications. This chapter armed you by giving you the following:

- An overview of the differences between Notes and other databases
- A fairly exhaustive listing of the types of database integration that can be done
- A list of questions to help you decide which integration method is good for you
- A description of the ways of implementing the integration
- A list of third products for database integration
- A detailed example of how to code database integration into a Notes application

VII

PART

Setting Up a Simple Notes Network

Initial Installation

by Don Child

IN THIS CHAPTER

CHAPTER

32

If you are familiar with installing and setting up a Notes Network in Notes R3, then you should be comfortable with installing and setting up a network in Notes R4. The process of setting up a simple Notes network in R4 is virtually identical to what it was in R3, with only a couple of differences that are not at all significant. There is a new format for the Public Address Book (what used to be called the public Name & Address Book), and a separate design for a Personal Address Book, an enhanced mail template, and an optional shared object mail database. There are also new options for the access control list (ACL) in the Public Address Book that enable you to delegate many of the administrative tasks. The other differences in setting up a Notes network are generally cosmetic.

Preliminaries

Before you can create a Notes network, you have to determine the naming structure for your Notes organization. This can have a profound impact on how you handle security internally, and how you communicate with other organizations. The naming structure of your Notes deployment is likely to follow the structure of your organization, from the organization's name down to its geographic distribution and departmental structure.

If you decide at a later time to change the way you have named your organization, it can affect how you communicate with every user in the organization, as well as affecting your external communications.

One advantage of Notes R4 system administration, though, is that the impact of a later name change has been greatly reduced. Notes now has an administrative agent that helps make a name change throughout the Public Address Book, and in all database ACLs. Regardless, you should still carefully consider your naming scheme.

The names you will have to establish, especially with the first server in the organization, include the following:

- The Server name uniquely identifies the server. To simplify administration, the name should be short and reasonably generic, in case the server gets moved at a later date. The name can include alphanumeric characters, spaces, underscores, ampersands, dashes, and periods. If you use spaces, you will have to include the server's name in quotation marks when referring to the server in commands entered at the server console. Although the administrative agent in Notes R4 makes it easier to change names, you should still assume that the name you give your server is something you are going to keep for the life of your Notes installation. If you communicate with outside organizations, consider identifying your company and your location in the name.

- The Organization name is the overall identity of your organization. As with the server name, a name without spaces simplifies administration. The organization name is also the name associated with the certifier ID, used in Notes security to stamp all user and server IDs as authentic. When a user sets up their workstation, they identify the server by name, including the organization name. For example, if the Server name is Consulting and the organization is Acme, then the server's full name is Consulting/Acme.

- The Domain name is the name that appears on the Public Address Book. Each Domain has its own Public Address Book, used for mail routing, and a common ancestral certificate. Administration is simplified if you have a single domain for a single organization. By default, the Domain name is the same as the Organization name.

- The Administrator's name is the name of the administrator of the server. If you want to use the full name including initials, enter a period after the initial if you want it to appear that way. During setup, a user ID for the administrator will be created, and the administrator's name will appear in the ACL for the Public Address Book, the administrator field for the Server document, and on the administrator's user ID. The administrator has responsibility for the Public Address Book, but does not necessarily have system-wide access to all databases, since individual databases are administered by the person with Manager access in the database Access Control List.

- The Administrator's password protects the administrator's user ID. The password in Notes is always case sensitive.

- The Organizational Unit names are created later, after you set up the initial server in your organization. Organizational Units enable you to delegate the certification process by creating other certifier IDs, and they describe the hierarchical nature of your Notes organization.

- The Network name is shared by a group of Notes servers that are on the same network and that can communicate directly using the same network protocol. If a Notes server runs multiple protocols, then it by definition belongs to multiple Notes networks. When you first set up Notes, the default name is Network1, or you can enter your own name. If possible, include the location and the protocol as part of the network name; for example, SFTCP might be the name of a TCP/IP network in San Francisco.

  The Network name, also referred to as a Notes Named Network (NNN), is used to group Notes servers that share a protocol and that are constantly connected. A user connected to their home server (where their mail file is located) can see all other Notes servers in the same NNN when they select File | Database | Open. A Notes server can be assigned to a different NNN even if it is constantly connected to another Notes server and shares a common protocol. To avoid confusion, you may want to create separate NNNs to group servers as they are used within your organization.

- The Organization country code is an optional, two-letter code used to distinguish the name of your organization from another organization with the same name in another country. The country code becomes part of a name in a hierarchical Notes organization—for example, Acme/US, Acme/CA (Canada), and Acme/UK.

You should spend some time planning out how Notes will be deployed in your organization, and develop a naming scheme that complements that deployment. It will make the organization easier to administer, and will ultimately enhance security within the organization. For example, if major divisions within your organization can be given names that make the divisions obvious, yet they should be kept generic in case they change. You could name Notes servers WestServer1 and EastServer1 instead of NewYork and SanFrancisco. What happens if you move your western office to Los Angeles? And give networks names such as SFTCP and SFSPX, to identify the location and the protocol. It is easier to change the name of a network than it is to change the name of a Notes server, therefore the San Francisco TCP/IP NNN can be named SFTCP, and if you move, just create a new NNN name—LATCP, for example.

With Notes R4, you are strongly advised to use a hierarchical organization. The structure of the hierarchy is like an organization chart with the name of the organization at the top. Beneath that, there can be one or more branches of organization units, with no practical limit to the number of branches directly beneath the organization. Each branch is headed by an Organizational Certifier. The branch can be up to four levels deep. Individual Notes users and Notes servers can be found at any level of the organizational structure. Figure 32.1 shows the hierarchical structure of a Notes organization.

FIGURE 32.1.

The hierarchical structure of a Notes network.

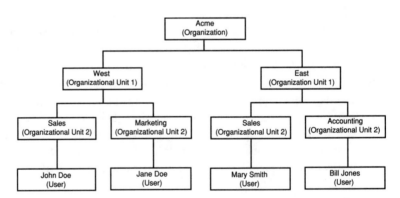

As far as Notes is concerned, a user's name is determined by his or her place in the hierarchy. For example, a user in the Sales department of the West branch of the Acme corporation might be named John Doe/Sales/West/Acme. From the name, you can deduce that John Doe was registered as a Notes user by an administrator with access to the Sales Certifier ID, which was created by the West certifier, which was created in turn by Acme.

Whenever the Notes administrator or certifier is registering a new user or a new server, they should have a copy of the Notes hierarchical structure handy to ensure that they are using the correct Certifier ID. It is the Certifier ID that determines where the user is within the hierarchical structure.

Installing Notes R4 Software

Installing the Notes R4 software is more or less automatic, especially if you have a CD-ROM drive. Notes can detect earlier versions of Notes and will install over the top of the existing installation. If this is a new installation, Notes will suggest a directory in which Notes should be installed.

If you accept the default installation, Notes will create a directory for its program files, and beneath that, a data directory. When a user looks for database files by selecting File | Database | Open from within Notes, they will see only the data directory and any other directories beneath it in the directory tree.

For the most part, installation is the same on all platforms, with the exception of the location of the NOTES.INI file. And certain files that are installed on a Notes server are not required on a Notes workstation—most notably the full HELP.NSF and many of the Notes template files. On workstations, a normal install includes Help Lite, a smaller version of the full help database.

Notes R4 has the following minimum and recommended hardware/software platforms, and supported protocols for Notes servers and Notes workstations:

- OS/2 Server: PC with Intel 486 or Pentium processor, 32MB RAM minimum, 48MB RAM recommended

  Operating System: OS/2 WARP version 3 or OS/2 WARP Connect version 3

  Protocols: AppleTalk, Banyan VINES, NetBIOS, NetWare SPX on OS/2, TCP/IP, Lotus Notes Connect for SNA Version 3.0a on OS/2, X.PC (supplied with the Notes software)

- Windows NT Server: PC with Intel 486 or Pentium processor, 48MB RAM minimum, 64MB RAM recommended

  Operating System: Microsoft Windows NT Advanced Server version 3.51, Windows NT Workstation 3.51

  Protocols: AppleTalk, Banyan VINES, NetBIOS, Novell NetWare SPX, TCP/IP, X.PC (supplied with the Notes software)

- Windows 95 Server: PC with Intel 486 or Pentium processor, 16MB RAM minimum, 24MB RAM recommended

  Operating System: Microsoft Windows 95

  Protocols: NetBIOS, NetWare SPX, TCP/IP (Banyan VINES on workstation only), X.PC (supplied with the Notes software)

- UNIX Server: HP 9000 Series running HP-UX 10.01. Sun SPARC system running Sun Solaris 2.4, 2.5, or 2.5.1. IBM RISC System / 6000 running IBM AIX version 4.1.3 or 4.1.4, all with 64MB RAM minimum, 96MB recommended.

  Protocols: Novell NetWare SPX, TCP/IP (native), X.PC (supplied with the Notes software)

■ NetWare Server: PC with Intel 386, 486, or Pentium processor, 64MB RAM minimum, 96MB recommended

Operating System: NetWare 3.12 or 4.1

Protocols: AppleTalk, NetWare SPX, TCP/IP, X.PC (supplied with the Notes software)

■ Windows Workstations: PC with Intel 486 or Pentium processor, 6MB RAM minimum, 8MB RAM recommended for Windows 3.1 and Windows for Workgroups 3.11, 8MB RAM minimum, 12MB RAM recommended for Windows 95, MS-DOS or PC-DOS 3.31 or later

■ Macintosh Workstations: Motorola 68030 or 68040 or PowerPC with 12MB RAM (for 680xx), 16MB RAM (for PowerPC) minimum, 20MB recommended for both

Operating System: Mac System 7.1 (for 680xx) or Mac System 7.5 (for PowerPC)

Protocols: AppleTalk, TCP/IP, X.PC (supplied with the Notes software)

These platforms were certified for Release 4.11 as of October 20, 1996, just prior to the release of Notes 4.5 to customers. It is anticipated that Release 4.5 will have similar requirements.

Setting Up the First Notes Server in an Organization

Setting up the first server in the organization is distinguished by the fact that you have no ID files of any sort and no Public Address Book (NAMES.NSF) before you start.

The process of creating these files is automatic after you have given Notes the information it requires. This is done through a series of dialog boxes, which are displayed during the setup process.

CAUTION

If you are setting up your first Notes R4 server in an existing Notes R3 network, the server should be registered in Notes R3 so the new Notes R4 server ID has a certificate that can communicate with the R3 servers in the organization. You should then run setup as if you were setting up an additional server, using the Server ID created by the Notes R3 certifier ID. Registering a server in Notes R3 is done by selecting File | Administration | Register Server from the Notes R3 workspace.

Running the Setup Process

To initiate the setup process, double-click on the Notes Client icon. Notes will prompt you to specify whether this is the first server you are setting up in your organization, or whether you are setting up an additional server. Indicate that this is the first server (assuming you are setting up a new organization. See the preceding Caution if you are setting up a Notes R4 server in an existing Notes R3 environment).

CAUTION

It may seem logical that you start the Notes server by clicking on the Notes Server icon. However, during the setup process (for certified Notes server platforms as of first customer ship), you have to start by clicking on the Client icon. A Notes server has a Notes server client that runs on the same hardware and provides a graphical user interface to the server software during setup, and during many of the tasks involved in administering the Notes system. For newly released Notes server platforms such as the NLM server, starting the setup process may be different.

During the setup process, you will be prompted to enter the following information in fields in a dialog box, shown in Figure 32.2. For the most part, this is the same information you already defined for your organization during planning:

- Organization name
- Administrator name
- Administrator password
- Server name
- Server password
- Communication protocol, and optional modem information

CAUTION

You also have the option to specify that the server is also the Administrator's personal workstation on some platforms. For some types of server, such as the NLM server and the Windows NT server, this option was not possible with Notes R3. Check your Notes Install guide if you are planning on using the Server as the Administrator's personal workstation.

FIGURE 32.2.

Setting up the first server in an organization.

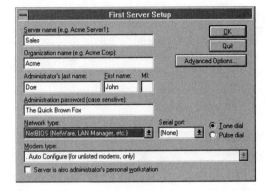

In a second dialog box, called Advanced Server Setup Options (see Figure 32.3), you can enter the following information:

- Domain Name: By default, the same as the Organization
- Network Name: Network1, by default
- Country Code
- Minimum Administrator password length
- ID files to be created during setup
- Logging options (what type of information to write to a Notes Log database to assist with troubleshooting)

FIGURE 32.3.

Entering advanced server setup information.

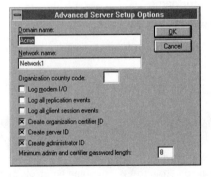

When you have entered all of the required information, Notes begins the setup process. This can take up to several minutes.

During the setup process, Notes will display messages on the status bar at the bottom of the workspace, so you can tell what is being done. By reading the messages, you will see that Notes does the following:

- Creates a file named CERT.ID, which is used to create certificates that have the same name as your organization
- Creates a server ID in a file named SERVER.ID
- Creates a user ID for the administrator
- Creates a Public Address Book for the domain
- Creates a Server record in the Public Address Book
- Creates a Person record for the administrator in the Public Address Book, and assigns the Administrator Manager access to the Public Address Book.
- Creates a mail database for the administrator
- Sets up the first communications port based on the default protocol that you specified
- Creates a Notes log database for the server
- Creates a mailbox database (MAIL.BOX) that Notes will use for mail routing

During the setup process, Notes will display a dialog box so you can enter the time zone in which you are setting up the server. In the time-zone dialog box, you also indicate whether daylight savings is observed at this location. This information is used by Notes to synchronize the time when communicating with servers and users in other time zones.

When the setup process is completed, the Notes workspace will be displayed.

On the desktop are database icons for the Public Address Book and the Notes Log for the server.

Before proceeding with the setup procedures, verify your port setup. To do this, select File | Tools | User Preferences, and click on the Ports icon. This was located under Tools | Setup under earlier versions of Notes.

> **CAUTION**
>
> Ports are initialized when the Notes server is started up. Therefore, if ports are set up or modified while the server is running, you have to exit and restart the server before the changes take effect. Therefore, as a general rule, you should verify that your port is correctly set up, and add any additional ports you want to use prior to starting the server software.

The setup process is now complete. You can start up the server.

Starting the Server

On platforms that allow both the Notes server and the Workstation to run simultaneously, the server can be started up with the Server client running, or you can close the Server's client window. Return to the operating system's graphical desktop and double-click on the Notes

Server icon. The system will switch to a text screen, and a number of messages will be displayed as the server starts up.

As the server starts, messages are displayed on the screen. If this is the first time the server has started, there are databases that get created automatically.

MAIL.BOX is created as a holding place for mail messages while they are awaiting delivery, and the server's Router task is started.

The Admin Proxy database is created and the administrative agent (ADMINP) is started. The Admin Proxy database holds administrative requests such as name changes. The administrative agent then checks this database and applies the changes throughout the Public Address Book and in the ACL of all applicable databases.

CATALOG.NSF is created. This is a list of databases that will be seen by users when they select File | Database | Open. By default, this list is updated automatically each night by the server software.

Various processes are started up. In addition to the administrative agent and the router, the Database Server process, the Index Update process, the Stats agent and the Replicator are started up. For a complete list of server tasks that are started up on your Notes server, refer to the NOTES.INI file for your server, and look for the "Server Tasks" line, which tells you which tasks are currently running.

When the server has been started up, users can access the server and the shared databases that reside on the server.

Creating Organizational Unit (OU) Certifiers

When the first server has been set up, most administrative functions are handled through the Administration control panel. (See Figure 32.4.) Display this screen by selecting File | Tools | Server Administration. This screen is new to Notes R4, consolidating all server administrative tasks in a single location.

In Notes R4, it is highly recommended that you use hierarchical certification. This increases security by ensuring that each user has a unique identity within your organization, and simplifies administration for functions such as cross-certifying with another organization. It is still possible to have a "flat," or nonhierarchical, organization in Notes R4 but by default, all certification—even with only a single, organization-wide certifier—is hierarchical. Refer to Chapter 36, "Troubleshooting the System," for more information.

Because hierarchical certification allows for up to four levels of organizational units, your naming scheme may require you to create OU certifiers before continuing.

FIGURE 32.4.

The Server Administration control panel.

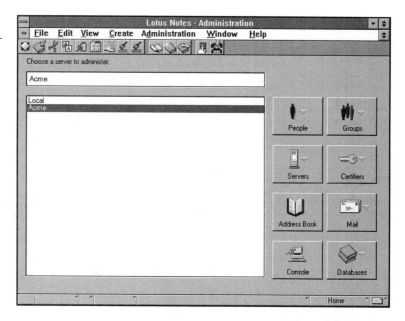

In the Administration Control Panel, select the name of the server you have already set up, then select the Certifiers button. This will display a drop-down menu, from which you should select Register Organizational Unit. The Register Organizational Unit Certifier dialog box will be displayed. (See Figure 32.5.)

FIGURE 32.5.

The Register Organizational Unit Certifier dialog box.

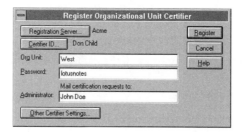

In this dialog box, do the following:

- Select the Registration Server. This is the server on which the Public Address Book will be updated when you create the new OU. The registration server should be one that replicates regularly with other servers in the organization, to ensure that the new information gets distributed throughout the organization without undue delay.

- Select the certifier ID that will be used to create this new OU. In a hierarchical name, the certifier ID name will display all of its own hierarchical certificates. For example, if your Organization certifier is Acme, and you create a new OU named West, then the new OU certifier will be named West/Acme, and this hierarchical certificate will be part of the name of every user registered by the West Organizational Unit certifier.

- Enter the name of the new Organizational Unit, up to 32 characters long.

- Enter the password for the OU certifier ID. Remember, the password is case-sensitive.

- Enter the name of the person to whom administrative requests should be sent. This is the person who registers new users and servers using this OU Certifier ID. The person must use Notes mail.

- You can optionally select the Other Certifier Settings to specify the license type (North American or International), the minimum password length (default eight), and enter a comment and location to appear as additional information in the Certifier document in the Public Address Book.

> **NOTE**
>
> North American licenses can only be used within the United States and Canada because the encryption technology used in the North American version has export restrictions. The encryption algorithm for the International licensed versions can be legally exported. The encryption technology is the only significant difference between the two versions. Encryption still works when one user is using a North American version, and another user is using an International version.

Requiring Additional Passwords for a Certifier ID

As an additional security measure for your organization, you may want to consider requiring multiple passwords to access the Certifier ID, thereby requiring that more than one person knows when a new person or server is being registered. With multiple passwords, you can have a team of administrators, each of whom has a valid ID, to access the ID. If you require at least two IDs before the ID can be used, then at least two administrators must be present to register a new user or server.

You can set up multiple passwords for any ID—certifier IDs, user IDs, or server IDs—from the Administration Control Panel. Click on the Certifiers icon and select Edit Multiple Passwords. Notes will ask you to select the ID file for which you want to edit the multiple passwords list, then will display the Edit ID File Password List dialog box. (See Figure 32.6.)

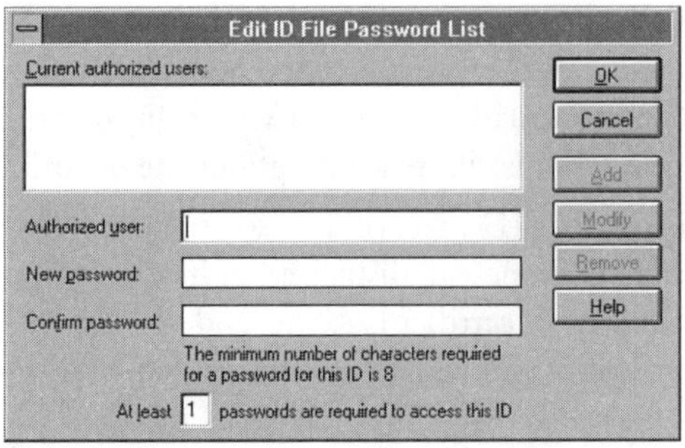

FIGURE 32.6.

Setting up multiple passwords using the Edit ID File Password List dialog box.

In this dialog box, have each authorized person enter the following:

- His or her user name
- A password. If you apply multiple passwords to an ID, any previous passwords become invalid
- Re-enter the password to verify that it has been entered correctly

When you are done, click on Add. The process is repeated for each person who will be using the ID. When all authorized users have entered their password, enter the number of passwords that will be required to access this ID. After that, you will be able to use the ID only if you have the correct number of passwords available.

You can remove a password from the ID list by selecting the user ID from which you want to remove the password, then selecting Remove. You must enter the password first to verify that you have authorized access to it, before you can delete the password. You can also modify an entry by highlighting the user name and clicking on Modify, then enter the original password, then the new password (entered twice to verify the accuracy of your typing).

> **CAUTION**
>
> You cannot use multiple passwords when you are using nonhierarchical names, nor can they be used with Notes R3.

> **TIP**
>
> If you want to always require the presence of multiple users when certain database functions are performed, try registering a fake user and put the fake user into the ACL. You can then have all members who should have access to the ID enter a password in the Edit ID File Password List dialog box, and indicate the number of passwords that are required to access the ID. If you have 10 passwords for an ID, for example, and only two passwords are required, then any two authorized users can access the ID by entering their passwords.

Setting Up an Additional Server

Setting up an additional server is virtually identical to the process with earlier versions of Notes. With the first server (or the "registration" server) running, you have to register the additional server based on the naming scheme you have already established. This creates a SERVER.ID file for the new server and creates a new Server document in the Public Address Book. You then access the server ID either over the network or from a diskette, and set up the server software—a process that is the same as setting up the first server in the organization, except that the certifier ID already exists and the organization's naming scheme has already been established.

To register a new server, click on the Servers icon from the Administration Control Panel, and select Register Server. Click OK to indicate that you have a server license for the new server.

Before you can register a server, you have to select which certifier ID you are going to use. In other words, you are defining where this new server will fit into your organization. Select the appropriate certifier ID or the Organizational Unit certifier ID, and enter the password. You also have to indicate which server is the Registration server if you are not using the Workstation desktop on the Notes server. You can also indicate whether you are setting up a server using a North American license or an international license, and you can change the expiration date for the server ID if you want. The license normally expires in 100 years, so you are only likely to change it if you want to ensure that the server is only used for a short duration.

Notes will display the Register Servers dialog box shown in Figure 32.7. In this dialog box, enter the server name, the password, the domain, and the name of the administrator for this server. Enter the minimum password length.

FIGURE 32.7.

*Registering an
additional server.*

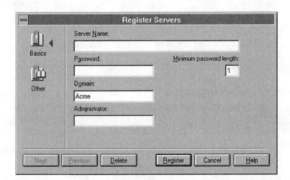

TIP

You may want to consider setting the required password length for the server to zero so the password can be cleared after the server is set up. If there is no password, the server can be restarted automatically from a batch or start-up file following a power outage, without requiring the presence of the system administrator.

Click on the icon marked Other to display the Additional Address Book information fields. In these fields, you can specify the server title to more specifically identify the server. This is a memo field that appears in the Server document.

You can also specify the network name. The network identifies which other servers and users will be using the same protocol, and it can view this server when users select File | Database | Open.

The Local administrator is the person assigned to ServerCreator and ServerModifier roles in the Server document. They do not have to be server administrator, but authority has been delegated to them so they can share the server-administration tasks.

You can also decide where to store the server ID until the server has been set up. You have the option of storing the ID as an attachment to the Server document in the Public Address Book, or you can store it in a file, either on a diskette or on the network.

CAUTION

The server ID is the identity of the server, and enables the server to authenticate with other servers and users in your organization. Therefore, you want to make sure that the server ID is protected by a password as long as it is exposed during transit. After the server has been set up, you want to ensure that the server is physically secure so the server ID cannot be stolen.

After the server has been registered, you set up the software in a process that mirrors the setup for the first server in the organization, with a couple of exceptions.

On Windows and OS/2 servers, you begin by double-clicking on the Notes workstation icon, as with the first server in the organization, but you tell Notes that you are setting up an additional server. You then have to enter the name of the new server exactly as it appears in the Server document in the Public Address Book, including the full hierarchy.

On UNIX, the software-install process is different (the installation processes are described in the Install Guide for Servers that ships with Lotus Notes R4), but after you get to specifying information for the server setup, the process is identical to the setup process for Windows servers. (See Figure 32.8.)

FIGURE 32.8.

*The Additional Server
Setup dialog box.*

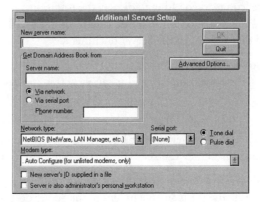

- Enter the name of a server that contains a copy of the domain's Public Address Book. This is necessary so the new server can get a copy of the Public Address Book as soon as a network connection is established.

- Select how the new server will communicate with the server that contains the Domain's Public Address Book—either via a network port, or via a serial port. If communication is via a serial port, you also have to indicate the phone number of the dial-up server. If you are using modem communications on the new server, you have to enter additional serial-port-setup information.

- Select the network-communication protocol that will be used by this server. The protocol must also be supported by the server on which the domain's Public Address Book is found. The Registration Server must also have the same protocol.

- Select where the server should look for the server ID file. If you specify that the server ID should be stored in the Server document of the Public Address Book, then the new server will look for its ID in the Public Address Book during setup. If you specify that the ID is in a file, you have to specify where the file is located during setup.

- The Advanced Options icon lets you specify what should be logged to the server's Notes Log. You can specify modem I/O, replication events, and client-session events.

- You can also specify the time zone for the new computer, and whether or not daylight savings time should be observed.

When you are done, Notes sets up the server based on the information you have given it. After the workstation software starts up, you can specify additional ports for the server if you want, and then start up the server by double-clicking on the server icon from the Program Manager.

Setting Up User Workstations

Setting up a user workstation is similar to setting up a server, in that you first have to register the user, then set up the workstation that they will be using.

Registering users does several things. For every user registered, Notes creates a user ID, which is used to authenticate with Notes servers and to provide access to Notes databases. A Person document is created in the Public Address Book so the Mail Router can send mail to the user. If the person is using NotesMail, a server-based mail file is created and Organization and Organizational Unit certificates are added to the user's ID. The Organizational Unit certificate is added only if the organization is using hierarchical naming.

There are a few things to consider before you begin registering users. First, you have to know how each user fits into the Notes organization so you can determine which certifier ID to use when creating the new user.

The certifier ID defines the user's place within the Notes organizational hierarchy. For example, suppose there is a new user named John Smith. He could be registered by the organizational certifier of the Acme Corporation, in which case, he would become John Smith/Acme. He could be registered by the West certifier, in which case he would become John Smith/West/Acme. Or he could be registered by the marketing certifier for the Western regional office, in which case he would become John Smith/Marketing/West/Acme. The hierarchical name can determine which databases are available to him, and how easy it is to communicate with other users within the organization.

Second, you have to decide how to register users. You can register them individually, for example when a new user joins your staff, or you can register them as a group using a text file, which might be preferable if you have to register a large number of users, and especially if their names are already available online, for example in a database or spreadsheet format that can be exported to a text file.

Third, you can customize their setup by predefining the desktop and workstation configuration they will see when they first set up their workstations. You can do this either by creating a User Setup Profile, new to Notes R4, or by customizing a DESKTOP.DSK file before they set up, or both.

Creating a User Setup Profile

User Setup Profiles are created in the Public Address Book. A setup profile is used when a group of users will all have the same communications setup. By creating a setup profile, you can apply the same configuration to a number of users at one time.

To create a setup profile, open the Public Address Book and switch to the Select Setup Profile view. Choose the action Add Setup Profile. Give the new profile a name, and, if appropriate, enter the name of the Internet server for the group. Enter the name and phone number of the default passthru server, and add the names and phone numbers of any remote dial-up servers. Enter the mail Domain for the group, then save your profile.

When you are setting up users, you will have an option of using a User Setup Profile. Select the profile you have just defined, and all of the communication parameters will be applied to that user.

Customizing the DESKTOP.DSK File Prior to User Setup

In the same way you set up a number of communication parameters, you can also set up a group of users so they have a standard suite of Notes databases on their desktop after they run workstation setup. This is done by creating a standard DESKTOP.DSK file and placing it in a Notes installation directory on a file server. Obviously, for this to work, all of the users should be on the same network, with the same path to the Notes databases that are placed on their desktop.

To create a DESKTOP.DSK file for installation, close the Notes workstation program if it is running, and go to an operating-system command prompt. The workstation software cannot be running, because the DESKTOP.DSK file is always in use when the Notes workstation program is running.

Rename DESKTOP.DSK something else (such as DESKTOP.OLD) in the Notes data directory on your local workstation, then copy DESKTOP.DSK from the Notes installation directory on your file server to your local Notes data directory. Restart the Notes workstation program with the new DESKTOP.DSK file and set it up the way you want it to appear for the users when they set up their workstations. In other words, name the folders, add databases to the desktop, set up replication schedules, add customized SmartIcons, and so forth, until the desktop looks exactly the way you want users to see it.

Exit the workstation program again and copy the modified DESKTOP.DSK from your Notes data directory back into the Notes installation directory on your file server. You can then rename your own desktop so you have your own DESKTOP.DSK file in your Notes data directory.

Registering Users Individually

You register users from the Administration Control Panel. Click on the People icon, and select Register Person. Select the certifier ID you want to use, based on your naming scheme. Notes will then display the Register Person dialog box.

Select the Registration Server. This is the server in the user's domain that contains a copy of the Public Address Book. You can also change the certifier ID at this point if you need to.

Select the Security Type, either North American or International. North American security uses a type of encryption technology that cannot be exported legally, so users who will be traveling overseas must use International encryption. Aside from encryption, there are no differences between the two versions.

You can also change the default expiration date for the User ID. The default expiration is two years, but you may want to set a shorter period for temporary employees, and you may want to extend the time for employees who are likely to be core members of your team for years to come.

After you accept the data in the first dialog box, Notes displays another Register Person dialog box with three icons so you can enter Basic, Mail, and Other information. On the Basic page, you enter the following information:

■ Enter the user's first, middle, and last names. The way you enter the user's name is the way it will be saved with their user ID. Then enter the password length and an initial password for the user.

TIP

If you use a generic password as a default, it can represent a security weakness if the user does not immediately change the default password to their own password. One way to overcome this potential weakness is to give the user a password that is so awkward to type that they will want to change to their own password as soon as possible. For example, give them a password such as cHANGE tHIS pASSWORD aSAP. The password can be up to 64 characters long and is case-sensitive.

■ Enter the license type. With Notes R4, there are three types of end-user license: a full developer license; a Notes desktop license, which lets you run Notes applications but does not enable you to make any design changes; and NotesMail (previously Notes Express), which lets you use Notes mail along with basic applications such as discussion databases.

■ Select the User Profile to use, if you have one defined for a group to which this user belongs.

Click on the Mail icon and select the mail type for this user. You can use Notes Mail, cc:Mail, another VIM mail program, or you can elect to have no mail program running with Notes. If you are using Notes Mail, enter the name of the user's mail database. Notes creates a database with a default name of the user's first initial plus up to seven characters from their last name, with an NSF extension—for example, JSMITH.NSF. If another user has the same name, Notes will prompt you to give the database file another name.

Select the user's Home server. This is the server on which the user's mail database will be created and stored. Click on a radio button to tell Notes whether you want the user's mail database created as soon as they are registered, or at the time they set up their workstation. Be aware that the user's mail database will be perceived as active by other users as soon as it is created, even if the user does not set up their workstation until later. Try to avoid a situation where the mail database is collecting unanswered mail because the user does not yet have access to their mail.

Click on the Other icon to enter memo-address information for the user, and to indicate whether to store their user ID in their person document in the Public Address Book, or on a diskette prior to workstation setup.

Most of the information for the user is entered by default, so even though there is a lot of information to be entered, it is usually a relatively simple process. When all information is correct, click the Register button to register the user.

Registering Multiple Users from a Text File

You can batch register new users from a text file. This is particularly handy if you can create a text file from an existing employee database. The text file must be formatted with semicolons delimiting the different data elements for each user, and a carriage return separating each record. The full information for each user, with one user per line, includes the following:

```
Lastname;Firstname;MiddleInitial;organization;password;Idfiledirectory;IDfilename;
➥homeservername;mailfiledirectory;mailfilename;location;comment;forwardingaddress
```

Although the lines wrap in the example, they would appear as a single line in a text file.

At a minimum, you must include the last name and the password. The ID file directory and the ID filename will be created automatically if you do not enter them. You should also include the user's first name to avoid duplicate names.

The following three examples show two records from a text file with minimum information for a flat naming scheme (name and password), two lines from a text file with different home servers defined, and a text file with one record with all information defined:

```
Edison;Thomas;A;;edisonpw
Pound;Ezra;;;poundpw

Edison;Thomas;A;;edisonpw;;;SCIENCE
Pound;Ezra;;;poundpw;;;POETRY

Edison;Thomas;A;sales;PASSWORD1;C:\USERID;TEDISON.ID;SCIENCE;MAIL;
➥TEDISON;Laboratory;tom_edison@lightbulb.com<RETURN>
```

After the text file has been set up, you can register the users from the Administration Control Panel. Click on People and select Register from File.

The process is identical to registering an individual user, but you will be asked for the name of the text file before Notes displays the main registration window.

If you save user IDs in the Public Address Book, the user ID will be attached to the user's Person document until they set up their workstation. The user ID stored in the Public Address Book must have a password of at least one character in length.

If the Notes user will be using cc:Mail or another type of VIM mail, you should include a forwarding address in the user's Person document to ensure that mail sent by other Notes users gets directed to the user's mail box. You can include a forwarding address during setup, or you can enter it into the user's Person document later. The forwarding address should include a full explicit path to the user—for example, `Jane Doe@Marketing@West@Acme@SanDiego`.

Running the Workstation Setup Program

After users have been registered, they are ready to run the workstation-setup program from their workstation. This is initiated by double-clicking on the Notes icon. If the workstation setup program has not been previously completed, it will begin automatically. Notes begins to build the workspace, but it will need certain information from the user before continuing. This information is entered in the Network Workstation Setup dialog box, shown in Figure 32.9.

FIGURE 32.9.
The Network Workstation Setup dialog box.

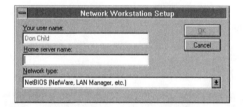

Notes requires the following information for user setup:

- Are you setting up a workstation that will communicate with the server via a network connection? If you will have no connection to a server, select No connection to server. If you are setting up remotely and will be communicating with a server, select either Remote connection (via modem) or Network and remote connections.

- If your administrator has supplied your user ID in a file on a diskette or over the network, select User ID supplied in a file and specify the full path so Notes can locate the file. Otherwise, Notes will look for your ID as an attachment to your Person document in the Public Address Book. Copy the user ID file to your data directory when prompted.

- Enter your full name exactly as it was entered by the person who registered you, and the password given to you by the administrator. Note that passwords are case-sensitive and may include spaces.

- Enter the full name of your home server. For example, if the server is Sales and it is in the Acme organization, your server's full name would be `Sales/Acme`. The home server is where Notes will look for the Public Address Book and your personal mail file.

Depending on the type of connection you selected in the first step, enter one of the following:

- The network protocol with which you will connect to the server
- The home server's phone number and dialing prefix (without any spaces in between), the modem type and port, and whether the phone is tone dial or pulse dial
- Whether you want to connect to the server via network or via phone during setup

When all the information is entered correctly, click OK; Notes will set up the workstation. Before the setup is completed, Notes will give you an opportunity to enter the time zone where you are setting up, and whether to observe daylight savings time. Notes uses this information to synchronize with Notes servers when you replicate.

If you are setting up Notes R4 as an upgrade from an earlier version of Notes, you may want to use your old DESKTOP.DSK file and other data files. If so, shut down the workstation, copy these files so they replace any files created during setup, then restart Notes.

If you had any difficulties during setup, you can rerun the setup by doing the following:

- Delete the newly created DESKTOP.DSK file.
- Edit the NOTES.INI file, deleting everything except the first three lines, so the file looks like this:

```
[Notes]
KitType=1
Directory=C:\NOTES\DATA
```

> **TIP**
>
> You can restart a server setup in the same way. However, make sure that the second line of the NOTES.INI file says `KitType=2` instead of 1. In addition, if you are reconfiguring the first server in an organization before any other servers have been set up, you should delete NAMES.NSF (such as the Public Address Book), MAIL.BOX, LOG.NSF, CATALOG.NSF, CERT.ID, SERVER.ID, USER.ID (the Administrator's user ID), plus any mail files in the MAIL subdirectory off the default data directory.

Restart Notes and make sure that everything was typed in correctly, and that your workstation is locating and able to communicate with the Notes server if you are getting your user ID from the Public Address Book.

After setting up a workstation for the first time, your desktop will have certain icons on it, depending on how you are set up. If you are on a network, you will have icons for the Public Address Book and your mail file. If you are remote, you will have replicas of those databases on your desktop, and a store/forward mailbox. If you are setting up as a disconnected workstation, you will also have a copy of a Personal Address Book with four default locations set up along with an outgoing mailbox. And if you were registered using a User Setup Profile, your location records may already be set up with the correct telephone numbers and protocols for dialing up and replicating from various locations.

The mail file may have been created at the time you were registered as a user, or the file may be created at the time of setup. This second option is useful for situations where you don't know which server will become the user's home server. They can select a server at the time they run the workstation setup program, and their mail file will be created on that server.

Setting Up Shared Files on a Network

One option for setting up Notes workstations is to place all of the Notes program files on a shared program directory. When this is done, each user will have only their personal data files on their local workstation, whereas all of the program files reside in a single location on the network. This saves disk space for all of the users but is likely to slow down the performance of Notes because it has to run over the network. The data files on the user's workstation include the user ID, the DESKTOP.DSK file, and any personal databases the user wants to store locally.

To set up Notes so workstations can run from a shared program directory, select Install on a file server during software installation.

> **CAUTION**
>
> Only workstations can run from a shared program directory. The Notes server requires all of its own program files on the Notes server workstation. If you want to offload any server files, you can use directory links to place databases elsewhere on the network. This does result in slower data access but frees up disk space on your Notes server. Be sure to prevent users from directly accessing databases on the network. Databases can be shared only if they are accessed through a Notes server.

Setting Up a Mobile Workstation

Setting up a mobile workstation is essentially the same as setting up a regular Notes workstation, but there are a few setup differences that you should be aware of. Foremost among these differences are Location documents in the Personal Address Book, the importance of setting up communications correctly, the creation of a local outgoing mailbox, and the creation of database replicas that the mobile user will want to replicate. Each of these topics is covered in detail in Chapter 9, "Using Mobile Notes on the Road."

Migrating from a Notes R3 Network to Notes R4

So far, all of the setup for a Notes network has assumed that the user is setting up a new Notes organization from scratch. But for many users, setting up Notes R4 means migrating from an earlier version of Notes—most likely Notes R3. Migration is a process that takes some planning, so that you can minimize any disruption as you make the upgrade. The recommended steps for upgrading from Notes R3 to Notes R4, in order, are:

1. Migrate Notes servers.
2. Migrate Notes clients.
3. Migrate nonessential applications.
4. Upgrade applications using R4 features.
5. Upgrade essential applications.
6. Develop new applications using R4 features.

The first three steps are summarized in the following sections. The last three steps involve Notes application design, and are described in detail in the chapters in Part III, "Developing Applications with Lotus Notes."

Upgrading the Notes Server to R4

The first step in the migration path is to upgrade servers from Notes R3 to Notes R4. This is the first step in the Notes migration primarily because it is likely to have the least impact on your organization. There are fewer Notes servers than there are clients, so you can get the servers upgraded one at a time before you begin to upgrade users. One server can be upgraded, and it can run for awhile to ensure that everything is going smoothly. Then a second server can be upgraded when you are sure that the first server is stable. The migration path can be taken one step at a time because Notes R3 clients are able to use databases, even though they are running on a Notes R4 server.

To upgrade a server, do the following:

■ Back up your Notes R3 in case you discover that, for some unforseen circumstance, you have to revert to your old system. There are specific files that you must back up if you want to recover your old setup, including DESKTOP.DSK, NOTES.INI, various ID files (server, certifier, administrator), NAMES.NSF (the Public Address Book), LOG.NSF, MAIL.BOX, and any other address books that you might have cascaded by placing them in the Names= setting of your NOTES.INI file. Certain files, such as DESKTOP.DSK and NAMES.NSF, remain open as long as the Notes server or workstation is running. Therefore, you will have to shut down Notes before these files are backed up.

- You should also back up any database files (*.NSF) and customized template files (*.NTF), plus any directory links (*.DIR). In fact, if you have the space available, it is advisable to back up your entire Notes directory structure. Then you can be assured of a complete recovery, should it become necessary.

- Verify that you have the recommended software and hardware for the upgrade, including the proper version of the operating system, and protocols supported by Notes. For example, on a Windows NT server, you must be running NT 3.51 or later.

- Install the Notes R4 software. If possible, install it to the same directory in which Notes R3 was installed to minimize the loss of links to other applications. However, you should be aware that some of the test build (beta) versions of Notes R4 sometimes had trouble when they were installed on top of existing Notes 3.x files, so you may want to consider deleting earlier versions of Notes, except for the data files and ID files. The install process is pretty much automatic, especially if you are installing from a CD-ROM drive. Select the type of install you are doing—Windows 32 bit for Windows 95 or NT, OS/2 for an OS/2 server. There are no 16-bit servers, so the 16-bit Notes on the install CD is for clients only.

- If you had customized templates in Notes R3, do not copy the R3 templates back over R4 templates that have the same name. Instead, add the customized features into the R4 templates. This ensures that Notes R4 can still take advantage of new features in the R4 templates.

- Upgrade the Public Address Book. When you open the Notes R4 client software on the server for the first time, the Public Address Book design will be refreshed with several new views. To ensure that the design reflects the latest changes to the Public Address Book template, open the Database properties box and switch to the Design page. Enter the name of the new template (StdR4PublicAddressBook) from which design changes should be inherited.

There are several steps that you can take to upgrade the Public Address Book. You can add administration roles to the address book, and apply delegation to selected document using Actions. You can update the indexes to R4 format by running iupdall, nupdall, or updall on NAMES.NSF for OS/2, Windows NT, and UNIX, respectively. You can convert the address book to R4 format by running icompact, ncompact, or compact on NAMES.NSF (again, for OS/2, Windows NT and UNIX respectively). If you had your Notes R3 replication set with the parameter ServerPushReplication=1 in the NOTES.INI file, you can edit the Connection document for this server and set the replication method to Pull-Push. Set up statistics and event monitoring for the new server by loading EVENT and REPORT. If you already have a STATREP.NSF database for recording statistics, change the database properties to inherit its design from the StdR4StatReport template, and delete the file EVTTYPES.NMF.

- Verify port setups in the User Preferences dialog box.

- Update Administrator Roles. This can be done now or later. The administrator roles let the Notes administration be delegated to users with lower access levels. For example, a user with Author access to the Public Address Book can be added to the UserCreator and UserModifier groups to let them create new users. Without the administrator roles, you would have to give them at least Editor access to be able to create new people in the Public Address Book, which would give them the ability to edit any document in the Public Address Book.

After the server has been upgraded, monitor it to ensure that everything is running smoothly, then upgrade other servers in the organization.

Upgrading Client Workstations

Upgrading client workstations is, in many ways, more of an educational challenge than it is a technical challenge.

When Notes R4 is installed in the same directory as a previous version of Notes, the personal Name & Address Book (in Notes R3 format) is automatically upgraded to a Personal Address Book in R4 format, and the outgoing mailbox is automatically upgraded, because the template from which it inherits data is a new Notes R4 template with the same name. Notes R4 will not overwrite existing IDs or the existing DESKTOP.DSK file, and user-specific settings are maintained. If the users want the full features of the R4 desktop such as the use of more than six tabbed pages, they should compact the desktop. This is done from the Information tab in the Desktop Properties box.

Users could easily continue using Notes R4 as if nothing had happened. They can still access the same databases and authenticate with the same servers. The databases will look different and some new features might confuse users at first, but they will see no immediate change in functionality. A couple of quick pointers will help them on their way to productivity:

- Show them the R3 Menu Finder on the pull-down Help menu. This will help them locate familiar functions in the new environment.

- Show them how to resize the panels on the View screen so they can preview documents and quickly locate views and folders.

- Show them the User Preferences panel. Most of the user-setup functions from Notes R3 have been consolidated into this single screen. As soon as users are comfortable with the new environment, they will be seasoned Notes R4 users.

Upgrading Notes R3 Mail Databases to Notes R4

Mail databases should be upgraded after the user workstations have been upgraded. Notes R4 mail uses a new mail template, StdR4Mail(MAIL4.NSF), which has several new features outlined in Chapter 7, "Using Applications and Mail on Your Desktop."

There are two ways to upgrade mail. You can use a mail conversion utility from the Server console, or knowledgeable individual users can upgrade their own mail files.

Before converting mail files, be sure to inform the users that they should copy any customized mail forms, views, or macros (agents) to a temporary database, if they want to preserve these customizations.

To run the conversion utility on multiple files, do the following:

1. At the server console, enter the command `tell router quit`. This will ensure that all mail is held in the Outgoing Mailbox until the conversion process is completed.

2. Enter the command `load convert` with any of the following optional flags:

   `-l` creates a text file listing all primary mail databases (not replicas) on the server. Use the flag along with the name of the file you want to create. This argument should be run separately, not at the same time as you run the `-f` argument.

   `-f` updates only databases listed in a text file previously created with the `-l` flag. You must also include the name of the text file, such as `load convert -f filename.txt`.

   `-r` searches the specified directory and all of its subdirectories.

   `-i` lets you create more than 200 categories or folders in your Notes R4 mail database. Two hundred is normally the top limit for an R4 mail database, but the convert utility changes categories into folders and subfolders. Therefore, if you have more than 200 categories, they will all be converted to folders. Notes will prompt you to enter the `-i` argument if a database has more than 200 categories. In this case, users must use an R4 workstation to access their mail after conversion, because Notes R3 will not enable them to open their mail if it has more than 200 folders.

   `-d` replaces design templates with the new template you specify, but it does not create folders or add categorized documents to folders.

   `-n` lists databases that would be converted by conversion utility, but does not convert the databases.

The following command would convert all databases in the \MAIL subdirectory, replace the design template with MAIL4.NTF, create (and populate with documents) folders and subfolders from all categories and subcategories in the old database, and place uncategorized documents into an incoming mail folder:

```
load convert mail/*.nsf stdnotesmail mail4.ntf
```

Individual users can upgrade their own mail databases by replacing the design template of their database with the MAIL4.NTF template and then running the agent Convert Categories to Folders.

Upgrading Applications to Notes R4 and Creating New Applications in R4

After all of your servers and users are running Notes R4, you can begin converting databases (Notes applications) to R4 format, and once the conversion is complete, you can begin creating new databases in R4 format. You should begin by converting nonessential databases; then, when all of them are converted and you are familiar with the process, you can move your mission-critical databases to Notes R4.

There are three ways to convert a Notes database from R3 format to R4 format: compact the database, make a replica of the database in R4, or make a new copy of the database in R4. Each one converts the database to R4 file format.

To convert a database back to R3 format, make a copy of the database using an R3 client, make a replica of the database using the R3 client, or compact the database using an -r argument. Better yet, save a backup copy of the original database before you convert any databases to R4 in the first place.

After databases are in R4 format, you can enhance them with R4 design features and functionality, as described in Part III, "Developing Applications with Lotus Notes," or you can develop new applications from scratch or from database design templates in Notes R4.

Summary

Setting up a simple Notes network involves developing a naming scheme for your organization, registering and setting up one or more servers, and registering and setting up users. The process varies only slightly from setting up a Notes network in Notes R3.

If you are upgrading to Notes R4 from an existing Notes network, you should convert servers first, enabling users to access R3 databases on R4 servers while you convert user workstations. When all workstations are running Notes R4, you can convert user mail files, then begin the process of converting and enhancing production databases, and developing new Notes R4 databases from scratch.

Replication and Its Administration

by Don Child

IN THIS CHAPTER

Lotus Notes is all about communications: exchanging information, making it available when and where it is needed. The when and where are handled by two processes: replication and mail routing. Replication makes information available on multiple servers, so that members of a workgroup can share information and work on a local copy of the database, no matter where they are physically located. And mail routing makes sure that information is brought to the attention of users when they need that information.

The word *replicate* means "to make a copy," and a replica is a reproduction or a copy. But within Notes, the word is much more precise in its meaning, going beyond the idea of some sort of a copy of a database, and beyond the notion of the periodic synchronization of data across a network and between locations. Replication, along with the related concept of mail routing, is key to understanding how Notes works.

Replication makes it possible for users to work on a local copy of a Notes database no matter where they are located. On the other hand, if a database is used only in a single location, then only a single copy of the database is needed. Regardless of whether or not a database is replicated, a document can be edited by more than one user at a time. There is no file or document locking. Notes manages potential conflicts through field-level replication (new in Notes R4) and by saving both copies of the document when a conflict cannot be resolved.

There are several components of replication that work together to make Notes such a robust groupware platform. The key components include the Replica task on the Notes server, the Access Control Lists and other design elements within the Notes databases, and the Public Address Book that helps connect everything together.

Understanding Replication

Replication is the periodic synchronization of databases—not just any database, but a database specifically created as a replica database. Replication can be a scheduled event between two servers, or it can be initiated by the system administrator on either server. Replication can also take place between a workstation and a server, either as an event scheduled on the workstation or as an event initiated by the user from a workstation. A Notes server cannot initiate replication with a workstation, and workstations cannot communicate directly with each other (peer to peer).

Synchronization takes place at the field level in Notes R4, so after the initial replication when a replica copy of a database is first made, subsequent replication only needs to synchronize information in fields where data has been added or modified since the last successful replication. This makes replication between two databases very fast.

To understand how replication takes place, we will consider three things:

- How the Replica task on the Notes server works
- What gets replicated
- How replication is initiated

How the Replicator Task Works

Replica is the name of a task that runs on the server. When the server is started up, Replica is also started, and it remains idle until there is a scheduled replication or a replication is initiated from the server console or the Notes workspace. As soon as a replication is initiated, Replica wakes up and begins to replicate with another server.

Server-to-Server Replication

For now, assume that replication is taking place between two Notes servers: Server A and Server B. You are directly connected to Server A and initiate a replication with Server B, which could be in the next room, across town, in the next state, or on the other side of the world.

Server A can do any of the following:

- *Pull-pull replication:* Server A pulls changes from Server B, and it tells Server B's replicator to pull changes from Server A. The two processes can take place simultaneously.

- *Pull-push replication:* Server A can pull changes from Server B then push changes back to Server B. In this case, only Server A's replicator is involved in the process, and it writes information in the replica databases on both servers. All the burden is on Server A, which could be a specialized hub server that does nothing but replicate, so other servers in the organization can more efficiently support other Notes functions.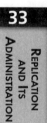

- *Push-only replication:* Server A pushes changes to Server B. Changes are not pulled or pushed back to Server A from Server B. This scenario is ideal for a hub-and-spoke server topology, where all changes are made centrally and are then replicated out to the spokes.

- *Pull-only replication:* Server A pulls changes from Server B. No changes are pulled by Server B or pushed by Server A back to Server B. This scheme lets all of the spoke servers do all of the work, while the hub server is left free to perform other tasks.

The new replicator Push function is only one of many improvements to the replicator function in Notes R4. For example, in Notes R3, the replicator was a single-threaded task, so a server's replicator could pull documents from only a single source at a time. Other servers requesting replication had to wait in a queue, which could hold up to five requests. With busy hub servers, requests would be dropped if the queue was already full. Notes R4 enables the system administrator to define additional replicator threads, so the number of simultaneous replications is now more likely to be limited by the bandwidth of the communications channel, rather than by any inherent limitation in the Notes Replicator. However, multiple replicators will place an additional processing burden on the Notes server, so the more replicators you have, the more slowing of processing speed you are likely to see on the server.

33

REPLICATION
AND ITS
ADMINISTRATION

The number of replicator tasks can be set in the new Server Configuration document, shown in Figure 33.1, or in the NOTES.INI for the server, or from the server console using the SET CONFIG command.

FIGURE **33.1.**

*Setting up multiple
replicators using the
Server Configuration
document.*

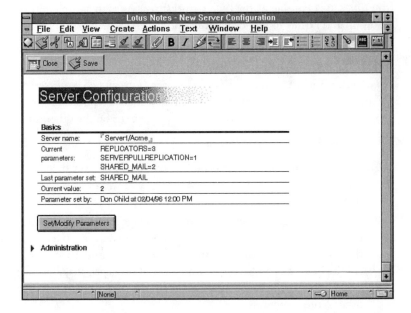

The Server Configuration document, new to Notes R4, makes it easy to manage configuration settings for a server. To display this document, open the Administration Control Panel (File | Tools | Server Administration…), select the server you want to configure, then click on Servers and select Configure Servers.

The Server Configuration Document shows all configuration settings for the selected server. To add a new configuration setting, click on Set new parameter. Notes will display a list of all server parameters that can be set by the administrator. Select REPLICATORS and set the value to the number of replicators you want to have available.

If you have already set a parameter and want to change it, click on Change existing parameter, highlight the parameter you want to change, and make your changes.

Workstation-to-Server Replication

The replication process between a workstation and server achieves the same results as in server-to-server replication, but there is one vital difference. The replicator on the server remains passive in workstation-to-server replication. Replication is initiated by the workstation, although the workstation has no Replicator task. The workstation does all of the work, copying changes from databases on the Notes server, and sending changes back to the server.

What Gets Replicated

Notes R4 is somewhat like those nested Russian dolls—you open one doll, and inside is another, and another, and another. Practically every element in Notes can be thought of as a container for an increasingly smaller object. The Notes kernel is the back end of Notes, and doesn't change. But the Notes User Interface, what you think of when you say that you have Notes on your computer, is the largest container.

Inside the Notes container are global elements—the workspace settings, user preferences, and the ever-important Public Address Book, which is the database that serves as a control center for the Notes organization and server-access settings. There are templates. Then there are all of the other databases.

Within each database there are many objects, but not necessarily just the user-created documents one would think of. There are other objects whose framework is hidden from the user, but these are elements that are nonetheless vital to the database. These include the access-control list (ACL), replication settings, and definitions for other database properties and design elements—including forms, views, subforms, Navigators, agents—each a specialized object. Within these objects, there is yet another level of properties, fields, and actions. And of course, within this framework, there are documents, defined as a related collection of data that fits into the fields on a form, and the properties of that data.

It would take too much time to copy all of this information every time replication occurs. Therefore, the replicator is very selective in the information it pulls from another database. Here is what happens when replication occurs between two Notes R4 servers using the Replicate command (pull-pull replication):

1. After one server calls the other to replicate, the two servers compare replica IDs on all databases to determine which ones they have in common (including database templates, which are specialized databases).

2. Databases are replicated in numerical, then alphabetical, order. The exception to this is the Public Address Book, replicated before all of the other databases are considered, because changes in the Public Address Book could affect what gets replicated, or even whether replication can take place. If the server-access fields or connection documents have been changed, it is possible that no further replication could occur.

3. For each database, design changes and database properties are pulled, including the access-control list from the database on the other server. The ACL is actually a design document, and is the first document pulled. If the ACL has changed on the other end, it could determine which documents can be pulled.

4. The replicator looks at the date and time of the last successful replication with this database, held in the Replication History window, which can be displayed from the Basics page of the Document Properties InfoBox. It compares this date to the

document-creation date for each document in the source database (the one being pulled *from*). If the document was created after the last successful replication, then it will be pulled.

5. If the document in the source database has been modified since the last successful replication, then there are several options related to field-level replication.

6. Each field in the document has a sequence number. If the field was modified since the last replication, then its sequence number is incremented by one. Notes compares the sequence number of each field in the source document with the sequence number in the same field in the target document. If a source field has a higher sequence number than the same field in the target document, then the contents of the field are pulled by the replicator and merged into the target document.

7. If the sequence numbers in a field in both databases are the same, the contents of the field are ignored.

8. If the field has been modified in both the source and target databases, the target-source document is pulled in as the main document, and the document from the target database is saved as a replication conflict. Both versions of the document are then available.

9. In the previous instance, the application developer can have Notes attempt to merge documents even if a potential conflict arises. This is done on a form-by-form basis. If two versions of the document were edited, they are merged as long as no fields conflict. The application developer also has the option to merge documents even though fields are in conflict, or to programmatically determine which of two conflicting fields should be saved. This is done by checking Merge Replication Conflicts at the bottom of the first page of the Form Properties InfoBox.

Notes has no file locking. Replication can take place even though users have documents open at the time of replication. Users will not even be aware that replication is taking place, unless they happen to notice some slowing in the processor speed, or the replication happens to be taking place between a database on their own workstation and the server. In that instance, they may notice system messages at the bottom of the screen, or be aware of a background task taking place on the workstation.

Replication History

Notes keeps track of the last time a Notes server successfully sent documents to each server with which it replicates, and the last time it received documents from other servers with which it replicates. For workstation-to-server replication, a history is maintained on the workstation for each server with which the workstation replicates. This history is used to determine what has changed, and therefore what should be replicated during the next replication event.

If you suspect that a database has become corrupted or you have been replicating selectively and now want to make sure you replicate all documents in a particular database, you can force Notes to do a full replication by clearing the replication history for the database. The replication history can be viewed by clicking on the Replication History button on the first page of the Database Properties InfoBox, or by pointing to the database icon and clicking the right mouse button, then selecting Replication History from the menu that is displayed.

Replicating Deleted Documents

Consider what happens when you delete a document. If you delete it in one database, then replicate with another database that still has that document, logic tells you that the document should get pulled back into the database, making it virtually impossible to get rid of a document unless it was simultaneously deleted on all replicas of the database. But that doesn't happen. Instead, here's what happens.

Notes creates what is called a deletion stub. The deletion stub retains the document ID number so other replicas will recognize that the document still exists. But they will also see that the document has been modified. Therefore, they will pull the deletion stub when they replicate, until all replicas of the database have the deletion stub instead of the document. The deletion stub can then be aged out of the database by setting a purge interval of something like 90 days (the default purge interval), long enough to ensure that the deletion stub has been replicated everywhere. If the purge interval is shorter than the replication cycle, purged documents can get copied back into the database, because the deletion stub is already purged.

CAUTION

The one caveat here is to teach people not to reactivate old replicas they have at home or on their laptops. If they haven't used a database for the last several months, have them delete the database and create a new replica. Then, when they replicate, they won't reintroduce documents to the database after the document stub has been deleted from all of the other replicas.

How Replica Databases Are Created

As already mentioned, databases must be replicas of each other before they can replicate. Being replicas of each other does not mean that the two databases are identical. It means that the two databases have the same Replica ID. Replica databases can be given different filenames, they can have different icons, and one can have only a subset of documents of the other, but they are still replicas as long as their Replica ID is identical. On the other hand, just because two databases have the same name and the same icon on different servers, they are not necessarily replicas of each other. The difference lies in how a database copy was created. Replica databases can be created in any of the following instances:

- One database was created using the command File | Replication | New Replica while the other database was selected on the desktop.

- Both of the databases are replicas of a common ancestor database; in other words, both are replicas created from a third database.

- Both of the databases were copied from the same install disk (or at least from two install disks that had identical files on them) during setup.

- One of the two databases was created by copying the other at the operating-system level, or both were copied from a common ancestor database at the operating-system level.

- A new replica of the Public Address Book gets created automatically when an additional server or workstation is set up on the network.

Consider what this means. If a database was created by selecting File | Database | New Copy from the pull-down menu, it is not a replica. It has a different Replica ID from the original database and cannot replicate with the original. From within Notes, the only way you can create a new replica is to add a database icon to your desktop, select that icon, then select File | Replication | New Replica.

You can tell if two databases are replicas of each other in a couple of ways. The first way is to look at their Replica IDs. The Replica ID is found on the Information page of the Database Properties InfoBox, and in the database catalog (CATALOG.NSF) on a Notes server. For the database selected in Figure 33.2, the Replica ID is 0A256296:006F7671.

FIGURE 33.2.

The Replica ID is found on the Information page of the Database Properties InfoBox.

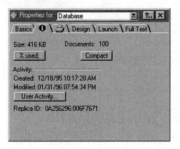

Every database has a Replica ID made up of two eight-character strings separated by a colon. If the Replica IDs for two databases match exactly, then they are replicas of each other. It does not matter what the databases are called. It does not matter that they might have a different subset of documents than another replica of the same database. It matters only that the Replica IDs are the same.

The other way to tell whether two databases are replicas is to place them both on your workspace, and select View | Stack Replica Icons. If the icons are stacked on top of each other (a small drop-down arrow will be displayed in the upper-right corner of the top icon), then they are replicas of each other. Sometimes you may have more than one replica of the same database on your desktop—for example, you may have a limited replica of a database that you use when you are on the road, and a complete replica of the same database for when you are working from home. This can be confusing, both to you and to Notes, so be sure you know which replica of the database is selected before you begin replication.

Databases cannot replicate until you have created a replica of the database. This is a task that only needs to be done once, before you replicate for the first time. Once the replica database has been created, keeping replica copies of the database synchronized is usually a matter of deciding how often to replicate, and establishing a schedule so the replication occurs automatically.

Selectively Replicating Database Elements

Now that you have determined which databases can be replicated, the next trick is to determine which elements of those databases you want to be replicated. Sometimes, a user does not want to replicate the entire database, but only a portion of it. Consider the mobile user connecting to the server via a long-distance phone call over a 9600 baud modem. They only want to replicate the information that is likely to be relevant to them, and, if possible, they would like to screen out the rest of the database.

There is a lot of flexibility in determining which parts of a database get replicated and which don't. For example, you can replicate selected documents or parts of documents. You can select the documents by formula, by view or category, or by date. You can replicate specific design elements. All of these selections are made from a single Replication Settings dialog box, displayed by highlighting the database and selecting File | Replication | Settings…. The first page of this dialog box, the Space Savers page, is illustrated in Figure 33.3.

FIGURE 33.3.

The Space Savers page in the Replication Settings dialog box.

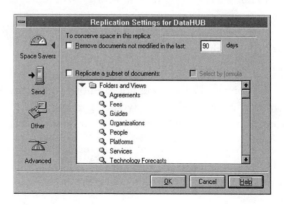

All of the selections on this page can be used to save space in the local replica of the selected database. The selections include:

- *Remove documents not modified in the last ninety (90) days.* If you select this, then replication will completely remove a document from the local replica if it was not modified in the number of days specified. This gets rid of older documents. As long as the documents still exist in another replica copy of the database, you can later change this setting and get the old documents back from the other replica.

- *Replicate a subset of documents.* If you select this, you can click on a view or folder, and only the documents in that view or folder will be replicated.

- *Select by formula.* You can select by formula only if you first click on Replicate a subset of documents. A formula screen will be displayed, and you can enter a selection formula in one of these formats:

  SELECT Author = *@UserName*, where *@UserName* returns the name of the current user

  or

  SELECT Form = "*formname*", where *formname* is the name of any form in the database.

  You can create formulas to select documents based on the content of any field, so long as the field is not a Computed for Display field, or a Rich Text field.

On the second page of the Replication Settings dialog box, you can specify what does *not* get sent from your local replica to the replica on the server.

If you elect to not send deletions made in this replica to other replicas, then you can safely delete documents locally, and not worry about the deletions being copied to other replicas throughout your organization.

If you elect to not send changes in database title and catalog information to other replicas of the database, you can change the title of your own local database or Database Catalog settings without affecting other replicas of the same database.

If you elect to not send changes in local security to other replicas, you can safely make changes to the local-access control without affecting other replicas of the same database. This is important if you want to enforce local security, but do not want to replicate your ACL changes to the server-based copy of the database.

On the third page of the Replication Settings dialog box, marked Other, you can disable replication of this copy of the database. For example, you might be making design changes on a replica that is sitting on one Notes server, and you want to ensure that the changes do not get replicated to replicas on other servers until your design changes have been thoroughly tested.

You can determine the replication priority of the database. Different replication schedules can be set up for databases based on their priorities. For example, you might want to replicate a high-priority database every two hours, whereas low-priority databases need to be replicated only once a week.

You can establish a cutoff date, and receive documents that were created or modified only after the cutoff date.

If you publish the database on a CD-ROM, you can specify the publication date. The database can then be published on that date. Users can make a copy of the database from the CD, and then they need to replicate only documents created or modified since that date.

The fourth page of the Replication Settings dialog box, labeled Advanced, lets a system administrator create selective replication settings for other servers from a central location. The Advanced page, which is used to administer replication settings from a central location, is shown in Figure 33.4.

Figure 33.4.

The Advanced page of the Replication Settings dialog box.

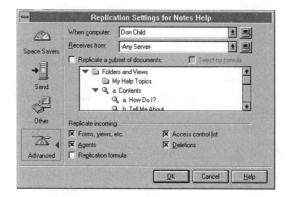

On this page of the Replication Settings dialog box, the administrator can specify selective replication settings between any two Notes servers in the Domain, or specify which server the local server should receive documents from.

You can also specify which database elements can be received from other databases during replication, including whether to accept incoming deletions from other databases.

The Role of the Access-Control List in Replication

Most people familiar with Notes are aware of how the access-control list (ACL) affects what a user can do in a database. Anyone with at least Reader access can read documents in a database. Users with Author access or higher can create documents, and can edit documents they have created. Editors or higher can modify any document in the database. Designers can make design changes to the database, and only Managers can make changes to the ACL. These settings are generally true, but there are options that can be set; for example in some instances authors cannot create documents, but they can edit documents for which they have been denoted as authors.

Servers are also included in ACLs. The server can be considered an agent for the user, an agent that goes out and retrieves data, creates documents, modifies documents created by the user.... Basically, the server can do anything the user can do, depending on how the ACL is set up.

Let's look at Server A and Server B again. The ACL on Server A lists Server B as a Reader. What can Server B do when replicating a database on Server A? Server B can read documents (in other words, can pull documents or accept documents that are pushed by Server A), but cannot send any new documents or modifications to Server A.

If Server B were an Author in Server A's ACL, then Server B could send new documents to Server A, and it could send modifications to documents that were originally created on Server B.

If an administrator on Server B wants to make changes to the ACL on a database that is being replicated to Server A, then Server B must be listed as a Manager in the ACL of that database.

Think of Notes servers as if they were people. If you want someone to act as a courier and deliver a message to someone you trust, then you have to trust the courier as well. If the courier cannot be trusted to carry the message, then the person on the other end will not receive the message. Likewise, if a Notes server does not have sufficient access privileges, then the local database manager will not be able to receive messages.

As a rule of thumb, always list internal servers (servers in a group known as LocalDomainServers, included by default in all database ACLs) as Managers in the ACL, and you will have no problems. If replication is scheduled serially, from Server A to Server B, then from Server B to Server C, Server C is limited by what Server B can do on Server A. Therefore, try to give all intermediary servers manager access unless there is an overriding reason not to. And with external servers (servers in a group known as OtherDomainServers, included by default in all database ACLs), you can limit their access using the ACL, if there is a reason to give them access to your servers.

Initiating Replication

Replication between servers is usually a scheduled event, set up in a Connection document in the Public Address Book. A schedule is devised to ensure that information is available to users when and where it is needed.

Replication between a workstation and a server can also be initiated with a scheduled call from a Location document or from the Replicator page.

Replication can be initiated manually by entering a command at the server console, from stacked icons on the workspace page, or by selecting File | Replication | Replicate.

Overall, there are a lot of options, but they boil down to three: scheduling a replication, initiating a replication with a console command, and initiating replication from the desktop.

Scheduling Replication from a Server

Scheduled replication from a server is initiated from a Server Connection document in the Public Address Book, with Replication selected as the task. In this document, you indicate the full name of the server doing the calling and the server to call during replication.

The Server Connection document, shown in Figure 33.5, has a couple of vital bits of information in it. At the top of the document is a definition of the connection type, and a definition of which server is the calling server and which is the server being called, along with the information necessary to make the connection between the two servers.

FIGURE 33.5.

The Server Connection document, used for scheduling replication and mail routing.

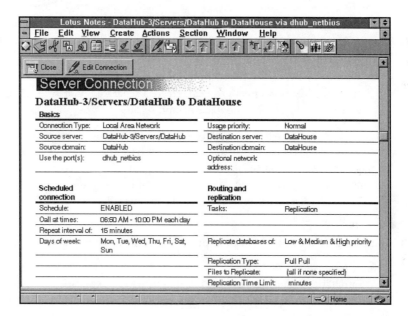

Beneath that is the scheduling section, which is the one you are interested in. This section has two parts to it: the schedule, and what gets done after the connection is made.

The schedule portion of the document includes the following fields:

- *Schedule:* Select Enabled to enable automatic replication.
- *Call at times:* You can enter one of the following:

    A specific time to call, such as 8:00 a.m. If the call is unsuccessful, Notes will keep trying at random and progressively longer intervals for one hour, then will quit trying.

    Multiple times to call, such as 8 a.m., 11 a.m., 2 p.m., and 5 p.m.. This is the same as when you enter a specific time, but there are multiple specific times.

    A time range during which Notes should continue to make connections based on the length of the repeat interval.

■ *Repeat interval of:* How long in minutes Notes should wait before replicating again after the completion of the last successful replication. This is used in combination with the Call at times field. For example, a repeat interval of 180 means that Notes will start trying to replicate exactly 180 minutes after the last successful replication ended. If the last replication started at 8 a.m. and ended at 8:06 a.m., Notes will start trying to replicate again at 11:06 a.m.

You can also enter a repeat interval of 0 (zero) in conjunction with a time range. Notes will start trying to connect with the other server at the beginning of the time range, and will keep trying throughout the time range until a replication is successfully completed. If a connection cannot be made immediately, Notes uses a randomized, exponential backoff algorithm to determine how soon to try again, until a successful connection is made. After a replication is successfully completed, Notes will stop trying until the beginning of the next time range.

■ *Days of the week:* The first three characters of the days of the week when this replication schedule is in effect. You can create a separate replication schedule for weekends, another for low-priority databases, and so on.

The other noteworthy part of the Server Connection document is the Routing and Replication section. In this part of the document, you have the option of setting up a document for Replication or for various sorts of Mail Routing, or for both replication and routing using the schedule you have just defined. If you select Mail Routing as one of the scheduled tasks, additional fields are displayed, so to avoid confusion we will discuss Mail Routing as a separate issue later in this chapter.

You have the following replication options for scheduled replication:

■ *Replicate databases of (high, medium, low) priority:* This lets you specify which priorities of databases you want to be replicated using this replication schedule. For example, you could set up three different replication schedules that would replicate high-priority databases once an hour, medium-priority databases once a day, and low-priority databases once a week. Each schedule would require a separate Connection document.

■ *Replication type:* You can set up replication using this schedule as Pull-Pull, Pull-Push, Pull-Only, or Push-Only.

■ *Files to replicate:* You can specify databases that are to be replicated using this schedule. Enter the exact filename for databases you want to replicate—for example, NAMES.NSF. Databases will be replicated in the order you specify. If you leave the field blank, all databases that have a replica on the other server will be replicated, assuming they haven't been screened out by the priority setting. All databases will be replicated in numeric, then alphabetical, order if specific databases are not selected. On the server that initiates the replication, Notes looks at the Replica ID for the specified database, and looks for a database with the same Replica ID on the other server. In other words, it doesn't matter if the filename of the database is different on the other server. The ability to specify which databases to replicate during a scheduled replication is new to Notes R4.

■ *Replication time limit:* You can specify a maximum replication time. If the time limit is reached, replication will stop. If you use this setting, you should be sure to select the most important databases to replicate first.

If you do not schedule replication, and do not force replication from the console or from the desktop, replication will never take place. Replication is not automatic.

Initiating Replication with a Console Command

As long as you have a way to connect to another server and you are authorized to do so, you can initiate replication between replica copies of a database using a console command. You can do this either from the server's text interface, or by displaying the console from the Administration Control panel. Because security dictates that Notes system administrators should use the workstation console rather than accessing the server directly, this section will illustrate the issuing of replication commands from the console on the workstation, shown in Figure 33.6.

Figure 33.6.

Initiating replication from a Remote Server Console.

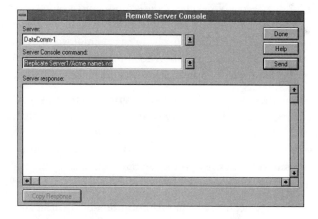

To enter a console command from a workstation:

1. Display the Administration Control Panel by selecting File | Tools | Server Administration....

2. Click on the Console icon to display the Remote Server Console dialog box.

3. Select the name of the server where you want to issue the replication command.

4. Enter the replication command in the Server console command field.

5. The server will initiate replication with the source server you have identified in the console command.

The Server response field will inform you when the command is sent, but for the most part, there is no active server response to be seen when you send a replication command from the remote server console. If the command was valid, the replication will take place as specified (assuming a successful connection was made and the targeted databases exist on the server you specified).

Server console commands consist of the replication command, the name of the server you want to replicate with, and, optionally, the names of any specific databases you want to replicate. Valid replication commands include Replicate (Pull-Pull replication), Pull, or Push. For example:

- `Replicate Server1/Acme` will do a full two-way replication with Server1/Acme.
- `Pull Server1/Acme names.nsf` will pull changes to the Public Address Book on Server1/Acme, but no other replication will occur.
- `Push Server1/Acme *.nsf` will send all changes in all replica databases from the initiating server to Server1/Acme, but no modifications will be pulled from Server1/Acme, and no modifications to Notes template files (*.ntf) will be sent.

Scheduling Replication from a Workstation

Replication between a Notes client workstation and a Notes server can be initiated only from the workstation. Scheduling the replication is similar to scheduling replication between servers, except that the replication schedule is maintained in Location documents on the workstation. There is a Server Connection document in the personal Address Book on the workstation, but it is used only to provide specific information for connecting with a server.

Because you can have several different Location documents, you can create replication schedules that are specific to the needs of each location. For example, you might want to replicate a number of databases to your Home location if you regularly telecommute from home. If you are traveling with a laptop computer, you will probably want to replicate only databases that you know you will need while you are on the road. When you switch to a different location from the status bar, you will automatically activate the replication schedule for that location.

The replication-schedule portion of a Location document is shown in Figure 33.7.

The fields are the same as the scheduling portion of the Server Connection document on the Notes server, shown previously in Figure 33.5. However, there are no options on the Location document to select which databases will be replicated. Instead, this is done from the Replicator page on the Notes desktop.

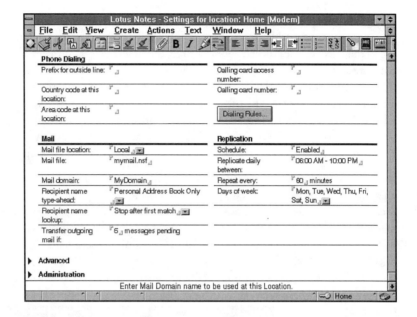

FIGURE 33.7.

Location document showing a replication schedule between the workstation and a server.

Initiating Replication from the Desktop

The last page on the workspace desktop is the Replicator page, which provides a centralized place to manage replication from a workstation. The Replicator page provides a graphical way to manage replication on the Notes workstation from a single screen, with each replica database potentially residing different servers. Replication takes place in the background, so you can continue working while replication occurs. To enable background replication, you have to run the DOS program SHARE.EXE from a DOS prompt before starting Windows. You can do this automatically by adding the following line to your AUTOEXEC.BAT file:

```
LOADHIGH C:\DOS\SHARE
```

With background replication enabled, you can continue working in Notes while replication takes place. If you elect to replicate a database using one-time options (for example, by highlighting the database icon and selecting File | Replication | Replicate, then selecting Replicate with options), the replication takes place in the foreground, and you must wait for the replication to finish before you can resume working.

Depending on the type of location you have set up, the basic elements of the Replicator page may vary slightly. For example, if you have a location record that gives you a remote network connection over TCP/IP, you would not need an option to automatically hang up the phone as you would with a modem connection. But whatever your location setup, you will have options to enable scheduled replication, to send mail, to replicate templates, and to replicate any databases that have a replica copy on the desktop.

The Replicator page shown in Figure 33.8 is for a TCP/IP connection. Each of the horizontal rows represents a possible action during replication. You can turn the action on or off by clicking in the checkbox on the left. For example, the first row is used to enable a replication schedule. The second row sends any mail that is held in the store/forward mailbox at the same time that a connection is made for replication. The third and fourth rows are databases that will replicate with the server. The fifth row will replicate template files that have been modified or added. And the last row is a database that is currently being replicated. When a replication event is in progress, a pointer icon indicates the database that is currently being replicated, and the status of the current database replication is illustrated at the bottom of the screen.

In Figure 33.8, Notes has estimated that the initial replication of HUBNAMES.NSF will take an additional 15 minutes to complete, based on the documents it has pulled so far and the total number of documents that remain to be pulled. However, Notes constantly recalculates as more documents are pulled in. In the replication illustrated, the actual replication took only an additional six minutes because most of the remaining documents were small ones. After the initial replication, regular replications are likely to take considerably less time; you are replicating only fields that have been modified and new documents that have been added.

FIGURE 33.8.

The Replicator Page, used to manage replication on the desktop.

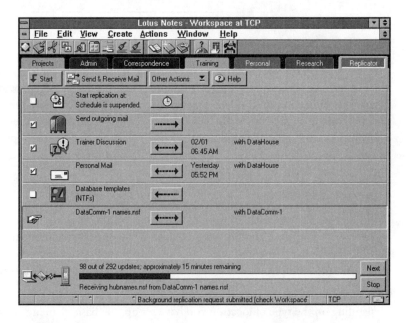

Notice that each row on the Replicator page has a checkbox, an icon, text, and a button. To the right of the button is more text, reporting on the status of the last replication. If you want a row to be a part of the next replication, make sure it is checked. Only checked rows are considered during replication.

The buttons on each row can be used to tailor the replication action on that particular row. For example, if you click on the button with the clock icon on the line that is labeled

"Start replication at," Notes will open up the current Location document so you can set up a replication schedule for that particular location. If you click on the button for a database, you can determine which server you prefer to look on for a replica of the database, whether to send documents, and whether to replicate full documents or only a summary and up to 40KB of text.

The database icons on the replicator page can be placed there in a couple of ways. If you manually replicate a database, either by selecting Replicate from the drop-down menu displayed by clicking on the arrowhead on a stacked icon, or by highlighting the database and selecting File | Replication | Replicate, then the icon will be placed on the Replicator page automatically. Or you can drag a database icon and drop in on the tab for the Replicator page. The original icon remains on the workspace page where you found it, and a row gets added to the replicator page for that database.

You can specify the order in which databases get replicated by pointing to a row and dragging it to a new location in the replication process. For example, in Figure 33.8, you might want to have your personal mail replicated before you send your outgoing mail. Highlight the Personal Mail row and drag it upwards, dropping it above Send Outgoing Mail. Then, if you should happen to lose your remote connection, at least you are likely to get your high-priority databases replicated.

If you want to remove a row from the Replicator page, highlight the row and press the Delete key. Notes will remove the database from the Replicator page. This does not affect the database icon on other workspace pages. You cannot remove the Start Replication at entry, the Outgoing mail entry, or the Templates entry, although you can uncheck these to make them inactive. If you delete entries such as Hang up from your Replicator page, you can add them back by selecting them from the Create menu.

Other options can be initiated from the Action buttons at the top of the Replicator page, from the Action menu, or by clicking the right mouse button. The buttons on the Action bar have the following effects:

- *Start:* Initiates replication. You can initiate replication manually at any time, whether or not you have set up a replication schedule.

- *Send and Receive Mail:* Routes mail that is held in your outgoing mailbox to the server, and retrieves any new mail from the inbox in your server-based mail file. No replication takes place. Mail routing is a completely different task within Notes, but the two tasks share enough functionality in common that they have been grouped together on the Replicator page, and on Connection documents.

- *Other Actions:* Lets you replicate all of your high-priority databases, replicate with a specific server, replicate only the database you have selected on the Replicator page, or send outgoing mail without replicating or receiving incoming mail.

All of these options on the Replicator page make the management of replica databases much simpler in Notes R4.

Managing Notes Mail

Notes Mail complements replication as a way to deliver information to users in a timely manner. Notes Mail uses the Public Address Book and a Mail Router process to deliver documents to user mailboxes and to databases that have been mail-enabled. The router can also deliver mail via gateways to routers in other Notes domains, and to other mail systems. As mentioned previously, the router process is distinct from the Replicator task, but shares enough functionality with the replicator that it is worth covering in conjunction with replication.

From the user's perspective, the Mail Router works just like it did in Notes R3, but to the system administrator there are new features, such as the option to use shared mail using a single-copy object store (SCOS). With SCOS, users receive summary data including addressing fields and the contents of the Subject field, along with a link to the body of a message in the shared object store.

It is the administrator's job to ensure that mail gets routed to users, and to manage the SCOS database if one is used. Before thinking about how to administer routing and the object store database, though, it might help to understand how Notes Mail works.

Notes Mail is easy to understand if you think about the functioning of the Post Office. You write a letter and put it into the mailbox. It gets picked up by the mail carrier and deposited at the central Post Office, where it is sorted according to which route the addressee lives on. If the mail is local, it gets sent out immediately (ideally) on the carrier's route, and put into the addressee's mailbox. If the addressee lives in another neighborhood, the letter goes into a bin. As soon as the bin is full (or sooner, if a truck is going that way), the mail is delivered to a branch office nearer to the addressee and is then delivered to the addressee's mailbox. On the other hand, if the addressee lives out of town, the mail goes to the airport and is sent to a Post Office in another town, where the local Post Office looks at the address, determines the route, and delivers the mail.

With Notes Mail, a task called the Mailer (running on a local workstation) looks up the addressee's name and address in the Personal or Public Address Book, or both, to see the user's name is valid, then puts the mail message into a database on the Notes server called MAIL.BOX.

The Mail Router then takes over. The Mail Router determines where the addressee's home server is located (the Notes server on which their mail database is stored) by looking at their Person document in the Public Address Book. The Router then puts the message into the user's mail database if the database is on the local server, or places it in the MAIL.BOX database on a server elsewhere in the same Notes Named Network, for the other server's Mail Router to deliver.

If the user's mail database is in another Notes Named Network, the Mail Router looks for a Server Connection document to determine how and when to route the mail. If there are multiple Connection documents, the least expensive and most direct route to the other server is used (in order of precedence, Notes routes via the local area network, a remote LAN service, a dial-up modem, and a passthru server).

If the addressee is in another Notes domain, the Mail Router has no way to verify the user's address in the Public Address Book. Therefore, the mail is routed to a MAIL.BOX file in the other domain using Connection documents and if necessary, gateways. At the other end, the router from the other domain picks up the message and delivers it.

To reiterate, this is the same process as with the regular U.S. Postal Service; only the names have been changed. The mail gets picked up from the mailbox by the carrier (the Router), who takes the mail to the Post Office. The mail is then rerouted for local delivery, or forwarded to another Post Office, where the address is verified, and the mail sorted and delivered.

Setting Up Mail Routing

The Mail Router sends mail to another location if the addressee's mail database is not on the local Notes server. Mail Routing is a one-way task, so there has to be a Server Connection document in each direction to ensure that mail gets delivered throughout an organization. With replication, only a single Server Connection document was required, because the Replicator could push documents to another server, but it could also pull documents from the other server. Since it was a two-way process, only one Server Connection was needed for replication connections.

Mail routing is dependent on the definition of a user's home server in the Public Address Book. The router looks in the user's Person document for information in five specific fields:

- *Mail System:* By default, it is Notes Mail, but you can also use Notes with cc:Mail, MS/Mail, or any VIM mail system.
- *Domain:* The domain in which a user is registered. If the domain is not the same as the domain for the Router, then the user is addressed as *username@domain*. The Router will assume the address is correct if it sees the @ symbol, since it cannot verify the address in its own domain's Public Address Book.
- *Mail server:* The server on which the user's personal mail database is stored.
- *Mail file:* The path and filename of the user's mail database file. Mail files are stored, by default, in a Mail subdirectory beneath the Notes data directory.
- *Forwarding address:* If the user is using a mail system other than Notes Mail, enter his full mail address in this field so the router can forward his mail to him.

If there is no mail-addressing information in a user's Person record in the Public Address Book, then they have to be addressed explicitly when mail is addressed to them.

A person does not have to be registered as a user in your organization to have a Person document. Users can create Person records in Personal Address Book, or names can be created in the Public Address Book solely for the purpose of mail routing.

Within a Notes Named Network (a group of Notes servers that are constantly connected and share the same communications protocol), Server Connection documents are not needed for mail routing to work. If a server is in another domain, or in a Notes network in the same domain but with no connection through a passthru or dual-protocol server, then a Server Connection document is needed to tell the router how to find the other server.

You can use the same Server Connection document that was used to schedule replication, but you may want to set up additional Server Connection documents so that mail routing takes place more often than replication. If you select Mail Routing as a task in the Routing and Replication section of the connection document, two additional fields are displayed.

- ■ *Route at once if:* lets you set a threshold for routing. For example, if the threshold is 5, then as soon as there are five messages in the outgoing mailbox, a connection will be made to route mail to the other Notes server, even if it is not yet time for a scheduled mail-routing connection.

- ■ *Routing cost* lets you enter a number (1-10) so you can prioritize which connection will be used to route mail. If a connection is over a local area network, there are no associated communication costs, so it has a cost of 1, which is the lowest cost. If you want a connection to be used only as a last resort, give it a routing cost of 10. The default for a remote connection via modem is 5.

The terms used in this discussion can be confusing to the Notes neophyte. Refer to Chapter 32, "Initial Installation," for a more detailed discussion of some of the terminology used. Also, refer to the Notes R4 Administrator's Guide, and Notes R4's online help for additional details.

Using a Shared-Mail Database

 By default, if mail documents are sent to groups of users, then each user has a copy of the same document stored in his or her personal mail file. This can eventually lead to storage problems as mail databases expand. To overcome this problem, Notes R4 lets the system administrator set up shared mail using a single copy object store (SCOS), which is a specialized database that holds non-summary data (the body of a mail memo and any file attachments) for all messages received by more than one user.

When the router receives a message addressed to more than one user on the same server, the message header (the To: and From: fields, and the Subject field) is placed in each user's mail file, along with a pointer to the object store. The body of the message is saved just once in the object store. When the user opens the memo from his or her desktop, Notes displays the header from the mail file and the non-summary data from the object store as a single message. The user is not even aware that the two parts of the document are stored in different places.

If a message is subsequently edited by a user, Notes places the entire message in his mail database and deletes any pointers to the original message.

Notes keeps track of how many users still have a header pointing to a particular object in the object store. When all users have deleted from their mail databases the header for a particular memo and there are no more pointers to the object store, there is no longer a need to keep the non-summary portion of the memo. A server task, Collect, runs automatically at 2 a.m. by default. This task deletes unused messages in the object store, deletes all links, and compacts the database to reclaim the unused space.

Security Considerations

A user's e-mail is confidential, protected by many of the same guarantees of privacy as a letter sent through the postal service (although there are legal precedents that indicate that the company owns your mail and everything in it). By default, the security for the user's mail file makes each user the manager of his own database, and no one else has access. However, the information in the object store is shared. To protect the confidentiality of the information in the object store, only the Notes router has access. No users can open the database, and the database does not show up in the database catalog, nor is it listed when the user selects File | Database | Open.

If a user encrypts incoming mail, the router encrypts incoming mail with the user's public key. Because others would not be able to read the encrypted, non-summary data, the object store will be bypassed for this user, and she will receive the entire memo in her mail file. On the other hand, if an encrypted message is sent to users, an encryption key is generated and included in the header portion of the message. The encrypted body of the message is stored in the object store in encrypted format, and the encryption key stored in the header is used to decrypt the body of the message when the user opens the mail memo.

Setting Up Shared Mail

If you are running a Notes R4 server and all of your users have Notes R4 client workstations, you can set up shared mail. You set up shared mail by issuing a server-console command to the router, which must be running. At the server console, type `Tell Router Use SHARED.NSF` where *SHARED.NSF* is the full name and path to the object store database you want to create.

The router will create the share mail database you have specified, along with another database called MAILOBJ.NSF, which goes into the Notes data directory. MAILOBJ.NSF is actually just a traffic director and keeps track of the links between the user mail files and the object store database.

After the object store database has been created, you may want to change the configuration for it. Select File | Tools | Server Administration... and from the Servers icon, select Configure Servers. The configuration for the Shared_Mail setting is given a default value of 2. This means that all mail is automatically placed into the object store, and users receive only header information, even if they are the only ones to receive the message. You might want to change the value of this setting to 1, which means that only shared messages are placed into the object store. A setting of 0 disables the object store. These settings can also be modified in the NOTES.INI file or by using a `Set Config` command at the server console.

When shared mail is set up, you can link existing mail files to the store. Otherwise, only new messages are placed in the store. To link a user's mail database to the shared-mail file, enter the server console command `Load Object Link` *USERMAIL.NSF SHARED.NSF* where *USERMAIL.NSF* is the name of the user's mail file and *SHARED.NSF* is the name of the object store database. You can enter a directory instead of a filename for *USERMAIL.NSF*, in which case all mail files in the directory would be linked. MAILOBJ.NSF keeps track of pointers, and if more than one user has the same memo, the non-summary portion of the memo will be put into the object store and only the header will be stored in the user's mail file. If a user has more than five documents that get linked, their mail database will be compacted automatically to reclaim unused space. You may want to link a few users at a time and monitor the growth of the shared mail file.

If the shared mail file grows too large, you can create another file by issuing the server console command `Load Object Create` *NEWOBJ.NSF* where *NEWOBJ.NSF* is the name of the new object store, then issue the command `Tell Router Use` *NEWOBJ.NSF*. MAILOBJ.NSF will still recognize older object-store databases. If you want to delete old object stores, there is a console command to unlink the old database and relink to the new one, after which the old database can be deleted. Refer to the Notes R4 Administrator's Guide that ships with Notes for details.

Moving and Unlinking User Mail Files

If you make a file copy of a user's mail database and place it on another server, the router can no longer resolve links to the shared-mail object store. Each mail file looks only at the object store on the home server, the server where the mail file is stored. All the user will see in a copy of the database is the summary data in the header of their mail messages.

The problem of moving a mail file is compounded if you delete the user's mail file from the original server, because deleting a mail file without unlinking it makes it so the object store database cannot be purged of the documents the user left behind.

To move a user's mail to another server if he is using shared mail, do the following:

1. Replicate (make a replica copy) of the user's mail database on the new server.
2. On the new server, issue the console command `Load Object Link` USERMAIL.NSF *NEWSHARED.NSF* where *NEWSHARED* is the name of the object store on the new server.
3. On the original server, issue the console command `Load Object Unlink` USERMAIL.NSF to delete pointers from MAILOBJ.NSF to the user's mail database.
4. Delete the user's mail database from the original server.

Collecting Garbage from the Object Store Database

The `Collect` server task, which by default runs at 2 a.m., purges unlinked messages from the object store. If users have deleted headers from their mail databases, MAILOBJ.NSF keeps track of how many other users are linked to the message. When there are no links remaining, the message gets purged. If you want to compact the database after obsolete messages have been purged, you have to use the `-COMPACT` option with `Collect`.

You can also run `Collect` manually from the server console on old object-store databases.

Shared Mail and Mobile Users

The shared mail database only works on a per-server basis, for mail databases that are stored on that server. Mobile users can still use shared mail, but only when they are accessing their mail directly from their home server.

If mobile users have a replica of their mail on their mobile or remote workstation, the entire message, summary information and the body, gets replicated to them, exactly as it did with earlier versions of Notes. If messages were copied from the server-based mail instead of being replicated, they would receive only summary information, and the pointers to the body of the messages would no longer function.

It is the same situation as when a mail database is moved to a new server. The database must be replicated, not copied. In other words, the new copy must be created using File | Replication | New Replica, or the mail database file must be copied at the operating system level. It cannot be created using File | Database | New Copy.

Summary

Information is distributed to Notes users through two separate processes—replication and mail routing—that share many of the same setup documents and fields for scheduling purposes.

Replication is the synchronization of two databases using the Notes server's Replica task for server-to-server replication, and a workstation task for workstation-to-server replication. Replication is not automatic. It must be initiated with a server console command, or scheduled using Server Connection documents in the Public Address Book. Replication between a workstation and a server can be scheduled using Location documents in the Personal Address Book on the workstation. Replication depends on the existence of replica copies of the same database. The replica copy must be created before replication can take place.

Mail routing is a separate task that is also scheduled in the Server Connection document in the Public Address Book. Mail routing is the same in Notes R4 as it was in Notes R3 from a user's perspective, but the system administrator has the additional option of setting up and managing shared mail to conserve disk space.

Security Overview

by Don Child

IN THIS CHAPTER

Most people are familiar with that shot from the TV sitcom *Get Smart*. Secret Agent Maxwell Smart walks down a long corridor blocked by numerous security doors, each one as heavy as the door to a bank vault. The doors magically swing open as he walks along, then slam behind him again as he exits at the end of the show. It makes a nice metaphor for Notes security, because there are a number of security doors that start by determining which users and other servers, if any, can talk to a Notes server. The security doors continue all the way down the long corridor to the individual field level. A user or another Notes server can be stopped at any one of those doors, and will not be allowed to progress any further. When properly enforced, Notes security is virtually unbreakable. The CIA has staked their own information security on that premise.

And with Notes R4, a couple of potential security risks in earlier versions of Notes have been answered. A person bent on defeating Notes security and stealing data from your Notes databases could make copies of databases using the operating system, if they could gain physical access to the Notes server. If they could get a copy of a database, they could open it locally on any Notes workstation. There was no access security on local databases. Notes R4 lets you enforce access security on all copies of a database, both locally and on the server.

If someone gets hold of a copy of a user ID and is able to guess the password, they have the full privileges of the user to whom the ID belongs. To access a Notes server and its databases, you must have a valid Notes user ID. If a user ID is left lying around on a diskette or on the hard drive of an unattended workstation, then it is relatively easy to steal. But guessing or stealing a password has been made more difficult in Notes R4 in several ways.

When you type in the password for your user ID, Notes displays a random number of Xs to make it difficult for the casual observer to determine how many characters there are in the password. That has not changed. But now, Notes also displays a series of hieroglyphic symbols as you type your password. The glyphs change with each keystroke, beginning with the fifth keystroke. These hieroglyphics make it more difficult for a technically sophisticated password thief. It is possible to develop a program that mimics the password dialog box and captures the password for later use. But every password generates a different pattern of glyphs. To mimic the password dialog box, the techno-thief would have to develop a different program for every user in the organization to match the exact pattern of hieroglyphics associated with each password. The process of mimicking a dialog box like this is called *spoofing*. Notes R4 has installed antispoofing.

In addition to the antispoofing hieroglyphics, Notes R4 makes it harder to try to guess a password. If a password is entered incorrectly, there is a timeout before you can try again. The timeout period gets longer in random intervals, hopefully frustrating the would-be password guesser. A third password-security feature is the ability to require multiple passwords for an ID.

 In Notes 4.5, additional password security has been added in the form of password expiration. The Notes Administrator can specify an expiration period or date for user ID files. If a password has expired, the user will be informed during authentication, and he will be required to select a new password before he can access the server. In addition, a list of previous passwords is maintained, and users can be prevented from reusing the previous *n* number of passwords.

An Overview of Notes Security

Two potential security weaknesses have been closed. But before looking more closely at passwords and IDs, let's step back and take a look at the overall security structure of Notes.

There are several levels at which security can be enforced, and at some levels, there is more than one type of security available to the Notes administrator or application developer. Each of the levels gets progressively more refined, moving from a macro level that entails the physical security of your network environment, right down to a highly granular level of security, a single field on a single Notes document.

Think of security as if you were building a pyramid. (See Figure 34.1.) The base level of security entails protecting the physical and logical access to the Notes server and the Notes network. As you move up the pyramid after you have a physically and logically secure network, you control access to the Notes server, then access to the database, access to the forms and views within the database, access to specific documents, access to sections within the document, and finally, you can control access to the fields within a document. At some of these levels there may be multiple security options, and in some instances, such as View access or Section access, what appears to be security feature is more accurately a way to enhance the usability of the database.

FIGURE 34.1.
*Levels of Notes security
defined as a pyramid.*

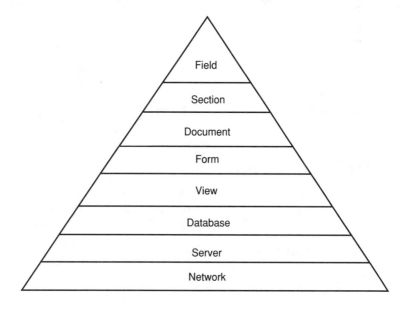

Network Physical and Logical Security

Network security includes the physical security of the Notes server. The Notes server should be located in an area where casual users cannot physically access it. As mentioned previously, you can locally encrypt databases and enforce access control locally, and you can protect ID files with multiple passwords, but physical-access security is still vitally important.

For Notes R4, you might also want to consider a couple of other, less obvious logical access-security issues. Notes R4's InterNotes products, the InterNotes Web Browser and the InterNotes Web Publisher, make Notes an ideal tool for Internet as well as intranet applications. But you will want to create a firewall, for example, by creating a Notes server specifically for handling all external communications, and ensure that you know what you are doing before you open your databases to the Internet.

Also, make sure that your users understand the need to physically secure their workstations. Notes provides the means to locally encrypt databases, and users should know the importance of protecting passwords. But even so, you will find user IDs on hard drives and diskettes, passwords pinned to the wall in too many cubicles, and databases that are not locally secured.

TIP

For the security of your Notes network, have in place a plan to ensure each of the following:

- Keep a backup of all your vital files.
- Do not rely solely on replication to another Notes server as a form of backup.
- Keep your Notes servers in a locked area that is accessible only to authorized personnel.
- Keep your Notes certifier IDs safe in a secure location.
- Do not leave Notes workstations logged in and running if they are in a publicly accessible area.

Notes Server Security

When a Notes server is first set up, Notes generates ID files that are used for security purposes. Those ID files are one of the primary focuses of this chapter because they are the cornerstone of Notes security. The ID files used with Notes include the following:

- The server ID, which gives each server its own unique identity.
- The administrator ID, which is a user ID that provides administrative access to the server before any other user IDs have been set up.

■ The certifier ID, which is used to register additional servers, organization certifiers, and users within the Notes organization.

■ The user ID, which is issued to each user in the Notes organization.

In the Public Address Book, Notes maintains a list of which user and server IDs are allowed to access a particular server. The use of these IDs in authentication and Notes server security is discussed in detail later in this chapter.

Database Security

Assuming you have gained access to Notes databases, you need to be aware of security at the database level. Databases can be secured in the following ways:

■ **Local encryption.** You can select simple, medium, or strong encryption from the Database Properties dialog box, or when you first create a database, to encrypt a database. To access an encrypted database, you must have the user ID that was used to encrypt the database in the first place. Since your user ID should be password protected, you would need both a user ID and a password to access an encrypted database. This is an excellent way to protect a database on a laptop computer.

■ **Access control list security.** Every database has an Access Control List (ACL) that defines which privileges users and servers have in the database. Although the ACL is usually thought of in terms of databases on Notes servers, Notes R4 provides a means to enforce ACL security on all replicas of a database, no matter whether the replica is on a Notes server or on a local workstation. The database manager (for instance, the person with Manager access in the ACL) can cause local ACL security to be enforced on all replicas of the database by placing a checkmark next to "Enforce a consistent Access Control List across all replicas of this database" on the Advanced page of the Access Control... dialog box.

Design and Document Security

The remaining security features are concerned with the design of the Notes database, and are generally refinements of access security. Not all of these features are true security measures, but each contributes to security in its own way. Among other things, they include the ability to lock the design of an entire database; the ability to determine who can use certain forms, and under what conditions; the ability to restrict the use of certain views; the ability to determine who can create or modify which fields on a document; the ability to restrict access to a section within a document; and the ability to hide a field under certain conditions, and for certain users. These features are the top part of the Notes security pyramid illustrated earlier in Figure 34.1. The use of these features is described in detail in chapters dealing with database design.

One other aspect of Notes security, encryption, is described later in this chapter.

34

SECURITY
OVERVIEW

The Place of Notes IDs in Security

Despite the layer upon layer of security features, the security that really counts within Notes is the interaction of the various Notes ID files with one another, and the interaction of the server and user ID files with ACLs. The remainder of this chapter looks at that interaction in greater detail.

Notes IDs

There are four types of ID files involved in security:

- The certifier ID, created when the first server is set up, provides a unique identity to every server and every user in a Notes organization. The certifier ID is used to create certificates that establish the authenticity of IDs for users and servers.

- The organizational unit (OU) certifier ID provides a way that your organization can expand its use of Notes. An OU certifier ID can be used to create new servers and users in your organization, delegating some administrative work. OU certifier IDs are hierarchical, so you will not find them in organizations that use a flat naming scheme.

- The server ID uniquely identifies a server within the organization. Each server has its own ID that contains certificates from the organization certifier ID or OU certifier ID used to create the server.

- The user ID uniquely identifies every Notes user in the organization. The user ID, like the server ID, holds hierarchical certificates. The User ID is used to authenticate with Notes servers, and to identify the user in various security roles such as database ACLs, server access lists, and in Reader and Author fields.

Server and User IDs

The server and user IDs are binary files that hold the name of the user or server, a Notes license number, a password (may be optional depending on how the administrator has defined the minimum password length on registration), a private key that is used to encrypt and decrypt data, and certificates that identify the server or user's place within the organizational hierarchy.

Think of the certificate as being like the official seal that is stamped onto your driver's license or passport. Because you recognize the authority that issued the driver's license, you accept the document as being valid. Without that authority, the document cannot be trusted. Likewise, when two IDs each have at least one certificate that they both recognize as valid, then the two IDs can potentially communicate with each other. There is no peer-to-peer communication between Notes users, so the previous sentence assumes that at least one of the IDs is a server ID.

Certifier and OU Certifier IDs

The certificates that are part of Notes security are created by a certifier ID. The certifier ID is central to Notes security, and it should be protected and kept secure. The certifier ID is the identity of your Notes organization, such that any user or server created using the certifier ID or any of its descendants is automatically trusted by all other servers and users in the organization. It may be a good idea to require multiple passwords to access the organizational certifier IDs and organizational unit (OU) certifier IDs, thereby ensuring that multiple administrative personnel are aware whenever the Notes certifier ID is being used.

The certifier ID is used to register new users and new servers, and to issue certificates that enable external organizations to communicate with you. If two server IDs or a user ID and a server ID have a certificate issued by the same certifier ID, then they can talk to each other.

When an OU certifier ID is used to issue a certificate, the certificate is hierarchical; that is, it contains a certificate from the organizational certifier ID plus certificates from any OUs higher up in the organization's hierarchy.

For example, the Sales OU certifier ID could be used to create a certificate for a new user, John Doe. John Doe's user name would identify the full hierarchy of certificates issued to him, in a format such as John Doe/Sales/Marketing/West/Acme, where Acme is the organizational certifier ID and West, Marketing and Sales are all OU certifier IDs. In this instance, Acme created the OU certifier ID West/Acme, which in turn created the OU certifier ID Marketing/West/Acme, which in turn created the OU certifier ID Sales/Marketing/West/Acme. A user can have up to four OU certificates in their hierarchical name.

The Role of Notes IDs in Protecting Server Access

When another server or a user attempts to initiate a dialog with a server, Notes validates the ID file, and then goes through a process known as *authentication*. The validation is a process of establishing trust. The server examines the ID of the server or user trying to establish a dialog, looking at the certificates. If the ID contains a certificate that has the same hierarchical ancestor ID as the server, then the ID can be trusted. If there is not a common ancestral ID, Notes will look at cross-certificates in the Public Address Book, and will trust the ID if there is a cross-certificate for the ID or any of its descendants.

When an ID is trusted by the server, the process known as authentication takes place. For example, Server1/Acme wants to authenticate the user John Smith/Acme before allowing John Smith access to the server. The dialog goes somewhat as follows:

> Server1/Acme: Here is my name and my public key. You can trust me, because I have an Acme certificate.

> John Smith/Acme: I have an Acme certificate too. Therefore, I trust you. Here is my name and my public key.

Server1/Acme: To make sure you aren't an impostor, let me give you a test. I'm thinking of a number between 1 and 10. I'll send you the number, and I challenge you to encrypt it with your private key.

John Smith/Acme: That's easy. I'll use my private key to encrypt the number. Now, here it is back.

Server1/Acme: Using your public key, I can see that you sent me back the same number, encrypted with my public key. Let's talk.

John Smith/Acme: Not so fast. I want to make sure you aren't an impostor. Now I'll send you a number.

The dialog is reversed until both IDs are satisfied with each other's identity, and communication is then fully established. The authentication remains in place as long as the session lasts, even when the user closes one database and opens another. But if the user or the other server logs off or changes IDs, the authentication is no longer valid, and server databases and server functions can no longer be accessed.

Cross-Certification

Every organization has its own certifier ID, and the organization certificate must be available as part of an ID before a user or another server can authenticate with any of the organization's servers. Within the organization, this does not present any problems; the organization certificate is part of every server ID and every user ID in the organization. But what about another organization that wants to communicate with you?

For example, the Acme Corporation is teaming up with a subcontractor, XYZ Corporation, on a project. They need to discuss project issues and share progress reports, e-mail, and so on. To communicate directly with Acme using Lotus Notes, XYZ needs a certificate that is recognized as valid by Acme, and Acme needs a certificate that is recognized as valid by XYZ.

In order to provide each other with valid certificates, they go through a process known as cross-certification if both organizations are using hierarchical naming. If either organization uses flat names, then flat certificates are exchanged to enable specific servers to communicate with each other. These two processes, cross-certification and exchanging flat certificates, are described next.

When you attempt to establish communication with a server in another organization, the first thing the server looks at are the certificates on your ID. If there are no certificates recognized as valid, Notes looks for a Cross-Certificate document. If there are no certificates or cross-certificates recognized by the server, you cannot authenticate, and therefore cannot access the server.

Cross-certification involves exchanging certificates between two organizations. You can cross-certify at the organizational level, at the organizational unit level, or at the user level. No matter which level you cross-certify at, both sides have to exchange certificates.

For example, suppose Jane Doe in the Sales Department at Acme has reason to access a server in the XYZ corporation. She sends a *safe copy* of her user ID to the Notes administrator of the XYZ organization, requesting cross-certification. The XYZ administrator certifies (using a certifier ID to create a certificate for) the safe ID. This creates a cross-certificate document in the XYZ Public Address Book, where the cross-certificate is stored. Meanwhile, XYZ has to be certified on the Acme side, so XYZ sends a safe copy of its organization certifier ID to Acme.

The organizational certifier or an OU certifier from Acme certifies the safe copy of the XYZ organizational certifier ID and stores it in a cross-certificate document in the Acme Public Address Book. Now each organization has a cross-certificate in their own Public Address Book. Jane Doe must also place a copy of the cross-certificate from XYZ in her Personal Address Book. When Jane Doe communicates with the XYZ server, the XYZ server looks in the XYZ Public Address Book and finds Jane Doe's cross-certificate, and therefore lets her continue with the authentication process.

In summary, the following cross-certificates are created during cross-certification so that a Notes user from XYZ can access a server in another organization (Acme):

- A safe copy of a user ID from XYZ is cross-certified by an Acme certifier ID and placed in the Acme Public Address Book as a cross-certificate.

- A safe copy of an Acme certifier ID is cross-certified by a certifier ID from XYZ and placed in the XYZ Public Address book.

- The user who needs to access an Acme server places a copy of the Acme cross-certificate (from the XYZ Public Address Book) into her Personal Address Book.

The safe ID used in the cross-certification process is not a complete ID. It contains just enough information to be able to collect certificates, but it is useless for any other purpose.

When a Notes server checks to see if another user or server ID is valid, it looks at the ID to see if it contains a certificate that can be trusted. Trust is established only if the other ID holds at least one certificate issued by a trusted certifier. Therefore, in the scenario described previously, Acme trusts Jane Doe because the Acme Public Address Book contains a safe copy of Jane Doe's ID, which has been cross-certified by an Acme certifier ID.

CAUTION

If you cross-certify at the Organization or Organization Unit level, you should use server-access restrictions to ensure that the other organization has access only to those servers you mean to let them access. If you want to access servers in another organization but do not want to allow them access, then make sure that you have restricted access to all servers in your organization. Note that if you cross-certify a specific user in another organization, all users in the other organization at that user's level or below can authenticate with your server.

How to Cross-Certify

How you cross-certify depends on the circumstances. There are four ways to cross-certify, all of them having the same goal—certifying a safe ID and placing it in a cross-certification document in the Public Address Book. The only difference lies in the mechanics. The four ways to cross-certify are described in the following four sections.

Using Notes Mail

1. Display the User ID dialog box by selecting File | Tools | User ID. Click on the Certificates icon and the Request Cross-certificate button.

2. Select the ID to be cross-certified. The ID must be a hierarchical ID.

3. The request is in the form of a mail memo. Address the request to the administrator in charge of certification in the other organization and send it.

4. The administrator in the other organization opens the request in her mail file, and from the Action menu selects Cross-certify Attached ID File, selects the certifier ID to use, and enters the password for the ID.

5. In the Subject Name field of the dialog box, the administrator enters the name of the certifier, user, or server being cross-certified. She can optionally change the default expiration date of the certificate, change to another certifier, or change the registration server (the server on which the cross-certificate will be created in the Public Address Book).

6. Click on Cross-certify to complete the process on this end. The same process must be repeated in the other direction before the complete cross-certification is effective.

Using the Postal Service

The first time two organizations exchange cross-certificates, they may not be able to communicate via computers until after cross-certificates have been exchanged. Therefore, they may need to use regular mail, as described here:

1. Display the Server Administration panel, and then select Administration | User ID.

2. Select the certifier ID or a safe ID certified by the certifier ID, and enter a password if necessary.

3. Select the More Options icon and click on the Create Safe Copy button. Name the safe ID something like ACMESAFE.ID and save it on a diskette. On a UNIX server, transfer the file to a diskette or through a utility such as FTP.

4. Send the safe copy of the ID to the administrator responsible for certification in the other organization. The administrator will repeat steps 4-6 in the Notes Mail cross-certification process.

Cross-Certifying by Phone

1. The administrator in charge of certification provides a public key for the ID that is to be certified. The public key for a user is stored in her Person document. It can be seen if you are in the edit mode. The public key is a lengthy number, but it can be read aloud over the phone and typed by someone on the other end.

2. A cross-certificate is generated in the Server Administration panel. Click on the Certifiers icon and select Cross-certify Key. Select the certifier ID and the registration server and click OK. If you want to store the cross-certificate in a Private Address Book, select Local as the registration server.

3. Enter the user, server, or certifier name associated with the ID you are certifying, and the public key of the ID. Both of these can be found in the User ID dialog box.

4. Repeat the process in the other direction.

Cross-Certifying on Demand

If a hierarchical user tries to access a hierarchical server in another organization and the user is not cross-certified, or if the hierarchical user tries to open signed mail and is not cross-certified, then Notes will prompt her, asking if she wants to cross-certify. She has the option of creating a cross-certificate for the root certifier of her organization, or declining to cross-certify, or of creating a cross-certificate for a certifier ID. She can then put the cross-certificate in the Public Address Book by selecting a registration server. Note that a user must have at least Editor access to the Public Address Book before she can do this.

How to Exchange Flat Certificates

Whenever possible, you should use hierarchical certification and communicate with other organizations through cross-certification. But there may be times when an organization with flat certification has to communicate with a hierarchically certified or flat certified organization. In this case, the two organizations must exchange safe server IDs, each of which is certified by the other organization, and then returned and merged into the regular server ID. To do this, the hierarchical organization must create a flat certifier to use in the process.

Safe IDs are created by selecting File | Tools | User ID from the server, ensuring that you are using the server ID. Click the More Options icon and select Create Safe ID. After the safe ID has been certified and returned, merge the certified safe ID back into the server ID from the same screen.

Because a certificate gives everyone from the other organization an open door into your Notes network, you should turn off Trust on certificates issued by certifiers outside your organization. With trust turned off, the other organization can communicate only with the particular server that has the certificate in its ID. This protects the rest of your organization from unauthorized intrusion by untrusted users.

Securing the Server Console with a Password

There is another aspect to server security that Notes administrators need to be aware of. On the Notes server, there are two icons for launching Notes. One icon launches the server process itself, and the other launches the Notes client workspace on the server. The administrator communicates with the Notes server process primarily by entering commands via a text-based console, or by using the same commands via a remote console from a Notes client, which can be the Notes client on either the server machine or a workstation. There is a special administrative window on the Notes R4 client that groups all administrative functions together, including certifying servers and users, and accessing the remote console function.

To prevent unauthorized individuals from using the server-console commands, the administrator can protect the console with a password. The Server document in the Public Address book already defines who has administrative rights, and can therefore use the remote-console function. But password protecting the console increases security, especially in the case where someone gains physical access to the server.

To secure the console, enter the following command:

```
SET SECURE password
```

where *password* is the password you want to use to secure the console. The console password does not have to be the same as the administrative password and, in fact, should not be the same.

The following commands cannot be used while the console is secured with a password:

```
LOAD
TELL
EXIT
QUIT
SET CONFIGURATION
```

To use these commands, you must remove console security by again entering SET SECURE *password*.

There is one small loophole here that can be sealed only by denying physical access to the Notes server. The password used to secure the console is stored as an environment variable in the NOTES.INI file. You can figure out what the password is by looking in the NOTES.INI file, or you can edit the file and delete the line that contains the console password. This is great for the forgetful system administrator, but does provide a back door for anyone attempting to gain direct-disk access to your server. In short, protect your server by securing the console, but do not turn around and hand out the key by allowing people physical access to your Notes server.

People Responsible for Notes Security

There are a number of individuals involved in Notes security at various levels, from the person who initially sets up the system to the individual who decides to encrypt an e-mail message. Some of the key security functions are described here, with a description of the person who performs that function.

At the most explicit level of security, as already mentioned, is the *individual user* who decides to encrypt a particular mail message, or a particular field within a message. The individual user plays another, more pivotal role, however—protecting her Notes user ID. The individual user should be taught that she must lock her ID out of the system whenever she gets up from her desk. If she leaves a workstation unattended without locking her ID (in other words, logs off Notes by pressing F5 or selects File | Tools | Lock ID), then anyone can access the server without having to locate a valid Notes ID and enter a password. It is as if she had installed new locks on her house, and then left the house without locking the door. She is the first line of defense when it comes to keeping intruders out of the Notes network.

The second line of defense is the *application developer*, the person who designs databases. The database is teaming with potential security features that the designer can choose to utilize or not. Some of these features include form and view formulas, enabling fields for encryption, hiding information under certain circumstances, creating sections that can be seen only by particular users, determining how users will enter data into fields, read and compose access, and so on. Not all of these are absolute security measures, but they do determine how easy it is to use the database and how much can be done by the casual user.

The other person involved in security at the database level is the *database manager*. Every database can have a different manager (the user with Manager access in the ACL). The manager is the one who determines which level of access individual users will have. If users have too high a level of access, the database is subject to misuse and could eventually become unwieldy from too many replicate-and-save conflicts, because there are too many people capable of editing the same documents.

At the system level, there is, in one sense, only one type of individual involved with Notes security—the *system administrator*. But this role can be broken down into two major divisions: the system administrator and the administration certifier, the person responsible for the certifier ID. Beyond that, there are specific administrative roles that can be delegated by the system administrator, roles that involve creating and editing a variety of documents in the Public Address Book.

34

SECURITY
OVERVIEW

The system administrator is the person or persons with Manager access to the Public Address Book. By default, the system administrator is the person who is named as administrator during the setup of the first server in the organization, although other users can later be assigned this role by the administrator. Common sense says that you should have more than one person capable of changing access privileges in the Public Address Book. If your lone system administrator gets hit by the proverbial bus on the way to work, you would have little choice but to break down your Notes network and set it up again from scratch, because nobody would be able to gain administrative access. If you had to set up the Notes organization a second time, you would probably be a little smarter, and assign a team of users to an administrative group.

Another administration role is that of *server administrator.* The server administrator can use the remote console to issue commands to the Notes server. Her Notes user name must be entered into the Administrators field on the server document, or she must belong to a group assigned the role of server administration.

A common approach to server administration is to create a group with a name something like ServerAdmin, and add to the group any users who should have administrative privileges on the organization's servers. Presumably, you would not add people to this group until they had been certified as system administrators or had at least taken system administration classes from a Certified Lotus Instructor (CLI). And then, you would want to trust them to use discretion when they make changes that can easily affect every user in the organization.

If you understand how a Notes network is set up and how servers and users are added to the Notes organization, then you realize the crucial role played by the *administration certifier.* This is the person responsible for the organization's certifier ID.

If the certifier ID falls into the wrong hands, you can no longer trust any of the users who access your servers. It cannot be overemphasized—you should keep your certifier ID (and one or more backup copies of it) safe from loss, safe from theft, and safe from unauthorized use. Consider keeping the certifier ID in a safe deposit box. Consider protecting it with multiple passwords so that at least two people have to be present in order to create new users or servers.

There is an alternate way to use the certifier ID in Notes R4—storing the ID in encrypted format on the server. This is discussed in detail in Chapter 35, "Administering Users, Servers, and Databases."

In addition to the administrative functions described previously, Notes R4 provides an easy way to delegate authority by creating and assigning *roles* to individual users. (See Figure 34.2.) As long as users have at least Author access, they can normally create documents or edit the documents they have created. The notable exception to this is the Public Address Book, where you would expect that only the system administrator could create or modify documents. But in a large organization, the administrator cannot be everything to everyone.

FIGURE 34.2.
The Public Address Book's ACL, where administrative roles can be assigned to a user.

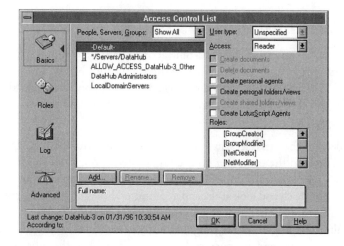

If the administrator delegated authority to others in earlier versions of Notes, then users ended up with greater access than they needed. For example, if someone were given the authority to certify new users, then she had to have Author access to the Public Address Book in order to create person documents. This means that she could create other types of documents in this vital database, making some system administrators reluctant to delegate such authority.

Modifier roles can be assigned to anyone with at least Author access in the ACL. Creator roles have to be explicitly assigned before individuals can perform those roles, regardless of their access privileges. Notes has eight default roles defined:

- **GroupCreator** is a user or group of users who can create new groups.

- **GroupModifier** is a user or group of users who can modify or delete existing group documents, but cannot create new groups unless assigned as a GroupCreator as well.

- **NetCreator** is a user or group of users who can create all documents except Person, Group, and Server documents.

- **NetModifier** is a user or group of users who can modify or delete all existing documents except Person, Group, and Server Documents.

- **ServerCreator** is a user or group of users who can create new Server documents.

- **ServerModifier** is a user or group of users who can modify existing Server documents.

- **UserCreator** is a user or group of users who can create new Person documents. The administration certifier would have to be assigned this role in order to perform his or her job of creating new users.

- **UserModifier** is a user or group of users who can modify existing Person documents.

Use these groups wisely; the Public Address Book is vital to your Notes organization. Plan out who will do what, and make sure that all roles are adequately covered by assigned roles. It is easy to give all managers an equally high level of access, but it may be a foolish approach.

34

SECURITY OVERVIEW

Encryption in Lotus Notes

Imagine, if you can, having full-time access to a supercomputer. You have managed to do an end run around all of the security features built into Notes, and you have a copy of someone else's Notes mail, an encrypted message. You also know by hearsay that the encrypted message holds the secret to eternal life. So you are going to use the supercomputer to decrypt the message.

To decrypt the message, you have to perform prime number calculations on a 170 digit number. You start the computer on the task of decrypting, and you go away for a vacation. You come back a month later. Still going. You go off to get married, have kids, raise the kids, and then come back and look at the supercomputer. Still going. Finally, when you are nearing your 100th birthday, you decide to pass the information on to your great-grandchildren so they can monitor the progress of the program. Forty generations later, as the 31st Century approaches, one of your descendants goes to the museum to look at the supercomputer. Still going.

This is an Energizer Bunny story if there ever was one. It could take that supercomputer until the 121st Century—that is not a typo—up to 10,000 years to crack the encryption technology used by Lotus Notes. No wonder the CIA uses Notes for their world-wide communications.

Understanding Public Key Encryption

Traditional encryption, the kind you see in spy movies, entails both the sender and receiver having access to the same secret key, which is used to encrypt a message on one end and decrypt it on the other end. If the secret key is intercepted, the message is no longer secure.

Notes uses another form of security called public-key encryption, based on RSA's Cryptosystem, using RC4 technology for domestic encryption, and RC2 encryption for international versions of Notes. The primary difference between RC4 and RC2 is the size of the keys. The RC4 key is 512 bits, whereas the international RC2 version is only 64 bits. Cryptographic products require an export license from the State Department, under the authority of the International Traffic in Arms Regulation (ITAR), which defines encryption devices as munitions. Presumably, they consider the 64-bit technology as being okay, even though it too is virtually unencyrptable. Public key encryption has become the de facto industry standard, because it supplements private key encryption, making it much more secure.

Here is how it works. Each person gets two keys—one public key and one private key. The public key is made publicly accessible, hence its name. The private key is kept secret, as part of the user ID in the case of Notes.

All encrypted communications use only public keys. The private key is never sent to anyone over the network, and it is never exchanged with anyone. You don't have to worry about the secret key being intercepted, you don't have to worry about someone eavesdropping on your communications. The encrypted message can move across publicly accessible channels, and the public key is easily obtainable. But the only person who can decrypt the message is the person who owns the private key associated with the public key that was used to encrypt the message.

Digital Signatures

With electronic documents, you cannot go to a notary public and have them put their seal on a document to verify that they witness your signature. But encryption does provide a way to exchange secure digital signatures that are recognized by many organizations as legally valid signatures.

A digital signature ensures that a document was actually sent by the person whose name appears on the document. In addition, the digital signature ensures that the document has not been tampered with since its creation.

A digital signature is created using the sender's private key. To sign a mail memo, create the memo and click on the Delivery Options button. Click on the Sign checkbox. Then, when the memo is mailed, your Private Key (not a full, usable private key, but just enough information to create the digital signature) will be encrypted and attached to the document.

When a user receives a document that has a digital signature attached, the sender's public key is retrieved from the Public Address Book to decrypt the signature. If the decryption is successful, the recipient can be sure that the document was sent by the person identifying themselves as the sender.

If someone in another Notes domain sends you a message, and you do not have their public key in any of your address books, you can still read the message. However, Notes will display a message box that says `You and the signer have no Certificates in common; signer cannot be assumed to be trustworthy`. Although you can still read the document, you cannot accept the digital signature as a legal signature. See the section "The Execution Control List (ECL)."

Encrypting Outgoing E-Mail

Using the same public key-private key encryption technology in a slightly different way from digital signatures, you can encrypt the e-mail you send to another user. For example, when a Notes user, Mary, wants to send an encrypted message to her co-worker Stuart, this is what happens.

1. Mary creates a memo using her Notes Mail. Before she sends the memo, she clicks on the Delivery Options button on the Action Bar, and checks Encrypt, and then sends the memo.

2. The Mailer on Mary's workstation looks for the Person document for Stuart in the Public Address Book Notes, and uses Stuart's public key to encrypt the memo. The memo is then sent via regular communication channels, which could be over a local area network, over a phone line, or over the Internet.

3. Stuart receives the memo. When he opens the message to read it, it looks just like any other memo. Notes used the private key that is part of Stuart's Notes user ID to decrypt the memo automatically at the time he opened it.

Encrypting Incoming Mail

The Mail page in the User Preferences box (File | Tools | User Preferences) has two checkboxes concerned with encryption. One checkbox causes all outgoing mail to be encrypted, so the user does not have to open the Delivery Options dialog box every time. If the addressee of a memo has a public key in her Person record in the Public Address Book, then mail to her is encrypted. If no public key is available, a message notifies the sender, and the memo is sent in unencrypted form if the sender okays that option.

The second checkbox in the User Preferences box enables encryption of all incoming mail. This option uses the recipient's public key to encrypt mail before it is stored. The mail cannot be read subsequently unless the user's Notes ID with its attached private key is available.

The system administrator can also encrypt mail for all mail files on a Notes server by setting the system parameter MailEncryptIncoming=1 in the server's NOTES.INI file.

What happens if an organization is using an optional shared copy object store (SCOS) database for storing the non-summary portion of shared e-mail messages? The user who elects to encrypt all incoming mail will not be able to use the shared object store. Instead, she will receive the full e-mail message, which will be stored in her personal mail database.

Encrypting All Network Data Over a Network Port

If your organization needs to ensure that all data transmissions over a particular network port are secure, you can elect to encrypt all data traffic through that port. This prevents someone with a network sniffer from intercepting messages. The messages get encrypted at the network port, and they remain encrypted while they are being transported. Once the traffic is received and stored on the other end, the data is no longer encrypted.

Data only needs to be encrypted on the sending end. A different encryption algorithm is used for this form of encryption. There is little difference in performance with this type of encryption, except that transmission speed may be slowed because the encrypted data cannot be compressed.

To set up encryption for a network port, open the Ports page of the User Preferences box (File | Tools | User Preferences), select a network port, and click on Encrypt Network Data.

The Role of Encryption in Authentication

Authentication between a user and a Notes server, or between two servers, utilizes encryption to verify the identity of the other party. The two exchange digital signatures that guarantee that the other party is not an impostor.

Consider for a moment what could happen with the earlier secret key encryption technology. If someone obtained the secret key by stealth, they could create a message and claim to be the legitimate user of the secret key. There was no way to guarantee the identity of the sender on the other end.

With public key-private key encryption, the digital signature exchanged between the two systems is guaranteed to be authentic. A short mathematical message is encrypted using the public key of the other system. The other system then decrypts the message with its private key, and sends it back in unencrypted format to verify that the right mathematical message was decrypted. The process is then reversed until both systems recognize each other as authentic.

This exchange of encrypted data takes place every time two Notes systems authenticate each other.

Encrypting Documents and Fields Within Documents

Field encryption can only be used at the option of the database designer. Fields on a form can be defined with a security option to enable encryption for the field. This is done in the Security Options field on the Options page of the Field Properties InfoBox.

The database designer can enable fields for encryption and can assign a default encryption key that will automatically encrypt the enabled field when a document is created and saved.

If no default encryption key has been assigned to the form properties by the designer, then users can decide whether to encrypt enabled fields or not. The brackets around encrypted fields are displayed in red to distinguish them from unencryptable fields, which by default have gray brackets around them.

When a document with encryption-enabled fields is saved, the user will be asked if she wants to encrypt the fields or not. If she says yes, then Notes will ask which encryption key should be used. The user can encrypt the fields on the document by selecting an encryption key. Any users who need to read the data in the encrypted fields need to have a copy of the encryption key assigned to the document, and they have to merge the encryption key into their Notes user IDs.

Creating, sharing, and merging encryption keys is described in the next section.

Encrypting an entire document is similar to encrypting fields within a document. Again, the database designer is responsible for enabling encryption. Once encryption has been enabled, a document may be encrypted automatically as soon as it is saved, or the user may have the option of encrypting the document, depending on how the designer has enabled the form with the document is created.

A document can be encrypted in any of the following ways:

■ A form attribute can be selected (on the security page of the Form Properties InfoBox) whereby the designer assigns one or more encryption keys to the form. Users must have one of those encryption keys before they can read documents created with the form.

■ The user can encrypt a document that has one or more fields enabled for encryption by displaying the Document Properties InfoBox and selecting an encryption key to apply to the document, using a field on the security page of the InfoBox.

■ The designer can include a field named SecretEncryptionKeys on the form. This field can be blank, enabling users to assign their own encryption keys, the field can have a default value that is the name of an encryption key, the field can be hidden or visible, and the field can use a formula to determine whether the field should be encrypted, based on the conditions set by the designer. If the conditions are met, the formula can insert the encryption key.

It is also worth reminding you that local databases can be encrypted from within the Database Properties InfoBox or when the database is first created. You have three methods of encryption—simple, medium, and strong. Simple encryption is simplest and provides the quickest access, and the encrypted database can be compressed. Medium compression is the default. A database with medium compression cannot be compressed, but it can be accessed faster than a strongly encrypted database, and should be sufficient for most uses. A strongly encrypted database has all of the security encryption can provide, but the strong encryption has a price in terms of database access and performance.

Creating and Sharing Encryption Keys

Encryption keys are created by selecting File | Tools | User ID. Enter your password to display the User ID dialog box, and then click on the Encryption Navigator to move to the encryption page. (See Figure 34.3.)

FIGURE 34.3.

The encryption keys page of the User ID dialog box.

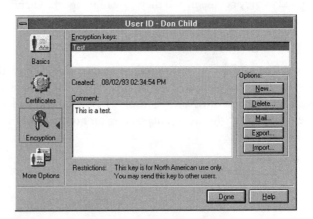

To create a new encryption key, click on the New button. Notes will display just the encryption key name field, a comment field, and give you the option of creating a key for North American use or for International use.

> **CAUTION**
>
> If you are sending encrypted documents to a user outside of the United States (including Hawaii and Alaska) or Canada, you must create an International encryption key to encrypt your data. International licensees cannot decrypt data encrypted with a North American license. However, a user with a North American license can decrypt data created with either a North American or an International encryption key.

To send the encryption key to another user so she can decrypt documents created using the key, click on the Mail button. An addressing dialog will be displayed. Address the user you want to send the encryption key to, and click on Send. The user will receive the key as an attachment in her e-mail, along with instructions to select Accept Encryption Key from the Actions menu. This will merge the encryption key into her Notes user ID.

If you want to export the encryption key to a file, click on the Export button. A dialog box will be displayed with a field where you can enter a password to protect the exported encryption key file. There is a second field where you must retype the password to confirm what you have entered. You can also click on a Restrict Use… button and enter the exact name of the only person who is authorized to use the exported key. When you have entered a password (required) and entered the optional name of the person who can use the key, click on OK. Notes will create an encryption key file named with a .KEY extension.

To import a key that has been sent to you as a file, you do the opposite of exporting. Click on the Import button and identify the file you want to import. Enter the password that protects the file, and Notes will display information about the encryption key in the file and give you the option to accept the key. Click on the Accept button to merge the key into your Notes user ID. Once the key is part of your ID, you can read any documents encrypted using that key.

Added Security Features for Internet Computing in Notes 4.5

There was an uproar among Lotus Business Partners when someone demonstrated an unavoidable security hole that he thought not enough people were paying attention to. Notes has complex documents that allow execution of embedded code. Someone can mail a document to you or post one in a database that, when opened, runs an embedded program. This type of embedded program is called a Trojan Horse because it sneaks past your defenses by taking advantage of the application's built-in design features.

This particular Trojan Horse was an "innocent" attention-getter that told you what type of system you were using. But it could just as well have been a hidden program that launched a computer virus. There is no way to know in advance what type of program code is embedded in a document, so Notes 4.5 gives you an option—actually, numerous options—for handling documents that potentially hold viruses, Trojan Horses, or embedded code of any sort. This is especially important when you're opening pages directly from the Internet (which has a reputation for being a bit anarchic) and storing them as Notes documents.

The Execution Control List (ECL)

You can determine what actions a Notes document can perform on your workstation by setting up the Execution Control List (ECL) as part of your workstation security. Using the ECL, you control how much of your system the embedded program can touch. If the document was created by a colleague, you can probably trust that person. If the document was retrieved from the Internet and you don't know the person or company who created it, maybe you should withhold your trust.

When you first open a document in Notes 4.5, Notes checks the ECL to see if the document's author is trusted to perform specific actions on your workstation, such as accessing the current database. If the author isn't listed in the ECL for that specific action, Notes displays the Execution Security Alert dialog box, shown in Figure 34.4.

FIGURE 34.4.

The Execution Security Alert dialog box appears when the document signer isn't trusted in ECL.

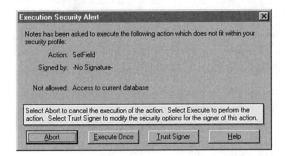

This dialog box has three options:

- If you click Trust Signer, the ECL will be modified to accept this action from this author in the future without warning you.

- If you click Execute Once, Notes will perform the action this one time, but you will be warned the next time a document from the same signer attempts to perform the same action.

- If you click Abort, the action won't be performed, but the document might still open if the action isn't essential.

You control what can be done on your workstation by documents that were created by others. You have considerable control over what actions can be executed on your workstation.

In addition to choosing to trust the signer of a document or to execute an action only once for that signer, you can define a variety of actions from the ECL. To view the ECL, select File | Tools | User Preferences and click the Security Options button on the Basics page. The ECL dialog box is shown in Figure 34.5.

Figure 34.5.

You select executable actions from the ECL dialog box.

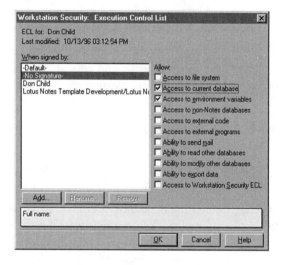

In many instances, you can use Default and No Signature to protect your system from intrusion by unwanted agents. The degree of protection is very much in your hands. It's a small price to pay for the rich complexity of Notes documents culled from enterprise systems, the Internet, and fellow Notes users.

TIP

One suggestion culled from the Lotus Web site (http://www.lotus.com) is to display an icon next to documents that contain attachments. To do this, create the following column formula:

```
@If(@IsAvailable($Title);n;"")
```

n can be any number between 1 and 170. Each number displays a different icon. (Chapter 13, "Developing Views," shows all 170 icons.) You can also view the icons online by looking under "Displaying an icon in a column" in the Notes Help database. Be sure that you have Display Values as Icons selected in the Column Properties box. Then you will be able to see in advance that a document has an attachment and can set up the ECL accordingly.

34

SECURITY
OVERVIEW

Java Applet Source Specification

Java applets provide another type of program that can be executed on your workstation, especially now that Lotus Notes 4.5 has a built-in Web Navigator that lets Java applets run. To prevent unwanted applets from executing on your workstation, you can define which locations are acceptable sources of Java applets. For example, you could decide not to retrieve Java applets unless they're hosted on Web servers located inside your firewall—for example, from your corporate intranet.

By default, all hosts can run Java applets on your system, but no hosts are allowed to access system resources such as password files, environment variables, and files, regardless of their ability to run applets.

You can modify the list of trusted Java applet hosts in location documents in your Personal Address Book.

In the Advanced section of your location document, locate Java Applet Security. Four fields are used to set Java Applet Security:

- Trusted hosts: Enter the IP address or domain name of hosts that can load Java applets on your computer. You can specify wildcards, as in `123.45.678.*` or `*.lotus.com`. Note that if a host name maps to multiple IP addresses or vice versa, intended hosts might not get included in your wildcard. If you leave this field blank, all hosts will be considered to have the type of access defined for network access for untrusted hosts.

- Network access for trusted hosts: This is the level of network access you want to give to trusted hosts. Options include the following:

    Disable Java: The trusted host cannot run applets on your system.

    No access allowed: Lets the host run an applet on your system but doesn't let it make network HTTP connections on any host.

    Allow access to any originating host: The applet can make network HTTP connections on the host from which the applet was retrieved.

    Allow access to any trusted host (the default selection): The applet can make network HTTP connections on trusted hosts only.

    Allow access to any host: The applet can make network HTTP connections on any host.

- Network access for untrusted hosts: This determines the level of access for all other hosts—those not selected as trusted hosts. Options are the same as the first three options just discussed. "Allow access only to originating host" is the default.

- Trust HTTP Proxy: This field is used if you specified an HTTP Proxy in the Web proxy field on the location document. Yes indicates that you want the proxy to resolve the host for you. Otherwise, you won't be able to resolve the host name or run Java applets.

Summary

Notes security can be designed and enforced on several different levels, beginning with the physical security of your entire system, the physical and logical security of your Notes servers, the security of your administrative processes, the security of individual databases, and clear down to the security of a specific field in a single document.

A key concept for Notes security is the hierarchical naming scheme, which is closely tied to the use of a certifier ID and its descendants. The certifier ID is synonymous with the Notes organization, and a certificate from the certifier ID identifies legitimate users and servers within the organization. In order to communicate with a Notes server, a user ID must have a certificate trusted by the server ID. If a user is from an outside organization, then they can be trusted if they have exchanged certificates with your organization through cross-certification—or, in the case of an organization with a flat naming scheme, by exchanging certificates via safe copies of IDs and merging those certificates into server or user IDs.

The task of administering Notes security belongs to all users in the Notes organization, but the primary responsibility lies with the system administrators, who are responsible for maintaining the documents in the Public Address Book. Administrative tasks can be delegated to other users from the Access Control List dialog box for the Public Address Book.

And no discussion of security would be complete without a discussion of the role of encryption in security. Notes provides a very robust security system that gives users access to some of the most powerful encryption tools available.

Administering Users, Servers, and Databases

by Don Child

IN THIS CHAPTER

CHAPTER

35

One aspect of Lotus Notes strikes most users at one time or another—there is rarely just one way to do something. Any Notes cookbook you see is likely to say, "To accomplish this, do A, or B, or C." There is a lot of latitude depending on the type of organization you have, and how you are using Notes. In that sense, this chapter serves as somewhat of a review of subjects that have been covered previously. This chapter is a cookbook for Notes R4 administrators. It describes some of the options for adding and deleting users from a Notes network, adding new servers or removing servers, and putting databases into or removing them from production.

With Notes 4.5, basic administrative functions are unchanged. But this doesn't mean that the server tasks are the same as with Notes 4.0. For one thing, the server is now called "Domino Release 4.5 Server, Powered by Lotus Notes." And many new "industrial-grade" features are available to any Notes organization through the Domino Advanced Services add-on. These Domino Advanced Services include clustering, server partitioning, detailed usage tracking, and billing. Domino also includes several new features for Windows NT users, such as a single logon for Notes and network services, redirecting the logging of Notes events to the NT Event Manager, directory synchronization between Notes and NT, and support for the Microsoft System Management Server.

The Notes organization can be very dynamic, in part as a result of using Notes. If a topic needs to be discussed, a discussion database can be created and deployed in a matter of minutes, and individual users can be added to workgroups made up of users from other locations around the world. It is the database designer's and the administrator's job to ensure that databases are correctly set up. In other words, the access control list and roles have to be thought out so they contribute to the security and usefulness of the database, and the database has to be distributed to servers in such a way that the users who need access can work on a local copy of the database.

The administrator can delegate much of the responsibility for maintaining this dynamic Notes organization. For example, he can delegate the right to create groups, but must monitor the Public Address Book to ensure that unnecessary groups do not proliferate. Creating ad hoc groups for ACLs can be facilitated by a good hierarchical naming scheme that allows for the use of wildcards, obviating the need to create groups.

And of course, as the Notes network changes its dynamics, servers may need to be brought online, or removed and changed to different uses. This is the job of a system administrator, working in conjunction with the administration certifier. The administration certifier, of course, is responsible for registering both new users and new servers.

This chapter looks at some of the options for achieving these changes in the growing and changing Notes organization.

Adding and Deleting Users

In Chapter 32, "Initial Installation," you saw how to add a new user to the Notes network during system setup. The process involved determining the place of the user in the Notes organization, selecting the correct certifier ID, and registering the user. After users were registered, they set up their workstation and were up and running.

Adding a User

If a new employee starts at your organization, the same basic process is followed. Perhaps the most important part of the process is figuring out where the new user will fit into the organization, because it can have profound implications when the user is registered.

For example, a new user, Luis Otero, has just joined the Acme Corporation. He will be working out of the San Francisco office, which falls under the responsibility of the West/Acme certifier. He will be working in the Sales office, so the ultimate responsibility for registering him as user on the system falls to the administration certifier responsible for the Sales/West/Acme certifier ID. The Acme Corporation has a Notes policy that says adding new groups will be minimized by using wildcards in the ACL of shared databases whenever possible.

He could have been registered by the top-level Acme certifier, but look at the ramifications. He would have been given automatic access to any databases that include */Acme in the ACL as a Reader or higher. That would include databases even if they were in the Accounting Department, Human Resources, and so forth. He would have been given too much access.

On the other hand, by registering him with the Sales/West/Acme certifier ID, you are ensuring that he is not accidentally included in access lists for the Accounting department's databases. Luis can now access the Sales databases, and the West databases, and the Acme databases using a wildcard */Sales/West/Acme that creates a de facto group for anyone with a certificate from the Sales/West/Acme certifier ID. And his name, for the foreseeable future, is Luis Otero/Sales/West/Acme. He can enter his name in a shortened form as Luis Otero/. The slash following his name means that the entire hierarchy, his full user name, is intended.

Notes refers to names in several different ways, which can get confusing. A fully canonical name includes location markers, for example CN=Luis Otero/OU=Sales/OU=West/O=Acme, where CN is the common name, OU is an organizational unit, and O is the organization. This is how Notes stores the name, with all of its components labeled. The abbreviated distinguished name is how the user might see it displayed, such as Luis Otero/Sales/West/Acme. However, many fields on Notes forms will contain input translation formulas that will simplify the name so only the common name is displayed, such as Luis Otero.

Now look in the Public Address Book at his Person record, shown in Figure 35.1. Registering him has automatically created the person record and displayed the common name in the Full User Name field. This means that he can be addressed by just his common name, and the Notes router will find his mail box. But the Sales office in the West branch of the Acme Corporation is pretty informal. Everyone goes on a first-name basis, and there are no other users going by the name Luis in the organization. So the administrator, or a person assigned to the UserModifier role, has gone in and edited the person document to include the first name, Luis, as an alias in the same field. So now, everyone can send him e-mail addressed simply to "Luis" and it will get to him.

FIGURE 35.1.

The Person record in the Public Address Book, showing a newly registered user's distinguished name and aliases.

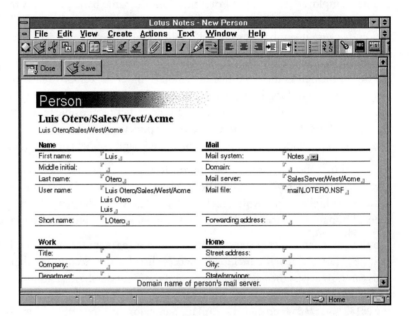

If the user is a member of a workgroup that crosses the boundaries of the hierarchical naming scheme or a workgroup that is somehow too eclectic to fit into a wildcard-naming scheme, he may have to be put into a group with special-access privileges.

For example, suppose there is a group reviewing and rewriting corporate white papers. The white papers are available to everyone in the organization as reference materials, but the wildcard group */Acme has only reader access to the database. The review team needs editor access so they can rework some of the papers. A group is created called Reviewers. When Luis Otero joins the company, they discover that he has a strong background in copy editing, so they want him to help out with the review process. A user with GroupModifier access to the Public Address Book will have to add Luis to the Reviewers group. After he has been added to the group, he opens a document in the database and double-clicks. Bingo. He is in edit mode and can begin editing the changes that have been made by other members of the Reviewer group.

On the other hand, Luis may be part of a temporary workgroup exploring the implications of discontinuing the sale of blue widgets. There are only three individuals in the workgroup, too small a number to make creating a group worthwhile. In this case, the database manager adds Luis' name directly to the ACL of the new database as an author.

> **CAUTION**
>
> If a group is created for an ad hoc instance like the one described previously, there is a caveat. If the group's purpose is no longer valid, and the system administrator deletes the group from the ACL, the group name may still remain in database ACLs. Anyone who is allowed to create a group in the Public Address Book can then create a group that includes his own name, thereby giving him access to all databases that still have that group name in the ACL.

The net result is that he ends up with his name appearing in several places throughout the Notes organization, in groups and ACLs as well as in the Public Address Book. So what happens when Luis receives a promotion and moves from the Sales office in San Francisco to the head office in Atlanta? His name, as far as Notes is concerned, is `Luis Otero/Sales/West/Acme`.

Renaming or Moving a User

Renaming or moving a user can be tricky. Consider that the user's name is part of his Notes identity, and his hierarchical name in effect lists the certificates he has that enable him to access servers and databases within the Notes organization. When a name is changed, the user risks losing the ability to access databases, both on the server and on his local computer. Once his name has changed or he has been recertified (for instance, been given a new certificate or set of certificates), his user ID is changed, so encrypted data may be lost. If a backup of the old ID was not saved that would enable them to decrypt the data, the encrypted data will be lost forever, unless someone else has a copy of the same data that he is willing to share. Later in this section, there is a list of what the effects are of various types of changes to a user ID.

We will follow Luis as his career moves along at Acme. First, let's suppose that the administration certifier who registered Luis made a mistake. He was a jazz fan, so he spelled the first name "Louis," as in Armstrong. Note that the same might apply commonly when an employee's name changes as a result of marital status.

Luis put up with the misspelling for the first few days because he was used to it. But soon enough, he wanted to correct the spelling. By then, his name could be found in multiple groups and database ACLs. Here is how he changes his name. He opens the User ID dialog box by selecting File | Tools | User ID, clicks on the More Options icon, and selects the Request New Name button. This displays the Change Name dialog box, shown in Figure 35.2.

Figure 35.2.

Change Name dialog box, used to submit a name change request to the administration certifier.

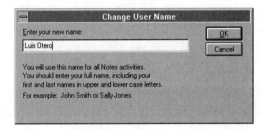

He enters his new name (first and last name, known to Notes as the common name, or CN, not the full hierarchical Notes name) and submits the request. The administrator receives the request in his mailbox. He opens the Public Address Book to the People view and selects the Person record of the person to be renamed—in this instance, Luis Otero. He then selects from the Action menu, Rename Person, selects the certifier ID that was used originally to certify the person, changes any defaults, and clicks Certify.

A record is made in the Certification Log and in the Administration Requests database. When the Administration Process runs on the server that night, all instances of the original name are replaced with the new name. The only place the name cannot be changed is in the Personal Address Book of individual users, and in databases on local hard drives. He still has all of his original certificates, but the common name component of his ID has changed.

Later, when Luis moves from one part of the company to another, the administration certifier also needs to move his name within the hierarchical naming scheme. This is done by recertifying him with his new hierarchical name. The name change is made in one place, then the Administration Process takes over and automatically changes the name throughout the Notes network. He still has the same common name, but now he has new certificates, which effects his ability to access data throughout the organization, including on his own desktop or mobile computer.

For example, our friend Luis is moving to Atlanta. He will become `Luis Otero/Sales/Main/ Acme`. By changing his name through recertification, he is automatically moved within the Notes organization, including a name change in his Person record in the Public Address Book, in all groups that his name has been added to, and in the ACL of all databases to which he has been added. If the name were not changed in all databases and groups, he could end up losing access to some databases.

To move a user within the hierarchical naming scheme:

1. Locate the user's Person document in the Public Address Book.

2. Select Rename Person from the pull-down Action menu.

3. Click on the Request Move to New Certifier button. You will have to select the original certifier ID and enter the password to verify that you have the authority to change the certification of the individual.

4. Select the name of the new certifier ID and submit your request.

   This much of the process is done by the original administration certifier, using the original certifier ID. The remainder of the process takes place using the new certifier ID, the one that will result in new certificates for the user ID being renamed.

5. In the Administration Requests database, select the name using the Name Move Requests view, and run the action Complete Move for Selected Entries.

6. Select the certifier ID that will be used to issue new certificates for the user, and enter the password.

7. If you want to, you can change default information such as the expiration date of the certificates, and you can enter a New Certifying Organizational Unit, which distinguishes the individual from others with the same name in the same organizational unit.

8. Click on Certify. The request will be submitted to the Administration Process.

The Administration Process, ADMINP, runs on the server as a task, and automates changing the hierarchical name throughout the Notes Organization.

The one thing that doesn't get changed is the user's mailbox. If Luis has moved to Atlanta, he doesn't want his home server—the one that holds his mailbox—to be in San Francisco. To move the mailbox to Atlanta, it should be replicated to the new home server in Atlanta, and the name of the home server should be changed in the Person record in the Public Address Book. Then, if shared mail is being used, the mailbox in San Francisco should be unlinked and then deleted, and the new mailbox in Atlanta should be linked to the object store in Atlanta. When Luis arrives at the office in Atlanta, he can use his renamed user ID, open his mail, and have access to local copies of all of the databases he is accustomed to.

> **CAUTION**
>
> After a user ID has been certified by a Notes R4 certifier, the ID can no longer be used to access a Notes R3 server. Do not move or rename users with an R4 certifier ID until all servers and clients have migrated to Notes R4; this avoids the possibility of incompatibility.

The Impact of Name Changes on a Mobile User

The Administrative Agent minimizes the impact of changes to a user ID on a Notes server. However, changing the user ID has consequences for the mobile user.

■ If the user changes his own name, rather than submitting a request to the administrative certifier, he will be unable to access any servers, encrypted databases, and encrypted documents. There is no back door. The system administrator cannot help. The data is irretrievably lost. Also, he cannot open local replicas on which the ACL is enforced. If his name is changed on the server by the administrative certifier, he can still access all databases on the server, but needs to either change his name on the ACLs of local databases, or wait for them to replicate with the server if ACLs are locally enforced.

■ If he is recertified but remains in the same organization, he loses access to local databases on which Access Control is locally enforced until the databases replicate with the server and get updated ACLs. He can still read locally encrypted databases and documents. However, as manager of his own mail database file, he can go in and change the ACL of that database locally.

Deleting a User

A user leaves the company. She has taken a job with another company and has given her notice. The usual separation interview is done, and her last day finishes. She turns in her Notes user ID. As the former employee walks out the door for the last time, the system administrator adds her name to a group that has been named NO_ACCESS. The group is included in the Not Access Server field on every server in the organization. As soon as the Public Address Book is replicated around the organization, the user will no longer be able to access any server, even if she had a valid Notes user ID.

> **TIP**
>
> Sometimes people will name the NO_ACCESS group something like OUTLAWS or EX_EMPLOYEES. Be aware that there is a stigma that goes with being called an outlaw. Give the group a neutral name, one that does not brand the people who must be added to the group.

The user turned in her Notes ID. But it is a binary file of only around 3000 bytes. Who says there is not another copy of the file floating around? Assume there are copies out there, and lock the user out of the system.

If the user has a hierarchical ID and you have set up the Administration Process on your system, you can delete the user from the system using the Administration Process. Open the People view in the Public Address Book, select the person to be deleted, and from the Action menu select Delete Person. You have the option of deleting the person from the Public Address Book immediately. Select this option, and all references to the person will be removed, including any groups they are in. Otherwise, the references will be removed when ADMINP runs.

A request is automatically sent to the Administration Request database, and, when ADMINP runs, the user's name is automatically removed from all database ACLs.

In addition, the user's mail file should be unlinked if you are using shared mail, then deleted.

If you feel there is a real security risk, you can force replication of the Public Address Book to all servers in the organization to ensure that the deletions are distributed throughout the organization as quickly as possible.

Administering Servers

Administering servers is rather an amorphous term, but essentially, it is the job of the system administrator to ensure that the server is running, and that it is running properly. In addition, the system administrator is occasionally responsible for bringing new servers into the organization, either by adding a new server, or by merging an existing server into your Notes network. This can come about as a result of a corporate takeover, or during consolidation of two or more local domains. The administrator may also have to split servers into separate domains.

Maintaining Server Configuration

There are two distinct areas of server configuration for which the system administrator has responsibility: documents within the Public Address Book, such as Connection documents and replication and routing scheduling; and the scheduling and running of server tasks.

The Public Address Book

What needs to be done when administering servers depends somewhat on how you want to use a new server. For example, if a server has mail files on it, you may want to set up shared mail, and you will want to schedule mail routing on the server. If, for some reason, the server has to be taken out of service, you will have to move the mail files and help the users change their mail setup. If the server is solely a multiprotocol communications server used for passthru, you will not have to worry about mail routing, but you will need to set up your passthru connections.

No matter how the server is to be used, there are certain documents in the Public Address Book that have to be set up correctly. After the Public Address Book is set up correctly, you will need only to edit or change information when new elements are introduced, such as a new server or a new communications protocol. Maintaining this information can be delegated to other users, as described in Chapter 34, "Security Overview."

There is no one checklist for which documents need to be maintained, because different servers may be used for different purposes. However, as a general rule, you want to ensure that you have the following documents and fields correctly set up, if your setup requires them:

■ **Server documents**: One must be set up for every server in your organization. The Server Name field, the Domain field, and the Administrators field are required, and get filled in automatically based on the information you supply when the server is first registered. Set up the names of the Routing Tasks you will be using to deliver mail from this server. Define telephone numbers or other connection information such as which passthru server to use in the Server Location section. Enable communication ports and define which Notes Named Network(s) the server belongs to in the Network Configuration section. Define which users and which other servers need to access the server, who cannot access the server, and which other servers to use as passthru servers in the Restrictions section.

■ **Connection documents**: Depending on your implementation of Notes, set up a Connections document for each of the following: Local Area Network connections (connections between different Notes Named Networks, which must have at least one server that has dual protocols, if required, so it can belong to both Notes Named Networks); Dialup Modem connections; Passthru Server connections; Remote LAN Service connections; X.25 connections; SMTP connections; X.400 connections; cc:Mail connections; and SNA connections. Be sure that you have a connection set up to your passthru server if you are setting one up.

In the Connections document, you should also define which types of routing and replication tasks the connection is being used for.

■ **Group documents**: Maintain a Deny Access group so that, if necessary, you can immediately lock a user or server out of your organization's servers by adding them to this group.

■ **Domain documents**: Maintain a Domain document for any domains you connect to. Do not forget to include FAX, pager, and Internet gateway domains, if you are using them.

■ **Mail-in Database documents**: Set up Mail-in Database documents for any databases that you want to have as a destination for mail-enabled forms, for example, an event-log database used to gather trouble-shooting documents from other Notes servers in your organization, and databases used in workflow applications.

■ **Program documents**: You can schedule server tasks using Program documents or using Server Configuration documents. For example, you can schedule a Program document for Updall, Fixup, Catalog, Design, and Statlog server tasks.

 Views such as **clusters** and **networks** come into play when you're managing larger Notes organizations with multiple domains and when you need fault-tolerant computing provided by Domino Advanced Services.

■ In other views, you also need to maintain **Person documents**, **Group documents**, and **Location documents**.

You want to ensure that your server is configured correctly, that all connections have been correctly specified, and that all tasks that are supposed to run on a periodic basis, such as replicating and mail routing, have been properly scheduled. It is the system administrator's job to ensure that information is getting to users and to other servers when and where the information is needed.

> **NOTE**
>
> Whenever you make changes to the configuration of the server, such as Configuration documents or changes to the NOTES.INI, or make changes to ports, you have to exit the server and restart it from the desktop by clicking on the server icon. When the server restarts, it will reinitialize and the new settings will take effect. Other changes can be made with the server running, and they take effect immediately.

Running Server Tasks

Administering the server also means ensuring that full-time server tasks such as the replicator and the mail router are started up when the server starts. In addition, other server tasks can be scheduled to run on a periodic basis either from the NOTES.INI file, from a Server Configuration document, or from a Program document. Tasks can also be run manually from the server console on an as-needed basis.

The tasks that you, as an administrator, want to ensure are running (again, depending on how a server is being used), include the following:

- Catalog: The Catalog task updates a database catalog (CATALOG.NSF) that is created on a server the first time the Catalog task runs. The catalog lists all databases that are available to users of that server. By default, Catalog is included in the ServerTasksAt1 setting, meaning that the task will run at 1 a.m.

- Compact: The Compact server task gets rid of unused white space in databases. Blocks of white space are left in the database after documents are deleted, and Compact recovers that white space. You can load Compact at the Server Console, or you can schedule it to run at a set time in the NOTES.INI file or a Program Document. The Compact task can be used with an -s flag plus a value to indicate the minimum percentage of white space before Compact runs on a database. For instance, Load Compact -s 15 will compact databases with at least 15 percent white space.

  When databases are compacted, you need at least the size of the database in free space on the disk. When Notes compacts the database, it makes a duplicate of the database, then copies all documents back into the original database space, minus any white space.

  Certain files cannot be compacted while they are open, such as the NAMES.NSF database (the Public Address Book), which is always open when Notes is running.

> **CAUTION**
>
> When Compact is run on a Notes R3 database, the database is converted to R4 format unless the database has been named with a .NS3 file extension. You can revert to R3 format by running Compact with an -r flag—for instance, Load Compact *DATABASE.NSF* -r, where *DATABASE.NSF* is the filename of the database to be reverted to R3 format.

- Design: The Design task updates the design of databases with changes that were made to the templates on which database design is based. The design template should be placed in the Notes data directory and should be replicated to all servers on which the database resides. The Design task runs by default at 1 a.m., and it should be followed by the Updall task to rebuild views changed during the Design task.

- Event: The Event task is an optional task that is used for event reporting. When Event is loaded for the first time at the Server Console or by putting it into the ServerTasks setting in the NOTES.INI file, an EVENTS4.NSF database is created automatically to collect server statistic and event documents. Events are specific, system-performance statistics that surpass predefined parameters.

- Fixup: The Fixup task fixes corrupted databases by locating corrupt documents and removing them completely from the database, including the document-deletion stub. If a replica of the database exists, the document can be replicated back into the database after the document has been completely deleted. Fixup runs at startup and fixes the Notes Log, but it does not locate and rebuild corrupted views. You can schedule Fixup to run using a program document or a NOTES.INI setting, but be aware that it takes significant CPU resources to run. Therefore, avoid running Fixup from the Server Console during the day unless it is necessary.

- Replicator: The Replicator task is started at system start-up by default, then remains idle until there is a scheduled replication, a replication request from the Server Console, or a request for a replication from another server. It is possible to have a database server that allows other servers to perform only pull-push replication, in which case the Replicator task would not be required on the host server. It can be turned off with a Server Console command (TELL ROUTER QUIT) or by removing it from the ServerTasks line in the NOTES.INI file.

- Reporter: The Reporter is similar to the Event task. The first time it is run, it creates a mail-in database called STATREP.NSF, and creates a Server to Monitor document in the EVENTS4.NSF database for the server on which you run Report. The Server to Monitor document specifies how often statistics are generated for the server, in intervals ranging from 15 minutes to 1440 minutes (once a day). You can also create an analysis report at a specified interval of daily, weekly or monthly. You can set up statistical reporting and analysis reporting across several servers in the organization by mailing statistical reports to a single STATREP.NSF database.

- **Router**: The Router task is used to route mail, including e-mail, as well as documents automatically generated by other tasks such as Event and Reporter, and by workflow applications that send documents to mail-in databases.

- **Updall**: The Updall task updates views and indexes on all databases on the server. As documents are added to databases, views need updating, and full-text indexes get out of date because new documents are not automatically added to the index. This task can be run on specific databases that may have damaged view indexes, as one way to repair the view. (Another way is to create a new replica of the database, then delete the original that has the damaged view index.) You can use a number of optional flags to control what gets updated:

  - -f updates full-text indexes without updating views.

  - -s updates full-text indexes that have an Immediate or Hourly update frequency, and scheduled update frequencies if the Updall task is initiated from a Program document.

  - -m is the same as -s, but it updates scheduled update frequencies even if no Program document exists for Updall.

  - -h updates full-text indexes only if they have Immediate or Hourly update frequencies.

  - -l updates all view and full-text indexes.

  - -x rebuilds full-text indexes.

  - The flags are all optional. Updall can be run with no arguments.

Running Server Tasks Using Program Documents

Server tasks can be run from the Server Console, from the NOTES.INI file, or from Program Documents. Program documents are created in the Public Address Book by selecting Create | Server | Program. A completed Program Document is shown in Figure 35.3.

The Program document can be used to schedule a variety of tasks and external programs. For example, in the Command line field, you could enter a DOS command filename to run an automatic backup on the system. Enter the name of the server on which the task or program should be run, and enable a schedule.

After a server is correctly set up so that tasks run on a scheduled basis, the server more or less runs itself. The system administrator will want to monitor the server daily by examining various logs, described in Chapter 36, "Troubleshooting the System," and Chapter 37, "Troubleshooting Networks and Modems."

Merging Networks and Domains

Setting up an additional server in an organization was covered in detail in Chapter 32. You register the server, run the setup program, verify your ports, modify connection documents, and set up access security. All of these changes are replicated throughout the organization, because they are all contained in the Public Address Book. But what about a server that is already set up, but is now being merged into an existing network of Notes servers?

Figure 35.3.

The Server Program document, used to schedule Notes tasks.

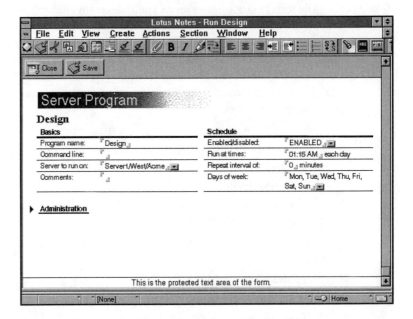

Consider the following scenario, common in these days. Your company, Acme, is using Lotus Notes R4 extensively. You discover a strategic advantage in merging with the XYZ corporation, who also uses Lotus Notes. For the sake of argument, let's assume that XYZ runs a real mixed environment of Notes servers and workstations. Half the company is running Notes R4 servers, and they have their own users who have been registered using a hierarchical R4 certifier ID. Another division in XYZ is using Notes R3 servers and R3 clients with flat names. They have cross-certified the R3 and R4 systems because they were not ready to move everyone to R4, and did not want to rename all of the users until everyone had migrated to Notes R4.

You would have to do all of the following to create a single, homogenous organization:

■ Rename hierarchically named users, then rename hierarchically named servers.

■ Rename flat-named users, then rename flat-named servers.

■ Merge or cascade Public Address Books.

> **CAUTION**
>
> Note that *rename* does not mean changing a user name from Smith to Jones or a server name from Server1 to Apollo. *Rename* means to give them a new identity within the Notes hierarchical organization. During the renaming process, some users may temporarily be unable to access databases they are accustomed to using. For that reason, it is imperative that you plan carefully before merging an existing server into another Notes organization.

Renaming a Hierarchically Certified Server

Renaming a hierarchically named R4 server is similar to the process of renaming (and recertifying) a user, already described. The administrator initiates the process, then the Administration Process completes the process automatically. The following occurs during the process:

1. The administrator opens the Server view in the Public Address Book, selects the server or servers to be recertified, and from the Action menu selects Recertify Server.

2. The request is automatically posted in the Administration Requests database on the server where the request was made, and in the Certification Log on the same server. If this is not the server listed as the administration server for the Public Address Book, then the Administration Requests database is replicated to the administration server.

3. The Administration Process on the administration server updates the Server Document in the Public Address Book with the new certificate (that is, the new hierarchical name), and the Public Address Book is replicated throughout the domain. The Administration Process automatically updates changed names whenever they are found in database ACLs, and in the ACL for the Public Address Book. The name is also updated in any documents in the Public Address Book where the name appears. One place that the name cannot be updated, however, is in databases on the hard drives of mobile users.

4. The server that has been recertified gets its new certificate from the Public Address Book.

Renaming a Server That Has a Flat Certificate

Renaming a server that has a flat certificate is essentially the same as renaming a server that already has a hierarchical name, except that you have to be aware that the Administration Process can only be run from a hierarchically named R4 server. Regardless, once the process is completed, the new hierarchical certificate is added to the flat server name. For example, Server1 would become Server1/West/Acme when it is recertified using the West/Acme certifier ID.

35

ADMINISTERING USERS, SERVERS, AND DATABASES

CAUTION

There are several steps involved in recertifying and merging two organizations, and the order in which they are done is vital to the success of the process. In this case, you are merging another organization into yours. Do the following, in order:

1. Back up the system Public Address Book and user and server ID files so you can recover in case you make a mistake.

2. Disable replication of the Public Address Book until the recertification is complete.

3. Take a certifier ID from your organization to the administration certifier in the other organization. Have him use your organization's certifier ID (or an OU certifier ID) to recertify all user IDs except his own. If he recertified his own ID, he could no longer access the server in his own organization to recertify it.

4. Have the certifier in the other organization use your organization's certifier ID (or an OU certifier ID) to recertify the servers in his organization.

5. If he is manually recertifying by creating a safe ID, having it certified, then merging the certified safe ID into the original server ID, shut down the server before merging the ID. Otherwise, there is a good chance you'll corrupt the server ID. When done, restart the server.

6. The administrator can then recertify his own ID.

7. At this point, everyone should be able to access servers in the new organization (the one whose certifier ID was used to recertify them), but they will not have full access to databases until ACLs have been updated.

When you have recertified all users and all servers in the organization, you have to update all instances of all user and server names in the Public Address Book including LocalDomainServer, Mail-in Database Documents, People documents, Monitoring documents, Groups, ACLs in all databases on servers, Server documents, Connection documents.... In short, you have a lot of work ahead of you, unless you have set up the Administration Process to run on your server.

TIP

Implement the Administration Process in the organization to be merged into yours, and run the process to update user names and server names. It will save a considerable amount of work. When everything has been updated by the Administration Process, you can merge Public Address Books.

Merging Public Address Books

The Public Address Book provides a unified identity for all of the Notes servers and users who share that Address Book. The Public Address Book is associated with a Domain used for mail routing. The Domain name and the organization name are usually the same.

If your organization is merging with another organization, as described previously, then the administrator will probably want to merge the Public Address Books to simplify administration. Otherwise, you would have to address some users within your own organization using an explicit path to the other domain—for example, John Doe/West/Acme@XYZ.

To merge two Domains, decide which Public Address Book will be used for the single Domain. Copy from the other Public Address Book into the primary one all Person and Server documents that you want to have in the merged Domain. Determine whether you will need any of the other documents, such as Connection documents and Group documents, and copy those as well, and edit them to reflect the setup in the new Domain. For example, make sure that the servers in the old Domain are now part of the LocalDomainServers group, and no longer part of the OtherDomainServers group. When all the documents you require have been copied over, recertify users and servers so that all users will be able to communicate within the single Domain. When everyone can communicate successfully, delete the old Public Address Book, or rename it and save it until everything has been thoroughly tested. Edit the Domain= line in the NOTES.INI file on servers that have moved from the old Domain so that the line reflects the name of the new Domain.

Splitting a Domain

There are occasions when you may want to split a single domain into multiple domains. For example, your company may have grown too large, and you decide to create multiple domains to more effectively delegate administration. Or you may be spinning off part of the organization.

Splitting a domain is essentially the reverse of merging two domains. Make a nonreplica copy of the Public Address Book, and delete person and server documents from each Public Address Book until it contains only the users and servers that belong in that Domain. Change the name of the mail domain in the relevant Person documents, and the name of the domain and the network in the Server documents.

Edit and create Domain and Connection documents for the new Domain to make sure the new Domain can communicate with the old Domain (if appropriate), change the administrator names, and edit the LocalDomainServers group. Edit the Domain= line in the NOTES.INI line, then shut down the server by typing e or q at the server console and start the server again by typing on the Server icon. This reinitializes the server with the new information in the NOTES.INI file. Once the server is running again, replicate the Public Address Book to other servers in the domain.

Setting Up the Administration Process

If you do not have the Administration Process running, you have to rename and recertify users and servers manually. This is done by creating a safe ID and sending it to the administration certifier, who certifies the ID with a new certifier ID. The new ID is then sent back and is merged into the original ID.

Manual recertification is a cumbersome process, especially if you are renaming or recertifying servers and users that are all within the same Notes domain, and you have an R4 server running in that domain.

 To take advantage of Notes R4's Administration Process (new to Notes R4), you have to set up the process on a Notes R4 server. Do the following to set up the process:

1. Create a certification log database. This is done by creating a new database using the Certification Log template on the Notes R4 server. Name the certification log database CERTLOG.NSF. This database keeps track of all users and servers in the organization, and which certificates they have.

2. Create an Administration Requests database. There is a template for this database on the R4 server. This database and its related administrative functions were not available in earlier releases of Notes.

3. If you do not have any hierarchically certified servers, manually certify one server with a hierarchical name. You have to do this because the Administration Process can be run only on a hierarchically named server.

4. In the Public Address Book, ensure that administrators have the authority to modify Person and Server documents.

5. In the ACL of the Public Address Book, specify an administration server.

6. Ensure that ADMINP is running as a task on the server.

When these steps have been competed, the Administration Process can be used to streamline the process of renaming and recertifying users and servers in your organization.

Assuming that you have recertified a server with a new hierarchical certifier ID, that server is now in your new organization. If the Public Address Book has been replicated throughout the organization, then other users and servers in the organization can authenticate with the new server, as long as they have a common ancestral certificate.

Troubleshooting Recertification

If you are having trouble after recertification or renaming, verify that everything is correct in the server setup, the same as you would do with a new server. Check that the correct ports are enabled, that other servers and users have been given access in the Server document, and that you have any necessary Connection documents set up. You should also remember that the changes made by Administration Process are replicated only within your Notes organization.

If you communicate with outside organizations, you should ensure that they have the new name and a safe copy of the new ID so they can create a cross-certificate.

You should also verify that the Administration Process has run correctly and has completed its processing. To do this, look in the Administration Requests database. When the Administration Process runs, it creates a response document showing which changes have been made. Two fields—the Action Completed On field and the Errors field—show whether the action was successfully completed. If there was an error, you can fix it, then select Perform Request Again to force the Administration Process to rehandle the request.

You can also check the Event Monitor and ACL Monitor documents in the Statistics & Events database for specific errors. These documents are described in Chapter 36.

Moving a Notes Server Within the Organization

Moving a server within an organization is virtually the same process as moving a person within the organization. The administrator requests certification for the server, and selects the new certifier ID. The Administration Process handles the remainder of the process, changing the name of the server throughout the Public Address Book.

Consider where the changes have to be made. If the server is a home server for some users, then the server name has to be made to the home-server information in each user's Person document. If the server is a passthru server or is the destination of a passthru server, then changes have to be made in the Security section of Server documents, and in passthru Connection documents. But (perhaps most important of all) when the server's name has changed, users who are accustomed to accessing the server will no longer have any access because they will no longer have a common ancestral certifier.

After the server has had its certifier changed, you have to recertify all users who need to access the server, assuming that the server has been moved into a new Notes organization.

If the server has previously communicated with its new organization, you may have to reprioritize ports. Notes attempts to use the first enabled communication port, and moves to the second port only if the first port is not available. Likewise, you may want to verify your lowest cost-routing connections. Moving to a new Notes organization could mean that communication alternatives not previously available can now be used. For example, you may be able to communicate using TCP/IP over a local network connection rather than having to dial in directly, now that the server is part of the organization you are calling.

Managing and Maintaining Databases

The database designer generally works on a local copy of the database while it is being designed, but when the database is ready for production and it is time to move it to the Notes server, the responsibility for the database is shared by the system administrator and the database manager. The database manager is responsible for seeing that database security is enforced and that users

35

**ADMINISTERING
USERS, SERVERS,
AND DATABASES**

have access to the data they need. The system administrator, on the other hand, is responsible for the impact of the database on the Notes system, and the impact of the system on the database.

Databases have to be monitored for usage and size. Corrupted databases have to be repaired and put back into production. View and full-text indexes need updating. Databases need to be moved to a new location, or replicated so they are accessible by users in other locations. These are the responsibility of the system administrator.

Moving Databases into Production

Databases have to be put into production where users can get to them. That means that a database may have to be replicated to other servers if the workgroup that will be using the database works in different locations.

Something you may want to consider when looking at testing databases is that you should test them on an R4 server, in addition to any testing you may do on a development workstation. You may want to do these tests on a separate server, set up solely for the purpose of testing. Then, when the tests are complete, you can move the database to a more secure production server.

Set Up Replication if Needed

The first duty of the system administrator is to ensure that a suitable replication schedule is set up for the database, if necessary. That includes scheduling the replication, ensuring that the correct Connection documents are available, and that Group documents are created in the Public Address Book, if there are any new groups in the access control list. The modifications to the Public Address Book then need to be replicated to the other servers, where users will be accessing the database.

Determine Where to Store the Database

The administrator also has to work with the database manager to determine where to store the database on each Notes server. The default location for all databases is in the Notes data directory, defined in the NOTES.INI file (for example, Directory=C:/NOTES/NOTEDATA). If you create a subdirectory for the database, the directory is automatically placed beneath the data directory. If you create a database and give it the name MYDATA/SALES.NSF, the database will be placed on the Notes server as C:/NOTES/NOTEDATA/MYDATA/SALES.NSF.

Directory Pointers

You can increase database security by placing databases in directories that are outside the Notes directory structure. You can use network security to limit direct access to the databases from the operating system, and block access for all Notes users except those given access in a directory pointer. Users will see the linked directory as a subdirectory under the Notes data directory, but they will not be able to access it unless they have been given access.

> **CAUTION**
>
> Using a directory pointer on Netware or OS/2 will tend to slow the system down. Also, if users can gain direct access to a Notes database without going through the Notes server, they have local access. On a UNIX server, do not use the 1n command to create a soft link, because this circumvents ACL security.

In Notes R4, you can protect yourself against users gaining local access to databases by enforcing access security on local databases.

To create a directory pointer, you need a text editor. Then do the following:

1. Create a text file in the default Notes data directory. Give the file a .DIR extension.
2. The first line of the text file is the complete path to the directory where you are pointing.
3. Subsequent lines are optional. Without any additional lines, any user can access the directory. If you create additional lines, they should contain the names of any groups who can access the directory being pointed to, and the full hierarchical name of any individual users who should have access to the directory. Anyone not listed in the directory pointer can see the directory but cannot access it.

For example, to point to a directory on the G: drive using a Novell Network, you could create a directory-pointer text file named ACME.DIR as follows:

```
>        G:/Projects/Acme
>        AcmeUsers
```

Database Pointers

Database pointers are similar to directory links, but they let you store a single database outside of the Notes directory structure. To the user, the database will look as if it is in the Notes data directory, and security will be handled by the access control list, as usual.

As with the directory pointers, create a text file using a text editor, and place the text file in the Notes data directory. Give the text file a name that has a .NSF extension, just like a Notes database. Then type a single line that has the complete path and filename to the database you are pointing to. For example, create a database pointer named WESTSALE.NSF, and a single line of text with the path, such as G:/Projects/Acme/WESTSALE.NSF.

Monitoring Databases

When databases are in production, they have to be monitored and maintained. Although many of the maintenance tasks can be scheduled to run automatically by setting parameters in the NOTES.INI file, in Server Configuration documents, or in Program documents, it is worth reviewing those that have specific functions in terms of database maintenance.

Fixing Corrupted Databases

Databasescan become corrupted during an improper shutdown of the system, or by an external program that accesses the database incorrectly. Whenever Notes detects a database that has been closed improperly, it examines every field in every document and deletes documents that are damaged. This ensures that the damaged document does not get replicated to other copies of the database. It may be that users can live with this simple solution, allowing Notes to automatically fix documents.

However, it is the system administrator's job to ensure that the system is running as efficiently as possible. The job of examining databases and fixing any corrupted ones takes time and system resources. This task can therefore be scheduled to run once for all databases on the server, and the task can be scheduled for the middle of the night, when there are few users on the system. The program that does this is the Fixup task, described earlier in this chapter.

Corrupted databases can be restored (after corrupted documents have been deleted) through replication, by manually copying and pasting the deleted documents from another copy of the database, or by deleting the database and replacing it with a backup copy.

Fixing Corrupted Views

Corrupted views can result in the information in documents and views being out of synchronization. Sometimes, you will be unable to open a view that is corrupted, there may be odd characters appearing in the view, documents may be missing, or you may find messages in the Notes log.

You can repair corrupted views in a couple of ways. First, you may be able to rebuild the view from the workstation by opening the view and pressing Shift+F9, or you can press Ctrl+Shift+F9 to rebuild or refresh all views in a database.

You can run the Updall task on a specific database and include an -r flag to rebuild the corrupted view. You would enter the following at the Server Console:

```
Load Updall filename -r
```

Other options include restoring a view by copying the view from a backup copy of the database, or you can create a replica copy of the original database.

TIP

You can create a new replica to fix corrupted views, but you want to make sure the users can still access the database without having to delete the old icon and reopen the new replica. To do this:

1. Back up the database with a corrupted view, and rename the copy.

2. Create a replica of the original database, giving it the same server and directory as the original, but give the new replica a different name temporarily.

3. Create the new replica immediately, and copy the ACL. Make sure that you replicate all documents—for example, turn off the indicator that replicates documents created only after a certain date.

4. Delete the original database, then rename the new replica with the filename of the original database.

Monitoring Database Size

Database size can be monitored in the Notes Log by examining the Database Usage, Database Sizes, and Usage By User views. Individual databases can be monitored by examining the Information page in the Database Properties box. You can also use the Statistics Reporting database and monitor whitespace in databases, or run Compact on databases that fall below a specific threshold.

> **CAUTION**
>
> Remember, if you are running in a mixed Notes R3 and Notes R4 environment, compacting a database in R4 converts it to a new file format. To ensure that R3 databases do not get compacted, rename them with an .NS3 file extension.

You can also set up quotas for database size, and generate warnings at thresholds you determine. This is done by clicking on the Databases icon on the Server Administration panel and selecting Database Quotas. Specify a size, and indicate whether to generate a warning in the Miscellaneous Events view of the Notes Log. When a size limit is reached, the administrator or database manager will have to remove unnecessary documents to create additional space. The Database Quotas function is new to Notes R4.

Monitoring Full-Text Indexes

Full-text indexes are updated by Updall. If your system is starting to run out of space, you may want to consider minimizing full-text indexes by deleting them and recreating them with more restrictive settings, or simply deleting them altogether. Full-text indexes can be deleted or recreated from the Full-text page of the Database Properties box. With some databases that are frequently used and searched, such as the Help database, the full-text index is a powerful tool. So consider carefully whether you really want to delete the index.

Making Databases Available to Users

Assuming users have access to a server, the administrator can make it easier for them to locate databases using two tools: the database catalog and the database library.

The Database Catalog

The database catalog CATALOG.NSF can be created on the server. The catalog is updated by the `Catalog` task, which by default runs at 1 a.m. The catalog lists all databases available on the server, unless the designer specifically indicates that the database should not be listed.

The Database Library

The database library is a new feature of Notes R4 that is similar to the database catalog, but it lists only those databases published to the library by the library's database manager (the librarian). When a user attempts to open a database from the library, Notes searches for the database using the replica ID; it will search first on the local hard drive, then on the user's home server, then on other servers. The first occurrence of the database will be opened.

A library is created by making a new database using the DBLIB4.NTF template. After creating the database, you can create a list of librarians in the Librarians view. You can publish a database in the library if you are a librarian and have the library on your desktop.

Highlight the database icon you want to publish and select File | Database | Publish.

Enter an abstract describing the database in the dialog box displayed by Notes. This creates a document for the database in the library.

If a user has only reader access to the database library and attempts to publish a database, a Notes Agent automatically generates mail to the librarian, who can then decide whether to publish the database. This has to be done, because a reader does not have access to create or modify documents on their own.

Updating Database Design

You can refresh the design of databases, if they are linked to a specific design template, by running the Design task. This is described earlier in this chapter.

Moving and Deleting Databases

You can move databases from one server to another by making a new replica copy of them. Before you make a new replica copy, determine whether the ACL needs changing for its new location. Also, determine if the database is used as a mail-in database, in which case you will have to edit the mail-in database document to reflect the new location. Notify users of the new location, then delete the original database, if you want, by highlighting the database and selecting File | Database | Delete.

Notes cannot delete databases that are currently being used, such as the Notes Log, the Public Address Book, and user mail files. You can, however, delete these files at the operating-system level. Users will still have icons for the databases on their desktops, but they will be unable to open the databases.

Enhanced Integration Features in Windows NT

Notes 4.5 has several enhanced features for organizations that have standardized on a Windows NT environment (3.51 and 4.0, on both Intel and Digital Alpha platforms). These features include single-password logon, directory synchronization so that the Public Address Book can be managed from Notes or NT, and NT event logging. Support for the Microsoft SMS (System Management Server) is also planned for Notes 4.5.

NT Single Logon

With the single-logon feature, you access the NT service using the NT password, and you then use the same password to unlock the Notes ID file. This gives the NT user secure access to all Notes messaging features, including data encryption and digital signatures from Notes or third parties, without having to log on to Notes separately. This feature is available only to Notes 4.5 users on NT workstations.

The single logon runs as a native NT service in the NT service control panel. Once a user logs onto NT with a valid password, he can log onto Notes and won't be prompted again for his Notes password. A request gets sent to the Single Logon Service to unlock the Notes ID file. When the unlocking is successful, the user is authenticated with the Notes server and can proceed as normal.

If you change your password on NT, Notes will automatically prompt you to change your password on Notes so that the passwords stay synchronized. You can then change your ID by selecting File | Tools | User ID | Set Password.

The single logon is not restricted to a single Notes ID. This provides another security model, allowing you to centrally administer security through the NT Server if you wish rather than use the Notes distributed public key/private key IDs.

If you run your Domino Server on the Window NT Server, you will still need to manually enter the password for Domino. The single logon works only with Notes clients on NT workstations.

Directory Synchronization Between Notes and NT

When new users are created and deleted in Notes 4.5, user accounts are automatically set up for Windows NT as well, and vice versa. You can manage user directories using the Windows NT User Manager for Domains or the Notes Public Address Book.

Directory synchronization is managed through a Notes menu that is installed in the Windows NT User Manager during the Notes installation. Using menu options, the Windows NT administrator can specify that new NT user accounts or existing accounts get added to the Domino Name and Address Book, and vice versa. The NT administrator can choose a Refresh option to create users in the Domino Address Book, or he can respond to a prompt when he exits from the Windows NT User Manager and have the Domino server create the new users at that time.

In order to maintain synchronization, the Notes Administrator must create users by registering them as new users in the Server Administration panel and delete users only from the Actions menu.

Event Logging in Windows NT

Events such as replication and mail routing are routinely logged in Notes as informational events, or as alarms in the event of a failure. When the Domino 4.5 server is running on a Windows NT workstation, the administrator can redirect logging to the Windows NT Event Logger. In this way, the NT administrator can monitor both Notes events and NT events from a single vantage point.

Log to NT Event Viewer is available as a notification option on the Event Notification form in EVENTS4.NSF. It is visible only if you have the Domino server running on Windows NT.

Once an event is logged to the NT Event Viewer, it can be seen under the Application view in NT. The source for Notes events will be listed as NotesEvent. The five levels of severity on Domino are reduced to three levels in NT, as follows:

- Fatal and Failure are grouped under Error.
- Warning (high and low) are grouped under Warning.
- Normal becomes Informational.

When you view an event in NT, you will see the same message you see on the Domino server.

NT SMS Support

SMS (Software Management System) is a Microsoft product that lets you manage networked PCs. SMS includes hardware and software inventory, software distribution and installation, diagnostic and remote-control tools, and network packet decoding.

The SMS relies on a Package Definition File (PDF), which is a text file with predefined workstation, sharing, and inventory property settings for a package. When a new package (that is, installation parameters for a software application) is created, you can define package properties using a PDF. Lotus planned to have PDFs available for Notes and SMS customers in late 1996 so that administrators could install or upgrade users to Notes 4.11a without having to visit each desk or rely on user intervention.

New PDFs will be posted for downloading on the Lotus Web site, on the Systems Management page at `http://www.lotus.com/systems`.

Summary

When the Notes system is up and running, the system administrator must perform administrative tasks to maintain and monitor the system. These tasks involve registering and managing system users, managing servers and their deployment, maintaining servers, and monitoring and maintaining databases. Many of these tasks can be set up to run more or less automatically, but they must be closely monitored by the administrator to ensure that the system is running smoothly as more users and servers are added and databases grow.

In addition to functions that are available using the Domino server, Notes 4.5 has the added capability of integrating logon and directory services, and event logging with Windows NT.

When you start making changes to user IDs and server IDs or start making configuration changes to your Notes servers, anticipate the possibility that you may have to roll back to where you were before the changes, and start over again. Always make a backup of any files that might be changed during administrative tasks. For example, you want to protect user and server ID files, the Public Address Book, and the NOTES.INI file, and minimize the possible impact of any mistake you make during these administrative processes.

Troubleshooting the System

by Sam Juvonen

IN THIS CHAPTER

CHAPTER 36

Although often bothersome, troubleshooting is a necessary skill in today's networked world of computer systems. As systems grow more powerful and increase user productivity, they usually require more knowledge from administrators and designers. Lotus Notes offers great leaps in productivity for workgroups. It carries with it much complexity, however, and its diverse array of components can challenge the best of administrators new to Lotus Notes.

This chapter takes a different approach in looking at troubleshooting. Instead of listing all of the possible error messages and their causes, which is outside the scope of this book, it looks at the tools available, the documentation, and the components of the system. Having a good understanding of the important components will enable you to troubleshoot a wider array of issues. When something goes awry, knowledge of the components and their relationships to one another is the best way to prevail against system problems. For particular error messages, look in the "Troubleshooting" view of the Notes Help database for the heading "Error Messages A-Z."

Tools

Let's take a moment to look at the various tools you have at hand in Lotus Notes. We'll look at the Notes Log database as well as the Statistics and Events server tasks.

The Notes server records into the Log various system activities as they occur. We'll look at the most helpful views of this database.

Statistics and Events are optional server tasks that you can enable to gather more information about a server's behavior (Statistics) and capture events of various severity's as they happen (Events).

The Notes Log

The Notes Log template (LOG.NTF) is used to create the Log database (LOG.NSF) on a server as it starts (if it doesn't exist). The server checks for the presence of this database each time it starts, so if you delete your Log database, the server will re-create another the next time it starts.

The Log shows information about all types of server activity that has been recorded by the server logger, which is an intrinsic process of the server, as opposed to a visible server task such as the replicator.

A Log database is created on each workstation, as well. Not surprisingly, less information is logged at a workstation than on a server. Users can look in their personal logs to see the results of modem activity that have occurred on their system (if the user has enabled logging for the modem port).

Replication Events

Each time Notes replicates between two servers or between a client and a server, the replication session creates a log entry using the Replication Event form. This event document lists what took place during the replication. Figure 36.1 shows an example of a Replication Event document.

FIGURE 36.1.

A sample Replication Event document from the Notes Log database.

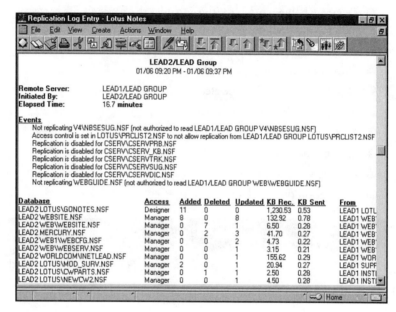

Detailed in the Replication Event are the following:

- The name of the receiving station
- The starting and ending time
- The names of the servers involved
- The duration of the replication
- A list of events that occurred
- A list of databases that were replicated

The amount of detail shown in a Replication Event document depends in part on the type of replication that occurred. For pull-pull replication, there are two event documents recorded, one for each receiving station; the information contained in the document pertains to databases that were read by the receiving station. For push-pull replication, there is one event document written; the controlling station writes the document. The information relates to both databases that were read from as well as those that were written to on the remote server.

The Events section contains entries for problems that occurred during replication. Commonly, entries report the inability to replicate all or part of a database due to settings—those in the

ACL that affect replication, for example, or the inability to establish or maintain a session with a server.

Databases that were examined and found to have nothing to replicate are not referenced in this document. If a database replicates documents, it is logged in the database list at the bottom of the document. This list reveals much information about the databases that replicated:

- Database being written to (this includes the name of the server or workstation and the path to the database file)
- Access level during write operation
- Number of documents added
- Number of documents deleted
- Number of documents updated
- Number of kilobytes received
- Number of kilobytes sent
- Remote server name
- Replication type: Pull or Push

> **NOTE**
>
> Notes 4 now reveals the direction of the replication with a parenthesized flag for each database.

A Pull operation indicates that the remote server is writing to the database. A Push operation indicates that the local station is writing to the database on the remote server. The access level relates to the station doing the writing.

Miscellaneous Events

Miscellaneous event documents are a running log of everything that passes through the server console. Both system-generated messages (as well as administration commands entered at the keyboard, along with the resulting output) are reflected chronologically in this type of document. Figure 36.2 shows a sample of a Miscellaneous Event document.

After a Miscellaneous Event document accumulates about 40KB worth of log entries, the server saves the document and begins a new one. The level of activity on a server determines how many documents will be written in any given period of time. The busier the server, the quicker the documents get full and the more documents get written.

These documents are best used when the time of an occurrence is known. Knowing the time, you can locate the documents that were written around that time and use them to determine what activities were occurring on the server.

36

FIGURE 36.2.

A sample Miscellaneous Event document from the Notes Log database.

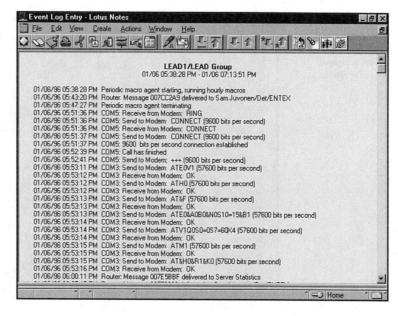

On a workstation, Miscellaneous events are written for all communication attempts made by the workstation over a network or a modem. The start and stop times reflect the period of the Notes session. Each time Notes is started, a new document is created.

The Log database is initially configured to purge documents that are older than seven days. It purges these "old" documents every two or three days (one-third of seven is the purge interval). You can change the setting under the Replication Settings for the Log database (File | Replication | Replication Settings).

Mail Routing Events

Mail-routing event documents are written into a server log file, but not into a personal log file. These documents are much the same as Miscellaneous event documents, where messages that occur on the server console are written to this document, but the entries reflect only those activities that are performed by the Mail Router. Figure 36.3 shows a sample of a Mail Routing Events document. These events are written into both the Mail Routing and the Miscellaneous events documents.

TIP

By setting the configuration parameter `MAIL_LOG_TO_MISCEVENTS=0`, the events will appear in only the Mail Routing Events documents, making them more vital and reducing the clutter in the Miscellaneous Events documents. Alternatively, you can set `LOG_MAILROUTING=0` to turn off logging of mail-routing events.

FIGURE 36.3.

A sample of a Mail Routing Events document from the Notes Log database.

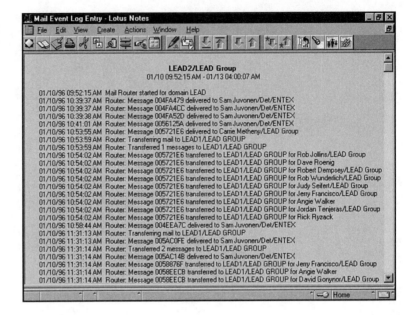

Phone Calls

Notes records information about the phone calls that are made using Phone Call documents. Both servers and client stations write these documents. Figure 36.4 shows a sample Phone Call document. Important information that can be gleaned from these documents includes the baud and carrier rates that were established; the volume of traffic that passed during the connection; and the error count of port errors, CRC errors and retransmissions. High error counts typically indicate line problems. High port errors indicate that the serial port is not functioning properly.

> **TIP**
>
> If the server answering the phone field is empty, the two stations never passed authentication. Communication was not established, which is most likely a line problem.

These documents can also be used to verify basic information such as the phone number being dialed. If the number appears to be incorrect, either it was entered incorrectly in a dialog box (if the call was initiated manually), or the connection document leading to this server contains the wrong number.

Statistics and Events

The Notes server has the capability of reporting detailed information about its behavior. These reports can be either of a general, statistical nature or focused on certain events that occur at random. Using this feature is optional, but through the regular usage and monitoring of statistics and events, you can often spot problems before they become serious and resolve them at that time.

FIGURE 36.4.

A sample Phone Call document from the Notes Log database.

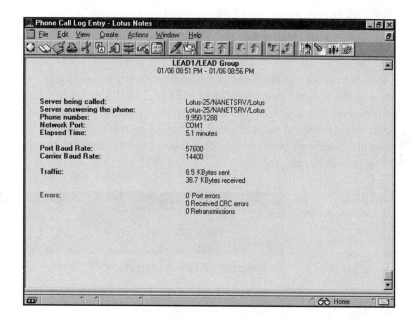

From Notes R3 to R4

In Notes R3, gathering statistics and events is accomplished using several databases. The EVTTYPES.NMF database contains all of the possible statistic types and event error messages. A statistics-collection database, STATREP.NSF, collects the statistic and alarm reports. The Public Address Book is used to configure the statistics and events to monitor. Trouble tickets are routed to an alarm-tracking database, ALARMTRK.NSF.

Notes R4 consolidates this process into a distinct administration process using only two databases. The EVENTS4.NSF database houses the definitions of the statistics and event messages and it is also the location for creating the documents that specify what you, as the administrator, wish to monitor. The STATREP.NSF database is used to collect the statistics and alarms as in R3. The Public Address Book is no longer involved in the configuration.

When upgrading an R3 server to R4, the Public Address Book may contain R3 statistics and event-monitor configuration documents. In EVENTS4.NSF, an action is provided that helps you clean up the Address book by removing the forms and views associated with the R3 statistics features. This action is designed for you to execute manually if and when you need it. You should run it only once in your domain. If you have no such configuration documents in your Public Address Book, then you may run this Agent without concern; otherwise, first create equivalent documents in the new database, delete the old documents, and only then use the action.

Configuring Statistics and Events

The server requires that additional tasks be loaded in order for it to report statistics and event documents into the Statistics Reporting database (STATREP.NSF). These tasks are called REPORT (the Reporter) and EVENT (the Event reporter).

The first time you load REPORT, the server will create a new Statistics Reporting database from the STATREP.NTF template that is included with the server.

The first execution of the Reporter task automatically creates a new Server to Monitor document in the Statistics and Events (EVENT4.NSF) database; inside this document is the name of the server that will be monitored, the mail-in name of the Statistics database, the statistics collection interval (in minutes), and the period for statistical analysis to be performed (daily, monthly, weekly, or never). Figure 36.5 shows a sample Server to Monitor document from the Statistics and Events database.

FIGURE 36.5.

The document that the Report task creates in the Statistics and Events database.

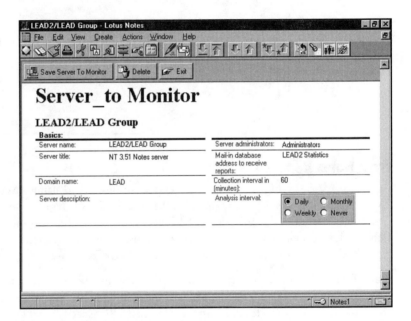

In order for REPORT and EVENT to launch each time the server is started, you will need to manually edit the NOTES.INI file. Find the `ServerTasks=` entry and add these two task names at the end separated by commas. For example:

```
ServerTasks=Router,Replica,Update,Report,Event
```

Documentation (Printed and Online)

Lotus Notes ships with an abundance of documentation, both printed and online. Because printed documentation often sits on a shelf far away from the problem site, let's look through the online documentation databases. These databases should be installed on at least one of your servers and readily accessible to all of your administrators.

Notes Help

It's not surprising that the Notes Help database, being the primary source of online information, is the largest of the online documentation databases. It is on the order of 20MB in size. This database should be full-text indexed for easiest access by you and your users. Inside, you'll find subjects ranging from using Notes to designing databases to administering the system.

Administration Help

Specifically for administrators, Administration Help (HELPADM.NSF) contains detailed information about planning, general administration, and network protocols. When you want specific details about configuring multiple protocols, for instance, this is the database to read. It includes sample configuration files that will prove very helpful.

Server Install Guide

This brief guide describes how to install the Notes server software on Windows, OS/2, and UNIX. Each chapter is roughly the same, because Notes behaves much the same way on any platform. Unique platform idiosyncrasies are pointed out, however.

Workstation Install Guide

This brief guide describes how to install the Notes workstation software on Windows, OS/2, and UNIX. It also discusses methods for distributing and sharing the Notes program files to workstations throughout your network.

Migration Guide

The Migration Guide focuses on migrating to the R4 environment from an established R3 network. Detailed are steps to plan your migration, upgrade servers, optimize performance, and upgrade applications.

Web Navigator Admin Guide

The Web Navigator Admin Guide explains how to configure the Web Retriever task (WEB.EXE) that is used to retrieve HTML pages from the World Wide Web, effectively making Notes clients a Web browser.

Notes Knowledgebase

A truly valuable resource is a frequently updated database titled the Lotus Notes Knowledgebase. Lotus produces and maintains this database, which is replicated through the Lotus Notes Network (LNN) (which is hosted and maintained by Lotus) and distributed periodically on CD-ROM. You can obtain your copy by calling Lotus to sign up on LNN or by purchasing the Knowledgebase directly from Lotus.

Global Assistance: Online Forums

You can find a plethora of information about Lotus Notes online, from public Internet forums to the World Wide Web to premium pay services such as CompuServe. These repositories are an excellent way to communicate with other users and administrators. In many locations you will find rich libraries of files that may help you in solving problems, deploying applications, and improving network or modem communications.

CompuServe LOTUSCOMM

CompuServe is one of the oldest and richest content-laden online resources available. Hundreds of online Forums exist on a vast array of topics. Many software vendors have a presence to support their products by answering questions, providing tips on using software, and even distributing updates. Forums are frequented by interested parties who want to learn more or to contribute by helping others.

Lotus has a forum dedicated to its communication products, Lotus Notes and cc:Mail. The LOTUSCOMM forum is an excellent place to meet new people who may have experienced issues that you are seeing for the first time. Many custom-database applications, modem files, and other related items can be found in the software libraries.

CompuServe also provides a unique Lotus Notes service that gives you e-mail gateways and server-storage space. You can use this service in lieu of deploying a large number of servers that must be geographically dispersed. Contact CompuServe for more information.

WorldCom

Wolf Communications hosts a Notes communications service called WorldCom. It provides e-mail gateways, server storage, as well as a wide variety of topical Notes databases. For differing rates, you can receive newswires, interactively communicate to Internet Usenet newgroups and replicate information databases.

LNOTES-L Usenet List

On the Internet—or, more specifically in this case, Usenet—you can find a dizzying array of newsgroups, which are much like CompuServe's Forums or dial-up, bulletin-board message areas. Equipped with a news reader, you can read and post messages related to specific topics.

The Lotus Notes newsgroup is named LNOTES-L. Notes users from around the world participate daily in this group.

Server Stability

If your server tends to crash frequently, how can you explore the possible causes? Notes has a process for creating a special file (NOTES.RIP) when a crash occurs. This file contains information about the state of the system at the time of the crash. Let's look at this process and an example of using the .RIP file to find the problem.

Server Crashes: .RIP Files or UNIX Core Dumps

At times a server or workstation may crash. Not all crashes are fatal to Notes, but most are. Isolated incidents, if rare, aren't worth worrying about, but a server that crashes repeatedly needs to be investigated. When a crash occurs, Notes invokes a program commonly known as Quincy (for QNC.EXE). Quincy generates, depending on platform type, either a NOTES.RIP file or, in the case of UNIX, a core dump file. This file is appended to, not overwritten, each time a crash occurs.

For Trivial Pursuit fans, a friend observed that the name Quincy comes from the popular 1980s TV show about a curious coroner (starring Jack Klugman), hence the use of the extension .RIP for the output file.

A .RIP file consists of several sections. While much of the file is in the form of a hex dump, you can determine the cause of many crashes with some careful reading. At the top of the file is some basic information such as the general condition that occurred, the amount of free memory (and if applicable, swap-file space). The contents of the registers are displayed, followed by the main section, the stack trace.

The stack trace has two parts. On the left is the hex dump of the stack contents. To the right of the hex dump is the ASCII representation of the hex codes. By perusing the ASCII section, you can often determine what program or task was executing. Not far below the name of the task, you can often find the filename of the database that was in use.

You may find that your server is generating .RIP files every morning just after 5 a.m. By looking at the .RIP, you may see that the UPDALL server task was running, and the last database referenced was the NAMES.NSF file. This may indicate that the Public Address Book (or the database that is referenced) has one or more corrupted views. You can often fix that problem by loading UPDALL with the -R switch to rebuild the indexes of that database:

```
LOAD UPDALL -R NAMES.NSF
```

Without looking at the .RIP file, you may have determined that, because your NOTES.INI contains UPDALL in the ServerTasksAt5 entry, UPDALL is causing the problem. You won't know, however, which database is causing trouble for UPDALL.

API Programs

Let's say your server is crashing every morning at 7 a.m. You peruse your configuration looking for the culprit. The .INI file yields no clues; you can't find a `ServerTasksAt__` entry for 7 a.m.

If your environment requires the development and use of custom API server add-in programs, you may encounter situations like this where the API program is causing the server problems.

Using the .RIP file and comparing the time with your Program documents in the Public Address Book, you might find that these seem to be the culprit.

Turn off one or more of the suspect API programs for a short period and determine whether the problem disappears. If so, your only recourse is to take this information back to the API developers and wait for a fix.

It would be a good idea to have API developers run their tasks on a development server that cannot affect the contents or schedule of your production servers. Often, though, these custom tasks behave well in a limited development environment and misbehave only in a loaded server. Try copying the databases being used by the API programmers to their server, complete with all the contents so that their code is tested under load. You might also enable many background macros and other server tasks to put the development server under a load to simulate your production server.

Server Issues

Let's now take a look at some issues in four categories regarding your servers: visibility, access, replication, and mail routing.

Visibility of your servers is manifested through the dialog boxes used on workstations. A user might want to open a new database (using File | Database | Open); how can you control which servers they can see in this dialog box?

How can you control access to your servers? If you expect to have access but are not allowed, what might the causes be? How can you resolve them?

As you maintain many databases, you might find that too few documents replicate. What controls do you have to configure that might correct the problem? Additionally, you might find that documents disappear after replication or that replication between servers is not occurring or it fails to finish. We'll look at the details surrounding these issues.

If mail isn't routing correctly, we'll look at all of the pieces that could be causing problems if not configured properly. For instance, the Public Address Book contains many different documents that can affect mail; we'll look at these. The router creates a Delivery Failure Report when a message cannot be delivered; we'll look at the information you can use from this document to find and correct the problem. We'll also talk about mail files and the MAIL.BOX database.

Server Visibility

What is happening if you suddenly see a different list of servers on your File Open dialog list than you normally expect?

First, let's talk about the File | Database | Open (or File | Open Database in R3) menu command, which works differently in R4 than in R3. Essentially, there are two different server lists in R4, whereas there is only one in R3.

> **TIP**
>
> You can also open a database by clicking the alternate mouse button somewhere on your workspace (not on an icon). Then choose the Open Database item from the resulting "context" menu that appears.

This command initially brings you to a directory of the Notes data directory on the local drive. Looking in the drop-down list will show you a list of servers, which is determined from the collection of icons that you have on your desktop and the list of server-connection documents in your Public Address Book. If you have icons from three different servers that you access via a network port somewhere on the desktop, and you have a connection document to another server that you communicate via a modem port, then the list will contain Local plus four other server names. This quick, local lookup means that the File Open dialog box and the server list will typically perform very quickly.

> **TIP**
>
> You may find that even after you've removed all icons that refer to a particular server, this server still shows up in the initial list. To remove this server name from the File Open list (if you have no references to it any longer, you probably won't need it in the list), do this: open the Server Connections view in your Personal Address Book and remove the connection document to that server.

The second server list appears when you choose Other... from the initial server list. If you are connected to a network or are online with your modem, this time Notes reaches out and asks your home server (or the one you're connected to via modem) for a list of available servers. The resulting list is then a combination of the first list and any other available servers to which you don't have local references. This is called a Name Server lookup; your home server is acting as Name Server, providing you with this list.

What determines the list that the server returns to you? The Notes Named Network settings in the server documents in your domain. The list will contain those servers that belong to the same Notes Named Network as your Name server. Notes builds the list by looking at all servers in the same Notes Named Network as the user's home server.

If a user's home server goes down, then Notes will use a "fallback" method to obtain the server list. The method used depends on the network protocol. In general, the workstation looks for another Notes server from which it can get its list. This list will reflect all of the servers in the same Notes Named Network as the "fallback" server; the list might be completely different than the one the user normally sees.

Server Access

Several factors control who can access a server. Authentication occurs between Notes ID files. Depending on how these files have been certified, access may not succeed. The Server document also contains entries governing access based on names that are entered in these fields. This section also will look at entries you can use in the NOTES.INI file to control access over specific ports.

Authentication and Certification

When two Notes entities (servers or workstations) attempt to communicate, the first hurdle is authentication. A comparison of Notes IDs reveals whether the two sides trust the other. There are two distinct methods of authentication. The first involves the older, nonhierarchical ID structure, where an ID file contains one or more certificates. The second involves the newer, hierarchical ID structure, in which an ID contains one certificate that gives it a hierarchical name, adding at least an organization name to the common name on the ID, and perhaps additional organizational units as well.

Flat Certification: Missing Certificates or Lacking Trust

During authentication, under nonhierarchical certification, these certificates are compared against those held by the other ID. The two must each find a trusted certificate in the other ID file. If this does not happen, authentication fails.

By examining the ID files and looking at the certificate lists, you can determine what must be done to resolve the situation. Either a certificate is missing, or the trust flag has been disabled on one or more of the certificates.

Expired Certificates

Every certificate given to an ID file has its own expiration date. By default, users expire in two years and servers expire 100 years after the date of certification. These initial values can be modified at the time the certificate is issued.

When the expiration date nears, starting at 90 days from expiration, Notes issues a message indicating the expiration date. For a server, this message appears at the console (and thus in a Miscellaneous Events document of the Log).

Once the expiration date is reached, the certificate is no longer valid, and unless there are other flat certificates available on the ID file that are also trusted, the ID becomes useless.

36

By simply recertifying the ID file, it once again becomes viable. If the expiration date has been reached, then the file must be physically transported to the administrator for recertification. It is easier to use Notes Mail in advance of the expiration date to send the ID to the administrator, who can then recertify it and send it back through Notes Mail.

Cross-Certification Problems

Authentication failure under the hierarchical scheme is easier to debug and resolve. The error message that results informs you of the nature of the problem. First, though, when will authentication work under the hierarchical structure? It will succeed when both IDs have a common ancestor, or when both IDs have been cross-certified to access the other organization. This chapter doesn't intend to explain the details of cross-certification, but rather to describe how to resolve the problem resulting from a lack of it.

For servers who lack cross-certification, you must decide at what level you wish to cross-certify, then proceed to accomplish that. The possible levels are

- Between server and server or workstation
- Between server and organization/organizational unit
- Between organization and organizational units

Cross-Certification at the Workstation

For users to communicate with a server in another organization, they need to hold a cross-certificate to that server or organization in their Personal Address Book. Without it, half of the puzzle is missing.

When a user attempts to communicate with such a server, Notes R4 now displays a message that explains the lack of cross-certificates and enables the user to fix their half of the authentication problem by issuing an appropriate cross-certificate in their Personal Address Book. (See Figure 36.6.) This cross-certificate is not the same as the organization-to-organization cross-certificate that exists in the Public Address book. It is usable only by the user who generates the document. Additionally, this works only when the two organizations have cross-certified at the organization and organizational-unit levels.

FIGURE 36.6.

The Cross Certify dialog box enables a user to add a cross-certificate to their Personal Address book.

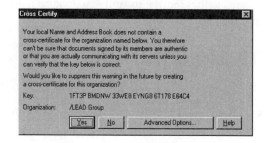

Even though the user can proceed with this "fix," it does not change the potential lack of a cross-certificate in the address book on the server. It is likely that the user still will not be able to access the server, unless that server has already been cross-certified with the user's organization.

Authorization: You Are Not Authorized To Access the Server

When this message appears, you know one fact: authentication has succeeded, and you are being denied access not because your ID file is invalid or because of cross-certification, but because the server document or a parameter in the server's NOTES.INI has an entry that specifies that you should be denied.

The key word in the message is authorized. A Notes term similar to "authorization" is "authentication." Authentication, however, is the verification process that takes place between two Notes ID files. Authorization is a comparison between the ID file accessing the server and the restriction parameters that have been configured on that server.

Server-Document Restrictions

Every server document has a Restrictions section, which contains a number of fields in which you can specify server-specific access rights for users and/or groups. Two fields on this document may be causing the authorization failure.

The Access Server field, if it is empty, allows access to any ID file that is certified under the same organization certifier, or to any ID that has been properly cross-certified. In other words, if authentication succeeds, then the ID is allowed access to the server. However, if this field contains one or more entries, then access is limited to those users or groups. If the ID attempting to access the server is not specifically listed and is not a member of a group that is listed, then it is denied access.

The other server document field that affects authorization is the Deny Access field. Entries listed here are specifically denied access. This field overrides any entries from the Access Server field, if any duplicate entries exist.

Each time you change the server access lists, the server must be shut down and restarted. Plan to use group names in these entries instead of individual names; then you can modify the group documents and the server will not need to be downed.

NOTES.INI Restrictions (Port Level)

Alternatively, there are some parameters not found on the server document that can be added to the NOTES.INI file and that also affect authorization. These entries are ALLOW_ACCESS_portname and DENY_ACCESS_portname. For example, to allow the group Developers access to the Dev1 server over the TCP/IP port, the entry would read:

```
ALLOW_ACCESS_TCPIP=Developers
```

To deny access to the OtherDomainServers group over the COM2 port, the entry would read:

```
DENY_ACCESS_COM2=OtherDomainServers
```

The `ALLOW_ACCESS_portname` parameter, like the Access Server field on the server document, allows access across that port to the listed users or groups only. The NOTES.INI file does not contain this entry initially; you will need to add it. If this parameter exists and your name is not specified (individually or via a group name), then you cannot use that port.

On the other hand, the `DENY_ACCESS_portname` field, if present in the .INI file, specifically denies access across that port to any user or group listed. This entry overrides the `ALLOW_ACCESS_portname` entry.

Depending on the various settings, you may be able to access the server over one port but not another.

Replication Issues

A number of factors control which documents replicate. The most important fact to know and remember is that most replication controls affect the documents that are being received, not those being sent. The controls for the documents being sent can be found in the remote database. Yet the controls, which are set locally, specify the name of the remote entity (server or workstation).

Too Few Documents Replicate

Think of this question when resolving replication issues: "What can the other entity do to this replica, based on the local settings?" Or, to simplify the question, become the database: "What can the other entity do to me?"

It is also important to remember that to Notes, servers are "people" too. Notes ID files simply give a license number a name that you reference in the system. It is not known or distinguished whether an entity is a server or workstation; it is identified simply as a trusted Notes name that has been granted a certain level of access to a database.

Servers and the ACL

A database's Access Control List is fairly straightforward. It contains a list of servers, people, or groups and assigns one of seven levels of access to each entry.

Realize, however, that every replica of every database has its own ACL. As you deploy many servers, it becomes important to consider the settings on each replica. You can think of the multiple replicas of a single database as an ACL topology; which server will be the master for design and ACL changes?

Consider this: how many replication hops are there from this ACL "hub" down to the last replica? That is, does the ACL "hub" copy replicate with all other copies, or does it replicate with some intermediary copies? At each intermediate step, these servers must have sufficient access in the next replicas to pass ACL and design changes.

You probably want to consider using the new R4 feature which enables you to maintain a consistent ACL throughout all replicas. To use this feature (under Replication Settings for a database), you set two items: the Administration server, and the checkbox labeled "Enforce consistent ACL across all replicas of this database." All other replicas must use the same settings. Then, any local changes to an ACL will be overwritten with the settings from the "master" database. The Administration server must be listed in this ACL with Manager access.

Servers and Author Access

You should generally avoid giving a server Author access. Because servers are not used to create and edit documents, they are not listed as the authors of documents. Notes will refuse to receive edits to a document from a user or a server if that name isn't listed in the document as the Author.

In the case of users, Author access is useful in preventing those who can make local changes to a document from passing those changes back illegally to the server replica. Servers, however, often are in the role of distribution Agents; that is, they pass documents (including changes) back and forth between them.

A server that is listed as an author will not be able to write changes to documents. This typically comes to an administrator's attention because certain users, in conversation, will determine that they aren't looking at the same document in their respective replicas. The user who edited the document will be confused as to why their associate is reporting that they don't see the changes.

Along with the Author access level, there are two important access flags that can also affect the number of documents that replicate. The `Create documents` flag allows the named entity to write new documents in the replica. The `Delete documents` flag allows it to write document-deletion stubs.

Selective Replication Formula

Databases may also control what is received based on one or more Selective Replication formulas. This formula, which is written much like the Selection formula for a view, will receive only those documents that meet the criteria specified in the formula.

A Selective Replication formula also acts as a Selection formula for the local database. Any local documents that do not meet the criteria are removed. If the formula is changed, then at the next replication, the set of allowed documents will also change. This may result in too many documents being received, or in too many documents being removed from the local replica.

To test your formula, consider using a selection Agent that contains the same formula to see if the correct documents are being marked for replication.

36

Document-Level Access Lists and Roles

The ACL is a broad classification of what a named entity can do. It applies across all the documents in the database. Notes also provides for document-level access lists. These lists can contain names of users, groups, or roles. They act to reduce the level of access for members of the database ACL, but do not grant more rights than those given in the ACL.

Document-level access lists can be applied in a number of ways. They are usually applied by designers, but users can also apply Read access lists to particular documents independent of the form design. Forms can have Create and Read access lists. Views and folders can have Read access lists.

If a user or server is listed in the database ACL but not in document-level access lists, then those documents may not replicate. It is important to remember server names when access lists are defined. This affects the planning of administrators, who must know of and educate users of the factors that affect replication; and designers, who must include a mechanism that enables servers to replicate documents regardless of the document-level access that users apply.

> **TIP**
>
> A useful method for ensuring that servers are allowed to replicate documents is to create one or more roles just for servers, then apply these roles throughout the database.

Time Limit

New to R4, a Connection document now contains a field specifying the maximum time limit allowed for replication. This can be used to efficiently schedule many replication jobs. At any particular time, however, it may appear to affect the amount of data that gets replicated. If a replication is halted for time considerations, those documents not replicated will have to wait for the next cycle. Depending on the frequency of replication with that server, users may find that new documents or changes aren't present at a particular time. You may get complaints about "failures" that are "fixed" with the next replication.

User Type

ACL entries are simply text strings that Notes compares against the name from an ID file or the text strings of names in group documents. This means that it is possible to create or modify a group in the Public Address Book with the same name as an ACL entry (say, LocalDomainServers), entering your username in that group, and then be allowed access to the database based on the group name entry. Notes doesn't know or care whether an ID is a server or a user. This is the reality in Releases 3 and 4. R4 does this for compatibility with R3 databases.

However, in R4 there is also a provision for specifying the type for an ACL entry. The choices for the User type are Person, Server, Mixed Group, Person Group, or Server Group. Figure 36.7 shows the settings and the icons that are used to represent the various types. This will prevent this kind of aliasing problem. Under R4 in a database where the User types have been applied, the LocalDomainServers group would be identified as a Server Group. If a username has been entered into this group, that user will not be allowed access based on the LocalDomainServers group. Notes will see that the user's ID is a user ID, and that the group should contain only server IDs, and therefore ignore the user name entry in the group. If LocalDomainServers is defined as a Mixed Group, though, then the user would be allowed.

FIGURE 36.7.

The Access Control List dialog box shows the User types and their representative icons.

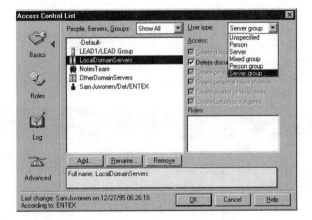

If you intend to use the server's workstation to perform administration tasks, then you will want to add that server to the ACLs of any databases you will work on, defining the server entry as "Unspecified," not "Server." The server ID as seen from the workstation process will be seen as a "User," and if you've told the ACL that that ID is a "Server," then you won't be allowed to make changes.

Databases on a server that has been recently upgraded will not automatically have user types assigned to the ACL entries. A button under the Advanced section can use your Public Address Book to detect the type for each entry by performing lookups.

Any databases where the R3 "trickery" has been applied may affect your replication after the user types have been applied. A user that is in a Server Group will no longer be allowed to replicate the database. You will need to move that user into a User or Mixed Group, or enter their name individually.

Documents Disappear After Replication

After a replication is complete, it is possible that documents present before replication began are now missing. Several factors can play a part in removing documents.

As discussed previously, a Selective Replication formula (if it has been modified since the last replication) may now not allow for certain documents that had been allowed by the prior formula.

For instance, suppose you have a Status field (whose values can be Open or Closed) and you also use a Selective Replication formula that selects only documents where Status=Open. If a document which had been Open replicated in, and was subsequently changed to Closed, the Selective Replication formula would cause this document to disappear from this replica copy after it replicated.

Secondly, there are a pair of Replication Settings that work in concert to keep a replica database small in size. These are known as the purge interval and the cutoff date. The purge interval is measured in a number of days. In R4, the setting is called Remove documents not modified in the last __ days. See Figure 36.8 for an example. The purge interval is the number that fills the blank. Every one-third of the number of days entered here, Notes will purge documents that are older than the purge interval. If the number is 30 days, then every 10 days Notes will trim documents that are 30 or more days old.

FIGURE 36.8.

The purge-interval setting for a database.

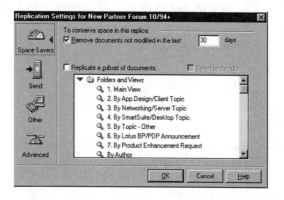

More specifically, every one-third of the purge interval, the cutoff date is updated. See Figure 36.9 for an example of the cutoff date. It is the setting in the cutoff date that determines the date boundary for removing documents. The cutoff date is identified as the field called Only replicate incoming documents saved or modified after _____, specifying a date and time.

In order to recover documents that have been purged, you can manually reset the cutoff date. Replicate again, and this cutoff date will be used as the date boundary for determining the documents to replicate. The purge interval will take over again, however.

If the replication cycle has completed propagating deletion stubs to all replica copies of the database, and the purge interval has passed, you can no longer recover documents; all copies have been deleted.

FIGURE 36.9.

The cutoff-date setting for a database.

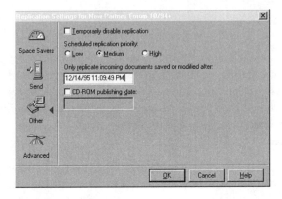

Another reason for losing documents is that they were actually deleted. If the ACL settings on the various replicas allow for deletions, then the deletion stub for a document will replicate to each copy of the database.

Replication Between Servers Not Occurring or Failing to Finish

If replication between a pair of servers continually fails or even fails to occur, what can you look for?

First, make sure that replication has not been disabled for this database. Look in the Replication Settings dialog box under the Other icon for an entry labeled "Temporarily disable replication." If this is enabled on either of the replica copies in question, then the database will not replicate.

Second, determine whether replication is failing to occur or failing to finish. By using the Notes Log, you can determine the answer. If the servers communicate asynchronously, you can check the Miscellaneous Events, Phone Call and Replication Event documents. For network replication, you can check the Miscellaneous Events and Replication Events.

TIP

To aid your search, try using the new Log Analysis feature in R4. This feature asks for one or more search string(s), then searches every document in the log and returns the results of the search in a Log Analysis database. By searching on the name of the remote server, you will see if the local server has made any attempts to communicate with it. Alternatively, you can browse the various documents in the Log by hand. In either case, there are certain elements to look for in determining the cause of the problem.

Let's investigate some reasons for the servers' failure to replicate. First, by looking at connection documents, determine which of the servers is supposed to make the call.

Verify that the parameters of the connection document are correct:

- Is the connection enabled?
- Is the port specified indeed the correct port?
- Are the source and destination server names spelled correctly?
- Is the phone number correct (including extra dialing rules)?
- Does the Tasks field contain the Replication task entry as it should, or does it just include Mail Routing?

TIP

A sneaky problem could be that there are one or more files specified in the Files to Replicate field. This precludes all other files from replicating. If these filenames are incorrect, no files will replicate.

If the network or serial port that is specified for the connection between the two machines isn't working, then replication will fail. See Chapter 37, "Troubleshooting Networks and Modems," for more information on communications problems.

Before two Notes entities can communicate, they must first authenticate. If the two machines are not certified under the same organization or cross-certified, it would be a breach of security to let replication occur. Miscellaneous Events and the Replication Events documents will reflect this security issue.

Additionally, servers may fail to obey their own schedule for the following reasons:

- A low memory situation exists.
- There is not enough disk space.
- The server activity load is too high to permit replication to take place.
- All allowable replicators are busy.

The first two of these conditions generate a message on the console (and thus in the Log). The second two just cause the replicator to skip the job without notification.

If the replication schedule is lengthy, it is possible that the server cannot get to the connection document in question before a new day begins or the end of the scheduled range has passed.

If you have schedules that overlap by one minute or more, then replication occurs randomly; replication might even skip parts of the schedules. This overlap might be between multiple entries in one document or between schedules specified on multiple documents.

Let's look at an example: You have Low priority databases scheduled to replicate between 1 a.m. and 5 a.m. (document #1), and Medium and High priority databases are scheduled between 5 a.m. and 11 p.m. (document #2). The overlap at 5:00 a.m. will cause a problem, so, at the least, change the schedule in document #1 to 1 a.m. to 4:59 a.m.

If you have multiple Connection documents telling your server to call another server, and the document that references databases of the same or lower priority tells the server to make a call, but another document is scheduled to make a call within the next hour, then the first replication is suppressed in favor of the document referencing the higher priority databases. What should you do? Spread your replications out further than one hour, or do as we did previously, so that lower priority documents won't be ignored. Give each a wider range so that at some point in their schedules, they are not within an hour of each other.

Let's look at another related issue. If you have Connection documents going in both directions for the same two servers at same time, then one server is going to call the other for replication, and the second schedule will be ignored.

Replication Conflicts

At times you or your users will notice replication conflict documents in some databases. These conflicts occur when a document is edited in multiple replicas between replications. When this database replicates, the replicator doesn't know how to resolve changes to both documents, so it creates a conflict document as a response to the other. The "winner," or main document, is the one which has been edited more recently or which has been saved more times.

More specifically, each document contains a sequence number and a sequence time. When you update a document, the sequence number increments by one and the sequence time is recorded from the system clock. Thus, the "winner" has the higher sequence number, or if these are the same, the more recent sequence time.

How can you resolve replication conflicts? First, resolve the conflicts in only one replica, or you will likely create more conflicts. Second, you will need to manually review both documents and decide upon a course of action. Can one document be saved and the other deleted? Do you need to use cut and paste to merge different information into one of them? Your review of the documents will tell you this.

To actually perform the resolution, it is best if you can keep the main document, merging all updates into it and then deleting the conflict response. If there are more changes to the conflict response and you would rather keep that document, then before doing any editing, edit this document and resave it. Resaving the conflict response will make the document a "main" document as is the winner. Then you can safely cut and paste and finally delete one of them.

How can you prevent conflicts?

Notes R4 has a new feature that reduces the likelihood of conflicts: field-level replication. In R3, every time a document was updated, even if it was just one small field that was changed, then the entire document had to be replicated again (which could be expensive if the document contained attachments or other large objects).

With field-level replication, in addition to the document's sequence number and time, every field has its own sequence number. When that field is modified and the document is saved, the field sequence number is incremented to one more than the previous document sequence number, and the document sequence number is incremented by one. The document sequence number is then equal to that of the field(s) that just changed.

During replication, in addition to comparing document sequence numbers, the replicator also compares field sequence numbers. If it turns out that different fields have been modified, then the potential exists for the documents to be merged instead of generating a conflict. The reason this is a potential instead of an automatic event is that the database designer must have enabled a Property called `Merge replication conflicts` for this form in the database.

Field-level replication speeds up replication, since less data will need to replicate, and it can also reduce the number of replication conflicts.

Another way to reduce replication conflicts is to cause them! This sounds contradictory, but let's explore it further. There is a feature found in both R3 and R4 called *document versioning*. This is a form property that tells Notes to create a new document each time a document is modified (in R4, look for the Versioning property on the Basics tab on the Form Properties InfoBox). This new document can either be created as a response document or it can become the new main document while the prior versions become responses (or siblings). In essence, you are creating a new "conflict," but this is a proactive step instead of a reactive step. This conflict, or version, gives you an audit trail.

When this method is used, if document is edited in multiple replicas, then all of the versions add up during replication and no replication conflict appears.

Clearing Replication History

When a replication is successful, Notes updates the Replication History in a database. You can see this history through File | Replication | History (R4 menu). If replication is occurring in both directions (as opposed to a Pull only or Push only), you will see two entries for a particular server: one for send and one entry for receive. Notes also stamps the time and date from the other server into the history on the current server.

The next time this database is replicated between these two servers, Notes takes this time stamp as the starting point to speed up the process.

In rare cases, documents may get saved during a replication, after Notes has determined the set of documents to replicate at that time. That document's time stamp will be slightly older than the history stamp that is written in the history upon the successful completion of that replication. At the next replication, Notes uses the history time stamp as the starting point, ignoring the document in question.

When will you find out about this? Notes doesn't announce this behavior; in fact, it doesn't know it happened. Typically, your users will discover that they aren't seeing the same set of documents in their respective replicas.

To fix the problem, you can clear the replication history by clicking the Clear button on the Replication History dialog box. Notes will inform you that clearing the history will make the next replication with all servers take much longer, and that you should only clear the history if you suspect a time problem as we've discussed. But by clearing the history, you will force the replicator to look at all documents without regard to a history time stamp, and the "lost" document(s) will "reappear."

The Mail Router

The Notes mail router is a server task (Router) that continuously looks for pending messages in the store-and-forward mailbox database (MAIL.BOX). When it finds a message waiting, it reads the address fields (SendTo, CCTo, and BCCTo) and attempts to forward the message. The router makes heavy use of the Public Address Book to resolve addresses.

Given the crucial nature of the Public Address Book, let's look more closely at the various documents that have a hand in the routing process.

The Router Process

For any given recipient, the router either finds that a domain name is included in the address (jim white @ acme) and it looks for a route to that domain (among the Connection documents in the Public Address Book). If the address doesn't contain a domain name, then the router looks for the appropriate person or group document in the Public Address Book. If it is a group, then the router repeats the steps detailed next for each person listed in the group.

When it finds the correct person document, the router determines the mail server where the user's mail file is stored. If it is the same server, then it writes the message directly to the mail file. If it is another server, then this router sends the message to the other server. This process happens with each router until the message reaches its destination.

Public Address Book

For Notes Mail to work, the Pubic Address Book must contain accurate data and have the right design. On your servers, this is usually the case. You'll have already set up the Address books in your domain; they will have at least Editor access in one or more directions, so that any new documents or modifications will be able to work their way through your domain to all of your servers. Because each server, at startup, builds its own routing table based on the documents it sees in its replica of the Public Address Book, it is imperative that data is pervasive in the domain.

If a Public Address Book should lose any of its views through modification of the design (a rare problem), you may find that mail-routing errors crop up. Certain views are critical for the operation of the server. Any view whose name begins with $ is a view that is being cached and can be assumed necessary for the server to operate. If a necessary view is deleted, you will see the message `NAMES.NSF does not contain a required view`.

A user who modifies the design of her Personal Address Book may also get this message when attempting to send mail.

Using File | Database | Replace Design, you can regain the lost design elements without hurting any of the documents. Before using this option, however, any new elements should be protected from getting deleted by the replacement process. The property Do not allow design refresh/replace to modify can be enabled to prevent it from being deleted.

To prevent the design from getting overwritten, you should use the ACL to prevent others from making changes.

Server Documents

Each server needs to find a Server document in the public Public Address Book that matches the name on its server ID. The Server document is used in the building of the routing table to specify the domain and named network(s) in which the server is operating.

The Domain field on the server document must be correct. A server will consider itself a mail router for that domain, and if this field is not correct, then the router will not send mail to users whose Person documents reflect the actual domain name.

Person Documents

Each Notes user needs to have a corresponding Person document in the public Public Address Book. This document tells the router how to send mail to the user's Notes mail file or how to forward messages to a foreign (non-Notes) mail destination. For Notes mail users, the following fields must be complete and correct for mail to reach the user:

- Mail system
- Domain
- Mail server
- Mail file
- Username
- Forwarding address

Incorrect or missing entries in one of these fields will cause delivery failures to occur; the router will not have enough information to complete the delivery.

The forwarding address overrides the other mail entries and sends all messages to that address. If it is invalid, all mail routing to that individual will fail. This address must be a proper Notes address, not an Internet address.

For example, instead of jwhite@company.com, if you have the SMTP Gateway or SMTP MTA installed, the proper address would be similar to jwhite@company.com @ *internetdomain*, where *internetdomain* is your SMTP Gateway's foreign domain name which is recognized by Notes.

The other gateway strips the Notes domain name and sends the message to jwhite@company.com over SMTP.

Multiple Documents

If a Public Address Book contains duplicates of user documents or person and group documents with the same name, the router will become confused when it tries to deliver mail to such a user. This will result in a delivery failure indicating that Public Address Book contains duplicate entries.

Connection Documents

Connection documents are vital for mail routing that takes place across servers in different named networks. Within the same named network, mail routing happens automatically; otherwise, connection documents are required, one for each routing direction. Invalid or missing entries in a connection document on a server can be enough to halt the routing of a message. Figure 36.10 shows the new R4 connection document.

FIGURE 36.10.

A new R4 connection document.

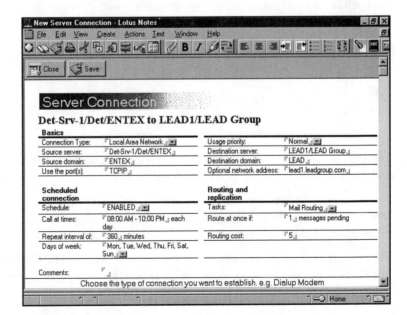

The Destination domain and Tasks fields are the most important entries on the form; these fields are used in a server's routing table as an indication that the server knows how to route messages destined for that domain. If this field is invalid, then the router immediately generates a failure for a message heading that way, because it sees no route to that domain, even though the server may be capable of calling the destination server and passing authentication.

Next, the Use the port(s) and Call at times fields are important. If a routing table indicates that there is a route to domain A, but these entries are invalid, then a condition worse (in terms of time) than a failure occurs; the message sits and waits in the store-and-forward MAIL.BOX file.

How can these fields be invalid? The Port field is invalid if it references a port name that cannot reach the destination server. The Call at times field is invalid if the listed entry doesn't conform to the proper conventions. The time values can be:

- ▪ A single time in the format HH:MM AM
- ▪ A list of times separated by semicolons or commas
- ▪ A single time range in the format HH:MM AM–HH:MM AM
- ▪ A mixed entry of times and ranges separated by semicolons or commas

The connection document essentially tells the router: "I know how to route in that direction, I just can't right now; maybe I will be able to soon." Why doesn't it return the message right away? Perhaps the entries are correct, and the remote phone is not answering or is busy because that server is down or is busy. When the destination server's phone begins answering again, then the message that was waiting will move along its route.

A connection that is improperly configured in this manner looks exactly like a properly configured connection! In a large domain, where there might be hundreds of connection documents, this problem could be hard to detect.

When a message sits for 24 hours, it will be returned as a Delivery failure due to the fact that the "delivery time expired." If it cannot be returned due to routing problems in the reverse direction, it becomes dead mail in the MAIL.BOX file on the server that determines that it can no longer route it further toward the original sender's mail file.

It is wise to use a monitoring tool such as NotesView, or to periodically update a drawing based on the connection documents in your domain, paying close attention to the spelling of these field entries. Such a drawing can alert you to an improperly tuned mail-network configuration and tell you where you need to apply corrective measures.

Location Documents

New in R4 is a document type called a Location. This is useful for users (especially telecommuters) to tell Notes where they are at any given time, so that certain resources can automatically be enabled or turned off appropriately.

On a Location document, the Home/mail server field must be accurate for a user's mail to work properly. If this or the dialing information is incorrect, then outgoing mail may sit in a user's MAIL.BOX file. These messages can easily be forgotten, especially if the user has become accustomed to the automatic transfer of mail (with a properly working location). The user thinks the message was sent, but doesn't know that it didn't leave his or her machine.

Because Location documents are not directly under the control of an administrator, this topic is one that is best covered thoroughly in your end-user training. Teaching laptop users to become road warriors means teaching them how to maintain the critical components of their own Notes system.

Adjacent and Nonadjacent Domain Documents

Adjacent Domain and Nonadjacent Domain documents are extremely simple. Yet the power they can wield can be great, and the results can be misleading.

Nonadjacent domains are used to simplify mail addressing. For users who frequently send messages to recipients who are more than one domain away, the addressing requires more than one domain name to be specified. For instance, to send mail to a user in the Lotus domain, the message has to pass through the Notes Net domain; the address would be Lotus User @ Lotus @ Notes Net. It would be simpler if the address could be entered as Lotus User @ Lotus. The Nonadjacent domain solves this by setting the Mail sent to domain to Lotus, and Route through domain to Notes Net. Now the router, when seeing that a message is destined for the Lotus domain, determines that it actually has to route to a server in the Notes Net domain.

If the either of these fields is incorrect, this won't work. If the Mail sent to domain field is wrong, then users will get an immediate delivery failure from the router because it can't find a route to the domain specified. In this example, there is no connection document to a server in the Lotus domain, so if the router can't find an appropriate Nonadjacent Domain document, the message fails to route. On the other hand, if the Route through domain entry is invalid, then the router finds the Nonadjacent Domain document but fails to find an appropriate connection document, and a Delivery Failure results.

Adjacent domain documents are new to R4. This document has been introduced so that mail routing does not become global merely because you communicate with a particular domain. For instance, just because you communicate with Lotus, your servers (under R3) may act as mail routers for messages that are not intended for anyone in your domain. You incur communication costs for users from other domains using your domain for routing. Perhaps you communicate with a customer, and that customer determines that you route mail to Lotus. They can then route mail to users at Lotus through your server without your consent or control.

Both the Adjacent and Nonadjacent Domain forms have two fields that essentially let you create mail-routing firewalls. You can specify that for a certain domain with which you communicate—say, Notes Net—you want to enable mail to be sent only to this adjacent domain from certain domains. Perhaps this would be one of your internal domains (if you have them). Enter the domain name in the Allow mail only from domains field.

Conversely, you can specify domains that will be restricted from sending mail to this adjacent domain; enter these domain names in the Deny mail from domains field. You can enter your customers' domain here; they will still be able to route mail with your domain, but if they try to route a message to this adjacent domain through yours, they will be denied.

You need only enter values in one field or the other. Entering a value in the Allow mail only from domains field denies all entries not listed.

When you put an entry into the Allow mail only from domains field, however, you have just limited it to that list. If you previously had users who were routing to that domain, they will now receive delivery failures due to the fact that they are not allowed that right any longer. Remember that you need to check these documents during your troubleshooting process; it may be that their message is not addressed correctly, but it could be that you have closed a routing hole they once benefited from.

Delivery Failure Reports

Delivery Failure reports are one of the most common ways to detect mail problems. By reading the reason for the failure that is specified in the document, more can be learned about the cause. For instance, it is possible to determine which server has the problem that stopped the routing by looking at the routing path that the message took. If you see that the message traveled along servers A, B, C, D, D, F, A, then you know server D has a problem. It got that far before it couldn't proceed. Server D may be out of memory, or it may have an error in a document in the Public Address Book. The Failure document may specify the exact error, or at least give a good clue.

Replicating the Public Address Book

In order for a domain to operate efficiently, the Public Address Book must be replicating correctly to all servers in your domain. Different replicas that are out of sync may cause problems; when one server performs actions based on the documents in its replica, but those actions require assistance from other servers that don't have the same settings, the process fails. Verify your Public Address Book ACLs on each replica.

Mail File

For mail to actually be delivered to a user's mail file, it must exist on the disk at the location specified in that user's Person document. The Mail file field expects a path to the filename. If the file has been moved or is named other than indicated in the Person document, mail delivery will fail, and a Delivery Report will be routed to the sender. Also, the server needs to have Write access to the file. Acceptable ACL settings are Depositor, Editor, Designer, or Manager. (The router writes new documents only to the mail file. For replication of this mail file with other servers, the Depositor level of access would not be appropriate, as editing changes to documents would not replicate.)

MAIL.BOX

The mail-router mail box (MAIL.BOX) is a critical database for mail routing. If this file is kept open by another process—say, a tape-backup program—Notes may not be able to write to the file and messages will not route. A message to this effect is generated in the Notes Log in a Miscellaneous Events document.

The default access to MAIL.BOX is Depositor, allowing all messages to be created here but not viewed or edited. To catch and correct problems, you will want to add your administration group to this ACL with Manager access. You can then see documents that have failed to route. When you open a message that has failed to route, you will see a failure reason. By monitoring this database, you can proactively watch for routing problems and fix them quickly. To send a message on its way after fixing a problem, you can run the Agent entitled Release Dead Messages.

NOTES.INI on the Server

On a Notes server, there are some settings in the NOTES.INI that require attention in times of trouble. The NAMES= setting is used to set up cascading address books for the router to use in determining the routing path to a user. If you have set up several address books (NAMES=NAMES,NAMES2,NAMES3) and then at some point the NAMES2 database gets deleted, the server will not look through NAMES3 because it fails to find NAMES2. Now that most of the configuration in Notes is performed in the address book, it can be easy to forget that your .INI files still need attention.

Summary

This chapter looked at the tools available, the documentation, and the larger components of the system. You learned more about the Notes Log and the Statistics and Event tasks. This chapter discussed the various resources available to you both in Notes and in the Notes community. It also discussed server stability and access issues. You learned more about the crucial points of replication and mail routing.

Troubleshooting is an inevitable part of administration, especially in larger systems. Having knowledge of the components and how they work together will enable you to resolve a wider array of issues.

Troubleshooting Networks and Modems

by Sam Juvonen

IN THIS CHAPTER

CHAPTER

37

Establishing and maintaining consistent communication between computers is often the most challenging aspect of a system. Modem communications are especially difficult to troubleshoot, given the fact that many components of telephony are simply out of our control: they belong to the phone companies. Network communications require a strong knowledge of protocols and hardware in order to successfully configure and later troubleshoot.

Lotus Notes makes extensive use of both networks and modems. Because Notes sits atop the communications infrastructure, problems with this layer of the system will no doubt affect its performance and reliability.

In this chapter you will find information about both network and modem troubleshooting. There are two main sections: the first section contains general information; the second section adds more details behind those mentioned in the first.

In order to find the cause of problems and resolve them, it pays to know all of the components of the system, both at the communications layer and at the Notes application layer. Many tools exist to aid in troubleshooting communications. For instance, cable and protocol analyzers can be a great help in pinpointing network problems.

Information for the User

So you have a laptop, and you've received Lotus Notes on your system. You need to communicate with the server at your office as you travel, but you are experiencing problems. This section is for you.

Let's look at the components of your system (your workstation, network hardware, and modem) and at the methods for using them to troubleshoot your communication problems. The methods that must be resolved are the following:

- How to communicate with the modem to reach a Notes server
- How to reach a Notes server (including from what locations)

To communicate with your modem, you need software that tells the modem to dial a number and establish a connection to another system. In this case you're focusing on Lotus Notes as that software, but many other types of software exist. For example, if you are a Windows 95 or Windows NT user, you may use a package called RAS (Remote Access Service) or Dial-up Networking to dial into an NT server at your office and access the network. The modem software that comes with Notes is designed only to dial into a Notes server. The workstation software cannot answer the phone, so clients cannot call one another peer-to-peer.

Modems come in three flavors: internal, external, or PCM/CIA card. Your software communicates with the modem through a serial port, also known as a COM port; typically, the port is named COM1 or COM2. To connect the modem to the phone system, you have a phone cord. This completes the hardware.

You should know that Notes has many different components that affect remote communication.

First, to communicate with your modem, Notes uses a modem file. A modem file is a text file that contains instructions Notes uses to tell the modem how to behave. When Notes is installed, 144 modem files get installed in the NOTES\DATA\MODEMS directory. The installation process does not discriminate among the modem files during installation; in fact, it doesn't ask you until later what kind of modem you have. These files don't take up much space, but you may want to use your favorite disk management tool (File Manager or Explorer) to reduce the number of modem files. You should be able to find your modem file from among these.

To use a modem, Notes must be told two things: which communications port to use and which modem file to use. To set this up, use the User Preferences box (from the File menu, click Tools followed by User Preferences). When you see this dialog box, click the Ports icon toward the lower-left corner of the window. Figure 37.1 shows the Ports section of the User Preferences dialog box.

FIGURE 37.1.

This is where you configure Notes to talk to your communications port.

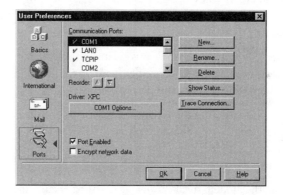

Here you can see from the check mark that COM1 is enabled, along with a port named LAN0. The port is enabled by either double-clicking the port name or selecting the port and clicking the Port Enabled option near the bottom of the window. Because the COM1 port is highlighted, notice that, below the Communication Ports list, the driver name indicates XPC and the button is labeled COM1 Options. When you select a port from the list, the button changes its label to reflect the selected port name.

Use the COM1 Options button to assign a modem file. Figure 37.2 shows the Additional Setup dialog box with the Modem type field expanded showing the list of modems. Identify your modem and choose it from the list.

Figure 37.2.

This is the Additional Setup dialog box for COM ports.

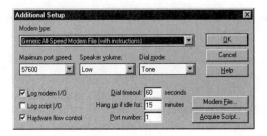

If you cannot find your modem in the list, try using either of the files titled "Generic All-Speed Modem File" or ". Auto Configure (for unlisted modems, only)". If, after selecting the modem file that matches your modem, you have trouble making a connection, you might find that one of these two modem files will improve that condition as well. You can find more information about modifying a modem file later in this chapter.

For troubleshooting purposes, it is also advantageous to select the Log modem I/O option and set the Speaker volume setting to Low on this Additional Setup dialog box. When the Log... option is on, Notes will write entries into your Notes Log database when it uses the modem. These Log entries tell you which commands Notes sent to the modem and how the modem responded.

Your personal Notes Log database was created on your machine during the configuration phase of the installation (when you specified your name and connection type). At the same time, your Personal Address Book was created, as well.

In the Log, look into the Miscellaneous Events view to see the documents created when you used your modem. You can also look in the Phone Calls view to see documents that record which server you dialed, the connection speed you achieved during that connection, and how many modem errors occurred.

In addition, the modem speaker can give you further clues in resolving a communications problem; if the phone number is incorrect, for instance, the speaker sound will let you hear why the modem at the far end is not being reached (you may hear voices instead of the usual modem warble!).

Also take a look at the Dial Timeout field. The default here is 60 seconds, but depending on where you are dialing from, this may not be enough time. If you notice that your calls are not able to complete and you see the message `Call timer expired`, you should increase this number, perhaps to 120 seconds. You may be in a location where the phone switches react slowly as your call is routed, and this may take sufficiently long that the 60 seconds is depleted before Notes can establish communications with the server.

If you tend to dial your Notes server and then walk away to do something else while it connects, you might forget to come back to your machine for a while, as your phone bill rises due to the active connection. You can prevent this by changing the Hang up if idle for: field from the initial 15 minutes down to 5 minutes. This feature hangs up the phone if no activity is detected on the line for that period of time. During typical replication, there should be activity within that time to keep the line active if there is work to be done.

Another useful troubleshooting device is the Show Status button on the User Preferences dialog (see Figure 37.1). Figure 37.3 shows the statistics that are reported in the COM Port Status dialog box.

FIGURE 37.3.

These statistics can help you determine the nature of a modem problem.

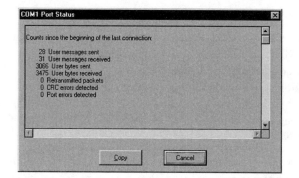

Let's say you have successfully dialed your server, but the response seems extremely sluggish during this particular connection. Looking at this status dialog, you may see that either or both of the Retransmitted packets and/or the CRC errors detected entries are well above zero. The user messages sent and received are probably rather low for the amount of time you've been connected. You most likely have a bad phone line or just a bad connection. Try hanging up and redialing. From some locations, where the actual line is of poor quality, you may have to decrease the modem speed to reduce the error rate. Head back to the User Preferences Port Options dialog to reduce the speed. (See Figure 37.2.)

The modem-file assignment tells Notes how to communicate with your modem. To actually use the modem, however, some configuration documents are required. These documents determine how to reach particular Notes servers, and which servers to dial from specific locations.

The Personal Address Book

When your copy of Notes was installed and configured, a Personal Address Book database was created for you. In this database, you can add names and e-mail addresses of people you intend to communicate with. This database is also the repository for two other types of documents that affect how your machine communicates with Notes servers.

The Connection Document

You determine how to reach a particular Notes server by configuring one or more Connection documents.

To actually connect to a server, your Notes client needs to know some key facts: the name of the server and its phone number. This information is entered into a Connection document. In your Personal Address Book, choose Create - Server Connection to create a new Connection document.

A Server Connection document tells Notes exactly how to reach the server, whereas a Location document references specific server names but does not specify how to reach them. In other words, a Location document depends on Connection documents to actually reach another server.

You can create one of four types of connections. The most common type of connection is called Dialup Modem. When you create a new connection, this type is entered automatically for you. The other types are Local Area Network, Passthru Server, and Remote LAN Service. Each connection type is used to define a path to a Notes server, and it implies that by following the rules defined by the parameters on the document, the server can be reached. Connection documents are required for dialup communications; they are not necessary, but may prove useful on a LAN.

How can a Connection document be useful in a LAN environment? They prove useful if you wish to connect to a server by name and its name cannot be resolved into its network address by your network routing system. For instance, you might need to connect to a server over IP whose name is not in the Domain Name server or in your HOSTS file (example: Home/Notes/Net, whose IP name is home.notes.net. This is a public server hosted by Iris Associates that you can connect to if your company is connected to the Internet). You can create a Connection document that specifies the name of that server along with its network address; Notes will then use that address to connect to that server.

Figure 37.4 shows a Connection document configured to call the server Columbia over COM1.

FIGURE 37.4.

This is a Connection document configured to call the server Columbia over COM1.

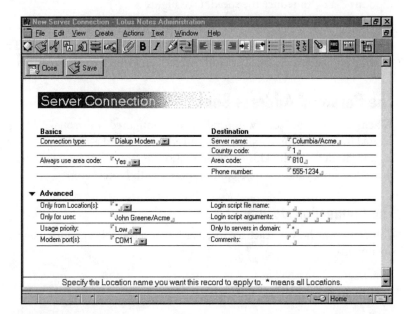

There are two ways to use the various phone-number fields. The most flexible method is to use each field individually, as opposed to entering the whole number into the Phone Number field. This enables you to customize the number easily as you change locations. For locations where area codes are always used when dialing numbers outside of your local zone, you can set Always use area code to Yes.

The Advanced section has two fields that limit the use of a Connection document. The Only from Locations field lists the locations that can use this Connection. Initially, the entry is *, which means all Locations. The Only for user field lists the ID file for the user who is allowed to use this Connection. This should contain your name (it's your Personal Address book). These two fields may affect the actual availability of a Connection document, so remember to look here when you are troubleshooting. On the other hand, if you leave them alone, they will not cause you any harm.

The Location Document

A Location document references your Connection documents. It tells Notes when to call one of the servers listed, either at your request or based on the schedule that you enable in this document. The primary server is the Home/Mail server. Normally the Passthru server will have the same name as the Home server, because your Home server is likely to allow Passthru routing to other Notes servers (so that you'll only have one phone call to make). See the section entitled "The Passthru Connection Document" for more information on Passthru.

The ports that a Location document enables determines the set of Connection documents that can be used. (See Figure 37.5.) Conversely, the Locations specified in the Only from Locations field under the Advanced section of a Connection document determine the locations that are allowed to use it. For example, if the Travel location enables the COM2 port, only those Connections that use COM2 will be used while the Travel location is selected; similarly, if the Office location enables COM2 and TCP/IP, the set of Connection documents will be those which use either COM2 or TCP/IP. A Connection that uses another port will not be considered. If this dependency is forgotten and these documents are improperly configured, you may see errors attempting to reach a server from certain locations.

In addition to the Dialup Connection, there are three other types of Connection documents. Although Dialup is the most common type that you'll create, the other types deserve some mention, so that you'll understand their role and, if need be, how they might affect your system when you are troubleshooting communications problems.

FIGURE 37.5.

The Location document enables the user to specify settings that take effect only for that location (such as the dialing rules).

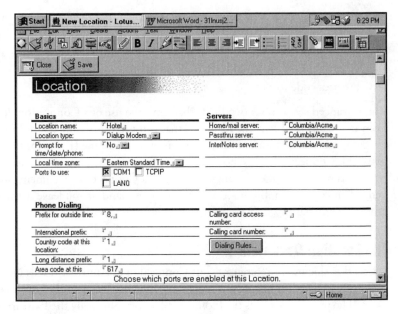

The Passthru Connection Document

This type of connection is used to tell Notes exactly how to get to a server that you will not dial directly. It may be a server that doesn't even have any modems attached to it, yet has important databases that you must access while away from the office network.

A Passthru is a simple document that specifies which server to route through in attempting to reach the ultimate destination server. Example: You need to dial the server Sales1, but it has no modems. You can, however, dial your mail server, Mail1, and Mail1 can reach Sales1 on the network. Create a Passthru connection document that specifies:

- Connection type: Passthru
- Passthru server name: Mail1
- Destination server name: Sales1

With this document in place, you can now attempt to access Sales1 by opening a database icon, using the File Open dialog, or having the Replicator tab attempt to replicate a database from Sales1. In each of these cases, your workstation will dial Mail1 and extend through that server to talk to Sales1. You do not need a Dialup connection document for Sales1.

When you use Passthru, a replica copy of a database can reside on only one server as opposed to being replicated to many different dial-in or Passthru servers. The Passthru server itself does not need to have any replica databases aside from the Public Address Book, which it needs to function within the Notes domain.

You might wonder what kind of an effect many Passthru sessions will have on your network. Specific benchmarks haven't been developed, but let's consider the components. On an Ethernet network with several Notes servers, some of them will have modems for remote Notes clients. If all of these modems were active at one time, the cumulative effect, due to modem speeds which are much lower than Ethernet speeds, will be relatively unnoticeable. The effect on the Notes server that is hosting the Passthru is minor as well, since Lotus reports that these sessions are "lite" sessions, consuming very few resources from Notes.

The Remote LAN Service Connection Document

Remote-network access is a common service requested by remote users of all kinds, including Notes users. In general, this service enables you to obtain access to the network and reach network services as if you were connected using a network interface card. This implies that you can perform many different kinds of tasks, including printing to network printers, accessing files from file servers, and communicating with many different types of servers: file servers, for instance, as well as any of the Notes servers that are reachable on the network.

Remote LAN Service is a type of Connection document you can enable in Notes that uses your remote network software to dial into your network as opposed to dialing into your Notes server. This service is similar to Passthru in that by dialing one number, you have access to multiple Notes servers. One reason that this service might be employed is to avoid having modems on any of the Notes servers. Instead of Dialup or Passthru connection documents, only Remote LAN Service documents would be needed. As long as your Notes server is reachable on the network (which, unless you're using NetBIOS, isn't likely to be a problem; NetBIOS users won't have difficulty unless the Notes server is on the far side of one or more routers). As of R4, the only supported remote access service is Microsoft RAS, although more services, such as Novell's NetWare Connect, are slated to be supported in a point release.

Under normal usage, you would use the service launcher itself (outside of Notes) to dial into the network, then use any application package, such as Notes, to access the network. When finished, you would manually hang up.

The Remote LAN Service connection in Notes allows access through this type of service to occur unattended and even follow a schedule that you define in your Location documents. Notes will dial the Microsoft RAS server, authenticate with that service via your user ID and password, proceed to access any Notes servers as necessary, and, finally, hang up.

Figure 37.6 shows a sample Remote LAN Service document configured to dial into a RAS server. The Remote connection name is the name of the service as defined by your machine. Notes asks RAS on your machine to use the connection by that name. The details of that connection are completed using the RAS software (under Windows 95 it is known as Dial-up Networking).

The most important point of using a Remote LAN Connection is this: even though you are reaching the network over your modem, the connection document in Notes specifies that a LAN port is being used. You do not need to have a COM port enabled under Notes.

FIGURE 37.6.

This is a sample Remote LAN Service Connection document.

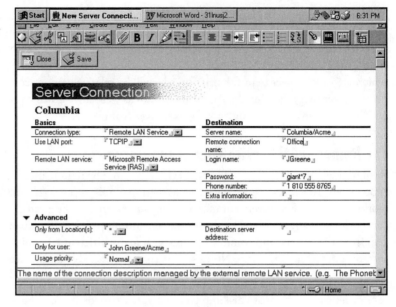

Figures 37.7 and 37.8 contrast the methods of Passthru and Remote LAN Service for accessing Notes servers.

FIGURE 37.7.

The Passthru method of routing.

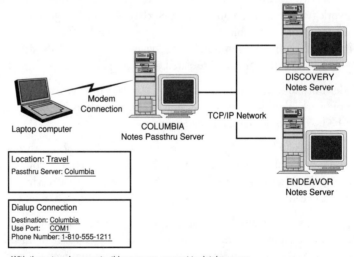

With these two documents, this user can connect to databases on Discovery and Endeavor. Attempts to access these servers will force a call to the user's Passthru server, Columbia.

FIGURE 37.8.

The Remote LAN Service method of routing.

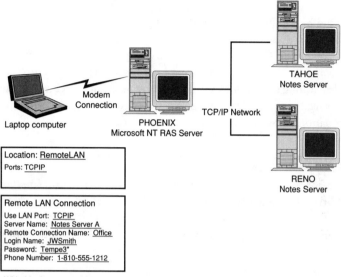

With this document, this user can connect to databases on Tahoe and Reno, both of which are using TCP/IP. The Dialup Networking definition "Office" dials the NT server Phoenix when an attempt is made to access Tahoe or Reno.

How do Passthru and Remote LAN Service compare? Passthru takes you directly to a Notes server, and enables you to reach additional Notes servers, but doesn't provide for other network services during that session (such as file or print services). Remote LAN Service connects you to your network, offering all services you would have in the office, but is somewhat slower to connect initially, as there is more negotiation to connect to the network than to connect to a Notes server. Overall, if you are only interested in accessing Notes, use Passthru; if you need other network resources, such as your calendar file from the file server, use Remote LAN Service.

The LAN Connection Document

When you access servers over a network, you reference Notes servers by their name. The resolution of their name into a network address that is understood by your network software is performed in different ways, depending on the protocol you are using. Usually, the network resolution method works just fine. In some cases, however, you may need to specify which port you wish to use to communicate with a particular server. The most common case would be that the server and your workstation both use the same set of multiple protocols, and you want to specify that you use a certain protocol rather than leave the decision to the Notes software.

This simple document specifies that in order to communicate with the specified destination server, Notes should use the specified LAN port.

This connection document should not generally come into play for the remote user unless the method of communication to the Notes server is through the Remote LAN Service connection. Under this condition, a real network protocol, such as TCP/IP, is being used in lieu of the modem, or XPC, protocol that is used by Notes when your workstation dials directly into the Notes server. This means that a Local Area Network connection document would be included among the set of connections being used and, if set incorrectly, could cause a problem. "Incorrectly" in this case means that the protocol specified in the connection is one that the destination server doesn't use.

Replicator Tab

The rightmost tab on your workspace is labeled Replicator. You'll use this tab to identify and prioritize the databases you wish to replicate. The settings on this tab are dependent on the Location you've chosen. For each Location, you can reconfigure the parameters for the databases that appear here. For example, if you are using the Office location, you might turn on replication for all of your databases, but for the Travel location you might only select your mail database (using the checkboxes to the left of each database). Figure 37.9 shows the Replicator tab.

FIGURE 37.9.

The Replicator tab helps you automate dial-up tasks such as replication and outbound mail transfer.

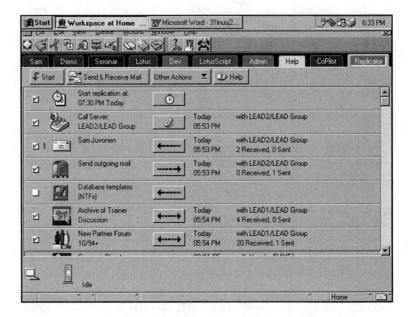

In the center, forming a column, are a series of buttons containing arrows. These represent the intended data flow during replication. For example, the Outgoing mail box typically has an arrow pointing to the right, indicating that this database will only send documents to a server, not receive them. By clicking on this button for a database, you can set the data-flow parameters. Specify whether to send and/or receive documents by selecting the respective options.

More importantly, you can also set the name of the server with which this database should replicate in the Replicate with server field. You may set each database to replicate with a different server.

Calling a Server

To force your machine to call a Notes server, you can select File | Mobile | Call Server. The list of servers presented is dependent on the chosen Location. If the call is not successful, and the error messages that are presented in the status bar aren't sufficient for determining the problem, try using the Trace Connection tool to determine the cause of the problem. Another tool you can use is the Trace Connection button. See the section "Using Trace Connection" later in this chapter for more details on Trace Connection.

Dependency Summary

To summarize the dependencies of the various dial-up components, the Replicator, the Call Server list, and the desktop icons are dependent on the Location documents. The Location documents depend on the Connection documents to actually reach a server. The Connection documents depend on your enabled ports and their parameters, such as the modem file. Connections may also depend on RAS or Dialup Network connections, which are configured separately. Figure 37.10 depicts this hierarchy.

FIGURE 37.10.
The hierarchy of dependent documents needed for communication with Notes R4 servers from a workstation.

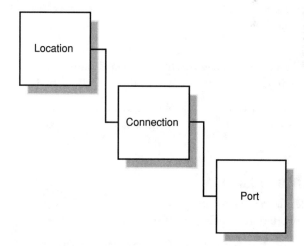

Information for Administrators

The documents described in the first section also apply to administrators. These same documents are found in the Public Address Book. In fact, there they are more detailed, because servers have a greater ability to schedule tasks than workstations do. The additional sections available in the public Connection documents pertain to scheduling replication and routing tasks.

NOTE

Many administrators are tasked with assisting users in addition to designing and maintaining the servers of a Notes network. If you have jumped right to this section, it would be a good idea to go back at some point and read the first section as well.

The Server Document

The server document must be configured correctly for the server to work on a network. The primary settings are found in the Port table in the Network section. The Port name, Notes Network name, and Network Address are all important parameters. When the server starts, it reads this table to establish its active protocols.

The Notes Address field is also important. If users are having trouble connecting to a server, check this field. Different protocols require varying specific entries to be made here.

For SPX and NetBIOS, simply enter the server name. NetBIOS functions without relying on an external service. SPX requires that a NetWare server be reachable to provide an SPX connection ID.

For TCP/IP you can enter either the server name or the actual IP address; the server-name entry will function adequately if the name-to-IP address-resolution mechanism is working satisfactorily on your network. If not, use the IP address itself.

For AppleTalk, if you use multiple zones, make sure you enter the server name at the proper zone (Notes1@ZoneAlpha) in this field; this will enable workstations in other zones to see the server.

Passthru Problems

If you decide to use Passthru, you may encounter problems related to your restriction settings or to network routing problems. We'll take a look at these issues first.

There are also four parameters which have counterparts in both the Server document and the NOTES.INI file; if you don't set a standard, such as always putting the entries in the Server document only, you might forget about settings you made that affect the behavior of Passthru.

Passthru Restriction-Related Problems

If you find that users and servers attempting Passthru cannot complete their connections, check the server documents' Passthru Use sections. The first three of the four fields in this section, if left empty, allow no one to perform those activities. The fourth field, Destinations allowed, is used by that server in determining the remote servers to which it may route via Passthru; if it is blank, there are no restrictions.

For other servers and users, you have control over three things: who can access this server via Passthru, who can route through this server via Passthru, and who can cause this server to call other servers while using Passthru. You must explicitly list users, servers, or, better yet, groups in order for any other entities to be able to use this server for Passthru. Make sure you use the distinguished names for people and server entries.

Another security measure that may affect Passthru is the field in the Security section of the server document named Compare public keys against those stored in the Address Book. Enabling this field forces this server to compare the public key contained in an ID with the public key stored in the Address Book document for that ID. Passthru will fail if this comparison fails. Although this is an authentication problem, it may at first appear to be a communication problem.

Passthru Routing Problems

A server that is being used for Passthru may not be able to determine the route to a destination server being requested. This may be due to several factors: the network name resolution systems are not functioning correctly, the Public Address Book doesn't contain enough information for Notes to determine the route, or this server may not be configured for Passthru.

Depending on your protocol, your network routing system has a method for resolving computer names into network addresses. If this system develops problems, when Notes asks for the network address for a server name, it won't get a response, and the server will not be reachable. In this case an error would be returned to the Passthru client saying that a route to the server that the user was attempting to reach could not be found.

If your Public Address Book doesn't have the required information, Passthru won't be able to find a complete path to the server the user is trying to reach. This might be due to a simple condition where the Public Address Book on the Passthru server hasn't replicated the most current documents from the hub server, or it might be that certain values were either forgotten or mistyped. Settings to look for include missing Connection documents for servers not directly reachable on the network, wrong values for the Passthru server field on the server document or users' Location documents, or invalid Passthru Connection documents.

Passthru Connection documents are usually not required, but if they are entered, they take precedence over the network name resolution process. If a server's address is changed, the server is physically moved to another network or it is renamed, and the Passthru Connection documents referencing that server must be changed.

Passthru Parameters in NOTES.INI

The parameters in Table 37.1 correspond to fields on the Server document. They are used only if you've created entries for them in the NOTES.INI file and their counterparts on the Server document are empty. If there is a conflict between the NOTES.INI setting and the Server document field, the Server document takes precedence.

Table 37.1. Passthru parameters and corresponding fields.

NOTES.INI Variables	Server Document Fields
Allow_Passthru_Access	Access this server
Allow_Passthru_Callers	Cause calling
Allow_Passthru_Clients	Route through
Allow_Passthru_Targets	Destinations allowed

Tools

Included with Notes R4 are several tools that provide you with useful information regarding network- and modem-related troubleshooting.

Log

The Log database is a great resource for recent historical information about the operation of a server. For network or dial-up troubleshooting, two views are important: Phone calls and Miscellaneous Events.

Phone Calls

Phone calls reveal statistics about an attempted or completed phone call. Use these documents to learn how your modems are behaving for different connections. You may find, for instance, that the server has repeated problems dialing a particular set of servers while the remainder appear to be functioning wonderfully. This can help you narrow down your investigation. Working with administrators from these other servers, you can attempt various solutions until you have the problem resolved.

Common problems that you can detect with Phone Call documents include:

- Retransmission errors, which indicate line problems or invalid modem configuration; try different modems or reducing the baud rate.
- The remote server is not answering, which indicates that you might have an invalid phone number or the other server is not available (or they may be having trouble, too!); make a voice call to verify the number or find the status of the other server.
- The carrier signal could not be established, which indicates that you may have line problems or your modem isn't configured properly, or your modem isn't compatible with the one being used at the other server. To fix this, try a different modem, try reducing the baud rate, or have the phone company analyze your line.
- The dial timer expired, which indicates that your `Dial timeout` parameter may not be set high enough for the propagation delay of the telco switches along the route between your server and theirs; try setting this parameter up to 120 seconds or higher.

Modem Problems and Phone Calls

First, check the Phone Calls view. If there are no phone calls, check the Miscellaneous Events documents, choosing a document that spans the time frame where you would expect an attempt to have been made. Look in this document (select Edit | Find | Replace) for the name of the destination server. If an attempt has been made, you will find an entry of the form `Network: Connecting to servername over portname`, where *servername* and *portname* will actually be the respective names in use.

If you find Phone Calls, first check the Server answering the phone field. If this is empty, the remote server never authenticated with the local machine.

If the Elapsed time indicates a number greater than zero, the two modems spent that much time trying to synchronize but couldn't.

Look at the Traffic and Errors sections at the bottom of the Phone Call. You will probably see that the traffic counts are low; this may be accompanied by port or retransmission errors. These indications could be the cause of line problems, modem settings, or modem-brand incompatibility. In any event, you know the server is trying to make the call and failing.

Miscellaneous Events

Miscellaneous Events documents are created as the server operates. Every message that crosses the console is logged in these documents. Because, by default, the log retains documents for seven days, you can look back through a week's worth of entries at any time.

Often it is useful to take the time stamp from a failed phone-call document and zoom into the Miscellaneous Event document for the same time period. If the Log Modem I/O option has been enabled, you will then see the modem commands that were sent to the modem. You might find, for instance, that the return code from the modem went unrecognized and that the call was terminated soon after.

Log Analysis (Search Tool)

You may be able to locate entries in your Log file more quickly by using the Log Analysis tool. This tool can be accessed from the Server Administration panel (select File | Tools | System Administration). It is essentially a search utility. You provide the word or phrase you want to find, and Notes generates an output database that contains a document for each reference that was found in the Log database.

You can search through the Logs of multiple servers and append the results in one database. Each search is performed separately, and when finished, you can browse the results database.

Console and Remote Console

When you are trying to determine facts about a communication problem, the server console or the remote console can provide you with some vital information. For modem troubleshooting, you'll want to use the SHOW PORT COMx command (just replace the *x* with the appropriate number). This gives you the same statistics that you can see under the Show Status button on the User Preferences dialog box for a COM port. Repeat the command over a period of minutes to determine the error rate.

The SHOW PORT COMx command returns information similar to this:

```
Answered incoming call from system Server Notes1/Acme

Counts since the beginning of the last connection:
    57600 Bit per second connection (port speed)
    28000 Bit per second connection (carrier speed)
       11 Currently active sessions
      411 User messages sent
     1802 User messages received
   217831 User bytes sent
   955060 User bytes received
        1 Retransmitted packets
        0 CRC errors detected
        0 Port errors detected
```

If you see any of the error counts, especially port errors, climb rapidly, and repeat the call. If this happens each time you make that call, you will need to use a process of elimination to find and resolve the problem. For port errors, check the cable, try a different port, or try a different modem. For retransmissions or CRC errors, try a different phone line, a different modem file, a different modem, or a different port.

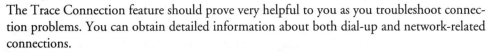

Using Trace Connection

The Trace Connection feature should prove very helpful to you as you troubleshoot connection problems. You can obtain detailed information about both dial-up and network-related connections.

The goal of using Trace Connection is to determine whether a path to a particular server can be found, and if so, how it was found. All of the current environment parameters are used during the trace attempt. For example, if you are currently using the Office location with the TCP/IP port enabled and the COM1 port disabled, the Trace feature will not attempt to make a phone-call connection based on a Dialup Connection document. It will use Remote LAN Connections and Local Area Network Connections as appropriate.

You can access Trace Connection through the Ports option on the File | Tools | User Preferences dialog box. Click the Trace Connection button to bring up this dialog box. Enter the name (or choose it from the list) of the server you are trying to reach, then click Trace. As Notes attempts to reach the server, it will report in the bottom list box how it is going about it and what success it is having at each step.

You can often find here that Notes is attempting to talk to a server or find a path that you didn't expect it to be attempting at that point. Often you can trace this back to an errant setting in one of your configuration documents (most likely a Location or Connection document).

If the server is unreachable on TCP/IP, an error is returned to you.

Figure 37.11 shows the Trace Connections dialog box.

FIGURE 37.11.

The Trace Connections dialog box.

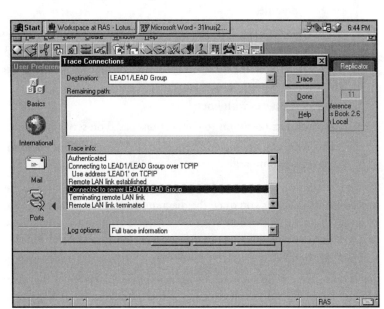

KnowledgeBase

A truly valuable resource is a frequently updated database titled the Lotus Notes KnowledgeBase. Lotus produces and maintains this database, which is replicated through the Lotus Notes Network (LNN) and distributed periodically on CD-ROM. You can obtain your copy by signing up on LNN or purchasing the KnowledgeBase directly from Lotus.

In this database you will find hundreds of Technotes and error messages. It also includes workarounds and, in some cases, file attachments that can help you.

Communication Element Hierarchy Chart

The Notes Public Address Book contains the documents that make communication possible. As you gather large numbers of these documents, it can be somewhat difficult to visualize the interrelationships. By drawing a hierarchy chart, you can quickly visualize the structure and detect problems that you wouldn't see by merely looking through the documents.

Follow these steps, drawing the boxes in tiers; that is, draw each box described in Step 1 in a horizontal line, then draw the boxes from Step 2 in another horizontal line below those drawn in Step 1, and so forth:

1. Draw a box for each Location document. Label each box with the name of the location. Indicate the names of the Mail server, the Passthru server, and the InterNotes server.

2. Draw a box for each Connection document. Label each box with the name of the server being called.

3. Draw a box for each Port that is enabled on the system. Label each box with the port name. To verify the active ports, check the User Preferences - Port section.

4. Draw a box for each Dial-up Networking (Windows 95) connection. Label each box with the connection name.

5. Connect the boxes with lines:

   ■ Connect Locations to connections based on server names.

   ■ Connect Connections to ports or RAS connections based on port names or RAS connection names.

If you can't draw a connecting line from one item to another, draw a short line that points to a question mark. After you draw the diagram, pay particular attention to any lines that point to question marks. Determine whether the question indicates a missing element that needs to be completed or whether the question is answered by a fact not indicated. You are trying to find any items which need to be completed.

Some questions can be answered by an item other than a Notes document. For instance, let's say you have a Location called Office, which uses your TCP/IP port. All three server fields indicate the Notes1 server. Further, you don't have any connections leading to Notes1 over TCP/IP. In your diagram, arrows lead from these three server entries to question marks. This is satisfactory because the item that resolves the link is your Domain Name Server (DNS), or a local HOSTS file. When you are using the Office location, you are connected to a LAN and the name-to-address resolution is successful. These arrows on your diagram actually have answers when you are connected to the LAN.

Any items that cannot be resolved this way, however, are points for concern. These items probably indicate areas that will be nonfunctional; you should focus your efforts toward adding the necessary documents to complete your diagram. (See Figure 37.12.) For instance, let's say that you have a Travel location that uses COM2 with all three server fields indicating Notes1. Your connection documents, however, do not include any that combine a destination server of Notes1 with a COM2 port. The arrows leading from this location document end in question marks. This problem cannot be resolved by an external entity. You need to either edit other connection documents so that they lead to Notes1 over COM2, or create new Dialup Connections that do so.

FIGURE 37.12.

A sample communica-tion hierarchy diagram.

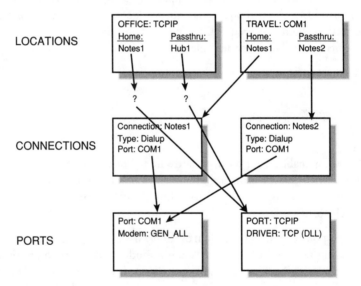

Modifying Modem Files

The Generic All-speed modem file (GEN_ALL.MDM) and the sample modem command file (TEMPLATE.MDM) are good files to read. They contain instructions on the parameters to modify to create a working command file.

Let's look at and demystify the contents of a modem file. The basic structure is that of an .INI file such as WIN.INI or NOTES.INI. The file consists of three paragraphs: [attributes], [commands], and [responses].

In the [attributes] paragraph, you specify the name of the modem, the maximum and default speeds, and whether the file controls a null modem. All modem files but two have the NULL MODEM parameter set to zero; the exceptions are the two null modem files NULL.MDM and NULLV1.MDM. The speeds are typically set to the highest that the modem will allow.

Some older modems don't work well at their advertised high speeds, and the modem files will limit those modems to a slower, more reliable speed for use under Notes. The MAXIMUM SPEED parameter effectively limits the modem to that speed; if you try to override with a higher speed setting—say, in the File | Mobile | Call Server dialog box—an error message will appear.

The important fields in this section are:

■ Maximum speed

■ Default speed

The [commands] paragraph is used to identify the modem-setup commands, volume-control commands, and RTS/CTS-control commands. There may be one or more SETUP parameters; they are executed in the order they appear. SETUP parameters may need to be modified in some command files. Your modem may not work correctly with all of the compression and error-correction commands in use. Use your modem's reference manual to examine each parameter specified in the Notes modem file against the allowed commands.

The most important fields in this section are the following:

■ Setup

■ RTS/CTS enabled

■ RTS/CTS ignored

RTS/CTS enables your modem hardware to control the flow of data. It is generally enabled, except when you are using a null modem. Look in your modem's user guide to confirm that the entries are correct. The entry should only be one or two flags (such as AT&K3 or AT&K3&R0).

The [responses] paragraph is often overlooked. Nothing will cause more stealthy problems than a missing response parameter. When a modem connects to another modem, it returns a response string back to your software. The software, recognizing the response, sets itself up accordingly. If the response is not recognized, however, the software behaves as if no response was received, often taking a minute or more to hang up for lack of dialog. The reason that this is a stealthy problem is that even by looking at the Log database you won't see any errors.

To detect and correct a response-parameter problem, look in the Log for the response string that is returned from the modem. Compare that string with the defined responses in the [responses] paragraph of your modem file. If you do not see that particular response string, or a response that matches it based on the wildcard (*), you will need to enter one or more new lines to accept this response.

A connect response line has the following syntax:

```
CONNECT, port speed, modem speed=CONNECT speed
```

For the connect speed, you can use the wildcard character * to indicate a variety of possible responses. For instance, CONNECT 28* would react to any of the following:

```
CONNECT 28800
CONNECT 28800/ARQ
CONNECT 28.8
```

For example, suppose you are trying to connect at a default speed of 57600. The modem hangs up after a minute of repeated attempts. Following the preceding steps, you notice that your modem is returning the string CONNECT 19200/ARQ. Examination of your modem file reveals no lines for the 19200 speed. Using another line (or set of lines) as an example, enter one or more 19200 responses:

```
CONNECT, 57600, 19200=CONNECT 19200
CONNECT, 57600, 19200=CONNECT 19200*
CONNECT, 57600, 19200=CONNECT 19.2*
CONNECT, 57600, 19200=CONNECT 19*
```

Server Issues

Let's look at a couple of common server issues that you'll probably encounter at some point. First, we'll discuss an error message: Server not responding. This occurs when your workstation cannot reach the server; we'll look at the reasons. Second, if you are having difficulty getting your server to start, we'll explore some possible reasons.

Message: Server not responding

This message occurs when the server is not reachable from a client or another server. The reasons for this message can vary depending on the protocol being used; sometimes it occurs when there are not enough network sessions.

For TCP/IP, the resolution of the server name to an IP address happens either through a local HOSTS text file or through a network Domain Name Service (DNS). If you are using the HOSTS file method, and the file is missing or has been edited in such a way that the server's name has been removed, the name resolution will fail. If you are using a DNS, check to see if the name table has been changed. Check the DNS to make sure it is operational. Try using the Ping utility to ping the server by name. If this fails, Notes will not be able to reach the server either. Resolve the DNS issue, and the server will reappear.

For SPX, the name resolution is handled by a NetWare server. If no server responds to the Notes request, the name never gets resolved into an SPX address, and the server becomes unreachable. Examine your NetWare servers for problems. Examine your Notes server for SPX connectivity outside of the Notes server task. Try rebooting the Notes server if all SPX functionality is available elsewhere.

For NetBIOS, determine whether you have ever been able to see the server. If so, ensure that no routers exist between the workstation and the server, or if they do, that they have the capability to route NetBIOS packets and that they have been configured to do so. Most routers cannot route NetBIOS. Try rebooting the server, if possible. If both the client and the server are running Novell's NetBIOS, they may not be running the same frame type.

Condition: Server Fails to Start

If your Notes server shuts itself down shortly after you start it, check for the following:

- The server document may have been corrupted or deleted. Without this document, the server cannot identify itself properly, and it may shut down.
- The server may not have been configured properly using the administrative client prior to launching the server task. Finalize the setup of the client first.

Modem Issues

In an ideal world, the modems you've configured for your Notes servers would always work. Let's take a look at a couple of issues you might encounter. If you walk up to your console and observe that the server seems to be continually querying a modem at all of the available speeds but never getting an answer, that modem is not operational. Or you notice that your modems just don't seem to be working, what can you do?

Your Server Is Cycling Through the Available Modem Speeds

If you see your server continually try to communicate with a modem, cycling through each of the speeds in order, your server isn't communicating with the modem. If a modem is not available but the port is enabled, the server will continually attempt to access the modem. If the modem is connected, cycle the power to it; if Notes still cannot access it, you may have a damaged port, or the system may just need to be rebooted. If this happens repeatedly, try using a different port, if one is available. Try another modem or modem cable. Consider replacing the port. Make sure that another task on that machine hasn't been configured to use that port, which would prevent Notes from having access to it.

Modem Connections Are Not Working

If you are experiencing a problem across multiple ports with a set of modems of the same brand, try checking the following:

- Look in the Miscellaneous Events documents for evidence that modem commands are being sent and acknowledged by the modems. Look carefully at the responses being received during any connection attempts with other servers.

- Examine the modem file (or switch to an alternate) for setup-string errors. Try simplifying the setup strings to one line that states SETUP=AT&F for factory-default settings.

- Check the settings on your modem. If it has DIP switches, compare the current settings with those recommended in the manual. Try setting the switches to the most basic settings described in the manual; you can slowly improve them after reaching a known good combination.

- Check the cable and the port. Try alternates if they are available.

Summary

By knowing the components that affect dial-up and network communications, you are in a position of strength when the time comes that you need to troubleshoot problems in these areas. Knowing the tools you have available enables you to quickly diagnose and even resolve these types of issues.

The components we looked at included documents in Public Address Book, the NOTES.INI file, along with preference and port settings.

We saw how the settings in these places affect overall server connectivity and network issues, modem-related problems, and Passthru-related problems.

For tools, we took a look at the various documentation available to you, and at the Log file with its Phone Call and Miscellaneous Events documents as well as the Trace Connections dialog box.

PART

VIII

Advanced Administration Topics

Managing a Large Notes Network

*by Sam Juvonen
and Marjorie Kramer*

IN THIS CHAPTER

As you might suppose, designing and managing a large Notes network takes some thought. Although building new Notes components into your organization can be accomplished piecemeal, the planning should be performed in advance of any serious implementation.

In this chapter, you explore many of the items that affect the design of your enterprise Notes network. Although, like snowflakes, no two networks are the same, many of the same issues must be considered in reaching your design goals. The goal of this chapter is to bring to your attention these details for consideration as you move forward.

Planning

Planning is key. The easy installation of a Notes server tends to oversimplify the importance of the early decisions you need to make. In fact, by using some of the examples provided in the dialog boxes, you can establish an unwieldy naming scheme. Use the following list as a guide:

1. Plan for teamwork. Use Notes to assist your administrative group. Establish open lines of communications and a clear process for establishing standards and resolving conflicts.

2. Plan your infrastructure. Your servers will behave better if you provide adequate hardware. Modem technology has greatly improved, yet many modem combinations still refuse to work or perform poorly together.

3. Plan your topologies carefully. Many aspects of Notes administration can be thought of as a topology. Because Notes doesn't draw pictures, develop topology maps for your team. It will help you make sense of the contents of your domain's Public Address Book.

4. Plan to monitor your system. Through careful monitoring you can often detect conditions that might lead to serious problems.

Teamwork: Distributing the Responsibility

Notes solves many problems with regard to information distribution. How widely spread are your offices or employees? Do your business units function as separate companies? You can choose to control your Notes environment centrally, or, more likely, you and your team of administrators will share the responsibility (perhaps geographically).

Developing Standards

The topic of standards encompasses nearly all the functionality of the system. Before you can create meaningful standards, you must have a firm grasp of the components of the system as well as the tools at your disposal. Though it is not within the scope of this chapter to lay out everything you need to develop a thorough standards document, you can take the high-level structure presented here to get you started.

Some of the more crucial standards to establish involve the entities that the public will see. Your server names are visible to others who connect to your domain; you use these names when you perform console commands such as REPLICATE SERVERNAME. Your domain names are visible to anyone sending e-mail to your users. Your organization name is visible to anyone reading documents you compose; it could be your mail memos or documents in a discussion database that replicates around the world. Think ahead and determine just how you want your company's name to be seen. Keep the names short and avoid spaces.

Distributed Management of the Public Address Book

In a large network, one administrator cannot manage the entire environment. Requests are often generated so rapidly that they mount quickly; fulfillment sometimes requires a local presence. A team of administrators must work together to fulfill requests and, ultimately, maintain the documents of the Public Address Book.

It has been observed, however, in established Notes networks, that local changes are often implemented without consideration for the impact on the other servers that depend on the same book. R3 does little to facilitate safe local changes. Enabling administrators to have Editor access to the book gives them free rein over all the documents. R4 adds tools to the Public Address Book to enhance its maintainability in a large, distributed environment.

Creating the Administrative Process for Managing the Public Address Book

To manage the maintenance of the Public Address Book, create a list of the types of changes (adds, modifications, and deletions) that will be necessary in your domain. Design a request and approval process that will facilitate the best balance of administration among all your administrators. Reaching agreement not only on the methods for maintaining the address book, but also on the resolution process for any related management issues (such as maintaining this request/approval process) will enable your administrative team to perform with confidence.

Documents: Adds, Moves, and Changes

If changes must be made to documents (such as groups) that can affect users and servers at other sites, consider forming a policy whereby change requests are submitted and reviewed before they are implemented. This review does not need to fall on one person, but instead can be put up for examination by all administrators. An administrator who notices a detrimental effect can voice the concern before the change is made. Review the various types of changes that may be made and classify them as to which can be made without review.

38

MANAGING A
LARGE NOTES
NETWORK

Creating a Request and Approval Process

You might consider creating an administrative facilitation database; it could contain a request/approval workflow process, a discussion section, tips and tricks, perhaps even a knowledgebase. It should define your company's standards for handling the routine chores of the Public Address Book. The request types should include creating and modifying users and creating and modifying groups. You can also use a similar procedure to promote new databases from test servers to production servers.

Notifications

Use NotesMail to notify administrators of a new request (include a DocLink). Once a request has been approved, a notification could be mailed to the requester informing of a change with regard to that request.

Granted and Rejected Requests with Reason and Suggestions

If your environment is one in which you have a hierarchical request process, use the mail platform to inform the requester of the decision. Offer suggestions if appropriate, especially for a rejection.

Designing Your Network

In a large Notes network design, you will evaluate the pros and cons of several different topics. Should you model your network after the political or geographic makeup of your company? How should you plan for your servers to communicate? How many domains would make sense for you? What should you consider in creating your hierarchical naming conventions? How should you configure the topologies for mail routing, replication and other features, such as passthru? As your Public Address Book grows in size and distribution, what are the effective ways to manage it? How should you plan for additional gateways or Mail Transfer Agents?

Let's consider each of these individually, realizing that many decisions on one topic hinge or bear on the decisions made in another area.

Naming Users and Servers

Notes provides a means to associate each resource (a user or server) with a component of your company. This is best accomplished using hierarchical names. Not only is it a convenience to know what part of your company a user is associated with, but it also enhances your company's security if you can isolate access to branches of your company. The rules of naming Notes users descends from X.500.

Although it is difficult to give hard and fast rules to what the hierarchies should be in your company, there are guidelines to follow. It is important to remember that hierarchies associated with users are flexible whereas hierarchies associated with servers are less flexible. The following are the rules of hierarchical naming:

- At least one level of naming must be established. This is referred to as the Organization or O.
- The country code is married to the Organization. It is a two-character, predefined value.
- After the O, the hierarchy can be four additional levels deep; each level is referred to as the Organizational Unit (OUn) where n is the level.
- Each user/server has a common name associated with it.
- The common name, organizational Units, and Organization define the name of the resource.
- Each level of the organization is associated with a discrete certifier ID.
- In order to secure your system, at least one level of OU should be implemented.

Consider the company G. S. Dunn, Inc. The firm has 45 employees worldwide. I would recommend that it use its "short form" name for the Organization, GSDUNN since it will be repeated over and over again in the domain. I would also recommend that they choose their locations as first-level OUs since the company is location based. Company officials chose HAM for Hamilton, TOK for Tokyo, and WIN for Windsor. Finally, I recommend that they use a separate OU for their servers. They chose SRV for servers. Ronald Kuver in Hamilton has the name Ronald Kramer/HAM/GDUNN. The servers are named sequentially by function. HUB01/SRV/GDUNN is the first hub server.

Using these rules, guidelines are simple. When setting up a naming scheme, remember that this is internal to the company. People communicating with members of your company via e-mail will use the common name of the person and domain name to get the mail to the user. Notes will resolve the name within your company to get to the destination.

Guidelines for Naming

No component should have a space in it. This would require referring to the resource with quotation marks around it when referring to this name at the server console, for instance.

The O name should be at least three characters long.

If country codes are implemented, refer to them in an OU to keep all IDs under the same certificate. Because the country code is associated with the Organization, a new Organization certifier (the top), has to be created for each country.

O names should be the "short form" of your company. Because this component is going to be referred to whenever a name is represented in Notes, it is cumbersome to use a long name. For

38

MANAGING A
LARGE NOTES
NETWORK

example, the company Helene Curtis is known as HCI internally. Instead of using Helene Curtis in every name, HCI is a better reference.

The total amount of characters in the OU levels should not exceed 15 for users. If you choose to have many (4) OU levels, make the names short. Remember that each time you refer to a resource in your domain you will be using the entire name, including the hierarchy. (The maximum characters used is 274, 80 max for CN, 32 max for each OU, up to 4 OUs, 64 max for Org, and 2 max for country.)

Servers should be isolated in their own branches of the hierarchy. Changing the name of the server is difficult because all users will have to change icons on their desktops.

Keep in mind that, internally, all resources will be able to authenticate (access each server/sign documents); externally, you can isolate branches of your hierarchy for authentication.

Designing a Scheme for Using the Guidelines

First, investigate other software packages in your company that use hierarchical naming (Novell 4.0, using Directory Name Services, for example). You can save time if you implement a plan similar to what is already being used.

You should treat servers and users separately. First, ask your users, "How do you know Joe Smith in your company?" Is it because he is in the marketing department or because he is in San Francisco? This should be your first level OU. For example, if the answer to the question is "We know him because he is in Sales," the first level should represent departments. Don't limit yourself to thinking of departments or location; companies have also implemented the first-level OU based on skill set. You may just have one OU level for users.

For servers, create an OU indicating that they are servers—for example, SVR. You may want to plan for external servers and internal servers by creating a second level separating the two. You don't have to implement the external servers' OU right away; if you have a plan, using it in the future will be easier.

The common name of the server should indicate its function in the company and a number for future growth.

Because some protocols used by Notes looks only at the common name of the server name, servers should be uniquely named in their common name. That is, don't depend on the hierarchy to define the server uniquely. As well, each server will have the fact that it is a server as a component of its name. It is unnecessary to include this in the common name of the server. For example, MKT1/SVR/WWCorp is an appropriate name, whereas MKTSVR1/SVR/WWCorp is redundant.

One of the main reasons to choose a good hierarchical naming scheme is to delegate responsibility to others. Most corporations are regional, with servers located in the regions as well as in corporate headquarters. If support is available for the regional users from the regions, it makes sense to have regional administrators responsible for their own mini-domain.

The global administrator can delegate the responsibility to a number of degrees. If all responsibility is to be delegated, meaning creating users, setting up servers, managing mail distribution, and ensuring replication, the global administrator can give the OU certifier for the region to the local administrator. This, along with delegation of authority in the Public Address Book (discussed later in this chapter) enables the local administrator to create IDs for users, enable them to access the servers they need to, and update connection documents. The global administrator should hold onto the server OU certifier and grant access to the server document to the appropriate local administrator.

This enables the global administrator to leave the regional tasks in the regions.

Planning Your Server Infrastructure: Server Types

Typically, Notes implementations start with servers performing one task, supply access to databases and routing mail. Once a critical mass of users starts using Notes, you may find a need to streamline your servers by function. You may want to consider this streamlining early in the process because certain efficiencies can be achieved. The types of servers to consider are Mail, Database, Passthru, External, and firewall.

Mail Servers

Mail servers provide access mail files only. The server will replicate with the rest of the domain to get the Public Address Book in synch. Otherwise, the mail server will have only mail databases located on it.

Using mail servers is the most efficient use of Single Copy Object stores (SCOS). SCOS stores the body of mail messages in a central database; the header (address) and pointer to the body are located in the individual mail files. Each mail file has just pointers and headers. If mail is centralized on one server, fewer SCOS databases are required. Use the SHARED_MAIL=2 parameter in the NOTES.INI file of the mail server. This enables all messages to go to the SCOS database.

In order to use the resources on a mail server efficiently, create a replication schedule that only replicates the Public Address Book between the mail servers and the rest of the servers in your domain.

Mail servers should be used in conjunction with passthru servers so that remote users need to make only one phone call to get their mail and databases.

Mail servers should be frequently backed up and be high-end machines to provide maximum access. Administrators need to have full access to mail servers. There should be at least one mail server per notes-named network so that users can access the server.

Database Servers

Database servers hold databases for users. What is on database servers depends on who is accessing the server. For example, if the marketing department accesses one server, all the databases for that department should be there.

Placement of database servers in your environment can enhance network traffic. If the databases are streamlined so that users are using servers closest to them with regard to the network, Notes will operate more efficiently.

Placement of databases on servers can also have an effect on the amount of disk space used by a database. If your replication topology requires databases to exist on the hub in order for it to be distributed to several spokes, you may want to reconsider placing a database on several spokes. Another consideration would be to implement a schedule for the database in question between spokes.

It is difficult to control how many users are accessing the databases. On busy servers, you may require certain users only to access the server to prevent slow access. For example, users with the last name A-F access one server; all others access another server for the same database.

You may want to consider placing reference databases on only a few servers for access.

Passthru Servers

If remote users access both database and mail servers, it may be necessary to implement passthru servers for dial-in purposes. This enables users to make only one call to access both their mail and the databases they need. A passthru server acts as an ambassador for the user and makes the connections for the user.

Passthru servers can be mail servers or database servers. Users specify their mail servers in the location documents of their mail files and the names of the servers to act as ambassadors. (See Figure 38.1.)

The receiving server must also have passthru enabled in order for it to act on behalf of the user to find the target server. (See Figure 38.2.)

When users call the mail server to get their mail, the passthru server is really called; then the connection is made by the passthru server. If the passthru server can connect to the database server, the user can indicate a database replication at the same time.

Passthru servers have a layer of security limiting who can use the server as an agent to get to other servers.

Passthru servers should have enough modems on them to enable efficient connectivity to the other servers.

FIGURE 38.1.

This user is configured to use the server PT01 for passthru.

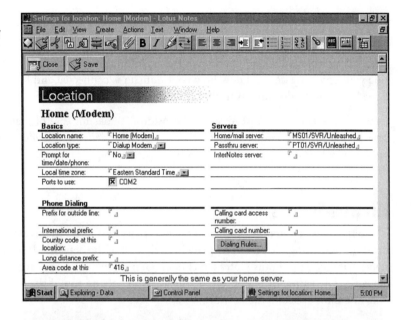

FIGURE 38.2.

Only the users or servers listed in the group PTAllowed can reach this server via passthru.

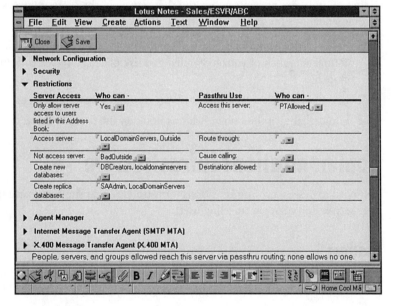

38

MANAGING A
LARGE NOTES
NETWORK

External Servers

Servers that communicate to outside organizations should be planned for in advance. The idea is to isolate nonsecret information on these servers to provide access to the pertinent information and, at the same time, not to risk company data.

External servers should be isolated in their own branches of the naming hierarchy you have in place so that you can provide access just to those servers easily through cross certification.

External servers should have bare-bones Public Address Book on them so that companies outside your company do not know how your domain is connected and how it is set up. This is done by changing documents in this server manually.

External servers contain cascading Public Address Books for ease of mail addressing to outside domains. When building external servers, plan for denying and allowing access to specific servers/people from outside companies by implementing them with entries in the allow and deny access groups.

Firewall Servers

The term firewall comes from Internet connectivity and refers to servers that allow access to data without letting the other company in to the rest of the network. It is important to understand that access to a Lotus Notes server does not mean that the user has access to the company network. The nature of Notes, providing access to data on top of the current network layer, does not allow access to the network.

A firewall in Notes prevents access to other servers in the Notes network. The following are recommendations for setting up a firewall Notes server:

- Cross-certify based on the server name only. As soon as you provide access to a complete branch of your hierarchy, you risk placing a server with insecure data in that branch.
- Use allow/deny access groups to limit who can access the server specifically.
- Limit what is in the Public Address Book on the firewall server.

Communications Infrastructure

You need to design a communications infrastructure that supports communications between your servers and between traveling users.

Modem

The most common method for connecting servers and users is to use modems. They are inexpensive and can use a well-established analog phone line system around the world.

Certainly for remote or laptop users, modems are still the most attractive option. Other methods, such as ISDN or X.25, require more hardware and software, not to mention support, to make them work.

It pays to bear in mind, however, that the analog system differs in quality around the world. As your users travel, they may dial back to your network from many locations where line quality is poor. You may have to suggest to some users that they reduce line speed to achieve a reliable connection.

ISDN

For servers or users at fixed remote sites, such as those who work from their homes, ISDN services are becoming attractive. Increasingly, providers are offering a wider array of ISDN services at lower price points.

ISDN is not to be taken lightly, however. The installation and support required to establish and maintain a single ISDN link can create a cost far greater than that imposed by the use of a modem. Until these procedures are simplified, ISDN should be considered only in cases where the costs are justified.

That said, Notes will perform wonderfully over ISDN. The Notes software knows only which protocol it is speaking; it isn't concerned with the underlying hardware that enables that protocol. You can run Notes over IP very effectively using ISDN.

WAN

Lotus Notes works well in a WAN environment. If your decision to implement a WAN hinges solely on Notes, however, it is often not worth the extra cost, because a Notes WAN can be implemented more cheaply with modem technology (depending on frequency and duration of calls).

A WAN still operates on certain network protocols. Again, Notes makes use of these protocols to communicate; it doesn't distinguish the underlying architecture. However, remember that Notes servers cannot be included in the same Notes Named Network unless they share the same protocol and are constantly connected (modem connections aren't sufficient).

Topology Types

A topology is a layout or schematic of a series of controls in a system. For Lotus Notes, this applies to many aspects of the system: mail routing, replication, and Passthru, to name a few. Let's look at some different types of topologies; they can be applied as appropriate against the various portions of a Notes system.

Peer-to-Peer

A topology where communications are established among a series of servers without designating a single master server can be called a peer-to-peer topology. For example, a New York server calls Dallas, which calls San Diego, which calls New York.

Peer-to-peer can be scheduled in an end-to-end fashion or as a mesh. This method is generally used when only a few servers are involved and a hub and spoke system would be overkill, perhaps requiring more hardware than necessary to meet the communication needs.

Though we use the term peer-to-peer, this does not apply to workstations. Just remember this: workstations cannot answer connection requests, they always initiate them. This implies that workstations cannot call one another.

End-to-End

In an end-to-end setup, servers call each other in an orderly fashion, making a series of calls to form a calling loop. For example, a New York server calls Dallas, which calls San Diego, which calls Chicago, which in turn calls New York. If a server goes down, however, the replication of databases around the loop is slowed significantly. For a document to replicate its way back upstream, for instance, it takes several more cycles. Note also that all servers have to have a replica copy of a database, and you should use the LocalDomainServers group or equivalent, assigning it Manager access in each replica.

Mesh

The Mesh method is an end-to-end schedule with a twist. Instead of calling only one other server, some of them make two or more calls, creating a crisscross pattern. If one server goes down, it does not affect the replication among the other servers.

With this method, the number of connection documents grows almost exponentially as the number of servers increases. It is practical only when you have a small number of servers (like 4 or 5).

Hub and Spoke

The most common and efficient topology in a large network is called hub and spoke. It is most prevalent largely due to its scalability.

The simplest hub and spoke arrangement is this: one server acts as the hub and coordinates the flow of information to other subhubs. The subhubs talk to production servers. As the number of production servers grows, more subhubs or even new layers of subhubs can be added to serve more production servers. The simplest arrangement is a single hub with 8 or 9 spoke servers.

One factor that is solved best by the hub and spoke method is the number of hops that a piece of data must make to travel from one end of the network to the other. Other topologies often require many more hops, slowing the communication process for the users, whereas this topology can move a mail message or a replicated document quickly anywhere within your network or even to other companies.

The principal benefits for using the hub-and-spoke model include:

- Centralized communication costs
- Enhanced security (hub will have restricted access)
- Centralized replication and backups
- Alleviates overlapping replication schedules

You may also want to consider implementing a backup hub server that replicates with the hub and that can quickly be reconfigured into becoming the hub server if the primary hub goes down.

The Domain and the Public Address Book

The glue of a Notes domain is the Public Address Book. The larger your network, the more crucial the management of this instrument. Your users will depend on it for addressing mail; your servers need it for identification, security, and task scheduling. Management of this book should be planned in advance so that emergencies can be avoided through routine maintenance.

Notes Domains

As you've learned, a Domain is defined as a group of servers that replicate their primary Public Address Books. The components of that domain are all defined in that Public Address Book. Each server knows its place in the network as well as the roles of, and communications paths to, each of the other servers.

However, this is not necessarily the best method for setting up a large network, although this doesn't imply that it is wrong. Simply stated, the evaluation of several factors can help you determine whether to use one domain or to split your organization into multiple domains.

Simplicity Versus Efficiency

A single Public Address Book eases mail addressing, but as this Public Address Book grows large, efficiency for each of the servers using that book decreases. For a barometer, Lotus scaled Notes R4 for 150,000 user documents, along with 20,000 group documents.

Multiple domains (each has its own Public Address Book) are each more efficient for lookups, but they make addressing harder; they require either a separate combined Public Address Book or cascaded books so that your users can find the names of recipients of their messages. Even so, users must continually switch between books as they look for a recipient's name. Addresses must include the domain name in addition to the user or group name.

Simplicity is better than efficiency (which may be marginal). Now that R4 can scale easily to large, multiprocessor platforms, using one Public Address Book can greatly simplify your administrative overhead.

38

MANAGING A
LARGE NOTES
NETWORK

Roles

The R4 Public Address Book provides various roles stratified to match the most common administrator functions in such an environment. The users and groups listed in the ACL are assigned to appropriate roles that grant them rights according to their assigned responsibilities. You can now enable some administrators to create and modify only groups but not users or servers; likewise, you can allow some to create users but not modify groups. In this way it is possible to distribute the maintenance responsibilities without releasing control to each and every administrator.

The roles that are new to the R4 Public Address Book are:

- GroupCreator: Allows creation of Group documents.
- GroupModifier: Allows modification of Group documents.
- NetCreator: Allows creation of all documents except Groups, Servers, and Person documents.
- NetModifier: Allows modification of all documents except Groups, Servers, and Users.
- ServerCreator: Allows creation of server IDs and Server documents.
- ServerModifier: Allows modification of Server documents.
- UserCreator: Allows creation of user IDs and Person documents.
- UserModifier: Allows modification of Person documents.

When you migrate a Public Address Book from R3 to R4, these roles do not exist, and you will find that you are not allowed to make any changes to the database. You will need to run two Agents that appear on the Action menu when you are in this database:

- Add Admin Roles to Access Control List
- Apply Delegation to All Selected Entries

The first Agent adds the roles into the ACL, and it also applies all the roles to any entries in the ACL that are Editor or higher; it gives the create-only roles to any entries that have Author with Create access. A message box appears that tells you how many of each type were corrected.

The second Agent is run against the documents in the database, and it adds the role names to a new field called DocumentAccess. This Agent only runs against those documents you have selected in a view; you might want to change the Agent definition so that it runs against all documents in the database before actually running it, to save yourself some time.

Public Address Book ACL

The ACL of the Public Address Book is an important item to manage. Because an ACL does not merge individual entries with other ACLs, but instead overwrites it (if allowed to via

Manager access), it is best if you make changes on one replica and let that ACL manage all other copies.

R4 offers a new ACL feature that provides for this: by setting the maintain-consistent ACL flag under the advanced section of the ACL dialog box, Notes will maintain the same ACL settings on all replica copies. Use this feature when you want to enforce the ACL even on a local copy of a database (on a laptop, for instance).

Understand, though, that even this is not true security; sharp-minded users can find ways around this. Educate your users so that they learn that this feature is really intended to help them understand what they can actually change on the server's copy. This will alleviate conditions where they make local changes only to find that their level of access on the server didn't accept those changes. Now they won't be able to make the changes locally, and it eliminates the guesswork.

When agreement has been reached as to a proposed change, it is still best to make the change on a "master" Public Address Book, such as the one on a hub server, and let that change flow down to other replicas.

In a widely distributed environment (both physically and administratively) you can, with care, determine in advance to allow certain changes, such as new user registrations, to occur on the local servers and replicate back up the hierarchy. Changes to group documents, however, can easily lead to replication conflicts; these are best made in only one replica.

Administration Groups

A new addition to the documents in the Public Address Book in R4 makes it easier to facilitate local changes in a distributed environment. Using the Administrators field, you can specify, per document, those groups that are allowed to modify it. This enables you to allocate specific sets of documents to the control of a local administrator; that person will be allowed to maintain those documents, yet you haven't relinquished control of the other documents.

For example, suppose you have an administrator in Wichita, Kansas. This person needs to have the authority to edit the documents for that branch. You can create a group for that branch and include that group name in the Administrators field on those documents that the Wichita administrator should be allowed to edit.

Mail Routing Topology

Let's look at how you can use NotesMail to configure your domain for efficient mail routing, which is key in satisfying your users.

Minimizing Hops

The simplest factor for efficient mail routing is the number of hops a message must make to reach its destination. This is not only a factor for speed, but troubleshooting as well. Each server has its own schedule for routing mail; two factors, the schedule and the message count threshold, determine how quickly messages route through a server.

The schedules are specified in Connection documents in the Public Address Book, along with the method of connecting (such as the COM port and phone number). You can specify days of the week, times to attempt connections (as either single times or ranges), and for time ranges, how often to call during the range.

The most efficient method of routing mail uses the hub and spoke topology. Messages travel one or two hops to the hub, then one or two hops down to the recipient's mail server.

Minimizing Cost

If some of your servers are connected via modem, you bear a communication cost for each phone call. Your goal is to make as few productive phone calls as possible. Instead of calling for each message that uses that route, you can let them accrue in the MAIL.BOX file, then pass them all at a scheduled time.

There is a field called Route at once if [ ] messages pending on the Connection document. By putting the threshold number in this field, the router will force a call if and when the threshold is reached. Otherwise, it will wait until the next scheduled calling time to route the messages.

Non-Adjacent Domains

To simplify addressing for your users, you can create non-adjacent Domain documents that enable the sender to specify the user's domain but not the intermediate domain needed to route the message. For example, let's say your design specifies that you will use an "external" domain for mail routing outside your company. A message intended for someone at another firm must be addressed to that user at that user's domain at your external domain (*User @ UserDomain @ ExternalDomain*). This tells the servers in your internal domain to first forward the message to the external domain, where a connection is found and established to the recipient's domain (*UserDomain*).

A non-adjacent domain document specifies that any message addressed to a particular domain must first pass through another domain (for example, to route to *UserDomain*, first route through *ExternalDomain*).

You can use other fields on a non-adjacent Domain document to secure the use of this feature. You may not want users from other domains to be able to take advantage of this route simplification, so you can specify who should or should not be allowed to route mail to this domain using the fields Allow mail only from domains or Deny mail from domains.

Adjacent Domains

Connection documents are the link between adjacent domains. R4 introduces a new Public Address Book document, the Adjacent Domain. This document is a security measure that enables you to close down mail routing holes that may exist due to explicit routing. If a user relies on a non-adjacent Domain document to route a message, the Allow and Deny fields you've set up there will allow or prevent the message from routing.

However, if a user explicitly routes a message (for example, `Tom White @ Domain A @ Domain B`), no non-adjacent Domain documents are consulted by the router. If you wish to prevent routing to `Domain A` from `Domain B`, you can create an Adjacent Domain document that prevents using `Domain B` to route to `Domain A`.

One reason for wanting this security would be to prevent users from other companies from using your mail infrastructure to route mail to other domains that are also connected to your domain. That is, the messages are not destined for users in your domain, but for users in another of your adjacent domains. By allowing for such activity, you may bear the communication costs for routing those messages.

Replication Topology

Your replication topology depends on many factors. Consider the number of databases that need to replicate, how much information each contains, what type of information is being replicated (documents containing large objects or documents containing only text fields), how often the databases need to replicate, and where they need to replicate.

Databases

Initially, users should be allowed to create databases freely. The reason is to get people interested in Lotus Notes and adjusted to using the product. Once the enterprise grows, however, data flow becomes more important. In a large enterprise, databases are not just placed on a server and accessed by users. You should consider the following:

- Who should access the database? Is it on the servers they need to access? Because replication is the means to distribute databases, allowing a database for users sometimes requires that the replica copies of the databases be located on several servers. If this is the case, ensure that all servers used to distribute the information also have the database. For example, in a hub and spoke situation, if the database is to be located on multiple spokes, it also needs to be located on the hub for distribution.

- Who needs to update the design? How will the design be implemented? Typically, changes to a design of a database are located in a database template, and the template is then used to propagate design changes. The person updating the design needs to have at least designer access to the database. The servers propagating the design changes need to also have designer access to the database.

- Who will be responsible for data distribution? This issue comes into play when a database is used as a reference, a company phone book for example. The user responsible for adding data to the database needs to have access to do so. Any server distributing data needs to have access as well.

- What other databases are required by the database? Notes enables you to look up data in other databases to provide information for the current database. Wherever the database is being used, the lookup database must also be available.

- What company standards for databases will be implemented? The person who creates a database needs to create it in such a way that the design can be modified easily by another designer. Standards for databases are difficult to have in place, because the perception is that they are restrictive. In the long run, however, the cost of maintaining the database will go down considerably if standards are followed. Standards have to be flexible and documented in order to get buy-in from the database developers in your company. A suggestion is to standardize basic elements, such as ACL standards, keyword listing standards, form names, and database names. As the first databases get implemented, document the design. Use the design documentation as a basis to develop new standards.

Implementing Databases

In a large enterprise, it is the administrator who places the database on a public server (hub) and who can be the gatekeeper for database design adherence. The job of the administrator primarily is to ensure that the database gets replicated throughout the environment correctly. Secondly, because the database is being checked anyway, the administrator can also ensure that the database adheres to company standards. You explore these roles later in the section. First, let's look at how a database gets posted on a server. The process in a large network should be as follows:

- The database is designed by the designer to meet users' needs.

- The database is staged on a server that few people can access for testing. Consider this your pilot of the database.

- The database is modified and versioned; then a template is drawn for future revisions. Versioning a database in an enterprise is important. Notes Database can be quite nebulous from a design perspective. It is very easy to "fix" something and end up ruining something else. When a change is made to a database, it should be documented and reported to the users. The scope of the change should also be considered.

- The database is implemented, which means that the database is placed in the environment in such a way that the data can be distributed to the users. In a hub spoke situation, the database is placed on the hub and replicas made on the spoke. It is at this point that the administrator checks the database for standards.

■ The database is published in a library for logical access. A Catalog is generated by the server and tracks all databases in a domain. A Library is a grouping of documents pointing to databases on the server. The group is decided arbitrarily.

Ensuring Data Flow

The ACL of any database needs to be standardized so that servers can replicate data appropriately. The rules are generally the following:

■ All servers changing ACLs need to have Manager access—this means servers where design changes originate.

■ All servers changing other design elements need to have Design Access. Servers where design changes originate need to have design access to the database.

■ All servers propagating documents should have editor access to the ACL.

■ All servers receiving data only should have reader access to the ACL.

■ A back door should be put in place to enable the administrator to change the ACL on the server. This back door is a group in the ACL that has manager access. The administrator need only add his name to the group in the Public Address Book to gain access to the database.

■ All ACLs for a database should be the same.

Using these rules, let's examine a possible scenario—a database used as a reference. The database is implemented in a hub and spoke topology on all spokes. A recommended ACL should have the hub as Manager, the spokes as Reader, default as Reader, the group of people updating as Author, and the back door group as Manager.

To make the job of the administrator easier, the ACL standard should be published so that the databases come with the ACLs set properly. The administrator needs only to check the access.

Not all databases need to go through this test in a distributed environment. If the database is located on only one server in the domain, it is unnecessary to check the ACL because data propagation is not an issue. In fact, if you have implemented a plan where administrators in regions are responsible for their own database replication on servers in their regions, they are responsible for the ACLs in their regions. It is only databases that go public that need to adhere to the ACL standards.

The standards should be published in a database available to all database developers. To aid in buy-in, the developers should be allowed to comment and change standards. The reason for publishing standards is to speed up implementation of databases. If a database is held at the checking phase, interest in it will diminish.

Publishing the Databases

Once a database is available, users need to access it. This can be done by the user accessing the server and loading the database. This becomes problematic in organizations where users move around in job functions frequently. Knowing which databases to access is half the battle when training a user to do a job. This is where database libraries come into play. (See Figure 38.3.)

FIGURE 38.3.

The Phone Book database has been published to a database library.

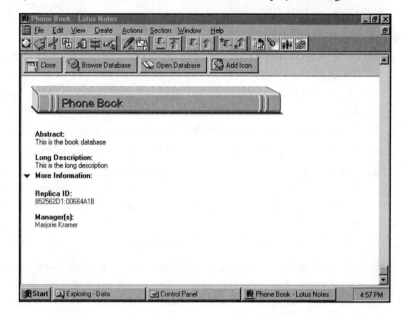

A database library is a collection of database links. You, the librarian, publish the database to a library. The users add the database library to their workspaces and use the links to load the icons to their workspace. (See Figures 38.4 and 38.5.)

FIGURE 38.4.

Publish the database in the library chosen from this list.

FIGURE **38.5.**

Inside the library, related databases are listed; they can be opened by using the Action bar.

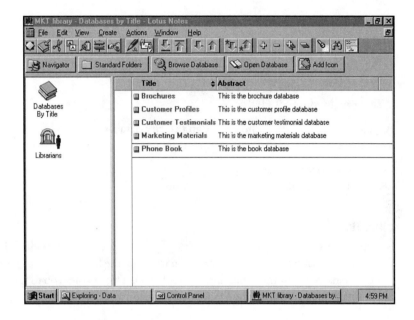

When new people start, they need only to add the database library icon to have access to the groups of databases in their locations.

Replication Controls

There are four replication controls that you can configure on a connection document to optimize and tune your replication topology: the overall schedule, the database priorities to replicate, specific filename(s), and a time limit on the call.

Scheduling

Determined through your connection documents, scheduling is an important facet of your replication topology. An overworked server often results from lack of schedule planning. Draw a timeline for each server depicting the calls for replication that it makes. Plot the starting times and durations of the various connections. Balance the calls against the busy times for that server. Use the Statistics Reporting database to determine the busy times using the Graph views.

Priority

A limited control is the database priority. Each database can be given a priority of High, Medium, or Low. Your connection documents can specify that only databases of certain priorities replicate. This setting applies to all the databases on the server. Managers can set the priority level. It is done by using the Properties dialog box of a database.

38

MANAGING A
LARGE NOTES
NETWORK

You might want to have one connection document for each priority level. Your choices for priority levels are:

- High
- Medium & High
- Low, Medium & High

As you can see from these choices, High priority databases will always be included, so you can use the first two choices to narrow down the number that replicate.

Database managers can set the priority of a database in the Replication Settings dialog box (File | Replication | Settings, in the Other section).

Specific Files

A better control, which is new in R4, is the field for specifying individual database filenames. One or more files can be listed, effectively narrowing the focus of the connection document to just the items in the list (no other files will replicate). This enables you to specify different schedules for each of your databases. Make sure you plot these on your timeline.

Time Limits

Given the varying nature of the data contained in Notes databases, another new feature in R4, time limits, gives you more control over your replication schedule planning. For each connection document you can specify a time limit in minutes. If this limit is reached during replication, the document in progress is finished and replication stops. Using this control, you can more closely plan and manage your replication timeline.

Replication of ACLs

It is important that you recognize and plan for replication of database Access Control Lists. The ACL behaves differently from normal documents in a database. The ACL is considered first in replication and is overwritten if a change is implemented. The initiating server's ACL is the one which is checked to see if there is a change.

The ACL is actually a "document" in the database, albeit not a data document that you can use in a view. During replication, the ACL replicates first in case any changes to the settings would prevent further replication. Through experimentation, it has been found that this operation behaves in a strange way. See the section "ACL Is a Push-Only Overwrite" for more details.

Central Management for Database ACLs

Plan to manage the ACL of every database. This doesn't mean that you need to manage each ACL yourself; it means that you should have a plan for each database agreed upon by your administrative team. Ideally, each database's ACL will be maintained on one server. If you plan to use the Administration Process, make use of the Administration Server setting on the ACL dialog box. This lets the Administration Process make changes to the ACL on the server specified in this field. Each replica of this database should have the same setting.

The Administration process consists of a server task (ADMIN.EXE) and a series of steps initiated in the Public Address Book by an administrator using the Actions menu. An administrator can initiate a change, such as renaming a user. That action writes a document into the Administration Requests database.

The Administration process server task sees that request, and it takes action on the Public Address Book. In the case of renaming a user, it puts the pending request into the user's Person document.

When that user next accesses the server, Notes alerts them to the pending request and asks them to accept the change. Upon accepting the change, another request is generated in the Administration Requests database and the Administration process server tasks takes action again, this time by propagating the new name throughout other documents in the Public Address Book.

Enforce a consistent Access Control List across all replicas of this database, under the Advanced section of the ACL dialog box. This does what it says: one replica copy is listed as Manager in all other replicas; on this copy only, enable this setting. The managing replica will force its ACL into every other replica, including those that reside on workstations or laptops.

This process should not be used on separate replica copies of the Public Address Book, but should be used on only one replica, that which is specified in the Administration Server field on the Replication Settings dialog box in the Advanced section. If this procedure is not followed, either the Administration process on the other servers will ignore the requests, or replication conflicts will result.

ACL Is a Push-Only Overwrite

The ACL is a special document that never suffers a replication conflict. If updated, it is completely overwritten; the entries from the winning ACL replace all entries in the "losing" ACL.

The interesting point to know about the flow of ACL changes is this: an ACL note is overwritten only by the initiator of the call for replication. In other words, if Server 2 calls Server 1, and the ACL in the Public Address Book on Server 1 has been changed, Server 2's ACL will not be overwritten, even though Server 2's ACL lists Server 1 as a Manager.

This fact is important, because if you are using a hub and spoke replication topology where your spoke servers call the hub, ACL changes made on the hub will not flow down to the subordinate servers unless the hub initiates the call. By having your hub servers call your spokes, you won't experience this problem.

Passthru Topology

Under R3, a Notes server was always an endpoint on a network; it performed no routing of protocols. Notes R4 introduces the concept of Passthru, which is essentially just that: protocol routing. By accessing a known, reachable Notes server, a Notes server or client can route through that server to reach another. This feature is fully configurable, including the capability of disabling it.

Dedicated Servers

Passthru allows for the first time for servers to be truly dedicated in their tasks. Under R3, for instance, although it is possible to establish mail-only servers and application servers, a difficulty always arises for remote users. With one phone call, the user can reach one server; if a database resides on a different server, it either must be replicated to the dial-in server or the user must hang up and redial that other server.

Task-Specific

With Passthru, however, by making only one phone call, the Notes server can route the caller to other Notes servers on the network. This enables you to segment your server types without wasting precious drive space for replica copies. A database can live on one server and be accessed easily by both network and remote clients.

Protocol-Specific

Another benefit of using Passthru is the capability of streamlining your protocols. Suppose that you have many users working under SPX, but a server in another area is using NetBIOS. Rather than enabling NetBIOS on the SPX users' machines, you can enable this protocol on a server running SPX. Via Passthru, the SPX clients can reach the NetBIOS server by routing through their normal SPX servers.

Let's take another powerful example. With R4 comes a server task called the Web Retriever, or WEB. This task reaches out to the World Wide Web and retrieves HTML pages, putting them into a Notes database called the Web Navigator. Access to the Web normally requires TCP/IP at the desktop; but by using Passthru in conjunction with this server task, your clients do not need TCP/IP. They can communicate with the Notes server over SPX while the server itself communicates with the Web via TCP/IP.

Segmenting your protocols can greatly reduce the expense of adding protocols to single-protocol desktops.

Mapping Your Passthru Topology

Draw a chart showing all your servers, their connections, and protocols. Determine which servers should allow Passthru. You can control Passthru with four fields on each Server Document: Access server, Route through, Cause calling, and Destinations allowed. As with other fields on a Server Document, use groups or wildcards rather than individual user or server names so that minimal changes will be required.

Wildcards are allowed. To allow all users, regardless of whether they have a Person Document in this Public Address Book, enter an asterisk (*); to allow all users under a particular organization or organizational unit, enter an asterisk followed by the proper hierarchical fragment (*/Sales/Worldwide Products).

Access Server

The Access server list defines the people, servers, or groups of users and/or servers that are allowed to access this server via Passthru; an empty list allows no one. Those items that are listed will be allowed to route mail and replicate databases using Passthru. This list does not affect the use of passthru from this server out to others.

Route Through

The Route through field defines whether this server is a Passthru server. If the list is empty, the server cannot be used for routing. The users, servers, or groups entered here are those that are allowed to use the Passthru feature.

Cause Calling

The Cause calling list specifies the users or servers that are allowed to use Passthru even if the routing requires that a phone call be made, because this usually causes an expense to be incurred at the server. This field gives you control over these expenses.

Destinations Allowed

At the Destinations allowed field you can specify the exact servers to which the listed entities will be allowed to route. If the list is empty, routing is allowed to any server to which this server can connect. If a call must be made, the Cause calling field precedes this list.

NotesNIC: A Global Opportunity

If you plan to extend your network and connect to Notes servers at other organizations, the typical method is to cross certify with that organization, then establish scheduled connections with them. This process must be repeated for any organization with which you want to communicate.

Another opportunity has arrived that greatly simplifies this process. The NotesNIC network is an Internet-based Notes network to which you can connect and achieve replication or mail-based communications with other companies.

To learn more, visit the web site www.notes.net or follow the NOTESNIC jump from the www.lotus.com page.

If you are connected to the Internet, you can actually connect to the Home/Notes/Net server by adding the address for Home.Notes.Net to your HOSTS file or Domain Name Server (DNS). To get the IP address, ping Home.Notes.Net. After you add this name, try to ping Home.Notes.Net; if this works, you can reach the server from your Notes client.

Once Home.Notes.Net is reachable, from Notes select File | Database | Open and enter the server name Home; alternatively, select File | Database | Open Special and choose the Home server from this list. You will have anonymous access to the server and will be able to open and browse the databases there. You can even sign up to NotesNIC through this Home server.

What is the real benefit? Once you sign up, your Internet domain (IBM.COM, for example) will be used to generate a new server ID whose common name is your domain name (IBM/NET). Using the /NET ID, you will create a server that is on your Internet segment. This server can communicate with any of the other servers in the /NET organization (one per company).

This server ID can be used to cross certify with any other users or servers internally. Thus, the /NET server acts as a Notes firewall server and enables communications (mail and replication) with any other similarly connected Notes server in the world.

In the end, you have a world-wide high-speed connection to other Notes servers on the Internet. Users from your organization can use passthru on your /NET server to reach information on your internal Notes network (but no one else can). These users need only a local Internet provider to reach their mail and replicate databases. Suddenly, the high-quality Notes security architecture can be put to world-wide use.

Incorporating Mail Gateways

 Lotus Notes R4 is prepared for, although it does not come with, three Mail Transfer Agents: X.400, SMTP, and cc:Mail. As of this writing, an R3 server is necessary to host a mail gateway.

The Lotus Mail Exchange Facility (LMEF) is a free piece of software that runs on a Notes R3 server for OS/2. The SMTP Gateway must be purchased separately; it also runs on the OS/2 server platform.

Until the new Mail Transfer Agents arrive on the scene, this implies that you still need an R3 server to host the gateway.

Monitoring Your Notes Servers

Be default, your servers will log messages and activities to the Notes Log file (LOG.NSF). Each server has its own log. You will quickly find that, although the log is extremely useful, you cannot get detailed performance information or notification of the events that occur. Using the log for troubleshooting requires that you peruse the documents (which are kept for the last seven days only) to find the messages that occurred at a given time.

To get assistance with monitoring the behavior of your servers in one place, turn to the Statistics and Events processes or even consider purchasing NotesView (an HP OpenView-based mapping and alerting tool).

Statistics and Events Server Tasks

Beyond the Notes Log file, Notes provides you with a way to collect statistics and trap events that occur on your servers. You can have this collection feedback to one central database from all your servers.

Statistics collection enables you to observe the behavior of a server over time, monitoring usage, disk space, memory, and tasks at specified intervals. Special graphing views in the Statistics Reporting database (STATREP.NSF) give you a visual representation of some of these statistics.

Simply collecting statistics will not provide you with alerts of trouble conditions. By creating Statistic Monitor or Event documents in the Statistics & Events database (EVENTS4.NSF), you can actually receive notification of thresholds that have been exceeded or of events as they occur.

NotesView

Although NotesView is an add-on product that carries additional cost, it is an excellent tool for monitoring the conditions across all your servers. The most useful feature of NotesView is its capability of monitoring server status and alerting you when a server goes down or fails to perform a task, such as mail routing.

Summary

As with any network, a Notes network has the potential to grow very large and to become unmanageable. By carefully planning the management of the system before you implement, you can ease the cost of ownership and provide truly useful groupware services for your company:

- Through teamwork, use Notes to assist your administrative group as you maintain and expand your environment.
- Create a good infrastructure. Your servers will behave better if you provide adequate hardware.
- Plan your topologies carefully, drawing topology maps for your team. It will help you make sense of the contents of your domain's Public Address Book.
- Plan to monitor your system so that you can detect conditions that might lead to serious problems.

Through careful planning and implementation, your groupware deployment can be a resounding success.

Migrating from Notes R3 to R4.x

by Marjorie Kramer

IN THIS CHAPTER

CHAPTER 39

You've purchased R4.x and are anticipating taking advantage of the new features in it. Perhaps you've even experimented with the new features and want to implement them. Nonetheless, in order to take full advantage of R4.x of Notes, you need to upgrade your environment to it.

The differences between the versions of Notes 4.x (4.0, 4.1, 4.11, and 4.5) are smaller than the differences between R3 and R4. Therefore, this chapter primarily covers the differences between R3 and R4.x. Depending on how entrenched R3 is in your environment, you have a large project or a medium-sized project ahead of you.

The number one question of migrators is coexistence. When I migrate a server to R4.x, what will be able to access it? When I migrate a database to R4.x, who will be able to use the new features? Fortunately, Notes R4 is quite flexible with regard to access. Generally speaking, servers in R4 are accessible to all Notes users. Users using R4 can access all types of servers. Usually, servers are upgraded first, then workstations accessing servers. This chapter reviews a methodology to migration. Table 39.1 summarizes what will coexist.

Table 39.1. Migration coexistance.

Workstation	Server	Database	Coexist?
R3	R3	R3	Yes
R4	R3	R3	Yes
R4	R4	R3	Yes
R4	R4	R4	Yes
R3	R4	R3	Yes
R3	R3	R4	No
R3	R4	R4	Yes/will get errors on unsupported features in database.

Components of a Migration

Migration is a multitiered process. In order to contain your project, consider what will be the "end" of your project. Is it over when all servers and workstations are using R4? Is it over when mail is converted to SCOS mail? Is it over when all database applications are using the features of R4?

In order to migrate a workstation or server, the software is installed, then the databases used to maintain a Notes Domain are converted to R4 (Names.nsf, log.nsf, mail.box). After this you have an operating R4 environment.

Once you are rolling in R4, you probably want to take advantage of the new features. Primarily, Single Copy Object Store, Admin process, and new design features. Implementing these features should be done one at a time, checking to see that your environment is stable.

We will discuss the following migration path considerations, followed by steps to migration.

Software Installation Options

Whether you are upgrading a server or a workstation, you should choose to overwrite files and upgrade CONFIG.SYS file during the installation process. This converts the current release of Notes to the new release of Notes completely.

For servers, there is only one way to access the new software—on a network drive or off the Notes 4 CD-ROM. The install program is run from the operating system prompt at the server.

For workstations, you have two choices, one being to install from CD or network as in server installation. The other option is to select upgrade by mail. (See Figure 39.1.) This is initiated by the administrator from a Release 4.x Public Address Book.

Figure 39.1.

Upgrading by mail.

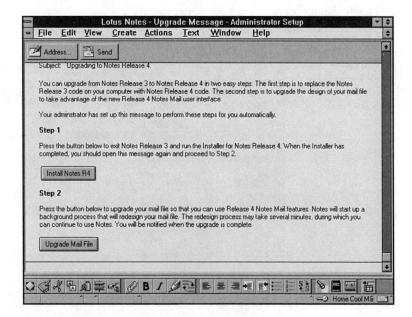

The upgrade by mail feature is initiated by the Administrator. Once the server is converted to Notes 4, the administrator selects Upgrade user from the Mail users view in the Public Address Book. The Admin specifies for each operating system the path to the NotesKit (install files for Notes) directory.

The R3 user receives a mail message pointing to the directory where the new release of Notes is located. The user merely clicks on the action button and starts the upgrade process. Once the software is installed, the mail message directs the user to upgrade his/her mail by clicking on a new button.

Since this process is initiated by a Notes form, it can be modified to match your system requirements.

Important Files

Once the software is on the machine, you are not done. Notes needs to use the "important" files in the R4 context. For servers, these files are Public Address Book, Log file, Catalog file, Statistics databases, and Events databases. For workstations, these files are Personal Address Book, desktop.dsk, and mail files.

Each of the important files should exist in the new design and the new file format. In order to convert a file, the first step is to use the new design. Select Yes to the question, "Do you want to upgrade..." when you first start the workstation. This will take the design of the current database and apply the new design to it. Otherwise, you can manually choose File | Database | Replace Design and select the appropriate database template. (See Figure 39.2.)

FIGURE 39.2.

Redesign of the Public Address Book using menu commands.

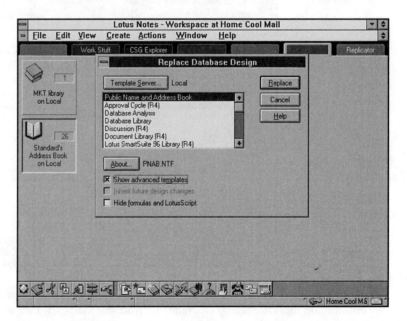

This process takes only the design elements—Views, Folders, Forms, and so forth—and converts them to the new R4 version. If you want the final stamp—the new icons—you must manually copy the icon to the database.

Update the design on only one replica. This will prevent multiple copies of the forms and views being transmitted.

In order for the database to be fully R4-compatible, the file format must be converted as well. This is generally done by creating a new copy of the database under R4, then recreating the indices. Because databases are typically replicated around the environment, it is best to use the compact method over copying the database to a new file using Notes. (See Figure 39.3.) This way the Replica ID is maintained.

FIGURE 39.3.

Properties of the Public Address Book, pointing to the new template.

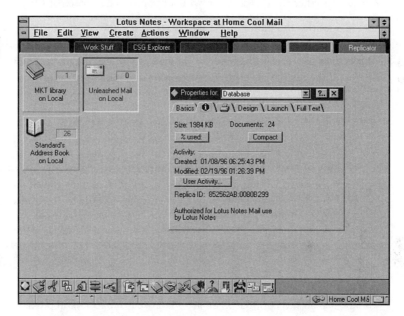

Although replication will update the design and documents of all occurences of the Public Address Book, the database is not an R4 version until compact is run on all versions of the Public Address Book.

The final step is done automatically. The process UPDALL is run automatically on the server. This will convert the indices of the database to R4 indices.

The Convert utility is used to change the settings on mail databases in batch mode. Convert will point the mail file to a new database template and change the file to use folders where categories are available. The syntax of Convert is the following:

```
load convert [-f] [-l] [-r] [-i] [-d] [-n] [drive:\directory]filename [oldtemplate
➡newtemplate]
```

-f uses database names listed in a text file and updates only those databases listed in the text file.

-l creates a text file listing all databases to be converted. Specify the destination file in the filename.

-r Searches the specified directory and all of its subdirectories.

The maximum folder conversion limit is 200. -i ignores this limit.

-d stops the folder creation.

-n lists the databases to be converted. Use this for testing.

drive specifies the drive letter on which the Notes databases or the text files exist.

directory specifies the directory on which the Notes databases or the text files exist.

filename specifies the name of the databases to convert. You can use wildcard characters to specify several databases. If you use the -f argument, *filename* specifies the name of the text file that contains a list of databases to convert. If you use the -l argument, *filename* specifies the name of the text file to create to store a list of database names.

oldtemplate specifies the old template name to convert—for example, STDNOTESMAIL. If you are using the -l argument, you cannot specify *oldtemplate*.

newtemplate specifies the filename for the template you want the databases to use.

The preceding code will take the filenames indicated and change the occurrence of the old mail template to the new mail template. Wildcards can be used here as well. For example, Mail can be referred to in the filenames option. Convert takes a while to run and should be done when the server is free.

> **NOTE**
>
> File conversions should be done on one server only. Otherwise, multiple copies of the new design elements will appear when the database is replicated. In practice, you convert one location of the database and allow replication to change the rest of the databases.

Where to Start

Now that the general steps are known, where do you start when migrating? You start by planning first for the migration. Because you generally don't upset users and change everything on a regular basis, migration is a good opportunity not only to migrate but also to reevaluate your Notes install base and methodologies. Notes R4 has many new features to take advantage of that should be considered before migration. Typically, the time line is to first stabilize your system software. If you are upgrading your operating system or network, now is the time to do this. While this is going on, plan for the upgrade. Then upgrade servers, then workstations.

Evaluate Replication

The first place to start is to evaluate the replication topology of your network. Is it running efficiently? Converting to R4 means that more replication options are available. The obvious option is multiple replication threads. If your server can handle it, you can provide the capability of spawning a new replicator thread when a request for replication is made. This requires 2MB of memory on your server. It is a more advanced feature that will be understood better when you are in R4. The number of replicators is defined in the NOTES.INI file, `Replicators=` parameters.

> **NOTE**
>
> If you specify more replicators than your system will support, only one replicator thread will be available.

Another, less obvious, option is to use Pull-Push replication. With Pull-Push replication, only one replicator is busy during the replication process: the calling server. If you are communicating in a hub spoke topology, this enables only the spokes' replicators to be busy during replication, freeing the hub's replicator for other purposes.

Finally, Notes R4 gives you the capability of scheduling replication for specific databases. Before migrating, evaluate the replication schedule of your domain to determine whether you should take advantage of the new features, then implement the schedule.

Evaluate Mail Topology

Although you probably won't be converting your mail files to SCOS mail during migration, you should consider and prepare for doing this in the future. SCOS mail is most efficient in environments where users have mail on one server, and it is not distributed on many servers. You should consider where the mail files are and where they should go before converting users.

Since SCOS mail is new to R4, there are not many statistics for how much space will be saved.

Connectivity for Users

Notes 4 provides the capability of using one server as the ambassador for all others using Passthru. A common complaint in R3 was that if the mail file and database files were located on different servers, two phone calls had to be made in order to get all the information necessary. Now, one server can take care of connectivity so that only one phone call needs to be made. Before converting to R4, you should consider which servers will act as a Passthru to other servers in the Notes network and set it up to do this.

Evaluate Standardizing User Access

Users now depend on location documents in their Personal Address Book. These location documents define how they will connect to servers. (See Figures 39.4 and 39.5.)

The source of location documents and setup is from the Public Address Book, profile documents.

FIGURE 39.4.

A location document for the user.

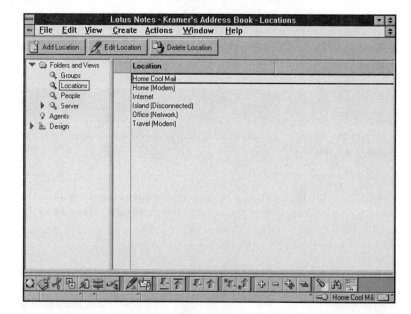

FIGURE 39.5.

Switching locations.

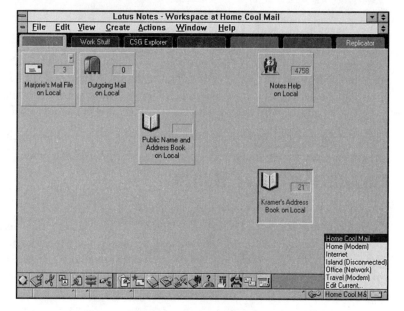

If it is standard operating procedure to access one Passthru server, create profile documents which indicate the Passthru document.

Hierarchical Naming

The Administrative Process automates conversion to hierarchical names. Like mail placement, you probably won't do a conversion to hierarchical names when creating your R4 environment. However, it is important to consider the names of things now while you are looking at your Notes environment from a global perspective.

The Next Steps

Now that you have evaluated your R3 environment and considered converting some of the current topologies to something that will take advantage of R4 enhancements, your next step is to survey the R3 environment.

Check Templates

Look for databases that will be directly affected by changing the design template of that database. Notes R4 has changed many templates you were probably using in your environment. You first want to evaluate closely what changes were made and whether the new versions will help you. There is no easy way of doing this. Templates which have changed are:

- The discussion template
- The mail template

Public Address Book

The second thing you want to do is evaluate your Public Address Book. Notes 4 has made many changes to the Public Address Book template that may affect what you have in your Public Address Book. In particular, you should investigate any changes made by other software packages. For example, the SkyTel Pager Gateway adds fields to the person document in the Public Address Book in order to make it operational. As well, views are used by other products to access information.

The other reason to investigate your Public Address Book is to evaluate who the administrators are and what access they have. In R3, many shops enabled their administrators by giving them at least editor access to the Public Address Book. In R4, this is no longer necessary. A series of roles are available for you to apply to the new Public Address Book. These roles enable the user who is author to create documents in the Public Address Book. (See Figure 39.6.)

FIGURE 39.6.

Roles in the ACL of the
Public Address Book.

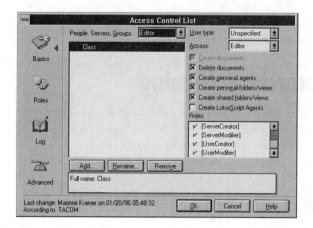

The roles refer to people who can create or modify groups, create or modify server documents, and create or modify group, user, and server documents. You want to look at people assigned to these tasks now and perhaps group them in the current R3 Public Address Book.

Finally, evaluate groups in the Public Address Book. Notes 4 enables you to organize the groups into three categories: Multi-purpose, Access Control List only (ACL), Mail only, and Deny List only. (See Figure 39.7.)

FIGURE 39.7.

Group document
in R4.

The reason for this categorization is to make the Public Address Book smaller. Only the ACL groups are considered when an ACL is evaluated. Groups by default are defined to be Multi-purpose. You may want to define your groups to fit into one of the categories R4 provides for you.

Migration Steps

Now that you know what to consider in migration, and some of the processes, here are the steps to migration:

1. Review templates and important databases.
2. Isolate the first server to migrate.
3. Install R4 on the first server.
4. Copy the Public Address Book template to another workstation for evaluation.
5. Compare the Public Address Book and the old Public Address Book.
6. Make changes to the Public Address Book template and implement on the server.
7. Start the workstation on the server.
8. Reconfigure the Public Address Book.
9. Compact the Public Address Book.
10. Change the Public Address Book location documents.
11. Migrate other servers.
12. Migrate workstations.
13. Change mail files.

Review Templates and Important Databases

Most companies change the templates to accommodate their environments. Notes R4 has completely rewritten the templates. Before upgrading, evaluate the effect of the change in the current templates to the old templates.

Isolate First Server to Migrate

Ideally, you can initiate the migration from a new server that is not being used currently. This is the server where you install the software and from which you convert the Public Address Book. If you can't use a separate machine, it is best to use a server that is not replicating regularly with the rest of your environment. To prevent replication, take the server out of the replication schedule by modifying the connection documents.

Change the ACL in the Public Address Book to prevent other servers from accessing the database. Deny access to the server in the Server Access List to all other servers.

Install R4 on First Server

Because the Public Address Book template is only available on an installed server, you must run the install program to get it. Run the install procedure on the server that is isolated. Do not run the workstation software until the Public Address Book template is evaluated and modified, if necessary. Running the workstation software changes the Public Address Book.

Copy Public Address Book Template to Another Workstation for Evaluation

The file PUBNAMES.NTF should be one of the templates installed on the server machine. Copy this file using the operating system and place it on a working workstation. Use the current Public Address Book template in your domain to create a new Public Address Book template for use in Notes R4. Copy the new Public Address Book template to the first server and use it.

Compare Public Address Book and Old Public Address Book

Use the current Public Address Book template in your domain to create a new Public Address Book template for use in Notes R4.

Make Changes to Public Address Book Template and Implement on Server

Copy the new Public Address Book template to the first server and use it.

Start Workstation on Server

A setup will follow. Redesign the Public Address Book when prompted.

Compact Public Address Book

Run a compact on the Public Address Book. (See Figure 39.8.) Update all the indices by loading UPDALL at the server console.

Figure 39.8.
Compacting a database.

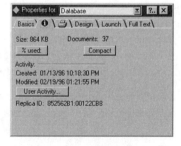

Add Public Address Book Location Documents

As per your planning steps, add location documents to the Public Address Book to help users set themselves up.

Migrate Other Servers

Once the first server is migrated, you will gradually add the additional servers to the environment. This is done first by installing the software. Then, set up the server. Replicate the new Public Address Book from the first server. Finally, change the template reference and compact the database.

Migrate Workstations

Use Upgrade by mail or point the users to the location of the new Release 4.x software. Have the users run INSTALL. The users should upgrade their Public Address Book.

Change Mail Files

Use the convert utility to migrate mail to the mail templates.

Database Migration

Once the workstations are migrated, you want to evaluate which databases to migrate over to release 4.x. Answer the following when considering your criteria for moving a database:

■ Will the database be used by R3 users? If so, keep it in R3 format. Remember migrating users may take longer than you think.

■ Will the new features of Notes R4 enhance the current application? R4 offers many new development features. In some current R3 applications, a simple compact on the database will be fine. In others, a complete rewrite of the database is required. A simple migration, followed by a complete rewrite, is a good idea.

■ Is the database a live database? Migration is a good time to get all the databases that are not being used by users and archive them. Use the database catalog usage view to evaluate this.

Database Migration Tactics

It is very difficult to get a handle on what to do to a database. It is simple to migrate a database—compact it. The first thing you should do is make your views efficient. On-the-fly column sorting will help to do this.

Typically, there are views that look the same except that they are ordered differently. (See Figure 39.9.)

39

MIGRATING
FROM NOTES
R3 TO R4.X

FIGURE 39.9.

Similar views sorted differently.

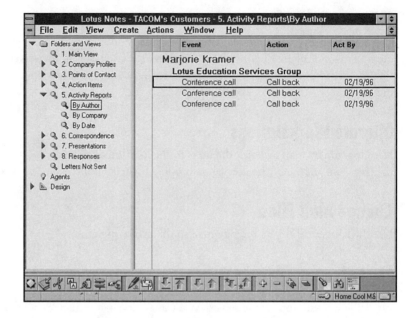

In Notes R4, you can use one view and on-the-fly sort to represent many views. (See Figure 39.10.)

FIGURE 39.10.

One view using sort on the fly.

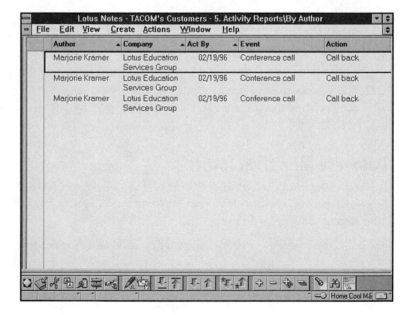

Keyword fields are automatically converted to show the indicator. (See Figure 39.11.) If you have used other hints, you may want to remove them, or you will have two indicators, the "hint" from R3 and the indicator from R4.

FIGURE 39.11.

Form with two indicators.

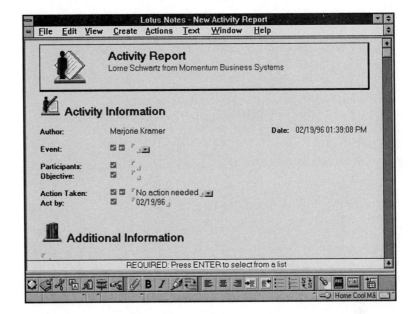

Notes will convert some @functions to be compatible with release functionality. For example, it will convert @command to @postedcommand. This is done during the compacting phase. @Postedcommand behaves as the @Command did in R3. They run after the rest of the formula runs. @command in R4 runs when it is hit in the formula.

Summary

With careful planning, a release 3.x to R4 migration should not impact your environment. My recommendation is to contain your goals—for example, make your goal to migrate all users and servers to R4, not to change all databases and upgrade to hierarchical at the same time. If you are currently assessing changing your operating system, do that now before upgrading to R4. Finally, let the migration be driven by your plan, not by the "immediate" needs of the users to have R4 right away.

Using Notes Between Different Companies

by Marjorie Kramer

CHAPTER 40

Lotus Notes provides easy communication in your company and outside your company. So far, this book has discussed how to enable Lotus Notes within your company. This chapter explores an in-depth outline of what it takes to enable Lotus Notes to communicate outside your company. It is important to remember that the intent of establishing outside communication is to create replica copies of databases in your company's domain and/or to establish mail routing between your company and another company.

Basically, you have to consider two things when communicating with outside companies:

- **Securing access.** Giving access to company information can be perceived to be risky; however, Lotus Notes enables and ensures access to information in a method defined by the administrator.

- **Establishing communication.** Enabling the appropriate schedule for phone calls can be difficult for a number of reasons.

Securing Access

Securing the communication really looks at two levels of security in Lotus Notes: access to the server and access to databases. In a perfect world, all companies would be able to isolate servers that communicate with the "outside world." Realistically, however, this is not the case. Due to the scalability of servers in Lotus Notes, it sometimes isn't cost-effective to use a completely different server to communicate. This chapter outlines the security issues involved with accessing the server and indicates switches you can place at each issue point. Table 40.1 indicates the security issue and security switch you can manage.

Table 40.1. Server security points.

Entry Point	*Security Switch*
Access to server	Server Access Lists
	Cross Certificates
	Trust & Flat Certificates
	Anonymous Access
Using Server to Pass Mail to Other Domains	Domain Documents
Access to the Public Address Book	Use Public Address Book Subset
	ACL in Public Address Book
Access to Databases	Database Settings
	ACL Settings
	Anonymous Access

Access to Server

As discussed in Chapter 34, "Security Overview," the first thing that a server does is consult with its approved access list by name (name check). The server then asks the requesting party to "prove" that they say who they are based on a common shared entity (authentication). Server Access Lists protect the server during the Name Check process; Certification Strategy protects the server during authentication.

> **NOTE**
>
> Server access is the foundation to secure the environment as it shuts out renegade users before they can gain access to databases.

Server Access Lists

Server Access Lists come in two formats, Allow and Deny Access. Allow Access enables you to define a known list of "accessors" who are allowed into the server during name check. The default is for all users to gain access. Deny Access enables you to define a known list of "denied accessors" who shouldn't be allowed into the server during name check. The default is for no users to be denied access. When each server is created, access from foreign sources should be considered when establishing denied and allowed access lists.

Access lists are defined in the Server Document and in the Notes INI fields. The fields Allow Users Note Listing in the Public Address Book, Allow Access, and Deny Access define who can be allowed access and who are denied access, respectively. The parameters ALLOW_ACCESS and DENY_ACCESS are the Notes.ini equivalents to the server document settings. If the information is in the server document and the NOTES.INI file, the server document settings "wins." You can also define more specifically who can be allowed into ports on your computer. ALLOW_ACCESS_LAN0 defines who can use port LAN0. These parameters are only available in the NOTES.INI file.

> **NOTE**
>
> If the entity is in both allow and deny access, the entity is denied access to the server.

The Allow and Deny Access references should be references to groups for managability. Because a changed entry in these fields does not take effect until the server is downed and reloaded, it is difficult to ensure that geographically dispersed servers are using the most up-to-date Allow and Deny Access entries. When you want to include a new entity in an Allow or Deny Access entry, update the group referred to in the entry. This will not affect what is in the field, just what is referenced.

The people/servers in the deny list should be those individuals who are known to you as being foreign. For example, if you once had communication with ServerA/DomainA, and now no longer need to communicate with this server, include the server in a group in the deny access list. The people/servers in the allow list should all be people in your domain, all servers in your domain (LocalDomainServers), and all people/servers not in your domain. Use a separate group to identify the individuals and servers not in your domain allowed to communicate with you. A default group, OtherDomainServers, is created automatically in each domain for your convenience.

Allow or Deny Access groups are identified in the NOTES.INI file (ALLOW_ACCESS= allow, and DENY_ACCESS= deny), or the Server/Server document in the Public Address Book. The entry in the Public Address Book takes precedence over the entry in the NOTES.INI file on the server. (See Figure 40.1.)

FIGURE 40.1.

Server document indicating restrictions.

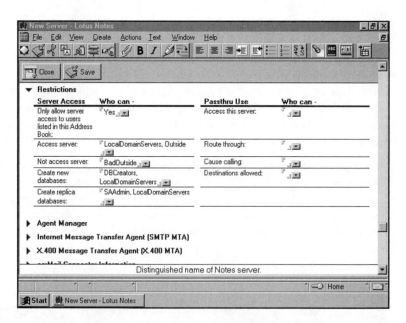

Once an allow/deny strategy is in place, every server connecting to your domain should be placed in the appropriate group. Notes will use Replication to distribute the change, thus securing your environment.

NOTE

Any server/workstation not allowed on another server will get the error message You are not Authorized to access this server.

Create Database and Create Replica Database access need not be considered in the context of communicating with other domains. These groups are used to define what people/servers can do in your domain. You will create the replica copies of the database, not the other domain.

Certification Strategy

Recall that deny/allow access protects the domain against known entities. That is, you know the name of the people/servers who are trying to get in, and you grant or deny them explicit access to your server. You don't always know the name of the person trying to get in or that the entity is trusted by the server in which it is trying to get access. For example, ServerA/DomainA is trying to access Server2/Domain2. A name check is done, and it passes. Server2/Domain2 does not know in fact that ServerA/DomainA is who it says it is. This is where authentication comes into play. In Chapter 34, authentication was described as a series of checks to verify that the two entities are who they say they are based on a trusted common factor, the certificate.

In order to establish communication between two domains, a certification strategy must be in place. If two hierarchically certified entities are authenticating, a cross certificate is necessary; otherwise, a common, trusted flat certificate is necessary.

Cross Certification Strategy

Cross certificates are generated in two directions. The first is what "they" will allow to authenticate with you. The second, where you will accept their request in your domain. When you receive a cross-certificate, you define where in your hierarchy you receive it—which servers can authenticate with the cross-certificate. When you send a cross-certificate, you define which servers from your domain will be able to authenticate with them. You have complete control over authenticating with other domains. For example, DomainA has the organization named AAA and the Organizational Unit named EXTSVR, where all servers are placed that are designated to communicate with outside domains. The server XX/EXTSVR/AAA is the server with the information for communication with DomainB. DomainB has the organization BBB and the organizational unit ESVR, where external servers are placed. The server 11/ESVR/BBB is designated to communicate with DomainA. The administrator from DomainB sends a cross certificate to DomainA. DomainA's administrator accepts this cross certificate and indicates it by using the Organizational Unit ID representing EXTSVR/AAA. DomainA's administrator sends a cross certificate back to DomainB's admin. DomainB's admin accepts this certificate using the Server ID 11/ESVR/BBB. In this exchange of cross certificates, DomainA allows the request from server 11/ESVR/BBB on all servers certified with EXTSVR/AAA. DomainB allows DomainA only on server 11/ESVR/BBB.

DomainA's admin knows that all servers in its OU, EXT/AAA, are secure; therefore, access is granted to all servers under the OU certifier. DomainB's administrator is not so sure and thus limits incoming and outgoing access to just the server 11/ESVR/BBB.

Your cross-certification strategy should be bidirectional. Consider which servers in your domain are secure. Are they under one OU or several? If you offer an OU Certifier Safe ID as a cross certificate, you have more flexibility in the future when moving databases. When receiving cross certificates, receive them under an OU certifier for flexibility. Notes R4, however, enables you to certify using a server/user ID to narrow down who can accept requests. (See Figure 40.2.)

FIGURE 40.2.

Cross certificate document of DomainA.

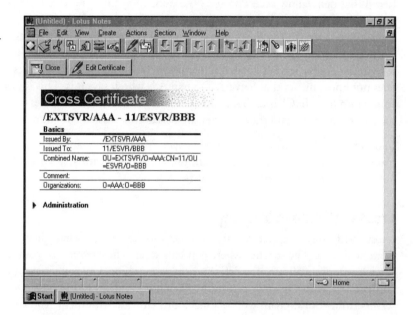

Flat Certificates

Flat certification exists in the Notes world. In order to authenticate with an ID that uses flat certificates only, the receiving server must have a flat certificate in common with it as well. An exchange of server safe IDs must take place with a stamping of the IDs to ensure there is a flat certificate in common because the certificate is in the ID, not the Public Address Book.

It gets tricky when you don't know where the certificate is. In this case, you should enable trust. The idea behind trust is that if you own the certifier ID, you know where it is going; therefore, you trust it. If you do not own the certifier ID, you don't trust it. Trust is a switch that can be turned on when accepting the ID, in the ID after it has been accepted, or when certifying an ID. (See Figure 40.3.)

Trust must exist in both directions, so, if it is used, both server IDs must be certified with the other domain's trusted certificate. When the server ID is merged, the other domain's certificate is not trusted (you don't own the certifier ID), but your domain's certificate is trusted (you own the certifier ID).

FIGURE 40.3.

Trust on an ID.

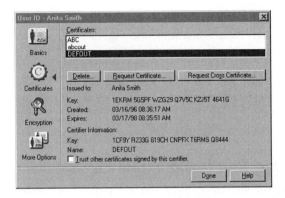

Using trust is a good idea only in situations where you are working with a competitor and are concerned about the security of the certifier ID it is using to stamp other server IDs. (If it stamps other server IDs with the same certificate, it has access to your domain.) Otherwise, use one flat certificate in common and rely on Name Check options when securing the server.

Anonymous Access

Sometimes it may be necessary to allow anyone (server/user) access to a server in your domain. This is done by enabling anonymous access on the server in question. (See Figure 40.4.)

FIGURE 40.4.

A server document with anonymous access enabled.

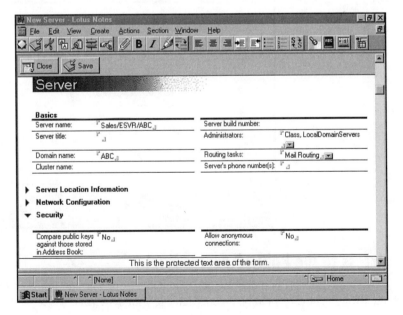

When a user/server attempts to access a server that allows anonymous access, it is tested by authentication. Then, when authentication fails, the user/server is allowed on the server. The name of the user/server is anonymous, which can be used to protect your databases. Use the name "anonymous" in your ACLs to reference users/servers using anonymous access on the server.

Anonymous access is the method used by public networks where it would be difficult to enable a name check and certification strategy.

Protecting Your Domain from Passing Mail

Once a connection is established (discussed later), your domain can act as a mail router to other domains to which it is adjacent. For example, my domain is connected to WorldCom, your domain is not. I establish a connection from my domain to your domain. Now you can explicitly pass mail from your domain to WorldCom via my domain. To prevent this, I would use a domain document in my domain for WorldCom, disabling your domain to route mail to WorldCom. (See Figure 40.5.)

FIGURE 40.5.

Domain document preventing routing of mail from your domain.

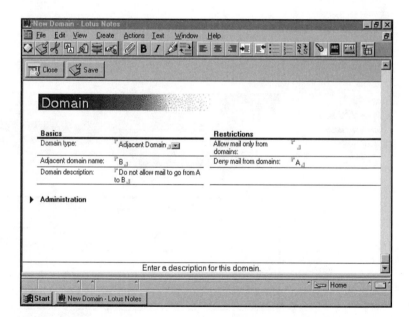

Access to the Public Address Book

The Public Address Book defines your domain. It has enough information that if it fell into the wrong hands, it could be used to damage your system.

Access to the Public Address Book Documents

The Public Address Book of your domain defines information that, if made public, could compromise the security of your domain. Information, such as server phone numbers, people phone numbers, and other connections within your domain, should not be made available to a foreign domain.

If you are concerned about compromising your domain's Public Address Book, create a subset of the Public Address Book that will enable your servers to communicate with outside domains, but not compromise the Domain's "secrets," then place this version on the isolated servers. The following list details some things you should consider when creating this database:

- The replica ID should be different.

- A replica of the Domain's Public Address Book should be on the server, hidden from view, with the outside domain group used as no access. This is so you can refer to it easily.

- Connection, people, and domain documents should be in the subset Public Address Book.

The Public Address Book's Access Control List

On the server connecting to other servers, you should enable the other servers to read documents, but not copy or replicate documents to their servers for the same reason brought out in the first item of the preceding bulleted list. (See Figure 40.6.)

FIGURE 40.6.

A sample ACL of the foreign Public Address Book.

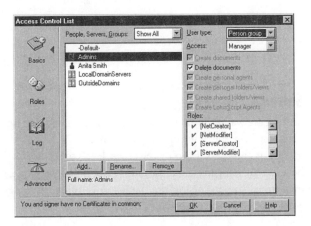

Access to Databases

Once the connection is established and verified, the connecting server/user has the capability of accessing any database on that server. There are two strategies you can take: hide the database or manage the ACL settings.

Database Information

Part of the information granted to a server accessing another server is the name of the directories and databases. This information can compromise security in your environment by indicating what you are using databases for, what companies you are working with, and the name of the database.

If this information is sensitive to your company you can implement the following:

- *Directory links.* These are text files that point to other directories and limit who can access the links. The file ABC.DIR, for example, contains the lines C:\COMPANYAC\Files\ and OtherDomains. The user sees [ABC] in the File Database Open dialog box. Notes accesses the C:\CompanyAC\Files directory and enables only members of the OtherDomains group to use this link.

- *Directory names.* These are fictitious names that don't give away the purpose of the directory. For example, name your data directories A, B, C, D rather than COADB, COXDB, and so forth.

- *Database properties.* Use database properties to hide databases from the File Database Open dialog box. (See Figure 40.7.)

Figure 40.7.

Database properties.

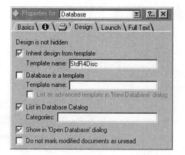

ACL Settings

The most secure way to limit access to data once an entity is on the server is to limit the access to the database by name or group. As you know, the ACL is used to control access to the database for both servers and users. Employ the access levels to secure databases. As a rule, all databases on a public server are fair game, so if the data is very sensitive, set the default to No Access to prevent unknown users from accessing the database. Employ the types of ACL entries to specify exactly what type of entry it represents. (See Figure 40.8.)

Defining the type of entry forces Notes to do an additional check to ensure that the entry is the type defined. This is used to prevent renegade access. For example, without this further definition, a group could be created with the same name as one of the entries. Anyone who has author access to the Public Address Book could add a name to this group and act as the entry in ACL.

This could happen if a user is not specifically specified. If a server named the same as a group enters the database, it won't get the group's access.

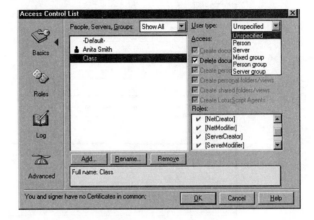

Secure Access Summary

When establishing a connection with another domain, you should ensure that the servers can authenticate, limit access to your servers using Name Check, and protect your Public Address Books and databases.

Establishing Communication

After you have ensured a secure environment, your next step is to establish the connection and pass data back and forth. Consider the following:

■ Creating the connection

■ Setting up databases to replicate

■ Setting up mail to route

■ Troubleshooting

Creating the Connection

When attempting to connect, the first question is who will call to update the data? This decision may already be made for your domain and this connection. If it is not, consider who will incur the cost of maintaining the data. The domain makes the call that will assume all the cost.

The connection is based on the connection document in the Public Address Book. (See Figure 40.9.)

FIGURE 40.9.

Server connection document.

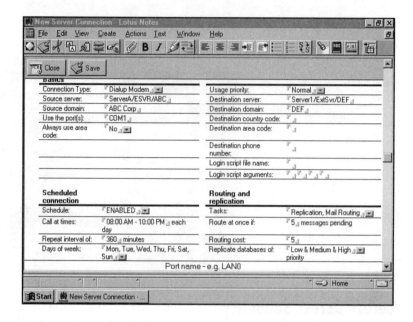

The connection document specifies how the servers will connect. This document is discussed previously. What you need to know is the fully distinguished name of the server and the phone number or how to connect to a service it already connects to, such as CompuServe.

> **NOTE**
>
> You can connect over the LAN; it is not as common, however. Typically, domains are in different companies.
>
> The connection should occur only between servers that can authenticate.

Between the two domains, their needs to be only one connection document if replication is occurring. If mail routing is occurring, two documents are necessary—one in one domain pointing to the other for mail routing, the other in the other domain for return. The schedule should recognize the fact that when replication is initiated, mail also goes.

Setting Up Databases to Replicate

The major cost of connecting to another domain is the initial synchronization of databases over the phone lines. Once the connection is established, the Notes Server needs replica databases that are on the other Notes Server. These databases can be generated as the target server as long as the administrator knows the name and server of the source database. Then, at the next replication, Notes will synchronize the databases. Alternately, the databases can be supplied on disk already established. The administrator copies the database to the server (using the operating system, not Notes, because this could change the replica ID). The next replication will synchronize the database. These steps are:

1. Gather the source server and filename.

2. Create a new replica using File | Replicate | New Replica.

3. Enter the name of the server and database.

4. Enter your location information.

Another issue with establishing the replica copies is ensuring that the groups and people and servers necessary for access to the database are established in the Public Address Book.

Setting Up Mail to Route

When establishing mail routing, the administrator must ensure that the server depositing mail onto your server has depositor access to the Mail.Box file.

The other consideration is how the mail will be addressed. The users depend on the Public Address Book to verify and determine the correct Address when mail is routed in their domains. When connecting to another domain, however, the story is different, because the target's Public Address Book is not available for verification. The administrators have several options. The first option is to aid the users in explicitly pathing a mail address. If you are in DomainA, and a connection has been established to DomainB, you can route mail to someone in DomainB (let's say John Doe) by using the address John Doe@B. You have to know John Doe's name, spelled correctly, and his domain name. The administrator can help you by creating a Domain document specifying the name of the domain. (See Figure 40.10.)

FIGURE 40.10.

Adjacent Domain document.

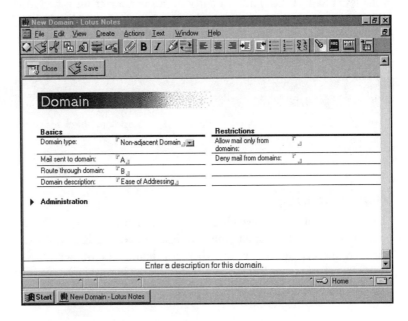

Another thing the administrator can do is create a separate database based on the Public Address Book and include in it all people documents to which people will e-mail regularly. (See Figure 40.11.)

FIGURE 40.11.

The person document with the minimum information needed for e-mailing.

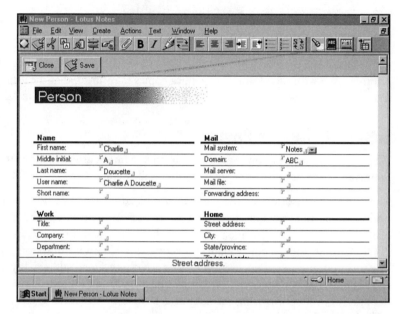

The administrator would then make this available to the server by using the NAMES= parameter in the NOTES.INI file. The first entry in this parameter must be NAMES.NSF, the Public Address Book, because Notes R4.x is hard-coded to refer to NAMES.NSF for security breakdowns; otherwise, what is being defined is other Public Address Books to use when an address cannot be resolved. (See Figure 40.12.)

NOTE

The user can also establish which Public Address Book to check for address verification in the Personal Address Book.

Troubleshooting

The most difficult part of establishing a connection is testing it. The two administrators involved should troubleshoot all problems together. New to R4.x is the trace connections capability. To test a connection to see where it is failing, use the server's workstation, select File Tools | User Preferences | Ports, and enable Trace Connections. (See Figure 40.13.)

FIGURE 40.12.

The location document with the server information completed.

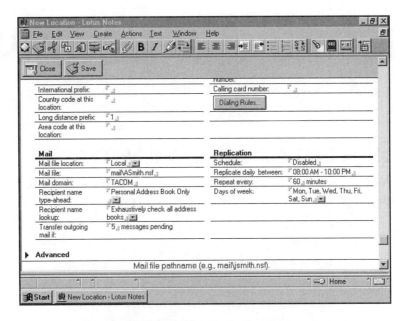

FIGURE 40.13.

Trace Connections.

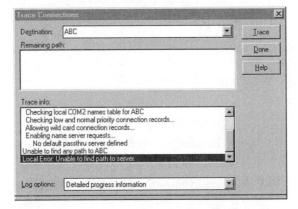

Trace Connections will attempt to connect to the target server and indicate where it fails.

Typically, it is not a port connection problem. The following items are things to check if the connection fails:

- Is the target server's name fully distinguished?
- Are there any spelling mistakes in the Allow group/deny group/connection documents?
- Is it in the allow access field?
- Is there a cross-certificate in the Public Address Book?
- Is the ACL appropriately set for connection? Can the other server access your server?

40

USING NOTES
BETWEEN
COMPANIES

> **NOTE**
>
> Both the administrators should speak when troubleshooting. Connection problems can go on for days over voice mail.

Steps for Connecting to a Server

You have explored concepts with regard to connections. To enable you to connect to a server, use the following steps, which have helped me in the past:

1. Set up a security strategy for servers in your domain communicating with servers in other domains:

   Isolate servers in an OU.

   Secure ACLs on Public Databases.

   Plan which OU you will use to issue a cross certificate.

   Create a subset of the Public Address Book to be used on outside servers.

   Create groups and place them in Deny/Allow Access groups of all your servers. Down your servers and reload them.

2. Gather information about the other domain/server:

   What is the server's name?

   What is the domain's name?

   What is the server's phone number?

   Who will be calling whom?

   Is this mail enabled?

   Do you want to allow the domain to route through yours?

   What groups are required?

   To whom will your users regularly e-mail?

3. Add the new server to the security groups that you have established.

4. Cross certify/flat certify.

5. Create Connection documents.

6. Test connection using server's workstation.

7. Establish replica copies.

8. Add the users to the second Public Address Book for name lookups.

9. Ensure that replica databases are loaded.

10. Enable users to use new databases.

Summary

Before you connect to other domains, you should secure a server in your domain first. Because it is not outlined formally elsewhere, here is a summary of what to do when connecting to another domain:

1. Determine which server will do the connecting in your domain.
2. Define how the other domain will connect (modem, service provider, and so forth).
3. Create a cross certificate for your domain.
4. Send the cross certificate to the other domain.
5. Accept the cross certificate from the other domain.
6. Add the other server to the server in your domain's document so that it can access your domain.
7. Add a connection document enabling replication and mail.
8. Create noninitialized replicas of databases.
9. Gather a Public Address Book from the other domain for mailing purposes.
10. Test the mail connection.

Lotus Notes R4.x is a multilayerd application encompassing connectivity and development. Throughout this book, we have represented everything necessary for you to implement, migrate, and secure your servers and outline and build your databases. This isn't easy, but this book should be your resource for the tasks at hand.

Epilogue

You've come to the end of your journey. I hope that you now see why the authors of this book and several million other Notes users are so enthusiastic about the product. Notes has begun to catch the attention of so many people that the enthusiasm is contagious.

You covered a lot of ground in this book. You saw how to use Notes, learned how to design applications using Notes, and discovered the important aspects of administering a Notes system. We tried to cover material that hasn't been covered well in other Notes books, such as Notes advanced development, telephony, Video and RealTime Notes, workflow, and connecting your company to other companies.

We also covered topics such as the Internet and how to set up Domino and the InterNotes Web Publisher. Although pundits predicted that the Internet would spell doom for Notes, the so-called death of Notes has turned out to be more of a splendid resurrection. In 1996, Notes added more Internet features and functions and became the Internet platform that other rival products were trying to catch up with.

In all, we tried to bring you the information you need to help you decide whether to use Notes, to effectively use and develop applications for Notes, and to deploy and administer your Notes network.

Although this is the end of our book on Lotus Notes R4.5, it's certainly not the final word on Notes. By the time you read this book, Notes 5.0 may already be out. With the advent of the Internet and the World Wide Web, Lotus has gone into hyperdrive and is trying to come out with major new functions within months instead of years. This has resulted in a dizzying rate of innovation.

On behalf of all the authors, I hope you have enjoyed and benefitted from this book. Best wishes in your Notes deployment.

—Randall A. Tamura

Business Partners, the User Group Connection, and Other Resources

by Rob Wunderlich

IN THIS APPENDIX

> **NOTE**
>
> In the interest of full disclosure, I must state at the outset that I work for a Lotus Premium Business Partner and a Lotus Authorized Education Center (LAEC). As such, I realize that some of my views might be somewhat tainted in favor of the "official" Business Partner network Lotus has set up.
>
> Although I will attempt to be as unbiased as possible, my vote is clearly with Lotus' Business Partner channel. In addition, as a founder of the Detroit Notes Professionals Association and a longtime board member of the Detroit Area Network User Group (http://www.danug.org), I'm somewhat biased toward user groups as well.

Let's say you've made the plunge into Notes, but you need some assistance. Where can you turn for help?

This appendix looks at several different paths you can take to get help with your problems. First, we'll look at the Lotus Business Partner Program in depth, using three different scenarios as examples. We'll also look at other resources that are available. We'll finish with a look at the assistance you can find at a User Group.

Lotus Business Partners

This section describes the scenarios I just mentioned. Three corporate managers faced with completely different tasks are encountering situations that might lead them to Lotus Notes and Lotus Business Partners.

Charlotte is sales manager of a small, family-run manufacturing company. She's looking for a method to track clients, prospects, and leads, and she's heard that Lotus Notes might be the answer. She's looking for what's commonly referred to as "sales force automation," with the potential for all 12 of her salespeople to use the system.

Samantha is spearheading her organization's e-mail initiative. There are nearly 500 people in the main office, and another 250 are spread across branch offices in all the major U.S. cities. She needs help in evaluating e-mail packages, and once a decision is made, she needs implementation assistance.

Eileen is vice president and managing partner in charge of corporate communications of an advertising agency and has been assigned the task of putting her firm on the Web. She needs a consultant who can lead her firm through the intricacies of connecting to the Internet and then make it happen. Yesterday.

Each of these women needs help. Each needs assistance not only in the form of consulting, but also implementation. And, although their three organizations couldn't be looking for anything more diverse, Lotus Notes might well be the answer for all three of them. Lotus Business Partners also can be involved in all three scenarios.

Whether you're faced with a 10-person departmental implementation of Lotus Notes or in charge of a 10,000-user corporate-wide Notes rollout, the tasks facing you might appear daunting. The good news is that there is help available—in the form of a worldwide network of consultants, developers, system administrators, instructors, and other service providers known as Lotus Business Partners.

Although the rest of this book is devoted to a product, Lotus Notes Release 4.5, this appendix is devoted to Lotus Business Partners. Along with the three scenarios just mentioned, we'll look at the following:

- What assistance a Business Partner can offer
- Some of the benefits and drawbacks of a Business Partner
- How to find a Business Partner who can satisfy your needs
- What the education channel has to offer

As a serious alternative, we'll take a quick look at what help User Groups can offer.

The Lotus Business Partner Program

A number of years ago, Lotus Development began a network of commercial and corporate developers, training companies, and service providers, including systems integrators, consultants, value-added resellers, systems analysts, instructors, and support organizations. These became known as Lotus Business Partners.

These organizations, in their own individual ways, were working with various Lotus products. The Business Partner program allowed them to work more closely with Lotus by providing them with the software, tools, information, training, and support they needed.

Although Lotus has packaged the Business Partner Program in flavors for developers, service providers, and training centers, there are three levels of "official" Business Partner:

- Member
- Qualified Partner
- Premium Partner

There are also Lotus Authorized Education Centers (LAECs), as well as certified independent instructors. And there are also several special levels of corporate partners.

> **TIP**
>
> Like so many other things surrounding Notes, everything you could possibly want to know about Lotus Business Partners can be found on Lotus' Web site. There are even forms to fill out if you're interested in becoming a partner. Check out http://www.lotus.com.

Let's take a quick look at the various levels of partner. After that, we'll discuss what you can expect from a relationship with a Business Partner.

Lotus Business Partner Member

This is the entry-level Business Partner. Although this isn't necessarily a negative, such a person probably is an independent consultant without much staff. However, this person gets access to Lotus software and support services just like the big guys. He gets access to Lotus support, various KnowledgeBases, and so on. He's also plugged into an amazing number of Lotus products and marketing information, as well as (periodically) some inside scoops on release dates and so on.

Lotus Qualified Business Partner

Technically, almost any firm working with Lotus products could become a Business Partner Member, but it's harder to become a Qualified Business Partner. The organization pays a modest amount of money to sign up, and it must fulfill some requirements, including having at least one Certified Lotus Professional (CLP) on staff. These CLPs are technical folks who've passed a number of tests to be certified as a Notes Application Developer or a Notes System Administrator, for example. In return for these more stringent requirements, the Qualified Partner gets pre-release software, marketing assistance, and additional support from Lotus.

Lotus Premium Business Partner

Becoming a Premium Partner is tougher than a becoming a Qualified Business Partner if for no other reason than you must have more than one CLP on staff—and there are sales-generation requirements as well. In addition, Premium Partners largely work with Lotus Notes, although not exclusively. Premium Partners get all the same information that regular Business Partners do, but they also have an inside track for support and marketing information. There are numerous people at Lotus who deal exclusively with the Premium Business Partners, so if you're working through a Premium Partner, chances are he can get more accurate information more quickly. Premium Partners get reevaluated each year, and if they don't measure up, they can get demoted to "plain" Business Partner status.

Lotus Authorized Education Centers (LAEC)

The LAEC channel represents training centers that focus on Lotus Notes training. In order to become an LAEC, a training center must have a Certified Lotus Instructor (CLI) on permanent staff and must agree to teach the authorized Lotus courseware.

Typically, the LAEC is also a Lotus Business Partner, although not always.

Our three women might end up needing the assistance of an LAEC in the end, but for the moment, they need a Business Partner who can help sort through the options and help procure and then implement the final solution. The implementation might simply be software installation. But in the case of the "hook us up to the Web" scenario, it might involve equipment purchases, configuration and installation, Internet connectivity, and Web site configuration—far more than simply Lotus Notes.

What to Expect from a Business Partner

There are numerous things that the three women—and you—can expect from a Business Partner. I've attempted to group them into some usable categories:

- Hard goods:
  - Product fulfillment
  - Equipment procurement
  - Dedicated resources (that is, people on-site)
- Assistance:
  - Installation and setup
  - Application development
  - System administration
  - Mentoring
  - Help line
- Training (whether LAEC or not):
  - End-user
  - Administrator
  - Developer

Hard Goods

The hard goods are fairly obvious. The Business Partner should be able to provide Lotus products, and possibly equipment, as well as assist you by offering dedicated resources (another way of saying they can lend you people).

Although it's certainly true that not all Business Partners can sell you software *and* hardware, there's an advantage to those who can, because you'll end up with an "I want a Notes server up and running" project handled by one firm. That firm will order the equipment, configure it as needed, install the software and configure *that* as needed, and make sure that everything is working correctly before handing it over to you. You'll lessen the possibility of the software guy and the hardware guy pointing fingers at each other when something doesn't work. Certain situations (such as the case of Eileen, who is looking for Internet connectivity) require far more on the part of the Business Partner than simply selling Notes.

Another commodity that most Business Partners offer is staffing, known as a *dedicated resource*. Even the smaller Business Partners often have one person who is continually farmed out to different customers to assist them with various projects. The rates for such resource people vary greatly, depending on the area of the country and the skill level needed. The case of Samantha might entail a dedicated resource serving as e-mail administrator for the first month, helping the in-house staff get everything set up and running smoothly.

Assistance

The assistance issue is harder to pin down, mostly because there are so many things that a Business Partner can help you with.

In some cases, the Business Partner might do an entire application development project and turn it over to the customer in a turnkey method. In other cases, the Business Partner might work with an organization's Notes people in a mentoring role to help them complete a project.

Regardless of the specific help you need, the Business Partner should be able to offer help in installation and configuration, system design, application development, Notes system administration, and hardware issues. (He might or might not be able to help with larger system integration issues—TCP/IP connectivity, for example. That might be an offshoot of a Notes project.)

Some Business Partners offer some sort of Help Line assistance, even if it's nothing more than an informal offer to call them if you have a problem. Others (such as my employer) offer 24-hour software support via an 800 number. Since Business Partners have access to the various Lotus KnowledgeBases, they often can track down answers quickly, particularly to the more simple problems.

All three of our scenarios will need assistance in one form or another, as well as training.

Training

Training is important, and it can come in many fashions.

Whether or not your Business Partner is an official LAEC, he probably will offer some training. In other words, even if he works strictly as an application developer, he should offer some amount of training to demonstrate how to use the application correctly. Even in the limited case of the 12-person sales department, each salesperson will need some training in how to use the system. For example, the e-mail rollout might require a three-week dedicated training schedule to instruct the staff on how to use e-mail.

The fully staffed LAEC organizations often have published schedules of public classes and might make instructors available to clients for customized training at the client's site. Also, different levels of courses might be offered. Some LAECs offer only the introductory Notes classes, and others offer the full range, up to and including LotusScript, cc:Mail Administration, and so on. Sometimes (but not always) the courses offered give an indication of the firm's expertise.

> **TIP**
>
> To find an LAEC in your vicinity, check the Lotus Web site (`http://www.lotus.com`). It lists LAECs, courses, certification requirements, and so on.

Some Business Partners offer Notes training but aren't LAECs. A number of third-party training courses are available, and many Business Partners take advantage of them. Some of the third-party courseware, although not produced by Lotus, is terrific. Many Business Partners use courseware from companies such as PTR, WordLink, and Kurchak and Associates. Other national training centers, such as New Horizons, have developed their own courses.

Also, just like many other software programs, Notes is the subject of CBT (computer-based training). CBT allows users to progress through the learning process at their own pace. Many Business Partners offer CBT for sale.

How to Choose a Business Partner

As the three women will discover, there's no surefire way to be certain that the Business Partner you're about to contract with is the perfect one, but there are many things you can do to ensure a good fit.

A large part of the process is to figure out what you *need;* the other major challenge is to figure out what the Business Partner *has.* Each of the three scenarios requires a different skill set from a Business Partner. The trick is to correctly match requirements with capabilities.

Keep in mind that Business Partners come in all shapes and sizes. What's right for Samantha's huge nationwide corporation might be totally inappropriate for Charlotte's mom-and-pop manufacturing operation. Some Business Partners are literally one-person shops. Others have dozens, if not hundreds, of consultants, developers, and administrators.

I suggest a five-step methodology in picking the correct Business Partner:

1. Know what you need.
2. Check out local Business Partners.
3. If appropriate, do a request for proposal (RFP).
4. Check with Lotus, and check out the "public offerings."
5. Check the local Notes user group.

These steps are described in the following sections.

Know What You Need

Before you start talking to a Business Partner, try to decide what you want. Having someone handle the complete project in a turnkey fashion might require one set of capabilities. On the other hand, if you want an occasional mentoring session with a seasoned developer, that might require a different set of capabilities.

Some Business Partners offer consultants who can help you figure out what you need. You can hire a consultant to help you develop the plan that you'll end up hiring someone else to implement. Some firms offer not only Notes consultants, but also business consultants who can help with organizational issues, process reengineering, overall technology initiatives, network and connectivity concerns, and other issues not directly pertaining to Notes itself. You can work with a business consultant to find the right Notes consultant.

In our examples, Samantha is the perfect candidate to use a consultant to help evaluate different e-mail packages and then set up an e-mail design that Business Partners could bid on implementing.

Check Out Local Business Partners

Find out who the local Business Partners are, what they've done, and what credentials they possess. See whether they have Lotus-certified personnel. Get references. Research current clients, previous experience, and applications delivered. Find out who your competitors used.

A huge listing of Business Partners is available from Lotus. You can visit their Web site at `http://www.lotus.com/partcat/` or call (800) 782-7876.

Call a couple of local partners and talk to them. They might even offer references for their competitors in case what they have to offer doesn't meet your needs.

Keep in mind that size *does* count. The needs of our three sample companies are diverse. It's unlikely that the partner who'd be perfect for Eileen's Web implementation project would also be interested in Charlotte's 12-person sales force. Samantha's nationwide e-mail project would need a partner with offices (or personnel) around the country.

If Appropriate, Do a Request for Proposal (RFP)

RFPs are common these days. They essentially equate to asking for bids on a project. Typically, as part of the RFP, the Business Partner will be required to document some of the credentials I noted earlier. In addition, the customer also defines the boundaries of the project at hand.

If you're not sure what questions to ask and how to frame an RFP, you can usually hire a consultant (perhaps even one of the potential bidders) to assist you in putting it together.

Although even Charlotte's 12-person project might involve a couple of bids, Samantha's e-mail project should garner attention from multiple bidders.

Check with Lotus, and Check out the "Public Offerings"

Granted, there's a possibility that the Lotus rep will recommend a Business Partner he had dinner with last night, but by and large, the Lotus reps are knowledgeable about the partners in their territory.

Lotus also has some national Business Partner representatives who are aware of what the partners in their areas are doing. You can call the Business Partner connection at (800) 782-7876.

Additionally, Lotus offers *The Notes Guide,* a compendium of partners and products. Most Lotus offices have copies. You can also obtain one by calling the number just listed.

Most Business Partners offer seminars or other "public offerings" that you can attend. Going to one of these seminars will quickly tell you whether the partner knows his stuff or not.

Check the Local Notes User Group

Notes User Groups are discussed at length near the end of this Appendix, but they bear mention here as a resource for finding Business Partners.

Many Business Partners are involved with local groups. They sometimes offer meeting space or advertising dollars, but they also are frequently involved as contributors to the group's programs. A quick check of presenters over the past few months would tell you which Business Partners are active in your area and probably would give you a good sense of what tasks they excel in.

In addition, typical user group people are extremely candid. They'll readily steer you toward the Business Partners they like.

How to Manage the Relationship with a Business Partner

Once you've decided what you need and who can help, you need to manage the relationship with the Business Partner. Don't take anything for granted. Like many things in life, there's often a gap between what the ad says and what the product delivers.

You can do several things to minimize potential problems in your relationship with the Business Partner:

- Be clear about what you're looking for.
- Get it in writing.
- Agree on payment terms.
- Build in a reevaluation time.

Be Clear About What You're Looking For

Earlier I mentioned that in the process of setting up the parameters for working with a Business Partner, you need to be clear about what you want.

One of the easiest ways to make sure that the Business Partner relationship works is to be completely clear about what you're expecting—for yourself and for the provider.

In some cases, you might want a partner to simply develop and deliver an application. In other cases, you might want a "dedicated resource" to work in your environment for a matter of months. Know what you really want before you end up asking for the wrong thing. Does Samantha want a dedicated resource as an e-mail administrator for the first six weeks of her project? Does Eileen want a Web site hosted locally, or would she prefer to use a "virtual host"?

Get It in Writing

As you hire the consultant, developer, or administrator, be sure the "deliverables" are clearly spelled out—in writing. Whether you create a wish list and have the partner sign off on it, or whether he creates a proposal you accept, be sure that the scope of the engagement is clearly delineated. Be sure that costs for "extras" are spelled out and that things such as overtime are either excluded or defined.

From a customer standpoint, this should eliminate much of the potential for unpleasant surprises. If you would like a printer user manual to accompany the application that's being developed, spell it out. Don't assume that the developer was going to do it anyway.

The agreement should include clearly delineated deliverables, timelines, the number of personnel to be assigned to the product, and what (if anything) the customer needs to do before the partner can begin working. If timing is an issue, even potential penalties for late delivery can be worked into the agreement.

In the case of Charlotte's 12-person staff, it's certainly likely that the application will need some customizing after they've worked with it for a few months. Have that final "tweaking" written in from the beginning. In the case of the national e-mail rollout, what's really expected in the branch offices? Does an engineer need to visit each branch, or are there branch people capable of plugging in a preconfigured post office? Get it in writing.

Agree on Payment Terms

Few, if any, vendors expect payment up front. But everyone needs to know they'll get paid. It's best to make sure—up front—that everyone agrees on the terms of payment.

As part of the agreement, make sure that a payment schedule satisfactory to both parties is worked out. Be sure that the payment schedule works as an incentive, not as a disincentive.

If there are any issues about premium time or additions to the contract, be sure to spell them out. If you need to accelerate the schedule, be sure the vendor is adequately compensated if he requires overtime or weekends.

Once you've agreed on payment terms, stick to your agreement. If the vendor delivers what he said he would, don't delay in getting him paid.

Build in Reevaluation Time

One of the most important aspects of a relationship with a Lotus Business Partner is to build in a time frame to assess the relationship itself.

Set a specific time frame to look at whether both parties are satisfied with the relationship. Is everything being delivered as promised? Is the quality of work what you expected? Are the assigned personnel of the caliber required?

If everything is going well, this reevaluation period will end up being a back-patting session. But, if not, it gives both sides an easy opportunity to set things right. As I mentioned, Charlotte's sales application will probably need some tweaking after a few months of use. Build in that reevaluation time up front.

With these guidelines in place, the relationship with the Business Partner will not only provide you with what you need, but will also be a pleasant experience all around.

Each of our three sample organizations was able to decide upon and work with the best Business Partner for them.

In the case of Charlotte's sales staff, it was a small Business Partner with a small staff who found a "canned" sales force automation application and made some minor modifications. In Eileen's Web site case, it was a one-office Business Partner with a multitude of capabilities. They designed the system; connected her to the Internet; set up a Web site, an elaborate firewall, and a Domino server; subcontracted the services of a graphic designer to assist in developing the look and feel of the Web pages; and even sold her several new computers to run all this on. Samantha, meanwhile, decided on NotesMail. Her project required the services of one of the few nationwide Business Partners who could have technicians on-site in each of the branch offices to install and configure the Notes servers.

A Word About LAECs, Lotus Education, and Certification

Thus far, we've focused on the partner who will offer development and administrative services. But there's another type of partner—one who offers Notes education. Each of our sample organizations will find that it needs training in one form or another.

Although many training organizations offer Lotus training of some sort, those offering "official" Lotus courseware and that are certified to work with Lotus are known as Lotus Authorized Education Centers (LAEC). Many LAECs also offer Microsoft or Novell training, but generally they don't offer training on the typical desktop applications.

LAECs are required by Lotus not only to have Lotus-certified instructors on staff, but also to teach Lotus-authored courses as opposed to third-party courses. As I noted earlier, some LAECs offer only the basic courses, while others offer the full gamut of classes. Regardless of the offerings, most publish schedules that are readily available.

The Lotus courses are directly related to the Lotus certification program. A Certified Lotus Professional (CLP) certification is becoming a sought-after commodity, much as some of the network certifications have been. With the advent of Notes 4.5, the courseware has taken on more of a "task" orientation than a "fact" orientation. In other words, both the courseware and the testing are more directly related to the business of getting a job done rather than memorizing a lot of obscure facts.

Lotus Education is aiming to eliminate "paper certification," wherein someone is certified but can't do the work. Some network certifications have been under fire because they require people to pass the tests based strictly on book learning without having the knowledge necessary to actually run a network.

Most LAECs can aim a CLP candidate in the right direction, offering classes and information about testing. You can obtain information about locating LAECs, course offerings, and the certification process by calling the Lotus Education Helpline at (800) 346-6409.

Other Resources for Assistance

You might be aware of the impressive number of books available on the subject of Notes. (And you obviously have picked the best one!)

But, in addition to books, there are also other resources. There are now numerous Notes periodicals, Web sites, conferences, seminars, and more.

Here are four Notes magazines I'm aware of:

- *The VIEW,* published by Wellesley Information Services, Inc.
- *Notes Advisor,* published by Advisor Publications
- *The Notes Report,* published by Lotus Publishing Corp.
- *Workspace for Lotus Notes,* published by the Cobb Group

Each of these magazines is packed with information, tutorials, and questions and answers.

Notes has also become the focus of several industry conferences. Many people have heard of Lotusphere, held in Orlando each January. But there is also a series of Notes Solution Symposiums held in various cities around the country, as well as other national seminar series and conferences that focus on groupware and Notes.

All of these additional resources are of tremendous value. Even the Web itself has become a resource. Although the next section of this appendix barely scratches the surface of Notes resources available on the Internet, check out those sites and see the wealth of information and experience that's available.

Notes Resources on the Web

The following sections describe Notes resources I've found on the Internet. This list is kept updated at `http://web1.leadgroup.com/iwpcourse/`.

> **NOTE**
>
> Countless Notes resources are available on the Web. The ones here are some that I've discovered and wanted to pass along. As with any printed list, these links are subject to change, but all were active at the time this appendix was written.

The Real Source

Lotus (main)	`http://www.lotus.com`
Lotus InterNotes	`http://www.lotus.com/inotes`
Lotus' Domino site	`http://domino.lotus.com`
Iris Associates	`http://www.iris.com`
Lotus Business Partners	`http://www.lotus.com/partcat/`

News and Networks

Notes Net Info Center	`http://www.notes.net/`
WorldCom	`http://www.worldcom.com/`

Notes Resource Sites

European Notes site	`http://pobox.com/~notes/`
Notes FAQ	`http://www.turnpike.net/metro/kyee/NotesFAQ.html`
Delta Notes Resources	`http://www-iwi.unisg.ch/delta/notes/index.html`

Notes Utility Vendors

ALI	`http://www.ali.com`
Brainstorm	`http://www.braintech.com`
Cambridge Software	`http://www.csg.com`
Campbell Services	`http://www.ontime.com`
CleverSoft	`http://www.cleversoft.com/cleversoft`
Collabra Share	`http://www.collabra.com/datashts/notes.htm`
Delta	`http://www-iwi.unisg.ch/delta/notes.html`
GroupQuest	`http://www.gqs.com/`
Ives Development	`http://www.teamstudio.com/info@jtassoc.com`
J&T	`http://www.jtassoc.com`
Mayflower	`http://www.maysoft.com`
Revelation	`http://www.revelation.com`
Thuridion	`http://www.thuridion.com/`
WorkFlow Designs	`http://www.wfdesigns.com/~workflow/`
WorldLedge	`http://bartok.jstechno.ch/worldb`

Notes Newsgroups

L-Notes-L	`http://www.disaster.com/lnotesl.html`
CompuServe	`GO LOTUSCOM`

Links to Links

Delta	`http://www.iwi.unisg.ch/delta/links/`

Business Partners and Other Notes-Related Sites

A complete Business Partner listing can be found at `http://www.lotus.com/partcat/`.

Andrew Pollack	`http://www.thenorth.com/`
Brad Cox	`http://web.gmu.edu/bcox/ElectronicCommunity/00LotusNotes.html`
ENTEX/Michigan	`http://web1.leadgroup.com`
Group Quest Software	`http://www.gqs.com/`
Meckler Media	`http://www.iworld.com/InternetShopper/1Lotus_Notes_related.html`
MPI FormGate	`http://www.mpi-sb.mpg.de/guide/staff/brahm/formgate/formgate.html`

Miguel Estrada	`http://www.maev.com/`
New Information Paradigms	`http://www.nipltd.com/`
Tile Home Page	`http://www.tile.net/`
Uptime Computer Solutions, Inc.	`http://www.uptime1.com/`

Search Sites

AltaVista	`http://altavista.digital.com`
Excite	`http://www.excite.com`
Lycos	`http://www.lycos.com`
WebCrawler	`http://www.webcrawler.com`
Yahoo	`http://www.yahoo.com`

There are countless other sites on the Internet that you can check out. Try a search at Yahoo or AltaVista for "Notes," and see how many hits you'll find!

As mentioned earlier, this list is kept updated at `http://web1.leadgroup.com/iwpcourse/`.

If you find a site of particular interest, send the URL address to `webmaster@leadgroup.com`, and we'll add it to the list.

Lotus Notes User Groups

I briefly discussed user groups earlier in this appendix. I'm a huge proponent of user groups in general and Notes groups in particular. Each of our three sample managers should get involved.

User groups initially sprang from the need of computer hobbyists to get together to swap disks, stories, and experiences. They've evolved over the years, and today there are probably as many "professional" user groups as there are hobbyist groups. Series of groups are devoted to things such as operating systems and networking (for example, NetWare Users International boasts chapters in 80 countries). Among the new breed of user groups are those devoted to Notes.

> **NOTE**
>
> Many user groups are very active but hard to find. You can check local newspaper listings for meeting information, but you're more likely to find user group information from local training centers, Business Partners, and so on.
>
> *continues*

continued

There are a couple centralized clearinghouses for user group contact information. The Association of PC User Groups (APCUG) is an international organization to which user groups belong. It can be found on the Web at `http://www.apcug.org`.

Another umbrella organization for user groups is the User Group Connection, a for-profit organization that assists user groups. Check it out on the Web at `htpp://www.ugconnection.com`.

As far as Notes-specific groups are concerned, guess what? Among the things you'll find on the Lotus Web site are a list of Notes user groups, complete with meeting and contact information. This list is updated regularly at `http://www.lotus.com`.

The Notes user groups are inappropriately named. They're not groups of Notes *users* at all; they're groups of Notes administrators, developers, VARs, trainers, and so on. They focus on issues of Notes deployment, training, products, and utilities. There's even a national association of Notes groups—the Worldwide Association of Lotus Notes Users and Technologists (WALNUT). You can contact them at (508) 466-6327.

Getting involved with a Notes user group in your area can be a rewarding experience. Most groups feature some sort of product presentation at each meeting, as well as a tutorial session in which various aspects of Notes are discussed. One of the most beneficial aspects of a user group is the user-to-user interaction. Someone will stand up and say, "I've been having a problem with such and such," and the entire group will pitch in to assist.

Lotus works closely with the various Notes groups, offering speakers, support, meeting space, and so on. The user group department at Lotus can steer you toward the group closest to you; call (617) 693-1870.

Summary

Working with a Lotus Business Partner can make your life easier, but it's important to find the right partner and to manage the relationship properly.

Use referrals from whatever sources you can find, and make sure that the terms of the relationship are clearly spelled out, including deliverables, time frames, and costs.

Find out about LAECs in your area, and get involved with the local Notes user group for additional support and information.

You're not alone! There's a network of service providers and training centers to help you, and user groups abound. If you're embarking on the Notes journey for the first time, you'll enjoy the company!

Each of the three women described in this appendix found a Business Partner to take care of her projects. These Business Partners were as diverse as the projects themselves, but each was a good fit.

I

INDEX

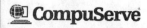

Lotus Notes 4 Administrator's Survival Guide

Andrew Dahl

Specific to system administrators, this book describes in detail the procedures and techniques necessary to run an efficient Lotus Notes environment. It specifies installation, configuration, system administration, and day-to-day maintenance techniques crucial to any Notes administrator. It provides unparalleled coverage of the physical components of the environment, and it offers tuning, optimization, and troubleshooting tips. The CD-ROM contains source code from the book and various demos from Notes-related software companies.

$55.00 USA/$77.95 CDN   *ISBN 0-672-30844-0*   *672 pages*
Accomplished - Expert   *Groupware*

Teach Yourself Microsoft Office 97 in 24 Hours

Greg Perry

An estimated 22 million people use Microsoft Office, and with the new features of Office 97, much of that market will want the upgrade. To address that market, Sams has published a mass-market version of its best-selling Teach Yourself series. This book shows readers how to use the most widely requested features of Office. It includes many illustrations, screen shots, and a step-by-step plan for learning Office 97. It teaches you how to use each Office product and how to use them together. You'll learn how to create documents in Word that include hypertext links to files created with one of the other Office products.

$19.99 USA/$28.95 CDN   *ISBN 0-672-31009-0*   *432 pages*
New - Casual - Accomplished   *Integrated Software/Suites*

Microsoft Office 97 Unleashed, Second Edition

Paul McFedries, et al.

Microsoft has brought the Web to its Office suite of products. Hyperlinking, Office Assistants, and Active Document Support lets users publish documents to the Web or an intranet site. It also completely integrates with Microsoft FrontPage, making it possible to point and click a Web page into existence. This book details each of the Office products—Excel, Access, PowerPoint, Word, and Outlook—and shows the estimated 22 million registered users how to create presentations and Web documents. You'll see how to extend Office to work on a network, and you'll learn about the various Office Solution Kits and how to use them.

$35.00 USA/$49.95 CDN   *ISBN 0-672-31010-4*   *1,330 pages*
Accomplished - Expert   *Integrated Software/Suites*

Red Hat Linux Unleashed

Kamran Husain, Tim Parker, et al.

Programmers, users, and system administrators will find this book a must-have for operating the Linux environment. Everything from installation and configuration to advanced programming and administration techniques is covered in this valuable reference. This book includes coverage of PPP, TCP/IP, networking, and setting up an Internet site.

$49.99 USA/$67.99 CDN   *ISBN 0-672-30962-9*   *1,176 pages*
Accomplished - Expert   *Operating Systems*

Paul McFedries' Windows 95 Unleashed, Premier Edition

Paul McFedries

This book discusses every new feature of Windows 95 in detail, leaving the reader fully informed and completely functional within the operating system. It also includes coverage of Microsoft Internet products such as Visual Basic Scripting Edition, Internet Studio, and Microsoft Exchange—coverage not found anywhere else. This book covers Internet topics, including the Microsoft Network, and discusses multimedia topics, internetworking, and communication issues. The CD-ROM contains an easy-to-search online chapter on troubleshooting Windows 95.

$59.99 USA/$84.95 CDN	*ISBN 0-672-30932-7*	*1,376 pages*
Accomplished - Expert	*Programming*	*Hardcover*

Intranets Unleashed

Dwayne Gifford, et al.

Intranets, internal Web sites that can be accessed within a company's firewalls, are quickly becoming the status quo in business. This book shows IS managers and personnel how to effectively set up and run large or small intranets. Everything from design to security is discussed.

$59.99 USA/$84.95 CDN	*ISBN 1-57521-115-7*	*906 pages*
Accomplished - Expert	*Internet/Intranets*	

Microsoft Internet Explorer 3 Unleashed

Glenn Fincher, Joe Kraynak, et al.

This comprehensive guide fully exploits the complete Microsoft Internet Explorer and ActiveX environment. It details the steps needed to use Internet Explorer to get around the Internet and to send and receive e-mail and news. You also learn how to use FrontPage and the Internet Assistants to create Web pages, and how to add interactivity to Web pages. This book shows you how to use Microsoft's Internet Assistants and FrontPage to create Web pages and teaches ways to add interactivity to Web pages with Visual Basic Scripting Edition and JavaScript.

$49.99 USA/$70.95 CDN	*ISBN 1-57521-155-6*	*1,088 pages*
Accomplished - Expert	*Internet/General*	

Netscape 3 Unleashed, Second Edition

Dick Oliver

This book shows you how to fully exploit the new features of this version of Netscape—the most popular Web browser in use today. You'll see how to install, configure, and use Netscape Navigator 3. You'll also learn how to add interactivity to Web pages using Netscape. The CD-ROM includes Netscape Navigator 3.

$49.99 USA/$70.95 CDN	*ISBN 1-57521-164-5*	*1,000 pages*
Accomplished - Expert	*Internet/Online Communications*	

Add to Your Sams Library Today with the Best Books for Programming, Operating Systems, and New Technologies

The easiest way to order is to pick up the phone and call

1-800-428-5331

between 9:00 a.m. and 5:00 p.m. EST.
For faster service please have your credit card available.

ISBN	Quantity	Description of Item	Unit Cost	Total Cost
0-672-30844-4		Lotus Notes 4 Administrator's Survival Guide (book/CD-ROM)	$55.00	
0-672-31009-0		Teach Yourself Microsoft Office 97 in 24 Hours	$19.99	
0-672-31010-4		Microsoft Office 97 Unleashed, Second Edition (book/CD-ROM)	$35.00	
0-672-30962-9		Red Hat Linux Unleashed (book/CD-ROM)	$49.99	
0-672-30932-7		Paul McFedries' Windows 95 Unleashed, Premier Edition (book/2 CD-ROMs)	$59.99	
1-57521-115-7		Intranets Unleashed (book/CD-ROM)	$59.99	
1-57521-155-6		Microsoft Internet Explorer 3 Unleashed (book/CD-ROM)	$49.99	
1-57521-164-5		Netscape 3 Unleashed, Second Edition (book/CD-ROM)	$49.99	
❑ 3 ½" Disk		Shipping and Handling: See information below.		
❑ 5 ¼" Disk		TOTAL		

Shipping and Handling: $4.00 for the first book, and $1.75 for each additional book. Floppy disk: add $1.75 for shipping and handling. If you need to have it NOW, we can ship product to you in 24 hours for an additional charge of approximately $18.00, and you will receive your item overnight or in two days. Overseas shipping and handling adds $2.00 per book and $8.00 for up to three disks. Prices subject to change. Call for availability and pricing information on latest editions.

201 W. 103rd Street, Indianapolis, Indiana 46290

1-800-428-5331 — Orders   1-800-835-3202 — FAX   1-800-858-7674 — Customer Service

Book ISBN 0-672-31004-X

What's on
the CD-ROM

The companion CD-ROM contains software developed by the authors, plus an assortment of third-party tools and product demos. This CD is designed to be explored using a CD-ROM Menu program. Using the Menu program, you can view information concerning products and companies and install programs with a single click of the mouse. To run the Menu program, follow the next steps.

Windows 3.1 Installation Instructions

1. Insert the CD into your CD-ROM drive.

2. From File Manager or Program Manager, choose File | Run.

3. Type *drive*\setup and press Enter. *drive* is the letter of your CD-ROM drive. For example, if your CD-ROM drive is drive D:, type d:\setup and press Enter.

4. Double-click the CD-ROM Product Browser icon in the newly created program group to access the software's installation programs or the source code on the CD.

5. To review the latest information about the CD, double-click the About this CD-ROM icon.

Windows 95 Installation Instructions

1. Insert the CD into your CD-ROM drive.

2. If Windows 95 is installed on your computer, and you have the AutoPlay feature enabled, a program group for this book will be automatically created whenever you insert the CD into your CD-ROM drive.

3. If AutoPlay isn't enabled, using Windows Explorer, choose Setup from the CD drive to create the program group for this book.

4. Double-click the CD-ROM Product Browser icon in the newly created program group to access the software's installation programs or the source code on the CD.

5. To review the latest information about this CD, double-click the About this CD-ROM icon.

> **NOTE**
>
> For best results, set your monitor to display between 256 and 64,000 colors. A screen resolution of 640×480 pixels is also recommended. If necessary, adjust your monitor settings before using the CD.